Handbook of Fan

Dorothy S. Becvar

Editor

Handbook of Family Resilience

 Springer

Editor
Dorothy S. Becvar
School of Social Work
Saint Louis University
St. Louis, MO 63103, USA

ISBN 978-1-4614-3799-4 (hardcover)   ISBN 978-1-4614-3917-2 (eBook)
ISBN 978-1-4614-8013-6 (softcover)
DOI 10.1007/978-1-4614-3917-2
Springer New York Heidelberg Dordrecht London

Library of Congress Control Number: 2012942607

Springer is part of Springer Science+Business Media (www.springer.com)

Preface

It seems appropriate to recall that early efforts to understand the ways in which families function typically made use of a deficit model, typically focusing on structure rather than on process. Such structural dimensions as family type (e.g., divorced, single parent) or father absence were thus the primary topics of concern. It is also important to note that this use of a deficit model was consistent with a national concern about family problems that goes as far back as the early days of this country, with forecasts of impending doom a common occurrence from then until now. However, beginning in the 1970s, many scholars began to acknowledge the limitations of a negativistic, structural approach to the study of families. Awareness of the fact that no one structure necessarily predicted success or failure grew, and studies of the characteristics of families who functioned well began to appear along with recognition that a variety of family forms could be supportive of healthy development. Beginning with a consideration of family strengths, more recently the focus has shifted to explorations of family resilience.

At the same time, as studies of family dynamics have continued to grow and evolve, there has been ever greater awareness of both the diversity and the complexity of families. Certainly such complexity is evident as we seek to understand family resilience. From efforts to define the concept, to methodological issues related to its study, to practice considerations relative to the facilitation of resilience in a variety of contexts, social scientists and mental health professionals are faced with enormous challenges. Indeed, the more we explore the more we may recognize that if our goal is to conduct research and/or interact with families in a manner that enables them not only to survive but also to thrive in response to life's vicissitudes, whether expected or unanticipated, the more a variety of perspectives will be essential to the fulfillment of this task.

In an attempt to respond appropriately to the various dimensions of this challenge, this volume purposely includes a variety of perspectives, some of which overlap to a degree, some of which take opposite points of view, but all of which help to shed light on many of the crucial concepts and processes that are subsumed by the term family resilience. Although some aspects of family resilience may not be addressed, as broad a sweep of relevant topics as is possible within one book also are examined. Finally, a variety of professional orientations are included as well, with chapters authored by a remarkable array of scholars representing the fields of counseling, education, human development and family studies, marriage and family therapy, nursing, psychology, social work, and medicine.

Content

Part I of the book, Resilience in General, includes discussions related to the evolution of a family resilience focus (Chap. 1), a consideration of methodological issues when attempting to study family resilience (Chap. 2), and ramifications of and approaches related to the inclusion of family resilience in clinical practice (Chap. 3, 4, and 5).

Resilience and Families, which is the focus of Part II, provides explorations of family resilience relative to stepfamilies (Chap. 5), military marriages (Chap. 6), parenting (Chap. 7), at-risk youth (Chap. 9), and high-risk situations (Chap. 10).

In Part III, Resilience and Ethnicity, resilience is investigated in the contexts of ethnic family systems in general (Chap. 11), Latinos families (Chap. 12), Native American families (Chap. 13), Black families (Chap. 14), and Korean families (Chap. 15).

Part IV, Resilience, Loss, and Grief, offers the reader discussions related to family resilience in the wake of loss (Chap. 16), as tolerance for ambiguity (Chap. 17), in response to peri-natal loss (Chap. 18), relative to parental death (Chap. 19), and in the process of aging (Chap. 20).

Resilience and Ability, the subject addressed in Part V, includes considerations of family resilience relative to children with severe disabilities (Chap. 21), in response to chronic illness (Chap. 22), in the context of children with autism spectrum disorder (Chap. 23), relative to mental health challenges (Chap. 24), and as strengthened through spiritual and religious resources (Chap. 25).

Finally, in Part VI, Resilience, Trauma, and Abuse, the topics addressed include family and community resilience relative to the experience of mass trauma (Chap. 26), resilience in African American adult children of alcoholics (Chap. 27), fostering resilience in daughters of battered women (Chap. 28), family resilience and sexuality (Chap. 29), and resilience in older women religious sexually abused in earlylife (Chap. 30).

Format

Authors were requested to include in their chapters the following elements: an introduction as well as the background of their topic; a discussion of the significance of the topic; a literature review related to the topic; a delineation of current issues relative to the topic; a consideration of clinical implications; a review of research implications; a case example if appropriate; and a conclusion. Thus, the reader will find that each chapter provides an in-depth exploration of the given topic. Indeed, another goal of this volume was to create a rich resource that would be meaningful to a diverse audience.

Dorothy S. Becvar
Saint Louis University, St. Louis, MO, USA

Acknowledgements

I would first like to thank the many contributors, without whom, needless to say, the production of this volume would not have been possible. I also want to thank my editors at Springer, Jennifer Hadley and Sharon Panulla, for their support during my 5 years as Editor of *Contemporary Family Therapy: An International Journal,* as well as for encouraging me to undertake the editing of this handbook. Finally, as always, I want to express my gratitude for the unwavering support of my husband, Ray, and my daughter, Lynne, as I continue my professional pursuits.

Dorothy S. Becvar

Contents

Contributor Bios

Yvonne Amanor-Boadu, Ph.D., is a Licensed Marriage and Family Therapist in private practice at Andrews & Associates, Inc., in Manhattan, Kansas. Her clinical and research interests are in the areas of partner violence and military families.

Jared R. Anderson, Ph.D., is an Assistant Professor in the Marriage and Family Therapy program at Kansas State University. His primary research interest is in marital quality across the life course, with a specific focus on military couples.

Kim M. Anderson, Ph.D., LCSW, is an Associate Professor in the School of Social Work at the University of Missouri. Her research interests include assessment of risk and resiliency in trauma populations and implementation of strengths-based mental health practice.

Mojdeh Bayat, Ph.D., is an Associate Professor in the College of Education at DePaul University. She has published in the areas of family resilience in autism, early childhood teacher education, and early childhood special education topics and methods.

Dorothy S. Becvar, Ph.D., LMFT, LCSW, is a Professor of Social Work at Saint Louis University, St. Louis, Missouri. Her previous books include *Soul Healing: A Spiritual Orientation in Counseling and Therapy, In the Presence of Grief*, and *Families that Flourish*.

Gary U. Behrman, Ph.D., is Director of the BSW Program, Lindenwood University, St. Charles, Missouri. His clinical and research interests include gerontology, post-trauma recovery, effective responses to crisis, and the functions of religion and spirituality in this process.

J. Maria Bermudez, Ph.D., LMFT, is an Assistant Professor in the Department of Human Development and Family Science at The University of Georgia. Her research focuses on Latino/a family dynamics and feminist and strength-based approaches to Couple and Family Therapy.

Pauline Boss, Ph.D., is a University of Minnesota Emeritus Professor, a practicing psycho- therapist, and author of the books *Ambiguous Loss, Loss, Trauma and Resilience*, and *Loving Someone Who has Dementia*.

Karen Caldwell, PhD, LMFT, Professor, teaches family therapy and counseling to graduate students at Appalachian State University in North Carolina.

Tracy Carr, Ph.D., MSc, BN, RN, is a Professor in the Department of Nursing and Health Sciences, University of New Brunswick Saint John.

Heejung Chun, Ph.D., is an Assistant Professor in Counseling and Educational Psychology at New Mexico State University. Her research interests include adolescent problem behaviors, resilience, academic achievement gap, immigrant paradox, and acculturation.

Marilyn Coleman, Ph.D., is a Curators' Professor of Human Development and Family Studies at the University of Missouri and is Affiliate Faculty with Women's and Gender Studies and a Fellow in the Center for Excellence on Aging and the Center for Family Policy and Research

James E. Deal, Ph.D., is Professor of Human Development and Family Science at North Dakota State University in Fargo. His primary area of interest is personality development in young children.

Laura G. DeHaan, Ph.D., is a Professor of Psychology at Calvin College in Grand Rapids, Michigan. Her primary areas of interest are adolescent alcohol use, family resiliency, and spirituality among adolescents and emerging adults.

Ginger Dickson, Ph.D., is an Assistant Professor at New Mexico State University, Las Cruces, New Mexico. Her research interests include multicultural and diversity issues in counseling, counselor training, public education, and culturally responsive teaching.

Ivelisse Torres Fernandez, Ph.D., is an Assistant Professor in Counseling and Educational Psychology at New Mexico State University. Her research interests include social–emotional learning, resiliency, multiculturalism, and social justice issues in psychology and education.

Rachel E. Foster is a Major in the US Air Force currently stationed at Joint Base Anacostia-Bolling in Washington, DC. Her primary research interests include family violence, attachment as it relates to child maltreatment, and individual and family resilience.

Lawrence Ganong, Ph.D., is Professor of Nursing and Professor and Co-Chair of Human Development and Family Studies at the University of Missouri. His primary research program has focused on postdivorce families, especially stepfamilies.

Abraham P. Greeff, Ph.D., Department of Psychology, University of Stellenbosch, Stellenbosch, South Africa.

J. Camille Hall, Ph.D., LCSW, is an Associate Professor in the College of Social Work at the University of Tennessee, Knoxville. Her research and clinical interests include risk and resilience factors that impact African American individuals, families, and communities.

Timothy S. Hartshorne, Ph.D., is Professor of Psychology at Central Michigan University. He has been researching CHARGE syndrome since 1993, motivated by the birth of his son with CHARGE in 1989. He focuses on understanding the challenging behavior exhibited by many individuals with CHARGE.

Dale R. Hawley, Ph.D., is a Professor in the Human Development and Family Studies Department at the University of Wisconsin-Stout. He is a core faculty member in Stout's Marriage and Family Therapy program.

Leslie D. Hollingsworth, Ph.D., ACSW, LMSW, is an Associate Professor in the University of Michigan School of Social Work, Ann Arbor, Michigan.

An Hooghe, M.A., a Clinical Psychologist, is a Marital and Family Therapist and trainer at Context, Center for Marital and Family Therapy, University Hospital, Leuven, Belgium. Her doctoral research focuses on grief in couples after the loss of a child.

Berquin Human is a Licensed Psychologist and accredited Cognitive Behavior Therapist working at the Priory Hospital in London, England. He specializes in the CBT treatment of anxiety and mood disorders.

Ppudah Ki is a doctoral student in Marriage and Family Therapy at the University of Connecticut, Storrs, Connecticut.

Judith L. Landau, M.B., Ch.B, D.P.M., is President of Linking Human Systems, LLC, and LINC Foundation, Inc., in Boulder, Colorado. She serves as Senior Advisor to New York University's Catastrophe Center, International Trauma Studies Program, and Community Resource Center.

Ariella Lang, R.N., Ph.D., is a Research Scientist at VON Canada, a national not-for-profit charitable home and community care organization. She is also a Chercheure Boursière funded by Fond de la recherche Santé Québec with joint appointments in Nursing at McGill University and Université de Montréal.

Cynthia A. Lietz, Ph.D., LCSW, is an Assistant Professor at Arizona State University's School of Social Work and a Faculty Affiliate with ASU's Family Communication Consortium. Prior to coming to ASU, she worked as a therapist and clinical supervisor with at-risk youth and families.

Jay A. Mancini, Ph.D., is the Haltiwanger Distinguished Professor in the Department of Human Development and Family Science at The University of Georgia, and Director of the Family and Community Resilience Laboratory. His research focuses on the intersections of vulnerabilities and resilience.

Hamilton I. McCubbin, Ph.D., Adjunct Professor, College of Education, Department of Educational Leadership and Counseling Psychology, Washington State University, Pullman, Washington and Professor and graduate faculty, Myron B. Thompson School of Social Work, University of Hawaii at Manoa, Honolulu, Hawaii.

Laurie D. McCubbin, Ph.D., Associate Professor, College of Education, Department of Educational Leadership and Counseling Psychology, Washington State University, Pullman, Washington.

Tasha M. Nacarato is a graduate student in School Psychology at Central Michigan University. She is in her second year of managing the CHARGE Syndrome Research Lab and also works at the Learning Acceleration Clinic where school children are helped to advance with reading and math.

Robert A. Neimeyer, Ph.D., is a Professor of Psychology, University of Memphis, where he also has an active clinical practice. His books include *Grief and Bereavement in Contemporary Society: Bridging Research and Practice*, and he is the Editor of the journal *Death Studies*.

Holly Nelson-Becker, Ph.D., LCSW, a Hartford Faculty Scholar in Geriatric Social Work, is Associate Professor at Loyola University Chicago. She has published extensively in aging and spirituality as well as end-of-life issues related to gerontological social work and resilience.

William C. Nichols, Ed.D., ABPP (Clinical). Fellow, Family Psychology (American Psychological Association). Former university professor and full-time independent practitioner in psychology and marital and family therapy. Author/editor of nine professional books.

Sandra Rigazio-DiGilio, Ph.D., Professor of Marriage and Family Therapy and Senior Scientist/Practitioner at the University of Connecticut, Storrs, Connecticut. Her research focus is the application of parental-acceptance-rejection theory and measures in relational and systemic therapy.

Rockey Robbins, Ph.D., (Cherokee/Choctaw) is an Associate Professor at the University of Oklahoma where he teaches multicultural Counseling and conducts research related primarily to the acculturation stress that American Indians experience.

Sharla Robbins, Ph.D., (Cherokee) is a Licensed Psychologist who works primarily with persons struggling with eating disorders. She is also a researcher who focuses on American Indian families.

Luke T. Russell is a Ph.D. student in the Department of Human Development and Family Studies at the University of Missouri. His primary research interest is in health and family dynamics in postdivorce relationships, remarriage, and stepfamilies.

Alyson Schafer, M.A., is a Psychotherapist and one of Canada's leading parenting experts. She is the "Ask an Expert" Columnist for *Today's Parent Magazine*, and sits on the Health Advisory Board for *Chatelaine Magazine*. Alyson is also a bestselling author of several books.

Peter Schuntermann, M.D., is a Clinical Instructor in the School of Medicine at Harvard University and practices psychiatry at Harvard Children's Hospital. His research interests include mental retardation, systems theory, developmental disabilities, resilience, and theory of mind.

Jonathan P. Schwartz, Ph.D., is Professor and Department Head, Counseling and Educational Psychology at New Mexico State University. His research interests include gender roles, the intersection of prevention and social justice, and bullying and intimate violence prevention.

Karolyn Senter, Ph.D., LPC, is a Mental Health Counselor on staff at the Student Health Services at Washington University in St. Louis, MO.

Ester R. Shapiro, Ph.D., is an Associate Professor, Psychology Department, Research Associate, Mauricio Gaston Institute, and directs the Community Engagement Core of the HORIZON Health Equity Center, University of Massachusetts, Boston.

Brad Stennerson, M.Ed., is in his second year of a Counseling Psychology doctoral program at the University of Oklahoma.

Sandra M. Stith, Ph.D., is a Professor and Director of the Marriage and Family Therapy program at Kansas State University. Her primary research interest is in partner violence and she has conducted research with the USAF Family Advocacy program since 1995.

Kasee K. Stratton is a doctoral candidate at Central Michigan University in School Psychology and a predoctoral intern at the Kennedy Krieger Institute at the John Hopkins School of Medicine. She focuses on families of children with developmental disabilities and complex behaviors.

Tina M. Timm, Ph.D., LMSW, LMFT, is an Associate Professor in the School of Social Work at Michigan State University. She specializes in research and clinical interventions related to issues of sexuality.

Michael Ungar, Ph.D., is the Founder and Co-Director of the Resilience Research Centre and Killam Professor of Social Work at Dalhousie University, Halifax Canada. He leads a team concerned with resilience and its application to practice across cultures and contexts in more than 20 countries.

Froma Walsh, Ph.D., is Co-Founder and Co-Director, Chicago Center for Family Health, and Mose & Sylvia Firestone Professor Emerita at the University of Chicago, School of Social Service Administration and Department of Psychiatry, Pritzker School of Medicine.

Part I

Resilience in General

Roads to Understanding Family Resilience: 1920s to the Twenty-First Century

William C. Nichols

We may be entering the *Age of Resilience*
Ganong and Coleman, 2002.

The evolution of family resilience includes changing meanings and multiple research and clinical interpretations and applications. In this chapter I trace the development of family resilience as a background to the chapters that follow. For clarity and continuity throughout this chapter a somewhat general statement regarding the terms related to resilience is provided.

Types of Resilience

Several types of resilience and associated topics that may be of interest to family therapists and other professionals concerned with family studies and interventions exist. Among them is individual resilience, which includes children's resilience, hardiness, salutogenesis, and other related topics. The notion of resilience arose from a focus on children and how they functioned in relation to their early life experiences. As noted in the literature, over time there was a shift from viewing families as the context for the individual's resilience to regarding families as a unit of resilience itself, and then to concern with resilience at the community level. These were not always clear-cut transitions: Caplan (1982) viewed the family as a support system to the individual family member (actually, this was an individual resilience system). Hawley and DeHaan (1996) conceptualized the role of the family as twofold, which can be regarded as being in both positive and negative terms. On the one hand the role of the family was to be protective, to support and undergird, and to encourage the resilience of the family members, while on the other hand that role included providing risks, that is, raising the vulnerability of family members by the possibility of abuse, exposure to disease, and other factors accompanying life in families.

Family resilience includes crisis and stress research, Reuben Hill's ABCX Model of family stress, family strengths research, and the various models of family resilience developed by Hamilton I. McCubbin and associates: the Double ABCX Model, Family Adjustment and Adaptation Response (FAAR) Model, T-Double ABCX Model, and the more recent Resiliency Model of Family

W.C. Nichols (✉)
755 West Lake Drive, Athens, GA, USA
e-mail: Nicholsw@aol.com

D.S. Becvar (ed.), *Handbook of Family Resilience*,
DOI 10.1007/978-1-4614-3917-2_1, © Springer Science+Business Media New York 2013

Adjustment and Adaptation. The McCubbins note that only in the 1970s did family stress researchers start studying "how family members interact with and support each other, what stress and capabilities family call upon to adjust and adapt, the specific roles and transactions the community plays and enacts in family coping and adaptation…" (McCubbin & McCubbin, 1992, p. 154).

Community resilience, which includes social support systems, is characterized by four themes. According to Landau and Saul (2004), these themes include building community and enhancing social connectedness as a foundation for recovery; using collective storytelling and validation of the trauma experience and response (which is broad enough to cover the many different experiences of the trauma); reestablishing the rhythms and routines of life and engaging in collective healing rituals; and coming through with a collective vision of the future with renewed hope.

Resilience-based policy includes the integration of resilience theory into policy formulation in various fields (adapted from Van Breda, 2001). When the range of contexts and influences, including family, extra-family groups, and associations such as work, school, persons, and larger social systems, is taken into account across the life span, we are dealing with an ecological outlook, as the work of Bronfenbrenner (1979) reminds us. The concept of a resilient ecological approach may be a bit difficult for general acceptance and certainly for formulating practical policy, but it is important, nevertheless.

Interestingly enough, there are some rough parallels in the development of family resilience and its introduction into clinical practice and the focus of treatment that occurred that led to family therapy, that is, individual therapy, concerns with relational entities such as the marital dyad, and family therapy with a focus on the family as a system, but that is material for another occasion. The focus here is primarily on the development of family resilience theory, with mention of some associated or ancillary areas.

What Is Family Resilience?

In response to the above question, there is a large amount of agreement shared by experts in the field, as the following descriptions and definitions of family resilience illustrate.

Indicating that family resilience "refers to coping and adaptational processes in the family as a functional unit," Walsh (2006, p. 8), more specifically defines it "as the capacity to rebound from adversity strengthened and more resourceful…" and further notes that it is "an active process of endurance, self-righting, and growth responses to crises and challenges" (Walsh, p. 4).

Family resilience is characterized by Hawley and DeHaan (1996) as: "…the path a family follows as it adapts and prospers in the face of stress, both in the present and over time. Resilient families respond positively to these conditions in unique ways, depending on the context, developmental level, the interactive combination of risks and protective factors, and the family's shared outlook" (p. 293).

McCubbin and McCubbin (1996) refer to family resilience as: "the positive behavioral patterns and functional competence individuals and the family unit demonstrate under stressful or adverse circumstances, which undermine the family's ability to recover by maintaining its integrity as a unit while insuring, and where necessary, restoring, the well-being of family members and the family unit as a whole" (p. 265).

Pauline Boss emphasizes that resilience: "…is more than 'bouncing back,' which implies regaining the status quo; rather, it means rising above traumatic and ambiguous losses by not letting them immobilize and living well despite them. Resiliency means flexibility, the opposite of brittleness, and movement, the opposite of paralysis" (p. 27).

While several significant ideas and factors are stated or implied in these definitions, two of the more important are stress and strengths, each of which has occupied researchers, practitioners, educators, and policy makers over the past several decades, first primarily in regard to individuals and increasingly with families. Tracing the origins regarding whence family resilience emerged and the paths it traversed within the space limitations of this chapter requires that the picture presented here be an illustrative rather than a comprehensive overview. Readers seeking more detailed descriptions are referred to such sources as Huang (1991), who reviewed family stress research from the 1930s to the 1990s, and Van Breda (2001), who compiled an extensive review of resilience theory literature. For a more comprehensive treatment of key family processes in resilience, applications to practice, and facilitating family resilience through crisis and extended challenges, there is no better source than Walsh (2006).

The Crisis and Stress Path Toward Family Resilience

With roots in the 1920s, during which Burgess (1926) described the family as a unity of interacting personalities in what Hansen and Hill (1960) called "The original statement now held classic in all family interactional frameworks," interest and research on family stress began to emerge. In the 1930s several studies of families in the period of the Great Depression, which began in late 1929 and essentially lasted through the decade, were undertaken. Major developments in the study of family resilience since 1930 have included, a shift from concern only with individual resilience to major attention to family resilience as well; movement away from regarding families as a source of dysfunction that members must overcome or rise above to viewing families as sources of strength and resilience; a move from viewing families solely as a context for the development of individual resilience to treating families as a unit with a focus on relational resilience; and progress in developing understanding of family-level constructs that cannot easily be identified from considering only individual members; and progress in measuring family-level constructs (adapted from Van Breda, 2001).

Early Family Stress Research

The early work that is pertinent here—including that of Angell (1936), Burgess (1926, 1937), Cavan and Ranck (1938), Morgan (1939) and others, such as Komarovsky's (1940) study of the unemployed man and his family—demonstrated how families dealt with the Depression and identified qualities of families that managed to successfully survive that critical experience. Burgess (1937) grouped crises that threaten to disrupt families into three categories: change in status, conflict among members in the conception of their roles, and loss of family members by departure, either by desertion, by divorce, or by death. Angell used the concepts of family integration and family adaptability. Koos (1946, 1948b) studied low income families in New York City and middle-class families in Rochester, New York and their troubles and problems, describing a roller-coaster profile of adjustment to crisis consisting of crisis→disorganization→recovery→reorganization (Koos, 1946; Chart in Hill, 1949, p. 14), and constructing a chart showing the interrelationship of causes in which an event does or does not become a crisis (Koos, 1948a, Chart in Hill, p. 106). Koos and Cavan emphasized family adequacy in dealing with crisis, with Cavan developing a scale for rating adaptation and integration.

The ABCX Family Crisis Model

The major development of the 1940s toward establishment of family resilience research and theory emerged from the work of Hill (1949), which furnished the basic reference point from which most subsequent family resilience theory and research ensued. Hill's focus was not on World War II itself but on families and their efforts to cope with the changes produced by war separation and reunion. Specifically, he studied 135 families (starting with an original goal of 822) with the objectives of sampling how families adjust in general by studying adjustment to the two crises of war separation and reunion; testing the findings of other studies of families in crisis in a new context; recording the variety of modes of adjustment to a set of previously unstudied family crises; and discovering the types of family organization and adjustment processes that render families most vulnerable or invulnerable to separation/reunion crises (Hill). Hill incorporated a number of findings from the depression-related studies of Angell, Cavan, and Komarovsky into his study for testing (Hill, pp. 17–21) and went beyond them in several other areas.

Hill's ABCX model, which evolved from the research, can be stated briefly in the following terms: A (the event/stressor) interacting with B (the family's resources for meeting the crisis) produces X (the crisis). The second and third determinants of the outcome—the family resources and C (the family's definition of the event)—are within the family itself and must be seen in terms of the family's structures and values. The hardships imposed by the event, which go to make up the first determinant, lie outside the family and are an attribute of the event itself (Hill, 1958). Later, slight revisions were made to the model by Hill (1958) and by Hansen and Hill (1960).

Besides laying a theoretical foundation that paved the way for the development of other models, Hill's ABCX Model significantly weakened the idea that stressors cause crisis by introducing several mediating variables into the process; identified two sets of variables (family definitions of the situation and resources) that lie within family control and thus suggested the possibility of improving family resilience; empowered/encouraged families subject to events/stressors over which they have no control (e.g., separation due to war, death, natural disasters) to resist going into crisis; and provided a framework for classifying findings of subsequent research such as studies of family strengths, which are part of the family's resources for meeting crises (the B factor in Hill's model) (adapted from Van Breda, 2001).

Development of Several Models After the ABCX Model

The 1970s and 1980s were marked by the work of Burr (1973, 1973/1982), a series of research papers published by Hamilton I. McCubbin and associates, and contributions by others, that led to modifications and expansions of the ABCX Model. During the same period a strong interest in family strengths description and research was evident, as well as in salutogenesis (a concern with health rather than pathology) and, in psychology, the emergence of positive psychology, all of which had direct or indirect effects on the emergence and development of family resilience emphases. The family strengths and related developments are taken up after following the path of model changes explicitly related to the ABCX model.

Wesley Burr's Contributions

Burr (1973; 1973/1982) provided significant contributions to the development of later research and theory construction by formalizing the work of Hill (1949, 1958), Hill and Hansen (1960), and earlier researchers such as Angell (1936), Komarovsky (1940), and Koos (1946) into a clear model. For example, Angell had brought in the terms family adaptability and family integration. Komarovsky had found in her study of families with unemployed men that differences in the family power structure brought differences in the amount of change when the family is exposed to a crisis, namely, that when the family power structure is based on coercion or fear, it changes more from contact with crisis than when the structure is rooted in legitimate personal or positional influence.

Taking such ideas and research findings into account, Burr set forth 25 propositions and portrayed the relationships among 23 variables, covering findings and theoretical ideas from Angell, Hill and Hansen, Koos, and others. Burr produced an interesting chart or figure (Burr, 1973/1982, p. 24), in which he laid out the place of each of the propositions, relating 14 of them to family vulnerability to stress (ability to keep the stressor from resulting in a crisis), seven to the regenerative power of the family (ability to recover from a crisis), and four related to change, amount of crisis in the family system, and power structure matters. The chart rather clearly depicts how he believes that vulnerability and regenerative power participate in determining both whether a family will undergo a crisis when it meets changes in the system and how adequately it will be able to recuperate from the crisis, clarifying what he saw as a significant distinction between vulnerability and regenerative power (Van Breda, 2001).

Double ABCX Model

From approximately the early 1970s until near the end of the decade, H. I. McCubbin and his various associates published a series of papers based on research that also resulted in identifying the need for alterations and improvements in the ABCX Model (cf., McCubbin, 1979; McCubbin, Dahl, & Hunter, 1976; McCubbin, Dahl, Lester, Benson, & Robertson, 1976; McCubbin & Patterson, 1983a, 1983b, 1983c). Among the findings were the following:

- Longitudinal studies revealed that there are more factors involved in dealing with crises than the ABCX model would indicate.
- Over time, families encounter normative stresses and strains and not simply single stressors.
- Families face the pileup of prior strains, hardships, and co-occurring stressors.
- When families face a crisis situation that requires change, their appraisal processes seem to be more complex than their definition of the situation and its degree of severity; rather, the family's appraisal involves an assessment of the total situation including the demands, resources, and capabilities.
- In crisis times families need and seek resources that are broader (e.g., social support), that change over time, and that often are created (e.g., policies and programs).
- Family crises are not generally catastrophic and typically do not result in a dysfunctional family situation, although they do call for alteration in the family's patterns of functioning.
- Most families seem to transition well and adapt to the crisis situation.
- Families facing crises change their established patterns of functioning and create a different family situation than previously existed.

The new Double ABCX Model set forth in 1983 (McCubbin & Patterson, 1983a) went beyond the Hill ABCX model by stressing the factors—especially coping and social support—that facilitate the family's adaptation to a crisis. That is, the new model also was concerned with what happens to the family after the crisis. The ABCX model dealt with the degree of the crisis, regarding successful families as those that reduced the crisis and minimized its disruptiveness on the family. As noted, the studies by McCubbin and associates found that most families recovered from the crisis and that some came through the stress more resilient and stronger than prior to the crisis. Some underwent a continued piling up of stressors, which resulted in either maladaptation (unhealthy adaptation) or bonadaptation (healthy adaptation), as mediated by the family's coping, by the family's perceptions of the crisis, by the pileup, and by existing or new resources.

A figure in McCubbin and Patterson (1982) portrays this conceptualization rather clearly and along a time line divided into Pre-Crisis, Crisis, and Post-Crisis periods (p. 46). The Pre-Crisis period depicts a (the stressor), b (existing resources), and c (family perception of a), the Crisis period x (the crisis itself), and the Post-Crisis period aA (the pileup of stressors)—which is mediated by coping, by perceptions (cC) of x, aA, and bB, and by existing and new resources (bB)—leading to Bonadaptation or Maladaptation (xX). The "c" factor in the ABCX Model had dealt solely with the family's perception of the "a" factor (the stressor). The total crisis situation is viewed as more extensive in the Double ABCX Model, consisting of "the stressor believed to have caused the crisis, as well as the added stressors and strains, old and new resources, and estimates of what needs to be done to bring the family back into balance" (McCubbin & Patterson, 1983a, pp. 15–16). This new model added five items to the older model, namely, the aA, bB, cC, xX, and coping patterns (McCubbin & McCubbin, 1996).

A major difference between the Hill model and the Double ABCX model was that the original considered the degree of crisis as the outcome; that is, families that minimized the degree of crisis or disruption in the family system were regarded as successful. However, "Reduction of crisis alone is an inadequate index of a family's post-crisis adjustment" according to McCubbin and Patterson (1983a, p. 17). McCubbin used the concepts of family adaptation and balance in describing outcome. Family adaptation was used to define "a continuum of outcomes which reflect family efforts to achieve a balanced 'fit' at the member-to-member and the 'family-to-community' levels" (McCubbin & Patterson, p. 20). Demand-capability balance results when member-to-family fit exists (demands of a member can be met by the family member, or the demands of the family unit can be met by members), and family-to-community fit prevails (demands of the family can be met by the community, or demands of the community can be met by the family). When there is a demand-incapability, the result is family stress and the need to restructure the family system.

In brief, the Double ABCX Model was an improvement given that it dealt with the post-crisis functioning of families instead of solely with their handling of the crisis itself, and by incorporating additional variables. As Van Breda (2001) further notes, the shifting of the outcome focus from crisis to adaptation reflects the evolving of the family resilience orientation of family stress researchers.

Family Adjustment and Adaptation Response (FAAR) Model

Research studies in the mid-1970s resulted in a revision of the Double ABCX Model termed the FAAR Model in 1983 (McCubbin & Patterson, 1983a; Lavee, McCubbin, & Olson, 1987). Viewed as "a natural extension of the Double ABCX Model with an emphasis on describing the processes involved in the family's efforts to balance demands and resources" (McCubbin & McCubbin, 1996, p. 5), the FAAR Model made seven additions to the Double ABCX Model. These included integrating coping into family stress theory and introducing the consolidation phase, adaptive coping strategies, adjustment coping strategies, a resistance phase in the family stress process, a restructuring phase in the family stress model, and the balance concept of family-to-member and family-to-community fit to the adaptation (xX) factor as a critical dimension of family adaptation (McCubbin & Patterson, 1983a; McCubbin & McCubbin, 1996).

Stated briefly, it was found through longitudinal studies that families go through three stages of adaptation, namely, resistance (in the pre-crisis/adjustment period of the Double ABCX), restructuring, and consolidation (appearing in the post-crisis/adaptation period). Restructuring in the FAAR Model is assigned to Level 1 Accommodation, and consolidation is assigned to Level 2 Accommodation (McCubbin & Patterson, 1983a). It works like this: When first exposed to a crisis (stressor), families tend to resist facing it or making adjustments in the family in response to the stressor. This brings on a state of maladjustment that leads to family crisis (Adjustment or Resistance Phase), which, in turn, increases the demand on the family for change, leading to the onset of initial restructuring by the family. Sometimes some family members do not support the changes being made and the demands are not well managed, leading to a family tendency to be disorganized and disjointed (Accommodation Level

1 of the Adaptation Phase/Restructuring Stage). Such disorganization sets the stage for additional changes aimed at securing a level of stability and coherence, as well as member-to-family and family-to-community balance (Accommodation Level 2 of the Adaptation Phase/Consolidation Stage) (McCubbin & Patterson, 1983a).

It is helpful in understanding the FAAR Model to recognize that the term adjustment is not the same as adaptation, but is used to refer to short-term responses by families that are adequate to manage many family life changes, transitions, and demands. McCubbin and Patterson (1983a), note several factors that can influence the adequacy of the adjustment endeavors, as follows:

- The nature of the stressor or transition involves (requires) a change in the family system.
- The nature, number, and duration of demands deplete the family's existing resources.
- The number and persistence of prior unresolved strains also tax the family's resources.
- The family's capabilities and resources are basically inadequate or underdeveloped to meet the demands.
- The family overtly or covertly seizes the opportunity to produce structural changes in the family unit as a way to promote family and member growth by allowing or facilitating a demand-imbalance or family crisis (McCubbin & Patterson, 1983a, p. 26).

McCubbin and Patterson (1983a) also provide a detailed description of the Family Adaptation Phase in terms of Family Accommodation: Level 1: Restructuring, and Level 2: Consolidation. The adaptation, as in the Double ABCX Model, can end up from bonadaptation on one end of the line to maladaptation on the other.

T-Double ABCX Model

The FAAR Model subsequently underwent additional development, which resulted in 1989 with the appearance of the T-Double ABCX Model, sometimes familiarly called the Typology Model of Family Adjustment and Adaptation. This new model was brought forth to stress the importance of family established patterns of functioning (deemed typologies) and family levels of appraisal as defenses against family dysfunction and positive factors in promoting adaptation and recovery from crisis. As was the case earlier, behind the emergence of the Typology model was information gained through the publication of additional research over several years during the 1980s, including the importance of family typologies as established patterns of functioning over the family life cycle; typologies as important established patterns of functioning as a factor in family adaptation; social class, ethnicity, and family typologies; and family problem-solving communication in family adaptation (McCubbin & McCubbin, 1989).

The T-Double ABCX Model made five additions to the FAAR Model: integrating family typologies (the T factor) into the model; integrating a life cycle perspective into family typologies and adaptation; introducing vulnerability (a V factor) due to pileup as a factor in adjustment and adaptation; clarifying the importance of the family life cycle in understanding both vulnerability and family resilience; and defining and including family schema as an additional level of family appraisal (CCC), thus emphasizing the importance of the family's shared views, values, and beliefs (McCubbin & McCubbin, 1996).

This new model, as with the FAAR Model, is divided into two phases—adjustment and adaptation (called pre-crisis and post-crisis in the Double ABCX Model). The Adjustment phase, with some additions, is like the original ABCX Model. The level of family adjustment in response to a stressor or transition into a crisis situation (X) (and into the adaptation phase or exhaustion) is determined by: A (the stressor event or transition and its level of severity)interacting with the V (family's vulnerability determined in part by the concurrent pileup of demands—stressors, transition, and strains—and by the pressures associated with the family life cycle stage), interacting with T (e.g., family typology: regenerative, resilient, rhythmic, balanced), interacting with B (family's resistance resources), interacting with C (family's appraisal of the event), interacting with PSC (family's problem-solving and coping repertoire and capabilities) (McCubbin & McCubbin, 1989, p. 8, slightly adapted).

The Typology Model's Adaptation phase also extends the treatment of this topic in the earlier models. Family adaptation describes the family efforts to get to a new level of balance and fit in response to a family crisis. Responses to stress by different types of families across the family life cycle also were examined during the 1980s (Olson, Lavee, & McCubbin, 1988).

Resiliency Model of Family Adjustment and Adaptation

Continued research from the mid-1980s to the early 1990s was a driving force once again in the emergence of still another model brought out by McCubbin and associates, namely the Resiliency Model of Family Adjustment and Adaptation (McCubbin & McCubbin, 1993, 1996). The Resiliency Model made five additions to the Typology and FAAR models by (1) adding relational perspectives of family adjustment and adaptation; (2) establishing and instituting patterns of family adjustment and adaptation; (3) integrating and including family problem-solving and family coping; (4) specifying four domains of family systems functioning: (a) interpersonal relationships, (b) development, well-being, and spirituality, (c) community relationships and nature, and (d) structure and function; and (5) specifying five levels of appraisal in relationship to patterns of function and problem-solving and coping (PSC): Schema (CCCCC), Coherence (CCCC), Paradigms (CCC), Situational Appraisal (CC), and Stressor Appraisal (C) (McCubbin & McCubbin).

The Adjustment and Adaptation Phases and the associated processes and factors have been depicted in a figure adapted from the work of the McCubbins by Van Breda (2001, p. 111). Several significant interacting components that influence the family's adjustment include: The Stressor (A) and its Severity (formed and influenced by the pileup of family, stresses, strains, and transitions existing at the time of the Stressor), which interact with the Family's Vulnerability (V), which interacts with the Established Patterns of Functioning (T) (i.e., the family's typology), which interact with the family's Appraisal (C) of the Stressor (the family's shared definition of the problem–i.e., as being a minor, a setback, a catastrophe), which interacts with the family's PSC strategies (adapted from McCubbin & McCubbin, 1996).

Families are viewed as striving to achieve and maintain harmony and balance, especially during times of change. Change brings imbalance, and on some occasions disharmony. Some families or family members may create imbalance in order to secure change. The demands placed on a family by a stressor also have the potential for providing alterations in the family system. Some stressors are normative, such as those generally experienced by families in the family life cycle. Nonnormative stressors (e.g., natural disasters, loss of a family member) tend to create more stress for families than normative stressors. The severity of a stressor depends on the extent to which it threatens the stability of the family unit, disrupts its functioning, or places significant demands on and tends to deplete the family's resources and capabilities (McCubbin & McCubbin, 1996).

Vulnerability of the family (the interpersonal and organization of the system) refers to how vulnerable a given family is to a particular stressor, and depends on the pileup of demands on the family (or within the family) and the normative problems associated with the particular stage of the life cycle of the family. Some examples of family development and issues normally faced at particular stages and appropriate interventions for dealing with problematic and normative transitional situations at those stages and with various conditions in the family life cycle are found in Nichols, Pace-Nichols, Becvar, and Napier (2000).

Family typology, first introduced in the McCubbin and associates research on the T-Double ABCX Model, refers to a family's habitual, predictable patterns of behavior. Established over time, the family's typology, once identified, can be used to predict the family's response to stress (McCubbin & McCubbin, 1989). Eventually, four broad categories of families were identified: Regenerative, Versatile, Rhythmic, and Traditionalist, under each of which were clustered four types of families. Each of the four types clustered under a general heading was defined along two dimensions dichotomized into high and low. Regenerative families were defined according to high or low Family Coherence and high or low Family Hardiness, resulting in Vulnerable Families, Secure Families, Durable Families, and Regenerative Families. Rhythmic Families, defined in terms of high or low Family Time Routines and high or low Valuing of Family Time and Routines, were comprised of Unpatterned Families, Intentional Families, Structuralized Families, and Rhythmic Families. Versatile Families were composed of families identified as high to low in Family Flexibility and high to low Bonding. These included Fragile Families, Bonded Families, Pliant Families, and Versatile Families. The fourth group was deemed Traditionalist Families, which were considered high to low on Family Celebrations and high to low on Family Traditions. The families under this general heading were Situational Families, Traditionalistic Families, Celebratory Families, and Ritualistic Families (McCubbin & McCubbin, 1996; see also Van Breda, 2001, p. 116, for a figure depicting all of these types).

Detailed discussion of the foregoing information regarding family typologies (T), family resistance resources (B), family appraisal of the stressor (C), family PSC, family bonadjustment, maladjustment, and crises (X), family adaptation (XX), pileup (AA) of demands on families, family types and newly instituted patterns of functioning (T and TT), family resources (BB), social support (BBB), family appraisal processes (C to CCCCC), family PSC, and related matters is found in several McCubbin and associates sources (e.g., McCubbin & McCubbin, 1989, 1993, 1996).

The Family Strengths Path

There has been a limited but intriguing search for family strengths over the past 5 decades that has complemented the interest in family resilience. Based on his research, Herbert Otto (1962a, 1962b, 1963) suggested 12 criteria for the assessment of family strengths, including the ability to provide for the physical, emotional, and spiritual needs of a family; be sensitive to the needs of family members; communicate effectively; provide support, security, and encouragement; initiate and maintain growth-producing relationships and experiences within and without the family; grow with and through children; engage in self-help and accept help when appropriate; perform family roles flexibly; use a crisis or seemingly injurious experience as a means of growth; create and maintain constructive and responsible community relationships in the neighborhood, school, town, and local and state governments; have mutual respect for the individuality of family members; and have a concern for family unity, loyalty, and interfamily family cooperation.

In the 1970s, Nick Stinnett and his associates at the University of Nebraska, among others, picked up the task of describing family strengths and dealing with how strong families can be empowered, with some continuing this work into the twenty-first century. See, for example, Stinnett and Sauer (1977), Stinnett, Chesser, and DeFrain (1979), Stinnett, Knorrr, DeFrain, and Rowe (1981), Curran (1981), Stinnett and DeFrain (1985), Schumm (1985), Dunst, Trivette, and Deal (1988), and Olson, McCubbin, Barnes, Larsen, Muxen, and Wilson (1988), whose research identified patterns of marital and family strength and family coping across the family life cycle. John DeFrain extended the family strengths emphasis across the globe (DeFrain, DeFrain, & Lepard, 1994; DeFrain, 1999), and into the twenty-first century with his consultation work in Australia (Geggie, DeFrain, Hitchcock, & Silberberg, 2000).

Besides Otto in the 1960s and Stinnett in the 1970s and 1980s, several others have offered definitions and some also have provided lists of family strengths, including Beavers (1976, 1977; Beavers & Hampson, 1990), Hanson (1986), Olson, Lavee, and McCubbin (1988), Trivette, Dunst, Deal, Hamer, and Propst (1990). Still others, such as Minuchin (1974) and Barnhill (1979), have added to the litera-ture and understanding of family strengths. Although the healthy family literature has been criticized as being largely descriptive and theory free (Ponzetti & Long, 1989), David Olson and associates (Olson, Larsen, & McCubbin, 1982) produced a Family Strengths Scale that is used to measure some components that relate to family strengths. The McMaster Model, developed in Canada, offers a research-based view of healthy family functioning (Epstein, Bishop, Ryan, Miller, & Keitner, 1993). Some elements from the broader area of family strengths have found their way into research models. For example, hardiness (Kobasa, 1979, 1982; Bigbee, 1992) is a part of both the individual resilience literature and family strengths emphases.

The Salutogenic, Healthy Perspective and Other Paths

Simultaneously with the family strengths approach, there were other emphases occurring that focused on health and positive elements with regard to both individual and family development and function-ing. Again, the reporting here is illustrative rather than exhaustive. Antonovsky (1979, 1987a, 1987b) introduced the concept of salutogenesis for understanding the development of health, a positive orien-tation instead of the pathogenic outlook that had largely prevailed previously, and he also contributed the perspective of a sense of coherence, which played a significant role in the continuing development of family resilience theory and research (Antonovsky 1993, 1998). At the same time, the emphasis in family therapy and related research as well as in the development of models pertaining to family resil-ience was moving away from viewing the family and parents as sources of problems toward their posi-tive contributions to resiliency. In addition, Martin Seligman, the "father of positive psychology," was studying and writing about learned helplessness and learned optimism (Seligman, 1975, 1990) and challenging psychologists to shift from a deficit-based to a strengths-based emphasis.

Consistent with the salutogenic and other related emphases has been the emergence of therapeutic approaches reflecting assumptions of family competence and resilience. These include Steve deS-hazer's solution focused therapy (de Shazer, 1985), Michael White's narrative therapy (White & Epston, 1989), and functional family therapy (Sexton & Alexander, 2003), an evidence-based thera-peutic model developed for work with at-risk adolescents and their families.

Other important but different paths contributing to the maturing of family resilience theory were the stress and trauma route undertaken by Charles Figley and others (Figley & McCubbin, 1983; McCubbin & Figley, 1983; Figley, 1989a, 1989b), as well as the work of David H. Olson. Olson, who had a long-term commitment to bridging the gap between research, theory, and practice, developed the familiar Circumplex Model of Marital and Family Systems (Olson, Russell, & Sprenkle, 1989) and continued to research and advocate its utility for the assessment and treatment of families (Olson, 1996). The circum-plex model integrates family cohesion, flexibility, and communication dimensions, which are important in several family therapy approaches. Carter and McGoldrick's (1980, 2005) adaptation of the family life cycle approach also has been highly influential among family therapists, bringing a combination of indi-vidual, family, and community emphases to bear.

Contemporary Resilience-Related Therapeutic Models

Several major therapeutic approaches reflecting the assumptions of family competence and resilience rather than emphasizing family pathology have emerged in the last quarter century. As mentioned above, these include solution-focused therapy, narrative therapy, and functional family therapy. In addition, two other more specifically focused examples represent contemporary approaches and recommended sources of introduction to the current state of family resilience-based therapy. I refer to the large body of work of Pauline Boss on stress and ambiguous loss—one of the major traumas and stressors commonly facing families, and the similarly extensive work of Froma Walsh on normal families, stress, and family resilience. Rather than attempting to describe and illustrate the details of each body of work and approach in this limited space, it seems more appropriate to cite some of the major and representative examples of Boss's and Walsh's writings and urge readers to explore or to examine them further on their own.

Among Boss's major and representative works are those on ambiguous loss and learning to live with unresolved grief (1999); family stress management (2002); therapeutic work with ambiguous loss (2006); and some edited readings (Boss, Doherty, LaRossa, Schumm, & Steinmetz, 1993; Boss & Mulligan, 2003).[1] Good introductions to Walsh's work on normal family processes are found in Walsh (1993); family resilience theory in Walsh (1996); practice and clinical applications in Walsh (1999, 2002a, 2002b) and Walsh and McGoldrick (1991); and her comprehensive treatment of family resilience in Walsh (2006).[2]

With the development of the resilience-related approaches mentioned here, family theory, family therapy theory, and family therapy practice have traveled a significant distance in the last half-century or so. Perhaps the greatest cumulative contribution has been emphasis on the importance of taking a balanced view of family resilience and strengths and the power of stress and trauma in therapy. When entering into a relationship with a family system, it seems well established to me that neither an extreme focus on pathology and an assumption of client inability or client helplessness nor an unrealistic "Pollyanna" view that assumes that the client system is so strong and resilient that it can be quickly and easily dealt with effectively with a dazzling array of interventions is appropriate. Instead, taking both sides into as realistic consideration as possible seems to be warranted by what has been learned and demonstrated to date.

Conclusion

In conclusion, this chapter has given a background, illustrated with examples, regarding how from a basic, rather vague conceptual beginning back in the 1920s, the conceptualization of family resilience has moved to its current position, which includes increasing specialization and expansion into more areas of life. As the complexity of life continues to expand and deepen and as our research and clinical practices are applied to more specific topics and areas and keep providing greater insights and deeper understandings, newer concepts and constructs are likely to continue to emerge. As is illustrated in the chapters that follow, the concept of family resilience will continue to be studied and applied in relation to individuals, families, society, and our planet. Welcome to the ever-expanding world of family resilience.

References

Angell, R. S. (1936). *The family encounters the depression*. New York: Charles Scribner's Sons.
Antonovsky, A. (1979). *Health, stress and coping*. San Francisco: Jossey-Bass.
Antonovsky, A. (1987a). *Unraveling the mystery of health: How people manage stress and stay well*. San Francisco: Jossey-Bass.

[1] This topic is addressed in depth in Chap. 17
[2] This topic is addressed in depth in Chap. 5

Antonovsky, A. (1987b). The salutogenic perspective: Toward a new view of health and illness. *Advances, 4,* 47–55.

Antonovsky, A. (1993). The structure and properties of the sense of coherence scale. *Social Science Medicine, 36,* 725–733.

Antonovsky, A. (1998). The sense of coherence: An historical and future perspective. In H. I. McCubbin, E. A. Thompson, A. I. Thompson, & E. J. Froner (Eds.), *Stress, coping, and health in families: Sense of coherence and resiliency* (pp. 3–20). Thousand Oaks, CA: Sage.

Barnhill, L. R. (1979). Healthy family systems. *Family Coordinator, 28,* 94–100.

Beavers, W. R. (1976). A theoretical basis for family evaluation. In J. M. Lewis, W. R. Beavers, J. T. Gossett, & V. A. Phillips (Eds.), *No single thread: Psychological health in family systems* (pp. 46–84). New York: Brunner/Mazel.

Beavers, W. R. (1977). *Psychotherapy and growth: A family systems perspective.* New York: Brunner/Mazel.

Beavers, W. R., & Hampson, R. B. (1990). *Successful families: Assessment and intervention.* New York: Norton.

Bigbee, J. L. (1992). Family stress, hardiness, and illness: A pilot study. *Family Relations, 41,* 212–217.

Boss, P. (1999). *Ambiguous loss: Learning to live with unresolved grief.* Cambridge, MA: Harvard University Press.

Boss, P. (2002). *Family stress management: A contextual approach.* Thousand Oaks, CA: Sage.

Boss, P. (2006). *Loss, trauma, and resilience: Therapeutic work with ambiguous loss.* New York: Norton.

Boss, P., Doherty, W. J., LaRossa, R., Schumm, W. R., & Steinmetz, S. K. (1993). *Sourcebook of family theories and methods: A contextual approach.* Thousand Oaks, CA: Sage.

Boss, P., & Mulligan, C. (Eds.). (2003). *Family stress: Classic and contemporary reading.* Thousand Oaks, CA: Sage.

Bronfenbrenner, U. (1979). *The ecology of human development.* Cambridge, MA: Harvard University Press.

Burgess, E. W. (1926). The family as a unity of interacting personalities. *The Family, 7,* 3–9.

Burgess, E. W. (1937). The family and sociological research. *Social Forces, 26,* 1–6.

Burr, W. R. (1973). *Theory construction and the sociology of the family.* New York: Wiley.

Burr, W. R. (1982). Families under stress. In H. I. McCubbin, A. E. Caugle, & J. M. Patterson (Eds.), Family stress, coping, and social support (pp. 5–25). Springfield, IL: Charles C Thomas (Original work published 1973).

Caplan, G. (1982). The family as a support system. In H. I. McCubbbin, A. E. Cauble, & J. M. Patterson (Eds.), *Family stress, coping, and social support* (pp. 200–220). Springfield, IL: Charles C Thomas.

Carter, E. A., & McGoldrick, M. (Eds.). (1980). *The family life cycle: A framework for family therapy.* New York: Gardner Press.

Carter, B., & McGoldrick, M. (Eds.). (2005). *Expanding the family life cycle: Individual, family, community.* Boston: Allyn & Bacon.

Cavan, R., & Ranck, K. (1938). *The family and the depression.* Chicago: University of Chicago Press.

Curran, D. (1981). *Traits of a healthy family.* Minneapolis, MN: Winston.

de Shazer, S. (1985). *Keys to solution in brief therapy.* New York: Norton.

DeFrain, J. (1999). Strong families around the world. *Family Matters, 53*(Winter), 8–13.

DeFrain, J., DeFrain, N., & Lepard, J. (1994). Family strengths and challenges in the South Pacific: An exploratory study. *International Journal of the Sociology of the Family, 24*(2), 25–47.

Dunst, C. A., Trivette, C., & Deal, A. (1988). *Enabling and empowering families.* Brookline, MA: Brookline Books.

Epstein, N. B., Bishop, D., Ryan, C., Miller, I., & Keitner, G. (1993). The McMaster model: View of healthy family functioning. In F. Walsh (Ed.), *Normal family processes* (2nd ed., pp. 138–160). New York: Guilford.

Figley, C. R. (1989a). *Helping traumatized families.* San Francisco: Jossey-Bass.

Figley, C. R. (Ed.). (1989b). *Treating stress in families.* New York: Brunner/Mazel.

Figley, C. R., & McCubbin, H. (Eds.). (1983). *Stress and the family: Coping with catastrophe* (Vol. 2). New York: Brunner/Mazel.

Ganong, L. H., & Coleman, M. (2002). Family resilience in multiple contexts. *Journal of Marriage and Family, 64,* 346–348.

Geggie, J., DeFrain, J., Hitchcock, S., & Silberberg, S. *Family strengths research project: Final report to the Australian Commonwealth Government Ministry of Family and Community Services, Canberry ACT.* (2000). Callaghan: University of Newcastle, Family Action Centre.

Hansen, D. A., & Hill, R. (1960). Families under stress. In H. Christensen (Ed.), *Handbook of marriage and the family* (pp. 782–810). Chicago: Rand McNally.

Hanson, S. M. H. (1986). Healthy single parent families. *Family Relations, 35,* 125–132.

Hawley, D. R., & DeHaan, L. (1996). Toward a definition of family resilience: Integrating life-span and family perspectives. *Family Process, 35,* 283–298.

Hill, R. (1949). *Families under stress: Adjustment to the crises of war separation and reunion.* New York: Harper & Brothers.

Hill, R. (1958). Generic features of families under stress. *Social Casework, 49,* 139–150.

Hill, R., & Hansen, D. A. (1960). The identification of conceptual frameworks utilized in family study. *Marriage and Family Living, 22,* 299–311.

Huang, I. C. (1991). Family stress and coping. In S. J. Bahr (Ed.), *Family research: A sixty-year review 1930–1990* (Vol. 1, pp. 289–334). New York: Lexington Press.

Kobasa, S. C. (1979). Stressful life events, personality, and health: An inquiry into hardiness. *Journal of Personality and Social Psychology, 37*, 1–11.

Kobasa, S. C. (1982). The hardy personality: Toward a social psychology of stress and health. In G. S. Sanders & J. Suls (Eds.), *Social psychology of health and illness* (pp. 3–32). Hillsdale, NJ: Lawrence Erlbaum Associates.

Komarovsky, M. (1940). *The unemployed man and his family*. New York: Dryden Press.

Koos, El. (1946). *Families in trouble*. New York: King's Crown.

Koos, E. L. (1948a). Families in crisis. In E. M. Duvall & R. Hill (Eds.), *The dynamics of family interaction*. Washington, DC: National Conference on Family Life (Mimeographed report.).

Koos, E. L. (1948b). *The middle-class family and its problems*. New York: Columbia University Press.

Landau, J., & Saul, J. (2004). Family and community resilience in response to major disaster. In F. Walsh & M. McGoldrick (Eds.), *Living beyond loss: Death in the Family* (2nd ed., pp. 285–309). New York, NY: Norton.

Lavee, Y., McCubbin, H. I., & Olson, D. H. (1987). The effect of stressful life events and transitions on family functioning and well-being. *Journal of Marriage and the Family, 49*, 857–873.

McCubbin, H. I. (1979). Incorporating coping behavior in family stress theory. *Journal of Marriage and the Family, 41*, 237–244.

McCubbin, H. I., Dahl, B. B., & Hunter, E. J. (1976). Research on the military family: A review. In H. I. McCubbin, B. B. Dahl, & E. J. Hunter (Eds.), *Families in the military system* (pp. 291–319). Beverly Hills, CA: Sage.

McCubbin, H. I., Dahl, B. B., Lester, G. R., Benson, D., & Robertson, M. L. (1976). Coping repertoires of families adapting to prolonged war-induced separations. *Journal of Marriage and the Family, 38*, 461–471.

McCubbin, H. I., & Figley, C. R. (Eds.). (1983). *Stress and the family: Coping with normative transitions* (Vol. I). New York: Brunner/Mazel.

McCubbin, M. A., & McCubbin, H. I. (1989). Theoretical orientations to family stress and coping. In C. R. Figley (Ed.), *Treating stress in families* (pp. 3–43). New York: Brunner/Mazel.

McCubbin, H. I., & McCubbin, M. A. (1992). Research utilization in social work practice of family treatment. In A. J. Grasso & I. Epstein (Eds.), *Research utilization in the social sciences: Innovations for practice and administration* (pp. 149–192). New York: Haworth Press.

McCubbin, M. A., & McCubbin, H. I. (1993). Families coping with illness: The resiliency model of family stress, adjustment and adaptation. In C. B. Danielson, B. Hamel-Bissell, & P. Winsted-Fry (Eds.), *Families, health and illness: Perspectives on coping and intervention* (pp. 21–63). St. Louis, MO: Mosby.

McCubbin, M. A., & McCubbin, H. I. (1996). Resiliency in families: A conceptual model of family adjustment in response to stress and crises. In H. I. McCubbin, A. I. Thompson, & M. A. McCubbin (Eds.), *Family assessment: Resiliency, coping and adaptation—inventories for research and practice* (pp. 1–64). Madison, WI: University of Wisconsin.

McCubbin, H. I., & Patterson, J. M. (1982). Family adaptation to crisis. In H. I. McCubbin, A. E. Cauble, & J. M. Patterson (Eds.), *Family stress, coping and social support* (pp. 26–47). Springfield, IL: Charles C. Thomas.

McCubbin, H. I., & Patterson, J. M. (1983a). The family stress process: The double ABCX model of adjustment and adaptation. *Marriage and Family Review, 6*(1/2), 7–37.

McCubbin, H. I., & Patterson, J. M. (1983b). The family stress process: The double ABCX model of adjustment and adaptation. In H. I. McCubbin, M. B. Sussman, & J. M. Patterson (Eds.), *Social stress and the family: Advances and developments in family stress theory and research* (pp. 7–37). New York: The Haworth Press.

McCubbin, H. I., & Patterson, J. M. (1983c). Family transitions: Adaptation to stress. In H. I. McCubbin & C. R. Figley (Eds.), *Stress and the family, Vol. 1: Coping with normal transitions* (pp. 5–25). New York: Brunner/Mazel.

Minuchin, S. (1974). *Families and family therapy*. Cambridge, MA: Harvard University Press.

Morgan, W. L. (1939). *The family meets the depression*. Minneapolis: University of Minnesota Press.

Nichols, W. C., Pace-Nichols, M. A., Becvar, D. S., & Napier, A. Y. (Eds.). (2000). *Handbook of family development and intervention*. New York: Wiley.

Olson, D. H. (1996). Clinical assessment and treatment interventions using the family Circumplex model. In F. W. Kaslow (Ed.), *Handbook of relational diagnosis and dysfunctional family patterns* (pp. 59–80). New York: Wiley.

Olson, D. H., Larsen, A. S., & McCubbin, H. I. (1982). Family strengths. In D. H. Olson, H. I. McCubbin, H. Barnes, A. Larsen, M. Maxen, & M. Wilson (Eds.), *Family inventories: Inventories used in a national survey of families across the life cycle* (pp. 121–132). St. Paul: University of Minnesota Press.

Olson, D. H., Lavee, Y., & McCubbin, H. I. (1988). Types of families and family response to stress across the family life cycle. In J. Aldous & D. M. Klein (Eds.), *Social stress and family development* (pp. 16–43). New York: Guilford.

Olson, D. H., Russell, C. S., & Sprenkle, D. H. (Eds.). (1989). *Circumplex model: Systemic assessment and treatment of families*. New York: Haworth Press.

Otto, H. A. (1962a). What is a strong family? *Marriage and Family Living, 24*, 77–81.

Otto, H. A. (1962b). The personal and family resource development programme: A preliminary report. *International Journal of Social Psychiatry, 8*, 185–195.

Otto, H. A. (1963). Criteria for assessing family strength. *Family Process, 2*, 329–338.

Ponzetti, J. J., & Long, E. (1989). Healthy family functioning: A review and critique. *Family Therapy, 16*(1), 43–50.

Schumm, W. R. (1985). Beyond relationships characteristics of strong families: Constructing a model of family strengths. *Family Perspective, 19*, 1–9.

Seligman, M. E. P. (1975). *Helplessness: On depression, development, and death.* San Francisco: W, H, Freeman.

Seligman, M. E. P. (1990). *Learned optimism.* New York: Random House.

Sexton, T. L., & Alexander, J. F. (2003). Functional family therapy: A mature clinical model for working with at-risk adolescents and their families. In T. L. Sexton, G. R. Weeks, & M. S. Robbins (Eds.), *Handbook of family therapy* (pp. 323–363). New York: Brunner/Routledge.

Stinnett, N., Chesser, B., & DeFrain, J. (Eds.). (1979). *Building family strengths: Blueprints for action.* Lincoln, NE: University of Nebraska Press.

Stinnett, N., & DeFrain, J. (1985). *Secrets of strong families.* Boston: Little, Brown, & Co.

Stinnett, N., Knorrr, B., DeFrain, J., & Rowe, G. (1981). How strong families cope with crises. *Family Perspectives, 15*, 159–166.

Stinnett, N., & Sauer, K. H. (1977). Relationship characteristics of strong families. *Family Perspective, 11*, 3–11.

Trivette, C. M., Dunst, C. J., Deal, A. G., Hamer, W., & Propst, S. (1990). Assessing family strengths and family functioning style. *Topics in Early Childhood Specialist Education, 10*(1), 16–35.

Van Breda, A. D. (2001). *Resilience review: A literature review.* Pretoria, South Africa: South African Mental Health Service. Retrieved August 9, 2010, from http://www.vanbreda.org/adrian/resilience.htm.

Walsh, F. (1993). Conceptualizations of normal family processes. In F. Walsh (Ed.), *Normal family processes* (Vol. 2, pp. 3–69). New York: Guilford.

Walsh, F. (1996). The concept of family resilience: Crisis and challenge. *Family Process, 35*, 261–281.

Walsh, F. (1999). *Spiritual resources in family therapy.* New York: Guildford.

Walsh, F. (2002a). A family resilience framework: Innovative practice applications. *Family Relations, 51*(2), 130–137.

Walsh, F. (2002b). Bouncing forward: Resilience in the aftermath of September 11, 2001. *Family Process, 41*, 34–36.

Walsh, F. (2006). *Strengthening family resilience* (2nd ed.). New York: Guilford.

Walsh, F., & McGoldrick, M. (Eds.). (1991). *Living beyond loss: Death in the family.* New York: Norton.

White, M., & Epston, D. (1989). *Narrative means to therapeutic ends.* New York: Norton.

Operationalizing Family Resilience as Process: Proposed Methodological Strategies

Laura G. DeHaan, Dale R. Hawley, and James E. Deal

Introduction

The notion that some families are able to function well, and even thrive, in the face of considerable stress has been the subject of considerable theoretical discussion as well as empirical study (Baldwin, Baldwin, & Cole, 1990; McCubbin, 1995; Walsh, 2006). Although the construct of family resilience holds much promise, there has not been universal agreement on how to conceptualize or assess this intriguing area of study. Previously, we explored conceptual and definitional issues relating to the notion of family resilience, paying particular attention to the idea that family resilience represents adaptive paths that a family exhibits both in the present and over time (Hawley & DeHaan, 1996). Such a process-focused approach necessitates a methodological framework to match these conceptual ideas. In this chapter we examine research design and analysis strategies, focusing on quantitative methods for measuring pathways of family resilience. We then examine the efficacy of our proposed method, with a sample test case of parents coping with the normative stressor of the birth of their first child. We believe that this proposed method, identifying differing trajectories of resilience, may play an important role in discovering factors instrumental in shaping adaptive pathways for families and may assist clinicians in both their research and practice. Our method is argued to align more closely with how family resilience is used clinically, that is, as a process, rather than as a trait.

Adapted and updated from De Haan, L. G., Hawley, D. R., & Deal J. E. (2002). Operationalizing family resilience: A methodological strategy. *The American Journal of Family Therapy, 30,* 275–291.

L.G. DeHaan (✉)
Department of Psychology, Calvin College, Grand Rapids, MI, USA
e-mail: ldehaan@calvin.edu

D.R. Hawley
Department of Human Development and Family Studies,
University of Wisconsin-Stout, Menomonie, WI, USA

J.E. Deal
Department of Human Development and Family Science,
North Dakota State University, Fargo, ND, USA

D.S. Becvar (ed.), *Handbook of Family Resilience,*
DOI 10.1007/978-1-4614-3917-2_2, © Springer Science+Business Media New York 2013

Literature Review

Family Resilience as Process

Cowan, Cowan, and Schulz (1996), in a discussion of risk research in developmental psychopathology, asserted that "psychopathology is not a static category but an ever-evolving set of processes that lead to pathways in and out of adaptation" (p. 9). They suggested that much of the research in this area has been causal in nature, seeking to determine the roots of resilience in single sample and control group studies that have relied on concurrent or retrospective designs. Similarly, Walsh (1996, 2003) indicated that resilience requires a developmental perspective concerned with how families deal with stress over time. She has contended that the pathway for each family is unique, negating the possibility of discovering a "blueprint for any singular model of 'the resilient family'" (1996, p. 269). She later argued (2007) that practitioners must maintain this focus on the pathways of recovery and family resilience, as the search for a "quick fix" may inhibit long-term recovery (p. 217). Family resilience also has been argued to "emerge" from previous stressors with an equal or even higher level of functioning (Patterson, 2002), also implying a long-term process.

The idea that families follow pathways in response to stress is not novel. The roller coaster model, first proposed by Koos (1946) and later refined by Hill (1949, 1958), provided an early theoretical framework for tracing family response to a crisis. Precipitated by a stressor event, this model suggested several stages that families often encounter: (a) a period of disorganization, which may be marked by increased conflicts, a search for effective ways of coping, and a general atmosphere of confusion, anger, and resentment; (b) a period of recovery during which family members discover new means of adjusting to the crisis; and (c) a period of reorganization wherein a family reconstructs itself at, above, or below its precrisis level of functioning. It is also possible that a family system will not recover from its period of disorganization, leading it to disintegrate. While the length of time needed to progress through this process may vary depending on what Koos and Hill have referred to as the angle of recovery, this model posited that most families pass through a similar series of events in the aftermath of a crisis. Burr and Klein (1994) tested this model, asking family members who had experienced a significant stressor to map retrospectively their perceptions of family functioning following a stressor relative to their perceptions of normal family functioning prior to the onset of the stressor. They discovered a variety of patterns that could be grouped into five basic categories: roller coaster, increased functioning, decreased functioning, mixed changes, and no change.

The roller coaster model offered a good start in identifying pathways of resilience. Based on our definition, resilient families are those who return to or surpass their precrisis levels of functioning in the reorganizational phase of the model. This model suggested that families progress through a series of stages. We concur with this notion, but also recognize that not all families will progress through the same stages or follow a given trajectory. Some, for example, may show an upward trend following the stressor, or as described by Walsh (2003), a process of "bouncing forward" (p. 410). Others, however, may vacillate between disorganization and recovery for a considerable length of time before reorganizing. An important research goal is to determine whether there are common paths that families may traverse following the onset of a stressor and to identify antecedents that help predict more adaptive paths.

Drawing from literatures such as those focused on family strengths (Silliman, 1994), and family stress (McCubbin & McCubbin, 1988, 1993), as well as research focusing on children within the framework of developmental psychopathology (Masten, 2001; Rutter, 1990), we proposed a definition of resilience that is offered again here:

> Family resilience describes the path a family follows as it adapts and prospers in the face of stress, both in the present and over time. Resilient families positively respond to these conditions in unique ways, depending on the context, developmental level, the interactive combination of risk and protective factors, and the family's shared outlook (Hawley & DeHaan, 1996, p. 293).

This definition focuses on several key elements. First, resilience should be considered not as a static construct or label applied to some families and not others, but rather as unique paths that families may follow in response to specific stressors. Second, it is important to consider resilience both in the present and the long term, as many factors that are initially protective or helpful to families may place a family at risk at a later time. Third, this definition implies that what resilience will actually look like and how it will be assessed will differ according to the particular stressor. For example, positive adaptation to loss of income and job-related stress during a farming crisis might include maintaining supportive parenting skills with children (Simons, Whitbeck, & Wu, 1994), while parental functioning was found to be less important than a high level of differentiation of self by mothers among children in low income urban environments (Skowron, 2005). Finally, this definition acknowledges the importance of risk and protective factors that are unique to each family. Individual and contextual factors will play a major role in how stressors are responded to and how pathways are developed.

Few studies have attempted to examine the process-oriented function of family resilience. One study of family resilience in response to child separation and reunification due to maltreatment (Lietz & Strength, 2011) used a narrative and qualitative approach in order to uncover processes of resilience over time. Other examples include short-term longitudinal studies examining factors leading to couple resilience in the face of economic pressure (Conger, Rueter, & Elder, 1999) and the effect of various protective factors as predictors of paternal engagement over time (Fagan, Palkovitz, Roy, & Farrie, 2009).

Family Resilience as a Trait

Much of family resilience research has concentrated on identifying a set of risk or protective factors related to family resilience. This process has borrowed from research on individual childhood responses to stress. Much research on child resilience has sought to identify traits associated with higher child adjustment. For example, Neighbors, Forehand, and McVicar (1993) found that mothers of adolescents with high cognitive competence (labeled resilient by those authors) reported significantly better relationships with their children than mothers of adolescents in the low cognitive competence group (labeled nonresilient). Adolescents with positive views about parental divorce and higher levels of family hardiness and communication were considered resilient (Shin, Choi, Kim, & Kim, 2010). Wyman et al. (1992) identified children as resilient if they were reported to have more stable family environments, more nurturant relationships with their parents, and more age appropriate and consistent family discipline. Among older adults, "trait resilience" weakened relationships between positive and negative emotions during times of stress (Ong, Bergeman, Bisconti, & Wallace, 2006, p. 38).

Studies that have operationalized *family resiliency* as a trait are also plentiful. Examples include a study of Hawaiian families with preschool children (McCubbin, Thompson, Thompson, Elver, & McCubbin, 1994), which identified family problem-solving communication and family hardiness to be associated with higher levels of family functioning. McCubbin (1995) also examined African American military personnel and their spouses to determine factors in their adjustment to overseas assignments. The family's fit into the military lifestyle, whether or not the spouse was employed, and the spouse's assessment of family time together emerged as important factors associated with adaptation. In another study, families with internationally adopted children were identified as more resilient if they exhibited higher levels of communication and problem-solving, maintaining a positive outlook, and spirituality (Buchanan, 2009). Similar traits (positive worldview, mobilizing resources, and family cohesion) were associated with higher levels of family resilience in families of children with autism (Bayat, 2007). Among single parent families, Greeff and Ritman (2005) identified factors such as perseverance, emotional expression, and self-confidence as individual characteristics of resilience.

Current Issues: Family Resilience as a Process

Although the previously mentioned studies have yielded results of much practical and theoretical import, they have been cross-sectional in nature, and have defined resilience as an outcome or a set of static traits whose presence or absence will define family functioning. These studies often attempt to measure family resilience at a given point in time through standardized instruments that assess characteristics associated with resilience or to create instruments that measure resilience as a static trait. This approach is at odds with both clinical and theoretical considerations that view family resilience as a process that changes over time and can follow multiple pathways.

Based on our desire to examine resilience as a process, the goal was not to develop a resilience scale assessing responses to every kind of stressor applicable to all families. Rather, our aim was to develop a method of examining family responses to a variety of situations, with the operationalization of resilience depending on the context and the examined stressor. The focus on long-term adaptation calls for a longitudinal design, which assesses families before, during, and after the occurrence of a particular stressor. The goal is also to identify common trajectories exhibited by families facing stressful situations, as well as uncover paths that are associated with adaptive outcomes in the long term. Families that are able to regain or surpass precrisis levels of functioning at some point after the stressor may be considered resilient; however, this process-oriented approach allows the paths followed towards healthy postcrisis to vary considerably.

Methodological Issues

Family as the Unit of Analysis

A continuing concern in family research involves choosing the proper unit of analysis. One can choose to assess families as units, as opposed to collections of perceptions from individual family members. There are several ways to gather data from more than one family member and transform individual reports into a construct serving as a proxy for family functioning. These range from fairly straightforward difference scores, additive scores, and ratios to slightly more complicated dispersion-based scores and dyadic-level correlations to the social relations model and other covariance-based techniques requiring knowledge of structural equations modeling techniques (for reviews, see Schumm, Barnes, Bollman, & Jurich, 1986; Thomas & Marcos, 1990; Thompson & Walker, 1982; Tiggle, Peters, Kelley, & Vincent, 1982; White & Brinkerhoff, 1981).

Perhaps the biggest problem with these strategies (and the most relevant to our suggested approach) is that they still assess perceptions of individual family members rather than directly assessing the family itself. We can ask family members, for example, to report on their perceptions of others, on their perceptions of dyadic relationships, on their perceptions of triadic relations, or on their perceptions of the family as a whole. Similarly, we can ask them to report on their perceptions of other family members' perceptions of the same things. However, we are still obtaining the reports of individuals; we are still gathering data at the individual level and extrapolating it to the family level. While such data obviously can be helpful, useful, and appropriate for a number of research questions, it is our belief that they are limited in their usefulness for the operationalization of family resilience. As Simon, Murphy, and Smith (2005) argue, not only individual contributions of family members play a role, but "qualities or characteristics of the family unit as a whole can influence resilience" (p. 429). This suggests that the family as the unit of analysis must be considered. That is to say, if family resilience is conceptualized as a family level variable, its operationalization must match this theoretical definition.

Research Design

Almost all of the above cited studies reported on data collected at a single point in time. In a review of research from developmental psychopathology, Cowan et al. (1996) stated: "[a] central ingredient of contemporary risk research is its emphasis on moving pictures rather than static snapshots" (p. 7). They went on to suggest that the study of resilience needs to focus on the paths that individuals follow in response to stressors, which are best captured in longitudinal designs. Patterson (2002) also maintains that longitudinal research designs are needed to understand how unique family factors interact over time.

The model presented in this chapter is one according to which resilience is viewed as a process that is visible only over time. This view is also found in the individual risk resilience literature. As Cowan et al. (1996) noted, "the active ingredients of a risk do not lie in the variable itself, but in the set of processes that flow from the variable, linking risk conditions with specific dysfunctional outcomes" (p. 9). They also stressed that resilience forms only in response to stress and that resilient individuals are not those who are able to avoid the negative outcomes of experiences of risk, but instead are those who are able to demonstrate positive adaptation in the face of hardship.

It is surprising, then, to find that the research methods typically utilized to investigate risk and resilience fail to incorporate this dimension. As Cowan et al. (1996) and Walsh (2006) have noted in their reviews, this literature tends to be very static, focusing on examining risk and protective factors and their relationship to outcome variables. Our definition, however, makes it essential to consider the family over time, to identify for each individual family a family trajectory on a specified variable over at least three time points: prior to the crisis point, at the time of the crisis, and some time (or times) after the crisis. It thus becomes possible to categorize families according to how they function on this variable: for example, high prior to the crisis, low during the crisis, but high following the crisis is descriptive of a resilient family; or, alternatively, high prior to the crisis, low during the crisis, and low after the crisis describes a nonresilient family. To reiterate, what is needed is a technique that can be applied to individual families to determine their trajectory across the specified time points.

With this as a goal, the statistical methods typically used to assess change over time are problematic. Traditional multiple regression designs and path or structural models utilizing autoregressive cross-lag designs (Falk & Miller, 1991) allow for the removal of earlier time points from later measures of the same variables, but do not allow for the examination of individual family trajectories. Instead, these models investigate change between individuals and families, not change within specific individuals or families. Inherent in this design is the belief that the variable being studied over time is essentially trait-like, that "the relative rank order of individuals remains the same over time unless altered by the effects of other variables in the model" (p. 278).

Path or structural models incorporating state variable developmental designs are an improvement in some respects. This design is not concerned with stability of rank order between families or individuals. It does not expect that the variable of interest will remain stable and does not partial out data from any prior time points. While it allows linkages between predictor and outcome variables at a variety of time points, however, it is still a technique that is applied at the group level and does not allow for the identification of the individual family trajectory that is essential for this perspective.

Repeated measures ANOVA and MANOVA designs allow for the examination of changes in mean levels of variables over time. In addition, the relation of such change to one or more predictor variables also can be examined. This can be done only at the aggregate level; however, examination of trajectory on a family-by-family basis is still not a possibility.

A recently emerging technique can move this design forward. The use of latent growth curves allows for the creation of a latent, or unmeasured, variable—much like a factor—that represents the average amount of change, or growth, from one time point to another within the data set. Formulas are available allowing for the computation of scores for individual respondents or families that represent the degree of deviation from the group as a whole (cf., McArdle & Epstein, 1987, for a more detailed presentation). A variation of this technique, the construction of manifest, individual growth curves, allows for the more direct evaluation of individual level change. As noted by Karney and Bradbury (1995), this technique involves fitting, for each individual or family, a regression line to the available data points. The slope of this line then represents the best indicator of change for that individual or family over time and can be reentered into a data set, with the predictors of outcomes of change examined.

Growth curve models represent a potential improvement (particularly, manifest individual growth curves) in that they allow for the examination of change at the individual or family level. They are limited, however, in that they represent this change with a single variable, that is, with the slope of the particular line fit to the data in use. The slope lets us identify, for example, those families whose trend over time is upward as opposed to those whose trend over time is downwards, but this is not a fine enough differentiation to be useful.

Consider the following four ways to receive a positive slope based on measurement at four time points (i.e., precrisis, crisis, postcrisis 1, postcrisis 2):
1. Scores at all subsequent time points are higher than those at the first time point
2. The time 2 score is lower than the time 1 score, with the time 3 and time 4 scores higher than time 1
3. The time 2 score is lower than the time 1 score, with the time 3 and time 4 scores higher than time 2
4. The time 2 score is lower than the time 1 score, the time 3 score is higher than the time 1 score, but the time 4 score is equal to the time 1 score

All of these will lead to a positive slope. While the absolute value of the slope will differ, interpretation of the magnitude of the slope leads one to make quantitative distinctions between these families, that is, all are improving over time, but some are improving at a greater rate than others. In fact, however, the differences between these families are qualitative ones: The patterns of scores that produce these slopes represent real differences in how families proceed through the crisis. Nevertheless, the level of detail needed to see this is masked by the growth curve procedure and its reliance on the slope as the best measure of change.

One possible solution to the dilemmas presented by these methods is the use of configural frequency analysis (CFA; von Eye, 1990). The CFA is a statistical procedure that analyzes subjects according to their configurations among a group of variables (i.e., high on the first, low on the second, mid-range on the third vs. low on the first, mid-range on the second, and high on the third). The group of variables used can be distinct, although conceptually related (i.e., adaptable, cohesive, conflictual), or they may be the same variable, measured at different time points. To use the procedure the researcher begins by dividing each variable into discrete categories. Each family or individual is then identified by its categorical position on that variable. An observational assessment of family adaptability might be obtained at two time points, for example. Using some a priori reasoning (i.e., conceptual definitions, prior research), the researcher defines categories of adaptability at each point, perhaps defining them as low and high. Using a numerical system of "0" for low and "1" for high, the following configurations are possible: 1, 1; 0, 0; 1, 0; 0, 1.

Using the CFA program, the number of families representing each of these configurations would be examined. Statistically, configurations that occur more often than would be expected by chance are identified (and termed "types"), as are configurations that occur less often than would be expected by chance (and termed "antitypes"). Identifying these groups is important for two reasons. First, their identification allows for the detection of categories representing trajectories or relationships that are statistically significant. Second, after so identifying these configurations, they can be used as typological variables for future analyses.

Certainly there are limits to CFA. First, the necessity to categorize data undoubtedly will be bothersome to some researchers. In this case, however, the categorization clearly represents a close conceptual tie to continuous data and, furthermore, is based on process, on change over time. These points would appear to make up for the limitations that typically may be inherent in categorical data. Second, it may be difficult to determine when to collect the last wave of data in order to ensure that most families had adequate time to recover from the stressor. It is also important not to err by collecting data at too many points, which would result in the creation of too many identifiable configurations.

Third, and perhaps most important, the use of CFA necessitates large samples; this is, however, more of a conceptual problem than a calculational one. Without a large enough sample, one may find either that the statistically significant types account for only a small portion of the total number of subjects, that the majority of the sample is distributed among statistically insignificant configurations, or both. In a recent study of temperament, looking at configurations among four variables and utilizing over 3,000 children, the researchers found four significant types and one significant antitype. Together, however, the significant configurations accounted for only 40% of the sample (Halverson, personal communication, July 1996).

Limited Test Case

Overview

To illustrate the CFA procedure and its potential use in studying family resilience, a test case is presented. Finding data appropriate for such an example was difficult. To fit, these data had to be family level and longitudinal. More specifically, data had to be collected prior to, during, and after a family crisis event. It was also important to find a data set large enough to allow multiple trajectories to be observed. Needless to say, few if any preexisting data sets fit this description. It was especially difficult to find preexisting data that was of ample size. As a result, a compromise data set was used, taken from a transition to parenthood study. In this data set, there was a crisis, albeit a normative one: the couple's transition into first time parenthood. Family-level data were not available for this data set, however, so data from individual husbands and wives were used. Data have been collapsed across gender and are presented for individuals.

Subjects

Subjects were drawn from a longitudinal study of the transition to parenthood and were assessed at three time points: second or third trimester of pregnancy, 6 months postpartum, and 12 months postpartum. These couples were recruited during their pregnancies primarily through obstetricians' offices, birthing classes, birthing centers, and through advertisements posted in baby and maternity shops. The child had to be the couple's first, there could be no children from a prior relationship, and they had to be involved in a committed relationship, either married or living together. Forty-six couples participated in the first wave of data collection; they attended a data collection session on a university campus where each member of the couple completed an extensive questionnaire packet and were videotaped together in a discussion of an area of marital disagreement. Complete data at all three time points were available from 37 husbands and 39 wives. Mean ages of these husbands and wives at time 1 were 31.1 (range = 19–44) and 29.4 (range = 19–40), respectively, with an average length of marriage of 3 years (range = 0–11 for husbands, 0–12 for wives). Educational levels were high, with most spouses having at least some college experience. The vast majority (34 husbands and 32 wives) were Caucasian.

Measures

Marital adjustment was assessed with the Dyadic Adjustment Scale (DAS; Spanier, 1976). The DAS is composed of 32 items that factor into an overall measure of relationship adjustment, which was used in this study. In addition, spouses also responded to a 20-item questionnaire that assessed amount of conflict between them (sample items include, "we almost never seem to agree"; "my spouse listens when I need someone to talk to").

Spouses responded to two questions regarding division of family tasks and of work outside the home. General satisfaction with the current division in each area was assessed with a 5-point scale (very satisfied to very dissatisfied).

Depression and anxiety were measured using the relevant subscales from the Symptom Checklist 90 (SCL-90; Derogatis, 1977). The SCL-90 is a widely used instrument that assesses problems with emotional well-being in nonclinical populations.

Expectations regarding the new child's effect on the parents' adult development, on general marital relations, and on marital conflict and cooperation were assessed using a series of scales developed by Belsky (1985). Finally, spouses indicated how risky they perceived this pregnancy to be, using a 4-point scale (no risk at all to high risk).

Configural Frequency Analysis

Based on both theory and available research (Crane, Allgood, Larson, & Griffin, 1990; Spanier, 1989), the DAS total scores were split into thirds in the following manner: scores ranging up to 97 were classified as low and scored a 1; scores from 98 to 116 were classified as mid-level and scored a 2; and scores 117 and over were classified as high and scored a 3. Using this categorization of the DAS and three waves of data made for 27 unique configurations. These configurations are listed in Table 2.1 based on the model presented in Hawley and DeHaan (1996), and they can be divided into six groups: resilient, stable (indicating a score of 333 or 222); resilient, growth (with a score of 223 or 233, and so forth); resilient, recovery (e.g., 323); nonresilient, stable (a score of 111); nonresilient, declining (such as 221 or 211); and nonresilient, temporary recovery (such as 121). The 73 individuals utilized for these analyses fit into these categories with the following distribution:

Resilient, stable: 32

Resilient, growth: 1

Resilient, recovery: 1

Table 2.1 Configurations for calculating resilient and nonresilient families based on three time points

Resilient, stable	Resilient, growth	Resilient, recovery
222	112, 123	212
333	113, 132	313
232	122, 223	213
	133, 233	323
Nonresilient, stable	Nonresilient, declining	Nonresilient, temporary recovery
111	211, 321	121
	311, 312	131
	221, 322	231
	331, 332	

Nonresilient, stable: 4
Nonresilient, declining: 33
Nonresilient, temporary recovery: 2

These data were then subjected to a configural frequencies analysis, which revealed the presence of three significant types: pattern 111, which is defined as nonresilient, stable; pattern 211, which is non-resilient, declining; and pattern 333, which is resilient, stable. Note that only 31% of the individuals fit into a significant type, severely limiting any follow-up analyses, and reemphasizing the need for large samples. Were the sample larger individuals or families in these three categories could be analyzed using ANOVA, MANOVA, multiple group comparisons, or other appropriate statistics to determine existing differences between them. With the limited sample size that we have, however, this is not pos-sible. Purely as an illustrative device, we split the sample into two groups, resilient and nonresilient. (We were unable to conduct ANOVA analyses, as only four individuals fit into the nonresilient, stable category.) We then conducted two series of t tests based on this group membership. In the first, data used were from the first time point of the study (i.e., the pregnancy, or precrisis, time point). Using these data allows for the examination of factors that predict which trajectory the individual will take, resilient or nonresilient. In the second, data used were from the third time point of the study (i.e., the 1-year postcrisis time point). Using these data allows for the examination of the consequences of the trajectory taken.

Looking at the precrisis data, and as would be expected from our definition of resilience, there were no significant differences between these two groups on initial DAS scores ($t=-1.5$, $p<0.14$). The nonresilient group did score significantly higher on the marital conflict measure (2.9 vs. 1.3; $t=2.22$, $p<0.03$) and was significantly less satisfied with the current division of work within the family (3.3 vs. 3.9; $t=-2.5$, $p<0.01$). Interestingly, the resilient group tended to view the pregnancy as being of slightly higher risk than did the nonresilient group (1.9 vs. 1.5; $t=-2.23$, $p<0.03$). No significant dif-ferences, however, were found on depression, anxiety, division of work outside the family, or expecta-tions regarding the new child's effect.

Looking at the postcrisis data, resilient individuals reported significantly less marital conflict (1.18 vs. 5.53, $t=4.94$, $p<0.000$) and significantly more marital satisfaction (111.11 vs. 91.95, $t=-5.95$, $p<0.000$). They also reported less depression at this time point, although this trend was only significant at the 0.10 level (0.57 vs. 987, $t=1.68$). Resilient individuals reported more satisfaction with the divi-sion of work within the family (3.5 vs. 3.1, $t=-2.12$, $p<0.04$) as well as the division of work outside the family (3.5 vs. 2.9, $t=-2.26$, $p<0.03$). Finally, the resilient group reported more positive effects of the child in the areas of general marital relations (4.5 vs. 3.6, $t=-4.24$, $p<0.000$) and marital conflict and cooperation (4.5 vs. 3.7, $t=-3.55$, $p<0.001$).

Discussion

Our goal was to develop a quantitative method of assessing family resilience that could be used to examine a variety of stressors and to propose a new strategy for examining family resilience. As the limitations of our data set show, the decision to use this strategy must be made before data are col-lected. It is doubtful that the use of secondary data sets will be possible for this approach, as few existing data sets (a) are longitudinal, (b) include data points that are both pre- and postcrisis, and (c) have family level data.

There are several advantages to our proposed perspective. First and foremost, this method allows for an examination of the processes connected with family resilience. Instead of affixing a label to some families and not to others, it is possible to examine the multiple paths families may take, as well as the adaptiveness of these paths. Families may look like they are coping adequately at one point in time, when in actuality their coping patterns are destructive in the long run. Conversely, another family may seem to be flailing at a particular point in time while an assessment of their functioning over time reveals a generally upward trend toward recovery. Findings like these are easily overlooked in cross-sectional research.

This methodology also allows a diverse set of both stressors and family situations to be studied sensitively. It acknowledges the unique responses of different ethnic and geographical groups to a given stressor, and that different paths may be highly adaptive in a particular context but less so in others. The development of a single resilience scale would not be as sensitive, in that all groups would be compared using the same criteria. Finally, this method allows for many different types of measurement (observation, interview, and so forth) to be used as both dependent and independent variables. These different lenses can further illuminate our understanding of familial trajectories taken in response to stress.

Clinical Implications

Recognizing what contributes to resilience in families has important ramifications for the clinicians who work with them. In recent years, there has been a movement toward strengths-based approaches in family therapy. An approach that recognizes resilience as a key ingredient is consistent with such models but goes a step further in suggesting that the strengths contribute to a family's resilience over time (Hawley, 2000; Walsh, 2006). Moreover, resilient families may not always exhibit characteristics associated with strong families. By definition, resilient families have faced potentially overwhelming stressors and have managed to survive and sometimes thrive. If a one-time assessment is made in a clinical context it may appear that such a family is troubled, and they, in fact, may be. But this does not take into consideration the progress this family has made over time nor does it factor in the possibility that the moment at which the family was assessed may have been a low point in their roller coaster journey toward healthier functioning. Whether a family is overcoming difficult odds in progressing toward a better level of functioning can only be seen through multiple assessments occurring over time. Clinical research that helps us ascertain factors associated with families who show resilient trends can aid therapists in knowing how best to intervene with clients who enter therapy. The research model presented in this chapter may provide a useful way to identify the most resilient families and can shed light on what contributes to their ability to be resilient.

Hawley (2000) has suggested that this type of research may be especially helpful in constructing preventive interventions.[1] Although therapy is often considered a reactive intervention implemented after previous attempts to resolve difficulties have failed, clinicians are increasingly recognizing the value of prevention. Since the method advocated here calls for measurement of family functioning prior to a stressor event, researchers can help clinicians identify what sort of precrisis resources a resilient family tends to have. Once these are identified, therapists and family life educators can work with families at the level of primary or secondary prevention to develop skills that help build resistance to the effects of stressors experienced by a family. An essential question, however, concerns which characteristics of families should be assessed over time to determine a family's path of resilience. The research model presented in this chapter offers a means of analyzing data collected over time but does not seek to identify the nature of that data. Walsh (2006) has identified a framework that may help fill that gap. She suggested three broad categories that should be investigated to assess a family's resilience: belief systems (i.e., what sense does a family make of adversity), organizational

[1] For more on this topic, please see Chap. 3.

patterns (i.e., connectedness, flexibility, and resources), and communication processes (i.e., clarity, emotional expressiveness, and problem-solving). Researchers employing the model presented here may find these qualities a good starting place to begin their assessment. As process research is less concerned with the final outcomes of therapy and more with what factors contribute to change, this approach has added clinical benefit.

Limitations of Case Example

There are several limitations with our research illustration that should be noted, particularly in the suitability of the chosen data set. Due to the small sample size, it was not possible to examine the unique features of each of the trajectories, the primary goal of our preferred methodology. Larger data sets are essential in order to have the necessary statistical power to examine each of the trajectories. It is also important for this type of research to include family-level scales of assessment, which can include observational and conjoint interview data. For this particular data set, it also would have been beneficial for the data collection to have spanned a longer period of time, as 12 months postpartum may not have been long enough for families to adjust to the transition to parenthood. Finally, using more than three data points would help establish clearer trajectories. However, additional data points add considerably to the complexity of this method. Four data points, for example, yield 81 potential patterns instead of the 27 patterns examined in this study.

Despite its advantages, there remain some challenges with this approach. It was difficult in some instances to categorize some of the possible configurations. For example, although individuals who were assessed as "111" met a definition of resilience in that they were functioning at the same level as before the crisis, we elected to classify them as nonresilient because their level of functioning was so consistently low.

The ranges in the categories were also considerable. Those with a score of "112" were put in the same group (resilient, growth) as those with a score of "233," even though their level of marital satisfaction obviously was quite different. This was done because of our emphasis on growth in functioning as an integral part of resilience. It will be important to test that assumption empirically at a later date. It is also of interest to test whether our six categories do in fact represent differing trajectories.

Research Implications

There are several areas of future research that would advance our understanding of resilient families. Longitudinal designs are necessary in order to examine how the processes related to family resilience develop in different contexts and with different stressors. An inductive strategy also will be helpful. Indeed, as we learn what helps families cope with specific transitions and stressors, it then may become possible to reach a more general understanding of family resilience.

It is also important to further distinguish between individual and family resilience, as well as to explore how the two are interconnected. Much of the theoretical work on family resilience has adapted research on individual resilience and applied it to families. Some of this work (Hawley & DeHaan, 1996; Walsh, 1996, 1998) has sought to identify singular characteristics of resilience in families. However, the question as to whether there are elements in resilience that are unique to family units (apart from individuals) is largely unexplored empirically. In particular, research strategies that focus on the family as a unit are needed. Self-report data that explore the connection between individual and family variables and resistance to stress over time yield important insights about individual perceptions of the role of family in resilience. But, observational data and conjoint interviews (to name two such approaches) can provide important insights about interaction patterns and family schemas that a family utilizes as it seeks to master the crises it faces. It will be important to determine the degree to which factors associated with resilience in families mirrors or contradicts factors associated with resilience in individuals.

Finally, research on family resilience must be sensitive to the context of a given family. It is probable that differences exist in the risk factors facing different ethnic, racial, and geographical groups, as well as how these groups express resilience.

Conclusion

Although discovering the nature of family resilience remains a challenging prospect, its potential payoff is considerable. Learning more about the *process* by which families in unique environments cope and thrive in the face of stress undoubtedly will help in designing interventions that truly can be effective. In order to uncover process, it is necessary to conduct longitudinal research sensitive to both the context of a family and the unique stressor under consideration. If this methodology were used, the resulting focus on process would align more closely with how family resilience has been conceptualized from its inception, as well as its current use in clinical practice. Identifying differing trajectories commonly used by families in the face of crises will aid in identifying factors helpful in shaping those trajectories.

References

Baldwin, A. L., Baldwin, C., & Cole, R. E. (1990). Stress-resistant families and stress-resistant children. In J. Rolf, A. S. Masten, D. Ciccehetti, K. H. Nuechterlein, & S. Weintraub (Eds.), *Risk and protective factors in the development of psychopathology*. Cambridge, UK: Cambridge University Press.

Bayat, M. (2007). Evidence of resilience in families of children with autism. *Journal of Intellectual Disability Research, 51*, 702–714.

Belsky, J. (1985). Exploring individual differences in marital change across the transition to parenthood: The role of violated expectations. *Journal of Marriage and the Family, 47*, 1037–1044.

Buchanan, T. (2009). Family resilience as a predictor of better adjustment among international adoptees. *Dissertation Abstracts International, 69*, 8-A.

Burr, W. R., & Klein, S. R. (1994). *Reexamining family stress: New theory and research*. Thousand Oaks, CA: Sage.

Conger, R. D., Rueter, M. A., & Elder, G. H. (1999). Couple resilience to economic pressure. *Journal of Personality and Social Psychology, 76*, 54–71.

Cowan, P. A., Cowan, C. P., & Schulz, M. S. (1996). Thinking about risk and resilience in families. In E. M. Hetherington & E. A. Blechman (Eds.), *Stress, coping, and resilience in children and families* (pp. 1–38). Mahwah, NJ: Erlbaum.

Crane, D. R., Allgood, S. M., Larson, J. H., & Griffin, W. (1990). Assessing marital quality with distressed and non-distressed couples: A comparison and equivalency table for three frequently used measures. *Journal of Marriage and the Family, 52*, 87–93.

Derogatis, L. (1977). *The SCL-90 manual 1: Scoring, administration and procedures for the SCL-90*. Baltimore, MD: Johns Hopkins University Press.

Fagan, J., Palkovitz, R., Roy, K., & Farrie, D. (2009). Pathways to paternal engagement: Longitudinal effects of risk and resilience on nonresident fathers. *Developmental Psychology, 45*, 1389–1405.

Falk, E., & Miller, N. (1991). A soft models approach to family transitions. In P. Cowan & M. Hetherington (Eds.), *Family transitions* (pp. 273–301). Hillsdale, NJ: Erlbaum.

Greeff, A. P., & Ritman, I. N. (2005). Individual characteristics associated with resilience in single-parent families. *Psychological Reports, 96*, 36–42.

Hawley, D., & DeHaan, L. (1996). Towards a definition of family resilience: Integrating individual and family perspectives. *Family Process, 35*, 283–298.

Hawley, D. R. (2000). Clinical implications of family resilience. *American Journal of Family Therapy, 28*, 101–116.

Hill, R. (1949). *Families under stress*. Westport, CT: Greenwood Press.

Hill, R. (1958). Generic features of families under stress. *Social Casework, 49*, 139–150.

Karney, B., & Bradbury, T. (1995). Assessing longitudinal change in marriage: An introduction to the analysis of growth curves. *Journal of Marriage and the Family, 57,* 1091–1108.

Koos, E. L. (1946). *Families in trouble*. Morningside Heights, NY: King's Crown.

Lietz, C. L., & Strength, M. (2011). Stories of successful reunification: A narrative study of family resilience in child welfare. *Families in Society, 92,* 203–210.

Masten, A. S. (2001). Ordinary magic: Resilience processes in development. *The American Psychologist, 56,* 227–238.

McArdle, J., & Epstein, D. (1987). Latent growth curves within developmental structural equation models. *Child Development, 58*(1), 10–133.

McCubbin, H. I. (1995). Resiliency in African American families: Military families in foreign environments. In H. I. McCubbin, E. A. Thompson, A. I. Thompson, & J. A. Futrell (Eds.), *Resiliency in ethnic minority families: African American families* (Vol. 2, pp. 67–98). Madison: University of Wisconsin Press.

McCubbin, H. I., & McCubbin, M. A. (1988). Typologies of resilient families: Emerging roles of social class and ethnicity. *Family Relations, 37,* 247–254.

McCubbin, H. I., Thompson, A. I., Thompson, E. A., Elver, K. M., & McCubbin, M. A. (1994). Ethnicity, schema, and coherence: Appraisal processes for families in crisis. In H. I. McCubbin, E. A. Thompson, A. I. Thompson, & J. E. Fromer (Eds.), *Sense of coherence and resiliency: Stress, coping and health* (pp. 41–67). Madison: University of Wisconsin Press.

McCubbin, M. A., & McCubbin, H. I. (1993). Family coping with health crises: The resiliency model of family stress, adjustment, and adaptation. In C. Danielson, B. Hamel-Bissell, & P. Winstead-Fry (Eds.), *Families, health, and illness* (pp. 21–64). New York: Mosby.

Neighbors, B., Forehand, R., & McVicar, D. (1993). Resilient adolescents and interparental conflict. *The American Journal of Orthopsychiatry, 63,* 462–471.

Ong, A. D., Bergeman, C. S., Bisconti, T. L., & Wallace, K. A. (2006). Psychological resilience, positive emotions, and successful adaptation to stress in later life. *Journal of Personality and Social Psychology, 91,* 730–749.

Patterson, J. M. (2002). Integrating family resilience and family stress theory. *Journal of Marriage and the Family, 64,* 349–360.

Rutter, M. (1990). Psychosocial resilience and protective mechanisms. In J. Rolf, A. S. Masten, D. Cicchetti, K. H. Nuechterlein, & S. Weintraub (Eds.), *Risk and protective factors in the development of psychopathology* (pp. 181–214). Cambridge, UK: Cambridge University Press.

Schumm, W. R., Barnes, H. L., Bollman, S. R., & Jurich, A. P. (1986). Self-disclosure and marital satisfaction revisited. *Journal of Applied Family and Child Studies, 35,* 241–247.

Shin, S. H., Choi, H., Kim, M. J., & Kim, Y. H. (2010). Comparing adolescents' adjustment and family resilience in divorced families depending on the types of primary caregiver. *Journal of Clinical Nursing, 19,* 1695–1706.

Silliman, B. (1994). *Rationale for resilient families concept paper*. National Network for Family Resiliency.

Simon, J. B., Murphy, J. J., & Smith, S. M. (2005). Understanding and fostering family resilience. *The Family Journal: Counseling and Therapy for Couples and Families, 13,* 427–436.

Simons, R. L., Whitbeck, J. L., & Wu, C. I. (1994). *Economic pressure and harsh parenting. Families in troubled times: Adapting to change in rural America*. New York: Aldine De Gruyter.

Skowron, E. (2005). Parent differentiation of self and child competence in low-income urban families. *Journal of Counseling Psychology, 52,* 337–346.

Spanier, G. (1976). Measuring dyadic adjustment: New scales for assessing the quality of marriage and similar dyads. *Journal of Marriage and the Family, 38,* 15–28.

Spanier, G. B. (1989). *Dyadic Adjustment Scale manual*. Toronto, Canada: Multi-Health Systems.

Thomas, W., & Marcos, A. C. (1990). Family variables: Conceptualization, measurement, and use. In W. Thomas & A. C. Marcos (Eds.), *New perspectives on family* (pp. 19–47). Thousand Oaks, CA: Sage.

Thompson, L., & Walker, A. J. (1982). The dyad as the unit of analysis: Conceptual and methodological issues. *Journal of Marriage and the Family, 44,* 889–900.

Tiggle, R. B., Peters, M. D., Kelley, H. H., & Vincent, J. (1982). Correlational and discrepancy indices of understanding and their relation to marital satisfaction. *Journal of Marriage and the Family, 44,* 209–215.

von Eye, A. (1990). *Introduction to configural frequency analysis: The search for types and antitypes in cross-classifications*. Cambridge, UK: Cambridge University Press.

Walsh, F. (1996). The concept of family resilience: Crisis and challenge. *Family Process, 35,* 261–281.

Walsh, F. (2003). Family resilience; strengths forged through adversity. In *Normal family processes: Growing diversity and complexity* (3rd ed., pp. 399–433). New York: Guilford Press.

Walsh, F. (2006). *Strengthening family resilience* (2nd ed.). New York: Guilford Press.

White, L. K., & Brinkerhoff, D. B. (1981). Children's work in the family: Its significance and meaning. *Journal of Marriage and the Family, 43,* 789–798.

Wyman, P. A., Cowen, E. L., Work, W. C., Raoff, A., Gribble, P. A., Parker, G. R., & Wannon, M. (1992). Interviews with children who experienced major life stress: Family and child attributes that predict resilient outcomes. *Journal of the American Academy of Child and Adolescent Psychiatry, 31,* 904–910.

The Ramifications for Clinical Practice of a Focus on Family Resilience

3

Dale R. Hawley

Introduction

The study of family resilience has exploded over the past two decades. Fueled by the mystery of why some people seem to thrive under challenging circumstances when others unravel, the study of resilience has sought to answer the question of what distinguishes individuals and families that rise above the fray of adversity. Findings in developmental psychopathology have provided insights into what contributes to resilience in children and the positive and negative effects of families on their development. Family stress theory and the study of family strengths have extended the exploration of resilience to the family level, searching for characteristics in the interactions among family members and with their outside environments that are consistent with successfully weathering crises and promoting growth. Gradually, a picture of resilience has emerged. Initially described in terms like "stress-resistant" and "invulnerable," families displaying resilience are now depicted in more subtle terms. Instead of viewed as "super families," they often are described as families who struggle and experience significant loss but who also are able to muster the resources to survive and to meaningfully integrate the challenges they face into the fabric of their lives.

As findings on family resilience have emerged, therapists have shown increasing interest in incorporating ideas from this literature. Dealing with families who encounter severe stress is their stock in trade. An understanding of processes and characteristics seen in those who successfully battle challenges is vital in their work. In this chapter I focus on translating what we have learned about resilience into clinical settings. I begin by setting a context for conceptualizing resilience by examining the literature, followed by a discussion of important issues for therapists to bear in mind as they work with families to develop resilience, and then provide a case study to illustrate how resilience can be seen in therapy.

Significance of the Topic

For many years the study of family processes focused on deficits. Researchers were interested in learning what contributed to harmful behavior in families. Similarly, clinical models in the developing field of family therapy adopted a medical model wherein they sought to determine the causes of poor

D.R. Hawley (✉)
Department of Human Development and Family Studies,
University of Wisconsin-Stout, Menomonie, WI, USA
e-mail: hawleyd@uwstout.edu

D.S. Becvar (ed.), *Handbook of Family Resilience*,
DOI 10.1007/978-1-4614-3917-2_3, © Springer Science+Business Media New York 2013

family functioning in order to apply interventions to counteract dysfunctional patterns of interaction. Concepts such as the double bind (Bateson, Jackson, Haley, & Weakland, 1956), marital schism and skew (Lidz, 1963), pseudomutuality and psuedohostility (Wynne, Ryckoff, Day, & Hirsch, 1958), lack of differentiation and fusion (Bowen, 1978), and rigid and diffuse boundaries (Minuchin, 1974) were seminal ideas that shaped early thinking in working with families. Families characterized by concepts like these were viewed as deviating from a norm to which they needed to return, while therapists were seen as experts who, as outside observers, could assess dysfunctional patterns and provide treatment.

Over the past few decades, the tendency to conceptualize families in therapy as deviating from a norm has gradually shifted. Influenced by postmodern thinking, dominant models in the field have embraced constructivist and social constructionist ideals. These assume that families (and the individuals who compose them) act based upon a reality they have constructed, one that is influenced by their own interpretation of experiences. As such, there is no norm from which families deviate; each one is unique. Rather than searching for dysfunctional ways in which the family operates, approaches such as narrative therapy and solution focused therapy encourage family members to identify and adopt alternative behaviors that are more satisfying than their current experience. Therapists take on the role of consultants rather than experts. The assumption is that families inherently have the capacity to shift to a better way of functioning and the role of the therapist is to help them discover it.

The notion of resilience fits like a glove with this paradigm. It focuses on strengths rather than deficits and assumes that families have the ability not only to survive difficult times but also to eventually thrive as they emerge from those experiences. It is an innately appealing concept, full of hope and optimism. Resilience tells a story of families who have overcome challenging circumstances to arrive as survivors. It dovetails with approaches to therapy focused on helping families identify strengths as a means of accessing more satisfying ways of functioning.

But there is also another side to resilience. It is not only about strengths but also about struggles. It can be conceptualized as a process families engage in when beset by adversity. From this perspective, families do not emerge from their difficulties unscathed. They are battle scarred and often weary, struggling to keep their heads above water as stressor upon stressor pours in upon them. Resilient families are not necessarily those who emerge from crises as bright and shining stars; they are those families who struggle well (Walsh, 2010). Theirs is a story of survival in the face of overwhelming odds. Therapy may be less concerned with helping them discover hidden strengths and more about allowing them to process and find meaning in their experiences.

An understanding of resilience encompasses both of these perspectives. Therapists who adopt a resilience-minded approach need to recognize both the inherent strengths and the challenging struggles of their clients.

Literature Review

Family resilience as a unique concept is fairly new to the field of family therapy. Hawley and deHaan (1996) identify three primary streams of research that have influenced the development of family resilience as a construct.[1] One is the study of family strengths. Reacting to a focus in the literature on deficits in family functioning, studies on family strengths were concerned with identifying characteristics common to well-functioning families. Early studies (Lewis, Beavers, Gosset, & Phillips, 1976; Stinnett & DeFrain, 1985) identified dynamics such as open communication, good conflict resolution skills, shared time together, and a balance between closeness and togetherness as traits typically found

---

[1] This topic is addressed in depth in Chap. 1.

in strong families. Over time, research in the area shifted toward searching for strengths in diverse family types. However, the basic thrust of this area of study remained the same: searching for ways in which families operated well instead of discovering why they were dysfunctional. This emphasis toward strengths and away from pathology has become an important movement in family therapy over the past several decades. Strengths-oriented approaches such as solution-focused therapy (deShazer, 1985) and narrative therapy (White, 2007; White & Epston, 1990) have become dominant models, and family strengths are frequently equated with resilience (Huber, 2002; Roberts & Escoto, 2002; Simon, Murphy, & Smith, 2005).

A second influence on family resilience comes from developmental psychopathology. This field has focused on factors that enable children who face significant adversity that might otherwise predict later disorders to survive and even thrive in adulthood. Research has stressed the balance of risk and protective mechanisms experienced by individual children. Risk mechanisms may be genetic (e.g., major illness, psychopathology) or environmentally based (e.g., poverty, divorce, exposure to abuse) (Rutter, 1999). Researchers generally agree there is an interactive effect among risk mechanisms, such that exposure to multiple factors exponentially increases the probability of developing a disorder. For example, a child with a physical disability who lives in poverty and whose family environment is marked by conflict and instability will be at greater risk than a child with the same disability living in a stable family and economic environment. The effects of risk mechanisms are mediated by protective mechanisms. These may be internal traits (e.g., intelligence, internal locus of control, confidence) or part of the child's social environment (e.g., ability to foster relationships, parental support, access to social and community resources). The basic thesis of this approach suggests that children with strong protective mechanisms are more likely to access them in order to buffer the effects of risk mechanisms and, thus, are more likely to be resilient.

A third stream in the development of family resilience is family stress theory. Originally proposed by Hill (1958), the ABCX model suggests the degree of crisis experienced by a family is determined by the nature and severity of the stressor event moderated by the number of resources at their disposal and their perceptions of the event. McCubbin and colleagues extended this model through a number of revisions (McCubbin & McCubbin, 1993; McCubbin & Patterson, 1983), culminating in their family resilience model. Patterson (2002) indicates that families experience a pile-up of demands at three levels—individual, family, and community—that are moderated by a variety of capabilities at those same levels. In addition, individual family members and the family as a collective unit develop meanings about these demands and their abilities as a family to withstand them. These perceptions influence their family identity, or how they view themselves from an internal perspective, as well as their family worldview, or how they see themselves as dealing with adversity relative to systems outside their family. Family stress theory proposes that resilient families are able to buffer the effects of demands at multiple levels by utilizing an array of individual, family, and social resources and by maintaining a view of themselves as a family that is able to overcome in the face of adversity.

While family stress theory has much in common with developmental psychopathology in that it sees resilience at least partially as a function of balancing stressors and strengths, it adds a component by recognizing resilience as a family level construct. In the resilience literature, family is often seen as a risk or a protective mechanism for individuals. Wolin and Wolin (1993), for instance, cite numerous clinical examples where individuals have overcome parental mental illness, alcoholism, and disorganization in their families of origin to display elements of resilience in adulthood. Similarly, Werner and Smith (1982, 1992), in their classic longitudinal study of resilient children, found divorce, alcoholism, violence, and other forms of abuse as primary risk factors. At the same time, the family also may function in a protective manner for children. Barnard (1994) identifies minimal conflict in the home during infancy, maintenance of rituals, and absence of parent–child role reversals as associated with resilience in individuals, while Wyman et al. (1992) discovered that resilient preadolescents tend to have positive relationships with their caregivers and experience stable family environments and consistency in discipline. While this recognizes family as an important factor in the degree to which an individual displays resilience, it does not describe the extent to which a family as a unit is resilient. Family stress theory conceptualizes resilience in a family as a function of how the family members interact to collectively apply their capabilities and definitions of the situation to a given set of stressors. Resilience is seen not only in individual terms but also as an outcome of family functioning.

Another notion associated with family stress theory is the roller coaster model (Hill, 1958; Koos, 1946). This model suggests that, in the aftermath of a significant stressor, families go through a period of disorganization marked by increased conflict and confusion, followed by a period of recovery where they seek new ways of adjusting to the crisis and, finally, a period of reorganization where they restructure themselves at a level below, at, or above precrisis functioning. While this does not describe the path followed by all families experiencing a crisis (DeHaan, Hawley, & Deal, 2002), it does suggest that recovery from a stressor event takes place over a period of time. Similarly, family resilience can be conceptualized as a process that occurs over time as opposed to a static trait. Hawley and DeHaan (1996) describe resilience as "the trajectory a family follows as it positively adapts and bounces back from stressful circumstances" (p. 293). They contend that the path of resilience followed by each family is different and that the only way to adequately assess resilience is to measure how a family responds over time. Walsh (2010) describes resilience as "adaptational pathways over time" (p. 155) that include events leading up to a crisis event through eventual family reorganization. These paths are influenced not only by normative events that occur in the course of the family's development but also by individual, familial, social, and cultural environmental responses to the stressor (Walsh, 2003). The interplay of all of these contexts results in a unique path of resilience for every family. As Walsh (1996) indicates, there is no blueprint for mapping resilience in families.

If we are concerned with examining the processes that families exhibit over time, are there particular processes to which we should give greater attention? Walsh (2006) proposes a framework of key family processes associated with resilient families. The first set is focused on the shared belief systems of family members. Rooted in cultural values and shared experiences, these beliefs undergird how families interpret stressor events. While individuals often maintain beliefs that differ from others in the family, resilient families also tend to have a common mythology that helps them survive and thrive in difficult times. Antonovsky (1987) describes this as a sense of coherence, an overarching belief commonly held among family members that, regardless of what is happening at the moment, in the end things will turn out well.

Walsh (2006) divides these shared beliefs into three categories. The first includes those related to how families make meaning of adversity. Do they view it as a challenge they share instead of an obstacle they must face as individuals? Do they tend to normalize and contextualize the events as natural, if distressing, experiences? Are they able to provide feasible explanations that allow them to shed blame and exert control over their circumstances? A second category is focused on maintaining a positive outlook. Do they maintain a sense of hope and perseverance in the midst of challenge? Are they continually affirming of one another? The final category is concerned with transcendent beliefs. Walsh asserts that when families are able to step outside themselves and place their crises within a larger spiritual and historical context this shift allows them to find meaning and purpose in their adversity. Taken together, the beliefs shared by family members provide a powerful buoy that helps keep them afloat in challenging times.

The second set of processes in Walsh's (2006) framework involves family organization. Flexibility allows families to develop fresh responses to novel stressors. Walsh contends that families cannot return to previous levels of functioning; they can only "bounce forward" (p. 85) to new, and hopefully adaptive, ways of functioning. Authoritative leadership and the ability to maintain stability in the midst of disruption help them do this successfully. Connectedness is concerned with the mutual support, commitment, and collaboration family members exhibit as they weather storms together as well as their capacity to maintain clear boundaries and respect for one another. A final aspect of organization involves the family's ability to access social and economic resources. Isolation and financial stress are prominent risk factors for families facing adversity. The burden is shared for families able to mobilize help from extended family, friends, and community resources while those with financial reserves, adequate health care, and workplace flexibility are less likely to experience the compounding effects of financial strain.

The final set of processes Walsh (2006) identifies deal with how the family communicates. Families with higher levels of resilience tend to be clear in their communication, possessing the capacity to discuss difficult topics. Open expression of emotion is not only allowed but encouraged as they work to make the family a safe environment for sharing a wide variety of feelings. Finally, resilient families tend to possess excellent problem-solving skills. They can engage in shared decision making, are able to resolve conflicts, and learn from previous decisions that went awry.

Walsh's (2006) model provides a useful framework for observing how families deal with challenges over time. While it remains to be tested empirically, therapists, researchers, and other practitioners can use it to evaluate how families respond before, during, and after a crisis. There is no formula that concisely measures resilience in families due to the complex interaction of risk and protective mechanisms and developmental, social, and cultural contexts (Walsh, 2003). However, by observing family belief systems, flexibility, connectedness, mobilization of resources, and communication patterns as they roll out over a period of time we can begin to develop a picture of how resilient a given family is when faced with adversity.

Current Issues

Like any developing concept, there are a number of issues that need to be considered as researchers and practitioners begin to apply family resilience. Several of these are concerned with refining conceptual clarity. Defining what is meant by resilience, distinguishing resilience as a family level construct, and understanding the developmental nature of family resilience are three key issues to address.

What Do We Mean By Resilience?

Resilience has become a widely used concept in recent years. A cursory review quickly reveals there is no shortage of definitions. Resilience has been variously described as "the capacity to rebound from adversity, strengthened and more resourceful" (Walsh, 2006, p. 4), "a relatively good outcome for someone despite their experience of situations that have been shown to carry a major risk for the development of psychopathology" (Rutter, 1999, pp. 119–120), and "continued normative development and the creation of positive outcomes in the face of adversity" (Pearlman, Schwalbe, & Cloitre, 2010, p. 203). Hawley and DeHaan (1996) identify several components shared by many definitions of resilience: (a) the presence of hardship; without adversity there is no resilience; (b) the property of buoyancy, an ability to bounce back from difficulties to levels at or beyond previous functioning; and (c) a salutogenic orientation that emphasizes wellness and strength instead of pathology.

While a plethora of definitions may not be an issue in general discussions about resilience, lack of definitional clarity does present problems when applying the concept. Patterson (2002) points out that researchers and practitioners tend to view resilience in different ways. Researchers often deal with populations that have been subjected to specific and significant risks beyond the normative stressors families experience as a part of their development process. Normally, exposure to such risks would predict a negative outcome, but some families—those deemed resilient—demonstrate better than expected outcomes. Resiliency research is interested in why those families seem to do better than expected. In particular, what are the protective mechanisms they exhibit that allow them to balance the risk mechanisms? Adapting Masten and Coatsworth (1998), Patterson sums this up by suggesting resilience research needs a level of risk that is associated with the expectation the family will not be successful, a clear family-level outcome measure, and an understanding of what protective mechanisms prevent poor outcomes.

Therapists, on the other hand, tend to view resilience as an orientation that focuses on strengths rather than deficits (Patterson, 2002). They are less likely to consider the severity of the adverse conditions as a precursor for resilience. While families exhibiting resilience may have experienced chronic or traumatic experiences such as poverty, war, or chronic illness, they also show resilience when dealing with less severe and normative stressors. This reflects a view that life, in general, generates a set of risks that families may struggle to overcome (Patterson). Therapists tend to focus less on the risk mechanisms that contribute to a family's functioning and more on the protective mechanisms that allow them to move in a positive direction.

Similarly, there are often differences in expectations that researchers and therapists have about outcomes associated with resilience. For researchers, the normative outcome for families dealing with a significant set of risk mechanisms is destructive. Families who do not go down this path, who manage to avoid falling apart, are seen as resilient. Therapists tend to be more optimistic about outcomes. Resilience often implies that families are able to overcome their hurdles such that they can operate at levels that stimulate continued and future growth. Walsh (2006) indicates that resilience is more than survival; it enables people to heal and live full, productive lives. Thus, words such as thrive and flourish (Becvar, 2007) are often used in conjunction with resilience.

Another difference between therapists and researchers concerns who is defined as resilient. In general, researchers adopt a categorical perspective, looking for differences between families who are considered resilient and those who are not. There is an applied aspect to this endeavor. If we can determine what distinguishes resilient from nonresilient families, we can educate and intervene in ways that will encourage better outcomes. In order to do this, however, a demarcation needs to be drawn between those families that are resilient and those that are not. Therapists tend to adopt a continuous perspective, assuming that all families are resilient though the degree to which they exhibit it varies. Walsh (2010) states: "We must be cautious not to frame resilience as a static set of traits or typology— some have it and others do not—or to label and dismiss as 'not resilient' those who are struggling at a particular time" (p. 151). For therapists, the goal is not to discover whether or not a given family is resilient; it is to help them uncover the strengths associated with resilience they already possess.

It is not surprising that therapists and researchers tend to view resilience in different ways since they have different purposes for observing families. In general, researchers are concerned with discovering clues as to what makes some families have better outcomes in the face of adversity than others, while therapists are focused on helping a particular family with a specific set of risk and protective factors set in a unique context develop healthier patterns of interaction. Perhaps the real question is "Does it matter?" Will adopting a common view of resilience alter the way in which therapists approach clients and in which researchers measure families?

Perhaps not. Regardless of the set of circumstances that brings clients to therapy, strengths-based clinicians are still likely to help them uncover and build on hidden resources and frame their stories in a more positive light. Researchers, driven by the goal of discovering what sets resilient families apart from other families, will still take a comparative approach. However, the widening gap between research and practice in family therapy is one reason this issue merits attention. As early as 1976,

Olson called for closer connections among theory, research, and practice in the family field. Commenting over 25 years later, Anderson (2003) and Crane, Wampler, Sprenkle, Sandberg, and Hovestadt (2002) noted that not much had changed. Researchers and practitioners of family therapy tend to fall into two different camps. Those who conduct research tend not to identify family therapy as their primary professional identity, while those who define themselves as family therapists appear to be more focused on clinical practices than empirical investigation. Although the trend toward disconnection between theory/research and practice appears to be continuing, reasons for narrowing the gap still exist. Ideally, practice and research inform one another. Therapists need a research base to strengthen and validate the effectiveness of their practice; researchers operating without input from therapists risk producing results that are irrelevant to practitioners. A beginning point for connection is developing a common understanding of what is meant by resilience that results in greater definitional clarity.

Viewing Resilience Systemically

Most of the work in resilience has focused on individuals. This stems from the search for resilience in children found in developmental psychopathology. As previously mentioned, family has typically been seen as a risk or protective factor in the development of individual resilience. More recently, however, resilience has also been identified as a family level construct (Hawley & DeHaan, 1996; Patterson, 2002; Simon et al., 2005; Walsh, 2006). Walsh (2006) describes family resilience as the way a family adapts and copes as a functional unit. She indicates that the importance of relationships in individual resilience has been evident in much of the research, but that typically it has been confined to dyadic relationships such as when a child seeks out an adult mentor, teacher, or coach as a significant guiding influence. Parents often have been viewed in pathological terms, more likely to be the source of risk rather than of protection (Walsh, 2003). Walsh (2006) advocates for a systemic orientation to resilience that not only considers the mutual influence family members have on one another but also takes a larger ecosystemic view into account.

Resilience is a complex concept. It is often described in terms of the interaction of multiple risk and protective mechanisms occurring in multiple contexts. This fits well with a systemic view that takes into account not only individual factors but also family level variables. As seen earlier, Walsh (2006) identifies a number of family level variables (e.g., flexibility, connectedness, communication) as key processes in resilience. These processes are primarily concerned with the interaction among members within their family boundaries. Patterson (2002) indicates that resilience in families also can be assessed at the intersection of the family and other environments with which it interacts. She suggests the degree to which a family is able to fulfill key functions, including nurturance, socialization, economic support, and protection of vulnerable members, is a measure of their resilience.

Another way of evaluating resilience in families concerns their shared beliefs (Walsh, 2006). A long-standing debate in the field is whether a family can truly have a shared view or if they can only have a collection of individual perspectives. Wamboldt and Wolin (1989) argue it is possible for both to exist. They distinguish family myths (differing views held by individual members) from family realities (family perspectives held in common), suggesting that family realities can serve as a template for family actions and decision making. Wamboldt and Wolin contend that family realities can only be assessed through observation of family interaction, but Patterson and Garwick (1994) suggest that such beliefs (what they call family world view) can be discovered in conjoint interviews. In any event, commonly held beliefs in a family can shape their perspectives on adversity.

All of this suggests that clinicians need to be aware of resilience at multiple levels of interaction. It is vital to take into account a variety of genetic and environmental risk and protective mechanisms faced by individuals experiencing a crisis, which doubtless includes the influence of family in some way. But therapists used to thinking systemically will also want to adopt a larger picture that considers the influence of internal family processes and how a family interacts with its various environments as a measure of its resilience.

Resilience as a Developmental Pathway

Influenced by a strengths-based orientation, therapists have tended to conceptualize resilience as a set of capacities possessed by a family (Patterson, 2002). This view is consistent with the description by McCubbin and McCubbin (1988) of resilience as "characteristics, dimensions, and properties of families which help families to be resistant to disruption in the face of change and adaptive in the face of crisis situations" (p. 247). From this perspective, resilience is a set of strengths families can access when they encounter times of adversity. Therapists, who initially evaluate families at a given point in time (that of entering therapy), often seek to uncover these strengths in order to help them find more satisfying ways of interacting as they move forward.

As noted previously, however, this view lacks a temporal component. Several have suggested that resilience is better conceptualized as a set of processes that can be observed effectively only as a family interacts over time (Hawley, 2000; Hawley & DeHaan, 1996; Patterson, 2002; Walsh, 2006). This takes into account what Walsh terms a developmental perspective. She indicates that most stressors are not one-time events but a set of changing conditions with a past and a future. In addition, families also experience developmental transitions at individual, familial, and social levels over the course of time (White, 2004). When a family is dealing with multiple stressors set within a context of development occurring at multiple levels, a complex trajectory is created that requires a response unique to that family.

Given the nature of these trajectories, families demonstrating resilience tend to be fluid in their responses to crisis. Coping strategies that worked at previous stages in their development may not be currently useful. Similarly, helpful responses in the short term may need to give way to other strategies that enable a family to continue to be adaptive over time (Walsh, 2003). For example, a family experiencing the life-threatening illness of one of its members may initially respond with a vigil where they congregate at the hospital to provide mutual support and assistance. If the illness turns into a chronic condition, however, they may adjust by taking turns providing support in order to keep any one family member from being overwhelmed. All of this suggests that therapists should recognize family processes as they occur over a span of time and not focus only on isolated moments in their history. At any given point a family may appear to be far from resilient, swallowed up by stressors that appear overwhelming. As Hawley and DeHaan note (1996), however, a risk factor at a particular point in time may later become a protective factor. It is the ebb and flow of how a family manages and overcomes adversity that tells their story of resilience and identifies their unique pathway.

Clinical Implications

As previously indicated, there is a tendency for family therapists to associate resilience with strengths; thus it is tempting to adopt a strengths-based approach such as solution-focused therapy as a clinical framework for helping families develop resilience. Indeed, there is much in strengths-based models that is a good fit for a resilience-oriented clinical approach. Most assume that all families have strengths that allow them to be resilient. Working with them to uncover those strengths in order to move past their current set of stressors is a hope-filled approach consistent with a view that suggests families can survive and thrive in the face of adversity.

Yet there are some nuances in resilience that suggest its development in families goes beyond traditional strengths-based models. Walsh (2010) indicates a resilience approach differs from a family strengths approach in that it seeks to help families utilize strengths in a context of adversity. In addition to accessing strengths, the severity of this adversity may call on families to explore previous stressors and antecedents, mobilize new resources, develop long-term strategies for modifying their interactions as a family, and balance competing demands from work, school, community, and other environmental contexts. In short, no single clinical model can be adopted as an approach to resilience. Rather than envisioning a resilience-based approach as a model, it may be better to see it as a lens that colors how therapists view and interact with families. As such, there are not unique techniques associated with it; in fact, practices associated with a variety of models are consistent with focusing on resilience in families. However, a number of principles that apply across models are useful in helping families develop resilience. In this section I identify several of these principles.

Assessment

A number of standardized instruments have been developed to assess various aspects of resilience including stressors, coping mechanisms, support, and strengths (Baruth & Carroll, 2002; Dunst, Jenkins, & Trivette, 1984; Koren, DeChillo, & Friesen, 1992; McCubbin, Thompson, & McCubbin, 1996). These are helpful tools for gathering a snapshot of functioning as families enter therapy, and therapists should consider using instruments such as these to evaluate family functioning from multiple perspectives. But they are limited in their capacity to assess the ongoing nature of resilience. A lot of resilient families do not appear so as they enter therapy. They may be battle scarred and worn out from a series of ongoing struggles. They may seem to have few strengths and resources because they have expended them in the course of dealing with their challenges. A one-time assessment of stressors and strengths associated with resilience fails to capture the full picture. Walsh (2006) asserts that assessment should be a holistic process that is broad and inclusive. To do this, assessment must consider the way in which a family functions over time, the multiple contexts of their lives, and the delicate balance between risk and protective mechanisms.

Assessment of family functioning over the course of time is consistent with a developmental view of resilience. Gathering data about the interactive nature of multiple stressors the family has experienced over time as well as exploring ways in which they have successfully dealt with them provides a map of their path of resilience. Therapists should expect to see times when families have struggled under the weight of those stressors as well as times when their family functioning has been less burdened. Resilient families often encounter novel circumstances that call for them to create new ways of interacting; this tends to be a difficult and messy process. Walsh (2010) points out that resilience does not mean families come through crises unscathed but that they struggle well, integrating these challenges into the fabric of their lives. An assessment of family resilience therefore must include the story of that struggle.

Families often enter therapy feeling stuck. The strategies that worked for them in the past will not necessarily work at this point in time because they are dealing with a novel set of circumstances; they are at a place they have never been before. But learning how they have gotten unstuck in the past when overwhelmed by brand new stressors provides therapists with important clues to the processes they can access to bounce forward to a new normal. This ebb and flow of effective family functioning is central to understanding how they demonstrate resilience. Much of this data can be gathered in a clinical interview that assesses the family's history and includes techniques such as genograms and timelines (Walsh, 2006).

Because stressors experienced by families often come from multiple sources, assessment needs to consider the multiple environments in which a family interacts and the resources each of those contexts offers. Consider, for example, a family where a teenage child has just been diagnosed with a chronic illness such as Type 1 diabetes. The child faces a major adjustment as she gets used to the rhythm of testing blood sugars and giving insulin shots on a regular basis, paying closer attention to food intake, and adapting to a new identity. But the family is also required to make changes, such as developing more routines around meals, learning the signs of low blood sugar, and developing a balance between allowing the child to manage her own illness and providing the help she needs. Changes also occur in the child's school environment. Teachers, nurses, and administrators need to be made aware of the unique needs associated with the physical care of diabetes as well as behaviors that may occur as the child adjusts emotionally to her new identity. The child's social network at school is also likely to be affected. She may experience stigmatization due to her "different" condition. The family is also thrust into a new relationship with the medical community that calls for making room for frequent appointments and regular monitoring of the illness. All of these environments present potential stress points and resources. It is important for therapists to gather input from any significant environment that impacts family functioning and to give attention to the interaction of those contexts.

A good example of multicontextual assessment is found in multisystemic therapy, or MST (Henggeler, Cunningham, Schoenwald, & Borduin, 2009). This is an intensive approach that often deals with intractable cases involving adolescents. Therapists include parents, teachers, correctional officers, coaches—in short anyone who has interaction with the child—in assessing his functioning in each of his environments. They then create a map outlining primary and distal influences (both negative and positive) on his behavior and identifying ways in which these contexts interact. While this approach centers on the effects of multiple influences on an individual, a similar sort of assessment can be done at a family level.

Finally, assessment for family resilience needs to consider the balance between risk and protective mechanisms at both an individual and a family level. Patterson (2002) suggests that therapists coming from a strengths orientation often minimize the impact of risk factors. Rutter (1999), one of the foremost researchers in individual resilience, echoes this notion in an article directed toward family therapists. He urges them to look carefully at both the overall level of risk experienced by a family and their sensitivity to risk. The former can be assessed by taking into account the accumulation of stressors a family experiences while the latter is seen through the effects of prior experiences and the degree to which a stressor negatively impacts the child and, thus, the family system. Rutter also suggests that therapists consider individual genetic factors as well as social factors in assessing resilience. While systemically minded therapists tend to look for patterns of interaction among family members, some individuals are genetically prone to risk.

Treatment Implications

The line between assessment and treatment is often arbitrary. Assessment is an ongoing process throughout therapy and, from a systemic perspective, intervention begins with the first session (and sometimes before). Nevertheless, several ideas about treatment within a family resilience framework are offered below: reducing risk and building protective capacities, developing a useful family schema, and nurturing rituals and routines.

Reducing Risk and Building Protective Capacities

Many models of family therapy take a dual approach that includes both addressing initial complaints by adjusting negative interactions and building capacities by helping family members develop new skills or utilize existing strengths. Approaches vary as to which end of this continuum should receive more weight, but both processes are generally seen as important. This is consistent with family stress theory, which asserts that outcomes are stable when there is a balance between demands on the family and their capabilities to meet those demands.

A criticism of strengths-based approaches associated with resilience is that they give too much emphasis to developing strengths and not enough to ameliorating the effects of risk factors. They are seen as trying to provide a quick fix and underestimating the negative effects of stressors. Rutter (1999) warns of the danger of negative chain effects on children and suggests that reducing these effects be of primary importance. He indicates that simply providing positive experiences is of limited value, but interventions that negate or counteract negative experiences, including those that shift cognitive and affective responses, are helpful. One reason for placing renewed emphasis on addressing the effects of risk mechanisms is that they are often rooted in traumatic events experienced by families that result in significant loss. Boss (2006) cites numerous examples from a variety of traumas experienced by families, ranging from losses related to the 9/11/02 terrorist attacks to dealing with Alzheimer's disease.[2] She indicates that the ambivalent nature of these losses makes it difficult for families to come to a point of resolution and urges therapists to help families grapple with the uncertainty of these experiences. Walsh (2006) also cites the importance of dealing with grief for families who have faced traumatic loss and catastrophes. The magnitude of trauma experienced by some families is simply overwhelming. Sometimes resilience means staying afloat instead of sinking. Providing an environment where families can process their losses is vital in helping them avoid drowning.

A particularly powerful source for helping families deal with loss is often found in their communities. Connecting with other families who have suffered similar tragedies provides a potent forum for allowing families to openly express their grief and draw on the wisdom of others who share a common experience. Therapists can play an important role in creating a bridge between families who have experienced similar traumatic events. This is most clearly seen in the response to major community disasters. Walsh (2006) and Boss (2006) give numerous examples of therapists intervening at community levels in the aftermath of major events such as 9/11, Hurricane Katrina, and conflicts in war-torn regions like Bosnia. Landau (Landau, Mittal, & Wieling, 2008; Landau & Saul, 2004[3]) has developed a model called the Linking Human Systems approach that is designed with community disasters in mind. The underlying philosophy of this approach is that enhancing human connection among victims of a crisis can help get them back on their transitional pathways. Coalition building, support, collective storytelling, reestablishing routines, and developing a vision for the future are all important processes in helping families and communities regain their demand–capability balance. This approach also can be helpful with groups of families whose traumatic events have not come in the form of public disasters. Families dealing with the death of a child, severe economic hardship following a job loss, or divorce also may benefit from a shared connection.

While it is important not to underestimate the degree of trauma experienced by families, building strengths is also a critical component in helping them develop resilience (Hawley, 2000). A strengths-based approach asserts that what sets resilient families apart are skills and assets that allow them to rise above adversity. Rather than focusing on deficits that contribute to their difficulties, therapists

---

[2] This topic is addressed in depth in Chap. 17.
[3] This topic is addressed in depth in Chap. 25.

help families identify and develop assets that enable them to overcome their struggles. Wolin and Wolin (1993) refer to this as the Challenge Model.

Strengths-based approaches generally assume that families already possess the strengths needed to combat adversity but that these may be hidden from view due to the overwhelming nature of the problem (Simon et al., 2005). Narrative therapy, for example, suggests that families enter therapy with a problem-saturated story that keeps them from identifying a more hopeful alternative story, one that is already at work in their lives but obscured from view (White, 2007; White & Epston, 1990). A primary focus of strengths-based approaches is helping families uncover and utilize hidden strengths. This is often done by highlighting positive exceptions to the dominant, deficit-oriented story and encouraging them to continue behaviors consistent with those exceptions (deShazer, 1985; White & Epston, 1990).

By its very nature, however, resilience also may call for families to develop new assets. While they likely have had successes in the past that they can learn from, part of what makes families resilient is their capacity to generate innovative responses to a novel set of circumstances. Increasing their range of flexibility, managing the balance between togetherness and separateness, maintaining mutual support, identifying and accessing social and economic support, and honing problem solving and conflict resolution skills are all potential growth areas for challenged families (Walsh, 2006).

In addition to uncovering and developing strengths, a crisis itself may offer opportunities for developing strengths that otherwise would not have been present. Walsh (2006) indicates a resiliency framework is distinguished from a family strengths approach in that it focuses on utilizing strengths in the context of adversity. For example, a family facing surgery and chemotherapy in the wake of a cancer diagnosis may discover a new level of connection with one another that was not present before cancer. They also may be forced to alter their routines in response to medical treatments and, in the course of this process, discover a pace of life that is more conducive to long term, healthy functioning. Therapists can help clients recognize and capture opportunities for growth that stem from adversity.

Maintaining a Positive Perspective

Boss (2001) suggests that the most powerful factor for families in successfully dealing with a crisis concerns how they perceive the situation. There is a link between a family's capacity to maintain a positive outlook in the face of a complex array of stressors and the likelihood of surviving and even thriving in that experience. Several factors seem to be associated with maintaining a positive outlook. One is a sense of coherence (Antonovsky, 1987), which is concerned with how family members make sense of the circumstances that beset them and whether they believe they have the capacity to deal with them. Numerous questions may be asked as they try to assign meanings to their adversity. Is there some reason they find themselves in this situation? Do they affix blame or is this an unfortunate but normative experience that "just happens sometimes?" Family members may wrestle with a question of justice: "This isn't fair—why did this happen to us instead of someone else?" They may even wonder if this set of events occurred in order to strengthen them in some unknown way. Similarly, they assess the degree to which they are able to manage the challenges with which they are faced. Do they have the resources needed to tackle the problem? Have they had experiences in the past that would predict success in dealing with this set of stressors? Families with a strong sense of coherence tend to view adversity as a challenge instead of a burden.

Hope is closely connected to sense of coherence. It involves a belief that, no matter how badly things seem to be going now, there is a light at the end of the tunnel (Graham, 2000). Hope looks into the future. Families drowning in a sea of suffering often have a hard time envisioning that things could ever be better. More resilient families are able to maintain a temporal perspective that allows them to cast an eye toward the future. While their family is currently being transformed by the crucible of their current experience, there will be a time when life will settle and they will regain a sense of stability.

A third factor is the belief that there is a meaning and purpose to life greater than ourselves, a quality sometimes referred to as transcendence (Becvar, 2007; Walsh, 2006). This belief places adversity into a larger context, recognizing that personal struggle is one thread in a greater tapestry. Spiritual beliefs and practices are central to a sense of transcendence. Prayer, meditation, communion with nature, and reflection on beauty found in the arts are rituals that can help center families in the midst of chaos. Although spirituality is not necessarily connected with organized religion, many families draw strength from the faith communities of which they are a part.

Therapists play an important role in helping families maintain a positive outlook in the face of crisis. Families often seek therapy because they have temporarily lost their bearings and are looking for help in regaining them. Therapy can serve as an anchor in the midst of uncertainty. Reminding families of past successes, probing with questions about meaning, and highlighting strengths that they have a hard time seeing are all clinical practices that can instill hope. Therapists not only can assist individual family members in making sense of adversity but they also can help them strengthen their family schema or collective view of the crisis (McCubbin & McCubbin, 1993) through conjoint interviews. Viewed systemically, resilience has a synergistic quality where a positive outlook shared among the whole family has the capacity to have a greater effect than those individually held by family members.

Rituals and Routines

Intense adversity throws even the most resilient families out of kilter. Familiar patterns of interaction, means of mutual support, and commonly held values may all be severely challenged as families seek to regain their equilibrium. The enactment of rituals and routines can be vital to families attaining a modicum of stability in the midst of chaos. These may range from daily events to periodic occurrences, but they help families maintain a sense of continuity that extends before and after the crisis period, linking the past with the future (Becvar, 2007; Imber-Black, Roberts, & Whiting, 2003).

Doherty (1997) identifies several purposes rituals serve for families. One is providing a sense of predictability. While they may vary in the degree to which they value structure, families tend to develop a predictable rhythm around which they operate in their daily lives. Significant stressors disrupt that rhythm. The onset of an illness, for example, may mean an influx of medical appointments, increased incursions into the family interior from outsiders, and altered schedules and activities for family members. All of these changes may be necessary but they have the effect of altering usual interaction patterns. Maintaining routines such as bedtime rituals or dinner times provides a sense of the familiar in the midst of upheaval. It also has the effect of connecting family members, a second purpose of rituals Doherty cites. Common participation in regular rituals builds emotional links that sustain family members in times of crisis.

Strengthening family identity is a third purpose of rituals (Doherty, 1997). Rituals are rich with meaning; they define who we are as families. All families share processes in common but they are distinguished from one another in the ways they carry out those processes, and these differences are marked by the rituals they choose to enact. Often rituals send a strong, symbolic message to both the family and to others about what they value. Whether they are about service to others, accepting differences, preserving a work ethic, maintaining faith, or myriad other ideals, rituals cement the values of families through actions. They provide an anchor point for families in the midst of confusing circumstances saying, in effect, "Regardless of what happens, this is who we are."

Rituals also can punctuate a crisis. Boss (2006) notes that the ongoing and ambiguous nature of loss means that, in some cases, families are not likely to reach closure. However, rituals can provide meaning to help them integrate the losses into their lives. In an editorial at the third anniversary of the

9/11 attacks, Imber-Black (2004) cites the need for authentic rituals. She describes examples of ways in which people who lost friends and loved ones in 9/11 have developed meaningful events apart from public memorials to remember their losses. Families who face adversity inevitably suffer loss. Part of resilience is being able to remember and honor what was lost, even in those cases where families thrive as they emerge from crisis.

Therapists play a key role for families in helping them maintain and develop rituals in the midst of their struggles. They can identify rituals that already exist in family life and assist families in finding ways to maintain them. They can work with families to develop strategies to maintain their boundaries when outside forces tend to encroach upon and disrupt family rhythms. They can encourage families to build new rituals in response to the new challenges they are facing and to develop ways of meaningfully honoring their losses. Whatever their role, helping families maintain rituals and routines is important in a resilience-based approach.

Research Implications

While there is a well-developed literature on individual resilience, research that focuses on the family as the unit of analysis is limited and clinical studies on family resilience appear to be largely nonexistent. Most of the literature on resilience-based clinical approaches describes principles for practice but does not evaluate how they affect either the outcomes or processes of therapy.

Thus, perhaps the first implication is that a line of research focusing on clinical intervention using principles rooted in resilience needs to be developed. This is probably easier said than done. As noted in the earlier discussion, there is a lack of agreement on what is meant by resilience and how it is operationally defined. Researchers intent on exploring this area will need to be clear about how they define resilience, how it is distinguished from family strengths research, and what variables will be used for measuring clinical practice. A good starting place may be Walsh's (2006) framework. Though untested at this point, it is an elegant model that lends itself to assessing both outcomes and therapeutic processes.

A second implication for research concerns whether resilience is viewed as a static trait or a developmental process. If conceptualized as a trait, it is expedient to develop standardized measures that capture the essence of resilience in families. DeHaan et al. (2002), however, have asserted that resilience is a developmental pathway and, as such, can only be measured using a longitudinal design that assesses functioning at various points in time. Rather than trying to measure assessment as a discrete characteristic, this approach looks at the paths families take over time on various measures of family functioning (e.g., conflict resolution, connectedness, flexibility). This appears to be a good fit for clinical outcome research that is focused on the degree to which families change over time, from the beginning to the end of therapy. However, it is limited in that most families enter therapy already in crisis. DeHaan, Hawley, and Deal's design assumes an assessment of precrisis functioning as a beginning baseline. Without it, determining which effects of change are due to resilience, therapy, or an interaction of both may be difficult.

Process research is less concerned with the final outcome of therapy and more in what factors contribute to change. It asks "What is there about therapy that works well with resilient families?" Once again, the starting point is defining what is meant by a resilient family; it is difficult to determine what is effective if we don't know whether we are observing such a family. Assuming this is done, the focus of the research is on therapeutic processes—are there certain interventions, therapist behaviors, assessment techniques, etc. that appear to be consistent with positive pathways in families deemed resilient? At this point, such research would be exploratory and would fit well with qualitative methods.

Case Study

Dan and Anita (pseudonyms), a couple in their mid-40s, had been dating for several months when they entered therapy. Both had been married before and reported acrimonious relationships with their ex-spouses. Each had three children from those marriages. Dan's youngest child was in the process of leaving for college and he indicated he had a good (if sometimes more distant than he wanted) relationship with all of his children. Two of Anita's children were adults and in relationships of their own. During the course of therapy one of them ended a relationship with her significant other, which resulted in increased child care responsibilities falling to Anita. In addition, she shared joint custody of her youngest child, Justin, who was in middle school, with her ex-husband. Justin dealt with a significant ADHD diagnosis.

Both partners were entering this relationship with considerable baggage from their previous marriages and families of origin. Anita indicated that her ex-spouse had been verbally abusive and was subject to fits of volatility. She reported having a distant relationship with her father, who seldom made efforts to connect with her despite repeated attempts on her part, a pattern that had existed since childhood. Dan indicated a history of instability during his growing up years. His mother was in and out of numerous relationships, he had little contact with his father, and he often had to fend for himself. His childhood was fraught with rejection, a pattern that carried over into his marriage. Although he had remained in an unhappy marriage for many years, he had felt a continual sense of rejection from his ex-wife.

Dan and Anita identified two goals as they entered therapy. They indicated that their relationship was getting serious and moving toward marriage, but that they were being cautious. Since both had experienced unsatisfactory marriages, they wanted to make sure this relationship was on solid ground. They also were aware of the potential impact of their relationship on their children and wanted help in moving ahead in a way that integrated them into the new family they were forming.

From the beginning of therapy it was clear that Dan and Anita shared a number of strengths. They were affectionate, laughed easily, and clearly enjoyed each other's company. Both were capable parents, particularly as they negotiated their roles with adult children and grandchildren. The therapist commented on these strengths on a continual basis and the couple seemed to recognize them. As therapy progressed, however, two significant issues became apparent. Though Dan wanted to be in this relationship with Anita, when he was stressed he would tell himself that she probably did not want him, based on his history of rejection. In order to avoid rejection, he would precipitate an argument and threaten to leave the relationship, thus rejecting her before she could do the same. This would provoke feelings of abandonment in Anita, causing her to placate Dan so that he would not leave. After a time (sometimes several days), this pattern would recede, but not before leaving both partners feeling tentative about the relationship. The second issue was related to distance regulation. Dan had been living in his own place for some time and, even in his previous relationship, had been used to significant amounts of time to pursue his own interests. Anita wanted to spend as much time together as possible and, although she recognized Dan's need for space, would sometimes make plans for their discretionary time that he felt encroached on "his time." This would create stress for Dan, leading to the onset of their rejection-abandonment pattern.

Over the course of therapy several things were done to address their concerns. The therapist identified the destructive rejection-abandonment pattern and worked with Dan and Anita to recognize signs that led to its appearance. Sessions often included a replay of conflicts to discover how this pattern had been displayed and to identify strategies for ways to short-circuit it. As time progressed, the couple became more adept at recognizing the pattern in its early stages and detouring around it.

They became more confident in their ability to manage this part of their relationship and began to develop a shared belief in their capacity to overcome this and other challenges they faced. This provided an opportunity for the therapist to comment on the couples' adaptability and to cite it as a relationship strength. Dan also sought individual therapy to address his feelings of rejection.

The couple also made some changes to regulate their time and space. Anita began checking in more closely with Dan regarding his schedule as she made plans that involved both of them, and Dan became better at communicating when he needed a break. This issue intensified when they eventually married and Dan moved into Anita's house. Initially he felt he was invading her space and had none of his own. The couple resolved this by designating a place in the basement as Dan's "man-cave" where he could go and spend time without interruption. Dan and Anita also became proactive in how they managed their discretionary time, creating routines that brought them together, which they both enjoyed.

As for the integration of their children, Dan and Anita were careful to proceed slowly with the development of their relationship to allow the children opportunities to get to know their parent's new partner. They were intentional about creating events that brought family members together, first with one side only and eventually with all of their children. Only one of the children, Justin, still lived with Anita on a half-time basis. Dan and Justin developed a healthy and respectful relationship. Dan saw his role as supporting Anita in her parenting and was clear that he had no intention to supplant Justin's father.

Dan and Anita continued in therapy for over 2 years, meeting on a biweekly basis at first, then tapering off to less frequent meetings. During the course of this time they went through a series of ups and downs. There were times when it appeared they were moving toward ending their relationship, particularly when they had frequent recurrences of the rejection-abandonment pattern. After about 18 months of therapy the couple married, but this did not signal the end of their struggles. Approximately three months after the wedding they came to a session reporting a recurrence of their previous difficulties. The therapist helped them identify the old relationship patterns that were at work and strategize about ways to alter the patterns. After several more months of sessions every 4–6 weeks, the couple indicated they were ready to discontinue therapy.

Adversity in the lives of families presents itself in a number of ways. Dan and Anita did not have the number or severity of stressors experienced by many families. They did not, for example, have to deal with a chronic illness, a child's death, or a catastrophe with lasting consequences. But they did have a pile-up of stressors as they entered therapy, including scars from previous marriages, messages of rejection and abandonment that had lingered over many years, dealing with ADHD in Anita's son, and supporting Anita's daughter and granddaughter through a disintegrating relationship. Over the course of therapy they exhibited a number of signs of resilience:

- They showed flexibility as they worked to break negative chain reactions found in the rejection-abandonment cycle by learning to recognize the signs associated with the onset of the cycle and altering their behaviors.
- They discovered a balance between personal and couple space that was appropriate for them and, in the process, regulated their emotional connection.
- They developed a set of rituals and routines that created emotional connections for themselves and established an identity for their blended family.
- They strengthened their shared belief in their ability to overcome negative interaction patterns that plagued their relationship.
- They accessed external resources by seeking couple and individual therapy and requesting more frequent appointments during times when their problem patterns became more persistent.

Over the course of therapy, Dan and Anita also displayed a path that followed a general upward trajectory in terms of overall functioning. Their resilience can be seen by stepping back and viewing their overall progress over a 2-year period. It was not a steady, upward path; as noted earlier, they experienced a series of ups and downs. In all likelihood, Dan and Anita will continue to experience times when they flourish and times when they struggle throughout the course of their relationship, but hopefully the resilience they demonstrated during the course of therapy will carry them through difficult times in the future.

Conclusion

Family resilience is an appealing concept. Its hopeful bent and positive orientation is valuable for therapists seeking to help clients mired in difficulties. Framing problems as passing challenges and clients as survivors who possess the strengths to overcome them can help families view their struggles as manageable and provide them with motivation to adapt. At the same time, there is a complexity to resilience that goes beyond a search for strengths. Family resilience involves a multifaceted web of risk and protective mechanisms, social, cultural, and developmental contexts, and perceptions of adversity. The most resilient families often may not appear to be resilient at all. In some cases, they are families who, in spite of incredible odds, have managed to stay intact. They may be limping and any strengths they possess may not be readily apparent but, after facing a torrent of stressors, they are still standing.

This underscores one of the challenges professionals face in applying resilience to families. The variety of ways in which the term is used clouds meaningful discussions to refine family resilience as a concept. To some, resilience is virtually synonymous with strengths that are possessed by all families in various degrees. For others, resilience in families is the exception instead of the rule. Experiencing formidable adversity is a prerequisite and only a minority of families can be truly described as resilient. Some conceptualize resilience as a quality possessed by families; others see it as a developmental pathway that can only be observed over time. Continued dialogue to come to greater definitional clarity would benefit all those who utilize resilience as a concept in their work with families.

In spite of these differing perceptions of resilience, it is a vital lens through which all therapists can view families. A therapist working from a resilience-based context searches for it in their clients. Families may or may not exhibit signs of resilience, but in cases where they do it is a powerful force for healing and provides therapists with ample opportunities for facilitating growth. Helping families balance risk and protective mechanisms, become adaptive, stay connected, utilize their resources, maintain routines, and develop shared, positive perspectives in the midst of troubles is consistent with almost any therapeutic approach. As therapists, we can serve as a conduit that allows families in adversity to bounce forward to new and more satisfying ways of functioning.

References

Anderson, C. (2003). Cassandra notes on the state of the family research and practice union. *Family Process, 42*, 323–329.

Antonovsky, A. (1987). *Unraveling the mystery of health: How some people manage stress and stay well*. San Francisco: Jossey-Bass.

Barnard, C. P. (1994). Resiliency: A shift in our perception? *American Journal of Family Therapy, 22*, 135–144.

Baruth, K. E., & Carroll, J. J. (2002). A formal assessment of resilience: The Baruth Protective Factors Inventory. *The Journal of Individual Psychology, 58*, 235–244.

Bateson, G., Jackson, D., Haley, J., & Weakland, J. (1956). Toward a theory of schizophrenia. *Behavioral Science, 1*, 251–264.

Becvar, D. S. (2007). *Families that flourish: Facilitating resilience in clinical practice*. New York: Norton.

Boss, P. G. (2001). *Family stress management: A contextual approach* (2nd ed.). Newbury Park, CA: Sage.

Boss, P. G. (2006). *Loss, trauma and resilience: Therapeutic work with ambiguous loss*. New York: Norton.

Bowen, M. (1978). *Family therapy in clinical practice*. New York: Jason Aronson.

Crane, D. R., Wampler, K. S., Sprenkle, D. H., Sandberg, J. G., & Hovestadt, A. J. (2002). The scientist-practitioner model in marriage and family therapy programs. *Journal of Marriage and Family Therapy, 28*, 75–83.

DeHaan, L., Hawley, D. R., & Deal, J. F. (2002). Operationalizing family resilience: A methodological strategy. *American Journal of Family Therapy, 30*, 275–291.

deShazer, S. (1985). *Keys to solution in brief therapy*. New York: Norton.

Doherty, W. J. (1997). *The intentional family: How to build family ties in our modern world*. New York: Addison-Wesley.

Dunst, C. J., Jenkins, V., & Trivette, C. M. (1984). The family support scale: Reliability and validity. *Journal of Individual, Community, and Family Wellness, 1*, 45–52.

Graham, J. M. (2000). Marital resilience: A model of family resilience applied to the marital dyad. *Marriage and Family: A Christian Journal, 3*, 407–420.

Hawley, D. R. (2000). Clinical implications of family resilience. *American Journal of Family Therapy, 28*, 101–116.

Hawley, D. R., & deHaan, L. (1996). Toward a definition of family resilience: Integrating life-span and family perspectives. *Family Process, 35*, 283–298.

Henggeler, S. W., Cunningham, P. B., Schoenwald, S. K., & Borduin, C. M. (2009). *Multisystemic therapy for antisocial behavior in children and adolescents*. New York: Guilford.

Hill, R. (1958). Generic features of families under stress. *Social Casework, 49*, 139–150.

Huber, C. H. (2002). Family resilience within individual psychology: Stay the same and change. *Journal of Individual Psychology, 58*, 211–213.

Imber-Black, E. (2004). Editorial: September 11, 2004: The third anniversary. *Family Process, 43*, 275–278.

Imber-Black, E., Roberts, J., & Whiting, R. A. (2003). *Rituals in families and family therapy*. New York: Norton.

Koos, E. L. (1946). *Families in trouble*. New York: King's Crown.

Koren, P. E., DeChillo, N., & Friesen, B. J. (1992). Family empowerment scale. In J. Touliatos, B. F. Perlmutter, & M. A. Straus (Eds.), *Handbook of family measurement techniques* (pp. 382–383). Thousand Oaks, CA: Sage.

Landau, J., Mittal, M., & Wieling, E. (2008). Linking human systems: Strengthening individuals, families, and communities in the wake of mass trauma. *Journal of Marital and Family Therapy, 34*, 193–209.

Landau, J., & Saul, J. (2004). Family and community resilience in response to major community disaster. In F. Walsh & M. McGoldrick (Eds.), *Living beyond loss: Death in the family* (2nd ed., pp. 285–309). New York: Norton.

Lewis, J. M., Beavers, W. R., Gosset, J. T., & Phillips, V. A. (1976). *No single thread*. New York: Brunner Mazel.

Lidz, T. (1963). *The family and human adaptation*. New York: International Universities Press.

Masten, A. S., & Coatsworth, J. D. (1998). The development of competence in favorable and unfavorable environments: Lessons from research on successful children. *American Psychologist, 53*, 205–220.

McCubbin, H., & McCubbin, M. (1988). Typologies of resilient families: Emerging roles of social class and ethnicity. *Family Relations, 37*, 247–254.

McCubbin, H., & Patterson, J. M. (1983). The family stress process: The Double ABCX model of adjustment and adaptation. *Marriage and Family Review, 6*, 7–37.

McCubbin, H. I., Thompson, A. I., & McCubbin, M. A. (1996). *Family assessment: Resiliency, coping and adaptation: Inventories for research and practice*. Madison, WI: University of Wisconsin Press.

McCubbin, M. A., & McCubbin, H. I. (1993). Family coping with health crises: The resiliency model of family stress, adjustment, and adaptation. In C. Danielson, B. Hamel-Bissell, & P. Winstead-Fry (Eds.), *Families, health and illness* (pp. 21–64). St. Louis: C.V. Mosby.

Minuchin, S. (1974). *Families and family therapy*. Cambridge, MA: Harvard University Press.

Olson, D. H. L. (1976). Bridging research, theory, and application: The triple threat in science. In D. H. L. Olson (Ed.), *Treating relationships*. Lake Mills, IA: Graphic Publishing.

Patterson, J., & Garwick, A. (1994). Levels of family meaning in family stress theory. *Family Process, 33*, 287–304.

Patterson, J. M. (2002). Integrating family resilience and family stress theory. *Journal of Marriage and Family, 64*, 349–360.

Pearlman, M. Y., Schwalbe, K. D., & Cloitre, M. (2010). *Fostering resilience and concluding the treatment*. Washington: APA.

Roberts, N. H., & Escoto, E. R. (2002). "Our child won't go to bed!": A functional assessment and intervention from a family resilience perspective. *The Journal of Individual Psychology, 58*, 245–249.

Rutter, M. (1999). Resilience concepts and findings: Implications for family therapy. *Journal of Family Therapy, 21*, 119–144.

Simon, J. B., Murphy, J. J., & Smith, S. M. (2005). Understanding and fostering family resilience. *The Family Journal, 13*, 427–436.

Stinnett, N., & DeFrain, J. (1985). *Secrets of strong families*. Boston: Little Brown.

Walsh, F. (1996). The concept of family resilience: Crisis and challenge. *Family Process, 35*, 261–281.

Walsh, F. (2003). Family resilience: A framework for clinical practice. *Family Process, 42*, 1–18.

Walsh, F. (2006). *Strengthening family resilience* (2nd ed.). New York: Guilford.

Walsh, F. (2010). A family resilience framework for clinical practice: Integrating developmental theory and systemic perspectives. In W. Borden (Ed.), *Reshaping theory in contemporary social work: Toward a critical pluralism in clinical practice.* (pp. 146–176). New York, NY, US: Columbia University Press, 2010.

Wamboldt, F., & Wolin, S. (1989). Reality and myth in family life: Changes across generations. *Journal of Psychotherapy and the Family, 4,* 141–165.

Werner, E. E., & Smith, R. S. (1982). *Vulnerable but invincible: A study of resilient children.* New York: McGraw-Hill.

Werner, E. E., & Smith, R. S. (1992). *Overcoming the odds: High risk children from birth to adulthood.* Ithaca, NY: Cornell University Press.

White, J. M. (2004). *Advancing family theories: Metaphors and methods.* Thousand Oaks, CA: Sage.

White, M. (2007). *Maps of narrative practice.* New York: Norton.

White, M., & Epston, D. (1990). *Narrative means to therapeutic ends.* New York: Norton.

Wolin, S. A., & Wolin, S. (1993). *The resilient self: How survivors of troubled families rise above adversity.* New York: Villard.

Wyman, P. A., Cowan, E. L., Work, W. C., Raoff, A., Gribble, P. A., Parker, G. R., et al. (1992). Interview with children who experienced major life stress: Family and child attributes that predict resilient outcomes. *Journal of the American Academy of Child and Adolescent Psychiatry, 31,* 904–910.

Wynne, L. C., Ryckoff, I. M., Day, J., & Hirsch, S. I. (1958). Pseudo-mutuality in the family relations of schizophrenics. *Psychiatry, 21,* 205.

Facilitating Family Resilience in Clinical Practice

4

Dorothy S. Becvar

Introduction

In this chapter I outline the basics of my clinical approach, which I refer to as a story about stories. According to my story, which is characterized by an ethical/respectful stance toward clients, the limits of what we can know are acknowledged; we recognize that there is no one right way that all people and families should be; pathologizing is avoided and the focus is on solutions rather than problems; shared expertise is emphasized; and the therapist is sensitive to language, conversations, and what is or is not privileged in those conversations, for example, power issues. Along with these aspects goes the requirement that the therapist stay abreast of new information, new stories that will aid in the therapeutic process relative to both the clients' goals and the facilitation of resilience. Indeed, my story continues to evolve and change as I continue to learn and grow.

My approach, or story, as I describe it today is grounded in three different but related theoretical perspectives: transcendental phenomenology (Husserl, 1965), second-order cybernetics (Bateson, 1972, 1979), and postmodernism (Gergen, 1991). Within this approach, all theories are understood as stories, with awareness that each may have utility relative to specific contexts. However, my assumption is that we cannot know any of them to be True in an absolute sense. Indeed, it is my belief that what Bronowski (1978) termed a "God's eye view" simply is not possible for us mortals.

The aspect of transcendental phenomenology to which I make recourse is its focus on basic assumptions, or the conditions of possibility that must be met in order to be able to make valid knowledge claims. For example, in order to say that something that occurred represented a self-fulfilling prophesy, we would have to be able to repeat the exact initial conditions and then see revealed the same outcome in order to know the truth of our claim. This, of course, is not possible. Similarly, the claim that we have an unconscious cannot be supported as True in that the unconscious is unknowable by definition. While each of these constructs may prove useful in practice, we are called to behave in a manner that is self-referentially consistent, and thus to be aware of and acknowledge the limits of our knowing, our claims of knowledge.

With a second-order cybernetics perspective (Bateson, 1972; Becvar & Becvar, 2009) we assume that recursion, mutual influence, and ongoing feedback loops characterize all relationships, including those between therapists and client systems. Subjectivity and self-reference are understood to be

D.S. Becvar (✉)
Saint Louis University, St. Louis, MO, USA
e-mail: becvards@slu.edu

D.S. Becvar (ed.), *Handbook of Family Resilience*,
DOI 10.1007/978-1-4614-3917-2_4, © Springer Science+Business Media New York 2013

inevitable, with the observer as part of the observed as he or she is always viewing what is out there through her own worldview or frame of reference. In other words, believing is seeing. Further, the therapist sees herself as *working within* as opposed to standing outside and *working on* clients and client systems. Rather than intervening, she engages in an ongoing mutual process of perturbation and compensation in the context of an autopoietic (self-generated), autonomous, or closed system (Maturana & Varela, 1987). She also assumes a both/and perspective, recognizing that there may be many valid ways of understanding as well as working with clients.

The third major theoretical perspective that undergirds my approach is postmodernism, with awareness of both social constructionism (Gergen, 1985, 1991) and constructivism (von Glasersfeld, 1988; Watzlawick, 1976). Social constructionism provides a macro focus, emphasizing the socialization processes by which we learn to speak and behave in accepted ways. Consistent with this orientation, facts are replaced by perspectives, or stories, and we recognize that the self is constructed in relationship. Constructivism, on the other hand, offers a more micro focus according to which we recognize that both the self and problems take shape and have meaning in the context of specific relationships. In general, a postmodern awareness invites us to see language as the means by which we come to know our reality and in our knowing simultaneously to create it. There is recognition that minds and objects are inseparable. Accordingly, we are invited once again to hold onto concepts lightly, and to consider our "knowing" with both skepticism and humor (Becvar & Becvar, 2009).

The above ideas and assumptions provide the foundation for my clinical approach. The building blocks that comprise the completed structure include various clusters of information, including the many stories about individuals, families, and contexts of which I believe the therapist needs to be aware in order to be an effective helper. First and foremost among these is information about the concept of resilience.

Significance of a Resilience Orientation

Depending on one's perspective, resilience refers to either the capacity and/or the demonstrated ability not only to bounce back from adversity but also to do so in a manner that indicates an increase in strength and resourcefulness. According to Walsh (1998, p. 4), resilience represents, "An active process of endurance self-righting and growth in response to crisis and challenge." Boss (2006) adds to this the idea that evidencing resilience connotes the experience of having been stretched as a function of how one experienced and responded successfully to a crisis or challenge.

It is crucial to note the widespread agreement on the part of researchers that resilience does not represent a static concept that can be described in terms of specific traits or characteristics. Rather, it refers to a fluid process that evolves over time (Conger & Conger, 2002; De Haan, Hawley, & Deal 2002; Hawley & De Haan, 1996; Kragh & Huber, 2002; Oswald, 2002; Patterson, 2002a, 2002b; Sandau-Beckler, Devall, & de La Rosa 2002; Schwartz, 2002; Walsh, 1998, 2003a). For families, as for individuals, this process is influenced by the context within which it emerges.

Coming from a second-order cybernetics perspective as I do, context becomes one of the most significant aspects to be considered when attempting to understand families as part of the process of facilitating resilience. According to Hawley and de Haan (1996, p. 293):

> Family resilience describes the path a family follows as it adapts and prospers in the face of stress, both in the present and over time. Resilient families positively respond to these conditions in unique ways depending on the context, developmental level, the interactive combination of risk and protective factors, and the family's shared outlook.

I do not disagree with the above quote. However, for me, the family's context is *comprised* not only of the other factors noted (i.e., developmental levels, the interactive combination of risk and protective factors relative to specific stressors, the family's shared outlook) but also includes structural and cultural variations, socioeconomic status, as well as the impact of both the system within which the family exists and the other systems with which it also interacts. I believe that all of these factors must be considered when helping families negotiate a path that leads to resilience.

Keeping this in mind, my intent is to help families flourish by assisting them in achieving their desired goals while at the same time facilitating resilience so that in the future they can manage more effectively on their own. My approach is thus two-pronged. Relative to the first prong, assisting clients to achieve their goals involves responding therapeutically to each unique family in ways that are designed specifically for that system. This entails knowledge of and the ability to make recourse to a variety of family therapy approaches and related interventions/perturbations that often have proven useful in my work. Brief overviews of some key concepts derived from many of the classic approaches as well as the more recently developed postmodern approaches to family therapy are reviewed below.

At the same time, concurrent with efforts to help clients achieve their goals, utilizing ideas and interventions/perturbations derived from various therapy stories, the therapist also is engaged in the process of facilitating resilience, the second prong of my approach. This entails, as appropriate, a focus on processes that have been found to characterize successful families. These processes contribute to the ability of families to evidence resilience. However, it is important to be aware that specific risk and protective factors must be considered relative to the unique context of each client system. An overview of both general and specific processes is provided following brief descriptions of some basic family therapy concepts that may support the process of helping clients achieve their goals.

Review of Family Therapy Concepts

Classic Approaches

The contextual family therapy of Boszormenyi-Nagy (1966; Boszormenyi-Nagy & Spark, 1973) emphasizes the impact of intergenerational processes in families. Especially significant in terms of his introduction of an ethical dimension, Nagy offered the concept of a ledger of indebtedness and entitlement, describing the idea that families would do well to achieve balance relative to the dimensions of trust and loyalty. Accordingly, the goal of therapy is the redefinition of the relational context in an ethical manner such that trustworthiness is a mutually merited phenomenon and a concern for future generations provides the impetus for health.

Bowen's (1976) genogram and the concepts of differentiation and triangulation, which are all part of his natural systems theory, provide several potentially useful ideas. The genogram, which involves visually depicting a minimum of three generations, enables a fuller understanding of the family's larger context. Considering the degree of differentiation of self from others as well as the degree of differentiation between emotions and the intellect may provide important information about family members and their relationships. Triangulation occurs in situations where one member of a dyad seeks a third party as an ally to support his or her position in a conflict with another member of the dyad. Helping family members to avoid such two against one situations may enable them to resolve their issues more effectively.

Whitaker's (1975) experiential approach reminds us of the potential of spontaneity, humor, and the unexpected to support the therapeutic process. According to Whitaker, the therapist goes crazy so the client may become sane, with a concurrent focus on growth for everyone involved, including the therapist. Although the specifics of his approach certainly may be difficult to replicate, Whitaker suggests the value of an experiential approach to therapy, parts of which may be utilized regardless of one's theoretical orientation.

An emphasis on patterns of interaction, or the structure and organization of the system, represent the primary focus of Minuchin (1974), who provided a means for mapping various family configurations. According to Minuchin, the family's structure is constrained both by characteristics generic to all families and those that are unique or idiosyncratic to each family.

Important aspects of the system's structure are the spousal, parental, and sibling subsystems, and crucial to their functioning is the degree to which boundaries are clear, rigid, or diffuse, and an appropriate hierarchy is or is not being maintained. The goal of therapy is to facilitate structural change so that new, more functional patterns may evolve. The use of positioning directs our attention to the information that can be gained and the progress that may be made as clients experience changes in the way they have organized themselves.

Satir (1964) believed that the natural movement of all individuals is toward growth, the potential for which everyone possesses; that mutual influence and shared responsibility are inescapable; and that therapy is characterized by an interactive process with clients. Her use of sculpting offers a way to allow clients to demonstrate how they are experiencing themselves in relationship to other family members. In addition, her emphasis on the importance of effective communication reminds us to focus on helping families to improve their skills in this area, perhaps utilizing the five stances of blaming, super reasonable, placating, irrelevant, and congruent that she described.

Haley (1963) focused initially on the levels of communication—digital/report and analogue/command—and then moved to a consideration of relationships, emphasizing the power tactics he felt were an inevitable aspect of human interaction. Strategic family therapy was created based on Haley's method-oriented and problem-focused approach to designing unique strategies for attaining clients' goals. He described the use of directives, paradoxical injunctions, or both, to shift the covert hierarchical structure in families as well as to replace symptomatic metaphors and behaviors with those that are more adaptive.

Behavioral family therapists encourage a focus on the goals of the client with an emphasis on working to achieve them. The use of caring days (Stuart, 1969, 1980) to help couples reconnect as they seek to improve their relationships is one suggested intervention. Another is skills training for parents in the realms of communication and child rearing. Cognitive behavioral approaches add recognition of the importance of beliefs and attitudes, or internal schema, in the creation and resolution of problems.

Postmodern Approaches

In addition to the interventions/perturbations from the classic approaches described above, the contributions of more recent postmodern approaches also provide significant ideas and concepts that may be useful in helping clients to achieve their goals. Andersen (1992) asked, "Why did we hide away our deliberations about the families?," which led to his creation of a reflecting team approach (Andersen, 1987) to therapy. Regardless of the presence or absence of a team, this approach ultimately suggests the inclusion of respect, transparency, a focus on language, and tentativeness relative to conclusions as the means to expand the ways in which situations may be viewed. Focusing particularly on the importance of reflecting processes, Andersen hoped to help clients reach new understandings and perceptions of themselves without imposing on them his beliefs or ideas about what they should look like.

Bill O'Hanlon's (O'Hanlon & Wiener-Davis, 1989) solution-oriented approach is an active, pragmatic process in which the therapist directs the conversation toward goal-oriented solutions, validates clients' experiences, suggests behaviors aimed at goal achievement, and emphasizes solution-oriented stories. Focusing on the framework of meaning according to which problems are defined and solutions are thus limited, O'Hanlon sees therapy as a conversational process that involves joining with the client, allowing the client to describe the problem, uncovering exceptions to the problem, normalizing, goal-setting, and searching for possibilities, all of which may enhance the therapeutic process.

Similarly, de Shazer (1985), along with his wife, Insoo Kim Berg, created a solution-focused approach according to which clients' goals, rather than their problems, are the focus. Believing that the therapist does not necessarily need to know the problem in order to help clients find a solution, de Shazer used scaling questions, the search for exceptions, creative misunderstanding, and other language games intended to help clients move from problem-focused stories to progressive narratives in an effort to create solutions. The hallmark of this approach is the Miracle Question:

> Supposing that one night there is a miracle and while you were sleeping the problem that brought you to therapy is solved. How would you know? What would be different? What will you notice different the next morning that will tell you there has been a miracle? What will your spouse notice? (de Shazer, 1985, p. 113)

Although aspects of narrative therapy certainly may be found in all of the postmodern approaches, the most widely recognized proponents of this approach are Michael White and David Epston (1990). Focused particularly on helping clients to create and live their own personal stories, rather than being lived by the more generic, meta-narratives of society, this approach involves helping clients to externalize, or separate the problem from themselves; searching for unique outcomes that reveal gaps in clients' problem-saturated stories; and facilitating the reauthoring of their lives. With an emphasis on language, both oral and written, the therapist speaks in terms of stories, encouraging clients to understand the storied nature of reality as the problems that brought them to therapy are resolved.

In an effort to move away from the extreme focus of earlier models on intervention and change, Anderson and Goolishian (1986) created a therapeutic conversations, or collaborative language systems approach. In this approach an attitude of not-knowing and the facilitation of caring, empathic conversations that are respectful and collaborative are the means for assisting in the cocreation of new stories that enable clients to live more meaningful lives. Based on the notion that it is the problem that creates the system, conversations in which problems are dis-solved and one's sense of self is reconstructed are encouraged.

Finally, regardless of theoretical or therapeutic orientation, Watzlawick, Weakland, and Fisch, in their book *Change: Principles of Problem Formation and Problem Resolution* (1974), provided a four-step procedure for change, applicable across approaches and recognizable as the basis of some of the more recently developed postmodern approaches briefly described above:

- Define the problem in clear, concrete terms
- Investigate the solutions attempted so far
- Define the concrete change to be achieved
- Formulate and implement the plan for change

Also outlined are the distinctions between first-order change and second-order change, or change that occurs within a system that itself remains unchanged, as opposed to change in the rules of the system, or thinking outside of the box. It is in the second-order change category that we may understand so-called paradoxical injunctions, or interventions that, although logical from another framework, appear illogical in the context of the client's current framework.

Processes Characterizing Successful Families

As noted above, while helping clients achieve their goals by utilizing ideas from the therapy approaches just described, helping families flourish also involves an awareness of and efforts to facilitate resilience. To do so requires knowledge of the various process dimensions found in successful families.

These processes contribute to the ability of families to evidence resilience. While no family is likely to demonstrate all of them, well-functioning families generally are characterized by a majority of the following: a legitimate source of authority; a stable rule system that is consistently followed; stable, consistent nurturing behaviors; stable childrearing patterns and couple-maintenance behaviors; a sense of family nationality and belonging; respect for individual differences; flexibility and adaptability; initiative and creativity; clear generational boundaries; a balance between separateness and togetherness; clear and congruent communication; spontaneity and humor; mutuality, cooperation, and collaboration; shared roles and responsibilities; permission to express all feelings; friendliness, good will, and optimism; belief in a larger force or a transcendental value system; an ethical sense of values; shared rituals and celebrations; a natural network of relationships outside the family; shared goals; and negotiation without intimidation (Becvar & Becvar, 2009).

Once again, the therapist must be well informed relative to ways that may support the attainment by clients of skills related to and success in the above areas. Indeed, the entire process of facilitating resilience involves bringing to bear a variety of information and accessing many theories/stories about how best to proceed. In addition to knowledge related to areas already discussed, this also involves the ability to assess and respond appropriately to various contextual factors.

Social Ecological, Cultural, and Contextual Factors

The ability to facilitate and/or evidence resilience is affected by a variety of contextual factors at many levels. Beginning with information related to families in general, first it is appropriate to consider the family's internal context. From my perspective, a family is whatever or however it defines itself to be. Rather than focusing on a specific structure, I have found it more useful to consider the processes characterizing the families. Consideration of those described above is involved at this point.

I also want to determine where family members are relative to both expected and unexpected developmental challenges they may be experiencing as these are two dimensions of the internal context that are likely to have an impact on the ability of families to evidence resilience. In the former category it is thus appropriate for the therapist to be able to make recourse to theories/stories related to physical development, cognitive development (e.g., Piaget, 1955), psychological development (e.g., Freud, 1900/1962), psychosocial development (e.g., Erikson, 1963), moral development (e.g., Gilligan, 1982; Kohlberg, 1981), spiritual development (e.g., Fowler, 1995), and family development, including life cycle stages and life cycle issues and tasks (Carter & McGoldrick, 1988). As the therapist is able to normalize and/or help families negotiate various challenges she may contribute to her ability to facilitate resilience as well.

Families also may be affected by such unexpected developmental challenges as the loss of a relationship, job, home, physical capacity, or something of value; denial of membership in a valued group; loss of respect or an experience of betrayal; loss of self-esteem; death of someone important; a parent being called to active duty or going to war; a parent taking a job away from home; a grandparent moving in with the family; or winning a large sum of money. In cases such as these, attention must be focused on dealing effectively with the particular challenge, which of course is an important aspect of facilitating resilience.

Relative to the family as a whole, context also includes both structural as well as ethnic/cultural variations and related considerations about which the therapist must be knowledgeable. While no one structure is necessarily better than another, the way the family is organized may have important ramifications relative to areas on which it is appropriate to focus. Such structural variations include divorced families with young children; blended/reconstituted families; adoptive families; multigenerational families;

single-parent families; and lesbian and gay families. Being sensitive to the unique needs and challenges faced by families in each category is essential when the goal is to facilitate resilience (Becvar, 2007).

To illustrate, we might consider and compare divorced families with young children with adoptive families in terms of the issues with which each group is likely to be dealing. For divorced families with young children, attention may need to be directed to facilitating the well-being of the custodial parent; shifting and redefining roles, responsibilities, and relationships; mourning the previous family and celebrating the new family; encouraging effective co-parenting; building new support systems; maintaining appropriate boundaries; clarifying custody and visitation arrangements; and avoiding the assumption that problems must necessarily occur as a function of the divorce. By contrast, for adoptive families the salient issues are likely to include such aspects as facilitating attachment; considering relationships with the child's birth culture; clarifying legal arrangements and specifying boundaries relative to the birth mother; assuming the best but being alert to signals that indicate problems; supporting children in cultural identity formation; celebrating difference; being honest with children in age-appropriate ways; and recognizing the potential desire of the child to seek information about his or her birth parents.

In addition to such structural variations, our very diverse society also includes many families influenced by differing ethnic and cultural heritages. This diversity includes American Indian and Alaska native families, Asian-American families (e.g., Korean-American, Chinese-American, Japanese-American, Filipino-American), African-American families, and Latino families (e.g., Mexican-American, Puerto Rican-American, Cuban-American), to name just a few. It is important to note that I do not believe that we can be expert relative to each of these groups. Further, although it may be useful to have information about characteristics said to be typical of each group (e.g., McGoldrick, Giordano, & Pearce, 1996), we must beware of the assumption that all families within a group are the same, recognizing as well that there generally is as much difference within groups as there is between groups. At the same time, I believe it is important to be particularly sensitive to issues pertaining to help-seeking behaviors that tend to be characteristic of various ethnic groups.

For example, in many traditionally oriented Asian-American families the family takes precedence over the individual, with the individual understood to be the product of preceding generations. Such families often have formal rules of conduct and they tend to be hierarchical and patriarchal in structure. Arranged marriages, when they occur, often are predicated on the continuation of the male line. Shame, obligation, social class, geographical origin, birthplace, and generation in the US are all important dimensions for these families. They also tend to be internally oriented regarding problem-solving, display reticence when it comes to the expression of feelings, and favor indirect expression of disagreement. Therefore, when working with Asian-American families it may be important to understand that therapy typically is a last resort as help-seeking behavior may bring a sense of shame and a fear of stigma. Further, establishing trust is essential as is respecting family roles. Avoiding direct confrontation and being aware that ambiguity may create anxiety also may be important even as it may be best for the therapist to act as a knowledgeable expert (Ho, 1987; Lee, 1996; Shon & Ja, 1982).

Needless to say, another important aspect of a family's context is its socioeconomic status. Awareness of the family's ability to access needed resources is essential if therapy is to be successful. According to Patterson (2002b), families have four core functions, including family formation and membership; economic support; nurturance, education, and socialization; and protection of vulnerable members. Certainly, not being able to provide adequate economic support to members has significant ramifications for and influences the degree to which the family is successful relative to the other three core functions.

The family's context also includes the nature and degree of interaction it has with other systems. Use of an ecomap (Hartman & Laird, 1983) enables the therapist to depict and understand the connections and types of relationships the family and its members do or do not have with such other systems as work, school, social services, the courts or juvenile justice system, extended family, friends, religious/ spiritual resources, and the larger community. This, in turn, enables the therapist to have a better sense of the family's larger network.

In addition to the above, perhaps one of the most significant contextual factors is the larger society within which families dwell. Although in the US family issues generate a great deal of conversation and controversy, we are not primarily a family-oriented society despite verbiage to the contrary. Rather, the value most cherished in this society is individualism (Becvar, 1983). In part as a function of our individualistic orientation, we are one of the few industrialized nations in the world that does not have an integrated, coherent family policy. Rather, what we have is a fragmented patchwork of policies that in many cases are less than adequate for assisting families in need. Consistent with a predominant fear of big government, money is allocated to states, which are responsible for creating policies, and states vary in terms of the money received and how it is spent. What is more, unlike policies in other countries, access to resources for children often requires parental participation. When parents don't follow through, the children do not benefit in terms of receiving needed services and resources.

What is more, as I have noted elsewhere (Becvar, 1983, 2007), the general tendency at all levels of our society, from policy makers to practitioners, has been to operate as error-activated systems, responding to crises when they occur, and being concerned primarily with problems and pathology rather than with prevention and health. Indeed, as Patterson (2002b, p. 233) has noted, "we have a long history of focusing on the causes of disease, deficits, and behavioral problems." Therefore, we tend not to be proactive in terms of preventive measures and the responses to crisis generally have not been strength-based.

The final consideration relative to context is that regardless of structure, culture/ethnicity, or other influential factors, from my perspective there is no such thing as *the* family. Rather, there are as many families as there are family members. That is, each member of the family has a different and unique story about the family relative to his or her personal experience and perspective on that experience. Therefore, my approach includes taking an anthropological stance to understanding each new family system with which I work. Behaving as not-expert and not-knowing, I am curious about my clients and invite them to teach me about what I need to know to help them. They have the greatest expertise regarding their family. I, in turn, bring to bear the theories/stories that I believe are most relevant for helping them to achieve their goals while at the same time attempting to facilitate resilience.

Clinical, Research, and Policy Implications

Similar to individually focused research on resilience, facilitating family resilience involves consideration of the risk and protective factors related to the specific family context or focal issue. That is, family members are at risk in specific ways depending on the particular challenges with which they are dealing. What is more, the protective factors that may enable them to handle such challenges also vary and are specific to the issues at hand. For example, the risk factors for families relative to the severe mental illness of one of their members (Marsh & Johnson, 1997) include grief for the one afflicted and for personal losses as well as grief related to the loss of hopes, dreams, and expectations; chronic sorrow related to a wide variety of losses and challenges; having to live on an emotional roller-coaster related to the relapse/remission cycle; empathic pain for the afflicted one's losses; the energy drain related to coping and caregiving; disruption in family routines; obstacles in the service delivery system; and the stigma of mental illness. The factors that help to protect the family members from the ill effects of such risks include sensitive understanding and an emphasis on normalizing on the part of professionals; a focus on the strengths and skills of everyone involved; education regarding the illness, the mental health system, and resources that may be available; effective communication and problem-solving skills; the ability to manage stress and resolve feelings of grief and loss; and a supportive family environment.

As with social policies, the focus of research until rather recently has been on individuals and individual resilience (Patterson 2002a, 2002b), and thus information about the many different challenges faced by families is somewhat limited. While research related to individual resilience continues, family resilience is now also receiving widespread attention. Indeed, research in this area is on the rise and promises to provide much new and needed information on the topic. Essential in this research is the consideration of relationship dynamics and contextual issues, which may not receive similar attention in individually focused research.

All families have an amazing complexity, as illustrated by the vast amount of information with which I believe it is appropriate to be familiar if one is to be able to provide effective services. However, when the client system falls into the vulnerable population category, then complexity increases exponentially. To illustrate, Aponte (1994) describes the circularity of problems experienced by what he terms "the new poor." According to his view families are seen as under-organized and thus unable to provide the appropriate support for their members. Lack of support is also characteristic of the communities in which such families reside, which in part accounts for the maintenance if not the cause of the family's under organization. What is more, social policies fail to provide the support needed by the community in order to support the families in that community. The cycle continues as problem families produce problem members who are unable to enhance the community, which is then unable to access needed resources. Aponte therefore suggests what he terms an eco-structural approach. This approach involves working not only with families and their members but also with the other systems with which they are involved, a position that I certainly support. There are thus at least four challenges with which policy makers must grapple if efforts to help families achieve their goals as well as to evidence resilience are to succeed.

First, those who are to provide services for members of vulnerable populations need to be extremely well trained and ideally have proven track records as well as reasonable experience as mental health professionals. Unfortunately, the reverse is often the case as new graduates and other novices are hired to fill positions in which they typically are underpaid and overworked. Appropriate supervision that might improve the situation is often lacking, and high rates of burn-out lead to frequent turnover in which the pattern tends to repeat.

Second, if mental health professionals are to be able to work not only with families but also with the other systems with which the families are involved, as Aponte (1994) advocates, there needs to be coordination between the service providers. Also required is a limited case load that allows for meaningful therapeutic interventions. Ideally, a team approach would be implemented in order to support the process.

Third, the creation of one-size fits all responses to the challenges faced by any family, let alone those that are particularly vulnerable, is doomed to limited success at best and failure and the exacerbation of problems at worst. As I have emphasized throughout the writing of this chapter, each family is unique and requires responses that are tailored to fit the needs and goals of that family. While there are some general aspects that all families may share, no two families are exactly alike.

Fourth, and perhaps most significant, is the challenge related to American ideology and the primary values characterizing this society. What I am suggesting relates to changes that I believe are necessary relative to orientation. In order to be as effective as possible when working with members of vulnerable populations, I believe we need to move from an individual focus to a focus on families, as well as moving from a problem-response mode to a preventive, strengths-based, solution focus.

Unfortunately, such challenges are not likely to be resolved in the near future. On the one hand they are likely to require more money, at least at the outset. However, over time I suspect that less money would be required as more solutions were achieved and more families were successful in evidencing resilience. On the other hand, a major overhaul of the system would require a sea change in the way we think about helping those in need. Nevertheless, each of us can do our part in small but nevertheless important ways.

We can focus on facilitating resilience clinically and conduct research that validates the effectiveness of our approaches in this realm. We can expand research efforts to have a broader understanding of the risk and protective factors relative to a wider array of contextual influences. And we can advocate for policies that would support more meaningful and effective responses to families in general as well as those in need (Zimmerman, 1975).

As I indicated at the outset, by describing my approach what I provide here is but a story, one that I have found to be useful. At the same time, I am mindful that this is but one of many possible stories that might describe ways to facilitate family resilience. However, what I believe all such stories may have in common is the following summation: Resilient families are successful in achieving their own goals. More than merely surviving, they thrive in response to the challenges of both expected and unexpected crisis and change. Resilience is facilitated as healthy processes in families are encouraged and supported. These are families that flourish (Becvar, 2007), as exemplified by the clients described below in a composite case example.

Case Example

Ted Rivers, a 45-year-old successful business man, contacted me a little less than a year after the death of his wife, Renee. Ted and Renee had been married for 15 years and had two sons, Sam, age 12, and Max, age 10. Ted's presenting concern was Sam's anger and acting-out behavior at school as well as Max's silence and withdrawal from various activities both at home and at school. During our first session, which included the boys, Ted reported that he had been working very hard to maintain some kind of stability for his sons since Renee's death. However, he felt like he was failing given reports from the counselors at his sons' schools regarding their behavior as well as their attitude toward him at home. He said that previously they had been a happy, loving family involved in many activities and that he had always gotten along well with the boys and enjoyed being a parent. Aside from normal childrearing issues, he and Renee had never had to cope with serious or inappropriate behavior from either Sam or Max, so he was very unsure about how to proceed. What he had tried included talking with the boys, both separately and together, taking away privileges, and even grounding Sam on occasion, but the problems seemed to be getting worse instead of better. What he really wanted was some advice about how to get things back to normal.

When I chatted with the boys, I first asked them about school, things they liked to do, things they did well. Not surprisingly, although they were certainly polite and well-behaved, their answers were short and they didn't disclose very much. When I asked them what they would like to see happen for themselves or for their family, neither could, or would, say.

In the course of the conversation that ensued I learned that "normal" in Ted's eyes would be life as it was before Renee died; that Sam thought his Dad wasn't around very much; that both boys thought he was a push-over because he often relented on punishments; and that Ted felt guilty and was afraid of being too strict given the fact that the boys had just lost their mother. When I asked about the circumstances of Renee's death and how they were dealing with their grief, the boys became nervous and fearful that their Dad would get upset. It seemed that they had been unable to talk together about how each was feeling and that it had almost become a taboo subject. Through the tears that the boys seemed to fear I learned from Ted that Renee, who had been a wonderful wife and mother, had been killed in an automobile accident the day after her 44th birthday, and that he had not been prepared for what they all were now facing. However, he was doing his best and he desperately wanted things to improve.

As we neared the end of the first session I had several stories running through my head related to typical responses to the death of a parent and the death of a spouse as well as the risk and protective factors found to characterize each of these experiences in addition to those related to unexpected death. That is, children the ages of Sam and Max tend to have reactions to the death of a parent that mimic those of adults and include increased fears about both their own mortality and that of the surviving parent (Raphael, 1983). At the same time, when a spouse dies, the surviving spouse's sense of security tends to be shattered, he or she may feel totally lost and bewildered, and he or she is likely to experience anger, frustration, and loss of control (Becvar, 2007). In the case of the death of a parent, the risk factors include great anguish; guilt; fears about one's own mortality; fears about the mortality of the surviving parent; depression; and mental and physical health challenges (Greeff & Human, 2004). Protective factors related to the death of a parent include emotional and practical support among family members; family hardiness; coherence; communication; flexibility; economic resources; positive personality characteristics/optimism; support from extended family and friends; and religious and spiritual beliefs and activities. The risk factors following the death of a spouse include pre-loss dependency both on the spouse and in general; an inability to find any meaning in a loss; views of the world as meaningless, unjust, and uncontrollable; low instrumental support (Bonanno et al., 2002), and an increase in mortality and depression for men (Stroebe & Schut, 2001). The protective factors following the death of a spouse include pre-loss acceptance of death and belief in a just world; emotional stability; conscientiousness; agreeableness; openness to experience; tendency to introspect; perceived confidence in coping; and religion/spirituality. Finally, in the case of unexpected death, risk factors include health consequences (Stroebe & Schut); challenges to the bereaved person's coping mechanisms (Rando, 1988); belief that one has little control over one's life; lack of social support; low self-esteem and ego strength; and guilt proneness and anxiety. The protective factors relative to unexpected death include high self-esteem; high internal control beliefs; secure orientation to attachment; religion/spirituality; and family and social support (Becvar).

Drawing on this information I first attempted to normalize the way each of these family members was feeling, letting them know that what was going on was pretty typical given their circumstances. I then affirmed the strengths that I perceived in this family including Ted's efforts to be a good parent and to provide for his family, the decision to come for help, the boys' desire to avoid upsetting their father, as well as the efforts of all to be supportive and caring. I then explained to Ted that the family would probably need to create a new normal, one that accommodated their loss and still enabled them to be successful and happy, although I acknowledged that this probably would take some time. In the meantime I suggested that it was important that Ted behave in such a way that the boys would know that he could handle them and that they would all be alright. Part of doing so was to assure the boys that they could talk about their mother with him, and that just because he was sad didn't mean that he wasn't going to be o.k. I emphasized the importance of creating and maintaining logical consequences in response to inappropriate behavior, and recommended that appropriate behavior be acknowledged as well. Finally, I suggested that Ted spend one-on-one time with each of his sons every day and that, if possible, he adjust his schedule so that he could be more available.

Over the course of the next several months I saw the Rivers on a weekly basis and during that time was able to learn more about their daily lives as well as their extended family. After doing a genogram with the family I suggested ways they could access support from grandparents as well as other relatives who were more than willing to lend a hand. I also encouraged Ted to inform the counselors at his boys' schools about their situation and the fact that they were getting help, and encouraged him to enlist their support by providing a safe space should either of the boys feel the need for a time out. I regularly asked Ted to tell me how the boys were doing and I asked the boys to tell me how their Dad was doing. I also devoted some time each session to conversations about grief and encouraged the family members to continue these talks at home. I suggested that the family think about how they wanted to handle birthdays, anniversaries, and other holidays. In addition, I suggested that they create a memory book dedicated to Renee, and that they add pictures and other items they thought would have been meaningful to her. I inquired about their religious/spiritual beliefs and learned that although they previously had attended weekly church services, they had not been going since Renee's death. Although this was an area that was important to Ted, he both dreaded going back and regretted his inattention to the boy's spiritual education. I therefore suggested that the three of them create a home church service that they have each Sunday, at least for the next little while.

As therapy progressed, both Sam and Max became more willing to participate and share their feelings. Their behaviors improved at school as well as at home and they reported that they really liked having time alone with their Dad. Eventually we began to space our sessions out over longer intervals as it became clear to all of us that the original goal had been attained. Not only that, but during our last session together Ted informed me that he and his sons had decided to volunteer at a summer camp for families who had lost one of their members. They felt that they had come a long way and now they wanted to help others do so as well. They certainly were evidencing resilience.

Conclusion

As I interact with clients such as Ted, Sam, and Max Rivers, I bring with me my theoretical orientation, which is a part of me both personally and professionally. In addition, my metaphorical storehouse of theories/stories that I can access as needed contains information about processes characterizing successful families; information about families in general as well as about specific families; information about how to encourage such healthful processes in families as effective communication, family enrichment, relationship enhancement, effective parenting, rituals and traditions, spontaneity and humor, goals, values and meaning, religion and spirituality; and information about resilience in context, all of which have been described briefly above. Also included, of course, is awareness of the various therapeutic strategies/interventions that may be useful for the particular family with whom I am working. As I select from this storehouse my path is illuminated by a series of guiding principles, described as follows.

The first of my guiding principles is to recognize that believing is seeing. This speaks to the importance of becoming aware of my personal stories, asking such questions as, "What am I telling myself about the client?" and "What other stories might I tell myself?" Such questions also lead to a consideration of the second guiding principle, which is to acknowledge the influence of the observer on the observed. I thus might ask myself, "How would my having a different story change what I am seeing?" and "How might the other person respond differently to my new stories?"

The third guiding principle is to recognize that I am participating in the creation rather than the discovery of realities. Important questions relative to this principle include, "Can I see how I am participating in creating problems?" and "Can I see how I am participating in creating solutions?" Answers to these questions are a preamble to the fourth guiding principle, which is always to act in a manner consistent with the behavior desired. In consideration of this principle I might ask myself, "What kind of response would I like?" and "What behaviors on my part are logical to the desired responses on the part of the other?"

My fifth guiding principle is to assess, analyze, and perturb with a solution focus. This includes suspending judgment in terms of evaluating good/bad or right/wrong and choosing instead to focus on shedding light upon the client's situation. This principle is also operationalized by becoming sensitive to language, for example, by checking out meanings and being careful of the way I express myself verbally. Reframing behavior speaks to the importance of helping clients to expand their views in recognition of the influence of perception on the creation of problems and solutions. Finally, affirming clients speaks to the importance of emphasizing the strengths that I believe are inherent in all people.

Thinking in terms of both/and rather than either/or represents my sixth guiding principle. That is, I operate on the assumption that all perspectives contain truth and that the more important consideration relative to a particular theory/story is its utility, which is to be decided relative to context. Thinking in terms of both/and also means that I see complementarity and connection, and I understand separateness as an illusion. Indeed, I believe that we are all involved in each other's destiny, and I attempt always to act in a manner that is consistent with this belief.

References

Andersen, T. (1987). The reflecting team: Dialogue and meta-dialogue in clinical work. *Family Process, 26*, 415–428.

Andersen, T. (1992). Reflections on reflecting on families. In S. McNamee & K. J. Gergen (Eds.), *Therapy as social construction* (pp. 54–68). Newbury Park, CA: Sage.

Anderson, H., & Goolishian, H. A. (1986). Problem-determined systems: Towards transformation in family therapy. *Journal of Strategic and Systemic Therapies, 5*, 1–13.

Aponte, H. (1994). *Bread and spirit: Therapy with the new poor.* New York: W. W. Norton.

Bateson, G. (1972). *Steps to an ecology of mind.* New York: Ballantine Books.

Bateson, G. (1979). *Mind and nature.* New York: Dutton.

Becvar, D. S. (1983). *The relationship between family and society in the context of American ideology: A systems theoretical perspective.* Unpublished doctoral dissertation, Saint Louis University, St. Louis, MO.

Becvar, D. S. (2007). *Families that flourish: Facilitating resilience in clinical practice.* New York: W. W. Norton.

Becvar, D. S., & Becvar, R. J. (2009). *Family therapy: A systemic integration* (7th ed.). Boston: Allyn & Bacon.

Bonanno, G. A., Wortman, C. B., Lehman, D. R., Tweed, R. G., Haring, M., Sonnega, J., et al. (2002). Resilience to loss and chronic grief: A prospective study from preloss to 18-months postloss. *Journal of Personal and Social Psychology, 83*(5), 1150–1164.

Boss, P. (2006). *Loss, trauma and resilience: Therapeutic work with ambiguous loss.* New York: W. W. Norton.

Boszormenyi-Nagy, I. (1966). From family therapy to a psychology of relationships: Fictions of the individual and fictions of the family. *Comprehensive Psychiatry, 7*, 406–423.

Boszormenyi-Nagy, I., & Spark, G. (1973). *Invisible loyalties: Reciprocity in intergenerations family therapy.* New York: Harper & Row.

Bowen, M. (1976). Theory in the practice of psychotherapy. In P. J. Guerin (Ed.), *Family therapy: Theory and practice* (pp. 42–90). New York: Gardner Press.

Bronowski, J. (1978). *The origins of knowledge and imagination.* New Haven, CT: Yale University Press.

Carter, E. A., & McGoldrick, M. (Eds.). (1988). *The changing family life cycle.* New York: Gardner Press.

Conger, R. D., & Conger, K. J. (2002). Resilience in midwestern families: Selected findings from the first decade of a prospective, longitudinal study. *Journal of Marriage and Family, 64*, 361–373.

De Haan, L., Hawley, D. R., & Deal, J. F. (2002). Operationalizing family resilience: A methodological strategy. *American Journal of Family Therapy, 30*, 275–291.

de Shazer, S. (1985). *Keys to solution in brief therapy.* New York: W. W. Norton.

Erikson, E. (1963). *Childhood and society.* New York: W. W. Norton.

Fowler, J. W. (1995). *Stages of faith: The psychology of human development and the quest for meaning.* New York: HarperCollins.

Freud, S. (1900). The interpretation of dreams. In J. Strachey (Eds.), The complete psychological works of Sigmund Freud. London: The Hogarth Press.

Gergen, K. J. (1985). Social constructivist movement in psychology. *American Psychologist, 40*, 266–275.

Gergen, K. J. (1991). *The saturated self.* New York: Basic Books.

Gilligan, C. (1982). *In a different voice.* Cambridge, MA: Harvard University Press.

Greeff, A. R., & Human, B. (2004). Resilience in families in which a parent has died. *The American Journal of Family Therapy, 32*, 27–42.

Haley, J. (1963). *Strategies of psychotherapy.* New York: Grune & Stratton.

Hartman, A., & Laird, J. (1983). *Family-centered social work practice.* New York: Free Press.

Hawley, D. R., & DeHaan, L. (1996). Toward a definition of family resilience: Integrating life-span and family perspectives. *Family Process, 35*, 283–298.

Ho, M. J. (1987). *Family therapy with ethnic minorities.* Newbury Park, CA: Sage.

Husserl, E. (1965). *Phenomenology and the crisis of philosophy* (Wuentin Lauer, Trans.). New York: Harper & Row.

Kohlberg, L. (1981). *The philosophy of moral development.* San Francisco: Harper and Row.

Kragh, J. R., & Huber, C. H. (2002). Family resilience and domestic violence: Panacea or pragmatic therapeutic perspective? *The Journal of Individual Psychology, 58*(3), 290–304.

Lee, E. (1996). Asian-American families: An overview. In M. McGoldrick, J. Giordano, & J. K. Pearce (Eds.), *Ethnicity and family therapy* (2nd ed., pp. 227–248). New York: Guilford.

Marsh, D. T., & Johnson, D. L. (1997). The family experience of mental illness: Implications for intervention. *Professional Psychology: Research and Practice, 28*(3), 229–237.

Maturana, H., & Varela, F. (1987). *The tree of knowledge.* Boston: New Science Library.

McGoldrick, M., Giordano, J., & Pearce, J. K. (1996). *Ethnicity and family therapy* (2nd ed.). New York: Guilford.

Minuchin, S. (1974). *Families and family therapy.* Cambridge, MA: Harvard University Press.

O'Hanlon, W. H., & Wiener-Davis, M. (1989). *In search of solutions: A new distinction in psychotherapy.* New York: W. W. Norton.

Oswald, R. F. (2002). Resilience within the family networks of lesbians and gay men: Intentionality and redefinition. *Journal of Marriage and Family, 64,* 374–383.

Patterson, J. M. (2002a). Integrating family resilience and family stress theory. *Journal of Marriage and Family, 64,* 349–360.

Patterson, J. M. (2002b). Understanding family resilience. *Journal of Clinical Psychology, 58*(3), 233–246.

Piaget, J. (1955). *The language and thought of the child.* New York: World Publishing.

Rando, T. (1988). *Grieving: How to go on living when someone you love dies.* Lexington, MA: Lexington Book.

Raphael, B. (1983). *The anatomy of bereavement.* New York: Basic Books.

Sandau-Beckler, P. A., Devall, E., & de La Rosa, I. A. (2002). Strengthening family resilience: Prevention and treatment for high-risk substance-affected families. *The Journal of Individual Psychology, 58*(3), 306–327.

Satir, V. (1964). *Conjoint family therapy.* Palo Alto, CA: Science and Behavior Books.

Schwartz, J. P. (2002). Family resilience and pragmatic parent education. *The Journal of Individual Psychology, 58*(3), 250–262.

Shon, S. P., & Ja, D. Y. (1982). Asian families. In M. McGoldrick, J. K. Pearce, & J. Giordano (Eds.), *Ethnicity and family therapy* (pp. 208–228). New York: Guilford.

Stroebe, W., & Schut, H. (2001). Risk factors in bereavement outcome: A methodological and empirical review. In M. S. Stroebe, R. O. Hansson, W. Stroebe, & H. Schut (Eds.), *Handbook of bereavement research: Consequences, coping, and care* (pp. 349–371). Washington, D. C.: American Psychological Association.

Stuart, R. B. (1969). Operant-interpersonal treatment of marital discord. *Journal of Consulting and Clinical Psychology, 33,* 675–682.

Stuart, R. B. (1980). *Helping couples change.* New York: Guilford.

Von Glasersfeld, E. (1988). The reluctance to change a way thinking: Radical constructivism and autopoiesis and psychotherapy. *Irish Journal of Psychology, 9,* 83–90.

Walsh, F. (1998). *Strengthening family resilience.* New York: Guilford.

Walsh, F. (2003a). Family resilience: A framework for clinical practice, *Family Process, 42*(1), 1–8.

Watzlawick, P. (1976). *How real is real?* New York: Vintage Books.

Watzlawick, P., Weakland, J. H., & Fisch, R. (1974). *Change: Principles of problem formation and problem resolution.* New York: W. W. Norton.

Whitaker, C. A. (1975). Psychotherapy of the absurd: With a special emphasis on the psychotherapy of aggression. *Family Process, 14*(1), 1–16.

White, M., & Epston, D. (1990). *Narrative means to therapeutic ends.* New York: W. W. Norton.

Zimmerman, S. L. (1979). Reassessing the effect of public policy on family functioning. *Social Casework, 59,* 451–457.

Community-Based Practice Applications of a Family Resilience Framework

5

Froma Walsh

Introduction

A family resilience practice framework is especially valuable in community-based intervention and prevention with families facing serious life challenges. How families approach and respond to their stressful conditions can foster positive adaptation, with potential for personal and relational growth for all members. In this chapter I first summarize the core practice principles of my research-informed Family Resilience Framework and identify key processes that practitioners can facilitate to strengthen family resilience. I then describe several community-based training and practice applications developed through the Chicago Center for Family Health (CCFH) to demonstrate the utility of a family resilience-oriented framework in a wide range of adverse situations: healing and recovery from crisis, trauma, and loss; navigating disruptive transitions or dislocations; thriving despite multistress, chronic conditions; and positive development of at-risk youth in vulnerable communities. Using varied formats, including brief consultation, family counseling/therapy, and multifamily groups, workshops, and forums, this collaborative resilience-oriented approach strengthens family functioning, relational bonds, vital community connections, and resources to meet future life challenges.

Individual Resilience in Systemic Perspective

Most resilience theory, research, and intervention approaches over the past 3 decades have been individually focused, reflecting dominant medical, neuroscience, and mental health paradigms (Luthar, Cicchetti, & Becker, 2000; Walsh, 1996, 2006). Influenced by the Anglo-American cultural ideal of the "rugged individual," early studies of resilience sought to identify innate or acquired personal traits that rendered some children invulnerable to the impact of parental pathology or extreme environmental conditions. An interactive view of resilience emerged as research was extended to a wide range of adverse conditions—such as growing up in impoverished circumstances, dealing with chronic illness, or recovering from catastrophic life events, war-related and mass trauma, and traumatic loss.

F. Walsh (✉)
Chicago Center for Family Health, Chicago, IL, USA

School of Social Service Administration and Department of Psychiatry, Pritzker School
of Medicine, University of Chicago, Chicago, IL, USA
e-mail: fwalsh@uchicago.edu

D.S. Becvar (ed.), *Handbook of Family Resilience*,
DOI 10.1007/978-1-4614-3917-2_5, © Springer Science+Business Media New York 2013

Resilience came to be seen in terms of the interplay of multiple risk and protective processes over time, involving individual, family, community, and larger sociocultural influences (Rutter, 1987; Walsh, 2003). Individual vulnerability, risk, or the impact of stressful conditions could be countered by positive mediating influences.

Relational Lifelines for Resilience

The crucial influence of significant relationships for individual resilience has stood out across studies (Walsh, 1996). Reports of children who managed to thrive despite a parent's mental illness or mal-treatment noted that their resilience was most often nurtured in strong, supportive bonds—particularly with mentors, such as coaches and teachers, who were invested in them. Yet, the narrow focus on parental deficits led many to dismiss families as dysfunctional and to look to outside resources to counter their damaging influence. In mental health and child development literature, families were seen to contribute to risk, but not to resilience.

Family systems theory, research, and practice have broadened our recognition of the potential fam-ily resources for individual resilience in the network of relationships, from parents and caregivers, to couple and sibling bonds and the contributions of extended family members (Ungar, 2004; Walsh, 1996, 2003). Widening our lens to include kinship networks within and beyond the household, family assessment and intervention aim to identify and involve family members who are—or could become—relational lifelines for resilience. Even in troubled families, strengths and potential can be found alongside vulnerabilities and limitations (Walsh, 2006).

The Concept of Family Resilience

The concept of family resilience expands focus beyond a dyadic view—seeing individual family members as resources for individual resilience—to a systemic perspective on risk and resilience in the family as a functional unit (Walsh, 1996). Building on studies of family stress, coping, and adaptation and research on well-functioning family systems, family resilience is seen to involve dynamic pro-cesses that foster positive adaptation of the family unit and its members in the context of significant adversity (Patterson, 2002; Walsh, 1996).

A basic premise is that stressful life challenges impact the entire family and, in turn, key family processes mediate the adaptation—or maladaptation—of all members *and* the family unit. The family's approach and response to adversity is crucial. Major stressors can derail the functioning of a family system, with ripple effects for all members and their relationships. Key processes, supportive bonds, and extrafamilial resources enable the family system to rally in times of crisis, to buffer stress, to reduce the risk of dysfunction, and to support optimal adaptation.

Family resilience can be defined as *the ability of families to withstand and rebound from disruptive life challenges, strengthened and more resourceful* (Walsh, 2003, 2006). The concept of resilience entails more than managing stress, shouldering a burden, or surviving an ordeal. It involves the poten-tial for personal and relational transformation and growth that can be forged out of adversity. Tapping into key processes for resilience, families that have been struggling can emerge stronger and more resourceful in meeting future challenges. Members may develop new insights and abilities. A crisis can be a wake-up call, heightening their attention to core values and important matters. It often becomes an opportunity to reappraise life priorities and it stimulates greater investment in meaningful relationships, as has been found in research on *posttraumatic growth* (Tedeschi & Calhoun, 2004). Studies of happy couples (Driver, Tabares, Shapiro, & Gottman, 2012) and strong families (Stinnett & DeFrain, 1985) report that through weathering a crisis together couple and family relationships were enriched and became more loving than they might otherwise have been.

Sociocultural and Developmental Contexts of Family Resilience

A family resilience framework is grounded in family systems theory, combining ecological and developmental perspectives to view family functioning in relation to its broader sociocultural context and multigenerational family life cycle passage. Risk and resilience are viewed in light of multiple, recursive influences involving individuals, families, larger social systems, and cultural variables. Symptoms of distress may be primarily biologically based, as in neurological vulnerabilities, and also influenced by sociocultural factors, such as barriers of poverty and discrimination that render some families or communities at higher risk. Symptoms of family members may be generated by a crisis event, such as a sexual assault, or by the wider impact of a large-scale disaster. Unsuccessful attempts to cope with an overwhelming situation exacerbate family distress. The family, peer group, community resources, school or work settings, and other social systems are seen as nested contexts for nurturing and sustaining resilience. A multidimensional, holistic approach (Falicov, 1995) addresses the varied contexts, identifies common elements in a crisis situation, and also takes into account each family's unique perspectives, resources, and challenges.

Family Transformations in Rapidly Changing Societies

The concept of family resilience is especially timely as our world grows increasingly turbulent and families face unprecedented challenges. With profound social, economic, and political upheavals over recent decades, families have been undergoing rapid transformation and redefinition (Walsh, 2012b). To understand family challenges and resilience, it is important to consider the implications of the following trends: (1) varied family structures and gender roles, (2) increasing cultural diversity and economic disparity, and (3) varying, expanded family life course. Efforts to strengthen family resilience must be attuned to this growing diversity and complexity in family life.

Varied Family Structures and Gender Roles

A broad spectrum of contemporary family structures has become "the new normal" (Walsh, 2012b). Increasingly, individuals and couples construct a wide variety of household, gender, and kinship arrangements. Most couples today are dual-earners and strive toward more flexible, egalitarian, and satisfying partnerships in the workplace and in family life; yet navigating job, household, and childrearing demands is highly stressful (Fraenkel & Capstick, 2012). A large body of research has shown that families can function well and children can thrive in a variety of family structures—including single-parent, step-, and gay/lesbian-headed families—that are stable, nurturing, and financially secure (Green, 2012; Walsh, 2012b). What matters most for strong families and the well-being of members are effective family processes.

Cultural Diversity and Economic Disparity

As societies become more culturally diverse, largely through immigration, families also are becoming increasingly multiethnic, multiracial, and multifaith, requiring a pluralistic practice approach to facilitate mutual understanding and the blending or honoring of differences among members (Walsh, 2010). The social ecology of risk and resilience must be considered. Harsh socioeconomic conditions and discrimination of minority groups heighten risks for vulnerable youth and families, especially for single-parent households with limited resources. A vast disparity between the rich and the poor affects growing numbers of families: precarious economic conditions, job dislocation, and persistent unemployment have a devastating impact on family functioning and stability, fueling conflict, violence, divorce, and homelessness. Conditions of neighborhood decay, poor schools, crime, violence, and inadequate healthcare worsen life chances for multistressed families, requiring multisystemic interventions to reduce risks and support resilience.

Varying, Expanded Life Course

Medical advances and the aging of societies have increased the number of four- and five-generation families, with concomitant stressful challenges of chronic illness and caregiving and fewer children to care for elders (Walsh, 2011a). With longer life expectancy, it is perhaps remarkable that over 50% of couples *do not* divorce, many celebrating 60th and 70th anniversaries. We need to understand how they weather the storms and evidence resilience in such long-lasting marriages. Still, two or more committed couple relationships over time are increasingly common, interspersed with periods of cohabitation and single living. Children and their parents are likely to transition in and out of several household and kinship arrangements over their life course. For resilience, families need to buffer transitions and learn how to live successfully in more fluid and complex arrangements.

Family Resilience in Developmental Context

A family developmental perspective views the family as a system moving forward over the life course of all members and across the generations. To understand and foster family resilience the following variables must be considered: (1) families navigate varied pathways in resilience with emerging challenges over time; (2) a pile-up of multiple stressors can overwhelm family resources; (3) the impact of a crisis may vary in relation to its timing in individual and family life passage; and (4) a family's past experiences of adversity and response can generate catastrophic expectations or can serve as models of resilience.

Varied Pathways in Resilience

Most major stressors are not simply a short-term single event, but rather, a complex set of changing conditions with a past history and a future course (Rutter, 1987). Family resilience involves varied adaptational pathways over time, from the approach to a threatening event, through disruptive transitions, subsequent shockwaves in the immediate aftermath, and long-term reorganization. For instance, in adaptation to loss, how a family approaches the death of a loved one, facilitates emotional sharing and meaning making, effectively reorganizes, and reinvests in life pursuits will influence the immediate and long-term recovery for all members and their relationships (Walsh & McGoldrick, 2004). Likewise, the experience of divorce proceeds from an escalation of predivorce tensions through disruption and reorganization of households and parent–child relationships; most experience transitional upheaval again with remarriage and stepfamily integration (Greene, Anderson, Forgatch, Degarmo, & Hetherington, 2012). In the wake of a major disaster, such as an earthquake, with widespread destruction of communities, families undergo many dislocations, losses, and setbacks in a long recovery process.

Given such complexity, no single coping response is invariably most successful; different strategies may prove useful in meeting emerging challenges. Some approaches that are functional in the short term may rigidify and become dysfunctional over time. For instance, with a sudden illness, a family must mobilize resources and pull together to meet the crisis, but later must shift gears with chronic disability and attend to other members' needs over the long haul (Rolland, 2012). Research on effective family processes for resilience over time in situations of loss, divorce, or illness can guide interventions.

Cumulative Stress

Some families may do well with a short-term crisis but buckle under the strains of persistent or recurrent challenges, as with prolonged unemployment or a progressive disease. A pile-up of internal and external stressors can overwhelm the family, heightening vulnerability and risk for subsequent problems. Multistressed, underresourced families, most often in impoverished minority communities, are often blamed for their difficulties. In contrast to problem-focused interventions, which can increase parents' sense of deficit and despair, strengths-oriented family therapy approaches affirm and enhance family confidence, competencies, and vision for the future (Aponte, 1994; Madsen, 2009; Minuchin, Colapinto, & Minuchin, 2006; Walsh, 2006).

Family Life Passage and Stressful Transitions

Functioning and symptoms of distress are assessed in the context of the multigenerational family system as it moves forward across the life cycle (McGoldrick, Carter, & Garcia-Preto, 2011). Well-functioning families tend to have an evolutionary sense of time and a continual process of growth, change, and losses over the generations (Beavers & Hampson, 2003). This perspective helps members to see disruptive events and transitions also as milestones on their shared life passage.

A family resilience practice approach focuses on family functioning and adaptation around stressful life events and transitions (Lavee, McCubbin, & Olson, 1987; Walsh, 2009a). Some researchers focus on variables in risk and resilience around predictable, normative stressors, such as the transition to parenthood (Cowan & Cowan, 2012). Most address family processes for resilience with unanticipated, untimely, and highly disruptive events and transitions, such as divorce (Greene et al., 2012), death of a child or early parental loss (Greeff & Human, 2004; Greeff & van der Merwe, 2004; Walsh, 2006, 2007), and situations of ambiguous loss, such as dementia or missing loved ones (Boss, 2006). There is growing interest in family resilience with serious health challenges and long term adaptation in chronic illness and disability, intertwined with individual and family development (Rolland, 2012; Walsh, 2011b).

Intergenerational Legacies

The convergence of developmental and multigenerational strains heightens distress and the risk for dysfunction (McGoldrick et al., 2011). When current stressors reactivate painful memories and emotions, family members may lose perspective, conflate immediate situations with past events, and either become overwhelmed by or cut off from unbearable feelings and contacts. We thus explore multigenerational anniversary patterns, as some families function well until they reach a developmental milestone that had been traumatic a generation earlier. We inquire about family stories of past adversity and how they influence future expectations, from catastrophic fears to a hopeful outlook. Legacies of resilience can be found in positive responses to past events, inspiring current efforts.

Assessing Family Functioning and Resilience

The assessment of family functioning is fraught with dilemmas (Walsh, 2012a). Views of normality and health are socially constructed and often culture-bound. Clinicians and researchers bring their own assumptive maps, which are embedded in cultural norms, professional orientations, and personal experiences, into every evaluation and intervention. Moreover, with recent societal transformations and a growing multiplicity of family kinship arrangements, no single model of family health or family resilience fits all families and situations. Over the past 2 decades, systems-oriented family process research has provided important empirical grounding for assessment of healthy family functioning (e.g., Beavers & Hampson, 2003; Epstein, Ryan, Bishop, Miller, & Keitner, 2003; Olson & Gorell, 2003). Yet most family assessment instruments have been normed on samples of white, middle class, intact two parent families with adolescents, then later applied to varied family forms and minority racial/ethnic groups. Family typologies tend to be static and acontextual; many offer a snapshot of interaction patterns within the family but lack multisystemic and developmental perspectives in relation to family challenges, resources, and constraints. Since families most often seek help in periods of crisis, clinicians must be cautious not to reflexively view distress or differences from norms as family dysfunction, for example, mislabeling as *enmeshed* a family's high cohesion/connectedness that may be ethnically normative, satisfying, and/or functional in dealing with their situation (Walsh, 2012a).

A family resilience metaframework offers several advantages. By definition, it focuses on family strengths under stress, during crisis, and when facing prolonged adversity (Walsh, 2003). It is assumed that no single model of healthy functioning fits all families or their situations. Families forge varied pathways through adversity. Functioning is assessed in context: relative to each family's values, structure, resources, and life challenges.

Individual and family symptoms of distress are assessed in sociocultural and developmental contexts. A family genogram and timeline are valuable tools to schematize relationship information, track systems patterns over time, and guide intervention planning (McGoldrick, Gerson, & Petry, 2008). To consider the role of family stressors in current distress or difficulties, particular attention is given to the timing of symptoms: their co-occurrence with recent, ongoing, or threatening stress events. For instance, a son's school dropping out may be precipitated by his father's job loss and related family tensions, although those concerns may not be mentioned initially. Frequently, individual symptoms coincide with stressful transitions, such as parental disability, that require boundary shifts and the redefinition of roles and relationships. It is crucial to attend to the extended kinship network beyond the immediate household, especially in divorced, single parent, and remarried families. We explore (1) the impact of stressful events on the family system, its members, and their relationships, (2) how the family has approached the challenging situation: their preparedness, immediate coping response, and long-term adaptational strategies, and (3) strengths and resources to support their resilience.

Whereas family assessments and the use of genograms most often focus on problematic family patterns, a resilience-oriented approach intentionally searches for positive influences: past, present, and potential. We inquire about ways a family dealt with past adversity, with interest in stories of resilience in family history and models of resilience in the kin network that might be drawn on to inspire efforts to master current challenges. We search for relational resources in kin and social networks, within and across households. We might encourage efforts to involve estranged noncustodial parents who have the potential to contribute to their children's well-being. We consider ways family members might contribute, each in their own ways, to shore up resources in troubled times or to rally as a caregiving team for an elder disabled parent. We also consider the role of companion animals for resilience, especially for those living alone, for military veterans returning home, or relative to a child's bond with a pet through family transitions with divorce or stepfamily formation (Walsh, 2009b, 2009c).

Table 5.1 Walsh: key processes in family resilience

Belief systems
1. Making meaning of adversity
Relational view of resilience
Normalize, contextualize distress
Sense of coherence: View challenges as meaningful, comprehensible, manageable
Appraise adverse situation: Causal/explanatory attributions; future expectations
2. Positive outlook
Hope, optimistic bias; confidence in overcoming barriers
Affirm, expand strengths and potential
Encourage active initiative and perseverance (can-do spirit)
Master the possible; accept what cannot be changed
3. Transcendence and spirituality
Larger values, purpose
Spirituality: Faith, contemplative practices, community; connection with nature
Inspiration: New possibilities; life dreams; creative expression; social action
Transformation: Learning, change, and positive growth from adversity
Organizational patterns
4. Flexibility
Open to change: Rebound, reorganize, adapt to new conditions
Stability: Continuity, dependability, predictability to counter disruption
Strong authoritative leadership: Nurture, guide, protect
Varied family forms: Cooperative parenting/caregiving teams
Couple/coparent relationship: Mutual respect; equal partners
5. Connectedness
Mutual support, collaboration, and commitment
Respect individual needs, differences
Seek reconnection, repair wounded bonds
6. Social and economic resources
Mobilize kin, social, and community networks; models and mentors
Financial security; balance work/family strains
Larger systems: Institutional, structural supports for families to thrive
Communication/problem solving
7. Clear, consistent messages
Clarify ambiguous information; truth seeking
8. Open emotional expression
Share painful feelings; empathic response
Pleasurable interactions, humor; respite
9. Collaborative problem-solving
Creative brainstorming; resourcefulness
Share decision-making; repair conflicts; negotiation; fairness
Focus on goals, concrete steps: Build on success; learn from failure
Proactive stance: Preparedness, planning, prevention

Family Resilience Framework: Mapping Key Processes

The Family Resilience Framework (Table 5.1) was developed as a conceptual map of key processes to guide assessment and intervention in clinical and community practice. This framework is informed by 3 decades of social science and clinical research on well-functioning family systems and on individual and family resilience. Synthesizing findings, nine processes for resilience are identified within three domains of family functioning: *family belief systems*, *organization patterns*, and *communication/ problem-solving*. These processes can be targeted to strengthen family capacities to rebound from crises and master persistent life challenges (Walsh, 2003, 2006). Interventions aim to build family strengths as problems are addressed, thereby reducing risk and vulnerability. As the family becomes more resourceful, members gain the ability to meet future challenges.

Family Belief Systems

Family resilience is fostered by shared beliefs that help members *make meaning* of their stressful situations, facilitate a *positive, hopeful outlook*, and offer *transcendent, or spiritual, values, practices, and purpose*. Families can be helped to gain a sense of coherence (Antonovsky & Sourani, 1988), recasting a crisis as a shared challenge that is comprehensible, manageable, and meaningful to tackle. Normalizing and contextualizing members' distress as natural or understandable in their crisis situation can depathologize their reactions and reduce blame, shame, and guilt. Drawing out and affirming family strengths in the midst of difficulties counters a sense of helplessness, failure, and despair as it reinforces shared pride, confidence, and a "can-do" spirit. The encouragement of family members bolsters efforts to take initiative and persevere in attempts to overcome barriers. For resilience, family members focus their energies on mastering the possible, accepting that which is beyond their control, and learning to tolerate uncertainties. Shared spiritual resources, such as transcendent values, deep faith, contemplative practices (e.g., prayer, meditation), and religious/congregational involvement can strengthen family bonds and resilience (Walsh, 2009d). Many find healing and resilience through communion with nature, creative expression in the arts, and collaborative social action to alleviate suffering or repair unjust and harmful conditions. Adversity can be transformative, yielding new life priorities, purpose, and positive growth.

Family Organization

Resilience is fostered by a *flexible family structure* (e.g., role functioning) for adaptation to meet life challenges. In navigating disruptive changes and structural reorganization, families need to *restabilize*, especially reassuring children and other vulnerable family members, by providing security, continuities, and dependability. *Strong leadership, mutual support, and teamwork* facilitate resilience. *Extended kin and social networks* can be mobilized as relational lifelines. Larger system supports (e.g., workplace policies and structures) are also essential. It is not enough to help vulnerable families to "overcome the odds" against them; it is crucial to "change the odds" to enable them to thrive (Seccombe, 2002).

Communication Processes

Resilience in families is facilitated through *clear, consistent information* about their adverse situation and options. *Open emotional expression* with mutual empathy strengthens bonds. *Pleasurable interactions, sharing fun, joy,* and *humor*, offer respite from suffering and struggle, revitalizing energies and bonds. In *collaborative problem-solving*, families in problem-saturated situations can be helped to envision a better future and take concrete steps toward achieving their goals. Families become more resourceful by learning from mistakes and shifting from a crisis-reactive mode to a *proactive stance*, anticipating and preparing to meet future challenges.

Community-Based Training and Practice Applications

A family resilience orientation can be applied usefully with a wide range of crisis situations, disruptive transitions, and prolonged life challenges. Interventions utilize principles and techniques common among many strength-based family systems practice approaches, but attend more centrally to the impact of significant stressors and aim to strengthen the family resources and potential for positive adaptation. This approach also affirms that families may forge varied pathways for resilience over time, as fitting their adverse situation and their values, resources, and challenges. Principles guiding this approach are outlined in Table 5.2.

Family resilience-oriented practitioners serve as compassionate witnesses and facilitators, helping family members to share with each other their experience of adversity, to overcome silence, secrecy, shame, or blame, and to build mutual support and teamwork. Appreciative inquiry, attending to family strengths in the midst of suffering readily engages families, who are often reluctant to seek mental health services out of concerns that they will be judged as disturbed or deficient. Instead, family members are respectfully regarded as essential members of the healing team for recovery and resilience. Where they have faltered, they are viewed as struggling with an overwhelming set of challenges and their best intentions are affirmed. Intervention efforts are directed to master those challenges through their shared efforts (Table 5.3).

In community-based services, a resilience-oriented systemic assessment may lead to individual, couple, family, and multifamily group modalities, or combined approaches, depending on the relevance of different system levels to intervention aims. Putting an ecological view into practice, family-centered collaborative efforts may involve peer groups, community agencies, the workplace, schools, healthcare providers, and other larger systems. Resilience-based family interventions can be adapted to varied formats from family consultations to brief or more intensive family therapy. Psychoeducational multifamily groups emphasize the importance of social support and practical information, offering concrete guidelines for crisis management, problem-solving, and stress reduction as families navigate through stressful periods and face future challenges. Therapists, coaches, or group leaders may help

Table 5.2 Family resilience: principles for clinical and community-based practice

Relational view of human resilience: Mutual support; collaboration; team effort
   Strengthen kin/social networks; community, cultural and spiritual resources
Shift from deficit to strengths view of families
   Challenged by adversity; potential for repair and growth
Grounded in developmental systemic theory
   Biopsychosocial–spiritual influences over life course, generations
Crisis events, major stressors impact family system; family response influences
   Recovery of all members, relationships, and family unit
Contextual view of crisis, distress, and adaptation
   Family, larger systems/institutional supports; sociocultural influences
   Temporal/developmental influences
   Timing of symptoms vis-a-vis family stress events
   Cumulative stressors, disruptive transitions, persistent adversity
   Varying adaptational challenges over time: Immediate–long term
   Individual and family developmental passage, multigenerational patterns
Varied pathways in resilience—no single model fits all families and situations
Interventions have prevention value: In strengthening resilience, families become more resourceful, proactive in meeting future challenges

Table 5.3 Practice guidelines to strengthen family resilience

Collaborative approach: Family members as partners in healing/recovery team
Convey conviction in their potential to overcome adversity through shared efforts
Appreciative inquiry; respectful language, framing to humanize and contextualize distress
View as understandable, common in traumatic or adverse situation (normal reactions to abnormal or extreme conditions)
Decrease shame, blame, pathologizing
Provide safe haven for sharing pain, fears, challenges
Show compassion for suffering and struggle
Build communication, empathy, mutual support of members
Identify and affirm strengths, resources alongside vulnerabilities, limitations
Draw out strengths and build potential for mastery, healing, and growth
Tap into kin, community, and spiritual resources—lifelines—to deal with challenges
View crisis, adverse experience as opportunity for learning, change, and growth
Shift focus from problems to possibilities
Gain mastery, healing, and transformation out of adversity
Reorient future hopes and dreams
Integrate adverse experience—and resilience—into individual and relational life passage

families to clarify specific stresses they are dealing with and to develop effective coping strategies, measuring success in small increments and maintaining family morale. Brief follow-ups and cost-effective workshops or forums can assist families at various steps or transitions along their journey, helping them to integrate what has happened and meet anticipated challenges ahead.

Community-Based Training and Model Programs

Over the past 20 years, this family resilience framework has guided the development of professional training, consultation, and services at the CCFH (http://www.ccfhchicago.org). Building partnerships with community-based organizations is at the heart of our mission to train and support health, mental health, and social service professionals, particularly those who work with low-income, minority and other underserved vulnerable groups. Toward this end, we work collaboratively to provide specialized staff training, organizational consultation, and program development. Our goal is to help these organizations create and sustain family-centered practices that identify strengths and build resilience. Collaborative programs have been designed and implemented to address a wide range of family challenges (Rolland & Walsh, 2006; Walsh, 2002a, 2002b, 2006, 2007) (see Table 5.4).

Several brief programmatic descriptions are offered here to illustrate the potential utility of this approach in community-based services to families facing adversity.

Stresses of Job Loss and Prolonged Unemployment

Job and income loss, as well as anxiety and uncertainty about prolonged unemployment, can be devastating for the entire family. They heighten risks for a cascade of other devastating losses, as bills cannot be paid or homes face foreclosure. The severe strains often fuel depression, substance abuse,

Table 5.4 Family resilience-oriented program applications: Chicago Center for Family Health (CCFH)

Recover from crisis, trauma, loss
Complicated family bereavement (J. Rolland, F. Walsh)
War-related trauma; military families (J. Rolland, F. Walsh)
Community disasters (e.g., Hurricane Katrina recovery) (F. Walsh)
Refugee trauma (Bosnian and Kosovar multifamily groups) (J. Rolland)
Ongoing complex trauma (Palestinian Community Mental Health) (F. Walsh, C. Whitney)
Relational trauma (M.J. Barrett)
Master challenges of multistress chronic conditions
Serious illness, disabilities, end-of-life challenges
(J. Rolland et al.) (e.g., *resilient partners* couples group with multiple sclerosis)
Navigate disruptive life changes
Job loss/transition: *Operation Able*—family resilience workshops (F. Walsh, P. Brand)
Divorce; stepfamily formation (L. Jacob)
Overcome barriers for positive development
At-risk youth: Family–school partnership for success (R. Fuerst)
Challenges of stigma, heterosexism for LGBT youth, couples, and families (B. Koff)
Family intervention for youth at high risk of gang involvement (J. Rolland, F. Walsh, and training team H. Aponte, W. Madsen)

intense marital conflict, relational abuse, and family breakup. Cumulative stresses over many months, in turn, reduce the ability of spouses and family members to support efforts toward reemployment. Parental roles also may need to be realigned.

One CCFH family resilience-based program was directed to the adaptation of displaced workers and their families when jobs were lost due to factory closings or company downsizing. Our Center was contacted to develop family resilience-based workshops and counseling services in partnership with a community-based agency, *Operation Able*, which specialized in job retraining and placement services. In one case, with the closing and relocation of a large clothing manufacturing plant, over 1,800 workers lost their jobs. Most were ethnic/racial minority individuals and/or immigrants with limited English and lacked education and skills for employment in the changing job market. All were essential breadwinners for their families; many were single parents.

Family resilience-oriented workshops were designed to address the personal and familial impact of losses and transitional stresses, attending to family strains, reorganizing role functions, and rallying family members to support the best efforts of the displaced worker. Workshop members and leaders identified discussion themes relevant to their challenges and focused on keys to resilience. For instance, they discussed constraining beliefs (e.g., "No one will hire me," "I feel worthless without a job and paycheck") and then identified strengths, such as pride in doing a job well, and their dependability and loyalty in work and family life. Parental roles needed to be realigned. In particular, for men whose sense of worth was diminished with the loss of the traditional male role as "breadwinner" it was important to broaden their contribution and value to their families. Fathers experienced new competencies and benefits through greater sharing of household and childrearing responsibilities. Single parents, depressed and depleted, were encouraged to reach out to "lifelines" in their kin network. For instance, they might involve their children's aunts, uncles, and godparents, as well as grandparents, by offering mutual support, such as exchanging childcare or eldercare time for respite from burdens.

Parents and children brainstormed creative ways to build in "family fun time" and to show daily appreciation of each other despite stresses. The bi-weekly family workshops offered encouragement to take initiative and persevere in job search efforts, and celebrated small successes as they strengthened family bonds and mutual support.

Family and Community Resilience with Trauma and Traumatic Loss

Family resilience-oriented intervention approaches are increasingly being applied to recovery efforts in situations of mass trauma, major disasters, and in regions suffering complex, ongoing trauma with war, political persecution, or prolonged displacement (e.g., Boss, Beaulieu, Wieling, & Turner, 2003; Cohen, Slonim, Finzi, & Leichtentritt, 2002; Girwitz, Forgatch, & Wieling, 2008; Hernandez, 2002; Knowles, Sasser, & Garrison, 2010; Landau, 2007; Landau & Saul, 2004; MacDermid, 2010; Walsh, 2002b, 2007). There is growing recognition among trauma and bereavement specialists of the intertwining of trauma, loss, grief, and resilience (Bonanno, 2004). In contrast to individually-based symptom-focused treatment programs, multisystemic resilience-oriented approaches build healing networks that facilitate child, family, and community resilience (Walsh, 2007). These programs, through family counseling, multifamily groups, and community forums, create a safe haven for family and community members to support each other in sharing deep pain, resilient responses, and positive strivings. They can help families and communities expand their vision of what is possible through collaboration, not only to survive trauma and loss, but also to regain their spirit to thrive.

Our Center also has served as a resource for consultation, professional training, and the development and implementation of family resilience-based services for communities, in the United States as well as internationally, that have suffered trauma and traumatic loss. Several experiences will be briefly described to illustrate the potential value of a family resilience orientation.

Long-Term Disaster Recovery in Louisiana Gulf Region

Most disaster recovery efforts involve short-term intervention in the immediate aftermath of the crisis event. Yet families and communities most often must deal with multiple long-term challenges and losses, disruptive changes, separations from loved ones, and prolonged displacement, as well as future uncertainties in recovery, rebuilding of their lives, and revisioning of their hopes and dreams. Currently, I serve as an ongoing consultant to the Porter Cason Institute, at Tulane University in New Orleans, to contribute to their efforts to develop collaborative, strengths-based, family resilience-oriented community mental health services to those suffering and struggling from the long-term effects of Hurricane Katrina. In St. Bernard Parish, where 100% of homes were lost in the flooding, over 100 families still remained in temporary trailers 5 years later. As one mother recounted, "We're alive, but we're not living." Community residents who have demonstrated resilience in their own recovery efforts are being involved as peer counselors in a collaborative program to serve families that are struggling.

In Plaquemines Parish, three-generation fishing families, many of whom were refugees from Southeast Asia, struggle to recover from the 2010 BP oil spill. Meaning-making of their situation and future planning have been confused and frustrated by repeated unclear and inconsistent information (key variables in belief systems and communication processes for resilience) by government and industry officials about future expectations: Will fish be safe to eat and will the fishing industry survive or be destroyed? Should the younger generation rebuild the family business or disperse to find new livelihoods elsewhere, breaking up the strong families that have supported their resilience over the years? Here professionals are urged to work not only with families in distress but also with the larger systems affecting their recovery, especially government authorities, to clarify and bolster future prospects for recovery, to post updated website information and resource contacts, and to hold community forums to facilitate communication and collaborative efforts.

Military Family Resilience

Military families suffer the impact of physical, psychological, and relational wounds with prolonged service in war, repeated deployments, highly stressful reentry transitions, and changing roles and relationships for spouses, parents, and bonds with children. Rising rates of posttraumatic stress disorder (PTSD), disabilities, traumatic brain injuries, substance abuse, suicide, violence, and divorce ripple through the entire family. The predominant treatment models for war-related trauma have been individually based and pathology focused, reducing symptoms of PTSD and related disorders. A family resilience framework situates the trauma in the extreme experience of war, and contextualizes intense distress as a normal reaction to abnormal conditions. Interventions address family stresses, strengthen bonds, and facilitate family support of a returning service member's resilient adaptation to "normal" life. The family resilience framework presented here (elaborated in Walsh, 2006) has been applied in military family resilience research (MacDermid, Sampler, Schwartz, Nishida, & Nyarong, 2008). It is widely used in training US Navy family life educators, chaplains, and therapists, and in services for military personnel and their family members. Family Resilience Programs, utilizing workshop and weekend retreat formats, are designed to help families navigate pre- and postdeployment challenges and to foster healing from injuries, trauma, and losses as they revitalize family relationships and revision future possibilities.

Resilience-Oriented Multifamily Groups for Bosnian and Kosovar Refugees

The value of a community-based family resilience approach with refugees from war-torn regions was demonstrated in projects developed by CCFH in collaboration with the Center on Genocide, Psychiatry, and Witnessing at the University of Illinois (Walsh, 2006; Weine et al., 2004). In 1998–1999, multifamily groups were designed for Bosnian and Kosovar refugees who had suffered atrocities and traumatic loss of loved ones, homes, and communities in the Serbian "ethnic cleansing" campaign. Our family resilience approach was sought out because many refugees were suffering posttraumatic stress symptoms but were not utilizing mental health services, feeling shamed and stigmatized by psychiatric diagnoses of PTSD and mental disorders and by the narrow focus on individual symptoms of pathology. The community responded enthusiastically to our family-centered resilience orientation to foster recovery and positive adaptation.

This program, called CAFES for Bosnians and TAFES for Kosovars (Coffee/Tea And Family Education & Support), utilized a 9-week multifamily group format. Families readily participated because the program tapped into the strong family-centered cultural values and was located in an accessible neighborhood storefront where they felt comfortable. Offering a safe and compassionate setting to share stories of suffering and struggle, it also affirmed family strengths and resources, such as their courage, endurance, and faith; strong kinship networks; deep concern for loved ones; and determination to rise above their tragedies to forge a new life. Their efforts were encouraged to bridge cultures and, to the extent possible, to sustain kinship ties and gain a sense of belonging in both old and new worlds (Falicov, 2007). To foster collaboration and to develop local resources, facilitators from their respective communities were trained to colead groups and to be available as urgent needs might arise. This approach was experienced as respectful and empowering.

Kosovar Family Professional Educational Collaborative

The success of the above program led to development of the Kosovar Family Professional Educational Collaborative (KFPEC), an ongoing partnership in Kosovo between their local mental health professionals and an American team of family therapy consultants under the auspices of the American Family Therapy Academy. The aim of this multiyear project was to enhance the capacities of mental health professionals and paraprofessionals to address the overwhelming service needs in their war-torn region by strengthening family coping and recovery in the wake of widespread trauma and loss. In describing the value of this approach, Rolland and Weine (2000) noted:

> The family, with its strengths, is central to Kosovar life, but health and mental health services are generally not oriented to families. Although "family" is a professed part of the value system of international organizations, most programs do not define, conceptualize, or operationalize a family approach to mental health services in any substantial or meaningful ways. Recognizing that the psychosocial needs of refugees, other trauma survivors, and vulnerable persons in societies in transition far exceed the individual and psychopathological focus that conventional trauma mental health approaches provide, this project aims to begin a collaborative program of family focused education and training that is resilience-based and emphasizes family strengths (p. 35)

The consultants, sharing a multisystemic, resilience-oriented approach to address family challenges, encouraged Kosovar professionals to adapt the framework and develop their own practice methods to best fit local culture and service needs. The approach emphasized the importance of meeting with families to hear their stories, bearing witness to atrocities suffered, and eliciting the strengths and resources in family belief systems, organization, and communication processes. Interviews revealed that their Islamic teachings and the inspiration of family models and mentors were powerful wellsprings in resilience.

In one family, the mother had listened to the gunshots as her husband, two sons, and two grandsons were murdered in the yard of their farmhouse. She and her surviving family members talked with team members in their home about what has kept the family strong:

> The surviving son in the family replied, "We are all believers. One of the strengths in our family is from Allah. Having something to believe has helped very much."
> *Interviewer*: "What do you do to keep faith strong?"
> *Son*: "I see my mother as our 'spring of strength' … to see someone who has lost five family members—it gives us strength just to see her. We must think about the future and what we can accomplish. This is what keeps us strong. What will happen to him (pointing to his 5-year-old nephew) if I am not here? If he sees me strong, he will be strong. If I am weak, he will become weaker than me."
> *Interviewer*: "What do you hope your nephew will learn about the family as he grows up?"
> *Son*: "The moment when he will be independent and helping others and the family—for him, it will be like seeing his father and grandfather and uncles alive again" (Becker, Sargent, & Rolland, 2000, p. 29).

In this family, the positive influence of belief systems and communication were striking, in particular, the power of faith, the inspiration of strong models and mentors, and the stories of resilience conveyed to the next generation. In many families, strong cohesiveness and adaptive role flexibility enabled members to assume new responsibilities to fill in for missing functions. Team members noted: "When cooking or planting everyone moved together fluidly, in a complementary pattern, each person picking up what the previous person left off…. Although their grief was immense, their resilience was remarkable." As one family member remarked: "Everyone belongs to the family and to the family's homeland, alive or dead, here or abroad. Everyone matters and everyone is counted and counted upon" (Becker et al., 2000, p. 29).

UNRWA Community Mental Health Programme: Gaza and the West Bank

Since my early Peace Corps volunteer experience in Morocco, much of my most treasured work involves training and consultation in many parts of the world to support collaborative, family-centered, strengths-based, community mental health services. One particularly meaningful experience for me was a 2007 brief training on Trauma, Bereavement, and Family Resilience for the Community Mental Health Programme of the United Nations Recovery and Work Agency (UNRWA), serving the Palestinian refugee communities in Gaza and the West Bank. The multiday training group experience in Ramallah fostered more open sharing by counselors and their supervisors of their professional challenges and strengths, brainstorming effective strategies, and planning team meetings for greater collaboration and mutual support in their work.

I had tremendous admiration for the courage and dedication of the Palestinian counselors, who work with children and families suffering from ongoing complex trauma and traumatic loss, as they and their families experience these same conditions and shattering losses. In our discussion, they found most helpful our application of the Keys to Family Resilience to their own resilience as counselors, especially the power of positive belief systems (as described above). They highlighted the importance of sustaining/restoring hope, as distinguished from optimism: faith that their positive efforts have the potential to make a difference for children's future despite pessimism about immediate prospects for an end to their occupation and recursive cycles of violence, trauma, and loss. With the larger political stalemate beyond their control, the key to resilience that most resonated with them was "mastering the art of the possible" and the quote: "Do all you can, with what you have, in the time you have, in the place you are." Spirituality, experienced in the deep and abiding Islamic faith of the Palestinian people, is their deepest wellspring for resilience, nourishing their spirit to thrive, their perseverance, and their transcendence.

I arrived in Jerusalem the day the 2007 war broke out between Israel and Lebanon. Due to the closing of the Gaza border, training with the Gaza counselors was arranged via videoconferencing between the United Nations offices in Jerusalem and Gaza City. The heartfelt appreciation of the counselors—for my caring about their efforts to alleviate the suffering of families in Gaza, where they have felt abandoned and cut off from the world—made the brief training experience all the more meaningful. It led to continued contact through email exchanges and a writing collaboration on spiritual sources of resilience (Wolin et al., 2009). This internet connection became a vital lifeline for several of them 2 years later, during the Israeli military incursion of Gaza, when they contacted me to relate their experience of the killings and atrocities, the terror felt by children, and the widespread destruction (including schools and the United Nations compound).

Such profound suffering and ongoing challenges faced by families and communities experiencing trauma and loss are not problems for a brief solution focus or therapist techniques for change; I was humbled by how little I could offer. Yet, such experiences have taught me that in our training and practice from a resilience orientation, it is our relationships with those we serve that matter most of all. Our connectedness with them, even in brief contact or through distance communication, can nourish their resilience, from our compassionate witnessing of experiences of suffering and struggle to our conviction in the human capacity for resilience.

Family-Centered Training: Preventing Gang Involvement/Promoting Positive Development of High-Risk Youth

Gang prevention programs in the United States have rarely involved families, influenced by the prevalent assumption in the juvenile justice field that families of high-risk youth are too dysfunctional and untreatable. Recognizing the potential positive role families can play to counter the draw of youths into gangs, the Los Angeles Deputy Mayor's Office for Gang Reduction and Youth Development contacted CCFH to provide a family-resilience oriented training program for case managers working with at-risk youth in neighborhoods with high gang activity. Our approach was valued for its collaborative team model and conviction that all families, individuals, and communities under stressful conditions have the capacity to change their lives. Youths' behavior and future aspirations are viewed in the context of their living situation, including consideration of family, peer, and larger socioeconomic and cultural influences. This approach shifts attention from traditional problem-focused deficit models to view "at risk" youth and their families "at promise," with the potential for positive growth and successful lives by strengthening supportive relational bonds and community connections. The training programs, conducted by a team of seasoned family therapists over the current year, includes a series of 2-day workshops and case consultation coaching sessions, focusing on two strategy components.

The vertical strategy component is based on a multigenerational life cycle model, using resilience-oriented genograms and coaching techniques to connect youth and their parents/caregivers to relational resources, or "lifelines" for resilience. The vertical strategy focuses on multigenerational family history, draws out stories of resilience in dealing with past adversity, and identifies positive models and mentors in the current extended family system to support long-term family resilience and engagement with at-risk youth for their successful development. We identify and involve family members who are—or could become—invested in the youth to support their best efforts, believe in their potential, and encourage them to make the most of their lives. Strength-based genograms and timelines also provide tools for youth and families to develop a stronger sense of identity, connectedness, and competence, and will increase their ability to overcome the challenges/barriers they confront.

The horizontal training component increases staff skills and alliance with each youth and family to strengthen their problem-solving abilities and foster their positive potential. Madsen's *Collaborative Helping Map* provides a useful practice tool to reduce problem behaviors and risk factors by refocusing on the youth's and family's positive future vision (hopes and dreams), obstacles to overcome, supports and resources to draw on, and steps toward desired aims (Madsen, 2009). Throughout, attention is given to social and economic challenges and to cultural and spiritual resources for resilience. Recognizing that the agency staff, like the families they serve, are multi-stressed and face overwhelming challenges of neighborhood violence, the training also draws out their strengths and resources and facilitates their collaboration for effective intervention and worker resilience.

Research Challenges and Opportunities

The very flexibility of the concept of resilience, the complexity of systemic assessment, and the varied applications and intervention formats pose daunting challenges for family assessment and intervention research. Given cultural and family diversity, and the probability that some processes may be more useful than others in dealing with varied challenges, findings from a particular study may not be generalizable to diverse populations and adverse situations. Despite the challenges, a number of recent and ongoing mixed-method and qualitative studies in many parts of the world are making progress in adapting to their context and aims the Family Resilience Framework presented here.

Conclusion

There is growing interest in the potential value of a family resilience framework in community-based practice. This approach involves a crucial shift in emphasis from family deficits to family challenges, with conviction in the potential inherent in family systems for recovery and growth out of adversity. This conceptual framework can be integrated usefully with many strengths-based practice models and applied with a range of adverse situations, with respect for family and cultural diversity. By targeting intervention and prevention efforts to strengthen key processes for resilience, families can become more resourceful in dealing with crises, weathering persistent stresses, and meeting future challenges. This approach fosters family empowerment, develops new and renewed competencies, and strengthens relational bonds.

References

Antonovsky, A., & Sourani, T. (1988). Family sense of coherence and family adaptation. *Journal of Marriage and the Family, 50,* 79–92.

Aponte, H. (1994). *Bread and spirit: Therapy with the poor.* New York: Norton.

Beavers, W. R., & Hampson, R. B. (2003). Measuring family competence. In F. Walsh (Ed.), *Normal family processes: Growing diversity and complexity* (3rd ed., pp. 549–580). New York: Guilford.

Becker, C., Sargent, J., & Rolland, J. S. (2000). Kosovar Family Professional Education Collaborative. *American Family Therapy Academy Newsletter, 80,* 26–30.

Bonanno, G. A. (2004). Loss, trauma, and human resilience. *The American Psychologist, 59,* 20–28.

Boss, P. (2006). *Loss, trauma, and resilience.* New York: Norton.

Boss, P., Beaulieu, L., Wieling, E., & Turner, W. (2003). Healing loss, ambiguity, and trauma: A community-based intervention with families of union workers missing after the 9/11 attack in New York City. *Journal of Marital and Family Therapy, 29*(4), 455–467.

Cohen, O., Slonim, I., Finzi, R., & Leichtentritt, R. (2002). Family resilience: Israeli mothers' perspectives. *American Journal of Family Therapy, 30,* 173–187.

Cowan, P., & Cowan, C. (2012). Normative family transitions, couple relationship quality, and healthy child development. In F. Walsh (Ed.), *Normal family processes* (4th ed., pp. 428–451). New York: Guilford.

Driver, J., Tabares, A., Shapiro, A., & Gottman, J. S. (2012). Couple interaction in happy and unhappy marriages: Gottman laboratory studies. In F. Walsh (Ed.), *Normal family processes: Growing diversity and complexity* (4th ed., pp. 57–71). New York: Guilford.

Epstein, N., Ryan, C., Bishop, D., Miller, I., & Keitner, G. (2003). The McMaster model: A view of healthy family functioning. In F. Walsh (Ed.), *Normal family processes* (3rd ed., pp. 581–607). New York: Guilford.

Falicov, C. (1995). Training to think culturally: A multidimensional comparative framework. *Family Process, 34,* 373–388.

Falicov, C. (2007). Working with transnational immigrants: Expanding meanings of family, community and culture. *Family Process, 46,* 157–172.

Fraenkel, P., & Capstick, C. (2012). Contemporary two-parent families: Navigating work and family challenges. In F. Walsh (Ed.), *Normal family processes* (4th ed., pp. 78–101). New York: Guilford.

Girwitz, A., Forgatch, M., & Wieling, E. (2008). Parenting practices as potential mechanisms for child adjustment following mass trauma. *Journal of Marital and Family Therapy, 34,* 177–192.

Greeff, A. P., & Human, B. (2004). Resilience in families in which a parent has died. *American Journal of Family Therapy, 32*(1), 27–42.

Greeff, A. P., & Van Der Merwe, S. (2004). Variables associated with resilience in divorced families. *Social Indicators Research, 68*(1), 59–75.

Green, R.-J. (2012). Gay and lesbian family life: Risk, resilience, and rising expectations. In F. Walsh (Ed.), *Normal family processes* (4th ed., pp. 172–195). New York: Guilford.

Greene, S., Anderson, E., Forgatch, M. S., Degarmo, D. S., & Hetherington, E. M. (2012). Risk and resilience after divorce. In F. Walsh (Ed.), *Normal family processes* (4th ed., pp. 102–127). New York: Guilford.

Hernandez, P. (2002). Resilience in families and communities: Latin American contributions from the psychology of liberation. *Journal of Counseling & Therapy for Couples and Families, 10,* 334–343.

Knowles, R., Sasser, D., & Garrison, M. E. B. (2010). Family resilience and resiliency following Hurricane Katrina. In R. Kilmer, V. Gil-Rivas, R. Tedeschi, & L. Calhoun (Eds.), *Helping families and communities recover from disaster.* Washington, DC: American Psychological Association Press.

Landau, J. (2007). Enhancing resilience: Families and communities as agents for change. *Family Process, 46,* 351–365.

Landau, J., & Saul, J. (2004). Facilitating family and community resilience in response to major disasters. In F. Walsh & M. McGoldrick (Eds.), *Living beyond loss: Death in the family* (2nd ed., pp. 285–309). New York: Norton.

Lavee, Y., Mccubbin, H. I., & Olson, D. H. (1987). The effect of stressful life events and transitions on family functioning and well-being. *Journal of Marriage and the Family, 49,* 857–873.

Luthar, S. S., Cicchetti, D., & Becker, B. (2000). The construct of resilience: A critical evaluation and guidelines for future work. *Child Development, 71,* 543–562.

MacDermid, S. M. (2010). Family risk and resilience in the context of war and terrorism. *Journal of Marriage and the Family, 72,* 537–556.

MacDermid, S. M., Sampler, R., Schwartz, R., Nishida, J., & Nyarong, D. (2008). *Understanding and promoting resilience in military families*. West Lafayette, IN: Military Family Research Institute at Purdue University.

Madsen, W. C. (2009). Collaborative helping: A practice framework for family-centered services. *Family Process, 48*, 103–116.

McGoldrick, M., Carter, B., & Garcia-Preto, N. (2011). *The expanded family life cycle: Individual, family, and social perspectives* (4th ed.). Boston: Pearson.

McGoldrick, M., Gerson, R., & Petry, S. (2008). *Genograms: Assessment and intervention* (3rd ed.). New York: Norton.

Minuchin, P., Colapinto, J., & Minuchin, S. (2006). *Working with families of the poor* (2nd ed.). New York: Guilford.

Olson, D. H., & Gorell, D. (2003). Circumplex model of marital and family systems. In F. Walsh (Ed.), *Normal family processes* (3rd ed., pp. 514–544). New York: Guilford.

Patterson, J. (2002). Integrating family resilience and family stress theory. *Journal of Marriage and the Family, 64*, 349–373.

Rolland, J. S. (2012). Mastering family challenges in serious illness, disability, and genetic conditions. In F. Walsh (Ed.), *Normal family processes* (4th ed., pp. 452–482). New York: Guilford.

Rolland, J. S., & Walsh, F. (2006). Facilitating family resilience with childhood illness and disability. Special issue on the family. *Current Opinion in Pediatrics, 18*, 1–11.

Rolland, J. S., & Weine, S. (2000). Kosovar Family Professional Educational Collaborative. *American Family Therapy Academy Newsletter, 79*, 34–35.

Rutter, M. (1987). Psychosocial resilience and protective mechanisms. *The American Journal of Orthopsychiatry, 57*, 316–331.

Seccombe, K. (2002). "Beating the odds" versus "changing the odds": Poverty, resilience, and family policy. *Journal of Marriage and the Family, 64*(2), 384–394.

Stinnett, N., & Defrain, J. (1985). *Secrets of strong families*. Boston: Little, Brown.

Tedeschi, R. G., & Calhoun, L. G. (2004). Posttraumatic growth: Conceptual foundations and empirical evidence. *Psychological Inquiry, 15*, 1–18.

Ungar, M. (2004). The importance of parents and other caregivers to the resilience of high-risk adolescents. *Family Process, 43*, 23–41.

Walsh, F. (1996). The concept of family resilience: Crisis and challenge. *Family Process, 35*, 261–281.

Walsh, F. (2002a). A family resilience framework: Innovative practice applications. *Family Relations, 51*(2), 130–137.

Walsh, F. (2002b). Bouncing forward: Resilience in the aftermath of September 11. *Family Process, 41*(1), 34–36.

Walsh, F. (2003). Family resilience: A framework for clinical practice. *Family Process, 42*(1), 1–18.

Walsh, F. (2006). *Strengthening family resilience* (2nd ed.). New York: Guilford.

Walsh, F. (2007). Traumatic loss and major disaster: Strengthening family and community resilience. *Family Process, 46*, 207–227.

Walsh, F. (2009a). Family transitions: Challenges and resilience. In M. Dulcan (Ed.), *Textbook of child and adolescent psychiatry* (pp. 675–686). Washington, DC: American Psychiatric Association Press.

Walsh, F. (2009b). Human-animal bonds: I. The relational significance of companion animals. Special section. *Family Process, 48*(4), 462–480.

Walsh, F. (2009c). Human-animal bonds: II. The role of pets in family systems and family therapy. *Family Process, 48*(4), 481–499.

Walsh, F. (2009d). Integrating spirituality in family therapy: Wellsprings for health, healing, and resilience. In F. Walsh (Ed.), *Spiritual resources in family therapy* (2nd ed., pp. 31–61). New York: Guilford.

Walsh, F. (2010). Spiritual diversity: Multifaith perspectives in family therapy. *Family Process, 49*, 330–348.

Walsh, F. (2011a). Families in later life: Challenges, opportunities, and resilience. In M. McGoldrick, B. Carter, & N. Garcia Preto (Eds.), *The expanded family life cycle* (4th ed., pp. 261–277). Needham Heights, MA: Allyn & Bacon.

Walsh, F. (2011b). Resilience in families with health challenges. In M. Kraft-Rosenberg & S.-R. Pehler (Eds.), *Encyclopedia of family health* (pp. 895–899). Thousand Oaks, CA: Sage.

Walsh, F. (2012a). Clinical views of family normality, health, and dysfunction. In F. Walsh (Ed.), *Normal family processes: Growing diversity and complexity* (4th ed., pp. 28–54). New York: Guilford.

Walsh, F. (2012b). The "new normal": Diversity and complexity in 21st century families. In F. Walsh (Ed.), *Normal family processes: Growing diversity and complexity* (4th ed., pp. 4–27). New York: Guilford.

Walsh, F., & McGoldrick, M. (2004). Loss and the family: A systemic perspective. In F. Walsh & M. McGoldrick (Eds.), *Living beyond loss: Death in the family* (2nd ed., pp. 3–26). New York: Norton.

Weine, S., Muzuravic, N., Kulauzovic, Y., Besic, S., Lezic, A., Mujagic, A., et al. (2004). Family consequences of refugee trauma. *Family Process, 43*, 147–160.

Wolin, S. J., Muller, W., Taylor, F., Wolin, S., Ranganathan, S., Saymah, D., et al. (2009). Religious perspectives on resilience: Buddhism, Christianity, Judaism, Hinduism, and Islam. In F. Walsh (Ed.), *Spiritual resources in family therapy* (2nd ed., pp. 103–124). New York: Guilford.

Part II

Resilience and Families

Resilience in Stepfamilies

Marilyn Coleman, Lawrence Ganong,
and Luke T. Russell

Introduction/Significance of the Topic

Stepfamilies are common in the United States. An estimated 40–50% of marriages are a remarriage for one or both partners (Cherlin, 2010), and although not all of these remarriages result in the formation of a stepfamily, a significant portion of them do. According to a recent study, 42% of a national sample of US adults and more than half (52%) of those younger than 30 had at least one steprelative (Pew Research Center, 2011). About 40% of US families have a stepgrandparent (Szinovacz, 1998). What is more, these statistics do not account for the growing number of stepfamilies created through cohabitation (Sweeney, 2007), an often-overlooked group.

A large percentage of Americans are currently living in stepfamilies and many more will be in the future if present trends in divorce, cohabitation, and remarriage continue. Despite the increasing prevalence of stepfamilies, however, being in a stepfamily is not something that people anticipate, which makes understanding stepfamily resilience especially important. A significant segment of the population can benefit from the growing body of knowledge about how to adapt to stress and crises in stepfamilies.

Literature Review

Interest in stepfamily resilience processes was slow in developing. In early studies, researchers focused primarily on identifying problems, and most examined differences between stepfamilies, households headed by single parents, and first-marriage nuclear families. The underlying assumption was that nuclear families represented the standard to which all others should be compared. Guided by this deficit-comparison approach, most researchers framed investigations from the viewpoint that divorce and remarriage damaged children and adults, and compared to individuals in continuously married families, stepfamilies were deviant and deficient (Ganong & Coleman, 2004).

Stepfamilies formed after the death of a parent have been common throughout history. Women died in childbirth, men were killed in farm accidents, and populations were ravaged by outbreaks of

M. Coleman • L. Ganong (✉) • L.T. Russell
Department of Human Development and Family Studies, University of Missouri,
Columbia, MO, USA
e-mail: ganongl@missouri.edu

D.S. Becvar (ed.), *Handbook of Family Resilience*,
DOI 10.1007/978-1-4614-3917-2_6, © Springer Science+Business Media New York 2013

flu and other deadly diseases. Researchers, however, did not show interest in stepfamilies until the late 1970s, when postdivorce stepfamilies began to outnumber those formed following bereavement. This interest was driven by perceptions of divorce and remarriage as societal problems, and so theories and research questions guiding the study of stepfamilies generally focused on problems, not resilience. This problem-oriented focus meant that much of the early study of stepfamilies was by clinicians (Ganong & Coleman, 2004; Sweeney, 2010). Although clinical views have been extremely useful in developing a scholarly understanding of stepfamily living, clinicians' knowledge generally was derived from work with stepfamilies with problems, which contributed to a problems-based paradigm of thinking about stepfamilies.

Over time, research designs became more sophisticated, but most stepfamily studies still are framed from a deficit-comparison perspective (for reviews of research over the past 2 decades, see Coleman, Ganong, & Fine, 2000; Sweeney, 2010). Stepchildren continue to be compared to children living with both of their parents, and they continue to do slightly worse on average than children in nuclear families and about the same as those in single-parent homes. Adults in stepfamilies also have been identified as at greater risk for problems than adults in first marriages although there is relatively little research to support this claim. Some researchers have found that mothers in stepfamilies experience higher rates of depression and role strain than do those in first marriages (Demo & Acock, 1996), and mothers have identified being caught in the middle between their children and their husbands as stressful (Weaver & Coleman, 2010). Remarried couples divorce at higher rates than do those in first marriages (Cherlin, 2010) and they do so more quickly, which many researchers and clinicians see as an indication of the greater stressors involved in remarriage. Consequently, a large body of research presents evidence that children and adults in stepfamilies face numerous challenges while the literature on stepfamily resilience is minimal.

What a deficit-comparison approach fails to address is *why* stepfamilies experience difficulties, *which* difficulties are normative to stepfamilies, and *what* coping skills are essential for successful stepfamily functioning. Additionally, researchers using the deficit-comparison approach often fail to note that the vast majority of stepfamilies and stepfamily members in their studies are functioning well and at levels similar to those in other family forms (Ganong & Coleman, 2004). It is increasingly important, therefore, that researchers and clinicians change their focus to a resilience perspective, with a goal of determining how stepfamilies and their members function effectively. In the remainder of this chapter, we examine both risk factors and resilience processes in stepfamilies. Before we review this literature, we first define stepfamilies.

Defining Stepfamilies

Stepfamilies are families in which at least one adult has biological or adopted children from a previous relationship (Ganong & Coleman, 2004). This definition can be applied to married or cohabiting heterosexuals as well as to gay and lesbian couples in which there are children from previous relationships or children who have been conceived through donor insemination or a surrogate. This definition also includes older stepfamilies and is not limited to households that contain children. Because of the wide variety of stepfamily forms, as we can we will use specific terms when describing stepfamilies. *Simple stepfamilies* are partnerships in which only one member of the couple has children from previous relationships. In *complex stepfamilies* both partners have children from previous relationships. In stepfamilies, children may reside in multiple households for various lengths of time or they may live together in one household full time. Stepfamilies in which stepfamily members reside with one another most of the time will be described as *residential relationships*, whereas *nonresidential relationships* are when stepfamily members are together for limited periods, such as on weekends or holidays.

Risk Factors in Stepfamilies

Risks Faced by All Families

Stepfamilies experience risks associated with normative developmental life transitions such as children entering adolescence or older adults becoming frail. Stepfamilies also face nonnormative stressors that are unrelated to family structure, such as acute or chronic illnesses of family members (Ganong, Doty, & Gayer, 2003; Kelly & Ganong, 2011), and they also deal with daily hassles just as other families do (Coleman, Fine, Ganong, Downs, & Pauk, 2001). Although understanding how stepfamilies cope with and adjust to normative risk factors is important, nonnormative risks and daily hassles are important to understand as well. Few scholars have examined how stepfamilies adapt in response to major developmental changes, nonnormative crises, or daily hassles.

Structural Changes as Risk Factors

Clinicians and researchers have long identified a number of stepfamily characteristics and experiences that may be considered as risk factors that add distress and strain to stepfamilies and stepfamily members. Many of these risk factors are related to the transition to stepfamily living. To understand these stressful transitions, however, one needs to examine risk factors associated with family life before the remarriage or repartnering.

Divorce-Related Risks

Many would describe the processes of divorce and subsequent remarriage or repartnering as significant risk factors in and of themselves. For example, family structure transitions involve risk factors such as relocations, new schools for children, new neighborhoods, and reduced contacts between some family members. Relocations alone involve losses of friends, neighbors, and familiar community resources, as well as alterations in routines. Following divorce, children may spend time in two parental households, finances become more complex, and there may be economic problems because of inadequate incomes and greater expenses in maintaining separate residences (Amato, 2010; Amato & Gilbreth, 1999).

In addition to the above risk factors, the most often cited challenges for children are uncertainty about the future, interpersonal conflicts (particularly between parents), parental adjustments to separation and divorce, and loss of contact with nonresidential parents (Sandler, Miles, Cookston, & Braver, 2008). Researchers generally agree that interparental conflicts and loss of involvement of nonresidential parents (usually fathers) are the primary risk factors that affect children whose parents divorce (Carlson, 2006).

For parents, major stressors include financial strains, hostility felt towards the former spouse, mental health risks (particularly depression), and having to reorganize coparental relationships (Evenson & Simon, 2005). Nonresidential parents often contend with creating ways to maintain relationships with children who live apart from them (Amato & Gilbreth, 1999; Amato & Sobolewski, 2004), while residential parents may be challenged by having more responsibility for childrearing than when there were two parents in the household (Kelly, 2007).

The extent to which adults and children adapt to life changes brought about by separation and divorce influences how well or poorly suited the family members will be to subsequent stepfamilies that are formed. That is, unfinished business from prior families intrudes into the lives of stepfamily members and affects their new stepfamily configurations (Sweeney, 2007).

Bereavement-Related Risks

There is clinical evidence that for postbereavement families failure to complete the emotional processes of grieving for the deceased creates a risk factor if this unfinished work is carried into subsequently formed stepfamilies (Visher & Visher, 1996). Children may be reluctant to accept a stepparent if they have not resolved their losses, and widowed adults may rush into new unions without carefully preparing. In fact, some widows and widowers remarry quickly to avoid the painful grieving process, which will likely affect subsequent stepfamily dynamics.

Risks Related to Nonmarital Reproduction

Households headed by never-married mothers generally have less income than households with two or more adults (Ispa, Thornburg, & Fine, 2006). Poverty affects schooling for children, housing, safety, access to community resources, and other factors that place single mothers and their children at risk for problems. If mothers have to work long hours to provide for their children, they may have little time to monitor them. Single parents are under-staffed, although some have help from nonresidential partners who are the parents of their children (Ispa et al.). Never-married unions are more unstable than marriages, so children of never-married parents often experience numerous household changes, which may include a series of social fathers introduced into their lives. Some low-income never-married mothers create complex cohabiting stepfamilies by reproducing with several men over time (Bzostek, 2008).

Stepfamily Structure as Risk Factors

Remarriage or repartnering represents another set of transition-related risk factors, with new household routines, new family members and roles, and often more relocations. Because many of the stepfamily risk factors are associated with transitions, a significant portion of research has focused on the transition period immediately following remarriage. Risks related to this period include: structural complexity, ambiguities, social stigma, and economic challenges.

Structural Complexity Risk Factors

Stepfamilies are more complex systems than are first-marriage nuclear families, families headed by one parent, or postdivorce families in which children link the households of two parents by going back and forth between them. The greater complexity of stepfamilies is partially due to the presence of more people in the family and household, which means there are more relationships, more new roles, and more changes, all of which can create greater stress for family members (Ganong & Coleman, 2004; Gerlach, 2001).

New family members. Incorporating new individuals into the household and family unit is a process that presents challenges to many stepfamily members. New relationships must be formed concomitantly with the nurturing of ongoing family ties. Finding time for new and old relationships can create strain, and there also may be jealousies. For example, when children feel they have lost time with a parent because that time is now being spent with the stepparent, they may act out in unexpected ways (Ganong, Coleman, & Jamison, 2011). Adding new family members also may alter children's birth order; an only child may have to share space and resources with stepsiblings, and the "baby" of the family may no longer be the youngest child. Such changes demand new ways of relating and even modifications of personal identities.

New roles. Some new roles in stepfamilies are associated with family positions. After parental remarriage a child becomes somebody's stepchild and perhaps someone else's stepsister. An adult becomes a stepparent and sometimes a stepgrandparent. Even ongoing family positions acquire new roles. For instance, Weaver and Coleman (2010) found that mothers in stepfamilies developed new roles as defenders, gatekeepers, mediators, and interpreters. Mothers described feeling a need to defend their biological children against perceived slights or unfair treatment from the children's stepfather, and others monitored the involvement among their husband's children and their own children (i.e., gatekeeping). Weaver and Coleman speculated that defending and gatekeeping were consequences of single-parent households where outsiders may have been seen as threats—a lack of trust of others was evident in some of the mothers' comments. Unfortunately, defending and gatekeeping reinforce stepparents' positions as outsiders and can negate positive relationship development.

Merging of family cultures. When families merge to create a stepfamily, family members often bring with them different values, rituals, and beliefs about how everyday life should be lived (Ganong & Coleman, 2004). Although merging of family cultures occurs to an extent in a first marriage, the newly first married couple typically has time to negotiate resolutions to these differences before they have children. For stepfamilies, merging cultures can be difficult because the parent–child bonds are older and more established than the adult couple bond. The newly remarried couple may be struggling to create a sense of what Papernow (2006) calls "we-ness" as a family unit, and these actions can be met with resistance from the children who liked the previous culture in their "old" family. Negotiating these challenges can be especially difficult if stepfamily members are unaware of the source of their discomfort. Both adults and children in stepfamilies often struggle to resolve what they may be experiencing as profound cultural clashes (Braithwaite, Baxter, & Harper, 1998).

To alleviate anxiety parents may try to reassure the children that nothing will change after the remarriage when, in fact, many things change. One parent may be quite lax about table manners and the other not. Children who have been allowed late phone calls from friends may balk when a stepparent who has to go to work early insists on a curfew for calls. One parent may think children should be given an allowance as a means of learning to manage money, the other parent may think children should work for any money given to them. The list of these "family culture" issues is endless, and all of them can create stress and ill will among the new family members (Ganong & Coleman, 2004).

Incongruent life course trajectories. Remarried couples tend to be more heterogeneous than first-married couples. That is, they are more likely than couples in first marriages to differ in age, education levels, race, ethnicity, and other demographic characteristics (Carter & McGoldrick, 2005). These differences can both create and contribute to challenges. For example, an older man with adult children may marry a younger woman who has young children. Because it has been years since he has had to deal with young children's noise and messes, he may find the children annoying and show little patience. Or, an older woman with grown children marries a younger man who wants children of his own. If she does not agree to have more children or is not able to do so, a serious rift could occur in the marriage.

Normative developmental changes and individual and family transitions occur in all families, but the complexity of these transitions greatly increases when life course trajectories are out of synch (e.g., a young mother of a toddler finds herself also dealing with the rebelliousness of a teenage stepchild with whom she has little relational history). Some stepfamilies adjust swiftly to incongruent life course trajectories, but others either struggle, make maladaptive changes, or fail to change at all. Inflexible responses to conflicts associated with incongruent life course trajectories can cause friction that produces high levels of stress, reduces family functionality, and damages the health of family members (Ganong & Coleman, 2004, 2006).

Ambiguities as Risk Factors

Stepfamilies are complex, but they are also characterized by a relative absence of social norms, social policies, laws, and clear language to help them figure out how to deal with the complexity (Cherlin, 1978). As a result of this societal ambiguity, Cherlin asserted that remarriage and the families formed by remarriage were *incomplete institutions*. There are few agreed-upon rules or models to guide them. In the absence of institutional guidelines, unrealistic expectations, a lack of preparation for stepfamily complexity, and the choice of inappropriate models for family life may result.

Unrealistic or conflicting expectations. Parents planning to remarry seldom seem to communicate their expectations (Ganong & Coleman, 1989) and often are caught off guard when their partners do not share their expectations (Orchard & Solberg, 1999). Nearly 83% of stepmothers in one study indicated that they had lowered their unrealistically high expectations about being a stepmother and living in a stepfamily (Orchard & Solberg). Stepparents who have not raised children may have unreasonable expectations for children, such as expecting a 2-year old to keep her room neat. Expecting a stepparent to instantly love a child he or she barely knows also is unrealistic; it takes time to build a relationship. Moreover, stepparents may feel they cannot openly share their ambiguous feelings about stepchildren with the children's parents, so resentments may smolder and create schisms in the stepfamily that are difficult to repair (Baxter, Braithwaite, & Nicholson, 1999; Weaver & Coleman, 2010). Gatekeeping and defending by remarried mothers may be partially due to their unmet, yet often unspoken, expectations about stepfathers' interactions with children. If maternal expectations are not expressed to the stepfather he may be left feeling like an outsider in his own home.

It is also clear that stepchildren's expectations for their stepfamilies may differ from those of parents and stepparents (Cartwright, 2005; Fine, Coleman, & Ganong, 1998). Children and adolescents have divergent perspectives from adults in all families, but the expectations gap between generations in stepfamilies can contribute to interpersonal conflicts and personal strain (Cartwright, 2005; Ganong et al., 2011).

Lack of preparation. Researchers indicate that both homosexual (Lynch, 2000) and heterosexual couples (Ganong & Coleman, 1989; Higginbotham, Miller, & Niehuis, 2009) do little to prepare for creating a new stepfamily household. Despite the growing availability of remarriage education classes and programs, the most common preparation for remarriage is talking with other people or reading articles in magazines, newspapers, and pamphlets (Higginbotham et al.). Many couples also cohabit as preparation for remarriage (Ganong & Coleman, 1989). Couples are reluctant to use remarriage preparation services because they believe attending such a program is unnecessary (Higginbotham et al., 2009). Whether this reflects denial of potential problems or lack of awareness of the challenges of stepfamilies is unclear. It is known that not preparing places stepfamilies at risk, and attending classes and programs has been associated with fewer conflicts, a normalization of stepfamily difficulties, and greater cohesion among stepfamily members (Higginbotham et al., 2009; Skogrand, Torres, & Higginbotham, 2010).

Inappropriate models: nuclear family ideology or the Brady Bunch. Stepfamilies may attempt to recreate the nuclear family as a model for themselves because, in the absence of clear norms to follow, stepparents and other stepfamily members experience role strain and even mental health problems (Fine et al., 1998; Saint-Jacques, 1995). It is easier to model behaviors you have observed than to create new ways to interact as a family. Lynch (2000) reported that even adults in gay and lesbian stepfamilies initially acted as if they were heterosexual nuclear families because they did not perceive other models available to them.

Recreating a nuclear family, however, is effective only when everyone in the stepfamily, including children and nonresidential parents, agree to it. If even one member of the family refuses to accept a stepparent as a replacement parent, a great deal of emotional energy will be expended trying to maintain the model (Ganong & Coleman, 2004). Not recognizing other ways to create stepfamily life is a stress-producing risk factor for most stepfamilies.

Social Stigma as a Risk Factor

The use of stepfamily positions in colloquial terms as negative descriptors of individuals or events reflects the stigma that stepfamilies still face. For example, the term "red-headed stepchild" is commonly used to describe someone who is abused, neglected, or unwanted—the prefix "step" is often construed as a pejorative (Ganong & Coleman, 2004). An article in the New York Times quoting Connecticut Senator Joseph Lieberman as he discussed a bill illustrates how even stepfamily members may find such terms ingrained in their speech (Samuelsohn, 2010):

> If you put it on as an amendment, it's like we're a stepchild. Excuse me for that, because I have some stepchildren who I love. It's like we're not the main event. We're a sideshow. That's a better metaphor.

The tropes of wicked stepparents or ugly stepsisters prevalent in fairy tales and folklore for centuries (Claxton-Oldfield, O'Neil, Thomson, & Gallant, 2005) continue in modern media (Claxton-Oldfield, 2000; Leon & Angst, 2005). These negative portrayals lead some stepfamily members to hide or deny their status (e.g., stepchildren using the stepfather's last name). Conversely, when not negatively portrayed stepfamilies often are projected idealistically as in the television series *The Brady Bunch*, where love developed quickly and problems were solved rapidly (Claxton-Oldfield). These media images send mixed messages to stepfamilies—one message is that stepparents are mean and stepchildren are abused and another message is that love and caring among stepfamily members should occur instantly. The inability to meet these impossible standards creates stress (Weaver & Coleman, 2005).

Economic Challenges as Risk Factors

Finances frequently are complex in stepfamilies. Money management problems and economic strains have been shown to influence stepfamily members' quality of life significantly (Addo & Sassler, 2010; Pasley, Sandras, & Edmondson, 1994). Conflicts may occur when partners' beliefs about saving and spending money vary (Coleman & Ganong, 1989; Pasley et al., 1994). A complicating financial issue in stepfamilies is the role of the legal system in determining child support amounts that might limit stepfamily members' sense of control over their own finances (Pasley et al.). A sense of financial control is further challenged when financial issues in one household (e.g., a child needs expensive braces) affects monetary decisions in another household (e.g., the foregoing of a family vacation). In complex stepfamilies money may leave the household to support children living elsewhere, and child support money may come into the household from a nonresidential parent. Decisions about whether or not to comingle "external" income from nonresidential parents with income earned by the step-couple may be difficult to negotiate. Financial stability may be especially problematic in cohabiting stepfamilies because cohabitation is more prevalent among low-income populations (Fein, Burstein, Fein, & Lindberg, 2003). The risks contributed by financial constraints and management techniques have the potential to disrupt couple relationships as well as negatively affect child outcomes in all stepfamilies (Addo & Sassler, 2010; Hetherington & Elmore, 2003).

Stepfamily Resilience

We have presented a multitude of potential stressors associated with living in a stepfamily. If the effects of living in stepfamilies were only negative, remarriage or repartnering would quickly end; however, this is not the case. Many stepfamilies resolve problems with relative aplomb. What are the protective factors that enable these stepfamilies to thrive? Hetherington and Elmore (2003) described three levels of protective factors affecting stepchild adjustment: individual, familial, and extra-familial. Individual protective factors include attributes of individuals such as temperament and age. Familial factors are variables regarding the development and maintenance of dyads such as parent–child and stepparent–stepchild relationships. Extra-familial factors include a family's interactions with social institutions such as schools and the legal system.

Individual Factors Contributing to Resilience

Personality Characteristics and Temperament

Clingempeel, Brand, and Segal (1987) hypothesized that tolerance for ambiguity and cognitive complexity might be individual factors that help stepfamily adults, particularly stepparents, adjust to the ambiguities of stepfamily roles and be able to think about and adapt to complex stepfamily situations. When we tested this hypothesis with a sample of remarried adults, however, we did not find an association among these individual factors and satisfaction with stepfamily life (Coleman & Ganong, 1990).

However, other personality characteristics may contribute to stepfamily resilience, such as an ability to delay gratification, persistence, or a calm temperament (Marsiglio, 2004). We found that some persistent stepparents who continued their efforts to befriend stepchildren despite continual rejection eventually "won" the affections of their stepchildren (Ganong et al., 2011). In another study, calm stepparents who let relationships with their stepchildren develop at a pace comfortable for the stepchildren succeeded in building close ties, while stepparents with take-charge personalities who tried to control the pace of relationship development engendered negative reactions from stepchildren (Ganong, Coleman, Fine, & Martin, 1999).

Stepparents with good interpersonal skills may be advantaged over the less socially skilled. For instance, stepparents who engaged in affinity-seeking behaviors early in the relationship and never stopped in those actions had close steprelationships, as did stepparents who engaged in activities with stepchildren that the children enjoyed rather than in activities built around the stepparents' interests (Ganong et al., 1999). Adults who can relate to adolescents or young children in ways the children appreciate and understand may be better able to develop affinity (i.e., warm friendships) and positive relationships that will weather daily hassles and other difficulties (Ganong et al., 1999; Hetherington & Elmore, 2003).

Adults willing to take on stepparenting responsibilities are more likely to have been raised by a stepparent or have accepting attitudes toward nontraditional families (Goldscheider & Kaufman, 2006), which suggests a selection effect into stepparenthood that may benefit stepchildren and remarriages. Stepparents with either a personal background or accepting attitudes are likely to be more prepared and have more realistic expectations.

Children's personalities also may be relevant. Stepchildren with a mature understanding of conflict resolution are better able to articulate their needs and communicate their frustrations to parents and stepparents than are emotionally immature stepchildren (Hetherington & Clingempeel, 1992). Deciding that steprelationships are worth the investment of time and energy also takes emotional maturity, especially when stepchildren do not perceive direct benefits to themselves, but rather that their loved ones are benefiting. Regardless of their maturity, stepchildren's receptivity to stepparents' efforts to befriend them is critical in developing positive relationships (Ganong et al., 1999).

Attachment Styles of Children and Adults

Clinicians and researchers have hypothesized that securely attached parents and stepparents could encourage better emotion regulation, be more responsive parents, and be more appropriate disciplinarians (Faber & Wittenborn, 2010), and that securely attached stepchildren may have easier transitions into stepfamily life and fewer behavior problems (Chapman, 1991). Securely attached remarried individuals are more likely to engage in relational repair strategies with their spouses than individuals with other attachment styles (Ragsdale, Brandau-Brown, & Bello, 2010); it remains unclear to what extent attachment styles contribute to resilience in stepfamilies. One investigator found that securely attached stepmothers related to their stepchildren no better than did anxious or avoidant stepmothers (Ceglian & Gardner, 1999). Only a few studies directly address how attachment styles influence stepfamily resilience, and further investigation may help clarify this relationship.

Dyadic and Family Resilience Processes

It is difficult to clearly distinguish between individual factors and some dyadic processes. For instance, parenting styles and communication skills may be seen as properties of individuals, but they also may be seen as reflecting dyadic and family processes (Diamond, Serrano, Dickey, & Sonis, 1996). A stepparent's style of relating to children may be related to the stepparent's personality and temperament (individual factor), but a child's reactions to a stepparent affect how a stepparent interacts with that child in the future. This makes stepparenting style in part a dyadic process. Similarly, clear communication between a stepparent and stepchild is a dyadic process, but one that is related to the individuals' abilities to send and receive messages. It may be more important to understand the interpersonal processes that contribute to resilience in stepfamilies than it is to distinguish between them and individual protective factors; Walsh (2002) has argued that dyadic and family processes form the crux of resilience in stepfamilies.

Stepparent–Stepchild Relationships

The steprelationship is critical in stepfamilies because problems related to raising stepchildren (e.g., discipline, finances) are found to be among the leading causes of conflicts in remarriage and even re-divorce (Coleman et al., 2001). There has been much more research on stepparent–stepchild relationships than on other stepfamily ties because difficult steprelationships place strains on the adult couple and put children at risk for developmental and behavioral problems (Michaels, 2007). Conversely, positive stepparent–stepchild relationships lead to better grades and fewer externalizing and internalizing behaviors among stepchildren (Hetherington & Clingempeel, 1992), as well as less depression and greater marital satisfaction for parents and stepparents (Bronstein, Stoll, Clauson, Abrams, & Briones, 1994; Greef & Du Toit, 2009).

Several investigators have reported that stepparents taking a supportive role with stepchildren and letting the biological parents do most of the disciplining is related to the closeness of steprelationships (Bray & Berger, 1993; Crosbie-Burnett & Giles-Sims, 1994; Hetherington & Clingempeel, 1992). Stepparents who eschew high control and low warmth (authoritarian) in their "parenting styles" in favor of high warmth and flexible control (authoritative) have better relationships with stepchildren (Fine et al., 1998; Golish, 2003; Henry & Lovelace, 1995), and their stepchildren are more likely to talk with them. Talking is important; individuals' predispositions to engage in everyday talk with stepfamily members are related to satisfaction with the remarriage for parents (Schrodt, Soliz, & Braithwaite, 2008) and bonding (Golish, 2003). Stepchildren prefer communication with stepparents that is open and flexible (Baxter, Braithwaite, Bryant, & Wagner, 2004; Henry & Lovelace, 1995), which is more likely with authoritative and permissive stepparenting styles.

Stepparents who try to develop friendships with their stepchildren report greater acceptance by stepchildren (Erera-Weatherly, 1996; Ganong et al., 1999; Svare, Jay, & Mason, 2004). Creating friendships with stepchildren is effective because it fits with what many stepchildren want from their stepparents (Fine et al., 1998) and with how they perceive stepparents when relationships are positive (Crohn, 2006). This suggests that stepchildren want to be close to stepparents, but they want to relate to stepparents in a role that emphasizes shared interests and companionship.

Engaging in age-appropriate activities that interest stepchildren is part of effective friendship building by stepparents (Ganong et al., 1999). For very young children, simply playing a favorite game with them is a way of developing friendship. With older children, getting to know them while engaging in a favorite game or sports activity contributes to building positive steprelationships. Building affinity and establishing a relationship between stepparents and stepchildren early in the courtship process of family formation is not enough, however. Once a positive relationship is developed, stepparents need to continue having fun with stepchildren, sharing common interests, helping them with problems, and other friendship-enhancing actions. Stepchildren become resentful when stepparents only work to build relationships with their stepchildren when they are "courting" the children's parent and who assume a disciplinarian role once married. In fact, Hetherington and Clingempeel (1992) found that when stepfathers began with warm and peer-like relationships with stepchildren but discontinued these actions over time the stepchildren engaged in more externalizing behaviors and had poorer adjustment.

In Erera-Weatherly's (1996) typology of stepparenting styles, only the *friendship style* was associated with positive relationships and individual well-being for all stepfamily household members. The friendship style did not engender as much competition from nonresidential parents, was accepted more readily by stepchildren, and resulted in closer steprelationships than did other styles. Orchard and Solberg (1999) also found that stepmothers who chose the *friend/supportive adult* model fared well. These research findings are similar to clinicians' advice to stepparents to befriend stepchildren and build positive, trusting relationships before attempting to discipline (Ganong, Coleman, & Weaver, 2002; Visher & Visher, 1996).

Friendship, however, is not the only model for steprelationships. In several qualitative studies, researchers have documented that stepparents and their spouses have created a variety of ways of "doing stepfamily" that appeared to work for them, at least from the adults' perspectives. Respondents in these studies reported that their interactions with stepchildren were the result of a complex process of trial and error in which the needs and wishes of all parties—children, parents, including nonresidential parents, and stepparents—were considered. Svare et al. (2004) identified two types of stepparent styles that worked well—the *third parent* (stepmothers only) and the *assistant parent* (mostly stepfathers)—that were characterized by stepparents engaging in parenting behaviors, but clearly doing so at the direction and will of the biological parent. This relationship pattern has been found by others under different labels. Weaver and Coleman (2005) called this a *mothering but not a mother* role, Orchard and Solberg (1999) described *another parent/mother-like* pattern of stepmothering, and a study of Canadian stepmothers identified the *extended model/added parent* style (Church, 1999). These styles may be similar to White and Gilbreth's (2001) *accumulation model* of stepparenting because stepparents did not replace an absent parent, but they became additional parents.

There is ample empirical evidence that stepparents often function in parent-like ways with stepchildren. Many stepparents invest as many resources (e.g., time, affection, encouragement, financial help) in their stepchildren to help them succeed as they do in their biological children (Schmeekle, 2007), and stepfathers may find ways to *claim* their stepchildren, even when the children have close ties with their fathers (Marsiglio, 2004). Claiming refers to behaviors that signify to stepchildren and to others that the stepfather cares about the child's well-being, intends to invest resources into helping the child grow and develop, and wants to create a close bond with the child.

Most stepparenting typologies include a style conceived to be identical to parenting (Church, 1999; Crohn, 2006; Erera-Weatherly, 1996; Svare et al., 2004). Although not always seen as a preferred mode (Erera-Weatherly, 1996), and rarely chosen by children (Crohn, 2006), this may be a resilient choice that results in close stepparent–stepchild bonds when stepchildren are extremely young when the stepparent enters the family and both parents support this mode (Ganong et al., 2011).

In contrast, some stepparents effectively create an *extended family* style of stepparenting that involves deliberately sharing childrearing responsibilities not only with the residential parent, but also with the nonresidential parent (Svare et al., 2004). Even though they were not always comfortable doing so, stepmothers and stepfathers made a point of including nonresidential parents and even grandparents in decision-making about the children because they believed it benefitted the child for everyone to have input. Some stepchildren likely would agree with this; Gross (1986) found that stepchildren in an *augmentation* group considered all parents and stepparents to be in their families.

Parent–Child Relationships

Although parent–child relationships appear to play an important role in resilience processes in stepfamilies, little attention has been paid to these relationships. One finding is that residential biological parents should continue to do things with their children alone (without the stepparents) (Thomson, Hanson, & McLanahan, 1994). In stepfather families, when mothers do fewer things with their children (such as talking with their children, working on a project, reading and helping children with their homework), the children misbehave more in school and exhibit more internalizing and externalizing behavior problems. Adolescents are more satisfied in their stepfamilies if they have positive communication with their parents (Henry & Lovelace, 1995). Additionally, the stepfather–stepchild relationship is better when mothers have good relationships with the children (Marsiglio, 1992), and stepmothers' adjustment is better when fathers are actively engaged in childrearing (Guisinger, Cowan, & Schuldberg, 1989).

Weaver and Coleman (2010) found that some roles mothers assumed in relating to their new partners and biological children positively influenced how steprelationships developed and how the family functioned. For example, mothers who described themselves as mediators settled disputes between stepfathers and stepchildren to keep the peace in their families. Although often stressful for mothers, being a mediator was an important role for them to enact, particularly early in the life of the stepfamily before steprelationships had formed solid bonds. Later, some mothers discontinued this role and found that communication and problem-solving between stepfathers and stepchildren eventually improved, although there were more disputes initially. Maternal mediating contributes to resilience because it helps stepfamilies adjust until steprelationship bonds are strong enough to withstand conflicts.

The most helpful role that mothers assumed was that of interpreter (Weaver & Coleman, 2010). Mothers interpreted children's emotions and behaviors to stepfathers, and they also interpreted the actions and motives of stepfathers to their children. This interpreter role may have worked because rather than allowing themselves to be triangulated into stepfather–stepchild problems, the mothers helped both stepfathers and stepchildren better understand one another.

Remarriage Relationships

As with other stepfamily relationships, remarriages are seldom studied from a resilience framework, but a few things are known about remarriage and resilience. First, sharing decision-making and marital power increases remarriage satisfaction for wives (Pyke, 1994). Second, resolving emotional attachments to former spouses and avoiding conflicts with them enhances marital intimacy in remarriages (Gold, Bubenzer, & West, 1993). Third, developing a strong couple bond and co-parenting team builds resilience (Michaels, 2007). Indeed, couples who disagree less about childrearing are more likely to report higher marital satisfaction and better marital quality (O'Connor & Insabella, 1999). This higher level of marital quality in turn reduces externalizing behaviors among children in stepfamilies. Higher remarital satisfaction also is related to greater stepparent–stepchild closeness (Bray & Berger, 1993). Fourth, remarried couples can handle their finances in multiple ways and still be satisfied with their relationships and their financial management practices. Pooling incomes works better for some (Addo & Sassler, 2010; Fishman, 1983), whereas separate accounts work well for others (Coleman & Ganong, 1989; Pasley et al., 1994). Fifth, remarriage expands older adults', especially men's, perceptions of kinship support for financial help, emotional support, and aid if they have an emergency (Curran, McLanahan, & Knab, 2003). Finally, couples should allow time to bond and grow closer (Cissna, Cox, & Bochner, 1990) without ignoring their children's needs for ongoing relationships with their parents.

Time in a stepfamily is a valuable and limited commodity. The remarried couple often feels a need to make up for previous relationships, and they have an understandable desire to spend time together privately. They must learn, however, to carefully balance their time together with concurrent demands of work and their children's and stepchildren's needs (Greef & Du Toit, 2009; Hetherington & Elmore, 2003). Clinicians assert that stepfamilies that can balance dyadic time in parent–child pairings and romantic pairings as well as family time and activities are less likely to experience destructive relational jealousy and competition among stepfamily members (Browning, 1994; Ganong et al., 2002; Visher & Visher, 1994).

Grandparents, Stepgrandparents, and Grandchildren

Developing resilience in stepfamilies is not limited to a single set of households or generations. Extended kin networks and stepgrandparents in particular also can play an expanded role in providing support and maintaining relationships within stepfamilies (Ganong, 2008; Ganong & Coleman, 2006; Greef & Du Toit, 2009). Although not replicated in other studies, Kennedy and Kennedy (1993) found that children in stepfamilies relied on the stability of the grandparent–grandchild relationship as they adjusted to stepfamily life. Stepgrandparents also can and do function as important characters for stepgrandchildren (Ganong, 2008). Some stepgrandparents are able to function as mediators when stepchildren and stepparents have conflicted relationships by acting as kinder, less demanding extensions of their biological child. In this way stepgrandparents may ease family tensions by warmly welcoming stepchildren and offering assistance. Clawson and Ganong (2002) found that adult stepchildren changed their views about older stepparents because of the stepparents' warm relationships with their stepgrandchildren. When they became aware of close relationships forming between their children and their stepparents, they reassessed their judgment of the stepparents.

Supportive extended kin networks that can provide both tangible benefits such as cheap or free childcare and intangible benefits such as emotional support and guidance can be invaluable in helping to foster closeness in family relationships (Clawson & Ganong, 2002; Greef & Du Toit, 2009). Extended kin relationships may be limited in their effectiveness and ability to provide support due to distance, but new technological advancements make staying in contact increasingly possible. Further research is needed to determine how extended kin networks and relationships might foster resilience.

Stepfamily Dynamics

Stepfamilies that allow school age and adolescent stepchildren to maintain close bonds with both nonresidential parents and residential stepparents have children with greater well-being than those in which children are close to only the nonresidential parent or the residential stepparent (King, 2006; White & Gilbreth, 2001). This *accumulation model* of stepparenting is better for children than the *loss* (nonresidential parent disappears) or *substitution* (stepparent replaces the nonresidential parent) models (White & Gilbreth). The benefits of accumulating stepparents may extend into young adulthood (Amato, 1994) and may be more beneficial for stepchildren living with stepmothers (King, 2007) than with stepfathers (King, 2006).

Rituals are features of almost all human groups and may vary from human sacrifice in pagan societies to what foods an American family eats for Thanksgiving dinner. Rituals are important in stepfamilies and those rituals brought from prior family units that incorporate and are accepted by new stepfamily members help create a sense of unity among stepfamily members (Braithwaite et al., 1998). Incorporating the old rituals conveys a sense of valuing the previous families and is a way of positively linking old and new families. New rituals developed in the stepfamily can make positive contributions toward forging a new stepfamily identity. Sharing major life events and sharing daily activities, and any event or experience that helps stepfamily members define themselves as a unit separate from others helps stepfamily members perceive that their stepfamily feels like a family (Baxter et al., 1999).

Some stepfamily resilience processes and protective factors may resemble those of first-marriage nuclear families (O'Connor, Hetherington, & Reiss, 1998). Coughlin and Vuchinich (1996) found that over time stepfather families with adolescent males began to problem solve more like nuclear families. Another resilience process shared by stepfamilies and other family structures is kinkeeping, the process of connecting family members with each other, negotiating disagreements and mediating disputes among family members, and monitoring how individual family members are doing. Stepmothers have been found to kinkeep by helping their husbands maintain connections with their nonresidential children (Schmeekle, 2007; Vinick & Lanspery, 2000). Vinick referred to these women as "carpenters" because they built relationships between their husbands and their husbands' children.

Extra-Familial Factors

Although the lack of institutionalization facing stepfamilies in legal, health, and education systems still holds true on a national level, there are a few local efforts to reverse this trend (Ganong & Coleman, 2004; Sweeney, 2010). The inclusion of more than two lines on forms requesting the names of a student's parents or emergency contacts is a simple step taken by some institutions to reduce the loyalty conflicts experienced by stepchildren who otherwise have to make a choice about which parent to include.

Interventions with stepfamilies also have increased in number and effectiveness. One example is DeGarmo and Forgatch's (2007) evaluation of an intervention with stepfathers. They found that the stepfathers' new skills (e.g., encouragement, effective limit setting, monitoring, interpersonal problem-solving, positive involvement) and new knowledge about stepfamilies contributed to reductions in children's depression and behavioral noncompliance months and even years after the intervention. As the number of families with steprelatives continues to remain a significant portion of the population, it is possible that institutional adjustments and support will continue to be developed.

Current Issues

Cohabiting Stepfamilies

Cohabitation is rapidly increasing in the United States and Europe (Kennedy & Bumpass, 2008), and the number of cohabiting stepfamilies is also quickly rising (Pew Research Center, 2011; Stewart, 2001). Cohabiting stepfamilies exemplify dynamics and difficulties similar to those found in stepfamilies formed through remarriage (Stewart), although the lack of legal ties can make economic concerns and financial management especially salient among cohabiting families because of issues related to child support, inheritance, and similar concerns (Addo & Sassler, 2010). Unfortunately, we know little from research about resilience processes and protective factors among cohabiting stepfamilies.

Gay and Lesbian Stepfamilies

Gay and lesbian couples have become increasingly visible, and all of them form stepfamilies if children from previous relationships or conceived through donor insemination are involved. Some gay male couples also adopt children (Coleman et al., 2000). The challenges of these families are similar to those of other stepfamilies—a lack of labels for relationships, few models of how family members should relate to one another, and stigma (Hequembourg, 2004; Lynch, 2000; Moore, 2008). Emotional support from friends and family is especially important for these highly stigmatized stepfamilies, and the more resilient ones are able to mobilize these resources in the construction of a supportive community. Emotional support from friends and family members plays a large part in reducing gay and lesbian parents' experiences of depression and anxiety (Oswald, 2002).

Because mothers more often get custody than fathers, we know more about lesbian stepfamilies than we do about gay ones (Crosbie-Burnett & Helmbrecht, 1993). Not surprisingly, both parents and stepparents are protective of the effects of coming out on children in the household, causing Lynch (2000) to label these stepfamilies as child centered. As an example, when children who had been comfortable with their parents' openness about gender in elementary school became less comfortable as adolescents, the couples followed the child's lead and downplayed their gender orientation (Lynch). Much of the research on gay and lesbian stepfamilies is framed from a deficit comparison perspective and this area requires continued investigation into resilience processes.

Clinical Implications

Familial Interventions

As we noted earlier, clinicians have long written about stepfamily dynamics, but not always from a resilience perspective. A resilience approach to working with stepfamilies is innately strengths-based (Hawley, 2000), and although focusing on family strengths and fostering resilience processes may be familiar to solution-focused and narrative family therapists, this concept is more novel within other clinical fields.

A simple intervention has been to validate and normalize stepfamily members' cognitions and experiences (Ganong & Coleman, 2004; Shalay & Brownlee, 2007; Visher & Visher, 1994). Normalization of experiences can help relieve anxiety experienced by stepfamily members and promote new frameworks for dealing with past difficulties (Shalay & Brownlee, 2007).

In addition to normalizing experiences, clinicians must work to balance the opposing societal ideology of first-marriage nuclear families and the stigma attached to remarriage and stepfamilies. Visher and Visher (1988) stressed that clinicians must constantly monitor and reevaluate their perceptions of what it means to be in a remarried family and ensure that as therapists they provide a validating and positive environment. Applying resilience to stepfamilies means focusing on family strengths and acknowledging diverse ways for families to accomplish goals and tasks (Hawley, 2000).

Conceptualizing resilience as a process means that applying resilience research to stepfamilies in a clinical setting often requires family-level interventions. This is difficult to do. According to Visher and Visher (1988), aligning schedules from multiple households makes family therapy and treating the entire suprasystem of stepfamilies challenging but worthwhile. Other clinicians would strongly disagree (Browning, 1994). Most clinicians, however, would agree that working with subsystems can help foster resilience and may be ideal when tensions and stress are high (Browning, 1994; Visher & Visher, 1994). Unlike in nuclear families, family interventions that rely on applying stress to the family system, whether to test boundaries or force change, can be perilous when relationships are new and lack the buffer provided by a shared family history (Browning). Parent–child and couple subsystems, on the other hand, are likely to retain more stability when prodded, and adjusting for dyadic work may be more conducive to promoting resilience (Browning, 1994; Ganong et al., 2002).

As Papernow (2006) has noted, newly formed stepfamilies lack "middle ground" or shared histories, experiences, and cultures, all of which facilitate being able to effectively problem solve and maintain relationships through conflicts and challenges. Families with a lot of middle ground don't have to think much about how to cope or problem solve, so clinicians need to help families thicken their middle ground. Papernow does this with psychoeducation about how stepfamilies differ from first-marriage families, slowing down the changes, helping to gently modify unrealistic expectations and fantasies about what should be happening, and helping stepfamily members build skills, such as authoritative parenting abilities.

Educational Interventions

Psychoeducational approaches to working with stepfamilies can foster resilience, and attempts to normalize stepfamily experiences can occur in either group or individual settings (Papernow, 2006; Shalay & Brownlee, 2007; Visher & Visher, 1994). Often what is most needed by stepfamily members is information and education. For example, new stepparents who previously had no children of their own can greatly benefit from child development basic knowledge (Ganong et al., 2002; Papernow, 2006). An understanding of how to differentiate between age-appropriate behaviors and misbehavior can go far in helping stepparents better understand their new stepchildren (Ganong & Coleman, 2004; Papernow, 2006). Biological parents can fill in specifics regarding their children's temperament and other personality characteristics, but learning about young children's and adolescents' abilities and developmental goals can help stepparents adjust their expectations. Understanding adolescent development can allow parents and stepparents to reframe a teenager's increasing disinterest in family life and combative arguments as attempts to assess his or her autonomy rather than rebellion and personal rejection. This developmentally informed reframing can foster family resilience by moving these stressful arguments from being destabilizing forces to learning opportunities and negotiations about what it means to begin transitioning to adulthood (Shalay & Brownlee, 2007).

Some stepfamily members would greatly benefit by learning simple communication techniques such as how to properly voice complaints and avoid criticizing language, or the importance of describing one's own feelings and thoughts by using I-statements, which can be taught both individually and in dyadic or group settings (Ganong et al., 2002; Papernow, 2006). Communication skills and mastering abilities such as being able to recognize when is and is not an appropriate time to start a sensitive discussion are important resilience processes that require both knowledge and practice.

Research Implications

Further investigation into the process of resilience in stepfamilies is still needed. Stepfamily research continues to be primarily posited from a deficit comparison rather than a normative-adaptive perspective. Over the last 2 decades, researchers and clinicians have gained a better understanding of how and why stepfamilies are different. Stepfamilies are complex and simple explanations of family dynamics are not sufficient for understanding stepfamily processes and the development of resilience (Ganong & Coleman, 2004).

More attention needs to be given to the role of biological relationships in stepfamilies. A large body of literature exists on parent–child relationships in nuclear families and postdivorce families, but little research has been done on how parent–child relationships operate in stepfamilies. Relationships among siblings in stepfamilies also have received little attention.

Investigating dyadic and systemic properties through observations and from data collected from multiple reporters will greatly benefit research on stepfamily resilience. A significant portion of stepfamily research relies upon survey responses from large, nationally representative samples, or qualitative in-depth interviews with convenience samples. Although these methods benefit one another and help begin to frame a coherent picture of stepfamily life, large-scale surveys struggle to capture the complexity of stepfamily life, and findings from small convenience samples make it difficult to know how generalizable the results may be. Ultimately, better quality research and a greater understanding of processes that promote resilience in stepfamilies will directly benefit stepfamilies themselves.

Conclusions

Stepfamilies remain an important and prevalent topic for both clinicians and researchers, and many questions remain unanswered. While the past several decades have allowed investigators to outline the wide variety of risks stepfamilies face, fewer studies have been conducted from a resilience perspective. We have highlighted *some* of the ways resilience can be developed in stepfamilies, but there are likely many others not yet discovered. Understanding resilience processes could be used by stepfamilies as well as the professionals and community agencies supporting them to enhance adjustment.

References

Addo, F. R., & Sassler, S. (2010). Financial arrangements and relationship quality in low-income couples. *Family Relations, 59*, 408–423.

Amato, P. R. (1994). The implications of research findings on children in stepfamilies. In A. Booth & J. Dunn (Eds.), *Stepfamilies: Who benefits? Who does not?* (pp. 81–87). Hillsdale, NJ: Erlbaum.

Amato, P. R. (2010). Research on divorce: Continuing trends and new developments. *Journal of Marriage and Family, 72*, 650–666.

Amato, P. R., & Gilbreth, J. G. (1999). Nonresident fathers and children's well-being: A meta-analysis. *Journal of Marriage and Family, 61*, 557–573. doi:10.2307/353560.

Amato, P. R., & Sobolewski, J. M. (2004). The effects of divorce on fathers and children: Nonresidential fathers and stepfathers. In M. E. Lamb (Ed.), *The role of the father in child development* (4th ed., pp. 341–367). Hoboken, NJ: Wiley.

Baxter, L. A., Braithwaite, D., & Nicholson, J. H. (1999). Turning points in the development of blended families. *Journal of Social and Personal Relationships, 16*(3), 291–313.

Baxter, L. A., Braithwaite, D. O., Bryant, L., & Wagner, A. (2004). Stepchildren's perceptions of the contradictions in communication with stepparents. *Journal of Social and Personal Relationships, 21*(4), 447–467.

Braithwaite, D. O., Baxter, L. A., & Harper, A. M. (1998). The role of rituals in the management of dialectical tension of "old" and "new" in blended families. *Communication Studies, 46*, 101–120.

Bray, J., & Berger, S. (1993). Developmental issues in step families research project: Family relationships and parent-child interaction. *Journal of Family Psychology, 7*, 76–90.

Bronstein, P., Stoll, M. F., Clauson, J., Abrams, C. L., & Briones, M. (1994). Father after separation or divorce: Factors predicting children's adjustment. *Family Relations, 43*, 469–479.

Browning, S. W. (1994). Treating stepfamilies: Alternatives to traditional family therapy. In K. Pasley & M. Ihinger-Tallman (Eds.), *Stepparenting: Issues in theory, research, and practice* (pp. 175–198). Westport, CT: Greenwood.

Bzostek, S. H. (2008). Social fathers and child well-being. *Journal of Marriage and Family, 70*, 950–961.

Carlson, M. J. (2006). Family structure, father involvement, and adolescent behavioral outcomes. *Journal of Marriage and Family, 68*, 137–154.

Carter, B., & McGoldrick, M. (Eds.). (2005). *The expanded family life cycle: Individual, family, and social perspectives* (3rd ed.). Boston: Allyn & Bacon.

Cartwright, C. (2005). Stepfamily living and parent–child relationships: An exploratory investigation. *Journal of Family Studies, 11*(2), 267–283.

Ceglian, C. P., & Gardner, S. (1999). Attachment style: A risk for multiple marriages? *Journal of Divorce and Remarriage, 31*, 125–139.

Chapman, S. F. (1991). Attachment and adolescent adjustment to parental remarriage. *Family Relations, 40*, 232–237.

Cherlin, A. (1978). Remarriage as an incomplete institution. *The American Journal of Sociology, 84*, 634–650.

Cherlin, A. J. (2010). Demographic trends in the United States: A review of research in the 2000s. *Journal of Marriage and Family, 72*, 403–419.

Church, E. (1999). Who are the people in your family? Stepmothers' diverse notions of kinship. *Journal of Divorce and Remarriage, 31*, 83–105.

Cissna, K. N., Cox, D. E., & Bochner, A. P. (1990). The dialectic of marital and parental relationships within the stepfamily. *Communication Monographs, 57*(1), 44–61.

Clawson, J., & Ganong, L. (2002). Adult stepchildren's obligations to older stepparents. *Journal of Family Nursing, 8,* 50–72.

Claxton-Oldfield, S. (2000). Deconstructing the myth of the wicked stepparent. *Marriage & Family Review, 30,* 51–58.

Claxton-Oldfield, S., O'Neil, S., Thomson, C., & Gallant, B. (2005). Multiple stereotypes of stepfathers. *Journal of Divorce & Remarriage, 44*(1/2), 165–176.

Clingempeel, W. G., Brand, E., & Segal, S. (1987). A multilevel-multivariable-developmental perspective for future research on stepfamilies. In K. Pasley & M. Ihinger-Tallman (Eds.), *Remarriage and stepparenting today: Research and theory* (pp. 65–93). New York: Guilford Press.

Coleman, M., Fine, M., Ganong, L., Downs, K., & Pauk, N. (2001). When you're not the Brady Bunch: Identifying perceived conflicts and resolution strategies in stepfamilies. *Personal Relationships, 8,* 55–73.

Coleman, M., & Ganong, L. (1989). Financial management in stepfamilies. *Lifestyles: Family and Economic Issues, 10,* 217–232.

Coleman, M., & Ganong, L. (1990). *Relationship of personality variables to stepfamily closeness.* In Presented at the national council on family relations annual conference, Seattle, WA, November 1990.

Coleman, M., Ganong, L., & Fine, M. (2000). Reinvestigating remarriage: Another decade of progress. *Journal of Marriage and Family, 62,* 1288–1307.

Coughlin, C., & Vuchinich, S. (1996). Family experience in preadolescent and the development of male delinquency. *Journal of Marriage and Family, 58,* 491–501.

Crohn, H. M. (2006). Five styles of positive stepmothering from the perspective of young adult stepdaughters. *Journal of Divorce & Remarriage, 46*(1/2), 119–134.

Crosbie-Burnett, M., & Giles-Sims, J. (1994). Adolescent adjustment and stepparenting styles. *Family Relations, 43,* 394–399.

Crosbie-Burnett, M., & Helmbrecht, L. (1993). A descriptive empirical study of gay male stepfamilies. *Family Relations, 42,* 256–262.

Curran, S. R., McLanahan, S., & Knab, J. (2003). Does remarriage expand perceptions of kinship support among the elderly? *Social Science Research, 32,* 171–190.

DeGarmo, D. S., & Forgatch, M. (2007). Efficacy of parent training for stepfathers: From playful spectator and polite stranger to effective stepfathering. *Parenting: Science and Practice, 7,* 331–355.

Demo, D. H., & Acock, A. C. (1996). Singlehood, marriage, and remarriage: The effects of family structure and family relationships on mothers' well-being. *Journal of Family Issues, 17*(3), 388–407.

Diamond, G. S., Serrano, A., Dickey, M., & Sonis, W. (1996). Current status of family-based outcome and process research. *Journal of the Academy of Child and Adolescent Psychiatry, 35,* 6–16.

Erera-Weatherly, P. I. (1996). On becoming a stepparent: Factors associated with the adoption of alternative stepparenting styles. *Journal of Divorce and Remarriage, 25*(3/4), 155–174.

Evenson, R. J., & Simon, R. W. (2005). Clarifying the relationship between parenthood and depression. *Journal of Health and Social Behavior, 46,* 341–358.

Faber, A. J., & Wittenborn, A. K. (2010). The role of attachment in children's adjustment to divorce and remarriage. *Journal of Family Psychotherapy, 21,* 89–104.

Fein, D. J., Burstein, N. R., Fein, G. G., & Lindberg, L. D. (2003). *The determinants of marriage and cohabitation among disadvantaged Americans: Research findings and needs.* Marriage and family formation data analysis project final report. Bethesda, MD: Abt Associates.

Fine, M. A., Coleman, M., & Ganong, L. (1998). Consistency in perceptions of the stepparent role among stepparents, parents, and stepchildren. *Journal of Social and Personal Relationships, 15,* 810–828.

Fishman, B. (1983). The economic behavior of stepfamilies. *Family Relations, 32,* 359–366.

Ganong, L. (2008). Intergenerational relationships in stepfamilies. In J. Pryor (Ed.), *International handbook of stepfamilies: Policy and practice in legal, research, and clinical environments* (pp. 394–420). Hoboken, NJ: Wiley.

Ganong, L., & Coleman, M. (1989). Preparing for remarriage: Anticipating the issues, seeking solutions. *Family Relations, 38,* 28–33.

Ganong, L., & Coleman, M. (2004). *Stepfamily relationships: Development, dynamics and interventions.* New York: Kluwer/Plenum.

Ganong, L., & Coleman, M. (2006). Patterns of exchange and intergenerational responsibilities after divorce and remarriage. *Journal of Aging Studies, 20,* 265–278.

Ganong, L., Coleman, M., Fine, M., & Martin, P. (1999). Stepparents' affinity-seeking and affinity-maintaining strategies with stepchildren. *Journal of Family Issues, 20,* 299–327.

Ganong, L., Coleman, M., & Jamison, T. B. (2011). Patterns of stepchild-stepparent relationship development. *Journal of Marriage and Family, 73*(2), 396–413.

Ganong, L., Coleman, M., & Weaver, S. E. (2002). Maintenance and enhancement in remarried families: Clinical applications. In J. Harvey & A. Wenzel (Eds.), *A clinicians' guide to maintaining and enhancing close relationships* (pp. 105–129). Hillsdale, NJ: Erlbaum.

Ganong, L., Doty, M. E., & Gayer, D. (2003). Mothers in postdivorce families caring for a child with cystic fibrosis. *Journal of Pediatric Nursing, 18*, 332–342.

Gerlach, P. (2001). *Building a high-nurturance stepfamily*. Philadelphia: Hibris Corporation.

Gold, J. M., Bubenzer, D. L., & West, J. D. (1993). Differentiation from ex-spouses and stepfamily marital intimacy. *Journal of Divorce & Remarriage, 19*, 83–95.

Goldscheider, F., & Kaufman, G. (2006). Willingness to stepparent: Attitudes about partners who already have children. *Journal of Family Issues, 27*, 1415–1436.

Golish, T. D. (2003). Stepfamily communication strengths: Understanding the ties that bind. *Human Communication Research, 29*(1), 41–80.

Greef, A. P., & Du Toit, C. (2009). Resilience in remarried families. *American Journal of Family Therapy, 37*, 114–126.

Gross, P. E. (1986). Defining post-divorce remarriage families: A typology based on the subjective perceptions of children. *Journal of Divorce, 10*, 205–217.

Guisinger, S., Cowan, P., & Schuldberg, D. (1989). Changing parent and spouse relations in the first years of remarriage of divorced fathers. *Journal of Marriage and Family, 51*, 445–456.

Hawley, D. R. (2000). Clinical implications of family resilience. *American Journal of Family Therapy, 28*, 101–116.

Henry, C. S., & Lovelace, S. G. (1995). Family resources and adolescent family life satisfaction in remarried family households. *Journal of Family Issues, 16*, 765–786.

Hequembourg, A. (2004). Unscripted motherhood: Lesbian mothers negotiating incompletely institutionalized family relationships. *Journal of Social and Personal Relationships, 21*, 739–762.

Hetherington, E. M., & Clingempeel, W. G. (1992). Coping with marital transitions: A family systems perspective. *Monographs of the Society for Research in Child Development, 57*, 1–242.

Hetherington, E. M., & Elmore, A. M. (2003). Risk and resilience in children coping with their parents' divorce and remarriage. In S. S. Luthar (Ed.), *Resilience and vulnerability: Adaptation in the context of childhood adversities*. Cambridge, UK: Cambridge University Press.

Higginbotham, B. J., Miller, J. J., & Niehuis, S. (2009). Remarriage preparation: Usage, perceived helpfulness, and dyadic adjustment. *Family Relations, 58*, 316–329.

Ispa, J. M., Thornburg, K. R., & Fine, M. A. (2006). *Keepin'on: The everyday struggles of young families in poverty*. Baltimore: Brookes Publishing Company.

Kelly, J. B. (2007). Children's living arrangements following separation and divorce: Insights from empirical and clinical research. *Family Process, 46*, 35–52.

Kelly, K., & Ganong, L. (2011). 'Shifting family boundaries' after the diagnosis of childhood cancer in stepfamilies. *Journal of Family Nursing, 17*, 105–132.

Kennedy, G. E., & Kennedy, C. E. (1993). Grandparents: A special resource for children. *Journal of Divorce and Remarriage, 19*, 45–68.

Kennedy, S., & Bumpass, L. (2008). Cohabitation and children's living arrangements: New estimates from the United States. *Demographic Research, 19*, 1663–1692.

King, V. (2006). The antecedents and consequences of adolescents' relationships with stepfathers and nonresident fathers. *Journal of Marriage and Family, 68*, 910–928.

King, V. (2007). When children have two mothers: Relationships with nonresident mothers, stepmothers, and fathers. *Journal of Marriage and Family, 69*, 1178–1193.

Leon, K., & Angst, E. (2005). Portrayals of stepfamilies in film: Using media images in remarriage education. *Family Relations, 54*, 3–23.

Lynch, J. M. (2000). Considerations of family structure and gender composition: The lesbian and gay stepfamily. *Journal of Homosexuality, 40*(2), 81–95.

Marsiglio, W. (1992). Stepfathers with minor children living at home: Parenting perceptions and relationship quality. *Journal of Family Issues, 13*, 195–214.

Marsiglio, W. (2004). When stepfathers claim stepchildren: A conceptual analysis. *Journal of Marriage and Family, 66*, 22–39.

Michaels, M. L. (2007). Remarital issues in couple therapy. *Journal of Couple & Relationship Therapy, 6*, 125–139.

Moore, M. (2008). Gendered power relations among women: A study of household decision making in Black, lesbian stepfamilies. *American Sociological Review, 72*, 335–358.

O'Connor, T. G., Hetherington, E. M., & Reiss, D. (1998). Family systems and adolescent development: Shared and nonshared risk and protective factors in nondivorced and remarried families. *Development and Psychopathology, 10*, 353–375.

O'Connor, T. G., & Insabella, G. M. (1999). Marital satisfaction, relationships, and roles. In E. M. Hetherington, S. H. Henderson, & D. Reiss (Eds.) (pp. 79–101). *Monographs of the Society for Research in Child Development, 64*(4, Serial No. 259). Malden, MA: Blackwell.

Orchard, A. L., & Solberg, K. B. (1999). Expectation of the stepmother's role. *Journal of Divorce and Remarriage, 31*, 107–123.

Oswald, R. F. (2002). Resilience within the family networks of lesbians and gay men: Intentionality and redefinition. *Journal of Marriage and Family, 64*, 374–394.

Papernow, P. (2006). Therapy for people who live in stepfamilies. *Family Therapy Magazine, 5*, 34–42.

Pasley, K., Sandras, E., & Edmondson, M. E. (1994). The effects of financial management strategies on quality of family life in remarriage. *Journal of Family and Economic Issues, 15*, 53–70.

Pew Research Center. (2011). *Pew social & demographic trends survey*. Washington, DC: Pew Research Center.

Pyke, K. D. (1994). Women's employment as a gift or burden? Marital power across marriage, divorce, and remarriage. *Gender and Society, 8*, 73–91.

Ragsdale, J. D., Brandau-Brown, F., & Bello, R. (2010). Attachment style and gender as predictors of relational repair among the remarried. *Journal of Family Communication, 10*, 158–173.

Saint-Jacques, M.-C. (1995). Role strain prediction in stepfamilies. *Journal of Divorce and Remarriage, 24*(1/2), 51–72.

Samuelsohn, D. (2010, June 9). Senate climate bill's boosters try smorgasbord strategy in bid for votes. *The New York Times*, Section B.

Sandler, I., Miles, J., Cookston, J., & Braver, S. (2008). Effects of father and mother parenting on children's mental health in high- and low-conflict divorces. *Family Court Review, 46*, 282–296.

Schmeekle, M. (2007). Gender dynamics in stepfamilies: Adult stepchildren's views. *Journal of Marriage and Family, 69*, 174–189.

Schrodt, P., Soliz, J., & Braithwaite, D. (2008). A social relations model of everyday talk and relational satisfaction in stepfamilies. *Communication Monographs, 75*(2), 190–217.

Shalay, N., & Brownlee, K. (2007). Narrative family therapy with blended families. *Journal of Family Psychotherapy, 18*, 17–30.

Skogrand, L., Torres, E., & Higginbotham, B. J. (2010). Stepfamily education: Benefits of a group-formatted intervention. *The Family Journal: Counseling and Therapy for Couples and Families, 18*, 234–240.

Stewart, S. D. (2001). Contemporary American stepparenthood: Integrating cohabiting and nonresident stepparents. *Population Research & Policy Review, 20*, 345–364.

Svare, G. M., Jay, S., & Mason, M. A. (2004). Stepparents on stepparenting: An exploratory study of stepparenting approaches. *Journal of Divorce and Remarriage, 41*(3/4), 81–97.

Sweeney, M. (2010). Remarriage and stepfamilies: Strategic sites for family scholarship in the 21st century. *Journal of Marriage and Family, 72*, 667–684.

Sweeney, M. M. (2007). Stepfather families and the emotional well-being of adolescents. *Journal of Health and Social Behavior, 48*(1), 33–49.

Szinovacz, M. E. (1998). Grandparents today: A demographic profile. *The Gerontologist, 38*(1), 37–52.

Thomson, E., Hanson, T. L., & McLanahan, S. S. (1994). Family structure and child well-being: Economic resources vs. parental behaviors. *Social Forces, 73*, 221–242.

Vinick, B. H., & Lanspery, S. (2000). Cinderella's sequel: Stepmothers' long-term relationships with adult stepchildren. *Journal of Comparative Family Studies, 31*, 377–384.

Visher, E. B., & Visher, J. S. (1988). *Old loyalties, new ties: Therapeutic strategies with stepfamilies*. New York: Brunner/Mazel.

Visher, E. B., & Visher, J. S. (1994). The core ingredients in the treatment of stepfamilies. *The Family Journal: Counseling and Therapy for Couples and Families, 2*, 208–214.

Visher, E. B., & Visher, J. S. (1996). *Therapy with stepfamilies*. New York: Brunner/Mazel.

Walsh, F. (2002). A family resilience framework: Innovative practice applications. *Family Relations, 51*, 130–137.

Weaver, S. E., & Coleman, M. (2005). A mothering but not a mother role: A grounded theory study of the nonresidential stepmother role. *Journal of Social and Personal Relationships, 22*, 477–497.

Weaver, S. E., & Coleman, M. (2010). Caught in the middle: Mothers in stepfamilies. *Journal of Social and Personal Relationships, 27*, 305–326.

White, L., & Gilbreth, J. G. (2001). When children have two fathers: Effects of relationships with stepfathers and noncustodial fathers on adolescent outcomes. *Journal of Marriage and Family, 63*, 155–167.

Resilience in Military Marriages Experiencing Deployment

7

Jared R. Anderson, Yvonne Amanor-Boadu,
Sandra M. Stith, and Rachel E. Foster

Introduction/Background

Separation due to deployment is a hallmark of married life for military couples. As a result of U.S. military engagement in the Middle East since 9/11, known as Operation Iraqi Freedom (OIF) and Operation Enduring Freedom (OEF), these separations resulting from military related deployments have become more frequent and longer. According to recent Department of Defense statistics, since September 11, 2001, over two million service members have been deployed, with nearly 800,000 deploying more than once. In total, U.S. troops have deployed 3.3 million times (Tan, 2009). Since 56% of the nearly 1.5 million service members are married and 71% of all officers in the military are married, the vast majority of military couples have experienced one or multiple deployments. The most dominant narrative related to the effects of military service in general, and specifically to deployment to combat zones, is that deployment harms personal well-being and marriages, often irreparably (Dao & Einhorn, 2010). However, there is also evidence that deployment seems to have little effect on marital stability (Karney & Crown, 2007), and many report that deployment strengthened their marriage (Kaiser Family Foundation, 2004). The purpose of this chapter is to begin to understand and describe how some marriages are able to be resilient following the stress of deployment.

There is little debate that deployments are stressful for individual service members, couples, and families. In addition, there is a growing body of research to support the notion that deployments can, at times, negatively affect the mental and physical health of service members, spouses, and children (Chandra et al., 2010; Mansfield et al., 2010; Thomas et al., 2010) and cause great strain on relationships (Galovski & Lyons, 2004; Monson, Taft, & Fredman, 2009). This strain on personal and family well-being can affect service member morale, effectiveness, and retention in the Armed Forces. As a result, the military has begun to increase spending to support military families and to find ways to strengthen both individual service member resilience and couple/family resilience in response to the stressors and strains of deployment (Casey, 2011; Lorge, 2007).

J.R. Anderson (✉) • S.M. Stith
Marriage and Family Therapy Program, Kansas State University, Manhattan, KS, USA
e-mail: jra@ksu.edu

Y. Amanor-Boadu
Marriage and Family Therapist, Manhattan, KS, USA

R.E. Foster
Joint Base Anacostia-Bolling, Washington, DC, USA

D.S. Becvar (ed.), *Handbook of Family Resilience*,
DOI 10.1007/978-1-4614-3917-2_7, © Springer Science+Business Media New York 2013

Significance of the Topic

There is very little empirical data related to the factors that promote resilience in military couples experiencing deployment. Part of this undoubtedly has to do with the significance of the negative effects that service members are experiencing, the ongoing nature of U.S. military involvement, and the tendency for social science to focus on disease and pathology rather than on strength and resilience. However, despite the stressors, strains, and even trauma related to deployment, the majority of military couples are, in general, resilient (Bell & Schumm, 2000; Kelley, Herzog-Simmer, & Harris, 1994). That is, they evidence the "ability to withstand and rebound from disruptive life challenges" (Walsh, 2003, p. 1). In the following sections, we provide a brief overview of the effects of deployment on individual service members, their spouses, and the couple relationship. We then apply data from interviews with seven *resilient* Air Force couples who have experienced deployment to a framework for understanding resilience in families developed by Walsh (2003). Next, we present a case vignette illustrating factors leading to resilience operating within a particular Air Force couple who have experienced multiple deployments. Finally, we present clinical and research implications related to resilience in military couples experiencing deployment.

Literature Review

Effects of Deployment on Army Personnel and Spouses

While the focus of this chapter is on how successful Air Force couples manage deployment, most of the previous research has focused on Army personnel and their spouses. A growing body of recent research suggests that deployment increases risk for Army personnel to experience a wide variety of mental health problems. For example, Vasterling et al. (2010) found that compared to nondeployed soldiers, deployed soldiers reported increased posttraumatic stress disorder (PTSD) symptoms from pre- to postdeployment after controlling for predeployment levels of PTSD symptoms. Thomas et al. (2010) surveyed 13,226 US Army soldiers from both active components and National Guard infantry brigade combat teams to determine the effects of deployment on mental health. They found prevalence rates of depression ranged from 5.0 to 16.0% and from 5.6 to 30.5% for PTSD depending on the definition (level of severity and functional impairment), assessment time frame (3 or 12 months following deployment), and duty component (active duty vs. National Guard). In general, prevalence rates were higher at the 12-month postdeployment assessment than they were 3-months postdeployment. In addition, between 8.5 and 14.0% of soldiers in their sample reported serious functional impairment due to either depression or PTSD symptoms. Finally, 50% of those soldiers who met criteria for depression and PTSD based on the strictest definitions also met criteria for alcohol misuse or aggressive behavior.

In one of the largest studies ($N = 88,235$) on the effects of deployment on mental health problems, Milliken, Auchterlonie, and Hoge (2007) reported that 20.3% of active duty soldiers and 42.4% of reserve component soldiers screened positive for a mental health problem requiring treatment. In addition, similar to previous research (Thomas et al., 2010), rates of mental health problems increased from initial postdeployment screening to follow-up, 6 months after reintegration. Finally, the research by Castro and McGurk (2007) sheds some light on the relationship between length and number of deployments and mental health risk. Soldiers who had deployed more than once were more likely to screen positive for PTSD (1.6 times), anxiety (1.2 times), and depression (1.7 times) than soldiers who had deployed only once. In addition, soldiers who were deployed for longer than 6 months were

1.5–1.6 times more likely to screen positive for PTSD, anxiety, or depression. Thus, recent research on soldiers deployed in OIF/OEF related conflicts clearly points to the elevated mental health risks of deployment and exposure to combat.

Research on the effects of deployment on the health of partners of soldiers (mainly wives) also finds negative mental health consequences, although spouses are the focus of far fewer studies related to the current military operations (i.e., OIF/OEF). For example, utilizing outpatient medical records of 250,626 wives of U.S. Army active duty soldiers, Mansfield et al. (2010) found that wives of soldiers deployed for 1–11 months received more diagnoses for depressive symptoms, sleep, anxiety, acute stress, and adjustment disorders compared to wives of soldiers who had not deployed. Further, wives of soldiers deployed more than 11 months had even higher rates of diagnosis for these same disorders. A majority of spouses also report stressors related to feelings of loneliness, difficulty communicating with their spouse while he is deployed, balancing work and family obligations, worrying for their husband's safety, and if they have children, raising and caring for their children while functioning as a "single" parent (Warner, Appenzeller, Warner, & Grieger, 2009).

Effects of Deployment on Couple Relationships

Research related to deployment and relationship functioning is primarily concerned with the effects of combat-related PTSD on spouse adjustment and relationship functioning (for recent reviews, see Galovski & Lyons, 2004; MacDermid Wadsworth, 2010; Monson et al., 2009). For example, couples in which a veteran has been diagnosed with PTSD have higher levels of relationship distress and greater relationship instability than couples where the veteran does not have PTSD (Cook, Riggs, Thompson, Coyne, & Sheikh, 2004; Riggs, Byrne, Weathers, & Litz, 1998). More recent studies that include active duty military members or partners evidencing PTSD symptoms rather than diagnosed PTSD have had similar results. For example, samples that include partners of Dutch peacekeepers (Dirkzwager, Bramsen, Ader, & Ploeg, 2005), active duty Army soldiers and spouses (Allen, Rhoades, Stanley, & Markman, 2010; Nelson Goff, Crow, Reisbig, & Hamilton, 2007), National Guard soldiers (Gewirtz, Polusny, DeGarmo, Khaylis, & Erbes, 2010), and spouses of National Guard soldiers (Renshaw, Rodrigues, & Jones, 2008) have all evidenced a deleterious link between higher PTSD symptoms and lower levels of relationship satisfaction. Therefore, across a diverse set of soldiers and partners that include veterans and active duty soldiers in at least three countries, there is emerging evidence that PTSD or PTSD symptoms are negatively related to relationship quality.

Positive Effects of Deployment

Given the toll that mental health problems such as PTSD can have on the well-being of individuals and families as well as on the readiness of military service members and their ability to continue their military service, it is not surprising that the overwhelming focus to date has been on the deleterious effects of deployment. Not discounting the stress and strain that deployment poses for military service members and their families, or the seriousness of the physical and mental health problems that can result from combat exposure, it is also true that the majority of military service members do not meet criteria for mental illness upon return from deployment and continue to maintain their marriages and family life. For example, Karney and Crown (2007), in the most comprehensive study to date related to deployment and marital stability, found that deployment was either not related to marital instability or was associated with greater levels of marital stability. Only for enlisted members and officers of the Air Force was number of days deployed associated with greater marital instability. In a survey of nearly

1,600 military spouses by the Kaiser Family Foundation (2004), 58% stated that their spouse's deployment had *strengthened* their marriage, while only 10% reported that the deployment had weakened their marriage (31% reported that the deployment "hasn't made much difference"). Spouses also overwhelmingly reported (84%) that they were more confident in their ability to take care of themselves and their family as a result of their husband's/wife's deployment, while less than a fourth (24%) reported that coping with their spouse's deployment constituted a major problem for them. Deployments also have been found to enhance military spouses' sense of mastery and accomplishment and this experience provided a context in which they developed new friendships. Service members also have reported positive effects of deployment. For example, Hosek, Kavanagh, and Miller (2006) report that soldiers found deployments to be a way for them to utilize their skills and training, to advance their careers, and to obtain higher pay. Finally, married U.S. Army soldiers ($N=519$) on a peacekeeping mission to Bosnia reported positive outcomes related to deployments, including the opportunity to make additional money (13.5%), self-improvement and time to think (9.2%), and an experience that improved their marital relationship (9.4%) (Newby et al., 2005).

Factors That Promote Resilience in Couples Experiencing Separation Due to Deployment

There are very few studies that directly investigate the factors that promote resilience in couples experiencing separation due to deployment. One recent study of 33 women married to U.S. service members investigated the strategies they employed in order to maintain their relationships with their spouses during their deployment (Merolla, 2010). Three broad maintenance strategies, including intrapersonal maintenance, maintenance in mediated partner interaction, and social network support emerged from the data. Intrapersonal maintenance referred to strategies and activities that the wives engaged in outside of partner interaction and included such actions as journaling, focusing on the self, positive thinking and fond reminiscing, and prayer. Maintenance in mediated partner interaction included communication through e-mail, webcam, instant messaging, etc., debriefing talk (sharing news and events of the day), verbally sharing affection and intimacy, talking about future plans for when the service member returned, and avoiding negative topics in order to maintain a positive connection. Finally, social network support (e.g., family, peer, military facilitated support) was a way for spouses to maintain a positive, hopeful outlook regarding the deployment by obtaining the emotional and tangible support they needed during their partners' absence. All three of these broad maintenance strategies assisted spouses in feeling close to their spouses and dealing with the stress of their spouses' absence. Previous studies also have found that flexible gender roles (Kelley et al., 1994), utilizing active rather than passive coping strategies (Jensen & Shaw, 1996), and accessing community and social supports (Martin, Vaitkus, Johnson, Mikolajek, & Ray, 1996; Norwood, Fullerton, & Hagen, 1996) are protective factors that positively influence family resilience or adaptation to the deployment of a spouse/parent.

Current Issues

The concept of family resilience, which can include couple resilience, has been a topic of growing interest among family researchers and practitioners. This has led to the development of specific frameworks to understand resilience in families (Patterson, 2002; Walsh, 1996, 2002, 2003), as well as reviews of protective factors derived from the larger literature on families that were presumed to foster family resilience (Benzies & Mychasiuk, 2008; Black & Lobo, 2008). Accordingly, we outline Walsh's framework for understanding family resilience and apply this framework to qualitative data obtained from interviews with resilient Air Force couples who have experienced deployment. We also present a case study in which we use Walsh's framework to highlight factors promoting resilience in one couple. The interviews used in this chapter are preliminary data from an ongoing study of Air Force couples who have success-fully navigated one or multiple deployments. We are conducting this study to learn the strategies and the skills these couples used to deal with the separation and reintegration related to deployment. That is, we are seeking to begin to learn what enabled them to be resilient. We begin by providing an overview of the specific context of deployment in the United States Air Force.

Deployments in the Air Force

Because America has been at war for almost 10 years now, the demand on those who serve in uniform is greater than it ever has been previously. The United States Air Force has over 330,000 active duty men and women (called Airmen) who stand ready to deploy in support of military operations all over the globe (Air Force Personnel Center, 2010). As of February, 2011, the Secretary of the Air Force, Michael Donley, reported that over 34,000 Airmen currently are deployed (Lyle, 2010).

Over the years Air Force deployments have varied in length and scope. Even in the first years after 9/11 most Air Force deployments ranged between 90 and 120 days. However, the Chief of Staff of the Air Force, General Norton Schwartz, announced a change in the fall of 2010, modifying the rotational deploy-ment baseline from 120 to 179 days. Now, according to Air Force officials, over 71 % of Airmen deploy outside the 120-day baseline making Air Force deployments longer than they ever have been previously (Hanson, 2010).

Currently, there are nine Air Force Career Groups that include: Operations, Maintenance/Logistics, Support, Medical/Dental, Legal/Chaplain, Finance/Contracting, Special Inves-tigations, Special Duty Assignments, and Special Reporting Identifiers. These nine groups are subdivided into over 295 Air Force Specialty Codes (also known as AFSCs) in the Air Force. These AFSCs identify the exact job for a given person serving in uniform. Traditionally, most people think of the Air Force's flying mission when they think of the Air Force. Certainly, the Air Forces' tremendous air and space operations are a hallmark of what this military service brings to the fight. However, there are many who serve in support of both the air and space operations during deployment as well as at their home stations.

Study Methods

Seven couples from three Air Force installations were interviewed for the current project. They learned about the study through flyers, email messages, and by word of mouth, asking for volunteer couples who have experienced at least one deployment and feel they have a strong and stable relationship. Spouses were given $25.00 for participating in a 60–90 min face-to-face interview in their own home to help researchers learn more about what they did to cope with deployment(s). Among the 14 indi-viduals in the project, ages ranged from 24 to 54 years, with a mean age of 32.4 years, and education ranged from high school graduates to those with a postgraduate degree, with the most common response being college graduate. Thirteen participants indicated their race as Caucasian/White, and one indicated Latino/a. Annual household income ranged from $40,000 to over $100,000, with a median income of $90,000–$99,999. Of the seven couples, two were dual military, in one couple the female partner was active duty and the male partner was civilian, in one couple the male partner was active duty and female partner was in the reserves, and in the remaining three couples, the male part-ner was active duty and the female partner was civilian. Four of the active duty participants were enlisted, and six were officers. Couples had experienced from 1 to 4 deployments, with most having returned from the most recent deployment sometime in the previous 4–8 months. Length of marriages ranged from 3 to 17 years; two of the couples interviewed had no children in the home, three couples had two children in the home, and one couple had four children in the home. In the findings section, fictitious partners' names begin with the same first initial so that the reader will be better able to determine which male is paired with which female.

Findings

A Framework for Understanding Couple Resilience

Walsh (2003) proposed a framework for understanding family resilience based on previous research in the area of individual resilience, and on ecological and developmental perspectives that expand this research into a more systemic conceptualization of family resilience. We use this framework to organize the feedback we received from resilient Air Force couples who had experienced deployment(s). This framework addresses three key areas thought to characterize family resilience: belief systems, organizational patterns, and communication/problem-solving processes. "Family belief systems" include the ways in which family members understand their experiences, "organizational patterns" are how the family structures itself around stressful events, and "communication/problem-solving patterns" describe how family members interact with each other in the face of stressful events. We found clear examples from the resilient couples in our study of each aspect of Walsh's framework.

Belief systems. Within the area of belief systems, Walsh (2003) suggests that resilience is promoted when family members are able to come together to make meaning of adversity in a way that: (1) includes a relational view of family strengths; (2) views stressors as normal or transitional; (3) views the stressor as something that is understandable and can be mastered; and (4) includes a shared understanding of the cause of the stressor. The Air Force couples we interviewed identified many relationship strengths that they felt contributed to their ability to deal well with deployments. For instance, Betty and Brian viewed their ability to trust each other as a strength that contributed to their ability to cope with the separations of deployment; as Brian stated, he "realized that she is going to stick with me, she hasn't left me yet, so I think that was a big strength for us," and Betty reiterated, "it is definitely a trust building experience, because if you don't trust the person you are with, with all the deployments it just wouldn't work. I know I can trust him with everything." Being able to recognize strengths in their relationship was clearly an important resource for each of our couples.

One way that the Air Force couples we interviewed had of normalizing their experiences was to remind themselves that others around them were dealing with similar challenges and to seek support from those who were going through similar things. For instance, Brian said,

> you got at least 50 other people on our flight that are going through the exact same thing you are, so you just get in touch with somebody else that is married or going through it. We just keep telling ourselves that there are other people who are going through the exact same thing and that we are going to be fine.

Additionally, Walsh (2003) suggests that having a positive outlook on the event, being optimistic or viewing the event as something that can be mastered, along with acceptance for the parts of the event that cannot be changed, contributes to resilience. Brian and Betty displayed this positive outlook combined with acceptance for the parts that could not be changed in this way:

> The big thing before we headed…before I headed out was, ya know we had a talk and when it pretty much came down to the end, we accepted the fact that, ya know it was, I was leaving… it was going to happen and we anticipated it and looked forward to it because we knew, like once I left that, ya know it was a matter of time and it was just like a countdown and the quicker I left, got it started, the sooner I'd be back. So…that's one thing… that I think that helped out a little bit…once I left it was only a matter of time before I'd be back so…

Acceptance of everything that comes along with a life in the military appeared to be vitally important for these Air Force couples in dealing with their deployments. Dorinda and Douglas described the importance of acceptance in terms of being able to be "understanding" of the way things happen in the military. Douglas stated, "understanding is big because in the military it happens, it happens and no sense for you being pissed off at me…," with Dorinda concurring,

> I mean it's not their fault that they're leaving, and it doesn't do any good to put the blame on him because he's already got enough to worry about… it's just kinda the way it goes, I mean it sucks, but you just suck it up and be like, 'that sucks' and grin and bear it.

Feelings of mastery appeared to come about as a result of dealing with multiple deployments, as couples noted that learning from each deployment experience, or looking back on the successful management of a previous deployment, helped them to feel more confident about their abilities to cope with future deployments. As Dorinda described it,

> But, of course, like the second or the third time around now you know what to expect and you know what you need to deal with, and you still have to go through the struggle of getting used to managing all of those extra chores and things, but at least you know a little bit better how to deal with it.

Finally, according to Walsh (2003), having a shared understanding of the stressor and connecting their experiences to something transcendent or beyond their present-day experiences in a way that allows family members to view new possibilities or see themselves growing through adversity is an additional contributor to resilience within the component of belief systems. Celeste viewed their deployment experiences as something that fostered growth in their relationship, something they could be proud of, "not that we didn't think that we would make it through but, when he actually got back we were really…really impressed with each other that…that we made it through, you know?" She further viewed this growth as something that was an added benefit of being in the Air Force, something that came along with other benefits for which she expressed gratitude,

> so, we made it through that and I can tell somebody my husband's been deployed and that makes me feel good knowing that…knowing that we support each other and things like that and…without the Air Force how could we make it [laughter] you know? They have such good benefits and everything. I think that it makes our family and our relationship as husband and wife stronger.

Gail talked of looking at "the bigger picture" as a way of keeping her own experiences in perspective and of appreciating the positives in her relationship. She stated,

> You get a different perspective on what's really important…I think that we were able to step back and look at the bigger picture…You know there is a lot of people out there that are losing their homes. We may lose a lot of money because we sold the house and the money is in this house. We may lose all that money but we still have our marriage and we can still earn money. I had to step back and look at those things…We made something positive out of it.

Organizational patterns. Within the area of organizational patterns, resilience is promoted when families are flexible, or able to "bounce forward" toward a new way of organizing themselves, while still maintaining some stability of family roles and responsibilities (Walsh, 2003). Additionally, Walsh proposes that families in which members are able to remain connected in relationships of mutual support that value individual needs and differences, and families that are able to mobilize social and economic resources to support their adaptations foster resilience in the face of adversity.

This flexibility in organization was often described by our Air Forces couples within the context of adjusting to changes in responsibilities throughout the deployment and reintegration cycle. George noted that flexibility had been common throughout their marriage: "We work together well, and we do what has to be done. We both share the responsibilities." Others described a gradual process of observing and adjusting to new roles following reintegration. For instance, Alexander stated:

Really, the first week [after returning home from deployment] was like looking, observe, and just ask "what do you need help with?" To be honest with you, I told myself a long time before, she has a routine and when you get there her routine still happens: eleven o'clock is still this, twelve o'clock is this, nap time now. We just, uh… kinda observed for a while. Try not to cut into everything and just stop everything. Figure out what's going on and how it's been working. Trying to adapt. I don't know if I adapted to her or she adapted to me.

Similarly, Brian talked of being unsure of his role in the relationship when he first returned from a deployment, wondering to himself, "maybe she doesn't need me as much" but described a similar process of observing how things were done, so that,

in that transitional couple of days, you see how…it's not so much that she'll pass it back on you, but you see how she did it and you slowly help her out with that and eventually start to take it over so then it becomes more routine, and you get back into things.

For the Air Force couples we interviewed another key strategy used for managing deployments appeared to be establishing ways to remain connected throughout the deployment, whether through phone calls, emails, the use of Skype, or sending care packages. Betty gave an example of the use of these methods of keeping connected in this way:

with Skype it's nice. It's kind of like having him in the same room but…he's highly infected so I can't touch him so…I just prop it up and sit there and talk to him and tell him about what's going on…

What seemed to be important in managing these connections was the ability for each partner to feel included in the other's experiences, to remain involved in each other's lives. For instance, Celeste spoke of the importance of keeping her spouse involved in this way:

But another thing that I thought was helpful to him anyways, to update him on anything new around here, so when he got back it wasn't like all these…I didn't think about it before though, you know, if they leave and then they come back and you got a new couch or you rearranged and you did this and they feel out of place because all these things have changed, and I took it upon myself to just tell him about little things here and there as they happened of…um buying something new or changing things around or whatever. That way when he got home he was already aware of all these things and it's not like he's coming in and so I did that and then I also keep a journal and that I wrote in everyday and then gave it to him as a gift when he got home so he could read and see, you know even though he was gone 120 plus days I thought of him every day. So he was still involved in our household even though he was gone.

Additionally, many of the couples talked of the ways that they mobilized networks of support involving family members or friends, or the ways in which they utilized Air Force programs for family members of the deployed to adjust to the deployment. For instance, Alicia talked about attending informational meetings that were helpful, saying:

His squadron did a meeting both times where they brought the spouses in and they did a slide show and answered questions and showed where they were going to stay and how they were going to get there and answered a lot of the unknown questions for you before they left. Like this is where they're going and this is how they get there and this is what their rooms look like…this is the internet service. Both times they did that. And so I do remember that, and I came home from it and I asked him questions.

Similarly, Betty made reference to a book, *Today's Military Wife*, that had been passed on to her from her sisters-in-law who also were married to active duty members, and both Gail and George talked about accessing information on the internet related to reintegration, and to reading books about couple communication. Participants made use of the information provided in these resources and also described the ways that they talked about this information with others around them. Other participants talked about support from family members, friends or neighbors, and specific Air Force programs that they utilized as resources in coping with the deployment.

Communication/problem-solving. Finally, within the area of communication/problem-solving processes, Walsh (2003) notes that resilience is fostered when communication is comprised of clear and consistent messages, encourages emotional expression with tolerance of differences and individual ownership of feelings, and collaborates in ways that are proactive, goal-oriented, and based on fairness and reciprocity. Betty and Brian described their communication in the reintegration period in a way that demonstrates some of this openness:

> Betty: We went around just kind of, you don't want to hurt each other's feelings, you don't want to step on any toes or anything so I know the first couple of days [were like that]. It is kind of after we talk about each other's experiences when we are away that really lets everything out and it's really nice. I know this last time we were in the car going to a hockey game, and I had questions. It had been a couple of days, and he was really open and honest about it, and I told him everything that went on so that really helped. It's probably that moment when everything just kind of clicked together.
> Brian: She asked a question that led to more questions, and before you know it, we were explaining everything that was going on. What we had felt, what had happened. We didn't get through everything, but we got through most of it. The tough stuff was done before we even got to the game, and went to the game and everything and watched that and then the next day we might have brought on another question which led to more questions, and it just took time. It wasn't something that we sat down and did, and like in an hour or two everything was done.

Similarly, Felicia and Frank described how open communication throughout their relationship helped them to deal with the stress of deployment by enabling them to openly share their struggles with each other. Frank stated, "We kept it all open, and I think that is probably our biggest strength because from day one, we were transparent with each other with our relationship. Just put it all out there." Felicia agreed, saying "I was forever calling him telling him about silly stuff that people [did].... There was no separation of life and work and that was really hard for me...and being so transparent with [husband], being able to have that was really helpful." Finally, Gail talked about the couple's use of open communication and collaboration in adjusting to her return from deployment, as for instance, "he would say, 'can you make supper?,' and I was like, 'sure.' But I never came in and said, 'this place is a dump' or 'the laundry's not done.' You...just let them ask you what to do. Tell them that you are tired. Tell them how you feel. Like I said, I think that made a big difference...."

Case Example

Dorinda and Douglas are a dual military Air Force couple. They have been together 19 years and married 15 years. Douglas has been in the Air Force 21 years and Dorinda for 14 years. Douglas has had four deployments including two combat tours (one involving 12 months in Iraq and the other 6 months in Afghanistan). Dorinda has had one deployment, but not to a combat zone. Douglas' most recent combat tour was with the Army through the Joint Expeditionary Forces. It lasted 1 year and took place 2 years before the research interview. Dorinda's tour lasted 4 months and took place within the past year. Many of the key processes in family resilience (Walsh, 2003) described earlier were evident in their interview. They are italicized here.

One thing that stood out throughout the interview was how much they laughed. Humor seems to be a resource they share (*Open emotional expression*). When asked to describe their marriage, Douglas said, "I think we are more like friends... its gotta be a partnership.... So we have stupid little rules.... Last one out of bed makes the bed, if one cooks the other does the dishes... You gotta work together" (*Connectedness*).

When asked to compare the impact of the various deployments on the family, they each talked about how the first tour, 12 years ago, was the most difficult. They had just moved to a new base and had no friends. They had a 4-year old and Dorinda was 8 months pregnant. They had 12-h notice before the deployment. Dorinda emphasized the challenges with the situation and Douglas emphasized the fact that, "the communication factors weren't as good then." While he was deployed, he worked 12 h a day, 6 days a week. Every morning he drove to the other side of the base to call and find out if the baby had been born. It was extremely difficult for both of them when they were unable to communicate. However, at that time Dorinda was near her family. She said that helped a lot (*Social and Economic Resources*). Douglas said that many of the wives of young Airmen with small children move back home, but it's more difficult once the children get in school. Both Douglas and Dorinda talked about how helpful it was during the first deployment that Dorinda sent videotapes of the baby and wrote letters every day (*Communication*). However, they also discussed a miscommunication. At first it seemed to Dorinda that Douglas was only focused on their son and not on her. When he sent a teddy bear, she thought it was for her and was disappointed that it was for the baby. They talked about how they learned over time that while it was important to express concern and care over the children, it was also important to express concern and care for the partner left behind (*Clarity*).

With the recent deployment to Iraq, they had time to prepare and worked together to make sure that their finances were in order and that someone would take care of Douglas' responsibilities (*Collaborative Problem-solving*). They also talked about being intentional in trying to spend time together before the deployment. Douglas talked about going to a baseball game out of town with the family and about spending time together doing things as a family, "rather than just sit here and watch TV" (*Open Emotional Expression*).

When asked about the challenges she experienced during his deployment, Dorinda talked about taking on all the family and home responsibilities when Douglas was deployed. They both laughed when Douglas said, "the nice thing about the deployments, it made my wife realize, 'Man he really does do something'" (*Make meaning of adversity*). Although it was still difficult to manage all the responsibilities, Dorinda felt that it was easier after experiencing several deployments since she knows what to expect (*Flexibility*).

Because they both had been deployed, they both talked about understanding how helpless they felt when their partner was struggling with a problem at home that they could not help resolve (*Empathy*). A major factor they each emphasized was the importance of maintaining communication while deployed (*Communication/Problem-Solving*). When Douglas was in Iraq, Dorinda had to pressure him to send pictures. He said, "There's nothing to send pictures of." Dorinda asked him to "send pictures of the dirt if you have to. The kids want to see where you're at, what you're doing and things like that" (*Clarity*). Dorinda also talked about how difficult it was when she saw "stories on TV and this blew up and that blew up." She said the kids would ask, "Is that where Dad's at?" She really felt better when she knew he was going to be on the road and he called her and told her he was back safely (*Clarity*). Douglas talked about how important communication from home was to him. He talked about how he regretted missing being home when his son's team played in the state tournament. Dorinda sent all the game videos and he appreciated that his son would call and wake him up and say, "OK, Dad, we won." It meant a lot to both Douglas and Dorinda that they stayed in touch (*Connectedness*). They talked about morale calls, which the Air Force allows for 60 min a week and also having had a cell phone for a period of time while he was in Iraq. They also emphasized that they were both flexible (*Flexibility*). It was not unusual that one or the other missed a call, but the caller sent an e-mail letting the partner know that he or she had tried to call.

When asked about reintegration after deployment, Douglas and Dorinda didn't seem to find it difficult. Again, they talked about keeping in touch and sharing with each other the challenges they were each facing during the deployment. Dorinda said, "We always keep in constant contact whether it be by phone, e-mail, whatever, constantly the entire time we're gone so we know exactly what's going on with the kids or at home, even issues at work" (*Clarity*). Another factor that they thought led to less reintegration problems was that they both saw themselves and their partners as flexible (*Flexibility*). They share duties.

When asked why they seemed to thrive, Dorinda said, "I think being understanding makes a huge difference" (*Open Emotional Expression*). Dorinda emphasized that it was important that partners "understand that, 'hey this is my job and I might have to deploy once every six months or once every other year' or whatever the case may be" (*Positive outlook*). Douglas emphasized that partners need to understand that "this is part of my life and this is what you're married to." Douglas also emphasized that "some of those folks who are active duty with a nonactive duty military wife need to educate them more about what's available and what's out there." Dorinda agreed and noted that it is important to:

> give them [spouses] access to the programs that are available on base. We've got a family readiness center that can help them, letting them know what programs are available. … There is tons of assistance, I mean free child care once a month…there is all kinds of things that people could take advantage of (*Social and Economic Resources*).

Dorinda also attributed their ability to thrive to her husband's empathy (*Open Emotional Expression*). She talked about one time when the batteries died in both cars and the washing machine had gone out and she was having problems at work. She said,

> I was so stressed and just out of the blue he sends me flowers and he never sends flowers. He thinks they are a waste of time because they die…. But he did and that was like, 'wow' he must know I'm at my breaking point if he's sending me flowers because that's a big thing for him to do (*Connectedness*).

When asked about how deployments had affected their relationship, Douglas said, "I think, as I was telling somebody, they may struggle, but it made us stronger, made us stronger that year in Iraq because you appreciate them more" (*Make Meaning of Adversity*). Dorinda added, "You don't realize what you're taking for granted, I guess and then all of a sudden you're gone. It's like, 'wow, the house is quiet.'"

When asked "what would you say is the key ingredient a couple needs to get through those deployments and come out strong?" Dorinda said, "I think you have to be flexible with each other. You have to be understanding and I think you have to communicate and that's, that's huge." Douglas said, "Yeah, and understanding is big because in the military it happens and it's no sense for you to be pissed off at me." Dorinda added,

> So, it's not their fault that their leaving and it doesn't do any good to put the blame on him because he already has enough to worry about. It's going to put him in a bad mood and then you're going to be at odds and it's not good to leave on bad terms, you want to leave on good terms, you wanna know that the other person is there supporting you at home when you're gone and vice versa (*Flexibility, Communication, Connectedness, Open Emotional Expression*).
>
> When asked for advice for a young couple about ready to deploy, Douglas said, It goes back to don't be afraid to ask for help, whether that's somebody in the unit. As the senior member we're not going to scrutinize. If you never mowed the grass before it's no big deal. I'll grab my son and we'll go do it. Just don't be afraid to reach out and ask for help.

Dorinda also emphasized the importance of the units reaching out to the spouse left behind. She said that during the last deployment of a year, she was constantly getting e-mails offering help: "That was huge for me. I was like; 'wow' you know at least I knew somebody was looking out for me even if I didn't accept the help I knew it was there" (*Social and Economic Resources*).

Clinical Implications

A number of clinical implications can be drawn from the findings of our study. Each of these participants, who were identified as having strong marriages after deployment, seemed to have strong marriages before being deployed. Service providers are encouraged to offer relationship strengthening programs to service members and their families before they face deployment. In fact, premarital programs or programs that help single service members make good choices in life partnership might be useful. A second factor that emerged from this data is the importance of good communication before, during, and after deployment. Couple therapy or couple education that enhances effective communication and builds empathy and open expression of feeling may enhance resilience. Additionally, these couples all spoke of being flexible and seemed to be able to handle both separation and reintegration gracefully. Clinicians who wish to work with service members to enhance resilience need to understand the deployment cycle and should focus on helping couples prepare for transitions. Finally, each of these couples spoke of the importance of social support for the family members who were left behind during deployment. Clinicians need to become familiar with services available in the community and on nearby installations and encourage the partner left behind to use these resources in addition to natural helping networks.

Research Implications

The research opportunities and needs are great, as there is little empirical research specifically directed at understanding resilience in military couples. Given that separation due to deployment is at best stressful and at worst traumatic, what are the factors that influence a couple's ability to maintain a healthy, satisfying relationship through one or multiple deployments? Prospective, longitudinal studies are needed that follow military couples through the deployment cycle (i.e., predeployment, deployment, reintegration after deployment) to determine the factors that influence relationship flourishing. These studies could take into account relationship functioning prior to deployment, as there is some evidence to suggest that struggling marriages are most at-risk for negative outcomes, including divorce, as a result of separation due to deployment (Bell & Schumm, 2000). How these individual, couple, and community resilience factors differentially influence enlisted active duty members vs. officers, female active duty members/civilian husbands vs. male active duty members/ civilian wives, and dual military couples would all be important foci for future research that could lead to implications for prevention and intervention.

Studies that track couples over time where the active duty member has been diagnosed with PTSD or traumatic brain injury (TBI) after returning from combat could elucidate the specific individual, relationship, and community factors that allow some couples to maintain a healthy, satisfying marriage despite these mental health concerns. For example, recent research on the effects of PTSD symptoms on relationship quality has shown that negative communication (i.e., problematic communication patterns), positive bonding (e.g., level of friendship, intimacy, fun, felt support, sensual/sexual relationship), and the parenting alliance partially mediated the association between soldier PTSD symptoms and marital satisfaction for both soldiers and spouses (Allen et al., 2010). These results point to the potential avenues for intervention, namely strengthening marital communication and couple bonding. Additional research into the factors that mediate or moderate the influence of PTSD and TBI on relationship quality and functioning would aid practitioners by pointing to potentially fruitful avenues of intervention.

Conclusion

Our study provides support for Walsh's (2003) framework for understanding family resilience. Each of the factors identified by Walsh (2003) as leading to family resilience was present in the resilient couples in our project. These couples highlighted the importance of their belief systems, organizational patterns, and communication/problem-solving processes in leading to their success in remaining strong through the stressful experience of military deployment. Couple therapists working with military couples should build on these factors in helping military couples prepare for deployment and/or deal with challenges faced during reintegration following deployment.

Acknowledgments This manuscript was supported by a grant to the third author from the United States Air Force Family Advocacy Program through a contract with U.S.D.A.

References

Air Force Personnel Center. (2010, December). Air force demographics. *Snapshot of the Air Force*. Retrieved February 26, 2011, from http://www.afpc.randolph.af.mil/library/airforcepersonnelstatistics.asp.

Allen, E. S., Rhoades, G. K., Stanley, S. M., & Markman, H. J. (2010). Hitting home: Relationships between recent deployment, posttraumatic stress symptoms, and marital functioning for Army couples. *Journal of Family Psychology, 4,* 280–288.

Bell, D. B., & Schumm, W. R. (2000). Providing family support during military deployments. In J. A. Martin, L. N. Rosen, & L. R. Sparacino (Eds.), *The military family: A practice guide for human service providers* (pp. 139–152). Westport, CT: Praeger.

Benzies, K., & Mychasiuk, R. (2008). Fostering family resiliency: A review of the key protective factors. *Child & Family Social Work, 14,* 103–114.

Black, K., & Lobo, M. (2008). A conceptual review of family resilience factors. *Journal of Family Nursing, 14,* 33–55.

Casey, G. W. (2011). Comprehensive soldier fitness: A vision for psychological resilience in the U.S. Army. *American Psychologist, 66,* 1–3.

Castro, C. A., & McGurk, D. (2007). The intensity of combat and behavioral health status. *Traumatology, 13,* 6–23.

Chandra, A., Lara-Cinisomo, S., Jaycox, L. H., Tanielian, T., Burns, R. M., Ruder, T., et al. (2010). Children on the homefront: The experience of children from military families. *Pediatrics, 125,* 13–22.

Cook, J. M., Riggs, D. S., Thompson, R., Coyne, J. C., & Sheikh, J. I. (2004). Posttraumatic stress disorder and current relationship functioning among World War II ex-prisoners of war. *Journal of Family Psychology, 18,* 36–45.

Dao, J., & Einhorn, C. (2010, December 30). Families bear brunt of deployment strains. *New York Times*. Retrieved January 4, 2011, from www.nytimes.com/2010/12/31/world/asia/31families.html.

Dirkzwager, A. J. E., Bramsen, I., Ader, H., & Ploeg, H. M. (2005). Secondary traumatization in partners and parents of Dutch peacekeeping soldiers. *Journal of Family Psychology, 19,* 217–226.

Galovski, T., & Lyons, J. (2004). Psychological sequelae of combat violence: A review of the impact of PTSD on the veteran's family and possible interventions. *Aggression and Violent Behavior, 9,* 477–501.

Gewirtz, A. H., Polusny, M. A., DeGarmo, D. S., Khaylis, A., & Erbes, C. R. (2010). Posttraumatic stress symptoms among National Guard soldiers deployed to Iraq: Associations with parenting behaviors and couple adjustment. *Journal of Consulting and Clinical Psychology, 78,* 599–610.

Hanson, J. (2010, September 10). Air force officials increase deployment times. *Air Force News*. Retrieved February 26, 2011, from www.af.mil/news/story.asp?id+123221320.

Hosek, J., Kavanagh, J., & Miller, L. (2006). *How deployments affect service members.* Santa Monica, CA: Rand National Defense Research Institute.

Jensen, P. S., & Shaw, J. A. (1996). The effects of war and parental deployment upon children and adolescents. In R. J. Ursano & A. E. Norwood (Eds.), *Emotional aftermath of the Persian Gulf War: Veterans, families, communities, and nations* (pp. 83–109). Washington, DC: American Psychiatric Press.

Kaiser Family Foundation. (2004). Military families survey. Retrieved December 15, 2010, from www.kff.org/kaiser-polls/upload/Military-Families-Survey-Toplines.pdf.

Karney, B. R., & Crown, J. S. (2007). *Families under stress: An assessment of data, theory, and research on marriage and divorce in the military.* Santa Monica, CA: Rand National Defense Research Institute.

Kelley, M. L., Herzog-Simmer, P. A., & Harris, M. A. (1994). Effects of military-induced separation on the parenting stress and family functioning of deploying mothers. *Military Psychology, 6,* 125–138.

Lorge, E. M. (2007, October, 17). *Army leaders sign covenant with families.* Army News Service. Retrieved December 15, 2010, from www.army.mil/-news/2007/10/17/5641-army-leaders-sign-covenant-with-families/.

Lyle, A. (2010, February, 21). SecAF takes stock of progress, future challenges. *Air Force News*. Retrieved February 26, 2011, from http://www.af.mil/news/story.asp?id=123243500.

MacDermid Wadsworth, S. M. (2010). Family risk and resilience in the context of war and terrorism. *Journal of Marriage and Family, 72,* 537–556.

Mansfield, A. J., Kaufman, J. S., Marshall, S. W., Gaynes, B. N., Morrissey, J. P., & Engel, C. C. (2010). Deployment and the use of mental health services among U.S. Army wives. *The New England Journal of Medicine, 362,* 101–109.

Martin, J. A., Vaitkus, M. A., Johnson, M. D., Mikolajek, L. M., & Ray, D. L. (1996). Deployment from Europe: The family perspective. In R. J. Ursano & A. E. Norwood (Eds.), *Emotional aftermath of the Persian Gulf War: Veterans, families, communities, and nations* (pp. 250–282). Washington, DC: American Psychiatric Press.

Merolla, A. J. (2010). Relational maintenance during military deployment: Perspectives of wives of deployed US soldiers. *Journal of Applied Communication Research, 38,* 4–26.

Milliken, C. S., Auchterlonie, J. L., & Hoge, C. W. (2007). Longitudinal assessment of mental health problems among active and reserve component soldiers returning from the Iraq war. *Journal of the American Medical Association, 298,* 2141–2148.

Monson, C. M., Taft, C. T., & Fredman, S. J. (2009). Military-related PTSD and intimate relationships: From description to theory-driven research and intervention development. *Clinical Psychology Review, 29,* 707–714.

Nelson Goff, B. S., Crow, J. R., Reisbig, A. M. J., & Hamilton, S. (2007). The impact of individual trauma symptoms of deployed soldiers on relationship satisfaction. *Journal of Family Psychology, 21,* 344–353.

Newby, J. H., McCarroll, J. E., Ursano, R. J., Fan, Z., Shigemura, J., & Tucker-Harris, Y. (2005). Positive and negative consequences of a military deployment. *Military Medicine, 170,* 815–819.

Norwood, A. E., Fullerton, C. S., & Hagen, K. P. (1996). Those left behind: Military families. In R. J. Ursano & A. E. Norwood (Eds.), *Emotional aftermath of the Persian Gulf War: Veterans, families, communities, and nations* (pp. 163–197). Washington, DC: American Psychiatric Press.

Patterson, J. M. (2002). Understanding family resilience. *Journal of Clinical Psychology, 58,* 233–246.

Renshaw, K. D., Rodrigues, C. S., & Jones, D. H. (2008). Psychological symptoms and marital satisfaction in spouses of Operation Iraqi Freedom Veterans: Relationships with spouses' perceptions of veterans experiences and symptoms. *Journal of Family Psychology, 22,* 586–594.

Riggs, D. S., Byrne, C. A., Weathers, F. W., & Litz, B. T. (1998). The quality of intimate relationships of male Vietnam veterans: Problems associated with posttraumatic stress disorder. *Journal of Traumatic Stress, 11,* 87–101.

Tan, M. (2009, December 18). A million soldiers deployed since 9/11. *Army Times, 12.* Retrieved December 15, 2010, from www.armytimes.com/news/2009/12/army_deployments_121809w/.

Thomas, J. L., Wilk, J. E., Riviere, L. A., McGurk, D., Castro, C. A., & Hoge, C. W. (2010). Prevalence of mental health problems and functional impairment among active component and National Guard soldiers 3 and 12 months following combat in Iraq. *Archives of General Psychiatry, 67,* 614–623.

Vasterling, J. J., Proctor, S. P., Friedman, M. J., Hoge, C. W., Heeren, T., King, L. A., et al. (2010). PTSD symptom increases in Iraq-deployed soldiers: Comparison with nondeployed soldiers and associations with baseline symptoms, deployment experiences, and postdeployment stress. *Journal of Traumatic Stress, 23,* 41–51.

Walsh, F. (1996). The concept of family resilience: Crisis and challenge. *Family Process, 35,* 261–281.

Walsh, F. (2002). A family resilience framework: Innovative practice applications. *Family Relations, 51,* 130–137.

Walsh, F. (2003). Family resilience: A framework for clinical practice. *Family Process, 42,* 1–18.

Warner, C. H., Appenzeller, G. N., Warner, C. M., & Grieger, T. (2009). Psychological effects of deployments on military families. *Psychiatric Annals, 39,* 56–63.

Family Resilience and Parenting

8

Ivelisse Torres Fernandez, Jonathan P. Schwartz,
Heejung Chun, and Ginger Dickson

Introduction

The concept of resilience has been studied for decades at both individual and family levels. When examining the concept of family resilience, the question arises as to what makes some families face difficult circumstances and come out stronger while others fail at this task? What we know is that families are constantly faced with multiple challenges (e.g., divorce, violence, economic hardship, mental and physical illnesses, immigration) that impact not only individual family members but also the family system as a unit. The dynamic nature of family functioning also impacts the development of resilience. What remains unclear as our understanding of the developing area of family resilience increases is the role of parenting.

An examination of the literature on family resilience indicates that research on specific aspects of family resilience tends to be limited (Kalil, Tolman, Rosen, & Gruber, 2003). Two main approaches tend to dominate the literature. The first one is characterized by examinations of the processes that occur within the family unit (Benzies & Mychasiuk, 2009; Conger & Conger, 2002; Patterson, 2002; Walsh, 1998, 2003). With the second approach the focus is primarily on the context in which children are raised and how families provide a protective environment that will buffer against adversity and, in turn, promote healthy development in children and adolescents (Armstrong, Birnie-Lefcovitch, & Ungar, 2005; McGillicuddy-De Lisi, De Lisi, & Van Gulik, 2007; Prevatt, 2003; Schwartz, 2002). Although it can be argued that the concepts of resilience can be applied to family functioning, a void in the literature is noted when examining the role of parenting practices in the promotion of family resilience. Therefore, considering the prominent role that parenting plays in the development of children and adolescents and the lack of literature regarding parenting and family resilience, in this chapter we attempt to shed light on how parenting practices may impact the development of resilience in families and discuss both clinical and research implications.

I.T. Fernandez • J.P. Schwartz (✉) • H. Chun • G. Dickson
Counseling and Educational Psychology, New Mexico State University,
Las Cruces, NM, USA
e-mail: jschwart@ad.nmsu.edu

D.S. Becvar (ed.), *Handbook of Family Resilience*,
DOI 10.1007/978-1-4614-3917-2_8, © Springer Science+Business Media New York 2013

Significance of the Topic

One of the factors that has consistently predicted positive outcomes in families is resilience. Family resilience refers to the family's ability to respond positively to an adverse event and emerge strengthened, more resourceful, and confident (Hawley & deHaan, 1996; McCubbin & McCubbin, 1993; Simon, Murphy, & Smith, 2005). The concept of family resilience emphasizes a family's strengths and resources; recognizes that no single model will fit all families; and acknowledges the notion that all families have the potential to grow and recover from adverse circumstances (Walsh, 2002). Since change is inevitable and part of the natural processes by which families evolve, it is critical that the field move beyond the traditional deficit model to highlight preventive methods that focus on families' strengths and assets in order to promote resilience.

The concept of parenting has been explored as a mediator/moderating factor in both family and individual outcomes (Conger & Conger, 2002; Darling & Steinberg, 1993; Driscoll, Russell, & Crockett, 2008; Manzeske & Dopkins Stright, 2009; Milevsky, Schlechter, Netter, & Keehn, 2007). As such, we recognize that parenting practices can buffer against risk factors and, in turn, promote resilience among families (Conger & Conger, 2002; Prevatt, 2003; Wahler, 2002). Indeed, parenting practices impact not only the physical, cognitive, and emotional development of children (Benasich & Brooks-Gunn, 1996; Huang, Caughy, Genevro, & Miller, 2005; Manzeske & Dopkins Stright, 2009) but also the overall functioning of the family unit. However, the literature has been limited when exploring the impact of positive versus negative parenting practices in the context of a risk and resiliency model. Acknowledging the issues discussed above, in the following section we provide a thorough review of the literature in the field. This review is divided into several sections to address the topics of resilience, family resilience, and parenting style and practices. We also provide discussions related to the processes characteristic of resilient families, the Family Stress Model, and cultural considerations.

Literature Review

Overview of Resilience

Resilience, or the ability to bounce back from adversity or challenging situations, has become the focus of numerous research studies over the past decades (Benard, 1991, 2004; Werner, 1993; Werner & Smith, 2001). An examination of the literature in the field indicates that the term resilience has been defined in multiple ways. For example, Walsh (2003) defines it as "the ability to withstand and rebound from disruptive life challenges" (p. 1). Luthar, Cicchetti, and Becker (2000) define it as a dynamic process of positive adaptation in the context of significant adversity. Cowan, Cowan, and Schultz (1996) expand the definition to highlight the role of individual and family resources and strengths (protective factors) related not only to how we respond to a crisis, but also to how we recover and learn from those experiences.

When examining the concept of resilience, Benard (1991, 2004) indicated that resilient children have four main attributes or characteristics: social competence, problem-solving skills, autonomy, and a sense of purpose. Social competence is considered an important indicator of children's overall adaptation and wellness and includes "the characteristics, skills, and attitudes essential to forming relationships and attachments to others" (Benard, 2004, p. 14). These skills are responsiveness, communication, empathy/caring, compassion/altruism, and forgiveness. Problem-solving skills refer to several abilities that include planning, flexibility, resourcefulness, critical thinking, and insight.

Autonomy, on the other hand, involves "an ability to act independently and to feel a sense of control over one's environment" (Benard, 2004, p. 20). Factors associated with autonomy include having a positive identity or sense of who you are; an internal locus of control and initiative; self-efficacy and mastery; adaptive distancing and resistance; self-awareness and mindfulness; and humor. Lastly, having a sense of purpose refers to the "deep belief that one's life has meaning and that one has a place in the universe" (Benard, 2004, p. 28). Factors associated with a sense of purpose include goal direction, achievement motivation, and educational aspirations; special interests, creativity, and imagination; optimism and hope; and faith, spirituality, and sense of meaning.

So, how can these core characteristics be applied to family resilience? In essence, if we examine the characteristics that have allowed families to thrive and succeed amidst difficult circumstances we could hypothesize that their members are skilled at social competence, have the ability to generate novel solutions to problems, foster autonomy in their members so they are highly confident in their skills and abilities, and lastly, have a clear sense of family cohesion and purpose. Resilient families' decisions are made to favor the family as a unit rather than to focus solely on individual family members.

Werner and her colleagues (Werner, 1993; Werner & Smith, 1992, 2001) conducted one of the earliest and most widely cited research studies on resilience. Findings were significant because they acknowledged the positive aspects in families that would support the development of resilience in children and youth. As Walsh (2003) highlighted "this approach fundamentally alters the deficit-lens from viewing troubled parents and families as *damaged* and beyond repair, to seeing them as *challenged* by life's adversities with potential for fostering healing and growth in all members" (pp. 2–3). Moreover, Werner's studies were also important because they placed the family, particularly parent–child relationships, at the forefront of protective factors.

In sum, most of the research on resilience has focused primarily on children and adolescents. However, most recently, research has emphasized the concept of family resilience. Family resilience acknowledges not only the impact of the family structure on the development of resilient children and youth, but also acknowledges the complexity of systems and environmental variables that influence the development of resilience (Benzies & Mychasiuk, 2009; Patterson, 2002; Walsh, 2002). Thus, considering the complex nature of resilience, we are advised to move from the deficit model, which advocates for "fixing dysfunctional children and families" to a more strength-based approach, which emphasizes strengthening the environment in which children and families function (Krovetz, 1999; Schwartz, 2002).

Family Resilience Theory

As previously discussed, the concept of resilience emerged from studies that examined the factors that enabled individuals to succeed amidst challenging situations and what differentiated those who were successful from those who were unsuccessful (Kalil et al., 2003). As we describe, these theoretical concepts have been adapted in order to understand family development and functioning.

The concept of family resilience refers primarily to the family's capacity to deal with and manage difficult circumstances, including the resources families possess that would enable them to face adversity and remain strong. As with the general concept of resilience, there are multiple definitions of family resilience. For example, McCubbin and McCubbin (1988) defined family resilience as "characteristics, dimensions, and properties of families which help families to be resistant to disruption in the face of change and adaptive in the face of crisis situations" (p. 247). This definition emphasizes the protective factors at the core of family strengths.

On the other hand, Hawley and deHaan (1996) defined family resilience as adaptive patterns families have displayed both presently and over time. The authors emphasized the need to examine family resilience both as a developmental construct and as a process rather than as a static set of qualities.[1] Furthermore, Walsh (1996) introduced the notion of relational resilience to describe family processes

---

[1] For more on this topic please see Chap. 2.

and how those processes are related to unique challenges faced by families. This concept emphasizes a developmental perspective geared to understand how families deal with crises and stress over time. Lastly, Patterson (2002) posits that family resilience could be better understood as the *process* by which families are able to adapt and function following adverse circumstances.

According to Walsh (1996, 2003), the concept of family resilience goes beyond seeing individual family members as potential resources for individual resilience to focusing more on how the family as a unit could serve as a protective factor. Some of these factors have been identified as: family cohesion, family belief systems, and coping strategies. Family cohesion refers primarily to the "bonding" among family members; in other words, how connected they feel with one another. Cohesive families are more willing to work for the "collective" benefit of the family. Family belief systems, on the other hand, recognize the impact of spirituality[2] and having a positive outlook on family outcomes. Although a controversial issue, there is support to the notion that "a family emphasis on religion may promote family cohesion and parent–child affect and reduce intra-family conflict" (Kalil et al., 2003, p. 30). Lastly, coping strategies refer to the psychological, financial, and social resources and skills families employ to deal with difficult circumstances. Coping skills tend to be associated with competence and resilience.

Overall, such a systemic view of resilience acknowledges that serious crises (e.g., death of a family member, divorce, unemployment of a family member) or persistent challenging times impact family functioning, but recognizes that families possess strengths and resources that can facilitate the successful recovery from these crises. How families cope with these issues is context specific, and mediated by myriad risk and protective factors. Context specific refers to how the resilience of families facing adversity will be greatly impacted by different individual, social, and cultural factors. For example, family members who possess certain coping skills (i.e., communication strategies, problem-solving skills) might be able to fare well in times of distress. Furthermore, families who have dealt successfully with crises in the past might be better prepared to deal with subsequent challenges. On the other hand, family risk and protective factors refer to those characteristics that will make families either more vulnerable to or buffer against the challenges that they may face. Examples of family risk factors include violence, poverty, single-parent homes, divorce, or death in the family, whereas family protective factors might include family cohesion, cultural values, and spiritual beliefs. Thus, the idea of family resilience is complex and multidimensional. Hence, a family resilience framework that combines both ecological and developmental perspectives appears to be the most effective. We therefore address next the characteristics of resilient families and then the Family Stress Model.

Processes Characteristic of Resilient Families

Several key processes in family resilience have been identified in the literature: (a) family's beliefs and expectations; (b) family's emotional connectedness; (c) family's organizational style; and (d) the quality of family learning opportunities (Amatea, Smith-Adcock, & Villares, 2006; Walsh, 2003). Within each domain the authors include several key features. Having a sense of purpose, a positive outlook, and a sense of personal efficacy are related to the first domain. Within the second domain, the authors indicate emotional warmth and belonging; openness; emotional sharing; clear communication; and collaborative problem-solving. Factors associated with the third domain are strong leadership and clear expectations; a firm but friendly parenting style; and a strong social network. Lastly, factors associated with the fourth domain include the development of family routines that support achievement, and provide explicit skill instruction.

---

[2] For more on this topic please see Chap. 25.

Families' belief systems exert a powerful influence not only in how a family makes sense of a crisis but also in terms of how they will deal with it. According to Walsh (2003), resilience is fostered by "shared, facilitative beliefs that increase options for problem solution, healing, and growth" (p. 6). Family emotional connectedness refers to the sense of mutual respect for differences, collaboration, and commitment among family members. The stronger the bond among family members the more resourceful and resilient the family unit is likely to be. On the other hand, family organizational style, or patterns of behavior are related to who is in charge, cohesion among members, and social and economical resources available. Resilience is fostered by a flexible structure, a high level of cohesion, and the availability of resources (Walsh, 2003). Finally, the quality of family learning opportunities highlights how families problem-solve and come up with solutions. Overall, family resilience is fostered when these processes are clearly understood and put into practice.

Other factors that are related to how families impact the development of resilience in families include parental empathy, high expectations, and opportunities for participation and contribution (Benard, 2004). Parental empathy refers to parents' ability to understand their children's points of view. In other words, parents who are able to understand their children's feelings and view points have the ability to provide warm, engaging relationships, thus creating home environments that promote mutual respect, safety, and healthy social–emotional development. Moreover, high expectations can be the "catalyst for helping a young person find her or his strengths" (Benard, 2004, p. 56). In the context of parenting, the provision of clear structure and guidance for expected behaviors sets the stage for preventing future difficulties and for fostering resilience in both the individuals and the family unit.

Furthermore, the levels at which parents provide opportunities for participation in and contribution to the family promote both responsibility and autonomy in children and youth. This level of responsibility and autonomy is determined by parenting style. According to Benard (2004), parents who create opportunities for children and adolescents to have some decision-making power and to solve problems on their own help meet their children's basic need of psychological autonomy. Thus, instilling a sense of autonomy and responsibility among family members provides a buffer against risk factors, particularly in difficult times.

Another way to conceptualize the processes characteristic of resilient families is to identify and analyze protective factors. This notion places a socio-ecological approach at the core of family resilience and acknowledges that multiple protective factors rather than singular individual factors better explain how families can deal successfully with challenges, even when difficult circumstances are present. According to Benzies and Mychasiuk (2009), family resilience is optimized "when protective factors are strengthened at all three interactive levels of the socio-ecological model" (p. 104). The three interactive levels are the individual, the family, and the community. For the purpose of this chapter we focus on family protective factors, which include family structure; intimate-partner relationship stability; family cohesion; supportive parent–child interaction; stimulating environments; social support; family of origin influences; stable and adequate income; and adequate housing.

According to Benzies and Mychasiuk (2009), smaller families, mature older parents, and dual incomes foster resilience among families. In addition, the quality of the relationship between the parents, the level of connectedness, and positive-parent child relations are also important factors. This last point is particularly important because it emphasizes the role of parenting in the development of family resilience. For example, research has indicated that warm, nurturing parenting behaviors protect children from the consequences of economic distress and contribute to positive outcomes for children in high-risk situations (Brennan, Le Brocque, & Hammen, 2003; Mistry, Vandewater, Huston, & McLoyd, 2002; Yeung, Linver, & Brooks-Gunn, 2002, as cited in Benzies & Mychasiuk, 2009).

Stimulating environments that foster learning, social supports, and cultural and familial values also have been identified as protective factors in the development of resilience in families. Lastly, having a stable source of income and adequate housing are considered protective factors because the lack or absence of all or some of these resources adds to family stress, thus increasing risk factors. Overall, an examination of protective factors provides an excellent framework for understanding the influence that the family system and its environment have on the development of resilience.

Family Stress Model

As previously discussed, from an ecological perspective (Bronfenbrenner, 1979), individual, family, and community systems mediate how a family copes with adverse or difficult times. When examining the role of risk and protective factors in the development of family resilience, the application of a socio-ecological model that acknowledges the complexity of interactions between families and multiple systems seems the most logical approach. Patterson's (1988, 2002) work in the area of family resilience and stress provides a useful framework to conceptualize the dynamics of family resilience.

Patterson (1988, 2002) utilizes the Family Adjustment Adaptation Response (FAAR) Model to describe a family resilience perspective. According to this model "families engage in active processes to balance family demands with family abilities as these interact with family meanings to arrive at the level of family adjustment or adaptation" (Patterson, 1988, p. 350). In other words, how families perceive their current demands can make them more or less vulnerable in terms of how they respond to these demands. Furthermore, how families have dealt with crises in the past is a predictor of resilience. The positive or negative resolution of conflict is a determinant factor.

Patterson (1988, 2002) also highlights four central constructs in the FAAR Model: family *demands*, which include normative and non-normative stressors, family strains, and daily hassles; *family capabilities*, which include tangible and psychosocial resources, and coping behaviors; *family meanings*, which include how the family members define their demands and capabilities, their identity as a family, and their world view; and *family adjustment or adaptation*, which includes the process of restoring balance between capabilities and demands at two different levels: family members and family unit, and family unit and the community.

In the case of parenting and resilience, the understanding of demands (expectations of how a child should be parented), and how parents have dealt with pressure previously (social, cultural, economic factors involved in parenting style), mediate outcomes related to positive parenting techniques. Thus, families are constantly balancing family demands and family capabilities as they interact with family meanings in order to obtain a level of adjustment and adaptation.

Parenting and Resilience

The role of parenting styles in fostering resilience has been analyzed from two perspectives: parenting styles as a risk factor and parenting styles that appear to predict positive outcomes in children and adolescents. Thus, regarding risk and protective factors in family functioning, "parenting styles rather than family structure has been found to be the main determinant of effective family functioning and adolescent well-being" (McFarlane, Bellissimo, & Norman, 1995). At the same time, research also tends to indicate that authoritative parenting is strongly associated with positive outcomes in children and adolescents. For example, Masten et al. (1999) found that parenting that combines warmth, firm expectations, and structure was a major protective factor for healthy development in children and youth.

Furthermore, Steinberg (2000) posited that an authoritative parenting style promotes healthy adolescent development and that, "adolescents raised in authoritative homes continue to show the same sorts of advantages in psychological development and mental health over their non-authoritatively raised peers" (p. 173). Lastly, research has indicated that, "parents who provide explanations influence children, especially adolescents, to internalize their values more effectively than parents who rely on power-assertive methods or withdrawal of love" (Hoffman, 1970, 1982, as cited in Baumrind, 1996, p. 410).

Baumrind's (1966, 1991) and Maccoby and Martin's (1983) work on parenting styles provided the context for understanding diverse parenting practices and their effects on children's development. In their work they describe four distinct parenting styles: authoritarian, authoritative, permissive, and neglecting. According to the authors, authoritarian parents are those who attempt to control the child at all cost and usually resort to harsh punishment and discipline to achieve their goals. Authoritative parents, on the other hand, are those who are firm with their children, but also allow some degree of flexibility. Permissive parents, although responsive to child needs, do not set any rules or expectations for behaviors and tend to be lenient in their discipline practices. Neglectful parents are those who are uninvolved and respond minimally to either the child's needs or the child's behavior.

Parents' behaviors also can be analyzed utilizing two specific dimensions: responsiveness and demandingness (Maccoby & Martin, 1983). Responsiveness refers to the "extent to which parents intentionally foster individuality and self-assertion by being attuned, supportive, and acquiescent to children's needs and demands" (Baumrind, 1996, p. 410). There are four facets of responsiveness: warmth, reciprocity, clear communication, person-centered discourse, and attachment. Demandingness, on the other hand, refers to "the claims that parents make on children to become integrated into the family and community by their maturity expectations, supervision, disciplinary efforts, and willingness to confront a disputative child" (Baumrind, 1996, p. 411). This dimension includes: confrontation, monitoring, and consistent, contingent discipline.

Effects of Parenting on Children's and Youth Outcomes

When examining the effects of parenting styles and practices on children and youth outcomes the literature suggests that it is important to distinguish between two concepts: parenting styles and parenting practices. According to Darling and Steinberg (1993), parenting style refers to a "constellation of attitudes toward the child that are communicated to the child and that, taken together, create an emotional climate in which the parent's behaviors are expressed" (p. 488), whereas parenting practices refers to "specific-goal-directed behaviors through which parents perform their parental duties" (p. 488). The authors suggest that parenting practices tend to have a direct impact on outcomes in contrast to parenting styles' influences, which tend to be indirect because they serve as a moderating variable.

Overall, Darling and Steinberg (1993) pointed out that it is how parents go about imposing and carrying out parenting beliefs and ideas (rather than the beliefs themselves) that impact the outcomes of children. Therefore, parents should be mindful about the long-term, detrimental effects that negative parenting practices will have on their child's development. Moreover, Brenner and Fox (1999) posited that parenting style is a moderator of parenting practices and how parents interact and discipline their children is context specific. Thus, in order to promote family resilience, clinicians should be aware of the impact of parenting styles and practices relative to how families react to adverse circumstances. If we aspire to create effective prevention strategies, it will be critical to determine what parenting styles and practices promote healthy development.

In a study examining the impact of parenting practices in children's adjustment, Prevatt (2003) found that the combination of family risk and protective factors as well as parenting practices was highly predictive of children's functioning. Negative family factors (i.e., family stress, family conflict, SES) and poor parenting were associated with negative child outcomes, whereas protective family factors (i.e., family cohesion, family social support, family moral–religious orientation) and positive parenting were associated with positive child outcomes. Prior studies in this area (Doll & Lyon, 1998; Frick, 1994) also have demonstrated the effects of negative parenting practices on children's outcomes. These research findings were consistent with those of Scaramella, Conger, and Simons (1999), which indicated that positive parenting behaviors influence the incidence of conduct problems during adolescence. That is, "effective parenting practices buffer the impact of transitional risks on increases in adolescent conduct problems" (Conger & Conger, 2002, p. 369).

In related studies, Conger, Cui, Bryant, and Elder (2000) concluded that nurturant-involved parenting predicted positive behaviors during adolescence and early adulthood. Furthermore, these in turn also predicted the development of supportive and stable romantic unions. Moreover, Conger, Neppl, and Scaramella (2001) found that young adults who were exposed to hostile parenting practices early on in their lives had an increased risk of failure as parents later in their lives. When specifically examining how parenting practices impact the development of resilience in these families, Conger, Conger, Elder, Simons, and Whitbeck (1992) found that a nurturant-involved parenting style predicted positive adjustment in terms of self-confidence, peer relationships, and school performance even under harsh economic conditions. Further more, nurturant-involved parenting also predicted lower levels of adjustment difficulties, including the development of antisocial behavior and other severe behavioral difficulties.

Several other studies have examined the impact of parenting in other areas of children's and youth's functioning. For example, Vitaro, Brendgen, Larose, and Tremblay (2005) conducted an investigation examining the role of parenting practices and beliefs on educational achievement. Overall, the authors found that the affective and disciplinary orientations of the parent play a role in high school graduation rates (increased the probability of graduation) by compensating for the overall risk associated with internalizing and externalizing behaviors. Thus, parenting practices might impact positively or negatively the educational attainment of children and youth. This is an important finding because academic success has been linked to positive outcomes in children, even for those who live in adverse circumstances.

Kerr, Capaldi, Pears, and Owen (2009) conducted an intergenerational study examining the influences of fathers' constructive parenting practices on children's outcomes. Constructive parenting practices were defined by the authors as "multiple aspects of parenting that contribute to positive child and adolescent adjustment" (p. 1257). Overall, the authors indicated that constructive parenting practices impact the parenting practices of the subsequent generations by supporting "youth achievement, self-esteem, and positive peer relations" (p. 1264). These findings are important because they highlight the intergenerational influences of parenting practices.

Other research studies have focused on the impact of parental stress and related parenting practices as well as the effectiveness of parenting programs. For example, Putnick et al. (2008) conducted an investigation to examine the impact of parental stress on parenting behaviors and how these impact adolescent self-concept. Overall, the authors found a link between parental stress and behaviors on adolescent self-esteem, particularly as it relates to parental involvement and autonomy granting.

Finally, it has been widely documented that "the quality of parenting children receive has a major effect on their development" (Sanders, 2008, p. 506). Specifically, risk factors including poor parenting, lack of warm and positive parent–child relationships, inadequate supervision, and lack of parental involvement have been related to increased risk of developing emotional and behavioral disorders (Coie, 1996; Loeber & Farrington, 1998). Therefore, the development of sound parenting programs appears to be a viable alternative to promote positive outcomes in families and in turn, resilience. Several studies have examined the impact of parenting programs on children and family's outcomes (Jouriles et al., 2010; Ortega, Beauchemin, & Burcu Kaniskan, 2008; Sanders, 2008; Springer, Wright, & McCall, 1997). Overall, these programs appear to be promising in terms of strengthening family resources and providing mechanisms through which families not only can improve their parenting practices, but also build on their own strengths and resources, all of which promotes the development of resilience.

Multicultural Considerations

Cultural values and beliefs play an important role in how parenting practices are implemented among diverse families. In this regard, Garcia Coll and his colleagues (1996) posited that "adaptive cultural practices influence parenting and child development directly and in some cases mediates the influences of social stratification on the development of children's competencies" (as cited in Lee et al., 2008, pp. 167–168). We thus summarize some of the research examining the intersection of culture and parenting practices as it relates to family resilience and healthy development.

According to Lee et al. (2008) the key issue when examining how cultural values and beliefs impact parenting practices is to be cognizant of how culture and socialization play a role not only in the goals of parenting, but also in the different dimensions that encompass parenting practices. From this perspective, the authors posited two main goals of parenting: first, to manage children's behaviors, and secondly, to transmit the cultural values, beliefs, and expectations for appropriate behaviors. So, how does culture and socialization influence parenting?

Hill and Tyson (2008) examined ethnic, socioeconomic status, and contextual predictors of parenting behaviors among African-American and European American families. The results suggested ethnic differences in parenting practices. According to the authors these differences could be accounted for primarily by contextual factors such as socioeconomic status and cultural beliefs. In another study examining cultural differences, Dwairy et al. (2010) surveyed adolescents in nine different countries in order to explore the development of psychological disorders and their relationship with parental factors across cultures. Overall, the authors found that "culture is an important factor associated with parenting styles and patterns" (p. 39). Furthermore, results indicated that psychological disorders vary across cultures as well as do the associations between parental factors and psychological disorders. Indeed, parental rejection was the only parental factor that was consistently associated with psychological disorders across all countries and cultures.

The results of research examining parenting practices among different ethnic groups in the United States tend to be mixed. According to some, the authoritative parenting style, characterized by a combination of firmness and warmth, appeared to produce the best outcomes for children and youth. For example, Steinberg (2000) reported that "minority youngsters raised in authoritative homes fare better than their peers from non-authoritative homes with respect to psychological development, symptoms of internalized distress, and problem behavior" (p. 175). By contrast, several other researchers have challenged the notion of the efficacy of authoritative parenting styles in Latino, African-American, and Asian American children and youth by favoring a more authoritarian parenting style that promotes the use of more control and structure (Domenech Rodriguez, Donovick, & Crowley, 2009; Hill & Tyson, 2008; Lee et al., 2008).

Domenech Rodriguez et al. (2009) conducted an investigation to examine parenting styles and dimensions in a sample of Latino parents with a focus on three parenting dimensions: warmth, demandingness, and autonomy. Regarding parenting dimensions, the authors found Latino parents scored high on warmth and demandingness, but not on autonomy granting. Regarding parenting styles, Latino parents appear to be protective, followed by the authoritative style. Furthermore, results indicated that "the four parenting categories only accounted for approximately one-third of the Latino families, suggesting that traditional parenting categories do not capture Latinos' parenting styles well" (p. 204).

Dumka, Gonzalez, Wheeler, and Millsap (2010) evaluated the role of parenting self-efficacy and parenting practices in predicting adolescents' conduct problems among Mexican American families. Results supported "parenting self-efficacy as an antecedent causal variable in relation to parents' positive control practices and adolescents' conduct problems" (p. 528). Overall, this study highlights the importance of including parent efficacy as part of both prevention and intervention efforts. In a related study, Leidy, Guerra, and Toro (2010) examined the relation between positive parenting, family cohesion, and child social competence among immigrant Latino families. Results from their study suggested that even under adverse conditions, parents who were able to communicate clearly with their children, have clear expectations, and maintain close family connections, had children "who showed improvement in social competence, particularly in the area of social problem-solving and self-efficacy" (p. 257). Overall, the authors indicated that the combination of positive parenting practices and family cohesion predicted gains in social competence in children, whereas family cohesion alone just predicted social problem-solving skills.

Lastly, research examining the effects of parenting practices among African-American and Asian American families has yielded interesting results. For the most part, studies point out that among these groups a more authoritarian parenting style appears to be more prominent than the authoritative style. For example, Chao (2001) reported that the use of an authoritarian parenting style by Chinese American parents had more positive effects among children when compared to other parenting styles. Furthermore, Wills et al. (2007) indicated that parents' authoritarian parenting practices were related to self-control and self-esteem among African-American adolescents, and that they served as a buffer against the development of problem behaviors. Further, support of kin also has been found to be important for African-American families and children. In this regard, Taylor (2010) investigated risk factors and resilience among low-income African-American families by exploring the role of parenting and kinship social support. Overall, the findings were consistent with other studies that suggested that "kinship social support is an important feature of family relations in African American homes, which may influence child-rearing practices and moderate the impact of stressful experiences on family relations" (p. 348).

A Final Note on Parenting and Resilience

Parenting practices are impacted by myriad factors, which in turn impact the development of resilience. For example, family's beliefs and expectations determine how families view the parenting process as well as the dynamics of the parent–child interaction (Ganiban, Ulbricht, Saudino, Reiss, & Neiderhiser, 2010; Sameroff, 2000). Furthermore, the ways parents communicate and express affection to their children also are influenced by parenting practices. Parenting styles and practices also impact the emotional connectedness among family members. Research in this area tends to suggest that authoritative parenting practices, those that promote firm expectations but also combine caring and love, produce the most positive outcomes (Masten et al., 1999; Steinberg, 2000). On the other hand, there is research suggesting that cultural factors may influence parenting practices and that other practices beside the authoritative type might be effective in promoting positive outcomes (Domenech Rodriguez et al., 2009; Leidy et al., 2010). In addition, research tends to indicate that parenting practices also impact children's academic performance as well as psychological well-being (e.g., Kerr et al., 2009; Vitaro et al., 2005).

Current Issues

As noted, the concepts of resilience and parenting have been widely examined in the literature. However, the notion of how parenting practices can be utilized to promote resilience in families has not been thoroughly explored and analyzed. Part of this issue emanates from the complexities involved when examining family dynamics and how those dynamics not only impact the development of resilience but also affect parenting styles and how parents respond when they encounter challenging circumstances. Pressing issues related to the concept of family resilience include questions about why some families succeed and other do not; the lack of integration in terms of risk and protective factors and how they influence outcomes; and the complexity of family dynamics and structure (Benzies & Mychasiuk, 2009).

In order to answer the question of why some families are resilient in the midst of adversity requires an in-depth examination of individual and environmental factors. As previously described, several key processes in family resilience have been identified in the literature: (a) family's beliefs and expectations; (b) family's emotional connectedness; (c) family's organizational style; and (d) the quality of family learning opportunities (Amatea et al., 2006; Walsh, 2003). Families who are able to mobilize these resources and believe they have the power to change their outcomes will be better able to cope. Another important factor to keep in mind is that families that focus on their strengths and resources rather than on their "deficits" will not only be more motivated to face challenging situations, but they will believe that they can handle difficult times.

Finally, the lack of integration of how risk and protective factors influence outcomes in families and the complexity of family dynamics also have been discussed by Benzies and Mychasiuk (2009). In this regard, the authors indicated that family resilience is "built upon complex interactions between risk and protective factors operating at individual, family, and community levels" (p. 109). Therefore, acknowledging the complex dynamics involved in the development of family resilience, it is imperative to conduct in-depth examinations not only of whether a family is resilient but most importantly, what makes them resilient. Such studies will require a close examination of the different resources and strengths the family possesses (protective factors), how those resources mediate at the different levels (individual, family, community), and how protective factors can be enhanced while also acknowledging the risk factors involved. It is these authors' assertion that a combination of families' strengths and resources and pragmatic education would be an excellent approach to foster family resilience through parenting.

A second issue that needs to be addressed is the connection between parenting practices and the development of resilience in families. As previously discussed, the literature tends to be vast when it comes to different parenting styles and children's outcomes (i.e., Conger & Conger, 2002; Prevatt, 2003; Wahler, 2002). However, the literature has been limited when exploring the impact of positive versus negative parenting practices in the context of a risk and resilience model. Furthermore, when examining the concept of parenting the current issues appear to be the cultural applicability of parenting styles and the implications they may have for research and practice. As demographics continue to change and the United States becomes significantly more diverse (U.S. Census Bureau, 2000), it will become increasingly important to understand that cultural influences lead to differing family dynamics. In this regard, prevention efforts should focus not only on helping families develop strong protective factors, but also on understanding how cultural values and beliefs impact parenting practices, as well as the development of resilience, and how families face adverse circumstances. Hence, understanding successful parenting practices that lead to resilience is imperative.

Overall, there is a need for additional research on the relationship between parenting and family resilience. Our understanding of the impact of parenting on the resilience of children is growing. Although we know certain parenting practices lead to positive outcomes, additional longitudinal research is needed on resilience in children. Additionally, how parenting practices contribute to the resilience of the family system as a whole is relatively unexplored. As increased attention is given to prevention (Trust for America's Health, 2009) it is important to understand the dynamics that lead to resilience in families.

Clinical Implications

Research demonstrates that interventions that impact parenting, such as parent management training, are popular and empirically supported (Kazdin, 2005), but they do not operate from a family resilience perspective. The concept of family resilience presents important implications for clinicians and mental health professionals because it shifts the traditional view of emphasizing deficits to a view that "affirms the family's capacity for self-repair" (Walsh, 1996, p. 268). According to Hawley (2000), when working with families four clinical implications need to be understood regardless of the therapeutic model being utilized. These implications include: focusing on strengths; assessing resilience as a developmental pathway; searching for commonalities in diverse paths of resilience; and developing a useful family schema.[3]

During the last decade there has been much discussion and debate regarding how traditional therapeutic models tend to focus on what is wrong or lacking in clients and families (a deficit model) instead of focusing on the resources and strengths that individual clients and families have that will enable them to succeed (strength-based approach). Family resilience is a strength-based approach because resilience "assumes that individuals and families exhibit a capacity to overcome difficult circumstances through the use of inherent and/or acquired resources and strengths" (Antonovsky, 1987 as cited in Hawley, 2000, p. 105). Therefore, any preventive efforts and programming geared to promote healthy parenting and resilience should consider parents as experts who are resourceful and capable of fostering positive outcomes in their children.

Another important clinical implication proposed by Hawley (2000) highlights the dynamic nature of resilience. In this regard, it is imperative that as clinicians we acknowledge that families develop and evolve over time and that previous experiences influence how families react to subsequent adversities. Therefore, if we aspire to use parenting practices as a vehicle to promote resilience it is imperative to conduct an in-depth examination of traditional parenting practices, outcomes (both individual and family level), and cultural nuances. Thus, it is important to rely on parents' prior experience and expertise relative to their children and their own cultural context.

Lastly, Hawley (2000) pointed out the importance of looking for commonalities in diverse paths of resilience and the development of a useful family schema. The way families develop resilience is individualized and context specific. Therefore, trying to develop a one-size-fits-all model to facilitate family resilience would not be the best approach. Instead, prevention and intervention efforts should focus on the critical examination of each family pathway to resilience and how this information can be combined with sound parenting practices that meet the specific needs of that family.

Protective factors are also an important aspect in buffering against risk factors as well as fostering the development of resilience in families (Alvord & Grados, 2005). Thus, prevention and intervention strategies should emphasize strengthening assets and protective factors. In implementing these strategies, practitioners should have an understanding of the specific individual, family, and environmental factors that place children and families at risk. Indeed, it is important to utilize interventions focused on resilience, and "prevention, education, and intervention efforts can be used to help families minimize the impact of stress to maximize proactive coping" (Yazedjian & Kramer, 2006, p. 388).

Benard (2004) posits that family support programs are the best way to promote family resilience and, in turn, positive youth development. Furthermore, by treating the family as the unit of change, family support programs emphasize the development of characteristics of resilient youth within the family unit since characteristics of resilient youth are also seen in resilient families (Patterson, 2002; Walsh, 1998). Therefore, preventive and intervention strategies geared toward promoting family resilience should move beyond the classical deficit model to incorporate a strength-based approach. In other words, the development of prevention strategies focusing on how healthy parenting practices could promote family resilience is critical. These prevention efforts must capitalize on families' assets and strengths because families are the experts on their problems (Schwartz, 2002).

There are few parenting interventions that directly take a family resilience perspective. When examining family resilience and parenting it is also important to explore the role of parent education

[3] For more on this topic please see Chap. 3.

programs in the development of family resilience. Schwartz (2002) proposes that if parent education programs seek to promote resilience then they should draw upon family's strengths rather than emphasizing their dysfunctionalities or "deficits" as parents. Furthermore, the author asserts that "mental health professionals' main expertise should be in eliciting parents' own expertise. Any past successes that parents have had at resolving relationship difficulties with their children are the best models for present and future successes" (p. 252). The model proposed by Schwartz is based on two basic steps; first, to identify what the parents are good at in terms of their parenting skills, and secondly, to help families to put those skills into practice in an effective manner. The goal here is to promote problem-solving and communication skills and collaboration among family members in order to reduce stress.

Research Implications

There is no question that there is a need to study the role of parenting practices in fostering family resilience. As noted in this chapter the literature addressing this issue is limited, but provides a basis for future research. Several needs come to mind:

- Prevention and intervention programs: their development and evaluation should focus on a strength-based approach for conceptualizing families, parenting, and pragmatic education.
- The role of culture on parenting and family resilience: as the demographics in the United States continue to change it is becoming imperative that any prevention or intervention efforts place multiculturalism, diversity, and social justice at the core of these efforts. Research should focus primarily on how family practices detract or foster the development of resilience among diverse families, what mechanisms impact or mediate the pathway to resilience, and what types of education might benefit parents while acknowledging that they are the experts on their own circumstances and that all families have strengths that need to be capitalized on.
- More research exploring the efficacy of current models: we have discussed several models of family resilience and parenting education. Although these models are not perfect there is good information coming out of research efforts. We could also build on what we currently know in order to enhance what we have while acknowledging that there is room for improvement.
- Other issues as outlined by De Haan, Hawley, and Deal (2002) include: how family is viewed and contextualized (unit of analysis vs. individual reports); longitudinal studies versus one point in time; statistical methods utilized to analyze results (multivariate regression, path analysis vs. latent growth curves). There is no question that research methodologies deserve to be discussed and analyzed; it is clear that the field has not reached a consensus in terms of what research methodologies might be more appropriate when examining family resilience and the impact of parenting practices in its development. Therefore, research focusing on the efficacy of certain methodological approaches is highly needed and recommended.

Case Example

The case of Maira and Joel is presented to demonstrate how clinicians can foster resilience in families facing stressful situations. Maira, a Hispanic woman, sought counseling for her only son, 10-year old Joel, who had been reprimanded three times in the past semester for acting out and instigating fights at school. She reported that Joel also had become increasingly antagonistic and disrespectful toward her at home. These acts of aggression were quite different from Joel's previous behaviors. Maira stated that Joel's acting out behaviors had begun 3 months after her husband, Daniel, was deployed for a second military tour. Daniel was injured during his first tour of duty, which had been very upsetting to Joel. However, having Daniel home to recuperate seemed to be comforting and reassuring to Joel. Maira stated that she felt unable to deal with Joel, because he was suddenly acting like a totally different child. Furthermore, Daniel had always assumed the role of the disciplinarian in the rare instances that Joel required re-direction in the past. Maira maintained a more nurturing and supportive relationship with Joel. Maira said that her father had talked to Joel about the incidents at school, but that only seemed to make Joel angrier.

Approaching the case of Maira and Joel from a family resilience perspective, counselors will want to address the dynamics of the family and their cultural values and beliefs, and with the guidance of Maira as the expert identify strengths that Maira and Joel can build on in order to develop resilience. First, the counselor can help Maira to conceptualize herself as an expert within a family system that is experiencing a challenging situation and an opportunity to become more resilient. For instance, the counselor might ask Maira to identify parenting practices that she had used before there were problems with Joel's behavior. This type of questioning will help her see herself as an effective parent capable of addressing current and future challenges. For instance, Maira's asking for help and her concern for Joel demonstrates her resourcefulness and willingness to work with him. Additional questioning about Maira's cultural values will help identify strengths upon which the family can build. For example, Hispanic families often rely on extended family members for support. Maira's father is an additional source of emotional support for Maira and Joel who can also serve as a male role model for Joel in the absence of Daniel.

Maira's increased awareness of her parenting abilities will enable her to continue to use practices that have worked in the past in order to communicate with Joel about his current situation. For instance, Maira can continue her nurturing and supportive stance with Joel in order to facilitate better communications. Through enhanced communications, Maira may be able to understand the issues that are contributing to Joel's behavioral changes and help him to learn more effective ways to express his fears of losing his father. Furthermore, as a resourceful parent, Maira may seek additional support for Joel through groups that are designed for youth whose parents are deployed. Building on their strengths, Maira and Joel can enhance their relationship and develop coping skills that can lead to increased resilience.

Conclusion

The purpose of this chapter was to present an overview of the literature on family resilience and parenting and to provide a close examination of how parenting practices can inform the development of resilience in families. Although it can be argued that the concepts of resilience in general can be applied to family functioning and resilience, a void in the literature is noted when examining the role of parenting practices in the promotion of family resilience. Thus, we attempted to shed light on how these practices may impact the development of resilience in families and have discussed both clinical and research implications.

Based on the literature presented in this chapter two concepts were analyzed: family resilience and parenting. The concept of family resilience emphasizes family's strengths and resources; recognizes that no single model will fit all families; and acknowledges the notion that all families have the potential to grow and recover from adverse circumstances (Walsh, 2002). The concept of parenting, on the other hand, has been explored as a mediator/moderating factor on both family and individual outcomes (Conger & Conger, 2002; Darling & Steinberg, 1993; Driscoll et al., 2007; Manzeske & Dopkins Stright, 2009; Milevsky et al., 2007). So how are these concepts interconnected?

The above authors assert that if we examine the characteristics that have allowed families to thrive and succeed amidst difficult circumstances we could hypothesize that their family members are skilled at social competence, have the ability to generate novel solutions to problems, foster autonomy in their members so they are highly confident in their skills and abilities, and have a clear sense of family cohesion and purpose. Resilient families' decisions are made to favor the family as a unit, rather than focusing only on individual family members. Therefore, we could use all these skills to enhance their parenting practices and in turn develop more resilience.

Overall, enhancing family resilience is a team effort, which involves the active participation of families and facilitation from professionals working with these families. Families and professionals alike need to focus on family strengths. By doing so, families are allowed the opportunity to explore their own dynamics and celebrate family resilience. Professionals must help encourage and facilitate this process so that is can become an exploratory way of understanding families and how they cope during difficult situations in their lives.

References

Alvord, M. K., & Grados, J. J. (2005). Enhancing resilience in children: A proactive approach. *Professional Psychology: Research and Practice, 36,* 238–245.

Amatea, E. S., Smith-Adcock, S., & Villares, E. (2006). From family deficit to family strength: Viewing families' contributions to children's learning from a family resilience perspective. *Professional School Counseling, 9,* 177–189.

Antonovsky, A. M. (1987). Object relations theory and interpersonal theory: Some comparative comments. *Psychoanalysis & Contemporary Thought, 10*(4), 533–555.

Armstrong, M. I., Birnie-Lefcovitch, S., & Ungar, M. T. (2005). Pathways between social support, family well being, quality of parenting, and child resilience: What we know. *Journal of Child and Family Studies, 14*(2), 269–281.

Baumrind, D. (1966). Effects of authoritative parental control on child behavior. *Child Development, 37,* 887–907.

Baumrind, D. (1991). Parenting styles and adolescent development. In J. Brooks, R. Lerner, & A. C. Peterson (Eds.), *The encyclopedia of adolescence* (pp. 758–772). New York: Garland.

Baumrind, D. (1996). The discipline controversy revisited. *Family Relations, 45,* 405–414.

Benard, B. (1991). *Fostering resiliency in kids: Protective factors in family, school, and community.* Unpublished manuscript.

Benard, B. (2004). *Resiliency: What we have learned.* San Francisco, CA: WestEd.

Benasich, A. A., & Brooks-Gunn, J. (1996). Maternal attitudes and knowledge of child-rearing: Associations with family and child outcomes. *Child Development, 67,* 1186–1205.

Benzies, K., & Mychasiuk, R. (2009). Fostering family resiliency: A review of the key protective factors. *Child and Family Social Work, 14,* 103–114.

Brennan, P. A., Le Brocque, R., & Hammen, C. (2003). Maternal depression, parent–child relationships, and resilient outcomes in adolescence. *Journal of the American Academy of Child and Adolescent Psychiatry, 42*(12), 1469–1477.

Brenner, V., & Fox, R. A. (1999). An empirically derived classification of parenting practices. *The Journal of Genetic Psychology, 160,* 343–356.

Bronfenbrenner, U. (1979). Contexts of child rearing: Problems and prospects. *The American Psychologist, 34,* 844–850.

Chao, R. K. (2001). Extending research on the consequences of parenting style for Chinese Americans and European Americans. *Child Development, 72,* 1832–1843.

Coie, J. D. (1996). Prevention of violence and antisocial behavior. In R. V. Peters, R. McMahon, R. V. Peters, & R. McMahon (Eds.), *Preventing childhood disorders, substance abuse, and delinquency* (pp. 1–18). Thousand Oaks, CA: Sage.

Coll, C., Crnic, K., Lamberty, G., & Wasik, B. (1996). An integrative model for the study of developmental competencies in minority children. *Child Development, 67*(5), 1891–1914. doi:10.2307/1131600.

Conger, R. D., & Conger, K. J. (2002). Resilience in Midwestern families: Selected findings from the first decade of a prospective longitudinal study. *Journal of Marriage and Family, 64,* 361–373.

Conger, R. D., Conger, K. J., Elder, G. H., Simons, R. L., & Whitbeck, L. B. (1992). A family process model of economic hardship and adjustment of early adolescent boys. *Child Development, 63,* 526–541.

Conger, R. D., Cui, M., Bryant, C., & Elder, G. H. (2000). Competence in early adult romantic relationships: A developmental perspective on family influences. *Journal of Personality and Social Psychology, 79,* 224–237.

Conger, R. D., Neppl, T., & Scaramella, L. V. (2001). *The intergenerational transmission of hostile parenting and conduct problems.* In Paper presented at the annual meeting of the Life History Research Society, St. Michael's, MD.

Cowan, P., Cowan, C. P., & Schultz, M. (1996). Thinking about risk and resilience in families. In E. M. Hetherington & E. Blechman (Eds.), *Stress, coping, and resiliency in children and families* (pp. 1–38). Mahwah, NJ: Erlbaum.

Darling, N., & Steinberg, L. (1993). Parenting style as context: An integrative model. *Psychological Bulletin, 113*, 487–496.

De Haan, L., Hawley, D. R., & Deal, J. E. (2002). Operationalizing family resilience: A methodological strategy. *American Journal of Family Therapy, 30*, 275–291.

Doll, B., & Lyon, M. A. (1998). Risk and resilience: Implications for the delivery of educational and mental health services in schools. *School Psychology Review, 2*, 348–363.

Domenech Rodriguez, M. M., Donovick, M. R., & Crowley, S. L. (2009). Parenting styles in a cultural context: Observations of "protective parenting" in first-generation Latinos. *Family Process, 48*, 195–210.

Driscoll, J., & Easterbrooks, M. (2007). Young mothers' play with their toddlers: individual variability as a function of psychosocial factors. *Infant & Child Development, 16*(6), 649–670. doi:10.1002/icd.515.

Driscoll, A. K., Russell, S. T., & Crockett, L. J. (2008). Parenting styles and youth well-being across immigrant generations. *Journal of Family Issues, 29*(2), 185–209.

Dumka, L. E., Gonzalez, N. A., Wheeler, L. A., & Millsap, R. E. (2010). Parenting self-efficacy and parenting practices over time in Mexican American families. *Journal of Family Psychology, 24*(5), 522–531.

Dwairy, M., Achoui, M., Filus, A., Rezvan, P., Casullo, M. M., & Vohra, N. (2010). Parenting, mental health, and culture: A fifth cross-cultural research on parenting and psychological adjustment of children. *Journal of Family Studies, 19*, 36–41.

Frick, P. J. (1994). Family dysfunction and the disruptive behavior disorders: A review of recent empirical findings. In T. H. Ollendick & R. J. Prinz (Eds.), *Advances in clinical child psychology* (Vol. 17, pp. 203–226). New York: Plenum.

Ganiban, J. M., Ulbricht, J., Saudino, K. J., Reiss, D., & Neiderhiser, J. M. (2010). Understanding child-based effects on parenting: Temperament as a moderator of genetic and environmental contributions to parenting. *Developmental Psychology, 47*(3), 676–692.

Hawley, D. R. (2000). Clinical implications of family resilience. *American Journal of Family Therapy, 28*, 101–116.

Hawley, D. R., & deHaan, L. (1996). Toward a definition of family resilience: Integrating life-span and family perspectives. *Family Process, 35*, 283–298.

Hill, N. E., & Tyson, D. F. (2008). Excavating culture: Ethnicity and context as predictors of parenting behavior. *Applied Developmental Science, 12*(4), 188–197.

Hoffman, M. L. (1970). Conscience, personality, and socialization techniques. *Human Development, 13*(2), 90–126. doi:10.1159/000270884.

Hoffman, M. L. (1982). Affect and moral development. *New Directions For Child Development*, 1683–103. doi: 10.1002/cd.23219821605.

Huang, K.-Y., Caughy, M. O. B., Genevro, J. L., & Miller, T. L. (2005). Maternal knowledge of child development and quality of parenting among white, African-American and Hispanic mothers. *Journal of Applied Developmental Psychology, 26*, 149–170.

Jouriles, E. N., McDonald, R., Rosenfield, D., Norwood, W. D., Spiller, L., Stephens, N., et al. (2010). Improving parenting in families referred for child maltreatment: A randomized controlled trial examining effects of project support. *Journal of Family Psychology, 24*(3), 328–338.

Kalil, A., Tolman, R., Rosen, D., & Gruber, G. (2003). Domestic violence and children's behavior in low-income families. *Journal of Emotional Abuse, 3*(1–2), 75–101.

Kazdin, A. (2005). *Parent management training: Treatment for oppositional, aggressive, and antisocial behavior in children and adolescents.* New York: Oxford University Press.

Kerr, D. C., Capaldi, D. M., Pears, K. C., & Owen, L. D. (2009). A prospective three generational study of fathers' constructive parenting: Influences from family of origin, adolescent adjustment, and offspring temperament. *Developmental Psychology, 45*(5), 1257–1275.

Krovetz, M. L. (1999). Resiliency: A key element for supporting youth at-risk. *The Clearing House, 73*(2), 121–123.

Lee, H. N., Ceballo, R., Chao, R., Hill, N. E., Mc Bride Murry, V., & Pinderhughes, E. E. (2008). Excavating culture: Disentangling ethnic differences from contextual influences in parenting. *Applied Developmental Science, 12*(4), 163–175.

Leidy, M. S., Guerra, N. G., & Toro, R. I. (2010). Positive parenting, family cohesion, and child social competence among immigrant Latino families. *Journal of Family Psychology, 24*(3), 252–260.

Loeber, R., & Farrington, D. P. (1998). Never too early, never too late: Risk factors and successful interventions for serious and violent juvenile offenders. *Studies on Crime & Crime Prevention, 7*, 7–30.

Luthar, S. S., Cicchetti, D., & Becker, B. (2000). The construct of resilience: A critical evaluation and guidelines for future work. *Child Development, 71*, 543–562.

Maccoby, E. E., & Martin, J. A. (1983). Socialization in the context of the family: Parent–child interaction. In P. H. Mussen & E. M. Hetherington (Eds.), *Handbook of child psychology: Vol. 4, Socialization, personality, and social development* (4th ed., pp. 1–101). New York: Wiley.

Manzeske, D. P., & Dopkins Stright, A. (2009). Parenting styles and emotion regulation: The role of behavioral and psychological control during young adulthood. *Journal of Adult Development, 16*(4), 223–229.

Masten, A. S., Hubbard, J. J., Gest, S. D., Tellegen, A., Garmezy, N., & Ramirez, M. (1999). Competence in the context of adversity: Pathways to resilience and maladaptation from childhood to late adolescence. *Development and Psychopathology, 11*(1), 143–169.

McCubbin, H. I., & McCubbin, M. A. (1988). Typologies of resilient families: Emerging roles of social class and ethnicity. *Family Relations, 37*, 247–254.

McCubbin, M. A., & McCubbin, H. I. (1993). Family coping with health crises: The resiliency model of family stress, adjustment, and adaptation. In C. Danielson, B. Hamel-Bissell, & P. Winstead-Fry (Eds.), *Families, health, and illness* (pp. 21–64). New York: Mosby.

McFarlane, A. H., Bellissimo, A., & Norman, G. R. (1995). Family structure, family functioning and adolescent well-being: The transcendent influence of parental style. *Journal of Child Psychology and Psychiatry, 36*(5), 847–864.

McGillicuddy-De Lisi, A. V., De Lisi, R., & Van Gulik, K. (2007). The effects of grade level, context, and family type on male and female adolescents' distributive justice reasoning. *Journal of Adolescence, 31*(1), 107–124.

Milevsky, A., Schlechter, M., Netter, S., & Keehn, D. (2007). Maternal and paternal parenting styles in adolescents: Associations with self-esteem, depression and life-satisfaction. *Journal of Child and Family Studies, 16*(1), 39–47.

Mistry, R. S., Vandewater, E. A., Huston, A. C., & McLoyd, V. C. (2002). Economic well-being and children's social adjustment: The role of family process in an ethnically diverse low income sample. *Child Development, 73*(3), 935–951.

Ortega, S., Beauchemin, A., & Burcu Kaniskan, R. (2008). Building resiliency in families with children exposed to violence: The safe start initiative pilot study. *Best Practices in Mental Health, 4*(1), 48–452.

Patterson, J. M. (1988). Families experiencing stress: The family adjustment and adaptation response model. *Family Systems Medicine, 5*, 202–237.

Patterson, J. M. (2002). Integrating family resilience and family stress theory. *Journal of Marriage and Family, 64*, 349–360.

Prevatt, F. F. (2003). The contribution of parenting practices in a risk and resiliency model of children's adjustment. *British Journal of Developmental Psychology, 21*, 469–480.

Putnick, D. L., Bornstein, M. H., Hendricks, C., Painter, K. M., Suwalsky, J. T., & Collins, W. A. (2008). Parenting stress, perceived parenting behaviors, and adolescent self-concept in European American families. *Journal of Family Psychology, 22*(5), 752–762.

Sameroff, A. J. (2000). Dialectical processes in developmental psychology. In A. J. Sameroff, M. Lewis, & S. M. Miller (Eds.), *Handbook of developmental psychopathology* (2nd ed., pp. 23–40). New York, NY: Kluwer Academic/ Plenum.

Sanders, M. R. (2008). Triple p-positive parenting program as a public health approach to strengthening parenting. *Journal of Family Psychology, 22*(3), 506–517.

Scaramella, L. V., Conger, R. D., & Simons, R. L. (1999). Parental protective influences and gender-specific increases in adolescent internalizing and externalizing problems. *Journal of Research on Adolescence, 9*, 111–141.

Schwartz, J. P. (2002). Family resilience and pragmatic education. *The Journal of Individual Psychology, 58*(3), 250–262.

Simon, J. B., Murphy, J. J., & Smith, S. M. (2005). Understanding and fostering family resilience. *The Family Journal, 13*(4), 427–436. doi:10.1177/1066480705278724.

Springer, J. F., Wright, L. S., & McCall, G. J. (1997). Family interventions and adolescent resiliency: The southwest Texas state high-risk youth program. *Journal of Community Psychology, 25*(5), 435–452.

Steinberg, L. (2000). The family at adolescence: Transition and transformation. *Journal of Adolescent Health, 26*, 170–178.

Taylor, R. D. (2010). Risk and resilience in low-income African American families: Moderating effects of kinship social support. *Cultural Diversity and Ethnic Minority Psychology, 16*(3), 344–351.

Trust for American's Health. (2009). *Poll: American public supports investment in prevention as part of health care reform.* Washington, DC: Trust for American's Health.

U.S. Census Bureau. (2000). *U.S. Census Bureau race data.* Retrieved June 14, 2011, from http://www.census.gov/ population/www/socdemon/race.html.

Vitaro, F., Brendgen, M., Larose, S., & Tremblay, R. E. (2005). Kindergarten disruptive behaviors, protective factors, and educational achievement by early adulthood. *Journal of Educational Psychology, 97*(4), 617–629.

Wahler, R. G. (2002). How do parents do it? *Journal of Child and Family Studies, 11*(3), 253–254.

Walsh, F. (1996). The concept of family resilience: Crisis and challenge. *Family Process, 35*(3), 261–281.

Walsh, F. (1998). *Strengthening family resilience.* New York: Guilford Press.

Walsh, F. (2002). A family resilience framework: Innovative practice applications. *Family Relations, 51*(2), 130–137.

Walsh, F. (2003). Family resilience: A framework for clinical practice. *Family Process, 42*(1), 1–18.

Werner, E. E. (1993). Risk, resilience, and recovery: Perspectives from the Kauai longitudinal study. *Development and Psychopathology, 5*, 503–515.

Werner, E. E., & Smith, R. S. (1992). *Overcoming the odds.* Ithaca, NY: Cornell University Press.

Werner, E. E., & Smith, R. S. (2001). *Journeys from childhood to midlife: Risk, resilience, and recovery*. Ithaca, NY: Cornell University Press.

Wills, T. S., McBride Murry, V., Brody, G. H., Gibbons, F. X., Gerrard, M., Walker, C., et al. (2007). Ethnic pride and self-control related to protective and risk factors: Test of the theoretical model for the strong African American families program. *Health Psychology, 26*(1), 50–59.

Yazedjian, A., & Kramer, L. (2006). Fostering family resiliency through community-based learning experiences. *Journal of Teaching in Marriage and Family, 6*, 373–397.

Yeung, W., Linver, M. R., & Brooks-Gunn, J. (2002). How money matters for young children's development: Parental investment and family processes. *Child Development, 73*(6), 1861–1879.

Michael Ungar

Introduction

I knew I'd survived my family's emotional neglect the day my brother called to tell me my father had died. As I hung up the phone, I have to be honest, I was tearless, calm, awash in this sudden release. Not exactly the emotions most people experience at a time like that. We're not supposed to admit that sometimes the death of a parent is something we welcome. But to be truthful, many of us who survive the chaos of troubled families need emotional distance to remain whole. Staring at the phone still in my hand after I'd hung up, all I could think was "Finally." Then I went back to work.

I may have doubted my own sanity that day, except that my father took with him to his grave an iceberg of emotional baggage. By the time he died, there was little left of the weathered thread that once connected us. I never knew what he felt about anything. Not his work. His relationship with my mother, his grandchildren, or me. I didn't need to go to the funeral. He had perished from my life except as a thought 20 years ago when I married. He didn't attend the celebration. He never even sent a card or a gift. For a few years I forgave him, believing it was my mother who had convinced him to stay home in his sagging suburban bungalow, with its white rain gutters slowly warping into a twisted grimace.

I thought, hoped, that he would eventually call and apologize. That he'd come and experience the warm earthy welcome of my new extended family. He never did, and I spent years blaming my mother. She was, after all, a hair-pulling, arm twisting, mean-spirited woman whose enormous girth made it impossible to hug her. Blaming her for my father's mistake kept me civil for the next 10 years. It was safer to blame the one who was physically abusive than the one who held darker secrets.

With some help I survived that ice factory with the ferocity of a matchstick struck hard enough to ignite, but not so hard that it snaps. I suspect my father was just as relieved as I was when I left home at 16. I was the one who made people yell at one another, or cry, or say something just a little more genuine. Without me there, conversations were cold like a northerly wind in January.

There are others like me who are survivors hidden beneath veneers of success. Mary Pipher, whose New York Times bestseller *Reviving Ophelia* (1994) a decade and a half ago gave voice to a desperate generation of young women, is one of them. It took Pipher many years to admit to her own lingering

M. Ungar (✉)
School of Social Work, Dalhousie University, Halifax, NS, Canada
e-mail: michael.ungar@dal.ca

D.S. Becvar (ed.), *Handbook of Family Resilience*,
DOI 10.1007/978-1-4614-3917-2_9, © Springer Science+Business Media New York 2013

depression and to chronicle the unintended, but heart wrenching neglect of a mother who attended medical school and a father serving in the military. At just 6 years of age, Pipher recalls being left to do the mothering for her two younger brothers. She says she never thought much about it at the time. She was even mildly proud of how she could cook hotdogs and look after her brothers when they cried.

There are many more like us. I. F. Stone, the iconic American journalist celebrated by the left for surviving the McCarthy blacklist of the 1950s, is another survivor. He opposed the Vietnam War and became one of the loudest voices of reason among hackneyed journalists who would forgo principles to do infomercials in the guise of news stories. According to his biographer (Guttenplan, 2009) I. F. Stone was born Isidore Feinstein and grew up in an emotionally cold home (is there a trend here?) with a neglectful father and a mother suffering from periodic nervous collapses. And yet he, just like me and Pipher, also overcame a bad start.

But does anyone really understand the dangers Pipher, Stone, and I faced? Like each of them, I, too, am trying to understand why I survived, and the role the family I've built with my wife and two children has played in my emotional resurrection.

Literature Review: Families and Youth "At Risk"

The terms "family at risk" and "youth at risk" have both been used to describe very specific populations such as those where a family member faces comorbid mental health challenges (my mother) as well as those who face normal developmental crises in contexts of poverty (Eyber & Ager, 2003). The ubiquitous use of the terms has made their nomenclature less useful as all families and youth will at some point during their psychosocial development be considered at risk. In this chapter, I narrow the construction of the terms family at risk and youth at risk to groups that face a significant level of chronic or acute stress that threatens their capacity to function well over time. These risks include threats posed by their social ecology (extended family, peers, school, and community relationships), physical ecology (the safety of their neighborhoods, the quality of their school, their access to health services, the toxicity of their environment, and the availability of public infrastructure like housing), and the sociopolitical, economic, and cultural exosystemic factors that influence the policy and public discourses according to which resources to young people, their families, and their communities are allocated. If I survived a family at risk, it is not just because of a personal invulnerability, but also is related to how my environment facilitated my growth and development.

Though their contexts are ecologically complex, almost universally youth in families who face significant risk rely on their families as mediators and moderators of stressful and threatening individual and environmental stressors. A family is typically biological kin, but it can also be relationships based on intimacy formed with non-kin others who fulfill the same functions of family: instrumental and emotional support, providing safety, the raising of children or caring for the elderly, and consumption and redistribution of resources like food, clothing, and housing. Ideally, the stronger and more capable the family system, the more likely it is to protect the young people in its care. As a protective factor, the family's presence can buffer the influence of noxious environments and prevent risks from accumulating in ways that challenge children's healthy developmental trajectories.

Youth at risk are those who face two types of stressors that their families help moderate (Carter & McGoldrick, 1989). Horizontal stressors are challenges related to accomplishing normative developmental tasks like transitioning to junior high school, developing peer connections, and preparing to contribute to the welfare of themselves and their families. Vertical stressors intersect with normal developmental pathways and present either acute or chronic exposure to risks that are exceptional given the youth's culture and context. These may include life events such as the early death of a parent, a physical impairment resulting from an unexpected injury, or exposure to war and the forced dislocation that often follows. In the case of both horizontal and vertical stressors the youth's family provides a source of protection against the effect posed by differential exposure to risk.

These family processes, by means of which the young person is protected from risk and positive development is encouraged, are understood as aspects of resilience (Ungar, 2010; Walsh, 2006). When a child's immediate family does not fulfill these functions other family-like systems (foster care providers, extended family systems, peer groups, non-kin adult caregivers, and the families' young people form later in life on their own) may provide the resources necessary for a child to overcome adversity. In this chapter, I define family and youth resilience ecologically, then explore four concepts useful to describing family resilience and its relationship to the protective processes that influence the lived experience of youth at risk. These concepts include: decentrality, complexity, atypicality, and cultural relativity.

A Social Ecological Definition of Resilience

Resilience itself cannot be measured. It is a meta-construct for processes of positive development that take place when individuals, families, or communities are affected by the cumulative disadvantage of multiple interrelated challenges. Resilience refers to the processes that we observe that contribute to successful adaptation. One cannot describe an individual as resilient as individual aspects of resilience are temporal and contextual. Instead, resilience is a process, observable by what a child or family does to make it more likely that they will do well when facing adversity. Understanding these processes, however, is difficult as their influence on the healthy development of family members depends on the context in which the processes associated with good coping (resilience) take place. For example, a protective process like a very close relationship with a caregiver who helps choose a child's friends or intervenes with bullies may be an aspect of resilience for a younger child who is developmentally challenged but be a disadvantage to the same child when she is an adolescent and needing to learn how to cope with peers on her own (Haynie et al., 2001). Likewise, in conditions of extreme poverty street youth may physically leave their families and live in the street as a strategy to secure better nutrition but still may rely on a connection with their caregivers for emotional security (Alia, Shabab, Ushijima, & Muynck, 2004). Both examples suggest that the processes that contribute to resilience are the result of the capacity of individual youth and their families to navigate their way to the resources they need to cope with adversity in ways that fit with the demands of their social and physical ecologies. The examples also show that resilience is a family's capacity to negotiate with others in their social ecology for the resources they require (like safety from bullying, or food) in ways that are culturally meaningful to them. These dual processes of navigation and negotiation suggest that resilience is not a quality of the individual, but a quality of the individual's interactions with others. For at-risk youth, their family can be both an ally in these navigations and negotiations, or a source of stress that thwarts the youth's efforts to cope effectively when challenged. In the latter case, other family-like systems may function as family substitutes (Skovdal & Campbell, 2010).

Resiliency is distinguished from resilience by its connotation of individual intrinsic capacity to survive (Masten & Obradović, 2006). While the notion of the rugged individual reflects popular discourse, research has identified no internal genetic or psychological structures that predispose youth to resilience that do not rely on environmental triggers to shape their expression. Epigenetics and neural plasticity are both processes that can stack the odds in favor of an individual youth surviving exposure to risks like bullying or having a predisposition towards antisocial behavior (Greenberg, 2006; Moffitt,

Caspi, Rutter, & Silva, 2001). In both cases, however, the capacity of the family will account for more of the explained variance in individual developmental paths than any individual characteristic. In this regard, the capacity of the family to shape a youth's social ecology is more important than the child's individual characteristic. Even in instances, like mine, Pipher's or Stone's, external relationships with mentors, coaches, teachers, the parents of friends, peers, or extended family members are typically the sources of support that make the processes associated with resilience (like remaining in school, opening life opportunities, and maintaining self-esteem) accessible. It is this decentered understanding of resilience that is the focus of this chapter.

Distinguishing Resilience from Strengths and Assets

Resilience is also different than strengths or assets, though all three concepts share much in common. All families, whether facing adversity or not, have strengths that are available to be shared with their youth. These strengths, when itemized, are called assets (Lerner & Benson, 2003) and typically are clustered into internalizing and externalizing resources that support positive development. Large studies of assets have shown that youth with more assets are likely to avoid problems like early sexual initiation, delinquency, and school drop-out (Donnon & Hammond, 2007; Theokas & Lerner, 2006). Among the assets that have been shown to be most important are many family-related factors such as parental monitoring of children, realistic expectations of a child's behavior, and a secure attachment to a caregiver. What is less clear is which assets are most protective for which children in which contexts. Long lists of assets, like Search Institute's decision to include 40 assets in their work (Benson, 2003), have no foundation in evidence-based research. The number of assets chosen was arbitrary. More recent research suggests that far fewer assets can account for differences in developmental outcomes, and that internal and external assets cannot be well differentiated (Theokas et al., 2005). Therefore, lists of family assets should be viewed with caution. We need to ask, were they generated through careful study of diverse families or hypothesized based on a read of the published literature? In the latter case, there is the very real danger of creating a tautology. Only those factors that have been previously reported in the literature are hypothesized as assets. Hidden aspects of family functioning, such as the coping strategies of immigrants (Solis, 2003; Yoshikawa & Kalil, 2011) that have not been identified because they are indigenous to one population whose voices are poorly represented in the literature may be overlooked in favor of qualities of the majority. To illustrate, it has only recently been noticed that African-American parents teach their children both to resist cultural hegemony and to "code switch" in order to succeed in the dominant culture. These are assets that function specifically for a cultural minority, but are not identified as assets in the positive development literature, largely because the conceptualization of assets has been shaped by one cultural group whose voices are the loudest in the published literature (American Psychological and Task Force on Resilience and Strength in Black Children and Adolescents, 2008).

Studies of families' resilience need to move beyond lists of assets that ignore culture and context. Understanding resilience as a social ecological construct suggests that families under stress will manifest particular patterns of behavior that are relevant to the context and culture in which they are living. While the language of strengths is ubiquitous among family therapists, strengths are not the same as resilience. Strengths that occur under stress will function differently than in more advantageous environments. To illustrate this difference, studies of families experiencing a divorce have shown that when the family is financially stable, the children safe, and the parents exercising restraint in how much conflict they show their children, divorce poses little risk to children's mental health. In such cases, children may experience some emotional upset, but as Greene, Anderson, Hetherinton, Gorgatch, and DeGarmo (2003) conclude from their review of the research literature, the social and familial strengths that 80% of children still enjoy after a divorce are sufficient to sustain normal development. In this case, a promotive factor such as non-conflictual parent communication is protective when a family is experiencing divorce. While every child benefits from caregivers who can avoid conflict, this quality of caregiver interaction is *more advantageous* to the child in a family that is experiencing a divorce than in a family that is not. The effect of this strength is even more accentuated for subpopulations of divorcing parents and their children living in urban poverty, or facing a dangerous disorganized community associated with poor quality government housing. In such cases, parents who ensure the limited financial stability of their children post-divorce (Nelson, Laurendeau, Chamberland, & Peirson, 2001), keep the children anchored to the same community they lived in before divorce, and exercise emotional restraint, are likely to prevent a negative chain reaction of life events. Just as a divorce exposes the socially marginalized child to greater disadvantage than her more advantaged peer, strengths (like continuity in the availability of both parents, or economic security) exert a disproportionately greater positive (compensatory; Luthar, Cicchetti, & Becker, 2000) effect on the disadvantaged child, buffering her from a potential barrage of social and economic forces that threaten well-being. The more facilitative the environment, the less children experience the impact of risk.

The Complexity of the Family Environment

A family's environment is typically conceptualized as a tiered ecology, a hierarchical series of interacting permeable levels like that described by Bronfenbrenner (1979). To this orderly placement of individuals inside families inside communities that are inside cultures, Belsky (1980) adds the ontogenic development of the parents (what they bring to child rearing based on their personal histories). It is these qualities that affect microsystemic interpersonal dynamics of the immediate family, mesosystemic interactions between families, schools, and the other services youth use, the macrosystemic influence of social institutions, government policy, and community structures on families, and the impact of exosystemic dimensions of culture, values, and broader social and economic forces around the family that shape individual family functioning. Though Bronfenbrenner reified an understanding of ecology popular in the 1970s, advances in ecological theory suggest that a family's ecology is not tiered, but chaotic, with much more interaction between the levels resulting in mutual influence. In fact, it is now understood that children affect parents and their parenting a great deal, meaning the relationship is reciprocal rather than hierarchical (Stern & Smith, 1999). Paralleling advances in post-structuralism and related epistemology, it is only the outsider (the observer) who naively assumes that a family's interactions with the systems around it can be artificially bounded. Resilience, as a complex process, is only weakly determined by any single set of well-defined factors or processes. Recent work by McCubbin and McCubbin (2005) with families of cultural minorities, Zautra, Hall, and Murray (2008) with communities, and Ungar et al. (2007) with youth across cultures suggests that there is a great deal of interaction between individuals and the multiple dimensions of their social and physical ecologies in ways that are difficult to predict.

For example, Ungar et al.'s (2007) mixed methods study of youth in 11 countries included qualitative interviews with 89 young people from which they identified a set of seven tensions (themes) that are resolved when youth develop successfully in challenging environments: relationships, identity, power and control, social justice, access to material resources, cohesion, and cultural adherence. Each theme is not discreet, nor is any one more important than another (the structure to the findings are non-hierarchical, non-linear). To illustrate, the researchers found that a young person who grew up in a conservative rural community and who self-identified as gay explained that his effective coping involved running away from home and finding a peer group of homeless youth who accepted him. This unconventional pathway to resilience brings with it relationships, a secure identity, experiences of efficacy, and a better sense of social justice than continuing to live with an emotionally abusive family and attending a school where the boy was marginalized because of his sexual orientation. Understood this way, resilience is the process of *navigation* and *negotiation* in complex ecologies that only the observer organizes into tiers. Youth themselves experience the multiple dimensions of their ecology as conflated. Exosystemic values of heteronormativity and parental ontogeny that shape their expectations regarding gender roles combine with the stress of mesosystemic interactions between a youth's peer group within which he is marginalized and one where he is accepted.

When resilience is understood as processes of navigation and negotiation, attention to the context in which these processes take place is needed. As Wyman (2003) notes, processes associated with children demonstrating competence can be both universal and specific to particular contexts. Building on findings from the Rochester Child Resilience Project that has followed two cohorts of ethnically diverse children, ages 7–9 and 10–12, since 1987, Wyman and his colleagues have shown that contexts are complex and interact. Researchers must account for differences in communities (e.g., availability of mentors), family settings (emotional tone, cohesion), and within-child qualities that shape interactions (temperament, attribution style, emotional regulation). This complexity helps us understand why some youth do better than others when confronting risk as well as the role their families play in mediating risk impact. As Wyman explains,

> The implication for research on risk and resilience is that studies should investigate differences in the *protectiveness* of social resources and competencies based on how those factors serve children in specific contexts to reduce dysfunctional processes and enhance children's coping and mastery (pp. 294–295).

Clarification is needed regarding how qualities of the child and protective processes fit together, as is understanding of patterns related to how children express competence across developmental systems (cognitive, relational, emotional regulation, etc.). Wyman hypothesizes regarding what a more ecological understanding of resilience shows: that the potential adaptive fit between a youth's characteristics and his or her environment will be narrower in more adverse environments with fewer opportunities. Indeed, "different definitions of children's competence may be required in highly adverse settings" (p. 296) if we are to understand how young people resolve the seven tensions discussed by Ungar et al. (2007). These seven aspects of resilience are explored in the Case Study provided towards the end of this chapter.

Four Principles for Resilience Among Youth and Families

Decenter

In his qualitative study of 65 adolescents and young adults who identify as gay or lesbian, LaSala (2010) presents a complex narrative of the influence families have on the success of their children to cope as a sexual minority in a world that promotes heteronormativity. LaSala documents young people's experiences of stigma and marginalization in communities that provide them with information only on how to be heterosexual. Youth, he shows, are very much oriented towards disclosing their sexual orientation to their families. Many of his research participants "wanted to disclose their sexual orientation to their mothers and fathers because they believed that their parents could provide the support they needed to cope with the challenges of being gay" (p. 55). This finding, LaSala notes, is unusual as typically youth disclose to their friends and look to them for support. The focus on the family is in part the result of youth being younger at the time of disclosure and the likelihood that they are still financially and emotionally dependent on their parents. The success of the youth's adjustment after disclosure will be in large part dependent upon the reactions of parents, and the instrumental and emotional supports they make available.

Patterns of family interaction such as this suggest that it is not individual qualities of the young person that predict coping under stress, but the ability of the youth's social ecology, in this case parents, to remain emotionally available as well as instrumentally supportive, and to advocate for the young person (supporting the youth's sexual orientation when confronted by others in the extended family, or in the wider community). The reaction by parents will, according to LaSala's participants, influence greatly the capacity of a youth to come out and still maintain a healthy network of relationships. This resilience is not an attribute of the individual. It is a capacity of the family that triggers more secure development and positive attachments during a youth's period of emerging adulthood.

This need for a decentered perspective also can be seen in the structure of interventions. As Dodge and Coleman (2009) explain, "Efforts to fix individual families without also attempting to fix their communities or the community-based structures that lead to maltreatment are unlikely in the long run to result in a reduction of the incidence of child abuse" (p. 1). The Durhan Family Initiative (DFI; Dodge, Murphy, O'Donnell, & Christopoulos, 2009) approaches child abuse as a community event, with an understanding that family dynamics and attitudes are affected by wider social values such as patriarchy. The Initiative reflects the earliest work on child abuse that provided a progressive ecological argument for its etiology. The 1962 article by Henry Kempe and his colleagues published in the *Journal of the American Medical Association* that identified the "battered child syndrome" (Kempe, Silverman, Steele, Droegemueller, & Silver, 1962) showed that systemic change was needed to address a phenomenon occurring within individual families. Specifically, Kempe et al. wrote of the need for professionals to report abuse in order to detect it earlier and prevent the sequelae of negative consequences. Contrast this work with studies of brain plasticity related to child abuse and neglect, and one sees that it is structural changes that change the family that are important to recover from abuse (Anda et al., 2006). This community paradigm (Daro, 2009) that situates families within a network of supports is more likely than individual interventions to mitigate risk for children and youth by creating safe and nurturing environments in neighborhoods where poverty and disorganization exacerbate rates of child abuse.

Significantly, the DFI showed good results in North Carolina where the baseline rate of child maltreatment in 2000–2001 was more than double the national average. Interventions included helping caregivers develop competence as parents, helping parents develop their ability to self-care and care for others, and providing more social support to parents to help them cope with everyday stressors associated with poverty, violence, and marital problems. The DFI also addressed neighborhood-level needs for good social relationships that could help monitor parents' behavior and provide models for good parenting, as well as childcare and informal sources for parenting knowledge. At the community level, professional resources were made available and linked to mental health services, childcare, and pediatric care. Changes in community culture helped to communicate to parents what is and is not acceptable behavior with regard to child management. Finally, at the level of policy, more financial, medical, and emergency relief services were made available to parents as part of a comprehensive system of care that was directed by parents and coordinated by professionals. Few of the resources went to increasing the capacity of children and youth to cope with their abuse. Significant reductions in the incidence of child abuse occurred over a 10-year period as a result of the DFI.

A decentered approach to resilience like this shifts our focus to the social and physical ecologies that *potentiate* positive development. Rutter (2009) makes a similar point in regard to gene–environment interactions. While a youth's particular genetic or personality traits can affect the environment's response to an adolescent (either evoking concern or provoking sanction when behavior is judged "abnormal"), the environment also triggers the youth to succeed in prosocial ways (as is shown in the case example). Rutter characterizes adverse environments as predisposing children to genetically mediated problems, with the necessity to focus on the origins of risk rather than their effects. The reverse is just as true. Genetic predispositions towards problems are less likely to be triggered when environments are optimized. In both regards, the family is partially responsible for variation in developmental paths. Though it has been argued that peers trump parents when it comes to influencing adolescents (Rich, 1998), evidence of reciprocity in these relationships suggests parents are still very important (Kuczynski, 2003). Qualitative studies in particular illustrate the strong parent–youth interaction, a possible artifact of their research design. Patterns of dependency are only pathologized when theories of normal development are informed by gendered interpretations such as Erikson's (1963) eight stages of man in which independence is emphasized. Research that measures independence as a dichotomous variable, with more independence correlated with successful development suppresses narratives of dependency privileged by youth themselves (Weingarten, 1998).

Thus, as Beckett et al. (2006) show in a study of orphans who suffer extreme early deprivation, and Moffitt et al. (2001) show in their longitudinal work with a single birth cohort, the environment has the capacity to account for much of a child's biological predisposition towards good or bad behavior. In other words, families can alter gene expression. The question remains, however, how much resilience is accounted for by individual characteristic and how much by the capacity of the family environment to stimulate positive development? The answers are still unknown, though narratives from those who are marginalized within social discourses, like LaSala's participants, routinely show that families in particular have the capacity to shape positive development far more than do individual traits. Further work is needed to understand, as Rutter suggests, "How genes get 'outside the skin' (as through gene–environment correlations and interactions) and environments get 'under the skin' (as through biological programming and effects on developmental perturbations)" (p. 50).

Atypicality

To understand resilience as a process among youth at higher risk, we also need to investigate how atypical patterns of family interactions are functional adaptations when resources are strained. Context influences the opportunities for resilience to be expressed. To illustrate, a qualitative study of 25 incarcerated girls found that many of the participants chose to maintain positive relationships with their fathers by using drugs with them (Lopez, Katsulis, & Robillard, 2009). Contrary to the expectations of the researchers, the girls did not characterize this process of adultification as something bad, nor did they feel manipulated into peer-like relationships with their fathers. Instead, they accounted for the act of doing drugs with their fathers as a way of accepting an invitation to connect, or soliciting a connection when drug use was initiated by the adolescent. In such cases, employing a principle of atypicality does not mean that all solutions are created equal. Dominant discourses that define appropriate father–daughter interaction and drug use as illegal mean that these girls' patterns of attachment will be seen as problematic. The point, however, is to understand these patterns as adaptive. Interventions to promote better, prosocial alternatives for father–daughter interaction are more likely to succeed when it is acknowledged that the antisocial pattern of drug use was oriented towards the positive goal of attachment. An equally effective substitute is needed. Treatment options that result in less contact between family members are likely to be resisted by both the girls and their fathers.

Atypicality shifts the focus from individual challenges viewed narrowly from the perspective of family outsiders to the way family members respond to the multiple demands of their social and physical ecologies. An example of atypicality that is very different from the one above is found in a study by Edwards and Steinglass (2001), who report on how 35 families (64 adults and 73 children) employed by the US State Department coped with the destabilization caused by an average of 5.7 household moves between overseas placements. Though studies of stress and life events suggest that multiple dislocations have a multiplicative negative effect on children (Tiet et al., 1998), these mobile families and children managed to construct their experience positively. Overall, the children did well. Vulnerability was increased only if one or more of the following three factors were present. First, children who are not

Caucasian were less likely to transition well if they experienced institutional racism or were denied the same status and privilege enjoyed by their white peers in the host culture. Second, younger children had more difficulty adjusting and showed more behavior problems, perhaps because of their lack of experience making the adjustment. And third, children who expected the transition to be difficult, and the social interactions that followed challenging, tended to have their expectations met and experienced more trouble adjusting to the required moves.

As both examples show, family research that hypothesizes a narrow set of outcomes associated with resilience may overlook patterns of coping that are responsive to unique social ecologies and the risks they pose. In this regard, it is important to negotiate the meaning of a family interaction. Assumptions of "normal" may inadvertently overlook sources of strength (McGoldrick, 2003; Walsh, 2003).

Complexity

Studies of resilience suggest that there is complexity in the interactions between individuals and environments that makes it very difficult to predict patterns of causality. Any single factor, like the age of a child, will dramatically affect experience and maturation when a child's family's exposure to risk increases (Rutter, 2008). There is even more need to account for complexity when we introduce cultural norms and expectations related to developmental milestones that transition the child into adolescence and emerging adulthood. Continuity between stages, and determination of which child is doing well, all depend on appreciation for the complex mesosystemic interactions between children, families, schools, and communities. Likewise, the direction of the influence is also complex, with children just as likely to influence parents as parents are to influence children (Ambert, 1992; Kuczynski, 2003; Sameroff & Chandler, 1975).

In the case of youth at risk and family systems, these complex patterns are evident in longitudinal studies of development. One example is provided by Laub and Sampson (2003) in their follow-up research using Glueck and Glueck's (1950) cohort of 500 male delinquents ages 10–17 and 500 non-delinquents first sampled in Boston in the 1930s. The sample, all from low income homes, matched by age, race/ethnicity, and IQ, originally were assessed at ages 14, 25 and 32. Data stored at Harvard University was revisited by Laub and Sampson in the early 1990s. They examined lifetime criminal records for all 500 offenders, and interviewed 52 that differed by engagement with the criminal justice system (persisters, desisters, and intermittent offenders). Results indicated that resilience is a process rather than a measurable stable outcome. Interpreted ecologically, Laub and Sampson reject the development argument that posits life as an orderly, staged unfolding of milestones, and instead

> embrace the notion that lives are often unpredictable and dynamic and that exogenously induced changes are ever present. Some changes in the life course result from chance or random events; other changes stem from macro-level shocks largely beyond the pale of individual choice (for example, war, depression, natural disasters, revolutions, plant closings, industrial restructuring) (p. 34).

Among the many factors that appeared to buffer the impact of these events and contribute to positive developmental gains was the consistency of an intimate relationship. The men who reported the least engagement in crime accounted for their change in behavior as partially a response to having found a partner (wife) who supported them and held expectations that they would cease their involvement in crime.

The principle of complexity introduces to the study of resilience among youth and families an understanding that solutions to risk are often temporal and multidimensional. When Saewyc and Edinburgh (2010) looked at how best to restore healthy developmental trajectories for sexually exploited young runaway girls, they offered a Runaway Intervention Program (RIP), a strengths-based home visiting, group support, and case management program staffed by nurses with experience treating trauma responses and lowering risk behaviors common to the sequelae of sexual violence. The 68 girls in the group aged 12–15 were compared to non-abused and abused urban ninth grade girls from the 2004 Minnesota Student Survey. The intervention group showed positive developmental gains among the girls 6 and 12 months after the intervention. Among the most significant findings were that the program was most helpful for the girls with the fewest personal, family, and school resources. Contrary to expectations, the girls who at time of entry into the program had better functioning families, higher rates of school engagement, higher self-esteem, and lower emotional distress were less likely to benefit from the program:

> Those with the lowest baseline school, family, or other adult connectedness, lowest self-esteem, and highest emotional distress actually improved the greatest amount, and those with the highest connectedness and self-esteem at baseline improved the least, suggesting RIP is more effective with those at high risk (p. 186).

Saewyc and Edinburgh suggest that the program's focus on key relationships in the teens' lives, like those with parents, as well as improvements in self-care and access to health care, are what made the difference. In other words, the complexity of the risks the youths faced interacted with the resources provided by the intervention. While we would have to speculate why the girls most at risk showed the greatest improvement in outcomes, such patterns appear often enough in the literature to suggest that interactions that engage youth and families in processes that contribute to resilience are complex and difficult to predict.

Cultural Relativity

What constitutes a threat to an adolescent's psychosocial development, and which behaviors are judged to be good outcomes for youth and families also vary across cultures. Respect for localized discourses of resilience challenges absolutist traditions in psychology that postulate the existence of characteristics across cultures that are biologically driven and universally measurable with only minor translation of key concepts. Youth at risk, in complex social ecologies, manifest patterns of coping that may be atypical relative to those assumed by cultural elites to represent good coping. An etic, or universal, approach to resilience has validity, but only to a degree. To illustrate this tension between the etic and emic perspectives of resilience, we can look at Achenbach's (2008) work, which has shown that patterns of behavior such as conduct disorder are remarkably stable across cultures and are almost universally viewed as problematic. The question, however, is not whether a monocular view of youth at risk demonstrates homogeneity across cultures, but whether other mechanisms that are culturally specific explain both negative and positive behavior. Achenbach's work tells us only that a phenomenon like conduct disorder is relevant to many different cultures, not whether there are other "hidden" aspects of resilience that may explain children's behavior (Ungar, 2004) but have been ignored during the exporting of dominant cultural (most often Eurocentric) perspectives.

What patterns of interaction between youth and families are most relevant to resilience? A report by the American Psychological Association's Task Force on Resilience and Strength in Black Children and Adolescents (2008) suggests that Black families teach their children ways to resist cultural hegemony and racism as strategies to sustain resilience. No scale for measuring resilience exists, and if it did one must wonder whether children from the dominant culture would score low on a measure of "resistance to cultural hegemony." The example suggests that the construction of resilience is not value neutral. A family's values and culture will influence which patterns of coping are honored and supported. Berry (1979) resolves this etic vs. emic debate by suggesting that a principle of universalism can contribute to respect for indigenous knowledge while at the same time allowing cautious juxtaposition of cultural practices. This works best when allowance is made for an analysis of the relative discursive power of those who decide which parenting practices are best in which contexts.

An interesting example of families negotiating for a more nuanced understanding of resilience is found in Tagalik's and Joyce's (2005) report on relationality among indigenous youth in Canada. They observe that the loss of traditional names is threatening cultural transmission. As families use non-traditional names (imported from the dominant non-Aboriginal culture) there has been a concurrent lack of interest on the part of elders in socializing youth to understand indigenous values.

Traditionally, an entire community shared responsibility for making a child "human." The elders reported that they felt young people today do not become human beings and lack socialization. Cultural resilience in Inuit society means anchoring children to their past and the values transmitted generation to generation. The loss of indigenous names is a symbol of a breakdown in the continuity of culture that is being caused by the actions of parents.

Clinical Implications

The challenge for family therapists and other mental health professionals is to understand processes that youth and their caregivers describe as facilitating resilience, even when those processes are contextually unique and culturally distinct from those of the dominant culture. While there are a few aspects of family functioning that are "universal by consent" (Leonard, 1995), such as the necessity for secure attachment with caregivers and safety within the home, families nurture the resilience of youth at risk through processes that are culturally distinct and responsive to the demands of social and physical ecologies that disadvantage young people. Family behavior such as monitoring of the young person outside the home, expectations regarding contribution to the instrumental and emotional needs of caregivers (adultification and parentification), and patterns of independence and dependence during adolescence are variable both between and within cultures. Clinical work with youth at risk and their families will necessarily involve understanding the way they navigate to resources and negotiate for those resources to be provided in a manner meaningful to them.

Guided by the four principles detailed above, family interventions can demonstrate this tolerance for diversity and equifinality in the processes associated with resilience. By understanding the potential for family processes to nurture and sustain resilience, as reflected in Walsh's (2006) and Becvar's (2007) work,[1] we decenter the individual. Solutions to problems become the consequence of interactions between individuals and social and physical ecologies, and the resources available therein.

Problems arise when therapists ignore the four principles:

- When we center therapy on the person we think only of individual solutions rather than the potential for change embedded in systems. We leave youth, rather than their families, schools, and communities, with the responsibility to solve problems. We avoid engagement in collective processes that build capacity under stress.
- When we expect simple solutions and truncate problems we miss the complex relationships that exist between problems and resources in stressful environments. We ignore the power dynamics that exist between youth, families, and social institutions that influence what solutions are seen as credible solutions that should be invested in.
- When we expect typical outcomes in stressful social ecologies, we miss the atypical solutions youth and families find to their problems.
- When we neglect cultural definitions of success, we overlook the strengths embedded in a family's cultural practices.

We could say that a clinical practice that is centered on individuals' burdens; that simple solutions limit possibilities; that valuing only typical solutions implies the inferiority of people's responses to diverse contexts; and that adhering to culturally normative solutions oppresses people who may have their own ways of coping. In clinical work with marginalized youth and their families, there is the danger of undermining people's attempts to nurture resilience if clinical interventions are burdensome, limiting, convey inferiority, and are culturally insensitive. This can be avoided when

---

[1] Please see Chap. 4 for a fuller discussion of this topic.

therapy contextualizes interventions to create a more social ecological practice (Ungar, 2011). Family therapy is likely to promote resilience when it is decentered (the burden for solutions is shared), complex (resources are unlimited), atypical (all solutions are of potential value), and culturally responsive.

To achieve a more responsive therapy, the therapist needs to bracket his or her knowledge as a tentative expression of the truth, especially when discerning processes that may protect youth from negative developmental trajectories. This complexity is evident when we look at family decisions. For example, returning to the case illustrations that begin this chapter, early parentification or home leaving may be advantageous to some youth if these atypical solutions bring with them opportunities for the young person to feel competent.

Another example of this complexity can be seen in the recent controversy over laws governing child neglect among recent immigrants from countries in Africa where there were long histories of war and time spent in refugee camps. A number of news reports have spoken of parents who have left 9- and 10-year-old children in charge of much younger siblings for extended periods of time after school and even overnight. Parents, desperate for employment, are often forced to take one or more low-paying jobs with inconvenient work schedules. There is simply not enough income to pay for childcare. To cultural outsiders, the situation looks like neglect. To the parents, it is a reasonable solution. Given the dangers they have experienced, and the relative safety of their homes and communities in North America, as well as cultural norms regarding children's capacities to care for their siblings, they do not perceive the same level of risk as do child welfare authorities. Complicating the situation further is that studies of children who assume domestic responsibilities often report that the experience provides them with a sense of self-worth and status within their families in situations where they otherwise may experience marginalization in their wider communities (Liborio & Ungar, 2010). In such instances, intervention is complicated by culturally specific constructions of youth as competent (resilient) and able to cope with manageable amounts of risk.

The reverse situation also may pose risks. As Luthar (2003) has shown in her research with families who have a combined household income of more than $300,000 annually, there may be a number of risks associated with economic advantage if it comes with high expectations for success and few responsibilities.

Each of these examples means that the resilience of youth and families at risk depends on slightly different access to resources and interventions. The onus is on both those sharing and those receiving to evaluate the meaningfulness of a proposed solution to a problem.

Research Implications

Concurrent exploration of more indigenous aspects of resilience is required if viable, evaluable alternatives to dominant culture solutions are to be shown effective. To return to Berry's (1979) point, the universalist must be both a realist and a constructionist. To understand development he or she must understand opportunity structures (the availability and accessibility of health-nurturing resources) and the meaning systems and negotiations that decide which resources are deployed and which interventions are most effective in specific contexts. Achieving this sensitivity to emic perspectives of family resilience among youth and adults will require mixed methods: the use of qualitative tools that capture the nuanced heterogeneity between young people, and the more generalizable quantitative methodologies that help us to understand the homogeneity of populations under stress and their coping strategies (Ungar, Liebenberg, Boothroyd, & Duque, in press). This use of multiple methods also may help us to avoid the imposition of a singular Eurocentric bias towards the indicators of positive functioning of families (Kagitçibasi, 2007).

Case Study

To explore the concept of resilience as it is described here, consider the case of a 12-year-old Latino-American boy, Eduardo, whose mother badly neglected him. The boy's mother was diagnosed with Fetal Alcohol Syndrome and her behavior has been chronically impaired with each of her three children. The two older children were both apprehended by Child and Family Services, but Eduardo, the youngest, was left with his mother until he was 10 years old, when she agreed to in-home supports. Eduardo's behavior became increasingly problematic and eventually he was placed in temporary care and custody though he has been desperate for his mother's attention. He frequently runs away from his foster home, always ending up at his mother's apartment. Each time, she takes him in and promises to parent him better, then within days calls her social worker to return Eduardo back to his foster home when his behavior becomes too unmanageable. Eduardo has a history of theft and is described as lacking impulse control or boundaries. What he wants he takes. As a result, he has changed foster care providers several times, his desire to attach quickly dissipating as he resists any imposition of rules by his caregivers.

Brief family therapy with Eduardo and his mother helps to identify Eduardo's need for attachment and facilitates a plan so that Eduardo can see his mother for short periods. This routine visitation helps Eduardo maintain an attachment with his mother. To improve his functioning at his foster home, Eduardo is enrolled in a highly structured day program. The structure and expectations help, especially when the day treatment staff members make a commitment to maintain Eduardo in their program no matter how bad his behavior becomes. Disciplinary strategies developed at the Center are employed at the foster care provider's home, creating consistency in Eduardo's environment. Within months his academic performance improves and his social worker arranges for him to have contact with his elder siblings. Within a year, a plan is developed to place Eduardo permanently with his uncle, who lives in a Spanish-speaking community in geographic proximity to the boy's mother. Eduardo, however, continues to attend the day treatment program for another year before transitioning back to the regular school system. By this point his mother has relocated to another city and married, but Eduardo's uncle agrees to keep the boy. The stability of the boy's treatment and education programming, and continuity of attachment within a kinship placement seems to provide enough support that Eduardo's behavior remains reasonably good.

Eduardo's experience shows that changes to the boy's social ecology at multiple levels facilitated sufficient changes in his behavior to make it more likely that Eduardo would succeed. In this case, family-like relationships were provided not only with the boy's mother, but also with foster care providers, the day treatment staff, siblings, and finally, the boy's uncle. Reciprocity in these relationships was such that small changes in Eduardo's response to structure and attachments made it easier for him to remain in a stable placement (the more he cooperated, the more his care providers could respond positively to him). In this case, resilience is a quality of both the boy and the boy's environment.

Conclusion

Youth and families who experience significant levels of risk report important interactions that can moderate or mitigate the impact of environmental stressors. Those interactions that promote resilience, however, are challenging to predict. A decentered approach to resilience, with an understanding of atypical solutions to problems, the complexity of social ecologies, and the need for cultural sensitivity, means that families can play an important though unpredictable role in the promotion of the resilience of their children. Thinking back to my own reaction to my father's death, its supposedly atypical expression may not be widely understood, but that does not mean it was not a way I sustained my own resilience in an emotionally neglectful family. Like Pipher, Stone, and many of the other youth mentioned in this chapter, solutions that bring resilience are always reflections of how individuals and families navigate and negotiate in challenging contexts. More study, however, is required if we are to understand systemically how processes related to resilience affect adolescent development in contexts where there is significant adversity.

References

Achenbach, T. M. (2008). Multicultural perspectives on developmental psychopathology. In J. J. Hudziak (Ed.), *Developmental psychopathology and wellness: Genetic and environmental influences* (pp. 23–48). Washington, DC: American Psychiatric Publishing.

Alia, M., Shabab, S., Ushijima, H., & Muynck, A. (2004). Street children in Pakistan: A situational analysis of social condition and nutritional status. *Social Science & Medicine, 59*, 1707–1717.

Ambert, A. (1992). *The effect of children on parents.* New York, NY: Haworth Press.

American Psychological Association, Task Force on Resilience and Strength in Black Children and Adolescents. (2008). *Resilience in African American children and adolescents: A vision for optimal development.* Washington, DC: American Psychological Association, Task Force on Resilience and Strength in Black Children and Adolescents. Retrieved July 2, 2010, from http://www.apa.org/pi/cyf/resilience/html.

Anda, R. F., Felitti, V. J., Bremner, J. D., Walker, J. D., Whitfield, C., Perry, B. D., et al. (2006). The enduring effects of abuse and related adverse experiences in childhood: A convergence of evidence from neurobiology and epidemiology. *European Archives of Psychiatry and Clinical Neuroscience, 256*, 174–186.

Beckett, C., Maughan, B., Rutter, M., Castle, J., Colvert, E., Groothues, C., et al. (2006). Do the effects of early severe deprivation on cognition persist into early adolescence? Findings from the English and Romanian adoptees study. *Child Development, 77*(3), 696–711.

Becvar, D. S. (2007). *Families that flourish: Facilitating resilience in clinical practice.* New York, NY: W.W. Norton.

Belsky, J. (1980). Child maltreatment: An ecological integration. *American Psychologist, 35*(4), 320–335.

Benson, P. L. (2003). Developmental assets and asset-building community: Conceptual and empirical foundations. In R. M. Lerner & P. L. Benson (Eds.), *Developmental assets and asset-building communities: Implications for research, policy, and practice* (pp. 19–46). New York, NY: Kluwer Academic/Plenum Publishers.

Berry, J. W. (1979). A cultural ecology of social behaviour. *Advances in Experimental Social Psychology, 12*, 177–206.

Bronfenbrenner, U. (1979). *Ecology of human development.* Cambridge, MA: Harvard University Press.

Carter, B., & McGoldrick, M. (1989). *The changing family life cycle: A framework for family therapy* (2nd ed.). Boston, MA: Allyn & Bacon.

Daro, D. (2009). The history of science and child abuse prevention: A reciprocal relationship. In K. A. Dodge & D. L. Coleman (Eds.), *Preventing child maltreatment: Community approaches* (pp. 9–28). New York, NY: Guilford.

Dodge, K. A., & Coleman, D. L. (2009). Introduction: Community-based prevention of child maltreatment. In K. A. Dodge & D. L. Coleman (Eds.), *Preventing child maltreatment: Community approaches* (pp. 1–8). New York, NY: Guilford.

Dodge, K. A., Murphy, R., O'Donnell, K., & Christopoulos, C. (2009). Community-level prevention of child maltreatment: The Durham Family Initiative. In K. A. Dodge & D. L. Coleman (Eds.), *Preventing child maltreatment: Community approaches* (pp. 68–81). New York, NY: Guilford.

Donnon, T., & Hammond, W. (2007). Understanding the relationships between resiliency and bullying in adolescence: An assessment of youth resiliency from five urban junior high schools. *Child and Adolescent Psychiatric Clinics of North America, 16*(2), 449–472.

Edwards, M. E., & Steinglass, P. (2001). Relocation as potential stressor or stimulating challenge. *Journal of Feminist Family Therapy, 13*(2/3), 121–152.

Erikson, E. H. (1963). *Childhood and society* (2nd ed.). New York, NY: W.W. Norton.

Eyber, C., & Ager, A. (2003). Poverty and youth. In S. C. Carr & T. S. Sloan (Eds.), *Poverty and psychology: From global perspective to local practice* (pp. 229–250). New York: Kluwer Academic/Plenum.

Glueck, S., & Glueck, E. (1950). *Unraveling juvenile delinquency.* Cambridge, MA: Harvard University Press.

Greenberg, M. T. (2006). Promoting resilience in children and youth: Preventive interventions and their interface with neuroscience. In B. M. Lester, A. S. Masten, & B. McEwen (Eds.), *Resilience in children* (pp. 139–150). Boston, MA: Blackwell.

Greene, S. M., Anderson, E. R., Hetherinton, E. M., Gorgatch, M. S., & DeGarmo, D. S. (2003). Risk and resilience after divorce. In F. Walsh (Ed.), *Normal family processes* (3rd ed., pp. 96–120). New York, NY: Guilford.

Guttenplan, D. D. (2009). *American radical: The life and times of I. F. Stone.* New York, NY: Farrar, Straus & Giroux.

Haynie, D., Nansel, T., Eitel, P., Crump, A. D., Saylor, K., Yu, K., et al. (2001). Bullies, victims and bully/victims: Distinct groups of at-risk youth. *Journal of Early Adolescence, 21*(1), 29–49.

Kagitçibasi, C. (2007). *Family, self, and human development across cultures: Theory and application* (2nd ed.). Mahwah, NJ: Lawrence Erlbaum.

Kempe, C. H., Silverman, F. N., Steele, B. F., Droegemueller, W., & Silver, H. K. (1962). The battered child syndrome. *Journal of the American Medical Association, 181,* 17–24.

Kuczynski, L. (2003). Beyond bidirectionality: Bilateral conceptual frameworks for understanding dynamics in parent-child relations. In L. Kuczynski (Ed.), *Handbook of dynamics in parent-child relations* (pp. 1–24). Thousand Oaks, CA: Sage.

LaSala, M. C. (2010). *Coming out, coming home: Helping families adjust to a gay or lesbian child.* New York: Columbia University Press.

Laub, J. H., & Sampson, R. J. (2003). *Shared beginnings, divergent lives: Delinquent boys to age 70.* Cambridge, MA: Harvard University Press.

Leonard, P. (1995). Postmodernism, socialism and social welfare. *Journal of Progressive Human Services, 6*(2), 3–19.

Lerner, R. M., & Benson, P. L. (Eds.). (2003). *Developmental assets and asset-building communities: Implications for research, policy, and practice.* New York, NY: Kluwer Academic/Plenum.

Liborio, R., & Ungar, M. (2010). Children's perspectives on their economic activity as a pathway to resilience. *Children and Society, 24,* 326–338.

Lopez, V., Katsulis, Y., & Robillard, A. (2009). Drug use with parents as a relational strategy for incarcerated female adolescents. *Family Relations, 58*(2), 135–147.

Luthar, S. (2003). The culture of affluence: Psychological costs of material wealth. *Child Development, 74,* 1581–1593.

Luthar, S. S., Cicchetti, D., & Becker, B. (2000). The construct of resilience: A critical evaluation and guidelines for future work. *Child Development, 71*(3), 543–562.

Masten, A. S., & Obradović, J. (2006). Competence and resilience in development. In B. M. Lester, A. S. Masten, & B. McEwen (Eds.), *Resilience in children* (pp. 13–27). Boston: Blackwell.

McCubbin, L. D., & McCubbin, H. I. (2005). Culture and ethnic identity in family resilience: Dynamic processes in trauma and transformation of indigenous people. In M. Ungar (Ed.), *Handbook for working with children and youth: Pathways to resilience across cultures and contexts* (pp. 27–44). Thousand Oaks, CA: Sage.

McGoldrick, M. (2003). Culture: A challenge to concepts of normality. In F. Walsh (Ed.), *Normal family processes* (3rd ed., pp. 61–95). New York, NY: Guilford.

Minnesota Student Survey. (2004). Retrieved July 2, 2010, from http://education.state.mn.us/MDE/Learning_Support/Safe_and_Healthy_Learners/Minnesota_Student_Survey/index.html.

Moffitt, T. E., Caspi, A., Rutter, M., & Silva, P. A. (2001). *Sex differences in antisocial behaviour.* Cambridge, England: Cambridge University Press.

Nelson, G., Laurendeau, M., Chamberland, C., & Peirson, L. (2001). A review and analysis of programs to promote family wellness and prevent the maltreatment of preschool and elementary-school-aged children. In I. Prilleltensky, G. Nelson, & L. Peirson (Eds.), *Promoting family wellness and preventing child maltreatment: Fundamentals for thinking and action* (pp. 220–272). Toronto, ON: University of Toronto Press.

Pipher, M. (1994). *Reviving Ophelia: Saving the selves of adolescent girls.* New York: Ballantine Books.

Rich, J. (1998). *The nurture assumption.* New York: Simon & Schuster.

Rutter, M. (2008). Developing concepts in developmental psychopathology. In J. J. Hudziak (Ed.), *Developmental psychopathology and wellness: Genetic and environmental influences* (pp. 3–22). Washington, DC: American Psychiatric Publishing.

Rutter, M. (2009). Understanding and testing risk mechanisms for mental disorders. *Journal of Child Psychology and Psychiatry, 50*(1–2), 44–52.

Saewyc, E. M., & Edinburgh, L. D. (2010). Restoring healthy developmental trajectories for sexually exploited young runaway girls: Fostering protective factors and reducing risk behaviors. *Journal of Adolescent Health, 46,* 180–188.

Sameroff, A. J., & Chandler, M. J. (1975). Reproductive risk and the continuum of caretaker casualty. In F. D. Horowitz (Ed.), *Review of child development research* (Vol. 4, pp. 187–244). Chicago: University of Chicago Press.

Skovdal, M., & Campbell, C. (2010). Orphan competent communities: A framework for community analysis and action. *Vulnerable Children and Youth Studies, 5*(1), 19–30.

Solis, J. (2003). Re-thinking illegality as a violence *against,* not *by* Mexican immigrants, children, and youth. *Journal of Social Issues, 59*(1), 15–33.

Stern, S., & Smith, C. A. (1999). Reciprocal relationships between antisocial behavior and parenting: Implications for delinquency intervention. *Families in Society, 80*(2), 169–181.

Tagalik, S., & Joyce, M. (2005). *Relationality and its importance as a protective factor for indigenous youth*. A publication of the Centre of Excellence for Children & Adolescents with Special Needs, Mental Health Task Force: Government of Nunavut. Thunder Bay, ON: Lakehead University, Centre of Excellence for Children & Adolescents with Special Needs.

Theokas, C., Almerigi, J. B., Lerner, R. M., Dowling, E. M., Benson, P. L., Scales, P. C., et al. (2005). Conceptualizing and modeling individual and ecological asset components of thriving in early adolescence. *Journal of Early Adolescence, 25*(1), 113–143.

Theokas, C., & Lerner, R. M. (2006). Observed ecological assets in families, schools, and neighbourhoods: Conceptualisation, measurement and relations with positive and negative developmental outcomes. *Applied Developmental Science, 10*(2), 61–74.

Tiet, Q. Q., Bird, H. R., Davies, M., Hoven, C., Cohen, P., Jensen, P., et al. (1998). Adverse life events and resilience. *Journal of the American Academy of Child and Adolescent Psychiatry, 37*(11), 1191–1200.

Ungar, M. (2004). *Nurturing hidden resilience in troubled youth*. Toronto, ON: University of Toronto Press.

Ungar, M. (2010). What is resilience across cultures and contexts? Advances to the theory of positive development among individuals and families under stress. *Journal of Family Psychotherapy, 21*(1), 1–16.

Ungar, M. (2011). *Counseling in challenging contexts: Working with individuals and families across clinical and community settings*. Belmont, CA: Brooks/Cole.

Ungar, M., Brown, M., Liebenberg, L., Othman, R., Kwong, W. M., Armstrong, M., et al. (2007). Unique pathways to resilience across cultures. *Adolescence, 42*(166), 7–310.

Ungar, M., Liebenberg, L., Boothroyd, R., & Duque, L. F. (in press). Assessing resilience across cultures using mixed methods: Construction of the child and youth resilience measure. *Journal of Multiple Methods in Research*.

Walsh, F. (2003). *Normal family processes* (3rd ed.). New York: Guilford.

Walsh, F. (2006). *Strengthening family resilience* (2nd ed.). New York: Guilford.

Weingarten, K. (1998). Sidelined no more: Promoting mothers of adolescents as a resource for their growth and development. In C. G. Coll, J. L. Surrey, & K. Weingarten (Eds.), *Mothering against the odds: Diverse voices of contemporary mothers* (pp. 15–336). New York: The Guilford Press.

Wyman, P. A. (2003). Emerging perspectives on context specificity of children's adaptation and resilience: Evidence from a decade of research with urban children in adversity. In S. S. Luthar (Ed.), *Resilience and vulnerability: Adaptation in the context of childhood adversities* (pp. 293–317). Cambridge, UK: Cambridge University Press.

Yoshikawa, H., & Kalil, A. (2011). The effects of parental undocumented status on the developmental contexts of young children in immigrant families. *Child Development Perspectives, 5*(4), 291–297.

Zautra, A., Hall, J., & Murray, K. (2008). Community development and community resilience: An integrative approach. *Community Development, 39*(3), 1–18.

Family Resilience in the Context of High-Risk Situations

Cynthia A. Lietz

Introduction/Background

Risk-focused research encompasses studies that test hypotheses that suggest the presence of a certain incident or quality increases the likelihood that a person will experience a negative outcome. Researchers commonly test risk models in health studies to identify predictors of various disorders. For example, understanding that smoking increases one's likelihood for lung cancer leads the medical field to identify smoking as a risk factor of this disease. Identifying risk is important for two reasons. First, recognizing risk offers implications for prevention. When risk factors are identified, preventing the presence of these factors can lead to improved health outcomes. Additionally, assessing one's level of risk may assist in diagnosis, as physicians can assess for disorders that may be predicted by one's personal and medical history.

Seeing the benefits of this approach, many leaders within the social sciences advocated for the adoption of the medical model, including its focus on risk identification and reduction. Rather than examining risk factors for various health disorders, social science researchers seek to identify risk factors that predict poor outcomes related to mental health or social functioning. For example, early studies were able to establish a connection between childhood experiences and one's risk for the development of addiction to alcohol or other drugs. Specifically, a body of literature suggests that growing up in a home with a parent who faces alcohol or drug addiction increases a child's likelihood for developing his or her own problems with addiction into adulthood (Chassin, Pitts, DeLucia, & Todd, 1999). Research based on risk models has contributed important knowledge to the social sciences as a set of risk factors have been identified, leading to important prevention and intervention efforts.

Despite the important contribution of this research, more recently researchers have recognized that risk factors are not the only predictors of functioning (Benard, 2004; Rutter, 2000; Werner & Smith, 2001). As research developed, social science leaders became interested in outliers, or the cases that failed to follow the expected trajectory based on one's risk. In other words, while researchers understand that being raised in a home with a parent facing addiction increases the likelihood that child will develop her own addiction issues, not all children raised in this situation end up experiencing this problem. What is different about these cases?

C.A. Lietz (✉)
School of Social Work, Arizona State University,
Tempe, AZ, USA
e-mail: clietz@asu.edu

D.S. Becvar (ed.), *Handbook of Family Resilience*,
DOI 10.1007/978-1-4614-3917-2_10, © Springer Science+Business Media New York 2013

This very question led many child development researchers to conduct studies regarding pathways toward resilience. The construct of resilience refers to situations in which individuals are able to avoid the negative outcomes associated with risk (Benard, 2004; Luthar, Cicchetti, & Becker, 2000; Rutter, 2000). Specifically, researchers are examining resilience when they look at individuals who are at high risk for a negative outcome but who maintain healthy functioning despite this risk. To explain these varied pathways, researchers interested in resilience measure not just risk factors, but also seek to identify protective factors, or the experiences and qualities that appear to buffer the negative effects of risk. Protective factors include strengths and resources that help individuals sustain functioning despite the challenges they face (Mandleco & Perry, 2000). Examples of protective factors include things like social support, a sense humor, and flexibility (Benard, 2004; Lietz, Lacasse, & Cacciatore, 2011; Werner & Smith, 2001), and are described in greater detail later in this chapter.

Resilience research was initially focused on child development and sought to identify the protective factors that help at-risk children avoid negative outcomes and grow into healthy adults (Garmezy, 1993; Rutter, 1987; Werner & Smith, 1982; Wolin & Wolin, 1993). More recently, researchers have become interested in applying the construct of resilience to family systems (Hawley, 2000; Lietz, 2006; McCubbin & McCubbin, 1996; Patterson, 2002; Walsh, 2003). Specifically, researchers have identified risk factors that can hinder the healthy functioning of a family unit. Family resilience researchers seek to examine the strengths or protective factors that help families to remain intact and functioning well despite facing a variety of risk factors known to predict family dissolution or discord.

The purpose of this chapter is to define family resilience in the context of high-risk situations. First, the literature is reviewed to describe the development of the construct of family resilience. Second, research regarding family risk factors is synthesized, providing information regarding some of the most challenging difficulties families face. Finally, the process of family resilience is presented by means of a typology that was developed through in-depth qualitative interviews with families who maintained and in some cases improved functioning despite their experience with multiple risk factors. The phases and corresponding family strengths are described, offering implications for clinical practice with families facing a variety of stressors.

Current Relevance of a Discussion of Family Resilience

A discussion of the risks and protective factors that impact family functioning offers important implications for practice and research. Considering the current economic situation, families are facing greater stress than ever before. More families are facing job loss and financial demands, requiring many to leave their communities to find affordable housing and new employment opportunities. At the same time, the social service system is stretched to capacity, leading to decreased services and support. While professional support services are hindered, personal support from extended family and neighbors is also challenged. When a family or neighbor faces a crisis, their support system typically rallies behind that family or neighbor. Because the current stressors facing families remain pervasive, the availability of this type of informal support is also limited. Finally, while financial strain and unemployment impact many, families representing all socioeconomic situations continue to face simultaneously both normative and non-normative stressors including but not limited to bereavement, health concerns, and the effects of natural disasters, creating the potential of a cumulative negative effect. Risk models simply inform us that these families are at risk for negative outcomes. More than ever, a resilience perspective that seeks to identify and build family strengths to support healthy coping and adaptation is critical to the health and well-being of our families and communities. Understanding the factors that buffer the negative effects of risk for families remains an essential part of clinical family practice.

Literature Review

The construct of resilience describes the ability to avoid negative outcomes associated with one's risk (Benard, 2004; Masten, 2001; Rutter, 2000). Luthar et al. (2000) define resilience as "a dynamic process encompassing positive adaptation within the context of significant adversity" (p. 543), while Walsh (2003) describes resilience as "the ability to withstand and rebound from disruptive life challenges" (p. 1). Early resilience research was influenced by Werner and Smith's (2001) seminal 40-year study of high-risk youth. These researchers conducted a longitudinal study that followed all 698 babies born on the island of Kauai in 1 year. One-third of the sample was identified as high-risk. These children (a) experienced perinatal stress, (b) were born into poverty, and (c) were raised in challenging circumstances including discord, addiction, or mental health issues of their parents. The sample of high-risk youth was recruited for participation and then assessed every 10 years. This study uncovered a set of protective factors, such as maintaining a relationship with at least one caring adult, that helped many of the children successfully overcome these challenges and ultimately developing into well-functioning adults. This important study prompted a growing interest in conducting research that examined how both risk and protection work together to better explain ongoing functioning (Garmezy, 1993; Garmezy, Masten, & Tellegen, 1984; Luthar, 1991; Masten & Coatsworth, 1998). This foundational research focused primarily on child development, specifically looking at how youth who experience high-risk circumstances cope with these challenges over time (Benard, 2004; Rutter, 1987).

More recently, the construct of resilience has been increasingly applied to family units. This perspective involves taking a systems approach to examine familial-level risk and protective factors that explain how families overcome negative effects predicted per a variety of adverse experiences (Allison et al., 2003; Black & Lobo, 2008; Hawley, 2000; Lietz, 2006, 2007; McCubbin, Balling, Possin, Frierdich, & Bryne, 2002; Patterson, 2002; Simon, Murphy, & Smith, 2005; Walsh, 2003, 2007). It is critical to note that having a supportive family is identified as a protective factor in the early child development literature, suggesting that healthy family functioning can predict positive outcomes for children. When speaking about family resilience in this chapter, this conceptualization does not reference the family's impact on the individual, but instead takes a systems approach, looking at the family as a collective unit whose outcomes are also of interest. Specifically, family resilience is a familial-level construct that looks at the family as the unit of analysis to understand the risk and protective factors that support healthy adaptation and functioning for the family as a whole.

Risk Factors

All families face a series of stressors throughout their life as a collective unit. Normative life transitions such as marriage, childbirth, retirement, and relocations, while representing positive events, still increase the demands on the unit. Concurrently, losses, such as the death of a parent, although at times expected and part of the normal family life cycle, also remain challenging for many. Even daily hassles or minor disruptions create strain on a family, particularly when the capabilities and resources to cope are diminished (Patterson, 2002).

In addition to normative life events, many families face adverse events that also can exert a negative effect on functioning. For example, when family members experience traumatic bereavement, serious chronic or terminal health disorders, major disasters, long separations, and ongoing financial hardships, these risk factors, particularly in the context of multiple stressors, can increase the likelihood that the unit will experience family discord and dissolution.

Traumatic Bereavement

Loss is a part of being a family. Normative losses are difficult for family members even when death is expected and part of the normal life cycle. However, the level of risk attributed to bereavement is enhanced when deaths are sudden, unexpected, or occur in such a way that they are traumatic for family members (Walsh, 2007). For example, Davies (2004) notes that the death of child is "recognized as the most intense and overwhelming of all griefs" (p. 506). The loss of a child due to stillbirth, SIDS, a health disorder, accidental death, or suicide incites emotional pain that can affect the psychological functioning of individual family members as well as the functioning of the family as whole (DeFrain, Martens, Stork, & Stork, 1990; Murphy, Johnson, Wu, Fan, & Lohan, 2003).

The loss of a child creates a crisis state for families requiring role adjustment and reorganization of the system (Fletcher, 2002). Ongoing parent–child interactions, sibling relationships, and connections between couples can be impacted by traumatic bereavement. Specifically, Murphy et al. (2003) found increased marital distress for parents bereaved through homicide, and noted that a sample of parents whose children died due to accident, homicide, or suicide reported higher levels of mental distress and trauma. Song, Floyd, Seltzer, Greenberg, and Hong (2010) report that research has identified an increase in marital distress for couples who face the loss of a child and demonstrate that the level of marital closeness affects the ongoing health-related quality of life for parents. Similarly, a review by Scwab (1998) suggests that while child death does not predict increased levels of divorce, many couples do experience strain on the marital relationship. Traumatic bereavement can increase a family's level of risk relative to a variety of outcomes.

Terminal and Ongoing Health Diagnoses

When a family member is diagnosed with a serious chronic or terminal health condition, the knowledge of the presence of the disease along with the increased time and financial demands can create a hardship for many family systems. McCubbin et al. (2002) assert that a childhood cancer diagnosis creates many new challenges for families, including multiple hospitalizations, painful treatments, and new role demands while the members must grapple with the possibility of mortality. Their review suggests that childhood cancer can put families at greater risk of post-traumatic stress symptoms (PTSS), decreased marital quality, and parental emotional distress. Similarly, Pai et al. (2007) found an increase in distress and perceived level of family conflict, particularly for mothers, during the year following a pediatric cancer diagnosis.

A study by Holmes and Deb (2003) suggests that the presence of a variety of chronic illnesses can exert negative effects on the family system and that these effects are increased when the family's financial resources and insurance coverage are lacking. Similarly, Midence (1994) asserts that marital conflict and strain are often increased for couples when caring for a child with a chronic health problem. Brown et al. (2008) reviewed literature related to the effects of chronic health conditions on the family and identified negative effects on the marital relationship, including decreased satisfaction with the sexual relationship and increased financial strain. Herzer et al. (2010) acknowledge that findings regarding the association between chronic health and family functioning are inconsistent, with some studies demonstrating negative effects of chronic health problems while other studies fail to establish this relationship. These inconsistent findings again highlight the importance of taking a resilience approach when considering risk. An examination of protective factors is needed to understand the variation in functioning for families facing difficulties such as chronic health issues.

Major Disasters

Landau and Saul (2004) define "major disaster as catastrophic or cataclysmic events that result in major disruption and/or massive and unpredictable loss" (p. 287). These events include natural disasters such as Hurricane Katrina and the 2010 earthquake in Haiti or acts of war or violence such as the attack on New York's Twin Towers. The devastation of these events can put communities and families at risk for diminished functioning on many levels. Landau and Saul suggest that major disasters cause families to face temporary or permanent separations. These unplanned separations can increase role strain and decrease cohesiveness. In addition, they report that communication may be hindered due to the disorganization and chaos present as a result of major disasters.[1] The effects of these stressors may be enhanced by increased financial strain and unmet housing necessities as families are faced with new barriers in their attempt to meet basic needs (Kilmer & Gil-Rivas, 2010).

Along with the disruption of predictable patterns of family interaction, Figley (1998) explains that family members also may suffer compassion fatigue when seeking to help loved ones who have experienced a traumatic event. Indeed, the caregiving burden can exert a strain on family relationships. Additionally, a review by Pfefferbaum and North (2008) suggests that family members experience a ripple effect when one or more experience a disaster. Specifically, they assert that the effects of trauma are enhanced for parents. That is, the negative effects for adults with children compared with adults with no children are increased due to the "physical, economic, and emotional burden of caring for children" in the wake of a major disaster (p. 4). Finally, parenting practices may be diminished due to the increased demands placed on the adults in the family during the days, months, and even years after a disaster (Pfefferbaum & North).

Military Involvement

In the development of the concept "Military Family Syndrome" it was theorized that there would be negative outcomes for children growing up in military homes (LaGrone, 1978). However, many disputed this conceptualization as lacking empirical evidence (Cozza, Chun, & Polo, 2005; Drummet, Coleman, & Cable, 2003), and further research has demonstrated that many military families are able to maintain healthy functioning and parenting practices despite the stress of deployment (Kelley et al., 2001; Palmer, 2008). Although research has found that many such families are functioning well, studies suggest some of these families are at risk for a variety of negative outcomes.

Lamberg (2010) concluded that military families may experience an increased risk for child maltreatment. Specifically, Rentz et al. (2007) conducted a time series analysis of child welfare data in Texas, demonstrating an increase in substantiated reports of child maltreatment that was twice as high the year after military members in this area were deployed while the rate for nonmilitary families remained consistent. In addition to child maltreatment, other family relationships can be impacted by the strain of deployment. For example, one recent study by McLeland, Sutton, and Schum (2008) found that a sample of military men reported lower levels of satisfaction with their marriages at both pre- and postdeployment phases compared to nonmilitary married men.[2] While many military families are able to cope with the challenges of deployment, the stress of deployment, particularly when families face multiple deployments in relatively short periods of time, can enhance role strain, increase marital and parent/child conflict, and decrease levels of family connectedness.

Financial Strain

Extensive literature on the topic establishes poverty as a risk factor that can impact the health and well-being of children, adults, and family systems. Wadsworth and Santiago (2008) explain that "economic stress is grueling and demoralizing, leading to depressed mood among parents. This distress then contributes to conflict among parents and other family members and, eventually, to less effective parenting" (p. 399). Specifically, lower socioeconomic status has been linked with marital distress and

---

[1] For more on this topic please see Chap. 26.

[2] For more on this topic please see Chap. 7.

parenting stress (Hayden, Schiller, & Dickstein, 1998), a finding confirmed by Herzer et al. (2010). Furthermore, poverty has been linked consistently to an increased risk of child maltreatment (Cancian, Slack, & Yang, 2010).

The impact of financial strain is often intermingled with other risk factors. For example, as mentioned earlier, some risk factors such as chronic health problems can increase financial strain (Brown et al., 2008). Concurrently, the presence of financial strain seems to enhance the negative effects of other risk factors (Holmes & Deb, 2003). Assessing for financial strain in the context of other risk factors thus is important for practitioners working with high-risk families.

Risk Exposure

Understanding that all families experience normative and non-normative stress, family theorists often discuss risk, not as a singular factor, but instead in relation to its cumulative effect on ongoing family functioning. In other words, at any one time, most families must manage challenges ranging from financial strain, job changes, relationship transitions such as children moving into adolescence, or a spouse leaving the workforce, to other challenges of the life cycle. At times, families also face adverse events such as health issues or unexpected traumatic loss. Family theorists have found that the effects of both normative and adverse experiences are increased by the number and degree of the stress that occur simultaneously. McCubbin and Patterson (1982) call this the "pile-up" factor to represent the idea that facing multiple stressors in close proximity increases the potential negative effects for the family.

When discussing level of risk as a familial-level construct, context becomes increasingly important. Consider the diagnosis of childhood cancer. This adverse event would represent a crisis state for any family. However, for a single father recently out of work and currently without health insurance, the potential negative effect is exacerbated considering the level of stress already placed on this system. Essentially, exposure to multiple risk factors increases a family's vulnerability to negative effects. Patterson (2002) asserts that a crisis leads to increased and potentially ongoing family distress when the demands exceed the capabilities and resources. As practitioners work with families coping with normative life changes and adverse life events, assessment should consider the cumulative effect of ongoing exposure to risk.

Protective Factors

Although risk-focused research has offered advances regarding identification of factors that predict poor outcomes, resilience research seeks to explain variability in functioning by considering the impact of both risk and protective factors. Protective factors are internal and external resources and capabilities that help children, adults, and families overcome adversity (Mandleco & Perry, 2000). Internal protective factors include personal traits such as humor or flexibility that are helpful as people cope with the difficulties in their lives. Benard (2004) classified internal protective factors found in previous child development literature into these categories: (a) sense of purpose, (b) problem solving, (c) autonomy, and (d) social skills. External protective factors, on the other hand, are the areas of support present in one's environment and include things like relationships with neighbors, friends, and faith organizations (Gilligan, 2004; Hartling, 2003). Despite early ideas suggesting resilience is an intrinsic personality trait and that some are hardier than others, current conceptualizations suggest that resilience represents the human capacity for growth and adaptation through the assistance of positive personal and relational influences (Benard, 2004; Hartling, 2003; Walsh, 2003).

When looking at resilience as a familial-level construct, researchers have identified some common protective factors found to foster family resilience, including: *Appraisal* or the meaning families attach to the difficulties they face; *Spirituality* or a belief system that provides comfort, meaning, and direction; *Communication* about the difficulties the family is facing; and *Flexibility* as exhibited by the family's ability to adapt and find solutions to manage the adversities faced (Allison et al., 2003; Defrain & Asay, 2007; Lietz, 2007; Patterson, 2002; Thomas, Chenot, & Reifel, 2005; Walsh, 2003). Researchers also have found reliance on a positive *social support* network through friends and family or through professional resources to be an important factor influencing resilience (Allison et al., 2003; Lietz et al., 2011). The following section provides a synthesis of four research studies that include in-depth qualitative interviews with families who rated high on risk, but who maintained and strengthened family functioning over time. Some material (in particular, the use of the qualitative quotes) is adapted from the articles describing these studies (Lietz, 2007, 2011; Lietz & Hodge, 2011; Lietz et al., 2011; Lietz & Strength, 2011). These stories of successful coping and adaptation highlight ten factors families identified as protective when dealing with adversity. Implications for clinical practice with high-risk families also are discussed.

A Typology of Family Resilience

The process of family resilience may be described by means of a typology that was developed from a set of in-depth qualitative interviews with families who were identified as being at high risk for family discord or dissolution. The first study identified a sample of families who experienced a series of risk factors yet simultaneously rated within the healthy range on a standardized measurement of family functioning (Lietz, 2006, 2007). This study led to the development of a typology (Fig. 10.1) that includes five phases and a set of protective factors (family strengths) that participants described when sharing their stories of resilience.

   To build upon this conceptualization, a second study was conducted that examined this process of family resilience in the context of child welfare (Lietz & Strength, 2011). Specifically, families whose children were removed due to being identified as high risk for child maltreatment, and who achieved successful family reunification, were interviewed. These stories of resilience affirmed the conceptualization of the process of resilience and uncovered an additional family strength that was incorporated into the typology. Although the situations faced by the families in the first study were quite different than those of the families involved with the child welfare system, the degree of consistency between their stories when referencing family strengths was striking. In other words, as seen in the following descriptions, similar family strengths were referenced despite the differences in the challenges faced. A third study was conducted using qualitative secondary data analysis to examine the strengths *social support* and *spirituality* in greater depth due to the salience of these particular family strengths in the child welfare study (Lietz & Hodge, 2011; Lietz et al., 2011). Finally, a fourth study looked specifically at the phase of *helping others* and explored the ways some resilient families engaged in pro-social behaviors (Lietz, 2011). This study offers additional detail to the typology around the benefits of such activities. The findings from these studies are synthesized in the following section to describe how ten family strengths (Table 10.1) were helpful to families facing high risk in different ways at different times.

Family Resilience: A Process

The families who participated in these studies were at high risk for family discord and/or dissolution due to the cumulative effect of facing multiple risk factors. Specifically, these families experienced a variety of risk factors ranging from poverty or other financial strain, chronic or terminal health disorders, substance abuse, raising children with developmental delays or other special needs, caregiving for elderly parents, and growing up in unhealthy family situations. Yet, despite their adversity, these families were able to cope with the difficulties faced such that they maintained and ultimately enhanced the functioning of their family unit. Similar to other conceptualizations (Hawley, 2000; Luthar et al., 2000),

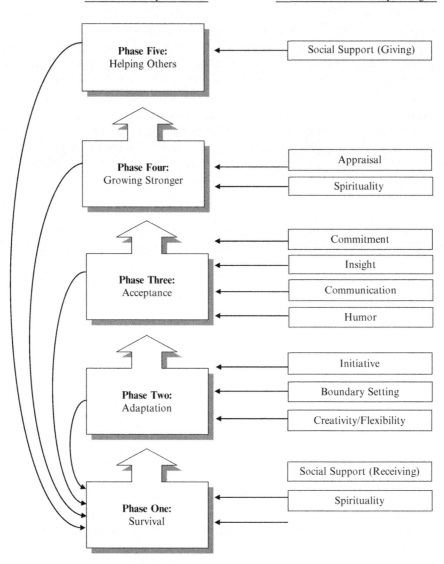

Phases of Family Resilience   Protective Factors/Family Strengths

Fig. 10.1 The process of family resilience (Lietz & Strength, 2011). Adapted with permission from *Families in Society* (FamiliesInSociety.org), a publication of the Alliance for Children and Families

Table 10.1 Family strengths

Appraisal	Finding meaning in the difficulties families face
Boundary setting	The ability and willingness to separate the family system from influences that are unhealthy
Communication	Verbal and nonverbal expressions of thoughts and feelings regarding the crisis
Commitment	A strong desire to keep the family together and strong
Creativity/flexibility	The ability to find multiple solutions to a problem and the willingness to try new things
Humor	The ability to be light-hearted despite the challenges a family faces
Insight	The ability to gain understanding into a family's difficulty
Initiative	The ability and willingness to take action meeting family needs
Spirituality	A belief system that provides direction and strength to the family
Social support	Giving and receiving emotional and practical help in the context of relationships with family, friends, and service providers

Adapted with permission from *Families in Society* (FamiliesInSociety.org), a publication of the Alliance for Children and Families (Lietz & Strength, 2011)

when discussing their stories of successful adaptation, these families describe resilience as a process. Coping and adaptation do not occur in a time-limited fashion but instead grow while responding to new needs and challenges that arise.

As a result of the process-oriented nature of family resilience, many families described both their struggles and the strengths that helped them to cope effectively in narrative format. These stories represent a history-taking of the events of their lives within their context that better depict the meaning families attach to their experiences. Indeed, as researchers and clinicians listen to stories of family resilience, paying close attention to the ways characters and events are situated within in-depth descriptions can offer important clues regarding what families find helpful when seeking to overcome adversity. These stories also help to illuminate a progression, demonstrating that their needs and the corresponding protective factors change over time and offering important implications for clinical practice.

When families who participated in these studies talked about stress and coping, they identified ten family strengths that were important in different ways at different times. These ideas are conceptualized into a series of five phases as depicted in Fig. 10.1. These phases included: (a) *Survival*, a time at which families were taking 1 day at a time trying to figure out how to keep their family going; (b) *Adaptation*, which included the changes that the families made in order to incorporate their new situation into their lives; (c) *Acceptance*, which was a time at which families recall coming to adopt the new situation as their new way of life; (d) *Growing Stronger*, the moments families recognized that their unit was growing stronger as a result of the difficulties faced; and (e) *Helping Others*, described as a need for families to help others as a result of overcoming adversity.

It is important to note that the use of the term "phase" does not mean that families must progress through these moments in a linear fashion. The arrows on the side of the figure represent the idea that as families progress, they are commonly thrown back into earlier phases as new crises occur. Additionally, there is not an assumption that all families start in the same place. Instead, the presentation of phases and the corresponding family strengths help to emphasize how coping and adaptation developed for these families over time.

Phase 1: Survival

The survival phase represents a point in time when families discussed just trying to make it through each day. Many families explained that before making adaptations to their family life or even coming to accept an adverse event (often occurring in the context of multiple other normative and non-normative life stressors), they simply had to figure out how to survive. The family strengths cited as most important during this time frame included spirituality and social support.

Spirituality. Many view spirituality as an individual's existential relationship with God or the Transcendent (Gallup & Jones, 2000; Gilbert, 2000). Religion, on the other hand, represents an expression of the spiritual relationship developed in community with others who share similar experiences of a transcendent reality (Canda & Furman, 1999; Derezotes, 2006; Hodge, 2005). Therefore, religious practices are encompassed within the larger construct of spirituality. Many participants cited their family's spiritual and religious practices as highly important to their ability to cope with and find meaning in their struggles.

During the survival phase, many families asserted that the practice of prayer was an essential part of surviving during the initial days of a crisis. For example, one couple shared their story of successful child welfare reunification. They described in detail the day they were both incarcerated for drug possession. Speaking about this moment, the mother stated:

> Then while I was in jail, the CPS [Child Protective Services] lady comes to tell me I will never see my kids again, and I just fell apart. I remembered my grandmother told me that whenever you really need God in your life, to pray. And that's when I started praying. Everything felt a little lighter at that point, and I was like, well, we've got to move in the right direction now, rather than the one that I'd been on.

This mother described the moment she and her husband lost custody of their children as the most devastating event of their lives. This adverse event occurred in the context of multiple other risk factors including financial strain, substance addiction, and a recent relocation leading to isolation of this family. It was the adverse event of the removal that created a crisis state for this family that was already stressed to a great degree. In this story, both parents acknowledge a desperation that led to a decision to start praying again. As seen in this mother's narrative, she situated prayer just before the statement, "everything felt a little lighter at that point," suggesting that the strength of spirituality, through the practice of prayer, represented a transition in their process of family resilience. Their story culminated in a successful completion of the case plan, return of the children, and ultimately this family now provides training to foster parents and professionals regarding how to engage families involved with the child welfare system. The first transition in their story of resilience toward these successful outcomes is situated at this moment, "And that's when I started praying" suggesting prayer was appraised as highly important.

It is important to note that while the spiritual practice of prayer was important for many families during the survival phase, spirituality was important again for families during the growing stronger stage as beliefs support the important activity of meaning-making. Practitioners should understand that while meaning-making is important for families later, during the survival phase families are not yet ready to attach positive appraisals to difficult circumstances. For example, one family lost a child to SIDs. This family talked about feeling angered when people would make comments such as "at least your daughter is in heaven" within just weeks of her death. Later this family stated, "Knowing she is in heaven brings comfort." However, during the first weeks following their loss, this family leaned on prayer, but did not look to spirituality for meaning-making or positive appraisal.

Spirituality has been identified as an important strength that is helpful for many families (DeFrain & Asay, 2007; Lietz & Hodge, 2011; Ungureanu & Sandberg, 2010; Walsh, 2007). While spiritual practices such as prayer and meaning-making are not applicable for all families, for those who identify as spiritual, offering an opportunity for culturally responsive practices such as these may be protective for high-risk families. To accomplish this, practitioners may want to consider conducting a spiritual assessment when working with a family in crisis to help identify whether the strength of spirituality may be relevant (Hodge, 2005). Once a spiritual identity is identified, offering services that are culturally responsive to the belief system would be indicated.[3]

Social support. Social support is generally recognized as an action or relationship that exerts some positive effect on a person or group of people. House (1981) identified four types of social support: affiliation or emotional support (a sense of belonging), instrumental support (a safe place for dialogue), informational support (practical aid), and appraisal (normalization and social comparison). When looking at a familial-level construct, families report both internal (support coming from within the family system) and external (support coming from outside the family system) sources as important. The importance of social support was expressed by families throughout their stories of family resilience. However, similar to spirituality, social support offered different benefits to families facing high-risk situations at different times. Later, during adaptation, the practical or tangible support was essential. However, during the survival phase, emotional support was critical.

External social support represents assistance coming from outside the family system and includes extended family, friends, support groups, and professionals. One mother discussed the value of support from her peers when she stated, "I have a really good support system through my friends. I think I wouldn't have been able to make the decisions I did without a solid support system." While friendships were important to some, others discussed social support from extended family such as the father who

---

[3] For more on this topic please see Chap. 25.

stated, "My parents live here in town, and they were very strong. They were adamant making sure everything works out right." Finally, support groups were important to many. The meaning of support groups was emphasized by one family who described the support group they began attending just 3 weeks after the death of their daughter. The father explained:

> I would definitely recommend getting into a support group of people who have been through it. Even with all our friends and family…when we looked at their eyes, and they looked back at us, it was hollow. They had no idea what in the hell we were talking about…The first time I showed up at this meeting and looked across the table, that guy, that girl, they knew exactly what I was talking about, because they had been through it. And that's when it changed for me.

In addition to external social support from extended family, friends, and support groups, families also reported receiving support from within the immediate family. One family discussed how they coped when their twins were born with serious, chronic medical problems. As the parents described the stress associated with the long-term caregiving of their twins, the father talked about the support he received from within the family:

> We've been fortunate to have some good friends and our [extended] families, but I really think that I've always looked into the family, my wife and even my kids. We've had some great bosses and friends that have really been helpful listening and stuff, but I guess when I hear significant, I think of a particular person that you can look at and say 'wow, that person really got me through this.' For me it's my family. For me it's my wife. We got each other through it.

Similarly, another couple talked about caregiving for their two children who were diagnosed with severe developmental delays. During the interview, the wife described the degree to which she leans on her spouse when she stated, "Oh goodness, I'm surprised he [her husband] doesn't have an eternal dent in his side from me. I am surprised he doesn't walk around with this concave side. I don't know what I would do without him."

When the idea of social support is discussed, there can be an assumption that social support comes from outside of the family as the members of the immediate family are all too stretched to support one another as they face a crisis. However, the families in this project were clear in saying that the primary support they received came from within their own families. Especially during the survival phase, these families reported that it was important that they looked within their own families for support in addition to seeking encouragement from outside the family.

These discussions offer important implications for practice. First, understanding that families appraise social support as highly critical to their successful coping and adaptation suggests that practitioners would do well to assess and build up the emotional and practical support provided to families. Strengths-based assessment (Early, 2001) that includes an evaluation of social support may be helpful in this regard (Dunst, Jenkins, & Trivette, 1984). The discussions by these families also emphasize the value of family services that lend professional support to families. Particularly when services were framed in the context of supportive therapeutic relationships, the external support provided was highly valued (Lietz et al., 2011). Additionally, as clinicians seek to build up external social support, it is also important to help family members look to one another for needed emotional support.

Phase 2: Adaptation

As families begin to move beyond the initial state of crisis as illustrated in the survival phase, they find quickly that they must make immediate changes to the way the family structures daily living. This phase of adaptation represents a time when such changes are made, even before a family truly may have come to accept the nature of their current circumstances. The family strengths discussed as most relevant during this time frame included initiative, flexibility/creativity, and boundary setting.

Initiative. The strength of initiative refers to a family's willingness to take charge and face a situation head on. Whether dealing with a medical problem, making funeral arrangements following a death, or responding to the crisis of child removal, families acknowledged the role their own initiative played within their stories of family resilience. For example, one family who faced traumatic bereavement spoke about the value of initiative. The father stated:

> My wife and I attacked it head on from the very beginning. We went to a support group immediately…With our children, if they want to talk about it, we talk about it. We don't hide anything from them. So, I think it was really important for us to deal with it immediately, head on, together.

Similarly, one family with three small children faced tremendous risk as the mother was battling cancer and the father was facing addiction to alcohol. The father talked about the importance of taking the initiative needed to make necessary changes. He stated:

> I was pleading on their behalf, don't punish them for my mistake, please don't take the kids from her, it's not her fault, it's mine. I'll do whatever. At that time, the investigator said, "how about in-home or inpatient therapy?", and I said, "I'll do it." And that day I was on the horn and finding help and literally that week we were off and ready to check in.

Another mother talked about initiative when she described her response to the child welfare case plan. She stated, "I just worked—overworked the program. Everything they told me to do, I did and more. They told me to jump through a hoop, I jumped higher. I called them and asked, 'Is there anything else you want me to do? I want my babies back.'" This type of initiative was important to many of these families as they began to make the changes needed to move forward.

Boundary setting. Another family strength discussed during the adaptation phase was boundary setting. One mother who was in recovery for alcoholism felt she was making improved choices for her family because she was "learning to put up healthy boundaries." Boundary setting refers to a family's ability to separate from unhealthy influences. While social support was highly important to these families, staying away from family and friends who were not supportive of the family in making changes was also identified as critical. One couple who was caregiving for their twins with serious chronic health issues discussed how their stress led to marital conflict. The father stated, "The only time that our marriage was really pulled apart was when the stress was pushing us into relationships with other couples that had unhealthy marriages, and we just kind of began to mimic them, but we realized it really quickly." The wife continued by explaining, "We talked about it one day and realized together at the same time that that was unhealthy. That we needed to disengage from these relationships, and so we did." As families make adaptations in response to stress, it is critical that the changes prompt positive coping, rather than an increase in unhealthy behaviors.

Similarly, one single mother who faced addiction to methamphetamines discussed the need to make adaptation to her family's peer group as she sought recovery. When referring to her current friendships, she stated, "I can probably count them on one hand, but they are sober, and they're doing what they should be doing, and that's where I want to stay." Finally, one couple discussed how their history of drug addiction led to extensive marital conflict, financial difficulties, and problems in their parenting. As they talked about making changes, the wife stated, "There's a lot of stuff that doesn't happen that used to happen just because we're not making stupid choices." Making healthy choices and separating from unhealthy influences allowed several of the families to make positive adaptations during their progression toward family resilience.

Creativity/flexibility. Creativity refers to the ability to find multiple solutions to a problem while flexibility is the willingness to try new things. According to Olson (2000), healthy family functioning requires a balance of both stability and flexibility in order to achieve the comfort that comes from predictability along with the ability to remain responsive to life changes. Working in conjunction with the family strengths initiative and boundary setting, creativity and flexibility help families facing adverse events respond to the needs created by adversity.

One mother who was in treatment for substance addiction shared a story regarding one way that she coped with loneliness while her child was placed in foster care. She stated:

> One thing I found helpful, when I would get the urge [to abuse drugs], when I would get triggers being alone, I would literally jump on the bus and ride around for hours. See, when you are by yourself, that's a trigger, and having all these people around me helped.

This mother was able to complete her program and make the changes necessary to be reunited with her daughter. This creative solution was situated in her story of resilience, representing an important transition that she felt contributed to her successful adaptation.

Similarly, one couple described a time when the family was caregiving for two elderly parents in the home, one diagnosed with Alzheimer's disease, while also facing a variety of other stressors. The wife talked about the strain on their marital relationship. She explained:

> I know something, it's very personal but…I was very self-conscious as far as having sex, because our parents were living here. You know, they're sleeping in the room next to you, and you feel very uncomfortable. And I can remember going home, and we still had his mother's apartment, so we would tell the kids we were going to the grocery store, and we would go over to his mother's apartment [Laughing].

In this story, the wife described this creative solution that she and her husband found to be able to achieve the privacy that was important for their relationship while still caring for their parents. Families are often required to make both immediate and long-term adaptations to the ways they function in response to many adverse events such as medical diagnoses, traumatic bereavement, and separations. Simon et al. (2005) advocate a "resilience-driven" approach that seeks to discover the family's interests, successes, and coping strategies. As practitioners work with families facing these stressors, identifying and fostering family strengths such as initiative, boundary setting, and creativity/flexibility may help families to make the necessary changes.

Phase 3: Acceptance

Once the families survived the initial crisis and began to make necessary adaptations, they discussed the importance of accepting the adversity, learning to adopt these difficulties as part of their new family life. When discussing how to accept their challenges, they identified four family strengths within their stories of family resilience. These included commitment, insight, communication, and humor.

Commitment. Family commitment refers to a powerful desire to keep the family together. Silberberg (2001) asserts that commitment "is showing dedication and loyalty toward the family as a whole. Strong families often view the well-being of the family as a first priority" (p. 54). As the families came to accept their current circumstances, facing their new reality was challenging for many. However, the family strength of commitment facilitated the units' willingness to move forward despite their difficulties. Speaking of commitment, one mother stated, "Our only focus in life was to get our kids back," while a father stated, "I'll do whatever I need to do to make this right." One mother talked about how important it was to remain focused on her five children as she sought treatment for her drug addiction. She stated, "It was my babies. I needed them back. I wasn't about to let them go to the state." Similarly, the single father who struggled with depression talked about his commitment to his two children. He stated, "My kids mean everything to me. I gotta do what I gotta do for them. That was my main focus. My kids come first no matter what."

These quotes illustrate the powerful role that commitment to family played in these stories of successful child welfare reunification. As clinicians work with families facing adversity, identifying and fostering commitment to the family unit may be particularly indicated. Activities that encourage families to discuss shared memories and articulate the family's unique identity help to establish boundaries around the family system that enhance levels of connectedness. Facilitating internal social support so that family members seek encouragement and tangible support from one another to foster levels of connection and commitment may represent additional interventions with at-risk families.

Insight. Insight refers to a family's ability to gain understanding of the problems they face. In many of these stories of family resilience, insight was situated as an element suggestive of a transition in the story.

One mother's transition from survival and adaptation to acceptance was apparent when she stated, "I started to be a mother more after I stopped doing drugs. And I realized I'm happier just being sober." Initially, this mother acknowledged that she engaged in substance abuse treatment because it was required in her case plan. However, once she started making progress, she developed new insight that allowed her to see the positive impact of recovery.

One mother talked about the insight received through her counseling. Although she acknowledged an initial resistance to receiving feedback, she came to accept the help. She explained, "Even though what she [the practitioner] said to me I didn't feel like hearing, it made me realize, I need to do this, I know what's right, and I need to do what's right." The insight gained through professional services allowed this mother to accept the idea that she needed to make changes within the family. Similarly, the family who lost their baby to SIDS also discussed how insight helped them to achieve acceptance. The father described this moment:

> I think just one day, I just talked to myself and realized that I had done everything that I could do. I was the best dad that I could be, and there was nothing I could have done about it. And, by being ready to let go, doesn't mean I've forgotten about her or that I don't love her. It just means that I am ready to move on.

The insight described by families accomplished two things. First, it demonstrated a progression toward acceptance. In addition, this insight was instrumental in helping these parents move forward, demonstrating the process of resilience. These discussions lend support to the value of clinical work with at-risk families. Counseling services can help to foster insight needed to help families develop new perspectives when coping with loss, trauma, and other high-risk situations.

Communication. As the families discussed accepting their situation, they identified communication as a family strength that helped them to achieve acceptance while also demonstrating that acceptance was indeed happening. Patterson (2002) suggests there are two types of family communication, affective and instrumental. Affective communication includes expressions of love, care, and concern and is essential for fostering a sense of family cohesion. Instrumental communication represents the patterns used to accomplish necessary tasks such as role assignment and rule setting. A family's ability to communicate care and concern effectively while accomplishing needed tasks is especially important as families face a crisis. One of the single mothers in the study said, "We communicate a lot. We are communicating, and we're getting along, and you can just feel it, just the energy in the house, you can tell when things are going good." Similarly, one of the children who participated in the family interviews was asked, what helps your family deal with problems? This 8 year old responded, "Well, we just like try to stop making the problem get worse, like by talking about it. We talk about the problems."

Many of these families talked about how increased communication helped them to accept what they were facing. The narrative tradition suggests that language is important in the construction of a family's story (White & Epston, 1990). As families use language to define their struggles, this acknowledgement fosters acceptance. Concurrently, as families speak about their problems, this communication also demonstrates that acceptance is happening. Again, these discussions support the potential benefits of clinical work with families such as these. Family therapy can offer a forum that creates space for families to find the words and courage to speak about the challenges they face.

Humor. The family strength humor refers to a family's ability to be light-hearted in the face of adversity. In these family narratives, humor was discussed as something that helped them come to accept their difficulties. Similar to communication, it also was a sign that acceptance was happening. It seemed that once families were able to make light of their situations, this activity eased their pain while also demonstrating that they were beginning to accept what they were facing. A father raising two sons with special needs stated, "If you don't have the humor in the family, then it's just too much. You need something to break the stress." His wife followed, asserting, "And it's too serious, the things that we deal with on a daily basis are very serious, and we have to find the silly things that get us through."

Similarly, the couple who cared for two elderly parents despite the wife's physical disability talked about what helped. The wife stated, "Sense of humor is probably one. I think that's helped us get through a lot of things. I mean really, it can relieve tension. I think a sense of humor is really helpful."

One family was caregiving for an elderly parent when their son was diagnosed with cancer. The father shared the following story regarding his father's stroke, and how he and his father used humor to begin to discuss and to accept the physical consequences of the stroke. Previously, the grandfather had cut his adult son's hair for many years. After the stroke, this changed, and the father used this exchange to demonstrate acceptance:

> He had his stroke, and he was paralyzed on his left side, and I went and got a haircut from somebody else, and I just said, "Dad, I'm sorry," I said, "I can't just go to a one armed barber anymore," and he laughed. He thought that was funny. We thought that was kind of funny, and I said, "now don't get jealous now [that] I've found another barber."

As professionals work with families facing adversity, it may be important to know that some families find humor helpful. This does not suggest that practitioners make light of difficulties. It is critical that families appraise the meanings attached to their difficulties and that they are given the ability to take the lead regarding light-heartedness. Clinicians can create space in sessions for humor while being cautious to speak about family difficulties with the utmost respect.

Phase 4: Growing Stronger

As families move past survival, early adaptations, and acceptance, the process of family resilience suggests that progress continues at a new level. Growing stronger represents a time during which families recognize and experience reinforcement for the changes they have made thus far.

Appraisal. The family strength most apparent during the growing stronger phase was appraisal, the meaning families attach to their experiences. Patterson (2002) asserts, "the meaning-making process is a critical component of family resilience, especially when the significant stress is due to adversity or trauma" (p. 244). When families experience loss and difficulty, yet find meaning in it, they seem better able to avoid the negative consequences typically associated with high-risk situations. For example, one mother described how she now views the incarceration of herself and her husband just before the holidays. She explained, "I just looked at it as a positive thing. This is what we needed. The best Christmas present I ever got was being in jail." Similarly, the father who struggled with alcoholism appraised his CPS involvement this way: "So, ultimately, yes, this was the most important thing to happen to me. I needed CPS to come in. As hard as it was to swallow, it had to happen, because it changed my life." Finally, the mother who faced homelessness and addiction stated:

> If it wasn't for CPS, I wouldn't be where I am now. I think I would still be stuck on drugs, because I was heavy into it. I now feel in my heart I've learned a lot and changed a lot, and I'm a different person now. So, it happened for a reason, that's what I believe.

These comments demonstrate the positive appraisals families attached to their child welfare involvement. At the same time, it is important to note that these families did not always see it this way. During the survival and even the adaptation phases, these families identified being angry, and most talked about "fighting" or "resisting" the child welfare case plan. However, family resilience is a process. Growing stronger is seen as families move from their initial anger and fear, to acceptance, and ultimately to a place where they appraise the situation positively, seeing a purpose in what they have faced.

Phase 5: Helping Others

As families appraised their difficulties in a positive way, many expressed reaching a moment at which they desired to help others, often seeking to reach out to other families who were facing struggles similar to their own. Some suggest that altruistic pro-social behaviors help families to find meaning in adversity (Lietz, 2011; Mandleco & Perry, 2000; Patterson, 2002). In other words, families described their participation in several pro-social behaviors as an effort to assist others while also helping themselves. Specifically, some participants provided public speaking or trainings to raise awareness about a social issue while others led support groups or volunteered for nonprofit organizations. Furthermore, some of the families engaged in fundraising for social causes or created foundations to honor a lost loved one. For example, one family was caring for a child diagnosed with developmental delays when they lost their third child to stillbirth. This family now provides support to other grieving parents through their participation in a nonprofit organization, a way of bringing meaning to their loss. Another mother's narrative described how her young son was killed in a violent crime. As this mother and her family sought to overcome the pain of this loss, they created a foundation in his name that fundraises for funeral costs for low income parents whose children die. Finally, one family who cares for their children who are affected by ongoing, serious health issues provides education to other parents through their website and speaking events about how to advocate for children within the healthcare system.

Giving social support. Social support was identified as the family strength associated with this phase. However, during this phase, social support was not about receiving, but instead represented the meaning families attached to the experience of *giving* social support. One couple was asked to speak at child welfare trainings regarding their experiences. Speaking about helping others, the father started by saying, "We want to be a part of something to try and give back somehow. And it helps us." The wife continued, "Maybe it'll help someone, maybe we're here to help someone." The couple raising children with severe developmental delays wrote a book to educate other parents about working within the educational system. When referencing this choice, the mother stated, "I can handle what I have went through, and I can accept what I went through, if I can pass that along and help somebody else." These stories of helping others illustrate how the process of resilience grows from the survival stage during which families are desperate to receive social support to a place of helping others in which it becomes their turn to give back.

Understanding that helping others may be protective for families facing adversity offers important implications for practice. As Simon et al. (2005) suggest, "a major goal of treatment is to encourage families to recognize and utilize their inherent capacity for growth and change" (p. 432). A strengths-based assessment may ask specifically about altruistic intention and behaviors as a strength that can help families positively appraise the difficulties they face. Social service organizations also may consider creating interventions that foster opportunities for helping. Although the findings of these studies do not suggest that all families will benefit from this practice, offering opportunities to help others may be beneficial for some high-risk families.

Clinical Implications

These findings offer important implications for clinical practice with families facing high-risk situations. First, practitioners should understand the importance of balancing their focus on risk with the identification and building of family strengths. While risk modeling helps to explain a family's vulnerability for discord and dissolution, many families sustain and even improve functioning despite exposure to both normative and non-normative risk factors. While the effects are cumulative and families experiencing multiple risk factors in a short period of time are at greater risk for poor functioning, the findings demonstrate that family strengths can help many families to overcome the negative effects of adversity. Remaining mindful of a resilience perspective may lead practitioners to adjust their approach when working with families facing high risk.

As practitioners adopt a family resilience perspective that integrates the effects of risk and protection in clinical work, findings also suggest they view resilience as a process that develops over time.

Being sensitized to the process-oriented nature of resilience can help practitioners to understand that families need different things at different times. In the time period during and just following an adverse event, families may not yet be ready for positively appraising loss or trauma. However, later on, meaning-making may be highly important to moving forward. Practitioners should assess risk and protection while remaining mindful that the timing of the intervention is as important as the activity attached to a particular intervention. Remaining aware and responsive to client preferences represents an essential part of a family resilience framework.

The process of resilience as described in the typology highlights the process-oriented nature of family resilience while identifying ten strengths families identified as helpful. Although strengths assessment should involve narrative interviewing that allows additional strengths to be uncovered, knowing these specific strengths were helpful for our sample of families may be relevant for others. Having an awareness of these particular strengths may help practitioners to become more sensitized to the ways these strengths are helpful, allowing clinicians to more easily identify and build such capacities with the families with whom they work. In addition, conducting a strengths assessment such that the family's strengths can be incorporated throughout the counseling is indicated per these findings.

Finally, a striking finding from our research was the conceptualization of social support as being something that stems from both within and outside of the family system, that involves both giving and receiving. The idea that social support is helpful remains pervasive within many areas of practice. This typology highlights the idea that while support from extended family, faith organizations, and one's community is helpful, support from within that family is also highly valued. Furthermore, while families lean on social support during their most desperate of times, these families also spoke about the benefits of providing social support through altruistic pro-social behaviors that simultaneously helped others while helping themselves. Such findings suggest that practitioners would do well to seek opportunities for giving and receiving social support within and outside of the family unit.

Research Implications

Further research is needed that continues to examine the protective factors families identify as helpful for healthy adaptation and coping when facing high-risk situations. Although the studies synthesized in this chapter offer important implications for clinical practice, more research is needed to explore family resilience in the context of various life stressors beyond the scope of these current studies. For example, despite a dramatic increase in the number of women deployed by the U.S. military in the recent OIF/OEF missions (Department of Defense, 2007), more research is needed that explores family reintegration when the member of the family who is returning is a woman (Manos, 2010). Ongoing research is needed that examines emerging areas such as these from a family resilience standpoint.

Furthermore, little work has been done that tests the effectiveness of adopting a resilience perspective within family practice. Although extensive research informs practice by identifying the strengths families discuss as helpful, more studies are needed that would conceptualize these research findings into a specified model of clinical practice that can be implemented with adherence to these practice principles and then tested regarding the model's impact on outcomes. One limitation of strengths-based practice is the need for more empirical work that evaluates its effectiveness (Lietz, 2009). As leaders within various helping professions advocate incorporating the best available evidence when making clinical decisions as a critical part of evidence-based decision making (Thyer & Myers, 2011), further implementation and testing of these findings would help to move the field forward in this area.

Conclusion

The concept of resilience is increasingly being applied as a familial-level construct. Understanding the risk factors that challenge family functioning and the protective factors or family strengths that support healthy coping is important for practitioners working in family practice. In this chapter, a set of risk factors that predict family break-up and discord was identified. When possible, prevention efforts should seek to avoid these negative impacts. However, when risks are unavoidable or already present, family practitioners can engage in the intervention of strength identification and building to support families in healthy coping and adaptation. The process of resilience highlights ten strengths that can help families in varied ways at different times to cope with risks or even improve functioning despite the challenges faced. Although further research is needed to examine both the implementation and outcomes of taking a resilience approach with high-risk families, these stories of resilience offer important implications for clinical practice with families facing high-risk situations.

References

Allison, S., Stacy, K., Dadds, V., Roeger, L., Wood, A., & Martin, G. (2003). What the family brings: Gathering evidence for strengths-based work. *Journal of Family Therapy, 25*, 263–284.

Benard, B. (2004). *Resiliency: What we have learned*. San Francisco, CA: WestEd.

Black, K., & Lobo, M. (2008). A conceptual review of family resilience factors. *Journal of Family Nursing, 14*, 33–55.

Brown, R., Wiener, L., Kupst, M., Brennan, T., Behran, R., Compas, B., et al. (2008). Single parents of children with chronic illness: An understudied phenomenon. *Journal of Pediatric Psychology, 33*(4), 408–421.

Cancian, M., Slack, K., & Yang, M. (2010). *The effect of family income on risk of child maltreatment*. Madison, WI: Institute for Research on Poverty, University of Wisconsin-Madison.

Canda, E. R., & Furman, L. D. (1999). *Spiritual diversity in social work practice*. New York: The Free Press.

Chassin, L., Pitts, S., DeLucia, C., & Todd, M. (1999). A longitudinal study of children of alcoholics: Predicting young adult substance use disorders, anxiety, and depression. *Journal of Abnormal Psychology, 108*(1), 106–119.

Cozza, S. J., Chun, R. S., & Polo, J. A. (2005). Military families and children during operation Iraqi freedom. *Psychiatric Quarterly, 76*(4), 371–378.

Davies, R. (2004). New understandings of parental grief: Literature review. *Journal of Advanced Nursing, 46*(5), 506–513.

DeFrain, J., & Asay, S. (2007). *Strong families around the world: The family strengths perspective*. New York: Haworth Press.

DeFrain, J., Martens, L., Stork, J., & Stork, W. (1990). The psychological effects of a stillbirth on surviving family members. *Omega, 22*(2), 81–108.

Department of Defense. (2007). *Demographics 2007: Profile of the military community*. Washington, DC: Department of Defense.

Derezotes, D. S. (2006). *Spiritually oriented social work practice*. Boston: Pearson.

Drummet, A., Coleman, M., & Cable, S. (2003). Military families under stress: Implications for family life education. *Family Relations, 52*(3), 279–287.

Dunst, C. J., Jenkins, V., & Trivette, C. M. (1984). Family support scale: Reliability and validity. *Journal of Individual, Family, and Community Wellness, 1*(4), 45–52.

Early, T. (2001). Measures for practice with families from a strengths perspective. *Families in Society, 82*(2), 225–232.

Figley, C. (1998). *Burnout in families: The systemic costs of caring*. Boston: CRC Press.

Fletcher, P. (2002). Experiences in family bereavement. *Family & Community Health, 25*(1), 57–71.

Gallup, G. J., & Jones, T. (2000). *The next American spirituality: Finding God in the twenty-first century*. Colorado Springs: Victor.

Garmezy, N. (1993). Children in poverty: Resilience despite risk. *Psychiatry, 56*(1), 127–136.

Garmezy, N., Masten, A., & Tellegen, A. (1984). The study of stress and competence in children: A building block for developmental psychopathology. *Child Development, 55*, 97–111.

Gilbert, M. (2000). Spirituality in social work groups: Practitioners speak out. *Social Work with Groups, 22*(4), 67–84.

Gilligan, R. (2004). Promoting resilience in child and family social work: Issues for social work practice, education and policy. *Social Work Education, 23*(1), 93–104.

Hartling, L. (2003). Strengthening resilience in a risky world: It's all about relationships. *Women and Therapy, 31*, 51–70.

Hawley, D. (2000). Clinical implications of family resilience. *American Journal of Family Therapy, 28*, 101–116.

Hayden, L., Schiller, M., & Dickstein, S. (1998). Levels of family assessment I: Family, marital, and parent–child interaction. *Journal of Family Psychology, 12*, 7–22.

Herzer, M., Godiwala, N., Hommel, K., Driscoll, K., Mitchell, M., Crosby, L., et al. (2010). Family functioning in the context of pediatric chronic conditions. *Journal of Developmental and Behavioral Pediatrics, 31*(1), 26–34.

Hodge, D. R. (2005). Spiritual life maps: A client-centered pictorial instrument for spiritual assessment, planning, and intervention. *Social Work, 50*(1), 77–87.

Holmes, A., & Deb, P. (2003). The effect of chronic illness on the psychological health of family members. *The Journal of Mental Health Policy and Economics, 6*, 13–22.

House, J. S. (1981). *Work stress and social support*. Reading, MA: Addison-Wesley.

Kelley, M., Hock, E., Smith, K., Jarvis, M., Bonney, J., & Gaffney, M. (2001). Internalizing and externalizing behavior of children with enlisted Navy mothers experiencing military induced separation. *Journal of the American Academy of Child and Adolescent Psychiatry, 40*(4), 464–471.

Kilmer, R., & Gil-Rivas, V. (2010). Responding to the needs of children and families after a disaster: Linkages between unmet needs and caregiver functioning. *Journal of Orthopsychiatry, 80*(1), 135–142.

LaGrone, D. M. (1978). The military family syndrome. *The American Journal of Psychiatry, 135*, 1040–1043.

Lamberg, L. (2010). Redeployments strain military families. *Journal of the American Medical Association, 300*(6), 644.

Landau, J., & Saul, J. (2004). Facilitating family and community resilience in response to major disaster. In F. Walsh & M. McGoldrick (Eds.), *Living beyond loss* (pp. 285–309). New York: W.W. Norton & Company, Inc.

Lietz, C. A. (2006). Uncovering stories of family resilience: A mixed methods study of resilient families, part 1. *Families in Society, 87*(4), 575–582.

Lietz, C. A. (2007). Uncovering stories of family resilience: A mixed methods study of resilient families, part 2. *Families in Society, 88*(1), 147–155.

Lietz, C. (2009). Establishing evidence for strengths-based interventions? Reflections from social work's research conference. *Social Work, 54*(1), 85–87.

Lietz, C. A. (2011). Empathic action and family resilience: A narrative examination of the benefits of helping others. *Journal of Social Science Research, 37*(3), 254–265.

Lietz, C. A., & Hodge, D. R. (2011). Spirituality and child welfare reunification: A narrative analysis of successful outcomes. *Child and Family Social Work, 16*(4), 380–390. doi:10.1111/j.1365-2206.2010.00752.x.

Lietz, C. A., Lacasse, J. R., & Cacciatore, J. (2011). Social support in family reunification: A qualitative study. *Journal of Family Social Work, 14*(1), 3–20.

Lietz, C. A., & Strength, M. (2011). Stories of successful reunification: A narrative study of family resilience in child welfare. *Families in Society, 92*(2), 203–210.

Luthar, S. (1991). Vulnerability and resilience: A study of high-risk adolescents. *Child Development, 62*(3), 600–616.

Luthar, S., Cicchetti, D., & Becker, B. (2000). The construct of resilience: A critical evaluation and guidelines for future work. *Child Development, 71*(3), 543–562.

Mandleco, B., & Perry, C. (2000). An organization framework for conceptualizing resilience in children. *Journal of Child and Adolescent Psychiatric Nursing, 13*(3), 99–111.

Manos, G. (2010). War and the military family. *Journal of the American Academy of Child and Adolescent Psychiatry, 49*(4), 297–299.

Masten, A. S. (2001). Resilience processes in development. *American Psychologist, 56*, 227–238.

Masten, A. S., & Coatsworth, J. D. (1998). The development of competence in favorable and unfavorable environments. *American Psychologist, 53*(2), 205–220.

McCubbin, H., & Patterson, J. (1982). Family adaptation to crises. In H. McCubbin, A. Cauble, & J. Patterson (Eds.), *Family stress, coping and social support* (pp. 26–47). Springfield, IL: Thomas.

McCubbin, H. I., & McCubbin, M. A. (1996). *Family assessment: Resiliency, coping and adaptation: Inventories for research and practice*. Madison WI: University of Wisconsin Publishers.

McCubbin, M., Balling, K., Possin, P., Frierdich, S., & Bryne, B. (2002). Family resiliency in childhood cancer. *Family Relations, 51*(2), 103–111.

McLeland, K., Sutton, G., & Schum, W. (2008). Marital satisfaction before and after deployments associated with the global war on terror. *Psychological Reports, 103*, 836–844.

Midence, K. (1994). The effects of chronic illness on children and their families: An overview. *Genetic, Social, and General Psychology Monographs, 120*(3), 311–327.

Murphy, S., Johnson, C., Wu, L., Fan, J., & Lohan, J. (2003). Bereaved parents' outcomes 4 to 60 months after their children's deaths by accident, suicide, or homicide: A comparative study demonstrating differences. *Death Studies, 27*, 39–61.

Olson, D. (2000). Circumplex model of marital and family systems. *Journal of Family Therapy, 22*(2), 144–167.

Pai, A., Greenley, R., Lewandowski, A., Drotar, D., Youngstrom, E., & Peterson, C. (2007). Meta-analytic review of the influence of pediatric cancer on parent and family functioning. *Journal of Family Psychology, 21*(3), 407–415.

Palmer, C. (2008). A theory of risk and resilience factors in military families. *Military Psychology, 20*, 205–217.
Patterson, J. (2002). Understanding family resilience. *Journal of Clinical Psychology, 58*(3), 233–246.
Pfefferbaum, B., & North, C. (2008). Children and families in the context of disasters: Implications for preparedness and response. *Family Psychology, 24*(2), 6–10.
Rentz, E. D., Marshall, S. W., Loomis, D., Casteel, C., Martin, S. L., & Gibbs, D. A. (2007). Effect of deployment on the occurrence of child maltreatment in military and non-military families. *American Journal of Epidemiology, 165*(10), 1–8.
Rutter, M. (1987). Psychosocial resilience and protective mechanisms. *The American Journal of Orthopsychiatry, 57*(3), 316–331.
Rutter, M. (2000). Developmental psychopathology: Concepts and challenges. *Development and Psychopathology, 12*(3), 265–296.
Scwab, R. (1998). A child's death and divorce: Dispelling the myth. *Death Studies, 22*, 445–468.
Silberberg, S. (2001). Searching for family resilience. *Family Matters, 58*, 52–57.
Simon, J., Murphy, J., & Smith, S. (2005). Understanding and fostering family resilience. *The Family Journal, 13*, 427–435.
Song, J., Floyd, F., Seltzer, M., Greenberg, J., & Hong, J. (2010). Long-term effects of child death on parents' health-related quality of life: A dyadic analysis. *Family Relations, 59*, 269–282.
Thomas, M., Chenot, D., & Reifel, B. (2005). A resilience-based model of reunification and reentry: Implications for out-of-home care services. *Families in Society, 86*(2), 235–243.
Thyer, B. A., & Myers, L. L. (2011). A quest for evidence-based practice: A view from the United States. *Journal of Social Work, 11*(1), 8–25.
Ungureanu, I., & Sandberg, J. (2010). "Broken together": Spirituality and religion as coping strategies for couples dealing with the death of a child: A literature review with clinical implications. *Contemporary Family Therapy, 32*, 302–319.
Wadsworth, M., & Santiago, C. (2008). Risk and resiliency processes in ethnically diverse families in poverty. *Journal of Family Psychology, 22*(3), 399–410.
Walsh, F. (2003). Family resilience: A framework for clinical practice. *Family Process, 42*(1), 1–18.
Walsh, F. (2007). Traumatic loss and major disasters: Strengthening family and community practice. *Family Process, 46*(2), 207–227.
Werner, E., & Smith, R. (1982). *Vulnerable, but invincible: A longitudinal study of resilient children and youth*. New York: McGraw-Hill.
Werner, E., & Smith, R. (2001). *Journeys from childhood to midlife: Risk, resiliency, and recovery*. Ithaca, NY: Cornell University Press.
White, M., & Epston, D. (1990). *Narrative means to therapeutic ends*. New York: W. W. Norton.
Wolin, S., & Wolin, S. (1993). *The resilient self: How survivors of troubled families rise above adversity*. New York: Villard.

Part III

Resilience and Ethnicity

Resilience in Ethnic Family Systems: A Relational Theory for Research and Practice

11

Laurie D. McCubbin and Hamilton I. McCubbin

Introduction

Theory building and research on resilient family systems has evolved over time, beginning with family stress theory focused on factors that protected the family system from entering into a crisis. With the addition of the postcrisis recovery processes of adjustment and adaptation, the foundation of family resilience theory was established (for an overview of over 2 decades (1976–2003) of family systems theory building and research see Hansen and Johnson (1979), McCubbin and McCubbin (1996a, 1996b), Patterson (1988, 2002), and Walsh (1996, 2002, 2003)). With the rapid development of psychological theories and research on resilient children and adults, family scholars drew from these theories and research methods to advance their own body of work on ethnic family systems and their resilience. Research on ethnic family systems followed along the psychology-guided pathway with the inclusion of dimensions of ethnicity as categorical variables inserted in the equation to explain variability in the chosen indices of resilience. Consequently, the in-depth study of ethnicity in family systems and the advancement of a systems theory of resilience have been limited.

The study of resilience in ethnic minority family systems continued to evolve as reflected in a three volume Sage book series: *Stress, Coping and Health in Families* (McCubbin, Thompson, Thompson, & Fromer, 1998a); *Resiliency in Ethnic Minority Families: Native and Immigrant Families* (McCubbin, Thompson, Thompson, & Fromer, 1998b), and *Resiliency in Ethnic Minority Families: African American Families* (McCubbin, Thompson, Thompson, & Futrell, 1998). These volumes, consisting of 37 chapters, were intended to foster this line of research and particularly to improve upon our identification and understanding of protective and recovery factors and processes related to ethnic

This publication was written as part of The Berry Fellowship awarded to the senior author by Washington State University, Pullman, Washington.

L.D. McCubbin (✉)
College of Education, Department of Educational Leadership and Counseling Psychology, Washington State University, Pullman, WA, USA
e-mail: mccubbin@wsu.edu

H.I. McCubbin
College of Education, Department of Educational Leadership and Counseling Psychology, Washington State University, Pullman, WA, USA

Myron B. Thompson School of Social Work, University of Hawaii at Manoa, Honolulu, HI, USA

D.S. Becvar (ed.), *Handbook of Family Resilience*,
DOI 10.1007/978-1-4614-3917-2_11, © Springer Science+Business Media New York 2013

family systems. While affirming the value of understanding ethnic family systems, these studies also revealed the limitations of the then current theories and research methodologies when applied to ethnic family systems. At one end of the spectrum of limitations was the dependence upon stereotypes to give meaning to the conceptualization, as well as the design, data collection, and interpretation of findings. At the other extreme were a dependence on Western and white middle class measures and a conspicuous absence of metrics grounded in the ethnic and cultural dynamics and processes of the populations being studied. In the middle of this continuum of weaknesses was the absence of constructs that reveal the dynamics of the ethnic family as a system embedded in a social and ecological context. Ethnic families in the US are, at a minimum, bicultural with indigenous ethnic and ancestral origins engaged (by forced immigration, migration and/or colonization) in survival and adaptation in a context that has its own schema of norms, expectations, beliefs, values, and traditions. It is our intention in this chapter to address these and other conundrums by introducing a Relational and Resilience Theory of Ethnic Family Systems (R&RTEFS).

Conundrums of Theory Development and Research on Resilience in Ethnic Family Systems

The study of ethnic family systems and the cultivation of theories to explain their resilience are accompanied by both challenges and opportunities that demand attention:

- First is the acknowledgement that ethnicity and culture within a family system have depth and meaning and are more than census-defined categorical variables (Asians, Polynesians, Native Americans, Hispanics, and African-Americans) to which stereotypes are attached
- Secondly, ethnic family systems have schemas or identities (values, beliefs, practices, and expectations) to guide their functioning and to which the family attaches meaning
- Third, ethnic family systems transform themselves and the ecological context in which they reside in response to the demands of the majority and dominant culture as well as normative and non-normative life events
- Fourth, ethnic family systems continue to increase in numbers and define themselves as being of bicultural or of mixed ethnic ancestries and thus challenge current assumptions about the perception of their homogeneity
- Fifth, families operate as systems in an ecological context with interdependent dimensions (e.g., schema or identity, patterns of functioning (POF), indices of system well-being) with a change in one dimension having reverberations and impact on other dimensions of the family system
- Sixth, family resilience involves processes of continuous adjustment, crisis management, and adaptation over time
- Seventh, the index of family systems' resilience is more than the physical and psychological well-being of individual members

Historical Foundation of Resilience in Ethnic Families

Inductive theory development (the concepts and propositions and the resulting framework evolve from research data, preferably from the populations to whom the theories are expected to be generalized) to explain the variability in the resilience in ethnic minority families in the US is rooted in the history of family stress research dating back to the 1930s. These beginnings have been traced, in part, to sociological research on families facing financial upheaval (Angell, 1936), war-induced

(World War II) separations (Hill, 1949, 1958), and prolonged war-induced (Vietnam) family separations of American prisoners of war and those missing in action (McCubbin, Dahl, Metres, Hunter, & Plag, 1975). Focused on family stress and coping and based on predominantly white middle class families, conceptual frameworks more often were referred to through acronyms such as ABCX—stressor (a), resources (b), appraisal (c), and crisis (x) (Hill, 1949); Double ABCX (McCubbin & Patterson, 1983)—post crisis factors—pile up (aa) resources and coping (bb), contextual appraisal (cc), and adaptation (xx); T-DOUBLE ABCX-typologies of family strengths and resources (McCubbin, 1988, 1990; McCubbin & McCubbin, 1988); FAAR (processes of adjustment and adaptation; McCubbin & Patterson, 1983; Patterson, 1988); and RMFAA (resilience processes of adjustment crisis transition and adaptation with an emphasis on schema and relational well-being [RWB]) (Marsella, Oliveira, Plummer, & Crabbe, 1998; McCubbin, Kehl, Strom, & McCubbin, 2010b; McCubbin, McCubbin, & Thompson, 1998). These frameworks have been applied to the study of family disruption and documentation of the variability in life changes, marital relationships, parent–child relationships, siblings, adolescents, rural families, military families, and to the study of family development and health problems over the life cycle and in rural families (see for example, Burr, 1973; Conger & Conger, 2002; Kosciulek, McCubbin, & McCubbin, 1993; McCubbin & McCubbin, 1996a, 1996b; McCubbin & Patterson, 1983; Olson, McCubbin, Larson, Barnes, & Muxem, 1983; Patterson, 1988).

With appropriate recognition of this body of work, built predominantly on white, middle class family systems, there remains a paucity of resilience-focused research and theory building on ethnic family systems. In the current context, this deficit may be linked to two discernable barriers. The first is the dominance of psychological research, theories, concepts, and measures of resilience focused on children (Garmezy, 1991), and the assumption that family systems are being studied when dyads (e.g., mother–child, father–child, sibling–child, mother–father) are emphasized (Luthar, Cicchetti, & Bronwyn, 2000). The survival of the family system operating as a unit has received limited attention in the study of resilience-oriented research. Secondly, theory building based on longitudinal research focused on the transformation of and system change in ethnic family systems as part of resilience has remained relatively uncharted (Werner, 1993, 2010; Werner & Smith, 1992).

The Evolving Paradigm of Resilience in Ethnic Family Systems

The Western European conceptualizations of risk and protective factors were focused on children and their ability to overcome adversity. With this centrality of the child and the individual, the nuclear family was characterized and studied as an influential factor embedded in an ecological context of layers of external influences ranging from the extended family to the neighborhood, community, and society. The family system was conceptualized and examined as subunits (marital dyad, siblings, father–child, and mother–child relationships). Consequently, resilience research evolved around their influence on physical, psychological, and social development as well as the individual resilience of its members, particularly children.

The durability, resilience, and survival of the family system were acknowledged but placed on the "backburner" of scientific inquiry. Fortunately, in an era of social change, immigrations, ethnic diversity, and increases in the number of offspring of ethnic ancestry, the interest in research on what makes ethnic family systems resilient has persisted. As the population of the US continues to evolve, with a steady increase in the number of ethnic minorities, particularly Hispanics, Asians, Polynesians, as well as multiethnic family systems (U.S. Census Bureau, 2000, 2010), the demand for knowledge about these populations has increased accordingly.

The Ethnic Family System and Resilience

A sustained interest in the resilience of ethnic minority family systems brings the social, behavioral, and physical sciences face to face with both challenges and opportunities to advance research and theory building. However, the foundation to advance ethnic family systems research must first be laid. Such a foundation recognizes the following:

- The need to clarify the distinction between and use of the core concepts of race and ethnicity
- The need to acknowledge and clarify when family units being represented in the study are of a single, bi, or multiple race or ethnicity and what single/bi/multirace/ethnicities are involved
- The need to recognize the system implications (pattern of functioning, schema, well-being) in those family systems of bi- or multiethnic/racial ancestry and their vulnerabilities as well their protective and recovery factors involved in promoting resilience
- The need to identify, address, and respect the uniqueness as well as variability in race and ethnicity, and acknowledge the underlying identities, cultures, values, beliefs, traditions, and practices as integral and influential elements within the family system
- The need to move beyond the scientific dependence of "dummy" variable classifications of race/ethnicity and give meaning and depth to each ethnic group or race
- The need to define and operationalize variables and measures related to race/ethnicity that reveal the uniqueness as well as variability in cultures and ethnicities for application in family systems research
- The need to advance the development and use of race/ethnicity-based concepts, propositions, theories, and research paradigms to guide investigations of ethnic populations, particularly family systems
- The need to reduce the scientific dependence on homogeneous ethnic stereotypes to guide the design, measures, constructs, and interpretation of race/ethnic data
- The need to advance the development and use of scientific research methodologies (e.g., involvement of ethnic families in the research process, decolonization) for systematic application in conducting research with these populations
- The need for scientists to acknowledge and address the depth and meaning of being "American" in the context of family research on racial/ethnic populations indigenous or immigrants to the US
- The need to recognize and understand that the development, influence, and change processes involved in a family's collective identity (culture(s), values, beliefs, expectations, and priorities) have an important role in determining and being influenced by the family's functioning and well-being
- The need to acknowledge and address the ever changing and evolving nature of racial/ethnic populations in the US and thus improve the knowledge base of social change and the processes of adaptation and transformation of these ethnic groups
- The need to recognize and incorporate the scientific, social, and theoretical significance of conceptualizing racial/ethnic minority families as responsive, proactive as change agents (acting as a single family and/or collectively as families) engaged in the change themselves as well as in the environment and social context as part of the resilience process

We conceptualize ethnic family systems as consisting of interdependent elements (individuals in family roles, agents of the family in the community), and as collectives with ancestral origins, POF, having a collective identity, and having responsibilities to maintain their commitment to the family and to harmonious relationships with the neighborhood, community, society, and the world. The family system is an evolving and changing entity as well as a respondent to structural and social (i.e., global, societal changes—social, legal, political, and economic) and cultural (i.e., traditions, values, beliefs, expectations) influences. The family system is also an actor or change agent in the adaptation and transformation processes of modifying the structure and identity of the family system. (Dubos, 1974; Papajohn & Spiegel, 1975; Spiegel, 1971, 1982). It is within this context of change, adaptation, and transformation that a R&RTEFS establishes its value.

Relational and Resilience Theory of Ethnic Family Systems

The R&RTEFS underscored in this chapter emerges from the authors' past and current history of empirical research, including meaningful observational experiences with ethnic minorities in the US, and particularly Hawaii, as well as with ethnic populations in Western and Eastern Europe, the Middle East (Israel, Kuwait, Qatar, Dubai, Abu Dhabi), New Zealand, and Asia (China, Okinawa, Hawaii, the Philippines). These experiences cultivated an awareness of the uniqueness and complexities of ethnic minority world-views, values, beliefs, identity, environment, and behaviors. The R&RTEFS addresses the following challenges:

- The limitations of a Western nuclear family perspective (ethnic diversity, cultures, meanings, and processes) when applied to ethnic family systems
- The value and applicability of culture-based theories, particularly indigenous theories, in explaining variability in family systems and their resilience
- The centrality of the family system, rather than the individual member, as a permeable entity encompassing the individual, the extended family (inclusive of individuals linked by ancestry and commitments), and its relationship to the neighborhood, community, society, and the world
- The inclusiveness, meaningfulness, and value of ancestors, past and present
- The importance of a sense of place and the meaning of land
- An emphasis on the congruence and alignment of the family systems' POF and the family schema (identity—incorporating culture and ethnicity and inclusive of values, beliefs, norms, and expectations)
- The importance of family RWB as a system-oriented criterion index of family system processes of adjustment and adaptation

The conceptual framework of the R&RTEFS traces its origins directly from the Resilience Model of Adjustment and Adaptation (McCubbin & McCubbin, 2005; McCubbin, McCubbin, Thompson, & Thompson, 1998) focused on ethnic family systems. The R&RTEFS places the family system (rather than the individual member) at the center of the ecological system (Bronfenbrenner & Ceci, 1994). As portrayed in Fig. 11.1, the family system has permeable if not fluid boundaries with meaningful relationships to its ancestral past and its respective values, beliefs, traditions, practices, and expectations. In the current context, the family system is proactive and has responsive relationships to changes at all levels (individual, neighborhood, community, society, and global) within the human ecology.

The conceptual framework is portrayed (see Fig. 11.1) as having three core and interacting elements, *family schema*, *family POF*, and *family* RWB, and involves the three core processes *of adjustment*, *crisis transition*, and *adaptation*. Before discussing these core processes it is important to introduce and discuss the three core and interacting elements of ethnic family systems involved in the three processes: *family schema* or identity, POF, and RWB.

Family Schema: Systems Identity

The concept of *family schema* (McCubbin, 2006; McCubbin & McCubbin, 2005) may be traced to the individual focused psychology literature on what Epstein (1973) and others (Rotter, 1954) refer to as psychologically constructed templates that provide expectations about the person and "allow individuals to act and respond with some confidence" (Tedeschi & Calhoun, 1995, p. 67). McCann and Pearlman (1990) referred to schema as a "frame of reference" comprised of attributions of causality and control as well as the munificence (trust, safety, and intimacy) of others (see also Bem, 1981; Fong & Markus, 1982; Taylor & Crocker, 1981). More pertinent to the current conceptualization of a family system's schema,

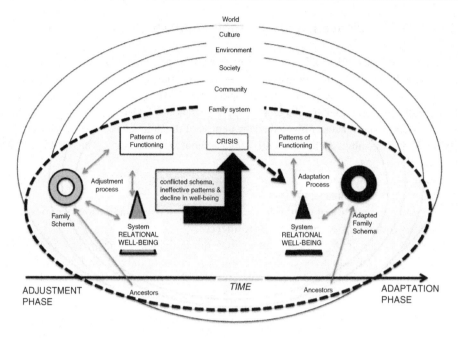

Fig. 11.1 Modified resilience model of adjustment and adaptation in ethnic family systems

emphasizing the centrality of ethnicity and culture, this concept also may be traced to the landmark work of Reiss' (1981) family construction of reality, Constantine's (1986) family paradigms, and Antonovsky's sense of coherence (1987, 1998; Antonovsky & Sourani, 1988).

In the context of ethnic family systems, a schema is defined as a structure of fundamental convictions and values shaped and adopted by the family system over time. A family's schema is designed to reflect the family system's unique character and identity and thus serves as an overarching shared informational framework against and through which family experiences are processed, evaluated, and meanings of life events are determined (Frankl, 1984). A family schema includes cultural and ethnic beliefs that evolve into an encapsulation of experiences that serves as a basis for actions and reactions to stimuli (Gates, 2010).

A family's schema influences and is influenced by family POF and RWB. In this process, a family schema cultivates one of its central functions—the development of family meanings. This aspect of schema involves the creation of family understandings, justifications, and a "perspective" on life experiences for the purpose of facilitating both family adjustment and family adaptation. For example, new POF intended to serve as family system adjustments and maintain RWB may be justified by family members faced with repeated separations of a father or mother due to deployments on military missions in Iraq and Afghanistan. A remaining parent (not deployed) may explain to a son: "In father's absence, you are the oldest and head of the family and I am counting on you." In a time of dwindling financial resources, a father may explain to a young child wanting toys or a daughter wanting clothes to feel a part of her schoolmates, "We all have to make sacrifices by giving up what we would like to have. Honey, we have less money now, and food and paying for our home have to come first."

In the situation of a family system-changing life event that disrupts the family's pattern of functioning and RWB, family schema becomes a vital element in the system's adaptation. In facing a father's death in military combat, a mother prepares the children for a life without their father as follows:

> Your father wanted to serve his country to allow us to be free. What happened was a risk your father knew was a possibility and it was his time when God called on him. Now, we need to work together to get through this. Your father would have wanted us to move on and I will need your help.

When moving on after a daughter's untimely death in a helicopter crash, a mother explains to the surviving siblings "Your sister wanted to be a special nurse on a medical helicopter. She was doing what she wanted when the helicopter crashed." In teaching a young child tolerance, while introducing a new pattern of functioning for that child, a mother offers compassion and understanding while explaining the meaning of a child's hurt about being called a "Negro" by her peers. A mother comments,

> Honey, I know what other children say to you is difficult and hurtful. Our skin color and race are part of our strengths as African-Americans. We are proud of who we are. These other children speak harshly because they do not know us and are afraid of people who are different from them.

These efforts to communicate "meanings" are intended to facilitate the system's transformation by placing the trauma in a broader context of experiences. These parental and spousal expressions are manifestations of the family's schema or identity intended to facilitate, affirm, and legitimize changes in family POF and improve upon the family's overall RWB.

In general, because family schemas evolve into a shared (actively or passively adopted) set of family values, beliefs, and expectations rooted in part in ancestral, culturally based, ethnic and/or racial perspectives, they serve as frameworks to guide the establishment of family POF and to align any changes or realignment of new patterns of family functioning. The cultural and ethnic/racial influences on family schema could include such values as respecting and maintaining one's ethnic heritage and honoring and respecting one's elders. They also might include convictions such as viewing land as a living entity as well as the family's responsibility for being a servant leader to the land. Valuing ethnic spoken and written language, dance, music, and traditions are part of family schemas adopted and transferred across generations. Not only does a family schema provide order and stability to family life, it plays an influential role in shaping and legitimizing the family's adopted POF, rules, boundaries, and expectations as a critical part of adaptation.

Ethnic origins and identity, an integral part of schemas, emerge by virtue of assumptions made about one's cultural legacy that is taught and given by parents to kin and are transferred across generations from their ancestors. When viewed from this perspective, ancestral ties may be based on genetics (DNA) and/or social origins (Keyes, 1981). One also comes to realize that ethnic family systems in the US may have multiple ethnic ancestries or origins. Thus, family schemas emerge because of different processes, inclusive of interethnic marriages, local and international adoptions, blended family systems, and a family system created by artificial insemination. This complexity is compounded by the fact that there is no invariable pattern according to which cultural differences will be used as emblematic of their ethnic difference. Language is often identified as a universal distinguishing feature, but not all ethnic groups/families have a distinctive language. Furthermore, colonization may bring extant multiethnic populations into the American context, as in the case of Mexican-Americans with Spanish-Mexican ancestral origins. Even cultural characteristics used as emblematic of ethnic identity depend upon the interpretation of the experience and actions of ancestors or forebears. These interpretations are often presented in the form of myths or legends in which historical events are accorded symbolic meaning. Ethnic origins and identity may be found in cultural traditions related to crises in everyday racism (Essed, 1991) as well as the life cycle inclusive of coming of age, marriage, illness and death (Braun, Pietsch, & Blanchette, 2000).

In exercising one or a combination of ethnic schemas, the family system seeks to align itself with others who share a common world view and identity, and also seeks to differentiate itself from others who may not share their world view. Because these are not mutually exclusive schemas, the family system may incorporate one or more identities and ethnic schemas and shift their priority and importance depending upon the context and the situation.

Family Patterns of Functioning

Central to family system adaptation is the family's selection, creation, and cultivation of relational POF designed and instituted to maintain the family system's stability, continuity, and survival. These patterns are intended to facilitate the family system's development and maintain mutually supportive and complementary relationships with the extended family, ancestors, the land, neighborhood, community, society, and the world. Focused on the family system, family scholars have identified specific patterns of system functioning. The Beavers (1977, 1982) framework focuses on the family interaction patterns of competence and style. Competence includes patterns of overt power, closeness, goal directed negotiations, clarity of expression, responsibility, and permeability. Style includes such system pattern as dependency, adult conflict, social presentation, and assertive/aggressive behavior. The Circumplex framework (Olson, 1989; Olson et al., 1983; Olson, Sprenkle, & Russell, 1979) focuses on the family system patterns of cohesion, change, and communication. The framework identifies 16 system types by using 4 levels of adaptability (chaotic, flexible, structured, and rigid), and 4 levels of cohesion (disengaged, separated, connected, and enmeshed), resulting in three clusters of family systems: balanced, midrange, and extreme. A third framework, developed by Moos (1974) and Moos and Moos (1984), recognized the system's role in determining an individual's health status. The environmental system includes the physical setting, organization factors, the human aggregate, and the social climate. The two central systems POF include the relationship dimension (cohesion, expressiveness, and conflict) and the system maintenance dimension (organization and control). A fourth framework focused on family systems' POF is the McMaster Model developed at McGill University (Westley & Epstein, 1969). The framework was designed as a clinical model (Family Assessment Device, FAD), with the primary function of the family system being to provide a setting for the development and maintenance of family members. The framework emphasizes structure, organization, and transactions focused on six dimensions: problem-solving, communication, roles, affective responsiveness, affective involvement, and behavioral control. The Family Assessment Measure (FAM) from the McMaster research group focuses on system POF, and specifically affective involvement, control, role performance, task accomplishment, and communication. A fifth framework focused on family system patterns developed at the University of Washington (Smilkstein, 1978, 1984; Smilkstein, Ashworth, & Montano, 1982) focuses on the system properties of adaptability, partnership, growth, affection, and resolve.

The Family Resilience Model of Adjustment and Adaptation (McCubbin & McCubbin, 1996a, 1996b) focused on family system POF and the capability to make and institute new, modified, or restored POF to achieve a positive level of system functioning (bon-adaptation). The resulting POF were two important family system properties: family system hardiness (sense of control, meaningfulness, and willingness to face challenges), and family system coherence (loyalty, pride, faith, trust, respect, and caring). Together these two patterns identified four types of family systems: regenerative, secure, durable, and vulnerable. Another set of family system POF was identified with properties of flexibility (open communication, willingness to compromise, active participation in decision-making) and bonding (system emotional closeness and connected as a unit). Together these two patterns identified the four system types of versatile, bonded, pliant, and fragile. A third set of family system POF included properties of family system traditions (adopt and maintain beliefs and values to pass on across generations) and family system celebrations (adopt and maintain an effort to punctuate and spotlight situations the family unit deems appropriate to emphasize). Together these two patterns identified four types of family systems: ritualistic, traditionalistic, celebratory, and situational. When considered in relationship to criterion indices of family satisfaction, and family well-being, the regenerative systems (with strong patterns of sense of control, meaningfulness, and a willingness to face challenges complemented by patterns of loyalty, pride, faith, trust, respect, and caring) were deemed the most resilient (McCubbin, Thompson, & McCubbin, 1996).

A study of lower income families of African-American ancestry revealed the importance of specific POF tailored to facilitate resilience in a high conflict and stressful context (McCubbin, 1995). This study of 184 African-American families (husband and wife pairs) located along the combat zone border of a foreign country, and in direct line of a potential enemy invasion, revealed that unique POF were developed and maintained. After taking into consideration rank (status and income), type of organization the family was affiliated with, conflict, maintenance, length of time in the conflict zone, and number of previous family deployments in a conflict zone, five family system POF involving family schema and POF were identified.

First, the more family patterns were designed to increase the family system's "fit" with the lifestyle of the military group and living in the military-base community, acceptance of the group's dangerous mission, and the value and meaning of the family's support role in the high risk situation, the more resilient the family system. Secondly, family patterns adopted to cultivate the family's (particularly spouse and children) ability to be self-reliant, the greater the system's overall resilience. Third, the greater the pattern of facilitating the spouse's employment and family income from the community, the greater the family's resilience. Fourth, the family pattern of insuring family time together and honoring commitments was critical to the system's resilience. Fifth, the family system's collective sense of ethnic identity that fostered community involvement and membership served to facilitate family adjustment and adaptation and thus system resilience.

These studies are highlighted as examples and are not intended to be exhaustive or prescriptive regarding what the ideal family patterns are or should be. Using these studies as examples, family patterns may be grouped into at least two different clusters. First are those system patterns one could consider as "core" to any family system such as patterns of flexibility, traditions and celebrations, and bonding. The second cluster of patterns is tailored to fit the circumstance and context, as was true in the study of African-American personnel and their families deployed in a high conflict zone. Research that takes variability in ancestral and ethnic origins into full account and reveals their influence on POF has much to offer to the advancement of resilience research.

Family Relational Well-Being

Given the dominance of individual measures of psychological and medical outcomes as core indices of resilience (Christopher, 1999), their application to the study of resilience involving the family system was less than optimum. The convenient linkage of family system to individual outcomes, while meritorious, did not address the scientific question regarding what would be more viable measures to reflect the resilience of the family as a unit. To address this question, the authors turned to Diener's (1984) work on well-being, Ryff's (1989) development of psychological well-being, Markus and Kitayama's (1991) writings on a collective sense of well-being, Keyes's (1998) research on social well-being, and Cross' (1998) and McGregor, Morelli, Matsuoka, and Minerbi's (2003) construct of RWB.

A "common sense" view of well-being is defined as a positive expression of individuals with Western values inclusive of high income, rewarding employment, advanced education, a quality marriage, healthy and developmentally appropriate children, good health, close friends, and social status in the community. Subjective "happiness" (Bok, 2010) is the closest to the "common sense" usage of well-being defined as the extent to which the level of positive affect outweighs the level of negative affect in an individual's life (Andrews & Withey, 1976; Diener, 1984; Deiner & Suh, 1997). This individualistic worldview emphasizes self-affirmation, aggressiveness, and achievement as markers of satisfaction and thus well-being (Diener, Suh, Smith, & Shao, 1995; Ellis, 1962; Rogers, 1961). In this regard, life satisfaction is normative and presupposes individualism and the adoption of values viewed as central to the Western culture.

The most prominent theory-based research focused on psychological well-being. Drawing from the work of personality theorists, Ryff (1989) framed psychological well-being as having six key dimensions: autonomy, environmental mastery, positive relations with others, purpose in life, personal growth, and self-acceptance. Well-being is achieved as one finds meaning and satisfaction in each of these areas. Her concepts include the underlying Western attributes of independence, internal locus of control and self-determination, the individual's ability to choose or create environments compatible with his or her aspirations and worldview, engaging in warm and trusting interpersonal relations, and having a sense of directedness and intentionality. It is assumed that there is a commitment to continual development of one's potential accompanied by a sense of responsibility to hold positive attitudes towards one's self.

A "collective" perspective of well-being emphasizes a self-effacing and self-negating worldview (Munro, 1985). This worldview is commonly associated with socialization in Eastern cultures. In this context, responsibility for the fulfillment of the social expectations of the community or society, rather than of the individual, is the priority. Personal achievement and attainment of goals also are valued in this collective context, but with a different emphasis. Such indices of recognition are intended to reveal the achievement of ancestral or family system values and beliefs. The community and/or family system receives the recognition for the achievements of its members and credits itself for its nurturance and support of the individual who fulfills familial and community expectations.

A relational worldview of family system well-being emerged from the collectivist perspective, and more specifically, from both the community-based studies of McGregor et al. (2003) and the transactional family systems theory of Spiegel (1971) and Papajohn and Spiegel (1975). McGregor and colleagues' investigation of rural indigenous communities cultivated a worldview of RWB, a conceptualization based on indigenous history and systems theory. Their central thesis is: "Well-being is synonymous with people-environment kinship and the organic relationship that bonds humans to the land" (p. 109). When this relationship is enhanced or disrupted the well-being of the people is impacted.

These theorists point to core beliefs in a relational worldview that the "land and ancestral spirits live" as they have provided for generations. This world view embraces the ecological conceptualizations of Bronfenbrenner and Ceci (1994) to include relationships with the community and society to cultivate a sense of place as a source of nurturance and energy and a context for the continuous transfer of cultural practices, values, beliefs, and a sense of community. In return, future generations benefit from knowledge of the life of the land, community, and society and embrace the natural elements of land, air, water, and ocean as interconnected and interdependent parts of their family system. It is in this context that community relationships are cultivated, economic development is nurtured, and cultural and spiritual practices give roots to cultivate the family system's shared sense of security and predictability.

This relational perspective is also integral to Papajohn and Spiegel's (1975, p. ix) transactional system theory, which is "based on the assumption that cultural, social, psychological, and social events constitute a field of transacting processes in which change in one part is related to change in the others." This framework emerged from case studies of ethnic minority families in an effort to advance our understanding of the family system adaptation as a target for primary prevention and/or therapeutic intervention. From their perspective, the family system engages in three adaptational processes each of which involves tension, conflict, and choices:

• Doing with an emphasis on development of all aspects of self vs. personal achievement
• Relational with an emphasis on interdependence and collaterality with group goals as a priority vs. individualism
• Relational harmony with Nature vs. man over nature or subjugation to nature

Operationalizing Relational Well-Being

To examine, and refine the construct of RWB, several investigators (McCubbin, Kehl, & McCubbin, 2007; McCubbin, McCubbin, Kehl, Strom, & Zhang, in press) conducted a study of 854 Native Hawaiians living in the Hawaiian Islands. The study involved the creation and psychometric testing of a 16-item measure to reflect RWB. The Relational Well-being index (RWBI) was constructed based on the literature and interviews with Native Hawaiians as well as with indigenous people residing in New Zealand and Okinawa, Japan. By administering this self-report measure to two randomly assigned groups ($N = 403$ and 408) and conducting a principal components exploratory factor analysis with tests of reliabilities, six dimensions of RWB were established. In this investigation, family RWB was operationalized as a dynamic and robust composite index of the degree to which the family system, operating within an ecological milieu, optimized (made as effective and functional as possible) its responsibility to maintain: (a) confidence and competence to survive; (b) cultural practices; (c) financial stability; (d) family commitment; (e) an investment in the community; and (f) access to quality health care.

We found that the family system operated to prioritize and cultivate depth and meaning relative to these six domains. In response to demands, and particularly to crises demanding change and adaptation, the family system gave higher priority or weight to select domains of RWB. For example, cultural preservation, financial stability, security, and family commitment may receive higher priority in the face of job loss while community involvement and health care remains at the same or is relegated to a lower level. In general, the domains of RWB may fluctuate depending upon the family's POF and its effectiveness in shaping the course of adjustment and adaptation. The family system's sense of financial stability (as characterized by having enough money to pay bills, save some money, and live within a budget) is complemented by the family's sense of survivability (e.g., the belief in being able to bounce back, having an optimistic outlook, confidence in facing hardships, stress management) and they appear to be uniformly important outcomes of mental health, physical health, and cumulative health risks.

These findings suggest that family systems operate to maintain a balance (positive and negative) in their overall sense of RWB. With this perspective in mind, the authors recognize that the introduction of RWB as a viable index of family system functioning presents an alternative conceptualization of family resilience. For example, family scholars (McCubbin & Patterson, 1983; Patterson, 1988) argued that family resilience was achieved when the demands on the family system (stressors and strains) were offset or matched with resources from within the family and the community. From a relational perspective, the family system achieves resilience through processes of adjustment, crisis management, and adaptation. Within each of the three processes, the family system shapes a complementary relationship between its family schema, POF, and RWB. The degree of harmony and balance achieved is determined by past experience and learned strategies, by professional guidance, community guidance, and trial and error. The search for complementary solutions includes changes in the family system's efforts to change the social and political context by removing the source of trauma and societal barriers, and improving the community by accessing support and increasing needed resources.

This relational perspective of resilience is built on the family system's ability to shift its POF, confirming its positive or acceptable alignment with the family's schema of agreed upon or altered values, beliefs, and practices, and confirm their positive or complementary impact on the family system's overall appraisal of its RWB. Depending on the intensity, scope, and severity of the trauma, resilience involves a process of finding the optimum congruence among the three family system properties (schema, POF, and well-being), with an emphasis on finding the optimum balance among the family's key indices of system-well-being (survival, financial stability, community relationships, family commitment, cultural practices, and health care).

Indigenous and immigrant populations change as a function of assimilation, adaptation, and preservation. The evidence is clear that these populations are called upon to establish themselves in the context of foreign and sometimes resistant host populations. To achieve a sense of "fit," these populations are called upon to find meaning, purpose, and a way of life in a different and sometimes subtle and not-so-subtle hostile host culture. Even in the face of colonization or oppression, the at-risk populations are called upon to subordinate their identity, culture, language, and traditions in order to survive (Dubos, 1974). On the other hand, it is equally true that families do preserve their cultures inclusive of language, beliefs, and values while adapting to a new and demanding social context (see Wright, Mindel, Thanh, & Habenstein, 2011). The transformation of special populations reveals the diversity in the adaptation process.

Ethnic Family System Processes of Adjustment and Adaptation

Ethnic family systems are not limited to being passive respondents to normative and non-normative life changes. When viewed in their historical context, ethnic family systems in the US bring with them an ancestral and current life history of traumatic upheavals that persist in their influence over time. Furthermore, given their minority status in the host or dominant culture these marginalized families are also active members and decision-makers engaged in continuous and dynamic *interaction* and relational processes focused on their survival, endurance, development, and resilience. These family systems achieve RWB by changing the family system (schema and POF) *and* changing the larger context. To achieve a family relational sense of well-being, ethnic families are called upon to engage and find meaning in their communities, society, and the world. They achieve survivability as well as harmony and balance in their RWB through processes of diffusion, acculturation, assimilation, and revitalization (McElroy & Townsend, 1979).

Family System Dissemination

The family system is involved in the intermingling, spread, and exchange of cultural items including foods, objects, values, behaviors, beliefs, and protocols between and among groups or cultures. Ethnic family systems are engaged in the process of revealing and sharing their beliefs, values, and practices to the host, surrounding, or dominant cultures with which they choose to engage in an effort to facilitate the cultivation of a "niche" in which to establish their identity, sense of control, and a sense of belonging (Antonovsky, 1987; Antonovsky & Sourani, 1988).

Family System Acculturation

Through coherence-building processes the family system creates opportunities or opens themselves to others to promote and sustain contact, interaction, relational exchanges, and to engage. In this context they engage in a *reciprocal* influence between/among two or more previously autonomous cultural groups and family systems. By their very nature as relational systems, family systems avail themselves of the experiences, values, beliefs, protocols, and practices of the host or dominant cultures. They may select and adopt elements of the host or other cultures into their family schemas and POF. For example, families may choose to adopt and/or integrate the diets and eating patterns of a mixture of the cultures they may be exposed to in a bi- or multiethnic family system, community, or society. Families also may choose to incorporate a particular set of values and practices, such as parental commitment to learn the language of the host culture, and commit them selves to cultivating an environment designed to promote academic achievement. They may adopt the practice of making sacrifices to give priority to the next generation and particularly their children's education and learning.

Family System Assimilation

By implementing a long-term and long-range psycho-socio-behavioral and political process, a family system may actively or passively choose to become fully identified with and assimilated into a particular host or dominant culture's values, beliefs, practices, and expectations. Their ancestral culture, beliefs, and practices are set aside, suppressed, or minimized. The ideals, values, beliefs, and practices of the host or dominant culture are embraced, emulated, and integrated into the family schema and POF. Assimilation may involve a range of ethnicities and cultures (e.g., American, Western European, Native American, Asian) depending upon the family system's exposure to the diversity within a particular community and society.

Ethnic/Cultural Revitalization

In an effort to establish stability and harmony as well as identity in a multiethnic or dominant culture, a family system may choose to resist and/or reject the influence and/or domination of a single culture or multicultures. In such a situation the family system may engage in active efforts to revitalize their chosen (the family system may have more than one ethnic/ancestral origin as in the case of multiethnic family systems) ancestral traditions, beliefs, language, practices, and values. For example, in the Hawaiian Islands, select subgroups of indigenous people of Hawaiian ancestry have chosen to reaffirm their sense of place, and reclaim their ancestral lands, customs, beliefs, practices, language, and ethnic identity. For these family systems the revitalization process has given meaning and depth to a family schema and associated POF committed to the Hawaiian ethnic identity.

Talking Story: Descriptive Portrayal Processes of Adjustment, Crisis, and Adaptation

Historically, ethnic family systems, particularly those of indigenous cultures, have passed on traditions, values, beliefs, norms, and expectations via "story telling." This practice is used in this chapter to depict the complex but distinguishable nature of family processes of adjustment (resistance), crisis (transition), and adaptation (recovery). The "talking story" example of job loss may be viewed as tragic as well as commonplace in the context of an unstable world economy.

James Yamamoto is a married, 47-year-old, second generation (the generation following his parent's immigration from Japan), Asian (Japanese) male with two children. Mark, age 21, the oldest, is a second year college student and aspiring musician of Hawaiian music, chants, and dance. His sister, Rachel, age 16, is a junior in high school and an aspiring actress. James is a 20-year employee of a stevedore company employing union (International Longshore and Warehouse Union, ILWU) dockworkers. His wife Jennifer, of Hawaiian-Caucasian ancestry, has been a homemaker for 21 years. Previously she was a sixth grade teacher in the public schools. Her transition from the work force occurred at the time of her marriage and under the firm guidance of her in-laws and their Japanese cultural schema of "wives' role as mother/wife, homemaker, and educator of their children."

Ancestral History

Both James and Jennifer place value on their ethnic origins, culture, and ancestry, Japanese (immigration) and Hawaiian (colonization) respectively. Consequently, their ancestral histories are relevant to understanding the family system processes of adjustment, crisis, and adaptation. James traces his heritage to Japan and his parents' migration to Hawaii (then a territory of the US) just before the Japanese 1941 bombing of Pearl Harbor, Hawaii, and the launching of US involvement in World War II. After starting a successful business and establishing a home in Hawaii, the Yamamoto family became the focus of an investigation along with about 10,000 other persons of Japanese ancestry. James' parents were among the estimated 1,250 Japanese Americans in Hawaii who were selected and detained on Sand Island on the island of Oahu. James's parents met in the camp and were married in 1948, 3 years following the end of the war. In general, the Japanese people, even though established as patriotic by their heroic performance in combat on behalf of the US, continued to be mocked, judged, and discriminated against.

Jennifer L. McGraw (Maiden name), more commonly referred to as "Leilani," her middle name, came from a working class family. Her father worked in the Pearl Harbor shipyard before, during, and after the war. Both of her parents were of Hawaiian ancestry. Her mother was employed at the local laundry and dry cleaning shop. Both of her grandparents lived with Jennifer in her parents' home, as was a common practice, because of the grandparents' limited income and without a permanent residence they could call their own. Jennifer described this as, "My parents took care of my grandparents and my grandparents took care of me. Thus my grandparents had a strong influence on my development." Her grandparents were both of Hawaiian ancestry and were fluent in the Hawaiian language, although they seldom used it except when they were teaching both Mark and Jennifer about the Hawaiian culture. Her grandparents felt strongly that the grandchildren should identify themselves as being exclusively of Hawaiian ancestry.

Both of Jennifer's parents were "activists" in the Hawaiian community and were passionate about raising the consciousness of both Hawaiians and Non-Hawaiians as to the historic trauma the Hawaiians experienced. The overthrow of a sovereign nation, which was Hawaii's status at the time of the US Government's overthrow, set a colonizing process in motion leading to the suppression of the Hawaiian culture and practices and elimination of the Hawaiian language. Jennifer's parents were committed to restoring the Hawaiian Monarchy and the return of lands (taken by the US Government) to the Hawaiian people. Jennifer grew up in this seemingly turbulent milieu, but chose to keep arms length from this very public conflict.

The Trauma

James's company was bought out by a major and larger international organization, and as part of the transition, several positions of the now merged company were eliminated. James was allowed to continue with the company, but with a 50% cut in pay. This difficult situation was accompanied by a reduction in family morale, shared fears about public ridicule, and a sense that the community would revive the historical traumas that they had worked so hard to overcome and rectify. For James and his parents, historical trauma included their incarceration during WWII and Japan's invasion of China, Korea, and the US. For Jennifer, her ancestors were colonized by the US, the Hawaiian Monarchy was overthrown by the US military, and also being of Caucasian mixture, her parents were rejected and marginalized. The concept of pileup of stressors and strains is appropriate in characterizing the Yamamoto's family plight.

Initial Family Relational Well-Being

Prior to this transition, the family's RWB reflected optimum depth and balance across all six relational-well-being dimensions, namely family commitment, survival, community involvement, health care, financial stability, and Asian cultural practices and traditions. There was alignment with the family's schema of valuing hard work, respect of elders, and cultures (Hawaii and Asian). The family schema, one of mixed ancestry, emphasized Japanese traditions, values, and beliefs, and includes caring for elders. Before marriage, James's wife, Jennifer, a college graduate, was employed on a full time basis as a sixth grade teacher in the public schools. She was also a performer (Native Hawaiian dancer) as part of a Hawaiian floorshow in a prominent hotel in Waikiki, a major tourist attraction in the Hawaiian Islands. Upon marriage, Jennifer became a full time homemaker while embracing the family schema of giving preference to her husband's ethnic (Japanese) practices and values and those of his parents. The Yamamoto family adopted POF consistent with the Asian system of male head of household and a schema encompassing strict discipline, a strong emphasis on education, and the supportive spouse.

Family System Adjustment

The Yamamoto family, while distraught by the social and economic setback, chose to make adjustments in their spending behavior, guided by the belief that their financial reserves were sufficient and managing resources with greater efficiencies was all that was necessary. They believed that through these adjustments they could and would maintain positive alignment and harmony with their current schema as well as what they believed to be an optimum level of RWB.

Family System Crisis

The family's tensions increased during this "status quo" period of adjustment. It was clear that they were having difficulty making ends meet and paying for the home mortgage. The situation worsened with Mark's announcement that he would be quitting college, was moving out of the family home, and would be living on his own at the end of the semester. He did not want to be a burden on the family system. Rachel was withdrawing emotionally and socially at school, fearful of criticism and exposure of the family's financial downturn. Mrs. Yamamoto offered to return to work. James rejected the idea while holding firm to the belief that they could make ends meet even with his dramatic reduction in salary. He fretted over the thought that friends, the community, and his parents would reject them. Furthermore, he believed that the family's commitment to Japanese traditions and expectations of him as breadwinner and his wife as homemaker must be maintained. Shame was too high a price to pay for any further changes in the family POF. Compromising the family's schema was out of the question. Family adjustments were not effective and the family's RWB—financial stability, family commitment, and community involvement—deteriorated in the process. System changes were necessary and the erroneous thinking that James would regain his status in the new management structure and all would return to "normal" was not enabling the family to move forward. The adjustments made were insufficient.

Family System Adaptation

The Yamamoto family unit needed to make system changes in their POF, modify the family's schema and expectations, and align the two changes along with the family's pattern of functioning. James consented to having Jennifer take advantage of a job offer to teach at the local public school. She joined their teachers union and was willing to work on a year-to-year contract. Job security was not guaranteed, but at this stage of adaptation it was valuable, particularly with the benefit of health care coverage. Her 9-month salary was nowhere near the 50% loss in James' income, but it was added income and allowed household payments to continue uninterrupted. Jennifer's role change from homemaker to employed spouse was accompanied by an increase in her community involvement. Encouraged by her peers and friends, Jennifer returned to dancing *hula* by joining a *halau* (a formal dance troupe) that called for more time learning the dances, chants, and the Hawaiian language. The added income was critical to adaptation, but as is often true with change, improvements may be, and in this case were, accompanied by added strain and conflict. James expressed unhappiness with Jennifer's outside activities in dancing, and struggled with the family secret as he had not informed his parents. With the parents' discovery of Jennifer's employment, James' sense of pride in upholding Japanese traditions and meeting his parents' expectations and family schema, his identification with the Japanese culture, was now a source of shame and strain.

On the docks, James immersed himself in work and actively took on the role of a spokesperson for management with the unions and the dockworkers. He was persistent in seeking to improve management's view of the workers and recognition of the value of strengthening benefits for the dockworkers. Management, in turn, looked to his negotiation skills to find common ground in union-management disputes. His leadership and affirmations for his new role became a source of pride and worth. With his new and recognized role in the organization, James took on the family system challenge of explaining and educating his parents regarding the legitimacy of the changes his family chose to adopt. James was affirmative in his support for these changes. Of equal importance, he communicated the meaning and value of these changes, which amounted to more than added income and consistent home payments as they also involved Mark's continuation in college and Rachel's active engagement in high school. The changes were reflective of the value the family attached to Jennifer's employment and involvement in activities that enriched her life and self-esteem. The grandparents eventually chose to reframe the situation as a positive reflection of their ancestral strengths that they attributed to their Japanese values and beliefs in family commitment, self-reliance, and self-sufficiency. These values, they believed, reflected their commitment to the Japanese culture involving self-discipline and dedication to work for the benefit of the family and the future of their children. However, parental acceptance and support of these changes in their family schema and patterns of behavior would take time.

In adaptation, the family system's RWB also changes, but only in select domains. Clearly, financial stability had improved, but the family is a long away from establishing optimum financial dependability and predictability. Family commitment also improved, with a shared acceptance and valuing of both James' and Jennifer's POF and modifications in cultural practices. In general, cultural practices were enhanced, with both the Japanese and the Hawaiian cultures and values gaining respect and inclusiveness in the family system. Family survival had improved, but not to the level that cultivated the belief that the family is no longer at risk. They maintained quality health. With both parents employed, availability for adolescent communication and family activities were reduced. Involvement in the workplace for both parents had created new demands and expectations, with both parents needing to share domestic tasks and responsibilities.

With improved family commitment, financial stability, cultural practices, and health care, but reduced sense of survival and community involvement, under the circumstances and in this context, the family system had improved its overall sense of RWB. This improvement was facilitated by a realignment of the family schema, with Jennifer's employment now affirmed and an overall successful change in the family system's POF.

Unfortunately, hardships persisted with events of everyday discrimination for both Mark and Rachel. They were called "names" because of their mixed ethnicity appearance. The parents were exposed to disquieting inquiries as to which culture the children belonged, and were subjected to being called "JAPS," referring to their ethnicity. These micro-aggressions also occurred within the family, with reference to faults, misbehaviors, or shortcomings being attributable to one or the other ancestral origins through statements such as, "that is the Hawaiian laziness in you," or "your Japanese passive-aggressive side is showing."

Intervention, Prevention, and Growth

We began this chapter with an observation and an inference: Ethnic minority families in America are resilient by virtue of their survival in the face of seemingly insurmountable odds. For many, if not most, ethnic groups in the US, survival was a necessity. The capacity to survive, an index of resilience, grew out of family systems enduring in the midst of war, threats of genocide, forced migrations, slavery, prejudice, discrimination, immigration as well as colonization, with the loss of language, culture, land, and sense of place. While this overstated observation of universal resilience has merit, the statement is intended to raise important scientific questions regarding how and through what processes and in what milieu family system resilience is cultivated, nurtured, and developed. The overstatement raises the challenge as to how we may facilitate the development of the appropriate competencies in present and future generations of ethnic, bi-ethnic, and multiethnic individuals and family systems without subjecting them to another historical trauma.

Our traditional approach to family appraisal and assessment is to differentiate and identify the extremes—the functional or healthy families from the ill and dysfunctional family systems (McGoldrick, Pearce, & Giordano, 1982). This traditional approach enables the therapy-oriented or "at risk trained" professionals to identify and classify the dysfunctional family systems they serve and for which the technology may be readily available. This strategy, however efficient it may be in identifying families in trouble, leaves the majority of struggling family systems without the much needed support network to overcome the odds and facilitate their transition and transformation to achieve RWB.

The R&RTEFS framework is designed to focus on identifying and validating the ethnic, bi-, and multiethnic family system competencies needed to make successful adjustments and to negotiate their way through crises, adaptations, and recovery. The knowledge base needed to influence and develop these family system competencies is at an embryonic stage of development and application. However, the knowledge base cultivated to date has been influential in leading to initiatives and programs designed to facilitate resilience (see, for example, Lee, 2010; Lerner, Sparks, & McCubbin, 1999; McCubbin, 2010; Root, 1992, 1996; Spickard, 1989; Wardle, 1999; Wardle & Cruz-Janzen, 2004; Wehrly, Kenney, & Kenney, 1999; Werner, 2010).

These scientists and educators take the position that all professionals (social workers, psychologists, teachers, physicians, psychiatrists, nurses, and administrators) should be able to provide "hurdle help," or "crisis interventions," to guide families through the struggles involved in transitions, adjustments, adaptation, and transformations they face. Professionals would benefit from adequate training in the unique cultural and ethnic characteristics of the family systems in populations they serve. Additionally, because these professionals are most likely to be involved with families under stress, they must also know and understand the latest information about working with mono, bi-, and multiethnic individuals and family systems. They are called upon to know and apply crisis-oriented interventions established to be "evidence based practices." Most important, these professionals are called upon to dismiss, or at least set aside, the common assumption that families that cross racial and ethnic boundaries are by their very nature dysfunctional and are thus more prone to social, academic, and interpersonal hardships than either the majority or those who live in mono-ethnic or single race family systems. The potential interventions range from therapy, crisis-intervention, and counseling to basic educational experiences in the home, preschool, middle school, high school, and higher education. The books, curricular content, materials, artwork, posters, and electronic media, as well as basic children's toys, should reflect the mono, bi-, and multiethnic nature of the populations served. These information pieces are for both those family systems and children who are part of such marginalized groups as well as the public in an effort to increase their awareness, sensitivity, and acceptance. The scientific community (Denzin, Lincoln, & Smith, 2010; Smith, 1999, 2000), inclusive of the authors of this chapter, is challenged by the need to understand and appropriately respond to the salience of ethnic diversity in the US based on knowledge of these populations. Our dependence on stereotypes of culture and ethnicities has not been helpful to the community served, and in turn, the scientific community has not cultivated the knowledge base needed to address the needs of the diverse ethnic populations that continue to increase, change, transform themselves, and migrate across the country.

The focus on family system resilience represents a substantive shift in our paradigms for research and intervention: The ethnic populations bring with them a deep and sustainable commitment to family life. The family systems, mindful of their ancestral roots, have combined these foundations with life experience to create and cultivate a wealth of knowledge and competencies. This chapter and the theory base for RWB and resilience are built upon the development and application of indigenous knowledge. It is the authors' expectation that the framework described here will facilitate research on ethnic populations and in so doing, advance our understanding of the meaning of ethnicity and its influence in the resilience of ethnic families. It is important to deemphasizing our long history of building theories to explain the variability in family dysfunction and to beginning to explain and predict why and how ethnic families, exposed to the same historical or situational trauma, are, in fact, resilient. The pressing questions continue to be:

- With a socialization history of exposure to and incorporation of cultural practices, beliefs, values, and POF, what ethnically based family processes come into play to protect the family system from a crisis leading to deterioration?
- What ethnically based family system processes come into play to facilitate the family's recovery (resilience) from a crisis?
- With family resilience defined as processes to protect the family from a crisis and to promote recovery in the face of a crisis, by what criteria and using what metrics would we determine whether the family processes were effective or ineffective, as well as which families were resilient and those who were not?
- In what ways and under what circumstances do ethnicity, culture, and identity (mono, bi-, and multiethnicity) shape the course and outcome of family RWB?

As a cluster, these questions represent a formidable challenge in posing clear expectations that family systems-focused resilience theory be advanced. It would be prudent for this advancement to be guided by a deeper knowledge of family system processes shaped by a valid understanding of the meaning of ethnicity and the cultural roots of all ethnic and multiethnic populations in the US and the world.

References

Andrews, F. M., & Withey, S. B. (1976). *Social indicators of well-being: Americans' perceptions of life quality*. New York: Plenum Press.

Angell, R. (1936). *The family encounters the depression*. New York: Scribner.

Antonovsky, A. (1987). *Unraveling the mystery of health*. San Francisco: Jossey-Bass.

Antonovsky, A. (1998). The sense of coherence: An historical and future perspective. In H. McCubbin, E. Thompson, A. Thompson, & J. Fromer (Eds.), *Sense of coherence and resiliency: Stress, coping and health* (pp. 3–40). Thousand Oaks: Sage.

Antonovsky, A., & Sourani, T. (1988). Family sense of coherence and family adaptation. *Journal of Marriage and Family, 50,* 79–92.

Beavers, W. R. (1977). *Psychotherapy and growth: A family systems perspective.* New York: Brunner/Mazel.

Beavers, W. R. (1982). Healthy, midrange and severely dysfunctional families. In F. Walsh (Ed.), *Normal family processes* (pp. 45–66). New York: Guilford Press.

Bem, S. (1981). Gender schema theory: A cognitive amount of sex typing. *Psychological Review, 88,* 354–364.

Bok, D. (2010). *The politics of happiness: What government can learn from the new research on well-being.* Princeton, NJ: Princeton University Press.

Braun, K., Pietsch, J., & Blanchette, P. (Eds.). (2000). *Cultural issues in end-of-life decision making.* Thousand Oaks, CA: Sage.

Bronfenbrenner, U., & Ceci, S. (1994). Nature-nurture reconceptualized in developmental perspective: A bioecological model. *Psychological Review, 101*(4), 568–586.

Burr, W. (1973). *Theory construction and the sociology of the family.* New York: Wiley.

Christopher, J. (1999). Situating psychological well-being: Exploring the cultural roots of its theory and research. *Journal of Counseling and Development, 77*(2), 141–152.

Conger, R., & Conger, K. (2002). Resilience in midwestern families: Selected findings from the first decade of a longitudinal study. *Journal of Marriage and Family, 64*(2), 361–373.

Constantine, L. (1986). *Family paradigms.* New York: Guilford.

Cross, T. (1998). Understanding family resilience from a relational world view. In H. I. McCubbin, E. A. Thompson, A. I. Thompson, & J. E. Fromer (Eds.), *Resiliency in ethnic minority families: Native and immigrant American minority families* (Vol. 1, pp. 143–157). Thousand Oaks, CA: Sage.

Deiner, E., & Suh, M. E. (1997). Subjective well-being and age: An international analysis. *Annual Review of Gerontology and Geriatrics, 17,* 304–312.

Denzin, N., Lincoln, Y., & Smith, L. (Eds.). (2010). *Handbook of indigenous methodologies.* Thousand Oaks, CA: Sage.

Diener, E. (1984). Subjective well-being. *Psychological Bulletin, 95,* 542–575.

Diener, E., Suh, M. E., Smith, H., & Shao, L. (1995). National and cultural differences in reported subjective well-being: Why do they occur? *Social Indicators Research, 34,* 7–32.

Dubos, R. (1974). *Of human diversity.* New York: Clark University Press.

Ellis, A. (1962). *Reason and emotion in psychotherapy.* Secaucus, NJ: The Citadel Press.

Epstein, S. (1973). The self-concept revisited, or a theory of a theory. *American Psychologist, 28,* 404–416.

Essed, P. (1991). *Understanding everyday racism: An interdisciplinary theory.* Newbury Park: Sage.

Fong, G., & Markus, H. (1982). Self schemata and judgments about others. *Social Cognition, 1,* 191–204.

Frankl, V. (1984). *Man's search for meaning: An introduction to logotherapy* (3rd ed.). New York: Simon & Schuster.

Garmezy, N. (1991). Resiliency and vulnerability to adverse developmental outcomes associated with poverty. *American Behavioral Scientist, 34,* 416–430.

Gates, H. L., Jr. (2010). *Faces of America with Henry Louis Gates Jr.* New York: Public Broadcasting Service (PBS).

Hansen, D., & Johnson, V. (1979). Rethinking family stress theory: Definitional aspect. In W. Burr, R. Hill, F. Nye, & I. Reiss (Eds.), *Contemporary theories about the family, (I)* (pp. 582–603). New York: Free Press.

Hill, R. (1949). *Families under stress.* New York: Harper & Row.

Hill, R. (1958). Generic features of families under stress. *Social Casework, 49,* 139–150.

Keyes, C. (Ed.). (1981). *Ethnic change.* Seattle, WA: University of Washington.

Keyes, C. L. M. (1998). Social well-being. *Social Psychology Quarterly, 61,* 121–140.

Kosciulek, J., McCubbin, M., & McCubbin, H. (1993). A theoretical framework for family adaptation to head injury. *Journal of Rehabilitation, 59,* 40–45.

Lee, S. (2010). Intermarriage trends, issues, and implications. In H. McCubbin, K. Ontai, L. Kehl, L. McCubbin, I. Strom, H. Hart, & J. Matsuoka (Eds.), *Multiethnicity and multiethnic families: Development, identity, and resilience* (pp. 15–42). Honolulu, HI: Leà.

Lerner, R., Sparks, E., & McCubbin, L. (1999). *Family diversity and family policy: Strengthening families for America's children.* Norwell, MA: Kluwer.

Luthar, S., Cicchetti, D., & Bronwyn, B. (2000). The construct of resilience: A critical evaluation and guidelines for future work. *Child Development, 7,* 543–562.

Markus, H., & Kitayama, S. (1991). Culture and the self: Implications for cognition, emotion, and motivation. *Psychological Review, 98*(2), 224–253.

Marsella, A., Oliveira, J., Plummer, C., & Crabbe, K. (1998). Native Hawaiian (Kanaka Maoli) culture, mind and well-being. In H. McCubbin, E. Thompson, A. Thompson, & J. Fromer (Eds.), *Resiliency in Native American and immigrant families* (pp. 93–114). Thousand Oaks, CA: Sage.

McCann, I., & Pearlman, L. (1990). *Psychological trauma and the adult survivor: Theory, therapy and transformation.* New York: Brunner/Mazel.

McCubbin, H. (1995). Resiliency in African American families: Military families in foreign environments. In H. McCubbin, E. Thompson, A. Thompson, & J. Futrell (Eds.), *Resiliency in ethnic minority families: African American families* (Vol. 2, pp. 67–97). Beverly Hills: Sage.

McCubbin, H. (2010). Emerging paradigms and conundrums of multiethnicity: A foreword. In H. McCubbin, K. Ontai, L. Kehl, L. McCubbin, I. Strom, H. Hart, B. Debaryshe, R. Ripke, & J. Matsuoka (Eds.), *Multiethnicity and multiethnic families: Development, identity, and resilience* (pp. 1–10). Honolulu, HI: Leà.

McCubbin, H., Dahl, B., Metres, P., Jr., Hunter, E., & Plag, J. (Eds.). (1975). *Family separation and reunion: Families of prisoners of war and servicemen missing in action.* Washington, DC: U.S. Government Printing Office.

McCubbin, H., Kehl, L., & McCubbin, L. (2007). *Relational well-being (I).* Honolulu, HI: Center for Training, Evaluation, and Research of the Pacific University of Hawaii at Manoa.

McCubbin, H., & McCubbin, M. (1988). Typologies of resilient families: Emerging roles of social class and ethnicity. *Family Relations, 37,* 247–254.

McCubbin, H., & McCubbin, M. (1996a). Resiliency in families: A conceptual model for predicting family adjustment and adaptation. In H. McCubbin, M. McCubbin, & A. Thompson (Eds.), *Family assessment inventories for research and practice: Stress, theory and resilience* (pp. 5–14). Madison, WI: University of Wisconsin.

McCubbin, H., McCubbin, M., Thompson, A., & Thompson, E. (1998). Resiliency in ethnic families: A conceptual model for predicting family adjustment and adaptation. In H. McCubbin, E. Thompson, A. Thompson, & J. Fromer (Eds.), *Resiliency in ethnic minority families: Native and immigrant families* (pp. 3–48). Thousand Oaks, CA: Sage.

McCubbin, H., Ontai, K., Kehl, L., McCubbin, L., Strom, L., Hart, H., et al. (Eds.). (2010). *Multiethnicity and multiethnic families: Development, identity, and resilience.* Honolulu, HI: Leà.

McCubbin, H., & Patterson, J. (1983). The family stress process: The double ABCX model of family adjustment and adaptation. *Marriage and Family Review, 6,* 7–37.

McCubbin, H., Thompson, A., & McCubbin, M. (Eds.). (1996). *Family assessment inventories for research and practice: Stress, theory and resilience.* Madison, WI: University of Wisconsin.

McCubbin, H., Thompson, E., Thompson, A., & Fromer, J. (Eds.). (1998a). *Stress, coping and health in families.* Thousand Oaks: Sage.

McCubbin, H., Thompson, E., Thompson, A., & Fromer, J. (Eds.). (1998b). *Resiliency in ethic minority families: Native and immigrant families.* Thousand Oaks, CA: Sage.

McCubbin, H., Thompson, E., Thompson, A., & Futrell, J. (Eds.). (1998c). *Resiliency in ethnic minority families: African American families.* Thousand Oaks, CA: Sage.

McCubbin, L. (2006). The role of indigenous family ethnic schema on well-being among Native Hawaiian families. *Contemporary Nurse, 23*(2), 170–180.

McCubbin, L., & McCubbin, H. (2005). Culture and ethnic identity in family resilience: Dynamic processes in trauma and transformation of indigenous people. In M. Unger (Ed.), *Handbook for working with children and youth: Pathways to resilience across cultures and contexts* (pp. 27–44). Thousand Oaks, CA: Sage.

McCubbin, L. D., McCubbin, H. I., Kehl, L., Strom, I., & Zhang, W. (in press). Family relational wellbeing: Indigenous theory and measurement. *Family Relations.*

McCubbin, M. (1988). Family stress, resources and family types: Chronic illness in children. *Family Relations, 37,* 203–210.

McCubbin, M. (1990). The typology model of adjustment and adaptation: A family stress model. *Guidance and Counseling, 6,* 6–22.

McCubbin, M., & McCubbin, H. (1996b). Family stress theory and assessment: The T-double ABCX model of family adjustment and adaptation. In H. McCubbin, A. Thompson, & M. McCubbin (Eds.), *Family assessment inventories for research and practice.* Madison: University of Wisconsin.

McElroy, A., & Townsend, P. (1979). *Medical anthropology in ecological perspective.* North Scituate, MA: Duxbury.

McGoldrick, M., Pearce, J., & Giordano, J. (1982). *Ethnicity and family therapy.* New York: Guilford Press.

McGregor, D., Morelli, P., Matsuoka, J., & Minerbi, L. (2003). An ecological model of wellbeing. In H. Becker & F. Vanclay (Eds.), *The international handbook of social impact assessment: Conceptual and methodological advances* (pp. 109–126). Northampton, MA: Edward Elgar.

Moos, R. (1974). *Family environment scale preliminary manual.* Palo Alto, CA: Consulting Psychologists Press.

Moos, R., & Moos, B. (1984). *Family environment scale manual.* Palo Alto, CA: Consulting Psychologists Press.

Munro, D. (Ed.). (1985). *Individualism and holism: Studies in Confucian and Taoist values.* Ann Arbor: The University of Michigan Press.

Olson, D. (1989). Circumplex model and family health. In C. Ramsey Jr. (Ed.), *Family systems in medicine* (pp. 75–94). New York: Guilford Press.

Olson, D., McCubbin, H., Barnes, H., Larsen, A., & Muxem, A. (1983). *Families: What makes them work?* Beverly Hills: Sage.

Olson, D., Sprenkle, D., & Russell, C. (1979). Circumplex model of marital and family systems 1: Cohesion and adaptability dimensions, family types and clinical applications. *Family Process, 18,* 3–28.

Papajohn, J., & Spiegel, J. (1975). *Transactions: The interplay between individual, family and society.* New York: Science House.

Patterson, J. (1988). Families experiencing stress: The family adjustment and adaptation response model. *Family Systems Medicine, 5,* 202–237.

Patterson, J. (2002). Integrating family resilience and family stress theory. *Journal of Marriage and Family, 64,* 349–360.

Reiss, D. (1981). *The family's construction of reality.* Cambridge, MA: Harvard University Press.

Rogers, C. (1961). *On becoming a person.* Boston, MA: Houghton-Mifflin.

Root, M. (1992). *Racially mixed people in America.* Thousand Oaks, CA: Sage.

Root, M. (1996). *The multiracial experience: Racial borders as the new frontier.* Thousand Oaks, CA: Sage.

Rotter, J. (1954). *Social learning and clinical psychology.* Englewoods Cliff, NJ: Prentice-Hall.

Ryff, C. (1989). Happiness is everything or is it? Explorations on the meaning of psychological well-being. *Journal of Personality and Social Psychology, 57,* 1069–1081.

Smilkstein, G. (1978). The family APGAR: A proposal for family function test and its use by physicians. *Journal of Family Practice, 6,* 1231–1239.

Smilkstein, G. (1984). The physician and family function assessment. *Family Systems Medicine, 2,* 263–278.

Smilkstein, G., Ashworth, C., & Montano, D. (1982). Validity and reliability of the family APGAR as a test of family function. *Journal of Family Practice, 15,* 303–311.

Smith, G. (2000). Protecting and respecting indigenous knowledge. In M. Battiste (Ed.), *Reclaiming indigenous voice and vision* (pp. 209–224). Vancouver, Canada: University of British Columbia Press.

Smith, L. (1999). *Decolonizing methodologies: Research and indigenous people.* New York, NY: Zed Books.

Spickard, P. (1989). *Mixed blood: Intermarriage and ethnic identity in twentieth century Americans.* Madison: University of Wisconsin Press.

Spiegel, J. (1971). Transactions inquiry: Descriptions of systems. In J. Papajohn (Ed.), *Transactions: The interplay between individual, family and society.* New York: Science House.

Spiegel, J. (1982). An ecological model of ethnic families. In M. McGoldrick, J. Pierce, & J. Giodorno (Eds.), *Ethnicity and family therapy* (pp. 31–51). New York: Guilford Press.

Taylor, S., & Crocker, J. (1981). Schematic basis of social information processing. In E. Higgins, C. Herman, & M. Zanna (Eds.), *The Ontario symposium on personality and social psychology* (Vol. 1, pp. 89–134). Hillsdale: Erlbaum.

Tedeschi, R., & Calhoun, L. (1995). *Trauma and transformation: Growing in the aftermath of suffering.* Thousand Oaks: Sage.

U.S. Census Bureau. (2000). *Racial and ethic classifications used in Census 2000 and beyond.* (2010). Retrieved January 10, 2011, from http://www.census.gov/population/www/socdemo/race/racefactcb.html.

U.S. Census Bureau. (2010). Retrieved May 30, 2012, from http://2010.census.gov/2010census/data/.

Walsh, F. (1996). The concept of family resilience: Crisis and challenge. *Family Process, 35,* 261–281.

Walsh, F. (2002). A family resilience framework: Innovative practice applications. *Family Relations, 51*(2), 130–137.

Walsh, F. (2003). Family resilience: A framework for clinical practice. *Family Process, 42,* 1–18.

Wardle, F. (1999). *Tomorrow's children: Meeting the needs of multiracial and multiethnic children at home, in early childhood programs and at school.* Denver, CO: CSBC.

Wardle, F., & Cruz-Janzen, M. (2004). *Meeting the needs of multiethnic and multiracial children in schools.* Boston: Pearson.

Wehrly, H., Kenney, R., & Kenney, M. (1999). *Counseling multiracial families.* Thousand Oaks, CA: Sage.

Werner, E. (2010). Risk and resilience: Lessons from the lives of children from multiethnic families. In H. McCubbin, K. Ontai, L. Kehl, L. McCubbin, I. Strom, H. Hart, B. Debaryshe, R. Ripke, & J. Matsuoka (Eds.), *Multiethnicity and multiethnic families: Development, identity, and resilience* (pp. 239–252). Honolulu, HI: Leà.

Werner, E. E. (1993). Risk, resilience and recovery: Perspectives from the Kauai longitudinal study. *Development and Psychopathology, 5,* 503–515.

Werner, E. E., & Smith, R. (1992). *Overcoming the odds.* Ithaca, NY: Cornell University Press.

Westley, W., & Epstein, N. (1969). *The silent majority.* San Francisco, CA: Jossey-Bass.

Wright, R., Mindel, C., Thanh, V., & Habenstein, R. (2011). *Ethnic families in America: Patterns and variations* (5th ed.). New York: Elsevier North-Holland.

Native American Family Resilience

12

Rockey Robbins, Sharla Robbins,
and Brad Stennerson

Introduction/Background

To write about Native American family resilience entails exploring critical aspects of European and Euro-American endeavors at subjugation from a neo-colonial perspective. Early in the history of this country, the social relations Native Americans had created were dismissed as uncivilized and inadequate. Consequently, colonizers felt justified to work toward disconnecting Native Americans from their histories and ways of interacting with each other and nature. The U.S. government legislated who lived on what reservations and how they were to serve the interests of the dominant society. In his Tribal Critical Race Theory, Braveboy (2006) contends that colonization is endemic to American society, that US governmental policies have been and continue to be rooted in imperialism and White supremacy, and that these policies are intimately linked around the problematic goal of assimilation. Duran and Duran (1995) argue that tribal people suffer from "a soul wound" as a consequence of wars, reservation subjugation, boarding schools, relocation, and termination. After Native Americans had been hunted and killed like vermin or rounded up and put on regulated spaces, they were then clothed with Western ideologies and moralities.

Throughout the colonizing process, Native Americans have interacted with and accepted many of the colonizers' ways, but they also have resisted physical, psychological, social, and cultural domination. This complex interaction has resulted in a multi-layered identity development. While focusing on Native American resilience does not necessitate a total rejection of Western knowledge and ways, it does involve keeping in mind that which is unique historically and traditionally about what constitutes Native American families. It is vital to select, arrange, prioritize, and legitimize the values and strengths that have enabled Native Americans to survive.

The near decimation of Native American peoples within only decades after Columbus' arrival, recently determined as even more devastating than believed even a generation ago (Mann, 2003), and six more centuries of colonial domination have not been enough to break the resilient wills of Native

R. Robbins (✉) • B. Stennerson
University of Oklahoma, Norman, OK, USA
e-mail: rockey@ou.edu

S. Robbins
President of OEDA, Norman, OK, USA
e-mail: sharlarobbins@yahoo.com

D.S. Becvar (ed.), *Handbook of Family Resilience*,
DOI 10.1007/978-1-4614-3917-2_12, © Springer Science+Business Media New York 2013

Americans. Many Native Americans retain traditions that can help their families to be strong, traditional, and resilient in the face of continued oppression. In this chapter, we consider what constitutes this resilience. In spite of the intolerable historical and present treatment by American society, somehow Native Americans have been able to continue and renew some semblance of family cultural traditions and health. Our goal is thus to look at the Native American family as it is today, as Native American family priorities and struggles are updated, with an awareness of where traditional families were yesterday and a vision of where they will be tomorrow.

In addition, we consider comments regarding family resilience made by a 40-year-old Muskogee (Creek) male client over the course of his 38 counseling sessions. We explore the commonalities among Native American families as well as look at the qualities of families and extended families that differentiate them from other groups, considering their unique tribal and individual struggles, obligations, commitments, role functions, and specializations. It is vital that we responsibly examine and refine the issues so that they represent the unique contemporary struggles of Native American families. Efforts are made to analyze the young man's comments in terms of Native Americans' perspectives. We especially consider the strengths his family drew upon to face difficult situations. Acknowledging the limitations for usage due to the unique needs and concerns of different tribes, we attempt to offer suggestions about how the information we uncover can be used to the benefit of Native American communities.

Significance of Native American Family Resilience

The strengths of Indian families are their spiritual qualities, which include values such as interconnectedness, relationships, harmony, respect, humility, and bravery. There are certain teachings that people will hear if they regularly attend Native American ceremonies or listen to elders. The authors cannot hope to be exhaustive in making a list of these teachings and consequently chose a few of the most frequently enumerated principles. Further, the principles mentioned here are not so easily defined, and when one tries to define them, one is always in danger of co-mingling colonial teachings with tribal perspectives. Nonetheless, we believe that the core beliefs found in Native American spiritualities have been key to the ability of Native American families to evidence resilience in the face of oppression.

For many Native Americans who practice traditional ways, spiritual principles are based on honoring relationships. The Lakota Sundance leader Howard Bad Hand (2002) explains that the words used for God in Lakota emphasize intimate interconnections and relationships. When entering or leaving the purification lodge participants say *mitawkuwe oyas'in*, "my blood relations inclusive of all." *Wakan Tanka*, or God, is translated as movement of blood flowing through a vein. *Tunkasila*, another word used in prayer, means "Grandfather." Still another word used in prayers is *Unci Maka*, translated as "living earth as mother to all." As these core concepts suggest, honoring relationships is the basis for many tribal spirituality philosophies. They serve to guide Native Americans in their interactions with nature and other human beings. Instead of seeing themselves as isolated individuals striving after selfish goals, they see themselves as a part of the family of Earth Mother and Sun Father, and this family extends beyond the nuclear family to everything, including persons who have gone on to the spirit world.

Such a philosophy has contributed to the unique personal relationships among extended Native American family members, the great reciprocal respect between children and their elders, and traditional childrearing practices that emphasize good role modeling based on this respect and nature. It is believed that if parents and grandparents respect and instill respect in their relationships with children, then it will be reciprocated, and also will lead to their respectful relationships with others. Collateral relationships, in contrast to the individualistic behaviors in mainstream family systems, offer a long-standing stability to Native American extended family systems. These values are still held dearly but differently according to contemporary tribal structures. For instance, kinship systems are important to take into account, and many Native American families are not defined by a father–mother–child organization. It is not unusual for Native American Indian homes to contain three generations of interrelated persons of all ages. Some families might be separated by distance but come together during ceremonies, rituals, and other tribal gatherings in addition to more narrowly defined extended family gatherings. They also may have honoring ceremonies to show appreciation for their youth or elders.

It is imperative that people working in helping professions respect the spiritual integrity of Native American family systems. Spirituality is the sinew that holds Native American families and communities together, and generosity is an important part of many Native Americans' spirituality. Almost all Native American tribes have "give-aways," presenting gifts to each other, thereby building social harmony in their communities. Most also have arduous spiritual practices, such as Sundances, scratchings, purification ceremonies, and vision quests. Native American spiritual practices have incorporated sweating as a form of spiritual expression, frequently involving preparatory ritual or prayer and used for rites of passage including birth, puberty, weddings, and death (Hibbard, 2005). Each tribe, and sometimes different clans, has specific protocols for their rituals. Many Native Americans attend Christian churches, but professional helpers should not assume that they have abandoned traditional principles (Diller, 2011).

For many generations, Native Americans have developed unique spiritual ways to cope with extreme external threats. A professional helper may misinterpret some of the profound inwardness and trust in the Creator that sustain them through such hardships as depression and pessimism, but a deeper look will reveal humility and bravery in the reticence that helps in facing painful hardships. Strong spiritual values have been passed on so that the present and future generations of Native American families can experience healthy living.

Traditionally, tribal membership was more than just living within a group or geographical region. Native people belonged to a family, clan or band, community, and tribe. From time immemorial, responsibility for the wellbeing of each other was communal and still is in some Native American communities. Parents never raised children alone; grandparents, aunts, uncles, other elders and adults, and siblings sometimes participated in the parenting process, transmitting information, knowledge, support, encouragement, and advice. Native American extended families nurtured, trained, and educated children. If a child could not live with parents, a relative was always present to take the child and treat him as if he were her own. In turn, every vulnerable elder or tribal member was cared for by younger members. Elders lived with and were cared for by family members. The community expected both children and elders to be treated with love and the greatest of care. Individual and collective identities were forged in the caring circles of extended families.

Literature Review

Overview of the Constitution of Native American Families

Most of those who write about Native American families begin by describing the extended family, but they would do well to consider the larger community within which the extended family operates. Traditional Native American families exist within complex and intimate transactions embedded in a community milieu. Often, Native American people have responsibilities in their communities to carry out a variety of roles in different rituals and community functions. One family may have kept sacred artifacts and carried out tasks for the entire community for many generations, or certain families may be singers or organizers of annual events. Therefore, if one is going to look at the Native American family, one must look at the Native American community as a totality. In spite of the appearance of social disorder and material deprivation, Native American families do try to help one another. These helping systems need to be explored and identified in order to establish a point of departure before professional programs and helpers begin intervening relative to the family patterns.

Extended Family

Mental health professionals are trained to work with persons whose primary relational system is the nuclear family, which tends to be programmed to raise autonomous, sometimes even individualistic human beings. This orientation contrasts dramatically with Native Americans in extended family systems whose identities are defined in terms of their participation: "Family ties define existence, identity. Individual family members feel close and binding connections with a broad network of relatives" (Diller, 2011, p. 242). Individuality may be deemed as having integrity only when it emerges in the context of mutual responsibility and interdependence. In other words, "Responsibility actually is a bilateral phenomenon in that it is adopted by and binding across generations. Every age cohort, regardless of gender, is accorded respect because each fulfills critical functions in the community" (Red Horse et al., 2000, p. 18).

Extended Native American families are often tightly-knit through second cousins, but usually people in tribal communities are aware of blood relations beyond this level. Parents and grandparents are likely to remind children repeatedly about their blood relations and clan lineage not only to support customs, obligations, and emotional connections, but also to avoid kinship marriages. Grandparents, aunts, and uncles are also more likely to assume primary care taking responsibilities for relatives' children. Sue and Sue (2008) report that in many Native American communities and families the parenting of children is communal and shared throughout the extended family, and it is not unusual for children to live in various households of the extended family while growing up. The survival of a healthy tribal community is a passion for many Native Americans who are willing to take on extra child care responsibilities.

The extended family kinship system varies from tribe to tribe. For instance, few Oklahoma Choctaws, one of the largest tribes, are able to identify their clan, though their neighbors, the Muskogee, are likely to be able to identify theirs. Nevertheless, Choctaws still have values and enact perennial roles that promote a communal system. For instance, one will readily find Choctaw extended families who weave supportive and interdependent relationships beyond first and second cousins. Children understand early that their actions are a reflection on their extended family, which serves to regulate individual behavior. Also, the belief that extended family members are to aid and protect one another is accepted as everyday practice. Referring to tribes in general, Morrison, Fox, Cross, and Roger (2010) write, "When these webs of interdependent relationships are intact, a sense of trust, commonality, and purpose unfolds, creating a sense of belonging. A sense of belonging is central to tribal sovereignty" (p. 104).

Grandparenting

Native American grandparents are more likely than those in the general population to accept the role of caretaker for their grandchildren because of generations of tribal historical traditions that have involved their incorporating significant participation in this role (Benally, 1999; Schweitzer, 1999). Indeed, Native American grandparents are almost three times as likely as the general population to report being responsible for a grandchild (3.6% compared to just 1.3% for all races combined) (U.S. Bureau of the Census, 2000a). Grandparents identifying themselves as Indian, tribally affiliated, and living in a rural area of an "Indian" state increases the likelihood of raising a grandchild by those 45 years old and older, regardless of being single or coupled (Mutchler, Baker, & Lee, 2007).

Grandparents represent an integral conduit for the transmission of Native American values, symbols, history, practices, and language. Shomaker (1989) reported that parents commonly send a child to live with grandparents for extended periods of time as a means of ensuring care for the child as well as a strategy to provide support and assistance to aging grandparents. On the other hand, Native American grandparents are also often utilized as safety nets for parents who are having difficulties. For instance, Native American parents may move to cities to seek employment, leaving children in the care of grandparents (Shomaker, 1989), or grandparents may take on full responsibility of grandchildren when parents are imprisoned, neglectful, substance abusers, disabled, or deceased (Burnette, 1997; Fuller-Thomson & Minkler, 2005; Pebley & Rudkin, 1999).

Robbins, Scherman, Holeman, and Wilson (2005) conducted a study with 20 Native American grandparents to uncover the specific ways and means in which they engaged in acculturative responsibilities. Reported strategies included storytelling, supporting grandchildren in their participation in tribal ceremonies, and direct teaching of tribal values. The values included: respect for nature, showing appreciation, courage, unselfishness, generosity, and bringing the family together. The study participants described their relations with grandchildren as being more egalitarian and less structured than parent/child interactions. Weibel-Orlando (1990), who conducted interviews with 28 Native American grandparents, classified five basic grandparenting types of interaction with grandchildren: (1) cultural conservator; (2) a model for ceremonial behavior; (3) custodial (full childcare responsibilities); (4) distanced, lack of contact with grandchildren; and (5) fictive (nurturing "nonbiological" grandchildren).

While most of the studies cited above report that Native American grandparents feel a sense of fulfillment in assuming a significant role, especially in regard to the love they feel, the opportunities to transmit tribal wisdoms, and responsibilities for grandchildren, many report financial hardship. Mutchler et al. (2007) reported that many Native American grandparents are not receiving services for which they and their grandchildren may be eligible, and that more effective efforts are needed to ensure broad awareness of and access to economic support and health programs.

Challenges Faced by Native American Families

Before discussing some of the difficulties that many Native American families are currently facing, it is important to consider that these issues are not to be viewed as failures of Native Americans, but rather as the results of colonialization and the lack of tribal self-determination. Three devastating methods of eradication through assimilation are addressed in the next section: the impacts of boarding schools, the process of removal and relocation, and the practice of cross-cultural adoption. The American Government has always represented its interventions with Native Americans as altruistic. Native American children were enrolled into Indian boarding schools that would lead to their equal participation in the market economy. But it was at the cost of relinquishing their tribal identities. Native Americans could leave their homes on reservations to be re-located to comfortable living conditions and high paying jobs. But they found their new homes to be squalid and their new jobs low paying and dreary. The American Government "helped" Native American foster children find new Euro-American families and homes that guaranteed "a better life." But many adoptees found themselves wrestling with identity issues for the rest of their lives.

Boarding Schools

The U.S. Congress first made provisions for Native American education in 1819, though it was not until after the Civil War that the US established the Carlisle Indian School in 1879 (Szasz, 1999). The government couched their talk of putting Native American children in boarding schools as being for the children's good. That marked the beginning of a full-scale effort to use education to rapidly assimilate Native Americans into mainstream culture. Native American children were forcibly removed and sent away beyond the reach of their parents to residential schools, which were systematically designed to destroy tribal language and any memories of traditional family life (Brave Heart & De Bruyn, 1998). Strict disciplinarians taught White ways. Many Native Americans who attended boarding schools identified with those disciplinarians, whom they deemed as powerful and/or as potentially meeting nurturance needs. They unconsciously introjected those persons' and associations' values, accommodating themselves to the oppressive environment and experiencing ongoing negative ramifications in regard to self-affirmation as well as in interactions with others (Robbins et al., 2006).

Boarding schools had an insidious effect on the Native American family and its cohesion. When children were taken out of their families and placed in boarding schools, they were separated from their grandparents, parents, extended family, aunts, uncles, community, and so on. For generations, many Native American children were robbed of the nurturing of their families and deprived of the opportunity to learn parenting skills and other cultural lessons that would enable them to raise healthy families on their own. The education institutions they were forced to reside in were, and are, harsh and brutal. As adults, the boarding school residents came home with many psychological issues such as low self-esteem, negative feelings about being Native, and deep self-hatred. Generations of such experiences have impacted Native American communities today. The consequence of the loss of Native cultures is that many Native Americans have come to internalize the stereotypes Whites hold about them. Many of the current family problems we have stem from the boarding school experiences. Indeed, boarding school experiences devastated the Native American extended family system.

Currently, there are 72 Indian boarding schools funded by the Bureau of Indian Affairs, serving over 10,000 students in the United States (U. S. Bureau of Indian Affairs, 2006). While current students report fewer atrocities and represent their schools more favorably than did past students, they continue to report feelings of intense anger, loneliness, cultural and tribal alienation, and hopelessness (Robbins et al., 2006)

Relocation

The Relocation Act beginning in the late 1940s was an effort by the government to encourage Native Americans to leave reservations and move to cities where they could work at jobs that might help them become more a part of the American mainstream. Unfortunately, many Native Americans lost traditional and kinship ties, or at least had them weakened with the move to cities. Many of us remember all too well seeing our Native brothers and sisters, down and out, homeless, hanging around bus stations and city parks. The government failed to understand that many rural Native Americans lacked the skills or values to survive successfully in urban environments where they were met with substantial discrimination and rejection (Diller, 2011). In addition, when family members began moving back and forth between the city and the reservation, great animosities and conflicts arose between urban Native Americans and reservation Native Americans. Whether successful or unsuccessful, urban Native Americans were often viewed as having "gone White" when they returned for ceremony and exhibited awkwardness and lack of understanding. These urban Native Americans would return such judgments by representing reservation and rural Native Americans as backward.

As with so many programmatic endeavors "to help the Indian," relocation had a devastating impact on Native families. If the children grew up and were educated in an urban area, they came to see themselves not as tribal people having inherited unique rituals, customs, or ways, but as urban Indians who did not know their language and rarely if ever practiced their spiritual ways. Colonial policies dressed in the humanitarian garb of inclusion worked as an instrument of domination. At the same time, this new generation was unaware that they were still objects of racist sentiment. Many have told us that they remembered early in their lives being embarrassed about their fathers, who may have been unemployed, might have misused alcohol, and were marginalized from tribal and mainstream society. Even those who assimilated successfully on the surface still had to contend with the knowledge that they were racially different. We have spoken with fathers and mothers who say that they saw assimilation and economic integration for their children as their eventual goals. They saw themselves as the sacrifice required for their children's success.

Currently 45–67% of Native Americans, or approximately 2.8 million, live in urban settings, including 65% of Native youth (U.S. Department of Health and Human Services, 2010; Urban Indian Health Institute, 2007). Many travel between urban and rural settings; family and rituals are reasons for urban Indians to return to rural settings, while work and education are the main reasons rural Indians travel into cities. Personal experience with many urban Native Americans has permitted one of the authors to hear stories that tell how they believed if only they lived in a city they could find work and security, but having moved into a city they found only low paying jobs or none at all, and lived in lodgings that were highly incommodious and inadequate. Some of the Native Americans who came to cities during relocation describe what the government represented as a humanitarian gesture as an instrument of assimilation. Now grown, they recall going to urban public schools where they began to think of themselves as different from Native Americans on reservations and even from their own parents. Some have said they were embarrassed that their fathers worked at low income jobs and often were dependent on their wives. When they were children they were especially ashamed to observe their parents' tentativeness with Euro-Americans, which they interpreted as fear. Eventually, some of their mothers divorced their fathers and married Euro-American men. They said they came to think of the dominant social values as normative and real until later in their lives when they themselves experienced unfair hurdles on their career paths and gained sufficient experience to begin to have an inkling of understanding of their parents' predicaments.

It is also important to note that there have been several developments in urban areas that have positively impacted Native Americans. Historically, Native Americans have been generously open in their interactions with other groups. Because this openness has been abused, trust was undermined to a great extent but not utterly annihilated. In cities across the United States, Native Americans of different tribes and indeed persons of other races have bonded together to form new systems of friendship relationships that function to support family functioning. In some tribal communities on reservations children's behavior is regulated by clan and other tribal members, biologically related or not (Harrison, Wilson, Pine, Chan, & Buriel, 1990; MacPhee, Fritz, & Miller-Heyl, 1996). Today, there are pan-Indian pow-wows and purification ceremonies. Many Native Americans have brought the notion of communal care for children into urban settings. There may be families of different tribes whose members all play on softball teams together, or who speak of all their group's children being the responsibility of all the parents. One of the authors has witnessed nonbiological parents assuming the responsibility of other parents' children for an entire summer. He has heard discussions where parents in these groups speak of not cheering for their own children more than the other children, adhering to the Native American perspective that all children are the responsibility of the entire community. Traditionally, the family extends to all clan and tribal members, whether biologically related or not.

Cross-Cultural Adoption of Native Americans

Just as the education process has been responsible for the dismantlement of many Native American families, child welfare policies contributed to the mass removal of children from American Indian homes. Between 1958 and 1967 the Child Welfare League of America and the Bureau of Indian Affairs created the "'Indian Adoption Project,' which instigated 'the rescue' of Native American children and their placement into non-Indian families (Red Horse et al., 2000, p. 17)." Throughout the twentieth century, many churches, in their evangelical zeal, made concentrated efforts to go into Indian boarding schools to adopt and convert Native American children. These children typically were kept ignorant of Native American tribal and cultural values and ways. This practice was not officially halted until 1978, when the Indian Child Welfare Act described placement preferences that reflect tribal social structures, giving tribes the legal status of a parent in child welfare proceedings in keeping with tribal beliefs that children are born in a community. Studies found that previously

25–35% of Native American children had been separated from their families and placed in foster homes, adoptive homes, or institutions, a rate five to eight times higher than that of other children, and that 90% of Native American children were being placed by states into non-Indian homes (George, Larson, Koeng, & McCullough, 2000). Though the number of such placements has been reduced drastically, the number of Native American children still getting placed in non-Native American homes remains proportionately higher than for other populations (Dana, 2000). Today, one will find few Native Americans who do not know other Native American adults who suffered the above fate or who do not suffer from mental disturbances related to identity issues. Many are still making diligent searches to find their families or the tribes from which they have descended.

One of the authors knows two Native American children in his urban neighborhood who have no idea what their tribe is. He also has met a young man who just found out about his biological heritage. He had been adopted into a Euro-American family. He recalls becoming cognizant that his skin was much darker, and after learning he had been adopted, he had assumed he was probably Hispanic. He was 21 when he finally was told that he was Native American. He had never been exposed to a single Native American perspective or ritual by his adopted family. He has struggled with identity issues and depression for most of his life. He is now seeking out experiences related to his tribal heritage. Many Native Americans who have been cross culturally adopted have reported difficulties related to finding out about their tribal heritages. They have reported feeling marginalized, and many report life-dissatisfaction (Harness, 2009). Such placements may result not only in identity confusion, social dysfunction, and unhappiness; they also may undermine unique tribal and cultural identities and limit the possibilities of passing along tribal rituals and values to future generations. It is crucial that helping persons who work with Native American families know about these psychological conflicts and also the political relationship that exists between Native Americans and state and federal governments. It also should be noted here that there are non-Native American parents who successfully encourage and support their adopted Native American children's learning and involvement about and with their tribes.

Such oppression, as described above, has had a significant effect on Native American family structures. Some native people have decided not to teach their children about their tribal culture, language, or traditions because they do not want their children to experience degradation and rejection from the outside world. Many have made the transition into dominant society, taking on mainstream values and religious beliefs and living happily. Some have managed to hang onto and practice cultural traditions and beliefs, learning from elders who have been able to share their wisdom with a younger generation. Other families mix traditional and dominant cultural ways. Native Americans are in transition, adjusting to changes in social structure and identity. Still, there is much healing that needs to take place. There is still oppression and discrimination to overcome in order to reclaim indigenous family values.

Other Current Issues

Poverty and Unemployment

Native Americans' income level is only 62% of the US average, and the poverty rate is twice as high (U.S. Bureau of the Census, 2006). The Bureau of Indian Affairs reported that unemployment on reservations is high, reaching up to 80%. More than 600,000 Native Americans live below the poverty level (Trosper, 1996).

For some, a partial buffer to poverty and unemployment is the fact that having possessions beyond what is necessary is a foreign concept in traditional tribal living. In the past, riches included freedom to cultivate or hunt on traditional lands, having animals offer themselves for the tribe to have meat and hides. These riches were shared among those less able to provide for themselves. Today, it is still a common practice for extended family members and other tribal members to engage in selfless sharing of resources with persons less fortunate than themselves.

Though many Native Americans still suffer from lack of financial security, as testified to by the statistics reported above, the tribal gambling industries have directly and indirectly provided many Native Americans with greater employment opportunities and with regular stipends. Some tribes have wisely invested these monies in ways that have helped families with child care, provided financial support for families to send their children to college, supported family counseling services, and have offered aid to grandparents and elders.

Couple Violence

Native Americans experience the highest rates of sexual and physical assault (Tjaden & Tahoennes, 2000). American Indian women are twice as likely to be victims of sexually violent crimes as women in other ethnic groups, and three and a half times more likely to be victims of physical and sexual assault than the national average (Amnesty International, 2007; Bhungalia, 2001). While these statistics include more than just violence within families, it is evidence that Native Americans exist in spaces where there is much violence and that there is an inordinate amount of violence in Native American marital relationships. Both Native American men and women report engaging in significant aggression, nonphysical intimidation, and low levels of physical aggression, such as yelling, threatening, and slapping, toward their spouses (Robbins, Stoltenberg, Robbins, & Ross, 2002). Robbins, Stoltenberg, Robbins, Lacey, and McWhirter (unpublished manuscript) reported that both Native American wives and husbands engage in more physical and psychological violence toward their spouse when they misuse alcohol. Native American husbands engage in more violence, both psychological and physical, toward their wives when they rate themselves as having high levels of historic trauma. This physical and psychological violence between spouses is bound to impact children's feelings of safety.

Traditional values and learning may offer buffers to domestic violence and lead to stronger marriages for Native American people. These include the importance of spirituality, receiving advice and counsel from family members, including the sharing of traditional stories (which taught values and provided guidance), having family members teach traditional roles and responsibilities within marriage, observing other couples (learning what problems to avoid and successes to follow), trying to be good examples for their own children, learning from spiritual leaders and counselors, and learning from each other. One of the authors was told recently by a Native American woman that on her reservation in the southwest, when she and her husband had had a physical altercation, elders had them make an appointment to appear in a particular building, where they were to sit silently and listen to older couples talk to them about their harmonious relationships for an entire day. She believed it helped. Curiously, Robbins et al. (unpublished manuscript) found that for Native American women, the possibility of family's or friends' revenge on their partner after a conflict mediated lower levels of physical aggression. This is an indication that protection of those physically weaker and in danger is an obligation of those who are stronger, reflecting traditional beliefs. While this in some ways is a sad commentary about how Native Americans may protect themselves, it may be a reality about which those in the helping professions who may have grown up in more secure environments need to become aware.

Alcohol Abuse

One hundred percent of Native Americans are affected either directly or indirectly by alcoholism. The lifetime prevalence of alcoholism among Native American people is estimated to be between 28 and

65% (Chester, Robin, Koss, Lopez, & Goldman, 1994). Among Native Americans, lower levels of parental monitoring and support have been risk factors for Native American adolescent misuse (Rogers & Fleming, 2004). Substance misuse is directly related to the disruption of Native American families. Fetal alcohol syndrome (FAS) is more common in Native populations, and can occur in 8.5 per 1,000 live births as compared to 2.2 per 1,000 in the general population (Gossage, 2002). Caretaker drinking behaviors are correlated with less effective parenting (DiClemente et al., 2001) and can increase the risk of early-onset drinking for children, both through modeling and less effective parenting (Walls, Whitbeck, Hoyt, & Johnson, 2007). As an example of intergenerational modeling, maternal grand-mothers of children with FAS had significantly higher rates of alcohol use than other grandmothers. They also experienced more alcohol-related medical problems (70.4%), including trauma (48.1%) and injuries (51.9%) (Kvigne, Valborg, Leonardson, Borzelleca, & Welty, 2008).

The presence of a nonparental adult who was willing to monitor youth behavior has been found to be a significant protective factor against adolescent Native American alcohol misuse (Rogers & Fleming, 2004). In addition, common practice in Native American communities when a parent drank has been for the children to go to a relative's home, knowing where to go to be safe. When the parent would sober up, he or she would go to the relative's house, be accepted and nourished with a meal, and take the children home (Morrison et al., 2010). Purifications (sweat) ceremonies also are currently being used successfully in many tribal treatment facilities to combat alcohol misuse.

Problem Gambling

Problem gambling has increased among American Indian populations, especially among women (Volberg & Abbott, 1997). Studies of general populations have shown that children of parents who gamble experience loss of emotional and financial support and exhibit inadequate coping skills, poor interpersonal relationship skills, and serious behavior problems (Darbyshire, Oster, & Carrig, 2001). Native American boys might be more negatively affected than girls by their mother's frequent gambling (MacPhee et al., 1996; Momper & Jackson, 2007).

The issue of organized gambling is complex. The 1988 Indian Gaming Act encourages gambling as a means to provide those Indian tribes who are poverty-stricken the ability to raise economic standards and better the standard of living for tribal people. Indeed, those who moved out of poverty because of the opening of a reservation gambling casino scored significantly higher on a measure of parenting adequacy and had children with fewer behavior problems than their counterparts who remained poor (Costello, Compton, Keeler, & Angold, 2003). Resources that encourage and enhance emotional and mental support for Native American mothers who engage in problem gambling might serve to counteract the negative effects (Momper & Jackson, 2007). Research has associated negative effects of Native American mothers' gambling on their sons' behavior, though it was conditioned by the availability of family support (MacPhee et al., 1996; Momper & Jackson, 2007).

Delinquency

In the United States, Native American youth experience the highest rates of interpersonal and self-directed violence. The annual violent crime rate for Native Americans aged 12 and up is reported to be approximately 2.5 times higher than the national rate (Greenfield & Smith, 1999). In 2005, more than 60% of incarcerated young offenders under federal jurisdiction were Native American (U.S. Bureau of Justice Statistics, 2006). Risk factors include family disintegration and lack of community support; loss of language and culture; racism; lack of teacher support and peer pressure at school;

availability of drugs and alcohol; lack of discipline from parents, uncles, and elders; and gangs and weapons (Mmari, Blum, & Teufel-Shone, 2010).

Protective factors that may buffer Native American youth from such risks as violence, crime, and incarceration include close connectedness with a parent or family member (U.S. Department of Health and Human Services, 2010), knowing their tribal languages (which enables learning of tribal ways and traditions), ceremonies and pow-wows, mentors and role models, religion and spirituality, and a sense of responsibility (Mmari et al., 2010).

Suicide

Native American youth, aged 15–24, have the highest rate of suicide of any racial or age group in the United States (Centers for Disease Control and Prevention, 2009). The rate of suicide for American Indian and Alaska Natives is far higher than that of any other ethnic group in the US, and 70% higher than the rate for the general population (U.S. Bureau of Justice Statistics, 2006). This crisis reflects the disenfranchisement of Native American people who are willing to die rather than endure their lives. Sadly, their families and communities feel as if they have failed, and they are left to grieve and endure the hardships.

Reducing the risk of suicide for Native American youth includes such protective factors as family and community support, having cultural and religious beliefs that discourage suicide and support self-preservation instincts, learning traditional forms of living, making tribal handicrafts, and attending tribal ceremonies and rituals (Substance Abuse and Mental Health Services Administration, 2010).

Clinical Implications

The points that might be drawn from the above literature review suggest similarities with other minority ethnic groups. Like other minority groups, Native Americans express an applied reference to spirituality that includes unique yet related perspectives about interconnectedness, harmony, and balance. Research also suggests that broad social forces and systems pervade the family's social environment, which requires that therapists make assessments and offer treatments that take into account the complex sets of contemporary influence and relationships. Also, similar to many other minority groups, the family includes biological members, extended and deceased, as well as significant others. Treatment must reflect the importance of these networks. Therapy is likely to include the client's support system, such as the extended family system, medicine persons, and significant others. Because so many Native Americans are connected to larger systems and agencies, some due to being victims of discriminatory acts and others because of their designations as "wards of the state," therapists should be prepared to work with case managers, advocates, probation officers, and group home workers.

Appreciation for unique beliefs and assumptions is necessary to ensure cultural competence. The above review of the literature suggests that the values of many Native Americans are likely to emphasize harmony, balance, interconnectedness, humility, and courage. Also, the above cited writers emphasize a focus on strengths, resilience, adoptability, and competence as opposed to pathology, addressing directly the negative influence of stereotyping and negative descriptions that minorities often internalize. Client values also may reflect the importance of social interactions, including ceremonies and rituals. It is crucial that therapists who work with Native Americans develop a referral list of appropriate persons who are tribally accepted leaders of spiritual rituals who might work in conjunction with them. In order for this to be conducted ethically, the therapist must adhere closely to professional guidelines and codes.

Research Implications

Research should focus on questions investigating family survival within an arena of institutional neglect, identifying strengths, assets, and resources among Native American extended family systems and communities. Such research could reveal effective coping and means toward achieving healing and health and describe the real world confrontation of problems by Native American families. We might ask questions such as: In what kind of extended family interactions and climates do children grow and experience healthy functioning? How do the elders give of their knowledge and in what situations do our families benefit most from it? As Native Americans we have to identify our strengths. This should be the focus of research first and foremost so that we might then find solutions to the problems that we ourselves must define. When appropriate and having gone through proper protocol, researchers also may examine the impact of traditional ceremonies upon family health.

All researchers must be wary of making Eurocentric conceptualizations when posing research problems related to Native Americans (or any other minority group). When designing their studies, researches should ask themselves if they have taken into account the changing coping styles adopted by oppressed groups to survive through their histories of victimization. What unique cultural characteristics and traits does the group value in relation to the social and political contexts in which they find themselves? As stressed throughout this chapter, culturally unique family strengths, such as adaptability should be emphasized. Further, family assessment instruments need further testing to advance construct validity.

Case Example

In this case example, narrative therapy techniques were adapted to facilitate work with an American Indian client. Narrative therapy might be defined simply as a therapeutic means to separate individuals or groups from unitary toxic knowledges that oppress them (White & Epston, 1990). As the therapist, I focused on "helping the clients tell their life stories, listening carefully for sparkling events that may help open up alternative stories" (Freedman & Combs, 1996, p. 107) rather than using problem solving techniques or interpretation. I utilized White and Epston's (1990) externalization of values internalized from socialization as well as culturally appropriate metaphors. I helped the client map not only his personal story (Denborough, 2008), but also his ancestors' stories. And I utilized supplementation, or the expansion of old stories, through the identification of contradictory details or oppositions in stories (Robbins & Harrist, 2004).

Chebon (fictional name), a 40-year-old, full-blood urban Woodland Native American and lifelong bachelor, came in declaring his problem to be "stress." He explained that he had had difficulty concentrating for over a month. The anxiety he was experiencing was impacting his performance at the factory where he had worked for 10 years. He also was frequenting the gambling casino more than usual, every weekday, before going home each night. He claimed to not "bet more than petty change," but it bothered him that until the past week he had previously gambled only about once a month and then with friends, not alone as now. When asked about any events that might have precipitated the stress, Chebon simply shook his head and said he just wanted to learn how he could curb his stress. When I tried to get a background history, he simply chuckled at the questions, shook his head, and refused to answer.

Over the first five sessions, for which he was always punctual, Chebon responded to cognitive-behavioral interventions, such as completing frequency charts regarding when and where he experienced the stress, and rating the level at which he experienced stress from highest (10) to lowest (1). He was able to determine that he felt the highest levels of stress at home but also felt high levels of stress when work was slow on the job. He felt the lowest level of stress when he was with his family on weekends. He spent every weekend either with his aunt, his cousin and her children, or his mother. He ate meals with them and took the kids bowling or to movies. On some weekends he drove 200 miles to "spend time with his mother." As an aside, he mentioned that he liked talking humorously with his mother and aunt in his Native language.

Around the tenth session, Chebon said that he had always felt some level of anxiety. Then he said he would like to tell me about his life. I told him that I would use narrative psychology techniques to help him "thicken" his stories with minute particulars that might elicit memories, which could result in emotional release (Robbins & Harrist, 2004). He said he grew up just outside a small Native American town. He fondly recalled painting a cow skull, and making stickball sticks and black and white stickballs with his grandfather when he was about 7 or 8. Then they put up the pole about 30 ft in the air, put a cow skull on its top, and launched the ball over and over again at the skull. He said his grandfather taught him how to call like a turkey while they played. He said that his grandfather "died fairly young because he drank too much and died around that time." He loved his grandfather very much "because he was really protective and was funny." I asked him to tell me more about playing stickball with his grandfather. At that point, he stopped talking, chuckled, shook his head characteristically, then said he had to leave.

For several sessions afterward we went back to fairly strict behavioral work, very concrete discussions about altering actions that caused stress. We also experimented with his timing himself as he attempted to spend longer and longer periods of time in necessary stressful situations at work, which demonstrated to him that he was more resilient than he had thought.

One session began with his telling me he had been going to "sweats" every Saturday night since just before he started counseling. I again attempted a supplementary question, asking him to describe his experience. He explained that since he had been an "urban Indian" he had had a hard time finding stickball games and getting to stomp dances so had begun going to sweats just outside of the city with a Plains Indian he had met at work. Instead of answering my question directly, he reflected a long time, smiling and shaking his head, and said he had been thinking that his high level of stress began when he started going to sweats.

Oddly, to me, his train of thought suddenly took still another direction. He said that when he was eight he found out that the woman he thought was his mother was really his aunt. He said that she had married a Euro-American man when he was 5. The rest of his family said it was for financial security. The man had two boys about his age, and he would force all of them to box each other until blood was drawn or force them to practice tackling each other over and over with no pads. He drank all the time and would whip them mercilessly with a belt almost every day for trivial reasons. One day, when he did not think Chebon was trying his hardest, he ran a tub of scalding hot water, took Chebon's clothes off, and forced him into the tub for punishment. Chebon was scalded so badly that when the woman he thought was his mother came home, she had to call the ambulance. Chebon was life-flighted by helicopter to the nearest city hospital.

One day during the weeks he stayed in the hospital, his biological mother, a woman whom he had always considered to be his aunt, told him who she was and that he would be going home with her. She said she had let her sister raise him because she was so young when she had him and had no financial support, had no job, and her mother was too poor to take care of another person in the family. He recalled not speaking for a few months while in his new home. He said he was angry at everyone except his uncle, who whipped the abuser a couple of times. When Chebon finished he said he felt great relief to be able to tell the story to someone.

Over the next few months his stress level was down and he spoke more casually in sessions. During his first 12 sweats he had not been able to endure the hot vapor more than two of the four rounds. I asked why he found it so hard to complete the four rounds. He said that the water vapor was hot. He paused shaking his head, put both hands on his left knee and burst into tears. After a few minutes, he raised his head and said he was going to tell his story about the "scolding hot water" to the people at the sweat lodge and ask for prayers to help him work through his "struggle" with the past. He added, "And my grandfather will help me." He later reported that he had made it through all four rounds with their support and prayers.

I thought Chebon would cease to come in for therapy after his "sweat" accomplishment, but he continued. We seemed to have little to talk about for a few sessions. He had ceased to gamble. He had joined an urban Native American stickball team. He had even committed to "going on the hill" for a *Hanbleceya*, or Vision Quest. When I asked him why he wanted to continue counseling, he said he was still "lonely."

He told me he had never even really had a "girlfriend." I asked him to tell me how his loneliness would look if I could see it. Confused at first, he eventually said that his loneliness looked like a woman. "How old?" "Little younger than me." "What does she look like?" "Brown and round. Indian." "What does this loneliness say to you?" "Nothin'."

After a few sessions, he said that one of his aunts had "tried to set him up with Indian girls before," but he could never take the risk of asking them out. After he was taken from the aunt he thought was his mother and her husband, he went to live with his birth mother, grandmother, aunt, and cousin. He explained that they never forgave the aunt for putting him in the abusive situation, and he had never seen her again. He said that everyone had talked so badly about her that even he eventually thought she must be a bad person. He told them that he never wanted to see her again.

We met until just after his Hanbleceya, which he successfully completed. His "good" aunt tried to set up a date for him with a "round and brown" woman, but he said he was going to have dinner with "the mother of my early childhood" first. He told me how he loved his whole family: aunts, mother, cousins, all of the nieces and nephews and grandfather. His last words in therapy were "I'm blessed."

Case Conceptualization

The main themes of Chebon's life story had to do with bravely dealing with stress, deception, sadism, lack of safety, poverty, gambling, alcohol, and loneliness. The sparkling moments he foregrounded dealt with the themes of humor, tribal traditions, tribal language, and ceremonial challenges. During his story's journey he was given support by his aunt, mother, cousins, and nephews, a Plain's Native American and the persons at the sweat lodge, and his grandfather, in both physical and spiritual forms. He drew upon inner resources such as bravery, trust, tribal spirituality, love, appreciation, harmony, and respect to help him move through his challenges. He and I actively worked at integrating his participation in Native American ceremonies and rituals with his counseling.

The first clinical implication one may consider from the case study is that the family therapy described entailed working directly with only one person. We have worked with many Native Americans in therapy, and having only Chebon in the room was an anomaly. Still, one should readily see that working with Chebon was not individual counseling. Chebon's entire identity was intricately interconnected to his family and community, and the themes that emerged in session were familial rather than individual. His family consisted of the larger friendship sweat community and his extended family, including the spirit of his grandfather, who spoke with him during the sweats. His ultimate goal came to be true harmony in his extended family, which was integral to eventually finding a girlfriend. He and his family were engaged in a struggle about how to deal with the disharmony that erupted when someone in their family married someone outside their race who harmed their child. Who were they to blame and what were they to do about the wrong committed?

The therapist benefited from gaining an understanding of what had helped Chebon's family and tribe survive, and then he worked to support and assist Chebon in revitalizing those activities, practices, and beliefs to benefit his health. Further, tracking family and tribal/cultural accommodations to external stress represents an important source of indicators of strengths inherent in Native American tribes and families, especially considering that the family system and culture have survived despite overwhelming and recurrent institutional disruption. Understanding life experiences, cultural values, and frames of reference informs culturally relevant approaches in therapy (Ancis, 2004).

Conclusion

Once one has heard the stories of the sicknesses, massacres, and cultural genocide Native Americans have been subjected to it may seem like a miracle that they have survived at all. But one might consider more deeply about what may have been the characteristics of their heroic resilience in the face of seemingly insurmountable odds. If they can be uncovered, the field of psychotherapy may expand its perspectives and approaches in its attempts to help people to cope and even grow in the midst of difficulties. We have discussed how, in spite of the traumatic experience of observing at close hand how land, water, forests, animals, and people were decimated and wasted, Native Americans have continued to espouse their deep appreciation of their kinships with all living things.

Our mental health fields can mirror the industrial/computer age that fosters individualistic/materialistic values, which are closely associated with the increasing alienation more and more people feel and the increasing violence that people express toward each other and nature, or we can learn from traditional Native Americans and begin to restore our kinship connections. The path toward humanization is not simply learning in a mathematical way that we fit into a family genealogical chart; rather it is feeling the connections with the heart. Native American resilience is based on a deep respect for everyone and all living creatures and things, which allows for a harmonious life within oneself as well as in social interactions. Health and harmony begin with awareness that we are all indigenous people, no matter what color, and that this mother earth connection makes us sisters and brothers.

The basis of healing for Native Americans is realizing our place in the ever-expanding concentric circles of our extended family and our responsibilities to each other, and especially to every child that is born. Family therapists are in a unique position to revitalize and organize Native American values, knowledges, and wisdoms, in the creation of new family treatment models. First, tribal people themselves must be given the space and opportunities to build upon their unique traditional beliefs, ceremonies, tribal identities, and language. Anchored in these traditional beliefs, we will observe how they reinterpret and even supplement traditional beliefs and ceremonies to speak to their current predicaments, often drawing from the wisdoms of Euro-American family treatment models. Of all forms of therapy, it is in the field of family counseling that tribal people have much to offer and learn. Out of such respectful interaction, our extended families can be rebuilt. With the restoration and revitalization of traditional knowledges and wisdoms, the seeds of hundreds of years of resilience can grow into a healthy tree of life.

References

Amnesty International Report. (2007). *Maze of injustice: The failure to protect indigenous women from sexual violence in the USA*. New York: Amnesty International USA.
Ancis, J. R. (2004). Culturally responsive practice. In J. R. Ancis (Ed.), *Culturally responsive interventions: Innovative approaches to working with diverse populations* (pp. 3–21). New York: Brunner-Rutledge.
Bad Hand, H. P. (2002). *Native American healing*. Taos: Dog Soldier Press.
Benally, R. K. (1999). Thinking good: The teachings of Navajo grandmothers. In M. Schweitzer (Ed.), *American Indian grandmothers: Traditions and transitions* (pp. 25–52). Albuquerque: University of New Mexico Press.
Bhungalia, L. (2001). Native American women and violence. *National NOW Times, 33*(5), 13.

Brave Heart, M., & De Bruyn, L. M. (1998). The American Indian holocaust: Healing historical unresolved grief. *American Indian and Alaskan Native Mental Health Research, 8*, 60–82.

Braveboy, B. M. J. (2006). Toward a tribal critical race theory in education. *The Urban Review, 37*(5), 425–446.

Burnette, D. (1997). Grandparents raising grandchildren in the inner city. *Families in Society, 78*, 489–499.

Centers for Disease Control and Prevention. (2009). *Suicide prevention: Youth suicide*. Retrieved, August 24, 2011, from http://wwwh.ede.gov/violenceprevention/pub/youthsuicide.html.

Chester, B., Robin, R. W., Koss, M. P., Lopez, J., & Goldman, D. (1994). Grandmother dishonored: Violence against women by male partners in American Indian communities. *Violence and Victims, 9*, 249–258.

Costello, J. E., Compton, S. N., Keeler, G., & Angold, A. (2003). Relationships between poverty and psychopathology: A natural experiment. *Journal of the American Medical Association, 290*, 2023–2029.

Dana, R. H. (2000). The cultural self as a locus for assessment and intervention with American Indian/Alaska Natives. *Journal of Multicultural Counseling and Development, 28*, 66–82.

Darbyshire, M., Oster, C., & Carrig, H. (2001). The experience of pervasive loss: Children and young people living in a family where parental gambling is a problem. *Journal of Gambling Studies, 17*, 23–45.

Denborough, D. (2008). *Collective narrative practice*. Adelaide: Dulwich Center Publications.

DiClemente, R., Wingood, G. M., Crosby, R., Sionean, C., Cobb, B. K., Harrington, K., et al. (2001). Parental monitoring: Association with adolescents' risk behaviors. *Pediatrics, 107*, 1363–1368.

Diller, J. V. (2011). Working with Native American clients: An interview with Jack Lawson. *Cultural Diversity: A Primer for the Human Services, 4*, 240–256.

Duran, E., & Duran, B. (1995). *Native American postcolonial psychology*. New York: State University of New York Press.

Freedman, J., & Combs, G. (1996). Gender stories. *Journal of Systemic Therapies, 15*(1), 31–44.

Fuller-Thomson, E., & Minkler, M. (2005). American Indian/Alaskan native grandparents raising grandchildren: Findings from the Census 2000 supplementary survey. *Social Work, 50*(2), 131–139.

George, L. K., Larson, D. B., Koeng, H. G., & McCullough, M. E. (2000). Spirituality and health: What we know, what we need to know. *Journal of Social and Clinical Psychology, 19*, 102–116.

Gossage, J. P. (2002). *Fetal alcohol syndrome among American Indians*. NIAAA Research Monograph no. 37.

Greenfield, L. N., & Smith, S. K. (1999). *American Indians and crime*. Washington: Department of Justice, Office of Justice Statistics.

Harness, S. (2009). *Mixing cultural identities through transracial adoption*. New York: Edwin Mellen Press.

Harrison, A. O., Wilson, M. N., Pine, C. J., Chan, S. Q., & Buriel, R. (1990). Family ecologies of ethnic minority children. *Child Development, 61*, 347–362.

Hibbard, W. S. (2005). *Reports of transpersonal experiences of non-native practitioners of the Native American sweat lodge ceremony*. Unpublished doctoral dissertation, Saybrook, San Francisco.

Kvigne, L., Valborg, L., Leonardson, G. R., Borzelleca, J., & Welty, T. K. (2008). Characteristics of grandmothers who have grandchildren with fetal alcohol syndrome or incomplete fetal alcohol syndrome. *Maternal and Child Health Journal, 12*(6), 760–765.

MacPhee, D., Fritz, J., & Miller-Heyl, J. (1996). Ethnic variations in personal social networks and parenting. *Child Development, 67*, 3278–3295.

Mann, C. C. (2003). *1491: New revelations of the Americas before Columbus*. New York: Alfred K. Knopf.

Mmari, K. N., Blum, R. W., & Teufel-Shone, N. (2010). What increases risk and protection for delinquent behaviors among American Indian youth?: Findings from three tribal communities. *Youth & Society, 41*(3), 382–413.

Momper, S. L., & Jackson, A. P. (2007). Maternal gambling, parenting, and child behavioral functioning in Native American families. *Social Work Research, 31*(4), 199–209.

Morrison, C., Fox, K., Cross, T., & Roger, P. (2010). Permanency through Wabanaki eyes: A narrative perspective from 'The people who live where the sun rises'. *Child Welfare: Journal of Policy, Practice, and Program, 89*(1), 103–123.

Mutchler, J. E., Baker, L. A., & Lee, S. A. (2007). Grandparents responsible for grandchildren in Native-American families. *Social Science Quarterly, 88*(4), 990–1109.

Pebley, A. R., & Rudkin, L. L. (1999). Grandparents caring for grandchildren: What do we know? *Journal of Family Issues, 20*, 218–242.

Red Horse, J. G., Martinez, C., Day, C., Day, P., Pupart, J., & Scharnberg, D. (2000). *Family preservation: Concepts in American Indian communities*. Seattle: Casey Family Programs.

Robbins, R., Colmant, S., Dorton, J., Schultz, L., Colmant, Y., & Ciali, P. (2006). Colonial instillations in American Indian boarding school students. *Educational Foundations, 20*(3–4), 69–88.

Robbins, R., & Harrist, S. (2004). American Indian contructionalist family therapy for acculturative stress. In J. Ancis (Ed.), *Culturally responsive interventions* (pp. 23–48). New York: Bruner-Rutledge.

Robbins, R., Scherman, A., Holeman, H., & Wilson, J. (2005). Roles of American Indian grandparents in times of cultural crisis. *Journal of Cultural Diversity, 1*, 46–56.

Robbins, R., Stoltenberg, C., Robbins, S., & Ross, M. (2002). Marital satisfaction and Cherokee language fluency. *Measurement and Evaluation in Counseling and Development, 14*, 134–146.

Robbins, S., Stoltenberg, C., Robbins, R., Lacey, K., & McWhittier, P. (unpublished manuscript). *Physical Aggression: The effects of alcohol and drug use, influence of parent relationship aggression, and historic trauma in an American Indian sample*.

Rogers, K. B., & Fleming, W. M. (2004). Individual, family, and community factors related to alcohol use among Native American adolescents. *Adolescent & Family Health, 3*(3), 140–147.

Schweitzer, M. M. (1999). *American Indian grandmothers: Traditions and transitions*. Albuquerque: University of New Mexico Press.

Shomaker, D. J. (1989). Transfer of children and the importance of grandmothers among the Navajo Indians. *Journal of Cross-Cultural Gerontology, 4*, 1–18.

Sue, D. W., & Sue, D. (2008). Counseling American Indian and Alaska Natives. In D. W. Sue & D. Sue (Eds.), *Counseling the culturally diverse: Theory and practice* (Rev. ed. 5, pp. 345–359). Hoboken, New Jersey: John Wiley & Sons, Inc.

Szasz, M. C. (1999). *Education and the American Indian: The road to self- determination since 1928*. Albuquerque: University of New Mexico Press.

Tjaden, P., & Tahoennes, N. (2000). *Full report of the prevalence, incidents, and consequences of violence against women: Research report* (NIJ Rept. No. NCJ 183781). Washington: U.S. Department of Justice, National Institute of Justice.

Trosper, R. L. (1996). American Indian poverty on reservations, 1969–1989. In G. D. Sandefur, R. R. Rindfus, & B. Cohen (Eds.), *Changing numbers, changing needs: American Indian demography and public health* (pp. 172–195). Washington: National Academic Press.

U.S. Bureau of Indian Affairs. (2002). *2001-2002 school year education directory*. Office of Indian Education Programs, U.S. Department of the Interior, Washington, D.C.: Author.

U.S. Bureau of Justice Statistics. (2006). *Race and crime in the United States*. Washington: U.S. Government Printing Office.

U.S. Bureau of the Census. (2000a). *Children under 18 living in their grandparents' household, by state*. Retrieved September 13, 2010, from http://factfinder.census.govt/BasicFactsServlet.

U.S. Bureau of the Census. (2006). *American Indian/Alaska Native data and links*. Retrieved July 13, 2010, from http://factfinder.Census.gov/home/aian/indix.html.

Substance Abuse and Mental Health Services Administration. (2010). *To live to see the great day that dawns: preventing suicide by American Indian and Alaska Native youth and young adults*. Rockville, MD: US Department of Health Human Services, SAMHSA, Center for Mental Health Services; 2010. Publication no. SMA 10–4480.

Urban Indian Health Institute. (2007). *Invisible tribes: Urban Indians and their health in a changing world*. Seattle: Author.

Volberg, R. A., & Abbott, M. A. (1997). Ethnicity and gambling: Gambling and problem gambling among indigenous peoples. *Substance Use & Misuse, 32*, 1525–1538.

Walls, M. L., Whitbeck, L. B., Hoyt, D. R., & Johnson, K. D. (2007). Early-onset alcohol use among Native American youth: Examining female caretaker influence. *Journal of Marriage and Family, 69*, 451–464.

Weibel-Orlando, J. (1990). Grandparenting styles: Native American perspectives. In J. Sokolovsky (Ed.), *The cultural context of aging*. Westport: Greenwood Press.

White, M., & Epston, D. (1990). *Narrative means to therapeutic ends*. New York: W.W. Norton.

Familias Fuertes: Family Resilience Among Latinos

13

J. Maria Bermudez and Jay A. Mancini

Introduction

Family life is vital to most Latinos. Family resilience thus is an important perspective for family scholars working with Latino families to adopt because of its focus on wellness and adaptability, in effect, punctuating the strengths common among Latino families. Toward the latter part of the twentieth century, conversations among family scientists and family therapists more and more included the concept of resilience. Researchers began examining family dynamics that provided a more accurate portrayal of family life, as well as in terms of providing professional support to families. Wolin and Wolin (1993) discussed both the "damage model" and the "challenge model" as they pertained to prevention and intervention, highlighting the significance of identifying and extracting the strengths families possess. Elevating aspects of strength and resilience is particularly important for working with families, who at first glance may be viewed as characterized mainly by needs and deficits, often an inaccurate and skewed portrayal. A strengths perspective views the glass as "half-full" rather than "half-empty." This is significant because families may present themselves in clinical settings as primarily having deficits rather than as possessing strengths and assets and living everyday life where negative and positive elements intersect.

Additionally, it is important to clarify that although there are distinctions between individual, family, and community resilience and there is substantial overlap, these forms of resilience are not the same (Hawley & DeHaan, 1996). Consequently, it is necessary for professionals and communities to assess how resilience my vary according to specific units of analysis or intervention. For example, the examination of family resilience without considering community resilience (as indexed by social support) leaves out important contexts that clearly influence family well-being (Mancini & Bowen, 2009). We also must assess how the interplay/intersections between these three locales of resilience operate as they relate to Latino families. Although we are primarily focusing on family resilience as the focus of analysis, we also discuss how cultural values, beliefs, attitudes, and practices can be integrated into a resilience framework for Latino families. For example, evidence shows that being bicultural and maintaining original cultural values contribute to positive mental health (Skogrand, Hatch, & Singh, 2009).

J.M. Bermudez • J.A. Mancini (✉)
Department of Human Development and Family Science,
The University of Georgia, Athens, GA, USA
e-mail: mbermude@uga.edu

D.S. Becvar (ed.), *Handbook of Family Resilience*,
DOI 10.1007/978-1-4614-3917-2_13, © Springer Science+Business Media New York 2013

Our discussion springs from Hawley and DeHaan's (1996) assertion that if we emphasize resilience in clients, then we will focus on strengths. Within this primary assertion, one assumes that if families possess qualities that enable them to withstand seemingly insurmountable barriers, then we should focus on the observable cultural norms and behaviors that contribute to Latino families' well-being. In this chapter, we thus pull together several threads that form a tapestry displaying *familias fuertes* (strong families). Building upon Walsh's model of family resilience (2002), Hawley and DeHann's work integrating lifespan and family perspectives (1996), and a review of the literature of family resilience among immigrant Latinos, our chapter provides a preliminary framework for understanding and supporting Latino families in therapy. Our goal in positing this emerging clinical framework is to account for various dimensions of family strengths among Latino families.

The Demography of Latino Families

Latinos comprise the largest and fastest growing ethnic minority group in the United States (14.8 % of total population). Most Latinos reside in California, Texas, Florida, and New York. Overwhelmingly, the majority of Latinos residing in the US are of Mexican origin (64 %), followed by Puerto Rican (9 %), other Hispanic (7.7 %), and Central American (7.6 %). Approximately 60 % are native born and 40 % are foreign born (US Census Bureau, 2006). Latino families in the US are most often younger and larger than their non-Latino counterparts (Ho, Rasheed, & Rasheed, 2004), with approximately 70 % under the age of 40.

With Latinos immigrating to the US from every country in Latin America and all over the world, the US has the most heterogeneous Hispanic population in history (McAdoo, Martínez, & Hughes, 2005). The reasons for immigrating to the US are similar to those of most other ethnic groups: the pursuit of the American dream, escape from economic hardship, political instability, limited opportunities for quality education, employment problems, and healthcare issues, as well as for a sense of safety and stability often lacking in one's country of origin. Nonetheless, when Latinos come to the US they experience multiple losses (Miller & Gonzalez, 2009), including leaving familiar customs, a dominant language other than English, friend and family networks, and a sense of belonging. Immigrant Latinos certainly enjoy the benefits of living in the US and they also have added to the rich diversity experienced here; however, the rewards have not come without a price and for many Latinos (immigrant and non-immigrant), everyday life continues to be hardship.

Adversity and Vulnerabilities

Given their marginalized status, Latinos residing in the US are especially susceptible to risk factors. Compared to the majority population, they are more likely to be uninsured, have lower socioeconomic status, live in unsafe neighborhoods, have lower graduation rates, less access to medical and mental health services, and quality education (Cardoso & Thompson, 2010; Domenech Rodríguez, Davis, Rodríguez, & Bates, 2006). These factors increase their risk of living in poverty, making it more difficult to rise out of a life of financial struggle for themselves and their families. Economic needs often force families to live apart as parents and partners may only find work in different locations. Family separation is common even when families immigrate together. Indeed, for Latinos, a main risk factor is the effect of immigration, which often creates a loss of familial and cultural support as well as a financial struggle. These challenges are compounded by the stress of navigating a new culture, strained family and work roles, limited access to resources, and a system filled with anti-immigrant sentiment and institutionalized racism (Domenech Rodríguez et al., 2006; Tummala-Narra, 2004).

Of particular note are transnational families (Glick, 2010). Transnational families differ from migrant families in that different family members are dispersed across various countries and borders at different times. Though transnational families are spread apart, they maintain a sense of togetherness and mutual responsibility. The comings and goings of transnational family members mean that transition, uncertainty, and challenges may become a way of life and less resolved than families who emigrate more traditionally. Although there are considerable hardships and challenges for many Latino families, there is also notable resilience that contributes to their sense of wellness and strength.

Common Themes of Resilience Among Latino Families

Cardoso and Thompson (2010) conducted a systematic review of the literature on common themes of resilience among Latino immigrant families. The importance of family and culture was clearly evident across the 42 articles reviewed. Common themes of resilience among Latino immigrant families were identified and four broad domains of risk and protective factors emerged: individual characteristics, family strengths, cultural factors, and community support. Each domain is essential to understanding resilience among Latinos families, despite the stresses of immigration, acculturation, discrimination, and pervasive socioeconomic disadvantage. Below we briefly discuss the four domains in order to help contextualize the formation of our clinical framework for family resilience among Latinos.

Individual Characteristics

Individual-level characteristics of resilience are often a combination of biological and psychosocial influences (Fraser, Kirby, & Smokowski, 2004). Given the above-mentioned risk factors threatening the well-being of Latinos living in the US, qualities such as self-esteem, self-mastery, and personal sense of agency are important attributes of competence that affect the quality of health and interpersonal relationships. Campbell (2008) conducted a study of Mexican immigrant women and found that these attributes led to a strong desire for employment, education, and autonomy. For children and adolescents, many studies have shown the empowering effects of positive ethnic identity. Other individual resilience factors were social competence, intellect, and motivation (Cardoso & Thompson, 2010).

Individual resilience is also reflected and culturally embedded in *dichos* (popular sayings or proverbs). *Dichos* are a fundamental aspect of Latino family discourse. They transmit intergenerational values, attitudes, and perceptions rooted in culture, and function as a reservoir of culturally based resilience, allowing family members to resist marginalization and to support and encourage each other (Espinoza-Herold, 2007). Many Spanish *dichos* reflect the spirit of maintaining a positive disposition, having a sense of determination, and spiritual beliefs that strengthen one's sense of resilience. They foster a sense of unity in the face of challenge and adversity, and the belief and pride in having the ability to be strengthened by life's challenges. For example, a common *dicho* my mother (M. B.) told me was *querer is poder*, which in English is "where there is a will there is a way." She had many *dichos* that encouraged me to reflect on my actions, to believe in myself, and to strive to be and do my best. Overall, it is challenging to disentangle individual traits from those traits embedded in culture and family. The overlap is evident as we discuss the other domains.

Family Strengths

Although family resilience was not the primary unit of analysis in studies examining resilience among Latinos, all of the resilience factors presented in the literature noted *familism*, family, and/or cultural factors as being the most salient resilience factors among Latinos. The concept of *familismo*/familism is a core value and belief in the centrality of family in the life of Latinos. It stresses family loyalty, interdependence over independence, and cooperation over competition (Falicov, 1998; Ho et al., 2004), and is thought to be the basis of the Cuban family structure (Bernal & Florez-Ortiz, 1982), the Mexican American family structure (Falicov, 1998; Mirandé, 1985), the Puerto Rican family structure (Comas-Díaz & Griffith, 1988; Garcia-Preto, 1982), and the Central and South American family structures (Hernandez, 1996; Korin, 1996). In general, Latinos strive to have cohesive families and expect that one's life will revolve around his or her extended family. The construct of familism continues to be salient for Latinos living in the US (Bermúdez, Kirkpatrick, Hecker, & Torres-Robles, 2010).

Other key factors related to family strengths are also evident. For example, Cardoso and Thompson (2010) cite family involvement, strong kin networks, and family support as being important resilience factors. Additionally, Latino parents who had a strong relationship with their children, supervised their children closely, and had open communication with them lead to resilience in Latino youth in immigrant families. These families cite cultural traditions as being protective factors. When examining protective factors that promote and hinder academic well-being among middle school children, Martinez, DeGarmo, and Eddy (2004) state that factors such as family pride and support, familism, parental respect, social support, and "familia" were especially important. They concluded that the parental relationship and a cohesive sense of family are key protective factors, and that the concept of *familia* is the most powerful protective force for many Latino children.

These findings are consistent with McCubbin, McCubbin, and Thompson's (1993) work related to the concept of family schema, a family's shared values, goals, priorities, expectations, and worldview. For example, a member of the Alvarez family knows what it means to be an Alvarez, and can likely articulate those collective values, behaviors, and approaches to life. In effect, family members are generally on the same page when it comes to the meanings they have as individuals and as a family group in their approach to everyday life. According to the authors, the stronger a family's sense of "we-ness," the stronger their family schema and family resilience.

Assessing for family strengths is also salient for children coping with a parent's depression. Specific guidelines have been offered for helping children overcome the effects of parental depression and build resilience (D'angelo et al., 2009). These guidelines include the importance of understanding the risk and resilience factors of Latinos in order to offer effective interventions. The authors note the importance of family in the Latino culture and the necessity of family-centered, strength based approaches. They also affirmed the importance of asking about the family's immigration/migration narrative, their hopes for their new life, and their current circumstances. By understanding the centrality of family and children in Latino cultures, one also can assess the extent to which family separation and the loss of support networks due to immigration and relocation relate to parental depression among Latinos.

There are also important links between resilience, Latino's cultural characteristics, and health outcomes. Hispanic cultural values (i.e., familism, *simpatia*, power distance, personal space, time orientation, gender roles) contributed to better health outcomes than for non-Hispanic Whites (Gallo, Penedo, de los Monteros, & Arguelles, 2009). Embracing familism as a value contributed to a familial stability, which was linked to better physical health behaviors, higher likelihood of seeking medical help, better psychological health, and lower perceived burden of stress. Religiosity and spirituality, which are strongly embedded in cultural values, also were associated with better health behaviors.

Cultural Factors

The ways in which families espouse resilience varies according to their cultural context (McCubbin, Thompson, & McCubbin, 1996). The role of culture is especially relevant in the development of resilience among Latino immigrant families (Cardoso & Thompson, 2010). Protective factors include the ideals of *personalismo*, which is an emphasis on positive interpersonal relationships, *respeto*/respect, loyalty, *consejos*/advice, *dichos*, and fatalism, which is a form of acceptance, especially of things that cannot change. Additionally, discussing migration experiences and maintaining cultural traditions are said to foster family resilience among Latinos (D'angelo et al., 2009).

Being bi-cultural also has been found to be an important resilience factor for Latino families. It is critical for Latinos to successfully navigate the norms and values of the dominant culture as well as to maintain the linguistic, social, and cultural aspects of their culture of origin. It is well documented that having a sense of ethnic pride, continuity, and cultural orientation are aspects of biculturalism. Being bicultural is essential for maintaining positive psychological and cognitive development, academic motivation, and successful family and community relationships (Cabrera & Padilla, 2004).

Additionally, education levels and health outcomes for Hispanics have been found to vary by race/ethnicity and country of origin. Kimbro, Bzostek, Goldman, and Rodríguez (2008) reported that Hispanics tended to fare better than other cultural groups despite their lower levels of SES, calling this the "Hispanic paradox." Consistent with previous research, foreign-born Latinos fare better than native-born for almost all health outcomes across different race/ethnicity groups. The authors state that immigrants tend to have better morbidity and mortality outcomes than native-born, attributing this to the "healthy migrant" effect. That is, people who immigrate may be healthier than those who remain in their home countries. Though not as obvious, socioeconomic status also has an effect on the health of immigrants. For example, in Mexico, the higher the people's SES, the greater the likelihood that they were linked to smoking, alcoholism, and obesity, with lower income Mexicans being healthier. What is more, lower levels of assimilation in the US also have been linked to better health outcomes. In addition to health outcomes, there are also important protective cultural resources that allow Latino youth to succeed in school despite their socioeconomic vulnerabilities (Ong, Phinney, & Dennis, 2006). Persistent parental support and greater levels of ethnic identity and family interdependence have influenced higher academic achievement.

Ethnic Identity

Having a positive ethnic identity is essential to resilience among Latinos. Latinos, especially new immigrant families, may feel recognizably different and many for the first time experience a shift in how others treat them due to their ethnicity, skin color, race, or social location. Not having the benefits of white privilege can be especially problematic for Latinos living in the US (Blume & De Reus, 2009), furthering their sense of marginalization and experiences of oppression. By focusing on risk *and* protective factors, it is possible to reduce negative outcomes and enhance resilience. For example, Mexican American youth showed how they used energy, creativity, and resilience in order to cope with cultural tensions, role conflicts, and identity formation (Holleran & Soyon, 2005). Keeping strong ties to one's ethnic culture is a key protective factor, as is a strong, positive ethnic identity; ethnic pride and appreciation of and growing up with traditional Mexican values and beliefs such as *familismo* (family closeness and loyalty) contribute to resilience. Also, focusing on maintaining positive attitudes toward life, even following traumatic events, and having social support are noted as important protective factors. Hispanic adolescents were found to be more resilient, when compared with their non-Hispanic Anglo peers, in response to uncontrollable stressors and parental alcoholism. The strength and availability of the Hispanic community and social support, strong positive ethnic identity, and familism were presented as a major probable explanation for such resilience (Holleran & Soyon, 2005).

Conversely, there is a strong relationship between ethnicity-related stressors and well-being among Latinos (French & Chavez, 2010). Experiences of discrimination have a negative effect on mental health for Latinos, especially as they relate to stereotype threat (confirmation concern) and conforming to the pressure of one's own cultural group. French and Chavez worked with a compensatory model and a protective model, focusing on four dimensions of ethnic identity: centrality, public regard, private regard, and other group orientation. They found that ethnic identity was positively associated with well-being and all four dimensions were most protective of well-being, with the fear of confirming stereotypes being the most problematic. Additionally, the centrality of ethnic identity to self-image and the feeling that others believed Latinos were good people also were associated with lower levels of depression, while being comfortable with other ethnic groups was related to lower depression and lower loss of control. Overall, the negative effect of the fear of confirming stereotypes overrode the protective nature of ethnic identity. Additionally, if students felt great pressure to conform around other ethnic groups, then the positives were nullified as well. In order to protect young Latinos' sense of well-being it is critical to help them overcome the fear of confirming stereotypes and nullify the pressure to conform. Family members, teachers, and community leaders can be pivotal in helping young Latinos strengthen their ethnic identity and lower their risks for confirming negative stereotypes.

Community and Social Support

Extended community support and networks are vital for continuity and resilience among Latino families (Hull, Kilbourne, Reece, & Husaini, 2008). Social networks improve overall well-being as well as offer several pragmatic functions such as assisting in food security and housing needs (Greder, Cook, Garasky, Sano, & Randall, 2009). Extended community networks have been found to be key in resilience as neighborhoods and community supports were influential in the psychological and behavioral outcomes of Latinos. Having a church community and extended and community networks also were important.

As with other cultural groups, active church/religious involvement is important and helps maintain cultural ties and offers social support; however, not all family, community, and social support is beneficial for everyone in the same way. For example, Kelly (2007) analyzed the role of religion among Mexican American immigrants and found that religion and religiosity had both protective and risk factors. Traditional strengths of the Mexican family culture, such as collectivism, respect for authority, and loyalty can be harnessed through an immigrant's religious participation. However, an essential aspect of religion as a protective factor (instead of a risk factor) for Mexican immigrant adolescents is the degree to which he/she shares religiosity with his or her parents.

Community and social support also has been found to be critical for Mexican American women survivors of intimate partner violence (IPV) (Roditti, Schultz, Gillette, & de la Rosa, 2010). Hispanic participants stayed in abusive relationships longer than women from other cultural groups, stating that Marianismo (using the Virgin Mary as a role model of the ideal women) and familismo can be a negative influence in this specific situation because they were often encouraged by their families to stay in the abusive relationship. Resilience in their case was linked more to formal social support from organizational sources (i.e., shelters, counseling) and also to informal social support from friends and neighbors, just not family. The authors note that acculturation decreases resilience, which is common to findings in other studies, and they also link increased resilience to decreased mood disturbance. However, the most important factor they note in relation to resilience is help seeking. Those who were willing to look for help and continue searching for ways out of their difficult situations were the most resilient and often found the most support.

Additionally, Contreras, López, Rivera, Raymond-Smith, and Rothstein (1999) examined the social support and adjustment among Puerto Rican adolescent mothers and the moderating effect of acculturation. They investigated the relationship between grandmother and partner involvement between adolescent mothers during the second or third year of parenting. Unacculturated Latina mothers were protected by their grandmother's involvement and exhibited fewer symptoms and less parenting stress. They also were more likely to implement Hispanic values and interdependence on family. Additionally, for less acculturated Latinas, partner support was significantly related to symptomology, but not parenting stress. Those who lived with their partners reported greater symptomology. Acculturated Latinas showed patterns similar to non-Latina Anglo Americans. More research is needed in the area of the role of family and social support, especially for single Latina/os parents living with extended family members.

Overall, the above-mentioned factors contributing to resilience among Latinos are evident across many of the studies reviewed. For example, the factors increasing resilience mentioned by Blanco-Vega, Castro-Olivo, and Merrell (2008) were parental and familial involvement, positive community support, and positive self-concept. The support of the host culture is also imperative in preserving and further developing the protective factors with which families arrive. For adolescent Latinos, positive ethnic identity, parental support and involvement, having a school community that supports and promotes strong cultural values, and community unity all engender a feeling of belonging and the capacity for academic success and community involvement. Latinos were more likely to thrive when they and others believed in their abilities and skills and had high self-esteem.

In summary, the common themes of resilience among Latino immigrant families identified four broad domains of risk and protective factors (i.e., individual characteristics, family strengths, cultural factors, and community support). Below we discuss how these data serve as a foundation for creating a theoretically informed framework for enhancing family resilience among Latinos.

Organizing Frameworks for Understanding *Familias Fuertes*

The primary goal of our chapter is to offer an emerging clinical framework that accounts for resilience among Latino families. Extant frameworks developed by Walsh (2002) and Hawley and DeHaan (1996) have been instructive for our thinking. When considering family resilience, Walsh's framework offers a sound foundation for adapting this clinical framework for work with Latino families. Her biopsycosocial systems model seeks to identify common themes related to a family's effective response to crisis. Three major themes are identified: (1) belief systems, the heart and soul of resilience; (2) organizational patterns, family shock absorbers; and (3) communication processes, facilitating mutual support and problem solving.

This framework serves as a conceptual map identifying key family processes that can help families strengthen their abilities to evidence resilience (Walsh, 1998, 2003, 2006). Walsh's (2002) article on innovative practice applications of her resilience framework notes her basic premise: "…stressful crises and persistent challenges influence the whole family, and in turn, key family processes mediate the recovery and resilience of vulnerable members as well as the family unit" (p. 130). Walsh adds that: "Family resilience involves more than managing stressful conditions, shouldering a burden, or surviving an ordeal. This approach recognizes the potential for personal and relational transformation and growth that can be forged out of adversity" (p. 130). Adversity takes many forms, and some families are faced with multiple challenges, some acute and others chronic. For example, Boss (2006) focuses on loss, trauma, and resilience, and discusses migration and immigration as common situations where families must adapt, adjust, deal with loss, reorganize, and redirect. Of particular importance is Walsh' exhortation of the importance of using ecological and developmental lenses when examining families, the former paying particular attention to what surrounds families, and the latter accounting for processes as they unfold over time.

A second resource for our own thinking is Hawley and DeHaan's (1996) work that integrates lifespan and family perspectives into the understanding of resilience. Up until the mid-1980s, much of the discussion on resilience was at the individual level rather than accounting for family systems.

Hawley and DeHaan contrasted individual and family resilience, discussed the merits of family resilience as a viable concept, and also began a discussion of clinical implications. They defined family resilience as "the path a family follows as it adapts and prospers in the face of stress, both in the present and over time. Resilient families positively respond to these conditions in unique ways depending on the context, developmental level, the interactive combination of risk and protective factors, and the family's shared outlook" (Hawley & DeHaan, 1996, p. 293).

Over the course of their discussion, they describe an individual resilience perspective as reflecting a pathologically oriented framework, whereas a family resilience approach elevates a wellness and adaptability framework. Hawley and DeHaan's orientation helps one to stay strength-based and avoid wandering into a family deficit way of thinking, which is particularly important when discussing families from marginalized social positions.

Toward a Clinical Framework of Family Resilience Among Latinos

Overall, the "common factors" for Latino family resilience offer an essential foundation for creating a resilience framework for Latino families living in the US (immigrant and non-immigrant). Our aim is to offer clinicians and other practitioners a preliminary model that reflects practices and beliefs that may enhance family resilience among Latinos. In our framework (see Table 13.1), we have used Walsh's three dimensions identifying a family's effective response to crisis (i.e., belief systems, organizational patterns, communication processes), and have added a fourth dimension, ethnic identity. Suggestions for clinical intervention, highlighting specific Latino cultural values, are embedded in this adapted framework. These cultural values have been noted consistently throughout the marriage and family therapy and the social science literature as being significant factors contributing to family resilience among Latinos. We offer suggestions for increasing attention to family resilience in assessment and intervention, especially as one considers within-group diversity among Latino families. Additionally, we consider future research directions for increasing our understanding of family resilience among Latinos.

Clinical Implications

There are several considerations we hope will help make our framework most useful to practitioners. First, we encourage therapists to use this framework in a fluid manner. It is meant to serve as a starting point that can be adapted and modified based on a family's specific context and/or goals for therapy. The four domains are informed by research and theory, however, the suggestions embedded within the framework can be added to extensively. We hope this framework enables therapists to work in a culturally sensitive manner that amplifies family resilience based on the cultural values and nuances unique for each family.

Therapists should be aware that clinical interventions will vary due to multiple contexts, social locations, and intersections of identity. For example, although there are many similarities among US born and immigrant Latinos, there are vast differences in their experiences relative to creating family resilience. Contextual differences are salient when considering the intersections of social locations. For example, US born Latinos/Hispanics/Chicanos may or may not have a strong ethnic identity. Depending on how long their families have been in the US, some US born Latinos may not embrace those values mentioned in our framework, at least maybe not to the extent that foreign born Latinos do. Other intersections of identity to consider are special needs families, gay/lesbian/bi-sexual/transgendered/queer led families, racially mixed families, and Latino families at all socioeconomic levels.

Table 13.1 Framework for enhancing family resilience among Latinos

Belief systems

  Make meaning of adversity

    Understand how fatalistic beliefs help Latinos normalize life experiences with dichos/sayings such as "así es la vida" (such is life)

    Understand how spiritual/fatalistic beliefs can help one accept of things that cannot change "que sera, sera" (whatever shall be shall be) or "si Dios quiere" (God willing)

  Positive outlook

    Foster an attitude that crisis is manageable; "no hay mal que por bien no venga" (there is always good that comes out of something bad); "querer es poder." (where there is a will there is a way)

    Assess values, beliefs, and positive influences that are embedded in the Latino culture

  Transcendence and spiritualism

    Understand the role that religion and spirituality have in each family member's life

    Understand the cultural value of spiritualism reflected in dichos, church attendance, religious practices, beliefs, and family rituals and routines

    Assess for beliefs in saints, spiritual realm, herbal remedies, and folk healers/"curanderos" and how they can be a resource for families

Organizational patterns

  Familism, connectedness, and reconciliation

    Assess the extent to which each family member feels loyalty to their family, loyalty for a specific family member, and who they define as family

    Be prepared to do a cultural genogram that does not reflect traditional family structures

    Assess for family unity, harmony, cut-offs, alliances, coalitions, resentments, family secrets, legacies, etc.

    Assess to what degree each family member sees their family as a protective and risk factor for resilience

  Cultural social support

    Be aware that many Latinos espouse a collectivistic mindset and expect others to be cooperative, helpful, respectful, and courteous; especially family and friends. They may have a sense of betrayal if their good actions or intentions are not reciprocated

    Assess the extent to which family members feel they belong to their community and their sense of agency or ability to voice their concerns and/or make improvements. Not all family members will have the same experiences for a multitude of reasons

    Assess the extent to which children are active in school, have a sense of belonging, and their parents feel free and able to participate in school functions and advocate for their children

    Inform families about community resources and encourage them to actively seek support from these networks that they may not feel entitled to

  Flexibility

    Use psychoeducation to teach families about life-cycle transitions, and the importance of balancing stability and flexibility during these changes

    Note the importance for immigrants to balance assimilation and stability for each family member; they will experience these processes differently

    Help family members accept and negotiate how assimilation differences affect their family functioning and relationships and amplify strengths for each one of them

  Personalism

    Always be mindful of this important cultural value promoting self and mutual respect

    Assess for all those in each family members' life that enhances their feelings of being accepted, cared for, loved, respected, and enables them to reciprocate those positive and respectful feelings

    Amplify those aspects of the family's life that helps them collectively and individually increase their sense of self-worth and contribution toward others

  Social and economic resources

    Assess for financial stability and family's risk for poverty

    Assess for children's educational resources and sense of safety, belonging, and support in their schools

    Assess the family's sense of obligation to support and provide for extended family members; be cautious not to pathologize their actions, but seek to understand their values and intentions

    Help family identify financial safety nets and the extent of their social capital

    Be cautious not to overly focus on materialism, unless this is what they value

(continued)

Table 13.1 (continued)

Communication/problem-solving

Dichos

Ask family about certain dichos that have given them a sense of strength, motivation, courage, and other feelings and actions that may be positive for them

Use these dichos/sayings as possibly relevant or important insights about family and cultural values that give them a sense of strength, perseverance, and overcoming

Clarity and open emotional expression

Help family members to examine ways in which they may be triangulating others into conflict as a way to decrease anxiety and maintain harmony. Assess how this may be helpful or harmful

When appropriate, offer suggestions for being direct in communication without being disrespectful

Teach the use of "I language" as a means to communicate needs, thoughts, and feelings in a sensitive and respectful manner

When appropriate, help couples and families acknowledge a possible tendency to avoid communications and conflict in order to keep the peace

Help family focus on communication that builds upon strengths

Understand the use of humor and teasing "choteo"/"bromiar" to decrease anxiety and tension and increase a sense of positive feelings and environment

Collaborative problem solving

Assess the family's style of resolving problems; do they have a preferred way? What aspects are culturally informed? What needs to change in order to increase a sense of well-being, family cohesion, and/or desired goals?

Use the value of family cohesion and interdependence as a means to increase collective problem solving

Engage parents, grandparents, or adults as leaders in the decision-making process, while also listening to the input of the children and other family members

Help family members identify individual and collective goals and assess how they may or may not be compatible

Identify negative or unsupportive influences for family members; a common dicho is "major solo que mal acompañado" (better off alone than in bad company). Assess how these influences may be affecting their resilience

Assess ways in which family members are taking a pro-active, assertive stance. Is this stance consistent with their values (i.e., depending on their acculturation level, educational level, adherence to traditional gender roles)?

Assess if violence, dominance, control, and aggression are means to resolve conflict

Ethnic identity

Embrace ethnic/cultural roots

Foster ideas, actions, and beliefs that support positive ethnic identity development and maintenance

Encourage family members, especially children and adolescents, to attend ceremonies, events, family rituals, and family gatherings that celebrate their family and culture

Do a cultural genogram that traces history as far back as possible, acknowledging pride/shame in mestizo heritage, and multiple family forms

Intersections of identities

Assess family differences in acculturation and assimilation and how these differences affect family members' sense of wellness and resilience

Acknowledge transnational families as having a legitimate family form, having unique challenges, and strengths

Foster family pride in heritage and bi-cultural or multi-cultural identity

Assess for other intersections of identity and social location adding or detracting from family resilience (race, white privilege, class, gender, sexual orientation, age, health problems, psychopathology/addictions, criminal history, employment status, educational level, language abilities)

Bi-culturalism/multi-culturalism

Help families embrace bi/multi-cultural identity and bi/multi-cultural way of life

With-in group differences

Do not essentialize Latinos as a homogeneous ethnic group

Assess how specific cultural traits from their country of origin strengthens their sense of family resilience

Be mindful of heteronormative assumptions; assess for similarities and nuanced differences in family resilience among gay and lesbian Latino families

The list of differences due to varying intersecting identities and social locations is vast, and careful assessments and interventions must be made in the most culturally sensitive and culturally responsive manner possible.

Lastly, we encourage family therapists and other practitioners to consider how our clinical framework for family resilience fits with their theoretical orientation to family therapy. It is our belief that as long as therapists consider their work strength based, they can work from clinical models that were not originally conceptualized as such. Given the focus on resilience, obvious compatible clinical models are the collaborative approach, solution focused, narrative therapy, and feminist informed family therapy. However, when carefully examining the four domains of family resilience among Latinos, we also suggest the use of more traditional models of family therapy that focus on family and cultural context, family process and structure, such as Bowenian family therapy, contextual family therapy, structural family therapy, strategic family therapy, and cognitive-behavioral family therapy. Regardless of the therapist's clinical approach, we hope our framework can inform clinical assessments and interventions with Latino families that will strengthen their sense of resilience.

Research Implications

There are also several considerations worth noting in regard to how this framework can be used to inform future studies specific to family resilience among Latinos. There is a clear need for social and behavioral scientists, as well as marital and family therapy researchers, to increase their emphasis on accounting for diversity, ethnicity, and family transitions. While we have only discussed migration and immigration factors as they apply to Latinos, we believe particular attention should be directed at those processes and how they contribute to or detract from a family's ability to have resilience. This is important to note because well-being is often challenged by transitions and changes due to the pressure to adapt and adjust, while at the same time preserving core family values and practices. There is a community context to these transitions that has been discussed by Glick (2010). She notes the significance of both sending and receiving communities for understanding how well or how poorly new immigrants fare. If context is important, and our discipline seems to say this is the case, then the nature of where you leave from and the nature of where you go to have a lot to say about how well you and your family will do. The four dimensions, highlighting clinical interventions, may also serve as an impetus for asking those process-related questions mentioned above.

We also believe there is insufficient research that takes a developmental view of process and progress as it pertains to Latino families, whether they are new to the receiving community or of a subsequent generation. Though this suggestion qualifies as the proverbial beating of the dead horse, there is little longitudinal research; therefore we may over-attribute the effects of new situations because we never had a clear sense of baseline. An important future research suggestion for this moment in time involves research on measurement. Current measures of family strengths, for example, were not designed with diversity in mind, ethnic or otherwise. Consequently, resilience measures, scales, and indicators may be poorly aligned with Latino family characteristics, dynamics, and processes, and therefore are unable to capture functional dimensions of family life among Latinos.

Additionally, there is another significant research implication that pertains to a core aspect of understanding resilience. In fact, this is *the* core research question: What differentiates families that do well from those that do not fare as well, even when circumstances and conditions are the same or similar? To answer this question requires a valid conceptualization of outcomes for Latino families (in quantitative research this is the effect variable), as well as conceptualizing valid explanations for variety in family outcomes (best suited to qualitative/narrative approaches). To date few research studies have accessed multiple methods to answer the important questions.

Conclusion

Overall, our aim was to pull together several threads that form a tapestry displaying *familias fuertes* (strong families). We built upon Walsh's (2002) model of family resilience, Hawley and DeHaan's (1996) work integrating lifespan and family perspectives, and a review of the literature on family resilience among immigrant Latinos (i.e., Cardoso & Thompson, 2010) to offer a preliminary framework for understanding and supporting Latino families. Our goal was to posit an emerging clinical framework that accounts for significant dimensions of family strengths among Latino families. Our hope is that our emerging framework will help strengthen our capacity as scholars, researchers, and therapists to understand and promote family resilience among Latino families.

References

Bermúdez, J. M., Kirkpatrick, D., Hecker, L., & Torres-Robles, C. (2010). Describing Latino families and their help-seeking experiences: Challenging the family therapy literature. *Contemporary Family Therapy, 32*(2), 155–172.

Bernal, G., & Florez-Ortiz, Y. (1982). Latino families in therapy: Engagement and evaluation. *Journal of Marital and Family Therapy, 8*(3), 357–365.

Blanco-Vega, C., Castro-Olivo, S., & Merrell, K. (2008). Social-emotional needs of Latino immigrant adolescents: A sociocultural model for development and implementation of culturally specific interventions. *Journal of Latinos & Education, 7*(1), 43–61.

Blume, L. B., & De Reus, L. A. (2009). Transnational families and the social construction of identity: Whiteness matters. In R. L. Dalla, J. Defrain, J. Johnson, & D. A. Abbott (Eds.), *Strengths and challenges of new immigrant families: Implications for research, education, policy, and service* (pp. 71–90). Lanham: Lexington.

Boss, P. (2006). *Loss, trauma, and resilience: Therapeutic work with ambiguous loss.* New York: W. W. Norton.

Cabrera, N. L., & Padilla, A. M. (2004). Entering and succeeding in the "culture of college": The story of two Mexican heritage students. *Hispanic Journal of Behavioral Sciences, 26*(2), 152–170.

Campbell, W. (2008). Lessons in resilience: Undocumented Mexican women in South Carolina. *Journal of Women & Social Work, 23*(3), 231–241.

Cardoso, J., & Thompson, S. (2010). Common themes of resilience among Latino immigrant families: A systematic review of the literature. *Families in Society: The Journal of Contemporary Social Services, 91*(3), 257–265.

Comas-Díaz, L., & Griffith, E. E. (Eds.). (1988). *Clinical guidelines in cross-cultural mental health.* New York: Wiley.

Contreras, J., López, I., Rivera, E., Raymond-Smith, L., & Rothstein, K. (1999). Social support and adjustment among Puerto Rican adolescent mothers: The moderating effect of acculturation. *Journal of Family Psychology, 13*, 228–243.

D'angelo, E., Llerena-Quinn, R., Shapiro, R., Colon, F., Rodriguez, P., Gallagher, K., et al. (2009). Adaptation of the preventive intervention program for depression for use with predominantly low-income Latino families. *Family Process, 48*(2), 269–291.

Domenech Rodríguez, M., Davis, M. R., Rodríguez, J., & Bates, S. C. (2006). Observed parenting practices of first-generation Latino families. *Journal of Community Psychology, 34*, 133–148.

Espinoza-Herold, M. (2007). Stepping beyond "Si se puede: Dichos" as a cultural resource in mother-daughter interaction in a Latino family. *Anthropology and Education Quarterly, 38*(3), 260–277.

Falicov, C. J. (1998). *Latino families in therapy: A guide to multicultural practice.* New York: The Guilford Press.

Fraser, M., Kirby, L., & Smokowski, P. (2004). Risk and resiliency in childhood. In M. Fraser (Ed.), *Risk and resiliency in childhood: An ecological perspective* (2nd ed., pp. 13–66). Washington: National Association of Social Workers.

French, S., & Chavez, N. (2010). The relationship of ethnicity-related stressors and Latino ethnic identity to well-being. *Hispanic Journal of Behavioral Sciences, 32*(3), 410–428.

Gallo, L. C., Penedo, F. J., De los Monteros, K., & Arguelles, W. (2009). Resiliency in the face of disadvantage: Do Hispanic cultural characteristics protect health outcomes? *Journal of Personality, 77*(6), 1707–1746.

Garcia-Preto, N. (1982). Puerto Rican families. In M. McGoldrick, J. K. Pearce, & J. Giordano (Eds.), *Ethnicity and family Therapy* (pp. 164–186). New York: The Guilford Press.

Glick, J. E. (2010). Connecting complex processes: A decade of research on immigrant families. *Journal of Marriage and Family, 72*, 498–515.

Greder, K., Cook, C. C., Garasky, S., Sano, Y., & Randall, B. C. (2009). Rural Latino immigrant families. In R. L. Dalla, J. DeFrain, J. Johnson, & D. A. Abbott (Eds.), *Strengths and challenges of new immigrant families: Implications for research, education, policy, and service* (pp. 345–367). Lanham: Lexington.

Hawley, D. R., & DeHaan, L. (1996). Toward a definition of family resilience: Integrating life- span and family perspectives. *Family Process, 35*, 283–298.

Hernandez, M. (1996). Central American families. In M. McGoldrick, J. K. Pearce, & J. Giordano (Eds.), *Ethnicity and family therapy* (2nd ed., pp. 214–224). New York: The Guilford Press.

Ho, M. K., Rasheed, J. M., & Rasheed, M. N. (2004). *Family therapy with ethnic minorities* (2nd ed.). Thousand Oaks: SAGE publications.

Holleran, L., & Soyon, J. (2005). Acculturative stress, violence, and resilience in the lives of Mexican-American youth. *Stress, Trauma & Crisis: An International Journal, 8*(2/3), 107–130.

Hull, P., Kilbourne, B., Reece, M., & Husaini, B. (2008). Community involvement and adolescent mental health: Moderating effects of race/ethnicity and neighborhood disadvantage. *Journal of Community Psychology, 36*(4), 534–551.

Kelly, M. (2007). Faith and rebellion: Protective and risk factors for the adolescent children of religiously observant Mexican-American immigrants. *Social Work and Christianity, 34*(3), 259–276.

Kimbro, R., Bzostek, S., Goldman, N., & Rodríguez, G. (2008). Race, ethnicity, and the education gradient in health. *Health Affairs, 27*(2), 361–372.

Korin, E. C. (1996). Brazilian families. In M. McGoldrick, J. Giordano, & J. K. Pearce (Eds.), *Ethnicity and family therapy* (2nd ed., pp. 249–267). New York: Guilford.

Mancini, J. A., & Bowen, G. L. (2009). Community resilience: A social organization theory of action and change. In J. A. Mancini & K. A. Roberto (Eds.), *Pathways of human development: Explorations of change* (pp. 245–265). Lanham: Lexington Books.

Martinez, C., Jr., DeGarmo, D., & Eddy, J. (2004). Promoting academic success among Latino youths. *Hispanic Journal of Behavioral Sciences, 26*(2), 128–151.

McAdoo, H. P., Martínez, E. A., & Hughes, H. H. (2005). Ecological changes in ethnic families of color. In V. L. Bengtson, A. C. Acock, K. R. Allen, P. Dilworth-Anderson, & D. M. Klein (Eds.), *Sourcebook of family theory & research* (pp. 191–212). Thousand Oaks: Sage.

McCubbin, H. I., McCubbin, M. A., & Thompson, A. I. (1993). Resiliency in families. In T. H. Brubaker (Ed.), *Family relations: Challenges for the future* (pp. 153–177). Newbury Park: Sage.

McCubbin, H. I., Thompson, A. I., & McCubbin, M. A. (1996). *Family assessment: Resiliency, coping and adaptation.* Madison: University of Wisconsin Publishers.

Miller, R. B., & Gonzalez, D. A. (2009). Migrating Latinas and the grief process. In R. L. Dalla, J. DeFrain, J. Johnson, & D. A. Abbott (Eds.), *Stengths and challenges of new immigrant families* (pp. 155–173). Lanham: Lexington.

Mirandé, A. (1985). *The Chicano experience: An alternative perspective.* Notre Dame: University of Notre Dame Press.

Ong, A., Phinney, J., & Dennis, J. (2006). Competence under challenge: Exploring the protective influence of parental support and ethnic identity in Latino college students. *Journal of Adolescence, 29*(6), 961–979.

Roditti, M., Schultz, P., Gillette, M., & de la Rosa, I. (2010). Resiliency and social support networks in a population of Mexican American intimate partner violence survivors. *Families in Society, 91*(3), 248–256.

Skogrand, L., Hatch, D., & Singh, A. (2009). Strong marriages in Latino culture. In R. L. Dalla, J. DeFrain, J. Johnson, & D. A. Abbott (Eds.), *Strengths and challenges of new immigrant families* (pp. 117–134). Lanham: Lexington.

Tummala-Narra, P. (2004). Mothering in a foreign land. *The American Journal of Psychoanalysis, 64*(2), 167–182.

US Census Bureau. (2006). *Statistical abstract.* Washington: U.S. Government Printing Office.

Walsh, F. (1998). *Strengthening family resilience.* New York: Guilford Press.

Walsh, F. (2002). A family resilience framework: Innovative practice applications. *Family Relations, 51*, 130–137.

Walsh, F. (2003). Family resilience: Strengths forded through adversity. In F. Walsh (Ed.), *Normal family processes: Growing diversity and complexity* (3rd ed., pp. 399–423). New York: Guilford.

Walsh, F. (2006). *Strengthening family resilience* (2nd ed.). New York: Guilford Press.

Wolin, S. J., & Wolin, S. (1993). *The resilient self: How survivors of troubled families rise above adversity.* New York: Villard Books.

Leslie D. Hollingsworth

Introduction/Background

Family scholars now seem to agree on a definition of family resilience—namely that resilient families are those that, confronted with adversity, get beyond it to grow and become stronger in the process. Rather than limiting conceptualizations of resilience to individual children who seem to be able to succeed in the face of adversity, or to explanations of "protective factors" that may insulate "at-risk" children from failure, recent emphasis has been on the resilient family in its own right.

Nowhere have issues of risk and adversity of families in the United States been discussed more than in terms of black families. The history of black families in the United States is a history of risk and adversity, beginning with the forced migration and enslavement of African people, the "Jim Crow" laws (National Park Service, n.d.) that perpetuated economic, educational, political, and social enslavement after the institution of slavery was no longer legal, and the inequities that maintain an image of black people as in need of protection and management by others.

The application of resilience theory to black families requires that family scholars and clinicians consider black families from a "both-and" perspective—one that recognizes both the adversity confronting them as individual families and as members of a racial minority group in the United States and the qualities by which many are able to thrive and prosper in spite of the adversity.

The adversity still faced by black people in the United States is easily accessed. Making up slightly over 13% of the U. S. population in 2009 (U. S. Census Bureau, 2009), black residents made up 14.2% of the unemployed (compared to 7.9% of white residents), 24.6% of those in poverty (compared to 8.6% of white residents), 18.9% of persons without health insurance (compared to 10.8% of white residents), only 12.8% of persons who had attained a bachelor's degree (compared to 21.0% of white residents), and 32.6% of married persons (compared to 55.9% of married white residents). Interestingly, from a family resilience standpoint, 63.9% of black Americans were in family households, a figure only slightly lower than the 65.7% of white Americans in family households (with family households defined as those in which at least one member is related to the person who owns or rents the occupied housing unit).

L.D. Hollingsworth (✉)
University of Michigan School of Social Work, Ann Arbor, MI, USA
e-mail: lholling@umich.edu

D.S. Becvar (ed.), *Handbook of Family Resilience*,
DOI 10.1007/978-1-4614-3917-2_14, © Springer Science+Business Media New York 2013

There are characteristics of resilient families that cut across racial groups and therefore apply to all families. However, the post-positivist, constructivist era of family studies has educated scholars and practitioners about the unique qualities that race and ethnicity bestow on families of specific racial and ethnic population groups as a result of their histories, experiences, and identities. Baldwin (1981) described a core personality system in black Americans that is expressed in what he refers to as "a congruent pattern of basic traits (beliefs, attitudes, and behaviors) which affirm African American life and the authenticity of African heritage (p. 62)." Four dimensions of competency believed to be reflected in this personality system of black people are: (1) awareness and recognition of one's African identity and heritage; (2) the prioritization of ideologies and activities that seek black survival, liberation, and proactive and affirmative development; (3) prioritization of activities that specifically facilitate self-knowledge and self-affirmation; and (4) a posture of resolute resistance toward forces that threaten the survival of black people generally. These descriptors clearly distinguish black Americans from other population groups. At least two of the competencies (the second and fourth) seem to speak to rising above adversity, as reflected in such language as "liberation and proactive and affirmative development" and "resistance toward forces that threaten the survival of black people."

The questions to be addressed in this chapter are fourfold: (1) How is it that many black families are able to succeed in the face of social, economic, educational, and political adversities in addition to adversities that confront them at the level of the individual family? (2) What characterizes such resilient black families? (3) What are the benefits of studying black families from the lens of resilience? (4) What are the barriers that interfere with such study?

Significance of the Topic

For about 18 of the last 20 years, I have taught courses on the family at the undergraduate and graduate levels. The undergraduate courses have included a basic marriage and family relationships course and a course on black families in America. An ongoing graduate course is a course in family therapy. For the past several years, in teaching the family therapy course, I've used the textbook edited by McGoldrick and Hardy (2008), *Revisioning Family Therapy: Race, Ethnicity and Gender in Clinical Practice*, now in its second edition, in addition to a clinical family therapy text. My utilization of this text is aimed at sensitizing students to issues of privilege, oppression, diversity, and social justice in studying and providing clinical services to families. Students consistently evaluate the course highly, particularly those aspects of the course related to race, ethnicity, and gender.

In spite of the positive response students have to the structure and content of this family therapy course, I've noticed a persistent theme among the mostly white American students who enroll in the class each semester. The students tend to think in terms of black families as oppressed, marginalized, and disadvantaged, and of themselves as privileged. They struggle to recognize the privilege they have in being white in America and to acknowledge how it differentiates their experience from families who don't share their experience. The recognition of the privilege associated with being white in America and the disadvantage associated with being black or a member of another racial minority group is important. The problem is that this dichotomy creates a hierarchy, however unintended—one in which the white students with privilege (preparing to become practitioners) provide services to the black people who lack such privilege. The picture one gets, therefore, is that the white practitioners are always at the top of the hierarchy, providing the services, and the black families are always at the bottom of the hierarchy, receiving the services provided. A chapter on the resilience of black families is important, therefore, for at least two reasons: first, having such a chapter emphasizes the fact that black families have an identity and a consciousness that is distinct from experiences of oppression, marginalization, and disadvantage, and second, such a chapter can distinguish what is known about the qualities and mechanisms by which such a transition in thought occurs.

Literature Review

Studies of resilience in black families frequently focus on the family factors that contribute to resilience in black children. Among many examples is Callaway's (2008) recent use of oral history methods to examine the family practices that contributed to resiliency skills used by five academically successful African American siblings who grew up in a small rural mining community in Appalachia between the 1940s and the 1970s. Other resiliency studies focus on the social and environmental conditions that make up many of the adversities with which black children or black families are confronted. A glipse at the works in McCubbin, Futrell, Thompson, and Thompson's (1998) edited volume - *Resiliency in African American Families* - yields topics related to the inner city life of black families, socialization and care-giving in black communities, black military families overseas, housing and neighborhoods of single-parent black women, inadequate prenatal care of black women, marital satisfaction of black couples, fatherhood, infertility, mother–daughter relationships in black families, and black families containing delinquent juveniles.

While all these topics demonstrate the contributions of black families to their children and the adverse conditions black families are often confronted with in the process, two chapters addressed qualities that characterize resilient families. Bagley and Carroll's (1998) chapter on "Healing Forces in African American Families" noted such qualities as: (1) immediate family and extended family support and other support networks; (2) religious involvement; (3) community participation; (4) a receptive attitude; (5) financial resources; (6) achievement and accomplishment experiences and self-esteem in members of the family; (7) an oral tradition; (8) racial awareness; (9) boldness and an attitude of challenge; (10) proactive behavior; (11) positive communication; (12) the availability of counseling as needed; and (13) compromise.

The chapter by McCubbin, Futrell, Thompson, and Thompson (1998) entitled "Resilient Families," emphasized the need to study resilience in black families (1) from a relational perspective and (2) with consideration given to (a) ethnic identity, values, and culture, and efforts to preserve these; (b) the community context and social milieu within which such families are embedded; (c) family relationships, community reciprocity standards, and social support; (d) flexibility and adaptability to change; and (e) parenting, marital relationships, and family meanings.

When nonblack persons hear descriptions of the qualities that characterize resilience in black families, the response is often "That's true of *any* family!" This is the essence of the dilemma surrounding the study of resilience in black families—how to acknowledge the central status of "family" for all families while simultaneously acknowledging those qualities that uniquely distinguish black families from families of other racial groups. Gregory's study (2001) of resiliency in black families addressed this seeming discrepancy by applying knowledge from research on families broadly and building on that knowledge in studying black families specifically. In his qualitative study of nine black families that had experienced "hazardous adversity" (p. 47) in the 12 years prior, he used constructivist inquiry to identify ways these families had coped with or adapted to their encounters. He found that the categorical framework that had emerged from Walsh's (1998) broader analysis of the research on family resilience applied to the black families in his study in certain ways (Table 14.1), and that there were five additional factors that characterized resilience in the black families in his study that were not distinguished or were less distinguished in Walsh's previous framework (Table 14.2).

The categorical framework organized by Walsh consisted of three domains: belief systems, organizational patterns, and communication processes. The belief systems of resilient families consisted of the experience of making meaning of adversity, developing or maintaining a positive outlook, and being able to transcend the immediate adversity while utilizing a sense of spirituality in doing so. The organizational patterns of resilient families were characterized by flexibility and connectedness and were influenced by social and economic resources. In addition, resilient families communicated clearly, were open in expressing emotions, and used collaboration in problem solving.

Table 14.1 A linkage of processes of resilient black families identified by Walsh (1998) and also manifested among resilient black families studied by Gregory (2001)

Processes in Walsh's categorical framework identified in families studied by Gregory	Manifestation in black families studied by Gregory
Positive outlook: hope, optimistic bias, confidence in overcoming odds. Courage and encouragement; affirming strengths and building on potential. Seizing opportunities; active initiative and perseverance. Mastering the possible while accepting what cannot be changed	Families were consistently positive
	Positive outlook expressed as courage
	Sense of determination
	Endurance as a source of pride and strength
	Hopeful, optimistic view of the future
	Acceptance of what cannot be changed
Transcendence and spirituality: larger values and purpose. Faith, healing rituals, congregational support. Inspiration—envisioning new possibilities; creative expression; social action. Transformation: learning, change, and growth from adversity	Ability to use adversities as catalysts for transformative learning
	Seeing life as a school and adversity as instructive
Making meaning of adversity: viewing resilience as relationally based. Normalizing or contextualizing adversity and distress. Sense of coherence—viewing crisis as a challenge; as meaningful, comprehensible, manageable. Explanatory attributions—questioning "how could this happen? What can be done"	Attempting to understand the context in which their crisis occurred and the systemic influences that help create the environment, occasion, and the event itself
	Understanding "why" may differ by family characteristics
	Reframing as a way of coping
Connectedness: mutual support, collaboration, and commitment. Respect for individual needs, differences, and boundaries. Seeking re-connection, reconciliation of wounded relationships	Becoming closer as a family in response to family crisis. Strong leadership giving rise to surviving and prospering. Becoming more reflective and connected to life/nature. Overcoming prior estrangement
Open emotional expression. Sharing a range of feelings. Mutual empathy; tolerance for differences. Taking responsibility for own feelings, behavior; avoiding blaming. Pleasurable interactions; respite; humor	Younger children were most emotionally expressive, uncensored; older children and some parents more likely to express negative feelings. Parents support family members' different feelings. Family interviews accented with tears, laughter, melancholy moments, cheerful remembrances, intense sadness, and hopefulness. Thin line between owning responsibility and assuming guilt, particularly among men. Strong sense of mutuality expressed as mutual empathy

Table 14.2 Processes of resilient black families identified by Gregory (2001) and not separately distinguished among processes of resilient families identified by Walsh (1998)

Resilience processes identified by Gregory and not previously identified or less distinguished by Walsh	Characteristics
Expression of empathy, compassion, and forgiveness	Tenderness in response to adversity. Compassion toward those responsible for the adverse event
The use of remembering	Remembering of ancestor and family history in supporting a sense of self and spirituality
The use of rituals	Participation in family rituals to honor and commune with the deceased loved one
The experience of gratitude and humility	Use of gratitude and humility to support the cognitive reframing that facilitates meaning making. Expression of gratitude for blessings. Perception of having been humbled through the adversity; of recognizing one's humanness
The experience of dreams and clairvoyant experiences	Families' use of dreams and other clairvoyant experiences to clarify issues, to console and comfort themselves, and to commune with deceased relatives

Resilient black families in Gregory's study were similarly characterized by a positive outlook, spirituality, connectedness, open emotional expression, and meaning making. In addition, the communication patterns of these families, when they were confronted with adversity, reflected empathy, compassion, and forgiveness (frequently toward the persons responsible for or associated with the adverse experience). They used rituals to help with transitioning through adversity and remaining connected. They used memories to validate their experience and the sense of who they were in the midst of adversity. They used gratitude and humility to help themselves reframe the adversity. They used dreams and clairvoyant experiences to resolve the grief associated with their experience of adversity.

Marks et al. (2008) conducted in-depth interviews with men and women in a purposive sample made up of 30 couples described by the civic and/or church leaders who referred them as having "strong, happy, enduring marriages." The study addressed the central research question, "How do some African American couples build strong, enduring marriages in the face of challenges and barriers?" (p. 174). Pervasive themes that were related to adversities described by the couples were the challenges of balancing work and family time and the challenges of providing needed support and care to extended family members. Central themes in overcoming such challenges were (1) relying on each other rather than persons outside the marriage; (2) acknowledging each others' differentness and using shared communication to resolve conflicts; and (3) having a joint commitment to and adherence to their faith, church participation, and religious beliefs. From a demographic standpoint, Marks et al. acknowledged the fact that, in addition to the longevity of their marriages, participants in their sample were between 42- and 75-years old (average age for women—53 years, for men—55 years), and that most lived in urban areas, were dual income families, had household incomes that were almost double the median income for black households at the time they were interviewed, had attained a high school education and, in many instances some college (wives more than husbands), and reported that both were religious. Interviewers' field notes were said to contain descriptors of the couples such as "positive," "upbeat," "quick to laugh," "great smile," and "joyous."

Case Example

Condoleezza Rice is widely known as former U. S. Secretary of State, current Senior Fellow at the Hoover Institution, Stanford University, and current professor of political economy in the Stanford University School of Business and professor of political science at Stanford University. In her book *Extraordinary, Ordinary People: A Memoir of Family* (Rice, 2010), she sums up her family life in Birmingham, Alabama, from the early 1950s in the following way: "…and like so many of their peers, [my parents] rigorously controlled their environment to preserve their dignity and their pride" (p. 2).

This is important information for those who seek to understand the resilience of black families who endure oppression, discrimination, and racism. In the face of demeaning and sometimes life-threatening circumstances related to their race, many black families were able to control the impact of these circumstances on them in a way that allowed them to grow and prosper. Such was the case of Mr. and Mrs. John Doty following their marriage on May 15, 1942. Their case example is derived from a content analysis (Patton, 2002) of the videotaped celebration of their 50th wedding anniversary and from personal memories and supplementary documents.

Mr. and Mrs. Doty (as they were known throughout the many communities they were a part of) were married during a period when so called "Jim Crow" laws (Jim Crow Laws: Texas, n.d.) were in effect—beginning in the 1880s and gradually subsiding, through the influence of the Civil Rights Movement, in the 1960s. In the State of Texas at the time of their marriage, laws existed that forbade shared accommodations between black people and white people in public schools, on trains, buses, and streetcars, in railway stations, in public parks and swimming pools, in public restrooms, and in public libraries. Voters were required to pay a poll tax—a restriction for many black families who could not afford it. Miscegenation laws prohibited (under threat of imprisonment) marriage between individuals of different races, and black persons were restricted from participation in any state Democratic Party elections. Their marriage occurred 2 years before the Brown vs. Topeka Board of Education case, outlawing segregation in public schools, was won and 6 years before Texas law gave the governor authority to close any schools where federal troops were being used to desegregate them.

Similar to Dr. Rice's parents, Mr. and Mrs. Doty maintained a protective shield around their family to whatever extent was possible. Although separate public drinking fountains marked "white" or "colored" were available, they reminded their children that "we don't drink 'colored' water," even though it meant going without until they returned home from whatever outing they had been on. Wherever possible, the family traded with local, black-owned neighborhood businesses rather than use separate entrances offered to black people who shopped at any of the larger, downtown stores. The Doty family's Friday nights were reserved for dinner at Joe's neighborhood fish restaurant where Mr. Doty, whose livelihood depended on tips he received in his work at the Downtown YMCA in Dallas, taught his children how to figure the amount of the tip to leave for their waiter. After Dr. Benjamin Mays, during a visit to the City, pointed out to black Dallas residents that they were sitting on one street looking at a movie on another street, the Dotys stopped frequenting that theater. (This particular theater, the only one in downtown Dallas black patrons were permitted to enter at all, required them to go in through a separate entrance where they watched the movie while sitting in the very back of the highest balcony. As Dr. Mays so accurately pointed out, the seating area for black patrons was so far up and so far back that the seats were literally on a different street than the one on which the screen was located.)

Mr. and Mrs. Doty raised their children in segregated South Dallas. In her remarks at the 50th Wedding Anniversary celebration, one of the attendees, a woman who had been a high school classmate and longtime friend of Mrs. Doty, spoke of the "great move to South Dallas." This referred to the period in the early 1950s when neighborhoods in South Dallas "opened up," meaning that black families were permitted to buy homes in areas that previously had been closed to them. Of course, once this happened, many realtors engaged in a practice of "redlining" in which white potential home buyers were steered away from the now "open" South Dallas neighborhoods, black potential home buyers were directed toward those neighborhoods, and white homeowners currently living in South Dallas neighborhoods were subtly (and sometimes not so subtly) encouraged to list their homes for sale quickly rather than risk the value of their property decreasing because of the influx of black residents. Rather than direct blame at the system of segregation and/or at the real estate practice that took advantage of it and kept it going, black families were blamed by whites who undoubtedly felt frustrated and helpless to stop what was basically a forced evacuation from their homes. During 1951, ten homes that had been purchased by black families in South Dallas were bombed.

How is it that in spite of such overt acts of discrimination, racism, and oppression, and in spite of the many social ills that continued to surround black families, relationships, and families such as that of Mr. and Mrs. Doty, are able to thrive over a lifetime? How is it that Mrs. Doty, the daughter of a single mother employed as a short order cook, became the first in her family to graduate from college in 1937. (At historically black Wiley College she was a member of the cohort of students who served on the debate team that became internationally known 70 years later in the movie "The Great Debaters.") How is it that, years later, after Texas universities were desegregated, she was able to qualify for admission to a Master of Education program at a large Texas public university, making the highest score that had ever been made in that university's history on the Miller Analogies Test (MAT), which was required for admission? How is it that, taking courses each summer, she became the first in her family to receive a Master's Degree? How is it that the Dotys were able to pay for their home, to provide three children with college educations—two with Master's degrees and one with the first PhD in the family? How is it that people in attendance at the anniversary celebration over and over again spoke of the inroads the couple had made in the larger community, of how they had served as models for others—individually and as a couple?

I would say they accomplished all this just as Dr. Rice's parents and many other black families did—by rigorously controlling their environment in a way that allowed their family and its members to maintain their dignity and their pride and not to allow what happened on the outside to define who they were or what they felt on the inside or what they accomplished. As a result of being restricted from interacting with whites during the period of segregation and discrimination, and as a result of avoiding participation in activities in which they would be treated or would perceive themselves as "second class," black families were able to create their own identities, self-respect, and sense of personhood. The emphasis of many contemporary black families on maintaining a black identity and a black community can be understood from the same perspective—as a way of ensuring their dignity and pride.

In analyzing the content of the videotape of Mr. and Mrs. Doty's 50th wedding anniversary celebration, I kept in mind the ten elements Gregory (2001) had identified earlier as characterizing resilience in black families—those that built on his application of the Walsh (1998) findings to the families he studied (Table 14.1) and those that emerged from interviews he conducted (Table 14.2). I incorporated those identified by Marks et al. (2008), which fit easily with the ten. This is what I found:

1. *Positive outlook*. I noticed that never once during the videotaped celebration did Mr. or Mrs. Doty, their children, or others who gave oral tributes mention the adversities. The one speaker who mentioned the "great move to South Dallas" mentioned it as a notable event in the history of their lives, even though the event had been surrounded by racism and prejudice. What came through instead was their courage, sense of determination, endurance, and optimism. There was no resentment; no blame; merely an acceptance of what could not be changed at the time it occurred.

2. *Transcendence and spirituality*. The couple and members of their cohort who were in attendance at the celebration seemed to have built on the learning that occurred through their experiences, transferring the knowledge gained to others. The middle-aged president of a black men's social club in which Mr. Doty had celebrated 50 years of membership 2 years earlier spoke of the role model Mr. Doty had been with regard to his own marriage. He shared that whenever he and his wife of 20+ years had a conflict, he reminded himself: "If Mr. Doty can do it, I can too!" He used the words "commitment," "foundation," and "education" in describing Mr. Doty.

The executive director of a city-wide organization for which Mrs. Doty was a founding Board member, spoke of the extent to which the couple had served as role models for many young couples, including his wife and himself. As a member of the neighborhood branch of a large national civic organization, this same speaker explained that Mr. Doty was always there [at meetings and other functions], always on time, always behind [the other members] to make sure they did what they were responsible for. He quipped: "Mr. Doty would never permit anybody to say: 'I'm fixin' to do this or I'm fixin' to do that!'"

Faith and a strong belief in God were also prevalent in comments about this couple. In a tribute to her parents on behalf of her sister, brother, and herself, Eleanor Doty explained that their parents' legacy was nurtured through instilling in their children Christian values and Christian virtues. Present for the celebration was the area Catholic church monsignor who led Mr. and Mrs. Doty through a renewal of their wedding vows, and the pastor of the church in which Mrs. Doty recently had been elected only the second female elder in the church's history, who gave a prayer of commitment. (Although married in the Catholic church where Mr. Doty was a member, the couple maintained their separate Catholic–Protestant memberships, even while educating their children in Catholic schools and supporting each other's involvement in their various church activities.)

Eleanor spoke of the couple's commitment to causes of righteousness and justice, their respect for all people, and their expectation of the same. Mrs. Doty was awarded the Silver Fawn Award for her work with the Boy Scouts of America. She served on the first Board of Trustees of Dallas' *Museum of African American Life and Culture* and as Board member of Jarvis Christian College and St. Anthony's Catholic School (where Mr. Doty was a long-time member). She was a 50-year-plus member of the Alpha Kappa Alpha Sorority. Mr. Doty was active in the South Dallas chapter of Kiwanis International and the Regular Fellows Men's Social Club. Both were avid tennis players—having met on one of the public tennis courts available to black people. Their children became active participants in the civil rights movement and other social movements as well as active civic, church, and community participants.

3. *Making Meaning of Adversity*. The fact that Mr. and Mrs. Doty and their family focused on opportunities rather than adversity is evidence of the way they reframed their experience. Addressing the manageable aspects of their lives rather than dwelling on those aspects they had no direct control over surely helped bring the family to the point of celebrating their marriage and their life.

4. *Connectedness*. Mr. and Mrs. Doty were strong leaders in their immediate and larger communities. Rather than dwelling on resentment and bitterness, they sought reconciliation and collaboration. Mrs. Doty was an active member of the ecumenical National Council for Christians and Jews and Church Women United, as well as the Christian Women's Fellowship of the Christian Church, Disciples of Christ locally and nationally. At the level of family, the Dotys were described as always having family and friends around; of emphasizing the necessity of fellowshipping with family, friends, and community; of displaying a special relationship with many different people. In one of her contributions to the devotional book *Go Quickly and Tell*, edited by Janet Sugioka, Mrs. Doty (1973a, 1973b, 1973c) writes:

> He was ill now, lonely and confined to a wheelchair. We had lost contact with him since he had married and moved away. A mutual acquaintance wrote that he asked about us often, so I wrote him a note. He called his friends to tell about his letter and the joy it brought him. He even called us to say, "Thank you." I was ashamed for having done so little so late, and I resolved then and there to take the time to minister to him and to all the other people in like circumstances whom I knew, by calling, writing, and visiting. (p. 145)

5. *Open Emotional Expression*. During her tribute to their parents, Eleanor spoke of remembering lots of humor, of laughing, learning to take things lightly, of having humor interjected into everything the family did. At the same time, she thanked their parents for "loving us despite our mistakes in judgment" and "for coming to our rescue even after we had arrogantly boasted our adulthood and independence."

6. *Expression of Empathy, Compassion, and Forgiveness*. This quality is summed up in an excerpt from another devotional written by Mrs. Doty (1973a, 1973b, 1973c) and entitled: "Thank God, I Can't Remember:"

> I was talking with two of my co-workers and the conversation turned to women's liberation and racism. I remarked that I felt victimized more because of my race than because of my sex. I started to relate an incident in which I had been deeply hurt by an individual of another race. Then I realized that I had forgotten what had actually happened and who was involved. 'I can't remember,' I said. "Thank God, I can't remember." Pray for the ability to forget the hurts that come our way. (p. 144)

7. *The Use of Remembering*. In another part of her tribute to their parents, Eleanor Doty commented: "Because of their undying love, we all have golden memories to forever treasure—of our earliest moments and a sense of history, of "from whence we came"—through articles, recordings, photos dating back to the 1920s and even earlier. Eleanor went on to reminisce about the time Mr. Doty showed her how to "properly stoop" when mini-skirts first came out, and of how he "just happened" to invite Mrs. Doty and her friend to the same concert Eleanor was going to on her first date. Still another devotional written by Mrs. Doty (1973a, 1973b, 1973c) describes the quality of remembering. It is entitled: "Old Friends Remembered:"

> Sometimes when we sit in church at worship, we hear a song or a specially worded prayer that reminds us of some beloved friend who has died. Our hearts are gripped with the remembering, as we recall the times that we have shared with them – good times and bad…. God blesses us through the lives of His children and through our memories of them when they have gone. Pray for the church and for all who serve. (p. 144)

8. *The Experience of Gratitude and Humility*. One of the speakers paying tribute to Mr. and Mrs. Doty described them as "simple people," continuing: "Yet, a lot of us have set the Dotys up as our models because they have high standards and we aspire to reach those standards." In her comments on behalf of her husband and herself, Mrs. Doty remarked: "Yes, we had troubles. We had disappointments." But the only examples she came up with were the difficulties of having three children and trying to have an argument after the couple had agreed never to argue in front of the children, and her frustration with the fact that Mr. Doty never wanted to buy anything "on time" (credit). If they couldn't pay for something outright, he didn't want to get it! As an afterthought, Mrs. Doty added: "Maybe that's why we're not in the poorhouse today!"

9. *The Use of Rituals*. I originally thought there was nothing in the videotape or supplementary documents that spoke to the Dotys' use of rituals in achieving resilience in the face of adversity. But then I realized that the 50th Wedding Anniversary celebration itself was a ritual—an opportunity to highlight their lives and memories as a couple and as a family, demonstrating their resilience in the process. Those attending included the Dotys' generational cohorts who had shared their many experiences; generations immediately behind them and for whom they served as role models; younger individuals and couples who, though not there yet, could still listen and learn and be a part of the process; and younger children who would always have somewhere in their memories, the knowledge that black families have long, enduring relationships and lives full of joy, laughter, and success as well as struggles.

10. *The Experience of Dreams and Clairvoyant Experiences*. I had difficulty initially in identifying anything in the anniversary videotape or supporting materials that spoke to this quality of resilient families Gregory (2001) had identified in the black families he interviewed. Eventually it occurred to me that the Dotys had a dream about the kind of family they wanted to create—a dream, like many of their era, about the importance of a college education for their children. That their relationship was the first step toward fulfillment of that dream is apparent in the sentiments expressed by Private John Doty in a letter to his wife on May 10, 1943, written from his post in Fort Huachuca, Arizona: "By the way, Sugar. Do you know what May 15th is? I hope I will get into town to send you something just to remind you that the best thing that ever happened in my life happened that day! All my love, Doty." The Doty's first daughter, Leslie Doty Hollingsworth, was born the month after this message was written.

Mrs. Doty died April 8, 2001 at the age of 83, 1 month before what would have been the 59th anniversary of their marriage. Mr. Doty died November 5, 2003 at the age of 94.

Current Issues

Ideological perspectives or value orientations tend to form the theoretical course by which family studies are conducted. Allen (1978) identified three such perspectives that have framed studies of black families: the cultural deviant perspective in which black families are viewed as pathological; the cultural equivalent perspective, in which black families are viewed as legitimate to the extent that their life-style is consistent with that of white families; and the cultural variant perspective, in which black families are considered as functional and as uniquely different from white families. Gregory refers to a 1988 review conducted by Bryant and Coleman (as cited in Gregory, 2001) of the content of 25 introductory marriage and family textbooks that revealed that none were written from the culturally variant perspective. Although first published in 1972 and updated 27 years later, Robert Hill's (1972; 1999) research and writing on the *Strengths of Black Families* continues to be cited as one of the major works about black families written from a strengths-based perspective.

Gregory also summarizes the work by Staples and Johnson (as cited in Gregory, 2001) in which these scholars trace the history of studies of black families in the United States across five periods: a "poverty-acculturation" period that emphasized the economic conditions that perpetuated the disorganization of the black family; a "pathology" period in which the deterioration of the black community was attributed to dysfunction in black families; a "reactive" period that put forth the proposition that black families were similar to white families except for their enslavement and subsequent impoverishment; a period of "black nationalism" that emphasized the strengths of black families and criticized the U. S. social, political, and economic system for the inequitable treatment of black families; and the "neoconservative" period which, while giving little attention to the impact of the social ecology on black families, began to study and identify the strengths of black families.

What stands out from this brief review of the history of black family studies is that, with a few exceptions, black families have been studied and presented in a way that emphasizes their limitations, ignores or minimizes the ecological conditions that surround and influence them, and/or overlooks evidence of overcoming adversity and achieving growth. This gives rise to at least two issues that currently serve as barriers to the recognition of resilience in black families—both having to do with the types of adversity resilient black families are confronted with and with which they must cope.

The first is the difficulty of US family scholars, clinicians, and others in considering black families from a multifaceted perspective. As Boykins and Toms (1985) proposed, black families are required instead to fit firmly into one category or another—into the category of indigenous Africans; into the category of U. S. minorities who are oppressed, marginalized, discriminated against, and/or victimized by racism; or into the category of mainstream members of US society academically, vocationally, and politically and therefore as no different from other families. Having black families function at two or more of these levels simultaneously becomes confusing and frustrating. Nonblack practitioners in human service professions may be unable to comfortably relate to black families from other than a minority position. They may make the mistake of one nonblack family therapist described by Hardy and Laszloffy (2008)—of assuming that resilience observed in one black family is an exception to the rule that labels all black families as oppressed, poor, and marginalized. They may join others in the US mainstream in objecting to programs (e.g., Affirmative Action programs) aimed at equalizing resources and opportunities across races, concluding from evidence of resilience in some black families that all black families have succeeded. Finally, they may make racism a focus of therapy for a black family when the family does not have that as a goal.

The second issue surrounding the topic of resilience in black families is what Hardy and Laszloffy (2008) refer to as *pro-racist ideologies*—"a generalized belief that espouses and supports the superiority of whites" (p. 227). As these authors point out, such ideologies are not intentionally racist. In fact, individuals who subscribe to them tend to see themselves as liberal and as the most unlikely of all Americans to be racist. Pro-racist ideologies get operationalized as an attitude that "my views are the right views; they have nothing to do with race." For example: The black student enrollment in one elementary school in a predominantly white school district was quickly becoming perceived as 'all black.' Desiring a more racially balanced student population in every school, the solution proposed by the School Board was to redraw the school district lines that determined what schools children would attend. Parents in a neighborhood of advantaged families whose children would be forced to leave their neighborhood schools and take the bus or be driven to schools in adjacent neighborhoods strongly objected. One parent seemed to represent the sentiment of the other parents by insisting that they were just typical liberal parents who didn't want their children bused to achieve what the parent thought of as some kind of quota. The implication was either that the increasing segregation of a school wasn't important or, if it was important, any inconvenience should be met by the black children. This parent never saw the inconsistency between considering herself or himself as liberal and unilaterally deciding how school policies should be formed.

Another example of pro-racist ideologies is the continuing unwillingness of white individuals across the United States, including individuals representing various human service professions, to acknowledge the feelings of many black persons regarding the transracial adoption of black children. In expressing their objection, black Americans called attention to the importance of children to black families, to the uniqueness of black families, and to the distinct processes used by black families to socialize their children in the development of a black identity, black consciousness, and personal resilience (Hollingsworth, 1999). Black citizens who asserted such views were accused, by white Americans, of discriminating against black children and by political action that resulted in policies that prohibited the consideration of race and ethnicity in adoption while facilitating transracial adoptions (Hollingsworth, 1998). Again, those persons who insisted that white parents should be free to adopt black children, in spite of objections in the black community, did not perceive their actions as having anything to do with racism—it was considered as simply the right thing to do!

One also may look at the objections of white Americans to the existence and public support of historically black colleges and universities (HBCUs) as an indication of pro-racist ideologies. The fact that the graduation rate of black students from these institutions is found on average to be much higher than that of black students from predominantly white institutions, and that some students thrive psychologically and socially from the group identity development available in HBCUs does not eliminate the objections of white Americans. Similar objections have been directed toward affirmative action programs; toward the establishment of social and professional organizations for black people (e.g., black fraternities, black sororities); toward the celebration of black identity events (e.g., black history month); and toward churches serving predominantly black congregations. (Sunday morning thus has been referred to by some as the country's most segregated time of the week.)

What makes these and similar incidents descriptive of pro-racist ideologies is the fact that they arise from perspectives their advocates consider to be the "right" perspectives. The issue of the "privilege" inherent in claiming ownership of the "right" perspective, or in freely imposing that perspective on others, never arises.

Clinical Implications

In discussing the future of family therapy from a family resilience standpoint, Walsh (1998) writes:

> What we need even more than new techniques are strength-oriented conceptual tools that guide intervention. The concept of family resilience offers such tools, and is distinct in its focus on surmounting crisis and challenge. Symptoms are assessed in the context of past, ongoing, and threatened crisis events, their meanings, and family coping responses. Therapeutic efforts are attuned to each family's particular challenges and family resources are mobilized to meet them. (p. 23)

A resilience-oriented approach recognizes that black families have been confronted with adversities related to being black in America and adversities associated with their individual family stresses. However, such an approach anticipates and accepts that black families have qualities that have allowed them to cope with and survive many of these adversities. The focus of assessment and intervention is on what qualities have worked successfully in the past (based on their own stories) and where there is interference with applying these qualities to current crisis events. Solution-based (Berg, 1994; de Shazer et al., 1986) and narrative (White & Epston, 1990) approaches to family therapy are conceptually consistent with such a resilience-oriented approach, although they have been less rigorously studied. Marks et al. (2008) have integrated knowledge acquired from their study of successful black marriages into undergraduate, graduate, and community-level family life education offerings. They report that the use of participants' narratives seems to elicit real discussions in these settings.

Moving from a "deficit" or "dysfunction" orientation to a resilience orientation in clinical practice with families may require an intentional paradigm shift. Many readers will be familiar with the exercise involving the "young girl–old woman" illusion, even though its origins are unknown (Weisstein, n.d.). Depending on how one "looks" at the picture, the viewer sees a "young woman" or an "old woman." The first time I was introduced to it, even though others were directing me toward seeing the alternate picture, I had literally to blink several times before I could see it. I had to blink several more times each time I transitioned from seeing the "young woman" to seeing the "old woman." After a number of "practices," I was able to move back and forth freely and intentionally between recognizing the two different images. Clinical practitioners can create a similar exercise. Once they succeed, they will be able to simultaneously recognize (1) the traumatic encounters a black family has had and how being black in the United States has exacerbated these encounters; (2) the unique methods the family has used to cope with such encounters—as a black family and as a member of an identity group of black people; (3) the ways black families have not only coped but have risen above and grown from the adversities experienced; and (4) the remaining obstacles and the assets available to the family for addressing them.

Research Implications

Researchers focused on black families increasingly are calling for qualitative or mixed method research. Gregory (2001) suggests that qualitative studies may be appropriate and even preferable for the study of the black family because they offer the opportunity for black families themselves to be heard from on issues salient to their survival and prosperity. His subsequent selection of constructivist inquiry as the research strategy used in his own study was consistent with this recommendation.

Walsh (1998) wrote similarly that "a redirection of research focus and funding priorities is needed, from studies of dysfunctional families and what makes families fail to studies of well-functioning families and what enables them to succeed, particularly in the face of adversity" (p. 22). She added that rather than proposing a blueprint for any singular model of "the resilient family," the search for family resilience "should identify key processes that can strengthen each family's ability to overcome the challenges they face in their particular life situations" (p. 22).

Finally, what was unique and relevant to the topic of resilience in black families was that Marks et al. (2008) "set out" to find and interview black couples that persons who might be considered experts perceived as having "strong, happy, enduring" marriages. In that regard, their approach might be considered a qualitative "panel study" of sorts. Because these researchers intentionally sought to learn about the qualities resilient couples saw as responsible for the satisfying and enduring quality of their relationship, they were able to collect this information. The fact that the researchers acknowledged the possible influences of the demographic characteristics of the couple suggests that a mixed method approach is realistic. In this context, it would also be interesting to examine what characteristics the "experts" who recommended the couples used to define "strong, happy, [and] enduring" marriages.

Conclusion

In summary, when resilience is defined as being confronted with adversity and surviving and prospering in spite of it, there certainly is evidence of it in black families. Adversity in the lives of black families can include racism, discrimination, and oppression as members of a racial minority group in the United States, as well as external and developmental stressors confronting them as families in general. Among successful strategies found in the research literature to characterize resilience in black families are: a positive outlook; spirituality (including a strong and shared faith) and the ability to transcend crises; viewing crisis as a challenge; relational connectedness and commitment; open expression of emotions (including humor, shared communication, gratitude and humility, empathy, compassion, and forgiveness, and a recognition that the same event can be met with diverse emotions); the use of memories; and the use of rituals as methods of strength and coping. Certain demographic factors, such as education and gender, also may contribute to resilience in black families.

Studying resilience in black families requires an intentional search for, and a focus on resilience, using qualitative methods informed by or supported by selected quantitative methods. Clinical practice with black families from a resilience perspective requires a multifaceted approach that assesses black families simultaneously from the standpoint of African American and mainstream American identities and according to past and current successes as well as adversities; perceiving current struggle as evidence of a breakdown in the otherwise competency to effectively manage the stress with which they are confronted. Barriers that can interfere with using a resilience-based approach can include (1) limiting research and practice to a deficit- or dysfunction-based model; (2) failing to consider black families from a multifaceted perspective (that is, mentally insisting that black families are either oppressed minorities, mainstream Americans, or ethnically African); and (3) operating according to "pro-racist ideologies" that put forth the superiority of whites.

Nonblack people, including nonblack practitioners and researchers, may find it difficult to believe that black families don't harbor resentment and rage for the oppression, prejudice, and discrimination they have been targets of because of their race. This has at times been referred to as arising from "white guilt," defined as guilt felt by white people because of the advantage and privilege they have received as a direct or indirect result of the oppression of black people. The assumption is that if white people can make amends for the treatment black people have received, they can be relieved of guilt. Such a perspective, even if well-meaning, perpetuates the victimization of black people since it requires that black people remain in a "one-down," "helpee" position. Shelby Steele is the Robert J. and Marion E. Oster Senior Fellow at the Hoover Institution, Stanford University. In his book *White Guilt: How Blacks and White Together Destroyed the Promise of the Civil Rights Era* (Steele, 2006), he refers to the efforts of white people to make amends for exploiting black people in order to establish their own moral authority. Black people indulge this process, according to Dr. Steele, by accepting the unequal position in which it places (and keeps) black people. Such a process inhibits the perception of black families as resilient. Three actions, taking place concurrently, are necessary if the resilience of black families is to be recognized. (This is within the context of the paradigm shift discussed earlier.)

First, black families must be recognized as competent and capable in their own right. Second, honest acknowledgement must be made of the external forces that oppress and disadvantage black people. (The focus, then, is not on the black people as victims of oppression but squarely on the forces that caused, and are perpetuating the oppression). Third, change efforts must be directed at the external forces that are responsible for oppression and disadvantage, not at the people who are oppressed (other than to assist in eradicating the elements that get in the way of success and coping).

The emphasis on the resilience of black people is not intended to suggest that resentment and rage have no place as a response to oppression and racism. The conscious awareness of inequality and injustice for any reason is an appropriate response and one that can motivate action for change. However, the concept of resilience as presented in this chapter is used to convey that black families are not, and have not in the past, been passive victims of their oppression but have instead used multiple mechanisms to thrive and succeed. The problem, as I close, is not the inability of black families to be resilient but the inability of mainstream family scholars and clinicians to look for and find that resilience. Hopefully this chapter will serve to widen the lens.

Finally, readers of the chapter may come away with the conclusion that the barriers to engaging in research and clinical practice in a way that acknowledges black family resilience are limited to white American family scholars and clinicians or that all white American family scholars are identical in their perspectives. As Hardy and Laszloffy (2008, p. 235) point out, all persons are socialized in a US society that is built on pro-racist ideologies; therefore it can be anticipated that all of us internalize these perspectives. The question, then, is not whether each of us operates from a pro-racist ideological perspective but in what way this occurs in our personal and professional lives. The answer undoubtedly differs for different individuals of all races. Hardy and Laszloffy suggest that we begin this process of self-examination and change by: (1) being aware that race matters; (2) recognizing the existence of pro-racist ideologies; (3) seeking and strengthening cross-racial experiences; (4) becoming acquainted with our own racial identity; (5) challenging our own pro-racist ideologies first, then challenging those of others; and (6) persisting in this effort in spite of criticism or rejection. This chapter will hopefully serve to motivate and guide this process.

References

Allen, W. R. (1978). The search for applicable theories of Black family life. *Journal of Marriage and the Family, 40*, 117–129.

Bagley, C. A., & Carroll, J. (1998). Healing forces in African-American families. In H. I. McCubbin, E. A. Thompson, A. I. Thompson, & J. A. Futrell (Eds.), *Resiliency in African American families* (pp. 117–142). Thousand Oaks: Sage Publications.

Baldwin, J. (1981). Notes on an Africentric theory of black personality. *Western Journal of Black Studies, 5*, 172–179.

Berg, I. K. (1994). *Family based services: A solution-focused approach.* New York: Norton.

Boykins, A., & Toms, F. (1985). Black child socialization: A conceptual framework. In H. P. McAdoo & J. L. McAdoo (Eds.), *Black children: Social, educational, and parental environments* (pp. 33–52). Beverly Hills: Sage.

Callaway, P. B. (2008). *'Don't you fall' resilient and academically successful African Americans' literacy and family involvement practices.* Available from Dissertation Abstracts International Section A: Humanities and Social Sciences (Publication No. AAI3315005).

de Shazer, S., Berg, I. K., Lipchik, E., Nunnally, E., Molnar, A., Gingerich, W., et al. (1986). Brief therapy: Focused solution development. *Family Process, 25*, 207–221.

Doty, E. H. (1973a). Old friends remembered. In J. Sugioka (Ed.), *Go quickly and tell* (p. 144). St. Louis: The Bethany Press.

Doty, E. H. (1973b). Only the lonely. In J. Sugioka (Ed.), *Go quickly and tell* (p. 145). St. Louis: The Bethany Press.

Doty, E. H. (1973c). Thank God I can't remember. In J. Sugioka (Ed.), *Go quickly and tell* (p. 144). St. Louis: The Bethany Press.

Gregory, W. H. Jr. (2001). *Resiliency in the black family.* Available from ProQuest Dissertations (UMI Number 3028768).

Hardy, K. V., & Laszloffy, T. A. (2008). The dynamics of a pro-racist ideology: Implications for family therapists. In M. McGoldrick & K. V. Hardy (Eds.), *Re-visioning family therapy: Race, culture, and gender in clinical practice* (pp. 225–237). New York: The Guilford Press.

Hill, R. B. (1972). *The strengths of Black families.* New York: National Urban League.

Hill, R. B. (1999). *The strengths of African American families: Twenty-five years later.* Lanham, MD: University Press of America.

Hollingsworth, L. D. (1998). Promoting same-race adoption for children of color. *Social Work, 43*, 104–116.

Hollingsworth, L. D. (1999). Symbolic interactionism, African American families, and the transracial adoption controversy. *Social Work, 44*, 443–454.

Jim Crow Laws (n.d.). Retrieved June 4, 2012, from http://www.jimcrowhistory.org/scripts/jimcrow/insidesouth. cgi?state=Texas.

Jim Crow Laws: Texas. (n.d.). Retrieved March 3, 2011, from http://www.jimcrowhistory.org/scripts/jimcrow/insidesouth.cgi?state=Texas

Marks, L. D., Hopkins, K., Chaney, C., Monroe, P. A., Nesteruk, O., & Sasser, D. D. (2008). "Together, we are strong:" A qualitative study of happy, enduring African American marriages. *Family Relations, 57*, 172–185.

McCubbin, H. I., Futrell, J. A., Thompson, E. A., & Thompson, A. I. (1998). Resilient families in an ethnic and cultural context. In H. I. McCubbin, E. A. Thompson, A. I. Thompson, & J. A. Futrell (Eds.), *Resiliency in African American families* (pp. 329–352). Thousand Oaks: Sage Publications.

McCubbin, H. I., Thompson, E. A., Thompson, A. I., & Futrell, J. A. (1998). *Resiliency in African American families.* Thousand Oaks: Sage Publications.

McGoldrick, M., & Hardy, K. V. (2008). *Re-visioning family therapy: Race, culture, and gender in clinical practice* (2nd ed.). New York: The Guilford Press.

National Park Service (n.d.). Jim Crow Laws. Retrieved June 4, 2012 from http://www.nps.gov/malu/forteachers/jim_crow_laws.htm.

Patton, M. Q. (2002). *Qualitative research & evaluation methods* (3rd ed.). Thousand Oaks: Sage Publications.

Rice, C. (2010). *Extraordinary, ordinary people: A memoir of family.* New York: Crown Archetype.

Steele, S. (2006). *White guilt: How blacks and whites together destroyed the promise of the civil rights movement.* New York: Harper Collins.

U. S. Census Bureau. (2009). *Current Population Survey, Annual Social and Economic Supplement, 2009.* Retrieved March 1, 2011, from http://www.census.gov/population/www.socdemo/race/ppl-bc09.html.

Walsh, F. (1998). *Strengthening family resilience.* New York: The Guilford Press.

Weisstein, E. W. (n.d.). *Young girl-Old woman illusion.* From MathWorld-A Wolfram Web Resource: Retrieved March 28, 2011, from http://mathworld.wolfram.com/YoungGirl-OldWomanillusion.html.

White, M., & Epston, D. (1990). *Narrative means to therapeutic ends.* New York: Norton.

Resilience Relative to Korean Families

15

Sandra Rigazio-DiGilio and Ppudah Ki

Our greatest glory is not in never falling, but in rising every time we fall.

Confucius

Introduction

The words of Confucius about the significance of regaining one's position after a fall are clearly evident at many levels of Korean culture.[1] Korea, like many of its Asian neighbors, was and still is influenced by Confucian notions of private and public life. The idea that one can be stronger by surviving catastrophe(s) is pervasive in the mythologies, religions, geopolitical history, and culture of Korea.

This drive to lift oneself up after a fall and to come back stronger, faster, and smarter is evident in resilient Korean families. History has shown, time and time again, that Korean families have the ability to pull together the necessary psychological, spiritual, interpersonal, and material resources to overcome adversities and to emerge with broader skills and knowledge, with a deeper sense of well-being; all necessary qualities to improve their lives and the lives of their kin.

Anthropologists are still not certain if resilience is an innate human quality that can be accessed during times of disaster (e.g., McCubbin & Patterson, 1981), or if it is a product of the interaction between humans and adversity (e.g., Cowen, Cowen, & Schultz, 1996; Lee et al., 2004; Walsh, 1998). In this chapter we do not penetrate the deep ontological nature of resilience, but rather draw from the concepts and definitions associated with resilience to identify sources of strength within Korean families that can be brought to bear in helping relationships.

For our purposes, we use the concept of family resilience put forth by Becvar and Becvar (2009), "The capacity of families …to rebound and go on is known as resilience, or the ability to meet and handle successfully both normal developmental challenges and unanticipated crisis and change" (p. 107). Viewing resilience as a capacity that can ebb and flow across different circumstances helps

---

[1] Note to clinicians: Thorough knowledge of the particular Korean families one is working with is critical if one is to interweave successfully the ideas expressed in this chapter with clinical conceptualizations of the ways resilience can be tailored to their specific cultural and contextual worldviews.

S. Rigazio-DiGilio(✉) • P. Ki
Marriage and Family Therapy, University of Connecticut, Storrs, CT, USA
e-mail: Sandra.Rigazio-DiGilio@uconn.edu

D.S. Becvar (ed.), *Handbook of Family Resilience*,
DOI 10.1007/978-1-4614-3917-2_15, © Springer Science+Business Media New York 2013

clinicians understand that their work is to increase the family's ability to engage in the change process as opposed to directing the change process from the position of an expert. As stated by Lee et al. (2004), by understanding family resilience as an enduring ability or capacity that is exhibited as family strength when responding to stress and problem solving, this construct can be measured, allowing practitioners to differentiate interventions that promote positive levels of family functioning. We thus review current research on family resilience specifically as related to families of Korean descent and provide culturally and contextually relevant considerations for assessment, treatment planning, and the therapeutic process.

A Positive Perspective on Family Resilience

Rather than assuming a deficit perspective, contemporary researchers are seeking to understand the protective factors that surround and imbue family life (Froman, 2010; Kim, Lee, & Yu, 2005; Lundman et al., 2010). The conceptualization of family resilience is primarily derived from current work in positive psychology (e.g., Steptoe, Dockray, & Wardle, 2009). Research suggests that there are marked associations between positive psychological states and health outcomes for family members. In addition to being beneficial for individuals at the biologic levels (e.g., lower cortisol output, more healthy heart rates, more normal blood pressure, lower inflammatory markers), positive affect also is associated with protective psychosocial factors such as positive social connectedness, perceived social support, collective optimism, and the increased proclivity to employ adaptive coping responses (e.g., Masten & Obradovic, 2008). As research on resilience advances, it builds on what has become known about the ways in which families cope with adversity and the processes they use for returning to prestressor levels of functioning. Building on this foundational knowledge base, investigators are now examining the ways in which families actually open their hearts and minds to move forward with newfound confidence, determination, hope, and visions for a better tomorrow and—in this process—becoming stronger through their interactions with stressor events. As our understanding increases, broader conceptualizations of family resilience are being brought to the forefront, such as the ways in which Lundman et al. (2010) conceptualize inner strength:

> It means to both stand steady, to be firm, with both feet on the ground and to be connected to family, friends, society, nature, and spiritual dimensions and to be able to transcend. Having inner strength is to be creative and stretchable (p. 251).

For systemic scientists and practitioners these conceptualizations can easily be broadened beyond definitions of inner strength as individual attributes to collective attributes that, for the purpose of this chapter, can be found in Korean family life.

Positive psychology has been influential in shifting the focus of analysis from the negative family correlates dealing with stress such as problematic family functioning and concordant levels of family stress, parent and child psychopathology, and conflicted parent–child relationships (Deault, 2010) to variables that might mediate protective factors for Korean families, such as a sense of cohesion, levels of attachment among family members, patience for attaining goals, and family member leadership (Lee et al., 2004). Taking a cultural and contextual perspective, positive psychology helps to broaden our lens to encompass the importance of sociocultural protective factors that promote adaptability and responsiveness in families. By understanding Korea's unique sociocultural history as well as the contemporary milieus within which Korean families survive and thrive, practitioners will be better able to: (a) appreciate the foundational qualities of Korean family resilience; (b) understand what features of family resilience are salient at any given moment and in relation to particular life experiences; and (c) incorporate this information into collaborative assessment, treatment planning, and therapeutic exchanges that access and support adaptability and responsiveness within the family.

Background

Developmental History

> Where we are today is a natural and logical consequence of our cultural and developmental histories.
>
> Ivey & Rigazio-DiGilio, 2009

Understanding the political and cultural history of Korea is essential to appreciating the role of resilience in the lives of Koreans. This brief overview of key historical and cultural aspects of Korean life is intended to provide contextual information that can be used to inform conceptualizations of how Korean clients view their past and current situations. This section is extended in order to identify critical historical and cultural elements that may provide insight into the worldviews of Korean clients. Also, realize that many libraries can be filled with books and articles describing and analyzing Korean history and this is but a brief overview intended to help understand how resilience may be manifested by Korean clients.

While anthropologists might differ about the exact population of the peninsula of Korea, it is hypothesized that peoples speaking the Tungusic branch of the Ural-Altaic language family first migrated from the Northwestern regions of Asia about 4,000 BCE (Beckwith, 2010). Current languages associated with the Ural-Altaic family include Mongolian, Finnish, and Hungarian and possibly Korean and Japanese. Linguistically, Korean is unrelated to Chinese and is similar to, but distinct from Japanese (Kwon, 2010). Early historical records indicate that at the dawn of the Christian era, two groups of languages were spoken in Manchuria and on the Korean Peninsula: the Northern or Puyo group and the southern or Han group.

The Korean language is spoken by over 48 million people spread all around the globe (Lee, 2010a). Korean is descended from Proto-Korean, Old Korean, Middle Korean, and Modern Korean. Korean is considered by linguists as a language isolate, meaning that connections to other language families is minimal. In this fashion, the language, people, and culture of Korea should be considered as distinct from that of its Asian neighbors, even though these countries share a long history together (Kwon, 2010). During the seventh century, the Silla dialect became the dominant language for the country. Since the Korean War, contemporary North–South differences in Korean have developed, including variance in pronunciation, verb inflection, and vocabulary (Lee, 1990), thus further differentiating the cultural and contextual histories of families living in Southern and Northern Korea (Hammal, 2010).

In terms of mythology, legend holds that Tan-gun, who was descended from the Gods, came to earth and created the first community in Old Choson in the northwestern part of Korea, near present-day Pyongyang, in 2333 BCE. The traditional Korean calendar dates back to this founding. Korean mythologies are replete with stories that reinforce the cultural message of perseverance and rebirth (Grayson, 1997). For example, the Korean creation myth holds that the father of Tan-gun was Hwan-ung, who was the son of Hwan-in, the God of all and the Ruler of Heaven, who transformed himself into a mortal to father Tan-gun. Tan-gun's mother was a bear who obediently followed Hwan-ung's directions to become human and was reborn as a "women of beauty." The power of rebirth thus is deeply woven into the Korean cosmogony.

Korean history is an intricate tapestry made up of the many major events by which it has been shaped as well as the numerous individuals, families, and clans who contributed to the country's survival (Ahn, 2003; Ch'oe, 1980; Park & Lee, 2008). Korea shares a common history with many of its South East Asia neighbors who were eventually incorporated into the Mongol Empire during the thirteenth century, including China, Korea, Vietnam, and Cambodia. All of these countries can trace the long road to political sovereignty through numerous internal campaigns for control over local territories to large-scale resistance, acquiescence, and eventual freedom from control by foreign governments (Yoon, 2005).

During the first two millennia CE, internal conflict among the three kingdoms—Silla, Koguryo, and Paekche—dominated life on the peninsula (Lee, 1988). Silla, in 668, became triumphant and unified the peninsula for the first time. In 935, the Koryo dynasty succeeded the Silla in laying claim to all of Korea. It was the term Koryo from which sixteenth-century Portuguese missionaries derived the western word "Korca." The Choson dynasty, which ruled Korea after the Koryo Dynasty, lasted from 1392 until the Japanese annexation of Korea in 1910 (Lee, 1988).

External wars and invasions by China, Manchuria, and Japan also occurred from the thirteenth to the nineteenth centuries (Lee, 1988). From 1231 until the early fourteenth-century Korea was under Mongolian rule, and the great Kublia Khan, who served as the supreme emperor, used Korea as a roadway to invade Japan on three different occasions. From the sixteenth century to the mid-twentieth century, Japan launched attacks on Korean ports and cities. From the seventeenth century to the dawn of the twentieth century, Korea enjoyed a certain degree of autonomy under the ultimate control of China. It was a time of feudal political power, and the Choson Dynasty maintained a strict social order that ensured their influence and control over the people and the resources of Korea—a control that lasted until the late 1800s. Since then, other foreign countries have attempted to "control" Korea, including France, Britain, the United States, and Russia, but it was Japan who finally annexed Korea in 1910 after gaining more power through the Sino-Japanese War (1894–1895), the Russo-Japanese War (1904–1905), and World War One (1914–1919) (Lee, 1988). During their colonial occupation, Japanese administrators used ruthless means in an effort to supplant the Korean language and culture, but to no avail (Park, 2010). International trade and commerce also were controlled to the benefit of Japanese merchants. These were methods the Japanese learned at the hands of the US during the mid-nineteenth century (Park). As a result of fending off the gunboat diplomacy tactics of these countries, Korean rulers initiated a closed-door policy resulting in the use of the phrase "Hermit Kingdom" to symbolize their nation (Barnett, 2006). Independence remained fragile during the second millennium.

During the first half of the twentieth century, Japan was given permission to control Korea by European Countries and the US as a means of curtailing Russian expansion to the East. At the end of World War II, the Potsdam Declaration divided Korea at the 38th parallel and permitted Russia to assume administrative control over North Korea and the US to assume administrative control over South Korea (Hammal, 2010). In 1950, in a move to reunite all of Korea, Northern Korea invaded Southern Korea, initiating the Korean War (1950–1953). The failure of this attempt to unify the country simply reinforced the separate control over the northern and southern parts of Korea by Russia and America (Hammal, 2010).

The period after the Korean War is known as the "Miracle on Han River" (1953–1996), during which time South Korea was transformed into the world's 15th largest economy (Ringen, Kwon, Yi, Kim, & Lee, 2011). This period was marked by rapid urbanization and industrialization, fueled by cheap labor. Additionally, during this time the Chaebol, or family-controlled corporations, were very influential in achieving government policy that furthered South Korea's wealth. Companies that started in the 1930s and 1940s became family controlled, and some ascended to major multinational status (e.g., Samsung, Hyundai, Kia, Daewoo, Lotte, LG).

At the heart of this great economic success were policies promulgated under General Park Chung-hee, who lead a successful coup d'état against the corrupt administration of Syngman Rhee and founded the Second Republic of South Korea (Ringen et al., 2011). Once again, the Koreans were to tolerate an authoritarian style of leadership that, while successfully catapulting South Korea's economy, did so by trampling on human rights and freedoms of expression, and by using extreme forms of torture to control enemies of the state and engender fear in the hearts of all Koreans. General Park was murdered at the hands of his closest friend in 1979, and the "Korean Economic Miracle" continued for another 20 years with a lesser degree of oppression and control.

In 1960, which was one year before Park gained control of Southern Korea, the Koreans experienced a student uprising that lead to the downfall of Syngman Rhee and the collapse of the First Republic of South Korea. There were then three more iterations of government in the 10-year period from 1979 to 1988, as democratic elections established the Sixth Republic of South Korea (Ringen, 2011). The rapidity of turnover in governments prompted the reversal of many of Park's dictates that restricted human rights.

While the South has had six iterations of government since 1948, the North has had a stable form of communist rule, which has not reflected the same economic advancements as those made in the South. The North shares over 5,000 years of common culture with Southern Korea, but the division since 1945 has resulted in significant differences in the quality of life. For example, while both countries have high expectations for the education of their future generations (i.e., there is a 99% literacy rate in the North and a 98% literacy rate in the South), the range of options available for children to achieve and exceed these expectations is far greater in the South than in the North (Hart, 1999). Economically, the per capita income in the North is approximately $2,000 (U.S.) and ten times that amount in the South. Life expectancies reflect these educational, economic, and other inequities. For example, family members living in the South can expect to live for 78.7 years while in the North life expectancy age is 63.8 years. Furthermore, the infant mortality rate in South Korea is 4/1,000 births as opposed to 51 deaths per 1,000 births in the North (Country Report, 2010). The stark differences in these data suggest that Korean families living in the North are under much more political, economic, and social stress than families in the South.

Cultural History

Korea shares much cultural history with the other countries that border the Yellow Sea, namely China and Japan (Kwon, 2010; Yoon, 2005). Together, these three countries account for more than one-quarter of the world's population and have over a long historical period constituted a cultural sphere characterized by the use of Chinese knowledge and science and Confucianism, with an ever increasing infusion of Western empiricism and thought (Park & Cho, 1995). Confucianism refers to the common value system of these three nations and is derived from the synthesis of traditional values espoused by Confucius and his followers and subsequently influenced by elements of Taoism, Legalism, Buddhism, Shamanism, and Mohism (i.e., advocating a utilitarian ethic) (Park & Cho). From a family perspective, although Buddhism, Taoism, and Shamanism have strong influences on individual moral and ethical conduct, it is Confucianism that has been most influential in shaping the behavior of Korean family life (Park & Cho; Sivananda, 2010): "The central pillar of Confucianism is the family. Indeed, family cohesion and continuity are taken as the foundation for sustaining the human community and the state" (Park & Cho, 1995, p. 117). A manifestation of this value is the pattern of universal marriage and childbearing in Korea.

Another legacy flowing from Confucianism is adherence to a patriarchal family structure. Aggressively advanced during the Chosun dynasty (1392–1910), the notion that the family takes precedence over individual members and that the family group is inseparably identified with the larger clan (Park & Cho, 1995) has flourished for over 600 years. The most important function of family members is to maintain and preserve the household within the traditional Confucian patriarchal system (Sivananda, 2010). This family structure, known as a stem family, has definite rules as to who can live with whom upon the death of the male head of household to ensure the continuity of the patriarchal system. It replaced a much more bilateral family system, in which a couple might live with either the woman's or the man's family, and both male and female offspring could inherit their parents' property (Deuchler & Jin-Sook, 1997).

According to Confucianism, the central familial relationship is not generational (i.e., between husband and wife), but rather intergenerational (i.e., between parent—usually male—and child—usually male). Thus, primary relationships between family members are not horizontal and equal (i.e., based on mutual love and equality), but are characterized by vertical filial piety (i.e., benevolence, authority, and obedience). Authority rests with the male head of the household and differences in status exist among other family members (i.e., there can only be one "excellent family member" who will receive the bulk of the family's resources as well as educational and economic opportunities that other family members will not benefit from). The hierarchical relationship between husband and wife was maintained by the "three obediences": A woman is required to obey her father, husband, and son, in that order (Sivananda, 2010).

Social organization according to Confucianism is tied together by a threefold mechanism: the domestic sphere (represented by the wife) is subordinated to the public sphere (represented by the father and son), who are, in turn, the sovereign's subjects (Chung & Das Gupta, 2007). Clan members thus monitored all aspects of family lineage and kept careful records of births (particularly males), family positions within the clans, secular and religious positions within the community, and aristo-cratic positions within the Chosun kingdom. Lineage membership thus determined much of a per-son's life chances (Chung & Das Gupta). The efficiency of the Confucian social structure rigidly reinforced this patrilineal kinship system by specifying very detailed descriptions of the roles and status of each member of a household and lineage, all under the unchallenged authority of the (male) head of the family.

Women were severely marginalized by these strict rules of patrilineal kinship and inheritance, which placed the father–son dyad in the public sphere and relegated women to the domestic sphere. Strict rules of lineage exogamy meant that wives would be outsiders in their husbands' village (Kim, 2001). As a result, women were socially isolated whereas men were surrounded by networks of social support. At marriage, a wife and her unborn children would be formally transferred to her husband's family. In this prescribed arrangement, only sons could care for their parents in this life and in their afterlives. A wife's primary duty was to bear sons to ensure the continuity of her husband's lineage (Chung & Das Gupta, 2007).

To infuse these notions into the lives of Korean families, the Confucians set out to obliterate Buddhism, with its emphasis on individual self-realization and salvation, which they felt detracted from the chief value of loyalty to family and state (Sivananda, 2010). They sought to replace this with a tightly structured system of kinship and political relations designed to promote stability and loyalty to a series of nested corporate groups: the household, the lineage, and the state, underpinned by pre-scribed rituals. Interestingly, Buddhism was not obliterated but rather was reframed as a cultural force that reinforced harmonious familial relationships across generations based on the same patriarchal Confucian principles of obedience, authority, and benevolence (Lee, 1988).

In 1950 these Confucian views of family hierarchy were enshrined in Korean Law. The Family Law provisions (1958) (as cited by Cho, 1994) stipulated: (a) that family headship must be held by the men in the line of the eldest son; (b) that inheritance should be through the male line; (c) that men must marry outside their lineage; (d) that women should be transferred to their husband's family reg-ister upon marriage; and (e) that the children belong to the father's lineage even in the case of divorce (Chung & Das Gupta, 2007). Later, at the end of the century, as the women's movement gained momentum along with the success of civil society movements demanding an end to military rule, there was enough sentiment to successfully obtain court judgments challenging the constitutional validity of key aspects of the Family Law (Chang & Song, 2010). Individual petitioners also were successful. For example, in 1997 the Constitutional Court of South Korea ruled it unconstitutional to prohibit marriage within the lineage. In this century, the South Korean Supreme Court ruled that women could remain members of their natal household after marriage, and that both women and men have equal rights and responsibilities to care for their ancestors (Kim, 2005). Eventually, in 2005, the government abolished male family headship and allowed parents who so wished to register their children under the mother's family name beginning in 2008.

The transition from stem families to nuclear families is currently increasing all over South Korea (Chang & Song, 2010). Data from 1990 suggests that traditional patriarchal stem family structures in South Korea were declining as the nation urbanized (Chung & Das Gupta, 2007). All parts of South Korea—across urban areas and rural communities—witnessed a decrease from over 30% of Korea's populace living in stem households in 1955 to only 9.5% of households in 1990 at the national level. In urban communities the decrease was from 20% to 8%, and in rural communities, from 34% to 14%. This rapid adjustment to alternative ways of raising families is indicative of the resilience inherent in Korean families (Cho, 1998; Chung & Das Gupta, 2007).

Spiritual Beliefs

Historically, religions have prospered in Korea. Buddhism blossomed in Koryo, Confucianism spread throughout the Chosun Dynasty, and Christianity is showing positive reception in the twentieth century (Lee, 1988). Again, as with other East Asian cultures, the beliefs of Confucianism, Buddhism, and Shamanism are evident at individual and family levels (Ahn, 2003). Most Koreans still practice many ancient rituals associated with these three paths to spiritual and moral enlightenment, but only Buddhism is viewed as a formal religion.

Today, in terms of spiritual preferences, South Koreans overwhelmingly prefer to view themselves as not belonging to a particular denomination (Chae, 2009). In fact, 46.5% of respondents in a 2005 national poll declared "no religion" as their affiliation, followed by 23% affiliating with Buddhism, and 18% and 11% affiliating with Protestant and Catholic religions, respectively. Today, the rise in mega-churches (i.e., Christian congregations numbering in the tens of thousands) is a testament to the vibrancy of Korean spirituality in that these congregations reinforce a sense of collectivism that feeds individual and family resilience (Chae).

There are a number of alternate religions (i.e., Jeungism, Daesunism, Cheondoism, Taoism, Confucianism, Won Buddhism) that some South Koreans practice. A small percentage of respondents (0.1%) indicated they practice Islam. Data from North Korea suggest that a large Christian population was emerging before 1945. However, because religious activity is now severely restricted, little information is known about the religious preferences of residents of North Korea. Christianity in South Korea reflects a hybridity of religious practices that meld traditional Confucianistic characteristics with modern day Protestant rites and theology to create a broader version labeled "Confucian Protestantism" (Chae, 2009).

Whether it is Buddhism, Confucianism, or Christianity, Korean people have relied on spiritual beliefs in times of adversity, and religion has been a consistent source of Korean family resilience. Box 15.1 offers a narrative by the second author that provides one illustration of the ways in which religion was able to support the elder generation to create paths for the next generation to move beyond traditional roles between men and women.

Fertility

Cotemporaneous with expansion of the economic system that previously had maintained women in low paying jobs until they had children was the widespread acceptance of birth control technologies.

Box 15.1 Spirituality and Korean Family Resiliency: The Impact of Christianity on the Second Author's Family

People describe my grandpa's death as martyrdom. Around 1885, the Christian missionaries came into Korea and distributed Bibles to local citizens and built up hospitals and schools. My grandpa was one of the first generation who accepted the gospel and converted to Christianity. He went to the theological school and worked for a Presbyterian church. However, during the period of Japanese annexation, Japan tried to force people to reject their own religious beliefs and adopt those that were mandated by the new government. Many Koreans who held Christian values and beliefs could not follow this coercive order, and since my grandpa had a firm belief in Christianity, he refused to bow down and he was jailed. After his imprisonment, he continued to be involved in the independence movement. He was an activist who worked for his country's liberation from Japan and for religious freedom from the communist government in the North. However, in 1950 when the Korean War broke out, the North Korean communist soldiers attacked the South and he was arrested by them and killed that day. Now, his work as a social activist and active pastor for social justice is recognized and he is enshrined in Memorial Hall for Christian Martyrs in Yong-in, a suburban city of Seoul. He was a strong leader who held steadfastly to his firm, righteous beliefs. His favorite Bible verse is engraved on his stone: "Do not be afraid of those who kill the body but cannot kill the soul. Rather, be afraid of the One who can destroy both soul and body in hell" (Matthew 10:28, NIV). Being influenced by my grandfather's beliefs and courage, my family learned to survive psychologically and spiritually by keeping the faith. Having beliefs and values in something more core and important in life helped our family not to be distracted by temporary false values, but to survive and be resilient from the difficulties and to help others as well.

After his death, my grandma influenced the whole family. At the onset of the war, she led many others from her community to seek sanctuary at Jeju Island, the only safe island in South Korea. She guided the group over many rivers, climbing numerous mountains, and finally brought them to Jeju where they stayed safe for 3 years. She was like a mother of everyone. She was a strong woman who sacrificed herself to care for everyone around her and demonstrated through actions her fervent religious values. She always motivated and encouraged people by finding strengths in them and supported them by telling them that they will have a better life in the future. She was greatly admired and respected, so at her funeral in 1999, almost a 1,000 people showed up and mourned. I believe that she was able to be the supporter for the whole community because she thought it was her responsibility as a Christian leader in the confusing era.

A massive family planning program initiated in 1962 greatly reduced the number of children born per woman from 6.0 in 1960 to 1.2 in 2009, the lowest birthrate worldwide at that time. The preference for having a son also diminished in the first decade of the twenty-first century. Chung and Das Gupta (2007) report that the stated preference for giving birth to a son decreased from 35% in 1991 to 19% in 2003 for women born between 1955 and 1964, and from 27% to 11% during the same time period for women born between 1965 and 1974. The authors attribute this significant shift in preference to the disintegration of the preindustrial social organization that occurred during the rise of industrialization and urbanization. Avenues opened up for obtaining livelihoods and social status that were independent of lineage membership and adherence to familial expectations. The accompanying urbanization resulted in people no longer being surrounded by patrilineal kin in their place of residence and work. This created possibilities for relationships between parents and children to be driven by affect rather than by rigid rules of gender and birth order. According to Chung and Das Gupta, all these changes, in combination, served to undercut the bases for son preference in South Korea.

The quest to secure a strong education for their Nation's children has prompted additional significant changes in the structure and functioning of Korean families. For example, it is not unusual for families to employ the "Wild Goose Father" solution whereby the mother travels with the child to enable him or her to participate in what are considered to be superior educational experiences, usually outside of Korea, for many years leaving the father and other family members at home (Choi, 2006; Kang, 2009; Kim & Chang, 2004; Lee & Koo, 2006). This practice is also a significant factor that has contributed to the reduction in childbirth evident in current-day South Korea.

Collectivism

Urbanization has not entirely ruled out the legacy of the Confucian system of clan control over geographic regions (Sivananda, 2010). The inner sense of belonging with others is important, even in urban areas. For many South Koreans their identity is defined by the relationships with their immediate and extended family (Chung, 2003). Individualism does not dominate the worldview, but rather the connections to nuclear and extended family members significantly inform the cognitive, emotional, and behavioral interactions of South Koreans (Lee et al., 2004). "Where are you from?" is an important and frequently asked question. Each province has unique characteristics that define it, and knowing where someone is from gives relief to South Koreans when they first meet. This deep sense of commitment to collectivism is directly connected to the overall sense of resilience on which South Koreans tend to rely (Kim, 2005).

Korean Diaspora

Worldwide, there are approximately seven million people who comprise the Korean Diaspora (Bergsten & Choi, 2003). In the mid-1860s, Korean families emigrated into Northeast China and Far East Russia. Over time, these early immigrates became the ancestors of over 2,000,000 Koreans living in China and another ½ million Koreans living in countries of the former Soviet Union (Saveliev, 2010). In the early twentieth century, Koreans were recruited or forced into service in Japan. When given the opportunity, many Koreans returned to both North and South Korea following World War II, yet today almost one million Koreans refer to Japan as their home (Chang, 2004).

Emigration to the U.S. exploded after the passage of the Immigration Reform Act of 1965. Today, the Korean population in the U.S. is over two million (Leong, 2003). Koreans live in all countries around the world. In each country, some families are returning to Korea and others are leaving South Korea (Lee, 2010a). Koreans, regardless of their geographic residence, economic well-being, and structure and proximity of family members, struggle to create their dream of success. Korean history has shown that individuals, families, clans, and communities who pick themselves back up after the fall are those who survive. Koreans worldwide know how to use personal, familial, and group resources to build the inner strength to move forward, even in times of great adversity, such as war, oppression, leaving one's family, and economic hardship (Ahn, 2003; Lee, Brown, Mitchell, & Schiraldi, 2008; Park & Lee, 2008).

Han: The Culmination of History and Culture

Han is a uniquely Korean concept that conveys a collective feeling of oppression and isolation in the face of overwhelming odds:

> For most Koreans, Han represents the core of their national ethos, and carries some five thousand years of the Nation's historical and cultural memories. This collective trauma has been handed down, in the form of specific emotions, from generation to generation (Shim, 2004, p. 220).

According to Shim, *Han* provides a window on the emotional landscape of the Korean people and indirectly helps reveal their worldview. *Han* is the consciousness of social injustice, unrighteousness, un-freedom, and inequities (Go, 1988).

This multilayered concept is usually expressed as negative emotions (i.e., unresolved resentment against injustices suffered, acute pain in one's spirit and body, sorrow, resentment, rancor) and is imbued with resignation, bitter acceptance, and a grim determination to wait until vengeance at last can be achieved (Ahn, 2003). In keeping with Korean tradition, *Han* is passive. That is, one must bear it. While it yearns for vengeance it never seeks it. *Han* is held close to the heart, hoping and patient, but never aggressive. The connotation that *Han* reflects dysphonic emotions was at its height during the first three-quarters of the twentieth century. The Japanese annexation of Korea in 1910, followed by the surrender of Japan in 1945 to the Americans (and not to the Koreans) continued the validity of *Han*. Further, having the country split to serve two masters (i.e., Russia, America) intensified the collective sense of utter hopelessness for a sovereign, fully intact Korea.

In the South, the rapid cultural transitions propelled by economic advances reaped by the "Miracle on the Han River" as well as the later movement toward greater human rights, redefined the meaning of *Han* in a more positive, resilient fashion (Ringen et al., 2011). This change was initiated by people involved in human rights, labor, and nationalist movements who—collectively—were able to overthrow President Park's dictatorial rule, bringing about the beginnings of a new, more democratic, less misogynistic, and less rule-bound social order. Today, *Han* can be viewed as bringing character out of oppression (Webster, 2001). *Han* is now considered a specific emotional coping style that many Koreans believe not only protects them from the negative effects of the chronic stress they have experienced as a people, but that also has built the character of the Korean people both nationally and individually. By accepting *Han,* the Koreans create not only the psychological resources to weather times of national as well as foreign government oppression, and to then spring forward and advance their well-being when conditions change—in other words, to recover after the fall (Ahn, 2003).

Significance

Korean families have "reinvented" themselves during the last century using the great strengths of family cohesion and loyalty mixed with ingenuity and innovation. The powerful patrilineal demands that ruled Korea for over 600 years have shifted radically, and South Korea is moving successfully toward a more balanced model of nuclear family headed by either a male or a female, or both. This is a major cultural transition that happened in a very short time period. It testifies to the resilience of the Korean family. They know what to do not only to survive but to thrive, often under the most extreme conditions of human oppression.

The survival skills mastered by resilient families during the "fallen" times of colonization are evident in today's research about Korean family resilience. While it is true today that the traditional Confucian image of the Korean family is becoming less influential in determining the structure of families, the deeply ingrained significance of the family still remains vibrant. The role of family is paramount within Korean culture, and the family is a primary source of resilience for its members. The many themes of the birth–rebirth narrative run deeply through the tapestry that is Korean history and are captured in the empirical literature concerning the definition and support of Korean family resilience.

Toward a Theory of Korean Family Resilience: A Review of the Literature

Korean family resilience is a little studied and poorly understood phenomenon. Researchers in South Korea and around the world have barely scratched the surface of information that would be helpful to inform culturally relevant practice. While all social science fields are publishing articles about Korean family life, the work that has advanced an empirical conceptualization of Korean family resilience is primarily emerging within the field of nursing. This research is being used to inform nursing practices in Korea, particularly with respect to guiding the ways in which nurses can interact with families so that the patient, family, and kin members are treated in culturally relevant ways that engender both realism and hope. Based on the research in this field, it appears that when cultural mores interfere with these interactions, nurses are learning ways to reflect upon and alter their perceptions and behaviors so as to minimize miscommunication and misinformation. This is especially true for Korean nurses who work in a system where physicians are not always forthcoming with family members (Yang, 2005).

One conceptual and empirical program of research being advanced to illuminate the understanding of Korean family resilience is being conducted within the College of Nursing at Seoul National University, led by Insook and Eun-Ok Lee. Based on McCubbin's and Patterson's (1981) initial conceptualizations, Lee, Lee, and their colleagues have derived a model that posits family resilience as "an enabling force for family functioning, especially in the context of family adjustment to stress" (Lee et al., 2004, p. 642). Specifically, family resilience is the proactive energy that is employed in the adaptation process and is a basis of individual and collective resources used by families during times of crisis to maintain family balance (Lee et al.).

Lee et al. (2004) have constructed and validated a 37-item Korean Family Resilience Scale based on 21 attributes identified through an extensive review of the extant literature on family resilience. A factor analysis revealed five factors that explained 56.4% of the variance among the 231 families in the study. Family cohesion accounted for 28.5% of the variance alone, with family maturity, the ability to use external resources, control, and the driving force for solving financial difficulties left to explain the other 28%. Psychometrically, the instrument had a Cronbach's alpha of 0.8039 and the Guttman split-half coefficient was 0.8184. Based on these results, Lee et al. (2006) noted that family coherence is the essential factor of Korean family resilience.

The conceptual model that informed instrument development organized the 21 attributes derived through the theoretical analysis into four dimensions following the fieldwork validation phase of this work: *Intrinsic Family Characteristics, Family Member Orientation, Responsiveness to Stress*, and *External Orientation*. Table 15.1 depicts the structure of these 21 attributes, as categorized into the four dimensions that comprise the Korean Family Resilience Model. Of the four dimensions, Lee et al. (2004) noted that the concept of an ability to use external resources, particularly those in the extended family, is a very important feature: "In South Korea, even when families live as nuclear families the extended family network is considered very important not only for interactions but also sharing resources" (p. 643).

Holroyd's (2005) critique of the work of Lee et al. emphasizes a broader issue about the work being done in the area of family resilience. Specifically,

Table 15.1 Korean family resilience model—four dimensions and attributes

Dimension	Attributes
Intrinsic family characteristic	Coherence
	Faith
	Positive outlook
	Mature thinking
	Family self-esteem
Family member orientation	Flexibility in reorganizing the family
	Attachment among family members
	Open communication and emotional expression among family members
	Mutual understanding
	Maintaining a balance in the family member demands
Externally directed	Economic resources
	Pro-activeness toward information
	Maintaining cooperative relations with health care professionals
	Ability to maintain good social relations
	Family member leadership
Responsive to stress	Adaptability
	Desire to maintain normal states
	Patience for attainment of goals
	Ability to control stress
	Readiness to accept critical situations
	Responsibility for causing trouble

Adapted from Lee et al. (2004)

the field of family resilience is still in an early stage of development and at present is more notable for its articulation of theory than for a large and consistent body of empirical evidence, and that, because of this lack of empirical evidence, some researchers question whether it has yet been demonstrated that the field of work on resilience at the family level has made its own unique contribution to the health professional knowledge (p. 638).

Lee and associates agree that the work on family resilience in general, and specifically relating to Korean Families, is just emerging, but that their research over years of studying this phenomenon indicates its significance for professionals working with Korean Families. Holroyd (2005) acknowledges that "the family resilience literature, with its focus on successful functioning in the context of adversity, has highlighted important ways in which families can draw upon protective factors, both within the family unit and in their wider environment" (p. 639). It is this ability to tap familial resources that is particularly associated with Korean families when they are dealing with stressful situations.

Lee et al. (2006) also highlight the differences in generational responses to stress. For older Korean families the values of their parents and grandparents might still be strongly held, but for younger Korean families those values are quickly losing influence over their behavior as Western culture and values gain more prominence. For example: (a) women are entering, staying at, and rising through all levels of the workplace; (b) the divorce rate is approximately 40% of all marriages; (c) premarital cohabitation is commonplace; and, (d) gay and lesbian groups are more visible (Han, Choi, & Lee, 2000).

Lee et al. (2006) contend that traditional Confucianism is no longer the dominant value structure in Korean families, but their research indicates that for some families, strict adherence to these traditional values is important, and for many families some of these values are maintained while others are rejected. Each Korean family, whether in Seoul, Pyongyang, Shanghia, or San Francisco, is unique and no generalization about old or young, rich or poor, urban or rural will apply to all. Therefore, culture-centered practitioners need to take the time to differentiate the aspects of traditional Korean culture that are salient for each Korean family they work with as well as what other values have become important outside of the culture-bound values adhered to in the past.

Based on their work over the past decade, Lee et al. (2006) state that Korean families do not differ greatly from families found in the West. As Korean society changes so, too, do Korean families. Younger generations are moving toward Western ideals of human rights and dignity and are not afraid to break away from traditional mores. The older generations still maintain traditional Confucian values. It is the conflict between generations that may be most problematic in terms of family harmony and functioning (p. 655).

Lee et al. (2004) present a well-grounded model of Korean Family Resilience and their corpus of work to date validates that Korean families, while very similar to families in the West, do have their unique coping styles that must be accounted for when working with them. The Korean Family Resilience scale provides one empirical instrument that can be used to measure a family's level of resilience as well as to inform interventions and prevention programs to assist Korean families, and the wider systems that define them, as they work to meet all of life's demands, especially during times of significant crisis.

The Power of Many

Families adapt to and/or influence their life space by increasing the protective factors that promote resilience at both individual and family levels. The Handbook of Ecology identifies three types of protective factors: (a) dispositional; (b) affective ties within the family; and (c) external support systems (Miller, Lerner, Schiamberg, & Anderson, 2003). Notice the centrality of the family in this typology. The family mediates both the individual development of its members (dispositional) and navigates the vicissitudes generated through interaction with the world beyond the immediate family (external support systems). Korean families are very skillful at tying affective relationships with external support systems during times of crisis (Lee et al., 2004; Lee & Bronstein, 2010). The extended family, reaching back to clan ties, is known to adapt various aspects of their lifestyle, when necessary, to help the family in crisis. This concept of multiple familial ties is important from both an adaptive and an evolutionary perspective. First, Hedonic capital, or the capacity for well-being and happiness, is increased by having multiple adults and other "family" members available to call upon throughout one's life. This large network is a wonderful gift that promotes adaptive behavior and good health:

> People with large social support networks and stronger social bonds with members of their networks have better physical and mental health, fewer illnesses and less depression, recover more rapidly from physical illness and psychological problems, and have a lower risk of death (Carr, as cited by Graham & Oswald, 2010, p. 378).

Yang (2005) reported that Korean families dealing with members in ICUs (intensive care units) expected extended family members to join "the ICU family" by visiting the patient, offering support to the primary caregivers, and engaging in practical help-giving activities. Based on research findings, Yang postulated that Korean familism plays a central role in family resilience. Even in South Korea, where the nuclear family structure is increasing every year, extended family networks are considered very important not only for interactions but for the sharing of resources (Lee et al., 2004).

The second benefit of a large extended family from an evolutionary vantage point is what biologists call kin selection. Hamilton (1964) is given credit for discovering that human genes have two paths to the next generation. The first is making the body that surrounds the gene more fit (i.e., the body is able to do something that is more adaptive). The second is indirect (i.e., the gene can be spread by benefiting other carriers of the same gene). In large extended familial networks, the probability of having genes that are the same as others is greatly increased.

Putting these concepts together, then, extended families both add happiness and provide an evolutionary edge for their members (Miller et al., 2003). Korean families, some of whom are able to trace their lineage back to the time of the Proto-Three Kingdoms (2338 BCE) and can count several hundred live family members, are well positioned to maximize the resilience benefits of extended family networks. It is the company of these others that encourages Koreans to grin and bear it during the hard times and to soar during the good times (Ahn, 2003; Lee, 1988).

Of course, just having large extended families is not enough to guarantee high levels of family resilience. The quality of communications and level of altruism among family members also determine the degree of happiness and evolutionary advantage. For example, Becvar and Becvar (2009) emphasize the significance of "clarity, open emotional expression, and the ability to solve problems collaboratively" (p. 107). In happy families, Becvar and Becvar explain, verbal and nonverbal communications are congruent, messages are acknowledged, and attention is direct. Discussion is neither chaotic nor characterized by the taking of rigid and inflexible positions. Family members are able to assert themselves, yet tend to agree more than disagree. Mind reading and intrusiveness are rare and disagreements are followed by friendly interactions. Echoing the findings of biologists, other family therapists, and evolutionary psychologists, Becvar and Becvar conclude that by practicing effective communication, family members model and thus encourage additional healthy processes.

Current Issues: What Does Korean Family Resilience Look Like

Lee et al. (2004) provided an illustrative case of Korean Family Resilience in their description of the "ideal" Korean family with a child who is chronically ill:

> [This family] had parents who had confidence in each other and communicated well. Whenever they made a decision, they always had a long and straightforward discussion about it. Previously, the sick child's father had rarely helped his wife with household chores, but this changed after the child became sick. When the child was in the hospital, the husband took care of him at the weekend so his wife could rest at home. The daughter moved to her grandmother, as her parents did not have time to care for her. She adapted to these new circumstances well. The parents had insufficient funds to care for the child, so their brothers and sisters gave them some money. The husband's coworkers raised a fund to finance the child's bone operation (p. 642).

This excerpt from the model case demonstrates how nuclear and extended family members flexibly changed roles, shared resources, and even altered living arrangements to accommodate to the needs of the child and the family. Using the full case study, Lee et al. (2004) compared and contrasted qualitative evidence derived from interviews with families living with children who have a chronic illness to classify 21 theoretically established characteristics of Korean Family Resilience. Their research identified four attributes that had not been accounted for in previous operationalized definitions of Korean Family Resilience, all of which can be considered when working with Korean families.

1. *Intrinsic family characteristics*, which include qualities such as coherence, faith, positive outlook, mature thinking, and family self-esteem.
2. *Family member orientation*, which includes flexibility in reorganizing the family, attachment among family members, open communication, mutual understanding, and maintaining a balance in the demands of family members.
3. *Responsiveness to stress*, which includes adaptability, desire to maintain normal states, patience for attainment of goals, ability to control stress, readiness to accept critical situations, and responsibility for causing trouble.
4. *External orientation*, which includes economic resources, proactiveness toward information, maintaining cooperation with health care professionals, the ability to maintain good social relationships and family member leadership.

These additional attributes can further inform the types of information culturally centered practitioners gather when working with Korean families to understand their reasons for seeking treatment, what they hope to gain, and the resources that can be made available during the therapeutic exchange and throughout the therapeutic process.

Clinical Implications

There are many normative and nonnormative events that interrupt a family's ideal trajectory. Unfortunately, we have little empirical research on Korean Family Resilience in particular and Korean family life in general. In this section, three major life events that have been reported in the literature are discussed to help illustrate clinical practices that may be considered when working with Korean families. The discussion of each life event includes current research that focuses on Korean reactions to these events.

Divorce

Divorce can be a very traumatic event for all members of the family in any culture. In South Korea, divorce was looked down upon for centuries. In fact, only recently have women gained the right to file for divorce. Since this right has been established, the rate of divorce has risen dramatically, especially in the last few decades. Based on 2003 South Korean census data, the divorce rate was nine times higher than it was in 1970 (Chung & Emery, 2010). It is estimated that one-quarter of South Korean women over the age of 20 will experience divorce by the time they are 59 years old (Han et al., 2000 as cited in Chung & Emery, 2010). Researchers have found that because of strong traditional cultural norms, divorced families are reluctant to openly discuss their family matters with others within and beyond the family, making it difficult to render a complete picture of just how divorce affects Korean family members (Shin, Choi, Kim, & Kim, 2010). This places Korean families in double jeopardy. Not only are members uncomfortable seeking solace and relational identity from nuclear and extended families, but their sense of cohesion—which Lee et al. (2004, 2006) identified as very important—is now disrupted. Here you can envision *Han* playing itself out in that the members of a divorced family may feel isolated and stressed. The culture-centered professional will consider ways to balance the cultural influence of *Han* and the need for members to reestablish a sense of self in relation to others to guide individuals and families to access currently under-utilized resources to promote resilience.

In South Korea, over 70% of divorces involve children, yet certain qualities of Korean culture (i.e., the family tradition of father custody, the removed role of the noncustodial parent, the pressure to remarry, the public humiliation associated with divorce) offer unique tests and perspectives on the consequences of divorce. Thus far, most research in the area of consequences of divorce for South Koreans has focused on individual reactions.

One window into the effects of divorce on Korean families is to examine the impact of such an event on children. The general research on children living in Western Cultures, particularly English-speaking countries, demonstrates that children manifest similar arrays of psychosocial needs (Chung & Emery, 2010; Kim et al., 2005; Shin et al., 2010). Studies of Korean children's reaction to the impact divorce had on their families suggest that:

> Compared to their counterparts from married families, South Korean children whose parents divorced: (1) reported increased internalizing and lower self-esteem on the average, but at the same time (2) the majority did not report severe maladjustment (they apparently were resilient), and yet (3) many otherwise resilient children reported painful feelings owing to their parents' divorce (Chung & Emery, 2010, p. 865).

The authors further explain that, "In comparison to children from married families, young people from divorced families also reported more troubled relationships with their biological and residential parents including both mothers and fathers" (Chung & Emery, 2010, p. 864), all aspects of relational life associated with *Han*.

The impact of divorce deeply affects all members of the immediate family, and in Korea, the extended family as well. Clinicians cannot take lightly, as they might for a couple from a country like America, the fact that divorce has deep-seated cultural messages that may or may not significantly impact Korean family resilience. Without probing this area, a clinician could mistakenly under diagnose the significance of a divorce somewhere in the family tree.

The Chung and Emery study (2010), as descriptive as it is, uses input from only South Korean adolescents and applies an individualistic perspective to explore the dimensions of the parent–child relationship. Recent work is contributing to a broader, more relational perspective. For example, Shin et al. (2010) apply a systemic framework to this line of research by translating McCubbin's Family Resiliency Model of Family Stress (McCubbin & McCubbin, 1988; McCubbin & Patterson, 1981) to Korean families. This was one of the first South Korean teams to examine the relationship between the impact of divorce on adolescent adjustment and family resilience. Using the five concepts of McCubbin's Model (i.e., family hardiness, problem-solving/coping skills, family communication, social support, family belief) with an individual measure of self-esteem, Shin et al. examined how well adolescents adjusted to divorce when living in different custodial arrangements. In their study, approximately 40% of the adolescents were living with their fathers, 41% with their mothers, and 19% were living with grandparents. Their findings revealed that for Korean youth significant relationships existed between positive adolescent adjustment and high levels of family hardiness ($p=0.001$), open family communication ($p=0.001$), and positive belief about divorce ($p=0.001$). Interestingly, contrary to existing findings (Sim, 2004; Yeh, Lee, Chen, & Li, 2000), they found that for this sample, problem-solving/coping by seeking help had a negative association with adjustment. The strongest predictor of Korean adolescent adjustment was the perception of divorce the family created before the divorce. That is, families who generally thought of divorce as a viable life option and believed that family members would succeed wherever they were living were less likely to experience adjustment problems. Most importantly, adolescents who blamed themselves for their family's problems or experienced the fear of being blamed were at increased risk for experiencing physical and psychological distress, manifested in symptoms of depression, anxiety, hostility, and developmental delays (Shin et al., 2010).

While this research indicated no differences in adolescent adjustment based on custodial arrangement, differences in family resilience factors were noted. Family units that included the child and the mother reported the highest scores in family hardiness and family communication and were more likely to perceive their family as successfully managing life stressors. On the other hand, families comprised of the child and the father or the child and the grandparents were less inclined to view their situation as warm and comforting or to view their family as effectively handling stressor events. The work by Shin and associates again reinforces the significance of divorce in Korean culture. When working with families of Korean heritage the full ramifications of divorce from personal, spiritual, familial, economic, and community (clan) perspectives must be explored in order to ascertain its impact on their sense of self. Divorce can have profound effects by depressing the capacity of the family to generate levels of protective factors at various points in time before, during, and after the legal proceedings.

Alcohol Abuse and Domestic Violence

A recent report finds that almost 22% of the adult Korean male population misuse or are dependent on alcohol (Korean Alcohol Research Foundation, 2005). Other estimates place the number of Korean children living with parents (and grandparents) who may be suffering from alcoholism at 37%, a full 22% higher than children of American parents. These high rates are attributed to many societal factors, such as the acceptability for men to drink heavily in social situations, the perception of alcohol as food (e.g., mak kol li is fermented rice wine), the rapid transition in the family model from stem to nuclear, the rapid pace of industrialization and modernization, the frequent opportunities to drink socially, and the accepting attitude of the public toward drunkenness (Lee & Cranford, 2008).

Given the high rate of alcohol use, clinicians must again probe deeply in this area. As the behavior is not viewed as discrepant from others' behavior with alcohol, Koreans may not appreciate or accept signs indicating that drinking is having deleterious effects on other family members, including the imposition of psychological and physical harm. Specific to Korean families, Lee and Cranford (2008) found that those characterized by stability, cohesion, organization, and preservation of routine and rituals were most conducive to promoting resilience among their members. Clinicians need to differentiate between the appropriate and inappropriate use of alcohol—from cultural and contextual lenses—in order to best work with Korean families to increase their sense of resilience. Therapeutic strategies associated with the research and practice with children, spouses, and siblings of alcoholics are appropriate to consider when working with Korean families in this area.

In terms of domestic violence, Confucianism socializes women to be dependent on their father before marriage, on their husband after the marriage, and on the son after the death of the husband. This is called "sam-jong-ji-do," which means a woman has three masters to obey in her life (Kim, 2005). Traditionally in Korean culture, in cases of domestic violence, battered women tend to hold their feelings instead of asking for help from the outside or discussing their experience and sharing their perspectives and feelings with nuclear or extended family members. A syndrome called "Hwa-byung" (Choi & Yeom, 2011) may develop that includes insomnia, fatigue, panic, fear of impending death, indigestion, anorexia, palpitations, and generalized aches and pains. The main reason cited for not seeking help, including counseling, by Korean women is the need to save face (Chae-myum). Again, the clinician working with Korean family members must probe for evidence of domestic abuse, especially when alcohol or other drugs are involved.

Physical and Emotional Distress and Disorder

The onset of an illness, either physical or emotional, for any family member is perceived or approached as a serious event that impacts not only the immediate and extended family, but also the wider community. Looking at how Korean families reacted to having a family member on an ICU, Yang (2005) found that the need for assurance from health care professionals was the most important. The families expressed a desperate need to grasp a thread of hope while trusting the expressed judgments and actions of the health care professionals working to care for their ill member. However, qualitative findings indicated that these families did not always feel they were provided accurate information about the condition of their ill member, as evidenced by comments such as "Doctors do not give us any clear answer. They keep saying, 'let's just wait and see'. They use medical language. What do we know about those difficult words" (p. 83).

The second strongest need expressed by Korean families was for information. Although family members hoped to obtain sufficient and realistic information from doctors and nurses, they did not find it forthcoming. The healthcare personnel appeared too busy to share the condition of their family member with them: "Although I have a question, the doctor in charge is not around…. The ICU nurses don't give me clear answers…. I feel so anxious because they do not explain in detail" (Yang, 2005, p. 84).

Next, the need to be physically close to their ill family member was very strong. Many participants missed work, school, and family duties to spend most of their time in the ICU family waiting room in order to see the patient every visiting opportunity. Family members reported that "we are eager to be here (ICU waiting room). It is very uncomfortable but we want to be close to the patient" (Yang, 2005, p. 84).

The ICU families deferred their own personal needs such as comfort and support to be close to their ill loved one, and Korean caregivers expected that nuclear and extended family members would also assist them. When appropriate support was extended it was greatly valued, as reflected in this excerpt from an interview: "My brother-in-law was a stranger to me. Going through this hardship together, I feel he is one of my family members. It is quite a fresh feeling" (Yang, 2005, p. 84).

Clinicians working with Korean families can draw from these findings to consider questions relative to assurance, specifically as this relates to the quality of the therapeutic relationship. Being sure to provide sufficient relevant and useful information can invite families to be active partners when addressing the types of role redistributions that may be necessary in response to the illness and its treatment.

Han et al. (2007) examined the impact of a family member's involvement with the mental health system in Seoul, including the effect of involvement in outpatient services on family functioning and resilience. Their data indicated that the quality of family support was the strongest predictor of family functioning. Over 55% of the variance found among participants was attributed to family communication and cohesion. Unlike families dealing with a physical illness, where the need for information was second, those dealing with a member who had been diagnosed with a psychiatric disorder had less of a need for information about the disease, and more of a need for family support, family hardiness, and family coping. The difference in reactions to physical vs. emotional health issues reveals important information for clinical practice. That is, it is essential to recognize that the priority of needs may vary in these two situations and that the quantity and type of information Korean families may need is dependent on the life stressor with which they are dealing. Given the dynamic processes Korean families manifest during times of crisis, it is important for clinicians to be able to identify which resources are most salient at any given time during the therapeutic exchange and to access these when moving to restore successful functioning.

Summary

The particulars of how clients are influenced by their inner familial dynamics and the external social expectations perceived and experienced can significantly influence the course of treatment for any family dealing with a crisis. For Korean families, the particulars in terms of where the family is positioned in the broader transition from stem to nuclear family are important. Each generation may have a specific disposition toward maintaining or rejecting traditional Korean family values and toward incorporating values from other geographic locations within which they are situated. Each generation will have a specific understanding of Han and its influence on the family. Each generation will need different configurations of support to work through issues related to substance abuse, domestic psychological and/or physical violence, medical issues, emotional traumas, and family disruption. Resilient Korean families strive for cohesion, role flexibility, and clear and effective communication both within the family and with key individuals (or groups) in the external environment. Mental health professionals who know how to surface the strengths associated with the particular Korean worldview a client or client system may display in treatment will be able to accelerate the therapeutic process. Culturally grounded therapists can use the attributes of family resilience identified by Lee et al. (2004) to be certain to conduct ongoing assessments and treatment decisions that are congruent with whichever needs are salient at any point in treatment and with whichever resilience attributes can be accessed to address these needs at different points throughout the therapeutic process.

Research Considerations

There is a rich, yet narrow vein of theoretical and empirical research in the area of Korean family resilience. The work of Lee et al. (2004) has established a foundational base that researchers can draw upon to design studies that describe and verify the existence of specific configurations of support that benefit all Korean families. We agree with Holroyd (2005) that the conceptualization and theory-building process is still in its infancy, but the potential for specific empirical investigation has never been more palpable. The explicit and implicit assumptions undergirding Lee et al.'s model should also be validated, extended, or modified. Targeted research in the area of Korean family resilience will add great knowledge to our theories of Korean family adaptation and could ultimately inform policy and practice. Adopting generic models or models founded on US populations of family resilience is not enough. Korean culture permeates the lives of Koreans, and the more specific clinicians can be in the identification of salutary aspects of this culture the more effective and relevant their work will be. Excavating the full landscape of Korean family resilience that Lee et al. have thus far identified will greatly add to the knowledge base of practice and could influence policy makers when designing support programs for families of Korean descent.

Simultaneous to this deep investigation of Korean family resilience theory, a research agenda that articulates how Korean families react to a variety of maladies that can afflict human and systemic existence should be initiated. The three areas covered in this chapter only scratch the surface of situations requiring Korean families to adjust their familial identifications and adopt new roles and interactions in order to survive and thrive. The many dilemmas that besiege families should be explored using Korean samples and reported widely, so that clinicians working with Korean families in China, Japan, the US, Europe, and elsewhere—where significant Korean populations exist—can refine their interventions to maximize the cultural legacy the family brings to the therapeutic relationship.

More case study and ethnographic studies are needed to elaborate on the research to date. Eventually, large-scale studies of Korean families will need to be designed to validate the major concepts of the Korean family resilience model (Lee et al., 2004). The qualitative studies can inform quantitative researchers about what specifically to include in terms of instrument design such as idiomatic language, conceptual factors, and particular research questions. Once validity and reliability of factors supporting and extending the Korean Family Resilience model have been proven in clinical trials, then particular treatment methods can be promulgated that will account for the role of culture and family history.

Finally, the ways in which some families are adapting to provide high quality education to their children can be investigated. This is the "wild geese family" where parents sacrifice their partner relationships and separate family for their children's advanced education (Lee, 2010b). While this gives rise to a host of difficulties for the wild goose fathers in terms of isolation and loneliness, it also has provided some positive aspects where the fathers reported that the relationship between partners improved due to the space they had and the increased frequency of good quality communication (Kim & Chang, 2004; Lee & Koo, 2006). These wild geese families are creating their own coping strategies to maintain family intimacy despite geographic separation, which includes communications, reallocation of household work, and new reinterpretations of personal and familial sacrifice (Kang, 2009), factors described by Becvar and Becvar (2009) as important to family resilience. The creative and dynamic interactive nature of these "wild geese families" should be investigated so that members of the helping professions working with such families will be well informed about interventions that promote, rather than diminish, family resilience.

Conclusion

Resilience is believed to be one of the human natures; all human beings possess this quality and can rebound from the fall to sublime life through the ability to develop interdependence with other people and openness to experiences (Walsh, 1998). Korean families have shown this resilience throughout their history. Whenever there was an invasion from other countries, Korean families experienced various difficulties including deprivation of properties and death of self, family, or community members. However, they always have been able to build themselves back up and to gather their power to keep their own spirits in order to resist the ideologies of the invaders. This resilient history is a great teacher for understanding the current Korean culture. By examining Korean history, the potential of future resilience in the Korean family is demonstrated in these current yet ever-changing environments.

Furthermore, at the personal level, the power for Koreans to evidence resilience comes from understanding their own family history and finding the meanings of their existence within that context. As is illustrated through the story shared by the second author, the importance of family history is engrained in Korean society as an influence of Confucianism. Therefore, knowing where they come from and valuing the interconnectedness of extended family is considered a great resource and asset. By grasping their own family history and tradition, individuals can understand the paths their families have traveled up to the current moment, and can use this understanding to create their own family narratives that integrate the resilience and ingenuity of other family members. Korean families are re-writing and re-telling their own family life stories—stories that will become the source of resilience and inspiration as they encounter normative and nonnormative events throughout their life time for themselves and for their future generations.

References

Ahn, B. (2003). Dominant ideologies and thoughts that shaped Korean history. *Korea Journal, 43*(4), 5–9.

Barnett, G. (2006). In 1866 the Koreans successfully knocked out America's first attempt to invade the 'Hermit Kingdom'. *Military History, 23*(9), 19.

Beckwith, C. I. (2010). Could there be a Korean-Japanese linguistic relationship theory? Science, the data, and the alternatives. *International Journal of Asian Studies, 7*(2), 201–219.

Becvar, D. S., & Becvar, R. J. (2009). *Family therapy: A systemic integration* (7th ed.). Boston, MA: Allyn & Bacon.

Bergsten, C. F., & Choi, I. (Eds.). (2003). *The Korean Diaspora in the world economy. Special report 15; Washington.* D.C.: Institute for International Economics.

Chae, B. K. (2009). Religion in the era of globalization: The potential of Confucian Protestantism of Korea. *The Korean Journal of Hyo Studies Association, 9,* 1–29 [in Korean].

Chang, K.-S., & Song, M.-Y. (2010). The stranded individualizer under compressed modernity: South Korean women in individualization without individualism. *The British Journal of Sociology, 61*(3), 539–564.

Chang, S. H. (2004). Overseas migration of Koreans in the colonial period and the historicality of repatriation. *Korea Journal, 44*(4), 5–29.

Cho, E. (1998). Caught in Confucius shadow: The struggle for women's legal equality in South Korea. *Columbia Journal of Asian Law, 12*(2), 125–189.

Cho, M. (1994). Korea: The 1990 family law reform and the improvement of the status of women. *University of Louisville Journal of Family Law, 33*(2), 431–444.

Ch'oe, Y. (1980). An outline history of Korean historiography. *Korean Studies, 4*(1), 1–27.

Choi, M., & Yeom, H. (2011). Identifying and treating the culture-bound syndrome of Hwa-Byung among older Korean immigrant women: Recommendations for practitioners. *Journal of the American Academy of Nurse Practitioners, 23*(5), 226–232.

Choi, Y. (2006). The phenomenon of "geese-families": Material separation between geese-fathers and geese-mothers. *Family and Culture, 18*(2), 37–65 [in Korean].

Chung, Y. (2003). The Korean Formation of the Modern Self. *Paper presented at the annual meeting of the American Political Science Association, Philadelphia Marriott Hotel, Philadelphia, PA Online.* Retrieved, 26 May, 2009, from http://www.allacademic.com/meta/p63284_index.html.

Chung, W., & Das Gupta, M. (2007). *Why is son preference declining in South Korea? The role of development and public policy, and the implications for China and India.* Policy Research Working Paper #4373. The World Bank.

Chung, Y., & Emery, R. (2010). Early adolescents and divorce in South Korea: Risk, resilience and pain. *Journal of Comparative Family Studies, 41*(5), 855–870.

Country Report. (2010, May). The domestic economy. *North Korea*, p. 17–19.

Cowen, P. A., Cowen, C. P., & Schultz, M. S. (1996). Thinking about risk and resilience in families. In E. Hetherington & E. A. Belchman (Eds.), *Stress, coping, and resilience in children and families* (pp. 1–38). Hillsdale, NJ: Lawrence Erlbaum.

Deault, L. C. (2010). A systematic review of parenting in relation to the development of comorbidities and functional impairments in children with attention-deficit/hyperactivity disorder (ADHD). *Child Psychiatry and Human Development, 41*(2), 168–192.

Deuchler, M., & Jin-Sook, P. (1997). The Confucian transformation of Korea: A study of society and ideology (1992). *Asian Journal of Women's Studies, 3*(1), 199–203.

Froman, L. (2010). Positive psychology in the workplace. *Journal of Adult Development, 17*(2), 59–69.

Go, E. (1988). Transcending Han. In K.-S. Suh (Ed.), *Stores of Han.* Seoul, Korea: Borhee Press.

Graham, L., & Oswald, A. J. (2010). Hedonic capital, adaptation and resilience. *Journal of Economic Behavior and Organization, 76*(2), 372–384.

Grayson, J. H. (1997). The myth of Tan'gun: A dramatic structural analysis of a Korean foundation myth. *Korea Journal, 37*(1), 35–52.

Hamilton, W. D. (1964). The genetical evolution of social behavior I & II. *Journal of Theoretical Biology, 7*, 1–52.

Hammal, R. (2010). Destined to fail? *History Review,* (67), 28.

Han, K., Lee, P., Park, E., Park, Y., Kim, J., & Kang, H. (2007). Family functioning and mental illness—A Korean correlational study. *Asian Journal of Nursing, 10*(2), 129–136.

Han, S. H., Choi, M. J., & Lee, J. S. (2000). The trend in divorce rate in South Korea during 1985–1966: Based on vital statistics data. *Journal of the Korean Society of Health Statistics, 25*(1), 1–10.

Hart, D. (1999). Creating the national other: Opposing images of nationalism in South and North Korean education. *Korean Studies, 23*(1), 68–93.

Holroyd, E. (2005). Commentary on Lee, I., Lee, E. O., Hesook, S., Young, S. P., Soon, M. and Youn H. P. (2004) Concept development of family resilience: A study of Korean families with a chronically ill child. *Journal of Clinical Nursing, 13*, 636–645.

Ivey, A. E., & Rigazio-DiGilio, S. A. (2009). Developmental counseling and therapy: The basics of why it may be helpful and how to use it. *Turkish Psychological Counseling and Guidance Journal, 4*(32), 1–11.

Kang, Y. J. (2009). Transnational life of Korean "Wild Geese Family": Coping strategies and family paths across time. *The Korean Journal of Community Living Science, 20*(2), 205–221 [in Korean].

Kim, J. H. (2005). *The effects of East Asian values, coping styles, social support on physical health among Korean American caregivers.* ProQuest Dissertations and Theses. University of Southern California, AAT 3220116.

Kim, T. H., Lee, S. M., & Yu, K. (2005). Hope and the meaning of life as influences on Korean adolescents' resilience: Implications for counselors. *Asia Pacific Education Review, 6*(2), 143–152.

Kim, Y. (2001). The predicament of modern discourses on gender and religion in Korean society. *Korea Journal, 41*(1), 114–136.

Kim, Y. H., & Chang, O. J. (2004). Issues of families that run separate household for a long time—The so-called "Wild Geese Family". *Journal of Korean Family Studies Association, 9*(2), 1–23 [in Korean].

Korean Alcohol Research Foundation (KARF). (2005). *Drinking culture in Korea.* Retrieved April 7, 2006, from http://www.kodcar.or.kr/karf_alcohol/a_culture01_01.asp?menu=culture. http://www.kodcar.or.kr/karf_alcohol/a_prevention01_01.asp?menu=prevention.

Kwon, I. (2010). The evolution of ancient East Asian writing systems as observed through early Korean and Japanese wooden tablets. *Korea Journal, 50*(2), 124–157.

Lee, H. (1990). Differences in language use between North and South Korea. *International Journal of the Sociology of Language, 82*, 71–86.

Lee, H. (2010a). "I am a Kirogi Mother": Education exodus and life transformation among Korean transnational women. *Journal of Language, Identity, and Education, 9*, 250–264.

Lee, H. H., & Cranford, J. A. (2008). Does resilience moderate the associations between parental problem drinking and adolescents' internalizing and externalizing behaviors?: A study of Korean adolescents. *Drug and Alcohol Dependence, 96*(3), 213–221.

Lee, H. S., Brown, S. L., Mitchell, M. M., & Schiraldi, G. R. (2008). Correlates of resilience in the face of adversity for Korean women immigrating to the US. *Journal of Immigrant and Minority Health, 10*, 415–422.

Lee, I., Lee, E.-O., Kim, H. S., Park, Y. S., Song, M., & Park, Y. H. (2004). Concept development of family resilience: A study of Korean families with a chronically ill child. *Journal of Clinical Nursing, 13*(5), 636–645.

Lee, I., Lee, E. O., Kim, H. S., Park, Y. S., Song, M., & Park, Y. H. (2006). To Holroyd, E. (2005) Commentary on Lee et al. (2004). *Journal of Clinical Nursing, 15*, 649–656.

Lee, J. (1988). Features of Korean history. *The Social Studies, 79*(4), 147–152.

Lee, J. (2010b). Education and family in conflict. *Journal of Studies in International Education. Advance online publication*. doi:10.1177/1028315310385462.

Lee, Y., & Bronstein, L. R. (2010). When do Korean-American dementia caregivers find meaning in caregiving?: The role of culture and differences between spouse and child caregivers. *Journal of Ethnic and Cultural Diversity in Social Work, 19*(1), 73–86.

Lee, Y., & Koo, H. (2006). "Wild geese fathers" and a globalized family strategy for education in Korea. *International Review of Development and Planning, 28*(4), 533–553 [in Korean].

Leong, R. C. (2003). Amerasia journal at the frontiers of Korean American studies. *Amerasia Journal, 29*(3), v–ix.

Lundman, B., Aléx, L., Jonsén, E., Norberg, A., Nygren, B., Santamäki Fischer, R., et al. (2010). Inner strength—A theoretical analysis of salutogenic concepts. *International Journal of Nursing Studies, 47*(2), 251–260.

Masten, A. S., & Obradovic, J. (2008). Disaster preparation and recovery: Lessons from research on resilience in human development. *Ecology and Society, 13*(1), 1–16.

McCubbin, H. I., & McCubbin, M. A. (1988). Typologies of resilient families: Emerging roles of social class and ethnicity. *Family Relations, 37*, 247–254.

McCubbin, H. I., & Patterson, J. (1981). Broadening the scope of family strength, an emphasis on family coping and social support. In N. Stinnett, B. Chesser, & J. DeFrain (Eds.), *Family strengths III: Roots of well-being* (pp. 177–194). Lincoln, NE: University of Nebraska Press.

Miller, J. R., Lerner, R. M., Schiamberg, L. B., & Anderson, P. M. (2003). *The encyclopedia of human ecology.* Santa Barbara, CA: ABC-CLIO Inc.

Park, C. S. (2010). Japanese rule and colonial dual society in Korea. *Korea Journal, 50*(4), 69–98.

Park, H., & Lee, S. (2008). A survey of data sources for studies of family and population in Korean history. *The History of the Family, 13*(3), 258.

Park, I. H., & Cho, L. J. (1995). Confucianism and the Korean family. *Journal of Comparative Family Studies, 26*(1), 117–134.

Ringen, S., Kwon, H., Yi, I., Kim, T., & Lee, J. (2011). *The Korean state and social policy: How South Korea lifted itself from poverty and dictatorship to affluence and democracy.* New York: Oxford University Press.

Saveliev, I. (2010). Mobility decision-making and new diasporic spaces: Conceptualizing Korean diasporas in the post-soviet space. *Pacific Affairs, 83*(3), 481–504.

Shim, J.-S. (2004). The shaman and the epic theatre: The nature of Han in the Korean theatre. *New Theatre Quarterly, 20*(3), 216–224.

Shin, S. H., Choi, H., Kim, M. J., & Kim, Y. H. (2010). Comparing adolescents' adjustment and family resilience in divorced families depending on the types of primary caregiver. *Journal of Clinical Nursing, 19*, 1695–1706.

Sim, M. K. (2004). Influence of resilience factors on adaptation in families of children with cancer. *Korean Journal of Child Health Nursing, 10*, 383–394.

Sivananda, S. S. (2010). Confucianism. *Chinese American Forum, 25*(4), 14–17.

Steptoe, A., Dockray, S., & Wardle, J. (2009). Positive affect and psychobiological processes relevant to health. *Journal of Personality, 77*(6), 1747–1776.

Walsh, F. (1998). *Strengthening family resilience.* New York: Guilford Press.

Webster, S. K. (2001). *Pursuing Han: A psychological investigation of Korean college student perceptions.* Seoul, South Korea: Fulbright Forum, Korean American Education Commission.

Yang, S. (2005). A mixed methods study of the needs of Korean families in the intensive care unit. *Australian Journal of Advance Nursing, 25*(4), 79–86.

Yeh, C. H., Lee, T. T., Chen, M. I., & Li, W. (2000). Adaptation process of parents of pediatric oncology patients. *Pediatric Hematology and Oncology, 17*, 119–131.

Yoon, H.-T. (2005). China's northeast project and Korean history. *Korea Journal, 45*(1), 142–171.

Part IV

Resilience, Loss, and Grief

Family Resilience in the Wake of Loss: A Meaning-Oriented Contribution

An Hooghe and Robert A. Neimeyer

Mimi's daughter Tierney was diagnosed with Trisomy 18, a genetic disorder, just a few weeks after her birth. Statistically these babies rarely survive beyond a year. Along with her husband, Doug, and Tierney's 5- and 7-year-old brothers, Reilly and Keegan, Mimi was devastated.

Mimi was determined from the time of Tierney's diagnosis to make her child's life matter, to have significance for all whom she touched, in the short time they had her. She explained to Reilly and Keegan that "90% of babies with Tierney's condition die before their first birthday," an expression that conveyed to their young minds that she would die before her birthday party—something they could not imagine. They therefore urged their mother to celebrate her birthday early, and the family began doing so each month, allowing the children generous input in suggesting how best to celebrate, decorating cakes, making goody bags, renting a bouncy castle for family friends to enjoy together. As the months added up, they began hopefully to plan the celebration of her living a full year, mindful of the fact that 90% of Trisomy families were denied that opportunity. With appreciation and empathy, the whole family and others in attendance wrote "letters to heaven" that they sent skyward on helium balloons to mark the occasion.

From a point shortly after Tierney's diagnosis, Mimi began to plan her daughter's funeral. Together with her sisters she selected appropriate music and songs, laughingly imagining having a concert rather than a conventional service. Working with a Catholic book on funeral planning, she encountered the idea of a pall, the covering over the casket, which would otherwise be as small and unadorned as a Rubber Maid box. Together with her family, she conceived the idea of making a quilt for the occasion, with Reilly and Keegan joyfully contributing drawings on fabric of all of

A. Hooghe
Context, Center for Marital and Family Therapy, University Hospital Leuven, Leuven, Belgium
e-mail: an.hooghe@uz.kuleuven.ac.be

R.A. Neimeyer (✉)
Department of Psychology, University of Memphis, Memphis, TN, USA
e-mail: neimeyer@mac.com

D.S. Becvar (ed.), *Handbook of Family Resilience*,
DOI 10.1007/978-1-4614-3917-2_16, © Springer Science+Business Media New York 2013

(continued)

the important events of the short life of their tiny sister, who they imagined as having the "super powers" appropriate to the angel she would soon become: "Power Baby" fighting monsters, "Spider Baby" climbing tall buildings with her special web, baby Tierney crying. Now, 4 years after her daughter's death, Mimi still cherishes and displays the quilt, imagining that she will be sewing it bit by bit for the rest of her life. As she says, "We were determined that it would be a beautiful thing that would cover the tragedy of losing her. My whole focus has been to see her as a beautiful thing, not a tragedy."[1]

As this case vignette illustrates, bereaved families often surprise us with their creative ways of dealing with a devastating loss. In relationship with one another and the broader community, family members can accommodate even the most dreadful experiences, endowing them with meaning while at the same time strengthening their collective resilience.

Introduction

For most people, the loss of a loved one through death is both painful and challenging. Losing someone with whom we have a relationship based on love sets in motion a series of bodily, emotional, cognitive, behavioral, and relational effects that ripple through our world in the days, weeks, months—and for many—years that follow, with subtler effects for some that can be observed for a lifetime. *Grief*, as we use the term, is the label given to the multitude of biopsychosocial experiences that arise in the aftermath of the loss, which can be distinguished from *bereavement*, the relatively "objective" fact of having lost a significant person, and *mourning*, the culturally shaped practices by which such loss is expressed and processed (Stroebe, Stroebe, Hansson, & Schut, 2001). People obviously grieve in their own ways, within their own world of meanings and relationships. Different contexts, different family systems, and different cultures give rise to richly varied ways of dealing with loss and ongoing life. At the same time, these diverse contexts impose their own assessment and valuation of ways of grieving (Paletti, 2008), in a sense "policing" grief to ensure that it stays within culturally acceptable bounds (Walter, 1999). While, for example, in some cultures withdrawal and muted depression is considered an acceptable response to the death of a loved one, these behaviors may be construed as pathognomic of complicated grief in another (Rosenblatt, 2011). Similarly, while an intense expression of grief emotions or an overt continuation of the bond with the deceased (even to the point of sensory experiences of that person's presence) is tolerable for some families or couples, such behavior can be viewed with suspicion in others. Generally, a contemporary Western conceptualization of grief emphasizes confronting the loss and subsequently moving on with life in a functional way without prolonged and disturbing "symptoms" (Harris, 2009).

Our goal in this chapter is to explore what is meant by *resilience* in the context of loss and grief, drawing on the predominantly Western literature to characterize this salutary response to loss and to consider its expression at both more individualistic and more systemic levels. Weaving clinical vignettes through our review, we conclude with several implications for therapists striving to respect and promote resilience within families, as well for researchers attempting to shed more light on adaptive processes when a member of a family or other small social system dies.

[1] Mimi's story and those of other parents who have lost children are featured in our colleague Todd Hochberg's video documentary, *Other Rituals: Parents' Stories of Meaning Making*, available at www.toddhochberg.com.

Significance of the Topic

The concept of family resilience relative to loss has been explored in both the grief and the family therapy literatures, but with remarkably little cross-referencing of key concepts and findings. We hope to bridge these two fields by summarizing what emerges from a review of each, and making a modest contribution to their integration.

The concept of resilience in grief literature[2] is relatively new and predominantly refers to an individual outcome without severe mental health or life adjustment problems after the loss of a loved one. For the majority of the twentieth century, the bereavement literature has concentrated primarily on grief symptomatology, from Freud's (1917/1957) early writing on "mourning and melancholia" onward. In this view, pathological grief became a clinical concern under one of two conditions: when survivors failed to "withdraw emotional energy from the one who died in order to invest it elsewhere," in theory continuing a form of "bondage" to the deceased, and alternatively, when the bereaved showed little by way of a grief reaction, giving rise to the suspicion that they were suffering from "denied" or "delayed" grief. A lack of empirical evidence to support this latter view ultimately led to the hypothesis that the absence of grief might not be an indication of pathology, but rather a sign of resilience (Bonanno, 2002). Hence, scholars in the field began to wonder why some bereaved were seemingly able to assimilate a significant loss into ongoing healthy functioning, while others experienced severely disabling conditions after the loss of a partner, a child, or a parent. Subsequently, factors predicting positive outcomes were explored empirically, and bereavement interventions were developed based on the promotion of resilience for the bereaved individual (Brown, Sandler, Tein, Liu, & Haine, 2007; Sandler, Wolchik, & Ayers, 2008) or family (Kissane, Lichtenthal, & Zaider, 2007).

From a family therapy perspective,[3] the theme of grief and bereavement is mainly approached from a family resilience viewpoint (Becvar, 2001; Boss, 2006; Greeff & Human, 2004; Shapiro, 1996; Walsh, 2006; Walsh & McGoldrick, 2004). In this literature, the concept of family resilience is situated in ecological and developmental contexts, considering how relational resilience processes vary with unfolding challenges and evolving family structures across the life cycle. In recent years, there also has been growing attention to the strengthening of a community in the aftermath of major disaster, such as the terrorist attacks in New York on 9/11/01 and Hurricane Katrina in 2005 (Bava, Coffey, Weingarten, & Becker, 2010; Landau, 2007; Landau, Mittal, & Wieling, 2008; Saul & Bava, 2009; Walsh, 2007).[4]

Literature Review

Resilience and Family Resilience in Grief Literature

Traditionally, grief literature and research have concentrated on those bereaved individuals struggling with ongoing life after the loss of a loved one. For much of the twentieth century, this resulted in a nearly exclusive focus on grief symptomatology and the refinement of the distinguishing features of what is now termed "complicated grief" (Shear, Simon, et al., 2011) or "prolonged grief disorder" (Prigerson et al., 2009). Until recently, clinical theorists have warned of both overreactions and underreactions to loss, thereby pathologizing all deviations from what is considered to be a "normal" grief

---

[2] We searched the two main journals in the field of grief (*Death Studies* and *Omega: Journal of Death and Dying*) from 2000 to 2010 for themes of resilience, supplementing this strategy with our knowledge of the broader literature, both classic and recent.

[3] We searched three main journals in the field of family therapy (*Family Process, Journal of Marital and Family Therapy,* and *Journal of Family Therapy*) from 2000 to 2010, for themes of resilience in relation to loss and grief.

[4] For more on this topic, please see Chap. 26.

trajectory (Boss, 2006). From this perspective it is believed that individuals who grieve normally should acknowledge the loss of a significant relationship and intensively work through the painful feelings inherent in doing so (the *grief work* hypothesis, Freud, 1917/1957). The absence of such an intense and painful grieving process has long been considered indicative of psychopathology (e.g., Bowlby, 1980; Rando, 1993; Worden, 1991), and thus the need for grief therapy.

The last decade, however, has witnessed a multitude of studies and meta-analyses questioning the assumptions of the grief work hypothesis (Bonanno & Kaltman, 2001), as well as the effectiveness of grief therapy for most bereaved people (Currier, Holland, & Neimeyer, 2007; Currier, Neimeyer, & Berman, 2008; Neimeyer & Currier, 2009). These comprehensive reviews of controlled studies have demonstrated that most bereaved persons, including children and the elderly, adapt to loss without debilitating symptomatology and without the need for specialized professional help to work through the grief. Similarly, Bonanno (2002, 2004) challenged the assumption that the absence of distress is a form of denial or grief inhibition, but instead might be indicative of resilience in the bereaved. He defines resilience as the capacity "to maintain relatively stable, healthy levels of psychological and physical functioning" following a highly stressful life event. Moreover, he contends that resilience is distinct from recovery, "as recovering individuals often experience subthreshold symptom levels, while resilient individuals, by contrast, may experience transient perturbations in normal functioning but generally exhibit a stable trajectory of healthy functioning across time" (Bonanno, 2004, p. 20). Ample research now demonstrates that the majority of bereaved people experience little to no major disruption in their psychological well-being and functioning (Bonanno, Moskowitz, Papa, & Folman, 2005; Bonanno, Wortman, & Nesse, 2004). With regard to this finding, the Changing Lives of Older Couples (CLOC) study (Bonanno et al., 2004), a large prospective study of spousal loss, distinguished five grief trajectories after the loss of a spouse: common (or adaptive) grief, chronic grief, chronic depression, depressed improved, and a resilient pattern.

Interestingly, the resilient trajectory proved most frequent (45.6%), characterized by low levels of depression at prebereavement as well as post (from 6 months to 4 years post loss), and low levels of other grief symptoms (e.g., yearning). Rather than representing a dysfunctional form of detachment, denial, or delay in the grieving process, a relatively stable low distress trajectory represented an adaptive pattern of coping with loss. Closely inspecting the prospective and longitudinal data from the CLOC study, Coleman and Neimeyer (2010) found that the resilient individuals appeared to be less likely to be thrown into a search for meaning relative to the death of the spouse. From a narrative perspective one could say that these individuals were able to integrate the loss into their existing self-narrative in a way that did not profoundly challenge the plot structure or thematic underpinnings of their previously viable life story (Neimeyer, 2006).

Besides the belief in a just world and an acceptance of death, other factors promoting resilience are often cited in the grief literature, such as the personality traits of hardiness (Bonanno, 2004; Mathews & Servaty-Seib, 2007) or dispositional resilience (Rossi, Bisconti, & Bergeman, 2007). This personal resource is characterized by "being committed to find a meaningful purpose in life, the belief that one can influence one's surroundings and the outcome of events, and the belief that one can learn and grow from both positive and negative life experiences" (Bonanno, 2004, p. 25). Moreover, factors such as self-enhancement (Bonanno, Papa, & O'Neill, 2002), repressive coping (Coifman, Bonanno, Ray, & Gross, 2007), social embeddedness, the flexible regulation of emotional expression (Mancini & Bonanno, 2006), and positive emotion and laughter (Bonanno, 2004) are considered important components of resilience in the aftermath of a significant loss. Finally, the experience of identity continuity is described as an important characteristic of the resilient individual (Bonanno et al., 2002). Whereas for some bereaved the loss of a loved one might feel as if a piece of themselves is missing, as if there were no thread of continuity between their lives before and after the loss, the resilient bereaved seem to have the capacity to maintain continuity in the self.

Beyond simply surviving or coping with a loss, it has been argued that many of the bereaved experience some kind of growth or positive transformation as part of the grieving process (Tedeschi & Calhoun, 2008). This posttraumatic growth following the struggle with grief refers to the emergence of new possibilities, an enhanced sense of personal strength, a greater appreciation of life, changes in relationships with others, and changes in existential and spiritual orientations. For example, in their study of bereaved parents, Lichtenthal, Currier, Neimeyer, and Keesee (2010) found that despite their grievous loss, fully 79% of the parents reported some form of benefit in the experience, the most common of which included a greater capacity to help others, increased compassion for human suffering, and a reduced tendency to take life for granted. Moreover, Coleman and Neimeyer (2010) reported that those widowed persons able to "make sense" of their loss at 6 and 18 months after the death reported high levels of well-being, pride, and satisfaction as much as 4 years following their bereavement. For Bonanno this might reflect resilient people's capacity for adaptive experiences and positive emotion (Bonanno et al., 2002), as opposed to merely limiting symptomatology. Just how such growth relates to resilience remains unclear, however, as Balk (2008) has questioned how transformation can be possible for the resilient person whose assumptive world has not been challenged, such that new understandings were not demanded and daily functioning returned quickly to baseline.

A rare extension of the largely intrapersonal approach to resilience in grief literature is the contextual resilience framework of Sandler et al. (2008), who emphasize the central role of person–environment transactions in the process of adaptation. From this perspective, reorganization of both individual and social environmental systems is needed to enable positive satisfaction of basic needs and developmentally competent role performance for the parentally bereaved child. Researchers using this model have found individual level protective resources such as coping efficacy, appraisal of threat, self-esteem, and control beliefs, in addition to family level variables such as caregiver warmth and discipline, and caregiver mental health (Haine, Ayers, Sandler, Wolchik, & Weyer, 2003; Haine, Wolchik, Sandler, Millsap, & Ayers, 2006; Lin, Sandler, Ayers, Wolchik, & Luecken, 2004).

Although in this model the risk and protective factors occur at the individual, family, community, and cultural levels, the outcomes on which these authors focus are still individual (e.g., mental and physical health problems, substance abuse, grief, life satisfaction, and growth for the bereaved child). Similarly, a study by Traylor, Hayslip, Kraminski, and York (2003) shows that family characteristics such as communication and cohesion shortly after the death of a family member are central in the grief process of its members, with individual outcomes being marked by subsequent reductions in grief when families are communicative and connected. Occasional writings in the grief literature consider resilience at the level of family relationships and culture (Kissane & Bloch, 2003; Nadeau, 1998, 2007; Shapiro, 2001, 2008). Shapiro (2008), for example, challenges the exclusive focus on reduced distress as the outcome of interest in bereavement studies. She suggests expanding attention to the outcomes of interest to include the bereaved themselves, which might be distinct for different bereaved family members. More than the level of functioning or the growth experienced by the individual, outcomes like marital satisfaction, sibling connection, family communication, mutual support, or shared meaning-making could be put forward as important outcomes of interest in their own right. For example, in her work on family meaning-making, Nadeau (2007) describes the importance for family grief and bereavement outcomes of the co-construction of meanings in a family around and after the death of a family member. As she concludes from her grounded theory study, "a family's ability to engage in meaning-making and the nature of the meanings that families co-construct are powerful determinants of how they will grieve and how well they will adapt to their loss" (Nadeau, p 13). Similarly, Kissane and Bloch (2003) underscore the importance of family communication, family cohesion, and conflict resolution for bereavement outcomes. In their family grief model, they formulate a typology of families based on their relational functioning. Two types of families are considered resilient in regard to coping with the impending loss of a family member: *supportive families*, characterized as highly cohesive, communicative, and free of conflict, and *conflict resolving families*, who experience transient conflict but are able to communicate and negotiate it together. Randomized controlled research suggests that neither of these families requires (or benefits from) professional intervention. In contrast, *sullen families* marked by poor communication, muted anger, and depression, and *intermediate families* characterized by mild reductions in communication and teamwork are quite responsive to professional therapy, using it to accommodate the loss of a family member with much less symptomatology. *Hostile families*, however, which are fractured by distance and conflict, are less responsive to family level interventions and instead are more likely to be helped in individual therapy (Kissane & Hooghe, 2011; Kissane, McKenzie, Bloch, Moskowitz, & O'Neill, 2006).

In summary, the concept of resilience in grief literature has grown against the background of the traditional assumption that mourning is best characterized in terms of grief symptomatology. As such, resilience is mostly defined as the relative absence of pathology in the years after the loss or even as the opposite of what is called complicated grief. Unfortunately, relational outcomes are only minimally considered. In recent years empirical research mainly has been focused on distinguishing features of the resilient individual or protective factors in the individual-context interaction that promote resilience for the bereaved. Although it is not prominent in the grief literature, a few studies have begun to point to contextual factors, such as family characteristics, that are important for the ability of the grieving individual to adjust to a new life following the loss.

Grief from a Family Resilience Perspective in Family Therapy Literature

For many years, the theme of death attracted only minimal attention in the family therapy literature (Walsh & McGoldrick, 2004). However, since its inception, a family perspective on grief has contrasted with a pathology-based, individual centered approach in adopting an explicit emphasis on resilient systems. Most authors in this field assume that all families have the intrinsic potential to deal with loss in a resilient way, and hence work towards maintaining or strengthening this process (Bava et al., 2010; Becvar, 2001; Boss, 2006; Greeff & Human, 2004; Kissane & Bloch, 2003; Landau, 2007; Landau et al., 2008; Saul & Bava, 2009; Shapiro, 1996; Walsh, 2007; Walsh & McGoldrick, 2004). Most prominent and influential is the work of Froma Walsh, who described a family and community resilience-oriented approach to recovery (2003; 2007). In this model she integrates her systemic approach to loss (Walsh & McGoldrick, 2004) with her framework for family resilience (Walsh, 2003). When families are challenged by the death of a family member, all family members are affected and the family as a whole is transformed. The loss alters the family structure and changes family organization and patterns of interaction. All members need to look for a new story that fits coherently into the family's life experience and belief system. Four family tasks should be accomplished for the long-term adaptation of all family members and the family as a functional unit: (1) a shared acknowledgement of the reality of death, (2) a shared experience of loss and survivorship, (3) the reorganization of the family system, and (4) the reinvestment in other relationships and life pursuits (Walsh & McGoldrick, 2004). These tasks of family bereavement involve processes in three domains of family functioning: belief systems, organizational patterns, and communication/problem-solving processes (Walsh, 2007). Echoing themes in the more individualistic grief literature, Walsh contends that the loss of a loved one can shatter one's belief system and that of the family. Through interaction with one another as well as others outside the system, families reconstruct their reality, including their sense of the loss, their suffering, and ongoing life. Families need to make meaning of the loss experience and regain hope in future possibilities. For some bereaved families their spiritual or religious values and practices bring solace and purpose. In addition, the organization and interactional patterns of a family might be disrupted. Flexibility to adapt to the multitude of associated changes, as well as stability in ongoing daily life is needed. Moreover, for most bereaved the experience of connectedness with family members and other support resources is vital in times of grief. Finally, Walsh (2007) underscores the importance of open communication and problem-solving processes for family resilience in dealing with loss. This includes clear, consistent information, emotional sharing and support, and collaborative problem solving following the loss experience. This model of family resilience to loss was also used by Boss (2006) in her work on ambiguous loss. Building and supporting family resilience in the tormenting situation of "an unclear loss that defies closure" (p. xvii), she pays attention to the belief systems of couples and families (e.g., to rethink power and control), their organizational patterns (e.g., to build community), and communication processes (e.g., to encourage dialectical vs. absolute ways of communication) (Boss, pp. 59–67). As the family literature is by definition context sensitive, so too is its approach to grief and resilience, considering the specific contextual features in identifying what is important to a particular family in a particular culture, at a particular time. However, it is noteworthy that these sophisticated systemic models, unlike the more individualistic work in the grief and bereavement literature, are largely undocumented by empirical research.

Clinical Implications

Although clearly formulating different approaches to resilience in the aftermath of loss, the grief literature and the family therapy literature underscore similar key processes for the therapist directed toward the strengthening of (family) resilience. Here we make a modest contribution to the bridging of these disparate literatures by discussing three processes: (1) the reconstruction of meaning or family meaning-making, (2) open communication or emotional sharing, and (3) relational connectedness. We illustrate these key processes with stories of the bereaved, in and outside a therapy setting. Finally, we elaborate on the importance of trust in the inherent resilience of the bereaved individual, family, and community in guiding therapeutic decisions—including when *not* to intervene.

The Reconstruction of Meaning

A central process in grief resolution is the reconstruction of meaning, understood as a partly verbal, partly tacit process that unfolds in a social field (Neimeyer, 2001). Clinicians can facilitate this process by making room for the sharing of different meanings related to the dying process, the death, the person of the deceased, and the changed life of all family members. More specifically, it is important to help families create a safe space in which to explore and share meanings related to blame, shame, and guilt connected to the loss, as well as the equally important opportunities to affirm love, draw on unique and cultural meanings and rituals that conserve a sense of continuity during transition, and honor the significance of their loved one in their joint lives. In transactions around the dying and following the death, family members seek partially communal, partially idiosyncratic significance in the loss and its implications for the future. The contexts for this social (re)negotiation of meaning can be as varied as discussing the meaning of dreams about the deceased and trying to make sense of the circumstances that led to the death. Alternatively, family members may attribute spiritual or philosophic meanings to apparent coincidences, such as hearing the loved one's favorite song on the radio on the anniversary of the death (c.f., Nadeau, 1998). Although much of this family meaning-making arises spontaneously without prompting by the therapist, it can nonetheless be woven into the dialogue of family therapy to foster patterns of resilient adaptation. At other times, explicit invitations to in-session or between-session tasks and rituals can promote adaptation, especially when families are struggling with the meaning of the death and the rupture of attachment with the deceased it occasioned.

One such therapeutic strategy is the *life imprint*, which involves the tracing of the durable legacy of the deceased in the lives of the living (Neimeyer, 2010; Neimeyer, van Dyke, & Pennebaker, 2009). Whether viewed in psychodynamic terms of the introjection of aspects of significant others into ourselves, in postmodern terms of the radical blurring of self and social system, or in simple behavioral terms of modeling, most schools of therapy recognize that our sense of who we are carries the imprint of our important attachment relationships. These can, of course, be perceived at many levels, ranging from our distinctive vocabulary of gestures and expressions, through our ways of speaking, telling a story or relating to others, on through to our central life pursuits, purposes, and personalities. Inviting all family members to reflect individually on those imprints that their loved one conferred on them as a between-session assignment and then share these in the subsequent session can prove to be an emotionally powerful intervention, one that helps them recognize and consolidate the living legacy of the other, who in a very real sense now lives in and through them. Equally important, recognizing the often different imprint left by the deceased on various family members also acknowledges the complexity and distinctness of each family relationship, opening discussion of the question of why, when family members have had the same loss, they do not necessarily have the same grief (Gilbert, 1996). Of course, it is important to recognize that not all imprints are positive, as survivors could also trace their tendency toward self-criticism or distrust of others to a demanding or emotionally unavailable parent, for example. Still, acknowledging such imprints can play a role in healing, as the therapist assists each family member in deciding which legacies to cherish and extend, and which to seek to release and transcend. In fact, it is not uncommon that negative relationships actually empower positive commitments, as when an adult child of an abandoning parent passionately commits to "being there" for his or her own children. In both these indirect ways and in the more direct importation of admirable qualities of the loved one into the self, using the life imprint method in the family setting provides a "counter-narrative" to the dominant story of loss, emphasizing what is retained as a resource for living, rather than relinquished as a result of the death (Hedtke & Winslade, 2003).

Pursuing the use of the life imprint in a joint therapeutic session, Cristina and her adult daughter Nuria each took a few minutes to write about the impact of Jose, the recently deceased husband and father of the family, on their sense of who they were as individuals. In subsequent sharing prompted by the therapist in the same session, Nuria looked on intently as Cristina described movingly how she now carried the confidence her partner had always had in her, as when he supported her desire to study for an advanced degree despite her own insecurity about her ability to do so, and how his undying love for her, even after they had lost an earlier child to stillbirth, instilled hope in her and let her embrace the decision to "try again." Cristina was then affirmed as Nuria, the product of this second attempt at building a family, related how the memory of her father's playful engagement with her through her youth, and his dying expression of pride in her as she entered womanhood, now gave her conviction to live passionately and to pursue her own ambitions. Through a veil of tears, each woman then gazed into the eyes of the other and embraced, feeling Jose's presence as another set of arms wrapped around them both.

A second resource for collective meaning-making in the wake of loss is *ritual*, which can give impetus to the social reconstruction of meaning by providing symbolic and communal validation of the changed reality of the bereaved, as well as tangible expression to their ongoing sense of connection to the deceased. Such rituals can be as prescriptively precise as a Buddhist *sutra* or a Jewish *shiva*, or as improvisational as relating stories of the loved one around the Thanksgiving table or at a family reunion. Frequently, however, in the therapeutic arena the use of ritual follows the dictum that *such practices need to be sufficiently open to individual interpretation to make them meaningful, and sufficiently structured to make them feasible.* Therapists therefore can assist families by prompting them to discuss how they might symbolically honor the place of their loved one in their lives, or signal their collective transition, taking care to construct an appropriate form of participation of each in the ceremony or activity they develop. As Walsh and McGoldrick (2004) caution, children and the frail elderly are especially likely to be marginalized in the presence of loss in a misguided effort to protect them, so that taking care to include rather than exclude them is a particular therapeutic goal. Most importantly, therapists need to recognize and respect that the most effective rituals are those that are adapted or invented by the clients, rather than crafted by the clinician (Lewis & Hoy, 2011). This does not mean, however, that the therapist cannot play a role in fostering discussion of ritual opportunities, or in the case of disaster work, creating a "safe space" within which families can create and perform their own "acts of meaning" in relation to a collective loss (Kristensen & Franco, 2011).

Holly and Tom's baby Ceclia was born at home on Mother's Day, and then rushed to the hospital. Her under-developed lungs and kidneys could not sustain her, and she died 15 h later in the arms of her parents, grandparents, and Tom and Holly's brothers and sisters, all of whom had a chance to meet her before her short life ended.

A practical man, Tom humbly went about his work to memorialize her. Cecelia's 4-year-old sister Grace was a strong impetus for him to do so, as he wanted her to have a loving memory of the little sister she had had all too briefly. As an amateur carpenter, Tom recalled the lumber he had cut a year before from a special black walnut tree that he helped a neighbor remove, a tree that he and his family had planted over 30 years before, and that he had cherished memories of playing in as a child. With the assistance of his lifelong friend, Tony, Tom carefully constructed a casket for his newborn daughter, lined with silk and furnished with a tiny pillow that Holly made to symbolically comfort her small body. Not being a man of words, Tom found that his hours of working quietly on his own or with Tony to plane, construct, and varnish the miniature coffin gave him the time and space he needed to reflect, and to spend time out of doors in what was his preferred environment. Following the funeral service, he returned to his work on the casket, cutting it in half to accommodate the urn that his company made for him to hold and lay to rest his daughter's ashes following her cremation. The other half, he reasoned, could be fashioned into a keepsake box for her sister when she got a little older, decorated in a way that would be appropriate to its new function.

Holly completed the circle of remembrance by planting another black walnut exactly 1 year later in Cecelia's memory with the assistance of her daughter Grace. Both Tom and Holly hoped the tree was one that she would play in one day, just as Cecelia might have done if she had had a chance to do so. The tree, they imagined, would get bigger and stronger each year, just like their love for their family. And both hoped that through her participation in the tree planting as in the funeral, they were also cultivating memories that Grace would take to heart, along with stories she might share one day with others (see note 2).

Open Communication and Emotional Sharing

It is generally assumed that the expression of one's emotional reactions to the loss is an important component of adaptive grieving (Harvey, 2000). "Storying" our experiences is a way to create coherence and to reorder our sense of self and our worldview, both of which can be threatened by loss.

Moreover, sharing grief experiences with family members in an open and honest way can be a key resource in adapting to loss, one that can contribute to stronger bonds and relational intimacy within the family. Emotionally connecting with significant others in grief can co-construct a shared reality and mutual support, as well as reinforce a sense of security, togetherness, and understanding of each other. Therefore, many family therapists underscore the importance of working with whole family systems in therapy, creating the opportunity for family members to connect in their grief, and enabling them to become more resourceful in facing future challenges. For Walsh (2006), therapists should "try to help family members to find ways to talk about the unspeakable" (pp. 190) and should "press reluctant members to take part" (p. 193).

Notwithstanding the value of sharing grief with family members, we argue for considering the complexity of communication in the context of bereavement (Hooghe, Neimeyer, & Rober, 2011). We see communication as a process between people over time, and want to explore the meanings of both talking and silence in a *dialectical, dialogical,* and *dynamic* approach. While the bereaved sometimes feel the desire to share how they are feeling and to *dialogue* with others in this grief, at the same time they often feel restraint in doing so in order not to be a burden to others, to spare loved ones the pain, to manage their own emotions, or to respect the impossibility of expressing their devastation in words. This tension between openness and closedness is also experienced on a relational level, in the communication between people. From a dialogical perspective, the story unfolds in the moment and all participants in the dialogue contribute to its unfolding (Bakhtin, 1986). Sometimes a bereaved family member initiates talking about the deceased, the death, or the grief, while the others are hesitant or not receptive at the time. The therapist is also part of this dialogue, often encouraging family members to share their grief, while sometimes honoring the need to create some breathing space in a "grief-suffocating climate," permitting some distance from the intensive raw pain experienced in the session. Moreover, communication is a *dynamic* process, so that every act of speech or silence must be understood in its context of time and space. Who is present in the therapy room, and who is not? What was discussed previously, and what is anticipated next? In clinical practice, rather than approaching grief communication as a necessary condition for all bereaved, we (Hooghe, 2009; Hooghe, et al., 2011) propose to explore the contextual factors, ambivalences, and relational tensions—in a word, the *dialectical* factors that shape the interaction—at a specific moment in the grieving process of the individuals and relationships involved. We therefore try to create a safe space and opportunity to explore with family members the possibility of sharing their grief experiences with others, or, as Fredman (1997) calls it, "talking about talking," while simultaneously acknowledging the difficulties of sharing and the good reasons family members might have to *not* share their experiences (Rober, van Eesbeek, & Elliott, 2006).

Marc and Sonja lost their only son Rik, when he was 13 years old. Since his death, 2 years ago now, they feel like they need to endure life, simply trying to get through every day. In their experience the best way to go on is to spend their days together, each remembering their child on his or her own. They feel a growing distance with most people in their social network because these former friends don't seem to realize and accept how their son is still a part of their lives. The first time they reluctantly came to therapy it was obvious that they very much doubted its usefulness. In this first session and parts of those that followed, the therapist intensively explored the possible value of psychotherapy for them, and more specifically, how it would be to share their grief with each other and with the therapist. How could psychotherapy or talking about their son be helpful? One thing was certain: no amount of talking would bring their son back. So what could be the meanings of "helping?" Exploring this further, Marc noticed that he was actually afraid that therapy would make him feel better, seemingly creating a further distance from their deceased son. At the same time they felt very close to Rik in

(continued)

(continued)

these sessions, being offered the time and space to remember him, to talk about him out loud. However, they both felt hesitant to verbalize how deeply wounded they felt inside, sometimes to the point that they doubted the value of living. Both feared that making this explicit might hurt the other, and make it more real for themselves. Being there together, listening to each other's immense pain, also felt frightening at times. To see the tears in each other's eyes, recognizing the pain, and knowing that there was so little they could do, was something they could only bear at times. The exploration and verbalization of these fears and hesitations to share their grief were important in creating a safer place for the therapy process, in which they also explored how they could "dose" their exposure to shared grief.

In the context of grief, talking about the deceased can be a way of both remembering and a way of integrating this memory into everyday life. Riches and Dawson (1998, 2000) use the concept of "conversational remembering," and propose that grief is, at least in part, a process through which the bereaved review and reorder significant events in the life of the deceased, in conversation with others, so as to produce a memory with which they can live. Although not the purpose of this approach, it is our experience that the opportunity to explore and share the meanings of talking and keeping silent about one's grief often creates the needed space for the bereaved family members to talk with each other, and connect in their grief process (Hooghe, 2009). In addition, the necessity of the spoken word in order to connect with others in grief can be questioned and expanded to nonverbal ways in which emotions can be expressed and shared as the previous vignette about Tom and Holly suggests.

Relational Connectedness

People rarely grieve in a vacuum, but instead do so in a network of relationships, family structures, social networks, and culture. Although the value of social support for the bereaved is subject to debate in grief literature (Stroebe, Zech, Stroebe, & Abakoumkin, 2005), it is generally assumed that these interpersonal connections, and more specifically family hardiness and cohesion (Greeff & Human, 2004; Kissane & Bloch, 2003), are paramount in the grieving process. In therapeutic practice, we aim to reinforce supportive connections with family members, so that families become more resourceful in meeting future challenges. In this way the family is empowered in its capacity for self-repair and in fostering resilience in all its members (Walsh, 1996). Therefore, as therapists we want to identify significant connections in the lives of the bereaved, as lifelines in their recovery process (Walsh, 2007). Who makes up the "psychological family" of the bereaved (Boss, 2006)? What are the natural support resources needed for resilience? In our work with the bereaved we look for ways to help them optimize reliance on and reinforcement of human connection in its most natural context, the family (Kissane & Hooghe, 2011). In this fashion both existing and new support resources are identified and reinforced.

A bereaved mother, Mieke, came to therapy following the loss of her son, Pieter. For the first session her husband, Koen, and daughter, Veerle, were invited to come as well, but only her husband accepted the invitation. Veerle, Pieter's twin sister, was not yet ready to talk about her loss, as Mieke explained. Koen made it very clear from the beginning that he came along to please his wife but that he would only do so once. Exploring his reluctance, he explained how talking was not a good way for him to deal with his loss, as it was too painful.

(continued)

(continued)

In addition, he was recently diagnosed with a brain tumor and would spend much of his time the next few months in the hospital for chemotherapy. For Mieke it was important to hear that his reluctance had to do with its being too anguishing, rather than his being unaffected by the loss of their son.

In the following sessions we explored the possibility of inviting Mieke's sister, Greet, to accompany her. In the presence of her supportive sister, an atmosphere emerged in which to comfortably share stories related to the loss of Pieter, as well as their fears about Koen's pending death. With her sister, Mieke shared her loneliness, her fears, and even began to plan for Koen's funeral. The therapist discovered that the two sisters developed their own ritual while driving to therapy. While the actual journey took only 20 min, they allowed a full hour. Laughingly, they admitted that they had their "own secret spot, somewhere down the road" to talk together on the way. After each session, they regularly treated themselves to an ice cream as a reward for their hard and emotional work. In this way, they connected for more than 3 h during each evening they came to therapy.

One week after the seventh session, Mieke called the therapist to say that Koen had died. The last days of his life had been "horribly painful, but also very connected and loving." At the funeral, Mieke expressed appreciation not only for the therapy, but especially for the wonderful connection with her sister, who had been beside her, often silently, in the last days of Koen's life.[5]

Working with the irreversibility of death and the raw pain of clients who have lost someone whom they loved deeply, therapists often feel powerless to lighten this kind of deep suffering. As this case illustrates, family members can be a rich support for each other not only in the sessions, but also, and even more importantly, in their shared world of everyday living.

Trusting Resilience

In the context of our qualitative research study on the sharing and not sharing of grief within the partner relationship after the loss of a child (Hooghe et al., 2011), we encountered a great deal of resilience in the bereaved couples we interviewed. Unlike the couples we see in our psychotherapy practice, most of these bereaved parents did not chose to pursue psychotherapy. Although they all acknowledged the pain of grief, they also stressed the importance of finding their own unique ways of dealing with it in the context of their natural support systems. For example, Gunter, one of the bereaved fathers, explained how it would not be a good thing for him to talk about his grief too much or share his pain in a therapy context, "I don't feel inhibited to talk about it, so I don't feel like I'm suppressing it. But I'm not searching for it either." He added that even the interview could hold the risk of things surfacing, while he and his wife have been doing well in the considerable time since the loss:

At this point we have a good coping trajectory of many years, and I think we are doing okay together.... It could be that we are a little strange, but we can live with it for the rest of our lives, without having too much burden from it.

---

[5]A more extensive discussion of this case also appeared in Kissane and Hooghe (2011).

A subtext of the foregoing material, from the research review through the description of therapeutic procedures to clinical and nonclinical vignettes, is that many of the bereaved adapt stoically, practically, or creatively to the hard reality of their loss, and do so without the intervention of professional therapists. And this is hardly surprising, given that human beings are "wired for attachment in a world of impermanence" (Neimeyer & Noppe-Brandon, 2011), and thus have evolved in a way that they are able to adapt capably to life's many unwelcome transitions. This fundamental adaptability underlies our capacity for resilience, even in the face of profound loss, as we revise our basic roles and goals in light of the changed life we now have. In doing so, we draw on both individual and communal resources, in effect reaffirming or reconstructing a self- and family-narrative that has been challenged by bereavement.

As ample data illustrate, resilience among the bereaved is more the rule than the exception, with a solid majority of those persons who lose a loved one adapting to their changed lives without debilitating and prolonged symptomatology (Bonanno, 2004; Bonanno et al., 2004). As a corollary of this fundamental postulate, dozens of randomized controlled trials of grief therapy demonstrate that it makes little contribution to the adjustment of the bereaved when offered "universally" to all who have lost a loved one (Currier et al., 2008; Neimeyer & Currier, 2009). Somewhat more evidence supports the helpfulness of professional therapy provided "selectively" to those persons suffering high-risk bereavement, such as children losing a parent, parents losing a child, or those whose loved ones have died by violent means—suicide, homicide, or fatal accident. However, the strongest case for the efficacy of grief therapy can be made when it is extended to "indicated" cases of complicated, prolonged, and debilitating efforts to accommodate the death, in which case it yields clear and consistent contributions to client well-being (Currier et al., 2008; Neimeyer & Currier, 2009). As work proceeds to identify the shared features of these effective interventions (Shear, Boelen, & Neimeyer, 2011), there is reason to hope that professional therapy can help provide to those clients struggling with life-limiting loss the additional resources required to help them achieve the hopeful adaptation that their more resilient counterparts demonstrate without clinical assistance.

Research Implications

As recent handbooks and research reviews demonstrate, a great deal of clinical relevance has been learned about grief and its vicissitudes in the last decade (Center for the Advancement of Health, 2004; Neimeyer, Harris, Winokuer, & Thornton, 2011; Stroebe, Hansson, Schut, & Stroebe, 2008). However, much of this research focuses on the "pathology" of grief, with much less attention being paid to those processes by which individuals adapt constructively to loss. Moreover, as was evident in our own research review, the great majority of those studies that do shed light on resilience among the bereaved focus on individualistic factors in adaptation, rather than on the systemic factors that promote or sustain it. In its starkest expression this contributes to a literature marked by the "accumulative fragmentalism" of dozens of individual-focused studies in the bereavement literature on factors correlated with adaptation to loss, but in the absence of an over-arching theory, juxtaposed with grand and sweeping models of family resilience following loss, which are minimally grounded in research. Clearly any useful research agenda should seek to close this gap by positing and pursuing the study of processes of adaptation that span the self and system, and that investigate outcomes defined at relational as well as individual levels.

What might be some questions that could be addressed within this frame? Although the paucity of research done to date on systemic factors in bereavement leaves ample room for imaginative investigators, a few illustrations might be offered. For example, how might couples collaborate to support one another as well as surviving children in the aftermath of the death of a child? How does emotion regulation occur between people as well as within people as they contend with severe grief?

How do meaning-making processes, whose role in predicting positive outcome is amply documented at individual levels, play out in the crucible of family communication? And what distinctive risks and resources exist for culturally distinctive groups as they strive to accommodate often violent loss against a backdrop of a history of racism on the one hand, and a supportive spirituality on the other? Some intriguing hypotheses about each of these and many other topics are suggested by thoughtful qualitative research done to date (Buckle & Fleming, 2010; Hooghe et al., 2011; Nadeau, 1998; Rosenblatt & Wallace, 2005), but much more remains to be done to craft clinically grounded and empirically informed models to assist therapists working alongside families facing loss.

Conclusion

Both our work as clinicians and our efforts as researchers confront us with the hard reality of death in human life, and with the equally real phenomenon of human resilience in its wake. At profoundly personal as well as intricately interpersonal levels, the clients with whom we sit share stories of devastation, and more often than not, gradual reconstruction of a livable life by dint of their own efforts, the support of their families, communities and cultural resources, and—gratifyingly—our own well-intended efforts to help. We hope that this chapter provides encouragement to other clinicians who find themselves facing the existential challenges of bereavement with their clients, as well as to researchers who seek to shed more light on the factors that foster and sometimes frustrate their adaptation in the aftermath of loss.

References

Bakhtin, M. (1986). *Speech genres and other late essays*. Austin, TX: University of Texas.

Balk, D. E. (2008). A modest proposal about bereavement and recovery. *Death Studies, 32*, 84–93.

Bava, S., Coffey, E. P., Weingarten, K., & Becker, C. (2010). Lessons in collaboration, four years post-Katrina. *Family Process, 49*, 543–558.

Becvar, D. S. (2001). *In the presence of grief: Helping family members resolve death, dying, and bereavement issues*. New York: Guilford.

Bonanno, G. A. (2002). Resilience to loss and chronic grief, a prospective study from preloss to 18-months postloss. *Journal of Personality and Social Psychology, 83*, 1150–1164.

Bonanno, G. A. (2004). Loss, trauma, and human resilience: Have we underestimated the human capacity to thrive after extremely aversive events? *The American Psychologist, 59*, 20–28.

Bonanno, G. A., & Kaltman, S. (2001). The varieties of grief experiences. *Clinical Psychology Review, 21*, 705–734.

Bonanno, G. A., Moskowitz, J. T., Papa, A., & Folman, S. (2005). Resilience to loss in bereaved spouses, bereaved parents, and bereaved gay men. *Journal of Personality and Social Psychology, 88*, 827–843.

Bonanno, G. A., Papa, A., & O'Neill, K. (2002). Loss and human resilience. *Applied and Preventive Psychology, 10*, 193–206.

Bonanno, G. A., Wortman, C. B., & Nesse, R. M. (2004). Prospective patterns of resilience and maladjustment during widowhood. *Psychology and Aging, 19*, 260–271.

Boss, P. (2006). *Loss, trauma and resilience. Therapeutic work with ambiguous loss*. New York: Norton.

Bowlby, J. (1980). *Attachment and loss* (Loss: Sadness and depression, Vol. 3). London: Hogarth.

Brown, A. C., Sandler, I. N., Tein, J., Liu, X., & Haine, R. A. (2007). Implications of parental suicide and violent death for promotion of resilience of parentally-bereaved children. *Death Studies, 31*, 301–335.

Buckle, J., & Fleming, S. (2010). *Parenting after the death of a child*. New York: Routledge.

Center for the Advancement of Health. (2004). Report on bereavement and grief research. *Death Studies, 28*, 489–575.

Coifman, K. G., Bonanno, G. A., Ray, R. D., & Gross, J. J. (2007). Does repressive coping promote resilience? Affective-autonomic response discrepancy during bereavement. *Journal of Personality and Social Psychology, 92*, 745–758.

Coleman, R. A., & Neimeyer, R. A. (2010). Measuring meaning: Searching for and making sense of spousal loss in late-life. *Death Studies, 34*, 804–834.

Currier, J. M., Holland, J. M., & Neimeyer, R. A. (2007). The effectiveness of bereavement interventions with children: A meta-analytic review of controlled outcome research. *Journal of Clinical Child and Adolescent Psychology, 36,* 253–259.

Currier, J. M., Neimeyer, R. A., & Berman, J. S. (2008). The effectiveness of psychotherapeutic interventions for the bereaved: A comprehensive quantitative review. *Psychological Bulletin, 134,* 648–661.

Fredman, G. (1997). *Death talk: Conversations with children and families.* London: Karnac.

Freud, S. (1957). Mourning and melancholia. In J. Strachery (Ed., Trans.), *The standard edition of the complete psychological works of Sigmund Freud* (Vol. 14). London: Hogarth Press. (Original work published 1917)

Gilbert, K. R. (1996). "We've had the same loss, why don't we have the same grief?" Loss and differential grief in families. *Death Studies, 20,* 269–284.

Greeff, A. P., & Human, B. (2004). Resilience in families in which a parent has died. *American Journal of Family Therapy, 32*(1), 27–42.

Haine, R. A., Ayers, T. S., Sandler, I. N., Wolchik, S. A., & Weyer, J. L. (2003). Locus of control and self-esteem as stress-moderators or stress-mediators in parentally bereaved children. *Death Studies, 27,* 619–640.

Haine, R. A., Wolchik, S. A., Sandler, I. N., Millsap, R. E., & Ayers, T. S. (2006). Positive parenting as a protective resource for parentally bereaved children. *Death Studies, 30,* 1–28.

Harris, D. (2009). Oppression of the bereaved: A critical analysis of grief in western society. *Omega, 60*(3), 241–253.

Harvey, J. H. (2000). *Give sorrow words.* New York: Brunner Routledge.

Hedtke, L., & Winslade, J. (2003). *Remembering conversations.* Amityville, NY: Baywood.

Hooghe, A. (2009). Talking about talking, hesitations to talk and not talking. *Context Magazine, 101,* 33–35.

Hooghe, A., Neimeyer, R. A., & Rober, P. (2011). The complexity of couple communication in bereavement: An illustrative case study. *Death Studies, 35,* 905–924.

Kissane, D., & Bloch, S. (2003). *Family focused grief therapy.* Philadelphia: Open University Press.

Kissane, D., Lichtenthal, W., & Zaider, T. (2007). Family care before and after bereavement. *Omega, 56*(1), 21–32.

Kissane, D., McKenzie, M., Bloch, S., Moskowitz, D. P., & O'Neill, I. (2006). Family focused grief therapy: A randomized controlled trial in palliative care and bereavement. *The American Journal of Psychiatry, 163,* 1208–1218.

Kissane, D. W., & Hooghe, A. (2011). Family therapy for the bereaved. In R. A. Neimeyer, D. L. Harris, H. R. Winokuer, & G. F. Thornton (Eds.), *Grief and bereavement in contemporary society: Bridging research and practice.* New York: Routledge.

Kristensen, P., & Franco, M. H. (2011). Bereavement and disasters: Research and clinical intervention. In R. A. Neimeyer, D. Harris, H. Winokuer, & G. Thornton (Eds.), *Grief and bereavement in contemporary society: Bridging research and practice* (pp. 188–201). New York: Routledge.

Landau, J. (2007). Enhancing resilience: Families and communities as agents for change. *Family Process, 46*(3), 351–365.

Landau, J., Mittal, M., & Wieling, E. (2008). Linking human systems: Strengthening individuals, families, and communities in the wake of mass trauma. *Journal of Marital and Family Therapy, 34*(2), 193–209.

Lewis, L., & Hoy, W. (2011). Bereavement rituals and the creation of legacy. In R. A. Neimeyer, D. Harris, H. Winokuer, & G. Thornton (Eds.), *Grief and bereavement in contemporary society: Bridging research and practice* (pp. 315–323). New York: Routledge.

Lichtenthal, W. G., Currier, J. M., Neimeyer, R. A., & Keesee, N. J. (2010). Sense and significance: A mixed methods examination of meaning-making following the loss of one's child. *Journal of Clinical Psychology, 66,* 791–812.

Lin, K. K., Sandler, I. N., Ayers, T. A., Wolchik, S. A., & Luecken, L. J. (2004). Parentally-bereaved children and adolescents seeking mental health services: Family, child, and stress variables that predict resilience. *Journal of Clinical Child and Adolescent Psychology, 33,* 673–683.

Mancini, A. D., & Bonanno, G. A. (2006). Resilience in the face of potential trauma: Clinical practices and illustrations. *Journal of Clinical Psychology, 62*(8), 971–985.

Mathews, L. L., & Servaty-Seib, H. L. (2007). Hardiness and grief in a sample of bereaved college students. *Death Studies, 3,* 183–204.

Nadeau, J. W. (1998). *Families making sense of death.* Thousand Oaks, CA: Sage.

Nadeau, J. W. (2007). Meaning-making in bereaved families: Assessment, intervention and future research. In M. Stroebe, R. Hansson, H. Schut, & W. Stroebe (Eds.), *Handbook of bereavement research: 21st century perspectives* (pp. 511–530). Washington, DC: American Psychological Association.

Neimeyer, R. A. (Ed.). (2001). *Meaning reconstruction and experience of loss.* Washington, DC: American Psychological Association.

Neimeyer, R. A. (2006). Widowhood, grief and the quest for meaning: A narrative perspective on resilience. In D. Carr, R. M. Nesse, & C. B. Wortman (Eds.), *Spousal bereavement in late life* (pp. 227–252). New York: Springer.

Neimeyer, R. A. (2010). The life imprint. In H. Rosenthal (Ed.), *Favorite counseling and therapy techniques.* New York: Routledge.

Neimeyer, R. A., & Currier, J. M. (2009). Grief therapy: Evidence of efficacy and emerging directions. *Current Directions in Psychological Science, 18,* 252–256.

Neimeyer, R. A., Harris, D., Winokuer, H., & Thornton, G. (Eds.). (2011). *Grief and bereavement in contemporary society: Bridging research and practice*. New York: Routledge.

Neimeyer, R. A., & Noppe-Brandon, G. (2011). Attachment at a distance: Grief therapy in the virtual world. In C. Sofka, K. Gilbert, & I. Noppe (Eds.), *Thanatechnology: Death, dying and grieving in the online universe*. New York: Springer.

Neimeyer, R. A., van Dyke, J. G., & Pennebaker, J. W. (2009). Narrative medicine: Writing through bereavement. In H. Chochinov & W. Breitbart (Eds.), *Handbook of psychiatry in palliative medicine* (pp. 454–469). New York: Oxford.

Paletti, R. (2008). Recovery in context: Bereavement, culture, and the transformation of the therapeutic self. *Death Studies, 32*, 7–26.

Prigerson, H. G., Horowitz, M. J., Jacobs, S. C., Parkes, C. M., Aslan, M., Goodkin, K., et al. (2009). Prolonged grief disorder: Psychometric validation of criteria proposed for DSM-V and ICD-11. *PLoS Medicine, 6*(8), 1–12.

Rando, T. A. (1993). *Treatment of complicated mourning*. Champaign, IL: Research Press.

Riches, G., & Dawson, P. (1998). Lost children, living memories: The role of photographs in processes of grief and adjustment among bereaved parent. *Death Studies, 22*, 121–140.

Riches, G., & Dawson, P. (2000). Daughter's dilemmas: Grief resolution in girls whose widowed father remarry early. *Journal of Family Therapy, 22*, 360–374.

Rober, P., van Eesbeek, D., & Elliott, R. (2006). Talking about violence: A micro-analysis of narrative processes in a family therapy session. *Journal of Marital and Family Therapy, 32*, 313–328.

Rosenblatt, P., & Wallace, B. (2005). *African American grief*. New York: Routledge.

Rosenblatt, P. C. (2011). The concept of complicated grief: Lessons from other cultures. Unpublished Manuscript, University of Minnesota.

Rossi, N. E., Bisconti, T. L., & Bergeman, C. S. (2007). The role of dispositional resilience in regaining life satisfaction after the loss of a spouse. *Death Studies, 31*, 863–883.

Sandler, I. N., Wolchik, S. A., & Ayers, T. S. (2008). Resilience rather than recovery: A contextual framework on adaptation following bereavement. *Death Studies, 32*, 59–73.

Saul, J., & Bava, S. (2009). *Implementing collective approaches to massive trauma/loss in western contexts: Implications for recovery, peacebuilding and development*. Retrieved from http://www.incore.ulst.ac.uk/pdfs/IDRCsaul.pdf.

Shapiro, E. R. (1996). Grief in interpersonal perspective theories and their implications. In M. Stroebe, R. O. Hansson, W. Stroebe, & H. Schut (Eds.), *Handbook of bereavement research: Consequences, coping, and care* (pp. 63–88). Washington, DC: American Psychological Association.

Shapiro, E. R. (2001). Grief in interpersonal perspective. In M. S. Stroebe, R. O. Hansson, W. Stroebe, & H. Schut (Eds.), *Handbook of bereavement research* (pp. 301–328). Washington, DC: American Psychological Association.

Shapiro, E. R. (2008). Whose recovery, of what? Relationships and environments promoting grief and growth. *Death Studies, 32*, 40–58.

Shear, M. K., Boelen, P., & Neimeyer, R. A. (2011). Treatment of complicated grief: Converging approaches. In R. A. Neimeyer, D. Harris, H. Winokuer, & G. Thornton (Eds.), *Grief and bereavement in contemporary society: Bridging research and practice* (pp. 139–162). New York: Routledge.

Shear, M. K., Simon, N., Wall, M., Zisook, S., Neimeyer, R., Duan, N., et al. (2011). Complicated grief and related bereavement issues for DSM-5. *Depression and Anxiety, 28*, 103–117.

Stroebe, M., Hansson, R., Schut, H., & Stroebe, W. (2008). *Handbook of bereavement research and practice*. Washington, DC: American Psychological Association.

Stroebe, M., Stroebe, W., Hansson, R., & Schut, H. (2001). *Handbook of bereavement research*. Washington, DC: American Psychological Association.

Stroebe, W., Zech, E., Stroebe, M. S., & Abakoumkin, G. (2005). Does social support help in bereavement? *Journal of Social and Clinical Psychology, 24*, 1030–1050.

Tedeschi, R. G., & Calhoun, L. G. (2008). Beyond the concept of recovery: Growth and the experience of loss. *Death Studies, 32*, 27–39.

Traylor, E. S., Hayslip, B., Kraminski, P. L., & York, C. (2003). Relationships between grief and family system characteristics: A cross lagged longitudinal analysis. *Death Studies, 27*, 575–601.

Walsh, F. (1996). Family resilience: A concept and its application. *Family Process, 35*, 261–281.

Walsh, F. (2003). Family resilience: A framework for clinical practice. *Family Process, 42*, 1–18.

Walsh, F. (2006). *Strengthening family resilience*. New York: Guilford Press.

Walsh, F. (2007). Traumatic loss and major disasters: Strengthening family and community resilience. *Family Process, 46*, 207–227.

Walsh, F., & McGoldrick, M. (2004). *Living beyond loss: Death in the family*. New York: Norton.

Walter, T. (1999). *On bereavement: The culture of grief*. Philadelphia: Open University Press.

Worden, J. W. (1991). *Grief counseling and grief therapy: A handbook for the mental health practitioner* (2nd ed.). New York: Springer.

Resilience as Tolerance for Ambiguity

17

Pauline Boss

Introduction

Marie's husband went hiking four years ago and vanished without a trace. Marie has come to believe now, four years after his disappearance, that she will never know where her husband is, or whether he is dead or alive. Some days she thinks he is dead; other days she thinks he started a new life somewhere else. It goes like that, back and forth. She wonders when it will be over. Never? All she knows for sure is this: She is not waiting anymore for him to come back. She is finally moving forward with her life despite not knowing.

Sal's wife was diagnosed with Alzheimer's disease. Sal is devastated as she sinks deeper into dementia. His feelings are conflicted and disturbing so he joined a group that meets each Saturday morning. There, he learns caregiving skills, and where to find help; and he makes some new friends who are also caring for someone who has dementia. He realizes that he is not alone in his despair and begins to see his situation as more manageable.

When a loved one disappears in body or mind, and when such loss has no resolution, the goal becomes resilience. Here, resilience is defined as tolerance for long periods of ambiguity, and the ability to thrive and even grow stronger despite the lack of clarity about a loved one's absence or presence. It means managing the anxiety that comes with not knowing. With dementia, for example, resilience means staying in a relationship, despite its rupture, rather than disconnecting and acting as if that person is already gone. With a physical disappearance, it means finding new hope in one's life despite the agony of having a loved one who disappeared without a trace and with no body to bury. With ongoing disappearances due to human and natural disasters, as well as the epidemic of dementia in our aging population, the experience of ambiguous loss is likely to hit many of us.

The goal of this chapter is to explain how people like Marie and Sal find the resilience to live well despite this traumatizing type of loss. We begin by defining ambiguous loss and then, with the examples of Marie and Sal, describe the process of how people find resilience despite stress and trauma and the lack of closure.

P. Boss (✉)
Professor Emeritus, Department of Family Social Science, College of Education and Human Development, University of Minnesota, 1985 Buford Avenue, 290 McNeal Hall, St. Paul, MN, USA
e-mail: pboss@umn.edu

D.S. Becvar (ed.), *Handbook of Family Resilience*,
DOI 10.1007/978-1-4614-3917-2_17, © Springer Science+Business Media New York 2013

Ambiguous Loss Defined

Ambiguous loss is a loss that remains unclear and without official validation. It has no resolution or closure. It can traumatize and immobilize people, but unlike PTSD, the threat and feelings of helplessness often continue for years, even a lifetime. The uncertainty can create chronic hyper vigilance, anxiety, and depression. The lack of information ruptures relationships, blocks coping processes, and complicates grief. In families, there is increased conflict, and often a termination of rituals, celebrations, and gatherings. But the important point for clinicians and researchers is this: The pathology after this unique kind of loss lies in the environmental context of ambiguity, not in individual or family deficits.

There are two types of ambiguous loss: physical and psychological. An example of *physical* ambiguous loss, like Marie's, is having a family member vanish without a trace, with no body to bury. An example of *psychological* ambiguous loss, like Sal's, occurs when a loved one's mind and memory disappear. The person is here, but not here in the way you normally expect him or her to be. With both types of ambiguous loss, the loss is ongoing and has no resolution.

While ambiguous loss is often catastrophic, it also can be found more commonly in family life today, for example, through military deployment, giving up a child for adoption, being in foster care, divorce or desertion, or simply leaving home. Here, family resilience means thriving despite not knowing who one's parent is, where one's child or family is, or where a loved one is as he or she is serving our country in dangerous and far away places.

More benign, yet immensely stressful, ambiguities of absence and presence also occur with life's transitions—a child grows up and leaves home, loved ones migrate to a new place leaving parents far behind, a frail elder leaves his mate for institutional care. For all of these reasons, ambiguous loss is more common than we may have thought.

Ambiguous Loss: Where Did the Term Originate?

In 1972, while training with Carl Whitaker, M.D., and psychiatric residents at the University of Wisconsin-Madison, I observed a consistent pattern in families who came for therapy: Families were intact, but fathers seemed absent. They were there, but not there—and they continually asked why we needed them in the session because "children were a mother's business." Back then, fathers were not expected to help with childrearing, but children were distressed by the ambiguity. As a doctoral student, I wrote about psychological father absence in intact families (Boss, 1972, 1986). Very soon, however, I expanded my conceptualization to include any family member who was *here, but not here*—and coined the term *ambiguous loss* (Boss, 1975, 1999, 2004a, 2004b, 2006, 2011).

This shift to ambiguous loss allowed a more inclusive framework; it could now apply to any family member and to diverse situations of ambiguous losses. The focus was now on perceptions of who was in or out of one's family—and the family became a psychological structure, not simply a physical entity (Boss, 1999, 2006, 2011).

Development of the Theory of Ambiguous Loss

The theory of ambiguous loss is a research-based theory that informs practice. I was curious about why some families managed to stay strong despite immense stress and trauma and others were not (see Boss, 1987, 2002, 2003).

Today, the original theoretical premise stands: Ambiguous loss is an immensely distressing loss because it defies resolution and has no closure. None of the usual markers exist to validate the loss—a death certificate, community rituals for disposing of remains, honoring and grieving the lost person. Perceptions about absence and presence remain unclear; close relationships are ruptured. In the sociological sense, the clarity needed for family boundary maintenance is gone; in the psychological sense, the clarity needed for meaning-making is almost unattainable.

The problem can be approached from the perspective of various disciplines. Ambiguous loss is a problem *sociologically* and *structurally* when roles are ignored, decisions put on hold, family members considered gone before death, and the usual gatherings and celebrations are canceled. The result is a family with nobody in it. But ambiguous loss is also a problem *psychologically* when feelings of helplessness and hopelessness lead to chronic sorrow and immobilization (Boss, 2004b; Boss, Roos, & Harris, 2011; Patrick-Ott & Ladd, 2010). In either case, family members feel alone and abandoned.

While the theory was born in the 1970s, it continued to be tested and applied to other kinds of ambiguous loss with families of the physically missing and the psychologically missing (Boss, 1977, 1980, 2008; Fravel & Boss, 1992) and with Alzheimer's disease and other illnesses or conditions that rob the mind (Boss, 2007; Boss, Caron, Horbal, & Mortimer, 1990; Caron, Boss, & Mortimer, 1999; Carroll, Olson, & Buckmiller, 2007.) (See also *Family Relations*, April 2007, special issue on ambiguous loss for 20-year review of literature.[1]) Today, like a Mobius strip, the process of observation, research, and refining theory continues.

Resilience[2]

When old wagon makers needed wood to build the wheels, it is said that they looked for the most weather-beaten trees because that wood was the strongest. A tree that could withstand the trauma and stress of wind and rain, bending back and forth without breaking, would be the most resilient. This is not unlike human resilience.

Coming from the stress perspective, resilience is the ability to bend (like a tree), or flex (like a suspension bridge), and thus withstand external pressures and strains without breaking down. It is the ability to bounce back to a level of functioning equal to *or greater* than before the stress or trauma. Like the tree bending back and forth and strengthened by withstanding harsh elements, many human beings also grow stronger from adversity. But there is more: When the pressure comes from ambiguous loss, the ability to sustain resilience relies not only on bending or flexing, or even tolerating the ambiguity, it requires the ability to imagine hope in a new way.

The father of a missing child forms a national network for finding the missing children of other families; the mother of a child with autism learns all she can about treatment and then forms a group to help other parents do the same. In the face of ambiguous loss, people discover unique ways to find hope. Frequently, they find it by giving hope to others, helping others avoid the pain they themselves have endured. They lessen their own pain, or move beyond it, by offering hope to others.

---

[1] *Family Relations* (April 2007), 56(2).

[2] This section was adapted from Boss (2006), Chap. 3.

History of Resilience

The history of resilience shows us that it is an interdisciplinary construct. Individual resilience emerged primarily from fields concerned with individual pathology, while studies of family resilience emerged from fields concerned with family stress and prevention.

Resilience in Psychology

In the early 1970s, psychologist Garmezy (1987) pioneered ideas about *competence* in the face of difficulty. He was studying children at risk for pathology because they had schizophrenic mothers. Surprisingly, some of the children thrived and did well in school (1985, 1987). He and his colleagues then studied children in poverty, another high-risk context, where he also found stress-resistant children (Garmezy & Rutter, 1985). The search was now for health (Garmezy & Masten, 1986), and in more recent years, the term *competence* was replaced with *resilience* (Masten, 2001). Subsequently, Masten linked resilience to positive psychology and emphasized that resilience is not unusual, but emerges from ordinary processes (Masten, 2001). She calls resilience "ordinary magic," implying that it is a common phenomenon, and she carries on this groundbreaking work today. Developmental psychologists increasingly see resilience as a process and favor the term *resiliency* to indicate development over time (Hetherington & Blechman, 1996).

Resilience in Sociology

In sociology, a pioneer in resiliency (who, like Garmezy, did not use the term) was Aaron Antonovsky. As a medical sociologist, he thought clinicians needed a broader, more preventive approach, rather than simply treating specific illnesses and disease. He identified psychological, social, and cultural resources that people use to resist illnesses and found that when people saw their world as understandable and manageable, that "sense of coherence" became the major factor in determining how well patients would manage stress and stay healthy (1979, 1987). Antonovsky then moved his work to the family level (Antonovsky & Sourani, 1988) and found that families also need a sense of coherence to master their problems. Yet, when loss remains ambiguous, it is difficult to make sense of the problem. Ambiguity blocks one's sense of manageability and coherence. Here, people must be prepared for *not* being able to solve the problem, and for living well nevertheless.

Family Resilience

The idea of family resilience has roots in family stress management and prevention. Family therapists Hawley and DeHaan (1996) define family resilience as:

> The path a family follows as it adapts and prospers in the face of stress, both in the present and over time. Resilient families respond positively to these conditions in unique ways, depending on the context, developmental level, the interactive combination of risk and protective factors, and the family's shared outlook. (p. 293)

If given time and community support, many families have this natural self-righting ability to recover and even grow stronger after trauma and loss. But it has been relatively recently that scholars have used the term *family resilience* (McCubbin & McCubbin, 1993; Walsh, 1998). While the individual focus remains today, most scholars now study it within the context of family and community—both of which can enhance or hinder resiliency. As family therapist Froma Walsh wrote: "Individual hardiness is better understood and fostered in the context of the family and larger social world" (1998, p. 24).

What we hope for is that members of a couple or family have reasonably compatible views about their problem. But with ambiguous loss, this is rarely the case. While I emphasize with clients that it is alright to see the situation differently at first, if over time there remains too much incongruence among beliefs within one couple or family, it will erode resilience. Disagreements and conflict lead to family or marital splits. To build teamwork, despite some differences in perceptions, becomes one of the first therapeutic tasks.

Research Update on Resilience

Since 9/11, and subsequent research, there are some surprising updates about resilience:

1. *Resiliency is more than recovery.* Most people have the ability to maintain a stable equilibrium despite loss and trauma.[3] What this means for clinicians is that not everyone requires individual psychotherapy after ambiguous loss. Resilient adults and children may prefer more family- and community-based interventions that offer peer group support and psycho-education. Individual and medical treatment should be reserved for the most vulnerable, those who are immobilized and traumatized or a danger to themselves or others (Bonanno, Papa, & O'Neill, 2001; Boss, 2006; Stroebe & Stroebe, 1991).

2. *Resilience is more common than we thought.* Grief therapists as well as trauma therapists have traditionally been trained to see pathology.[4] While there are exceptions, resilience is often overlooked. According to Bonanno (2004, 2009), the vast majority of people exposed to loss and trauma "... show the type of healthy functioning suggestive of the resilience trajectory" (2004, p. 22).

3. *There are multiple and unexpected pathways to resilience.* For some people, even repression is a functional way of coping (Bonanno, Noll, Putnam, O'Neill, & Trickett, 2003). For others, laughter and optimism help (Bonanno et al., 2003). Still others find resilience through prayer or beliefs in a higher power that make them invulnerable (Bonanno, Field, Kovacevic, & Kaltman, 2002). They believe, for example, that God would not give them any problem they could not manage. In addition, researchers are finding that pathways to resilience also vary by age, gender, genetics, and environment.

---

[3] Bonanno defined resilience as "the ability of adults in otherwise normal circumstances who are exposed to an isolated and potentially highly disruptive event, such as the death of a close relation or a violent or life-threatening situation, to maintain relatively stable, healthy levels of psychological and physical functioning" (2004, p. 20). Bonanno (2004) confirms Walsh's earlier (1998) premise that resilience is more than the absence of psychopathology. Even during times of adversity, it means continuous healthy functioning with regenerative growth and positive emotions (Bonanno et al. 2001).

[4] The focus on pathology was perhaps influenced by Bowlby (1980), who saw positive emotion after loss as denial. Previous researchers found that 65% of self-identified grief therapists believed that the absence of grieving was pathological (Middleton, Moylan, Raphael, Burnett, & Martinek, 1993; Osterweis, Solomon, Green, & Institute of Medicine, Committee for the Study of Health Consequences of the Stress of Bereavement, 1984). The update is this: There is no basis for the assumption that the absence of grief is pathological or that its absence is always followed by delayed grief reactions. In fact, there is solid evidence that resilience to loss is enhanced by positive emotion (Bonanno, 2004; Bonanno & Keltner, 1997; Wortman & Silver, 1989). What these researchers found, however, is that those who did well after loss were ready to accept the death, believed in a just world (Boss, 2002), and had instrumental support. Although immediately after loss, there were some emotional pangs, intrusive thoughts, and ruminations, they did not, in resilient people, endure or interfere with daily functioning and affect (Bonanno, 2004; Bonanno, Wortman, & Nesse, 2004). What this tells us is that Bowlby was wrong. Some people—resilient people—experience loss and trauma without disabling negative emotions.

4. *The family and community can be a source of resilience or a barrier to it.* Resilience is a complex relational process that is influenced by the environment, and one's family and community are the nearest environments (Boss, 2006; Boss, Beaulieu, Wieling, Turner, & LaCruz, 2003; Landau & Saul, 2004). Reports after the Oklahoma City bombing, New York's 9/11, and the South Asian tsunami support the idea that a sense of community can help individuals and families heal after loss (Boss, 2006, Boss et al., 2003). But if the family or community stigmatize and discriminate against the traumatized family member, they then become barriers to resilience. (cf. Robins, 2010)

Implications for Therapy and Intervention

The clinical goal with ambiguous loss is to move people from helplessness to hope. When a loss has no resolution, the only window for hope lies in one's perceptions about the ambiguity and the inability to know all the answers.

For people like Maria and Sal, the possibilities for hope reside in the resilience of becoming comfortable with ambiguity and uncertainty. While doing this is not easy in a culture that values mastery and problem solving, I have seen many individuals and families who were able to do so. The following guidelines are meant to help clinicians as well as researchers discover this kind of resilience. They are not intended to be prescribed in a certain order or formally manualized. Rather, these six guidelines are meant to *guide tailor-made therapies and interventions* to fit a diversity of people who, like Maria and Sal, are experiencing different types of ambiguous loss. (For detailed discussion of each guideline, see Boss, 2006, 2011).

Six Guidelines for Resilience[5]

1. Finding Meaning

   Without meaning, both grief and coping processes are frozen, and there is no hope to move forward with one's life. What I have learned from working with individuals and families whose loved ones are missing is that they feel they have to struggle more with the social norms that push for closure than they do with the loss itself. Until recently, the prevailing notion was that mourners should get over a loss and do so relatively quickly. While this is unreasonable with any kind of loss (Becvar, 2001), it is impossible with ambiguous loss.

   In the absence of closure, there are several ways to find meaning. The first is to name the problem. People can't understand or cope with a problem until they know what it is. It helps if it has a name. With ambiguous loss, this is what I say: "What you are experiencing is ambiguous loss; it is one of the most difficult kinds of loss because there is no closure. This isn't your fault. The ambiguity is the culprit."

   Next, to find meaning, reactions to ambiguous loss are normalized. While symptoms may look like depression or trauma, externalizing the cause helps people know that it is not their weakness that is causing their symptoms. As they see that even strong people are brought down by ambiguous loss, their perceptions of guilt and blame lower, and resilience can build.

   Meanwhile, I urge clients to try a more dialectical way of thinking. I call it "both-and thinking." I provide some examples: "I feel *both* that my loved one is dead *and* maybe not." "I feel my loved one is *both* here *and* gone." "I feel like I am *both* married *and* a widow." Family members catch on

---

[5] This section was adapted from Boss (2006), Chaps. 4–9.

quickly to this way of thinking and will add their own ideas to the list. They come to see that with ambiguous loss, resilience means holding two opposing ideas in one's mind at the same time (Boss, 1999/2000, 2006, 2011).

In this process of finding meaning it is also important for people to continue with their usual family rituals, celebrations, and gatherings. But while there are rituals in every culture and religion for dealing with death, there are none or few for dealing with ambiguous loss. Some Nordic communities have annual funerals for fishermen lost at sea, and in New York after 9/11, funerals often were held with a favorite artifact in the coffin instead of remains. It is from these examples that people can learn to create their own rituals that will acknowledge a loss that remains unclear.

When people gather together for rituals of loss, they are more able to hold the contradictions of absence and presence.[6] Whether we do this quietly or with song and dance, family dinners, or community events such as Memorial Day parades, regular gatherings and celebrations symbolically connect us with loved ones both present and absent. My mother's recipes still appear at our holiday dinners, and my father's painting still decorates the wall of the dining room.

It is at times of holidays and rituals that family members are also here in one's heart and mind, not just physically. This helps families of missing persons realize that they already have the capacity to live with the paradox of absence and presence. They begin to see some meaning in ambiguous loss.

2. Tempering Mastery

Tempering mastery means that some people, depending on culture, have to increase or decrease their sense of mastery and control in order to live well with ambiguous loss. For the most part, I have worked with people who are confident that they can solve problems, so they must lower their sense of mastery in order to live with a loss that has no solution. International Red Cross workers, however, have found that in some cultures where families and community stigmatize wives whose husbands had been kidnapped, these women are often ostracized and thus must increase their mastery in order to survive (Robins, 2010). Depending on cultural context, individuals and families with missing loved ones must find a way to regain their strength and status to move forward despite unresolved loss. It helps to externalize the blame and shame. In therapy or family meetings, the goal shifts to that of mastering one's internal self and to actively reconstructing how one lives and with whom. This can be by living in community with a family of choice, for example, other women who have been similarly ostracized by their marital family (Robins, 2010). Human connection is essential for healing.

3. Reconstructing Identity

When there is ambiguous loss, one's identity changes. People ask: "Am I still a wife if my husband no longer knows who I am?" "Am I still connected to my ex-mate after we are divorced?" "Am I still a daughter or son if I now take care of my parents?"

When long held identities are shaken, they need to be redefined. In therapy and in family meetings, we talk about roles, who does what, and how this has changed. We talk about rules, who was supposed to do what, and how this has changed; we talk about rituals, who used to lead them, and who does now, and what this means. In sum, the questions asked center on: Who are you now that your loved one has disappeared? This takes time to discover and is best done in the company of others—whether with a therapist or a group of trusted peers who do not discriminate, stigmatize, isolate, and above all, insist that the only identity is one's former identity.

---

[6] The capacity of rituals to express powerful contradictions simultaneously makes them especially relevant to the mourning process (Imber-Black, 2004).

4. Normalizing Ambivalence

Ambiguity leads to ambivalence. When a family member disappears, physically or psychologically, and information is not available to clarify the loss, mixed emotions tend to follow: "I want to find him alive; but now I would be glad if they just find his body because then I would know for sure." "I hate her for causing me so much pain; No, I love her." "I wish she could die because her life is so miserable now; but I want her to live." This is not psychiatric ambivalence, but rather, *sociological ambivalence*, caused by an external social situation. Explaining this to clients helps relieve their guilt and uncover their latent ambivalence, especially about negative feelings. Using narrative means, we normalize negative feelings, but not harmful actions. People begin to see their conflicted feelings as caused by the ambiguity, and they are better able to manage them. This lowers the probability of abuse or neglect.

5. Revising Attachment

Because ambiguous loss is a relational problem, relational interventions are most effective to revise one's attachment to a person who is missing, either physically or psychologically. This again requires dialectical thinking: "I love someone who is both here and gone, and that is how it is." In therapy—and often better, in interaction with peer groups—people gradually see the need for revision, moving from despair to action, a process necessary for change. The goal is to stay connected both to the lost person and to new friends and peers who can be more fully present. It is not disloyalty if, for example, the spouse or adult child of a dementia patient goes out to dinner regularly with a friend and also regularly visits and cares for his or her loved one who is psychologically gone.

In addition, people must differentiate between what is permanently lost from what is still here, grieve the former, and celebrate the latter. Staying involved with a loved one who is emotionally gone while finding new attachments is a way to stay resilient. With ambiguous loss, it is essential for the people left behind to have some relationships that are clear so that they can maintain a relationship that is not.

6. Discovering Hope

Without meaning there is no hope; without hope, there is no resilience. Hope, however, must be based on a reasonable appraisal of the situation. Yet, reasonable appraisal is extremely difficult when a loss remains ambiguous. In such situations, people have to discover some new hope.

Hope is defined as belief in a future good. It implies the expectation of fulfillment. It also implies a belief that suffering can stop and that comfort is possible in the future. This view of hope reflects a mastery-oriented view of the world (Boss, 1999/2000, 2006). That is, it reflects an assumption that things will turn out, *as we want them to*—as if ego wants its own way (Boss, 2006). Clinically, my concern rises when people hold on to old hopes too long. The wife of a dementia patient insists that her husband will get well even after ten hospitalizations and myriad doctors say he is in the last stages of Alzheimer's disease (Olson, 2011). Her hope is now delusional. Such false hope erodes resiliency and has no benefit for anyone involved.

The goal for realistic hope is more than a conviction that things will return to the status quo, the way they used to be before the disappearance of mind or body. New hope emerges when people listen to others, hear their stories, and gradually reshape their own narrative, one with a different ending than they had originally hoped for. The wife of a missing sailor now hopes for peace and productivity in her new life as a poet; the father of a brain injured soldier sees there is still opportunity for doing things together—going to ball games, having a beer together with friends, working together to keep up the lawn and garden.

Because happy endings are rare with ambiguous loss, letting go of old hopes and dreams is essential for resilience. Some say spirituality or religious faith helps. Others say that what helps is an optimism that things will work out. Others remain comfortable with the ambiguity for reasons that are more philosophical and existential. They are able to live life as it comes, in the moment, and worry less about finding sure answers. What I have learned, however, from the thousands of families I have worked with is this: People find resiliency in vastly different ways, and each can lead to some new version of hope.

Research Implications

At present, research suggests that resilience is both an individual and a family phenomenon; thus, researchers should take into account both the individual and family processes. As always, I define the family broadly, and often it means the community. The most recent advances in thinking about resilience conceptualize it at the community level (Landau & Saul, 2004; Robins, 2010; Saul, 2003).[7] While it can impede recovery, community connectedness also can promote lasting recovery after traumatic loss. While therapists can help, our connection is relatively temporary, as we do not go home with the people we treat. Distressed people yearn for their own community and family because that is where human attachment is more lasting.[8]

To determine whether family resilience is more than the sum of individual family member resilience, more research is needed.[9] While I propose it is both, I think the more important questions are: Who is the family? Is it the biological or marital unit? Or is it a family of choice, one that is more psychological? Is it a help or hindrance to coping and resilience? Is the community or tribe or clan the family? What kinds of human connections are most helpful to a particular individual? One can apply these questions to cases of ambiguous loss as a major test of resilience.

Clinicians can contribute to the research process by using their observations to generate new hypotheses about how family resiliency is enhanced or blocked. They also may have valuable ideas about when family, community, or culture get in the way of individual resilience and health.

Studies about resilience provide hope. Wolin and Wolin (1993) used the term *survivor's pride*, finding that if something bad happens to a person, a positive meaning or attribution can, as the saying goes, turn lemons into lemonade. But researchers also must be aware of the downside of resilience.

Cautions About the Idea of Resilience

Being resilient is not always desirable, especially if it is always the same persons who are expected to bend—the poor and disenfranchised worldwide, often women, and people of dark color. People with less privilege, power, or agency are often the ones who must adapt to the wishes of others. Resilience, therefore, is not itself always a sufficient goal. Sometimes protest, working for change, or even rebellion are better than continuing to endure injustice or abuse. In such cases, researchers and clinicians must see the need for change as another form of resilience and not pathologize a person's refusal to be resilient in the usual way.

We recognize and support the resilience of children of poverty or war, for example, but at the same time, we should do what we can to eliminate such trauma and loss for children. We must be

---

[7] For more on this topic, please see Chap. 26.

[8] This was evident for families of the missing after 9/11, Hurricane Katrina, and the South Asian tsunami, and more recently in East Timor and Nepal as discovered by field workers for the International Committee of the Red Cross (ICRC) (Bhawan & Baneshwor, 2009; International Committee of the Red Cross (ICRC), 2010; Robins, 2010).

[9] This shift to a resilience focus continues today with a research emphasis on assets, compensatory factors, protective factors, and competence in developmental tasks (Wright & Masten, 2005). Contemporary psychologists have studied how people stay resilient across the life span with risk factors such as poverty, homelessness, divorce, physical illness, and mental illness (Cowan, 1991; Hauser, 1999; Hauser, DiPlacido, Jacobson, Willet, & Cole, 1993; Masten, 2001). For example, in Hauser's (1999) longitudinal study of clinical and nonclinical adolescents (now mature adults), he found that attributing a positive meaning to the earlier experience of institutionalization accounted for the adult health and resilience.

cautious about adopting a resilience model that supports the status quo without seeking to change the stressor itself. We must not be content with human resilience as the only answer, but also promote the health of a community and society in which human beings can more easily thrive.

Regarding ambiguous loss research, I refer the reader to Boss (2007) where I explicitly explain why researchers must know, based on their research question, whether they are studying the phenomenon of ambiguous loss or its structural outcome, boundary ambiguity; whether they are social constructionists or neo-structure functionalists, and whether they need quantifiable data, qualitative data, or both. Also, see good examples of ambiguous loss and boundary ambiguity research in the special edition of *Family Relations* (April 2007).[10]

Case Example

What was the process that Maria and Sal used to get to a place of resilience as characterized by a tolerance for ambiguity? Both requested to see me because they had read my book (Boss, 1999/2000) and thought they were dealing with an ambiguous loss. Indeed, they were. Having a loved vanish without a trace, as did Maria, and having a mate whose mind and memory were vanishing, as did Sal, were both valid examples of ambiguous loss. When clients arrive, labeling their own problem like this, we move on to the meaning of the situation and its symptoms of stress and unresolved loss.

Maria reported frequent and very disturbing nightmares, always about her missing husband. It was as if her brain was working overtime to find a solution to the mystery of his whereabouts. We talked about her dreams as a metaphor for what she might never know for sure. After a year or two, she began to see a change in them. She said her dreams were becoming less frightening. In fact, they were now often comforting. As her husband appeared farther and farther away, and neither of them were struggling to reach the other, she said she felt more released and peaceful. Meanwhile, we worked on many levels, and it was Maria's dream work that helped her find meaning in her loss and new hope. Not everyone finds his or her resilience through dream work, but this was the method she chose. While we worked on many issues in our time together, Maria told me that it was talking about her dreams that helped her most in finding meaning and a new identity for a life on her own. I see Maria only occasionally now. She reports that she still dreams, especially around the anniversary of her husband's disappearance. She has, however, come to accept such reminders of loss and pain as part of what her life will be like forever. I hear a bit of pride when she says this, and I ask her to say more. She says she has become a stronger person for her suffering. For her, that means hope.

Sal arrived in my therapy office also saying he had experienced an ambiguous loss. He said his sadness was overwhelming and he could barely function. This was a problem because he was the primary caregiver for his wife, who was now in deep dementia. He was ashamed that he could not do the work as he wished. He loved his wife and wanted to do a good job. His identity centered on being a good problem solver and a master of his trade, which as an engineer, involved fixing things. He felt guilty for feeling like grieving while his wife was still alive. And he felt alone. After normalizing his symptoms, we focused primarily on his value of mastery that was now thwarted, and how he could separate what could be improved from what could not. What was permanently lost needed to be grieved, and he did not know how to do that. In addition to our therapy about grieving along the way and letting go of perfection, he joined a weekly group to hear the stories of other caregivers and to gradually tell his own. It was there, from a lecture, that he heard about the oscillation of grief, and he said that those words hit him as an engineer. It was the first time he understood his own feelings of

---

[10] *Family Relations,* April 2007, 56(2).

sadness. Sal is still caring for his wife today, but uses professional help when he goes out to golf with friends. He is still sad at times and rightly so. But now he knows that his sadness does not mean failure, nor does his need to grieve or go out with friends mean disloyalty to his still-living wife. He has become more philosophical, he says, because he can now accept the idea that his wife is both here and gone. He doesn't have to fix it.

Conclusion

From a relational perspective, resilience related to ambiguous loss means not being undone by a less-than-perfect relationship. It comes when people no longer expect absolute presence or absence. You may have guessed that Marie was resilient and likely to have a good life despite the occasional pangs of sadness about her missing husband. Indeed, that was the case. I saw her only at times when the anxiety and sadness were renewed—for example, when her daughter married and there was no father to walk her down the aisle. It was, she said, both a sad and happy time. She felt so alone and her grief was raw again. Even resilient people have bad times, but the important point is that they recover relatively quickly and continue to live their lives in an optimistic and functional way.

Sal found his resilience in the Saturday morning caregiver group and with his golfing buddies, whom he saw weekly. Both allowed him to go the distance with his ill wife, even when she no longer knew who he was. When she died, he no longer attended the Saturday group, but he continued to see socially some good friends he had made there, and of course, he continued to meet his golfing buddies who were now like family to him.

With ambiguous loss, the therapeutic goal is not to produce a solution, because there is none,[11] but instead to adapt, approximate, revise, adjust, and find a way to live and thrive despite the ambiguity. Being resilient means finding meaning and hope despite the anxiety and pressure of *not* having a solution.

The ambiguous loss theory, now considered middle range theory, is proving useful to both clinicians and researchers because it names a new kind of loss, provides a more refined view of loss and grief, and in both research and clinical applications, allows for more diversity in type of loss and in culturally different settings. Rather than being limited to one specific disease or disaster, professionals and researchers can focus on ambiguity that includes a broader category of illnesses or tragedies for any time loved ones go missing in body or mind. This more general framework guides researchers and clinicians to better understand and intervene with a more nuanced kind of loss, one clouded by mystery and ambiguity. With the theory of ambiguous loss, we now have a broader lens for understanding resilience under extreme circumstances of loss and grief.

References

Antonovsky, A. (1979). *Health, stress, and coping: New perspectives on mental and physical well-being.* San Francisco, CA: Jossey-Bass.

Antonovsky, A. (1987). *Unraveling the mystery of health: How people manage stress and stay well.* San Francisco, CA: Jossey-Bass.

Antonovsky, A., & Sourani, T. (1988). Family sense of coherence and adaptation. *Journal of Marriage and Family, 50,* 79–92.

Becvar, D. S. (2001). *In the presence of grief: Helping family members resolve death, dying, and bereavement issues.* New York, NY: Guilford.

---

[11] Although therapies that build resilience can be called "strength-based approaches," they are not synonymous with solution-focused therapies.

Bhawan, M., & Baneshwor, N. (2009). *Families of missing persons in Nepal: A study of their needs*. Kathmandu, Nepal: International Committee of the Red Cross (ICRC).

Bonanno, G. A. (2004). Loss, trauma, and human resilience: Have we underestimated the human capacity to thrive after extremely aversive events? *American Psychologist, 59*(1), 20–28.

Bonanno, G. A. (2009). *The other side of sadness*. New York, NY: Basic.

Bonanno, G. A., Field, N. P., Kovacevic, A., & Kaltman, S. (2002). Self-enhancement as a buffer against extreme adversity: Civil war in Bosnia and traumatic loss in the United States. *Personality & Social Psychology Bulletin, 28*(2), 184–196.

Bonanno, G. A., & Keltner, D. (1997). Facial expressions of emotion and the course of conjugal bereavement. *Journal of Abnormal Psychology, 106*(1), 126–137.

Bonanno, G. A., Noll, J. G., Putnam, F. W., O'Neill, M., & Trickett, P. K. (2003). Predicting the willingness to disclose childhood sexual abuse from measures of repressive coping and dissociative tendencies. *Child Maltreatment, 8*, 1–17.

Bonanno, G. A., Papa, A., & O'Neill, K. (2001). Loss and human resilience. *Applied and Preventive Psychology, 10*(3), 193–206.

Bonanno, G. A., Wortman, C. B., & Nesse, R. M. (2004). Prospective patterns of resilience and maladjustment during widowhood. *Psychology and Aging, 19*(2), 260–271.

Boss, P. (1972). Father absence in intact families. In *Research and Theory Section*. Presentation at the annual meeting of the National Council on Family Relations, Toronto, Canada, November 1972.

Boss, P. (1975). Psychological father presence in the missing-in-action (MIA) family: Its effects on family functioning. *Proceedings: Third annual joint medical meeting concerning POW/MIA matters*, (pp. 61–65). San Diego, CA: Naval Health Research Center, Center for Prisoner of War Studies.

Boss, P. (1977). A clarification of the concept of psychological father presence in families experiencing ambiguity of boundary. *Journal of Marriage & Family, 39*(1), 141–151.

Boss, P. (1980). The relationship of psychological father presence, wife's personal qualities, and wife/family dysfunction in families of missing fathers. *Journal of Marriage & Family, 42*(3), 541–549.

Boss, P. (1986). Psychological absence in the intact family: A systems approach to the study of fathering. *Marriage & Family Review, 10*(1), 11–39.

Boss, P. (1987). Family stress. In M. B. Sussman & S. K. Steinmetz (Eds.), *Handbook of marriage and the family* (pp. 695–723). New York, NY: Plenum.

Boss, P. (1999). *Ambiguous loss: Learning to live with unresolved grief*. Cambridge, MA: Harvard University Press (Original work published 1999).

Boss, P. (2002). *Family stress management: A contextual approach*. Thousand Oaks, CA: Sage (Original work published 1988).

Boss, P. (Ed.) (with Mulligan, C.). (2003). *Family stress: Classic and contemporary readings*. Thousand Oaks, CA: Sage.

Boss, P. (2004a). Ambiguous loss. In F. Walsh & M. McGoldrick (Eds.), *Living beyond loss: Death in the family* (2nd ed., pp. 237–246). New York, NY: Norton.

Boss, P. (2004b). Ambiguous loss research, theory, and practice: Reflections after 9/11. *Journal of Marriage & Family, 66*(3), 551–566.

Boss, P. (2006). *Loss, trauma, and resilience: Therapeutic work with ambiguous loss*. New York, NY: Norton.

Boss, P. (2007). Ambiguous loss theory: Challenges for scholars and practitioners [Special issue]. *Family Relations, 56*(2), 105–111.

Boss, P. (2008). A tribute, not a memorial. *SIGMOD Record, 37*(2), 19–20.

Boss, P. (2011). *Loving someone who has dementia*. San Francisco, CA: Jossey-Bass

Boss, P., Beaulieu, L., Wieling, E., Turner, W., & LaCruz, S. (2003). Healing loss, ambiguity, and trauma: A community-based intervention with families of union workers missing after the 9/11 attack in New York City. *Journal of Marital and Family Therapy, 29*(4), 455–467.

Boss, P., Caron, W., Horbal, J., & Mortimer, J. (1990). Predictors of depression in caregivers of dementia patients: Boundary ambiguity and mastery. *Family Process, 29*(3), 245–254.

Boss, P., Roos, S., & Harris, D. L. (2011). Grief in the midst of uncertainty: An exploration of ambiguous loss and chronic sorrow. In R. A. Neimeyer, H. Winokuer, D. L. Harris, & G. Thornton (Eds.), *Grief and bereavement in contemporary society* (pp. 163–175). New York, NY: Routledge.

Bowlby, J. (1980). *Loss: Sadness and depression, Vol. III. Attachment and Loss series*. New York, NY: Basic.

Caron, W., Boss, P., & Mortimer, J. (1999). Family boundary ambiguity predicts Alzheimer's outcomes. *Psychiatry: Interpersonal & Biological Processes, 62*(4), 347–356.

Carroll, J. S., Olson, C. D., & Buckmiller, N. (2007). Family boundary ambiguity: A 30-year review of theory, research, and measurement. *Family Relations, 56*(2), 210–230.

Cowan, P. A. (1991). Individual and family life transitions: A proposal for a new definition. In P. A. Cowan & E. M. Hetherington (Eds.), *Family transitions. Advances in family research series* (pp. 3–30). Hillsdale, NJ: Erlbaum.

Fravel, D. L., & Boss, P. G. (1992). An in-depth interview with the parents of missing children. In J. F. Gilgun & K. Daly (Eds.), *Qualitative methods in family research* (pp. 126–145). Thousand Oaks, CA: Sage.

Garmezy, N. (1985). Stress-resistant children: The search for protective factors. In J. E. Stevenson (Ed.), *Recent research in developmental psychopathology* (pp. 213–233). Oxford, UK: Pergamon.

Garmezy, N. (1987). Stress, competence, and development: Continuities in the study of schizophrenic adults, children vulnerable to psychopathology, and the search for stress-resistant children. *The American Journal of Orthopsychiatry, 57*(2), 159–174.

Garmezy, N., & Masten, A. S. (1986). Stress, competence, and resilience: Common frontiers for therapist and psychopathologist. *Behavior Therapy, 17*, 500–521.

Garmezy, N., & Rutter, M. (1985). Acute reactions to stress. In M. Rutter & L. Hersov (Eds.), *Child psychiatry: Modern approaches* (2nd ed., pp. 152–176). Oxford, UK: Blackwell Scientific Press.

Hauser, S. T. (1999). Understanding resilient outcomes: Adolescent lives across time and generations. *Journal of Research on Adolescence, 9*(1), 1–24.

Hauser, S. T., DiPlacido, J., Jacobson, A. M., Willett, J., & Cole, C. (1993). Family coping with an adolescent's chronic illness: An approach and three studies. *Journal of Adolescence, 16*(3), 305–329.

Hawley, D. R., & DeHaan, L. (1996). Toward a definition of family resilience: Integrating life-span and family perspectives. *Family Process, 35*(3), 283–298.

Hetherington, E. M., & Blechman, E. A. (1996). *Stress, coping, and resiliency in children and families*. Mahwah, N.J.: Erlbaum.

Imber-Black, E. (2004). Rituals and the healing process. In F. Walsh & M. McGoldrick (Eds.), *Living beyond loss: Death in the family* (2nd ed., pp. 340–357). New York, NY: Norton.

International Committee of the Red Cross (ICRC). (2010). *Needs of families of the missing in Timor-Leste*. Keybayoran Baru, Jakarta Selatan: Author.

Landau, J., & Saul, J. (2004). Facilitating family and community resilience in response to major disaster. In F. Walsh & M. McGoldrick (Eds.), *Living beyond loss: Death in the family* (2nd ed., pp. 285–309). New York, NY: Norton.

Masten, A. S. (2001). Ordinary magic: Resilience processes in development. *American Psychologist, 56*(3), 227–238.

McCubbin, M. A., & McCubbin, H. I. (1993). Families coping with illness: The resiliency model of family stress, adjustment, and adaptation. In C. Danielson, B. Hamel Bissell, & P. Winstead-Fry (Eds.), *Families, health, and illness* (pp. 21–64). St. Louis, MO: Mosby.

Middleton, W., Moylan, A., Raphael, B., Burnett, P., & Martinek, N. (1993). An international perspective on bereavement related concepts. *The Australian and New Zealand Journal of Psychiatry, 27*(3), 457–463.

Olson, J. (2011 January 20). Ruling delayed on Al Barnes' medical decisions. *Star Tribune*, pp. B2, B5

Osterweis, M., Solomon, F., Green, M., & Institute of Medicine, Committee for the Study of Health Consequences of the Stress of Bereavement. (1984). *Bereavement: Reactions, consequences, and care*. Washington, DC: National Academy Press.

Patrick-Ott, A., & Ladd, L. D. (2010). The blending of Boss's concept of ambiguous loss and Olshanky's concept of chronic sorrow: A case study of a family with a child who has significant disabilities. *Journal of Creativity in Mental Health, 5*(1), 73–86.

Robins, S. (2010). Ambiguous loss in a non-Western context: Families of the disappeared in postconflict Nepal. *Family Relations, 59*(3), 253–268.

Saul, J. (2003). Promoting community recovery in lower Manhattan after September 11, 2001. *Bulletin of the Royal Institute for Inter-Faith Studies, 5*(2), 69–84.

Stroebe, M., & Stroebe, W. (1991). Does "grief work" work? *Journal of Consulting and Clinical Psychology, 59*(3), 479–482.

Walsh, F. (1998). *Strengthening family resilience*. New York, NY: Guilford.

Wolin, S., & Wolin, S. (1993). *The resilient self: How survivors of troubled families rise above adversity*. New York, NY: Villard.

Wortman, C. B., & Silver, R. C. (1989). The myths of coping with loss. *Journal of Consulting and Clinical Psychology, 57*, 349–357.

Wright, M. O., & Masten, A. S. (2005). Resilience processes in development: Fostering positive adaptation in the context of adversity. In S. Goldstein & R. Brooks (Eds.), *Handbook of resilience in children* (pp. 17–37). New York, NY: Kluwer Academic/Plenum.

Bereavement in the Face of Perinatal Loss: A Hardiness Perspective

Ariella Lang and Tracy Carr

Background

Perinatal loss is a frequently and potentially life-transforming event for bereaved parents and families following the death of a baby. In this chapter, perinatal loss is defined from the parents' perspective as the death of a *baby* via ectopic pregnancy, miscarriage, stillbirth, neonatal, or infant death (Callister, 2006). Across North America and other developed countries the death rate of babies less than 1 year of age is approximately 5/1,000 (Statistics Canada, 2010; Åhman & Zupan, 2004). Although there are no published statistics on the demise of fetuses prior to 20 weeks gestation or who weigh less than 500 g, it is estimated that as many as 15–20% of pregnancies end in miscarriage (Johnson & Puddifoot, 1996; Puscheck, 2010; Seibel & Graves, 1980).

Compared to other types of mourning, like for the loss of a parent or a sibling, the loss of a child is associated with a grief experience that is particularly severe, long-lasting, and complicated, with symptoms fluctuating in intensity and duration (Rando, 1986; Zeanah, Danis, Hishberg, & Dietz, 1995). Among health-care professionals and society at large, however, perinatal loss is generally viewed as a less traumatic or prolonged experience than the death of an older child, and may not be publically acknowledged (Black & Sandelowski, 2010; Lang, Edwards, & Benzies, 2005; Lang et al., 2011). Perinatal loss, due to the concurrent physical absence of and psychological presence of the fetus or infant, also has been described as an ambiguous loss (Boss, 2004; Cacciatore, DeFrain, & Jones, 2008; Lang et al., 2011). This sense of ambiguity has the potential to be further compounded by the disenfranchisement of the parents' grief by society's dismissal of such a short-lived or even "unborn" life (Lang et al., 2011).

The death of a fetus or infant has a significant impact on many aspects of the health of bereaved parents and other family members. Bereavement is "the entire experience of family members and friends in the anticipation, death, and subsequent adjustment to life [surrounding] the death of a loved one" (Christ, Bonanno, Malkinson, & Rubin, 2003, p. 554). Experiences of loss, grief, and

A. Lang (✉)
Research Scientist, Victorian Order of Nurses (VON) Canada, Montreal, QC, Canada
e-mail: ariella.lang@sympatico.ca

T. Carr
Department of Nursing and Health Sciences, University of New Bruswick - Saint John (UNBSJ),
Saint John, NB, Canada
e-mail: tcarr@unbsj.ca

D.S. Becvar (ed.), *Handbook of Family Resilience*,
DOI 10.1007/978-1-4614-3917-2_18, © Springer Science+Business Media New York 2013

bereavement are unique, dynamic, and wide-ranging in spite of the ubiquitous presence, commonality, and universality of death in our lives (Moules, Simonson, Prins, Angus, & Bell, 2004; Stroebe, Hansson, Stroebe, & Schut, 2001).

For the most part, the focus of inquiry into perinatal loss has been on the deleterious outcomes of the physical and mental well-being of each spouse (Badenhorst, Riches, Turton, & Hughes, 2006; Christ, et al., 2003; Murray, Terry, Vance, Battistutta, & Connolly, 2000; Hughes & Riches, 2003; Turton, Hughes, Evans, & Fainman, 2001), as well as on the adverse effect on the quality of existing and future family relationships (Gilbert & Smart, 1992; Najman, et al., 1993; Wing, Clance, Burge-Callaway, & Armistead, 2001). Other studies have revealed the deleterious effects, including increased morbidity and mortality, that the death of a loved one can have on the health of the bereaved (Bonanno & Kaltman, 2001; Christakis & Allison, 2006; Christakis & Iwashyna, 2003; Genevro, Marshall, & Miller, 2003; Joanna Briggs Institute (JBI), 2006; Li, Laursen, Precht, Olsen, & Mortensen, 2005; Lillard & Waite, 1995; Schulz & Beach, 1999). Although it is still unclear which groups of bereaved individuals are most vulnerable, there is agreement that a loved one's death affects the health and well-being of all who are bereaved (Lang, Gottlieb, & Amsel, 1996; Lang, Goulet, & Amsel, 2004; Stroebe et al., 2001). Evidence indicates that the bereaved can suffer from a range of physical, emotional, social, and financial concerns (e.g., elevated risks of depression, increased somatic complaints, increased medication and substance abuse, increased absenteeism and disability days (Lang et al., 1996, 2004; Stroebe et al., 2001; Badenhorst, Riches, Turton, & Hughes, 2006; Hughes & Riches, 2003)). Bereavement is also associated with a heightened risk for mortality, especially in the early weeks and months after loss, as well as with higher rates of hospitalization than for the nonbereaved, including psychiatric admissions (Christakis & Allison, 2006; Erlangsen, Jeune, Bille-Brahe, & Vaupel, 2004; Li et al., 2005; Qin & Mortensen, 2003).

One of the most difficult aspects of parental bereavement is that the loss strikes both parents simultaneously and confronts them with an overwhelming sense of loss. In addition to being difficult to accept, it is beyond the parents' control and forces them to create new meanings about life and relationships, possibly altering how they feel about themselves, each other, and other family and close relationships (Lang et al., 2004). There is suggestive evidence that the differences in the way mothers and fathers grieve and perceive the situation can result in misunderstandings (Black & Sandelowski, 2010; Callister, 2006; Krueger, 2006; Lang et al., 1996; Lang & Gottlieb, 1993). Difficulties in the synchrony of the spouses' grief reactions and a lack of effective communication within the family are believed to play a major role in contributing to marital discord (Dyregrov & Dyregrov, 2004; Gottlieb, Lang, & Amsel, 1996; Lang & Gottlieb, 1993; Lang et al., 1996; Schwab, 1992). These misunderstandings can affect the family's functioning as well as the couple's marital relationship, thereby decreasing the ability of each to be a primary source of support for the other (Callister, 2006; Dyregrov & Dyregrov, 2004; Krueger, 2006; Lang & Gottlieb, 1993; Lang et al., 1996). This difficult situation has temporal implications in that the bereavement process and the harmful consequences of the loss will be felt throughout the parents' lifetime. Yet, in contrast, some parents report that they were able to make sense of their own existence following such a tragedy. Their loss had brought them closer together and strengthened their marital relationship (Gilbert, 1989; Gottlieb et al., 1996; Lang & Gottlieb, 1993; Lang et al., 1996; Lang & MacLean, 2007).

To date, we have not been able to understand which elements contribute to ease or intensify the damaging consequences following the death of a fetus or infant. Critical for health professionals caring for the bereaved is the persistent question of why some family systems endure and sometimes even thrive when faced with normative transitions or situational stressors like the death of a baby, while other families deteriorate and disintegrate. In this chapter we explore this question. We begin with an overview of the literature with a focus on the concept of hardiness as it relates to perinatal loss. Hardiness as a predictor of health and well-being is then situated within the Lang's model for the Promotion of Health and Well-being in Bereaved Individuals and Families (Lang et al., 2004; Lang et al., in press), which places emphasis on individual and family strengths rather than on the negative effects of perinatal loss. We also raise some current issues pertaining to bereavement care following perinatal loss, and discuss the implications for practice, research, and policy.

Literature Review

Conceptually, resilience and hardiness are often confused in the literature. Opinions differ regarding whether resilience reflects the ability to maintain a stable equilibrium (Bonanno, 2004; Davydov, Stewart, Ritchie, & Chaudieu, 2010; Earvolino-Ramirez, 2007; Gillespie, Chaboyer, & Wallis, 2007) or whether like hardiness, it also includes the notion of thriving or personal growth to a level beyond where the individuals or family was situated prior to the traumatic or life transforming event. We thus begin by addressing the differences and similarities between these two concepts.

Resilience

According to some authors, resilience to loss and trauma pertains to the ability of individuals and families in otherwise normal circumstances who are exposed to an isolated and potentially highly disruptive event such as the death of a fetus or infant to be able to "bounce back" or "rebound" to the level of functioning and well-being that they enjoyed prior to the death of their baby (Bonanno, 2004; Davydov et al., 2010; Earvolino-Ramirez, 2007). Resilience refers to a broad cluster of personal characteristics that facilitate the ability to cope despite trauma. These characteristics include optimism, self-enhancement, repressive coping, positive affect and a sense of coherence (Agaibi & Wilson, 2005; Antonovsky, 1993; Bonanno, 2004; Levine, Laufer, Stein, Hamama-Raz, & Solomon, 2009; Tedeschi & Calhoun, 2004). Collectively, these characteristics permit individuals to emerge from trauma with fewer psychological wounds and relatively unchanged. Indeed, concept analyses of resilience by different authors consistently describe it as quality of bouncing back and moving on in life after adversity is present (Bonanno, 2004; Davydov et al., 2010; Earvolino-Ramirez, 2007; Gillespie et al., 2007). This conceptualization conjures up the image of an elastic returning to its original state after being stretched. More recent conceptualization of resilience, particularly within the family therapy literature (Becvar, 2007; Boss, 2006), have moved beyond the notion of merely bouncing back to include the idea of emerging even stronger than before and experiencing personal growth. Gillespie et al. (2007), for example, define resilience as the ability to transcend adversity and transform it into an opportunity for growth.

Hardiness

Like more recent definitions of resilience, the concept of hardiness moves beyond the elastic band metaphor and refers to the individual's ability to attain a higher level of health and well-being following a stressful event such as a perinatal loss (Lang et al., 2001, 2004; McCubbin & McCubbin, 1993; Patterson, 1995). Hardiness stems from agriculture, referring to a plant's ability to survive and grow in a given climate and withstand adverse conditions (Seymour, 1936). Kobasa (1979) was the first to describe hardiness in humans as a set of three specific attitudes that mediate the stress response; she termed these challenge, commitment, and control. Kobasa viewed these existential dimensions as especially relevant to one's ability to rise to challenges of the environment and turn stressful life events into possibilities or opportunities for personal growth and benefit.

Hardiness has been studied in various populations (Duquette, Kerouac, Sandhu, Ducharme, & Saulnier, 1995; Lambert & Lambert, 1987; Lee, 1983; Wiebe, 1991). In psychology, researchers have studied college students to describe the relationship between a "hardy personality" and physical and emotional health (Ganellen & Blaney, 1984; Wiebe, 1991), and more recently they have examined the relationship between hardiness and a specific stressful life event such as childbirth (Priel, Gonik, & Rabinowitz, 1993) and the death of a spouse (Campbell, Swank, & Vincent, 1991). Among bereaved widows, hardiness predicted resolution of grief over and above the widow's age, time since the death (1 month–25 years), and general mental health; as the level of hardiness increased, the level of grief in widows decreased.

Hardiness also has been studied in a multitude of contexts. Some examples include management (Duquette et al., 1995; Wolf, 1990), adaptation to chronic illness (Pollock, 1986; Pollock, 1989), and family adaptation to stressors (McCubbin, McCubbin, & Thompson, 1987). Wolf (1990), who suggested ways that nurse executives could develop hardiness in themselves and their staff, believed that the hardy individual tends to focus on opportunity (challenge) as a stimulus for growth rather than on danger as a threat to security, and often referred to the Chinese symbol for crisis, which contains the symbols for both danger and opportunity.

> A concept analysis within the context of perinatal loss has defined hardiness as: a personal resource characterized by a *sense of personal control* over the outcome of life events and hardships such as the death of a fetus/infant, an *active orientation* toward meeting the challenges brought on by the loss, and a belief in the ability to *make sense of one's own existence* following such a tragedy. (Lang et al., 2001, p. 502)

When stressors are unavoidable the hardier person may interpret the situation differently, thereby being better able to meet the challenges of life head on and work through the negative effects of stress. A hardier person may experience personal growth in the face of adversity (Lang et al., 2001, 2004; Lang & MacLean, 2007; Maddi et al., 2002). Hardiness is actually a precursor to coping. Whereas coping refers to "cognitive and behavioral efforts to master, reduce, or tolerate the internal and/or external demands that are created by the stressful transaction" (Folkman, 1984, p. 843; Folkman & Moskowitz, 2000), hardiness is a person's inclination to cope with situations created by stressful circumstances like a perinatal loss, as well as the tendency and willingness to do so (Lang et al., 2001). This concept analysis also described the defining attributes of hardiness. Defining attributes are those that are essential to the presence of the concept and allow the broadest insight (Walker & Avant, 1995). The defining attributes of hardiness, namely, *sense of personal control, active orientation, and meaning making,* are described in Fig. 18.1.

For many, finding meaning in existence is fundamentally a spiritual enterprise (Black & Sandelowski, 2010; Davis, Wortman, Lehman, & Silver, 2000; Davydov et al., 2010; Van & Meleis, 2003), and hardiness in perinatal loss, for some, may be tightly connected to one's spirituality. Spirituality is understood as the essence of a person; a quest for meaning and purpose in life; forgiveness; inner strength; and connectedness to self, others, nature, and/or a higher power (Carr, 2008; Como, 2007; Demerath, 2000; Farran, Paun, & Elliott, 2003; Tanyi, 2002). The terms spirituality and religion are related but not necessarily tethered concepts. Religion encompasses belief systems, rituals, doctrines, and symbols. One's religious beliefs and practices are either chosen or handed down through individual cultural heritage and are part of an organized and formal experience (Carr, 2008; Como, 2007; Demerath, 2000; Farran et al., 2003; Tanyi, 2002). Religion can offer a means of expressing, nurturing, and understanding one's spirituality. However, one can be spiritual without being religious and vice versa (Carr, 2008; Como, 2007). Bereaved parents' spiritual beliefs about the meaning of life and death, existence of life after death, and the purpose of suffering can profoundly influence how they cope with their loss (O'Brien, 1999). Attending to and fostering spirituality as a personal resource may, in turn, foster hardiness and its associated positive consequences among the bereaved.

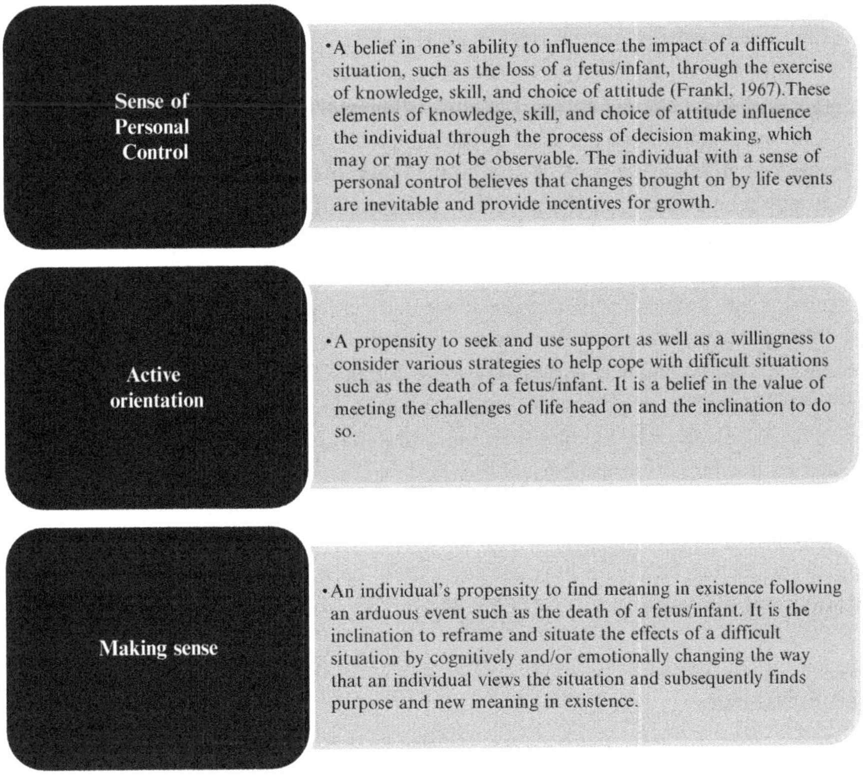

Sense of Personal Control
- A belief in one's ability to influence the impact of a difficult situation, such as the loss of a fetus/infant, through the exercise of knowledge, skill, and choice of attitude (Frankl, 1967).These elements of knowledge, skill, and choice of attitude influence the individual through the process of decision making, which may or may not be observable. The individual with a sense of personal control believes that changes brought on by life events are inevitable and provide incentives for growth.

Active orientation
- A propensity to seek and use support as well as a willingness to consider various strategies to help cope with difficult situations such as the death of a fetus/infant. It is a belief in the value of meeting the challenges of life head on and the inclination to do so.

Making sense
- An individual's propensity to find meaning in existence following an arduous event such as the death of a fetus/infant. It is the inclination to reframe and situate the effects of a difficult situation by cognitively and/or emotionally changing the way that an individual views the situation and subsequently finds purpose and new meaning in existence.

Fig. 18.1 Defining attributes of hardiness (Lang et al., 2001)

The consequences of hardiness within the context of perinatal loss include self-actualization, ability to transcend, and well-being (Lang et al., 2001). *Self-Actualization* is the realization of one's own potential, often resulting in a sense of personal growth. Many bereaved parents declare that although the experience of losing their baby caused them great anguish and they did not stop missing and feeling connected to their baby, it also enabled them to find new and deeper meaning in their life and in their relationships (Büchi et al., 2007; Gilbert, 1989; Lang & MacLean, 2007; Tedeschi & Calhoun, 2008). Indeed, some bereaved parents report that as a result of their loss, they experienced emergence of new possibilities, increased personal strength, changes in spiritual orientation, and appreciation for life (Büchi et al., 2007; Black & Sandelowski, 2010; Tedeschi & Calhoun, 2008). Some also reformulated their outlook on life and living as well as reevaluated their relationships, which included the loss of old friends while forging new relationships with others (Gottlieb et al., 1996). Thus, although the pain and feelings of loss and bereavement can wax and wane over one's lifetime (Stroebe & Schut, 2001), these can occur alongside experiences of personal growth and a deeper understanding of one's place and purpose in the world (Tedeschi & Calhoun, 2008). This growth is also not necessarily linear. A person can go back and forth in the course of life (Teixeira, 2008).

Over time, bereaved parents who have learned to draw on their hardiness acknowledge their *ability to transcend* the death of their baby as well as to weather the countless challenges that they are subsequently compelled to face (Lang et al., 2001). *Transcendence* can be understood as a level of awareness through which one can achieve new experiences and perspectives beyond the present, ordinary, physical boundaries. Spirituality and transpersonal connections (e.g., with God, nature, a deceased love one, a Higher Power) are indicators of the human capacity for transcendence (Chiu, Emblen, van Hofwegen, Sawatzky, & Meyerhoff, 2004).

The intrapersonal, interpersonal, and transpersonal strategies used to deal successfully with stressful situations in the past may help to reinforce bereaved parents' ability to transcend a stressful event such as the tragic loss of their baby. Transpersonal strategies, for example, can move the individual beyond the boundaries of the present and ego-self to spiritual concerns and connections that tap into healing possibilities and potentials. Transpersonal connections with the self, loved ones, nature, God, and/or a Higher Power can embrace the spirit or soul of the other through the processes of caring and healing and being in authentic relation, in the moment (Lukose, 2011; Smith, 1995). Parents who have the ability to transcend realize that change is inevitable and are confident that the challenges—known and unknown—that lie ahead can be dealt with successfully (Lang et al., 2001). Some research has shown an inverse relationship between self-transcendence and depression (Teixeira, 2008).

A final consequence of hardiness is a *sense of well-being* (Lang et al., 2001). Well-being encompasses feelings of vitality, balance, and realizing the potential health of the person as a whole (Bishop & Yardley, 2010). Like the other consequences, this becomes more noticeable over time. Bereaved individuals who have learned to tap into their hardiness may attain a sense of well-being and a higher level of health by attributing meaning to their experience, changing what they believe they can while coming to terms with what they perceive to be unchangeable, as well as achieving self-actualization and ultimately a sense of personal growth. In other words, individuals who have learned to draw on a personal resource such as hardiness have the capacity to optimize their level of health and well-being in myriad ways and situations.

Research Evidence

Program of Research

A program of research focused on prevention and health promotion for bereaved families and spanning nearly 25 years is the backdrop to this section. It stems from Lang's clinical practice with bereaved families following perinatal loss and is dedicated to improving the care provided to the bereaved from a systems change approach. Earlier work examined the relationship between grief reactions and marital intimacy following infant death (Gottlieb et al., 1996; Lang & Gottlieb, 1993; Lang et al., 1996). Subsequently, a theoretical model was tested longitudinally with this population (Lang et al., 2004). The objective of that study was to test an explanatory model of health for bereaved individuals and families following perinatal loss. This model was influenced by Boss' (2002) Crisis Model of Family Stress (CMFS), in turn based on Hill's (1958) ABC-X Model of Family Stress Theory. In contrast to the CMFS, Lang's model focused on health and well-being as the outcome (X). It is a model that centers on individual and couple strengths rather than on the deleterious consequences of perinatal loss, which have been the predominant emphasis of previous studies (Smith & Borgers, 1989; Theut et al., 1989). Some of the key findings from this study consequently led to more in-depth qualitative analyses specifically related to hardiness (Lang & MacLean, 2007) as well as ambiguity and disenfranchisement (Lang et al., 2011).

This first longitudinal study to support an exploratory model of health, including the importance of hardiness as a predictor of health and well-being, involved 110 bereaved couples (husbands and wives) who lost their *baby* during pregnancy or the first year of life. Other than the diverse ethnocultural aspect of the study's participants, the socioeconomic status was comparable to other bereavement studies. Mothers' ages ranged from 19 to 43 with a mean of 31.5 (SD=4:8), while fathers' ages ranged from 20 to 47 with a mean of 33.7 (SD=5:4). Couples had been married or living together from less than 1 to 23 years (M=6:4 year, SD=4:3). More than 45% had completed a university education, while 50 (23%) listed their high school diploma as the highest level of education completed.

Table 18.1 Measures used to test the Lang's model for the Promotion of Health and Well-being in Bereaved Individuals and Families (Lang, Goulet, & Amsel, 2004)

	Elements of model	Measure	Subscales
A (the event or stressor)	A Perinatal Loss	____	____
B (resources)	B (internal resources—hardiness)	Lang & Goulet Hardiness Scale (Lang et al., 2003)	Sense of personal control, active orientation, and making sense (45 items)
	B (external resources—marital and social support)	Support behaviors inventory (Brown, 1986)	Emotional, instrumental, informational, and appraisal support behaviors (11 items)
C (appraisal of the event)	C (appraisal of the event)	Subjective appraisal ratings of stressors (Fillion et al. 1996)	Negative consequences, positive consequences, loss, danger, failure, challenge, control, coping capability, unknown, and importance (10 items)
X (outcomes—health and well-being)	X (individual grief reactions)	Perinatal grief scale (Potvin, Lasker, & Toedter, 1989)	Active grief, difficulty coping, and despair (33 items)
	X (marital satisfaction)	ENRICH marital satisfaction scale (Fowers & Olson, 1993)	Marital satisfaction and idealistic distortions (15 items)
	X (family adaptability and cohesion)	FACES II (Olson & Tiesel, 1991)	Each spouse rated how he or she perceives their family (30 items)

Conducted in Montreal, Quebec, slightly less than half of the participating couples were French Canadian, 10% were English Canadians, while nearly one-third were "other" Canadians, a mélange from various ethnic backgrounds (i.e., Greek, Italian, Lebanese, Chinese). Thirteen percent were immigrants who had recently arrived in Canada from around the globe (i.e., Europe, Africa, South America, Haiti). In contrast with bereavement studies reported in the literature, the diverse ethnocultural portrait of these participants reflected the current Canadian mosaic in Montreal.

Couples were visited in their homes at 2 (T_1), 6 (T_2), and 13 months (T_3) following their loss during which they completed a battery of questionnaires measuring the elements of the model with psychometrically sound instruments that are summarized in Table 18.1.

Lang's model for the Promotion of Health and Well-being in Bereaved Individuals and Families

Lang's model for the Promotion of Health and Well-being in Bereaved Individuals and Families is composed of A: An Event (perinatal loss), B: Resources (internal—hardiness and external—marital and social support), and C: Perceptions and Meaning Making (appraisal of the event), all together leading to X: Outcome (health and well-being). A pivotal element of this model is the "family as the focus of care," reflecting the importance of caring for the bereaved individually and together within the context of the family.

(A) Perinatal loss

The bereavement experience triggered by a perinatal loss is the "event or the stressor." It is an event of sufficient magnitude to instigate change in the family system, and has the potential for producing stress (positive or negative) for family members. The bereavement experience depends on perceptions, resources, and the context in which the death occurs. Grief waxes and wanes throughout a person's lifetime, and dealing with the loss and secondary consequences of a death are potential sources of anxiety (Stroebe & Schut, 1999). Bereaved family members do not achieve closure after a death, but rather struggle to reconcile a new normal life without the physical presence of their loved one. There is also a significant discrepancy in the types of grief that are experienced, as well as in their intensity, duration, and expression (Christ et al., 2003; Stroebe & Schut, 1999).

(B) Resources (internal and external)

Resources, both internal as well as external, are potential "individual/personal and collective strengths." They may be characteristics, traits, competencies, or means of a person, family, or community. Lang's model includes the concept of hardiness, an important predictor of health in bereaved individuals, as the internal resource for coping with grief (Lang et al., 2004).

Marital and social supports underpin the external resources for the bereaved. External resources also help to protect against psychological suffering in stressful situations such as bereavement, and reconcile some of the stress of important life transitions (Rubin & Malkinson, 2001; Schaefer & Moos, 1998). Variations and examples of such external supports may include the following: family resources (i.e., cohesion, adaptability (Olson, 2000; Olson & Gorall, 1993)), level of marital satisfaction (Kelly & Conley, 1987; Kurdek, 1995), degree of family functioning (Davies, 1986; Sawin & Harrigan, 1994), communication (Caelli, Downie, & Letendre, 2002; Kavanaugh & Paton, 2001; Saflund, Sjogren, & Wredling, 2004; Satir, 1972), and community resources (i.e., characteristics, competencies, means of persons, groups, institutions outside of the family).

(C) Perceptions and meaning making

Perceptions and meaning making encompass the idea of family members' "appraisal" of the event and its subsequent impact on them and their relationships. Perception is a powerful factor that is instrumental to coping, and in turn, health and well-being (Lang et al., 2004). Family members' perceptions and the meanings that they attribute to the death and their bereavement experiences may be dissimilar from one another, and are often different from that of an objective outsider (Becvar, 2001; Boss, 2002). Although a person can be alone in his or her grieving, we must recognize that family, friends or others around him or her often influence that individual's grieving process. Family members, individually and collectively, attribute their own meaning and reality to the event, regardless of the facts (Boss, 2002).

(X) Health and well-being

Health and well-being are the "outcomes" in this model. Health and well-being have both individual/personal as well as relational elements that are affected by the interplay between bereavement, resources, and meaning making. Similarly, health and well-being also impact the other components of the model in a responsive and dynamic fashion. Furthermore, health and well-being are the desired outcomes for individuals, couples, families, and communities. The nature and level of health and well-being are assessed in the context of what is appropriate and optimal for a particular individual, family, or community and are based on individual and collective choices, judgments, and perceptions.

Family: The Focus of Care

Family, as the focus of care, is the core and anchoring element of the model. Family is the context in which individuals learn about health and how to mobilize resources, strengths, and potentials in order to reach their goals (Feeley & Gottlieb, 2000).

Caring

Caring is the connective and flexible cord woven throughout and that unifies the elements of the model. Caring as defined in Swanson's (1993) Caring Theory, is "a nurturing way to relate to a valued other, towards whom one feels a personal sense of commitment and responsibility" (Swanson, 1991, p. 161).

Swanson (1993) characterizes caring as being composed of five overlapping processes: maintaining belief, knowing, being with, doing for, and enabling. *Maintaining belief* is a fundamental belief by the clinician in family members and their capacity to make it through events and transitions, such as

LANG'S MODEL FOR THE PROMOTION OF HEALTH AND WELL-BEING
IN BEREAVED INDIVIDUALS AND FAMILIES

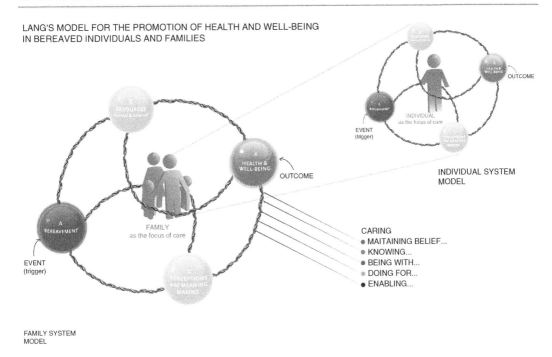

Fig. 18.2 Lang's model for the Promotion of Health and Well-being in Bereaved Individuals and Families

the death of their baby, and to face a future with meaning. *Knowing* refers to knowing in general about health, loss, and bereavement; and knowing about the family's specific situation and lived reality (e.g., the type of loss and spiritual or cultural context). *Being with* consists of having an emotional and authentic presence, attentive listening, offering reflective responses. It is the availability and ability to endure and share with another's reality. *Doing for* pertains to comforting bereaved family members, anticipating their needs, and protecting them from undue harm while preserving their dignity. It is about providing safe arenas for people to bring about their own healing. Finally, *enabling* denotes facilitating passage for family members through transitions and unfamiliar events, such as death and bereavement, coaching and clarifying, maintaining a focus on important issues, offering feedback, and validating the realities of others.

Results

In addition to being equally relevant to both mothers and fathers, the robustness of the model was evident across time. Moreover, hardiness emerged as a consistent and important predictor of health. Its strength and endurance at baseline (2 months), in particular, makes it a pivotal element of the model for bereaved parents, both as individuals and as a couple. It is assumed that each individual exhibits some degree of hardiness, which may be more or less obvious depending on the situation and the time frame (Lang et al., 2001). Furthermore, the change in hardiness scores over time, as measured by the Lang Goulet Hardiness Scale (Lang, Goulet, & Amsel 2003), indicates that hardiness is not a personality trait but rather a personal resource, potentially amenable to change (Maddi et al., 2002; Ouellette, 1993), suggesting it could be learned and reinforced. The findings from this study contributed to the model evolving into its current state (Fig. 18.2) and becoming the foundation for the development of a Bereavement Care Primer for Systems Change (Lang et al., in press) to be implemented in hospitals as well as home and community settings.

Box 18.1

T_1: "Can you tell me a little about what happened?"
T_2 and T_3: "Can you tell me about what has been happening since the last time we met?"

Hardiness in Depth

Given that hardiness consistently emerged as the single strongest predictor of health in bereaved mothers and fathers, both individually and as couple over time, how hardiness manifested in this population was explored in greater detail (Lang & MacLean, 2007). In addition, the experiences and perceptions of bereaved parents (husbands and wives) with "high hardiness" (HH) were compared to those with "low hardiness" (LH). Following completion of the questionnaires, each of the 110 couples took part in a co-joint semistructured interview that was audio-taped. At T_1 (2 months) couples were asked only one major question, which was about their experience with and their perception of their loss (Box 18.1). At subsequent visits, their reflections focused on their experiences and perceptions since the previous interview and once again only one major question was asked.

For the purpose of this in-depth analysis of hardiness, a subgroup of ten couples was selected: five in which both husband and wife scored high on the Hardiness Scale and five in which both husband and wife scored low. The demographics for this subgroup were consistent with the larger sample ($N = 110$), including the type of loss that ranged from first trimester pregnancy loss to sudden infant death syndrome (SIDS). The tapes from all three time points (T_1, T_2, T_3) were transcribed verbatim for each couple. Categories identifying hardiness and its components emerged from the data. As a first step, categories related to hardiness were explored with the extreme cases subjected to triangulation and disconfirmation procedures.

Bereaved couples in the HH group and LH group were found to diverge along the dimensions of sense of personal control and making sense but not with respect to active orientation. HH and LH couples discussed these issues in different ways and at different times. Even though both groups spontaneously described elements of hardiness within their narratives, HH couples generally expressed them more frequently and at greater length and depth than did couples with LH (Lang & MacLean, 2007). Some examples from HH include:

> I realize that there is nothing I could have done to change it so it wasn't in my power…it just happened and it was either we accept it and moved on or we didn't accept it and we stalled and made it more difficult for each other. …the grieving process takes a long time…every month that goes by you learn something new about yourself and how much you can accept and deal with something.

HH couples were more adept at attaining or regaining a sense of personal control while the LH couples were often not as successful. For example:

> Zero positive … ridiculous… like finding something spiritual, please! I find it ludicrously irritating that someone would want to waste their time finding something good in this situation…there is nothing good about finding your son dead in his crib… anybody who finds good in it was probably "####" up to begin with that they needed something like this to happen to find spirituality.

LH couples sometimes stayed trapped in their capacity to move on, fixating on elements of the experience where they felt most out of control. They tended to stay centered on events or perceptions that caused them pain and more often discussed themes of wanting but not receiving acknowledgement from others for their loss and grief, hurtful comments by others, and discussions of "the glass being half empty rather than half full."

As their stories unfolded, elements of hardiness emerged for each bereaved parent, at each data collection point, regardless of their score on the LGHS or the age of the baby at the time of its demise (Lang & MacLean, 2007). This evidence is compelling given that the narratives were not designed to elicit aspects of hardiness and no specific questions pertaining to hardiness were asked during the interview. Moreover, it offers further confirmation that hardiness does change over time (Lang et al., 2003; Lang, Goulet, & Amsel, 2004; Lang & MacLean, 2007), lending support to the argument that it is a personal resource, potentially amenable to change, and not a personality trait. It also reinforces the increasing evidence that personal resources may play a greater role than originally thought in the way people deal with such unexpected and important stressful situations (Campbell et al., 1991; Orr & Westman, 1990). Indeed, hardiness has been shown to be an effective personal resource, which can diminish potentially negative effects of life stress (Duquette et al., 1995; Lang et al., 2004; Maddi et al., 2002). Rather than responding to stress only when it is unavoidable, individuals who have learned to draw this resource forth seek out change, and instead of suffering the harmful effects of stress, are able to thrive in the face of adversity. The testimonials from these bereaved couples offer insights that help to illustrate and reinforce hardiness as an important predictor of health that may help to explain disparities observed in the responses of parents to the death of their baby.

Current Issues

As noted at the outset, the death of a fetus or infant is a prevalent and often a life transforming event. Yet, more often than not, bereaved parents and families do not receive appropriate care even though widespread consensus on the need for care and support exists in the literature and among professionals in the field (Lang et al., 2005). Reports of changes in hospital protocols have led to a false sense of security about the quality of care provided to parents experiencing the death of their baby as the few bereavement programs that have been evaluated have used only specially trained grief workers to offer the interventions (Murray et al., 2000; Swanson, 1998). Indeed, in a systematic review to determine the effectiveness of support interventions after perinatal death, Chambers and Chan (2004) reported that no studies met their eligibility criteria for inclusion and erroneously came to the conclusion that routine management of perinatal death over the past two decades has evolved to an extent where "the provision of empathic caring environment, and strategies to enable the mother and family to accept the reality of the death, are now part of standard nursing and social support in most of the developed world" (p. 1). Extensive clinical and research experience and other authors suggest otherwise (JBI, 2006; Lang et al., in press). For example, some have detailed that caregivers' lack of knowledge about the physical, emotional, social, and spiritual impact on individuals and families after perinatal loss, together with a sense of discomfort with bereavement, frequently spills over into caregiving, rendering it inadequate and often detrimental (Lang & MacLean, 2007; Ujda & Bendiksen, 2000). Furthermore, health and social care providers as well as society at large tend to underestimate the long-term impact that a perinatal death can have on a family, often resulting in interventions that are short term, limited, and possibly inappropriate.

Family members may not know about, want, or know how to seek bereavement care. They often perceive that time heals all wounds (Moules et al., 2004) and that grief is something to be endured personally and outside the health and social care system. People and society as a whole hold beliefs about death and grief that can facilitate or constrain bereavement experiences. When clinicians enter into relationships with family members around death, they also enter into relationships with the grief experiences of the family members, in addition to their own personal experiences with sorrow (Becvar, 2001). Clinicians, like most members of society, often are not comfortable with death and with those who are bereaved. They need to overcome their uneasiness and have confidence in the merit of their role and the potential impact of their caring interventions. Bereavement care does not just begin after a death but also includes the time leading up to, surrounding, and following the death. There are no prescribed stages of grief and there is no "right" way to grieve. Every individual has his or her own unique way to manage and cope with the death of a loved one. Thus, it is critical that clinicians be aware of their own personal losses and how the experiences of the bereaved can impact these losses and their ability to provide appropriate care (Genevro et al., 2003; JBI, 2006; Lang et al., in press).

Clinical Implications: Primary Bereavement Care

Caring for the bereaved is vital in order to sustain and promote the health of individuals, families, and communities. To date, the focus of bereavement care "interventions" has centered on those who present with complications rather than on primary prevention intervention (Genevro et al., 2003; JBI, 2006). For example, most people do not seek health care nor do they perceive their experience of bereavement to be one requiring professional help, despite the possible intensity of suffering. However, there is an acknowledged need for nurses and other health-care providers to attend to all who are bereaved (Gottlieb et al., 1996; JBI, 2006; Lang et al., 2004; Lang & MacLean, 2007; Williams, O'Brien, Laughton, & Jelinek, 2000).

Primary bereavement care is a relatively new term, first coined within the Bereavement Care Bereavement Care Primer for Systems Change (Lang et al., in press). It reflects the necessity to shift the bereavement care approach to prevention and health promotion rather than intervening only when negative consequences are revealed. It is also imperative to highlight that the "work" of primary bereavement care is not an additional task for nurses and other clinicians to perform in our present resource-challenged health-care system. Primary bereavement care is defined as capturing and creating opportunities to be with and support individuals and families in their experiences of grief and mourning surrounding the death of a loved one (Lang et al., 2011). It includes actively and openly acknowledging and validating both the death and people's experiences of bereavement; providing appropriate and discerning "anticipatory guidance" about grief reactions; ensuring a network for continuity of care as well as appropriate resources (time, staffing, experts/teachers, physical space, funds); and developing and implementing primary bereavement care-centered initiatives and policies (Lang et al., in press). Regardless of where and by whom care is provided, "a compassionate approach by all professional and non-professional staff is consistently reported by the bereaved as having a positive impact on their bereavement…[and that] conversely, approaches which do not relay such compassion can impact negatively" (JBI, 2006). The aforementioned evidence upholds the notion that it behooves us to connect with all who are bereaved in a caring, preventive, and upstream manner, and confirms the need for primary bereavement care—specifically through family-centered approaches, tailored interventions according to needs in all settings, and assurance of continuity of care. Thus, the human and financial costs of providing support for the bereaved should be set against the potential long-term personal and societal costs of not providing bereavement support (JBI, 2006).

Family-systems, crisis, and communication theories provide an empirical and theoretical evidence base for primary bereavement care practices (Boss, 2002; Stroebe et al., 2001; Tedeschi, Park, & Calhoun, 1998; Wright & Leahy, 2005). For most bereaved individuals, care in the form of general, supportive types of interventions that are appropriate and meaningful around the time of death, regardless of setting, can be provided by all nurses given their ubiquitous presence around the death of a baby. For others, additional care may constitute more in-depth, focused, secondary and tertiary prevention activities that are essential for "at risk" family members, and for which specialized education and practice are crucial. A key component of this care is to adapt to the uniqueness and individuality of the

Table 18.2 Practice, education, and research recommendations

Practice recommendations	Education recommendations	Research recommendations	Policy and community development
1. Proactive nursing practice includes bereavement care with family members 2. Nurses acquire the knowledge, skills, attitudes, and aptitudes to approach bereavement care with compassion 3. Nurses ensure continuity of care for the bereaved 4. Organizations value and support bereavement care with family members 5. Organizations recognize and support the nurses who provide bereavement care 6. Organizations ensure continuity of care for the bereaved by building and sustaining connections and relationships with other health and human services	1. Nurses develop, nurture, and evaluate an ongoing awareness of themselves in relation to bereavement and bereavement care, both personally and professionally 2. Nurses are committed to ongoing professional development of their knowledge, skills, attitudes, and aptitudes in bereavement care 3. Academic nursing programs (entry-level and advanced) include education about bereavement and bereavement care 4. Organizations include education about bereavement and bereavement care in all orientation and continuing nursing education initiatives, regardless of practice settings (i.e., emergency, obstetrics, medical/surgical, out-patient clinics, etc.) 5. Organizations utilize the Bereavement Care Primer for Systems Change for quality and safety improvement initiatives	1. Nurses stimulate and advance research about bereavement and bereavement care as an integral part of their daily practice 2. Nurse researchers who study bereavement and bereavement care seek opportunities to share research outcomes and new knowledge and their applicability to the practice setting. Nurse researchers also seek opportunities to listen to and learn from the voices and experiences of practicing nurses 3. Organizations assist in developing and advancing research about bereavement and bereavement care	1. Nurses and organizations, in partnership, advocate for changes in public policy 2. Nurses and organizations, in partnership, facilitate and promote intersectoral, interdisciplinary, and stakeholder collaboration to support the health of bereaved individuals, families, and communities

experiences and needs of bereaved family members. Given the evidence of potential negative health consequences following the death of a loved one and the recognized need for support, primary bereavement care must be integral to and prioritized on health-care agendas and services, particularly in nursing practice.

In partnership with the Victorian Order of Nurses (VON), Lang (PI) and her colleagues used a collaborative approach to cocreate the Bereavement Care Primer for Systems Change (Lang et al., in press). The primer is composed of recommendations targeted at different levels of system change (i.e., practice, education, research, policy/community development) and is based on the Long's model for the Promotion of Health and Well-being in Bereaved Individuals and Families. Research suggests that evidence-informed guidelines are a valuable part of knowledge translation strategies (Francke, Smit, de Veer, & Mistiaen, 2008; Davies, Edwards, Ploeg, & Virani, 2008; Hakkennes & Dodd, 2008). Although these recommendations for systems change are directed at nurses, they are also applicable to the wider interdisciplinary team. The major recommendations of this primer are summarized in Table 18.2.

Using primer and the Lang's model for the Promotion of Health and Well-being in Bereaved Individuals and Families as a guiding framework, health and social care providers can play a significant role in promoting hardiness in individuals and families experiencing perinatal loss. Clinicians can enable bereaved parents to attain a sense of personal control through the following:

(a) The exercise of knowledge, skill, and choice of attitude
(b) An active orientation in seeking and utilizing available supports
(c) A willingness to consider different strategies to cope with difficult situations

(d) Facilitating their propensity for positive reframing, thus guiding them through their search following an arduous event such as the death of their baby

These caring processes are directed at the whole person and in many ways overlap with processes associated with spiritual care (Carr, 2008). In the spiritual care of the bereaved, perhaps the most important intervention is the "presence of a caring other who is willing to be there and to share in the grief and the pain" (O'Brien, 1999, p. 281). This need for presence may be especially true in perinatal loss, when the family or individual experiences disenfranchised grief; that is, when their loss is not publically acknowledged, openly mourned, or socially supported (Doka, 1989). In these circumstances, the bereaved may turn to transpersonal connections, such as those with God or a Higher Power. Health-care providers can play an important role in listening, giving their true presence, acknowledging the loss and grief, and supporting such transpersonal connections.

Although key elements of hardiness, such as finding meaning and having the ability to transcend the experience, may be facilitated by spiritual and religious beliefs, caregivers must not attempt to impose such beliefs. For example, one would not say, "This must have been God's will" (O'Brien, 1999, pp. 283–284) or offer empty reassurances, such as "I understand;" "It will all be okay;" "Life could be worse;" "Everything happens for a reason;" "Count your blessings;" and so forth (Wright, 2005, pp. 155–156). These are judgmental statements that can do harm. It is critical, instead, that parents' suffering, as it is uniquely experienced, be acknowledged and that we invite, listen, and witness their stories of suffering and loss (Wright). We can encourage their stories by using questions to open dialogue about their bereavement, such as "What have you been feeling since the funeral?" "What sorts of memories keep coming back?" "Have you had trouble going on?" (O'Brien, 1999, pp. 285–286). We can acknowledge their loss and suffering by statements, such as "This time in your life is really tough;" "What your family is experiencing is a real loss;" "I can only imagine how difficult it must be for you and your family" (Wright, 2005, p. 150). By having their grief acknowledged and the opportunity to tell their story, the bereaved can find their own meaning (Frank, 1994).

Research Implications

Given the evidence for potential negative health consequences following perinatal loss as well as other types of death of a loved one, and the documented need for support to help individuals and families in a preventative and health promoting fashion, bereavement care must be integral to health-care agendas and services. Primary bereavement care should be a priority. A recent seminal report highlighted "the need for improved linkages between bereavement research and practice in order to determine and promote the most appropriate and meaningful care for [the] bereaved" (Genevro et al., 2003, pp. 11–12). In addition to ensuring that the most relevant research questions are addressed, strong reciprocal relationships among researchers, practitioners, as well as clinical and policy decision-makers are keys to the effective short- and long-term adoption of evidence into practice, and are the basis for building capacity for systems change (Graham et al., 2006; Lindstrom, 2003; Lomas, 1997; NCDDR, 2006).

Primary bereavement care can play a pivotal role in fostering hardiness among individuals and families experiencing perinatal loss. Yet, research suggests that the focus of bereavement care tends to be on tertiary rather than primary prevention strategies. There is a need, therefore, for research using a systems approach to explore how acute and home/community care organizations can establish and maintain policies and practices that support a primary bereavement care approach as an evidence-informed standard, while examining and responding to factors that support or impede this change process.

There are numerous examples of system-level factors that create either an absence or a fragmentation of support services for the bereaved. For example, caring for the bereaved does not consistently fall under the agenda of one particular segment of the health/social system, one professional group, or jurisdiction of any governmental body. This fragmentation contributes to lack of continuity of care and often leads to disjointed secondary and tertiary bereavement services as well as a lack of primary care services.

Research is currently underway to map out how both acute and home/community care organizations use recommendations from the Bereavement Care Primer of Systems Change to improve the care and services that they provide to individuals and families following the death of a loved one. This proposed research will encompass a variety of patient care populations, including those faced with a perinatal loss. The ultimate goal of this research is the establishment of a national consensus and set of standards for primary bereavement care in multiple settings and jurisdictions. The persisting challenge is to understand and galvanize effective strategies for knowledge translation (KT) and sustainability of evidence-informed practice within organizations and the larger health and social care system. This requires a large system change through effective KT strategies with key stakeholders across sectors and regions. A systems approach is essential to successfully begin the process of integrating primary bereavement care as an evidence-informed standard, while examining and responding to factors that support or impede this change process.

Model Case Example

To conduct research and provide care with the aim of improving health outcomes following a perinatal loss, it is helpful to have an illustrative example of what those positive health outcomes can look like. To see how, for example, key internal resources, such as hardiness, can be learned and fostered over time, and how they can operate to help families experience eventual growth, well-being, and self-actualization following a personal tragedy. The following is an example derived from clinical practice illustrating how all of the defining attributes of hardiness can function toward positive health outcomes and growth following the death of a baby.

Rachel and Edgar are parents who, 2 years earlier, lost their 4-month-old son Joseph to Sudden Infant Death Syndrome (SIDS). For the first few weeks Rachel was unable to function. She cried inconsolably, hardly interacting with anyone, including her surviving 3 year old twins, Erin and Zoe. Edgar, feeling the social pressures on a man to be strong, pushed his own grief aside and eventually coaxed his wife out of bed and back into family life. With the support and nurturing that Rachel was willing to accept, primarily from her husband, she slowly began to consider life without Joseph. She decided that although Joseph was dead he remained a part of her family. While looking at family photos 1 year after their loss, Rachel and Edgar explained to the twins, in a way that 3 year-olds would understand, why their brother was gone. On the anniversary of the death, they took Erin and Zoe to visit the cemetery and encouraged them to ask questions about Joseph. Rachel was willing to seek out information and support to help herself and her family cope with the loss. Seeking out the resources available to bereaved parents, she joined a support group for SIDS families. Rachel says that she realizes how life can change at any time and therefore she makes every effort to enjoy each day to the fullest. She says that she has reassessed her priorities in life and as a result has strengthened her relationship with those who are most important to her.

This short sequence exemplifies a hardy individual in Rachel. Having weathered the storm over the past 2 years, she believes that change in life is inevitable and often unpredictable, and she chooses to nurture and appreciate what she has. Although the loss of her son was beyond her control, Rachel has chosen her attitude over time by becoming active in helping herself, her family, and others through this difficult time while still allowing herself to feel her own pain. She demonstrates an inclination to seek and accept help from others. Her active orientation is also reflected in her willingness to consider different coping strategies to help herself and her family, such as joining a support group and including and helping her 3-year-old twins in the grieving experience. Presently, she makes sense of her existence by her propensity to reframe and situate the effects of her loss on herself and her life. Rachel says that she has learned over time to reassess her priorities in life and, as a result, has strengthened her relationships with the people who are most important to her. She seems to have attained a higher and more meaningful level of connectedness with her family by investing in each day to the fullest.

Conclusion

The concept of hardiness has been studied in many different contexts and settings. In this chapter we explored hardiness as a key resource and precursor to coping that can help families endure and even thrive following the death of a fetus or infant. This represents a shift from traditional approaches, which have tended to focus on the deleterious effects of perinatal loss rather than on the potential for recovery and growth. The concept of hardiness is closely related to more recent definitions of resiliency that go beyond the notion of bouncing back to status quo. Instead, in response to life stressors, hardy individuals can achieve a higher level of health and well-being, the ability to transcend, and engage in self-actualization (Lang et al., 2001). As a personal resource, hardiness is characterized by a sense of control, an active orientation, and the ability to make sense of one's own existence. A hardy individual is more inclined to embrace life's challenges, work through stressors, and experience growth in the face of adversity. In the context of perinatal loss, evidence was presented in this chapter demonstrating that hardiness as a personal resource can diminish the negative effects of this traumatic life event. How this can occur and what it can look like was then presented in a model case example, which illustrated all of the defining attributes of hardiness.

Research indicates that hardiness is not an inborn trait, but rather a personal resource that can be learned and reinforced (Lang et al., 2001, 2003, 2004; Maddi et al., 2002; Ouellette, 1993). Using the primer and Lang's model for the Promotion of Health and Well-being in Bereaved Individuals and Families as guiding frameworks, health-care providers can play an important role in promoting hardiness in individuals and families experiencing perinatal loss. To do this, care approaches need to move beyond attending only to those who present with complications. Instead, primary prevention interventions must become the standard of care. Such interventions need to occur at practice, education, and policy levels, and must be championed by direct care providers, the organization in which the care is provided, as well as the larger health and social care system. The Bereavement Care Primer for Systems Change is an evidence-based tool that provides recommendations for such interventions. Research is now needed that explores at a systems level how organizations in both acute and home/community settings can establish and maintain primary prevention as the standard rather than the exception for bereavement care. Factors that support or impede this shift also need to be investigated.

To successfully implement primary prevention strategies and foster hardiness among individuals and families around perinatal loss, organizations and the larger health and social-care system must value and support bereavement care. They need to ensure that appropriate resources are available (e.g., time, staffing, space, funds), to acknowledge that the care provider's own well-being is vital to successful bereavement care, and to develop and implement bereavement initiatives and policies (Lang et al., in press). Doing so will help more individuals and families develop hardiness as a personal resource and thereby experience growth rather than disintegration following a perinatal loss.

References

Agaibi, C. E., & Wilson, J. P. (2005). Trauma, PTSD, and resilience: A review of the literature. *Trauma, Violence & Abuse, 6*, 195–216.

Åhman, E., & Zupan, J. (2004). Neonatal and perinatal mortality: Country, regional and global estimates. Geneva: World Health Organization. Retrieved December 14th, 2011 from http://whqlibdoc.who.int/publications/2007/9789241596145_eng.pdf733.

Antonovsky, A. (1993). The structure and properties of the Sense of Coherence Scale. *Social Science & Medicine, 36*, 725–733.

Badenhorst, W., Riches, S., Turton, P., & Hughes, P. (2006). The psychological effects of stillbirth and neonatal death on fathers: Systematic review. *Journal of Psychosomatic Obstetrics and Gynaecology, 27*(4), 245–256.

Becvar, D. S. (2001). *In the presence of grief: Helping family members resolve death, dying, and bereavement issues.* New York, NY: The Guilford Press.

Becvar, D. S. (2007). *Families that flourish: Facilitating resilience in clinical practice.* New York: W. W. Norton.

Bishop, F., & Yardley, L. (2010). The development and initial validation of a new measure of lay definitions of health: The wellness beliefs scale. *Psychology and Health, 25*(3), 271–287.

Black, B., & Sandelowski, M. (2010). Personal growth after severe fetal diagnosis. *Western Journal of Nursing Research, 32*(8), 1011–1030.

Bonanno, G. A. (2004). Loss, trauma, and human resilience. *The American Psychologist, 59*, 20–28.

Bonanno, G. A., & Kaltman, S. (2001). The varieties of grief experience. *Clinical Psychology Review, 21*, 705.

Boss, P. (2002). *Family stress management* (2nd ed.). Thousand Oaks, CA: Sage Publications.

Boss, P. (2004). Ambiguous loss. In F. Walsh & M. McGoldrick (Eds.), *Living beyond loss: Death in the family* (2nd ed., pp. 237–246). New York: Norton.

Boss, P. (2006). *Loss, trauma, and resilience: Therapeutic work with ambiguous loss.* New York: Norton.

Brown, M. A. (1986). Social support during pregnancy: A unidimensional or multidimensional construct? *Nursing Research, 35*(1), 4–9.

Büchi, S., Mörgeli, H., Schnyder, U., Jenewein, J., Hepp, U., Jina, E., et al. (2007). Grief and post-traumatic growth in parents 2–6 years after the death of their extremely premature baby. *Psychotherapy and Psychosomatics, 76*, 106–114.

Cacciatore, J., DeFrain, J., & Jones, K. (2008). When a baby dies: Ambiguity and stillbirth. *Marriage and Family Review, 44*(4), 439–454.

Caelli, K., Downie, J., & Letendre, A. (2002). Parents' experiences of midwife-managed care following the loss of a baby in a previous pregnancy. *Journal of Advanced Nursing, 39*(2), 127–136.

Callister, L. C. (2006). Parental loss: A family perspective. *The Journal of Perinatal & Neonatal Nursing, 20*(3), 227–234.

Campbell, J., Swank, P., & Vincent, K. (1991). The role of hardiness in the resolution of grief. *Omega, 32*(1), 53–65.

Carr, T. (2008). Mapping the processes and qualities of spiritual nursing care. *Qualitative Health Research, 18*(5), 686–700.

Chambers, H. M., & Chan, F. Y. (2004). Support for women/families after perinatal death (Cochrane review). In *The Cochrane library* (Vol. 2). Chichester, UK: Wiley.

Chiu, L., Emblen, J. D., Van Hofwegen, L., Sawatzky, R., & Meyerhoff, H. (2004). An integrative review of the concept of spirituality in the health sciences. *Western Journal of Nursing Research, 26*(4), 405–428.

Christ, G., Bonanno, G., Malkinson, R., & Rubin, S. (2003). Bereavement experiences after the death of a child. In M. Field & R. Berhman (Eds.), *When children die: Improving palliative and end-of-life care for children and their families* (pp. 553–579). Washington, DC: National Academy Press.

Christakis, N. A., & Allison, P. D. (2006). Mortality after the hospitalization of a spouse. *The New England Journal of Medicine, 354*, 719–730.

Christakis, N. A., & Iwashyna, T. J. (2003). The health impact on families of health care: A matched cohort study of hospice use by decedents and mortality outcomes in surviving, widowed spouses. *Social Science & Medicine, 57*, 465–475.

Como, J. M. (2007). Spiritual practice: A literature review related to spiritual health and health outcomes. *Holistic Nursing Practice, 21*(5), 224–236.

Davies, B. (1986). Manifestations of levels of functioning in grieving families. *Journal of Family Issues, 7*(3), 297–313.

Davies, B., Edwards, N., Ploeg, J., & Virani, T. (2008). Insights about the process and impact of implementing nursing guidelines on delivery of care in hospitals and community settings. *BMC Health Services Research, 8*(29), 1–15.

Davis, C. G., Wortman, C. B., Lehman, D. R., & Silver, R. C. (2000). Searching for meaning in loss: Are clinical assumptions correct? *Death Studies, 24*, 497–540.

Davydov, D. M., Stewart, R., Ritchie, K., & Chaudieu, I. (2010). Resilience and mental health. *Clinical Psychology Review, 30*, 479–495.

Demerath, N. J. (2000). Varieties of sacred experience: Finding the sacred in a secular grove. *Journal for the Scientific Study of Religion, 39*(1), 1–11.

Doka, K. J. (1989). Disenfranchised loss. In K. J. Doka (Ed.), *Disenfranchised grief: Recognizing hidden sorrow*. Lexington: Lexington Books D. C. Health & Co.

Duquette, A., Kerouac, S., Sandhu, B. K., Ducharme, F., & Saulnier, P. (1995). Psychosocial determinants of burnout in geriatric nursing. *International Journal of Nursing Studies, 32*(5), 443–456.

Dyregrov, A., & Dyregrov, K. (Eds.). (2004). *In living with loss over time—Bottle it up or talk it through?* Edmonton, AB: SIDS International Conference.

Earvolino-Ramirez, M. (2007). Resilience: A concept analysis. *Nursing Forum, 42*(2), 73–82.

Erlangsen, A., Jeune, B., Bille-Brahe, U., & Vaupel, J. W. (2004). Loss of partner and suicide risks among oldest old: A population-based register study. *Age and Ageing, 33*, 378–383.

Farran, C. J., Paun, O., & Elliott, M. H. (2003). Spirituality in multicultural caregivers of persons with dementia. *Dementia, 2*(3), 353–377.

Feeley, N., & Gottlieb, L. N. (2000). Nursing approaches for working with family strengths and resources. *Journal of Family Nursing, 6*(1), 9–24.

Fillion, L., Hurwitz, B. E., Fletcher, M. A., Graves, J. S., Klimas, N. G., & Schneiderman, N. (1996). *Reliability and validity of the SARS in assessing the cognitive appraisal of HIV status*. Paper presented at the Fourth International Congress of Behavioral Medicine, Washington, DC.

Folkman, S. (1984). Personal control and stress and coping processes: A theoretical analysis. *Journal of Personality and Social Psychology, 46*, 839–852.

Folkman, S., & Moskowitz, J. T. (2000). Stress, positive emotion, and coping. *Current Directions in Psychological Science, 9*, 115–118.

Fowers, B. J., & Olson, D. H. (1993). ENRICH marital satisfaction scale: A brief research and clinical tool. *Journal of Family Psychology, 7*(2), 176–185.

Francke, A. L., Smit, M. C., de Veer, A. J. E., & Mistiaen, P. (2008). Factors influencing the implementation of clinical guidelines for health care professionals: A systematic review. *BMC Medical Informatics and Decision Making, 8*(28), 1–15.

Frank, A. W. (1994). Interrupted stories, interrupted lives. *Second Opinion, 20*(1), 11–18.

Ganellen, R. J., & Blaney, P. H. (1984). Hardiness and social support as moderators of the effects of life stress. *Journal of Personality and Social Psychology, 47*, 156–163.

Genevro, J. L., Marshall, T., & Miller, T. (2003). *Report on grief and bereavement research*. Washington, DC: Centre for the Advancement of Health (CFAH).

Gilbert, K. R. (1989). Interactive grief and coping in the marital dyad. *Death Studies, 13*, 605–626.

Gilbert, K. R., & Smart, L. S. (1992). *Coping with infant or fetal loss: The couple's healing process*. New York: Brunner/Mazel.

Gillespie, B. M., Chaboyer, W., & Wallis, M. (2007). Development of a theoretically derived model of resilience through concept analysis. *Contemporary Nurse, 25*, 124–135.

Gottlieb, L. N., Lang, A., & Amsel, R. (1996). The long-term effects of grief on marital intimacy following infant death. *Omega, 33*(1), 1–19.

Graham, I. D., Logan, J., Harrison, M., Straus, S. E., Tetroe, J., Caswell, W., et al. (2006). Lost in knowledge translation: Time for a map? *The Journal of Continuing Education in the Health Professions, 26*(1), 13–24.

Hakkennes, S., & Dodd, K. (2008). Guideline implementation in allied health professions: A systematic review of the literature. *Quality & Safety in Health Care, 17*, 296–300.

Hill, R. (1958). Generic features of families under stress. *Social Casework, 49*(2), 139–150.

Hughes, P., & Riches, S. (2003). Psychological aspects of perinatal loss. *Current Opinion in Obstetrics and Gynecology, 15*, 107–111.

Joanna Briggs Institute (JBI). (2006). *Literature review on bereavement and bereavement care*. Garthdee, Aberdeen: The Joanna Briggs Collaborating Centre.

Johnson, M. P., & Puddifoot, J. E. (1996). The grief response in the partners of women who miscarry. *The British Journal of Medical Psychology, 69*, 313–327.

Kavanaugh, K., & Paton, J. B. (2001). Communicating with parents who experience a perinatal loss. *Illness Crisis and Loss, 9*(4), 369–380.

Kelly, E. L., & Conley, J. J. (1987). Personality and compatibility: A prospective analysis of marital stability and marital satisfaction. *Journal of Personality and Social Psychology, 52*(1), 27–40.

Kobasa, S. C. (1979). Stressful life events, personality, and health: An inquiry into hardiness. *Journal of Personality and Social Psychology, 37*, 1–11.

Krueger, G. (2006). Meaning-making in the aftermath of sudden infant death syndrome. *Nursing Inquiry, 13*(3), 163–171.

Kurdek, L. A. (1995). Predicting change in marital satisfaction from husbands' and wives' conflict resolution styles. *Journal of Marriage and the Family, 57*, 153–164.

Lambert, C. E., & Lambert, V. A. (1987). Hardiness: Its development and relevance to nursing. *Image—The Journal of Nursing Scholarship, 19*, 92–95.

Lang, A., Duhamel, F., Fleiszer, A., Sword, W., Aston, M., & Gilbert, K. (in press). *Bereavement Care Primer for Systems Change*. Ottawa, Canada: Victorian Order of Nurses (VON) Canada.

Lang, A., Edwards, N., & Benzies, K. (2005). A "false sense of security" in caring for bereaved parents. *Birth, 32*(2), 158–159.

Lang, A., Fleiszer, A., Duhamel, F., Sword, W., Gilbert, K., & Corsini-Munt, S. (2011). Perinatal loss and parental grief: The challenge of ambiguity and disenfranchisement. *Omega: Journal of Death and Dying, 63*(2), 183–196.

Lang, A., & Gottlieb, L. (1993). Parental grief reactions and marital intimacy following infant death. *Death Studies, 17*(3), 233–255.

Lang, A., Gottlieb, L. N., & Amsel, R. (1996). Predictors of husbands' and wives' grief reactions following infant death: The role of marital intimacy. *Death Studies, 20*(1), 33–57.

Lang, A., Goulet, C., Aita, M., Giguere, V., Lamarre, H., & Perreault, E. (2001). Weathering the storm of perinatal bereavement via hardiness. *Death Studies, 25*(6), 497–512.

Lang, A., Goulet, C., & Amsel, R. (2003). Lang and Goulet hardiness scale. *Death Studies, 27*(10), 1–30.

Lang, A., Goulet, C., & Amsel, R. (2004). Explanatory model of health in bereaved parents post fetal/infant death. *International Journal of Nursing Studies, 41*(8), 869–880.

Lang, A., & MacLean, L. M. (2007). Hardiness in bereaved parents following fetal or infant death. In P. T. Wong, L. C. Wong, M. J. McDonald, & D. W. Klaassen (Eds.), *The positive psychology of meaning and spirituality: Selected papers from meaning conferences*. Abbotsford, BC: INPM Press.

Lee, H. J. (1983). Analysis of a concept: Hardiness. *Oncology Nursing Forum, 10*(4), 32–35.

Levine, S. Z., Laufer, A., Stein, E., Hamama-Raz, Y., & Solomon, Z. (2009). Examining the relationship between resilience and posttraumatic growth. *Journal of Traumatic Stress, 22*(4), 282–286.

Li, J., Laursen, T. M., Precht, D. H., Olsen, J., & Mortensen, P. B. (2005). Hospitalization for mental illness among parents after the death of a child. *The New England Journal of Medicine, 352*(12), 1190–1196.

Lillard, L. A., & Waite, L. J. (1995). Til death do us part: Marital disruption and mortality. *The American Journal of Sociology, 100*, 1131–1156.

Lindstrom, R. R. (2003). Evidence-based decision-making in healthcare: Exploring the issues through the lens of complex, adaptive systems theory. *Healthcare Papers, 3*(3), 29–35.

Lomas, J. (1997). Improving research dissemination and uptake in the health sector: Beyond the sound of one hand clapping. Hamilton, ON: McMaster University Centre for Health Economics and Policy Analysis. Policy Commentary C97-1. Retrieved December 14th, 2011 from http://www.chsrf.ca/knowledge_transfer/pdf/handclapping_e.pdf.

Lukose, A. (2011). Developing a practice model for Watson's Theory of Caring. *Nursing Science Quarterly, 24*(27), 27–30.

Maddi, S. R., Koshaba, D. M., Persico, M., Lu, J., Harvey, R., & Bleecker, F. (2002). The personality construct of hardiness. *Journal of Research in Personality, 36*, 72–85.

McCubbin, M. A., & McCubbin, H. I. (1993). Families coping with illness: The resiliency model of family stress, adjustment, and adaptation. In C. D. Danielson, B. Hamel-Bisseil, & T. Winstead-Fry (Eds.), *Families, health, illness: Perspectives on coping and intervention* (pp. 21–63). St. Louis, MO: C. V. Mosby.

McCubbin, M. A., McCubbin, H. I., & Thompson, A. I. (1987). Family Hardiness Index. In H. I. McCubbin & A. I. Thompson (Eds.), *Family assessment inventories for research and practice* (pp. 123–130). Madison: University of Wisconsin-Madison.

Moules, N. J., Simonson, K., Prins, M., Angus, P., & Bell, J. M. (2004). Making room for grief: Walking backwards and living forward. *Nursing Inquiry, 11*(2), 99–107.

Murray, J. A., Terry, D. J., Vance, J. C., Battistutta, D., & Connolly, Y. (2000). Effects of a program of intervention on parental distress following infant death. *Death Studies, 24*, 275–305.

Najman, J. M., Vance, J. C., Boyle, F., Embleton, G., Foster, B., & Thearle, J. (1993). The impact of a child death on marital adjustment. *Social Science & Medicine, 37*(8), 1005.

NCDDR. (2006). *Overview of international literature on knowledge translation*. FOCUS Technical Brief (14). Retrieved May 1, 2007 from http://www.ncddr.org/kt/products/focus/focus14/.

O'Brien, M. E. (1999). *Spirituality in nursing: Standing on holy ground*. Toronto, ON: Jones and Bartlett Publishers.

Olson, D. H. (2000). Circumplex model of marital and family systems. *The Association for Family Therapy and Systemic Practice, 22*, 144–167.

Olson, D. H., & Gorall, D. M. (1993). Circumplex model of marital and family systems. In F. Walsh (Ed.), *Normal family processes* (3rd ed., pp. 514–544). New York, NY: Guilford Press.

Olson, D. H., & Tiesel, J. W. (1991). *FACES II update: Linear scoring and interpretation*. St. Paul: Family Social Science, University of Minnesota.

Orr, E., & Westman, M. (1990). Does hardiness moderate stress, and how?: A review. In M. Rosenbaum (Ed.), *Learned resourcefulness: On coping skills, self-control, and adaptive behavior* (pp. 64–93). New York: Springer.

Ouellette, S. C. (1993). Inquiries into hardiness. In L. Goldberger & S. Bregnitz (Eds.), *Handbook of stress: Theoretical and clinical aspects* (2nd ed., pp. 77–100). New York: The Free Press.

Patterson, J. M. (1995). Promoting resiliency in families experiencing stress. *Pediatric Clinics of North America, 42*(1), 47–63.

Pollock, S. E. (1986). Human responses to chronic illness: Physiologic and psychosocial adaptation. *Nursing Research, 35*(2), 90–95.

Pollock, S. E. (1989). The hardiness characteristic: A motivating factor in adaptation. *Advances in Nursing Science, 11*(2), 53–62.

Potvin, L., Lasker, J., & Toedter, L. (1989). Measuring grief: A short version of the perinatal grief scale. *Journal of Psychopathology and Behavioral Assessment, 11*(1), 29–45.

Priel, B., Gonik, N., & Rabinowitz, B. (1993). Appraisals of childbirth experience and newborn characteristics: The role of hardiness and affect. *Journal of Personality, 61*, 299–315.

Puscheck, E. E. (2010). *Early pregnancy loss.* Retrieved September 17, 2010 from http://emedicine.medscape.com/article/266317-overview.

Qin, P., & Mortensen, P. B. (2003). The impact of parental status on the risk of completed suicide. *Archives of General Psychiatry, 60*, 797–802.

Rando, T. A. (1986). The unique issues and impact of the death of a child. In T. A. Rando (Ed.), *Parental loss of a child* (pp. 5–43). Champaign, IL: Research Press Company.

Rubin, S. S., & Malkinson, R. (2001). Parental response to child loss across the life cycle: Clinical and research perspectives. In M. S. Stroebe, R. O. Hansson, W. Stoebe, & H. Schut (Eds.), *Handbook of bereavement research: Consequences, coping, and care* (pp. 219–240). Washington, DC: American Psychological Association.

Saflund, K., Sjogren, B., & Wredling, R. (2004). The role of caregivers after a stillbirth: Views and experiences of parents. *Birth, 31*(2), 132–137.

Satir, V. (1972). *People making.* Palo Alto, CA: Science and Behavior Books.

Sawin, K. J., & Harrigan, M. (1994). Measures of family functioning for research and practice. *Scholarly Inquiry for Nursing Practice: An International Journal, 8*(1), 5–144.

Schaefer, J. A., & Moos, R. H. (1998). The context for posttraumatic growth: Life crises, individual and social resources, and coping. In R. G. Tedeschi, C. L. Park, & L. G. Calhoun (Eds.), *Posttraumatic growth: Positive changes in the aftermath of crisis* (pp. 99–125). Mahwah, NJ: Lawrence Erlbaum Associates.

Schulz, R., & Beach, S. R. (1999). Caregiving as a risk factor for mortality: The caregiver health effects study. *The Journal of the American Medical Association, 282*, 2215–2219.

Schwab, R. (1992). Effects of a child's death on the marital relationship: A preliminary study. *Death Studies, 16*, 141–154.

Seibel, M., & Graves, W. L. (1980). The psychological implications of spontaneous abortions. *The Journal of Reproductive Medicine, 25*(4), 161–165.

Seymour, E. L. D. (1936). *The gardening encyclopedia.* New York: W. H. Wise & Co.

Smith, E. D. (1995). Addressing the psychospiritual distress of death as reality: A transpersonal approach. *Social Work, 40*(3), 402–413.

Smith, A. C., & Borgers, S. B. (1989). Parental grief response to perinatal death. *Omega, 19*(3), 203–313.

Statistics Canada (2010). *Infant mortality rates, by province and territory (both sexes).* (Table 102-0504). Retrieved December 14th, 2011 from http://www5.statcan.gc.ca/cansim/a26?lang=eng&retrLang=eng&id=1020504&paSer=&pattern=&stByVal=1&p1=1&p2=37&tabMode=dataTable&csid=.

Stroebe, M. S., Hansson, R. O., Stroebe, W., & Schut, H. (2001). *Handbook of bereavement research: Consequences, coping, and care.* Washington, DC: American Psychological Association.

Stroebe, M. S., & Schut, H. (1999). Meaning making in the dual process model of coping with bereavement. In R. A. Neimeyer (Ed.), *Meaning reconstruction and the experience of loss* (pp. 55–73). Washington, DC: American Psychological Association.

Stroebe, M. S., & Schut, H. (2001). Risk factors in bereavement outcome: A methodological and empirical review. In M. S. Stroebe, R. O. Hansson, W. Stroebe, & H. Schut (Eds.), *Handbook of bereavement research* (pp. 349–372). Washington, DC: American Psychological Association.

Swanson, K. M. (1991). Empirical development of a middle range theory of caring. *Nursing Research, 40*(3), 161–166.

Swanson, K. M. (1993). Nursing as informed caring for the well-being of others. *Image—The Journal of Nursing Scholarship, 25*(4), 352–357.

Swanson, K. M. (1998). Research-based practice with women who have had miscarriages. *Image—The Journal of Nursing Scholarship, 31*(4), 339–345.

Tanyi, R. A. (2002). Toward clarification of the meaning of spirituality. *Journal of Advanced Nursing, 39*(5), 500–509.

Tedeschi, R. G., & Calhoun, L. G. (2004). Posttraumatic growth: Conceptual foundations and empirical evidence. *Psychological Inquiry, 15*, 1–18.

Tedeschi, R. G., & Calhoun, L. G. (2008). Beyond the concept of recovery: Growth and the experience of loss. *Death Studies, 32*, 27–39.

Tedeschi, R. G., Park, C. L., & Calhoun, L. G. (1998). *Postraumatic growth: Positive changes in the aftermath of crisis.* Mahwah, NJ: Lawrence Erlbaum Associates Incorporated Publishers.

Teixeira, M. E. (2008). Self-transcendence: A concept analysis for nursing praxis. *Holistic Nursing Practice, 22*(1), 25–31.

Theut, S. K., Pedersen, F. A., Zaslow, M. J., Cain, R. L., Rabinovich, B. A., & Morihisa, J. M. (1989). Perinatal loss and parental bereavement. *The American Journal of Psychiatry, 146*(5), 635–639.

Turton, P., Hughes, P., Evans, C. D., & Fainman, D. (2001). The incidence and significance of post traumatic stress disorder in the pregnancy after stillbirth. *The British Journal of Psychiatry, 178*, 556–560.

Ujda, R. M., & Bendiksen, R. (2000). Health care provider support and grief after perinatal loss: A qualitative study. *Illness Crisis and Loss, 8*(3), 265–285.

Van, P., & Meleis, A. I. (2003). Coping with grief after involuntary pregnancy loss: Perspectives of African American women. *Journal of Obstetric Gynecologic and Neonatal Nursing, 32*(1), 28–39.

Walker, L. O., & Avant, K. C. (1995). *Strategies for theory construction in nursing* (3rd ed.). Norwalk, CT: Appleton & Lange.

Wiebe, D. J. (1991). Hardiness and stress moderation: A test of proposed mechanisms. *Journal of Personality and Social Psychology, 60*, 89–99.

Williams, A., O'Brien, D., Laughton, K., & Jelinek, G. (2000). Improving services to bereaved relatives in the emergency department: Making healthcare more human. *The Medical Journal of Australia, 173*, 480–483.

Wing, D., Clance, P., Burge-Callaway, K., & Armistead, L. (2001). Understanding gender difference in bereavement following the death of an infant: Implications for treatment. *Psychotherapy, 38*, 60–72.

Wolf, G. A. (1990). Promoting executive hardiness. *The Journal of Nursing Administration, 20*(1), 10–11.

Wright, L. M. (2005). *Spirituality, suffering, and illness: Ideas for healing.* Philadelphia, PA: F.A. Davis Company.

Wright, L. M., & Leahy, M. (2005). *Nurses and families—A guide to family assessment and intervention* (4th ed.). Philadelphia, PA: F. A. Davis Company.

Zeanah, C. H., Danis, B., Hishberg, L., & Dietz, L. (1995). Initial adaptation in mothers and fathers following perinatal loss. *Infant Mental Health Journal, 16*(2), 80–93.

Family Resilience Relative to Parental Death

19

Abraham P. Greeff and Berquin Human

Introduction

The experience of loss due to the death of a family member constitutes an individual crisis as well as a family crisis, making the experience the most stressful life event that families face (McKenry & Price, 1994). All families will encounter the death of an immediate family member—a powerful experience that shakes the foundation of family life and leaves no member unaffected (Jordan, Kraus, & Ware, 1993; Walsh, 1998). It has long been known that certain individuals are much more competent than others in coping effectively with such situations. What about families? The death of a parent generally is considered to be one of the most stressful experiences that people encounter in the course of their lives (Shuchter & Zisook, 1993), one that calls on the family to utilize all its resources in order to adapt successfully and maintain normal family functioning.

In the past few years, the perspective that families, like individuals, may be seen as resilient as they cope with the challenges in their lives has received increasing attention from scholars all over the world (Masten & Powell, 2003; Patterson, 2002). Within the field of mental health, a definite paradigm shift from pathology-based to health-oriented, or strength-based approaches, is growing and gaining momentum. Integral to this health-oriented paradigm is resilience, the ability to rebound after being stressed or challenged, as well as being able to rise above adversity and to survive. Family resilience theory and applied research emphasize the role that family characteristics, behavior patterns, and capabilities play in cushioning the impact of stressful life events and in assisting the family in recovering from crises (McCubbin, Thompson, & McCubbin, 1996).

Few studies have focused on resilience in single parent families (Heath & Orthner, 1999). Research that focuses on resilience provides acknowledgment and encouragement of resilient thinking and behavior, which have a reciprocal effect on the family and the community of which the family forms

A.P. Greeff (✉)
Department of Psychology, University of Stellenbosch,
Stellenbosch, South Africa
e-mail: apg@sun.ac.za

B. Human
The Priory Hospital Roehampton, London, Priory Lane, Roehampton, London,
SW15 5JJ, United Kingdom
e-mail: BerquinHuman@priorygroup.com

D.S. Becvar (ed.), *Handbook of Family Resilience*,
DOI 10.1007/978-1-4614-3917-2_19, © Springer Science+Business Media New York 2013

a part (Der Kinderen & Greeff, 2003). Lack of knowledge and understanding in this regard call for attention, and researchers and practitioners are urged to utilize the available resources to identify strengths, despite adversity, and to develop those valuable protective and recovery qualities present in families.

Significance of the Topic

Death in a family is a source of profound stress and calls on the family to utilize its resources in order to cope adequately with the situation and to maintain balance and harmony. Certain characteristics of family members' interactive processes and patterns of functioning allow them to face adversity and challenges in their lives, and to survive well. Most literature dealing with family relations does not contain adequate information about coping mechanisms for dealing with the loss of a family member.

Generally, research on death has focused on the experience of death and dying and its negative implications for the family (Janosik & Green, 1992). This is largely due to the deficit-oriented approach that has been the dominant paradigm in the field of mental health. Much of the research on families and health has tended to pathologize families, implicating the family in the cause or maintenance of nearly all problems in individual functioning (McKenry & Price, 1994). This focus on family pathology originated from early family therapy research, in which the focus was on how family dysfunction could cause mental illness, and from medical research that searches for pathogens and other "causative" factors.

More recently, the strengths and resilience of families have been emphasized. Antonovsky (Antonovsky & Sourani, 1988) developed the salutogenic paradigm, according to which it is proposed that stressors are part of human existence, and that it is as important to investigate successful coping (origins of health) as it is to investigate the origins of pathology. Rather than looking at factors associated with deficits, salutogenesis is concerned with discovering characteristics that contribute to healthy functioning in families (Hawley & DeHaan, 1996). This is an optimistic and forward-looking perspective. Families are viewed as challenged rather than damaged, an approach that questions the myth of the problem-free family and focuses on family regeneration and capacity for self-repair.

Resilience is associated with a salutogenic orientation toward psychological health. Derived from Latin roots, resilience means "to jump (or bounce) back" (Silliman, 1994, p. 2), thus implying an ability to return to an original form after being bent, compressed or stretched, as well as being able to rise above adversity and to survive stress (Hawley & DeHaan, 1996; Walsh, 1996): "Family resilience describes the path a family follows as it adapts and prospers in the face of stress, both in the present and over time" (Hawley & DeHaan, 1996, p. 293). Family resilience theory emphasizes the role that family characteristics, behavior patterns, and capabilities play in cushioning the impact of stressful life events and in assisting the family in recovering from crises (McCubbin et al., 1996). The challenge is to identify resilience factors that enable families to move through bereavement by adapting and adjusting successfully despite the loss, with the ultimate goal being to be able to nurture, develop, and utilize these qualities when experiencing adversity.

Literature Review

In the literature, grief is conceptualized most often as an individual response to loss, with little attention being paid to family processes. In the years of research on families under stress, the focus of most work has been on the identification, conceptualization, measurement, and validation of the protective and recovery factors operative in resilient individuals (Dugan & Coles, 1989; Luthar & Zigler, 1991; Masten, Best, & Garmezy, 1990; Simeonsson, 1995; Werner-Wilson, Zimmerman, & Whalen, 2000).

Clinical attention to bereavement has focused on individual mourning processes, much more than on the grief reactions of the family (Walsh, 1998).

Although the grieving process is a normal response to death, there can be physical, psychological, and social consequences for the surviving family members that can be viewed as stressor experiences (Burnell & Burnell, 1989). It has been estimated that one third of all major bereavement leads to problems for which professional help may be required (Raphael, 1984). The bereaved often experiences heightened levels of social and emotional adjustment problems (Nelson, 1982), and parental loss in childhood has been considered a risk factor in adult psychopathology (Mäkikyrö et al., 1998).

As a result of this individual approach, the mental health field has failed to appreciate the impact of loss on the family as an interactional and functional unit. Although the individuals—with their unique differences, reactions, emotions, and needs—who constitute the family deserve attention, serious consideration should be given to the family going through and being confronted by challenges unique to its developmental stage in the family life cycle (McGoldrick & Carter, 2003; Walsh & McGoldrick, 2004).

Characteristics of Parental Loss and Its Impact on Families

The death of a parent is always a significant event in a family's life, with diverse implications and consequences for the remaining members of the family and for the family as a unit. What were the roles within the family? What were the nature and quality of the relationships? What vacuums were left within the different contexts? How ready and able are the family members to integrate this loss into their current and future life? Many more questions arise, given the individual differences that exist among the family members with regard to gender, developmental stage, and connectedness to the deceased. Becvar (2001) provides an extensive discussion of various possible family permutations and impact on and implications for the survivors. It is necessary, however, to briefly emphasize different developmental stages in which the specific family members will experience the impact of the loss distinctively as a result of their positions in the family.

During childhood, responses to the loss may be expressed as uneasiness and tears (infants); some distress over a longer period, as well as requests that the "lost" parent should return (slightly older infants); experiencing guilt about their parent's death, or acting as if this loss is not permanent (5–8-year-olds); an increase in fear about one's own mortality and that of the other parent, and irritability and defiant behavior (8–12-year-olds); and intense emotions and sudden outbursts (adolescents). During this bereavement period, clear and direct communication is important, while the remaining parent should assure the children of their importance and place in the "new" family (Becvar, 2001).

The impact of the loss of a parent during adulthood may vary, depending on the ages of the children and the parent, and the nature of their relationships. Unresolved issues may come to the fore that the child needs to pay attention to; alternatively, the presence of a supportive and understanding parent may be missed. At the same time, the death of the parent may draw the family together or, inversely, may cause new and unexpected conflict and tensions among the survivors.

Irrespective of the age or gender of the deceased parent, or of the remaining parent and child(ren), the grief is intense and widely affects those left behind. Combined with structural changes and challenges, the loss poses emotional and psychological demands on those involved, which reverberate in the surviving family.

The questions that need to be answered are: How can the family keep on functioning despite the structural change due to the death of a parent? What adjustment and adaptation challenges are the family confronted with? And, what qualities, strengths, or resources need to be activated that would help the family with the adaptation processes?

A Brief Theoretical View

Family resilience theory goes beyond a contextual view of individual resilience to a family-system level, focusing on relational resilience in the family as a functional unit (Walsh, 1996). Resilience is conceptualized as the combination of individual characteristics and relationship patterns of interactions within the family. It is thus necessary to recognize that both individual and relational factors are operating and that these must be considered simultaneously.

McCubbin et al. (1996) were the pioneers in shifting the focus of resilience from the internal and external factors associated with the individual, to an examination of resilience as it is experienced in families. Their Resiliency Model of Family Adjustment and Adaptation, developed by McCubbin et al., is an attempt to explain why, when faced with transitions and crises, some families are able to recover while other family systems fall apart and deteriorate under the same circumstances. According to this model, resilience is defined as "the positive behavioral patterns and functional competence individuals and the family unit demonstrate under stressful or adverse circumstances, which determine the family's ability to recover … [by] restoring the well-being of family members and the family unit as a whole" (McCubbin, Thompson, Thompson, & Futrell, 1999, p. 142). Within this framework, resilience is viewed as involving two distinct, but related, family processes. The first is *adjustment*, which involves the influence of protective factors in facilitating the family's ability and efforts to maintain its integrity and functioning and to fulfill developmental tasks in the face of risk factors. A family experiencing a stressor will thus be motivated by the tension created by the crisis to adjust its patterns of functioning in order to restore harmony and balance. The second process is *adaptation*, which involves the functioning of recovery factors that promote the family's ability to "bounce back" from and adapt as a result of family crisis situations. Adapting entails the process of altering the environment, the community, and the family's relationship with the community in order to restore the family's harmony, balance, and well-being (McCubbin et al., 1996).

Family resilience research has focused on addressing the central and complex issues of determining what protective factors are critical to family adjustment in the face of specific risks or clusters of risk factors, as well as what recovery factors are critical to family adaptation in the face of specific family crisis situations. McCubbin et al. (1996) emphasize that, while families have been studied in both the adjustment and the adaptation phases of the Resiliency Model, few results have indicated a need for separate emphasis on either. Instead, as McCubbin, McCubbin, Thompson, Han, and Chad (1997) have reiterated, family systems call upon and utilize all their resources in crisis situations. In view of this, the Resiliency Model depicts the entirety of the family system's responses to stress—the interaction of family problem-solving and coping, family resistance resources, social support, and family coherence—as the family attempts to restore stability.

Qualities, Resources, and Processes Associated with Family Resilience

The death of a parent can cause a major shift in a family's worldview, with reverberations for both the immediate reorganization and the long-term adaptation of the disrupted family. How families make sense of a crisis, such as the loss of a family member, and endow it with meaning is crucial for familial resilience (Antonovsky & Sourani, 1988). A family's sense of loss can be influenced by its sense of coherence, defined as a global orientation to life that is comprehensible, manageable, and meaningful. A strong sense of coherence fosters confidence in the family's ability to clarify the nature of problems so that they seem ordered, predictable, and explicable. Demands placed on the family are believed to be manageable by mobilizing useful resources, including relational resources. Stressors are viewed as challenges that the family is motivated to deal with successfully. Viewing a crisis as comprehensible, manageable, and meaningful can assist a family in adapting to events that affect and transform family and social structures (Patterson & Garwick, 1994). A high sense of family coherence can promote stability and health, thereby helping families to reach higher levels of reorganization and adjustment after the crisis (Antonovsky & Sourani, 1988). Underlying each of these three components of sense of coherence are core processes that facilitate adjustment and adaptation to the crisis.

Communication is one of the core processes that facilitate families in their adjustment and adaptation to the crisis caused by parental loss and smooth progress to making the loss comprehensible (Greeff & Human, 2004). Sharing the experience of death, dying, and loss can promote both immediate and long-term adaptation for family members, strengthening the family as a functional unit (Walsh, 1998). Open and honest communication is an essential element in grief resolution (Gilbert & Smart, 1992; Jordan et al., 1993; Wolin, 1998). Indeed, the ability to communicate openly and honestly is of vital importance for family resilience over the entire course of the loss process, but particularly in the face of transitional difficulties in the immediate aftermath (Walsh, 1998). To communicate means to share and to foster good relationships with others. Although understanding is an important component of communication, it does not imply agreement with everybody about everything. People may differ about issues, but still communicate effectively with one another. Furthermore, it is not necessary to talk about issues all the time. It is important to listen, and to try to understand what the other person is attempting to convey. According to Baer (1999), positive and open communication fosters family functioning by allowing family members to share their changing needs with one another. In this process it is important to express emotions explicitly and willingly (Greeff & Human, 2004).

In the aftermath of loss, intense emotions may surface at different moments, including complicated and mixed feelings of anger, disappointment, abandonment, helplessness, relief, guilt, and confusion. Because of the change in family composition and structure, ambiguity in messages about blurred boundaries and role expectations may surface, all of which can foster depression and block mastery of challenging situations (Boss, 1991).[1] Family members' abilities to express and respond to their needs and concerns, and to negotiate system changes to meet new demands at crisis points, are crucial to family resilience (Walsh, 1998). Clear, open and direct communication between family members, empathy for one another's positions, tolerance of conflict, and a readiness to grapple with differences when they occur are essential factors that increase the resilience of the family in dealing with a loss (Bloch, Hafner, Harari, & Szmukler, 1994). Such communication facilitates family adaptation and strengthens the family as a supportive network for its members. For example, in a study on the adjustment of children after the loss of a parent, it was found that children who experienced open communication with the surviving parent reported fewer depressive symptoms and a decrease in anxiety (Raveis, Siegel, & Karus, 1998). Similarly, Anderson et al. (1992) found that for adolescents facing risk factors open communication with parents was seen as a strong protective factor that predicted adjustment. Thus, sharing of information and open expression of feelings about the deceased foster comprehension of the loss experience, and healthy adaptation to parental loss therefore is more likely to occur (Raveis et al., 1998).

Manageability is the second core element of family sense of coherence and can be described as the family's efforts to reach and maintain an equilibrium that will lead to balance, harmony, and recovery after the initial crisis. The death of a parent invariably changes the structure of the family and distorts established patterns of interaction. In order to obtain a state of equilibrium that is conducive to balance, harmony, and recovery, the family is compelled to reorganize and reinvest in other relationships and life pursuits, and to change its patterns of functioning, including roles, rules, meanings, and lifestyles (Bloch et al., 1994). This process of management is influenced by the family's ability to be

---

[1] Please see Chap. 17 for an in-depth discussion of this topic.

flexible. Flexibility is the capacity to change when necessary, an element that encourages high functioning in couples and families (Satir, 1988).

Families that have lost a member through death commonly experience an immediate period of rapid disorganization, which is disorienting and chaotic. Change is alarming, mainly because the family members fear they might lose control of their lives in a runaway process that might leave them even worse off than they are in their present predicament. Family resilience requires the ability to be flexible enough to counterbalance stability and change as family members go through crises and challenges (Walsh, 1998). Some families allow for too much change and become chaotic. A chaotic and disorganized family structure will make it difficult for the family to maintain enough stability and continuity to manage the transitional upheaval. Other families allow too little change after the family structure has been altered by loss. An overly rigid family structure will resist modifying its set patterns to make the necessary accommodations to loss (Walsh). A flexible balance between stability and change maintains a stable family structure, while also allowing for change in response to life's challenges (Beavers & Hampson, 1993; Olson, 1993). Manageability is fostered not only by the family's ability to be flexible but also by the ability to maintain set patterns of functioning. During times of crisis, disruption in set patterns of functioning such as rituals and daily routines can intensify the upset and confusion. Rituals and routines provide a sense of stability that can help a family to manage the transitional upheaval. They also provide a family with a sense of continuity over time by linking past, present, and future through shared traditions and expectations (Walsh, 1998). Daily routines, such as family dinner and bedtime stories, can provide the family members with regular contact and order (Hochschild, 1997). Rituals to mark the loss of a life and a loved one, such as a funeral and anniversary visits to the grave, can bind the family together by sharing grief and receiving comfort in the supportive network of the community of survivors (Imber-Black, Roberts, & Whiting, 1988).

The third core element of a sense of coherence is the meaningfulness of a crisis within the broader context of life. The beliefs of families who have lost a parent shape their definition of the current situation and help them to develop coping strategies that are associated with positive psychological outcomes (Patterson & Garwick, 1994). Families can cope with crisis and adversity by making meaning of their experience through linking it to their social world, to their cultural and religious beliefs, to their multigenerational past, and to their hopes and dreams for the future. Beliefs shape who we are and how we understand and make sense of our experience (Walsh, 1998). Belief systems include values, convictions, attitudes, biases, and assumptions, which combine to form a set of basic premises that trigger emotional responses, inform decisions, and guide actions.

Families develop shared belief systems that are connected to cultural values and are influenced by their position and experiences in the social world over time (Falicov, 1995). Such shared belief systems organize the experience to enable family members to make sense of crisis situations. The dominant beliefs in a family system have a very strong influence over how a family as a functional unit will deal with adversity. Core family beliefs, such as "We never give up when the going gets tough" or "Men don't cry," are fundamental to family coping strategies (Walsh, 1998). Accordingly, a family's belief system can be facilitative and increase options for problem resolution, healing, and growth, or it can be constraining, which leads to problems and restricts options (Wright, Watson, & Bell, 1996).

Religious and spiritual beliefs can provide meaning and purpose in times of crisis (Beavers & Hampson, 1990). Religions are organized belief systems with shared moral values and involvement in a religious community (Wright et al., 1996). The original root of the word religion—"religio," to bind together—has dynamic significance. During times of loss, religion may help bind together the fragments of one's life, restoring some sense of coherence and meaning (Parrot, 1999). Research has shown the important role played by religion and spirituality in the coping process. For example, Frantz, Trolley, and Johll (1996) examined the role of religion and spiritual beliefs in the grieving process and found that 77% of their subjects said that their religious and spiritual beliefs were significantly related to their positive coping and future outlook and of considerable help in their grief. Congregational support can be particularly helpful during a crisis. Reed and Sherkat (1992) reported that church attendance reduced depression significantly by raising the self-esteem of individuals; however, this occurred only if attendance enhanced social integration, the social support was put to use, and the support was expressed with affection. It was also found that reading about and believing in God helped widows cope with the loss of their loved one (Brubaker, 1990).

Spirituality, on the other hand, can be equated with internal values that provide a sense of meaning, inner wholeness, and connection with others. It can be described as a nontraditional, noninstitutionalized religiousness, or as the human quest for personal meaning and mutually fulfilling relationships with people, the nonhuman environment, and for some, with God (Angell, Dennis, & Dumain, 1998). Angell et al. view spirituality as a human need for solace and direction; essentially, it is a fundamental source of resilience. If spirituality is a source of resilience, it undoubtedly plays a prominent role in the ability of the family to bounce back after a tragedy. A belief in a supreme being or in oneness with nature is an example of spirituality, both of which can be experienced within or outside of formal religious structures. Spirituality is a fundamental form of resilience in that it provides the individual with the ability to understand and overcome stressful situations . In support of previous research, Greeff and Ritman (2005) identified faith as a characteristic of individual resilience in 52% of the participants in their study. This is consistent with the findings of Greeff and Human (2004) that 77% of families participating in their study identified religion and spiritual support as important coping resources, which led to an understanding and an acceptance of the loss of a parent.

Family hardiness is an adaptation resource that is characterized by the internal strengths and durability that a family unit demonstrates during times of crisis. A family's sense of commitment to overcoming the crisis, its efforts to be active rather than passive, and its sense of being in control of the crisis are all components of hardiness. These characteristics of hardiness, as a stress-resistant and adaptation resource in a family, may act as mediating factors in mitigating the effects of stressors and demands and facilitate the necessary adjustment and adaptation over time (McCubbin et al., 1996).

A family's sense of commitment to overcoming the crisis, which is one dimension of hardiness, can be expressed in the cooperation between family members. When family members cooperate, they strengthen their ability to overcome adversity by forming relational resilience. That is, relationships are strengthened when a crisis is viewed as a shared challenge to be confronted together. This affiliation between family members can create an atmosphere of trust in times of trouble, and this can foster resilience. As Beavers and Hampson (1990) have proposed, families are best able to weather adversity when members have an abiding loyalty to and faith in one another, rooted in a strong sense of trust. This "togetherness" also can lead to an emotional bonding between family members, described as family cohesion (Olson, 1993; Sigelman & Shaffer, 1995). Cohesion creates the opportunity for family members to turn to one another for emotional and practical support, and for collaboration during times of crisis. Each member of the family can participate in easing family burdens or providing comfort, and each is helped by being included in a functional way.

The comfort and security provided by warm, caring relationships can help buffer stressors (Walsh, 1998). However, it is important that family members counterbalance unity, mutual support, and collaboration with the separateness and autonomy of the individual member. Patterns of either extreme family enmeshment or disengagement can become problematic. Enmeshed families often demand absolute togetherness and become intolerant of individual differences, which are seen as threats to group survival. In contrast, disengaged families tend to avoid the pain of loss by way of distancing and emotional cut-off, leaving members isolated in their grief. Adaptation to loss is enhanced when families balance closeness and commitment with respect and tolerance for separateness and individual differences (Walsh).

Another dimension of family hardiness is the sense of being in control of the crisis. This characteristic can facilitate or constrain the adaptation response to the stressor. How a family appraises the crisis, the distress, and its recovery resources, influences its sense of being in control (Lazarus & Folkman, 1984). Consequently, adaptation to a crisis situation is influenced by the views families hold about their successes and failures. It has been reported that highly resilient families view mistakes or failure as experiences from which to learn, rather than as occasions of defeat. They attribute mistakes to factors they can change, such as not enough effort or an unattainable goal. The more competent a family feels, the more it feels in control of the situation (Walsh, 1998). In contrast, families lacking in resilience attribute their mistakes to their own deficits and believe that these deficiencies cannot be changed.

A family's determination to be active and to persevere in the face of overwhelming adversity is another dimension of the family hardiness construct. However, this active perseverance must be counterbalanced by an awareness of what can be controlled during a crisis and accepting what cannot. Resilience requires acceptance of limitations and shortages, and then putting one's best efforts into what is possible. Mastering a crisis can be seen in terms of ongoing processes. Family members may not be able to control the outcome of a situation, but they can make choices and find meaningful ways to participate actively in the process of unfolding events. They can change aspects they can influence. For example, when no treatment options remain and death is at hand, family members can actively choose ways to participate in care giving, the relief of suffering, and preparation for death. In such ways they make the most of the time they have together and find comfort in loving one another well in the face of loss and grief (Walsh, 1998).

Support from relatives, friends, and the community can facilitate adaptation to the death of a parent or other family member. Family isolation and a lack of social support and community connections make loss more difficult to bear and contribute to dysfunction under stress. Relatives, close friends, and social networks provide both practical assistance and vital community connection. They also provide information, concrete services, support, companionship, and relief. Very importantly, they provide a sense of security and solidarity (Walsh, 1998). Community activities and religious affiliation, such as participation in church activities, social clubs, and community outreach programs, foster individual and family well-being. Reed and Sherkat (1992) found that the opportunity for, as well as the using and quality of social support, can significantly enhance self-esteem and reduce depression. Having someone available when one needs support makes the future look more hopeful; being satisfied with the support received promotes positive feelings.

Economic resources also can buffer the family's experience of loss and have a positive influence on family adaptation (Walsh, 1998). This is especially true if finances have been drained by costly, protracted medical care, and/or if economic resources were lost with the death of a parent. Socio-economic status is an important factor in determining healthy family adaptation and functioning because it determines the capacity of the family to control and support children and other family members through a crisis situation and related developmental changes. For example, Raveis et al. (1998) found that bereaved children in families with higher incomes and with parents that perceived their finances as adequate were less likely than those from less affluent families to exhibit sleep disturbances, and that they had fewer difficulties in concentration and fewer learning problems over a 2-year follow-up period. With regard to socio-economic status, research has provided evidence that parental education has a direct bearing on the parents' ability to provide the family with adequate exposure to knowledge and problem-solving skills (Heath & Orthner, 1999).

Individual resilience also may have an effect on family resilience (Hawley & DeHaan, 1996). Greeff and Human (2004) found that 49% of the families in their study rated individual characteristics—for example positive personality characteristics such as optimism—equally as important as family hardiness and intrafamilial support in helping to get through the stressful period after a parent had died, while 28% of the families in Greeff and Van der Merwe's (2004) study of resilience in single parent families created by divorce indicated that positive attitudes towards the family's future helped them through their difficult adaptation processes. In their research conducted in the Western Cape, South Africa, Greeff and Ritman (2005) found that optimism was one of the individual characteristics that a family could use as a resource to enhance its resilience when dealing with the crisis of losing a parent.

Beavers and Hampson (1993) found that high-functioning families in the United States held a more optimistic view of life. Walsh (2003) identified a positive outlook, consisting of hope, optimistic bias, and confidence in overcoming the odds, as one of the key processes in family resilience and emphasized the importance of hope, initiative, perseverance, and encouragement between family members during the recovery from crisis. Cheavens, Feldman, Woodward, and Snyder (2006) described hope as a vehicle that enables individuals to explore that which makes their lives worth living. It is important to emphasize the agency component of hope, as it is precisely this aspect that differentiates hope from optimism (Bryant & Cvengros, 2004).

Optimism can be defined as a generalized (cross-situational) expectancy of a positive outcome (Snyder, 1995). It generally is viewed as being situated at one end of a continuum, with pessimism at the other end. As a coping style, optimism is believed to influence individuals' psychological and physical well-being, with hope functioning merely as a closely related construct. As such, optimism and hope are frequently used interchangeably in the psychological literature. However, in a study conducted by Bryant and Cvengros (2004, p. 296), the findings indicated that "hope has more to do with general self-efficacy than does optimism," and "optimism has more to do with positive reappraisal coping than does hope." Accordingly, these authors suggest that optimism holds stronger implications for individual cognitive appraisals of personal outcomes than hope, which is more strongly tied to individual beliefs about personal capabilities. Thus, the agency component embedded within the construct of hope necessarily implies a sense of personal responsibility for goal attainment, which is not true for optimism. Therefore, Bryant and Cvengros suggest that hope focuses more directly on expectations about the personal attainment of *specific* goals, whereas optimism focuses more broadly on the expected quality of future outcomes in *general*. As indicated, however, hope and optimism are closely related or are nearly identical constructs. Indeed, most, if not all, of the findings attributed to hope also have been found to be applicable to optimism.

Bonanno et al. (2002) found that coping resources played a crucial role in moderating the adjustment and adaptation to interpersonal loss. Included among these resources are personality traits associated with coping efficacy. Hawley and DeHaan (1996) are of the opinion that both long- and short-term coping styles are necessary for true resilience, with a specific focus on continued adaptability and flexibility in the long term. Other character traits, such as conscientiousness, agreeableness, openness to experience, the tendency to introspect, and perceived confidence in coping, are also noted as being able to serve as buffers against interpersonal loss (Bonanno et al., 2002).

Wolin and Wolin (1993) have identified seven individual protective characteristics that contribute to resilience. These include insight, independence, relationships, initiative, humor, creativity, and morality. Hoopes, Hagan, and Conner (1993) state that one of the primary characteristics of a resilient person is optimism, defined as a tendency to focus on the positive aspects of a situation. It is, however, important to distinguish between optimism and being easy-going and adaptable. Many studies on individual resilience have found that traits such as a happy, easy-going, and adaptable temperament are helpful, although not essential, for building resilience (Walsh, 1996). Individuals with an adaptable temperament were found to be more likely to use positive emotions rather than negative emotions when faced with adversity. It was also found that an adaptable temperament promotes character traits such as agreeableness and flexibility, which in turn contribute to resilience (Dumont & Provost, 1999; Frederickson, 2001).

In Summary

From our review of the literature it is plausible to conclude that family resilience in crisis situations depends on the degree of successful adaptation achieved by the family. Supportive family communication, internal strengths such as a family's ability to collaboratively face a crisis, and to be active rather than passive foster a family's hardiness. The view that a family has of a crisis, seeing it as comprehensible, manageable, and meaningful, fosters family coherence and resilience. Very importantly, external support from relatives, friends, and the community can facilitate adaptation to the death of a family member.

The experience of a death is not the same for an accident victim, a person with AIDS, a person who commits suicide, and someone who dies instantaneously of a heart attack. Neither is the experience of bereavement the same for their survivors (Papalia & Olds, 1992). As indicated, the gender and developmental stage of the surviving family members, and the nature and quality of the relationships with the deceased and with one another, all combine in complex ways to leave the surviving members with their unique feelings, thoughts, abilities, and potential to adapt to their new circumstances. Yet all people are human, and just as there are commonalities in our lives, there are commonalities in adjusting and adapting to the death of a loved one.

Healing and resilience in the face of loss depend not only on individual characteristics but also on a combination of family qualities, dynamics, and processes. Therefore, a systemic framework is crucial to examining the reverberations of the loss of a mother or father. An understanding of the challenges of family adaptation to loss and the key interactional processes in recovery can guide theory, research, practice, and interventions to strengthen families after the loss of a parent.

Current Issues

Grieving about a parent is an individual issue, which takes place within the context of a family unit, in which each member is connected in a unique way to the others. The pain and loss that is experienced must be handled, worked through, and given meaning by the individual in order to continue with life. All of this, for each family member, happens within the realm of a dynamic family environment constituted by the history, processes, values, and world view prevalent in that particular family. This complexity of interactive and interlinked factors needs to be considered and addressed when conceptualizing family resilience after the loss of a parent. However, there are currently issues regarding the family's role and function after the loss of a parent that are receiving attention from researchers and practitioners.

Various types of single parent families are becoming more and more common, which necessitates the focused attention of family scholars. From a salutogenesis perspective, the question that needs to be answered is, "What qualities or characteristics of single parent families created by the death of a parent would help them to cope and continue with life in a way that strengthens the family unit, as well as each of the members?" In relation to families in which a parent has died, care should be taken so that the bereavement process occurs within the parameters of the adapting and evolving family unit, which should remain, or become for the first time, the secure base for future development.

Once family resilience qualities have been identified, explored, and described in sufficient detail and clarity, the next step is to go further and start developing interventions or procedures to enhance the identified qualities in families. This requires sufficient knowledge and an understanding of both family dynamics and the principles underlying the development of intervention programs, which need to be tailor-made to the specific needs of target families. In this way, primary prevention can be implemented that will not only benefit families in their immediate bereavement, but may contribute in a substantial way to the adaptation of the family in the long run.

Clinical Implications

The intensity of the loss will be related to the nature of the relationships the deceased parent had with each family member and the various roles and functions that he or she fulfilled. The individual members constitute the family unit. Care should be taken by the clinician to ensure that each one of the remaining family members obtains the understanding and support that his or her circumstances require. A sudden death means that the family did not have time to prepare for the loss, to finish unfinished business, and to say goodbye to the parent. On an individual level, the focus should be on the affected children and the remaining adult.

With regard to the child(ren), extensive research has been and continues to be conducted by the Family Bereavement Program (FBP) at Arizona State University (Sandler et al., 1992, 2003), and initial findings have been published on the effect of the FBP program on the grief experienced by children (Sandler et al., 2010). Child-related issues that need the attention of clinicians are the child's self-esteem, adaptive control beliefs, coping skills, expression of emotions, a positive parent–child relationship, parental warmth, parent–child communication, effective discipline, parental distress, positive family interactions, and the child's exposure to negative life events. Other child-related factors to bear in mind are the child's developmental level and gender, the cause and type of death, the time since the death, and the cultural background of the family (Haine, Ayers, Sandler, & Wolchik, 2008).

For the remaining spouse, the impact of the death will be determined, inter alia, by the meaningfulness and quality of the couple relationship. The loss and healthy adjustment to the bereavement are described in several different models. Shuchter and Zisook (1993) present the following six dimensions of grief that need to be adapted in very unique ways: (1) emotional and cognitive experiences; (2) coping with the loss; (3) continuing the relationship with the deceased spouse; (4) own functioning; (5) social and intimate relationships; and (6) own identity. Bonanno and Kaltman (1999) proposed four aspects that need to be addressed for successful adaptation to the loss. These include (1) the contextual variables that influence adjustment to the death, for example age, gender, and social support; (2) the subjective meaning of the loss; (3) the changing representation of the lost relationship with the deceased; and (4) coping and emotion-regulating strategies. Neimeyer (2006) in a constructivist approach emphasizes the multiple ways to reconstruct the life story after the loss. The aforementioned approaches suggest different, but relevant, aspects or ways that might be the focus of clinical engagement with the remaining spouse.

Grief reactions and family adaptation depend on the way the family is organized. First, family flexibility in terms of clear structures with regard to family rules and roles and an understanding of what is expected of each member will play a role in the adaptation process. Second, the level of communication will determine the extent to which there will be internal support and the amount of cohesion, or closeness, experienced by the members. If this bond is strong enough, each member may get the necessary support and understanding to work through the grieving process in his or her own way.

Viewing a family purely in pathological terms undermines its potential for repair and growth. A resilience approach, viewing families in distress as challenged and not as damaged, emphasizes and promotes growth and prosperity. Therapists generally have neglected those elements in families that, if they were understood, would have the potential to become levers that could actualize and expand the behavioral repertoire of the family members and the family unit (Masten & Powell, 2003; Walsh, 2003).

What processes, qualities, and resources need to be activated or utilized in order to adapt to the loss and the new family structure? One of the key elements in adaptation during the grieving process is the capacity of the family members to communicate their emotions and thoughts that have been provoked by the death of the parent. Not only will it facilitate the grieving process but it will open up possibilities for growth in existing relationships, which may become more intimate and meaningful. Also sharing feelings and thoughts with the extended family, friends, and neighbors will evoke understanding and support, which may be needed and helpful in the changed future.

Although limited research is available on the resilience qualities of families who have lost a parent, and given the many different types of single parent families created due to the death of a parent, the following could become the focus of interventions (Greeff & Human, 2004), thereby enhancing the adaptation process: (1) encouraging members to support one another on an emotional and practical level; (2) identifying the leading remaining family member (probably the remaining parent) and encouraging him/her to reach out to other family members, showing them how to accept the situation and how to be optimistic about the future; (3) encouraging the family members to practice open and honest communication; (4) identifying and utilizing the support of extended family members and friends; (5) encouraging religion and spirituality practices—if this is appropriate for the family; (6) identifying the family's internal strengths, encouraging them to work together, to depend on each other, and to be committed to the family; and (7) fostering a belief that the family is in control of its own future and life events.

A specific example of an individual quality that can be developed in a family is optimism. All professionals (e.g., nursing staff, social workers, psychologists, educators) who come into contact with families in distress should identify and encourage optimism in individual family members, thereby increasing the optimism of the family unit as a whole. This, in turn, will increase family adaptation and functioning. Developing optimism can be achieved by paying attention during an intervention to at least two important aspects. First, the members of the family should develop a vision of their future. If a vision of this nature arises from the family itself, it will provide the desired focus and direction in terms of which the members of the family can think, act, and live. Second, the members of the family should experience and believe that they have the necessary qualities and abilities to be co-constructors of their own future.

A specific approach that can be utilized on an individual and family level to achieve this objective is solution-focused brief therapy (SFBT). This therapeutic approach emphasizes both of these aspects and can be used successfully to bring about greater optimism and hope in families (Bannink, 2007; De Jong & Berg, 2001). The overarching aim in SFBT is to change the way people talk about their problems and to become more optimistic about the future. Solution-focused talk initiates change, which provides the foundation for improved interactions, which in turn reinforce and expand the client's positive outlook on and expectations about life.

Research Implications

Studying families that have coped well with loss by death is important, because few studies have focused on the coping patterns and sources of resilience in single parent families (Heath & Orthner, 1999). Research of this nature can add to our understanding of why some families are resilient and how they are able to embrace family crises as manageable challenges rather than seeing them as insurmountable tragedies. Furthermore, there is a paucity of research looking at how the family as a unit may be resilient and how that may affect therapy (Hawley, 2000). This calls for more studies, since the concept of resilience can be presented as a valuable framework to guide research, intervention, and prevention efforts.

Identifying and understanding key processes can help clinicians to mobilize untapped resources, thereby enabling distressed families to cope more effectively through their mutual support and collaboration (Walsh, 1996). Examining resilience factors will add to current theories and also will reveal the limitations of various resilience models. These limitations then can be addressed and theories and frameworks can be refined and improved. The capacity for resilience is innate and, as such, we are able to develop social competence, problem-solving skills, a critical consciousness, autonomy, and a sense of purpose (Benard, 1995). Research on resilience has the possibility of giving families going through grief-related life transitions a sense of purpose and a belief in the future, including goal direction, educational aspirations, achievement motivation, persistence, hopefulness, optimism, and spiritual connectedness.

It is imperative that further research be undertaken to cross-validate existing theories and findings in different study populations. A proactive, health-focused paradigm is of particular value in developing countries, where resources are limited. At a time when there is some concern about the demise of the family unit, it is becoming more important than ever to recognize existing strengths and to understand those processes that enable families to weather change and to rebound as a strengthened unit from life's challenges.

Family intervention programs should be directed toward the goal of reinforcing the family as the critical unit for mitigating the stresses and strains of modern life, and providing stability in a fast-changing world. Planning interventions that focus on these normal family processes may be an effective way to approach families that have lost a parent.

An Example of Research Within a Specific Population

To add to the literature on family resilience in single parent families due to the death of a parent, Greeff and Human (2004) investigated the processes and factors associated with family adaptation in 39 such families using the theoretical framework of the Resiliency Model of Family Adjustment and Adaptation developed by McCubbin et al. (1996). A mixed-method approach was utilized, with the parent and an adolescent child representing the family. Self-completion questionnaires were filled out independently by the parent and child, while an open-ended question, requesting the respondents' opinions about which factors or strengths they believed helped their family through the stressful period, was put simultaneously to the two family representatives.

Combined responses to the open-ended question were obtained from all 39 participating families. Responses that implied recovery attempts by the family, or that were identified as supportive, recovery-enhancing resources, were identified and organized into two main categories. These were identified as internal resources, which included all the support obtainable within the immediate family, and as external resources, which included all the support the family obtained outside of its immediate boundaries.

It was found that, within the boundaries of the surviving family, intrafamilial assistance, such as emotional and practical support amongst the members, was the primary resource that helped families cope with the loss (indicated by 79% of the families). This form of support was followed by the individual characteristics of family members (e.g., personality, reaching out to others, acceptance of the situation by one leading family member) (49% of the families) and open and honest communication (indicated by 38% of the families). The most important coping resources outside the boundaries of the surviving family were support from extended family members and friends (95% of the families), followed by religion and spirituality (activities such as going to church and prayers, and beliefs) (indicated by 77% of the families). Third was professional support (e.g., psychologists, clergy), indicated by 26% of the families.

The quantitative results support existing theories and previous research on resilience (Garvin, Kalter, & Hansell, 1993; McCubbin et al., 1996; Werner & Smith, 1993), and add some details. In only a few instances did the parents and adolescents differ in the identification of resilience factors. The following variables showed significant correlations with family adaptation: for the parents and the children, family hardiness (their family's internal strengths, and their ability to work together and to depend on each other), and commitment to the family (the family's ability to collaboratively confront their challenges with an identifiable sense of commitment to the family). In addition, according to an analysis of the children's data, an orientation that the crisis was a challenge, a belief that the family was in control of its own future and life events, seeing the community as a source of support, and the utilization of a passive appraisal coping style were also indicative of better family adaptation. Of note is the somewhat contradictory finding that, although the adolescents identified their family's innovative and active stance toward the loss and its ability to experience and learn new things from the loss as a resilience enhancing factor, they also identified a passive appraisal coping style as a resilience enhancing factor. In summary, both the parents and the adolescents identified their family's internal strengths, and their ability to work together and to depend on each other as fostering resilience.

An analysis of the biographical data indicated that neither the age of the parent or the adolescent, nor the number of years the couple had been married prior to the loss, nor the number of years that had elapsed since the death of the parent, was associated with the adaptation of the family unit. This can be of relevance for inclusion criteria in future studies. A limitation of this study is that the sample utilized represented only a small sector of the heterogeneous South African population. Furthermore, cultural backgrounds, with their unique beliefs about the death of a parent, the manner in which the parent died and its effect on the family, and the pre-morbid functioning of the family, also were omitted. Future studies should consider these factors in order to further explore and validate resilience resources.

This study contributes to an understanding of resilience factors that assist family adjustment and adaptation to the loss of a parent. The usefulness of a salutogenic perspective can be extended through the exploration and validation of resilience variables. Families that have lost a parent can utilize already existing recovery-enhancing resources and become more resilient.

Conclusion

To lose a parent is one of the very natural, but also very upsetting, life events experienced by human beings. Except for the personal loss and consequent implications, there are the more systemic changes, which require adjustments and adaptations by all those involved. The question that arises is, what are those processes, qualities, and resources that help families to adapt to their new circumstances?

Each family member experiences the loss of a parent in a very unique way. Bereavement should be experienced in the safe and supportive environment of the restructured family. It is within this "new family" that an altered future unfolds; one in which the needs and expectations of all members should be met; and in which the entire family should keep on functioning.

Current research has identified family qualities and resources that are associated with family adaptation after the loss of a parent. Given the many individual factors (e.g., age, gender, relationship with deceased) and family factors (e.g., family developmental stage, family structure, financial resources) that have an effect on the family's ability to adapt, it is clear that much more focused research based on homogenous family populations needs to be done. As a result, more will be known about those family resilience processes and qualities that are present in different family populations that help families to adjust and adapt to challenges due to the loss of a parent.

References

Anderson, L., Beinashowitz, J., Grossman, F. K., Finnin, L., Flaherty, M., & Sakurai, M. (1992). Risk and resilience in young adolescents. *Journal of Youth and Adolescence, 21*, 529–550.

Angell, G. B., Dennis, B. G., & Dumain, L. E. (1998). Spirituality, resilience, and narrative: Coping with parental death. *Families in Society, 79*(6), 615–630.

Antonovsky, A., & Sourani, T. (1988). Family sense of coherence and family adaptation. *Journal of Marriage and the Family, 50*, 79–92.

Baer, J. (1999). The effects of family structure and SES on family processes in early adolescence. *Journal of Adolescence, 22*, 341–354.

Bannink, F. P. (2007). Solution-focused brief therapy. *Journal of Contemporary Psychotherapy, 37*, 87–94.

Beavers, W. R., & Hampson, R. B. (1990). *Successful families: Assessment and intervention*. New York: Norton.

Beavers, W. R., & Hampson, R. B. (1993). Measuring family competence: The Beavers systems model. In F. Walsh (Ed.), *Normal family processes* (2nd ed., pp. 73–103). New York: Guilford Press.

Becvar, D. S. (2001). *In the presence of grief: Helping family members resolve death, dying, and bereavement issues*. New York: Guilford Press.

Benard, B. (1995). Fostering resilience in children. *ERIC Digest*. Retrieved August 27, 2001, from http://www.npin.org/library/pre1998/n00418.html.

Bloch, S., Hafner, J., Harari, E., & Szmukler, G. I. (1994). *The family in clinical psychiatry*. Oxford: Oxford University Press.

Bonanno, G. A., & Kaltman, S. (1999). Toward an integrative perspective on bereavement. *Psychological Bulletin, 125*, 760–776.

Bonanno, G. A., Wortman, C. B., Lehman, D. R., Tweed, R. G., Haring, M., Sonnega, J., et al. (2002). Resilience to loss and chronic grief: A prospective study from preloss to 18-month postloss. *Journal of Personality and Social Psychology, 83*(5), 1150–1164.

Boss, P. (1991). Ambiguous loss. In F. Walsh & M. McGoldrick (Eds.), *Living beyond loss: Death in the family* (pp. 237–246). New York: Norton.

Brubaker, T. H. (1990). *Family relationships in later life*. London: Sage.

Bryant, F. B., & Cvengros, J. A. (2004). Distinguishing hope and optimism: Two sides of a coin, or two separate coins? *Journal of Social and Clinical Psychology, 23*(2), 273–302.

Burnell, G. M., & Burnell, A. L. (1989). *Clinical management of bereavement: A handbook for healthcare professionals*. New York: Human Sciences.

Cheavens, J. S., Feldman, D. B., Woodward, J. T., & Snyder, C. R. (2006). Hope in cognitive psychotherapies: On working with client strengths. *Journal of Cognitive Psychotherapy: An International Quarterly, 20*(2), 135–145.

De Jong, P., & Berg, I. K. (2001). *Interviewing for solutions*. San Francisco, CA: Brooks/Cole.

Der Kinderen, S., & Greeff, A. P. (2003). Resilience among families where a parent accepted a voluntary teacher's retrenchment package. *South African Journal of Psychology, 33*(2), 86–94.

Dugan, T., & Coles, R. (Eds.). (1989). *The child in our times: Studies in the development of resiliency*. New York: Brunner/Mazel.

Dumont, M., & Provost, M. A. (1999). Resilience in adolescents: Protective role of social support, coping strategies, self-esteem, and social activities on experience of stress and depression. *Journal of Youth and Adolescence, 28*(3), 343–363.

Falicov, C. J. (1995). Training to think culturally: A multidimensional comparative framework. *Family Process, 34*, 373–388.

Frantz, T. T., Trolley, B. C., & Johll, M. P. (1996). Religious aspects of bereavement. *Pastoral Psychology, 44*, 151–163.

Frederickson, B. L. (2001). The role of positive emotions in positive psychology. *American Psychologist, 56*(3), 218–226.

Garvin, V., Kalter, N., & Hansell, J. (1993). Divorced women: Factors contributing to resiliency and vulnerability. *Journal of Divorce and Remarriage, 21*(1/2), 21–38.

Gilbert, K., & Smart, L. (1992). *Coping with fetal or infant loss: The couple's healing process*. New York: Brunner/Mazel.

Greeff, A. P., & Human, B. (2004). Resilience in families in which a parent has died. *American Journal of Family Therapy, 32*(1), 27–42.

Greeff, A. P., & Ritman, I. N. (2005). Individual characteristics that contribute towards resilience in single parent families. *Psychological Reports, 96*, 36–42.

Greeff, A. P., & Van der Merwe, S. (2004). Variables associated with resilience in divorced families. *Social Indicators Research, 68*(1), 59–75.

Haine, R. A., Ayers, T. S., Sandler, I. N., & Wolchik, S. A. (2008). Evidence-based practices for parentally bereaved children and their families. *Professional Psychology: Research & Practice, 39*(2), 113–121.

Hawley, D. A. (2000). Clinical implications of family resilience. *The American Journal of Family Therapy, 28*(2), 101–116.

Hawley, D. R., & DeHaan, L. (1996). Toward a definition of family resilience: Integrating life-span and family perspectives. *Family Process, 35*(3), 283–298.

Heath, D. T., & Orthner, D. K. (1999). Stress and adaptation among male and female single parents. *Journal of Family Issues, 20*(4), 557–585.

Hochschild, A. (1997). *Time bind*. New York: Holt.

Hoopes, L. L., Hagan, S., & Conner, D. (1993). *Change resilience: A cognitive resource approach*. Unpublished manuscript, Organizational Development and Research, Atlanta, GA.

Imber-Black, E., Roberts, J., & Whiting, R. (Eds.). (1988). *Rituals in families and family therapy*. New York: Norton.

Janosik, E., & Green, E. (1992). *Family life, process and practice*. Boston: Jones and Bartlett Publishers.

Jordan, J. R., Kraus, D. R., & Ware, E. S. (1993). Observations on loss and family development. *Family Process, 32*, 425–440.

Lazarus, R., & Folkman, S. (1984). *Stress, appraisal, and coping*. New York: Springer.

Luthar, S., & Zigler, E. (1991). Vulnerability and competence: A review of research on resilience in childhood. *American Journal of Orthopsychiatry, 61*, 6–22.

Mäkikyrö, T., Sauvola, A., Moring, J., Veijola, J., Nieminen, P., Järvelin, M. R., et al. (1998). Hospital treated psychiatric disorders in adults with single-parent and two-parent family background: A 28-year follow up of the 1966 Northern Finland birth cohort. *Family Process, 37*(3), 335–345.

Masten, A., Best, K., & Garmezy, N. (1990). Resilience and development: Contributions from the study of children who overcome adversity. *Development and Psychopathology, 2*, 425–444.

Masten, A. S., & Powell, J. L. (2003). A resilience framework for research, policy and practice. In S. Luthar (Ed.), *Resilience and vulnerability: Adaptation in the context of childhood adversities* (pp. 1–25). Cambridge: Cambridge University Press.

McCubbin, H. I., McCubbin, M. A., Thompson, A. I., Han, S., & Chad, T. (1997). Families under stress: What makes them resilient. *AAFCS Commemorative Lecture*. Retrieved July 5, 2001, from http://www.cyfernet.org/research.resilient.html.

McCubbin, H. I., Thompson, A. I., & McCubbin, M. A. (1996). *Family assessment: Resiliency, coping and adaptation—inventories for research and practice*. Wisconsin: University of Wisconsin Publishers.

McCubbin, H. I., Thompson, E. A., Thompson, A. I., & Futrell, J. A. (1999). *The dynamics of resilient families*. London: Sage.

McGoldrick, M., & Carter, B. (2003). The family life cycle. In F. Walsh (Ed.), *Normal family processes* (3rd ed., pp. 375–398). London: Guilford Press.

McKenry, P. C., & Price, S. J. (1994). *Families and change: Coping with stressful events*. London: Sage.

Neimeyer, R. A. (2006). Widowhood, grief, and the quest for meaning: A narrative perspective on resilience. In D. Carr, R. M. Nesse, & C. B. Wortman (Eds.), *Spousal bereavement in late life* (pp. 227–252). New York: Springer.

Nelson, G. (1982). Coping with the loss of father: Family reaction to death or divorce. *Journal of Family Issues, 3*(1), 41–60.

Olson, D. H. (1993). Circumplex model of marital and family systems. In F. Walsh (Ed.), *Normal family processes* (2nd ed., pp. 104–137). New York: Guilford Press.

Papalia, D. E., & Olds, S. W. (1992). *Human development* (5th ed.). New York: McGraw-Hill.

Parrot, L. (1999). Grieving the death of a spouse. *Journal of Psychology and Christianity, 18*(4), 330–337.

Patterson, J. M. (2002). Integrating family resilience and family stress theory. *Journal of Marriage and the Family, 64*(2), 349–360.

Patterson, J. M., & Garwick, A. W. (1994). Levels of family meaning in family stress theory. *Family Process, 33*, 287–304.

Raphael, B. (1984). *The anatomy of bereavement*. London: Hutchinson & Co.

Raveis, V. H., Siegel, K., & Karus, D. (1998). Children's psychological distress following the death of a parent. *Journal of Youth and Adolescence, 28*(2), 165–180.

Reed, M. D., & Sherkat, D. E. (1992). The effects of religion and social support on self-esteem and depression on the suddenly bereaved. *Social Indicators Research, 26*, 259–257.

Sandler, I. N., Ayers, T. S., Wolchik, S. A., Tein, J.-Y., Kwok, O.-M., Haine, R. A., et al. (2003). The family bereavement program: Efficacy evaluation of a theory-based prevention program for parentally bereaved children and adolescents. *Journal of Consulting and Clinical Psychology, 71*, 587–600.

Sandler, I. N., Ma, Y., Tein, J.-J., Ayers, T. S., Wolchik, S., Kennedy, C., et al. (2010). Long-term effects of the family bereavement program on multiple indicators of grief in parentally bereaved children and adolescents. *Journal of Consulting and Clinical Psychology, 78*(2), 131–143.

Sandler, I. N., West, S. G., Baca, L., Pillow, D. R., Gersten, J. C., Rogosch, F., et al. (1992). Linking empirically based theory and evaluation: The family bereavement program. *American Journal of Community Psychology, 20*, 491–521.

Satir, V. (1988). *The new peoplemaking*. Palo Alto, CA: Science & Behaviour Books.

Shuchter, S. R., & Zisook, S. (1993). The course of normal grief. In M. S. Stroebe, W. Stroebe, & R. O. Hansson (Eds.), *Handbook of bereavement* (pp. 175–195). Cambridge, UK: Cambridge University Press.

Sigelman, C., & Shaffer, D. (1995). *Life-span and human development* (2nd ed.). California: Brookes/Cole.

Silliman, B. (1994). Resiliency research review: Conceptual & research foundations. *National Network for Family Resiliency*. Retrieved July 24, 2001, from http://www.cyfernet.org/research/resilreview.html.

Simeonsson, R. (1995). *Risk, resilience, and prevention: Promoting the well-being of all children*. Baltimore: Brookes.

Snyder, C. R. (1995). Conceptualising, measuring, and nurturing hope. *Journal of Counseling & Development, 73*(3), 355–360.

Walsh, F. (1996). The concept of family resilience: Crisis and challenge. *Family Process, 35*(3), 261–281.

Walsh, F. (1998). *Strengthening family resilience*. New York: Guilford Press.

Walsh, F. (2003). *Normal family processes: Growing diversity and complexity* (3rd ed.). New York: Guilford Press.

Walsh, F., & McGoldrick, M. (Eds.). (2004). *Living beyond loss: Death in the family* (2nd ed.). New York: W.W. Norton.

Werner, E. E., & Smith, R. S. (1993). *Vulnerable but invincible: A study of resilient children*. New York: McGraw-Hill.

Werner-Wilson, R. J., Zimmerman, T. S., & Whalen, D. (2000). Resilient response to battering. *Journal of Contemporary Family Therapy, 22*(2), 161–187.

Wolin, S. J. (1998). *Project Resilience*. Retrieved June 15, 2000, from http://www.projectresilience.com/framesconcepts.htm.

Wolin, S. J., & Wolin, S. (1993). *The resilient self*. New York: Villard Books.

Wright, L., Watson, W. L., & Bell, J. M. (1996). *Beliefs: The heart of healing in families and illness*. New York: Basic Books.

Resilience in Aging: Moving Through Challenge to Wisdom

Holly Nelson-Becker

Introduction

Individuals at older ages have had many opportunities to develop resilience through challenges and adverse events across the life course. Do they all develop their capacity for resilience, or do some more vulnerable older adults "break" emotionally or mentally with the passage of time? Can one intentionally develop this capacity? In this chapter I discuss the meaning of resilience in aging and posit a practice-based definition. I also present a strengths-based perspective of aging well and positive aging, enhanced by the life course perspective. I address the unique capacity of intergenerational relations to build resilience in families. Empirical support for biopsychosocial emotional and spiritual factors that promote resilient outcomes is explored. A resilient approach also can be carried through the end of life, when attention may turn to death preparation. Finally, I present narrative gerontology and metaphor as models for assessing and expressing resilience in practice.

The Meaning of Resilience

There are many ways to understand the meaning of resilience in the context of aging. In fact, in the literature pertaining to aging, death, and dying there is currently some definitional drift in the discussion of what resilience is and is not. One type of definition establishes it as the universal capacity to avoid, reduce, or surmount adversity (Monroe & Oliviere, 2007; Newman, 2004). However, is avoidance of adversity a skill, or instead a misfortune if adversity is one of the singular mechanisms by which people grow and become more skilled and compassionate beings? Can individuals reduce adversity itself or merely its effects? Is resilience an outcome in the absence of adversity or significant life challenge? Is there resilience without some object or event against which to rebound? Is resilience an innate trait or a process by which one learns to meet the exigencies of life? If it is a process, then to what extent is context—the amalgam of sociohistorical variables in the life course—responsible for a resilient outcome? These are just a few of the questions this topic poses.

H. Nelson-Becker, PhD, LCSW. (✉)
Loyola University Chicago School of Social Work, 820 North Michigan Avenue,
Chicago, IL 60611, USA
e-mail: hnelsonbecker@luc.edu

D.S. Becvar (ed.), *Handbook of Family Resilience*,
DOI 10.1007/978-1-4614-3917-2_20, © Springer Science+Business Media New York 2013

Older adults carry this capacity, demonstrated across decades of determination and drive, but resilience expressed in human terms vs. those of physics does not typically return them to their former state. Soft objects thrown against a hard surface bounce back; people absorb the shock and change. They are different in ways profound and small. A victim of a street assault may change a routine path, but also may act in response to a fundamental shift in worldview. This individual may no longer be friendly toward strangers and may be cautious where he/she once was bold. However, he/she also may now advocate around issues related to social injustice and the long-term poor. Older people search for a new equilibrium through what now is often known as posttraumatic growth (Park, Mills-Baxter, & Fenster, 2005) or stress-related growth (Davis & Nolen-Hoeksema, 2001; Park & Fenster, 2004). This phenomenon is not unique to aging. Resilience has been associated with risk in younger populations. To the young, resilience offers protection from such harms as poverty, violence, and depression (Masten, 2001). Rather than an extraordinary quality, it may be a normative response. Understanding what helps people function under conditions of high adversity at all ages may lead to successful strategies for practice (Fraser, Richman, & Galinsky, 1999; Fry & Keyes, 2010). With resilience, people exposed to adversity adapt in positive healthy ways; however, when adversity meets vulnerability, people become more susceptible to risks.

Cumulative Adversity and Recovery or Resolution

During the life course, cumulative adversity for some and cumulative advantage for others result in diverging trajectories and increasing inequality over time (Hatch, 2005; Ong, Bergeman, & Baker, 2009). Three key points from Halfon and Hochstein's (2002) work on the life course and health are relevant to this discussion: (1) different health trajectories are the product of cumulative risk, resiliency, protective factors, and other influences that may be programmed into behaviors during critical and sensitive periods; (2) health is the consequence of numerous interacting determinants that operate in various changing contexts (e.g., biological, behavioral, social, economic) over time; and (3) historical events, in addition to biological, psychological, and cultural issues, influence the health of both individuals and populations. As individuals age along the life course, they enter and exit different social contexts in accord with life transitions. In fact, aging-related losses may be experienced as secondary to effects of earlier trauma (Bar-Tur & Levy-Shiff, 2000). However, the "resource reservoir" can be drained by repeated losses just as it can be replenished. More resources or different use of available resources are required at older ages to mediate loss (Baltes, 1993).

Resilience also has been defined as maintenance, recovery, or improvement in mental and physical health following a loss experience (Ryff, Singer, Love, & Essex, 1998). At older ages, maintenance of physical health is primarily achieved through attentiveness and activity, rather than expectations that the body will continue to function as well it always has without effort. Maintenance involves action instead of inaction. Balk (2008) argues that the term recovery is often unnecessarily discounted in favor of resilience. Recovery is about recapturing the self and one's humanity. Rather than a process or outcome, it is viewed as a necessary period of time where one progresses in building ability, skill, and function following illness or injury. For aging, this can occur singly in one domain when another domain such as cognitive or sensorimotor ability might experience decline. Resolution is a term preferred by Tedeschi and Calhoun (2008) over recovery from loss. They believe the latter term is often too narrowly associated with addiction and does not acknowledge the possibility of positive change. Similar to Ryff et al.'s idea of improvement, such change is often visible in terms of awareness of personal strength, the value of life, and an altered existential or spiritual orientation.

Contexts of Resilience

Resilience denotes the ability to successfully cope in the midst of great difficulty (Nelson-Becker, 2004, 2005). Few lives are untouched by tragedy. Across the lifespan, older adults have faced multiple challenges to well-being, and for the most part, have transitioned well. However, this is not only an individual problem and response pattern. The ecological model (Germaine, 1973) suggests there is an element of historical location involved in the types of challenges that societies face together that determines specific challenges for the older adults who live in those times. Additionally, family patterns either promote or build barriers to resilience (Becvar, 2007; Walsh, 1998); cultural models imply that resilience is expressed with different nuances in Eastern and Western contexts (Ng et al., 2006). For example, a qualitative study of stroke survivors in Hong Kong showed that most participants successfully created a resilient poststroke self through facing spiritual suffering and relying on social and spiritual resources, some of which were culturally specific (Chow & Nelson-Becker, 2010). Protective factors at all interactive micro, mezzo, and macro levels lead to healthy outcomes. Thus a systems approach to resilience relies on exploring sociohistorical, cultural, and family-level factors that impede or promote resilience.

On an individual level, resilience often includes meaning-making. Self-constructed narratives from earlier life stages may no longer represent current understanding of experience. As older people begin to appreciate their lives from larger perspectives, subjective meaning may change and experiences that were not well understood at the time may be integrated into the concept of the self. Authentic enduring change generated from stressful events includes a shift in values, mastery and coping, social interaction levels, spirituality, and appreciation of life (Ardelt, Landes, & Valliant, 2010). Coping repertoires may expand as loss is confronted in small daily events: one can no longer unscrew an aspirin bottle, or reach the highest shelf, but a helpful younger neighbor may live next door. While loss alters the self-schema, hope intervenes and gives renewed freshness as one reconfigures both the pragmatic and the subjective experiences of daily life. The integration of learning from all life stages—wisdom—signals less need for individual achievement in the world and a greater focus on contribution. In fact, wisdom in aging signals the choice to focus efforts on singular activities and maintenance of meaningful social connections rather than the scattershot participatory approach to living common in younger years when individuals are still finding their way. At older ages, resilient people have found it.

Forgiveness also may play a role in resilience, with multidimensional foci on forgiveness of self, others, and unexpected events (Strelan & Covic, 2006). First, some perception of hurt or pain must be a precursor to stimulate this process. There must be a reason for forgiveness to be needed. It is possible to heal at an individual or group level (Holocaust survivors have forgiven Nazi captors), and this can lead to stronger mental health. This act involves both a process of releasing resentment and of offering compassionate responses to the offender (McCullough, Pargament, & Thoresen, 2000), although there are many levels in between. A compassionate response may be reflected in a transformed emotional state or in a behavioral expression. There is no consensus on the endpoint of forgiveness (Strelan & Covic, 2006), nor is there consideration for how forgiveness occurs in varying cultural contexts or across cultures. However, forgiveness may be the ultimate act of resilience.

Properties of Resilience in Older Ages and a Practice-Based Definition

In older adulthood, resilience opens unexpected doors to possibility. While death draws nearer, it is often more acceptable, not the threat it was at younger ages. Pain and loss may be present, but they also offer learning opportunities. Resilience is this capacity for late-life growth. Although it is best

Table 20.1 Resilience properties in aging

Framework	Resilience element
Past history—personal and social	Resilience capacity in older ages is based on interactive styles learned and practiced in earlier life stages
Present-environmental assets	Resilience involves effective use of current available resources in multiple environments and contexts
Variability by vulnerability	Resilience is not constant, but varies according to areas of vulnerability and unprocessed/unhealed loss
Variability by place	Resilience is context specific, reflecting different interpretive meanings according to geography and culture
Growth capacity	Resilience is the ability to achieve posttraumatic or stress-related growth from adverse events or conditions
Future-formulating hope	Resilience contains a component of hope in the future and the ability to envision that preferred future
Transcending limits	Resilience acknowledges limits, but finds ways to move beyond them or step outside of them

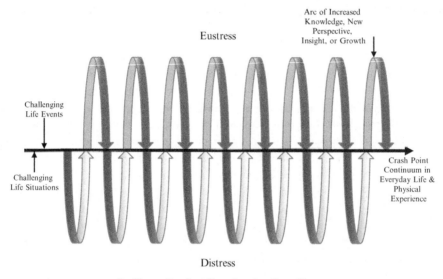

Fig. 20.1 Resilience Measurement

learned at younger ages, it is still present and sometimes increasingly expansive in later years. Resilience is the ability to access one's inner wisdom and strength enhanced by time and experience. In Table 20.1, The Resilience Properties in Aging is a framework showing several life areas where resilience is constructed. These segue from past, present, to future time horizons, areas of variability by vulnerability and place, contexts for planned and unplanned life span growth, and interstitial points of limit leaping also called transcending boundaries. The latter element acknowledges limits but also makes room for creative paths to achieve goals or desires as in Baltes' (1993) model of selective compensation with optimization (discussed in the Strengths Perspective section of this chapter). Based on this framework, resilience in older ages is defined here as the ability to achieve growth through life challenges based on personal history and environmental assets, a capacity for generating hope, and the ability to transcend boundaries in optimal ways.

The model presented in Fig. 20.1, Resilience Quotient Transforming over Time, identifies a resilience model that takes into account challenging events and situations over the life course. In a life, there are multiple points of distress and eustress (positive stress), both of which lead to new understanding and insight. The crash point continuum reflects the concrete level in tangible physical reality where distress and joy are immediately perceived through the senses. While the arcs themselves may be of varying length, representing different degrees, the drawing portrays how the effects rotate forward with the flowing of time. For simplicity they are drawn at the same level of height and depth. Each arc encapsulates the learning achieved from prior points in time. Though difficult to portray visually, it is also important to understand that while learning always moves forward, at times people do make choices that in their actions seem to contradict forward movement. Self-doubt, suffering, and fear can cause individuals to remain at the same point or to slip backward to an earlier developmental location. Resilience capacity is informed by many variables that shift as time passes.

Strengths-Based Perspectives and the Life Course

There are a variety of perspectives, now coming into sharper focus in various professions, that attend to client strengths. Several of these relate specifically to aging. The strengths approach (Kivnick & Murray, 2001; Nelson-Becker, Chapin, & Fast, 2009; Ronch & Goldfield, 2003; Saleebey, 2009), aging well (Kahana & Kahana, 1996; Valliant, 2002), successful aging (Rowe & Kahn, 1998), positive psychology of aging (Cohen, 2005; Gergen & Gergen, 2003), and the life course perspectives (Elder, 2001) all tend to take a malleable view of the aging process. By contrast, the pathologically oriented approach to treatment assumed the professional held the power and was responsible for the course and success of helping activities, consequently engendering a more passive response in those served.

The Strengths Perspective in Aging

For the professional helper, the strengths approach constitutes not only the actions that create spaces for an equal relationship, but also a way of being with clients that promotes their resilience. Yes, life is fraught with problems and difficulties, but that is the nature of life. It is not effective to denounce what is, although for many individuals that might be a beginning step to acknowledging a concern. Instead, there is an understanding that the key knowledge a client needs often lies within but for various reasons, usually relating to pain, uncertainty, lack of self-confidence, and fear, those pathways of self-understanding have become blocked or are inaccessible. In the strengths model, the professional becomes an expert consultant on the journey who affirms client power, knowledge, and responsibility for choice (self-determination) (Ronch & Goldfield, 2003; Saleebey, 2009). If childhood or later trauma has been experienced, it is not viewed as predictive of what the individual client can achieve.

Eliciting the individual narrative is essential to understanding perceptions, so the helper can come to know the client from the inside out, rather than the outside in. Of course a necessary precondition comes from establishing a therapeutic relationship. Instead of holding a problem or deficit focus, the professional assumes a potential and possibility focus that affirms individual hopes and aspirations. Arguably for older adults, these hopes and aspirations may need to be redefined within physical constraints. The selective optimization with compensation (SOC) approach acknowledges that older adults may need to adapt to changing biological conditions (Baltes, 1993). However, they can still select activities that are important to them and enjoy their participation by creatively compensating for what they no longer can accomplish. The classic example given by Baltes is a concert pianist who changes his repertoire to fewer selections that are more frequently practiced, so recitals can still be enjoyed by the audience and older performer.

In older adulthood, individual difference is salient. Ageist views promoted by society in recent decades often depicted older adults as victims of functional deterioration with few choices or signal events to anticipate. Aging was viewed as a period of unmitigated decline leading to death. Now, we know that older adults who retire often choose to return to different forms of work or to engage in volunteering, thereby enhancing their productivity for a modern society concerned with those benchmarks. Literature on productive aging has helped to soften ageist views and to broaden former stereotyped stances (see for example, Hinterlong, Morrow-Howell, & Rosario, 2007; Morrow-Howell, 2010). Older adults are more likely to be healthier at older ages than were their own parents or grandparents (Federal Interagency Forum on Aging-Related Statistics, 2010). Still, for others, resilience in meeting life challenges may not fit definitions of active engagement. Rather it may involve reassessment of life and sharing of vitality that constitutes a wisdom approach; this may or may not include active components (Tornstam, 1996). Many older adults acknowledge that they wished they had made more enlightened choices in younger years, but are accepting of their behavior in a way that can model the value of self-forgiveness for younger generations.

Possibilities for new commitments and recommitment or re-engagement remain available in later life. Professional practitioners can help foster a reconstructive process to reinforce the innate strengths that older adults possess. Rather than utilize problem-saturated vocabularies, professional practitioners can incorporate needs-based language. Thus, in contrast to asking what problems clients bring, which sets the initial orientation and tone of the interview, clients can be asked to express their needs. This transformational language (from problems into needs) implies that actions may be taken to meet needs. Asking questions about needs uncovers a different set of solutions than does asking about problems, suggesting remedies that may be longer lasting as they address more fundamental issues. Further, a problem focus will sometimes only elicit a focus on deficits, attention to what is missing rather than what is present. Hopefully, the work will extend from there, but it may not, leading to anger and frustration as outcomes. A needs-based focus, in contrast, can lead to an exploration and inclusion of the strengths, knowledge, skills, abilities, and adaptive capacities of the individual and community (Nelson-Becker et al., 2009; Saleebey, 2009).

In the case of older people, community members in the form of neighbors, friends, and fellow parish, congregation, or mosque members, sometimes offer significant regular assistance. Neighbors will pick up grocery items for an older neighbor or help shovel snow. Co-religionists may offer transport to services to maintain social connection and foster worship opportunities. These examples all constitute informal helping patterns, but can be encouraged when older clients are too embarrassed to ask for such help. Formal help would include everything from connections to aging agencies that serve the needs of older adults (such as AAAs), to hiring assistance with household tasks. This form of assistance can be vital to help older adults remain in their homes despite functional limits, since disability risk tends to increase with age (Federal Interagency Forum on Aging-Related Statistics, 2010). Requesting formal help is not giving up or giving in to real concrete needs. Rather it is an astute recognition of change and a resilient approach to living at older ages.

Based on the above points, six principles have been suggested by Nelson-Becker et al. (2009) that are important in attending to strengths and resilience in older adults: (1) all individuals have strengths at every stage of life and under all conditions; (2) all experiences, even negative or unexpected ones, may present opportunities for growth; (3) traditional diagnosis and assessment often make assumptions that limit rather than expand capacity; (4) collaboration with older adult clients can motivate them to achieve their aspirations; (5) any environment has resources to be uncovered or co-constructed; and (6) a civil society engages in care for all of its members. Thinking in terms of older adult strengths enables the social worker or other mental health practitioner to counter the mentality of limitation predominant in our ageist Western culture. As the social worker or other professional begins to work from this ideological position, the effect is transformational for clients. They begin to think in terms of promise and possibility; they are motivated to expand capacity in whatever direction (internal or external) they prefer. They do not accomplish this alone, but through building on and accessing the resources for resilience that are abundant within true community life. These are the messages endorsed in the six older adult strengths principles presented.

Aging Well

Aging well consists of a holistic approach where individuals adapt both themselves and the environment in ways that reduce harm and maximize benefit (Kahana & Kahana, 1996). This readily occurs when the losses typically associated with aging, such as a decrease in physical ability, social networks, and sometimes mental acuity, ensue. Aging well is both a goal or outcome and a process.

In his investigation of adult development, Valliant (2002) and his team interviewed three cohorts across nearly six decades, where possible. Valliant's method comprised a panel study. A panel study is one of the most powerful forms of research, because it asks people what they are thinking at moments over time, rather than asking them to assess their life from a single position. The latter method often is dependent on memory biases. What were some of his findings? While many participants experienced difficult life situations—one woman in his sample had a mother who exploited her financially from a young age, told her she wished she had not been born, and prevented her from doing the things that gave her joy—many of them found mentors who modeled for them what their own parents could not. He also found that a capacity for gratitude and forgiveness healed relationships and helped people connect well with others. In retirement, fostering innate creativity and playfulness, and making younger friends as long-term friends died, meant more to perceiving happiness than did the size of one's income. Finally, one's subjective sense of healthiness was more important than outside measures of health. In speaking of one study respondent, Valliant (2002) suggested, "If for seventy-seven years you can always look on the bright side, maybe it starts to become true" (p. 316).

While the above features of the sample were indicators of healthy aging, alcohol abuse was also present in this high functioning, principally Harvard and Stanford-affiliated sample (Valliant, 2002). Alcohol abuse was consistently a factor for those people who did not age well, and alcoholism was a principal problem in damaging possible future social support. In these older cohorts, alcohol was more commonly abused than other illicit drugs. In earlier writing, Valliant (1993) suggested that defenses may be adaptive responses, even though they may be assessed otherwise by outsiders. His designation of mature coping included altruism, humor, suppression, and sublimation. When seen as part of a life history approach, ego defenses were viewed as important to realizing health and creativity.

Successful Aging and Positive Aging

The current cohorts of older adults (ages 65 through centenarian status) are the first to be so long-lived. There are several reasons for this effectiveness in biological aging, one of which relates to advances in medical knowledge and treatment. However, another known factor is that older individuals have some control over the aging process through nutrition, exercise, and mental health choices (Rowe & Kahn, 1998). Although critiques have been mounted of Rowe and Kahn's limited definition of what it means to successfully age (low risk of disease, high mental and physical function, and active engagement), especially regarding who would meet their criteria and who could not, developing a model that included a positive image of the aging process was groundbreaking. Cohen (2005), too, advanced this view through his study of creativity and brain plasticity at older ages. Positive aging and resilience have been promoted for many years by social constructionists Gergen and Gergen (2003).

In fact Ken and Mary Gergen edit a periodic online publication entitled *The Positive Aging Newsletter* that promotes both research findings and practice approaches for reconstructing loss and improvising the path to optimal aging.

The Life Course and Resilience

The life course perspective (Elder, 2001) breaks open the conceptualization of the life journey in new ways. This is accomplished through consideration of the many variables that can enhance resilience. In a sense, older ages are very rich in variable acquisition, and the life course perspective forms a backdrop to understanding resilience in aging. This paradigm describes chronological age, historical timing, and cohort effects as important assessment tools. Often referred to as age, period, cohort, this constellation of factors helps professionals understand different permutations of historical and geographic location, degree of personal control, ways the past shapes the future, the timing of life events (e.g., whether a woman marries for the first time at age 20 or age 50), and linked lives—the social component of aging over time. All of these factors can either create resilience or a greater sense of burden.

Families, Older Adults, and Building Resilience

Our families of origin and families of procreation have become the primary ground where resilience is learned. It is often in these fields where hardship is first experienced. Older adults, like any age group, learned to deal with tensions inside the family context. Alcoholic parents, siblings who were disabled and received most of the family's attention, parenting disciplinary styles that were often restrictive if not abusive, sexual abuse or sexual inappropriateness, and depression, suicide, and other forms of mental illness in the family are a few of the common difficulties encountered. Beyond these, families also experienced tensions from the outside. Many had to face unemployment and underemployment in the Great Depression, leaving underage children scrambling to help support the family financially. Some family members never returned from World War II or came home broken either physically or emotionally, unable to contribute to the family's welfare.

The message given to older people at younger ages was to "be strong" and "deal with it." Often they also were expected to keep any perceived failure hidden. As a result, there was a lot of shame mixed with the reality of deprivation. Rather than learning self-acceptance and healing from heart-breaking sorrow, they were more likely to conceal and cover their troubles. Personal accounts from older adults sharing their life narratives either in therapeutic contexts or in research studies often include a glistening tear. Generally, they faced tough times and are proud of survivorship. Joyce Carol Oates writes her advice to other older widows, "Of the widow's countless death-duties there is really just one that matters: on the first anniversary of her husband's death the widow should think, 'I kept myself alive' " (2011, p. 416). Surviving, rather than healing, was often the unspoken goal.

Within families, there is an intergenerational strength that particularly connects grandparents and grandchildren. Grandparents model compassion and caring for their grandchildren. They often physically care for grandchildren when the parents must work or be away. Sometimes they parent grandchildren on the basis of slim social security checks. However, they also are the recipients of care. Although middle-aged women are the primary caregivers for their older relatives, increasingly grandchildren are beginning to take that role (Dellmann-Jenkins, Blankemeyer, & Pinkard, 2000). While older adults may teach grandchildren to read, grandchildren show their grandparents how to surf the internet and appreciate changing tastes in popular culture. In the safety of families, grandparents or other older relatives can learn to share vulnerabilities. They encounter new opportunities to learn resilience if they did not learn it in earlier decades, but also have unique opportunities to contribute to their family. They heal. The give and take between the generations both strengthens individual family members and affirms for older members a sense of their value.

Resilience Across Biopsychosocial Emotional and Spiritual Factors

In the direct practice professions, particularly social work, there is an applied focus that values the person in his/her environment. Resilience becomes not just an abstract concept but guidance for living. Social workers and other professionals assess the holistic interactions across individuals and within the inner self-concept. While it is useful to look at resilience holistically as in the perspective and family sections earlier, in this section I look more closely at the particular domains in which resilience unfolds.

Biological Resilience

Biological resilience involves innate genetic hardiness as well as an approach to healthy aging that includes such universally recommended parameters of self-care as attention to diet, exercise, and social support. These three factors were identified by the McArthur study as vital in the health of older adults (Rowe & Kahn, 1998). Controlling food choices and the type and amount of time given to exercise will vary according to individual needs and preferences, but studies continually note that these voluntary factors are critical to achieving satisfying health outcomes in older ages and more resilience in coping with change (Van Leuven, 2010). Older adults who perceive themselves as healthy tend to be more engaged in their lives and universally express their desire to age in place instead of moving into assisted living or nursing care facilities (Mendes de Leon, Gold, Glass, Kaplan, & George, 2001; Van Leuven, 2010). A metaphor for other forms of healing can be drawn from the example of wound healing. In this complex process of self-repair, macrophages remove bacteria in the inflammatory stage and cells migrate to the area, depositing fibroblasts, collagen, and other needed material in the repair stage. As maturation and remodeling continue, the tensile strength builds as fibers are rearranged and cross linked (wound healing, Wikipedia, http://en.wikipedia.org/wiki/Wound_healing). This is a self-righting process where the body leads the way in rebuilding where it can, though at older ages this process is sometimes slower or diminished.

Physical bodies do not always come back to their preillness or preinjury state. Imagine an older bike rider who hits an unexpected bump over a protruding railroad track tie. She falls, dislocating her shoulder and tearing muscle. While her shoulder does eventually heal, during the healing time she has walked in a way that favors the sore side of her body and the muscles accommodate her new way of walking. Soon, though released from medical care, she finds she can no longer walk without a slight tilt in her balance. The body is resilient but may achieve a new form of normal.

Environmental press suggests that there is an optimum level of daily activity and environmental interaction to suitably challenge the physical capacity of older adults (Lawton, 1983). Too little and the older adult will lose physical strength and ability, but too much, and older adult bodies may stress organs, fall, or encounter another mishap. One part of maintaining biological resilience then involves using current capacity and reaching just a bit beyond it, yet not moving to a point where the body experiences tension and disease. A number of researchers have studied factors that specifically contribute to longevity and have found that continuing involvement in physical activity from middle to older ages along with social engagement, persistence, and motivation are significant to achieving longer life (Friedman & Martin, 2011; Perls & Silver, 1999).

Psychological Resilience

Psychological resilience occurs when individuals encounter difficult situations and life challenges; they evaluate options and take a problem-solving approach consistent with the classic Lazarus and Folkman (1984) model of stress and coping. Lazarus and Folkman (1984) define coping as "constantly changing cognitive and behavioral efforts to manage specific external and/or internal demands that are appraised as taxing or exceeding the resources of the person" (p. 141). In this model, when perceptions of stress reach an uncomfortable level, individuals are motivated to take action to relieve the discomfort and improve the situation, if possible. The role of cognitive appraisal is primary in shaping responses that reflect the individual's relation to the environment.

Individuals are motivated to decrease stress and improve the situation as they perceive it. First, action will be taken when it is relevant to key goals. Second, assessment of *which* immediate action to take centers on goal congruence, benefit potential, or harm reduction. Emotions are both motivation and response throughout the coping process (Folkman & Moskowitz, 2004). At the initial recognition of a threat (primary appraisal), negative emotions can be overwhelming and interfere with instrumental (action-focused) coping, so a preliminary task is to down-regulate these emotions that potentially thwart needed action. Secondary appraisal is an assessment of available psychological, material, spiritual, and social resources, weighing options and asking the question, "How should I respond?" This question also entails a values component that attempts to foresee conceivable consequences. Coping is not a one-time action but a process that "evolves and unfolds" as response opportunities are evaluated and alternatives tested to achieve a new state of systemic equilibrium (D'Zurilla & Nezu, 2007; Lazarus, 1993). Secondary appraisal thus involves understanding options for coping and expectations about what will happen.

Increasing the probability of favorable outcomes, even for those factors outside of their immediate control, can positively affect well-being for older persons. Expectancy of a positive outcome is also known as hope (Folkman & Moskowitz, 2000). Further, future-oriented coping strategies seek to proactively prepare for events (Schwarzer & Knoll, 2003). Such tasks as completing advance directives in the event of life-limiting illness are a future-oriented coping activity. At the same time, there is a contextual aspect to coping that indicates some types of behavior are more normative than others within culture. For instance, some Asian older adults prefer to let family members make end-of-life decisions on their behalf instead of individually completing advance directives (Ko & Lee, 2010). Coping repertoires are also dynamic and may be effective at one time or place and not others.

Culture also affects development of a coping repertoire. One surprising finding from a qualitative study of coping styles in 75 low-income community-dwelling African American and European American Jewish older adults was that coping styles did not vary by type of problem (Nelson-Becker, 2004). Instead of the problem appraisal determining a best-fit coping response, older adults preferred a primary coping style that they applied to all types of life challenge. Principal forms of coping included use of religious, social, or personal resources. A hierarchy of coping styles emerged across these two ethnic groups, with African Americans generally preferring religious coping, then social coping, and finally personal coping styles ("I depended on myself," "I was strong."). European American Jewish study participants generally preferred personal coping styles, followed by social coping, with religious coping forms their last choice. The influence of the problem was less salient than the influence of ethnicity and culture.

Optimism is another psychological resilience mechanism that is similar to coping in its expectations for positive outcomes (Scheier & Carver, 1985). This mechanism serves a helpful function in supporting coping efforts. However, there may be a down side to having too much optimism. Oishi, Diener, and Lucas (2007) suggest that extremely high levels of happiness may coincidently hinder people from achieving desired goals because they stop too soon. They may be satisfied with less than they had really preferred and thus refrain from making the many adjustments needed to reach an objective. Still, a meta-analysis by Diener and Chan (2011) indicated that both longitudinal and prospective studies give evidence that subjective well-being influences health and contentment in generally healthy populations. Effect sizes suggest an increase in longevity as high as 4–10 years. There is uncertainty about the way subjective well-being may affect specific illnesses, although positive moods, hopefulness, and humor seem to improve health measures such as blood pressure, length of recovery, and longevity.

Overall, resilience is demonstrated through the ways older adults cope psychologically with problems and challenges. Encounters with stressful events can create vulnerabilities that then either underlie future maladaptive responses to stress or lead to a type of inoculation response that reinforces self-efficacy and self-esteem (Windle, Markland, & Woods, 2008). Factors such as curiosity, creativity, self-confidence, sense of competence, and self-acceptance may function as types of core or reserve capacities even when physical health, for example, may diminish or change.

Social Resilience

Socially, resilience draws on such factors as social network size, closeness of social contacts (who and for what one can ask assistance), and frequency of contact (Lubben & Gironda, 2003). Older adults with larger or denser social networks will experience higher levels of social support: this may lead to greater resilience capacity. Emotional support, such as esteem and empathy, and instrumental support, such as information or capital, each meet different kinds of needs. These forms of support provide an older adult with greater fluidity when facing a difficulty. Social factors are particularly important in aging because negative life events (e.g., hospitalization, death of significant friends and family members) often result in weakened social connection.

Reciprocity dynamics, whether an individual overbenefits or underbenefits from social transactions, are also factors in resilience. When a person overbenefits (receives more than she/he gives), feelings of guilt and dissatisfaction may arise (Litwin, 1999, 2001). When an individual consistently underbenefits from the interaction or social transaction, he/she may feel burdened, for example, a caregiver in a caregiving dyad. Caregivers usually attend to the physical needs and sometimes emotional needs of another individual, with little opportunity for their own self-care. Social skills, too, may not be effective to meet needs, such as the case when an older adult carries a lifelong history of introversion leading to diminished social interaction. Loneliness, a risk factor for depression, can then result. Evidence suggests that more diversified social networks tended to show older adults more frequently in giving rather than receiving roles; however, extended family networks led to mutual exchanges (Litwin, 1999, 2001). In some cases, older adults in religious networks more often benefitted from exchanges (Litwin, 1999, 2001). Although support in itself is valuable, perceived social control within relationships may matter more (Bisconti & Bergeman, 1999). Perceived social control, the ability to engage support if needed, may foster resilient responses to loss.

Socioemotional Selectivity Theory (SST) suggests that the time perspective of older adults (e.g., perception of less future time available rather than assumptions of chronological age alone) accounts for a reorganization of goals (Lockenhoff & Carstensen, 2004). With a limited future horizon, older adults limit social networks to contacts that are more satisfying and emotionally fulfilling. They consciously select their social environments. Ultimately, they cull support networks of more distant or peripheral social partners, a process that begins in middle age. This process implies that diminished social networks do not occur through death of social network members alone. This pragmatic approach to aging suggests that older adults do exhibit social resilience, although loneliness and social isolation can be difficult to mediate when a long-term partner dies.

Emotional Resilience

Emotional resilience involves the capacity to change one's social construction of a situation and thus one's emotional engagement with it. An ability to successfully manage ambiguity and uncertainty also may form part of emotional resilience, whereas fear of failure and reluctance to try new things can *interfere* with the development of resilient approaches to life. Changing one's reaction or emotional stance to difficult situations (e.g., moving from anxiety, fear, and depression to acceptance and engagement) is the preferred approach if one cannot alter the situation itself (D'Zurilla & Nezu, 2007), such as receiving a medical diagnosis of cancer. In fact, SST posits that emotion-focused coping strategies take priority over problem-focused coping in older ages (Carstensen & Mikels, 2005; Lockenhoff & Carstensen, 2004). Emotion-focused coping governs emotional pain and may involve such strategies as denial, venting anger or worry, seeking support in social contacts, or locating a positive interpretation of an incident (Stanton & Franz, 1999). Frequently, emotion-focused coping is viewed as passive and a somewhat negative choice, but that may not be true in aging. When the time horizon is short, older adults seek to regulate emotions by avoiding negative social partners, consequently attending to relationships that benefit them emotionally. Perception of what will enhance positive affect and lead to greater meaning is chosen over what may cause undesirable disturbing feelings or increased social distance. Because of the diminishing time perspective in older ages vs. an expansive perspective in younger ages, attention centers on achieving emotionally meaningful life goals.

At younger ages, goals tend to center on information acquisition. Results from one study comparing older and younger individuals suggest that older people recall more positive images than younger people (Charles, Mather, & Carstensen, 2003). Biomarkers such as cortisol levels, blood pressure, and immune functioning can change due to emotional responses to stress. Overall, a resilient approach seeks to maximize benefits and diminish the power of stressful or negative encounters. A study of cumulative adversity in Holocaust survivors and comparison groups suggested that the survivors were relatively resilient physically and cognitively in coping with later adversity, but they showed emotional vulnerability, particularly relative to depression (Shrira, Palgi, Ben-Ezra, & Shmotkin, 2010). Older adults do report higher levels of success in managing positive and negative emotional states than younger persons. This includes controlling visible emotional signs and maintaining a neutral state. Tempers may be less prone to flare, for example, and older adults have been shown to display greater flexibility in adjusting their emotion-regulatory strategies (such as passive or active ones) to meet the demands of the situation (Kessler & Staudinger, 2009).

Spiritual Resilience

Spiritual resilience suggests the capacity of the human spirit to respond in growth-oriented ways to some of the most difficult challenges of life, particularly those associated with aging and loss experiences. Spirituality is not easy to define because different professions perceive it in different ways and many spiritual experiences are beyond the power of language to easily capture. Further, any definition, rather than confining the term in narrow ways, should be inclusive enough to encompass an ongoing expansion of understanding. As individuals age, developmental processes may enlarge the capacity to learn more about this fundamental life aspect. In social work, spirituality is used as an inclusive term that contains religious expressions.

Spirituality may be defined as that which gives meaning, purpose, and moral guidance to life and reflects an individual's or group's deepest or most central understanding about the reality of life (Nelson-Becker & Canda, 2008). It may include theistic, atheistic, nontheistic, and polytheistic forms, among others. Intense spiritual experiences, such as those mystics report, may cause one to transcend former boundaries and undergo a sense of connection with generations who lived long ago as well as with those yet to be born. In a qualitative study of 79 minority older adults who were asked to define spirituality and religion separately, spirituality was often mentioned as "a feeling inside, in the heart, or embedded in Being" (Nelson-Becker, 2003). It also was seen as a connection with God, having forgiving relationships with others, the way one lives life, and communication with nature (Nelson-Becker, 2003). Spiritual resilience is holding an ability to be nurtured by one's inner spiritual self, outer spiritual relationships, and to live with ambiguity, trusting the goodness of the universe in times when that goodness or light might be only dimly perceived.

At older ages spirituality may more typically be conflated with definitions of religion since at younger ages most older people did not consider them to be distinct forms (Nelson-Becker, 2005). Religion includes belief, faith, tradition, and an ethical code adhered to by a group and transmitted over time. Approximately 84% of adults ages 60–69 in the US say they affiliate with Christian religions; an additional 5 % affiliate with other world religions, such as Hinduism, Buddhism, and Islam (Pew Forum on Religion in the Public Life, 2007). These percentages increase slightly for adults age 70 and older. With projected demographic changes, world religion membership is likely to grow. Religion remains a strong potential resource for many of the current older cohorts.

There are many kinds of loss in aging; these range from losses in physical or sensory ability, the loss of "home" and familiar locales if one transitions to new housing arrangements, to losses of significant others and family members (Boss, 2007; Goldsworthy, 2005; Hooyman & Kramer, 2006). The latter form of loss includes reconstructing one's life to be worthy of continuing when some of the most meaningful relationships are no longer available. Often, the movement from a loss orientation to a restoration orientation is an oscillating process (Stroebe & Schut, 1999). Bereaved individuals move back and forth between feeling the loss deeply and creating new meaning. They survive and then eventually can reconnect to life in new ways. In handling loss, there is no linear downward or upward trajectory. The bereaved individual is plunged into an environment where what was familiar and comfortable becomes unfamiliar and strange. Commonly, the older person enters a process of questioning what is real and what is true, which tears apart the fabric of what was once accepted as part of everyday life (Nelson-Becker, 2006).

While some older adults rely on a religious faith that has sustained them over time, others enter a time of spiritual doubt or spiritual struggle that may lead them through what feels like a wasteland with no resources. In a sample of 481 patients assessed prior to cardiac surgery, findings indicated that Interleukin-6, a biomarker of age-related functional decline, might increase for those who had more religious struggle (Ai, Kronfol, Bolling, & Nelson-Becker, 2008). Those who acknowledge life as a spiritual journey suggest that this time of doubt and struggle is critical to deepen understanding and widen a grasp of the richness of all existence through examination of life at its most fundamental levels. It is not a process that one would ever choose, but the pain usually diminishes, leaving behind something wonderful.

Resilience at the End of Life

At older ages the end of a lifetime draws nearer, if individuals are healthy enough and fortunate enough to live to that point. Religious and spiritual views mediate the fear of death at older ages for those who consider themselves to be religious and/or spiritual (Daaleman & Dobbs, 2010), but society often has medicalized dying in a way that keeps people out of touch with their own dying experience. We have marginalized the ability to talk about death and dying in the Western culture. When social workers or family members attempt to sort out advance directives and final wishes with older clients before an illness, the topic is often changed.

Outsider perspectives of what illness and death look like and mean are important, but insider perspectives—how older adults view their own impending death and their life alongside it, are less often considered (Nelson-Becker, 2006; Wrubel, Acree, Goodman, & Folkman, 2009). Partly this occurs because these types of conversations are difficult to hold. There are few models on how to hold them within families and usually when they do occur, they are quite uncomfortable. There are a few rare individuals who are ready to initiate talk about their dying plans and more than that, to share self-reflections on what their life has meant. However, more often a social worker or other clinician is essential to help facilitate these important family conversations, to help older adults say what must be said. These conversations need to occur in the moment-to-moment normal routines of end-of-life challenges. They balance grief work, saying good-bye, thank you, and I'm sorry, with a fuller reflection on life purpose and hope in the context of dying. The source of that hope may be spiritual or religious, may be existential found meaning, or may be simply to have lived a life colored with its own uniqueness and beauty. When I presented my resilience at the end of life study in Hong Kong in 2008, I was asked what I thought was the most important task of those dying. An intuitive response came to me that seems true to me still. "They need to give and receive love" was my answer. The key task is no more difficult nor any less simple than this. This is what it means to die well. Perhaps there are yet plans and dreams that will ever remain unfinished, but the parts of a life that mattered most were both said and done. Life can only be lived spontaneously and experimentally.

The process of living and how one approaches life matters greatly, but the process of learning how to die well matters, too. As suggested earlier, it is uncommon for older adults to speak about how they want to die and what they want to accomplish prior to that moment. The Buddhists believe that preparing for one's death is a way to build resilience. Meditating on death and the impermanence of all life gives enhanced meaning to life and our own interdependence (Sogyal, 1992). Entering hospice care at a point where one can work with and learn from one's dying can facilitate dying well. The life world one creates and the meaning one makes is singular and meaning making continues—even as Death encircles close.

Narrative Gerontology and Metaphor

Narrative gerontology offers a promising method to enhance resilience. In a narrative framework, older adults form stories about significant occurrences over their lifetimes. These may include shocking and traumatic events, or glimpses of daily life that permitted more subtle exploration of meaning. As older adults reminisce and reflect on events in their lives, their responses then and now to these often emotionally infused and emotionally imprinted episodes may become clearer. Learning happens when older adults can bridge the distance and explore new perspectives that were invisible to them at earlier points in time. Therapeutic life review carries the goals of finding meaning, reorganizing, and integrating through an evaluation of life experiences over the life span (Butler, 1963; Randall & Kenyon, 2001). Identifying dominant discourses and the way one's particular life story was shaped by these larger narratives provides a rich forum in aging. For instance, in my study of African American and European American older adults (Nelson-Becker, 2003), it was curious that discrimination was not identified as a life challenge. It was present there in the stories participants told; however, since it was part of the dominant discourse, it was also accepted as the way things were. It seemed these older adults could not see how their lives might have unfolded differently. This then, became a sad indictment of power used wrongly. In problem-saturated life stories, this particular structural issue was not much discussed.

Creating a personal biography gives older adults the courage to look at experiences of suffering, both why they occurred and the role they played in the context of a person's life (Black & Rubinstein, 2009).

But the narrative needs to move beyond this exploration of challenge and suffering to discernment of what is worth sharing with others, particularly as a legacy to younger generations. Is it practical knowledge about how to live a life? Is it something useful about the culture and/or religious or spiritual context in which one moves? Is it wisdom? In this way reciprocity between the generations is honored and the capacity for greater understanding is enhanced as time moves forward.

Metaphor as Resilience Tool

Why is metaphor particularly useful in finding the way to resilience? Metaphor, as a part of narrative gerontology, structures our conceptual understanding and is often a container for meaning (Lakoff & Johnson, 2003). Because it is so much a part of our communication, we do not always acknowledge the role that metaphor plays. (There was one, did you catch it?). Metaphors orient us ("I feel *up* today") and describe our ontological experience ("The *pressure* of the job was overwhelming"). The language of metaphor helps us discover and say what cannot be said easily. Through metaphor we can "speak about those thin places where the sacred hovers tantalizingly just beyond our fingertips. These are tip-of-the-tongue places, the stammering places where everyday language refuses its normal fluency and stutters to a stop" until metaphor "bridges the gaps into new awarenesses" (Finnegan, 2008, p. 119). At times, illness or calamity threatens to shatter us. Metaphor helps us move through those difficult places and times and share our story with others. Metaphors take us deeper than our own words would otherwise sometimes go:

> I call it [the illness] the invader. I've given it a name because it came into my life uninvited and unannounced and it's decided it's going to camp here. I can't get rid of it. It's like a house guest you don't want (Research participant cited in Nelson-Becker, 2006).

However, it is important to remember that metaphors only point the way to resilience, they are not the way. They gift us with a way to express our struggle and our pain, our hope and our yearning, our confidence and courage, our buoyancy and boldness as they crash against our disbelief and doubt. In crossing desert places, whether that crossing be short or long, metaphor gives us a way to see beyond our immediate vision; it gives us a song of sustenance, when all else fades away. Metaphors help us touch our grief in moments when that grief seems too hard to bear. As Ricoeur (1991) has mentioned, metaphor mediates meaning. Metaphors can open windows to the soul and unfreeze what was frozen there, engendering creative methods and imaginative means for people to find their way back to a new place. Resilience is not about a return to where one has been, but breathing a new breath into life. This process for many signals one of the many recursive turns in spiritual development.

Resilience in Aging: Narrative Case Example

The following case example of Genevieve Jones (name changed) from one of my research studies demonstrated a resilient approach to life. She was 85 at the time of the interview. In this illustration, aspects of biological, psychological, social, emotional, and spiritual resilience are portrayed.

> My mother died at an early age of an accident. I was no child at that time, but still I felt very much alone. I was about 17. There was no other male figure in my life, so it was just me and my stepfather. That was a hard time. It was during the Depression years and it was very hard. But somehow or other you cope. I don't know what it is, but you cope. My own hardiness got me through. My family was all spread around. Everyone was in a bad position I guess at the time. My mother and I were sort of close. She'd had a bad life too. She wasn't the real affectionate mother like we are nowadays or maybe even then. She was always there, but she couldn't help me with a lot.

A year after she died, I got married. It was a new thing in my life. It was a good marriage in the beginning, but somehow it didn't continue. Through that marriage I had three daughters which I'm grateful for. It was hard after the divorce—a working mother living alone with three kids, you know? Money wasn't that easy to get. Somehow I managed through it, thank God.

One time—lunch money was hard—I got them money through the AFDC and that wasn't really a heck of a lot. I didn't get any support from my ex-husband for the children. That's about the gist of it. I was working then, too, so it was kind of hard. I wasn't a stay-at-home mother. Disciplining the kids was hard. It wasn't easy. At times we had very little to eat. This is the way I was brought up. My mother never had too much when she was alive. I had one brother who lived with an aunt. I didn't see him often because they always lived in the suburbs. It was a lonely way, but I have good friends and we were all in the same position. My friends provided emotional support.

I went to two years of high school because at that time you were allowed to take just two years. At that time I learned nothing, because I took the wrong course. Instead of taking a business course, I took a general one, so there was nothing there that helped me and jobs were very scarce anyway. I worked at little jobs but they weren't worth much. I worked in a hot dog store close to our house. I worked at Marshall Fields—it sounds classy but believe me it wasn't—I worked a lot of years. It wasn't hard work, but it was late hours and transportation was tough. I didn't have a car and I didn't have a credit card. Can you believe it?

As you get older your health is a little less. You worry whether anything will come out of it, whether you'll be alright or you won't. I have had arthritis since I was seven. Sometimes I feel like a tiger inside an old cat's body. I am now getting around, able to walk better, but I do have difficulty walking. Therapy helps and religion helps me because I know I can handle it. My friends have also helped me.

I just talked to my stepdaughter and she said to me, 'We try to call you and you are never home!' I don't know that any calls are so important. If so, they'll call again. I retired in 1979 from a manufacturing firm, but I just did paperwork. I retired because my second husband wanted to go to Florida to live. I only had a couple more years and I would have gotten a pension, but he didn't want to stay, so we went to Florida. We took our social security at 62 and that meant less money. My second husband died twenty years ago. He was a wonderful husband, but I've had to struggle financially since then. However, I would depend on myself and was able to do things for myself. I was lonesome, but I was able to do things. Now I enjoy volunteering. I deliver meals and volunteer at the resale shop. My arthritis doesn't keep me inside!

I solve problems through using the scriptures in the Bible—I don't beseech God. Whatever it is will happen and He knows. 'Be thankful and the good will come to us,' that is what I believe. Giving thanks in difficult situations has always helped me to persevere. I try not to ask God for things that are unnecessary. I don't ask God about my health, 'cause that's His problem. He already knows before I even tell him. He knows what time he's going to take me back to him. I pray to God for things that I feel are necessary, not unnecessary things.

Genevieve Jones lived a life that was difficult by modern standards. It was especially difficult because of the loss of her mother when she was emerging as a young woman, an early marriage that was unsuccessful, low level jobs due to inadequate educational opportunity and scarcity of jobs, and long-term arthritis. However, she enjoyed her children and she ultimately met a man she loved who became her second husband. They didn't have much money, but she enjoyed their life together. At the time of the interview, rather than feel sorry for widowhood and near-poverty, she volunteered. She had friends whom she valued and she had some contact with her daughter-in-law. Although she didn't consider herself highly religious, she did use religious resources in ways she saw as being very practical. While she may not have achieved success, fortune, or fame, she was content. Her approach to living was a resilient one.

Conclusion

In this chapter I have sought to build a comprehensive picture of resilience at older ages. Some would argue that, by definition, older adults who must manage a multitude of unexpected challenges miss out on any opportunity for resilience to return them to previous levels of functioning. However, examination of biological, psychological, social, emotional, and spiritual resilience—it is hoped—has demonstrated that, as at any age, older adults have singular opportunities to learn, develop, and to construct potency of character. In some ways, on the verge of physical diminishment, appreciation for the ancient ideals of truth, beauty, and goodness may deepen. Focus on spiritual values may increase. Much of this is meant to be learned, shared, and passed on in families. Wisdom may be the legacy left for those who have the good fortune to hear the life story narratives of these custodians of time.

References

Ai, A. L., Kronfol, Z., Bolling, S. F., & Nelson-Becker, H. (2008, November). *Existential crisis or spiritual struggle may influence interleukin-6 before open-heart surgery.* Paper presented at the 61st annual Gerontological Society of America, National Harbor, MD.

Ardelt, M., Landes, S. D., & Valliant, G. (2010). *The long term effects of WWII combat on later life wisdom and well-being moderated by generativity.* Paper presented at the 63rd annual meeting of the Gerontological Society of America, New Orleans, LA.

Balk, D. (2008). A modest proposal about bereavement and recovery. *Death Studies, 32,* 84–93.

Baltes, P. B. (1993). The aging mind: Potential and limits. *The Gerontologist, 33*(5), 580–594.

Bar-Tur, L., & Levy-Shiff, R. (2000). Coping with losses and past trauma in old age: The separation-individuation perspective. *Journal of Personal and Interpersonal Loss, 5,* 263–281.

Becvar, D. (2007). *Families that flourish: Facilitating resilience in clinical practice.* New York: W.W. Norton.

Bisconti, T. L., & Bergeman, C. S. (1999). Perceived social control as a mediator of the relationships among social support, psychological well-being, and perceived health. *The Gerontologist, 39*(1), 94–103.

Black, H. K., & Rubinstein, R. L. (2009). The effect of suffering on generativity: Accounts of elderly African American men. *Journal of Gerontology Social Sciences, 64B*(2), 296–303.

Boss, P. (2007). Ambiguous loss theory: Challenges for scholars and practitioners. *Family Relations, 56*(2), 105–111.

Butler, R. N. (1963). The life review: An interpretation of reminiscence in the aged. *Psychiatry, 26,* 65–76.

Carstensen, L. L., & Mikels, J. A. (2005). At the intersection of emotion and cognition: Aging and the positivity effect. *Current Directions in Psychological Science, 14*(3), 117–121.

Charles, S. T., Mather, M., & Carstensen, L. (2003). Aging and emotional memory: The forgettable nature of negative images for older adults. *Journal of Experimental Psychology, 132*(2), 310–324.

Chow, E., & Nelson-Becker, H. (2010). From spiritual distress to spiritual transformation: Stroke survivor narratives from Hong Kong. *Journal of Aging Studies, 24,* 313–324.

Cohen, G. (2005). *The mature mind: The positive power of the aging brain.* New York: Basic Books.

D'Zurilla, T., & Nezu, A. (2007). *Problem-solving therapy: A positive approach to clinical intervention.* New York: Springer.

Daaleman, T. P., & Dobbs, D. (2010). Religiosity, spirituality, and death attitudes in chronically ill older adults. *Research on Aging, 32*(2), 224–243.

Davis, C. G., & Nolen-Hoeksema, S. (2001). Loss and meaning: How do people make sense of loss? *The American Behavioral Scientist, 44*(5), 726–741.

Dellmann-Jenkins, M., Blankemeyer, M., & Pinkard, O. (2000). Young adult children and grandchildren in primary caregiver roles to older relatives and their service needs. *Family Relations, 49*(2), 177–186.

Diener, E., & Chan, M. (2011). Happy people live longer: Subjective well-being contributes to health and longevity. *Applied Psychology, 39*(1), 1–43.

Elder, G. (2001). Life course. In G. L. Maddox (Ed.), *The encyclopedia of aging* (3rd ed., pp. 593–596). New York: Springer.

Federal Interagency Forum on Aging-Related Statistics. (2010). Older Americans 2010: Key indicators of well-being. In *Federal interagency forum on aging-related statistics.* Washington, DC: U.S. Government Printing Office.

Finnegan, J. (2008). *The audacity of spirit: The meaning and shaping of spirituality today.* Dublin: Veritas Publications.

Folkman, S., & Moskowitz, J. T. (2000). Positive affect and the other side of coping. *The American Psychologist, 55,* 647–654.

Folkman, S., & Moskowitz, J. T. (2004). Coping: Pitfalls and promise. *Annual Review of Psychology, 55,* 745–774.

Fraser, M., Richman, J., & Galinsky, J. (1999). Risk, protection, and resilience: Toward a conceptual framework for social work practice. *Social Work Research, 23*(3), 131–143.

Friedman, H. S., & Martin, L. R. (2011). *The longevity project: Surprising discoveries for health and long life from the landmark eight-decade study.* New York: Penguin Group.

Fry, P. S., & Keyes, C. L. M. (Eds.). (2010). *New frontiers in resilient aging: Life-strengths and well-being in late life.* New York: Cambridge University Press.

Gergen, M., & Gergen, K. (2003). Positive aging: Living well as the best revenge. In J. Gubrium & J. Holstein (Eds.), *Ways of aging* (pp. 203–224). New York: Blackwell.

Germaine, C. B. (1973). An ecological perspective in casework practice. *Social Casework, 54*, 323–330.

Goldsworthy, K. (2005). Grief and loss theory in social work practice: All changes involve loss, just as all losses require change. *Australian Social Work, 58*(2), 167–177.

Halfon, N., & Hochstein, M. (2002). Life course health development: An integrated framework to developing health, policy and research. *The Milbank Quarterly, 80*, 433–479.

Hatch, S. L. (2005). Conceptualizing and identifying cumulative adversity and protective resources: Implications for understanding health inequalities. *The Journals of Gerontology Psychological Sciences and Social Sciences, 60B*, S130–S134.

Hinterlong, J., Morrow-Howell, N., & Rosario, P. (2007). Productive engagement and late life physical and mental health: Findings from a nationally representative panel study. *Research on Aging, 29*(4), 348–370.

Hooyman, N. R., & Kramer, B. J. (2006). *Living through loss: Interventions across the life span*. New York: Columbia University Press.

Kahana, E., & Kahana, B. (1996). Conceptual and empirical advances in understanding aging well through proactive adaptation. In V. Bengston (Ed.), *Adulthood and aging: Research on continuities and discontinuities* (pp. 18–41). New York: Springer.

Kessler, E., & Staudinger, U. (2009). Affective experience in adulthood and old age: The role of affective arousal and perceived affect regulation. *Psychology and Aging, 24*(2), 349–362.

Kivnick, H. Q., & Murray, S. V. (2001). Life strengths interview guide: Assessing elder clients' strengths. *Journal of Gerontological Social Work, 34*(4), 7–32.

Ko, E., & Lee, J. (2010). Completion of advance directives among Korean American and non-Hispanic White older adults. *Research on Aging, 32*(5), 618–644.

Lakoff, G., & Johnson, M. (2003). *Metaphors we live by*. Chicago: University of Chicago Press.

Lawton, M. P. (1983). Environments and other determinants of well-being in older people. *The Gerontologist, 23*(40), 349–357.

Lazarus, R. (1993). Coping theory and research: Past, present, and future. *Psychosomatic Medicine, 55*(3), 234–247.

Lazarus, R., & Folkman, D. (1984). *Stress, appraisal, and coping*. New York: Springer.

Litwin, H. (1999). Support network type and patterns of help giving and receiving among older people. *Journal of Social Service Research, 24*(3/4), 83–101.

Litwin, H. (2001). Social network type and morale in old age. *The Gerontologist, 41*(4), 516–524.

Lockenhoff, L., & Carstensen, L. (2004). Socioemotional selectivity theory, aging, and health: The increasingly delicate balance between regulating emotions and making tough choices. *Journal of Personality, 76*(6), 1395–1424.

Lubben, J. E., & Gironda, M. W. (2003). Centrality of social ties to the health and well-being of older adults. In B. Berkman & L. Harooytan (Eds.), *Social work and health care in an aging society: Education, policy, practice, and research* (pp. 319–350). New York: Springer.

Masten, A. S. (2001). Ordinary magic: Resilience processes in development. *The American Psychologist, 56*(3), 227–238.

McCullough, M. E., Pargament, K. I., & Thoresen, C. E. (Eds.). (2000). *Forgiveness: Theory, research, and practice*. New York: Guilford Press.

Mendes de Leon, C. F., Gold, D. T., Glass, T. A., Kaplan, L., & George, L. K. (2001). Disability as a function of social networks and support in elderly African Americans and Whites: The Duke EPESE 1986–1992. *The Journals of Gerontology Series B Psychological Sciences and Social Sciences, 56*, S179–S190.

Monroe, B., & Oliviere, D. (Eds.). (2007). *Resilience in palliative care: Achievement in adversity*. Oxford, UK: Oxford University Press.

Morrow-Howell, N. (2010). Volunteering in later life: Research frontiers. *The Journals of Gerontology Series B Psychological Sciences and Social Sciences, 65B*(4), 461–469.

Nelson-Becker, H. (2003). Practical philosophies: Interpretations of religion and spirituality by African-American and Jewish elders. *Journal of Religious Gerontology, 14*(2/3), 85–99.

Nelson-Becker, H. (2004). Meeting life challenges: A hierarchy of coping styles in African-American and Jewish-American older adults. *Journal of Human Behavior in the Social Environment, 10*(1), 155–174.

Nelson-Becker, H. (2005). Religion and coping in older adults. *Journal of Gerontological Social Work, 45*(1/2), 51–68.

Nelson-Becker, H. (2006). Voices of resilience: Older adults in hospice care. *Journal of Social Work in End-of-Life and Palliative Care, 2*(3), 87–106.

Nelson-Becker, H., & Canda, E. R. (2008). Research on religion, spirituality, and aging: A social work perspective on the state of the art. *The Journal of Religion Spirituality and Aging, 20*(3), 177–193.

Nelson-Becker, H., Chapin, R., & Fast, B. (2009). The strengths model with older adults: Critical practice components. In D. Saleebey (Ed.), *The strengths perspective in social work practice* (5th ed., pp. 161–180). Boston: Allyn & Bacon.

Newman, T. (2004). *What works in building resilience?* Ilford, UK: Barnado's.

Ng, S. M., Chan, T. H., Chan, C. L., Lee, A. M., Yau, J. K., Chan, C. H., et al. (2006). Group debriefing for people with chronic diseased during the SARS pandemic: Strengths-focused and meaning-oriented approach for resilience and transformation (SMART). *Community Mental Health Journal, 42*(1), 33–52.

Oates, J. C. (2011). *A widow's story: A memoir.* New York: HarperCollins.

Oishi, S., Diener, E., & Lucas, R. (2007). The optimum level of well-being: Can people be too happy? *Perspectives on Psychological Science, 2*(4), 346–360.

Ong, A. D., Bergeman, C. S., & Baker, S. M. (2009). Resilience comes of age: Defining features in later adulthood. *Journal of Personality, 77*(6), 1777–1804.

Park, C. L., & Fenster, J. R. (2004). Stress-related growth: Predictors of occurrence and correlates with psychological adjustment. *Journal of Social and Clinical Psychology, 23*(2), 195–215.

Park, C. L., Mills-Baxter, M. A., & Fenster, J. R. (2005). Post-traumatic growth from life's most traumatic event: Influences on elders' current adjustment. *Traumatology, 11*(4), 297–306.

Perls, T., & Silver, M. (1999). *Living to 100: Lessons in living to your maximum potential at any age.* New York: Basic Books.

Pew Forum on Religion in the Public Life. (2007). *US Religious Landscape Survey: Chapter 3. Religious Affiliation and Demographic Groups.* Retrieved April 15, 2011, from http://religions.pewforum.org/reports#.

Randall, W. L., & Kenyon, G. M. (2001). *Ordinary wisdom, biographical aging and the journey of life.* Westport, CT: Praeger.

Ricoeur, P. (1991). *From text to action.* Evanston, IL: Northwestern University Press.

Ronch, J. L., & Goldfield, J. A. (Eds.). (2003). *Mental wellness in aging: Strengths-based approaches.* Baltimore, MD: Health Professions Press.

Rowe, J. W., & Kahn, R. L. (1998). *Successful aging.* New York: Pantheon Press.

Ryff, C. D., Singer, B., Love, G. D., & Essex, M. J. (1998). Resilience in adulthood and later life. In J. Lomranz (Ed.), *Handbook of aging and mental health: An integrative approach* (pp. 69–96). New York: Plenum.

Saleebey, D. (Ed.). (2009). *The strengths perspective in social work practice* (5th ed.). Boston: Allyn & Bacon.

Scheier, M. F., & Carver, C. S. (1985). Optimism, coping, and health: Assessment and implications of generalized outcome expectancies. *Health Psychology, 4*, 219–247.

Schwarzer, R., & Knoll, N. (2003). Positive coping: Mastering demands and searching for meaning. In S. J. Lopez & C. R. Snyder (Eds.), *Positive psychological assessment: A handbook of models and measures* (pp. 393–409). Washington, DC: American Psychological Association.

Shrira, A., Palgi, Y., Ben-Ezra, M., & Shmotkin, D. (2010). Do Holocaust survivors show increased vulnerability or resilience to post-holocaust cumulative adversity? *Journal of Traumatic Stress, 23*(3), 367–375.

Sogyal, R. (1992). *The Tibetan book of living and dying.* San Francisco: HarperCollins.

Stanton, A. L., & Franz, R. (1999). Focusing on emotion: An adaptive coping strategy? In C. R. Synder (Ed.), *Coping: The psychology of what works* (pp. 90–118). New York: Oxford University Press.

Strelan, P., & Covic, T. (2006). A review of forgiveness process models and a coping framework to guide future research. *Journal of Social and Clinical Psychology, 25*(10), 1059–1085.

Stroebe, M. S., & Schut, H. (1999). The dual process model of coping with bereavement: Rational and description. *Death Studies, 23*, 197–224.

Tedeschi, R. G., & Calhoun, L. G. (2008). Beyond the concept of recovery: Growth and the experience of loss. *Death Studies, 32*, 27–39.

Tornstam, L. (1996). Gerotranscendence: A theory about maturing into old age. *Journal of Aging and Identity, 1*(1), 37–50.

Valliant, G. E. (1993). *The wisdom of the ego: Sources of resilience in adult life.* Cambridge, MA: Harvard University Press.

Valliant, G. E. (2002). *Aging well.* New York: Little, Brown, and Company.

Van Leuven, K. (2010). Health practices of older adults in good health: Engagement is key. *Journal of Gerontological Nursing, 36*(6), 38–46.

Walsh, F. (1998). *Strengthening family resilience.* New York: The Guilford Press.

Windle, G., Markland, D., & Woods, R. (2008). Examination of a theoretical model of psychological resilience in older age. *Aging & Mental Health, 12*(3), 285–292.

Wrubel, J., Acree, M., Goodman, S., & Folkman, S. (2009). End of living: Maintaining a lifeworld during terminal illness. *Psychology and Health, 24*(10), 1229–1243.

Part V

Resilience and Ability

Family Resilience Relative to Children with Severe Disabilities

21

Timothy S. Hartshorne, Alyson Schafer,
Kasee K. Stratton, and Tasha M. Nacarato

Introduction

All births change the dynamics of a family, sometimes in ways the parents never anticipated. The web of relationships multiplies in complex patterns of interaction. Roles of family members often shift with the addition of new needs, demands, and expectations. Parenting can be exciting and meaningful, but it is also hard work. Most parents endure the hard work because of the hopes and joys of watching their children grow and change and develop into people who in their turn will make their way in the world. Of course, it does not always turn out the way parents anticipated. Children do not always fulfill their parents' expectations. But the hope can linger because it should be possible.

When a child is born who has severe disabilities identified at birth, the dynamics change. Hopes and dreams appear dashed at the start. The web of relationships is not very balanced. The needs and demands that shape new role arrangements are far different than anyone could have imagined. And there is an abiding fear that this child will never be able to make his or her way in the world.

So what is the impact on the family? In 1973, Mitchell wrote:

> The impact of a handicapped child on a family is never negligible, usually damaging, and sometimes catastrophic. A few families with great spiritual strength may be bound more firmly together by the experience, but in most, the stresses imposed far outweigh any benefit (p. 267–268).

Similarly, Murphy (1982) reviewed the literature on the family of a child with disabilities prior to 1982, and cites many very discouraging articles describing the constant anxiety, lowered self-esteem, depression, neuroses and psychoses, and a lack of enjoyment of parenthood that many parents presumably experience.

This view has changed in recent years. In 2002, Hastings and Taunt made the following statement: "First, families of children with disabilities report positive perceptions in addition to negative

T.S. Hartshorne • T.M. Nacarato
Central Michigan University, School Psychology,
Mount Pleasant, MI, USA
e-mail: harts1ts@cmich.edu; tim.hartshorne@cmich.edu

A. Schafer
Private Practice, Toronto, Canada

K.K. Stratton
Kennedy Krieger Institute, John Hopkins School of Medicine,
Baltimore, MD, USA

D.S. Becvar (ed.), *Handbook of Family Resilience*,
DOI 10.1007/978-1-4614-3917-2_21, © Springer Science+Business Media New York 2013

perceptions and stress, and there is some data to suggest that positive perceptions are common" (p. 121). In fact, Scorgie, Wilgosh, and Sobsey (2004) note that, "Increasingly, parents are asserting that, despite the considerable and on-going stresses involved in parenting a child with a disability, their experiences have been personally transformative" (p. 85). Did the authors in the 1970s miss something, or has the experience changed over time? We suspect it is a bit of both.

Sometimes You Find What You Are Looking For

Professionals encountering parents who have just learned that their baby has severe disabilities are quite likely to find very stressed and upset individuals. The early frequent advice to institutionalize the child was an attempt to reduce that stress so that parents could lead a "normal life." Early researchers wanted to measure the experience of stress in order to better understand it, and one of the most widely used instruments was the *Questionnaire on Resources and Stress* (Holroyd, 1974), particularly its short form (Friedrich, Greenberg, & Crnic, 1983). This true–false instrument tallies possible sources of stress such as: constant demands for care, feeling tense out in public, being upset with how life is going, problems with communication, and having to give up things the parent wanted to do in life. However, several authors have noted problems with this approach (Clayton, Glidden, & Kiphart, 1994; Glidden, 1993; Hartshorne, 2002). Consider, for example, this item: "I worry about what will happen to _____ when I can no longer take care of him/her." While all parents must worry about their children as they grow up and move out on their own, this is a particular concern for parents of children with severe disabilities. But consider the implications of a parent choosing "false" for this item. Under what circumstances would a parent of a child with severe disabilities NOT worry about the child's future? As Hartshorne (2002) notes, that would suggest total denial of the realities of the circumstances. While the instrument scores a "true" for the item as indicative of parental stress, a "false" suggests a parent who is not very in touch with reality. So, for many of the items, honest answers based on an understanding of the reality of the child's condition result in scores indicative of high stress. Because most parents are not in denial, researchers inevitably have found this experience of having a child with severe disabilities to be highly stressful, and may have missed the truly resilient parent who clearly understands the situation but is able to manage it and perhaps even transcend it.

How Has It Changed?

Consider the following changes:
- Passage of Public Law 94–142 the *Education of All Handicapped Children Act* mandated an appropriate, public education for all children.
- Advances in medical care have kept more children alive with improved health.
- Advances in health technology such as cochlear implants have helped to compensate for some of the disabling conditions.
- The internet and email have allowed parents to link with other parents of children with the same or similar diagnosis for support, encouragement, and advice.
- An increase in the number of identified genetic syndromes has allowed more parents to have an actual diagnosis for their child's condition.
- An increased emphasis on inclusive education and community settings has meant that children with disabilities are more likely to know and be known by their peers.
- Raising a child with a severe disability is not the same prospect today as it was 40 years ago.

Review of the Literature

Over the years there have been several reviews of research on families with a child who has disabilities. The earliest, noted earlier, was by Murphy (1982). She reviewed 52 studies, only 16 of which were actual research, and only 8 included a control group. Murphy summarizes the literature with this quote from Howell (1973): "those who work in the field of habilitation with children are well aware of the neuroses and psychotic breaks of parents, dissolution of marriages, and adjustment problems of siblings, as well as significant behavioral problems of the handicapped child himself" (p. 203). The literature described parents with very low self-concept, depressed, beset by constant anxiety, with marital stress, and conflicts over life decisions and personal needs. The families struggled to find appropriate services such as schools, child care, and medical care.

Some of the work reviewed by Murphy addressed sibling reactions. Deviant behavior in the siblings was related to family size and social class. Brothers seen in a clinic had more behavior issues than sisters, but girls were subjected to more household responsibility. Interestingly, siblings of children with mild disability tended to be more disturbed than siblings of children with more severe disability.

While some authors saw acceptance as a potential outcome of working through the issues of raising a child with disabilities, the research tended to find chronic sorrow as more characteristic. A problem cited was the lack of a culture or tradition for supporting and raising children with disabilities. Murphy noted that most researchers have focused on problems and deficits as opposed to strengths.

Scorgie, Wilgosh, and McDonald (1998) reviewed 25 studies published between 1988 and 1995 pertaining to stress and coping. Six of the studies included control groups. Coping was viewed differently in different studies. Some looked at the characteristics of parents who cope well, while others viewed coping as the end of a process from crisis to adaptation, and for still others coping was understood as the absence of stress. The authors organized their review around four variables: family, parent, child, and external.

The research on family variables was mixed on socioeconomic status (SES), with some studies finding SES mostly unrelated to family stress and adjustment, while others found families of higher SES to have better access to resources and coping strategies. Family cohesion was found to mediate stress and predict lower levels of distress and higher marital satisfaction. Family hardiness, the construct most related to resilience in this review, was found to be related to positive family outcomes. Hardy families tended to perceive stressful events as challenging, as opposed to devastating, and they employed more coping strategies and had larger support networks than less hardy families. The ability of the family to produce a variety and greater number of solutions to difficulties was found to support challenges with schools, child care, and dealing with toileting, dressing, and eating. Family roles and responsibilities were reported to be more demanding as parents coped with meeting their child's needs, and could lead to role restriction, particularly for the mother. Findings on family composition were mixed. Two parent families were generally better at coping than single parent families, although one study found single parents were just as adept through greater utilization of support systems.

Four parent variables were examined. First, the quality of the marital relationship was found to be a strong predictor of family well-being. Second, mothers with more of an internal locus of control experienced more adaptive functioning and access to social support. Third, fathers who felt more competent to meet their child's needs had less stress, which seemed to impact the mother as well. Finally, lack of time due to increased caretaking duties was a problem that detracted from activity and contact with other children and spouse.

Four child variables also were summarized in this review. The impact of severity of the disability and the age of the child were inconclusive. It is possible that characteristics such as prognosis, behavior problems, issues of communication, and lack of progress are more important. Parents of a female child tended to adjust better than parents of a male child, perhaps because of the father's view of a son, or because boys may have more behavior problems. Further, a negative temperament along with emotional unresponsiveness in the child appeared to affect family adaptation.

Finally, Scorgie et al. (1998) reviewed findings related to stigmatizing social attitudes, social network support, and collaboration with professionals. The ability of the parents to respond to inconsiderate remarks or behavior from others was associated with reduced levels of stress. Research is clear on the importance of social support. Many parents have encountered professionals who are difficult to deal with, suggesting the importance of better training of professionals who work with severe disability.

The review by Scorgie et al. (1998), unlike Murphy's (1982), was more focused on the variables influencing parental coping outcomes, rather than documenting how poorly parents cope. Yau and Li-Tsang (1999) reviewed articles over a 20-year period ending in 1994, overlapping both Murphy (1982) and Scorgie et al. (1998, 2004); however, their review was focused on adjustment and adaptation, which they summarized in two categories. The first category pertained to the attributes of an adjusted family. These include the presence of a small, intense social support network, the availability of adequate resources for meeting crises, being a two-parent family with few children, having higher SES, which supports coping with the extra care-taking demands, and living in a community that accepts the child and family. The second category contains characteristics of adaptive functioning parents. These include personal resources such as higher education, being well adjusted, having positive and realistic expectations for the child, less preoccupation with negative thoughts and able to creatively respond to challenges, and better problem-solving skills. A strong spousal relationship, good rewarding parenting skills, and an involved father who communicates well with his child were all important. Finally, participation in a parent support group has been found to be helpful.

Two additional reviews have been more focused. Ylven, Björck-Åkesson, and Granlund (2006) reviewed the literature for evidence regarding positive functioning in families with children with disability, including 30 studies from 1985 to 2004. They noted that only four of those articles had positive aspects of family functioning as the focus, suggesting the continued influence of a deficit orientation. A majority of the articles came from a stress and coping orientation, but nine came from a family systems perspective. The focus of the review is on sorting out the constructs of family problem solving, sense of coherence, coping, and adaptation.

The other review, by Blacher, Neece, and Paczkowski (2005), is of articles primarily from 2004. The authors note that while research continues to focus largely on the "impact" of the child on the family, there is much more interest in the contexts of family well-being such as poverty, stressful life events, and culture. An interest in siblings has developed, as well as in parenting practices.

In summary, the literature generally has considered the kind of impact a child with severe disabilities has on the family. Early on it was concluded that the impact was devastating. However, over the years the focus has shifted so that the impact is now viewed as potentially positive, and the literature is focused more on identifying those factors that make for a positive impact.

Current Issues

Broberg, Blacher, and Emerson (2009) edited a special issue of the *Journal of Intellectual Disability Research* on resilience. The three articles included provide a useful picture of current issues in resilience and families of children with severe disability.

Positive Psychology

The recent trend toward a positive psychology focused on adaptation, strengths, and abilities is the foundation for Lloyd and Hastings' (2009) study of hope as a resilience factor. They adopt a two-component model of hope from Snyder, Rand, and Sigmon (2002) that includes hope agency, or the perception that goals can be met, and hope pathways, or the ability to plan ways to achieve goals. While the authors hypothesized, based on theory, that high levels of both hope agency and hope pathways would be associated with the highest level of parent adjustment, hope pathways were only a resilience factor for maternal depression. Hope agency was a resilience factor for both mother and father psychological adjustment. What is significant about this study is its emphasis on what makes a difference for mothers and fathers in having a positive coping experience.

Stress Over Time

The stress experienced by parents of children with disabilities is unlikely to be static over time, but rather to vary in response to events and experiences of the family members. Gerstein, Crnic, Blacher, and Baker (2009) measured daily parenting stress at 6-month intervals from child ages of 36–60 months. The authors found that for mothers the experience of daily stress increased over these months, whereas for fathers it stayed the same. Marital quality was found to be a compensatory variable for both mothers and fathers, but surprisingly, parent–child relationship was not. The authors found some interesting crossover influences. For example, the psychological well-being of the mothers was related to less parenting stress in the fathers, and fathers' well-being was associated with a smaller increase in mothers' stress over time. Also, an early positive father–child relationship led to less of an increase in mother stress over time. These are complex findings. The variables that influence how parents are able to cope with the experience of a child with disabilities over time are multifaceted and overlapping, and it will take considerable research to sort out the critical variables.

Adults

Most of the literature on parenting children with severe disabilities has focused on younger children and adolescents. Adult children have been somewhat overlooked, but for many parents, raising a child with disabilities is a lifelong endeavor and commitment. Hill and Rose (2009) extended research on how child, environmental, and parental characteristics impact parent stress in mothers of adult children over 30 years of age. Child characteristics of adaptive behavior and behavior difficulties were associated with mother stress, as was the mother's rating of how supportive her social support system has been. For parent characteristics, the extent to which they enjoyed their role was associated with stress, as was a measure of locus of control. From regression analysis, the two parent characteristics of parenting satisfaction and locus of control accounted for the most variance in stress. Mediation analysis found that while the child's adaptive behavior and family support were correlated with stress, these relationships were mediated by parenting satisfaction.

Clinical Implications: A Model of Resilience

The idea that families of children with severe disabilities very often show considerable resilience has been noted by a number of authors (Broberg et al., 2009), although definitions of resilience are often quite variable and sometimes absent. Influenced by Hill's (1958) ABCX model of stress and coping, we conceptualize resilience as the process of creating positive perceptions of, and the ability to identify and marshal the resources needed for managing highly stressful events and circumstances. In this section, we review the ABCX model as a means of indicating the kind of support that may be most useful to families.

In the ABCX model, A is the stressor event, B represents the resources available, C is the perception of the event, and X is the coping outcome. Orr, Cameron, and Day (1991) used path analysis to identify a possible sequence of events and determined that the perception comes before the identification and use of resources. In other words, after the birth of a child with severe disabilities, parents will attribute meaning and develop a perception of that event, and this perception will lead them to avail themselves of resources that may assist them with coping. As Orr and colleagues point out, the provision of resources to parents before they have perceived a need for them is not helpful. Because we view the perception of the event and the ability to identify and use resources as fundamental to resilience, we examine each of these in more detail.

Perception of the Event

People rarely view an event the same way. Interpretation always colors perception, and how people interpret or perceive is a product of several factors. We discuss three of these: intrapersonal factors, contextual factors, and the approach of professionals.

Intrapersonal Factors

Intrapersonal factors include such constructs as personality and temperament. It is reasonable to assume that different personalities react to stressful events consistent with their personality. Vermaes, Janssens, Mullaart, Vinck, and Gerris (2008) considered the impact of the "Big-Five" personality factors, extraversion, emotional stability, agreeableness, openness to experience, and conscientiousness (Goldberg, 1992), on parenting stress in parents of children with spina bifida (a wide range of spinal cord malformations caused by the incomplete closure of the embryonic neural tube). They found that emotional stability was the strongest predictor of amount of stress for both parents, but that for mothers their extraversion and openness to experience, and for fathers their level of agreeableness, also contributed to explaining the variance in parenting stress. Furthermore, the personality factors were stronger determinants of stress than characteristics of the child's physical condition. The authors note that extraversion, emotional stability, and agreeableness have been suggested to be part of a construct called positive affectivity. Parents whose personality views experience through positive emotions are likely to respond very differently to the birth of a child with severe disabilities than other parents, and to be more resilient.

Personality provides the filters through which we experience events. Viewed this way, personality includes the organization of each person's understandings of his or her world, his or her ideas and schemata, or what is called lifestyle by Adlerians (Manaster & Corsini, 1982). According to Zeitlin, Williamson, and Rosenblatt (1987), the appraisal of stressful experience is based on beliefs, values, and expectations that have developed over time. This notion has been elaborated upon in a model developed by Park and Folkman (1997) and their concept of global meaning: "Global meaning encompasses a person's enduring beliefs and valued goals. Global meaning influences people's understanding of the past and the present, and it influences their expectations regarding the future" (p. 116). Global meaning develops over time as experiences are integrated into an "organizing subjective perspective" from infancy through adolescence, but is increasingly stable as the person ages.

Park and Folkman (1997) discuss three beliefs that contribute to global meaning: beliefs about the world, about the self, and about the self in the world. A person may, for example, believe the world is a benevolent place where bad things do not happen to good people. The person may believe there is justice and fairness in the world. On the other hand, the person may believe in an uncaring world where there are few rewards. Beliefs about self may revolve around issues of self-worth and personal control over events and outcomes. Beliefs about self in the world encompass thoughts about what one must do given the kind of world lived in and the amount of control over events and outcomes: "because the world is fair, and I am a capable person, I only have to look for the solution because it is out there," or "living in a world where you cannot count on anything, and being a person who tends to be ignored by others, I will do best by isolating myself."

A second component of global meaning according to Park and Folkman (1997) is goals, or purpose; the motivational aspects of meaning: "Meaning described in terms of purpose refers to beliefs that organize, justify, and direct a person's striving" (p. 119). Experience is then viewed in terms of its likelihood of facilitating or impeding the direction of a person's life. Goals are not always conscious, but they may come into awareness better when an event is viewed as potentially impacting them.

Global meaning is relatively stable, and in that sense, is much like the construct of personality. Events are considered in terms of a person's global meaning, and in most cases are fit or assimilated into the structure of global meaning. Certain events may challenge the attempt of the individual to assimilate into global meaning and ultimately may impact and modify global meaning. Park and Folkman (1997) describe situational meaning as the interaction of global beliefs and goals with the circumstances of a particular event.

To briefly illustrate, consider the birth of a child with severe disabilities. The meaning of this situation is influenced by how it interacts with the beliefs and goals of the parents. In terms of beliefs, a parent might believe that living is comprised of problems and therefore they must be fixers. Thus, they are not surprised to be confronted with this birth, but are shaken because it appears to have no solution. In terms of goals, a parent might have very clear goals around what their children will be like and accomplish, and so see this birth as the door slamming shut on their entire image of the future and goals for that future, and also find that nothing can be done to fix it. Resilience comes from changing either the situational meaning or the global meaning. Where the parent sees the birth as a problem to be solved with no solutions, the situational meaning can be changed to identifying strategies or actions that may lead to some short-term solutions. Where the parent believes his or her goals have been defeated, situational meaning can be changed to seeing how the new situation still may allow the possibility for meeting future goals, albeit by way of a different path than previously envisioned. The resilient parent is able to make these shifts to situational meaning so that there is no loss to the global meaning encompassed by the beliefs and goals.

Resilience also may come from changing the global meaning. Thus, the belief that everything must be able to be fixed can be changed to a belief that everything must be explored and understood. Likewise, with certain goals for the future, goals can be changed from what was once seen as important to new, suddenly appealing, goals related to making a difference in the life of a child with disabilities, or changing the systems that support persons with disabilities and their families. While changing situational or global meaning is not always easy, professionals may be helpful in supporting parents through this process of reorienting their perceptions.

Contextual Factors

Social context. The mother of a 15-year-old boy with severe disabilities did not know what to say when her brother-in-law referred to him as a "retard." The parents of a boy who was born without thumbs were not sure how to answer when members of their church asked them what sin they thought they may have committed that led to this tragedy. The mother of an infant born with a severe heart condition, stomach anomalies, and swallowing difficulties found she could no longer be around her group of close friends who all had babies born about the same time.

Parents take their cues from their social setting when developing perceptions of their infant with severe disabilities. Through such social referencing (Bandura, 1986), parents look to others to sense how they should react to the situation. Parents of an infant being discharged to home from neonatal intensive care heard the nurse say, "These parents are going to do great with this child." They were not as confident as the nurse, but it influenced how they thought about bringing their baby home for the first time.

Bonding context. While the term "attachment" is usually thought of as a child's affectional bond with the parent, the term "bonding" is often used to describe the parent's bond with the child. The bonded relationship is central to the model of parent outcomes after the birth of a child with disabilities developed by Scorgie et al. (2004). They note that this bond is formed as early as when the parents first find out the mother is pregnant. "Long before birth, parents are forming images of themselves, their baby, and the future life they will share together..." (p. 93). These preexisting attributes and expectations interact in the model with the actual attributes of the child once born.

There is limited research on how the birth of a child with severe disabilities affects bonding. Difficulties on the part of the child in sending the kinds of messages to mothers that they can interpret as emotional attachment may influence the parents' bonding process (Capuzzi, 1989). In a survey of 25 parents of children with CHARGE syndrome (a genetic syndrome characterized by a variety of sensory and physical anomalies), Reda and Hartshorne (2008) found that while ten felt bonded at conception or birth, six said it took weeks or months, or was still not well established. Presumably, the parents' perception of being closely bonded to the infant, regardless of disability, is significant for how they cope and develop resilience.

Knowledge context. We live in the information age where knowledge is easily available online. Some parents tap into this and learn as much as they can about their child's condition. They also may join support groups and foundations and become active in conferences. This can be disconcerting to some professionals. For example, a parent kept telling her child's physician about what she had learned about her child's condition on the internet. The physician asked her to stop getting on the internet and to just trust his judgment.

Sometimes a little knowledge is a dangerous thing, and parents sometimes are led to believe that treatments and cures are possible where there is no evidence to support this possibility. On the other hand, knowledge is also power, and having the sense that one has power shapes the perception of the event as more manageable.

Experience context. Scorgie et al. (2004) note that "many parents bring to their child's diagnosis powerful images of disability that have been formed through past experiences with persons with disabilities or through societal beliefs about disability" (p. 96). A professor gave a presentation based on the work of one of his students called "Parenting Children with Severe Disabilities." Three years later he became the father of a child with severe disabilities.

Those who went to school prior to the passage of the *Education for All Handicapped Children Act* of 1975 (Pub. L. No. 94–142) rarely encountered children with disabilities. These children were tucked away in separate buildings or isolated classrooms or in many cases not in school at all. Increasingly today even children with severe disabilities are attending school and are included in regular classrooms, and so their peers are growing up side by side and will have a far different experience of disability than the older generations. Fewer parents of a child with severe disabilities will never have known such a person before.

Experience will still vary, but those parents who have been exposed to disability in the past or even present will have a very different perception of the birth of their own child than will those with no experience. Of course there is no guarantee that the previous experience was positive.

Resilient parents are those who are able to create contexts that empower them in raising their child. They find a positive social support group, come to know their child in a way that creates a bond, learn as much as they can about their child's condition, and quickly acquire as much experience as they can in meeting the needs of their child.

Professionals. Professionals are supposed to know. So parents, in trying to make sense out of what has happened, will look to professionals for cues as to how to perceive their situation. As noted by Taanila, Jarvelin, and Kokkonen (1998), the initial information parents receive from physicians, nurses, and other hospital staff, "shapes the image that the parents create of their child and his or her future, and this in turn affects their attitudes towards the child and the nature of their interactions with him or her" (p. 506). In other words, professionals can play a significant role in supporting parent resilience.

Lazarus and Folkman (1984) listed several situational factors that can influence parent perception and that, according to Hartshorne (2002), can be influenced by professionals. One of these is novelty. For most parents of children with severe disabilities, this is a novel situation. They may have had some idea about what taking a typical child home from the hospital would be like, or might even have experienced that, but this is something new. You do not usually come home from the hospital with a baby and an apnea monitor, suction machine, and nasal feeding tubes. The novelty can be reduced when the parents are given a tour of the neonatal intensive care unit before the birth, when they are introduced to other parents with a similar experience, and when professionals are able to connect what the parents already know about infants to what new information and knowledge they need to acquire.

Another factor is predictability. Predictable shock is less aversive than is unpredictable shock. Parents will have many questions about the future they and their child face. This can be tricky for professionals because they want to be able to answer parent questions, but quite often really do not know the answers. Some professionals lay out the worst-case scenario for parents. This is not typically helpful, nor is it useful to sugar coat things. Parents want and deserve the facts as known, and what to look for in making future assessments. They also can benefit from some consideration of how they might handle the unpredictable.

A third factor is event uncertainty, or not knowing whether a particular event will happen or not. Will the hurricane strike the coast or not? Will my child need heart surgery? Will my child ever walk, or talk, or eat? With a hurricane, you can follow the weather reports. With a child you need to learn to read the signs along the way. Professionals can help parents to read these signs and can be very encouraging when the child shows any kind of progress.

Temporal uncertainty is a related factor, but in this case the event is going to happen, you just do not know when. For some conditions death is inevitable, and the child may only be expected to live a certain number of years. Professionals need to help parents to live in the present so that they can appreciate the child under their care. Professionals also can help parents to look for significant markers for the child's progress toward his or her future.

Ambiguity is a fifth factor. Human beings tend not to like ambiguous situations where they do not know exactly what they are dealing with. Parents want structure in their world as they try to make meaning out of it. Parents therefore want answers: do we need heart surgery, who is the best physician for kidney problems, when should my child start school, and what kind of program would be best for my child? While professionals may believe they know the answers to these questions, in many cases it is important that parents take control in finding the answers that make sense to them. This process of making sense out of the ambiguity is what allows parents to start taking control and find the resilience within themselves.

Summary. The perception that parents develop regarding the meaning of having a child with severe disability will be critical to how they adjust and cope. This perception is influenced by the parents' personalities, the contexts in which they live, and the attitude of professionals. Resilience develops when parents view their circumstance as something they can manage. Professionals will likely have an influential role to play in this process.

Identification of Resources

Based on the perception of the event, parents next are faced with the decision of what to do about it. Central to this, according to Zeitlin et al. (1987), is the identification of internal and external resources for managing stress. Lazarus and Folkman (1984) have proposed five categories of coping resources.

Three of these could be considered internal resources: problem-solving skills, general and specific beliefs, and health/energy/morale. The other two are external resources: material resources and social support networks. Burden and Thomas (1986) proposed a list of five needs: information, support, advice, access to resources, and opportunity for social interaction. The Family Needs Survey (Bailey & Simeonsson, 1988) used six categories of need: information, support, explaining to others, community services, financial needs, and family functioning. Because of its central importance and firm research base, we focus here more specifically on social support.

Social Support

The role of social support in assisting individuals and families in times of stress is well established (Greenblatt, Becerra, & Serafetinides, 1982; Hartshorne, 1991; Kane, 1988). Researchers also have investigated the nature of various networks of support and how they function in providing assistance. Such assistance typically is categorized as either emotional or instrumental support. The former includes such activities as visiting, sympathizing, listening, and caring. The latter may include material, financial, or informational aid. Together, they provide the external resources needed for meeting stressful situations.

White and Hastings (2004) summarized the literature on social support and parent coping with a child who has severe disabilities. Spousal support, or satisfaction with the marital relationship, support from extended family members, particularly grandparents, informal sources of support such as friends and religious groups, and the use of respite care services have all been associated with reduced stress. In their own study, White and Hastings found that parent perception of the helpfulness of informal support was associated with well-being, whereas professional support, while associated with child need, was not. Also, practical support, such as assistance with household chores, was associated with well-being, while emotional support was not, although the authors point out this might be because their sample was of parents of adolescents, and these parents' emotional needs might already have been met in the past.

Dunst, Trivette, and Cross (1986) found the presence of supportive social networks for parents of mentally retarded, physically impaired, and developmentally at-risk children to be associated with better personal well-being, both emotional and physical. Most impressively, the children with disabilities of parents with supportive social networks were more likely to make developmental progress over the course of a year. In addition, parents with more supportive networks perceived their children as having fewer physical limitations, being more socially accepted by others, and having fewer negative behavior and personality characteristics.

According to Dunst, et al. (1986), "There is general consensus among social systems theorists that social support networks function to nurture and sustain linkages among persons that are supportive on both a day-to-day basis and in times of need and crises" (p. 403). However, the mechanisms for how social support influences well-being are not well understood (DeLongis & Holtzman, 2005). Some people may more naturally have a well-developed social network to draw upon, while others may find a way to tap into support during times of crisis. Network orientation and seek and find are two variables that may impact the use of social support and that would reflect parent resilience.

Network orientation. Not everyone utilizes social support when confronted with a stressful situation. The propensity to utilize social support when undergoing stress has been called "network orientation" (Tolsdorf, 1976; Vaux, Burba, & Stewart, 1986); the individual is oriented toward tapping into the networks of support that may be available: "It involves a set of beliefs, attitudes, and expectations regarding the usefulness of the social network in providing help with all kinds of life problems" (Larose, Bernier, Soucy, & Duchense, 1999, p. 226). Network orientation is influenced by a person's past experience with social support: was it useful, harmful, uplifting, discouraging, etc. (Vaux et al., 1986)?

It also may derive from personality factors related to affiliation, trust, and nurturance. Several studies have found it to be associated with attachment style (Larose et al., 1999; Wallace & Vaux, 1993). If coping with stress is related to the utilization of resources, a negative network orientation would predict general problems with coping and would interfere with resilience.

Seek and find. Kane (1988) proposed that families exist within a web of relationships including relatives, friends, neighbors, and community services, all of which may be prepared to provide support. But some individuals and families appear to be better prepared to identify these supports than others. To begin with, in order to seek and find social support an individual must have some degree of social skill and interpersonal trust (Mortenson, 2009). Some individuals have a deeper commitment and involvement with various aspects of social life, including family, friends, work, and social activities (Eschleman, Bowling, & Alarcon, 2010). Such "hardy" individuals may be more likely to cope well with stress because they already have a wide network of support or because they are socially attractive and so find it easy to acquire support (Eschleman et al., 2010). Of importance is that some people are more skilled than others in developing networks of support that can be drawn upon in times of crisis. But also, these individuals may have the skills to create a specific network of support in the face of a particular stressor. In other words, when faced with the birth of a child with severe disabilities, some parents will already have the skills to seek out and gather the supports they need in order to cope well.

Seek and find skills also apply to the identification of other resources. Consider the list from Bailey and Simeonsson (1988): information, support, explaining to others, community services, financial needs, and family functioning. Some parents already know how to access the information they need. They are able to figure out where to turn for various sources of support, and they know how to be supportive of one another. Explaining to others becomes easier as they learn more about the condition and obtain experience. States and communities vary in the way resources are structured and provided to families of children with severe disabilities. The information as to what services are available and how to access them may be hard to find, but some parents are constantly tuned into possibilities. Financial needs may be embarrassing, but learning to accept all possible sources of financial support is important. Families are unlikely to consistently function perfectly. Identifying needs within the family, and resources that can support those needs, keeps families functioning well. More resilient parents are likely to be more active in seeking out and following up on resources that are available to them. Professionals can assist by helping parents to link with resources, and by making the kinds of supports helpful to parents in this situation less hidden so that parents are able to find them.

Coping Outcome

Eschleman et al. (2010) looked at hardiness, a construct similar to resilience, and found that hardiness was positively associated with certain personality traits and negatively associated with others. Hardiness was negatively associated with stressors, strains, and regressive coping, but positively associated with social support, active coping, and performance. This suggests that when faced with the birth of a child with severe disabilities, parents who are able to take a more positive and optimistic perspective (due in part to personality factors), and who are able to marshal social support resources (due to appropriate active coping), are likely to cope better and be more resilient than parents unable to do these things.

Earlier we discussed Park and Folkman's (1997) model of situational and global meanings, and how certain events that go against one's beliefs and goals may require a shift in these two kinds of meaning, or what these authors call meaning making. Situational meaning changes as the individual makes reattributions concerning the event. The anticipation of the birth of a child is generally very positive, with parents sometimes dreaming up a whole life time for the child. When the child is born with disabilities, that imagined future for both parents and child is changed. But over time parents may make reattributions that make the situation a better fit with beliefs and goals. Hartshorne (2002) cites a mother who illustrates this process, commenting on her family 3 years after her daughter with disabilities was born:

> We imagined that by Kindergarten she'd be a regular kid who just had some trouble walking and stuff. Well, she's almost three and she's sort of 'normal' in many ways, but very 'different' in other ways. She seems totally normal to me—which means I've adjusted my concept of normal.

There are two reattributions related here, the first that the daughter would somehow become normal by Kindergarten, and then the second that while she is different she is "normal" to the parent. Park and Folkman maintain that reattribution is involved throughout the process of coping.

The second kind of change proposed by Park and Folkman (1997) is relative to global meaning—a change in the way the parents view themselves, the world, and themselves in the world. Scorgie et al. (2004) refer to this as transformation: "Increasingly, parents are asserting that, despite the considerable and on-going stresses involved in parenting a child with a disability, their experiences have been personally transformative" (p. 85). Taunt and Hastings (2002, p. 411) summarize some of the positives that parents have described:

- Pleasure and satisfaction in providing care for the child
- The child is a source of joy and happiness
- The child provides a challenge or opportunity to learn and develop
- A strengthened family and/or marriage
- A new or increased sense of purpose in life
- Development of new skills, abilities, or new career opportunities
- Family members have experienced personal growth
- Expanded social and community networks
- Increased spirituality
- A changed perspective on life

Coping in this sense is not simply maintaining homeostasis, but can be a positive, life-changing experience (King, Zwaigenbaum, King, Baxter, Rosenbaum, & Bates, 2006).

Coping is truly a dynamic process. We have suggested it to be an outcome of perception and resources. Really, it is a continuous process influenced by perceptions that are initially based on personality and global meaning, but that in the resilient parent change over time. The identification of resources also is an ongoing process as needs shift over time. Resources also can change perceptions through positive social support. A child with severe disabilities will confront parents with stressful situations throughout that child's life. Situational and global meanings will always be confronted and need change. Resilience is not something one acquires once and for all. The resilient parent is the parent who actively copes with events by reattribution and meaning making, leading very often to transformations in their lives.

Courage vs. Denial

Earlier we discussed the *Questionnaire on Resources and Stress* and some of the problems with the interpretation of results, because truthful answers on the part of the parent indicate higher degrees of stress. Resilient parents have developed the courage to face the reality created by having a child with severe disabilities. It takes courage to maintain confidence in your ability to deal with the reality of any situation, as best you can. Hartshorne (2002) describes the "courageous paradox," where parents learn to accept the reality of their child's situation with no need for it to be any different, while simultaneously doing everything they can to assist their child in developing as far as he or she can. Accepting the reality reflects a *perception* of their child as fully acceptable as he or she is. Working to help their child develop his or her potential reflects the search for *resources*. Resilient parents who express their acceptance of their child as he or she is may give the impression of having given up, but in fact they have the courage to not place their personal needs for a perfect child onto their child with disabilities. On the other hand, resilient parents who are fighting for services they believe their child needs in order to develop new skills and abilities may be viewed as totally in denial and unrealistic, when in fact they are demonstrating the courage to not give up on their child's potential, but to keep pushing for more resources. Resilient parents are able to do both of these: to perceive their child as acceptable as is and to seek resources for greater development. One without the other would reflect the possibility of a parent who has given up or one who can never accept the reality of the situation. Such a parent would be subject to much more stress and would not be resilient.

Fathers and Siblings

While the title of this chapter refers to "Family Resilience," most of what has been discussed pertains to parents, and because most of the research on parents is completed by the mother, much less is known about the impact on fathers and siblings (Blacher, Glidden, & Hastings, 2010). But disability affects the entire family, and the resilience of each member is critical.

Fathers

The experience of fathers has not been completely ignored. However, the role of fathers within the family has been changing over time toward more active parenting, but often with little preparation and social support, making parenting itself a stressful experience for fathers (McBride, 1989). In fact Houser and Seligman (1991) found that fathers of adolescents with or without intellectual disability did not differ in levels of stress. While some early studies found that mothers of children with disabilities experienced more stress than fathers (Beckman, 1991; Moes, Koegel, Schreibman, & Loos, 1992), more recent research has found equal levels of stress (Keller & Honig, 2004). However, there are differences in the sources of stress. Keller and Honig found mothers to be more stressed by the child's demandingness and neediness for care, while fathers struggled with feelings of attachment. Fathers seemed more affected by the child's physical, intellectual, and emotional characteristics. These authors speculate that the child with disabilities may contrast with the father's expectations of the ideal child. This is consistent with our model of a stressful experience being influenced by the father's perception of the event.

Regarding resources, a few studies have looked at the father's utilization of social support. Beckman (1991) found that for both mothers and fathers the use of informal supports was related to lower levels of stress. Formal supports were found to be related to less stress for fathers, but not for mothers. Keller and Honig (2004) found that both parents rated the usefulness of social support as only sometimes helpful. Fathers regarded social support as more helpful when they also perceived their child as more acceptable. Mothers utilized social support more when they perceived their child's needs as less demanding.

What are the characteristics of the resilient father of a child with severe disabilities? Hartshorne has led a number of groups for fathers of children with severe disabilities. During the first group he facilitated, the fathers spent about a half an hour talking about problems with medical insurance—a concern about resources. During the second half hour he managed to get them shifted to sharing how their child's disability affected them. One father said it had entirely changed his life. Before his child with disabilities was born he already had two children—with whom he rarely spent any time. The father said most of his time was spent either working or drinking. But after his child with disabilities was born he recognized (perceived) that this was not going to work. He stopped drinking and he cut back his hours at his job, and now he spends lots of time with all three of his children. In subsequent groups, Hartshorne has asked fathers to relate the most positive thing that has happened to them due to having a child with disabilities. Typical responses: I spend much more time with my family; My wife and I have become closer; I have a changed sense of what is really important in life; I have learned how to do actual care for my children; I have started to slow down and to appreciate what I have in life; I enjoy my family so much more.

Siblings

Thoughts about the experience of siblings of children with severe disabilities have followed a course similar to those about the experience of parents. Based on clinical work, the early consensus was that having a brother or sister with severe disabilities was very problematic for siblings, often leading to mental health problems. Subsequent research explored who among siblings might be the most vulnerable, brother, sister, youngest, oldest, etc. (Cuskelly, 1999). An important difficulty is that much of the literature is based on parent report rather than on direct information from the siblings. Neece, Blacher, and Baker (2010), for example, looked at the impact of the child with disabilities' behavior problems on siblings, finding that behavior problems accounted for most of the variance in sibling impact. But their measure of sibling impact was a seven-item scale answered by both parents.

Not all siblings are in the same situation. Some are older than the child with disabilities, and some younger. In some cases there are multiple siblings in the home, and in others only one. Some siblings may have many friends outside the home, and others may have few. Siblings can also vary in temperament, cognitive ability, goals, and ambitions, etc. These differences complicate research.

Two meta-analyses have been conducted that have interesting implications. One (Rossiter & Sharpe, 2001) was of siblings of children with intellectual disabilities. The study found a small, negative effect. This effect was greater for adult reports vs. child self-reports. The second study was a meta-analysis of studies of siblings of children with a chronic illness (Sharpe & Rossiter, 2002). Again they found a small, negative effect that was greater for studies based on parent report than sibling self-report.

A more recent study by Giallo and Gavidia-Payne (2006) found the following factors to predict sibling adjustment: socio-economic status (SES), past attendance at a sibling support group, parent stress, family time and routines, family problem solving and communication, and family hardiness. Children look to their parents to know how to react to a situation. Parents who are resilient in the raising of a child with severe disabilities are likely to provide positive models for their other children.

Parenting

Central to the experience of raising a child with severe disabilities is the problem of how to parent. Parenting any child is not easy, but there is virtually nothing in the parenting literature regarding strategies for parenting a child with severe disabilities. Parents feel most vulnerable when they do not know how to respond to their child's behavior. When the behavior is unusual and complex, and typical strategies seem not to apply, parents can feel at a loss and experience an increase in stress, threatening their resilience.

Parenting Skills

The task of parenting poses a challenge to everyone. Confusion reigns over how best to respond to common misbehaviors and provide competent child guidance in a variety of parenting situations. It is hard enough to decipher child behaviors and find discipline strategies when you have a typically developing child, but the process can feel totally overwhelming for parents of children with disabilities when more variables are presented, such as "Does he understand?" "Is she in pain?" "What is he asking for?"

Three decades of research on parenting styles concludes that authoritative parenting is positively related to the best outcomes in children (Simons & Conger, 2007). This style of parenting offers children both firmness and kindness. However, when Woolfson and Grant (2006) studied stress and parenting styles of parents raising children with developmental disabilities (DD), they discovered that the authoritative style, so highly touted in the research for nondisabled children, was actually associated with significantly *higher* stress scores for parents as measured by the *Parenting Stress Index Short Form*. What leads to good outcomes in the child appears associated with poor outcomes in the parents.

Woolfson and Grant (2006) observed that parents of children with disabilities were more likely to be permissive as their child aged, increasingly abandoning an authoritative style over time. Are these parents forgetting how important it is to practice good parenting? That is doubtful. Raising a child with a disability comes with its own unique challenges.

The Challenge of Being Firm

The daily life of a parent raising a child with a disability is more time and energy taxing and often occurs in the absence of access to outside support. The unabating demands of such simple tasks as toileting and feeding may require a Herculean effort and leave parents more tired and weary. No parent can effectively enforce rules consistently when they are compromised themselves. Parental exhaustion should not be confused with ignorance. A 14-year-old boy with severe disabilities has a basket full of his favorite toys. He enjoys pulling toys out of the basket one by one, and after looking at a toy will usually throw it before he selects the next. If the parents insist, he will gather up the toys and put them back in the basket, but as simple as this may seem, it is easier for these exhausted parents to just let him alone, and then pick up the toys themselves later in the day.

The Challenge of Being Friendly

Children with a disability may not have the same capacity for connecting emotionally or socially with their parents, leaving them larger amounts of time to be autonomous. If a parent discovers that the child enjoys playing with a gadget, the parent will be so happy to have discovered something that captures his or her child's interest and so may allow the child to play endlessly, forgoing the parent's own social interactions.

Lack of interest in socializing should not be confused with neglect. In fact, the pendulum might err on the other side: spoiling. If you discover an activity or toy that excites and pleases your child, you are more likely to provide these. If they enjoy bubbles, an endless limit of bubbles ensues. Some of the objects may take on compulsive qualities for the child and so he or she has a huge collection of koosh balls, balloons, toy helicopters, or even vacuum cleaners, all purchased by parents eager to create positive experiences for their child, or wishing to avoid terrible tantruming on the part of the child, often in public.

In both of these examples we can see the motivation for the parents' actions. They are kind hearted and responsive to their situation. How can they be faulted? Yet guilt reigns, and worries about how their parenting is affecting their child's development remain a burden to the concerned parent. They know they should set limits, but may find any attempt to do so too aversive.

Rather than measuring parenting success as the ability to adopt the practices recommended by the authoritative style, the parent of a child with a disability is better served by evaluating his or her parenting confidence. When parents have confidence in their own abilities to face the challenges of parenting in a responsive manner they can parent creatively rather than aiming for a "perfect" or "formulaic" prescribed approach. A sense of agency in their parenting skills gains them confidence and assurance that they are handling things well. This is the desired quality needed in order to be a resilient parent.

   The resilient parent, armed with confidence, is able to see what the unique needs of the situation call for and respond in an adaptable manner that best seeks to help the child gain both autonomy and mastery in his or her self-development as well as guidance toward social integration. All the while, the parent is mindful of the needs of himself or herself as well as those of others in the family. Picking up the tossed toys themselves is a decision that honors the importance of parents' own need for ease at the end of a taxing day. Even purchasing that eleventh vacuum cleaner avoids the tantruming melt down that is so embarrassing and may not seem worth the price.

   Parents are apt to take their child's behavior personally; feeling affronted by them, or a growing sense of futility and failure when they cannot control their child. The use of positive or negative reinforcers may seem impossible because it is so difficult to find any that work. Children who are tube fed do not find food terribly reinforcing. Children who prefer to entertain themselves rather than interact socially are not impacted by the withdrawal of attention or time out. However, confidence can be restored once parents are given a new conceptual framework or lens to view their child's behavior and embrace a more holistic stance.

   Alfred Alder's Individual Psychology (Manaster & Corsini, 1982) invites parents to see behavior as neither good nor bad, but instead to understand behavior as being born out of the child's unique creativity and as being adaptive in nature. All behaviors have a purpose and serve to accomplish something important and vital to the child, albeit sometimes through mistaken or disruptive means. Adler invites us to first study and understand the usefulness or the purpose the behavior serves for the child. Once the child's purpose is discovered, we can better help him or her reach his or her goals with less disturbance to others, or in more community minded, co-operative ways.

   For example, a young boy plunges his hands into his pudding and smears it on the table, his face, and sometimes the floor and walls. Rather than reprimanding the child for misbehaving, the parents recognized the child's action was not actually a problem, but rather their son's creative *solution* for the need for more tactile stimulation. The parents were able to see that he was not being disrespectful or trying to make life difficult for them. The parents honored his high sensory needs not by indulging him in wasting food, but by substituting shaving crème for the pudding instead. Being able to understand the child's purpose and then taking steps to meet the child's needs in ways that were less disturbing, gave the parents greater confidence about their parenting skills and responsiveness.

   Similarly, a young girl with obsessive-compulsive behaviors would douse herself in water before taking her clothes off. Her parents addressed the need to end flooding of the bathroom floor by prohibiting her access to the water. The creative girl found a new solution for her need for wet clothes by urinating in them instead. It could easily discourage a parent who views these behaviors as unnecessary and who feels defeated by his or her lack of success in eradicating the child's behavior. However, the parent is working at cross purposes with the child's goals. By honoring the child's ritual and sensory need for moisture before getting undressed, the parents allowed her to douse herself with water, but required her to do so while standing in the bathtub where it would not make an undue mess and would respect orderliness in the home. Over time, the amount of water was reduced until she only required a small amount that she could administer herself at the sink. Working with the child and understanding the merit of her actions, the parents felt confident that they understood their child and were parenting in the right direction.

   Resilient parents, armed with confidence, also feel more at ease with themselves as being "good enough" parents, rather than perfect parents. They manage their parenting challenges in a number of ways, including the following:

   They choose their battles wisely. Child guidance and correction requires an ongoing effort. Parents who can selectively decide which matters need their immediate attention and which issues are best left for another day are able to sustain their energy and effectiveness. Adopting the longer view of parenting allows for more grace and a wider berth in dealing with children every day. Tossed toys is something that is a nuisance, but ultimately not life threatening. If a 20 min melt down can be circumvented by parents making a small concession, so be it.

They are consistent when it matters. Children gain a sense of security when they experience a world that is predictable. Having a few rules that are always enforced is better than having too many rules that are inconsistently enforced. Three such examples would be: You cannot bang your head against the bathtub, you cannot pull other people's hair, and you cannot put your hands in your food.

They give freedom of choice. Every person has a desire to be self-directed and to have choice in matters that affect him or her in accordance with his or her ability. We often are unaware of the diminished opportunities we provide children in general to be autonomous, and that is especially so with children who have disabilities. A concerted effort must be made to allow children to be in command of their own choices of activities so long as they are reasonable; we should encourage their independent pursuits that follow their interests.

They know that children who feel good, do good. Children who are well rested, well nourished, comfortable, and content will be easier to get along with. Children who are tired, hungry, or in pain will not be as easy. It is important to recognize when children are compromised and cranky so we can be responsive in helping them return to a more fully resourced state.

In sum, parents need the support of professionals who are able to recognize the challenges they face in parenting and the ongoing threat to their sense of competence as parents. Pointing out the obvious is not helpful: if you are inconsistent in having your child put away his toys he is unlikely to comply on any consistent basis; if you keep buying a helium balloon every time she demands one, she will continue to demand. Parents know this. What they need help with is how to make these parenting "errors" with confidence because they mean survival for the parent; they need help in understanding how some of the "misbehaviors" are creative solutions on the part of the child; and they need support in finding ways to guide their child to more healthy, socially cooperative solutions.

Research Implications

The focus of this chapter has been on severe disability, but this concept has remained undefined. The literature that we have reviewed has not been consistent in terms of the population of interest, and has likewise often been undefined. By lumping different categories of disability together, we may be guilty of over-generalization. This is a problem that has plagued research from the beginning when it was based on parents showing up in mental health clinics. Even studies that are syndrome specific may fail to explore the differences. For example, King et al. (2006) interviewed parents of children with autism and Down syndrome but did not distinguish between them in their results. Griffith, Hastings, Nash, and Hill (2010), on the other hand, did explore differences between these same two groups and the relationship between maternal well-being and child behavior problems. There are hundreds of identified syndromes that may create somewhat different profiles of challenges for parents, and more research is needed to identify these.

In a similar vein, the research has only begun to differentiate the challenge to parents over time, from birth, through preschool, school, and into adulthood. While differentiating the experience of mothers and fathers is more common, much more is needed to understand the unique challenges faced by fathers. Siblings too require more attention.

We have mentioned some of the problems with the *Questionnaire on Resources and Stress,* but in general too little attention is given to the quality of the measures used in the research and its potential to bias results. Each instrument is intended as a measure of a particular construct, but the construct validity of the instruments is rarely reported. This is due in part to a lack of consistency or agreement on what instrument is the best measure of the construct under investigation. Even stress is measured by different instruments.

On the other hand, the research sophistication has increased dramatically, particularly in the last decade. There is an increased use of model testing (e.g., Hill & Rose, 2009; Lloyd & Hastings, 2009), and the number of variables has become quite complex, reflecting the complexity of the parent and family experience. More studies are including control groups. Blacher et al. (2005) summarize their review of research from 2004 as follows:

> Missing from the literature this year is any overarching theory of family well-being that spans ages, life-course stages, phenotypes, and culture. Investigators increasingly use more sophisticated research designs, however, incorporate appropriate control groups, and present a more expansive, contextual view of families and intellectual disability. (p. 512)

Case Example

The days after Ashley was born were a complete blur to Kathy and David and their son, Jonathon. Immediately after Ashley's birth significant medical complications and multiple congenital anomalies were apparent. Genetic testing was suggested immediately by Kathy's physician. Over the first few days of Ashley's life she was transported to two different hospitals. Kathy and David recall riding the elevator at one of the hospitals shortly after they had been informed that Ashley would need heart surgery. Although her survival was their primary concern, they both said to each other, "It will be okay, no matter what happens." Kathy describes her family's resilience as "…continuously rolling with the punches…we do what needs to be done for Ashley's immediate care, and try to keep our regular life going on as well. We have needed supports."

Supports and Timing

Shortly after Ashley was born the obstetrician sent a mom from the community who had several children with disabilities to meet with Kathy. While the gesture was helpful, Kathy recalls only the woman sitting at her bedside talking. She does not recall who she was or what she said. These first few days were too overwhelming given Ashley's needs and adjustments in the family. Over time, as Ashley's health improved, the greatest need for Kathy and her family was (and continues to be) the need to be connected, supported, and to have the power of information:

> I am thankful that Ashley was born after the Internet! I am thankful we had a computer, Internet access, computer experience, and an education to make use of the resources available. Being well connected in the disability world has been helpful. If I didn't know something, I knew who to call to find out.

"We have needed support—support for questions and emotional support," stated Kathy when asked about the family's greatest needs. Finding an online support group for Ashley's diagnosis provided connections to other families and "people who knew what I was thinking, how I was feeling, and accepted me every step of the way." Further, as Ashley continues to grow and Kathy has had to make tough decisions, often against the status quo, for Ashley's medical and educational care and social interactions, the strength of the online community serves as "an army of supporters"—particularly when faced with a room full of professionals who do not seem to understand Ashley. The Internet also has allowed Kathy to stay current with the world of disability, through state organizations, conferences, and medical updates.

Certain professionals have been influential and memorable individuals in Ashley and Kathy's life. When Ashley was a newborn, one home health nurse helped the family during the "traumatic times" with what Kathy describes as "far beyond the call of her nursing duties." At times she even cried with

Kathy during challenging moments (e.g., changing Ashley's feeding tube). Ashley's pediatrician provided home and cell phone numbers with the order to call directly after hours. When Ashley was a baby, therapists were patient with Kathy during therapies and while she continued to ask the same questions over and over again. If she could not fit in everything the therapists suggested, they seemed to understand and were patient. Certainly there were professionals who were not helpful and Kathy states, "Those (professionals) who got in the way have been forgotten because I went right past them."

What Has Changed?

Social Support/Friendships

The social support and circle of friends that Kathy and her family had prior to Ashley's birth have changed. The daily interactions and the circumstances of their children are different. The friends are busy with "other normal stuff," while Kathy's family is busy with activities like doctors' appointments. Today, their friends come in many forms, mostly through individuals they have come to know due to their involvement with Ashley (e.g., therapeutic riding instructor) and the families on the Internet group who are available at any time.

Extended family continues to be an important support. All extended family members are accepting, loving, and supportive of Ashley and the family. The nearest grandmother geographically has been to nearly every surgery with Ashley and Kathy, allowing David to continue his work schedule. Having support, understanding, and acceptance from family members has been critical in keeping Kathy and the family going during challenging times.

Personality

"I am drastically different than I would have been (before Ashley was born), but it's hard to describe how," Kathy stated. Although Kathy maintains the same priorities in life and continues to do "regular things," her personality and lifestyle also have changed significantly. Some aspects of her personality, however, have simply shifted directions. For example, Kathy was once an active and networking leader of a parent initiative to protest large kindergarten classes for her older son, and now she is an outspoken and active mother working within the field of disability. What is her drive? Kathy remains driven by anything that will benefit Ashley's life and the life of other individuals with disabilities.

Ashley's family has reorganized their hierarchy of needs. Housekeeping, organization, clean closets, and well-manicured nails have been replaced with organizing doctors' appointments, understanding Ashley's education, exploring the differences and similarities of all individuals, and how we develop equality in this world. Ashley's birth has also resulted in a huge turn in Kathy's career path. When her oldest son was young, she was a child care provider and then a classroom teacher. Once Ashley was born, her care was too significant to continue working a typical 40 hour work week. Working within the field of disability, as a trainer/consultant and advocate for a state School of the Deaf Outreach department, now allows Kathy to have a more flexible schedule and, most importantly, understanding if she must leave work for a school meeting or a visit to the Low Vision Clinic. Kathy remarks that her satisfaction now comes from her work. She is continuously supporting and impacting other families, professionals, policymakers, and the like regarding the field of disability and special education.

Family Dynamics

All family members have been impacted drastically since Ashley was born. Kathy describes focusing so much on the priorities of Ashley's care that she feels she left to have a baby and never really came home to Jonathon. For the first 5 weeks of Ashley's life, Kathy spent nearly all of her time at the hospital. For the following year or two, Ashley and Kathy were continuously involved in therapies, doctor appointments, and surgeries. Despite these demands, Kathy has tried to find balance and be mindful of her attention to Jonathon; however, she believes life will never be what it would have been without Ashley's condition.

Kathy and David's marriage also has been challenged as all of Kathy's attention focused "100% on Ashley during her first 2 years of life." Making time together has been important and Kathy and David try to make date nights as often as possible. They also have experienced the stress of having a child with disabilities in different ways. Kathy has grown even more understanding of others in the disability field, yet she and David have lost opportunities to spend quality time together to "stay in touch with one another." Ashley and Jonathon also have many differences. There is a 6-year age difference between siblings and they function more like only children than as "buddies" or companions. They do not share the same interests or activities; however, they both care about each other.

Kathy credits her family for their strength and adaptation to challenges. Over the years, they have learned that when in crisis they must all come together to do what is necessary to meet the challenge. Kathy's positive attitude also helps: "I think we all feel strength in knowing that our family can make it through anything and that we are all there for each other. We adjust for each other." Ashley's family believes it is necessary to have resources to help: family support, an outside support group, access to helpful resources and information to explore options, and caring physicians who are willing to discuss informed options and opportunities for the family.

Responding to Challenges

Kathy says her family is not afraid to face head on the challenges brought before them. They face each day with optimism and try to prepare for future circumstances, although priorities and preparation may have to change at times based on each new challenge. Kathy indicated that her family makes as much of an informed decision as possible and they "reserve the right to adjust the decision as needed." Kathy also has come to recognize that with each challenge in life she is more than a bystander. She must be aware of her emotional responses but not let them take over. Additionally, Kathy has found spiritual strength: "Ashley brought me to God. The whole process is a long story, but I went from being unsure about the existence of God to having a strong relationship with Him. I now get through things by giving it up to Him. Letting go has been a huge gift," stated Kathy.

Kathy sees her development as an advocate as key to her family's resilience. When Ashley was first discharged from the hospital, with an intense schedule of feedings (every 2 hour around the clock), Kathy realized she could not keep up. Making the decision to speak up about Ashley's care resulted in an appeal to the insurance company for night nursing care, which ultimately helped Kathy and the family's adjustment. When surgeons began to look at Ashley through a narrow view, Kathy questioned the surgeon's approaches and insured she had enough information to make an informed decision regarding Ashley's care. Kathy's advocacy has continued as Ashley has grown, and Kathy has written a column for the newspaper about her experiences and how to advocate.

In response to the circumstances Ashley's condition has brought into her life, Kathy says:

I have definitely learned to step outside my comfort zone, grow, and change, whether I want to or not. That has transferred into all areas of my life. I have also learned to have faith. I may not be able to imagine how I will get through the next challenge, but I have faith that I will get through it somehow. Then, I can stay alert and aware through the journey.

Conclusion

Resilience in families of children with severe disability should never be considered the exception. While it can be a tremendous challenge to the meanings parents and siblings have constructed for their lives, reattributions led by changes in perceptions and the availability of resources can create new meanings and transformations. Researchers must focus their attention on the factors that facilitate such transformation. Professionals should recognize the tremendous impact of their actions. Parents want factual information, access to resources, and recognition that resilience does not mean parenting perfection. The courageous paradox means parents will be simultaneously working on their acceptance and enjoyment of the present, while doing everything they can to change the future. The best professionals will recognize resilience in these parents and appreciate the opportunity to be a supportive part of this process.

References

Bailey, D. B., & Simeonsson, R. J. (1988). *Family assessment in early intervention*. Columbus, OH: Merrill.

Bandura, A. (1986). *Social foundations of thought and action: A social cognitive theory*. Upper Saddle River, NJ: Prentice-Hall.

Beckman, P. J. (1991). Comparison of mothers' and fathers' perceptions of the effect of young children with and without disabilities. *American Journal on Mental Retardation, 95*, 585–595.

Blacher, J., Glidden, L. M., & Hastings, R. (2010). Families research—no longer monochromatic. *Journal of Applied Research in Intellectual Disabilities, 23*, 1–2.

Blacher, J., Neece, C. L., & Paczkowski, E. (2005). Families and intellectual disability. *Current Opinion in Psychiatry, 18*, 507–513.

Broberg, M., Blacher, J., & Emerson, E. (2009). Editorial for JIDR special issue on resilience and people with intellectual disabilities. *Journal of Intellectual Disability Research, 53*, 955–956.

Burden, R., & Thomas, D. (1986). A further perspective on parent reaction to handicap. *The Exceptional Child, 33*, 140–145.

Capuzzi, C. (1989). Maternal attachment to handicapped infants and the relationship to social support. *Research in Nursing & Health, 12*, 161–167.

Clayton, J. M., Glidden, L. M., & Kiphart, M. J. (1994). The questionnaires on resources and stress: What do they measure? *American Journal on Mental Retardation, 99*, 313–316.

Cuskelly, M. (1999). Adjustment of siblings of children with a disability: Methodological issues. *International Journal for the Advancement of Counselling, 21*, 111–124.

DeLongis, A., & Holtzman, S. (2005). Coping in context: The role of stress, social support, and personality in coping. *Journal of Personality, 73*, 1633–1656.

Dunst, C. J., Trivette, C. M., & Cross, A. H. (1986). Mediating influences of social support. Personal, family, & child outcomes. *American Journal of Mental Deficiency, 90*, 403–417.

Eschleman, K. J., Bowling, N. A., & Alarcon, G. M. (2010). A meta-analytic examination of hardiness. *International Journal of Stress Management, 17*, 277–307.

Friedrich, W. N., Greenberg, M. T., & Crnic, K. (1983). A short-form of the questionnaire on resources and stress. *American Journal of Mental Deficiency, 88*, 41–48.

Gerstein, E. D., Crnic, K. A., Blacher, J., & Baker, B. L. (2009). Resilience and the course of daily parenting stress in families of young children with intellectual disabilities. *Journal of Intellectual Disability Research, 53*, 981–997.

Giallo, R., & Gavidia-Payne, S. (2006). Child, parent and family factors as predictors of adjustment for siblings of children with a disability. *Journal of Intellectual Disability Research, 50*, 937–948.

Glidden, L. M. (1993). What we do not know about families with children who have developmental disabilities: The questionnaire on resources and stress as a case study. *American Journal of Mental Retardation, 97*, 481–495.

Goldberg, L. R. (1992). The development of markers for the big-five factor structure. *Psychological Assessment, 4*, 26–42.

Greenblatt, M., Becerra, R. M., & Serafetinides, E. A. (1982). Social networks and mental health: An overview. *The American Journal of Psychiatry, 139*, 977–984.

Griffith, G. M., Hastings, R. P., Nash, S., & Hill, C. (2010). Using matched groups to explore child behavior problems and maternal well-being in children with Down syndrome and autism. *Journal of Autism and Developmental Disorders, 40*, 610–619.

Hartshorne, T. S. (1991). The friendship life task and family-life satisfaction. *Individual Psychology, 47*, 477–481.

Hartshorne, T. S. (2002). Mistaking courage for denial: Family resilience after the birth of a child with severe disabilities. *Journal of Individual Psychology, 58*, 263–278.

Hastings, R. P., & Taunt, H. M. (2002). Positive perceptions in families of children with developmental disabilities. *American Journal on Mental Retardation, 107*, 116–127.

Hill, R. (1958). Genetic features of families under stress. *Social Casework, 49,* 139–150.

Hill, C., & Rose, J. (2009). Parenting stress in mothers of adults with an intellectual disability: Parental cognitions in relation to child characteristics and family support. *Journal of Intellectual Disability Research, 53,* 969–980.

Holroyd, J. (1974). The questionnaire on resources and stress: An instrument to measure family response to a handicapped family member. *Journal of Community Psychology, 2,* 92–94.

Houser, R., & Seligman, M. (1991). A comparison of stress and coping by fathers of adolescents with mental retardation and fathers of adolescents without mental retardation. *Research in Developmental Disabilities, 12,* 251–260.

Howell, S. E. (1973). Psychiatric aspects of habilitation. *Pediatric Clinics of North America, 20,* 203–219.

Kane, C. F. (1988). Family social support: Toward a conceptual model. *Advances in Nursing Science, 10,* 18–25.

Keller, D., & Honig, A. S. (2004). Maternal and paternal stress in families with school-aged children with disabilities. *The American Journal of Orthopsychiatry, 74,* 337–348.

King, G. A., Zwaigenbaum, L., King, S., Baxter, D., Rosenbaum, P., & Bates, A. (2006). A qualitative investigation of changes in the belief systems of families of children with autism or Down syndrome. *Child: Care, Health and Development, 32,* 353–369.

Larose, S., Bernier, A., Soucy, N., & Duchesne, S. (1999). Attachment style dimensions, network orientation and the process of seeking help from college teachers. *Journal of Social and Personal Relationships, 16,* 225–247.

Lazarus, R. S., & Folkman, S. (1984). *Stress, appraisal, and coping.* New York: Springer.

Lloyd, T. J., & Hastings, R. (2009). Hope as a psychological resilience factor in mothers and fathers of children with intellectual disabilities. *Journal of Intellectual Disability Research, 53,* 957–968.

Manaster, G. J., & Corsini, R. J. (1982). *Individual psychology: Theory and practice.* Chicago: Adler School of Professional Psychology.

McBride, B. A. (1989). Stress and fathers' parental competence: Implications for family life and parent educators. *Family Relations, 38,* 385–389.

Mitchell, R. G. (1973). Chronic handicap in childhood: It's implications for family and community. *The Practitioner, 211,* 763–768.

Moes, D., Koegel, R. L., Schreibman, L., & Loos, L. M. (1992). Stress profiles for mothers and fathers of children with autism. *Psychological Reports, 71,* 1272–1274.

Mortenson, S. T. (2009). Interpersonal trust and social skill in seeking social support among Chinese and Americans. *Communication Research, 36,* 32–53.

Murphy, M. A. (1982). The family with a handicapped child: A review of the literature. *Developmental and Behavioral Pediatrics, 3,* 73–82.

Neece, C. L., Blacher, J., & Baker, B. L. (2010). Impact on siblings of children with intellectual disability: The role of child behavior problems. *American Journal on Intellectual and Developmental Disabilities, 115,* 291–306.

Orr, R. R., Cameron, S. J., & Day, D. M. (1991). Coping with stress in families with children who have mental retardation: An evaluation of the double ABCX model. *American Journal on Mental Retardation, 95,* 444–450.

Park, C. L., & Folkman, S. (1997). Meaning in the context of stress and coping. *Review of General Psychology, 1,* 115–144.

Reda, N. M., & Hartshorne, T. S. (2008). Attachment, bonding, and parental stress in CHARGE syndrome. *Mental Health Aspects of Developmental Disabilities, 11,* 10–21.

Rossiter, L., & Sharpe, D. (2001). The siblings of individuals with mental retardation: A quantitative integration of the literature. *Journal of Child and Family Studies, 10,* 65–84.

Scorgie, K., Wilgosh, L., & McDonald, L. (1998). Stress and coping in families of children with disabilities: An examination of recent literature. *Developmental Disabilities Bulletin, 26,* 22–42.

Scorgie, K., Wilgosh, L., & Sobsey, D. (2004). The experience of transformation in parents of children with disabilities: Theoretical considerations. *Developmental Disabilities Bulletin, 32,* 84–110.

Sharpe, D., & Rossiter, L. (2002). Siblings of children with a chronic illness: A meta-analysis. *Journal of Pediatric Psychology, 27,* 699–710.

Simons, L. G., & Conger, R. D. (2007). Linking mother-father differences in parenting to a typology of family parenting styles and adolescent outcomes. *Journal of Family Issues, 28,* 212–241.

Snyder, C. R., Rand, K. L., & Sigmon, D. R. (2002). Hope theory: A member of the positive psychology family. In C. R. Snyder & S. J. Lopez (Eds.), *Handbook of positive psychology* (pp. 257–276). New York: Oxford University Press.

Taanila, A., Järvelin, M., & Kokkonen, J. (1998). Parental guidance and counselling by doctors and nursing staff: Parents' views of initial information and advice for families with disabled children. *Journal of Clinical Nursing, 7,* 505–511.

Taunt, H. M., & Hastings, R. P. (2002). Positive impact of children with developmental disabilities on their families: A preliminary study. *Education and Training in Mental Retardation and Developmental Disabilities, 37,* 410–420.

Tolsdorf, C. (1976). Social networks, support, and coping: An exploratory study. *Family Process, 15,* 407–417.

Vaux, A. C., Burba, P. C., & Stewart, D. (1986). Orientation toward utilization of support resources. *Journal of Community Psychology, 14*, 159–170.

Vermaes, I. P. R., Janssens, J. M. A. M., Mullaart, R. A., Vinck, A., & Gerris, J. R. M. (2008). Parents' personality and parenting stress in families of children with spina bifida. *Child: Care, Health and Development, 34*, 665–674.

Wallace, J. L., & Vaux, A. (1993). Social support network orientation: The role of adult attachment style. *Journal of Social and Clinical Psychology, 12*, 354–365.

White, N., & Hastings, R. P. (2004). Social and professional support for parents of adolescents with severe intellectual disabilities. *Journal of Applied Research in Intellectual Disabilities, 17*, 181–190.

Woolfson, L., & Grant, E. (2006). Authoritative parenting and parental stress in parents of pre-school and older children with developmental disabilities. *Child: Care, Health and Development, 32*, 177–184.

Yau, M. K., & Li-Tsang, C. W. P. (1999). Adjustment and adaptation in parents of children with developmental disabilities in two-parent families: A review of the characteristics and attributes. *The British Journal of Developmental Disabilities, 45*, 38–51.

Ylven, R., Björck-Åkesson, E., & Granlund, M. (2006). Literature review of positive functioning in families with children with a disability. *Journal of Policy and Practice in Individual Disabilities, 3*, 253–270.

Zeitlin, S., Williamson, G. G., & Rosenblatt, W. P. (1987). The coping with stress model: A counseling approach for families with a handicapped child. *Journal of Counseling and Development, 65*, 443–446.

Nurturing Family Resilience in Response to Chronic Illness: An Integrative Approach to Health and Growth Promotion

Ester R. Shapiro

Introduction: Learning From Family Lived Experiences of Chronic Illness

In 1995, Ann Burack Weiss published a paper in *Social Work* describing how her personal and professional experiences in family chronic illness caretaking, the enormous gap between practitioner biomedical education and the real-life challenges that families and caretakers faced, and their often overlooked strengths, inspired her to collect chronicles of family caretaking. In *The Caregiver's Tale: Loss and Renewal in Memoirs of Family Life* (2003), she recommends selected memoirs educating practitioners about family lived experiences with chronic illness. Her book is used in the field of medical humanities to help physicians' empathically connect to patients' illness experiences through narratives and other creative arts (Charon, 2008). In a volume on family systems and health, McDaniel, Hepworth, and Doherty (2003) asked contributors to present their frameworks and practice in light of a personal experience of facing family chronic illness that informed their work. Other writers have depicted efforts to move beyond "technocratic" medical models of illness and cure to offer "humanistic" biopsychosocial or "holistic" perspectives emphasizing cultural and spiritual worldviews of illness and wellness (Davis-Floyd, 2001; Walsh, 2006).

These interdisciplinary writings affirm that stories of lived experiences can educate and inspire us in striving for systemic transformations to nurture the family resilience at the heart of health. Yet Steinglass (2006) notes that promising family medicine and primary health approaches initiated as policies responsive to 1960s social movements and designed to link personal and social health were undermined by ideologies and economics supporting individual, de-contextualized, symptom-oriented care. At this time (June 2012), we stand on thresholds of crisis and tipping points for change. US and global chronic illness prevalence, challenges of co-chronicity, and vast social and economic illness burdens have resulted in calls for transformation of social conditions and systems of care that offer more favorable contexts for family and community-based health promotion and resilience. Achieving change requires linking knowledge based on both lived experiences and research evidence with critical perspectives on social determinants of health and flourishing, as well as with strategies for effective advocacy. However, dominance of biomedical illness models in health care delivery and reimbursement, in widely endorsed cultural beliefs and policies (Carman et al, 2010), and in researcher and provider training

E.R. Shapiro (✉)
Department of Psychology, University of Massachusetts,
Boston, MA, USA
e-mail: ester.shapiro@umb.edu

D.S. Becvar (ed.), *Handbook of Family Resilience*,
DOI 10.1007/978-1-4614-3917-2_22, © Springer Science+Business Media New York 2013

presents significant challenges to change. Martin and Petersen (2009) argue that achieving new models of chronic illness care requires "reflexive synthesis" of patient-centered perspectives and scientific worldviews of evidence-based medicine, exploring the social construction of chronicity as a sociopolitical discourse influenced by economic and power relations. Wood and Miller (2005) suggest that advancing family systems approaches to health requires both investment in theoretically guided research and challenges to "dominant paradigms" emphasizing individual symptoms, noting examples in developmental psychopathology and positive psychology as offering paradigm-shifting areas of theoretically based research incorporating developmental systems and the study of strengths.

This chapter provides critical interdisciplinary reviews towards a "reflexive synthesis" of ecosystemic models and participatory research, practice, and advocacy methods as tools in applying family health, growth, and resilience perspectives in family-centered chronic illness care. Increasingly, interdisciplinary literatures use complex adaptive systems theories to study linked processes contributing to child, adult, family, and environmental resilience, wellness, and flourishing when facing challenges. Further, resilience resources are viewed not as abilities of a lucky few but as capabilities emerging from unequal social distribution of adverse exposures and access to valuable resources, shifting perspective from individual good fortune in "beating the odds" to social responsibility in "changing the odds" (Seccombe, 2002). Exploring family resilience in response to chronic illness can contribute uniquely to this re-visioning by synthesizing well-established interdisciplinary, ecosystemic literatures within family, developmental, public health, and community sciences studying health promotion, resilience, and flourishing with participatory research and empowerment practice methods emphasizing ethical perspectives on inclusion, on social distribution of risk factors and protective resources, and on accountability for health equity. This synthesis links US and global initiatives in health promotion to family-centered chronic illness care through an intergenerational, ecosystemic lens emphasizing families as partners in collaborative care. Health and mental health are viewed holistically, integrating treatment, problem prevention, and health promotion across systems and linking social policies and their embodiment through impacts on shared, evolving family lives. This approach emphasizes empowerment education and resource rights advocacy for families struggling to meet the demands of chronic illness care while protecting capacities for growth.

Case Example: Intergenerational Impacts of Chronic Illness in My Own Immigrant Family

My own personal apprenticeship in learning from the enduring generosity of family resilience as a living legacy began in our extended Eastern European Cuban Jewish household in Havana, already transplanted from the Russian Polish border in my paternal grandparents' generation and soon to move to Miami in the aftermath of the Cuban revolution. Our intergenerational household was organized around managing my grandfather Eliezer/Lazaro's chronic neurological disorder, consequent to an accident in early adolescence when he was kicked in the head by a horse, leaving a visible hoof-shaped dent on his right forehead. In a family life filled with vivid, practical, conflicting, and contested stories illustrating how we survived unrelenting confrontations with politics and history, *Abuelo* Lazaro's unfolding chronic illness story was simultaneously ever-present yet invisible and unnamed, part of an implicit family agreement to protect his dignity by never speaking of his neurological impairment. Instead, we grew up hearing a paradigmatic story of my grandparents' marriage and family life as a romantic love story on the shifting borders of Russia and Poland, now Byelorussia. This dominant story, in which chronic illness was a minor theme, highlighted the love, loyalty, courage, and ingenuity that would become foundational to our family's resilience in confronting wars, revolutions, economic hardship, and multiple immigrations.

As a young man, my grandfather survived loss and dispersal of his once-secure Russian Jewish landowning family in the 1917 Bolshevik revolution, with grief exacerbating his seizure disorder. Slipping over the border to evade military service, he proposed to my *Abuela* Bashe/Bertha, who had fallen enduringly in love with the handsome, elegant young scion of a well-off, stable family even when his circumstances radically changed. He insisted they immigrate immediately, but she persuaded him to start their family in Poland as her deeply religious mother refused to leave. They finally immigrated to rural Cuba in 1936 with 11-year-old Consuelo, 9-year-old Noel, and my 5-year-old father, Jaime, just one step ahead of the impending holocaust. Stresses of loss and dislocation worsened his legendary temper and seizures. Yet, cunningly and laboriously, initially with the collaboration of her three children, then enlisting her daughters-in-law and growing grandchildren, my grandmother created a family life where no matter the turmoil and upheaval, my functionally limited, emotionally expressive, at times explosive grandfather was sheltered from family stresses, served scrupulously healthy meals, received the best possible medical care, and enjoyed privileged status as head of household and working man. She cared for him beyond his death in his 80s to her own death a decade later, his spirit by her side.

My father, their youngest son, proudly recalled that shortly before my birth in 1952 my grandfather had one of the first corpus callosotomies, a pioneering surgery performed by his Havana physicians and curing his seizure disorder while significantly controlling his outbursts. My 21-year-old father and his 24-year-old brother were already running the family business, launching their own families as we, too, faced revolutions and upheavals while caring for an unacknowledged invalid at the heart of our family lives. These complex family relationships, embracing multifaceted contradictions of love and loyalty, tender affection and hair-trigger outbursts of rage, generosity and resentments, formed shared, unfolding family legacies while impacting each uniquely due to roles, relationships, and developmental timing. My Aunt Consuelo shared a very different story of the consequences of her father's illness in her life due to her age, gender, and family life cycle timing. Her lively, engaging temperament and exotic beauty bloomed dangerously in adolescence across cultures, prior to her father's neurosurgery and near the height of his outbursts. Her sexual curiosity matched by persistent romantic attention from powerful men in their close-knit rural Cuban town led to passionate escapades that my father was assigned to monitor and inform on, triggering her father's violence and urgently demanding resolution. At age 16, she was married to my Uncle Isaac, a recent Polish Jewish refugee whose lifelong violent temper and obsessive loyalty to his sister were interpreted as consequences of being sole family survivors of the holocaust. As my grandparents and father told me this story, Consuelo's dangerous disobedience forced the family to arrange an appropriate marriage. Only after both his parents' deaths could my father acknowledge his father's condition and admit that his mother's imposition of extended family togetherness on her sons while extruding her daughter seemed necessary to family survival yet also exacted enduring consequences.

These experiences taught us to respect the centrality of health as a foundational family resource, one depending as much on societal and family commitments as on individuals. In 50 years of family political disagreements over Cuba's revolution, our single agreement is shared respect for Cuba's commitment to universal access to health care. Growing up between cultures, I learned to appreciate how our multifaceted, evolving family stories were responsive to changing circumstances, operating as powerful, flexible adaptive strategies, and constructively channeling emotions and purposefully guiding choreographies of what only appeared to be private individual actions. Our family actions and meanings created necessary stability in the face of potentially overwhelming changes, protecting family functioning as demands of chronic illness intersected with family life cycle transitions and changing cultural contexts. Our intergenerational extended family patterns of care, bridging gender and generations, remain characteristic for ethnically diverse and immigrant families caring for ailing elders who contribute to as well as receive care (Gallant, Spitze, & Grove, 2010).

Translating Lived Experiences of Family Resilience and Health into Frameworks for Research, Practice, and Advocacy

These multifaceted intergenerational family experiences of hardship, struggle, and resilience form the foundation for my own work, appreciating considerable strengths families bring to life course challenges and consequences of shared responses for altered life pathways and future possibilities. I view family health and mental health as critically important positive adaptive resources, which family members strive to protect through both overt and implicit actions and meanings. Chronic ill health, with its anticipation of enduring compromises and potential decline, can initiate life changes with cascading stresses, sometimes forcing families to change established responses to shared life course demands. These demands lead to complex, multifaceted responses that even when private imply consequences for the family as a unit: sacrifices made openly or secretly, with loving generosity that also can be tinged with resentment, new responses forged with creativity and courage that also can contain profound exhaustion and terrible fear of the future. As our own families and those we work with teach us, calamities of chronic illness may take over family life at moments of crisis that become turning points. Yet chronic illness cannot remain the whole story, or all else the family strives for will be consumed by its demands. As families adapt and co-create "the new normal," we can join them at multiple points of entry to recognize and affirm the realities of their suffering and fears, while also identifying health- and growth-promoting family resilience resources. In my own interdisciplinary work exploring the intergenerational family life cycle as a resource for shared health and growth, I have expanded sources informing how family adaptations to both expected change and unanticipated challenges can preserve capacities for flexible responding that promotes resilience. Beginning with feminist family and developmental systems integrations of individual and relational perspectives on how families face adversities while protecting shared development (Shapiro, 1994), I have incorporated culturally informed, community-based, and social justice approaches integrating health promotion, problem prevention, and symptom-reduction interventions that make the most of family life cycle transitions as health- and growth-promoting opportunities (Shapiro, 2002, 2008a).

Critical assessment of frameworks and their implications in enhancing or impeding access to needed health resources themselves operate as important resilience resources for patients and families as well as for providers, researchers, and policy makers. As Ungar (2010) suggests within culturally informed family resilience, Wallerstein (2006) within community-based participatory health, and Prilleltensky and Prilleltensky (2005) within critical health and community psychology, patients, families, and communities seeking to improve health and wellness must navigate environments for needed resources while critically assessing barriers and joining with others to insist on resource rights. Advances in medical research and acute care save and prolong more lives, but with an inconsistent commitment to the quality of those lives. Global comparative perspectives on chronic illness care, holistic health and mental health promotion, and health and human rights can help us gather frameworks, research evidence, and practice models that transcend the limitations of our particular setting and discipline (Perry, Presley-Cantrell, & Dhingra, 2010; Wellard, 2010).

The Center for Disease Control ([CDC], 2011) reported that nearly half the US population meets criteria for at least one chronic illness, and one third for two or more. Globally, the World Health Organization ([WHO], 2008) estimated that by 2020 chronic diseases could account for 73% of deaths and 60% of global disease burden. Exclusively biomedical approaches are unsuited to chronic illness care, as they isolate individuals from family and social resources, emphasizing physician expertise while viewing patients and families as passive recipients of care. Inappropriate application of medical specialty oriented care contributes to crises of cost, quality, and equity (Berwick, 2002; Health and Human Services, 2011; WHO, 2008). Following US and global health promotion and human development frameworks, we view health not just as absence of illness but as the presence of wellness and human rights at the highest possible attainable standards of health; recognize multisystemic social determinants of health, with only 10–15% attributable to direct health care, 10% to genetic endowment, and as much as 75% attributable to ecological burdens and resources throughout life. According to these models, health outcomes also are determined by education, housing, employment, and environmental quality; health care organization, quality, and access favoring primary care; and individual, family, and community engagement in promoting positive health outcomes while preventing and treating illness (Wellard, 2010; WHO, 2008). These models mobilize empowered multisector partnership to reduce risks and decrease chronic illness burdens.

Both US and global health promotion approaches to chronic illness care are consistent with holistic person and family centered, multisystemic strengths-based perspectives on health and mental health emphasized by the literature on family resilience. However, they contradict US symptom-oriented care emphasizing technological solutions, what Kleinman (1988) termed "the culture of medicine." Clarke (2010) describes "biomedicalization" as an ideology promoting medical interventions for problems of everyday life, treating "diseases" of menopause, or medicating children to manage behavior problems that would be best addressed through family and community supports. Consistent with these critiques, Berwick (2002, 2009) offers a guide to health care reform emphasizing patient and family-centered, systems-minded, and knowledge-based care. Berwick was appointed to lead Medicare/Medicaid while implementing the Affordable Care Act, which prioritizes partnerships in prevention as well as health care delivery, monitoring outcomes to achieve quality, effectiveness, and equity. Regrettably, as of this writing, both the Affordable Care Act and Berwick's directorship have become controversial because they challenge this "dominant paradigm" and threaten the status quo.

Individualized, decontextualized health care interventions place disproportionate burdens on families coping with chronic illness demands. They require managing visits to multiple providers, adherence to complex medications, and compliance with intrusive interventions without challenging medical authority. They may require draconian personal "lifestyle" solutions without consideration of patient context such as conditions of employment, neighborhood characteristics, co-occurring illnesses, or other family needs and constraints. Finally, they count on families, particularly women, to provide support services that are invisible and unsupported within biomedicine but are essential to patient and family health outcomes and quality of life (Singer, Biegel, & Ethridge, 2009). Feminist studies of work and family refer to "the third shift" (Gerstel, 2000) and "shadow workforce" (Bookman & Harrington, 2007) as women become responsible for health and disability-related family caretaking within eroding health and social service systems. Singer et al. (2009) recommend integrating knowledge across family chronic illness and disability studies to better support family caregivers. Disability studies argue that resilience and recovery require partnerships for empowerment at multiple systemic levels, including critical analysis of social stigma, identification of barriers to resource rights promoting health as measured by person and family centered quality of life, and legal advocacy for universal access to these rights (Rosenthal, Kosciulek, Lee, Frain, & Ditchman, 2009).

Ecosystemic Approaches to Resilience in Developmental, Family, and Community Sciences

Emerging interdisciplinary theories with associated research exploring ecosystemic health and development perspectives offer ways to conceptualize and study positive adaptation and resilience in response to ordinary growth and change as impacted by adversities across bio-psycho-social-environmental domains addressing interrelated health and growth outcomes. These include ecologies of human development in child psychology (Bronfenbrenner, 1979; Masten & Obradovic, 2008; Sandler, 2001), developmental psychopathology and resilience (Cicchetti & Cohen, 2005; Luthar & Brown, 2007), developmental contextualism (Lerner, Jacobs, & Wertlieb, 2003; Ungar, 2011), family systems theory (Becvar & Becvar, 2009), life-course developmental perspectives on health, growth, and well-being or flourishing (Brim, Ryff, & Kessler, 2004; Elder, Johnson, & Crosnoe, 2003; Keyes, 2007), ecosystemic public health (Krieger, 2001; Lu et al., 2010), family resilience (Becvar, 2007; Ungar, 2010; Walsh, 2006), holistic health integrating mind, body, spirit, and community (Bell et al., 2002; IOM, 2009; Martin & Sturmberg, 2009), and holistic environmental resilience studies (Capra, 2005). Ecosystemic approaches understand human health and development as adaptations within complex living systems characterized by constant change, involving transactions in relationships and environments evolving over time across biological, cognitive, emotional, behavioral, interpersonal, institutional, and environmental domains (O'Brien, 2005). From cellular to cultural, systems are embedded, interdependent, and constantly interacting, best understood using the two dimensions of time and environment or setting (Rolland & Walsh, 2006). Depending on our theoretical and practice disciplines and settings, we may join a system to promote change at a macro-systems—community, population, or policy—level, or at a micro-systems—individual or family—level. Regardless of entry and purpose, we strive to identify leverage points and promote linkages associated with more favorable intersections between contexts and their embodiments (Krieger, 2001; Wandersman, 2003), never forgetting that violent neighborhoods or exposure to carcinogens result in real bodies burdened by health consequences of harm.

Because complexity sciences view outcomes as dynamic and probabilistic rather than controllable and predictable, they use multimethod quantitative and qualitative research to identify variables and processes associated with desired positive outcomes for a particular dimension of health or development. In identifying valued outcomes, ecosystemic developmental approaches highlight systemic capacity to respond flexibly to future challenges of change. These models recognize the value of developmental thresholds and transitions as offering meaningful opportunities to introduce resilience and growth promoting resources (Shonkoff & Phillips, 2000). Interventions during critical transitions centered on the family's own goals and recognizing individuality and interdependence help families struggling with adversities renew a sense of shared purpose and negotiate more favorable growth-promoting relationships within and outside the family (Shapiro, 2008a). Complex systems perspectives argue that adaptations cannot be neatly categorized as successful or maladaptive without considering contexts and consequences for development. As assumed in the Family Adjustment and Adaptation Resiliency model ([FAAR], Patterson, 2002), responses deemed necessary and appropriate during an immediate adjustment phase may not necessarily serve longer term adaptation. Yet immediate adaptive strategies can become habitual and thus limit family responses to new demands.

Complex adaptive systems approaches to chronic illness care (Bell et al., 2002; Martin & Sturmberg, 2009) view transactions between individual lived experiences of health and social environments as dynamic adaptations in an "emergent present." Narratives of past experiences interface with evolving contexts to organize adaptive responding shaping illness trajectories. Across these literatures, ecosystemic thinking appreciates the interdependence of emotion regulation and meanings associated with health- and growth-promoting adaptations. Individualized interventions mobilizing multisystemic resources can promote new forms of adaptive self-organizing associated with improved health outcomes (Griffiths et al., 2010). Holistic and ecosystemic approaches emphasize allodynamic processes, including short-term allostasis and long-term allostatic load (McEwen & Gianaros, 2011). This concept offers a biological systems understanding of efforts required in returning biological processes to stability after exposure to stressors or changes, modeling how stressful environments become embodied as illness conditions while remaining amenable to change throughout life. At the same time, these approaches link genetics, biology, health, and development to qualities of societies as well as particular "localities" as settings for health and development, linking genes and neurons to families and neighborhoods both in childhood (IOM, 2009; Shonkoff & Phillips, 2000) and later life (McEwen & Gianaros, 2011). Intersections of timing and contexts create dynamic circumstances as potential pathways that, once initiated, become stable and self-organizing while remaining amenable to change. Due to the dynamic complexity of stressors and resources, environments may be more or less health and growth promoting, at the same time that individuals and families may navigate high-risk or resource-rich environments differently depending on appraisals and beliefs that offer stability while remaining responsive to new circumstances.

Ecosystemic frameworks present significant challenges to predominant biomedical research methods (Bell et al., 2002; Ungar, 2011; Wandersman, 2003). Ungar suggests that ecosystemic resilience research requires a paradigm shift using the four guiding principles of decentralization of the individual, recognition of complexity, atypicality or uniqueness of pathways, and cultural relativity. Ecosystemic health and development researchers study specific mechanisms contributing to outcomes of interest, while recognizing that selection of independent, moderating/mediating, and dependent variables relies on discipline-based agreements guiding how best to reduce complexity of interrelated phenomen a allowing for systematic study (O'Brien, 2005). Outcomes of interest can be guided by biomedicalization to focus on pathology, or can assess both disease burden and positive processes such as wellness or flourishing (Keyes, 2007). Both negative and positive factors contributing to multifaceted outcomes can cluster and cascade, creating "vicious circles" of associated stressors or "virtuous circles" of associated positive resources promoting resilience. These convergences and contingencies are not fully captured by statistical research modeling. Further, well-controlled studies do not translate directly to real-life settings, what researchers concerned with contextualizing evidence-based practice term ecological validity (Bernal, 2006; Henggeler, Schoenwald, Bourdin, Rowland, & Cunningham, 2009).

Ecosystemic interventions use research evidence to target developmental turning points in light of multiple systems that can transform developmental contexts. For example, Lu et al. (2010) integrate ecosystemic and life-course perspectives in public health to map interventions with the potential to change persistent inequalities in birth outcomes for black and white women by strengthening positive health (i.e., prenatal care, gender and race sensitive services), family relational (i.e., father involvement), and social processes (i.e., equal pay for women's work). Ecosystemic health and development perspectives guide assessment and intervention for unique individuals and families in specific settings strategically, selecting leverage points and identifying linkages in the "web" or "map" of risk and protective factors, including relevant organizations and institutions supporting change. At the same time, these perspectives suggest ethical principles guiding relationships of parts to whole at multiple levels: inclusive knowledge based on dialogues that recognize and respect differences within a cultural context, with special attention to those most vulnerable; respect for diversity as protecting future, flexible responses to change; and monitoring sustainability while evaluating when lack of reciprocity and failures of accountability may damage future chances for the system as a whole (Capra, 2005; Prilleltensky & Prilleltensky, 2005; Wandersman, 2003). Because power inequalities in social relationships can lead to deliberate or inadvertent abuses, ecosystemic approaches turn to participatory and partnership methods to identify qualities of relationships, addressing and resolving conflicts while protecting communities and their constituents. Articulating impacts of cultural practices and social inequalities affecting within-family power asymmetries becomes especially important in family resilience studies, as gender and generation create power imbalances and potential vulnerabilities that can be exacerbated by chronic illness. Positive parenting, supported across literatures as a powerful protective factor (Masten & Obradovic, 2008; Sandler, Schoenfelder, Wolchik, & MacKinnon, 2011), requires marital, extended family, and societal support sensitive to dilemmas of gender inequality. Many cultures give children and elders opportunities to contribute, and families experiencing adversities are motivated to assist others within and outside the family in ways associated with resilience (Lietz, 2011). Resilient families draw from diverse cultural traditions to protect gendered mutuality and wellness of parenting adults as they take responsibility for dependent members.

Participatory and Inclusive Methods as Tools in Promoting Resilience

While ecosystemic health and development perspectives guide us to look at relationships between parts and whole in adaptive processes of change, they do not themselves address processes of power and collaboration. Participatory and inclusive methods, which are used in both research and practice, create knowledge about problems and solutions through communities of inquiry and partnerships that include all those potentially affected (Minkler, 2004; Wandersman, 2003). Further, these approaches prioritize the voices and knowledge of those closest to the problem, including those affected, their family caretakers, and their most hands-on direct care providers, who are often also the most powerless within society and systems of care. Using the language of disabilities rights, these approaches say to researchers, practitioners, and policy makers, "nothing about us without us" (Berwick, 2009). Finally, participatory methods emphasize shared outcomes monitoring as tools for advocacy and accountability, helping to identify ineffective interventions or unfair distribution of resources (Wandersman, 2003). Freire's participatory education, widely used in educational and health promotion settings (Wallerstein, 2006), suggests that "Concientización" or consciousness raising regarding problems and barriers impeding access to resources needs to be followed by "annunciation" or a vision of what should be and steps towards its actualization, creating a "pedagogy of hope" as a potent resilience resource. Participatory methods are implicitly ecosystemic, connecting individual knowledge to dialogues in relationships of mutual teaching and learning, and connect these in turn to societal distribution of material resources and shared meanings. These methods are compatible with scientific research design but deliberately democratize steps in posing meaningful, ecologically valid research questions applicable to practice and policy settings and promoting equity. Wandersman (2003) argues that community science expands biomedical prevention science by including community members and other "stakeholders" in "Getting to Outcomes" using a ten-step partnership process posing research questions while highlighting community accountability. Bell et al. (2002) suggest that effective evidence-based practice integrating holistic health and biomedicine requires integration of patient-centered care principles and partnerships in identifying and monitoring desired outcomes. These researchers and others find that using patient and family centered quality of life measures to establish and monitor goals is associated with more effective practice.

As an example in family and community-based chronic illness care, the Children's Hospital Resource Mother's Project (St. James, Shapiro, & Weisbrun, 1999) combined ecosystemic and home-based peer outreach and empowerment approaches to prevention in a program supporting young reproductive-age women with PKU (phenylketonuria) who needed to implement a strict protein-restricted diet prior to pregnancy to protect the fetus from early, devastating neurological damage. Yet, hospital-based nutrition programs, requiring involvement of girls at the time they initiated sexual activity, failed to change dietary habits, with dire consequences for their infants. Mothers of children with PKU, who had learned the rigors of the diet and understood lived experiences of implementation, were trained as outreach educators to work with these young women, their partners, and extended families, using an individualized, ecosystemic, supportive education approach to increase adherence to the strict protein-restricted diet prior to and during pregnancy needed to protect birth outcomes. The study, with both quantitative and qualitative components, found that ecological contexts of PKU from the girls' early childhoods, especially family income and education, resulted in two trajectories, one with higher risks leading to increased, enduring challenges, and one with greater resources protecting health and growth. The individualized home-based approach permitted shaping individualized educational interventions to address these different contexts for development, increasing adherence for all participants. The intervention significantly increased dietary adherence when compared to matched controls, as measured by maternal PKU blood levels and infant head circumference. Additionally, the home-based supportive education approach increased these chronically ill young mothers' self-confidence in their capacity for mothering. Finally, the Resource Mothers, many of whom had postponed professional development due to their daughter's chronic illness needs, described program participation as having inspired them to seek additional professional development.

In sum, ecosystemic frameworks on health interventions, used with participatory methods, include those most affected by problems and seek solutions through partnerships with practitioners, community-based organizations, and policy makers, offering powerful tools for changing contexts to promote family health and resilience. Expanding family peer support can strengthen empowered use of health care relationships, resource navigation and advocacy, improving health and well-being while transforming contexts and forming new, more favorable pathways for shared development.

Family Resilience and Chronic Illness: Review of the Relevant Literatures

Family Systems and Health: Contributions to Family Resilience Studies

Systemic family research and therapy literatures have a long history of focusing on positive family processes and strengths in chronic illness care, both in primary care and specialized health settings. A review of this broad literature, also termed medical or pediatric family therapy, is beyond the scope of this chapter. However, promoting family resilience in chronic illness care requires solid grounding in this work as it contributes to re-visioning family systems informed, holistic health care supporting provider reflexivity and partnerships (Bacigalupe, 2011; Campbell, 2003; Kazak, 2006; McDaniel, Campbell, Hepworth, & Lorenz, 2005; Wood & Miller, 2005). The Family systems and health field studies family-based health- and-growth promoting as well as health-and-growth com-promising characteristics for individuals facing both acute and chronic illness. Family responses are seen as dynamic, multifaceted, and evolving in response to changing circumstances. In pioneering work studying family adaptive responses to chronic illness, Cole and Reiss (1993) described "representing" or meaning-making and "practicing" or everyday behaviors as key family protective processes. Further, Cole and Reiss understood multifaceted meaning-making processes as themselves dynamic adaptive strategies, influenced by specific chronic illness demands, in turn influencing family coping.

The family systems and health literature also has provided empirical reviews of family contributions to positive health outcomes, exploring family processes contributing to a continuum of positive and desired or negative illness outcomes. Campbell (2003) reviewed family interventions for physical disorders in four clinical areas: family caregiving of elders, childhood chronic illness, spouse involvement in chronic adult illness, and family involvement in health promotion and disease prevention. This review found that family support, sense of connection, and spousal and familial sharing of positive emotions were important protective processes associated with improved health outcomes. The review also noted that family conflicts or expressions of negative emotions such as criticism for continuing risky behaviors were associated with negative health outcomes. Campbell found empirical support for three types of family interventions: educational interventions enhancing family knowledge of illness and illness-specific family support; family psycho-education informed by a broader family systems perspective on positive family relationships, specifically targeting illness knowledge as well as family protective factors; and family therapy. Fisher (2005) reviewed theoretical bases and empirical support for family interventions in chronic disease, identifying family emotional regulation and meaning-making as primary adaptive strategies, suggesting that these result in secondary adaptive strategies relative to altering family routines and problem solving. Wood and Miller (2005) reviewed the research literature on family functioning impacting individual health. These authors argue for theoretically grounded, ecosystemic research on mechanisms by which family processes influence health outcomes, exploring a Bio-Behavioral Family Model highlighting parent/child attachments, quality of couples' relationships, and family emotional climate as offering critical links between biological processes and health outcomes. Their review identifies the importance of protecting family routines and rituals disrupted by illness and medical management, especially for children; recognizing family stressors as biosocial pathways to illness; nurturing positive emotions in loving relationships; and reducing negative emotional cycles or conflicts to improve health.

Hartmann, Bazner, Wild, Eisler, and Herzog (2010) conducted a meta-analysis of research on family involvement in the treatment of adult patients with chronic medical conditions. Their study identified 52 relevant randomized control trials, primarily for cardiovascular conditions including stroke, cancer, and arthritis. Interventions were primarily relationship-focused family interventions and educational interventions. Both types of family interventions showed modest but statistically and clinically significant effects, with somewhat greater effects for relationship-focused family interventions. In addition, family systems and health literatures have focused on dyadic relationships as they contribute to chronic illness coping, increasingly studying these longitudinally for couples' coping with the chronic illness of an adult partner (Berg & Upchurch, 2007) and parents coping with a child's chronic illness (Alderfer et al., 2008). These reviews apply frameworks and research methods and identify variables complementing theory and research in family resilience and health.

Family Resilience in Family Studies: Positive Adaptation Under Stress

Two major approaches to family resilience form the foundation for work on family resilience in response to chronic illness, a family research strand with foundations in family sociology and family health psychology, and a family therapy strand (Patterson, 2002). In family sociology, the Resiliency Model of Family Stress, Adjustment and Adaptation proposed by McCubbin and colleagues (McCubbin, Thompson, & Thompson, 1999; Patterson, 2002) was based on Hill's original family sociology perspective on family crisis, stress, and coping focused on precrisis family resources. McCubbin et al. (1999) developed the Double ABCX model of Family Adjustment and Adaptation to build on this model while incorporating variables influencing family responses after the crisis. This model views family outcomes in response to stress as resulting from dynamic interaction of these factors: illness and disability as family stressors among other stressors; resistance resources such as psychological or economic resources that can counterbalance stressors; family appraisal of the illness and disability; and family coping strategies. These factors result in a crisis, with immediate adjustments focused on the illness, which then challenge the family to implement changes restoring balance and capacities to meet future challenges associated with positive longer termed adaptation. McCubbin et al. (1999) were distinctive in their family resilience writings for making cultural diversity central in understanding challenges families faced. Patterson (2005) applies the FAAR model to explore how family-meaning making promotes coping with a child's chronic illness.

Walsh's (2006) three-tiered theoretical model of family resilience emerges from a family systems and health perspective and interest in normal family processes as families face both anticipated and unexpected challenges throughout the family life cycle. Her family resilience framework highlights three factors: (1) *belief systems*, or how families view their circumstances, (2) *organizational patterns*, or how families are structured, and (3) *communication*, or how families problem solve relative to the adversities in their lives. Walsh theorizes that belief systems primarily impact family resilience through shared meaning-making processes, collective revisioning and renewal of hope, and spirituality. Organizational patterns primarily impact family resilience through flexible family structures such as family routines and rituals, family connectedness, and mobilization of extended kin and social and economic resources. Finally, Walsh theorizes that communication can promote resilience through effective and trusting emotional sharing and collaborative problem solving. Overall, Walsh's model uses a strength-based ecosystemic lens to identify how families mobilize individual, interpersonal, and community resources to grow and even flourish in responding to adversities. Her work also incorporates a family life course perspective, looking at how families "bounce forward" and re-organize so as to protect ongoing shared development.

Black and Lobo (2008) conducted a conceptual review of the family resilience construct within interdisciplinary social science and health literatures, recommending areas of assessment and intervention for family nursing practice. They note that the family resilience literature has not offered a measurement of the construct, in part because positive family adaptation draws from multiple levels of family ecology difficult to capture in a single scale. They distill a set of resilient family characteristics which include: *positive outlook*, with qualities of confidence, optimism, and humor; *spirituality* as a shared source of meaning for stressors; *family member accord*, with qualities of cohesion, nurturance, authoritative discipline, and avoidance of hostility and conflict; *flexibility* with stable family roles responsive to situational and developmental change; *family communication*, characterized by clear open emotional expression and collaborative problem solving; *financial management*, including both competence and family warmth in the face of financial problems; *family time*, making the most of togetherness with daily tasks; *shared recreation*, which reinforces cohesion, adaptability, and learning; *routines and rituals*, activities promoting close family relationships and stability during crises; and *support networks* for sharing resources outside the family. Their review emphasizes the importance of assessing tasks of everyday life to ensure they remain stable sources of family organization and provide opportunities for conveying positive emotions.

In her mixed-methods study of family resilience, Lietz (2006) interviewed six resilient families selected from a large survey who scored high on measures of risk and on positive family functioning. She used the qualitative method of narrative reconstruction to develop a model of family resilience, highlighting five evolving stages: (1) survival, (2) adaptation, (3) acceptance, (4) growing stronger, (5) helping others. In addition, she identified ten protective factors, including: (1) morality/spirituality, (2) taking charge, (3) external and internal social support, (4) communication, (5) boundary setting, (6) creativity/flexibility, (7) humor, (8) insight, (9) appraisal, and (10) giving social support.[1]

Complementing family resilience perspectives, Parke (2004) reviews family development research noting three areas of systematic study that demonstrate a significant impact on positive family adaptation: (1) family myths, (2) family stories, and (3) family routines and rituals. Parke describes myths as enduring stories and beliefs passed on relatively unchanged and influencing family processes through communication of deeply rooted cultural values, providing continuity across generations. Family stories, in contrast, offer foundations for collaborative problem solving, as family members participate in and contribute to story development. Kiser, Baumgardner, and Dorado (2010) underscore the healing power of collaborative family storytelling in overcoming legacies of trauma by encouraging multiple perspective taking and empathic listening and providing intergenerational support.

Decades of research on routines and rituals have suggested the important role these aspects of family life can have on family resilience (Fiese et al., 2002). Routines involve specific time commitments and are repeated over time, meeting primary needs while providing stability and conveying care and affection. Examples of family routines include activities such as dinnertime and bedtime practices. Rituals, on the other hand, involve rich symbolic communications and provide ceremony connecting the present to past legacies and future possibilities. Rituals provide meaning to family interactions and

---

[1] For more on this topic, please see Chap. 10.

can come in the form of family gatherings or celebrations such as holidays, traditions such as birthdays, and transitions and rites of passage such as weddings and funerals. Fiese's review highlights the health-promoting aspect of routines and rituals as indicators of family values, organization, and communication, preserving basic survival practices while conveying positive feelings of commitment and belonging vital to coping with hardships. Indeed, one focus of the literature on family resilience and chronic illness examines how families protect existing and create new routines and rituals to meet illness demands, creating new stabilities, opportunities for renewal, and images of the future in responding to both initial diagnosis and continuing disruptions and losses.

Family Resilience and Chronic Illness

While the broad research literatures on family resilience in response to stressors or crises yield valuable insights into family responses to crises of health, chronic illness as a family stressor presents highly specific demands and immediate challenges in creating a "new normal" while accommodating an evolving illness experience. In the family resilience and chronic illness literature, Rolland and Walsh (2006) offer a perspective on family resilience in response to childhood and adolescent chronic illness, synthesizing Rolland's family systems-illness model (1994) and Walsh's family resilience model (2006). In his family systems-illness model, Rolland argues that understanding family responses to chronic illness begins with what he terms the "psychosocial characteristics" of the illness, its medical qualities, and course—which can be progressive, constant, or relapsing/episodic, the degree of disability or impairment, and the specific treatment demands and prognosis as they impact on the individual and family. As a second dimension, psychosocial illness characteristics impinge on ongoing family life course and developmental processes. As a third dimension, Rolland suggests that family cultural and illness beliefs shape how families respond to the psychosocial demands of illness and integrate them into ongoing family development. In considering family responses to a chronic illness, the authors apply Walsh's multidimensional family resilience framework, highlighting the three key domains of family belief systems, organizational patterns, and communication and problem solving. These domains can be usefully applied in identifying resources promoting family resilience when facing the highly specific stressors presented by psychosocial illness characteristics as they interface with family life cycle demands. Integrating these two models offers a valuable framework for understanding family responses to a chronic illness diagnosis and its evolving course, beginning with realistic illness demands and specific ways these may challenge and nurture family strengths and resilience resources. Rolland and Walsh's useful synthesis highlights that family resilience in chronic illness care must begin with the best possible understanding of diagnosis and underlying medical condition, its impact and course, and its potential treatment.

Lee et al. (2004) present a conceptual framework for understanding family resilience in response to a chronically ill child, based on a review of characteristics identified in the family resilience literature, interviews with 11 parents of a chronically ill child in the pediatric oncology unit of a hospital in South Korea, studies of family resilience in maternal chronic illness, and synthesis of concepts from these sources. Their conceptual review suggests that chronic illness can be understood as a family stressor, with dimensions of family resilience buffering stress in ways that preserve critical domains of family functioning, including affective, structural, control, cognitive and external relationships. Their mapping of family resilience characteristics is congruent with the literature review in most instances, though some intriguing differences in emphasis emerge. Congruent areas of family resilience they identified included *intrinsic family characteristics* (coherence, faith, positive outlook, mature thinking, and family self-esteem); *family responsiveness to stress* (adaptability, desire to maintain normal states, patience for attainment of goals, ability to control stress, readiness to accept critical situations, and responsibility for causing trouble); and *family member orientation* (flexibility in reorganizing the family, attachment among family members, open communication and emotional expression among family members, mutual understanding, and maintaining balance in family member demands). Lee et al. (2004) highlighted a dimension termed *externally directed* as strongly represented in their interviews, but not emphasized in the published literature. The externally directed dimension included economic resources, pro-activeness toward information, maintaining cooperative relations with health care professionals, ability to maintain good social relations, and family member leadership in connecting to external resources. They proposed that for Korean families, extended family networks are especially important for family support as well as in mobilizing external resources. Because most of the published literature has focused on family responses to generalized stress rather than chronic illness coping, they suggest their family interviews may have elicited greater emphasis on the importance of externally directed family resources in illness settings. Other dimensions, such as recognizing the support and leadership of family elders as brokers to the outside world of resources, may be more salient for Korean and other collectivistic cultures yet also may illuminate the value of extended families and filial respect as resilience resources for all families.

Rosenthal et al. (2009) explored family resilience in adaptation to chronic illness and disability through the McCubbin et al. (1999) Resiliency Model of Family Stress, Adjustment and Adaptation reviewed earlier. In applying this model, these authors emphasized the importance of focusing on the configuration of stressors and resources contributing to longer term adaptation, rather than immediate, reactive adjustment to the demands of stressors and drawing on existing coping patterns without major change. Rosenthal and colleagues emphasize that while burdens of chronic illness and disability can lead to strains and maladaptation, successful coping with these challenges can lead to significant growth and maturation or "bonadaptation." The risk factors they identify include characteristics of the illness such as diagnosis, visibility, and severity; functional independence; and psychological stress due to disability related problems or daily hassles associated with the illness and impairments. They identify resistance or protective factors including stress processing, appraisal, and coping strategies; individual factors including temperament, competencies, and self-efficacy; and socioecological factors including family environment, social supports, and practical resources. They also highlight the importance of family-based peer social support, that is, families sharing experiences, supportive resources, and coping strategies in struggling and coping with illness and disability.

Ungar (2005, 2010, 2011) presents a cultural perspective on family resilience emerging from work with youth at risk for mental health problems. His approach highlights experiences of oppression and discrimination experienced by African American and other families, and the important role played by families in protecting children from the destructive impacts of inequality by educating them to be critically aware navigators of their social environments to safely access resources. Further, he notes that culturally diverse groups have culturally meaningful preferences for valued resources, and clinicians working with diverse families need to learn to negotiate these worlds and become advocates for culturally meaningful resources, ensuring that social environments respect cultural preferences.[2] In health care settings, culturally meaningful negotiation of resources can include strong preferences for family accompaniment and inclusion where Western norms would favor greater individual privacy or integration of culturally and spiritually based healing practices.

As noted throughout this review, multimethod family resilience research contributing to theoretical synthesis and practice applications requires assessment of variables including resilience processes and desired health and mental health outcomes. While the field of family resilience has not generated a

---

[2] For more on this topic, please see Chap. 9.

psychometrically reliable and valid scale measuring this construct, useful psychometrically tested instruments can be found in the broader field of family health and mental health assessment. Alderfer et al. (2008) conducted a literature search and a Division of Pediatric Psychology expert review of observational and self-report family assessment tools relevant to pediatric chronic illness from general family assessment, dyadic assessment, and child chronic illness care. Scales measuring constructs found in the family resilience literature designated well established include Fiese et al.'s observational coding of narrative coherence and relationship beliefs (Pratt & Fiese, 2004) and McCubbin and McCubbin's (1999) self-report Coping Inventory for Parents, with items measuring Family Integration, Maintaining Social Support, and Medical Communication and Consultation in responding to a child's chronic illness. Additionally, key variables contributing to family resilience include measures of dyadic functioning in couples, parent child, and sibling relationships and may be useful in exploring research questions such as couple's coping with chronic illness over time (Berg & Upchurch, 2007). In the adult resilience literature, Freiborg, Hjemda, Rosenvinge, and Martinussen (2006) have constructed an eco-systemic scale with individual characteristics such as optimism and self-efficacy, as well as key contextual variables of family cohesion and social support. Observational measures are time and resource intensive, but focus on family variables directly. Self-report measures of family functioning may ask individuals to report for the family as a unit, or collect this data from multiple family members, sometimes aggregating results or computing correlations indicating degree of agreement. Given these measurement challenges, and adding these to challenges of research design in studying dynamic, ecosystemic processes prospectively, qualitative research complements quantitative approaches with valuable insights into family experiences and adaptive coping.

Family Resilience and Specific Chronic Illnesses: Selected Review

The construct of family resilience is increasingly used to study specific illnesses in both child and adult literatures, arguing that attention to positive family processes promotes both positive health outcomes for affected individuals and positive mental health outcomes for families. While a full review is beyond the scope of this chapter, highlights from this literature suggest important future directions for research and practice. One pioneering family therapy work focusing on infected adults in the early HIV/AIDS epidemic was Gillian Walker's *In the Midst of Winter: Counseling Families, Couples and Individuals with AIDS infection* (1991). She described her work with families in the Bronx experiencing adverse ecologies associated with specific pathways of infection, including men who had sex with men, intravenous drug users, and the incarcerated, relative to what at that time was a devastating stigmatized illness and death sentence. Walker used a compassionate systemic and narrative therapy approach emphasizing family perspectives on suffering and problem-solving strategies, identifying the considerable strengths clients brought to coping. Currently, HIV/AIDS has been transformed into a chronic illness for all those with access to treatment. With roots in advocacy for disproportionately affected sexual minorities and racial and ethnic minority communities, the HIV/AIDS field has used socially informed ecosystemic and participatory approaches to care. Swendeman, Ingram, and Rotheram-Borus (2009) synthesize literatures on chronic illness self-management in the three categories of physical health, psychological functioning, and family/social relationships, exploring specific themes in application to HIV/AIDS. They note that unique family issues include challenges of disclosure and secrecy regarding gender and sexualities, which can be especially sensitive for serodiscordant couples or those experiencing stigma due to racial or religious discrimination.

The study of family resilience in response to asthma has been the focus of a substantial family health literature. In a 2008 special issue of *Family Process*, editor Fiese (2008) suggests that the study of asthma highlights general systems topics such as integrating individual needs into the family group, developmental trajectories of risk and resilience, family interaction patterns that can be constructive and supportive or burdensome and destructive, and cultural adaptation required for effective family care. Since 2008, the national burden of asthma has increased, affecting 1 in 10 children and 1 in 12 adults, and disproportionately affecting children living in poverty and ethnic minority children, adults, and families. Asthma is a condition that often can be controlled with a combination of medication and avoidance of environmental triggers, requiring a high degree of cooperation and control and affecting the lives of family members. Asthma is also very sensitive to emotional stressors with a strong mind/body dimension, and historically literatures in family health psychology over-emphasized dysfunctional family patterns such as conflict or over-control. The literature on family-based responses to asthma offers good examples of transformation from decontextualized family blaming to an emphasis on family strengths and the need for systemic supports in coping with challenges, recognizing the unique burdens for families living in poverty or coping with racism and discrimination who are disproportionately affected. Fiese, whose research focuses on family rituals and routines (Fiese et al., 2002) and family narratives in everyday life and in family illness (Pratt & Fiese, 2004), has explored how asthma disrupts daily routines including sleep as well as family caretaking demands (Fiese et al., 2008). They found that the mother's experience of caretaking burden in carrying out routines of everyday life demanded by asthma care could negatively affect family interactions, which in turn increased child anxiety and negatively affected child and family quality of life. Wamboldt et al. (2008) explored negotiations in families with an asthmatic child and an adult who smokes, noting the importance of realistic understanding of smoking as an asthma trigger. Recommendations for interventions emphasize family, school, and community-based psychoeducational approaches educating children and families about realistic illness and wellness management, while also improving family communication, protecting daily routines and rituals, and reducing conflicts along with promoting sharing of positive emotions.

Both child and adult chronic illness can disrupt family routines and rituals. Buchbinder, Longhofer, and McCue (2009) work with families where an adult has cancer, focusing on how this illness disrupts family routines and rituals. They conducted a qualitative study of families with young children and a diagnosis of cancer in one of the parents, requiring re-organization of family life to accommodate invasive, exhausting, and time-consuming treatments. Their study documented the extraordinary creativity and resilience with which adults as partners considered the needs of the cancer patient and the needs of their young children (ages 2–9). Despite significant upheavals in their family lives, these adults were sensitive to the impact of these disruptions on their children, and made meaningful choices such as timing chemotherapy to preserve family routines at meals and bedtimes, or including children in ritualizing medical milestones. Families were also creative in incorporating new family routines including hospital visits and recovery from surgery or chemotherapy, giving children opportunities to understand and contribute to care. The authors note that cancer can pull families apart, yet also offers experiences that can strengthen families and bring them together. This work illustrates how broad family resilience-building principles need to be specifically anchored in illness demands and family characteristics for unique individuals and families.

Retlaff (2007) explored resilience-related narratives of two-parent families with a child living with Rett's syndrome, a neurogenetic disorder primarily affecting girls and resulting in severe neurological disability as well as chronic illness. Drawing from a quantitative survey sample of 50 families recruited through a parent self-help organization, they used scores on Antonovsky's Family Sense of Coherence Scale (Antonovsky and Sourani, 1988) to select 6 families, 3 in the highest scoring and 3 in the lowest scoring quartiles, conducting home interviews with both parents. In the group reporting high coherence, narratives they termed "Story of the Refound Balance" emphasized the value and positive meaning of being able to rise to the demands of their special needs child. These families told stories of striving for balance in their family lives, finding ways to care for themselves and each other, feeling closer as a couple, and experiencing enhanced development as a person "with a big heart for people with disabilities." In the second type, termed "Story of the Long Tedious Walk Uphill," families told a story of a child-focused family experiencing significant burdens due to their child's needs, but finding com-

fort and pride in rising to these challenges. This group conveyed a greater sense of personal deprivation, and wives described "being like a single mother." Families who "refound balance" reported good
support from friends as well as each other, whereas more burdened families described less support
from both family and friends. Burdened families anticipated greater future problems, whereas "refound
balance" families used the phrase "she is just my child" to signal greater acceptance. While five of the
six families had other children, siblings were not mentioned in family themes. Bellin and Kovacs
(2006) review the literature on siblings of youths with chronic illness, noting that siblings are overlooked in research and clinical interventions yet face unique stressors due to illness demands as well
as growth in competencies. They recommend a multisystemic approach nurturing sibling disease
knowledge and personal competencies, addressing common misconceptions and emotions including
guilt and fears, and enhancing family and peer communication and support.

Although Rett's syndrome is a rare illness, Retlaff's (2007) work complements and illuminates
family resilience processes for other families coping with a child's disability, including autism and
other developmental disorders. Levine (2009) describes resilience narratives and strategies of 15 single mothers coping with a child's chronic disability. These included shifting from received social and
medical information to empowered, authoritative knowledge, transforming definitions of themselves
from inadequate to successful caretakers, and refusing to define their children as "disabled" in ways
that were stigmatizing and obscured their humanity and strengths.

Implications for Theory, Research, Practice, and Policy

This chapter's reflexive synthesis across multidisciplinary literatures suggests some exciting new
developments furthering the field of family resilience and health, within both family systems and
ecosystemic health promotion practice. Synthesizing ecosystemic family resilience frameworks using
participatory and inclusive methods that incorporate ethical lenses on the consequences for shared
development and on empowerment and resource rights offers a more multifaceted understanding of
the family dialogues, social contexts, and cultural beliefs and practices permitting families to mobilize
resilience resources when facing chronic illness. This integration suggests new directions for research/
practice partnerships that recognize the continuum of ecosystemic stresses and frameworks for responsive health- and growth-promoting interventions. Kazak (2006) and colleagues propose a pediatric
psychosocial preventative health approach to collaborations in pediatric family systems medicine,
using a social ecological model with public health prevention to identify resilient and at-risk families
facing specific challenges of pediatric illness. They suggest that most families confronting pediatric
illness are "distressed but resilient," meeting criteria for "universal" care including education and
family-to-family parent and sibling support reinforcing competencies. At the same time, some families experiencing acute distress with some risk factors can be offered "targeted" or brief interventions
addressing distress while also working to reduce identifiable risks within the pediatric care setting.
The smallest group demonstrating highest distress with high risk factors considered a "treatment"
group can be offered specialized behavioral health care. Kissane and Hough (2011) propose a similar
intervention approach for families experiencing adult cancer based on research identifying risk and
resilience factors. Their brief therapy program offers stepped interventions supporting family cohesion and communication while reducing conflict and isolation. These integrative health promotion/
prevention/intervention models emphasize the importance of conducting multifaceted family assessments and individualized interventions to reduce distress, disruption, and conflicts while mobilizing
positive resources including health care and community resources, family-based peer support and
education, as well as more traditional family therapy when needed.

This review suggests an important role for ethical and social justice perspectives in supporting family resilience. The lens of intergenerational family ethics offered by contextual therapy (Boszormenyi-Nagy & Krasner, 1986) complements work in family systems and resilience by specifically addressing family fairness in chronic illness care as it impacts posterity. Contextual therapy uses philosopher Martin Buber's principles of I/Thou relationships and dialogues of mutual empathy to explore the fairness of intergenerational give and take in light of historical and current contexts of suffering as well as their future consequences for all affected. This approach helps us evaluate fairness and balance in family responses to chronic illness and guides communication by recognizing differences and evaluating the consequences of family adaptations in the future. If a parent decides to keep a stigmatized illness secret, or to focus on a sick child at the expense of a partner or siblings, he or she can be helped to better understand histories and current circumstances as well as individual and family consequences. Siblings can be acknowledged as family helpers without having their own lives and needs completely consumed, and their relationships with their parents can be strengthened by more open communication and problem solving of divergent needs. Applying ethical and empowerment perspectives supporting family articulation of desired goals and resource navigation and advocacy, we can help families access social resources that create new contexts more conducive to experiencing and expressing positive emotions, addressing conflicts in culturally congruent, constructive ways, and affirming family intimacy. Mobilizing resources supporting desired goals, families can better co-create more positive and hope-filled family narratives, preserve family routines and rituals with energy and affection, and empathically attend to others in the family, offering more help to an exhausted, resentful overextended spouse, a frightened or burdened sibling, or a chronically ill member concerned with his or her growing dependence and family burden. Including family and social ethical perspectives also contributes to culturally sensitive assessments of shared understanding of the illness and its course, attention to shifts in family practices due to the realities of the illness, and attention to nurturing and strengthening ties with extended families and social networks.

Family experiences of chronic illness differ in impact depending on whether one or more children or adults are affected, their ages and family life cycle stages, and tasks of everyday life intertwined with chronic illness experiences and treatment demands, which may require complex medical management such as HAART protocols for HIV/AIDS or dietary restrictions for diabetes management to prevent disease progression. Restorative sleep and nutritious meals vital to health can be challenging to achieve when physical pain, disruptive medical procedures, and guilt or fear intrude on family routines. While multisystemic health approaches are well established in pediatric care literatures, the importance of relationship support and positive emotions in health is leading to greater recognition of family factors in adult health psychology literatures (Barskova & Oesterreich, 2009; Stanton, Revenson, & Tennen, 2007; Swendeman et al., 2009). Chronic illness self-management, based on a patient-centered perspective on resources supporting self-efficacy, has the potential for integration with a family systems and health perspective. A family-centered approach to disease management is emerging, primarily among family advocacy groups (Rosenthal, 2009). Intergenerational health promotion and resilience perspectives will become even more important as extended families share experiences of co-occurring disorders in multiple family members.

Further, it is important to evaluate how family cultural and spiritual illness beliefs complement or contradict provider understandings and recommendations for care, to conduct culturally and spiritually competent assessments, and to create meaningful partnerships for care both within and outside the health care system. The clash between diverse cultures and the "culture of medicine" is explored in Fadiman's (1998) compelling account of a Hmong family's experience seeking care for their young daughter Lia and the difficult attempts to control epilepsy. In *The Spirit Catches You and You Fall Down* she explores clashing cultural beliefs and miscommunications regarding the child's illness, which tragically interfered with her health, while signaling places where bridges were possible. Fadiman recommends Arthur Kleinman's cultural interview (Kleinman, 1988), exploring the family's culturally based understanding of the illness as offering a very different starting point for culturally sensitive care. Encouragingly, this text has become required reading in provider training programs because it offers a multifaceted understanding of family cultural and spiritual beliefs as they clash with the "culture of medicine," and ways providers can grow personally and professionally in learning from diverse families to offer sensitive chronic illness care.

In health care systems that emphasize individual illness and compliance with medical authority, implementing family resilience perspectives requires alliances and partnerships specific to the research and practice setting. This chapter's reflexive synthesis offers a guide in evaluating the key components of the research approach or intervention perspective offered from within a particular discipline or setting. Does the approach focus specifically on family relationships, and does it consider meaningful sub-groups such as couples, parents/children, and siblings? Does assessment include tools for sensitively eliciting perspectives of patients, family caretakers, and directly involved providers? Does the approach consider life-course developmental concerns in cultural context, their spiritual and sociopolitical components, and potential differences in acculturation within the family? Does the approach train practitioners to conduct cultural and spiritual inquiries through dialogues and personal reflection? Does it provide institutional support for interdisciplinary partnerships promoting access to needed resources? These questions facilitate use of ecosystemic and participatory approaches in developing interventions nurturing family resilience and wellness in chronic illness settings. Because both the families we encounter in diverse settings and the specific demands of chronic illness are complex and evolving, it becomes challenging to translate research into practice responsive to the family's unique circumstances. Some practitioners work in specialized health settings such as pediatric cancer wards or adult pain clinics, while others work in primary care or community health and mental health practice settings. Implementing resilience-building recommendations in practice will always require individualized family-based assessments sensitive to settings, timing in the illness trajectory, timing in the family's shared life course, and interdependent developmental consequences. This work is best conducted through interdisciplinary partnerships for referrals and follow-up.

Collaborative family-based assessment is foundational to nurturing family resilience. Regardless of family and practice contexts, the family assessment presents us with opportunities to explore family-centered quality of life in light of lived experience of the illness and its consequences. Falicov (2000) suggests that in culturally informed, multisystemic interventions, family therapists join with families in co-creating a new, more favorable "ecological niche" for shared development. Multifaceted assessments will include the family's understanding of the illness and the resource demands the illness places on their everyday family lives. Assessments will require sensitive interviewing regarding the impact of the illness on individual family members, beginning with the biological demands of the illness itself for the suffering individual and for family caretaking.

Boszormenyi-Nagy's intergenerational family ethics in contextual therapy (Boszormenyi-Nagy & Krasner, 1986) can be useful in working with families using "multidirected partiality," that is, connecting empathically with all members while exploring issues of family fairness in family give and take as a result of both developmental and illness needs. Also useful at the evaluation phase is goal-oriented assessment, asking family members what they would like to accomplish individually and collectively, and using these goals for continuous evaluation of progress toward desired outcomes. Literatures reviewed in this chapter suggest that family narratives offer powerful tools in sustaining family connections and in navigating resources that transform illness into meaningful journeys filled with possibility and purpose even when facing enduring losses. From the moment we initiate conversations with families we co-create a new story, and the way we tell it together will have a powerful impact. Family therapy has rich, strengths-based narrative traditions showing us how to listen for family strengths that promote resilience from the beginning (Allison et al., 2003; Madsen, 2009; White, 2008). However, the illness-specific resilience literature also suggests that assessments must include what

Rolland and Walsh (2006) term the "psychosocial characteristics" of the illness itself. It is especially important for assessments not to rush families toward a positive or strengths-based account at a point when they are grappling with fear and pain. Rather, we listen from the outset with our human as well as our professional recognition of suffering and its family challenges. At this phase we also become alert to differences and potential conflicts within the family. Strengths-based assessments help us evaluate family communication regarding the illness, its meanings, the challenges it presents as well as the opportunities for shared empathy, positive emotions, and mutual support. Exploring differences and arriving at mutual understandings can lead to negotiations of differences in ways that can lead to new problem-solving strategies, shifting family practices to better nurture family resilience. Promoting family resilience requires hearing from all affected, respecting culturally based gender and generational expectations, while giving all, including chronically ill members and young children, opportunities to both give and receive support. Finally, family resilience frameworks emphasize ways practitioners can assist families as they navigate and negotiate critical resources, recognizing that families with adequate material resources and extended family and social support can better mobilize resilient adaptive strategies within the family.

The importance of patient-family and community-centered health education promoting empowerment emerges across literatures, emphasizing the need to link knowledge to resource advocacy. Interventions can become spaces of mutual learning ensuring that families understand the illness, its individual and family impact, and available resources. The literature also guides us to use family-to-family supports in helping family members navigate illness demands and mobilize resources for hope and recovery. One exciting new resource emerges in increased access by chronically ill and their families to internet-assisted and social-networking based mutual help and advocacy (Bacigalupe, 2011; Fox & Purcell, 2010; Nicholas, 2010). Fox and Purcell (2010) found disproportionate barriers to internet access for the chronically ill, but note its growing use by this population and powerful ways to gain and share information while building connections. Bacigalupe and Nicholas both note that family peer-to-peer education, support, and advocacy can be enhanced as social networking tools help families progress from relatively passive though valuable health information navigation to family-centered, empowered mutual support and shared advocacy.

Conclusion

This review of research on family resilience as it contributes to chronic illness care suggests the need for interdisciplinary, mixed-methods research incorporating global perspectives on health promotion and including families themselves in creating and reviewing the knowledge base for care. With collaborative care partnerships and family-centered goal-oriented assessments, families themselves will identify areas of concern. Clinical practice promoting family resilience in chronic illness care is based on developmentally informed family systems and health perspectives, while integrating work from narrative, co-constructionist, and meaning-making approaches to individual, family, and community-based practice (Pare & Larner, 2004; White, 2008); from culturally and spiritually informed, ecosystemic treatment approaches in family therapy linking individuals, families, and communities (Bernal, 2006; Falicov, 2000; Landau, 2007; Lightburn & Sessions, 2005; Madsen, 2009); and from positive psychology and posttraumatic growth orientations (Chou, Lee, Datalano, Ditchman, & Wilson, 2009; Layne, Warren, Shalev, & Watson, 2008; Lindey & Joseph, 2008; Snyder & Lopez, 2009). Individualization of ecosystemic intervention principles helps resolve tensions between the use of specific empirically supported treatments and attention to meaningful common factors from positive development, health promotion, and treatment literatures (Shapiro, 2008a; Sprenkle, Davis, & Lebow, 2009). Henggeler's Multi-Systemic Therapy, developed for home-based treatment of youth with conduct disorders, implements individualized ecological assessment for a diagnosed condition using evidence on the continuum of symptom specific as well as broad health and growth promotion processes. Emphasizing empowerment partnerships and linking of multisystemic resources, they use best available research to reduce youth symptoms such as anger management, resolve family problems such as parental substance abuse or discord, and enhance positive developmental resources including family support and school success (Henggeler et al., 2009).

Partnering with families requires that we become reflective practitioners rigorously exploring our own biases based on research and practice training as well as personal, social, and cultural perspectives (Shapiro, 2008b). Aware of our own dilemmas in living with illness, and barriers we confront even with professional prestige and knowledge, we can better understand and partner with diverse families, empathize with their considerable challenges, nurture their inspiring resourcefulness, and advocate for needed change in systems of care. We begin by listening deeply to multifaceted family experiences of illness and wellness, looking broadly at the knowledge base, addressing symptoms while promoting health, and sharing these in accessible ways, critically examining access barriers, and joining with others in advocating for universal access to care for illness and opportunities for wellness. This work also requires that we expand our roles, becoming teachers and advocates as well as researchers and providers. One important strategy for revisioning care will be education and training of all sectors of society. The public and policy makers, as well as health researchers and providers, will need to evaluate health information critically, assessing barriers to change. The Center for Advancing Health offers one example of a health information clearinghouse focused on behavioral health and promoting patient engagement, equity, and policy change through knowledge of the evidence base. The Center's founder, Gruman (2007), has written about her own struggles with acute and chronic illness as inspirations for her work.

When we begin our work with what families know and what families need, we shift the way we ask questions and build knowledge. Using this lens, we can design interventions that offer comfort and reduce distress while also going further in building on strengths and expanding resources, relationship processes, and capacities that promote wellness and support growth. Family resilience in response to chronic illness recognizing our human interdependence and its consequences requires shared learning, emotionally based communication, and positive activities associated with sustaining everyday family lives and future plans. Treatment targeting illness symptoms and reducing suffering will be more effective with greater attention to family emotions, meanings, and goals, making chronic illness one factor among many rather than overwhelming family life. This approach to assessment and intervention makes the most of the "ordinary magic" promoting positive adaptation to change throughout the life cycle, while recognizing extraordinary capacities for health and growth in the face of challenges that can be nurtured by our family relationships.

Acknowledgments Work on this chapter was supported by the NIH Research Grant 5-P20-MD002290-05, HORIZON Center: Healthy options, research, interventions & community organizing funded by the National Institute of Minority Health and Disparities (NIMHD).

References

Alderfer, M., Fiese, B., Gold, J., Cutuli, J., Holmbeck, G., Goldbeck, L., et al. (2008). Evidence-based assessment in pediatric psychology: Family measures. *Journal of Pediatric Psychology, 33*(9), 1046–1061.

Allison, S., Stacey, K., Dadds, V., Roeger, L., Wood, A., & Martin, G. (2003). What the family brings: Gathering evidence for strengths-based work. *Journal of Family Therapy, 25*(3), 263–284.

Antonovsky, A., & Sourani, T. (1988). Family sense of coherence and family adaptation. *Journal of Marriage and Family, 50*, 79–92.

Bacigalupe, G. (2011). Is there a role for social technologies in collaborative health care? *Family Systems and Health, 29*(1), 1–14.

Barskova, T., & Oesterreich, R. (2009). Post-traumatic growth in people living with a serious medical condition and its relations to physical and mental health: A systematic review. *Disability and Rehabilitation, 31*(21), 1709–1733.

Becvar, D., & Becvar, R. (2009). *Family therapy: A systemic integration* (7th ed.). Boston: Allyn and Bacon.

Becvar, D. S. (2007). *Families that flourish: Facilitating resilience in clinical practice*. New York: Norton.

Bell, I., Caspi, O., Schwartz, G., Grant, K., Gaudet, T., Rychemer, D., et al. (2002). Integrative medicine and systemic outcomes research: Issues in the emergence of a new model for primary health care. *Archives of Internal Medicine, 162*, 133–140.

Bellin, M., & Kovacs, P. (2006). Fostering resilience in siblings of youths with a chronic health condition: A review of the literature. *Health and Social Work, 31*(3), 209–216.

Berg, C., & Upchurch, R. (2007). A developmental-contextual model of couples coping with chronic illness across the adult life-span. *Psychological Bulletin, 133*(6), 920–954.

Bernal, G. (2006). Intervention development and cultural adaptation research with diverse families. *Family Process, 45*(2), 143–151.

Berwick, D. (2002). A user's manual for the IOM report, "Crossing the Quality Chasm". *Health Affairs, 21*(3), 80–90.

Berwick, D. (2009). What patient-centered care should mean: Confessions of an extremist. *Health Affairs, 28*(4), w555–w565.

Black, K., & Lobo, M. (2008). A conceptual review of family resilience factors. *Journal of Family Nursing, 14*(1), 33–55.

Bookman, A., & Harrington, M. (2007). Family caretakers: A shadow workforce in the geriatric health system? *Journal of Health Politics, Policy and Law, 32*(6), 1005–1041.

Boszormenyi-Nagy, I., & Krasner, B. (1986). *Between give and take: A clinical guide to contextual therapy*. New York: Bruner Mazel.

Brim, O., Ryff, C., & Kessler, R. (2004). *How healthy are we? A national study of well-being at midlife*. Chicago: University of Chicago Press.

Bronfenbrenner, U. (1979). *The ecology of human development: Experiments by nature and design*. Cambridge, MA: Harvard University Press.

Buchbinder, M., Longhofer, J., & McCue, K. (2009). Family routines and rituals when a parent has cancer. *Family Systems and Health, 27*(3), 213–227.

Burack Weiss, A. (1995). The caregiver's memoir: A new look at family support. *Social Work, 40*(3), 391–396.

Burack Weiss, A. (2003). *The caregiver's tale: Loss and renewal in memoirs of family life*. New York: Columbia University Press.

Campbell, T. (2003). The effectiveness of family interventions for physical disorders. *Journal of Marital and Family Therapy, 29*(2), 263–281.

Capra, F. (2005). *Ecological literacy: Educating our children for a sustainable world*. San Francisco: Sierra Club Books.

Carman, K., Maurer, M., Yegian, J., Dardess, P., McGee, J., Evers, M., et al. (2010). Evidence that consumers are skeptical about evidence-based health care. *Health Affairs, 29*(7), 1400–1406.

Centers for Disease Control. (2011). Health disparities and inequalities report. *Morbidity and Mortality Weekly Report, 60*(Suppl), 1–113.

Charon, R. (2008). *Narrative medicine: Honoring the stories of illness*. New York: Oxford.

Chou, C., Lee, E., Datalano, D., Ditchman, N., & Wilson, L. (2009). Positive psychology and psychosocial adjustment to chronic illness and disability. In F. Chan, E. da Silva, & J. Chronister (Eds.), *Understanding psychosocial adjustment to chronic illness and disability: A handbook for evidence-based practitioners in rehabilitation* (pp. 207–242). New York: Springer.

Cicchetti, D., & Cohen, D. (2005). *Developmental psychopathology*. New York: Wiley.

Clarke, A. (2010). *Biomedicalization: Technoscience, health and illness in the U.S.* Durham, NC: Duke.

Cole, R., & Reiss, D. (1993). *How do families cope with chronic illness?* Hillsdale, NJ: Erlbaum.

Davis-Floyd, R. (2001). The technocratic, humanistic and holistic paradigms of childbirth. *International Journal of Gynecology & Obstetrics, 75*(1), S5–S23.

Elder, G., Johnson, M., & Crosnoe, R. (2003). The emergence and development of life course theory. In J. Mortimer & M. Shanahan (Eds.), *Handbook of the life course* (pp. 3–19). New York: Plenum.

Fadiman, A. (1998). *The spirit catches you and you fall down*. New York: Farrar, Strauss and Giroux.

Falicov, C. (2000). *Latino families in therapy: A guide to multicultural practice*. New York: Guilford.

Fiese, B. (2008). Breathing life into family processes: Introduction to the special issue on families and asthma. *Family Process, 47*(1), 1–5.

Fiese, B. H., Tomcho, T. J., Douglas, M., Josephs, K., Poltrock, S., & Baker, T. (2002). A review of 50 years of research on naturally occurring family routines and rituals: Cause for celebration? *Journal of Family Psychology, 16*(4), 381–390.

Fiese, B. H., Winter, M. A., Anbar, R. D., Howell, K. J., & Poltrock, S. (2008). Family climate of routine asthma care: Associating perceived burden and mother-child interaction patterns. Family Process, 47, 63–79.

Fisher, L. (2005). Using family models in health research: A framework for family intervention in chronic disease. In W. Pinsof & J. Lebow (Eds.), *Family psychology: The art of the science* (pp. 549–571). New York: Oxford.

Fox, S., & Purcell, K. (2010). *Chronic disease and the internet. Pew internet and American life project.* Washington, DC: Pew Research Center. Retrieved May 1, 2011, from http://pewinternet.org/Reports/2010/Chronic-Disease.aspx.

Freiborg, O., Hjemda, O., Rosenvinge, J., & Martinussen, M. (2006). A new rating scale for adult resilience: What are the central protective resources for healthy adjustment? *International Journal of Methods in Psychiatric Research, 12*(2), 65–76.

Gallant, M., Spitzc, G., & Grove, J. (2010). Chronic illness self-care and the family lives of older adults: A synthetic review across four ethnic groups. *Journal of Cross-Cultural Gerontology, 25,* 21–43.

Gerstel, N. (2000). The third shift: Gender, employment, and care work outside the home. *Qualitative Sociology, 23*(4), 467–483.

Griffiths, F., Borkan, J., Byrne, D., Crabtree, B., Dowrick, C., Gunne, J., et al. (2010). Developing evidence for how to tailor medical interventions for the individual patient. *Qualitative Health Research, 20*(12), 1629–1641.

Gruman, J. (2007). *Aftershock: What to do when the doctor gives you—or someone you love—a devastating diagnosis.* New York: Walker and Company.

Hartmann, M., Bazner, E., Wild, B., Eisler, I., & Herzog, W. (2010). Effects of interventions involving the family in the treatment of adult patients with chronic physical diseases: A meta-analysis. *Psychotherapy and Psychosomatics, 79,* 136–148.

Health and Human Services. (2011). *Action plan to reduce racial and ethnic health disparities: A nation free of disparities in health and health care.* Washington, DC: Office of Minority Health. Retrieved May 1, 2011, from http://minorityhealth.hhs.gov/npa/files/Plans/HHS/HHS_Plan_complete.pdf.

Henggeler, S., Schoenwald, S., Bourdin, C., Rowland, M., & Cunningham, P. (2009). *Multisystemic therapy for antisocial behavior in children and adolescents* (2nd ed.). New York: Guilford.

IOM. (2009). *Integrative medicine and the health of the public.* Washington, DC: National Academies Press.

Kazak, A. (2006). Pediatric psychosocial preventative health model (PPPHM): Research, practice and collaboration in family systems medicine. *Family Systems and Health, 24*(4), 381–395.

Keyes, C. (2007). Promoting and protecting mental health as flourishing: A complementary strategy for improving national mental health. *American Psychologist, 62,* 95–108.

Kiser, L. J., Baumgardner, B., & Dorado, J. (2010). Who are we, but for the stories we tell: Family stories and healing. *Psychological Trauma, 2*(3), 243–249.

Kissane, D., & Hough, A. (2011). Family therapy for the bereaved. In R. Neimeyer, D. Harris, H. Winokuer, & G. Thornton (Eds.), *Grief and bereavement in contemporary society: Bridging research and practice.* New York: Routledge.

Kleinman, A. (1988). *The Illness Narratives.* New York: Basic Books.

Kralik, D. (Ed.). (2010). *Translating chronic illness research into practice.* Hoboken, NJ: Wiley.

Krieger, N. (2001). Theories for social epidemiology in the 21st century: An ecosocial perspective. *International Journal of Epidemiology, 30,* 668–677.

Landau, J. (2007). Enhancing resilience: Families and communities as agents of change. *Family Process, 46*(3), 351–365.

Layne, C. M., Warren, J., Shalev, A., & Watson, P. (2008). Risk, vulnerability, resistance, and resilience: Towards an integrative conceptualization of posttraumatic adaptation. In M. J. Friedman, T. M. Kean, & P. A. Resick (Eds.), *PTSD: Science & practice—A comprehensive handbook* (pp. 497–520). New York: Guilford.

Lee, I., Lee, E., Park, Y., Song, M., Park, Y., & Kim, H. (2004). Concept development of family resilience: A study of Korean families with a chronically ill child. *Journal of Clinical Nursing, 13,* 636–645.

Lerner, R. M., Jacobs, F., & Wertlieb, D. (Eds.). (2003). *Applying developmental science for youth and families: Historical and theoretical foundations. Volume 1, Handbook of applied developmental science: Promoting positive child, adolescent, and family development through research, policies, and programs.* Thousand Oaks, CA: Sage.

Levine, K. (2009). Against all odds: Resilience in single mothers of children with disabilities. *Social Work in Health Care, 48,* 402–419.

Lietz, C. (2006). Uncovering stories of family resilience: A mixed methods study of resilient families—Part I. *Families in Society, 87*(4), 575–582.

Lietz, C. (2011). Empathic action and family resilience: A narrative examination of the benefits of helping others. *Journal of Social Service Research, 37,* 254–265.

Lightburn, A., & Sessions, P. (2005). *Handbook of community-based clinical practice.* New York: Oxford.

Lindey, P., & Joseph, S. (2008). *Positive psychology in practice.* New York: Wiley.

Lu, M., Kotelchuck, M., Hogan, V., Jones, L., Wright, K., & Halfon, N. (2010). Closing the black-white gap in birth outcomes: A life-course approach. *Ethnicity and Disease, 20*(S2), S2-62–S2-76.

Luthar, S. S., & Brown, P. J. (2007). Maximizing resilience through diverse levels of inquiry: Prevailing paradigms, possibilities and priorities for the future. *Development and Psychopathology, 19,* 931–955.

Madsen, W. (2009). *Collaborative therapy with multi-stressed families.* New York: Guilford Press.

Martin, C., & Petersen, C. (2009). The social construction of chronicity: A key to understanding chronic care transformations. *Journal of Evaluation in Clinical Practice, 15,* 578–585.

Martin, C., & Sturmberg, J. (2009). Complex adaptive chronic care. *Journal of Evaluation in Clinical Practice, 15*, 571–577.

Masten, A. S., & Obradovic, J. (2008). Disaster preparation and recovery: Lessons from research on resilience in human development. *Ecology and Society, 13*(1), 9–24.

McCubbin, H., Thompson, E., and Thompson, A. (1999). *The dynamics of resilient families*, Thousand Oaks, CA: Sage.

McDaniel, S., Campbell, T., Hepworth, J., & Lorenz, A. (2005). *Family-oriented primary care*. New York: Springer.

McDaniel, S., Hepworth, J., & Doherty, W. (Eds.). (2003). *The shared experience of illness*. New York: Basic Books.

McEwen, B., & Gianaros, P. (2011). Stress-and allostasis-induced brain plasticity. *Annual Review of Medicine, 62*, 431–435.

Minkler, M. (2004). *Community organizing for health*. New Brunswick, NJ: Rutgers.

Nicholas (2010). The potential of technology for providing social support for people and families. In D. Kralik (Ed.), *Translating chronic illness research into practice* (pp. 143–162). Hoboken, NJ: Wiley.

O'Brien, M. (2005). Studying individual and family development: Linking theory and research. *Journal of Marriage and Family, 67*, 880–890.

Pare, D., & Larner, G. (2004). *Collaborative practice in psychology and therapy*. New York: Haworth.

Parke, R. D. (2004). Development in the family. *Annual Review of Psychology, 55*, 365–399.

Patterson, J. (2002). Integrating family resilience and family stress theory. *Journal of Marriage and Family, 64*(5), 349–360.

Patterson, J. (2005). Weaving gold out of straw: Meaning-making in families who have children with chronic illnesses. In W. Pinsof & J. Lebow (Eds.), *Family psychology: The art of the science* (pp. 521–548). New York: Oxford.

Perry, G., Presley-Cantrell, L., & Dhingra, S. (2010). Addressing mental health promotion in chronic disease prevention and health promotion. *American Journal of Public Health, 100*(12), 2337–2339.

Pratt, M., & Fiese, B. (2004). *Family stories and the life course: Across time and generations*. New York: Routledge.

Prilleltensky, I., & Prilleltensky, I. (2005). Beyond resilience: Blending wellness and liberation in the helping professions. In M. Ungar (Ed.), *Handbook for working with children and youth: Pathways to resilience across cultures and contexts* (pp. 89–103). Thousand Oaks, CA: Sage.

Retlaff, R. (2007). Families of children with Rett syndrome: Stories of coherence and resilience. *Family Systems and Health, 25*(3), 246–262.

Rolland, J. (1994). *Families, illness and disability: An integrative treatment model*. New York: Basic.

Rolland, J., & Walsh, F. (2006). Facilitating family resilience with childhood illness and disability. *Current Opinions in Pediatrics, 18*, 527–538.

Rosenthal, D., Kosciulek, J., Lee, G., Frain, M., & Ditchman, N. (2009). Family and adaptation to chronic illness and disability. In F. Chan, E. da Silva, & J. Chronister (Eds.). *Understanding psychosocial adjustment to chronic illness and disability: A handbook for evidence-based practitioners in rehabilitation*. New York: Springer Publishing.

Sandler, I. (2001). Quality and ecology of adversity as common mechanisms of risk and resilience. *American Journal of Community Psychology, 29*(1), 19–61.

Sandler, I. N., Schoenfelder, E. N., Wolchik, S. A., & MacKinnon, D. P. (2011). Long-term impact of prevention programs to promote effective parenting: Lasting effects but uncertain processes. *Annual Review of Psychology, 62*, 299–329.

Seccombe, K. (2002). "Beating the odds" versus "changing the odds": Poverty, resilience, and family policy. *Journal of Marriage and Family, 64*, 384–394.

Shapiro, E. R. (1994). *Grief as a family process: A developmental approach to clinical practice* (2nd ed.). New York: Guilford Press (in preparation).

Shapiro, E. R. (2002). Chronic illness as a family process: A social-developmental approach to promoting resilience. *Psychotherapy in Practice, 58*(11), 1375–1384.

Shapiro, E. R. (2008a). Whose recovery, of what? Relationships and environments promoting grief and growth. *Death Studies, 32*, 40–58.

Shapiro, E. R. (2008b). Culture and socialization in assessment and intervention. In D. Balk (Ed.), *Handbook of thanatology* (pp. 189–201). Northbrook, IL: Association for Death Education and Counseling.

Shonkoff, J., & Phillips, D. (2000). *From neurons to neighborhoods: The science of early childhood development*. Washington, DC: National Academies Press.

Singer, G., Biegel, D., & Ethridge, B. (2009). Toward a cross-disability view of family caretaking. *Journal of Family Social Work, 12*(2), 97–118.

Snyder, C. R., & Lopez, S. J. (Eds.). (2009). *The handbook of positive psychology* (2nd ed.). New York: Oxford University Press.

Sprenkle, D., Davis, S., & Lebow, J. (2009). *Common factors in couple and family therapy: The overlooked foundation for effective practice*. New York: Guilford.

St. James, P., Shapiro, E., & Weisbrun, S. (1999). The resource mothers program maternal phenylketonuria. *American Journal of Public Health, 89*(5), 762–764.

Stanton, A., Revenson, T., & Tennen, H. (2007). Health psychology: Psychological adjustment to chronic disease. *Annual Review of Psychology, 58*, 565–592.

Steinglass, P. (2006). The future of family systems medicine: Challenges and opportunities. *Family Systems and Health, 24*(4), 396–411.

Swendeman, D., Ingram, B., & Rotheram-Borus, M. (2009). Common elements in self-management of HIV and chronic illnesses: An integrative framework. *AIDS Care, 21*(10), 1321–1334.

Ungar, M. (2005). *Handbook for working with children and youth: Pathways to resilience across cultures and contexts.* Thousand Oaks: Sage.

Ungar, M. (2010). Families as navigators and negotiators: Facilitating culturally and contextually specific expressions of resilience. *Family Process, 49*, 421–435.

Ungar, M. (2011). The social ecology of resilience: Addressing contextual and cultural ambiguity of a nascent construct. *The American Journal of Orthopsychiatry, 81*(1), 1–17.

Walker, G. (1991). *In the midst of winter: Counseling families, couples and individuals with AIDS infection.* New York: Norton.

Wallerstein, N. (2006). *What is the evidence on effectiveness of empowerment to improve health?* Copenhagen: WHO Regional Office for Europe (Health Evidence Network report). Retrieved April 1, 2011, from http://www.euro.who.int/Document/E88086.pdf.

Walsh, F. (2006). *Family resilience* (2nd ed.). New York: Guilford Press.

Wamboldt, F., Balkissoon, R., Rankin, A., Szefler, S., Hammond, S., & Glasgow, R. (2008). Correlates of household smoking bans in low income families of children with and without asthma. *Family Process, 47*, 81–94.

Wandersman, A. (2003). Community science: Bridging the gap between science and practice using community-based models. *American Journal of Community Psychology, 31*(3/4), 227–242.

Wellard, S. (2010). Globalization of chronic illness research. In D. Kralik (Ed.), *Translating chronic illness research into practice* (pp. 1–16). Hoboken, NJ: Wiley.

White, M. (2008). *Maps of narrative therapy.* New York: Norton.

Wood, B., & Miller, B. (2005). Families, health and illness: The search for pathways and mechanisms of effect. In W. Pinsof & J. Lebow (Eds.), *Family psychology: The art of the science* (pp. 493–520). New York: Oxford.

World Health Organization. (2008). *Social determinants of health.* Geneva: World Health Organization.

Enhancing Resilience in Families of Children with Autism Spectrum Disorder

Mojdeh Bayat and Peter Schuntermann

Introduction

Among the variety of developmental and physical disabilities that have been studied, certain of these have been known to affect families more (drastically) than others. Autism spectrum disorder (ASD) is such a disability. In the current *Diagnostic and Statistical Manual of Mental Disorders* (DSM-IV; American Psychiatric Association [APA], 2000), the term ASDs is used to describe five related neurodevelopmental disorders contained within the diagnostic classification of pervasive developmental disorders (PDD). That is, ASD is an umbrella term that refers to a range of disorders affecting multiple areas of development: social–emotional development, communication, sensory processing, cognition, and behavioral domains. The highly variable manifestations of autism can range from a nonverbal child with severe cognitive impairment and aggression or self-injurious behaviors to a college student with above-average intelligence and a successful academic and work record (Muhle, Trentacoste, & Rapin, 2004).

Because autism influences various areas of development, families of children with autism are faced with a unique set of stressors related to a variety of dysfunctions and behavioral characteristics, unlike families of children with other disabilities that face only one or two specific dysfunctions. In fact, the issues faced by families of children with autism remain constant even in those families who have children with high-functioning autism (HFA), where the degree of dysfunctions is mild (Roa & Beidel, 2009). In this chapter we describe the concept of family resilience as it relates to families of children with ASD by first presenting contemporary and lifecycle issues in these families, then describing the factors of resilience in families of children with ASD, and finally making recommendations for practice.

M. Bayat(✉)
College of Education, DePaul University, Chicago, IL, USA
e-mail: mbayat@depaul.edu

P. Schuntermann
School of Medicine, Harvard University, Boston, MA, USA

D.S. Becvar (ed.), *Handbook of Family Resilience*,
DOI 10.1007/978-1-4614-3917-2_23, © Springer Science+Business Media New York 2013

Significance of the Topic

There has been a dramatic increase in the number of children diagnosed within the ASDs during the last 2 decades. In 2007, the Center for Disease Control and Prevention (CDC) reported that the number of children who are diagnosed with ASD is approximately 1 in every 150 children (Center for Disease Control and Prevention, 2007). Other studies have reported this number to be from 1 in 125 to 1 in 91 children; this includes 1 in every 58 boys, which is four times higher than in girls (Baron-Cohen et al., 2009; Nicolas, Carpenter, King, Jenner, & Charles, 2009). The CDC has estimated that every year, approximately 26,670 children would be diagnosed with ASD (CDC, 2007). Compared to other disabilities, ASD is more common than Down syndrome (1 out of every 800 births), childhood cancer, diabetes, and AIDS combined (CDC).

In recent years, the media's attention to autism and its causes has lead not only to an increase in public awareness about ASD, but to fueling a controversy that continues to be rekindled periodically. The controversy began with a study conducted in England and published in *The Lancet* in 1998, claiming a link between the MMR (measles, mumps, and rubella) vaccine and the onset of autism in 12 children (Wakefield et al., 1998). In the following years after the publication of this study, other studies followed that proposed either the vaccine itself or *thimerosal*, a mercury-based preservative and additive used in the vaccines, was the element responsible for causing autism in children (Gier & Gier, 2003; Goldman & Yazbak, 2004). These studies were later discredited for scientific inaccuracy, methodological flaw, and conflict of interest on the part of the investigators (Offit, 2008). In fact, in 2010, *The Lancet* issued a retraction of the original study from its records (The Editors of Lancet, 2010). Yet this controversy seems to continue to consume much energy on the part of the parents and other family members of children with ASD.

Because ASD has various degrees of severity, it has been difficult to pinpoint a single cause or a single treatment. Treatment options available for autism are numerous. An internet search for "autism treatment" yields over 2,200,000 results. These options vary from biomedical, pharmacological, and dietary intervention, to educational and therapeutic methods. Many of these treatment options give parents a hope for a "cure" and "recovery" from ASD.

Factors influencing parental decisions in choosing a treatment are complex and multidimensional. For example, severity of impairment and the age of the child are two factors that might influence parents' decision. Another factor is the source of information. Parents are more likely to choose a treatment when other parents recommend it or testify to the treatment efficacy after having used it with their own child (Green, 2007). For example, a group of biomedical treatment options, such as a gluten- and casein-free diet, have gained popularity among parents because some celebrity parents and activists have testified to their efficacy in primetime TV or other media despite being considered "fads," "alternative," "pseudoscientific," and "unsubstantiated" (Offit, 2008; Zane, Davis, & Rosswurm, 2008). The testimonials of these parents vary from drastic treatment effect to an actual "cure" and "recovery" from autism (Kirk, 2008; McCarthy, 2008). The majority of unsubstantiated treatments, such as dietary interventions, chelation, or Relationship Development Intervention (RDI®), are expensive and time consuming (Zane et al., 2008). In addition, some treatments, such as chelation, have been recognized as dangerous to the child (Mitka, 2008).

There are educational and therapeutic interventions as well as pharmacological and medical approaches. Though some of these treatments have an empirical basis, others have no scientific evidence to support them. Some interventions require parental commitment around-the-clock. For example, applied behavior analysis (ABA) is an educational intervention with strong empirical validity (Lovaas, 1987; Lovaas & Smith, 2003). However, for it to be effective, parents have to invest a considerable amount of time, energy, and financial resources. Lovaas's (1987) study of a group of children with autism indicates that when ABA is implemented early in the child's life for at least 40 hours per week, and when it involves parents carrying out therapy in the absence of the therapist, it may lead to an improvement of the child to a degree where a diagnosis of ASD might no longer be applicable. Other more recent treatment models, such as Floor Time™ or DRI (developmental, individual differences, relationship-based) models (Greenspan & Wieder, 1998, 2006), also require parents to carry out play-oriented therapy sessions with the child several times throughout the day. Although parents of children with autism seem to be tireless in their fight for cause and cure for autism, exhaustion, disappointment, and depression are common early on during the diagnosis and identification of treatment (Keenan, Dillenburger, Doherty, Byrne, & Gallagher, 2010).

Literature Review

Families of Children with ASD and Lifecycle Issues

Asperger syndrome and childhood disintegrative disorder are not usually identified until late childhood. Currently, two disorders, autism and PDD-NOS, can be assessed as early as 18–36 months (Maston & Sipes, 2010). However, traditionally, autism has not been diagnosed before the toddler years. Research is underway to identify specific markers that might be apparent earlier. Thus far, our understanding of early behavioral signs of autism is based on a series of home video studies conducted in the early and late 1990s, which showed that there were a number of symptoms of autism that distinguished infants with ASD from typically developing infants long before diagnosis (Adrien et al., 1991, 1993; Dawson, Hill, Spencer, Galpert, & Watson, 1990; Hobson & Lee, 1998; Osterling & Dawson, 1994; Wimpory, Hobson, Williams, & Nash, 2000). According to these studies, infants with ASD often display a variety of avoidant behaviors during their early development. These behaviors include an initial lack of eye contact and positive affect in face-to-face interaction with their caregivers during the first months of life, repeated failure to raise their arms to be lifted up, a lack of pointing and joint attention, and failing to greet parents and others or wave good-bye. Furthermore, these home videos showed that infants with ASD seem to lack any enjoyment in lap or interactive games, and early on begin showing atypical use of toys and objects, and stereotypical motor mannerisms, like hand-flapping (Hobson & Lee; Osterling, Dawson, & Munson, 2002; Wimpory et al.).

While atypical developmental patterns might be present in some infants from the beginning, in other infants there is a regressive pattern that usually occurs after a period of 1 or 2 years of typical development (Landa, Holman, & Garrett-Mayer, 2007). Furthermore, in another group of infants with ASD, it was concluded that the behavioral characteristics of autism may appear after 6 months of age (Kagan, 2008). In general, there is an assumption that the biology of autism is present in these children even when the behavior characteristics are not (Rogers, 2009).

Given a lack of interactive behaviors in infants with ASD, some parents of children with ASD, especially mothers, report a tremendous amount of stress as a result of a lack of reciprocal behaviors in their infants (Stehli, 1991). In addition, parents may experience exhaustion due to lack of sleep and rest because of the unusual patterns of sleep in infants with autism, who may sleep no more than 3–4 hours per night (Norton & Drew, 1994). A child with ASD usually has difficulties coping with changes and recognizing danger. This frequently creates major challenges for families when deciding whether to relocate or making career decisions.

About 90% of parents recognize something might be wrong in their children by about 24 months, when abnormalities in language become apparent (De Giacomo & Fombonne, 1998). Because autism is often diagnosed after this age, the experiences of the parents are different from those of parents whose children's disability is apparent from birth. Parents of children with autism may gain validation of their sense that their child's development was not typical, while conversely, the true implication of the disorder may not be apparent to them initially. It may take some time before the families come to terms with the reality of how the disorder may change their lives (Schuntermann, 2002).

On the other hand, because of the public's increasing awareness of ASD, there is a possibility of a false-positive diagnosis of autism, where parents suspect their child has autism but the child may in fact have another disorder (Harrison Elder & D'Alessandro, 2009). Indeed, professionals have been reluctant to give an autism diagnosis before age 2, because during infancy and toddlerhood developmental delays look similar in characteristics, and sometimes it is difficult to distinguish general characteristics of one disorder, such as speech delay, from another disorder, such as autism. Therefore, it is important that expert consultation be sought early on to avoid confusion and misdiagnosis. Using specific screening instruments, trained professionals are able to detect a possibility of autism at around 14–18 months. For example, the Checklist for Autism in Toddlers (CHAT) is a screening instrument that uses parent report and observation of the child at 18 months, and presents a number of items that might suggest a possibility of autism in the infant (Baron-Cohen, Allen, & Gillberg, 1992; Baron-Cohen et al., 2000). The Modified Checklist for Autism in Toddlers (M-CHAT) (Robins, Fein, Barton, & Green, 2001) is the advanced version of this screener designed to be used with toddlers in the United States. Early intensive intervention has been found to be crucial for improving long-term outcome and moderating the severity of ASD (Eikeseth, 2009; National Research Council, 2001). Children with autism who are identified early are less likely to be mute and more likely to improve and to become independent in later years (Howlin, 2005).

After the diagnosis, a major task of the family includes securing appropriate education and therapeutic services, as well as establishing and maintaining relationships with service providers. On one hand, this requires a flexible family structure, demanding the understanding and cooperation of all family members to achieve a positive outcome. On the other hand, it requires the service provider's ability to mobilize a family's resources and establish a relationship with the family members based on collaboration and partnership. It is naïve to assume both of these qualities would be present in both the families and service providers. As a result, one of the common early issues for families of children with autism is specific stress and hardship related to navigating the intervention system to establish a treatment and educational program for their child. Thus, parents might experience a period of intense stress, which becomes more severe as they struggle to come to terms with the disorder itself while also attempting to secure appropriate services for their children (Marcus, Kunce, & Schopler, 1997).

During the child's elementary school years, although struggles with school settings are typical, parents seem to experience a relatively good period (Bayat, 2005; Marcus et al., 1997). This may be due in part to the fact that needed services have been secured for the child and the parents have adjusted to the demands of the disorder, having established some stability in their daily routines (Bayat; Marcus et al.). The child may stay in the same elementary school or program for 5–7 years and have the same teacher for the majority of this time, furthering this sense of stability (Marcus & Schopler, 1987). Additionally, the child may show some improvements in sociability, emotional control, and attention span (McAdoo & DeMyer, 1977). For most families, this period is a time to build consistent routines and daily living skills. Typically, the child might show gains in such skills, and the family, who previously had been frustrated when teaching cognitive tasks to their child, may find this time gratifying (Bayat).

In spite of the early gains that may have been made, the adolescent years often prove to be particularly stressful. As the adolescent becomes physically larger, violence becomes a significant problem, especially in families that have children with aggressive behaviors. This makes parents and siblings especially vulnerable (Gray, 2002). In addition, parents face new challenges as a result of the child's interaction of hormonal and physical changes. Manifestation of openly expressed aggressive behaviors and sexual awareness—which is exacerbated by dysfunctions in communication, social understanding, and cognition—is typical in adolescents with severe ASD (Marcus et al., 1997). At this time, families of children with severe ASD face issues such as the chronic nature of their children's basic deficits, finding age appropriate services, dealing with the community, and facing the fact that the disability is life-long (Bayat, 2005).

Families of children with high functioning autism and those with Asperger syndrome are particularly concerned about the lack of friendship in their adolescents (Bayat, 2005). A period of depression and under-activity has been mentioned in adolescents and young adults with ASD, which might be a reaction to the adolescent's unfulfilled need for friendships and peer relationships (Mesibov, 1983). In general, parental emotional exhaustion and emotional drain is typical during the child's adolescence (Gray, 2002).

Adulthood also presents specific stressors and difficulties for families. At this time, the formal school years have come to an end and families often find themselves having to deal with an adult with no occupation and/or practical working skills (Gray, 2002). It becomes increasingly challenging for families to occupy the adult with ASD—especially in the case of those who are nonverbal or have intellectual disabilities—where, for many years, the child's life routine has focused around going to school from the morning to the late afternoon. Securing appropriate services, including supervised living and working arrangements, are problems for which families struggle to find agreeable solutions during this phase—especially considering the decline of institutionalization and a lack of appropriate services in the United States and Canada (Bayat, 2005; Gray). Therefore, families of children with autism experience an intense stressful period when their children reach adulthood. One of the major issues at this time is the family's concern about the future of the adult with autism in light of the growing age of the parents (Bayat; Gray).

Other Factors Affecting Familial Adjustment

In addition to the lifecycle issues described, families may deal with other stressors at different periods of time, such as unusually high levels of emotional distress, anxiety, depression, and anger (Gray, 2002). In a study conducted by Olson and Hwang (2001), depression was found to be more pronounced in mothers of children with ASD as compared with depression in mothers of children with intellectual disabilities. Mothers of children with ASD also had higher levels of depression compared with fathers of children with autism. For example, mothers of children with ASD tend to have moderate to serious limitations on their careers, since they are usually the ones who stay home and care for the child after diagnosis (Gray, 2002). Mothers are also more likely to report severe distress due to their increased involvement in child rearing and exposure to negative social reactions by outsiders (Bayat, 2005). In general, parents of children with autism tend to suffer depression more severely as compared to parents of children with other disabilities (Ryde-Brandt, 1990; Sanders & Morgan, 1997).

Social stigmatization, extreme psychological distress, and parental isolation resulting from outside reactions are issues of serious concern. Social isolation and rejection are more pronounced in parents of children with ASD who have aggressive and/or obsessive behaviors. However, the perception of stigma appears to vary with the sex of the parent (with mothers feeling more stigmatized), severity of autism, and age of the child (Gray, 2002). Although stigmatization usually worsens as the child gets older and physically larger (Gray), over time parents seem to care less about society's perceptions regarding their child (Gray, 1993).

Another important issue in having a child with ASD is the financial cost to the families. Although there is no consistent body of research on the financial cost of having a child with ASD, available studies point to significantly higher costs of education, medical treatment, and supportive services as compared to having a child with another disability, such as Down syndrome or an intellectual disability

(Jacobson, Mulick, & Green, 1998; Marcus, Rubin, & Rubin, 2000). Aside from the typical costs of medical treatment or education for children with autism, it is important to consider the broader economic picture in terms of loss of employment and income (which is sometimes the case for one or both of the parents in order to provide in-home therapy for the child), other out of pocket expenses, lost leisure time, and special care (Jarbrink, Fombonne, & Knapp, 2003).

Looking at the life processes in families of children with autism, studies consistently show that family members report higher levels of stress than do those families of children with other disabilities, such as Down syndrome, intellectual disabilities, cystic fibrosis, or other medical conditions (Bouma & Schweitzer, 1990; Kasari & Sigman, 1997). The manifestations of autism—atypical or lack of communicative behavior, social relatedness issues, cognitive delays, and atypical or aggressive behaviors, lack of supportive services, and prolonged dependency of the child—affect family members more severely as compared with other disabilities. In fact, it has been argued that autism should be regarded as a chronic illness, since the effects of autism on families are seen as almost identical to those of having a child with a serious and chronic medical illness (Gray, 1994).

Siblings of Children with Autism

Crocker (1997) was among the first to draw attention to the dilemma of the siblings of children with developmental disabilities, especially to the nature of their attachment and relationships with their parents, as well as to the nature of their inter-sibling relationship. The latter is especially important, since the quality of the inter-sibling relationship often contributes to the overall adaptation of the family. Particular issues of concern about the siblings of children with disabilities are parental preoccupation and siblings' experience of neglect. These may contribute to siblings' vulnerabilities (Lobato, Miller, Barbour, Hall, & Pezzullo, 1991).

Research on the effects of having a sibling with ASD has provided variable results (Schuntermann, 2007). Some studies point to the neurotypical siblings demonstrating emotional and behavioral problems, although these have been judged to be not severe, or not to reach clinical levels (Dunn, 1992). When comparing the social competence and self-confidence of siblings of children with autism with those of siblings of children with Down syndrome, brothers of children with autism, especially when the brothers are younger than the affected children, have been found to have more psychosocial and peer problems (Hastings, 2003). One study found that the degree of language impairment in the children with autism correlated negatively with their siblings' adjustment, and that the severity of the degree of the disability in the child with autism was related to poor adjustment in the sibling (Pilowsky, Yirmiya, Dopplet, Gross-Tsur, & Shalev, 2004).

Bagenholm and Gillberg (1991) reported high levels of loneliness, problems with peers, attention difficulties, and conduct problems in siblings of children with ASD. In another study of 90 siblings, Kaminsky and Dewey (2001) assessed 30 siblings of children with autism matched with 30 siblings each of children with Down syndrome and typical children. They found that siblings reported reduced intimacy and less nurturance in families of children with autism compared to siblings in families of the other two groups.

In a later study, these authors found that the same findings were not duplicated once support services were provided for the family members (Kaminsky & Dewey, 2002). In this study the siblings were older than the child with the disability, and the majority of the siblings and their families attended support groups. These support groups provided realistic information about autism and Down syndrome, facilitated problem-solving activities, and enhanced social support.

Siblings may express concerns about their own physical or psychological wellbeing (Rolland, 1993; Schuntermann, 2009). They may not fully accept that one's health and wellbeing at a young age may be taken for granted (Safer, 2002). Some siblings may worry about "catching" some of the problems of their siblings with disability (Safer; Schuntermann). Other siblings may feel called upon to "act normal," perhaps as a result of perceived family expectations and self-appraisal (Schuntermann). Siblings of brothers or sisters with autism may be vulnerable to negative self-perceptions of their own social competence. For example, Schwartz (2003) found that the autistic child's social skills offered significant predictive value in determining a sibling's perception of his or her own social competence. In his study, the degrees of severity of autism and of parental stress were found to be vulnerability factors, whereas parental self-esteem and sibling self-esteem were seen as protective factors.

ASDs have strong genetic bases (Brent & Geschwind, 2009; Folstein & Rosen-Sheidley, 2001), and siblings are at a somewhat increased risk for subclinical characteristics known as the "broad phenotype." These might include mind-reading difficulties, attention-deficit disorder, and language-based learning problems (Ben-Yizhak et al., 2010; Dorris, Espie, Knott, & Salt, 2004; Gamliel, Yirmiya, Jaff, Manor, & Sigman, 2009), and symptoms of anxiety and depression in adolescents (Orsmond & Seltzer, 2009). There may be an increased risk for siblings if these conditions go unnoticed at home or escape clinical attention (Schuntermann, 2009). Finally, adult siblings may strive to find ways toward realistic self-acceptance and adaptive solutions (Willey, 1999).

Current Issues

The Concept of Family Resilience and Families of Children with ASD

The emerging picture of the lifecycle of families of children with autism is one that is grim and filled with stressors and negative life-altering factors, as just reviewed. However, this view has shifted during the last decade, due to the research in the fields of social work and family therapy (cf. Walsh, 1996, 1998, 2003) focusing on family resilience, as well as contributions from the field of positive psychology (cf. Antonovsky, 1987; Seligman & Csikszentmihalyi, 2000), culminating with this decade being termed as the "age of resilience" (Ganong & Coleman, 2002). Today a disability such as ASD no longer carries one-dimensional, deficit-focused assumptions; it has instead been replaced by a fresh, multidimensional perspective of strengths and challenges. In fact, there are a number of interacting factors and resilience processes in these families that may help them function well and grow stronger despite their child's autism.

Family resilience is considered a construct at the level of the family unit. As formulated by Walsh (2010), family resilience involves struggling with, and effectively working through and learning from adversity. Walsh (1998) articulated several key factors in family resilience, such as making meaning out of adversity, affirming strength and keeping a positive outlook, and having spirituality and a belief system. In advancing her family resilience model, Walsh (2010) has articulated resilience to mean more than the ability to bounce back from adversity unscathed. Rather, from her point of view, resilience "involves struggling well, effectively working through and learning from adversity, and integrating the experience into the fabric of individual and shared life passage" (Walsh, p. 149).

Family resilience is not merely a collection of "resiliences" held by individual family members (Hawley, 2000). Walsh (1996) believes that families take their own unique pathways to resilience. In her concept of "relational resilience," she emphasizes family processes and the manner in which families link these processes to their unique challenges, both immediate and long-term. Walsh (2006) also points to family processes that mediate the impact of stress for all members and their relationships and can influence the course of many crisis events, such as having a child with autism in the family. Family resilience sets the focus on the family as a functional unit, the family's interpersonal and developmental dynamics, their histories, and supra-ordinate values such as loyalty and responsibility.

Although studying resilience in families of children with ASD is relatively new, there is evidence both in research and in clinical practice that many families of children with ASD meet the criteria by which Walsh defines resilience, and possess key processing factors of and capabilities for resilience (Bayat, 2007; Schuntermann, 2009). In one of the first surveys on resilience in families of children with autism, Bayat (2007) found that about 40% of the families of children with autism described feeling stronger as a result of living with the affected child: they became less judgmental, more patient, and more compassionate. Bayat identified specific resilience processes, including the capacity to balance an appreciation of strengths against the developmental challenges (positive meaning-making) to grow closer as a family, to find greater appreciation of other people, and to gain spiritual strength through the process of living with an autistic child.

Understanding the process of meaning-making is central in promoting resilience in families of children with ASD. The role of perceptions and meaning-making in resilience is best understood by integrating family resilience and family stress theory (Patterson, 2002). Patterson (1988), in her Family Adjustment and Adaptation Response Model (FAAR), explains the process of coping and resilience in families of children with disabilities. According to this model, the process of meaning-making in the family is central to the family's ability to successfully cope and adapt to the demands of the disability. In fact, the way the family member makes meaning out of the disability determines whether he or she is able to utilize the family's resources (protective factors), arrange its structure, and ultimately balance—or fail to balance—the family's resources against the demands and stressors (risks) of having a child with a disability. In some cases, the event is only experienced as stressful according to the meaning that one attributes to the event.

In the Bayat (2007) study of family resilience in autism, not only did parents of children with autism frequently make positive meaning about having a child with autism, but the process of meaning-making in these families often was intertwined with spirituality. Another study similarly found that parents considered having been chosen to parent a child with ASD had occurred by divine intervention (Levine, 2009).

Resilience and Siblings of Children with Autism

The findings in family resilience studies are consistent with research on the resilience of children who have lived through sustained hardships other than growing up with a brother or sister with a developmental disability. This literature identifies important individual attributes including good judgment, social competence, self-agency, and intelligence (Hauser, Allen, & Golden, 2006; Masten, 2001; Sroufe, Egeland, Carlson, & Collins, 2005; Werner & Smith, 1982). Family strengths supporting resilience generally are based on the qualities of relationships. Siblings grow up in their families amidst "relations of relationships" (Dunn, 2005). Sibling roles and relationships are intricately engaged within the fabric of their families (the family-systems perspective), indirectly through triadic interactions with their parents (differential parental treatment), and directly with the other siblings (inter-sibling relationships). In addition, there are the bidirectional influences with extended family members, and beyond the family, with friends, peers, and institutions in the community.

Empirical findings suggest that close family relationships, good boundaries (Wood, 2001), effective communication, and consistent, workable family rules (Dugan, 1989), communal behavior, friendliness, and helpfulness (Yunger, Corby, & Perry, 2005), along with the capacity to reach out for support from friends, teachers, or members in the extended family, are qualities that support coping and resilience in the child (Dugan, 1989; Hauser et al., 2006; Sroufe et al., 2005; Werner & Smith, 1982). Similar protective factors have been identified in longitudinal studies (Fergusson & Horwood, 2003; Werner & Smith, 1982). Nurturing parent–child relationships (Masten et al., 1999) as well as affectionate sibling relationships (Gass, Jenkins, & Dunn, 2007) and, potentially, grandparents, may serve as moderators of stress (Hayslip, Shore, & Henderson, 2000; Jenkins & Smith, 1990). On the other hand, children who are easier temperamentally elicit more positive reactions from those in their environment, a phenomenon referred to by Rutter and Taylor (2010) as evocative-gene environment correlation.

> Social competence, a major area of research in resilience, includes children's abilities to develop positive relationships, to effectively coordinate and communicate actions and feelings in relation with others, to construct and communicate shared meaning through language and play, and to be increasingly able to control and to adjust their emotions (Fabes, Gaertner, & Popp, 2006, p. 297).

Self-regulation in the presence of hardship is strongly associated with outcome measures in the areas of mental health, behavior, academic achievement, and social competence (Buckner, Mezzacappa, & Beardslee, 2009). Positive peer relationships and good friendships are seen as protective factors in resilience research. They enhance self-worth and coping skills, and possibly diminish psychosocial risk and vulnerability (O'Dougherty, Wright, & Masten, 2005).

Friendships may provide compensatory psychosocial and adaptive support for siblings of children who are on the spectrum. On the other hand, the siblings' friendships also may be risk-enhancing since school-age children—away from home and with friends—are more exposed to events arising from their school and neighborhood, especially as the children age and then engage in more unsupervised activities (O'Dougherty et al., 2005).

Clinical and Research Implications

A Resilience-Based Approach to Intervention for Families of Children with ASD

An overarching goal in working with families that have a child with autism—as Werner's (2005) explanation might be applied—is to shift the balance between vulnerability and resilience. Innovative strategies—both for research and for interventions—will spring from a systems level approach that aims for the simultaneous assessment of multiple domains of variables both within and outside the developing person (Cicchetti & Curtis, 2007). Such information is central to the goal of designing preventive interventions with strategic timing and targeting by clinicians, communities such as schools and other agencies, and by policy makers (Masten & Cicchitti, 2010; Rutter, 2009).

With a view to capturing these multilevel dynamics, Luthar, Sawyer, and Brown (2006) proposed guidelines for the selection of risk and protective processes in future research on resilience. This model focuses on the family as a unit, such as the family's life context (e.g., societal prejudices, service provision for the child's behavior problems), risk modifiers that are amenable to change through external interventions, and areas that tend to be relatively enduring in the life situation. Luthar and colleagues emphasized that critical attention needs to be given to indices that generate other assets. These are factors that set into motion "cascades," wherein they catalyze other protective processes. For example, when a child's behavior problems improve, there will be less negative impact on the family, which results in increased positive family interactions and activities. Cascades, or developmental cascades, refer to an ingenious paradigm in resilience research that conceptualizes the functionality of protective and risk factors over time.

Masten and Cicchitti (2010) recently elaborated developmental cascades as the cumulative consequences for the development of many interactions and transactions occurring in developing systems. These result in spreading effects across levels, among domains at the same level, and across different systems or generations. Thus, the consequences of the developmental cascades alter the course of development. Developmental cascades may be positive or negative in their consequences with respect to adaptive behavior. Negative cascading may result when a child has a disability or a chronic condition. For example, as was reviewed in an earlier section, cascading may originate with the compromised functioning of a child with autism to far-reaching consequences for the entire family, the extended family, and the availability of resources in the community.

More importantly, however, positive cascading also occurs. Ecological resources associated with parenting are linked to individual self-regulatory behaviors (Lewin-Biza, Bowers, & Lerner, 2010). For example, competence may lead "upward" to further competencies, where "one good thing leads to another." Bidirectional cascading also may begin at the level of overall family functioning "downward" to the level of adaptation of children over time.

Yunger et al. (2005) described self-regulatory and proactive behaviors, such as assertiveness, leadership, curiosity, and pursuit of special skills as agentic behaviors. Therefore, a parental agentic behavior, such as exercising problem solving skills, supports the functioning level of the child with autism and other siblings in the family. Thus, innovative prevention and intervention programs designed for the family should aim to set in motion cascades that will enhance factors of resilience in the family.

A cascading intervention program aiming to promote resilience in families of children with ASD should be designed at multiple levels and consist of several components in order to address the various factors influencing the lifecycle of these families. An emphasis on implementation of each component depends on the severity of the child's disorder, the time in the lifecycle of the family, the structure of the family, and the need for support of one member as opposed to the other. Siblings of children with ASD and their capacity for resilience merits special attention and intervention in this regard.

An Intervention Model for Siblings

Levels of developmental cascades as they relate to the family may be envisioned beginning with neurotypical siblings of the child with autism and their levels of adaptive functioning. Intervention models currently emerging are focusing on the population of at-risk children, and have yet to be formulated for siblings of children with developmental disabilities and their families. Most models aim at several levels of the cascades. These evidence-based preventive intervention programs for at-risk children and adolescents are strength-based programs that emphasize capacity building (Beardslee, Ayoub, Avery, Watts, & O'Carroll, 2010; Maton, Schellenback, Leadbeater, & Solarz, 2004). For example, the Beardslee Preventive Intervention Program (Beardslee, 2003; Beardslee, Wright, Gladstone, & Forbes, 2007) is a manual-based intervention involving parents and children with long-term preventive effects for children at risk for depression. This program has been adapted to include preschoolers and their families in a Head Start Center in Boston (Beardslee et al., 2010), children of low-income Latino families (D'Angelo et al., 2009), and as a multilevel public health intervention for children displaced by war in Uganda (Betancourt, Speelman, Onyango, & Bolton, 2009).

Strategies of intervening at multiple systemic levels for proactive and preventive interventions are similarly promising for families who have a child with ASD and their siblings. Schuntermann (2009) developed guidelines for a clinical model of preventive intervention for siblings based on time-limited, focused conversations utilizing a semi-structured interviewing technique. This intervention can be implemented in individual sessions combined with family sessions or in sibling groups with collateral parent groups.

The Schuntermann (2009) model addresses the family system and its subsystems: inter-sibling relationships, parent–child relationships, differential parental treatment, and possible involvement of grandparents. In addition, going beyond the family context, other factors such as school adjustment and peer relationships and recreational activities also are addressed. During a discussion session, siblings talk about their own self-perceptions and possible concerns about their own life stages into adulthood (especially in adolescence). Goals for these sessions include supporting siblings' overall relatedness to the affected children, enabling siblings to overcome difficulties of being entrenched in negative interactions, and generally enhancing siblings' capacities for taking a reflective stance.

In this model, there is an orientation toward problem solving, the effective and modulated expression of feelings, self-regulation, and practicing social sensitivities such as empathic listening and being accepting of the feelings of others. Family support and support found in friendships and peer relationships are also discussed. The framework for these discussions was adapted from Allen, Fonagy, and Bateman (2008), with their format of mentalizing interventions with adults, and from Bateman and Fonagy (2006), with the paradigm of mentalization as an ongoing developmental process of understanding oneself and others.

Recommendations for Practice: A Multilevel Program for Parents of Children with ASD

An intervention program for parents of children with ASD should take into account the severity of autism, the functioning level, the age of the child, and the timing of the intervention during the family's lifecycle. In other words, a family's needs and resources might vary at different points in time, for example during diagnosis vs. later in life.

During the diagnosis process, a major need for the family is the identification of an appropriate treatment and related services for their child with ASD. As was mentioned, parents of children with ASD are likely to be influenced by the experiences of other parents (Green, 2007). Indeed, expanding the family's network of friendship with other parents and siblings in similar situations has been found to be an important source of support and empowerment for these families (Taunt & Hastings, 2002).

Accordingly, one important component of a comprehensive support program aiming at promoting resilience for parents of children with ASD is parent-to-parent information-sharing groups. Such groups could help families of children with ASD take on an appropriate level of advocacy and activism as they see fit (Ryan & Runswick, 2009). In this component of the program, the professional roles should consist of consultation on evidence-based treatments available. In addition, professionals should be able to locate and provide information to address various family questions about the disorder itself, public and private educational services, and other issues that might arise after the diagnosis (Harrison Elder & D'Alessandro, 2009).

Some family members of children with ASD deal with depression and psychological distress (Bouma & Schweitzer, 1990; Norton & Drew, 1994; Olson & Hwang, 2001). Although focusing on strengths is central to a resilience-based approach, reducing risk is also important. Therefore, an intervention and support program for parents should include addressing depression and other psychological distress in family members through referral or direct intervention if possible.

Depending on the severity of ASD in the child (e.g., presence of aggression, level of language, cognitive development), any cascading program also should include a behavior support plan for the child at home. Positive behavior support (PBS) is an intervention framework that provides behavioral methods for supporting children and adults with disabilities to reduce inappropriate and aggressive behaviors, to achieve educational outcomes, and to have a better quality of life with their families (Ruef, Poston, & Humphrey, 2004). Providing PBS for the child at home to improve social behaviors and reduce inappropriate behaviors could help families manage their daily life in order to lessen stressors that might be related to a specific behavioral characteristic of autism.

Since the process of meaning-making is central in promoting resilience in parents, providing professional support to guide the family members to form their own narratives about their experiences is one of the most important aspects of support. Similar to Schunterman's (2009) model described for siblings, discussion and interview sessions with parents should aim at helping them explore the meaning of having a child with autism. Such sessions could be conducted at various times and over certain periods with the family, since meanings are dynamic, have multiple levels, and shift over time (Levine, 2009; Patterson, 2002). For example, in the first level parents might make meaning about autism as a disorder and what it might mean for the child and the family. In the second level, parents might construct meaning about their identity as a family. At this time, parents of a child with ASD might decide on family members' roles, specifically in relationship with the child's treatment and new demands. Finally, parents may construct meaning about their view of the world. Helping parents make specific and global meaning about having a child with autism may help them cope with the situation, promote resilience, and ultimately cascade successful family functioning.

Finally, since spirituality and meaning-making often are entwined, professionals should be respectful of the family's articulation of their belief system. Spirituality is a key family dimension that promotes family adaptation as a unit, and might buffer the family during a crisis (Walsh, 2003). Therefore, when applicable, spirituality is one aspect of resilience that could be capitalized on to help foster the family's resilience. Acknowledgement of and respect for the family's belief system is one way of utilizing this resource. Families also could be encouraged to use their spirituality as an already present resource to draw upon (Greeff & Loubser, 2008).

Conclusion

In this chapter we have analyzed the contemporary and lifecycle issues faced by the family members, including siblings, of children with ASD. We also have presented a rationale for a multilevel intervention program that aims at promoting resilience in all family members. This program focuses on supporting positive family processes, and strategies are designed to enhance the resilience of families and their individual members by augmenting family-protective factors. The multilevel cascading intervention program includes an intervention model for sibling groups. The sibling model targets and seeks to develop important individual-protective factors in children and youth as identified in resilience research, which thereby secondarily enhances family resilience. Other components of the program aim at providing support for parents, through the provision of research-based information, mental health referral and intervention, positive behavioral support for the child with ASD, and parent–professional interview sessions—in which parents are encouraged to make meaning about having a child with ASD.

References

Adrien, J. L., Faure, M., Perrot, A., Hameury, L., Garreau, B., Barthelemy, C., et al. (1991). Autism and family home movies: Preliminary findings. *Journal of Autism and Developmental Disorders, 21*, 43–49.

Adrien, J. L., Lenoir, P., Martineau, J., Perrot, A., Hameury, L., Laramande, C., et al. (1993). Blind rating of early symptoms of autism based upon family home movies. *Journal of the American Academy of Child and Adolescent Psychiatry, 32*, 617–626.

Allen, J., Fonagy, P., & Bateman, A. W. (2008). *Mentalizing in clinical practice*. Washington, DC: American Psychiatric Publishing.

American Psychiatric Association. (2000). *Diagnostic and statistical manual of mental disorders: DSM-IV-TR, text revision* (4th ed.). Washington, DC: American Psychiatric Association.

Antonovsky, A. (1987). *Unraveling the mystery of health*. San Francisco: Jossey-Bass.

Bagenholm, A., & Gillberg, C. (1991). Psychosocial effects on siblings of children with autism and mental retardation: A population-based study. *Journal of Mental Deficiency Research, 35*, 291–307.

Baron-Cohen, S., Allen, J., & Gillberg, C. (1992). Can autism be detected at 18 months? The needle, the haystack, and the CHAT. *The British Journal of Psychiatry, 161*, 158–163.

Baron-Cohen, S., Scott, F., Williams, J., Bolton, P., Matthews, F., & Brayne, C. (2009). Prevalence of autism-spectrum conditions: UK school-based population study. *The British Journal of Psychiatry, 194*, 500–509.

Baron-Cohen, S., Wheelwright, S., Cox, A., Baird, G., Charman, T., Swettenham, J., et al. (2000). Early identification of autism by the Checklist for Autism in Toddlers (CHAT). *Journal of the Royal Society of Medicine, 93*, 521–525.

Bateman, A. W., & Fonagy, P. (2006). *Mentalization-based treatment for borderline personality disorders.* New York: Oxford University Press.

Bayat, M. (2005). *How family members' perceptions of influences and causes of autism may predict assessment of their family quality of life.* Doctoral dissertation. Available from ProQuest Dissertation and Thesis database (UMI No. 3180946).

Bayat, M. (2007). Evidence of resilience in families of children with autism. *Journal of Intellectual Disability Research, 51*(9), 702–714.

Beardslee, W. (2003). *When a parent is depressed: How to protect your children from the effects of depression in the family.* Boston: Little, Brown and Company.

Beardslee, W. R., Ayoub, C., Avery, M., Watts, C. L., & O'Carroll, K. (2010). Family connections: An approach for strengthening early care systems in facing depression and adversity. *The American Journal of Orthopsychiatry, 80*, 482–495.

Beardslee, W. R., Wright, E., Gladstone, T. R., & Forbes, P. (2007). Long-term effects from a randomized trial of two public health preventive interventions for parental depression. *Journal of Family Psychology, 21*, 703–713.

Ben-Yizhak, N., Yirmia, N., Seidman, I., Alon, R., Lord, C., & Sigman, M. (2010). Pragmatic language and school related linguistic abilities in siblings of children with autism. *Journal of Autism & Developmental Disorders, 41*(6), 750–760. doi:10.1007/s10803-010-1096-6. December 10, 2010.

Betancourt, T. S., Speelman, L., Onyango, G., & Bolton, P. (2009). A qualitative study of mental health problems among children displaced by war in Northern Uganda. *Transcultural Psychiatry, 46*, 238–256.

Bouma, R., & Schweitzer, R. (1990). The impact of chronic childhood illness on family stress: A comparison between autism and cystic fibrosis. *Journal of Clinical Psychology, 46*, 722–730.

Brent, B., & Geschwind, D. (2009). Genetic advances in autism: Heterogeneity and convergence on shared pathways. *Current Opinion in Genetics & Development, 19*(3), 271–278.

Buckner, J., Mezzacappa, E., & Beardslee, W. R. (2009). Self-regulation and its relation to adaptive functioning in low income youths. *The American Journal of Orthopsychiatry, 79*, 19–30.

Center for Disease Control and Prevention (CDC). (2007). *Autism developmental disabilities monitoring network.* Retrieved from http://www.cdc.gov/ncbddd/autism/documents/AutismCommunityReport.pdf. December 10, 2010.

Cicchetti, D., & Curtis, J. (2007). Multilevel perspectives on pathways to resilient functioning. *Development and Psychopathology, 19*, 627–629.

Crocker, A. C. (1997). The impact of disabling conditions. In H. M. Wallace, R. F. Bieh, J. C. MacQueen, & J. A. Blackman (Eds.), *Mosby's resource guide to children with disabilities and chronic illness* (pp. 22–29). St. Louis: Mosby.

D'Angelo, E., Llerena-Quinn, R., Shapiro, R., Colon, F., Rodriguez, P., Gallagher, K., et al. (2009). Adaptation of the Preventive Intervention Program for depression for use with predominantly low-income Latino families. *Family Process, 48*, 269–291.

Dawson, G., Hill, D., Spencer, A., Galpert, L., & Watson, L. (1990). Affective exchange between young autistic children and their mothers. *Journal of Autism and Developmental Disorders, 18*, 335–345.

De Giacomo, A., & Fombonne, E. (1998). Parental recognition of developmental abnormalities in autism. *European Child & Adolescent Psychiatry, 7*, 131–136.

Dorris, L., Espie, C., Knott, F., & Salt, J. (2004). Mind-reading difficulties in the siblings of people with Asperger's syndrome: Evidence for a genetic influence in the abnormal development of a specific domain. *Journal of Child Psychology and Psychiatry, 45*, 412–418.

Dugan, T. (1989). Action and acting out: Variables in the development of resilience in adolescence. In T. Fugan & R. Coles (Eds.), *The child in our times: Studies in the development of resilience* (pp. 157–176). New York: Brunner/Mazel.

Dunn, J. (1992). Sisters and brothers: Current issues in developmental research. In F. Boer & J. Dunn (Eds.), *Children's siblings relationships: Developmental and clinical issues* (pp. 1–17). Hillsdale, NJ: Erlbaum.

Dunn, J. (2005). Commentary: Siblings in their families. *Journal of Family Psychology, 19*, 654–657.

Eikeseth, S. (2009). Outcome of comprehensive psycho-educational interventions for young children with autism. *Research in Developmental Disabilities, 30*, 158–178.

Fabes, R., Gaertner, B., & Popp, K. (2006). Getting along with others: Social competence in early childhood. In K. McCarthy & D. Phillips (Eds.), *Blackwell handbook of early child developmen* (pp. 297–316). Malden: Blackwell.

Fergusson, D. M., & Horwood, L. (2003). Resilience to childhood adversity: Results of a 21-year study. In S. Luthar (Ed.), *Resilience and vulnerability: Adaptation in the context of childhood adversity* (pp. 130–155). New York: Cambridge University Press.

Folstein, S. E., & Rosen-Sheidley, B. (2001). Genetics of autism: Complex aetiology for a heterogeneous disorder. *Nature Reviews Genetics, 2*, 943–955.

Gamliel, I., Yirmiya, N., Jaff, D. H., Manor, O., & Sigman, M. (2009). Developmental trajectories in siblings of children with autism: Cognition and language from 4 months to 7 years. *Journal of Autism and Developmental Disorders, 39*, 1131–1144.

Ganong, L. H., & Coleman, M. (2002). Family resilience in multiple contexts. *Journal of Marriage and Family, 64*, 346–348.

Gass, K. R., Jenkins, J. M., & Dunn, J. (2007). Are sibling relationships protective? A longitudinal study. *Journal of Child Psychology and Psychiatry, 48*, 167–175.

Gier, M., & Gier, D. (2003). Thimerosal in childhood vaccines, neurodevelopmental disorders, and heart disease in the United States. *Journal of American Physicians and Surgeons, 8*, 6–10.

Goldman, G., & Yazbak, F. (2004). An investigation of the association between MMR vaccination and autism in Denmark. *Journal of American Physicians and Surgeons, 9*(3), 70–75.

Gray, D. E. (1993). Perception of stigma: The parents of autistic children. *Sociology of Health & Illness, 5*, 102–120.

Gray, D. E. (1994). Coping with autism: Stresses and strategies. *Sociology of Health & Illness, 16*, 275–300.

Gray, D. E. (2002). Ten years on: A longitudinal study of families of children with autism. *Journal of Intellectual and Developmental Disability, 27*, 215–222.

Greeff, A., & Loubser, K. (2008). Spirituality as a resiliency quality in Xhosa-speaking families in South Africa. *Journal of Religion and Health, 47*, 288–301.

Green, V. (2007). Parental experience with treatments for autism. *Journal of Developmental and Physical Disability, 19*, 91–101.

Greenspan, S. I., & Wieder, S. (1998). *The child with special needs: Encouraging intellectual and emotional growth*. Reading, MA: Perseus.

Greenspan, S., & Wieder, S. (2006). *Engaging autism: Using the Floortime approach to help children relate, communicate, and think*. Cambridge, MA: Da Capo Lifelong Books.

Harrison Elder, J., & D'Alessandro, T. (2009). Supporting families of children with autism spectrum disorders: Questions parents ask and what nurses need to know. *Pediatric Nursing, 35*(4), 240–253.

Hastings, R. P. (2003). Brief report: Behavioral adjustment of siblings of children with autism. *Journal of Autism and Developmental Disorders, 33*, 99–104.

Hauser, S. T., Allen, J. P., & Golden, E. (2006). *Out of the woods: Tales of resilient teens*. Cambridge, MA: Harvard University Press.

Hawley, D. R. (2000). Clinical implications of family resilience. *American Journal of Family Therapy, 28*, 101–116.

Hayslip, B., Shore, R., & Henderson, C. E. (2000). Perceptions of grandparents' influence in the lives of their grandchildren. In B. Hayslip & R. G. Glen (Eds.), *Grandparents raising grandchildren: Theoretical empirical and clinical perspectives* (pp. 35–46). New York: Springer.

Hobson, R. P., & Lee, A. (1998). Hello and goodbye: A study of social engagement in autism. *Journal of Autism and Developmental Disorders, 28*, 117–127.

Howlin, P. (2005). Outcomes in autism spectrum disorders. In F. R. Volkmar, R. Paul, A. Klin, & D. J. Cohen (Eds.), *Handbook of autism and pervasive developmental disorders* (3rd ed., Vol. 1, pp. 201–222). Hoboken, NJ: Wiley.

Jacobson, J. W., Mulick, J. A., & Green, G. (1998). Cost benefit estimates for early intensive behavioral intervention for young children with autism—general model and single state case. *Behavioral Intervention, 13*, 201–226.

Jarbrink, K., Fombonne, E., & Knapp, M. (2003). Measuring the parental, service and cost impacts of children with autistic spectrum disorders: A pilot study. *Journal of Autism and Developmental Disorders, 33*, 395–402.

Jenkins, J. M., & Smith, M. (1990). Factors protecting children living in disharmonious homes: Maternal reports. *Journal of the American Academy of Child and Adolescent Psychiatry, 29*, 60–69.

Kagan, J. (2008). In defense of qualitative changes in development. *Child Development, 79*, 1606–1624.

Kaminsky, L., & Dewey, D. (2001). Sibling relationships of children with autism. *Journal of Autism and Developmental Disorders, 31*, 399–410.

Kaminsky, L., & Dewey, D. (2002). Psychosocial adjustment in siblings of children with autism. *Journal of Child Psychology and Psychiatry, 43*, 225–232.

Kasari, C., & Sigman, M. (1997). Linking parental perception to interactions in young children with autism. *Journal of Autism and Developmental Disorders, 27*, 39–57.

Keenan, M., Dillenburger, K., Doherty, A., Byrne, T., & Gallagher, S. (2010). The experiences of parents during diagnosis and forward planning for children with autism spectrum disorder. *Journal of Applied Research in Intellectual Disabilities, 23*, 390–397.

Kirk, S. (2008). *Hope for the autism spectrum: A mother and son journey of insight and biomedical intervention*. London: Jessica Kingsley Publishers.

Landa, R., Holman, K. C., & Garrett-Mayer, E. (2007). Social and communication development in toddlers with early and later diagnosis of autism spectrum disorder. *Archives of General Psychiatry, 62*, 1007–1014.

Levine, K. A. (2009). Against all odds: Resilience in single mothers of children with disabilities. *Social Work in Health Care, 48*, 402–419.

Lewin-Biza, S., Bowers, E. P., & Lerner, R. M. (2010). One good thing leads to another: Cascades of positive youth development among American adolescents. *Development and Psychopathology, 22*, 759–770.

Lobato, D., Miller, C., Barbour, L., Hall, L., & Pezzullo, J. (1991). Preschool siblings of handicapped children: Interactions with mothers, brothers, and sisters. *Research in Developmental Disabilities, 12*, 387–399.

Lovaas, I., & Smith, T. (2003). Early and intensive behavioral intervention in autism. In A. E. Kazdin & J. R. Weisz (Eds.), *Evidence-based psychotherapies for children and adolescents* (pp. 325–340). New York: Guildford Press.

Lovaas, O. I. (1987). Behavioral treatment and normal education and intellectual functioning in young autistic children. *Journal of Consulting and Clinical Psychology, 55*(1), 3–9.

Luthar, S., Sawyer, J., & Brown, P. (2006). Conceptual issues in studies of resilience. Past, present, and future research. *Annals of the New York Academy of Sciences, 1094*, 105–115.

Marcus, L. M., Kunce, L. J., & Schopler, E. (1997). Working with families. In D. Cohen & F. Volkmar (Eds.), *Handbook of autism and pervasive developmental disorders* (2nd ed., pp. 631–649). New York: John Wiley and Sons.

Marcus, L. M., Rubin, J. S., & Rubin, M. A. (2000). Benefit-cost analysis and autism services: A response to Jacobson and Mulick. *Journal of Autism and Developmental Disorders, 30*, 595–598.

Marcus, L. M., & Schopler, E. (1987). Working with families: A developmental perspective. In D. Cohen, A. Donnellan, & R. Paul (Eds.), *Handbook of autism and pervasive developmental disorders* (pp. 499–512). New York: Wiley.

Masten, A. S. (2001). Ordinary magic: Resilience processes in development. *American Psychologist, 56*, 227–238.

Masten, A. S., & Cicchitti, D. (2010). Editorial: Developmental cascades. *Development and Psychopathology, 22*, 491–495.

Masten, A. S., Hubbard, J., Gest, S. D., Tellegen, A., Garmezy, N., & Ramirez, M. (1999). Competence in the context of adversity: Pathways to resilience and maladaptation from childhood to late adolescence. *Development and Psychopathology, 11*, 143–169.

Maston, J., & Sipes, M. (2010). Methods of early diagnosis and tracking for autism and pervasive developmental disorder not otherwise specified (PDDNOS). *Journal of Developmental and Physical Disabilities, 22*, 343–358.

Maton, K. L., Schellenback, C. J., Leadbeater, B. J., & Solarz, A. (Eds.). (2004). *Investing in children, youth, families, and communities*. Washington, DC: American Psychiatric Association.

McAdoo, W. G., & DeMyer, M. K. (1977). Research related to family factors in autism. *Journal of Marriage and Family, 41*, 236–244.

McCarthy, J. (2008). *Mother warriors*. New York: Penguin Group.

Mesibov, G. B. (1983). Current perspectives and issues in autism and adolescence. In E. Schopler & G. B. Mesibov (Eds.), *Autism in adolescents and adults* (pp. 37–53). New York: Plenum.

Mitka, M. (2008). Chelation therapy trials halted. *Journal of the American Medical Association, 300*, 2236.

Muhle, R., Trentacoste, S., & Rapin, I. (2004). The genetics of autism. *Pediatrics, 113*(5), 472–486.

National Research Council. (2001). *Educating young children with autism*. Washington, DC: National Academy Press.

Nicolas, J., Carpenter, L., King, L., Jenner, W., & Charles, J. (2009). Autism spectrum disorders in preschool-aged children: Prevalence and comparison to a school-aged population. *Annals of Epidemiology, 19*(1), 808–881.

Norton, P., & Drew, C. (1994). Autism and potential family stressors. *American Journal of Family Therapy, 22*, 67–76.

O'Dougherty, B., Wright, M., & Masten, A. S. (2005). Resilience processes in development. In S. Goldstein & R. B. Brooks (Eds.), *Handbook of resilience in children* (pp. 17–37). New York: Kluwer Academic/Plenum.

Offit, P. (2008). *Autism's false prophets: Bad science, risky medicine, and a search for a cure*. New York: Colombia University Press.

Olson, M. B., & Hwang, C. P. (2001). Depression in mothers and fathers of children with intellectual disability. *Journal of Intellectual Disability Research, 45*, 535–543.

Orsmond, G., & Seltzer, M. (2009). Adolescent siblings of individuals with an autism spectrum disorder: Testing a diathesis-stress model of sibling well-being. *Journal of Autism and Developmental Disorders, 39*, 1053–1065.

Osterling, J., & Dawson, G. (1994). Early recognition of children with autism: A study of first birthday home videotapes. *Journal of Autism and Developmental Disorders, 24*, 247–257.

Osterling, J. A., Dawson, G., & Munson, J. (2002). Early recognition of 1-year-old infants with autism spectrum disorder versus mental retardation. *Development and Psychopathology, 14*, 239–251.

Patterson, J. M. (1988). Families experiencing stress: I. The family adjustment and adaptation response model. II. Applying the FAAR model to health-related issues of intervention research. *Family Systems Medicine, 6*, 202–237.

Patterson, J. (2002). Integrating family resilience and family stress theory. *Journal of Marriage and Family, 64*(2), 349–360.

Pilowsky, T., Yirmiya, N., Dopplet, O., Gross-Tsur, V., & Shalev, R. (2004). Social and emotional adjustment of siblings of children with autism. *Journal of Child Psychology and Psychiatry, 45*, 855–865.

Roa, P. A., & Beidel, D. C. (2009). The impact of children with high-functioning autism on parental stress, sibling adjustment, and family functioning. *Behavior Modification, 33*(4), 437–451.

Robins, D., Fein, D., Barton, M., & Green, J. (2001). Modified checklist for autism in toddlers (M-CHAT). *Journal of Autism and Developmental Disorders, 31*(2), 131–144.

Rogers, S. (2009). What are infant siblings teaching us about autism in infancy? *Autism Research, 2*(3), 125–137.

Rolland, J. S. (1993). Mastering family challenges in serious illness and disability. In F. Walsh (Ed.), *Normal family processes* (pp. 444–473). New York: Guilford.

Ruef, M., Poston, D., & Humphrey, K., (2004). *PBS Putting the "positive" into behavioral support: An introductory training packet* (2nd ed.). Lawrence, KS: City: Beach Center on Disability, The University of Kansas. Retrieved from http://www.beachcenter.org/Books/Chapters/PDF/PuttingPositivePart1.pdf. December 10, 2010

Rutter, M. (2009). Resilience reconsidered: Conceptual considerations, empirical findings, and policy implications. In J. P. Shonkoff & S. J. Meisels (Eds.), *Handbook of early childhood intervention* (2nd ed., pp. 651–682). New York: Cambridge University Press.

Rutter, M., & Taylor, E. (Eds.). (2010). *Rutter's child and adolescent psychiatry*. Malden: Blackwell Publishing.

Ryan, S., & Runswick, C. K. (2009). From advocate to activist? Mapping out the experiences of mothers of children on the autism spectrum. *Journal of Applied Research in Intellectual Disabilities, 22*, 43–53.

Ryde-Brandt, B. (1990). Anxiety and defense strategies in mothers of children with different disabilities. *Journal of the British Psychological Society, 63*, 183–192.

Safer, J. (2002). *The normal one: Life with a difficult or damaged siblings*. New York: The Free Press.

Sanders, J. L., & Morgan, S. B. (1997). Family stress and adjustment as perceived by parents of children with autism and Down syndrome: Implications for intervention. *Child and Family Behavior Therapy, 19*, 15–32.

Schuntermann, P. (2002). Pervasive developmental disorder and parental adaptation: Previewing and reviewing atypical development with parents in child psychiatric consultation. *President and Fellows of Harvard College, 10*, 16–27.

Schuntermann, P. (2007). The sibling experience: Growing up with a child who has pervasive developmental disorder or mental retardation. *Harvard Review of Psychiatry, 15*(3), 93–108.

Schuntermann, P. (2009). Growing up with a developmentally challenged brother or sister: A model of engaging siblings based on mentalizing. *Harvard Review of Psychiatry, 17*(5), 297–314.

Schwartz, R. C. (2003). Resiliency in siblings of autistic children. *Dissertation Abstracts International, 64*(5B), 2420.

Seligman, M. E. P., & Csikszentmihalyi, M. (2000). Positive psychology: An introduction. *American Psychologist, 55*, 5–14.

Sroufe, L. A., Egeland, B., Carlson, E. A., & Collins, W. A. (2005). *The development of the person. The Minnesota study of risk and adaptation from birth to adulthood*. New York: The Guilford Press.

Stehli, A. (1991). *The sound of a miracle: A child's triumph over autism*. New York: Doubleday.

Taunt, H. M., & Hastings, R. P. (2002). Positive impact of children with developmental disabilities on their families: A preliminary study. *Education and Training in Mental Retardation and Developmental Disabilities, 37*, 410–420.

The Editors of Lancet. (Eds.). (2010). Retraction: Ileal-lymphoid-nodular hyperplasia, non-specific colitis, and pervasive developmental disorder in children. *The Lancet, 375*(9713), 445.

Wakefield, A. J., Murch, S. H., Anthony, A., Linnell, J., Casson, D., Malik, M., et al. (1998). Ileal-lymphoid-nodular hyperplasia, non-specific colitis, and pervasive developmental disorder in children. *The Lancet, 351*, 637–641.

Walsh, F. (1996). The concept of family resilience: Crisis and challenges. *Family Process, 35*, 410–420.

Walsh, F. (1998). *Strengthening family resilience*. New York, London: Guilford Press.

Walsh, F. (2003). Family resilience: Strengths forged through adversity. In F. Walsh (Ed.), *Normal family processes* (pp. 399–421). New York: The Guilford Press.

Walsh, F. (2006). Foundation of a family resilience approach. In F. Walsh (Ed.) (2nd Ed.). *Strengthening family resilience*, (pp. 3–26). New York, NY: Guilford Press.

Walsh, F. (2010). A family resilience framework for clinical practice: Integrating developmental theory and systemic perspectives. In W. Borden (Ed.), *Reshaping theory in contemporary social work: Toward a critical pluralism in clinical practice* (pp. 146–176). New York, NY: Columbia University Press.

Werner, E. (2005). What can we learn about resilience from large-scale longitudinal studies? In S. Goldstein & R. Brooks (Eds.), *Handbook of resilience in children* (pp. 91–105). New York: Springer.

Werner, E., & Smith, R. (1982). *Vulnerable but invincible: A longitudinal study of resilient children and youth*. New York: McGraw Hill.

Willey, L. H. (1999). *Pretending to be normal*. Philadelphia: Jessica Kingsley.

Wimpory, D. C., Hobson, R. P., Williams, J. M. G., & Nash, S. (2000). Are infants with autism socially engaged? A study of recent retrospective parental reports. *Journal of Autism and Developmental Disorders, 30*, 525–536.

Wood, B. L. (2001). Physically manifested illness in children and adolescents: A biobehavioral family approach. In A. Josephson (Ed.), *Current perspectives on family therapy* (pp. 543–562). Philadelphia: W.B. Saunders.

Yunger, J. L., Corby, B. C., & Perry, D. G. (2005). Dimensions of attachment in middle childhood. In K. Kerns & R. Richardson (Eds.), *Attachment in middle childhood* (pp. 89–114). New York: The Guilford Press.

Zane, T., Davis, C., & Rosswurm, M. (2008). The cost of fad treatments in autism. *Journal of Early and Intensive Behavior Intervention, 5*, 44–51.

Dorothy S. Becvar

Introduction

Traditionally, treating individuals with mental health challenges has involved a singular focus on intrapsychic processes, or the internal workings of the mind, consistent with the view that the illness resides within the person. However, during the 1950s and 1960s, a variety of models for working with families rather than only individuals began to emerge (Becvar & Becvar, 2009), with much of the early research examining families that included a member diagnosed with schizophrenia (Bateson, Jackson, Haley, & Weakland, 1956; Wynne, Ryckoff, Day, & Hirsch, 1958). Unfortunately, however, many of these studies of schizophrenia had the perhaps unintentional effect of blaming families for the problems experienced by one of their members.

In part as a response to the backlash to this early research, the focus began to shift to a consideration of the burden, both objective and subjective (Hoenig & Hamilton, 1966), that families experienced when caring for a mentally ill member. Indeed, as noted by Jewell, Downing and McFarlane (2009, p. 869), "In studies conducted as early as the 1950s and 1960s, it was found that family members experience stress in dealing with a loved one with mental illness," and that such stress had an impact on many aspects of family life. These research findings, in turn, led to a search for evidence-based approaches, such as psychoeducation, that were focused on the needs described by families (Lefley, 2010). From such a perspective, "The main goal in working with families is to help them develop the knowledge and skills instrumental in promoting the recovery of their family member while eschewing family dysfunctional etiological theories of the past" (Jewell, et al., 2009, p. 870). Conclusive data derived from more than 25 years of research now indicate that when families' needs are met, patient outcomes improve (Cohen, et al., 2008; Colom, et al., 2009; Lefley, 2010).

In addition, since the 1930s, a group of social scientists has focused on examining and describing the traits of families who were able to deal with various difficulties successfully (Becvar, 2007). In the 1960s and 1970s, particular emphasis consistent with this focus was given to two areas: family stress, coping and adaptation, and family strengths (De Haan, Hawley, & Deal, 2002; Hawley & DeHaan, 1996; Walsh, 2003). More recently, the concept of resilience has emerged as an important area of

D.S. Becvar (✉)
School of Social Work, Saint Louis University,
3550 Lindell Boulevard, St. Louis, MO 63103, USA
e-mail: becvards@slu.edu

D.S. Becvar (ed.), *Handbook of Family Resilience*,
DOI 10.1007/978-1-4614-3917-2_24, © Springer Science+Business Media New York 2013

study for researchers as well as a significant focus for clinicians (Haggan, 2002). While early efforts relative to the concept of resilience were concerned primarily with the health and successful functioning of individuals (Patterson, 2002b), there is now a growing body of literature whose focus is resilience in families.

In the family-oriented literature there is widespread agreement about the need to understand resilience as involving processes that are fluid, evolve over time, and are influenced by context, rather than as describing a phenomenon that can be defined by static traits and characteristics (Conger & Conger, 2002; De Haan, et al., 2002; Hawley & DeHaan, 1996; Kragh & Huber, 2002; Oswald, 2002; Patterson, 2002a, 2002b; Sandau-Beckler, Devall, & de La Rosa, 2002; Schwartz, 2002; Walsh, 1998, 2003). Also generally captured by the concept of family resilience is recognition of its importance both in enabling resistance to change-induced disruption as well as in fostering the ability to adapt when faced with a crisis. Further, resilience typically refers to a quality of buoyancy, or the capacity of families to repair themselves and to rebound from difficult situations even stronger than they were before such challenging situations were encountered.

At the same time, questions remain regarding whether resilience is "an internal quality, an outcome, a process, [or] an acquired skill" (Cohen, Ferguson, Harms, Pooley, & Tomlinson, 2011, p. 111). In addition, there has been some disagreement between clinicians and researchers regarding whether a family must experience and successfully withstand a crisis, for example, some kind of hardship or exposure to significant risk, before use of the term resilience becomes appropriate. According to Patterson (2002a, 2002b), clinicians have tended to equate family strengths, competence, and the ability to deal with life's challenges with resilience if and when such challenges arise. By contrast, researchers "have been more interested in outcomes to explain unexpected competent functioning among families (and individuals) who have been exposed to significant risk(s)" (Patterson, 2002a, p. 349). Patterson therefore advocates for the use of the term *resiliency* to describe a capacity that would be available should a crisis occur, and the term *resilience* to describe specific processes that emerge in response to significant stress.

Such a distinction may or may not be useful, depending on one's perspective and orientation. However, in either case there are several important dimensions of resilience that are worthy of emphasis. First of all, the paths followed by families as they negotiate challenges and regain their balance vary widely (De Haan, et al., 2002; Walsh, 2003). How this path is forged for each family is a function of the particular set of protective factors, risk factors, contextual factors, and circumstances characterizing each unique situation (Hawley & DeHaan, 1996). What is more, the ability to evidence resilience in one situation does not guarantee its presence in another situation, or in response to other stressors (Patterson, 2002a; Walsh, 2003), nor is there one single coping strategy that is necessarily always effective. Additionally, a both/and perspective that acknowledges deficits and problems as well as strengths and skills is inherent in a resilience orientation (Roberts & Escoto, 2003; Schwartz, 2002). Indeed, "family resilience further shifts the tendency to perceive family health or normality as residing in mythologized, problem-free families to seeking understanding how families can and do survive and regenerate even in the midst of overwhelming stress and crises" (Kragh & Huber, 2002, pp. 294–295). In summary, Walsh (2003, p. 6) emphasizes that, "While no single model of family health fits all, a family resilience perspective is grounded in a deep conviction in the potential for family recovery and growth out of adversity."

Thus, as with other forms of diversity, it is important to keep in mind the proviso that each family is unique, and therefore will evidence resilience in a manner logical to its particular context. At the same time, however, general patterns or trends have been found to characterize various groups of families, with each group varying in terms of what is experienced as supportive or helpful in dealing with particular kinds of challenges. Hence the importance of a focus on resilience relative to mental health challenges, making clear the distinct risk and protective factors that have been found to be pertinent to families as a whole as well as to various configurations based on the particular symptomatic family member. A concurrent emphasis on the dimensions of this problem as well as of the larger social context within which it occurs also is critical.

Significance of the Topic

Statistics from the National Institute of Mental Health (2008) indicate that the lifetime prevalence of a mental health disorder is 46.4% of the US adult population, with the average age of onset reported to be 14. During a 12-month period, 26.2% of the adult population experiences such a disorder, and of these, 22.3% (or 5.8% of the total adult population) fall into the severe category. Kessler et al. (2005) further conclude that "About half of Americans will meet the criteria for a *DSM-IV* disorder sometime in their life, with first onset usually in childhood or adolescence" (p. 593).

At the same time, only 41.1% of those with a mental health disorder are receiving any type of service, and 32.7% of this group (or 13.4% of those with a mental health disorder) are receiving treatment labeled as minimally adequate. In addition, according to the most recent statistics available, only 6% of the total health budget of the US is allocated to mental health (World Health Organization, 2005). Worldwide, the statistics are even graver, with the authors of the *Mental Health Atlas* (World Health Organization, 2011, p. 10) noting in their executive summary that:

- Resources to treat and prevent mental disorders remain insufficient
- Resources for mental health are inequitably distributed
- Resources for mental health are inefficiently utilized
- Institutional care for mental disorders may be slowly decreasing worldwide

In the US the greatest source of funding for those with a mental illness is private insurance, followed by tax-based revenues, and then the patient or his or her family. However, approximately one-sixth of the population does not have health insurance. The prevalence of mental illness as well as the realities of financial support—or the lack thereof—along with the long-term effects of deinstitutionalization thus have had a significant impact on the role of the family relative to mental health challenges.

Deinstitutionalization targeting individuals with mental illness began in the 1950s, followed about 15 years later by a focus on those diagnosed with a developmental disability (Stroman, 2003). This movement occurred in response to a variety of factors including criticisms of the poor conditions of public institutions as well as increasing awareness of both the prevalence and the costs associated with mental illness; the production and incorporation of more effective drugs that reduced symptoms and enabled more independent living options for those with mental illness; support by President Kennedy of federal policies that increased the funding of both research focused on preventing developmental disability and cognitive impairment as well as community facilities for those with mental illness; growing public approval of the shift to local community care as a response to mental illness that was more humane than previously was the case; changes in public opinion about those with mental health challenges as a function of a variety of advocacy efforts focused on reducing the stigma associated with these disorders; and the desire of both federal and state governments to counteract the increasing costs associated with hospitalization. Although well-intended, along with several other unanticipated consequences, "One outcome of the deinstitutionalization movement was increased responsibility of the family in managing their relative's mental disorder" (Richardson, Cobham, Murray, & McDermott, 2010, p. 28).

Indeed, the family has become the primary caregiver for those who have a mental health disorder (Abelanda & Helfrlich, 2003). For example, more than half of those who have been hospitalized for psychiatric care return to their families following discharge. What is more, given that most of those whose diagnosis falls into the severe category typically have been experiencing problems for many years, they generally have been unsuccessful in their attempts to assume the roles and responsibilities expected of other adults of their age who have similar intellectual abilities. They therefore are most likely to be cared for by their families (Saunders, 2003). With this situation in mind we turn now to a consideration of the literature related to mental health challenges and the facilitation of resilience in families experiencing such challenges.

Literature Review

I begin this literature review with a focus on the impact of mental illness on the family in general relative to both risk and protective factors, or indicators of family resilience. I then proceed by looking at the distinct contexts of mental illness that are created when different family members are the persons experiencing mental illness. In this latter category I include childhood mental illness, adult child mental illness, and parental mental illness. The studies included in this review are discussed in chronological order and represent the sum total identified by a search for articles published during the last 15 years that related to family resilience and mental health challenges.

The Family Experience of Mental Illness

In their search to explore the potential for resilience in families dealing with mental illness Marsh and Lefly (1996) surveyed a national sample (*n* = 131) of members of the National Alliance for the Mentally Ill (NAMI) that included the full range of close family relationships. By way of introduction to their study the authors note that grief for the patient, for the caregiver's losses, and for the impact on the family lies at the core of the subjective burden experienced by those facing the challenge of mental illness. Other dimensions of this burden include chronic sorrow, the emotional roller-coaster experience, and empathic pain for the patient. In terms of objective burden, the challenges include coping with often bizarre behaviors on the part of the patient and other daily caregiving responsibilities, dealing with the limits of the mental health system, and living in the context of a stigmatized illness. Indeed, despite survey questions focused on positive factors, nearly 40% of the respondents in this study voluntarily included negative comments related to family burden. At the same time, family resilience, individual resilience, and patient resilience were all reported by a majority of the participants. Family resilience factors included bonds and commitments; strengths and resources; growth and development; contributions; and gratifications. Individual resilience factors included the ability to make contributions; improved personal qualities; growth and development; enhanced coping effectiveness; gratifications; and better perspectives and priorities. Patient resilience factors included positive personal qualities; recovery; and contributions to the family, others with a mental illness, the mental health system, and society. The resources reported by participants that enabled them to adapt to the challenges of mental illness included the quality of the family and individual family members; membership in NAMI; the assistance of professionals as well as friends, neighbors, and co-workers; religion; and hobbies.

In a subsequent qualitative survey of families dealing with severe mental illness in one of their members, Marsh and Johnson (1997) enumerated the various risk factors, or subjective burden, found to have been experienced by their participants: grief for the one afflicted as well as for personal losses; sadness in response to symbolic losses related to hopes, dreams, and expectations; chronic sorrow as a function of ongoing experiences and challenges; life on an emotional roller-coaster as a function of repeated intervals of relapse and remission in the person with the mental illness; empathic pain for the afflicted person's situation; energy drain related both to coping with symptomatic behavior and to caregiving responsibilities; disruption in family routines; obstacles in the service delivery system; and stigmatization. At the same time, however, they found that many families and their members were able to acknowledge an enhancement in various areas of their lives as a result of their involvement with mental illness. Such enhancements involved family relationships, knowledge and skills, advocacy efforts, and participation in a family member's improvement. Personal resilience also included increases in compassion, contributions to the life of the family, and coping mechanisms, as well as the adoption of "healthier perspectives and priorities" (p. 231).

In their effort to identify resilience factors, Jonker and Greeff (2009) studied families in South Africa who were living in underprivileged areas and caring for a member with mental illness. The authors note the findings of others that caregivers face challenges related to support of the ill person both physically and emotionally; their own emotions relative to the situation; family and social relationships; financial strain; and discrimination and stigma related to the illness. Caregivers thus may feel guilt because they are healthy, mourn for themselves as well as for the person who is ill, lose a sense of freedom, be fearful given the lack of predictability and behavioral manifestations of mental illness, and worry about their own vulnerability in the mental health domain. Nevertheless, the qualitative findings of this study, which focused on adaptation as an indication of resilience, revealed three general categories: internal resources, external resources, and patient-related factors. Internal resources included religion and spirituality, caregiver characteristics related to perception, attitude, hope and acceptance, and such family characteristics as practical and emotional support, and love. External resources identified were related to support from the extended family, friends, and neighbors, as well as community resources. Patient-related factors included acceptance and understanding of self and illness, and positive behavior on his or her part. In addition to providing some support for these findings, the quantitative analysis revealed the significance of communication, whether negative or positive, in terms of the ability of the family to adapt. That is, "Positive, supportive communication patterns…indicated a relatively strong positive linear relationship with family adaptation, whereas negative, inflammatory communication patterns…had an even stronger negative relationship with family adaptation" (p. 870).

Saunders (2003) completed a review of the social science literature on families living with severe mental illness. Included in her review were 46 journals or books with a total of more than 400 articles. The domains identified were family coping, caregiver burden and psychological distress, caregiver resiliency, caregiver depression, social support, client behavioral problems, and family functioning. In addition to a reiteration of the findings of the studies considered above she summarized her findings as follows:

> Families living with a member with a chronic illness, such as severe mental illness, constantly adjust and adapt as the illness of the family situation changes…. Adjustment and adaptation to a chronic illness may result in an increase in family emotional and physical illness…and impaired family functioning…. Severe mental illness affects all aspects of family functioning, and all family relationships and roles are altered, sometimes permanently…. These alterations include finances, employment, social life, physical health, marital and family relationships, and daily household activities. Furthermore, changes in family identity may be experienced. (2003, p. 189).

In closing, Saunders notes her findings that such challenges were offset when families were able to use effective problem-solving skills and coping strategies and when they had adequate social support.

More recently, in a qualitative study conducted in Australia, Cohen et al. (2011) interviewed 15 individuals who had been caregivers of persons with a mental illness from between 2 and 25 years. Negative risk factors reported by the respondents included a lack of knowledge about their relative's illness; the strain or breakdown of family relationships, including lack of support, cohesion, and understanding; communication problems between the person with the illness and the caregiver as well as within the family; the sense that their never-ending journey "is long and arduous" (p. 119); and the need to give up other parts of their lives that previously were important. On the other hand, the researchers also identified several coping strategies and indicators of resilience including spiritual resources; involvement with music; meditation; gardening; and community support. They conclude that their study demonstrates "the importance of individual attributes, the family, and the social environment in determining resilient outcomes" (p. 123).

A somewhat different approach characterized a quantitative study by Gonźalez-Pinto et al. (2011), who conducted a study in Spain in an attempt to learn whether positive family factors could be protective against the development of psychosis in persons with a genetic risk. The authors describe the relationship that is assumed to exist between psychotic disorders and a neurodevelopmental disorder, but also note that psychotic disorders do not occur in all of those who are vulnerable. The findings of their study include, first of all, that there was an association between a lower level of psychosis and family environment, and secondly, that the influence of family environment was greater for those with a family history of psychosis than for those without such a history. Such findings support the conclusions of others that "a positive family environment is associated with greater improvements in negative symptoms, disorganized [sic] symptoms and functioning among individuals identified as being at imminent risk of becoming psychotic" (p. 28). Conversely, the researchers found that there was greater risk of psychosis for those whose family environment was experienced as negative.

Childhood Mental Illness

Mendenhall and Mount (2011) reviewed the literature related to the impact on parents of a child with mental illness. They report the dimensions of both caregiver strain and caregiver enhancement found to characterize parents relative to the following domains: mental and emotional, health, social, work, and family environment. In the mental and emotional domain caregiver strain may involve high levels of stress, worry, grief and sadness, and mental illness on the part of the parent. In the health domain, parents may experience decreases in their overall status, in their energy, and their self-care. In the social domain, risk factors include lack of personal time, embarrassment, stigma, a decreased social life, neglected friendships, and guilt for socializing. In the work domain, having inadequate child care, the need to leave the workforce, the shift to part time work, distractions while working, lack of support from co-workers, and absenteeism may all contribute to caregiver strain. The authors also describe manifestations of caregiver enhancement relative to three domains. In the mental and emotional domain parents may experience increases in their emotional and mental strength, in their views of themselves as effective parents, and in identifying and getting treatment for their own mental illness. In the social domain parents may benefit from expanded personal and social networks and positive involvement in the community. Similarly, their family environment may include enriched relationships and greater family unity. The authors note that the degree to which the dimensions of caregiver strain and/or enhancement is manifested is affected by the following predictors noted in past research:

- Level of child's symptomatology
- Level of child's impairment
- Type of mental illness
- Caregiver age
- Perceived amount of social support
- Externalizing behavior problems
- Race and ethnicity (p. 185)

Brown, Howcroft, and Muthen (2010) studied the experience of parents whose child had been diagnosed with attention deficit/hyperactivity disorder (AD/HD). Conducted in South Africa using a mixed methods approach, the study included 44 caregiver participants, and had an explicit focus on resilience. Resilience factors identified by the quantitative analysis included social support, family hardiness, personal strengths, dependability, cooperation, creativity, affirming communication, and openness to learning. Family adaptation was facilitated as members spent time together and also were able to deal effectively with problematic issues. The findings of the qualitative analysis indicated that social support, adhering to a treatment regimen, having information and knowledge about the illness, a supportive family unit, family times and routines, acceptance of the disorder, open and honest communication, implementing behavioral interventions both at home and in the school, parental mutuality, religious beliefs and behaviors, and financial resources were reported by participants to be factors that were important in enabling them to deal well with their child.

Adult Child Mental Illness

One parent in a study of the impact of adult child mental illness (Marsh, 1992, cited in Marsh & Lefley, 1996) described her reactions to the experience of having an adult child with mental illness as follows:

> The problems with my daughter were like a black hole inside of me into which everything else had been drawn. My grief and pain were so intense sometimes that I barely got through the day. It felt like a mourning process, as if I were dealing with the loss of the daughter I had loved for 18 years, for whom there was so much potential. (pp. 3–4)

Two articles detail the dimensions of this impact in ways that repeat the conclusions of those who have considered mental health challenges relative to the family in general. However, in neither article is family resilience specific to the experience of adult mental illness mentioned. In their review of existing research, Richardson et al. (2010) focused on grief, which has been found to be a significant aspect of parents' subjective burden. They note that:

> Parents' grief may be associated with a profound sense of loss; loss of their premorbid, healthier child, loss of hopes and dreams for their child's future, loss of former familial relationships, loss of perceived parental competence and loss of security and certainty. (p. 29)

In addition to the possible negative consequences of such grief, the authors do also note that grief may be less severe when the relationship between the parent and the child is characterized as having a secure attachment style.

MacFarlane (2011) proposes that family centered care has the potential to achieve the best outcomes for both the person with a mental illness and his or her family. While noting both the significant burden experienced by the family of a mentally ill person as well as the benefits for the patient of support by the family, the latter is focused on only as a means to enhance the former, without mention of family resilience. One can infer, however, that when the family is supported appropriately by the mental health system it is more likely to manifest resilience.

Parental Mental Illness

The following quote speaks to the impact of being raised by a parent with mental illness: "An adult offspring wrote about 'my loss of a healthy mother, a normal childhood, and a stable home" (Marsh & Lefley, 1996, p. 3). Similarly, according to another adult:

> My father's paranoid schizophrenia meant we moved frequently, because he felt the conspiracy was closing in on him. He battered my mother, because he felt she was part of the conspiracy. I was too frightened to go to her aid. I couldn't have friendships with peers because my father felt they might 'poison' my mind against him. (Marsh & Lefley, 1996, p. 4)

Relative to the experiences described above, three articles focused on families in which a parent was mentally ill. Dunn (1993) interviewed nine adults regarding their experience of growing up with a mother who was psychotic. She notes previous research indicating that confusion, isolation, and pain characterize the childhood of those in this situation, indicating they are at risk both genetically and environmentally. That is, the child's development may be impacted by inadequate or inappropriate interactions in the relationship with the parent with a mental illness; problems in the marital relationship; tensions between other members of the family; lack of social connections and supports; fear of being harmed; and financial problems. The themes the author identified in her analysis of the data included abuse and neglect at the hands of the mother; isolation within the family as well as from friends and families; guilt and loyalty issues; negative experiences in contacts with the mental health system; and supportive relationships with others outside the family. At the same time, "as children, study participants described consciously overcoming feelings of shyness, feeling of being different from other, and fear of reprisal from their mother in order to put themselves in safe and affirming situations with supportive peers and adults" (p. 186), and as adults, all but one had sought therapy for themselves, were working, and had satisfactory relationships with others. Pinpointing the dynamics of their resilience, however, was beyond the purview of this study.

Drawing from an "urban, low-income, and predominately ethnic minority" sample, Mowbray, Bybee, Oyserman, MacFarlane, and Bowersox, (2006, p. 3) interviewed 157 women with serious mental illness who had at least one adult child. A large majority (approximately 80%) of the adult children, who ranged in age from 18 to 30, were reported by their mothers to be either working, going to school, or receiving some kind of training. Most mothers indicated that their relationships with their adult children, 70% of whom lived nearby, were satisfactory. At the same time, other findings were not so favorable:

- About one-third of the adult children had not completed high school
- Fifty-four percent had a major psychological, drug or alcohol, or legal problem
- Only 12% of the 40% who had young children were in a committed relationship

Therefore, given the psychosocial risks for children of mothers with a mental illness, particularly bipolar disorder, the authors recommend that greater attention by professionals be given to the parenting behaviors of their female patients.

Finally, Zeman and Bulia (2008) studied the practice wisdom of 36 social work professionals relative to their work with custodial parents diagnosed with a mental illness. The authors note that with the mental health reform movement came the right, previously denied, of parents with a mental illness to retain custody of their children if they so chose. Given this reversal in approaches, they advocate the use of a strengths perspective when attempting to understand and work with members of this group. Such a choice is based on prior research indicating that, "fulfilling the parenting role has a positive impact. It serves as a part of the custodial parents' recovery from their mental illness and supports their higher level of functioning to the extent that parents thrive" (p. 54). Zeman and Bulia's findings indicated that resilience for both parent and child was fostered by their attachment to one another as well as by the parents' ability to make a distinction between their own and their child's experiences. The participants also noted that social support, particularly from extended family members, was critical. Relative to family functioning, it was felt that children who took on some of the parenting responsibilities often became more independent, although estrangement could occur when the parent was symptomatic. Further, for custodial parents, self-care often improves at the same time that treatment may be avoided in order for the parents to maintain the relationships they have established with their children. The conclusion is that individuals with mental illness also may be effective as parents, especially when there is a focus on strengths and potentials.

Current Issues

A major issue that I believe is in need of further attention is the prevalence of mental illness, which in and of itself poses significant challenges for society. These challenges are magnified in a context of less than adequate support from the health care system. This situation, in turn, has lead to an increase in the roles and responsibilities of the family as well as the burden that these roles and responsibilities entail. However, despite the importance of the family in terms of both caregiving and patient progress, "Research repeatedly demonstrates that families of adults experiencing mental illness are routinely ignored or excluded from the assessment and treatment process" (MacFarlane, 2011, p. 59).

A second major issue from my perspective, therefore, is the need for inclusion of the family in treatment protocols, and such protocols should go beyond a focus on support for the person diagnosed with a mental disorder. While support for the patient certainly is essential, so also is support for the family. Despite the rather modest attention that social scientists have given to family resilience relative to mental health challenges, it is clear that both patients and families have the potential to learn and grow from their shared experiences. As they do so, everyone, including the larger society benefits.

However, an old, and yet still current, larger issue is a function of the American ideological context (Becvar, 1984). That is, part of the tradition that we in the US hold most dear is a belief in individualism (Becvar & Becvar, 2009). Consistent with this value, the individual rather than the family or the community has for centuries been at the heart of all our social and political speculation. Indeed, although in the US family issues often generate a great deal of conversation and controversy, ours is not primarily a family-oriented society. In part as a function of the emphasis on individualism, we are one of the few industrialized nations in the world that does not have a coherent family policy. What we do have is a fragmented patchwork of often contradictory policies that leave much to be desired in terms of support for families. Consistent with a predominant fear of big government, money is allocated to states, which are responsible for creating policies, and states very in terms of the money received and how it is spent.

In addition and perhaps related, in this country the predominant orientation at all levels, from policy makers to practitioners, has been to operate as error-activated systems, responding to crises when they occur, and being concerned primarily with problems and pathology rather than with prevention and health (Becvar, 1984). Thus, as Patterson (2002b, p. 233) has noted, "we have a long history of focusing on the causes of disease, deficits, and behavioral problems." We do not have such a history when it comes to thinking about prevention. With these issues in mind, we turn now to a consideration of the ramifications for clinicians.

Clinical Implications

Blair (2003) describes a model aimed at fostering family resilience in general created by Richardson, Neiger, Jensen, and Kumpher (1990). According to this model, families that are dealing with a crisis go through stages of reintegration—dysfunctional, maladaptive, and homeostatic—that eventually may culminate in the manifestation of resilience as they reach a level of reintegration greater than before the crisis occurred. Blair builds on this model, suggesting that families generally progress from lower to higher levels of reintegration in the process of coping with various challenges, and during this process may at times become stuck before achieving resilient reintegration. Helping clients along the way involves making connections with each family member and facilitating their understanding of each other's perceptions; encouraging collaboration among family members; promoting the expression of emotions as appropriate; acknowledging individual and family strengths; and supporting the process of meaning-making throughout.

Ungar (2010) offers a "social ecological model of resilience" (p. 432), which emphasizes the need for sensitivity to context and culture when creating strategies with and for clients. Accordingly, therapists encourage client engagement by ensuring the availability of and access to resources as well as by advocating for clients and helping them to advocate for themselves. In addition, therapists choose interventions that are meaningful to the client, and as appropriate, adapt them to meet the unique needs of each client system.

Focusing more specifically, Mendenhall and Mount (2011) describe the varying formats of psychoeducation that may be available to families with a mentally ill child. They indicate that all are focused on the needs of the caregiver in an effort to improve family health and functioning. It is their conclusion that, "To alleviate family strain, increase caregiver enrichment, and improve chances of child recovery, practitioners working with children with mental illness should incorporate not only caregivers but also siblings and extended family into a family-focused, strengths based treatment when appropriate" (p. 188).

Similarly, MacFarlane (2011, p. 59) notes that many agencies are adopting a family centered care approach, one that "takes advantage of the many benefits of family involvement and also offers needed support to families with a mentally ill member." Such an approach focuses on creating respectful, collaborative partnerships characterized by open communication and accommodation of the unique culture of each client and his or her family. Families are given appropriate support, information, and education in order to enable them to function more effectively.

As part of their emphasis on a strengths based approach, Zeman and Bulia (2008) recommend "focusing assessments and interventions involving custodial parents with mental illness on identifying existing family patterns of resilience, social support, family functioning, self-care, and their experience of the symptoms" (p. 61). Such an approach enables full participation by everyone involved in the recovery process, as well as the experience of caring relationships and high expectations, all of which are significant protective factors relative to resilience in the context of mental illness. While such a strength-based approach certainly makes sense, Dunn (1993) adds the suggestion that the children of a parent or parents with mental illness may benefit from both age appropriate information about the illness and participation in multiple family support groups. She further cautions therapists regarding the loyalty conflicts and guilt such children may experience as well as the need to help the parents become more effective. Noting the importance of external supports, she suggests that clinicians encourage these children to create meaningful relationships with extended family members, school personnel, friends, and the families of friends.

As the various studies considered in this chapter indicate, the potential for resilience certainly exists and may be enhanced through a sensitive understanding of what the family is experiencing, and an emphasis on normalizing typical reactions (Marsh & Johnson, 1997). A focus on the strengths and skills of everyone involved also is important, as is the need to offer education regarding the illness, the mental health system, and available resources. Enhancing skills in the areas of effective communication, problem-solving, and managing stress, in addition to resolving feelings of grief and loss are all crucial.

Throughout the process of attempting to facilitate resilience it is critical that clinicians respect structural, cultural, and contextual variations in families. It is also important to be aware that family members do better when they understand how to deal with the symptoms of mental illness and are able to respond appropriately when a relapse appears to be imminent. Indeed, a supportive family environment in which expectations are realistic and the needs of all members are recognized and accommodated bodes well for the emergence of resilience in the face of serious mental illness.

However, although we have begun to learn more about this topic, there remains a great deal of room for additional research to enhance understanding and guide practice, which is the topic of the section that follows.

Research Implications

There appear to be many aspects of resilience relative to mental illness that are in need of attention by researchers. For example, in their study of adult children of parents with severe mental illness, Mowbray et al. (2006) found that, "Mother's bipolar disorder was a significant independent predictor of adult child problems, controlling for child age, gender, and race" (p. 106). However, following a review of the literature they noted the absence of, as well as the need for, studies that compare the effects on adult children of different diagnoses, and those that seek explanations for the more negative outcomes that may occur in the context of a parental bipolar disorder. I would also infer from such findings and conclusions that more research that focuses on the best ways to facilitate resilience relative to specific mental illness diagnoses is needed. Similarly, Brown et al. (2010) take note of the limited amount of research on family resilience relative to childhood ADD/ADHD as well as the need for greater attention in this area.

Richardson et al. (2010), who reviewed the literature on parental grief in response to adult child mental illness, also found very few studies that considered this issue. Of those found, a variety of methodological issues of concern were identified. These included an emphasis on cross-sectional rather than longitudinal studies; the ethnic homogeneity of participants; recruitment of participants from support groups; and the frequent use of measurement instruments that had not been validated. In addition to ameliorating such issues, the authors also note the need for research that examines the theories of grief and loss that are most applicable and relevant for this population; a focus on the impact on parents of mental illness in a young child; and the risk factors for such parents. I would add to this list the need for greater attention to protective factors and the facilitation of resilience.

Mendenhall and Mount (2011), who considered both risk factors and parental enhancement in families with a mentally ill child, share a concern similar to that of Richardson et al. (2010). Mendenhall and Mount (p. 183) note that, "The research on caregiver strain and burden focuses mainly on caring for adult children with mental illness, children with chronic illness, or the elderly." The lack of research related to having a child with mental illness occurs despite the fact that approximately 10.7% of parents in the general population are dealing with the burdens associated with such a situation. The authors indicate further that very little attention has been devoted to "caregiver enrichment" as a function of caring for a mentally ill child.

Although there certainly has been an increase in studies focusing on strengths and potentials for growth as opposed to problems and pathology, Saunders (2003) also describes a lack of attention relative to cultural sensitivity when helping families with a mentally ill member. She cites questions in need of attention related to cross-cultural variations, specifically as related to ethnic minority populations; the need for psychoeducational models that are culturally and socially sensitive; and an expansion of studies related to both caregiver burden and caregiver resilience. Relative to the latter concern, longitudinal studies of the long-term impact of mental illness on caregivers and their changing needs for support over time are also needed.

Indeed, there seems to be a great deal of room for research related to all aspects of resilience. The findings of future studies, in turn, might provide important information for professionals who work with mentally ill patients/clients and their families. I would suggest further that always there needs to be awareness on the part of both researchers and clinicians of the potential for positive outcomes and for the manifestation of resilience in such families, as illustrated in the following case example.

Case Example

Over the years I have worked with the Owens family on several occasions, typically with long periods in between when my services were not deemed necessary because they were doing well on their own. When they first came to see me, Marjorie (66) and Stan (70) sought assistance related to dealing with their youngest child, Sam (age 36), who at 20 had been diagnosed with schizophrenia. Sam had responded well to medication up to that point, with only minor setbacks, which his parents had been able to manage with the help of Sam's psychiatrist as well as the support of various social services and other family members. Sam had been employed in a sheltered workshop for several years and even had long periods of time when he was able to live on his own. However, at the time of our first meeting, he had had a serious relapse and needed to be hospitalized. It seems that Sam had been feeling so well that he decided to go off his medication. His psychotic symptoms returned, as did his bizarre behaviors. However, after a fairly brief stay in the hospital and some adjustments in his medication he seemed to be doing much better.

As the time of discharge was fast approaching, and it looked like Sam would now be living with Marjorie and Stan, at least for a little while, they wanted my assistance in planning for the next chapter in their lives. In addition, Sam's siblings, Charles (age 38), Barbara (age 40), and Albert (age 42) were frustrated about the situation and fearful regarding the toll that constant caregiving was going to take on their aging parents. This situation was complicated by the fact that none of the three older children lived nearby, although they did visit as often as they could, which seemed to be helpful.

Over the next several months Marjorie and Stan and I worked together to establish regular routines and rules for Sam, including medication supervision and expectations regarding appropriate behaviors, particularly related to hygiene and relationships with his parents and siblings. Sam also was assisted by his case worker to pursue and make arrangements to return to his previous employment at the sheltered workshop. At the same time, the parents and I brainstormed together regarding housing options and I encouraged Marjorie and Stan to seek alternative living arrangements for Sam. I also helped them access information on the internet regarding signs of an impending relapse so they could seek medical attention immediately if and when they became apparent.

Although we had a few brief encounters over the next 10 years, always along the same lines, the couple reported that they were doing well and seemed to be handling various challenges effectively. Sam had been placed in a community supported group home and his parents continued to have frequent contact with him. He was once again employed and seemed to be managing satisfactorily. After 10 years, however, I was contacted again. Several months prior to their call, Sam had had another relapse with subsequent hospitalization, and while in the hospital it was recognized that he had some cognitive impairment. Marjorie and Stan therefore had decided to have him move back in with them once he was discharged. Although their intentions were the best and they had worked well together to support Sam, the caregiving roles and responsibilities, along with Sam's erratic behavior, were taking a toll on their relationship. In addition, Sam's three older siblings and their families were refusing to visit because of his behavior, and they also had become even more concerned about their parents. Marjorie and Stan also were worried about what would happen after they died and wanted to plan for Sam's care while they still could.

I had several suggestions for Marjorie and Stan, which they soon put into practice. I felt very strongly that the couple needed some time to be able to focus on each other and their relationship without Sam and his care as the only topic of conversation. After conducting a search they were able to locate an assisted living center that would provide affordable respite care for Sam on an as needed basis, and the couple agreed to take advantage of it regularly, and especially during holidays when other family members would be visiting. While Sam was away, they were to do some of their favorite activities together. Then, in order to make the rest of the time go more smoothly, I encouraged them to give Sam some simple household responsibilities that ideally would help to improve his self-esteem and their relationship with him as he made a contribution to the family. I also suggested that they locate a support group for Sam, which they did with the help of NAMI. Finally, during the next holiday gathering I suggested that they hold a family meeting to plan for Sam's future.

At the family meeting, during which Sam was at the assisted living center, Stan explained his financial situation and preparations relative to his son's future care. He then expressed the need for Sam's siblings to take over the responsibility for finding a place where Sam could live that was close enough to one of them so that regular contact and monitoring could be maintained. Charles, Sam's next oldest sibling, who is a lawyer, agreed to do so. He lived midway between Barbara and Albert and felt comfortable handing the financial arrangements. Each of the others agreed to help whenever needed and would arrange to visit on a rotating regular basis.

A check up several months later revealed that Marjorie and Stan had regained the stability and pleasure that had been the primary characteristic of their long-term marriage. The arrangements for Sam had eased their minds tremendously and his contributions to the family had improved his relationships with his parents. Sam was back at his job on a part-time basis and seemed to be doing quite well, all things considered.

Conclusion

There is no question that the challenges faced by families with a mentally ill member are many and typically they are relentless, with their severity often, but not always, increasing over the lifespan (Segal, Qualls, & Smyer, 2011). Nevertheless, such families can and do evidence resilience, as demonstrated in various research studies and illustrated in the above case example. However, it is probably fair to surmise that resilience is more likely to occur when these families are supported appropriately. This includes the need for professionals to have as full an awareness as possible of the various risk and protective factors relative to families in this category.

At the same time, it is important to note that, even when available, not every family has the requisite knowledge and ability to access services and resources in the way that Marjorie and Stan were able to do. And not every family would have other members who would heed the call for help as readily as did Sam's siblings. Nevertheless, the adoption of a resilience perspective by professionals would increase the likelihood of its occurrence and there is no doubt that more families with a mentally ill member would be able to handle the associated challenges in a manner that enabled them to thrive, rather than just survive.

References

Abelanda, J., & Helfrlich, C. A. (2003). Family resilience and mental illness: The role of occupational therapy. *Occupational Therapy in Mental Health, 19*(1), 25–39.

Bateson, G., Jackson, D. D., Haley, J., & Weakland, J. (1956). Toward a theory of schizophrenia. *Behavioral Science, 1*, 251–264.

Becvar, D. S. (1984). *The family and society in the context of American society: A systems theoretical perspective.* Unpublished doctoral dissertation, St. Louis University, St. Louis, MO.

Becvar, D. S. (2007). *Families that flourish: Facilitating resilience in clinical practice.* New York: W. W. Norton.

Becvar, D. S., & Becvar, R. J. (2009). *Family therapy: A systemic integration* (7th ed.). Boston: Allyn & Bacon.

Blair, R. G. (2003). Understanding and fostering family resilience. *Family Preservation Journal, 7*, 43–56.

Brown, O., Howcroft, G., & Muthen, T. (2010). Resilience in families living with a child diagnosed with hyperactivity/attention deficit disorder. *South African Journal of Psychology, 40*(3), 338–350.

Cohen, L., Ferguson, C., Harms, C., Pooley, J. A., & Tomlinson, S. (2011). Family systems and mental health issues: A resilience approach. *Journal of Social Work Practice, 25*(1), 109–125.

Cohen, A. N., Glynn, S. M., Murray-Swank, A. B., Barrio, C., Fischer, E. P., McCutcheon, S. J., et al. (2008). The family forum: Directions for the implementation of family psychoeducation for severe mental illness. *Psychiatric Services, 59*(1), 40–48.

Colom, F., Vieta, E., Sánchez-Moreno, J., Palomino-Otiniano, R., Reinares, M., Goikolea, J. M., et al. (2009). Group psychoeducation for stabilized bipolar disorders: 5-Year outcome of a randomized clinical trial. *The British Journal of Psychiatry, 194*, 260–265.

Conger, R. D., & Conger, K. J. (2002). Resilience in midwestern families: Selected findings from the first decade of a prospective, longitudinal study. *Journal of Marriage and Family, 64*, 361–373.

De Haan, L., Hawley, D. R., & Deal, J. F. (2002). Operationalizing family resilience: A methodological strategy. *American Journal of Family Therapy, 30*, 275–291.

Dunn, B. (1993). Growing up with a psychotic mother. *The American Journal of Orthopsychiatry, 63*(2), 177–189.

González-Pinto, A., Ruiz de Azúa, S., Ibáñez, B., Otero-Cuesta, S., Castro-Fornieles, J., Graell-Berna, M., et al. (2011). Can positive family factors be protective against the development of psychosis? *Psychiatry Research, 186*, 28–33.

Haggan, P. (2002). Family resilience through sports: The family as a team. *The Journal of Individual Psychology, 58*(3), 279–289.

Hawley, D. R., & DeHaan, L. (1996). Toward a definition of family resilience: Integrating life-span and family Perspectives. *Family Process, 35*, 283–298.

Hoenig, J., & Hamilton, M. (1966). The schizophrenic patient in the community and his effect on the household. *The International Journal of Social Psychiatry, 12*, 165–176.

Jewell, T. C., Downing, D., & McFarlane, W. C. (2009). Partnering with families: Multiple family group psychoeducation for schizophrenia. *Journal of Clinical Psychology, 65*(8), 868–878.

Jonker, L., & Greeff, A. P. (2009). Resilience factors in families living with people with mental illness. *Journal of Community Psychology, 37*(7), 859–873.

Kessler, R. C., Berglund, P., Demler, O., Jin, R., Merikangas, K. R., & Walters, E. E. (2005). Lifetime prevalence and age-of-onset distributions of *DSM-IV* disorders in the national comorbidity survey replication. *Archives of General Psychiatry, 62*, 593–602.

Kessler, R. C., Chiu, W. T., Demler, O., & Walters, E. E. (2005). Prevalence, severity, and comorbidity of 12-month *DSM-IV* disorders in the national comorbidity survey replication. *Archives of General Psychiatry, 62*, 617–627.

Kragh, J. R., & Huber, C. H. (2002). Family resilience and domestic violence: Panacea or pragmatic therapeutic perspective? *The Journal of Individual Psychology, 58*(3), 290–304.

Lefley, H. P. (2010). Treating difficult cases in a psychoeducational family support group for serious mental illness. *Journal of Family Psychotherapy, 21*, 253–268.

MacFarlane, M. M. (2011). Family centered care in adult mental health: Developing a collaborative interagency practice. *Journal of Family Psychotherapy, 22*(1), 56–73.

Marsh, D. T. (1992). *Families and mental illness: New directions in professional practice.* New York: Praeger.

Marsh, D. T., & Johnson, D. L. (1997). The family experience of mental illness: Implications for intervention. *Professional Psychology: Research and Practice, 28*(3), 229–237.

Marsh, D. T., & Lefley, H. P. (1996). The family experience of mental illness: Evidence for resilience. *Psychiatric Rehabilitation Journal, 20*(2), 3–13.

Mendenhall, A. N., & Mount, K. (2011). Parents of children with mental illness: Exploring the caregiver experience and caregiver-focused interventions. *Families in society: The Journal of Contemporary Social Services, 92*(2), 183–190.

Mowbray, C. T., Bybee, D., Oyserman, D., MacFarlane, P., & Bowersox, N. (2006). Psychosocial outcomes for adult children of parents with severe mental illness: Demographic and clinical history predictors. *Health and Social Work, 31*(2), 99–108.

National Institute of Mental Health. (2008). *Prevalence of serious mental illness among U.S. adults by age, sex, and race* [*Website*]. Retrieved October 25, 2011, from http://www.nimh.nih.gov/statistics/SMI_AASR.shtml.

Oswald, R. F. (2002). Resilience within the family networks of lesbians and gay men: Intentionality and redefinition. *Journal of Marriage and Family, 64*, 374–383.

Patterson, J. M. (2002a). Integrating family resilience and family stress theory. *Journal of Marriage and Family, 64*, 349–360.

Patterson, J. M. (2002b). Understanding family resilience. *Journal of Clinical Psychology, 58*(3), 233–246.

Richardson, M., Cobham, V., Murray, J., & McDermott, B. (2010). Parents' grief in the context of adult mental illness: A qualitative review. *Clinical Child and Family Psychology Review, 14*, 28–43.

Richardson, G., Neiger, B., Jensen, S., & Kumpher, K. (1990). The resiliency model. *Health Education, 21*(6), 33–39.

Roberts, N. H., & Escoto, E. R. (2002). "Our child won't go to bed!": A functional assessment and intervention from a family resilience perspective. *Journal of Individual Psychology, 58*(3), 245–249.

Sandau-Beckler, P. A., Devall, E., & de La Rosa, I. A. (2002). Strengthening family resilience: Prevention and treatment for high-risk substance-affected families. *The Journal of Individual Psychology, 58*(3), 306–327.

Saunders, J. C. (2003). Families living with severe mental illness: A literature review. *Issues in Mental Health Nursing, 24*, 175–198.

Schwartz, J. P. (2002). Family resilience and pragmatic parent education. *The Journal of Individual Psychology, 58*(3), 250–262.

Segal, D. L., Qualls, S. H., & Smyer, M. A. (2011). *Aging and mental health* (2nd ed.). West Sussex, UK: Wiley-Blackwell.

Stroman, D. (2003). *The disability rights movement: From deinstitutionalisation to self-determination.* Lanham, MD: University Press of America.

Ungar, M. (2010). Families as navigators and negotiators: Facilitating culturally and contextually specific expressions of resilience. *Family Process, 49*(3), 421–435.

Walsh, F. (1998). *Strengthening family resilience.* New York: Guilford.

Walsh, F. (2003). Family resilience: A framework for clinical practice. *Family Process, 42*(1), 1–18.

World Health Organization. (2005). *Mental health atlas 2005: Global results.* [Adobe Digital Editions version]. Retrieved October 25, 2011, from http://www.who.int/mental_health/evidence/atlas/global_results.pdf.

World Health Organization. (2011). *Mental health atlas 2011.* [Adobe Digital Editions version]. Retrieved October 25, 2011, from http://whqlibdoc.who.int/publications/2011/9799241564359_eng.pdf.

Wynne, L. C., Ryckoff, I. M., Day, J., & Hirsch, S. I. (1958). Pseudomutuality in the family relations of schizophrenics. *Psychiatry, 21*, 205–220.

Zeman, L. D., & Bulia, S. (2008). Practice wisdom on custodial parenting with mental illness: A strengths view. *Journal of Family Social Work, 10*(3), 51–65.

Strengthening Family Resilience Through Spiritual and Religious Resources

25

Karen Caldwell and Karolyn Senter

Introduction/Background

How do families not only survive but thrive when faced with adversity, hardship, loss, or trauma? What processes of endurance, growth, meaning-making, and healing are at the heart of resilience? Walsh (1998) defines resilience as "the capacity to rebound from adversity strengthened and more resourceful... the qualities of resilience enable people to heal from painful wounds, take charge of their lives, and go on to live fully and love well" (p. 4). Spirituality and religion can be significant resources in individual and family resilience. A spiritual or religious worldview provides beliefs, values, practices, and relationships that can strengthen resilience. These powerful forces also can increase suffering and block recovery, making it vital to understand their processes and influences on individuals and families.

Definition of Spirituality Contrasted with Religion

Spirituality and religion are complex, multidimensional phenomena, and no simple definition can suffice for either. They are so intertwined that until the twentieth century, religion and spirituality were not considered to be separate things (Wulff, 1997). Scholars have proposed several alternative explanations for this development. One explanation is that the rise in secularism and growing disillusionment with religious institutions, particularly in Western societies, during the 1960s and 1970s resulted in spirituality acquiring distinct meanings and connotations as separate from religion (Turner, Lukoff, Barnhouse, & Lu, 1995). For example, some individuals consider themselves spiritual although they are not affiliated with a particular religious group. Another explanation involves the "deinstitutionalization of religious reality" (p. 14) in the world views of Western people (Hunter, 1983).

One particularly useful definition of religion is offered by Koenig, McCullough, and Larson (2001). They write that religion is:

K. Caldwell (✉)
Appalachian State University,
North Carolina, USA
e-mail: caldwllkl@appstate.edu

K. Senter
Washington University, St. Louis, MO, USA

D.S. Becvar (ed.), *Handbook of Family Resilience*,
DOI 10.1007/978-1-4614-3917-2_25, © Springer Science+Business Media New York 2013

...an organized system of beliefs, practices, rituals, and symbols designed (a) to facilitate closeness to the sacred or transcendent (God, higher power, or ultimate truth/reality) and (b) to foster an understanding of one's relationship and responsibility to others in living together in a community. (p. 18)

By contrast, spirituality is understood as an overarching construct, "a dimension of human experience involving an active investment in transcendent values and practices" (Walsh, Balint, Smolira, Fredericksen, & Madsen, 2009, p. 601). Similarly, Aponte (2002) has defined spirituality as, "The transcendent aspect of life that gives to our lives meaning (philosophy and/or theology), morality (ethics and/or virtue and sin), and spiritual practice and community (social network and/or faith community along with the spiritually transcendent)" (p. 282). In consideration of these components, it is clear that spirituality can be experienced both inside and outside of religious affiliation.

Significance of the Topic

Religion plays a role in the identity of most adults in the U.S. with fully 84% still identifying with a major religion (Newport, 2010). The diversity of religious and spiritual orientations practiced in the U. S. includes over a dozen major religious traditions, which can be subdivided into hundreds of distinct religious groups (Pew Forum on Religion & Public Life, 2008). About 65% of U. S. adults have labeled themselves "religious and spiritual," 15–20% label themselves "spiritual but not religious," and 5–10% indicate they are "religious but not spiritual" (Marler & Hadaway, 2002). Further, a trend towards spiritual pluralism is increasingly part of the religious and cultural mix of the U. S. today (Walsh, 2010).

Harold Koenig (1999) reviewed hundreds of research studies on the impact of religion on health. His findings were surprising to clinicians who believed, with Freud and others, that religion is like "a poison" (Freud, 1927, p. 88). Koenig concluded that people involved in mainstream religious groups live longer, have fewer strokes, less heart disease, better immune function, and lower blood pressures. In fact, *not* having religious involvement has a negative effect on mortality. Rates of drug abuse, alcoholism, divorce, and suicide were lower among religiously involved individuals compared to the population at large. Other reviewers of the literature have drawn similar conclusions. For example, Worthington, Kurusu, McCullough, and Sandage (1996) concluded that people who practice religion are less likely to suffer from depression and anxiety than the population at large. When they do develop these conditions, they recover more quickly.

What are the processes through which religious and spiritual belief could provide these health benefits? Koenig (2005) identified a number of pathways by which religious belief and practice could improve mental health. Religious beliefs promote a positive worldview, help make sense of difficult situations, give purpose and meaning, enhance social support, promote other—directedness, help release the need for control, encourage forgiveness and thankfulness, and provide hope. These processes can provide benefits to individuals, families, and their communities. What is more, several religious practices have been linked to positive physical health benefits. Meditation, prayer, and participation in devotional services have been associated with lower levels of anxiety and depression, higher self-esteem, better interpersonal relationships, and a more positive outlook on life (Koenig, 2005).

Literature Review

From a socio-ecological perspective, both individual's qualities of resilience as well as those of the family and environmental systems are important and mutually interconnected influences (Bronfenbrenner, 1979). Much of the resilience literature has focused on the individual level of resilience, although studies of family resilience have become more prevalent accompanied by a strength-focused approach to clinical services (Walsh, 2003). For example, early researchers of resilience in children focused on personal traits of resilience such as emotional and behavioral regulation and self-mastery, but predictors of resilience also included effective parenting, prosocial peer relationships, and access to community resources (Masten, 2004).

However, stressors and crises impact the entire family, not just individual family members. Protective processes foster resilience while maladaptive responses increase vulnerability and risk for individual and family distress. There are multiple pathways to resilience, and cultural and contextual factors are keys to understanding which individuals and families will overcome adversity and which will fall apart. Accordingly, religious and spiritual beliefs are best understood in their cultural context. For example, research on the diverse group of Latinos in the U.S. has emphasized the importance of the cultural tradition of *familism,* which includes the obligation to take care of nuclear and extended family members (Bermúdez, Kirkpatrick, Hecker, & Torres-Robles, 2010; Padilla & Villalobos, 2007). Among a number of protective factors that have been identified as contributing to family resilience (Benzies & Mychasiuk, 2009), those that are influenced by spiritual and religious resources include stable family structures with intimate-partner relationship stability, family cohesion, supportive parent–child interactions, social support, and the ability to cope with crises effectively.

Stable Family Structures and Family Cohesion

Several themes and trends emerge from literature reviews of peer-reviewed research on the role of religion and spirituality in family relationships (Mahoney, 2010; Marks, 2006). However, methodological issues constrain the conclusions that can be drawn from research published since the 1980s. Most of the studies relied on one or two items, such as religious attendance or general importance of religion, to assess family members' religiosity. These global indices of individual religiousness yield small differences between groups. Future studies with conceptually based and fine-grained measures of spiritual beliefs and practices could better describe what aspects of religion and spirituality sustain family resilience.

A consistent theme in the literature is that greater religiousness facilitates the formation and maintenance of family relationships, but very little research exists on how religion may help or harm distressed or clinic-referred families. Another methodological issue is the lack of family and religious diversity in published research. Most study samples are of White, traditional, two parent families identified as Christian, or Latter Day Saint. Very little research on the relationship between religion and family resilience has included nonnuclear families, interfaith families, non-Christian religions such as Judaism and Islam, or families of color (Mahoney, 2010; Marks, 2006).

Despite these limitations in research design, the construct of "religion" has emerged as a statistically significant factor in numerous studies. Stable intimate-partner relationships have been identified repeatedly as fostering family resilience. Religious attendance or items rating religion as important have been linked to increased marital satisfaction and lower risk of divorce, as well as lower rates of infidelity and domestic violence (Mahoney, 2010). In addition, religious activities such as shared religious holiday rituals and home-based family worship have been linked with marital satisfaction, higher commitment to marriage, and increased family satisfaction (Marks, 2006). There is some evidence that there may be a self-selection factor operating in these studies, that is, marriage-centered persons may be more likely to be religiously involved because most religions are marriage and family oriented. For example, a 12-year longitudinal study by Booth, Johnson, Branaman, and Sica (1995) found that marital satisfaction frequently precedes religious involvement.

Data linking religious involvement with marital benefits are based on same-faith marriages, while studies of interfaith marriages report higher divorce rates than for same-faith couples. Interfaith couples form a significant and growing percentage of married couples. A recent survey found that 27% of married people are in religiously mixed marriages, a figure that rises to 37% if marriage between different Protestant religious groups is included (Pew Forum on Religion & Public Life, 2008). Couples in which spouses are dissimilar in religious attendance and biblical interpretations were found to have higher levels of conflict, particularly over money and housework (Curtis & Ellison, 2002). In the rare situation (7.5%) in which marked differences exist in spouses' biblical beliefs, Ellison, Bartkowski, and Anderson (1999) found that conservative men married to more liberal women were more likely to be aggressive than men married to women with similar biblical beliefs.

Specific spiritual practices also have been studied for their influence on family relationships (Mahoney, 2010; Marks, 2006). Several studies of the role of prayer in managing conflict have found positive effects on communication processes such as perspective taking and reduced emotional negativity for both married people and for college students who are dating (Butler, Stout, & Gardner, 2002; Fincham, Beach, Lambert, Stillman, & Braithwaite, 2008). On the other hand, several studies also suggest that the use of private prayer can be destructive to the marital relationship if a spouse detours anger towards the spouse onto God or if spouses align with God against each other to win verbal disagreements (Gardner, Butler, & Seedall, 2008; Marsh & Dallos, 2000). Prayer and subjective spiritual growth also have been found to be unrelated to infidelity (Atkins & Kessel, 2008). One study found that compulsory family worship may be more detrimental for children than no family worship at all (Lee, Rice, & Gillespie, 1997).

Parent–Child Relationships

The relationships between parenting processes and religious beliefs have been the focus of numerous studies (Mahoney, 2010). One consistent theme from the literature is that spiritual beliefs consistent with a conservative Protestant ideology are associated with the use of corporal punishment, while other spiritual views on parenting increase other disciplinary strategies. Concern that biblically conservative parents are excessively authoritarian has been offset by Wilcox's (1998) national survey that tied biblical conservatism to greater parent physical affection towards children.

Several studies have found a relationship between higher religious attendance and greater parental physical affection towards children. This implies that diverse religious traditions offer spiritual resources that facilitate positive parenting in nondistressed families. Three rigorous longitudinal studies found that greater general religiousness appears to lower the risk of child physical abuse (Brown, Cohen, Johnson, & Salzinger, 1998; Carothers, Borkowski, Lefever, & Whitman, 2005; Cox, Kotch, & Everson, 2003). Studies of low-income or minority mothers also have found that higher general religiousness correlated with lower parental distress and positive parenting practices (Cain, 2007; Carothers et al., 2005; Dumas & Nissley-Tsiopinis, 2006; Hill, Burdette, Regnerus, & Angel, 2008; McEvoy et al., 2005; Sparks, Peterson, & Tangenberg, 2005; Wiley, Warren, & Montanelli, 2002). An additional consistent theme in the literature is that greater individual religiousness of a parent or adolescent predicts greater satisfaction in the adolescent–parent relationship (Regnerus & Burdette, 2006; Snider, Clements, & Vazsonyi, 2004).

Spiritual Coping and Family Crises

Most studies on spirituality and religious coping have focused on individual coping mechanisms. Positive religious coping involves a secure relationship with God, a belief that there is meaning in life, spiritual connectedness with others, and forgiveness (Pargament, 1997). Negative religious coping involves a less secure relationship with God, a tenuous or ominous view of the world, interpersonal religious discontent, and appraisal of God's power as malevolent. Studies of spiritual methods of coping with natural disasters and illness report that maladaptive spiritual coping is less common than adaptive spiritual coping (Pargament, 1997, 2007). However, maladaptive spiritual coping consistently predicts poor outcomes. While religious and spiritual coping with nonfamily related crises has been studied extensively, very little research has examined how specific spiritual beliefs and behaviors may operate when family crises arise. One study of specific coping methods and parenting found that mothers who experienced struggles with a faith community about parenting or a spiritual struggle with God reported lower parental satisfaction (Dumas & Nissley-Tsiopinis, 2006). In research focused on spiritual coping with the family crisis of domestic violence, a number of qualitative studies have identified specific spiritual coping strategies that can empower victims to leave or reconcile with an offender (Yick, 2008).

Several studies have examined parents' religious and spiritual coping mechanisms in dealing with the death of a child (Brotherson & Soderquist, 2002; Gilbert, 1992; Higgins, 2002; McIntosh, Silver, & Wortman, 1993). Two of these qualitative studies found some couples used positive and some used negative religious coping (Brotherson & Soderquist, 2002; Gilbert, 1992). In a quantitative study with a large sample of parents whose child had died, parents with a belief in an afterlife and frequent church attendance had lower levels of depression after the death of a child (Higgins, 2002). However, other variables such as gender, age, and education had a stronger relationship with depression than religiosity. Another study found that religion, in and of itself, was not associated with better adjustment, but greater participation in religious activities was related to greater social support, which in turn predicted a better adjustment (McIntosh et al., 1993).

Results from studies of the relationship between spiritual coping and the family crisis of divorce imply that divorce may be experienced as a spiritual trauma. Krumrei, Mahoney and Pargament's (2009) study of adults' postdivorce adjustment found most of their sample experienced spiritual struggles with the divorce and used adaptive spiritual coping strategies. In a study of young adults in college who recalled a parental divorce in the prior 5 years, students reported greater psychosocial distress when they also reported having spiritual struggles and when they viewed the divorce as a sacred loss (Warner, Mahoney, & Krumrei, 2009). Students' use of spiritual coping strategies usually identified as positive also was linked to greater current distress. Future research on the religion-family connection clearly needs to examine both specific religious and spiritual processes as well as family processes in diverse family forms, including both distressed and nondistressed families. Indeed, the connection between spiritual and religious resources supporting family resilience appears to be complex.

Current Issues

One of the most significant issues now receiving attention in the realm of spirituality and religion is mindfulness. Mindfulness as a construct studied by Western researchers refers to the ability to attend to present moment experience with a nonjudgmental quality (Kabat-Zinn, 2003). This is in contrast to automatic processing modes of mindlessness in which sensations, thoughts, emotions, and actions go unnoticed. Research in the West on the relationship between mindfulness and health has burgeoned over the past 3 decades beginning with the publication of studies finding positive results for chronic pain sufferers who participated in mindfulness-based stress reduction (MBSR) programs (Kabat-Zinn, 1982). Other programs in mental health treatment that have integrated mindfulness include dialectical behavioral therapy (DBT), mindfulness-based cognitive therapy (MBCT), and acceptance and commitment therapy (ACT). The mindfulness practices in these programs have roots in Buddhist, Christian, and other Eastern meditative traditions although the spiritual and religious foundations of the practices are not necessarily discussed with program participants. This secularization of mindfulness practices has made the treatment models accessible to a wider range of clients than otherwise possible, but there is some question about the ramifications of removing mindfulness practices from their original spiritual/religious context (Dimidjian & Linehan, 2003).

Outcome studies have found mindfulness-based therapies to be effective for a range of human problems including anxiety, personality disorders, eating disorders, and addiction (Greeson, 2009). Dispositional mindfulness and outcomes of mindfulness interventions are consistently associated with a number of measures of emotional well-being. Within the last 10 years, the focus of mindfulness research has expanded to study the potential mechanisms and moderators underlying mindfulness-based treatment outcomes (Lau & Yu, 2009). For example, changes in biologic systems, cognitive mechanisms, and affect regulation are being explored (e.g., Farb et al., 2010; Jha, Stanley, Kiyonaga, Wong, & Gelfand, 2010; Lazar et al., 2005). Mechanisms of action in the inverse relationship between mindfulness and psychological distress include a mediating role for rumination and nonattachment (Coffey & Hartman, 2008; Jain et al., 2007; Ramel, Goldin, Carmona, & McQuaid, 2004), experiential avoidance (Lavender, Jardin, & Anderson, 2009), and cognitive reactivity (Raes, Dewulf, Van Heeringen, & Williams, 2009). Self-regulation of emotions through greater emotional awareness, acceptance, and the ability to correct or improve unpleasant mood states are additional pathways suggested by other researchers (Baer et al., 2008; Feldman, Hayes, Kumar, Greeson, & Laurenceau, 2007).

The self-regulation of emotion, acceptance, and awareness that are associated with mindfulness have powerful implications for family relationships. Preliminary studies support the positive role that mindfulness can have in relationships given the importance of healthy emotional functioning in establishing and maintaining intimacy (Cordova, Gee, & Warren, 2005). Several studies have found mindfulness to be positively associated with secure attachment and negatively correlated with anxious and avoidant attachment in adults (Shaver, Lavy, Saron, & Mikulincer, 2007; Walsh et al., 2009). Wachs and Cordova (2007) found a positive association between mindfulness, marital quality, and the repertoire of emotional skills in a sample of married couples. Mindfulness has been fund to be related to higher relationship satisfaction, greater capacity to respond constructively to relationship stress, and better communication quality in dating college students (Barnes, Brown, Krusemark, Campbell, & Rogge, 2007). A randomized controlled trial of couples participating in a mindfulness-based relationship enhancement program found significant improvements in relationship satisfaction and relationship distress (Carson, Carson, Gill, & Baucom, 2004). Three potential mediating factors for the relationship quality improvements were examined: acceptance, relaxation, and participating in self-expanding activities (Carson, Carson, Gill, & Baucom, 2007). The self-expanding activities surpassed acceptance and relaxation as the principal mediator of the mindfulness-based program.

Connections between attachment theory and research are currently being explored. From his work in interpersonal neurobiology, Siegel (2007) argues that mindfulness training improves brain functioning related to the ability to attune to the behavior and emotions of others. Several researchers have focused on how mindfulness can improve attachment between parents and their children by increasing a parent's ability to regulate emotions and be more emotionally attuned to his or her children (Altmaier & Maloney, 2007; Dumas, 2005; Reynolds, 2003). Initial studies of several clinical programs intended to increase mindfulness in parents have been found to be effective. These include programs for parents and children with autism, developmental disabilities, or attention-deficit/hyperactivity disorder (Singh, et al., 2006, 2007, 2010). A pilot study on integrating mindfulness into a preexisting drug prevention program found greater improvements in parent–adolescent relationships in the mindfulness treatment group compared to two different control groups (Coatsworth, Duncan,

Greenberg, & Nix, 2010). By contrast, a mindfulness parenting program focused on postdivorce parent–child relationships did not find changes in the quality of the parent–child relationship (Altmaier & Maloney, 2007). Cohen and Semple (2010) conclude from their review of the literature on mindful parenting programs that initial evidence supporting their effectiveness is promising, and they call for further research.

Clinical Implications

Given the vital role that spiritual and religious practices play in health and resilience, clinicians are well advised to attend to these issues. A good first step for clinicians is to follow the advice of the aphorism, "Know Thyself." Therapists' own attitudes and experiences with spiritual and religious practices obviously will impact their comfort, confidence, and competence in relating with clients around these issues. Common recommendations for developing therapists' self-awareness related to spiritual and religious issues include acknowledgement of the personal morality and ethics of the therapist as well as development of skills for discussing one's own as well as clients' spiritual and religious influences (Carlson, Erickson, & Seewald-Marquardt, 2002; Haug, 1998; Patterson, Hayworth, Turner, & Raskin, 2000). Recent research results provided tantalizing evidence that the spiritual practice of therapists could impact the outcome of psychotherapy. In a randomized, double-blind, controlled study, the patients of psychotherapists-in-training who practiced Zen meditation showed greater symptom reduction than did a comparison group of patients treated by psychotherapists-in-training who did not meditate (Grepmair et al., 2007).

Knowledge and skills in addressing spiritual and religious issues in clinical practice are developed in the same ways that other multicultural skills grow through information, practice, and supervision. Clinicians are encouraged to become knowledgeable about clients' faith traditions, and maintain an awareness of the growing diversity of cultural and spiritual beliefs that characterize families in the U.S. This includes awareness of how ethnicity and religion can be linked with faulty stereotypes. For example, in contrast to media portrayal of Arab Americans as radical Muslims, most Arab Americans are Christian, and only one-third are Muslim. Most Muslims in the U.S. are largely assimilated and have moderate views on most issues (Pew Forum on Religion & Public Life, 2007).

Approaching clients respectfully involves maintaining awareness of similarity and differences between therapists' and clients' beliefs, practices, and values (Keeling, Dolbin-MacNab, Ford, & Perkins, 2010). Individual beliefs may vary greatly from the majority view. If possible, clinicians are encouraged to develop relationships with the religious or spiritual leaders that clients look to for direction and guidance. Not only may these leaders inform clinicians about the tenets of their faith, they may be invaluable sources of support for clients.

A narrative therapy perspective directs clinicians to ask clients about their religious and/or spiritual metaphors and stories. Griffith and Griffith (2002) encourage clinicians to inquire about metaphors and stories rather than beliefs unless a strong sense of trust and safety already has been established in the clinical relationship. Just as it is easier to avoid discussions of politics or religion when initiating conversations with new acquaintances, the same is true in a clinical relationship. Beliefs assert "truth" while metaphors and stories speak to experience. When beliefs differ, conflict can happen more easily. A narrative therapy approach focuses on externalizing problematic beliefs, and a number of narrative therapy methods can be applied to problems involving religious or spiritual beliefs (Freedman & Combs, 1996; White, 1995).

As a therapeutic relationship develops, it is important to explore respectfully spiritual or religious concerns that may contribute to suffering or facilitate healing. Spiritual resources that might contribute to healing and resilience include mindfulness practices, prayer, meditation, rituals, stories of spiritual or religious values, social relationships available through the faith community, beliefs about God or a higher power, or guidance from spiritual or religious leaders.

Research Implications

Hundreds of studies in the past several decades have addressed the question of how religion and spirituality affect family relationships, and numerous studies have addressed issues of family resilience. While there is growing acknowledgement of the importance of religion and spirituality in families, there is a noticeable need for more research on how general religiousness or specific beliefs may assist families in crisis. For example, while there are numerous studies of individual religious and spiritual coping, there are few studies of the interpersonal aspects of religious and spiritual coping. Mahoney (2010) found no studies on religion and coping with infidelity, child physical abuse, and serious marital or parent–child distress. Most studies connecting higher levels of general religiousness and the maintenance of family ties use single item measures of religious affiliation or attendance at religious services. Future studies with conceptually based and fine-grained measures of spiritual beliefs and practices could better describe what aspects of religion and spirituality sustain family resilience. Both qualitative and quantitative studies are needed with diverse family forms.

Recent research into the positive impact of mindfulness practices on family relationships is encouraging. The mechanisms through which mindfulness is associated with well-being also may help explain the effectiveness of other spiritual practices that develop present moment awareness and a nonjudgmental attitude towards inner experience. Research into the effectiveness of mindfulness-based interventions to improve family relationships and psychotherapy outcomes is still in the beginning stages but holds great promise.

Case Example

Spiritual and Religious Resources for Leaving an Abusive Relationship

Culture, spirituality, and religion all affect the family crisis of domestic violence. Qualitative studies on the role of spirituality and religiosity with culturally diverse domestic violence survivors have surfaced a number of themes common to the experiences of survivors (Yick, 2008). These themes are: (a) strength and resilience stem from a spiritual or religious base; (b) tensions result from religious or spiritual definitions of "family" and the reality of abuse; (c) tensions also develop from religious or spiritual definitions of gender role expectations; (d) individuals experience a spiritual vacuum and then reconstruction as part of the spiritual journey, and must recover a sense of spirit and self; (e) new interpretations of "submission" are developed; (f) forgiveness is a part of the healing process; and (g) social activism results. The following case illustrates these themes. The composite case was created from interviews with nine women who successfully interrupted the cycle of domestic violence (Senter & Caldwell, 2002).

Michelle is a 50-year old African-American woman, divorced, with two children. She left an abusive relationship 20 years ago. She had high hopes and expectations at the start of her marriage, which made it difficult for her to acknowledge the truth about her circumstances. Her dreams for a happy life with her husband along with her religious beliefs encouraged her to stay married at any cost. She tried desperately to make the relationship work despite mounting evidence that it was unworkable. Her husband became violently abusive immediately after they returned from their honeymoon, and the violence increased in frequency and intensity throughout the course of the relationship. Michelle attributed her decision to stay married mainly to a misinterpretation of scriptures. Receiving a different interpretation helped her to acknowledge the truth about the relationship:

> I found out that I had stayed in a situation that I didn't need to stay in because of my misinterpretation of the duties of a submissive wife. So I tolerated and put up with my husband's abuse thinking I was doing scripturally the correct things because I thought the definition of submissive meant doormat.

Michelle eventually came to the painful realization that she did not have the power to make her husband happy no matter what she did or how hard she tried. When one of her children was injured as a result of her husband's attack on her, she found the strength to initiate divorce proceedings.

Michelle's self-esteem plummeted during her time in the abusive marriage and it took years before she was able to reverse the damage that was done. Part of what made it difficult for her to leave was that she felt totally controlled and valueless as a result of living for years in a negative and invalidating environment. She had convinced herself that she did not deserve better and that there was no way out. An essential part of leaving was her willingness to receive and act on the advocating voices of others. These advocates included family, friends, ministers, and co-workers who all assisted her in seeing herself and her circumstances through a different lens. She recalled how her friends as well as her new minister and his wife offered their voices to assist her in recovering her self-worth:

> I would say that a tremendous help was the pastor and his wife. The more they let me know that it was alright for me to have my opinion, that it was alright for me to think on my own, and that I had the right to agree to disagree with my husband, the more I realized that I didn't have to stay in the marriage.

When Michelle left her abusive husband and filed for divorce, she experienced a wide range of emotions. There were feelings of empowerment and freedom as she made adjustments to a new way of living. There was also fear, anxiety, and trepidation as she contemplated moving forward alone. She transitioned from being controlled to being in control, and taking charge of her life was not an easy task. In the process, Michelle confronted a multitude of difficulties including a sick child, financial debt, a house in foreclosure, parenting problems, lack of confidence, pressure from her former husband, emotional distress, loneliness, depression, physical illness, and the contemplation of suicide.

Expressing herself openly in the abusive relationship often provoked the wrath of her abuser, so Michelle learned to keep her feelings hidden to avoid conflict. Once free of the abuse, the healing process required her to acknowledge and honestly express all of her suppressed thoughts and emotions. She was angry with herself for accepting less than she deserved and angry at her husband for making her feel like she was responsible for his violent behavior. She was also angry at all of the people in systems in society that asked why she stayed instead of asking why he was allowed to get away with the abuse. Her most difficult expression of anger was towards God for all her prayers for deliverance during the marriage and afterwards that seemingly went unanswered. God's perceived lack of response provoked questions like: "Why God?"; "Why are you doing this to me?", "Why aren't you hearing me?", "Why aren't you helping me?" These questions not only reflected Michelle's anger and frustration but also feelings of powerlessness, abandonment, and deep despair.

Her sense of loss was intense. Like many other women who have left abusive relationships, Michelle experienced the paradox of desperately wanting out of the relationship while missing it at the same time. Leaving her husband freed her from the abuse but it also meant the loss of her dreams for her marriage and her family. Her choices to find a mate, get married, and have a family were influenced by social, religious, and emotional factors. Her expectations for herself and those of society created an identity as a woman, a mother, a wife, and a good Christian. When Michelle left her marriage, she lost a sense of who she was in addition to losing the familiarity of her old life. She had to grieve the loss of her status in society, loss of status in her place of worship, and loss of status in the way she perceived herself.

As a mother, Michelle had to deal with some guilt regarding her children. Except for the final event that precipitated her separation, her children were spared a lot of the violence, and, as a result, they were able to hold onto the idealized images of their parents. The divorce was hard on them and this made Michelle question occasionally whether she had done the right thing:

> Every purple moon I kind of think maybe I should've handled it a little bit better, but I think I still would have done the same… Children have to go through their process. And although it was a scary environment, and we were all scared all the time, they had this fantasy Bill Cosby household in their minds, so of course, when I left it was like… Mommy what did you do to mess things up and make Daddy leave?

She eventually had to release the guilt associated with the belief that she had, in some way, ruined her children's lives and trust that she had made the best decision for the preservation of her family. Her new way of being and thinking got easier over time, but when things got particularly tough, she turned to her faith community for support.

Once Michelle recognized just how much the abuse had broken her spirit, an integration process began, which allowed her to awaken, explore, experiment, and engage in practices that were previously denied to her. She chose not to go to counseling, but instead found assistance in understanding herself through the use of self-help activities. She read books avidly, including the bible and other spiritual literature, listened to audiotapes, and watched inspiring television programs. She identified a variety of different authors, prophets, spiritual healers, and religious leaders as important resources in her recovery process. She also acknowledged the mentoring she received from her new pastor as extremely valuable.

Michelle attempted to practice the rituals of her faith on a regular basis during her marriage but it was difficult. She recalled how challenging it often was for her to participate in religious and spiritual activities because her husband would tease and make fun of her, calling her names like "Holy Joe" in an effort to discourage her from doing what she loved. He was successful at times in planting seeds of doubt in her mind about the importance of her commitment to God, and there were times when she wondered if God really did love her.

Michelle's relationship with God evolved as she continued to grow. Early in her process, her religious beliefs strongly influenced her choice to remain in the abusive relationship. She recalled how her attempts at marriage counseling facilitated by several ministers left her feeling blamed and responsible for her husband's actions:

> The religiosity part, I think actually kept me there a lot longer, and of course now, it wouldn't at all. I think over the years religion has changed its view on domestic violence as opposed to 20 years ago, but I am sure that was a part of it. I also think probably at this point I just happen to be in a church that takes a very strong stand against it. As a matter of fact, one of the pastor's sermons was about this; it wasn't just an aside that he mentioned during his sermon. His sermon was about domestic violence and don't do it and if you are a victim, its okay to leave. That's very different from the feedback I got from the pastors 20 years ago.

The following depiction of Michelle's relationship with God further demonstrates maturation in thought:

> I'm probably more spiritual and more in touch with God now than I was then. Back then it was probably more begging and praying to God, please get me out of here or please make things change or things like that. And sometimes when they didn't change, I'd become very angry … but now I just feel a much closer relationship with God, and I feel it's a more adult relationship as opposed to a child praying to a parent for help or rescue.

Accepting responsibility was a very important step in the movement away from her abusive relationship. Michelle came to a point in her journey where she had to take full ownership of her life, which was very empowering. She stopped the practice of blaming others, including God, for the choices she had made. She found strength in believing in her abilities to succeed, and self-encouragement helped her to become even more accountable. She conceded that some people may have received more encouragement to believe in themselves than others, but acknowledged that it was not impossible to arrive at a place where the truth could still be self-affirmed:

> I never, ever feel that what happens to us in our lives is some kind of punishment for who we are or what we did. We're responsible for the things we've done or not done, but God does not rain this stuff down on us to make our lives miserable. It's just what I believe, and I believe that if you reach down inside of you, you can come out of things by believing in yourself and knowing that God always believes in you!

Spirituality and corresponding religious beliefs play an important role in Michelle's life now. She holds an image of God as a wise, loving, compassionate helper and protector, and she willingly accepts the responsibility and consequences of her choices. Her feelings for God are so emotionally charged that she's often moved to tears when she thinks about God's presence in her life.

Michelle replaced old beliefs with new understandings about the abuse she suffered. This new understanding extended to her ex-husband as well. During the relationship, it was difficult to see beyond the cruel, irrational, and unpredictable behavior of the abuser. Only after a great deal of time passed was Michelle able to let go of the past through forgiveness of herself and her abuser. She recalled the most important thing that allowed her to forgive her ex-husband: "Well, I put myself in his place, and I thought about how he grew up, and maybe he, too, was abused and he couldn't express it any more than I could, and then I began to forgive him."

Reflections on this Case

A number of implications for clinical practice are apparent in this case. Practitioners working with domestic violence victims may want to assess the extent to which a victim's spirituality or religion is a source of strength. Collaborations between clinicians and faith communities are needed to develop culturally competent practices in working with domestic violence. Sometimes women remain in abusive marriages because of internalized notions of a "good wife" and a "good mother" that are reinforced by spiritual or religious leaders. Clinicians can facilitate explorations of how external constraints and internal beliefs shape their clients' perceptions of abuse, power, and gender roles. Practitioners may work with survivors in examining spiritual and religious beliefs, rebuilding a sense of self, as well as clearly delineating the differences among forgiving, forgetting, and condoning abusive behavior.

Michelle evidenced resilience as she emerged from the crisis of domestic violence to create a reorganized family structure that allowed her personal healing and strengthened the nurturing and supportive relationships with her children modeled on patterns of nonviolent behavior. Transformation was possible for her through her examination of her religious and spiritual beliefs about power, gender roles, and healthy family relationships. Changes in her relationships to her family and her religious community were facilitated through the affirmation she found in new, supportive religious leaders.

Conclusion

Spiritual and religious resources certainly can support family resilience, but this is a complex issue. Spiritual and religious resources can contribute to stable family structures with intimate-partner relationship stability, family cohesion, supportive parent–child interactions, and enhanced social support. Religious traditions offer resources that facilitate positive parenting in nondistressed families. Other protective factors facilitated by religious and spiritual practices include a positive worldview that supports coping with difficult situations and gives purpose, meaning, and hope. Spiritual practices that build mindfulness can lead to lower levels of anxiety and depression as well as better interpersonal relationships. Spiritual and religious factors also can create greater risks, especially in circumstances in which individual beliefs vary from the majority view, when individuals are engaged in a spiritual struggle with God, or when religious beliefs related to power and gender roles support ongoing abusive relationships. The religious and spiritual diversity of families in the U.S. creates challenges for clinicians who wish to address these issues with skill and sensitivity. Complexity characterizes not only the experiences of diverse families and their individual members but also the interplay of therapists' and clients' spirituality in clinical settings.

References

Altmaier, E., & Maloney, R. (2007). An initial evaluation of a mindful parenting program. *Journal of Clinical Psychology, 63*, 1231–1238.

Aponte, H. J. (2002). Spiritually-sensitive psychotherapy. In F. Kazlow (Series Ed.) & R. F. Massey, & S. D. Massey (Vol. Eds.), *Comprehensive handbook of psychotherapy: Vol. 3. Interpersonal/Humanistic/Existential* (pp. 279–302). New York: Wiley.

Atkins, D. C., & Kessel, D. E. (2008). Religiousness and infidelity: Attendance, but not faith and prayer, predict marital fidelity. *Journal of Marriage and Family, 70*, 407–418.

Baer, R. A., Smith, G. T., Lykins, E., Button, D., Krietemeyer, J., Sauer, S., et al. (2008). Construct validity of the five facet mindfulness questionnaire in meditating and nonmeditating samples. *Assessment, 15*(3), 329–342.

Barnes, S., Brown, K. W., Krusemark, E., Campbell, W. K., & Rogge, R. D. (2007). The role of mindfulness in romantic relationship satisfaction and responses to relationship stress. *Journal of Marital and Family Therapy, 33*(4), 482–500.

Benzies, K., & Mychasiuk, R. (2009). Fostering family resiliency: A review of the key protective factors. *Child and Family Social Work, 14*, 103–114.

Bermúdez, J. M., Kirkpatrick, D. R., Hecker, L., & Torres-Robles, C. (2010). Describing Latinos families and their help-seeking attitudes: Challenging the family therapy literature. *Contemporary Family Therapy, 32*(2), 155–172.

Booth, A., Johnson, D. R., Branaman, A., & Sica, A. (1995). Belief and behavior: Does religion matter in today's marriage? *Journal of Marriage and the Family, 57*, 661–671.

Bronfenbrenner, U. (1979). *The ecology of human development: Experiments by nature and design.* Cambridge, MA: Harvard University Press.

Brotherson, S. E., & Soderquist, J. (2002). Coping with a child's death: Spiritual issues and therapeutic implications. *Journal of Family Psychotherapy, 13*, 53–86.

Brown, J., Cohen, P., Johnson, J. G., & Salzinger, S. (1998). A longitudinal analysis of risk factors for child maltreatment: Findings of a 17-year prospective study of officially recorded and self-reported child abuse and neglect. *Child Abuse and Neglect, 22*, 1065–1078.

Butler, M. H., Stout, J. A., & Gardner, B. C. (2002). Prayer as a conflict resolution ritual: Clinical implications of religious couples' report of relationship softening, healing perspective, and change responsibility. *American Journal of Family Therapy, 30*, 19–37.

Cain, D. S. (2007). The effects of religiousness on parenting stress and practices in the African American family. *Families in Society-the Journal of Contemporary Social Services, 88*, 263–272.

Carlson, T. D., Erickson, M. J., & Seewald-Marquardt, A. (2002). The spiritualities of therapists' lives: Using therapists' spiritual beliefs as a resource for relational ethics. *Journal of Family Psychotherapy, 13*(3/4), 215–236.

Carothers, S. S., Borkowski, J. G., Lefever, J. B., & Whitman, T. L. (2005). Religiosity and the socioemotional adjustment of adolescent mothers and their children. *Journal of Family Psychology, 19*, 263–275.

Carson, J. W., Carson, K. M., Gill, K. M., & Baucom, D. H. (2004). Mindfulness-based relationship enhancement. *Behavior Therapy, 35*, 471–494.

Carson, J. W., Carson, K. M., Gill, K. M., & Baucom, D. H. (2007). Self-expansion as a mediator of relationship improvements in a mindfulness intervention. *Journal of Marital and Family Therapy, 33*(4), 517–528.

Coatsworth, J., Duncan, L., Greenberg, M., & Nix, R. (2010). Changing parent's mindfulness, child management skills and relationship quality with their youth: Results from a randomized pilot intervention trial. *Journal of Child and Family Studies, 19*(2), 203–217.

Coffey, K. A., & Hartman, M. (2008). Mechanisms of action in the inverse relationship between mindfulness and psychological distress. *Complementary Health Practice Review, 13*(2), 79–91.

Cohen, J. A. S., & Semple, R. J. (2010). Mindful parenting: A call for research. *Journal of Child and Family Studies, 19*(2), 145–151.

Cordova, J. V., Gee, C. B., & Warren, L. Z. (2005). Emotional skillfulness in marriage: Intimacy as a mediator of the relationship between emotional skillfulness and marital satisfaction. *Journal of Social & Clinical Psychology, 24*(2), 218–235.

Cox, C. E., Kotch, J. B., & Everson, M. D. (2003). A longitudinal study of modifying influences in the relationship between domestic violence and child maltreatment. *Journal of Family Violence, 18,* 5–17.

Curtis, K. T., & Ellison, C. G. (2002). Religious heterogamy and marital conflict: Findings from the national survey of families and households. *Journal of Family Issues, 23*(4), 551–576.

Dimidjian, S., & Linehan, M. M. (2003). Defining an agenda for future research on the clinical application of mindfulness practice. *Clinical Psychology: Science and Practice, 10*(2), 166–171.

Dumas, J. E. (2005). Mindfulness-based parent training: Strategies to lessen the grip of automaticity in families with disruptive children. *Journal of Clinical Child and Adolescent Psychology, 34*(4), 779–791.

Dumas, J. E., & Nissley-Tsiopinis, J. (2006). Parental global religiousness, sanctification of parenting, and positive and negative religious coping as predictors of parental and child functioning. *International Journal for the Psychology of Religion, 16*(4), 289–310.

Ellison, C. G., Bartkowski, J. P., & Anderson, K. L. (1999). Are there religious variations in domestic violence? *Journal of Family Issues, 20*(1), 87–113.

Farb, N. A. S., Anderson, A. K., Mayberg, H., Bean, J., McKeon, D., & Segal, Z. V. (2010). Minding one's emotions: Mindfulness training alters the neural expression of sadness. *Emotion, 10*(1), 25–33.

Feldman, G., Hayes, A., Kumar, S., Greeson, J., & Laurenceau, J. (2007). Mindfulness and emotion regulation: The development and initial validation of the Cognitive and Affective Mindfulness Scale-Revised (CAMS-R). *Journal of Psychopathology and Behavioral Assessment, 29*(3), 177–190.

Fincham, F. D., Beach, S. R. H., Lambert, N. M., Stillman, T., & Braithwaite, S. (2008). Spiritual behaviors and relationship satisfaction: A critical analysis of the role of prayer. *Journal of Social and Clinical Psychology, 27*(4), 362–388.

Freedman, J., & Combs, G. (1996). *Narrative therapy: The social construction of preferred realities.* New York: Norton.

Freud, S. (1927). *The future of an illusion.* Garden City, NY: Doubleday.

Gardner, B. C., Butler, M. H., & Seedall, R. B. (2008). En-gendering the couple-deity relationship: Clinical implications of power and process. *Contemporary Family Therapy: An International Journal, 30*(3), 152–166.

Gilbert, K. R. (1992). Religion as a resource for bereaved parents. *Journal of Religion and Health, 31*(1), 19–30.

Greeson, J. (2009). Mindfulness research update: 2008. *Complementary Health Practices Review, 14*(1), 10–18.

Grepmair, L., Mitterlehner, F., Loew, T., Bachler, E., Rother, W., & Nickel, M. (2007). Promoting mindfulness in psychotherapists in training influences the treatment results of their patients: A randomized, double-blind, controlled study. *Psychotherapy and Psychosomatics, 76,* 332–338.

Griffith, J. L., & Griffith, M. E. (2002). *Encountering the sacred in psychotherapy: How to talk with people about their spiritual lives.* New York: Guilford Press.

Haug, I. (1998). Spirituality as a dimension of family therapists' clinical training. *Contemporary Family Therapy, 20*(4), 471–483.

Higgins, M. P. (2002). Parental bereavement and religious factors. *Omega: Journal of Death and Dying, 45,* 187–207.

Hill, T. D., Burdette, A. M., Regnerus, M., & Angel, R. J. (2008). Religious involvement and attitudes toward parenting among low-income urban women. *Journal of Family Issues, 29,* 882–900.

Hunter, J. D. (1983). *American evangelicalism: Conservative religion and the quandary of modernity.* New Brunswick, NJ: Rutgers University Press.

Jha, A. P., Stanley, E. A., Kiyonaga, A., Wong, L., & Gelfand, L. (2010). Examining the protective effects of mindfulness training on working memory capacity and affective experience. *Emotion, 10*(1), 54–64.

Jain, S., Shapiro, S. L., Swanick, S., Roesch, S. C., Mills, P. J., Bell, I., et al. (2007). A randomized controlled trial of mindfulness meditation versus relaxation training: Effects on distress, positive states of mind, rumination, and distraction. *Annals of Behavioral Medicine, 33*(1), 11–21.

Kabat-Zinn, J. (1982). An outpatient program in behavioral medicine for chronic pain patients based on the practice of mindfulness meditation: Theoretical considerations and preliminary results. *General Hospital Psychiatry, 4*(1), 33–47.

Kabat-Zinn, J. (2003). Mindfulness-based interventions in context: Past, present, and future. *Clinical Psychology: Science and Practice, 10*(2), 144–156.

Keeling, M. L., Dolbin-MacNab, M. L., Ford, J., & Perkins, S. N. (2010). Partners in the spiritual dance: Learning clients' steps while minding all our toes. *Journal of Marital and Family Therapy, 36*(2), 229–243.

Koenig, H. G. (1999). *The healing power of faith.* New York: Simon & Schuster.

Koenig, H. G. (2005). *Faith and mental health: Religious resources for healing.* West Conshohocken, PA: Templeton Foundation Press.

Koenig, H. G., McCullough, M. E., & Larson, D. B. (2001). *Handbook of religion and health.* Oxford: New York.

Krumrei, E. J., Mahoney, A., & Pargament, K. I. (2009). Divorce and the divine: The role of spirituality in adjustment to divorce. *Journal of Marriage and Family, 71*(2), 373–383.

Lau, M. A., & Yu, A. R. (2009). New developments in research on mindfulness-based treatments: Introduction to the special issue. *Journal of Cognitive Psychotherapy: An International Quarterly, 23*(3), 179–184.

Lavender, J. M., Jardin, B. F., & Anderson, D. A. (2009). Bulimic symptoms in undergraduate men and women: Contributions of mindfulness and thought suppression. *Eating Behaviors, 10*(4), 228–231.

Lazar, S. W., Kerr, C. E., Wasserman, R. H., Gray, J. R., Greve, D. N., Treadway, M. T., et al. (2005). Meditation experience is associated with increased cortical thickness. *Neuroreport, 16*(17), 1893–1897.

Lee, J. W., Rice, G. T., & Gillespie, V. B. (1997). Family worship patterns and their correlation with adolescent behavior and beliefs. *Journal for the Scientific Study of Religion, 36*(3), 372–381.

Mahoney, A. (2010). Religion in families, 1999-2009: A relational spirituality framework. *Journal of Marriage and Family, 72*(4), 805–827.

Marler, P. L., & Hadaway, C. K. (2002). "Being religious" or "being spiritual" in America: A zero-sum proposition? *Journal for the Scientific Study of Religion, 41*(2), 289–300.

Marks, L. (2006). Religion and family relational health: An overview and conceptual model. *Journal of Religion and Health, 45*(4), 603–618.

Marsh, R., & Dallos, R. (2000). Religious beliefs and practices and Catholic couples' management of anger and conflict. *Clinical Psychology and Psychotherapy, 7*(1), 22–36.

Masten, A. (2004). Regulatory processes, risk, and resilience in adolescent development. *Annals of the New York Academy of Sciences, 1021*, 310–319.

McEvoy, M., Lee, C., O'Neill, A., Groisman, A., Roberts-Butelman, K., Dinghra, K., et al. (2005). Are there universal parenting concepts among culturally diverse families in an inner-city pediatric clinic? *Journal of Pediatric Health Care, 19*, 142–150.

McIntosh, D. N., Silver, R. C., & Wortman, C. B. (1993). Religion's role in adjustment to a negative life event: Coping with the loss of a child. *Journal of Personality and Social Psychology, 65*(4), 812–821.

Newport, F. (2010, May 21). *In U.S., increasing number have no religious identity*. Retrieved from Gallup, Inc. website: http://www.gallup.com/poll/128276/Increasing-Number-No-Religious-Identity.aspx.

Padilla, Y., & Villalobos, G. (2007). Cultural responses to health among Mexican American women and their children. *Family and Community Health, 30*(1S), S24–S33.

Pargament, K. I. (1997). *The psychology of religion and coping: Theory, research, practice*. New York: Guilford Press.

Pargament, K. I. (2007). *Spiritually integrated psychotherapy: Understanding and addressing the sacred*. New York: Guilford Press.

Patterson, J., Hayworth, M., Turner, C., & Raskin, M. (2000). Spiritual issues in family therapy: A graduate-level course. *Journal of Marital and Family Therapy, 26*(2), 199–210.

Pew Forum on Religion & Public Life. (2007, May). *Muslim Americans: Middle class and mostly mainstream*. Retrieved December 13, 2010 from http://religions.pewform.org.

Pew Forum on Religion & Public Life. (2008, February). *U. S. religious landscape survey: Religious affiliation diverse and dynamic*. Retrieved December 13, 2010, from http://religions.pewforum.org/reports.

Raes, F., Dewulf, D., Van Heeringen, C., & Williams, J. M. G. (2009). Mindfulness and reduced cognitive reactivity to sad mood: Evidence from a correlational study and a non-randomized waiting list controlled study. *Behaviour Research and Therapy, 47*(7), 623–627.

Ramel, W., Goldin, P. R., Carmona, P. E., & McQuaid, J. R. (2004). The effects of mindfulness meditation training on cognitive processes and affect in patients with past depression. *Cognitive Therapy and Research, 28*(4), 433–455.

Regnerus, M. D., & Burdette, A. (2006). Religious change and adolescent family dynamics. *Sociological Quarterly, 47*, 175–194.

Reynolds, D. (2003). Mindful parenting: A group approach to enhancing reflective capacity in parents and infants. *Journal of Child Psychotherapy, 29*(3), 357–374.

Senter, K. E., & Caldwell, K. (2002). Spirituality and the maintenance of change: A phenomenological study of women who leave abusive relationships. *Contemporary Family Therapy, 24*(4), 543–564.

Shaver, P. R., Lavy, S., Saron, C. D., & Mikulincer, M. (2007). Social foundations of the capacity for mindfulness: An attachment perspective. *Psychological Inquiry, 18*(4), 264–271.

Siegel, D. (2007). *The mindful brain*. New York: W. W. Norton.

Singh, N. N., Lancioni, G. E., Winton, A. S., Fisher, B. C., Wahler, R. G., McAleavey, K., et al. (2006). Mindful parenting decreases aggression, noncompliance, and self-injury in children with autism. *Journal of Emotional & Behavioral Disorders, 14*(3), 169–177.

Singh, N. N., Lancioni, G. E., Winton, A. S. W., Singh, J., Curtis, W. J., Wahier, R. G., et al. (2007). Mindful parenting decreases aggression and increases social behavior in children with developmental disabilities. *Behavior Modification, 31*(6), 749–771.

Singh, N. N., Singh, A., Lancioni, G., Singh, J., Winton, A., & Adkins, A. (2010). Mindfulness training for parents and their children with ADHD increases the children's compliance. *Journal of Child and Family Studies, 19*(2), 157–166.

Snider, J., Clements, A., & Vazsonyi, A. (2004). Late adolescent perceptions of parent religiosity and parenting processes. *Family Process, 43*, 489–502.

Sparks, A., Peterson, N. A., & Tangenberg, K. (2005). Belief in personal control among low-income African American, Puerto Rican, and European American single mothers. *Journal of Women and Social Work, 20*, 401–415.

Turner, R. P., Lukoff, D., Barnhouse, R. T., & Lu, F. G. (1995). Religious or spiritual problem: A culturally sensitive diagnostic category in the DSM-IV. *Journal of Nervous and Mental Disease, 183*(7), 435–444.

Wachs, K., & Cordova, J. V. (2007). Mindful relating: Exploring mindfulness and emotion repertoires in intimate relationships. *Journal of Marital and Family Therapy, 33*(4), 464–481.

Walsh, F. (1998). *Strengthening family resilience*. New York: Guilford Press.

Walsh, F. (2003). Family resilience: A framework for clinical practice. *Family Process, 42*(1), 1–18.

Walsh, F. (2009). Religion and spirituality in couple and family relations. In J. H. Bray & M. Stanton (Eds.), *The Wiley-Blackwell handbook of family psychology* (pp. 600–612). Malden, MA: Wiley-Blackwell.

Walsh, F. (2010). Spiritual diversity: Multifaith perspectives in family therapy. *Family Process, 49*(3), 330–348.

Walsh, J. J., Balint, M. G., Smolira, D. R., Fredericksen, L. K., & Madsen, S. (2009). Predicting individual differences in mindfulness: The role of trait anxiety, attachment anxiety and attentional control. *Personality and Individual Differences, 46*, 94–99.

Warner, H. L., Mahoney, A., & Krumrei, E. J. (2009). When parents break sacred vows: The role of spiritual appraisals, coping, and struggles for young adults' adjustment to parental divorce. *Psychology of Religion and Spirituality, 1*(4), 233–248.

White, M. (1995). *Re-authoring lives: Interviews and essays*. Adelaide, SA: Dulwich Centre Publications.

Wilcox, W. B. (1998). Conservative Protestant childrearing: Authoritarian or authoritative? *American Sociological Review, 63*(6), 796–809.

Wiley, A., Warren, H. B., & Montanelli, D. (2002). Shelter in a time of storm: Parenting in poor rural African American communities. *Family Relations, 51*, 265–273.

Worthington, E. L., Kurusu, T. A., McCullough, M. E., & Sandage, S. J. (1996). Empirical research on religion and psychotherapeutic processes and outcomes: A 10-year review and research prospectus. *Psychological Bulletin, 119*(3), 448–487.

Wulff, D. M. (1997). *Psychology of religion: Classic and contemporary* (2nd ed.). New York: Wiley & Sons.

Yick, A. G. (2008). A metasynthesis of qualitative findings on the role of spirituality and religiosity among culturally diverse domestic violence survivors. *Qualitative Health Research, 18*(9), 1289–1306.

Part VI

Resilience, Trauma, and Abuse

Family and Community Resilience Relative to the Experience of Mass Trauma: Connectedness to Family and Culture of Origin as the Core Components of Healing

26

Judith L. Landau

Introduction

The family is the integral unit of society, and the wellbeing and resilience of families and their communities[1] are inextricably linked. While most families and communities are inherently competent and resilient, when they experience three or more transitions (such as socioeconomic challenges or natural disasters) in a brief period of time they are likely to be stressed to the point of becoming symptomatic if there is imbalance between the stressors and the resources available to help them deal with the issues (Landau, 1982). How such stressors are handled is greatly influenced by the degree of connectedness to family and culture of origin. Our approach, using the Linking Human Systems Models, increases connectedness and awakens resilience at the individual, family, and community levels.

Literature Review

Traumas and Transitions Begin at the Individual and Family Levels

Individuals and families all experience a variety of traumas and transitions over their lifetimes; they each may have very different reactions to similar events. For example, for some people the beginning of a pregnancy is a celebration; for others it may be traumatic. Likewise, the death of an elder family member can be a sad, but manageable event if the death was expected or a major trauma if the elder died in tragic circumstances. In addition to such internal individual and family stressors, also ever-present are many community-wide threats that can affect people: socio economic change, natural and human-made disasters, migration and, more recently, the global financial crisis, and climate change. These challenges can be further exacerbated by inequalities of gender, wealth, resources, privilege, and power.

---

[1] The term "community" includes the natural support system: extended family, friends, neighbors, healthcare providers, clergy, employers, co-workers, etc.

J.L. Landau (✉)
LINC Foundation, Inc.,
Boulder, CO, USA
e-mail: JLandau@linkinghumansystems.com

D.S. Becvar (ed.), *Handbook of Family Resilience*,
DOI 10.1007/978-1-4614-3917-2_26, © Springer Science+Business Media New York 2013

For both individuals and families, these stressors can lead to increased incidence of substance abuse and other addictions, post-traumatic stress disorder (PTSD), sexual risk-taking, violence, poor eating and health habits, depression, suicide, and chronic or life-threatening illness. Moreover, while traumatic events primarily affect individuals and families, they do not occur in isolation. The effects ripple out into the community, touching friends, neighbors, schools, congregations, healthcare providers, and other support systems. On the community level, trauma can also breed prejudice, marginalization, and abuse of power.

The effects of trauma can persist for generations. When the balance of stressors and resources is disrupted by an unpredictable or massive loss, individuals, families, and communities may develop unconscious adaptive behaviors and coping strategies. One member or subgroup may develop symptoms that draw the group's attention away from the loss and toward resolving the new problem. These coping mechanisms serve to shield the family or community from the pain of loss. Because the adaptation is successful, it is transmitted through the generations and across families and communities, despite its being redundant and therefore dysfunctional. Examples of such intergenerational effects of trauma can be seen in several large populations. Among U.S. Viet Nam veterans, for example, more have died of addiction or suicide than were killed in the conflict (Sitikoff, 1999). Prior to the Holocaust, rates of PTSD (Dasberg, 1987, 1994) and addiction among Jewish people were extremely low; rates are now consistent with most other populations (Danieli, 1997; Hass, 1995).

As with individual and family loss and trauma, the consequences of community-wide stressors are seldom confined to those most directly affected (Bava, Coffey, Weingarten, & Becker, 2010; Bell, 2004; Garmezy & Rutter, 1983; Landau-Stanton & Clements, 1993; Rutter, 1987; Walsh & McGoldrick, 1991). The ramifications of large-scale trauma can jeopardize entire national economies and geopolitical dynamics. Despite the seeming independence of those large-scale traumas—such as natural disasters, chronic illness, trauma, addiction, and violence—the meaningful systemic connections between them all have been well documented; the aggregate situation is often described as a syndemic (Milstein, 2002; Singer & Clair, 2003). According to an extensive study by the National Institute of Mental Health (2002), early intervention can vastly reduce the impact of mass violence.

Healing from Trauma and Transition Also Starts with the Family

To deal with the effects of trauma on all of these levels, we need to start with the family. A family's heritage and values have profound bearing on the stresses it encounters, as well as how it handles them. Feeling connected or attached to family and culture of origin is correlated with reduced risk-taking behaviors as well as a reduction in family and societal violence, addiction, depression, suicidality, post-traumatic stress, and other chronic or life-threatening conditions (Landau, Cole, Tuttle, Clements, & Stanton, 2000). Therefore, facilitating family, cultural, and community ties and enhancing access to family and community resources can be protective against the impacts of trauma. Such connectedness fosters resilience and reduces the short- and long-term effects of stress in families and communities.

On the syndemic level, the most effective strategies for combating trauma are those that mobilize a broad range of social systems for long-term, systemic, and sustainable healing. Again, these systems depend on the inherent resilience of individuals, families, and communities; that resilience allows them to overcome tragedy and heal, and ensures that future generations survive and are strengthened by the hardships they endure.

I define community resilience as a community's inherent capacity, hope, and faith to withstand major trauma, overcome adversity, and prevail, usually with increased resources, competence, and connectedness.

My approach, the Linking Human Systems (LHS) Models, helps individuals, families, and communities to heal after trauma by actively increasing connectedness at the individual, family, and community levels, drawing on their inherent resilience and capacity to heal. In this chapter, I discuss the use of the LHS. Models as a way to help empower individuals, families, and communities to bind their own wounds. The models help these parties to see how they can recognize and extend their social support systems, empowering them to leverage their collective power to overcome adversity and sustain long-term change—with a minimum of time and effort on the part of outside professionals (Landau, 2007; Landau-Stanton, 1986). The LHS Models are intended for intervention with individuals, families, and communities that have experienced rapid, untimely, and unpredictable transition or loss. Such upheaval can arise from many sources: natural and human-made disasters, widespread drug abuse, AIDS and other pandemics, economic and political upheaval, urbanization and isolation of the nuclear family, and poverty.

In the next section, an overview of the significance of this topic is provided. Following that is a discussion of the theoretical background and principles of the LHS Models and the fundamentals of their implementation, including practical tips on the application of some useful tools, such as: (a) the assessment tools that enhance continuity and connectedness and evaluate resources and vulnerabilities, and (b) the tools that can identify community members who can act as natural agents for change. These community members—we refer to them as family and community links—are integral to the entire process; they allow us to rely on the family as the foundation that facilitates the entire LHS process.

Significance of the Topic

LHS Interventions target individuals, families, or communities as the object of change, utilizing individual, group, or multiple community links. The practical methods of mapping, assessment, and intervention presented consider all levels of individual, family, and community involvement, paying attention to health, spirituality, culture, and lifecycle stage. Assessment of available resources and vulnerabilities, protective factors, and goals encourages and facilitates collaboration across natural and artificial support systems for building resilience, rather than perpetuating vulnerability and long-term problems for individuals, families, and communities.

Also discussed are studies and clinical vignettes of the LHS Models in action that illustrate how they have helped families and communities facing trauma to heal and grow stronger. These examples illustrate the benefits of working with family or community links to build positive attachments.

As a society, when disaster strikes we tend to tally the number of people killed or injured, number of homes lost, and dollars spent on emergency aid. But seldom do we measure the more subtle costs, such as increases in depression, anxiety, substance abuse, risky sexual behavior, and domestic abuse. And rarely do we talk about the impact of these effects across extended families, neighborhoods, and generations. Yet it is crucial that we do so, helping families and communities harness their inherent resilience and optimize the use of their resources that can minimize the scope of damage in the immediate wake of a trauma, as well as in the years to come (Landau, 2004; Landau & Weaver, 2006).

Current Issues

Trauma Is All Too Common

Every day, millions of people all over the world are subjected to traumas of one type or another: one of every five veterans returning home from Iraq or Afghanistan is suffering from PTSD or major depression, according to the Wounded warrior Project (Liang & Boyd, 2010)., and a recent study found that the children of those deployed in Iraq and Afghanistan are 10% more likely to be hospitalized for a mental or behavioral health problem, compared to other children (MedlinePlus HealthDay News, 2011).

Globally, more than 43 million people were forcibly displaced—forced to leave their homes because of persecution, conflict, or other critical events—at the end of 2009, according to the latest statistics available. That number includes 15 million refugees (those who were forced to leave their countries of origin) as well as 27 million people who were internally displaced (UNHCR, 2010; WHO, 2009). According to the United Nations High Commissioner for Refugees, 2009 was the worst year for voluntary repatriation in 20 years, with ongoing conflicts in Afghanistan, Somalia, and the Democratic Republic of Congo showing "no signs of being resolved."

Natural disasters in 2010 alone killed more than 297,000 people worldwide, affected more than 217 million others, and caused $123 billion in economic damages. The Haiti earthquake claimed more than 222,000 lives, and in Russia, more than 55,000 deaths were attributed to extreme temperatures, floods, and wildfires. The year 2010 saw 385 natural disasters worldwide and was the deadliest in at least 2 decades (Guha-Sapir, Vos, Below, & Ponserre et al., 2010).

On March 11, 2011, Japan was decimated by an earthquake and tsunami that left 15,000 dead and 8,500 missing (T. Tamura, personal communication, May 29, 2011). The damage spread for thousands of miles along the coastline. The Fukushima area is still in danger of nuclear contamination, and resources are scarce. With more than 91,000 citizens living in evacuation shelters 3 months following the disaster, the Japanese Red Cross considers mental health a serious concern, particularly in a country with one of the highest suicide rates in the industrialized world (Hosaka, 2011). Suicide rates in Japan in May, 2011, increased 20% from the previous year, topping 3,000 for the first time in 2 years (Lah, 2011).

Substance abuse, depression, and suicide are frequent consequences of major trauma as well as being traumatic to individuals and families in their own right. In the United States, about 22.5 million people in 2009 were classified as substance-dependent or substance abusers (Substance Abuse & Mental Health Services Administration, 2010). Millions more of their family members, co-workers, and friends are dealing with the emotional and financial stressors resulting from those peoples' addictions (SAMHSA). Some of these stressors include 65–99,000 deaths from addiction, relational breakdown, and the enormous cost of medical care, unemployment, criminal justice system involvement, and addiction treatment. A large percentage of people presenting frequently to a primary care provider with minor illnesses and ailments are those living with the ongoing stress and intermittent acute trauma of addiction.

These statistics present brief snapshots of various types of traumas and disasters. Of course, we know that the effects of such events can remain for years. As the Inter-Agency Standing Committee's report (2007) about responses to disasters stated, "The psychological and social impacts of emergencies may be acute in the short-term, but they can also undermine the long-term mental health and psycho-social well-being of the affected population" (p. 2).

The Linking Human Systems LINC Community Resilience Model

The Underlying Principles and Philosophy of the LINC Model

The principles underlying the LINC Community Resilience Model arose in part from events in my own life. The first contributing factor was my childhood, which was spent in South African communities that endured severe deprivation and political oppression. Through tribal stories and healing rituals, the people of these communities instilled in me a deep conviction in the inherent resilience of people and in the essential worth of community connectedness.

Second, a seminal event occurred when I was 3 years old. At that time, a diphtheria epidemic struck my village; scores of people died and I was very ill (Landau, 1997). Our family doctor came to visit often during the crisis. He treated all members of our family as friends and colleagues, even respecting the childish chatter of my 3-year-old self. He represented safety to us at a very scary time. When he was there, my parents were relatively calm; once he left, they were anxious once again. He was exceedingly helpful during that crisis. But, I later wondered, could he somehow have helped my parents to develop a structure that would have made them feel safer when he was not there? Could he have helped them to access their own competence and resilience, which would have helped them weather the trauma?

Many years later, I realized that my approach to therapy was profoundly influenced by my illness and by the behavior of our family physician at that time. That ordeal taught me that professionals need to actively respect and acknowledge the knowledge, competence, and values of the families with whom they work. They need to work to reinforce the natural support systems of those families, including their healthcare providers, and they need to avoid secrecy and isolation, while helping the families address unresolved losses.

My work over the years has taken me very far, geographically, from where I spent my childhood. But the fundamental concept of my working philosophy remains what I learned as a child at the feet of the African storytellers: that a community's capacity to heal depends on the peoples' connectedness with one another and with their family and cultural histories.

The Impact of Transition on Communities

More than a century ago, Emile Durkheim (1897) showed that crisis throws a society into disequilibrium, rendering it temporarily incapable of exercising its usual regulatory function. This leads to a sense of hopelessness and despair, which Durkheim labeled anomie. Contemporary science has since confirmed that in times of stress, our response at every level, from molecular to interpersonal to societal, is to disconnect. During such times, our psychological sense of connection between the past, present, and future—what I term the Transitional Pathway—is easily disrupted (Landau, 1982).

Numerous researchers also have shown that experiencing multiple transitions (whether normal, predictable lifecycle events or unexpected traumas) within a short period can create stress (Boss, 2001; Figley & McCubbin, 1983; Garmezy & Rutter, 1983; Holmes & Rahe, 1967). In my own research, I have found that experiencing three or more stressors—again, normal lifecycle events or unexpected traumatic events—within a short period of time can cause disruption not just to each individual, but also to the larger family and community systems. People adjust to the stress of such changes by moving in different directions, at different rates. This asynchrony in responses between individuals and the subsystems they belong to (such as their immediate families), or between subsystems and larger community systems, I have termed transitional conflict. Left unaddressed, transitional conflict can lead to a variety of dysfunctions, including depression, suicidality, addiction, violence, post-traumatic stress, and risk-taking behaviors that can lead to HIV/AIDS (Landau, 2004; United Nations Programme on HIV/AIDS and World Health Organization, 2009). If resources are insufficient to balance the stressors, such symptoms almost invariably will result. And the more intense, unpredictable, or traumatic the stressors, the more likely it is that they will lead to major dysfunction.

In addition, for each person directly impacted by a mass trauma, there are many others—relatives, friends, neighbors, co-workers—who also are affected. A longitudinal study of the 1995 Oklahoma City bombing, for example, showed that for every one person directly impacted by the event, five others showed symptoms of stress or PTSD years later (Brom, Danieli, & Sills, 2005). The AIDS pandemic also provides a vivid illustration of how disease can devastate communities, extending far beyond those who are directly affected. Worldwide, in 2009, 33 million people were living with HIV, the virus that causes AIDS (UNHCR, 2010). About 2.6 million more were infected with the virus that year, and 1.8 million died of AIDS. Each of those millions of people is likely to have family, friends, and co-workers who also have been affected by the individual's diagnosis in some way (UNHCR).

Terrorism and other violent events can have especially pervasive consequences, primarily because of the suddenness, unpredictability, and magnitude of loss. In the months after the September 2011 terrorist attacks in New York City, for example, almost one-third of respondents reported increased rates of cigarette, alcohol, or marijuana use (CASA, 2003; Vlahov, Galea, Ahern, Resnick, & Kilpatrick, 2004), PTSD, and depression (Galea et al., 2002). According to McKernan (2006), increases in substance abuse occur by several different mechanisms: (a) increase in use to cope with stress seen amongst the general population, particularly amongst those suffering from PTSD and depressive symptoms, and in high-risk groups such as first responders, (b) those on the verge of substance abuse or dependence cross over, (c) those actively addicted increase their use, and (d) those in recovery relapse.

Sixty days after the attacks, cases of acute myocardial infarction had increased by 35%, and cardiac arrhythmias had increased by 40% (Feng, Karri, & Reddy, 2003). Abuse of drugs and alcohol rose by 29% within a year (CASA, 2003). In addition, when tragedy strikes the uncertainty about whether those missing are alive or dead creates its own stress—what Boss (1999) terms ambiguous loss.

Reconnecting the Transitional Pathway

Clearly, trauma to individuals can affect family members and others in a community. But influence also flows the other way. Family support can moderate the effects of trauma on individuals, even as the traumatized individual's experiences continue to influence the family (Catherall, 2004; Herman, 1992; Hobfoll, 1989, 1998; Matsakis, 1998; Norris, Stevens, Pfefferbaum, Wyche, & Pfefferbaum, 2008; van der Kolk, 1996). For example, a 1-year follow-up of 383 Israeli soldiers suffering combat stress reactions showed that family support was related to lower PTSD levels (Solomon, Mikulincer, Freid, & Wosner, 1987). Brewin, Andrews, and Valentine (2000) found that trauma severity and social support were among the strongest predictors of adjustment and PTSD symptomatology in various civilian and military samples; more social support generally led to less PTSD. These studies highlight the importance of family resources in dealing with the impact of trauma. Indeed, communities across time have found ways to share their stories of resilience, enabling subsequent generations to survive trauma and often emerge with increased strengths and resources (Hobfoll, 1989, 1998).

In order to understand the apparent resilience operating in families suffering from alcoholism after massive or unpredictable loss, I was able to explore the intergenerational story of 37 families with addiction by developing a five- to seven-generation genogram. The objective was to go back to the time before the beginning of the addiction in order to explore what had occurred around that time (Garrett & Landau, 2007). I found that the force of resilience in all families that drives them toward survival and health is the same force that drives them to develop adaptive behavior at the onset of major loss and grief. What happens is that a family member becomes addicted in an unconscious attempt to maintain family survival. The addicted person essentially carries the grief to allow the others to continue daily living and then that person starts to drink or use in order to assuage the heavy burden of the grief. Needing to attend to the consequences of the addictive behavior keeps the family close and prevents them from feeling the pain of intense loss and sorrow. The cycle also slows down the natural process of transitions, so that the family does not have to face the usual life cycle stages of separation until the grieving is done.

Once this has happened, the driving force of health and healing, "Family Motivation to Change," pushes, frees, or allows a member of the family, a natural change agent or family link, to lead the family out of grief and addiction into health and recovery (Garrett & Landau, 2007). The initial protection of the family starts unconsciously as one member of the family is drawn to offer him/herself as the sacrifice to serve as the diversion for a loved one from acute pain and grief, as described above. The motivating force functions to prevent the loved one from suffering grief to the extent that s/he might choose to join those lost in death. Each time that the alcoholic starts to succeed at a job, at leaving home, or at any other life cycle transition, the depression, grief, or overwhelming loss of the person s/he was protecting is likely to return. At this point, the alcoholic is highly likely to relapse, to save the loved one once again. It is only once the grief is resolved throughout the extended family that the alcoholic can succeed to traverse the life cycle transition with success and move into recovery for the long term. At this stage, the same protective, driving, Family Motivation to Change force serves to bring first one member, then the rest of the family, into recovery. Continued, unresolved grief results in the alcoholism being transmitted across and down the generations until the grief is resolved and a family member leads the family into healing. However, we discovered that we do not have to wait for the family's natural resolution of grief through the passage of time but can intervene at any place on the genogram and in the timeline to help families access their resilience to resolve the grief and avoid the consequences of serious loss. This resilience is demonstrated by the family's ability to resolve transitional conflict caused by the multiple stressors they have endured, and their successful navigation of subsequent transitions. Further, they have learned from past experiences, understand their impact on the present, and integrate these lessons into their choices for their future.

How then, I wondered, might professionals tap into these inherent family strengths to help individuals, families, and communities to survive trauma? How could professionals use those strengths to help reconnect transitional pathways that had been disrupted by trauma?

With my colleagues, I began investigating by looking at the role of connectedness in protecting people from risk-taking activities associated with many of the stress-related conditions that follow major trauma. We studied the relationship between connectedness to family and culture of origin and the level of sexual risk-taking in two samples of women—women attending a clinic focused on sexually transmitted diseases (STDs) and women in an inner-city Hispanic community organization. In both communities, we found that two measures correlated with reduced sexual risk-taking: knowledge of stories about grandparents or great-grandparents was a robust predictor of lower sexual risk-taking, and having at least monthly contact with extended family members was strongly associated with lower levels of sexual risk-taking (Landau et al., 2000). These measures also held up independently.

In a later study of adolescent girls who were attending a mental health clinic (for issues related to depression, anxiety, and sexual abuse), we analyzed intergenerational family stories, identifying themes of resilience (i.e., ancestors overcoming adversity) vs. vulnerability (i.e., depression, family violence, addiction). We found that knowing a story with a theme of resilience was most protective. However, knowing any family story, even if it contained themes of vulnerability, was more protective than knowing no story at all (Tuttle, Landau, Stanton, King, & Frodi, 2004). These findings suggest that being able to draw on the rituals, strengths, stories, scripts, and themes of past generations helps people to reconnect their transitional pathways. This enables families to reunite their communities, enhancing their collective resilience.

Our research has found that resilience—in many forms—is a key factor in overcoming trauma. Resilience was first understood as an innate characteristic that resided within individuals, with scant attention paid to families or communities. Indeed, the earliest studies of resilience were limited to children. More recently, a growing emphasis on family and community resilience not only acknowledges that the family can be a resource for individuals in times of stress, but also recognizes the family as a functional unit in itself and the family as the essential unit of community resilience (Bell, 2001; Boss, 1999, 2001; Falicov, 1991; Figley & McCubbin, 1983; Garbarino & Kostelny, 1996; Johnson, 2002; Karpel, 1986; Landau, 1982, 2004; Landau & Saul, 2004; Rolland, 2004; Walsh, 1998, 2003; Walsh & McGoldrick, 1991; Wolin & Wolin, 1996; Wynne, 1991; Wynne, McDaniel, & Weber, 1986).

The Linking Human Systems Models

The therapeutic approaches we developed, based on this research and other work, are the LHS models, which evolved in part from Transitional Family Therapy (TFT) (Horwitz, 1997; Landau & Garrett, 2006; Landau, 1982; Landau-Stanton & Clements, 1993; Seaburn, Landau-Stanton, & Horwitz, 1995; Watson & McDaniel, 1998). The TFT approach to therapy, which I began to develop in my research and practice in South Africa in the 1970s, was further honed with colleagues in the early days of the University of Rochester's Division of Family Programs.

TFT takes a systems perspective, recognizing that to address the concerns of families effectively, therapists must understand the social networks of those families, as well as the historic, geographic, economic, and cultural contexts in which they exist. Network or ecosystemic approaches have been widely used in family therapy since the 1970s, following the seminal work of Speck and Attneave (1973). Interested readers might also see earlier works of Auerswald and others (Anderson & Goolishian, 1988; Auerswald, 1968; Imber-Black, 1988; McDaniel, Hepworth, & Doughtery, 1992; Mirkin, 1990; Rueveni, 1979; Wynne et al., 1986). TFT employs an integrative, "here and now," trans-generational and ecosystemic approach that mobilizes the extended social system from the outset of therapy, highlighting past and present sources of resilience (Seaburn et al., 1995). TFT is also grounded in the idea that individuals, families, and communities are intrinsically healthy and competent. With appropriate guidance, they can access their inherent resilience to resolve their own problems.

The core philosophy of the LHS Models is that building a sense of continuity from past to future helps people navigate the present with greater awareness of their choices (Landau, 2007; Landau et al., 2000; Landau, Mittal, & Wieling, 2008; Landau-Stanton, 1986; Landau-Stanton, Griffiths, & Mason, 1981; Suddaby & Landau, 1998). LHS Intervention Models are designed specifically to resolve transitional conflict by creating resolution and synchrony across the system. The goals are to engage the entire system in the process of change, eliminate blame, reduce shame and guilt, and iden-tify and access naturally available resources for healing.

The LHS Models achieve these goals through a well-defined intervention process that is guided by a professional therapist or interventionist. Each intervention includes: assessment of the issue, relation-ships, and resources available using a variety of tools; identification of individuals who will serve as integral family and community links throughout the process; and prescribed steps for moving toward healing. A variety of LHS Intervention Models are available for use, depending on the issues and com-munities being addressed; they can be carried out at the level of individuals, families, or communities (see Table 26.1).

It is important to note that LHS Intervention Models are process-driven rather than content-driven. Process-driven interventions are replicable anywhere because the process is provided in consultation with the affected parties, and the content belongs to the context and culture of the situation at hand. These programs are essentially redesigned each time, using the process in each context and cultural situation, so they belong to the local target population. Involvement of external professionals is initially intensive, but brief; it is gradually reduced over time, empowering local people to take over and be suc-cessful in their own right. Content-based programs, conversely, often cannot be effectively replicated in different contexts and cultures and tend to require intensive and lengthy professional involvement.

Table 26.1 Link approach visual model (Landau et al., 2008)

Linking Human Systems Models		
Theoretical model	Intervention methods	Transitional assessment tools
Transitional family therapy	ARISE (A Relational Invitational Sequence for Engagement)	Transitional Genogram Transitional Field Map
	LIFE (Link Individual Family Empowerment Invitational)	Transitional Field Map Multisystemic Level Map Transitional Strategic Polarization Map
	LINC Community Resilience	Transitional Field Map Multisystemic Level Map Transitional Strategic Polarization Map Structural Pyramid Map

Continuity and Connectedness

LHS Intervention Models focus on continuity and connectedness. Every intervention begins with an assessment process intended in part to help re-establish the continuity between past, present, and future for a family or community. During this process, stories and histories emerge that shed light on the social, cultural, and historical context of the situation at hand, as well as on the ways in which families and communities confront their problems. This enables people to gain perspective on the complex systems in which they live and to see their families or communities in a fresh light. The process diffuses blame and anger and makes room for more constructive interactions that draw upon a full range of resources and strengths (Landau, 2007; Landau-Stanton, 1986; Watson & McDaniel, 1998).

The assessment process also sets the stage for enhancing connectedness within the extended family, the community, and the natural support systems, a critical aspect of fostering resilience (Bell, 2001; Bowlby, 1969; Johnson, 2002; Main, 1995). By re-establishing continuity with their forebears, people are reminded how their predecessors weathered difficulties and are reassured about their own competence (Landau, 2004; Seaburn et al., 1995). Building connectedness by enlarging and mobilizing natural support systems provides people with resources–tangible and intangible–that enhance their ability to overcome adversity (Hobfoll, 1989, 1998; Melton, Holaday, & Kimbrough-Melton, 2008). Achieving a strong sense of connectedness promotes a feeling of solidarity among family and community members. This eliminates counterproductive we/they dichotomies.

The role of connectedness in protecting against vulnerability was well-illustrated in the two research studies mentioned earlier: knowing stories about grandparents or great-grandparents and having at least monthly contact with extended family members were strongly associated with lower levels of sexual risk-taking. Knowing any story, even if it contained themes of vulnerability, was more protective than knowing no story at all. These findings suggest that being able to draw on the resilience of past generations helps people explicate and reconnect their transitional pathways. Then they can make informed choices about where to go and how to get there.

Assessment Tools for Linking Human Systems Intervention Models

LHS Intervention Models rely heavily upon assessment tools that are designed to evaluate the following: (a) whether the connectedness and continuity of the Transitional Pathway has been disrupted, (b) whether strengths and themes of resilience, rather than vulnerability, are being mobilized in the struggle with hardship, (c) what the overall level of stress is, (d) how stressors and resources are balanced, and (e) whether family and community resources are available, accessed, and utilized.

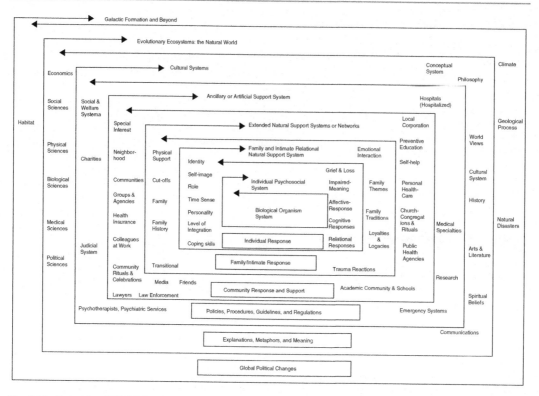

Fig. 26.1 Transitional Field Map (Landau-Stanton & Clements, 1993)

The assessment tools use a number of geographic, sociological, and therapeutic maps (Landau, 1982, 2007; Landau et al., 2008; Landau-Stanton & Clements, 1993).

The Transitional Genogram depicts important family genealogy, themes, scripts, events, relationships, conflicts, and strengths across as many generations as possible. It also maps belief systems in the sociocultural context (Landau, 1982, 2007; Landau-Stanton & Clements, 1993).

The Transitional Field Map provides a schematic representation of a family or community's members, problems, resources, events, themes, and histories in every level of the network, including biological and individual psychosocial systems, natural and ancillary (artificial) support systems, and cultural and ecosystems (Landau-Stanton & Clements, 1993). The Transitional Field Map also serves to underscore that each level within a system (family, community, culture, and context) affects the others (Fig. 26.1).

The Multisystemic Levels Map examines in further detail "slices" of the Transitional Field Map that focus on past and current events in the community, sources of resilience, and other features of the community's response to loss or trauma that may guide decisions about intervention (Fig. 26.2) (Landau & Saul, 2004).

The Structural Pyramid Map assists in the detailed design of an intervention (Landau, 2007). This map represents all members of the family or community, including target individuals, family members, extended family groups, schools, neighborhoods, local authorities and political leaders, and professionals. It highlights those with special skills and leadership positions, as well as majority and minority populations, to help ensure that everyone in the system is informed, there are no secrets, authority is acknowledged, and all potential change-makers are included. This detailed process provides insight not only to outside professionals attempting to guide families or communities toward healing, but also to the families and communities themselves.

Multisystemic Levels Map: Terrorist Attacks, New York City, 9/11/2001					
Systemic Level	Traumatic Event(s) Impact (Severity and Duration)	Protective Factors Resources and Resiliency	Symbolization and Narrative System	Problematic Reactions to Event(s) ane Long-Term Sequelae	Interventions and Prevention
Biological System • Physical • Nervous system • Endocrine	Death, injury, CNS response Respiratory problems from debris	Levels of physical fitness and health, youth, stress inoculation, mind-body-spirit practices	Somatic expression, dreams	somatic symptoms, respiratory and health problems	Pharmacological agents, mind-body-spirit regulatory practices and Intervention, physical self-care
Individual Psychological Systems • Cognition • Emotions • Behavior • Relations	Loss, Insecurity, disruption or routine, & role, fear and anxiety Dissociation, altered time	Personality and coping skills, identity, self-image, cognitive skills, relational behavior, affect regulation	Recall and constructions of dreams and Intrusive memories, and multiple personal meanings	Anxiety, depression acute stress symptoms, PTSD, grief reactions Aggression and Suicidality, alcohol and substance abuse	Individual counseling and therapy, stress-relieving Interventions, psychoeducation, enhancing intrinsic strengths, facilitation of postraumatic growth Psychological and emotional self-care Recreational, physical, and artistic activities
Social System • Family and intimate relations • Natural support system: Local community-church, neighborhood, school, work, other groups • Ethnic/national/global • Ancillary support system- emergency, hospital, welfare	Separation and loss, change in relational behavior and bonding, stress on family and other social groups, displacement, disruption of role and routine increased connectedness & bonding communication breakdown, media response Activation of ancillary support system	Family support, competence of natural supports, community organization and support, history of family and community community self-mobilization, organization and support. National and international support Ancillary support	Collective narration with family, friends, neighborhood, and community National and global narratives	Disruption of family life cycyle, neighborhood relations Flight from city and severing of social attachments Displacement of families and work organizations stress due to loss of Income, housing, employment Intrusion of ancillary support systems	Family, group, and network counseling and therapy Mobilization and facilitation or natural support systems try ancillary support systems. Peer support networks Building on long-term preventive groups and methods Organizing community forums; enhancing social connectedness for communication, problem-solving, and resource-accessing
Cultural System • Meaning systems • Knowledge systems • Language and symbols • Identity • Rituals and practices	Shattered world assumptions, sense of Invulnerability and safety	Creation of rituals Religious and spiritual solace, patriotism sources of coherent world view, arts and literature, communication	Interpretation of collective narration, of old and new rituals, contextualizing and memorializing, creation of new symbols, 9/11 as a temporal marker	Increasing rigidity and resort to primitive belief systems, discriminatory responses to Arab & Musilm minorities	Changing cultural belief systems from vulnerability to resilience Facilitation of new rituals and practices focused on communal grieving, revitalization, and concillation, cultural legacy, and mission
Ecosystemic Environment • Physical and natural world • Economic & Political context	Environmental destruction and hazzard Mobilization of rbetoric	Economic and political resources, physical	Impact of environmental, economic, and political change on symbolic system	Disruption or utilities, transportation, and communication Exaggerated political responses (Patriot Act and curtaiment of civil rights)	Clean-up of environment, plan for reconstruction war on terrorism, preemptive strikes

Fig. 26.2 Multisystemic Field Map, example following the New York City September 11, 2001, terrorist attacks (Landau & Saul, 2004)

Family and Community Links as Natural Change Agents

A fundamental goal of the assessment process is to identify the natural change agents who will serve as family and community links throughout the intervention. Central to the LHS approach is the recruitment and coaching of individual members of the family or community who can bridge the gap between the professional and the family or community in need (Landau, 1981, 1982, 2007; Landau et al., 2008). Ideally, these family and community links, referred to hereafter as Links, are acceptable to and respected by all members of the group. A Link's ability to convene representatives from all levels of the family or community structure is critical to the success of the LHS Intervention Model, so it is important to avoid selecting leaders who cannot garner broad support or who might derail the process for their own aggrandizement or personal gain. The Link should be a person who is unbiased and is able to view the problem from multiple perspectives. The Link should avoid affiliating with only one position or faction and artificially driving the decision-making process and subsequent action. Links may function individually or in pairs or larger groups.

Soon after the assessment in which the Link is selected, the professional begins coaching the Link to assist the family or community in resolving its problems. This reinforces the Link's confidence in his or her expertise about the family or community. A central advantage of utilizing Links is that the Link facilitates the professional's access to social systems that might otherwise resist outside "interference," or that might invite intervention during a crisis but quickly discontinue participation once the crisis is resolved. Working with Links is particularly useful for professionals attempting to intervene within "closed" social systems, such as traditional extended families and clans, or highly educated and sophisticated communities. Harnessing the power of a Link maintains respect for the traditions, strengths, pride, and privacy of a family or community and capitalizes on the group's capacity for healthy change and survival.

Principles of the Linking Human Systems Models

Whether executed at the level of individuals, families, or communities, the LHS approach is guided by the following principles:
- Involve all components of the extended social system.
- Ensure representation of each layer of the Transitional Field Map.
- Ensure invitation, authority, permission, and commitment from family or community members or leaders who are widely accepted by the larger system.
- Ensure access to biological, psychological, and spiritual resources.
- Directly relate the program to the group's goals, future directions, and best interests.
- Develop and prioritize realistic tasks from the goals and then devise practical projects.
- Build on existing resources, assigning projects to appropriate resources.
- Provide the process, remaining peripheral and encouraging the group to take responsibility for the content, goals, and actions.
- Attribute success of the program where it belongs – with the individual, family, or community.

Linking Human Systems Models in Action

Family and community links can implement prevention and intervention at the individual, family, and community levels in a wide array of circumstances.

Individual Level: The ARISE (A Relational Invitational Sequence for Engagement) Intervention and Continuum of Care

The ARISE Intervention and Continuum of Care starts with an invitational, nonconfrontational, gradually escalating intervention process designed to engage a problem individual and his or her family in treatment for a minimum of 1 year. The person with a problem is invited to participate in the process; the goal is long-term individual and family healing and recovery (Landau & Garrett, 2006, 2008). The ARISE Intervention is applicable to destructive behaviors such as substance abuse and addiction, as well as process or behavioral compulsions such as gambling, gaming, over-spending, Internet compulsion, sexual acting-out, cybersex, and eating disorders. It is also applicable for those struggling with chronic or life-threatening physical, mental, or emotional/spiritual issues (Landau et al., 2000; Landau et al., 2004).

The goal of an ARISE Intervention is to use the least amount of effort needed to motivate a substance abuser into treatment, stepping up the level of pressure gradually to match the intensity of resistance from the addicted individual. The collaboration between the Interventionist and the family relies on the understanding that, while the Interventionist is the expert on the interface between families and addiction, the family is the expert on itself. Throughout the process, the family is encouraged to take into account what they think will work. They also are encouraged to offer a selection of choices to the addicted individual so as to reduce the likelihood of a rebellious response. The dual focus of the ARISE Intervention is on engaging the addicted individual in treatment and supporting the family in healing from the effects of living with addiction for a long time. The power of the ARISE process lies in the collective motivation of the Intervention Network to bring about change (Fernandez et al., 2000). As the family's behavior changes, the substance abuser inevitably follows suit because as the family system changes, so do the individuals within it. We typically find that if there are additional family members with substance abuse or other behavioral compulsions, they also embark on the recovery process.

The ARISE Continuum of Care consists of three phases: Phase A, comprising the actual Invitational Intervention, mobilizes the Intervention Network toward motivating the addicted individual into treatment. Incremental pressure is applied until this is achieved. Phase B is a transitional phase, averaging 6 months, in which the Intervention Network supports the loved one through treatment and into early recovery. The goal is treatment completion, family relational improvement, grief resolution, and relapse prevention. Phase C, lasting 6–12 months, aims at the family's becoming a family living in long-term recovery, with long-term individual and intergenerational family recovery and healing. It focuses on reinforcing the family's behavioral changes and on healthy behaviors and lifestyle.

Phase A: Invitational Intervention

Level 1: The First Call. Phase A starts when a concerned person contacts a Certified ARISE Interventionist. The first call or contact is either a brief phone consultation or visit during which the Interventionist coaches and empowers the caller to mobilize the support system as an Intervention Network to invite the addicted individual to a First Meeting. Pivotal to Level 1 is development of the Recovery Message, which explicitly states the understanding of where the addiction started in the family and the intent to keep it from progressing into future generations. The Recovery Message is used to help families understand the addictive pattern across generations, to relieve guilt, shame and blame, and to bring hope for the future health of the family. It is the central component of the invitation to the Intervention and always draws on the strengths, survival, and love in the family.

At the first meeting, members of the Intervention Network share their concerns and ask the individual to enter treatment. The meeting commences whether or not the addicted individual chooses to attend. A primary focus of Phase A is getting the commitment from the family to enter and commit to the recovery process. At Level 1, 56% of individuals enter treatment.

Level 2: Strength in numbers. Level 2 begins only if the substance abuser has not entered treatment and the Intervention Network wants to escalate their effort. This typically occurs after 2 to 5 meetings or 6 months. The addicted individual's participation is continually encouraged, though his or her refusal does not deter the Intervention Network from their work. Strategies evolve over the course of these sessions and the network grows in strength as a group, allowing it to deliver a consistent message to the individual. All decisions are made by the majority of the Intervention Network. This prevents isolation and the vulnerability of any member to the one-on-one manipulation characteristic of addiction. After two to five Level 2 meetings, 80% have entered treatment.

Level 3: The formal ARISE Intervention. Fewer than 2% of families need to proceed to Level 3. At this level, the Intervention Network sets strict limits and consequences for the problem person, expressed in a loving and supportive way. By this time, the substance abuser has been given and refused many opportunities to enter treatment. Since the substance abuser has been invited to every meeting, this final limit-setting approach is a natural consequence and does not come as a surprise. The Intervention Network commits to supporting each other in the implementation of the agreed upon consequences.

Phase B: Supporting Treatment and Early Recovery

Once the substance abuser enters treatment, or 6 months has elapsed, Phase B begins. The Intervention Network continues meeting to support the recovery process. It is important for the encouragement and support of the family to take place over a period of time and through the difficulties and stress that invariably arise during this transitional period. The Network collaborates with the addicted individual and his or her treatment providers to ensure that the group addresses the following topics as they pertain to each member of the network: physical, mental, emotional, and spiritual health; relapse prevention and psychoeducation about addiction; family, social, and fellowship support; and financial and career vitality.

Phase C: Living in Recovery

Phase C focuses on the individual and family living in recovery. This includes relapse prevention, attendance at self-help meetings, continued family therapy and psychoeducation, and grief resolution.

Table 26.2 Outcome Comparison between National Institute on Drug Abuse (NIDA) study and a Real World Data from Stanley Street Treatment and Resources (SSTAR) (Landau, 2010)

Variable	NIDA ($n=110$)		SSTAR ($n=39$)	
	No.	%	No.	%
Engaged in treatment or self-help	91	83	31	80
Relationship of first caller				
Parents	44	40	18	46
Spouse/partner	34	31	7	18
Offspring	4	4	2	5
Other relatives	21	19	12	31
Nonrelatives	7	6	0	0
Gender of first caller				
Female	76	69	30	77
Male	34	31	9	23
Average Intervention Network size	3	–	2.5	–

Of primary importance is developing awareness of the details of family communication, relationships, patterns, and activities of daily living to ensure that difficult issues are discussed openly and without secrecy so that the family can learn to grieve, heal, celebrate, relax, and have fun together.

Research Findings

A clinical study was conducted through the National Institute on Drug Abuse (NIDA) on the cost-effectiveness of the ARISE Intervention for engaging resistant substance abusers in treatment or self-help. The primary outcome variable was dichotomous: did the substance abuser, within 6 months from the first call, engage in treatment or self-help by physically either (a) showing up and enrolling in treatment, or (b) attending self-help meetings. Results showed an 82.7% success rate. In a study of 110 individuals, 86 engaged in treatment while 5 engaged in self-help (Landau et al., 2004). Half of those who entered treatment did so within 1 week of the initial call, 76% within 1 week, and 84% within 3 weeks. The engagement rate did not differ across preferred substance of abuse, the level at which engagement occurred, or demographic variables such as age, gender, or race.

The outcome/effort scale (OES) was used to refine the above dichotomous outcome score (engaged vs. nonengaged) on the premise that a successful engagement achieved with less clinician time and effort should be viewed as a more positive outcome than a successful engagement that entailed greater clinician time/effort. Conversely, an unsuccessful engagement in which the First Caller refused even to attempt ARISE should be viewed as more negative than an unsuccessful case in which at least some effort was made. A score was thus assigned to each case using a five-point scale: First Caller refused ARISE (−2); ARISE was attempted but failed (−1); engagement success at Level 3 (1); engagement success at Level 2 (2); engagement success at Level 1 (3). On average, professionals spent less than 90 minutes coaching concerned friends and family members to mobilize their networks to motivate addicted subjects to enter treatment. The mean amount of time required was 88 minutes with a median of 75 minutes.

A recent "real world" study on ARISE conducted by Stanley Street Treatment and Resources (SSTAR) replicated the results from the NIDA study with an 80% engagement rate (see Table 26.2). A 1-year follow-up study by SSTAR demonstrated a 61% sobriety rate with an additional 10% improved (see Table 26.3) (Landau & Garrett, 2008). SSTAR also recently conducted a pilot study in which the ARISE Intervention was initiated by the addicted individuals themselves while in detox. The goal was to determine how effective the ARISE Intervention is at ensuring that after detox these patients engaged in secondary and tertiary care. The study participants, of whom 55% were homeless, ranged from 5 to

Table 26.3 Data from Real World Study at SSTAR of Sobriety Status at the 1-Year Mark (Landau, 2010)

Variable ($n=90$)	No.	%
Engaged in treatment	68	76
Engaged in secondary care	36	53
Sobriety status		
Sober at last contact	41	45.5
Period of sobriety w/ relapse	14	15.5
Reduced use	9	10
No change	11	12
No information	15	17

12 prior admissions to detox, with an average of 10 prior admissions. The study found that 82% of the participants went on to a secondary level of care; of those, 100% went on to a tertiary level of care; 91% reported that they were active in Narcotics Anonymous (NA) or Alcoholics Anonymous (AA). At the time of last contact; at 12 months, 55% had not relapsed. Of those who had, 80% were back in treatment (P. Emsellem, personal communication, October, 21, 2009).

Family Level: Link Individual Family Empowerment

Link Individual Family Empowerment (LIFE) focuses on helping families work together to revise their themes of vulnerability to themes of resilience (Landau et al., 2008). The LIFE Intervention is a formal, 8-session program; it focuses on enhancing positive connectedness to family and culture of origin, in line with our earlier findings that frequency of visits to extended family and knowledge of intergenerational stories of family resilience is correlated with reduced risk-taking. It also grew from studies on connectedness and self-protective behavior (Landau, 2007; Landau, Cole et al., 1995; Landau et al., 1996). In those studies, we found that the actual stories of families who interpreted their themes as vulnerable were not so different from those that others interpreted as resilient. The difference was in perspective: the children who perceived their families as being overcome by disaster, horrible events, or abuse took greater risks, while those children who had the same stories but perceived them as stories of success and overcoming adversity were resilient. Helping children to see their family's intergenerational strengths and positive themes can change their perceptions of their own capacity for positive change, as well as that of their families. This serves to build self-advocacy and hope, bringing positive connectedness to the nuclear, as well as the intergenerational, family and the expectation of achievement and positive change.

Six of the sessions in a LIFE Intervention focus specifically on creating positive connectedness by working with the Links to explore intergenerational family stories of vulnerability and resilience, helping recreate ritual and celebration so the perspective is positive (Imber-Black & Roberts, 1992; Landau et al., 2000; Tuttle et al., 2004; White & Epston, 1990). Two of the sessions, typically the final ones, focus on the specific need, problem, or goals of the particular family.

The original LIFE study was a qualitative, developmental study conducted in Rochester, New York, and Taipei, Taiwan (Landau et al., 1996). Its focus was to prevent the spread of HIV/AIDS in the immediate and extended family and in the neighborhood. Links in this case were HIV-positive family members who were best connected to other family members and neighbors. Single- and multi-family LIFE Interventions have since been applied in a number of contexts, including child abuse and domestic violence (the Bronx, New York), addiction (Argentina and Kosovo), and cultural transition (refugee families in Kosovo and the United States). A current federal study at the University of Rochester is applying the LIFE Intervention Model to inner-city abused women to empower them to prevent further abuse, STDs, and HIV in themselves and families.

Community Level: LINC Community Resilience

A LINC Community Resilience Intervention involves an entire community or its representatives in assessing a situation and designing its own intervention (Landau, 2007). This type of intervention can be used within a community or by governments and organizations as a way to prepare for and/or resolve the consequences of mass disasters (Landau, 2004, 2007; Landau et al., 2008; Landau & Saul, 2004; Landau & Weaver, 2006).

The intervention uses a series of maps to assess demographics, attitudes, customs, family structures, and important events in the community. Following this assessment, community forums are organized, each representing a comprehensive cross-section of the population. In larger communities (more than 6,000 people), LINC Community Resilience Interventions begin with consultants who train local professionals to assist in facilitating the intervention so that the entire community may be reached.

Following LINC guidelines, members of the community are divided into small discussion groups, each representing a cross-section of the community. The groups identify the strengths, themes, scripts, and resources that are available within the community and discuss what the concept of resilience means to them individually, as well as to their families and community. Each group then develops overarching goals for the future. Groups usually embrace the goals set by the collective, but they also usually add several of their own. They discuss ways in which their available resources can be applied to each small and easily achievable task that is derived from one of the goals.

The groups then work as collaborative teams to select their community Links; these are people from within their own group whom they trust and with whom they can communicate easily. Links are identified as people who would make good leaders, and who are able to bridge the gap between the community and outside professionals. Members of the collaborative teams then identify practical tasks from their goals and arrange work groups to achieve them. The number of Links depends in part on the size of the community. Medium-sized communities (populations of 6,000–50,000 people) select, on average, 3 to 5 Links; larger cities (50,000–1 million people) select 8 to 10 Links, each of whom coordinates multiple projects.

Clinical and Research Implications

A recent SAMHSA report (2010) summarized current evidence-based interventions for mass trauma and supported the critical need for empirically based systemic interventions. The global context of mass trauma resulting from war and organized violence encompasses an array of historical, social, economic, and political contexts. These must be carefully understood for professionals to develop meaningful programs of intervention with communities exposed to traumatic events and the related mental health consequences. Psychotherapists must respond to the increasing needs of traumatized families around the world by developing preventive and clinical interventions that are evidence-based, culturally relevant, and context-specific.

Currently, there are few evidence-based treatments directed at family or community levels for treatment after mass traumatic events. There are a number of highly effective preventive interventions focused on issues such as refugee mental health and HIV/AIDS. However, there is little work directed toward a better understanding of how to intervene effectively with families in their communities when they have been affected by mass trauma. The body of work presented in this chapter represents one of these approaches; it has been implemented across different trauma contexts and with different populations around the world.

The Linking Human Systems Models are examples of intervention and research that are ecologically based, are grounded in people's generative inner strengths and experiences, and that cut across all levels of a system that might be tapped into as a potential resource for rebuilding personal resilience and strength after mass trauma.

Case Examples: Assessing Resilience in Operation

A Family in Crisis

The following illustrates how we go about assessing resilience in a family situation. The situation involved a family in Finland. A 25-year-old man in the family had assaulted his wife. Their family was appalled and had threatened to put him in prison. The couple was referred for therapy by the prison diversion program because this was his first episode of violence.

To begin, to assess the practical aspects of resilience we used the Family Resilience Questionnaire (Landau & Weaver, 2006), which helps us to:

- Find out what resources are available within the families and community as a whole.
- Explore how the resources are being accessed and utilized so that we can estimate the balance between stressors and resources.
- Establish whether connectedness and continuity of the Transitional Pathway has been disrupted.
- Find out whether the families and communities know their stories about past adversities and how they overcame them.
- Establish whether clusters of strengths and themes of resilience rather than vulnerability are being mobilized.

In this situation, we were able to discover the following:

- Both spouses had extended families who loved them and wanted to help. Both families lived in the same neighborhood.
- The husband was reluctant to ask for help from his family, although he was struggling to support his young wife who was still at university. He was not talking to anybody, including his wife, about the stress of his own job or his financial difficulties. He was also not sharing with anyone his concerns about his mother's recent diagnosis of breast cancer.
- When we explored the history, it became clear that during 90 years of war, almost every family in Finland had lost several men. The Transitional Pathway had been disrupted. The rule about the many years of war was silence, and no resolution had occurred despite the fact that the war was over and the men were no longer being killed or were missing.
- The wife's grandfather had died in World War II, and her husband had also lost several male family members. The dominant culture's and this family's way of dealing with this ongoing and immutable situation was with total silence. Nobody talked about the missing men or the unresolved grief. However, in both families, similarly to most other Finnish families, in an attempt to adapt to the loss of the men and maintain healthy function of their families, the women had taken over many of the men's roles and had become extremely strong and competent.
- Now that the situation was different and the men were no longer going to war and being missing or killed, the strengths that had been mobilized and been adaptive in the past were no longer relevant or needed. Now, the current generation of young men objected strenuously to the women's behavior. They acted out against what they perceived as overbearing control and a lack of their own autonomy. They felt almost redundant and were extremely resentful of their mothers, sisters, and wives. The rate of addiction and sexual risk-taking had increased along with domestic violence and petty urban crime.

In this case example, it was clear that the family members really loved each other and were very connected. However, the husband felt helpless, isolated, and angry. Once he understood the history, and that the change in roles originally had been adaptive, he was able to understand his mother's and wife's behaviors. Once this occurred, he found that he could share his concerns about his finances, his future, and his overwhelming sense of obligation. Together, he and his parents, parents-in-law, and wife were able to design their future.

A Community in Crisis

After a lengthy period of severe political unrest and upheaval in Argentina from the late 1970s that culminated with a serious economic crisis in 1990, I was invited to perform a wide-scale survey to assess the problems in the community. The survey showed that there was an increase in the prevalence of addiction and HIV/AIDS in Buenos Aires Province (with an urban and rural population of 12 million). To combat these problems, health officials invited us to help develop a province-wide, community-based program focused on both prevention and intervention.

We first trained professionals and paraprofessionals to use the assessment and intervention protocols of the LINC Model. Then, we developed pre- and post-program surveys and used a series of maps to assess demographics, attitudes and customs, family structures, and important events in the communities. Following this assessment, we organized community forums, each representing a comprehensive cross-section of the population. There, members of the community (sometimes as many as 5,000) developed their own concept of resilience, using such words as trust, faith, confidence, hope, loyalty, spirituality, and survival. Following LINC protocol guidelines, they divided into small discussion groups, each representing a cross-section of the community. Each group developed overarching goals for the future, embracing those set by the ministry but also adding several of their own. The groups then worked as collaborative teams to select their community Links—people from within their own groups whom they trusted and with whom they could easily communicate, whom they thought would make good leaders, or links between their community and us as outside professionals. They then identified workable tasks from their goals and arranged work groups to achieve them.

Some of the activities and groups that developed in different communities in Buenos Aires Province included: a partnership of police, school personnel, parents, and community residents to expel drug dealers from the neighborhood; support of a preexisting formal organization, Padré a Padré, designed to serve parents of children struggling with issues of substance abuse or addiction (this organization grew into a nationwide initiative that continues to meet); a program for evening education for literacy, business skills, and handcrafts; and a social group for children and families of the military to become integrated into the communities in which they were stationed. Within 2 years, there was a 400% increase in the admission to treatment of young people struggling with alcohol or drug abuse—most of whom were brought to and supported in their treatment by family members.

Summary and Conclusion

The Linking Human Systems Models and the specific methods that developed from it are examples of ecologically based, culturally informed, multi-level, multi-informant systemic interventions to assist populations affected by mass trauma. These populations are vulnerable to developing a host of psychological, emotional, and relational disturbances, including the increased incidence of risk-taking behaviors often associated with traumatic events. As described earlier, systemic interventions incorporating comprehensive biopsychosocial dimensions to assist communities after mass trauma are virtually nonexistent. The Linking Human Systems Models are powerful in their ability to promote healing and reconnection by accessing the inherent strengths within families and communities. We would argue that if more mental health professionals and paraprofessionals were prepared to assist families in identifying their own strengths and resilience post-trauma, the escalation of maladaptive behaviors, emotional and relational disturbances, and severe psychological symptoms could be prevented and/or ameliorated.

The author is working collaboratively with an international group of scholars who are involved in communities affected by war and disaster and the resulting situations of mass trauma. We are currently designing a small-scale study to implement and test LIFE in some of these communities around the globe in order to develop solid and empirically-based support for this approach. We know of no other group of family therapists currently undertaking this type of research with mass trauma. Our long-term vision is to collaborate with this team of scholars to develop a multi-phased and multi-component tiered system of interventions that integrates: (a) an individual evidence-based intervention, (b) a parenting intervention, (c) a family-level intervention, and (d) a community-level intervention. We believe that the Linking Human Systems Models offer promise as an overall approach for guiding family and community interventions.

References

Anderson, H., & Goolishian, H. A. (1988). Human systems as linguistic systems: Preliminary and evolving ideas about the implications for clinical theory. *Family Process, 27*, 371–393.

Auerswald, E. H. (1968). Interdisciplinary versus ecological approach. *Family Process, 7*, 202–215.

Bava, S., Coffey, P., Weingarten, K., & Becker, C. (2010). Lessons in collaboration, four years post-Katrina. *Family Process, 49*, 543–558.

Bell, C. C. (2001). Cultivating resiliency in youth. *The Journal of Adolescent Health, 29*, 375–381.

Bell, C. C. (2004). *Sanity of survival: Reflections on community mental health and wellness*. Chicago: Third World Press.

Boss, P. (1999). *Ambiguous loss*. Cambridge, MA: Harvard University Press.

Boss, P. (2001). *Family stress management: A contextual approach*. Thousand Oaks, CA: Sage.

Bowlby, J. (1969). *Loss, sadness, and depression*. London and New York: Hogarth.

Brewin, C. R., Andrews, B., & Valentine, J. D. (2000). Meta-analysis of risk factors for posttraumatic stress disorder in trauma-exposed adults. *Journal of Consulting and Clinical Psychology, 68*(5), 748–766.

Brom, D., Danieli, Y., & Sills, J. (2005). *The trauma of terrorism: Sharing knowledge and shared care, an international handbook*. Binghamton, NY: Haworth Press.

CASA. (2003). Survey of 1,000 American teens ages 12–17 released Wednesday, February 21, 2001 by The 17 National Center on Addiction and Substance Abuse at Columbia University.

CASA. (2003, August). National Survey of American Attitudes on Substance Abuse VIII: Teens and Parents.

Catherall, D. R. (2004). *Handbook of stress, trauma and the family*. New York: Brunner-Routledge.

Danieli, Y. (1997). As survivors age: An overview. *Journal of Geriatric Psychiatry, 30*, 9–25.

Dasberg, H. (1987). Psychological distress of Holocaust survivors and offspring in Israel, forty years later: A review. *The Israel Journal of Psychiatry and Related Sciences, 24*(4), 243–256.

Dasberg, H. (1994). Kindliches Verfolgungstrauma und spaete Trauerreaktion. Falldarstel/ung. In H. Stoffels & H. Stoffels (Eds.), *Terrorlandschaften derSeele* (pp. 115–124). Regensburg: S. Roderer-Verlag.

Durkheim, E. (1897). *Suicide: A study in sociology*. London: Free Press.

Falicov, C. J. (Ed.). (1991). *Family transitions: Continuity and change over the life cycle*. New York: Guilford Press.

Feng, J., Karri, V., & Reddy, C. V. R. (2003, November). *Heart attacks rose at the Brooklyn Hospital after terrorist attack*. American Heart Association Scientific Sessions. Orlando, FL.

Fernandez, A. C., Begley, E. A., & Marlatt, G. A. (2006). Family and peer interventions for adults: Past approaches and future directions. *Psychology of Addictive Behaviors, 20*, 207–213.

Figley, C. R., & McCubbin, H. I. (Eds.). (1983). *Coping with normative transitions. Stress and the family*. New York: Brunner/Mazel.

Galea, S., Ahern, J., Resnick, H., Kilpatrick, D., Bucuvalas, M., Gold, J., et al. (2002). Psychological sequelae of the September 11 terrorist attacks in New York City. *The New England Journal of Medicine, 346*, 982–987.

Garbarino, J., & Kostelny, K. (1996). What do we need to know to understand children in war and community violence? In R. J. Apfel & B. Simon (Eds.), *Minefields in their hearts: The mental health of children in war and communal violence* (pp. 33–51). New Haven, CT: Yale University Press.

Garmezy, N., & Rutter, M. (1983). *Stress, coping and development in children*. New York: McGraw-Hill.

Garrett, J., & Landau, J. (2007). Family motivation to change: A major factor in engaging alcoholics in treatment. *Alcoholism Treatment Quarterly, 25*(1/2), 65–83.

Guha-Sapir, D., Vos, F., Below, R., & Ponserre, S. (2010). *Annual disaster statistical review 2010: The numbers and trends*. Brussels, Belgium: Center for Research on Epidemiology of Disasters (CRED), Université catholique de Louvain.

Hass, A. (1995). *The aftermath: Living with the Holocaust*. Cambridge, UK: Cambridge University Press.

Herman, J. L. (1992). Complex PTSD: A syndrome in survivors of prolonged and repeated trauma. *Journal of Traumatic Stress, 5*(3), 377–391.

Hobfoll, S. E. (1989). Conservation of resources: A new attempt at conceptualizing stress. *The American Psychologist, 44*, 513–524.

Hobfoll, S. E. (1998). *Stress, culture and community: The psychology and philosophy of stress*. New York: Plenum Press.

Holmes, T. H., & Rahe, R. H. (1967). The social readjustment scale. *Journal of Psychosomatic Research, 11*(2), 213–218.

Horwitz, S. H. (1997). Treating families with traumatic loss: Transitional family therapy. In C. Figley, B. Bride, & N. Mazza (Eds.), *Death and trauma: The traumatology of grieving* (pp. 211–230). London: Taylor and Francis.

Hosaka, T. (2011). *Japan disaster victims face mental health risks*. Associated Press. Retrieved June 10, 2011, from http://www.google.com/hostednews/ap/article/ALeqM5h2xqNSKRUgh1yGFQ_hh5tngnkfvw?docId=c75b4f6c5b 1040d58540fb76ebc4d063.

Imber-Black, E. (1988). *Families and larger systems: A family therapist's guide through the labyrinth*. New York: Guilford Press.

Imber-Black, E., & Roberts, J. (1992). *Rituals for our times: Celebrating, healing, and changing our lives and our relationships*. New York: HarperCollins.

Inter-Agency Standing Committee. (2007). *IASC guidelines on mental health and psychosocial support in emergency settings*. Geneva: IASC.

Johnson, S. M. (2002). *Emotionally focused couple therapy with trauma survivors: Strengthening attachment bonds*. New York: Guilford Press.

Karpel, M. A. (Ed.). (1986). *Family resources: The hidden partner in family therapy*. New York: Guilford Press.

Lah, K. (2011). *Japan suicide rates hit 2-year high in May*. CNN World. Retrieved June 8, 2011, from http://www.cnn.com

Landau, J. (1981). Link therapy as a family therapy technique for transitional extended families. *Psychotherapeia, 7*, 382–390.

Landau, J. (1982). Therapy with families in cultural transition. In M. McGoldrick, J. K. Pearce, & J. Giordano (Eds.), *Ethnicity and family therapy* (pp. 552–572). New York: Guilford Press. Translated and republished in Réseaux-Systèmes-Agencements (1983).

Landau, J. (1997). Whispers of illness: Secrecy versus trust. In S. H. McDaniel, J. Hepworth, & W. Doherty (Eds.), *Stories in medical family therapy*. New York: Basic Books.

Landau, J. (2004). El modelo LINC: una estrategia colaborativa para la resiliencia comunitaria. *Sistemas Familiares, 20*(3), 87–102.

Landau, J. (2007). Enhancing resilience: Families and communities as agents for change. *Family Process, 46*(3), 351–365.

Landau, J. (2010). ARISE-Intervention: Die Einbindung von Suchtabhängigen/Substanzmissbrauchern und ihren Familien in die Behandlung und Langzeit-Recovery. *Familiendynamik, 36*, 2–11.

Landau, J., Cole, R., Tuttle, J., Clements, C. D., & Stanton, M. D. (2000). Family connectedness and women's sexual risk behaviors: Implications for the prevention/intervention of STD/HIV infection. *Family Process, 39*, 461–475.

Landau, J., Cole, R. et al. (1995). *Link individual family empowerment (LIFE): A method for facilitating family resilience through re-storying the Transitional Pathway*.

Landau, J., Finetti, J. C., Jaffe, R., Speice, J., Tuttle, J., Espaillat, E., et al. (1996). *Manual for the link-individual family empowerment to reduce risk of HIV/AIDS and other sexually transmitted diseases*. Rochester, NY: University of Rochester School of Medicine and Dentistry.

Landau, J., & Garrett, J. (2006). *Invitational intervention: A step-by-step guide for clinicians helping families engage resistant substance abusers into treatment* (1st ed.). Las Vegas, NV: BookSurgePublishing.com.

Landau, J., & Garrett, J. (2008). Invitational Intervention: The ARISE model for engaging reluctant alcohol and other drug abusers in treatment. *Alcoholism Treatment Quarterly, 26*, 147–168.

Landau, J., Garrett, J., Shea, R., Stanton, M. D., Baciewicz, G., Brinkman-Sull, D., et al. (2000). Strength in numbers: Using family links to overcome resistance to addiction treatment. *The American Journal of Drug and Alcohol Abuse, 26*(3), 379–398.

Landau, J., Mason, J., & Griffiths, J. A. (1982). The extended family in transition: Clinical implications. In F. Kaslow (Ed.), *The international book of family therapy* (pp. 360–369). New York: Brunner/Mazel.

Landau, J., Mittal, M., & Wieling, E. (2008). Linking human systems: Strengthening individuals, families, and communities in the wake of mass trauma. *Journal of Marital and Family Therapy, 34*(2), 193–209.

Landau, J., & Saul, J. (2004). Facilitating family and community resilience in response to major disaster. In F. Walsh & M. McGoldrick (Eds.), *Living beyond loss* (pp. 285–309). New York: Norton.

Landau, J., Stanton, M. D., Brinkman-Sull, D., Ikle, D., McCormick, D., Garrett, J., et al. (2004). Outcomes with the ARISE approach to engaging reluctant drug- and alcohol-dependent individuals in treatment. *The American Journal of Drug and Alcohol Abuse, 30*, 711–748.

Landau, J., & Weaver, A. M. (2006). The LINC model of family and community resilience: New approaches to disaster response. *Journal of Family and Consumer Sciences, 30*(2), 11–14.

Landau-Stanton, J. (1986). Competence, impermanence, and transitional mapping: A model for systems consultation. In L. C. Wynne, S. McDaniel, & T. Weber (Eds.), *Systems consultations: A new perspective for family therapy* (pp. 253–269). New York: Guilford Press.

Landau-Stanton, J., & Clements, C. (1993). *AIDS, health, and mental health: A primary sourcebook*. New York: Brunner/Mazel.

Landau-Stanton, J., Griffiths, J. & Mason, J. (1981). The extended family in transition: Clinical Implications. *Psychotherapeia, 7*(4), 370–381.

Liang, B., & Boyd, M. (2010). PTSD in returning wounded warriors: Ensuring medically appropriate evaluation and legal representation through legistrative reform. *Stanford Law & Policy Review*. Retrieved from SSRN: http://ssrn.com/abstract=1685868 October 1, 2010.

Main, M. (1995). Recent studies in attachment. In S. Goldberg, R. Muir, & J. Kerr (Eds.), *Attachment theory: Social, developmental, and clinical perspectives* (pp. 407–474). Hillsdale, NJ: Analytic Press.

Matsakis, A. (1998). *Trust after trauma: A guide to relationships for survivors and those who love them*. Oakland, CA: New Harbinger.

McDaniel, S. H., Hepworth, J., & Doughtery, W. (1992). *Medical family therapy: A biopsychosocial approach to families with health problems*. New York: Basic Books.

McKernan, B. (2006, November). *Substance Abuse and Mental Health Services Administration Disaster Technical Assistance Center: Lessons Learned from the 2005 Hurricane Response*. Paper presented at the American Public Health Association's 134th Annual Meeting.

MedlinePlus HealthDay News. (2011, May). Retrieved June 4, 2011 from http://www.nlm.nih.gov/medlineplus/news/fullstory_112265.html.

Melton, G. B., Holaday, B. J., & Kimbrough-Melton, R. J. (2008). Strong communities as safe havens for children. *Family & Community Health, 31*(2), 83–185.

Milstein, B. (2002). *Introduction to the syndemics prevention network*. Atlanta: Center for Disease Control and Prevention (CDC).

Mirkin, M. P. (Ed.). (1990). *The social and political contexts of family therapy*. Boston: Allyn and Bacon.

National Institute of Mental Health. (2002). *Early mental health intervention reduces mass violence trauma. NIMH Press Office Report*. September 5, 2002.

Norris, F., Stevens, S. P., Pfefferbaum, B., Wyche, K. F., & Pfefferbaum, R. L. (2008). Community resilience as a metaphor, theory, set of capacities and strategy for disaster readiness. *American Journal of Community Psychology, 41*, 127–150.

Rolland, J. S. (2004). *Families, illness, and disability: An integrative treatment model*. New York: Basic Books.

Rueveni, U. (1979). *Networking families in crisis*. New York: Human Sciences.

Rutter, M. (1987). Psychosocial resilience and protective mechanisms. *The American Journal of Orthopsychiatry, 57*, 316–331.

Seaburn, D., Landau-Stanton, J., & Horwitz, S. (1995). Core intervention techniques in family therapy process. In R. H. Mikesell, D. D. Lusterman, & S. H. McDaniel (Eds.), *Integrating family therapy: Handbook of family psychology and systems theory* (pp. 5–26). Washington, DC: American Psychological Association.

Singer, M., & Clair, S. (2003). Syndemics and public health: Reconceptualizing disease in bio-social context. *Medical Anthropology Quarterly, 17*, 423–441.

Sitikoff, H. (1999). The postwar impact of Vietnam. In J. W. Chambers II (Ed.), *The Oxford companion to American military history*. New York: Oxford UP.

Solomon, Z., Mikulincer, M., Freid, B., & Wosner, Y. (1987). Family characteristics and post-traumatic stress disorder: A follow-up of Israeli combat stress reaction casualties. *Family Process, 26*(3), 383–394.

Speck, R. V., & Attneave, C. (1973). *Family networks*. New York: Pantheon.

Substance Abuse and Mental Health Services Administration. (2010). *Results from the 2009 national survey on drug use and health: Volume 1. Summary of national findings*. (Office of Applied Studies, NSDUH Series H-38A, HHS Publication No. SMA 10-4586Findings). Rockville, MD.

Suddaby, K., & Landau, J. (1998). Positive and negative timelines: A technique for restorying. *Family Process, 37*, 287–298.

Tuttle, J., Landau, J., Stanton, M. D., King, K. U., & Frodi, A. (2004). Intergenerational family relations and sexual risk behavior in young women. *The American Journal of Maternal Child Nursing, 29*(1), 56–61.

United Nations High Commissioner's Report [UNHCR]. (2010). *The 2009 statistical yearbook*. Geneva: Author.

United Nations Programme on HIV/AIDS and World Health Organization. (2009). *AIDS epidemic update* (UNAIDS/09.36E/JC1700E). Retrieved June 4, 2011, from http://www.who.int/hiv/data/en/.

van der Kolk, B. (1996). *Traumatic stress: The effects of overwhelming experience on mind, body, and society*. New York: Guilford Press.

Vlahov, D., Galea, S., Ahern, J., Resnick, H., & Kilpatrick, D. (2004). Sustained increased consumption of cigarettes, alcohol, and marijuana among Manhattan residents after September 11, 2001. *American Journal of Public Health, 94*, 253–254.

Walsh, F. (1998). *Strengthening family resilience*. New York: Guilford Press.

Walsh, F. (2003). Family resilience: A framework for clinical practice. *Family Process, 42*, 1–18.

Walsh, F., & McGoldrick, M. (Eds.). (1991). *Living beyond loss: Death in the family*. New York: Norton.

Watson, W., & McDaniel, S. (1998). Assessment in transitional family therapy: The importance of context. In J. W. Barron (Ed.), *Making diagnosis meaningful: Enhancing evaluation and treatment of psychological disorders* (pp. 161–195). Washington, DC: American Psychological Association.

White, M., & Epston, D. (1990). *Narrative means to therapeutic ends*. New York: Norton.

Wolin, S., & Wolin, S. J. (1996). The challenge model: Working with the strengths of children of substance abusing parents. *Child and Adolescent Psychiatric Clinics of North America, 5*, 243–256.

World Health Organization [WHO]. (2009). *Annual disaster statistical review 2009*. Geneva: Centre for Research on Epidemiology of Disasters CRED.

Wynne, L. C. (1991). An epigenetic model of family processes. In C. J. Falicov (Ed.), *Family transitions: Continuity and change over the life cycle* (pp. 81–106). New York: Guilford Press.

Wynne, L., McDaniel, S., & Weber, T. (Eds.). (1986). *Systems consultation: A new perspective for family therapy*. New York: Guilford Press.

Resilience Despite Risk: Understanding African-American ACOAS' Kin and Fictive Kin Relationships

J. Camille Hall

Introduction/Background

Parental alcoholism is fast becoming an epidemic within the United States; millions of children grow up with at least one alcohol-dependent or alcohol-abusive parent (National Institute on Alcohol Abuse and Alcoholism (NIAAA), 2007). Research findings have shown that for every eight Americans, one is the child of an alcoholic (Grant, 2000; Mupier, Rodney, & Samuels, 2002). Indeed, parental alcohol abuse does not just impact the alcoholic or alcohol abuser, it also has been found to be disruptive to the entire family, including the children (COAs) (Dube et al., 2001). Adult children of dysfunctional families, where parental alcoholism is present, are typically referred to as adult children of alcoholics (ACOAs). It is suggested in various research studies that while alcoholic parents may love and support their children (Amodeo & Griffin, 1997, 2009), severe alcohol abuse negatively affects parental performance (Hall, 2010; Mulia, Yu, Greenfield, & Zemore, 2009). As a result, the parent's maladaptive parenting style is likely to lead to the development of child psychopathology (Kumpfer & Bluth, 2004; West & Prinz, 1987).

Several researchers also suggest that families with alcoholic members often are confused about the exact ways in which alcoholism has compromised their lives (Black, 2001; National Institute on Alcohol Abuse and Alcoholism, 2007). The (NIAAA) contends that the clinical literature focusing on the more dramatic events associated with alcoholism gives a misleading picture of its impact on the family. In addition, parent–child interactions tend to be more impaired in families with an alcoholic parent(s) (Hall, 2010; Walker & Lee, 1998; Werner, 1985; Werner & Johnson, 2000). Furthermore, in two-parent homes the alcohol-dependent parents as well as the non-alcohol-abusing parents significantly impact the children (Black, 2001; Hall, 2010; Kelley et al., 2007). The non-alcohol-abusing parent tends to become preoccupied with the alcoholic's behavior and overall welfare (Black, 2001; Kelley et al., 2007; Rodney, 1996). Therefore, s/he may struggle to provide their children with an emotionally supportive and healthy home environment (Hall, 2008; Kelley et al., 2007).

Evidence has been found that suggests that neither COAs nor ACOAs are destined to suffer from poor mental health. A large population of COAs grow up and function adequately, develop positive self-esteem,

J.C. Hall (✉)
University of Tennessee, Knoxville, TN, USA
e-mail: jhall39@utk.edu

D.S. Becvar (ed.), *Handbook of Family Resilience*,
DOI 10.1007/978-1-4614-3917-2_27, © Springer Science+Business Media New York 2013

481

and do not suffer from psychopathology or alcohol abuse and/or dependence themselves (Black, 2001; Giglio & Kaufman, 1990; Hussong, Zucker, Wong, Fitzgerald, & Puttler, 2005; Rodney, 1996). Although there is limited research available on the resilience of African-American COAs and ACOAs, several research studies have concluded that external support (e.g., kinship social support, community involvement) may serve as protective factors (Hall, 2005, 2007, 2008; Rodney & Mupier, 1999; Walker & Lee, 1998).

Kin and fictive kin networks informed by African-Americans' cultural legacy, sociopolitical history, and their patterns of migration and acculturation were created in response to their experience with inhibiting environments (e.g., alcoholic parentage, slavery, racism) (Hill, 1999; Hill-Collins, 1997; Stack, 1974). The strategy of relying on extended and fictive kin relationships reflects cultural legacies that emphasize the value of extended family and interdependence (i.e., collectivism) (Stack, 1974; Wilson & Tolson, 1990). African-Americans are more likely than Whites to live in extended family households that provide varied forms of social support (Hill). The results from a study comparing African-American ACOAs' and non-ACOAs' social support, coping responses, and self-esteem indicated that ACOAs who had kin/fictive kin relationships are more resilient (Hall, 2007). When compared to non-ACOAs, these ACOAs reported fewer problems with alcohol consumption, satisfactory appraisal and resolution of problems, and positive self-esteem (Hall, 2008; Rodney, 1996). Findings from empirical and theoretical literature suggest that "external support" is a key component in fostering resilience for at-risk populations (e.g., children of alcoholics) (Amodeo & Griffin, 1997, 2009; Hall, 2010; Rodney & Mupier, 1999). Understanding the concept of fluidity in the extended family household structures can be pivotal in the study of ACOAs' resilience.

Literature Review

Alcoholism and African-American Alcoholics

There is now a burgeoning interest in alcoholism among African-Americans (National Institute on Alcohol Abuse and Alcoholism, 2007). The NIAAA contends that alcoholism almost certainly ranks as the number one mental health problem, if not the most significant of all health problems, in Black urban communities. Alcohol is the world's most commonly used drug (NIAAA, 2007). Unlike most addictive substances, alcohol is legally available with minimal governmental regulation, does not require a prescription, is openly and frequently advertised, and is relatively inexpensive. Alcohol-related problems include economic losses resulting from time off of work owing to alcohol-related illness and injury, disruption of family and social relationships, emotional problems, impact on health, violence and aggression, and legal problems.

Determining the incidence of alcoholism in any community is difficult and largely depends on the definition one uses. Mulia et al. (2009) note that African-Americans report significantly higher numbers of drinking consequences and alcohol-dependence symptoms than do Whites. According to the reports by the National Institute on Alcohol Abuse and Alcoholism (2007) and the Substance Abuse and Mental Health Services Administration (SAMSHA, 2005), African-Americans and Whites report similar rates of frequent heavy drinking, but African-Americans are more likely to die of alcohol-related illnesses and injuries such as cirrhosis of the liver and alcohol-related automobile accidents.

The results from research studies on alcohol consumption among racial/ethnic groups indicated that African-American men with relatively low incomes were significantly more likely than their White counterparts to report high rates of alcohol-dependence symptoms; the reverse was true for African-American and White men with relatively high incomes (Mulia et al., 2009; National Institute on Alcohol Abuse and Alcoholism, 2007). Alcohol studies on African-Americans make up a small but growing body of research. A report by the NIAAA summarized research regarding drinking patterns in African-Americans as follows: (1) African-Americans report higher abstention rates than do

Whites; (2) African-Americans and Whites report similar levels of frequent heavy drinking; (3) rates of heavy drinking have not declined at the same rate among African-American men and women as among White men; and (4) variables, such as age, social class, church attendance, drinking norms, and coping behaviors may be important in understanding differences in drinking and drinking problem rates among African-Americans and Whites. Fetal alcohol syndrome, which is first manifested in infancy, emotional problems and hyperactivity in childhood, emotional problems and conduct problems in adolescence, and the development of alcoholism in adulthood (Grant, 2000; Ksir, Hart, & Ray, 2008) all affect COAs.

Adult Children of Alcoholics

Currently, there is a move to classify ACOAs' identifiable and diagnosable characteristics as a separate clinical syndrome in the *Diagnostic and Statistical Manual of Mental Disorders* (DSM-IV-TR; American Psychiatric Association, 2000). COAs tend to encounter many serious problems as they attempt to fulfill the demands of adult life. The clinical literature has suggested that ACOAs also may be at risk for emotional and interpersonal problems (Black, 2001). ACOAs have reported more alcohol-related deaths, frequent divorces, significantly less communication with their parents, and greater frequency of parental arguments and violence in their families of origin (Greer & Chwalisz, 2007; Porter & Pryor, 2007). Limited data are available regarding the development of resilience among this population; very few studies have targeted the African-American population. Although it is clear that many ACOAs experience difficulties within their families, it is also clear that many factors can contribute to positive adjustment outcomes. Extended family and/or social support networks found in African-American family systems are known protective mechanisms for at-risk children (Hall, 2005, 2008; Masten, 2001; Werner & Johnson, 2000). Research regarding the impact of kin/fictive kin relationships on fostering resilience among African-American ACOAs is scarce.

Researchers suggest that COAs may be at risk for developing a variety of self-esteem issues, depressive symptoms, coping problems, family dysfunction, and perceived lack of control over events in their environment (Dube et al., 2001; Hall, 2007; Scharff, Broaida, Conway, & Yue, 2004). Family circumstances define the nature and extent of the trauma, making a detailed examination of family resilience important. In addition, as noted above, COAs' adjustment to the alcoholic member and their attempts to cope with and survive the realities of alcoholism may be mediated by kin/fictive relationships within the family. Because it is clear that not all COAs are maladjusted, understanding the role of family (i.e., kin/fictive kin relationships) may provide important insights relative to the way it helps buffer the stress of parental alcoholism.

Which parent and how sick s/he is seems to be an important consideration. If the mother is an alcoholic, the household is usually more chaotic and the children suffer more, especially if the father escapes the drinking problem by overworking (Black, 2001). When the mother is an alcoholic, the oldest child may be turned into a surrogate housekeeper and companion, giving rise to the problems that accompany pseudo-adulthood (Chase, Deming, & Wells, 1998; Veronie & Fruehstorfer, 2001). This is especially true for African-American children living in an alcoholic home (Hall, 2005). In many cases, younger siblings in the home form a secure attachment to the eldest female (Bakermans-Kranenburg, van IJzenoorn, & Kroonenberg, 2004; Hall, 2007). This child is respected and held in high regard because of his/her ability to take care of everything and perform well. African-American ACOAs in this role also earn respect in the community (Hill, 1999). Further, Hill asserts that the feeling of being responsible is a source of satisfaction for those providing assistance or support to the family. McCubbin, Thompson, Thompson, and Futrell (1998) pointed out that the African-American female, because of culture, will also assume the role of a hero in healthy family functioning and is unlikely to seek help for her problems because of the rewards of praise from the family for being responsible.

Children in alcoholic homes live with chronic embarrassment and they also tend to develop a lack of trust (Black, 2001; Chen & Weitzman, 2005). One or both parents seemingly fail to nurture the child; hence, the child discovers his or her parents cannot be depended on (Black, 2001; Hall, 2007; Haughland, 2005). The availability of caring and emotionally supportive family, friends, siblings, teachers, and neighbors (i.e., kin/fictive kin relationships) helps to mediate stressors for African-American ACOAs (Hall, 2005). Several researchers (Chassin, Carle, Nissam-Sabat, & Kumpfer, 2004; Durant, 2005; Hall, 2007; McCubbin et al., 1998) have found that, in the presence of stressful life events, the odds of child maltreatment decreased as social support increased. Participants in Hall's (2008) study of African-American ACOAs reported that their problems decreased when family members (i.e., kin and fictive kin) provided support. Many college student ACOAs also have reported better adjustment and satisfactory academic achievements when kin and fictive kin provided support (Hall, 2007; Rodney & Mupier, 1999).

African-American Risk and Resilience Factors

The literature is replete with references to the strength and resilience in African-American families. Yet, African-American families continue to receive an abundance of negative press with regard to crime, violence, female-headed households, joblessness, and alcohol and other drug use, while the positive aspects have not received comparable attention. In a socially stratified society, social position variables determine access to critical resources. The social mechanisms of racism, prejudice, discrimination, and oppression make meeting family needs a much more difficult task for families of color (Boyd-Franklin, 2003; Denby, 1996; Foster, 1983). The physical, material, and social contexts that surround families and children have an enormous impact on parenting and socialization.

Recently female-headed households accounted for 48% of African-American families (Bureau of Labor Statistics, 2008). Although African-American children of female-headed households are not necessarily in one-adult households, they are two to three times more likely than White children to be raised in extended-family households. The families of African-American children are three times as likely to be poor compared to the families of White children (26.6%). The educational attainments of African-Americans are lower than Whites (e.g., 35% of Whites aged 25–34 have graduated from college, compared with 18% of African-Americans). Although less obvious than the income differential, family structure and maternal employment patterns as contextual factors are important in the determination of whether and what types of child care arrangements are needed by families (Wilson, 1989). Family roles are influenced by adaptive culture, and these roles can have implications for resilience. This is especially true for at-risk African-Americans, especially those plagued with parental substance abuse (i.e., ACOAs).

Children of alcoholics may rely more heavily on family and kin networks for child care, etc., whereas more acculturated families may rely more heavily on center-based or other formal care settings (Boyd-Franklin, 2003; Carter & McGoldrick, 2005; Foster, 1983). Cultural and contextual factors that influence early socialization experiences and goals for African-American children are different from those of their White counterparts (Garcia-Coll et al., 1996). It thus is important to consider how these factors foster resilience.

Among African-American families, egalitarian distribution of labor between husbands and wives has its base in historical demands that are still ongoing but at odds with societal belief systems about traditional male and female roles (Hill, 1999). The increasing demands and responsibilities of mothers detract from quality care of children, creating spillover stresses especially when substance abuse (e.g., parental alcoholism) is added to the equation. African cultures have been characterized as placing a greater premium on the values of collectivism and spirituality than Western European countries (Billingsley, 1992;

Hill, 1999). Families use these primary cultural values to inform their parenting practices. Collective economics, provision of financial supports, and expected absorption of child care responsibilities appear to be more common in the extended family life of African-American families.

The open structure and fluidity of the extended family household provide opportunities for the care and well-being of children. Fluidity in family living is not synonymous with instability (Boyd-Franklin, 2003; Foster, 1983). Rather, it is a cultural ideal that presumes the family unit exists beyond the boundaries of households; augmentation of household configurations is not unexpected and can be desired. Within this cultural ideal, parenting is perceived as a communal family duty. Although research is limited in this area, care giving within the extended family structure may be positively associated with child development for ethnic minority children (Wilson, 1989). For example, attachment security between African-American infants and their mothers has been found to be positively affected by the presence and involvement of their grandmothers (Flaherty, Facteau, & Garner, 1995). Infants of adolescent mothers have been viewed as typical recipients of the buffering effects of their grandmothers, although this circumstance may not always be true. Comparisons of outcomes for children in care with extended family with those in care with individuals outside the family circle, either by choice or necessity, may be especially relevant in the studies of the effects of child care for children of color, specifically, African-American ACOAs.

Attachment Relationships, Commitment, and Shared Values

According to Ainsworth (1967), personality theorists beginning with Sigmund Freud as well as those who followed him believed that a mother is a child's first significant attachment figure. The essential bond that a mother and child share is said to develop over the course of the infant's first year of life. In African-American families, although a secure attachment base is commonly established with the mother, it is common for infants and children to have multiple caregivers (Jackson, 1993; Jaeger, Hahn, & Weinraub, 2000). Whether the child develops a strong interpersonal relationship with his/her mother, father, or other caregiver in his/her life, this relationship can serve as a protective factor and can foster resilience (Kumpfer & Bluth, 2004). Multiple attachment relationships formed by kin and fictive kin caring for children began during slavery. According to Bowlby (Ainsworth, 1967), a warm and continuous relationship with a caregiver promotes psychological health and well-being throughout the life in a manner according to which children learn who their attachment figures are, how available they are, and how they may be expected to respond. Hence, many COAs may have multiple attachment figures (e.g., kin/fictive kin relationships) available and thus are better able to withstand the deleterious effects of parental alcoholism.

A number of factors associated with family resilience have been identified (e.g., collectivism, spirituality, social support, egalitarian family roles). The discussion of these factors in this section is given special emphasis regarding their importance for children of alcoholics. As mentioned above, children of families and communities of African descent traditionally interact with multiple caregivers, consisting of kin and fictive kin (Billingsley, 1992). This interaction gives meaning to the definition of family and the ways in which extended family members assist in the socialization and care of the young. "My family," "my folks," "my kin," "my people," are terms used by African-Americans to identify blood relatives and to denote relationships with special friends or "cared for" individuals who are not related by blood. Thus, family is a group of people who feel they belong to each other, although they may or may not live in the same house.

Among the strategies that African-Americans have employed successfully to strengthen the family is their approach to childrearing. Three aspects of African-American childrearing are offered as examples of successful strategies to preserve the family unit: (1) shared parenting, (2) pride in children, and

(3) "nurturing firmness" in discipline. Regarding the first of these, the use of "collective" or "shared" parenting is an African cultural residual employed by African-American families (Hill, 1999; Hill-Collins, 1997; Stack, 1974). This practice is exemplified by the extensive involvement of the entire family in childrearing, the use of older siblings in care giving, and intergenerational support (usually grand-mother or aunt to a younger mother). Black women's experiences as blood mothers, "other mothers," and community "other mothers" reveal that the mythical norm of a heterosexual, married couple, nuclear family with a non-working spouse, and a husband earning a "family wage" is far from being natural, universal, and preferred; rather, it is deeply embedded in specific race and class formations (Hill-Collins, 1997). Women-centered networks, inclusive of mothers, sisters, aunts, godmothers, and grandmothers, have been a force as well as an unchanging presence in African-American family life. Such networks fulfill varied roles: nurturer, financial provider, teacher, caregiver, and community and family stabilizer. These roles are indicative of the self-reliance, resourcefulness, and strength that are inherent in Black motherhood. The flexibly of Black motherhood becomes the foundation for promoting resilience.

The centrality of grandmothers is critical in bolstering African-American family functioning. Flaherty et al. (1995) found seven key functions of grandmothers in their study of multigenerational African-American families: managing, caretaking, coaching, assessing, nurturing, assigning, and patrolling. Grandmothers are often the glue that holds generations of family members together. Thus, grandmothers can easily become surrogate parents to children of alcoholics. They are referred to for guidance in both major and minor family matters. Such importance is not granted to the grandmother simply because of African-Americans' regard and respect for elders, but also because she epitomizes endurance, wisdom, and spirituality.

Various scholars have found that many grandmothers, sisters, aunts, or cousins act as "other mothers" by taking on child-care responsibilities for one another's children (Billingsley, 1992; Hatchett & Jackson, 1999; Hill-Collins, 1997). In 1999, Hill wrote that the presence of "other mothers" in Black extended families and community role modeling offers powerful support for the task of strengthening Black selfhood. Hill-Collins (1997) adds that boundaries between biological mothers and other women who care for their children are fluid. Hence, a child living with an alcoholic parent can receive the nurturance and support needed to become resilient. Further, McCubbin et al. (1998) noted that without the agency of caregivers from outside the nuclear families, many Black children would live significantly briefer and less comfortable lives. These practices continue in the face of social pressures.

Juxtaposed with the role of motherhood, the parameters of fatherhood are broad in the African-American community. Uncles, ministers, deacons, elders of the church, and male teachers can all be viewed as father figures. These men play a significant part in solidifying the foundation of African-American communities (Boyd-Franklin, 2003; Hatchett & Jackson, 1999). Contrary to popular belief, many biological fathers embrace their fatherly duties with sincerity and thoroughness. In their discussions of father–child interaction in the African-American family, Billingsley (1992) and Hill (1999) noted that given economic and social supports, African-American fathers welcome the responsibilities of childrearing. Black fathers, like fathers of all ethnic groups, take an equal part in the childrearing decisions in the family. The father's main relationship and interaction pattern appears to be nurturing, warm, and loving toward his children. In the case of the dubious father who may require extra incentive to fulfill his rightful responsibilities, elders or male fictive kin fill in the gaps by encouraging and redirecting him toward familial matters of importance. They also serve as role models, caretakers, tutors, and informal counselors for the youth of the community. Unselfish efforts such as these are performed to facilitate interest and shore up successful possibilities for young people who are victims of social, economic, and educational disenfranchisement. Several African-American men's groups provide opportunities for cathartic release and curative redirection.

When specifically examining alcoholic homes, research findings suggest that the alcoholic parent typically is not emotionally present to offer a stable and supportive care giving relationship to the children; therefore, the children must rely on the presence of a stable and supportive care giving relationship with the non-alcohol abusing parent (Hall, 2007; Walker & Lee, 1998). If the aforementioned kin/fictive kin relationships are present in the child's life, researchers suggest it is the most important protective factor known to produce resilient outcomes among COAs (Hall, 2005, 2010; Rodney, 1994; Rodney & Mupier, 1999; Walker & Lee, 1998).

Relationship Between Social Support, Family Resilience, and ACOAs

Resilience refers to the ability to adapt successfully to adversity, trauma, and threat. It involves attitudes, behaviors, and skills that can be cultivated, taught, and practiced. Resilience is not an end state but a dynamic process of interdependent forces—at the individual, family, group, and community levels—that continually shape and reshape the organism (cf., Masten, 2001). Werner and Johnson (1999), writing on resilient ACOAs, cite a number of possible protective factors including:

- Plenty of attention from the primary caretaker during infancy
- No additional births into the family in the first 2 years of life
- Absence of conflict between the parents during the first 2 years of life
- Average or above IQ
- Being achievement oriented
- Having an internal locus of control
- Believing in self-help
  Other studies (Hall, 2004, 2010; Werner, 1999) have identified three additional protective factors:
- "Easy" temperament, good problem-solving and communication skills, and an area of competence valued by the person or society.
- Socialization practices within the family that encourage trust, autonomy, initiative, and affectionate ties to a stable, caring, competent adult, whether a parent, grandparent, older sibling, or other kin.
- External support systems in the neighborhood, school, or the church that reinforce self-esteem and self-efficacy and provide the individual with a positive set of values.

Current Issues

The childrearing strategies of African-American families are protective of the child against the antagonistic environment located beyond the community and in some cases within the family. The importance of fostering naturally occurring social supports for African-American children of alcoholics is crucial for resilience. Naturally occurring support that resides in families, friends, rituals, and traditions is embedded in the kin/fictive kin relationships found in African-American culture. Symbolically, the family is the source and the reflection of the African-American culture. The family has also been the source of strength, resilience, and survival. The value of group effort for the common interest is taught as an enduring strategy for the survival of the African-American community, as opposed to an individual effort for private gain (Foster, 1983). Stack and Burton (1993) refer to this concept of group effort as "interdependent lives" in their description of the family life course perspective of the kinscripts framework. Although shared roles between husbands and wives may be a relatively new phenomenon within the dominant, middle-class culture, this egalitarian practice has been an enduring tradition in African-American families (Hill, 1999). The sharing of roles lessens the pressures associated with raising a family and ultimately promotes family cohesion and strength (Hill).

These similarities cut across specific religious beliefs and across cultures whether the patterns are from the Caribbean, Africa, or were the result of enslavement within the United States (Hill, 1999; Logan, 2000). The common cultural patterns that have contributed to the resilience of African-American families are: supportive social networks, flexible relationships within the family unit, a strong sense of religiosity, extensive use of extended family helping, and strong identification with their racial group. They pertain to the empowerment that comes when as many as are able to earn a living, meet their families' basic needs, and have a little bit left over to help others in the extended family who may need temporary assistance. As the extended family circles widen and overlap, the entire community would theoretically be covered. In addition to contributions, it is common practice within African-American families to make small loans with token or no interest to one another on a short-term basis. This may seem at first to be in conflict with the group-effort ethic, but it actually extends that ethic. The ability "to get it from each other" is highly valued because underlying the exchange of funds is the strength that comes from self-reliance and the demonstration of trust between family members.

Many African-American families continue to place a high value on respecting and obeying elders. In addition to honoring the special status of elderly persons, a high value is also placed on obedience to parents as well as other older persons, including an older sibling. Another value found within the African-American culture that has a lasting legacy in strengthening the family unit is spirituality or religion (Haight, 1998). From its inception, the African-American church has been the place where community members learned the values and responsibilities of leadership and organizational skills, since in the past these experiences were not available in the larger society. The church often serves as a vehicle of renewal and solace. In addition to providing spiritual guidance, church activities (e.g., church "welfare" programs, libraries, nurseries, preschools, Saturday and Sunday schools) intensify the bonding and solidarity of African-American families. Many African-American ACOAs utilize tangible resources provided by local churches (Hall, 2007).

It bears repeating that a discussion of African-American family characteristics that help to enhance the family system and protect ACOAs is incomplete without the mention of the strong sense of communalism that is prevalent in most African-American families, about which much has been written. Communalism focuses on two points, family support structures and community support structures. Two key elements in family support structures that enrich African-American families are kinship networks and egalitarian family units. African-American families tend to rely on kin/fictive kin relationships in maintaining the family unit. The findings from a study of African-American college students ($n=100$) indicate that both non-ACOAs and ACOAs utilized family and community support available through kin/fictive kin relationships (Hall, 2010).

Case Study

Louise (fictitious name), a 23-year old, African-American college student, was a client at the counseling center for which I volunteered several years ago. She was a plus-sized woman, casually dressed, wearing light makeup, and well groomed. Louise was articulate and well mannered. She reported feeling sad and uninspired to complete her studies. Her affect and mood were congruent with clinical depression, with no homicidal and/or suicidal ideations. She reported a family history of parental alcoholism and currently was sharing an apartment with a friend off campus. She had been living independently since she was 17 years old. Her relationships with her stepmom and father were considerably strained, and except on holidays, she rarely saw them. Louise reported that her relationship with her mom, the non-custodial parent during childhood, had blossomed. A thorough psychosocial history revealed a history of childhood sexual abuse by an elder male cousin and some experimentation with drugs and alcohol. She denied substance abuse and/or dependence, and her above-average GPA, as well as her college and community service supported this reality. A complete physical examination screened out biological etiology for depression. However, she delayed anti-depressant medication and decided to participate in a 14-week series of psychotherapy sessions. Initial sessions consisted of a battery of psychological testing to rule out personality disorders, etc.

The next three sessions focused on her disruptive and "chaotic family life," after which Louise was more reflective and began talking about some of the "good times" she had during childhood. She reported having considerable guilt about the fact that she was able to "escape the family drama and avoid ruining what little chance she had to live a 'normal' life." Upon further exploration, she also reported that both of her parents were alcoholics. She said, "My stepmom was the breadwinner; dad vs Dad was unable to keep a job because he drank too much. I never knew what to expect from day to day. It was like growing up in a three ring circus." The latter comment seemed curious and I asked her to say more:

> My dad was like Dr. Jekyll and Mr. Hyde, it was comical, I mean sort of. More like strange, every day I didn't know what to expect from him. Some days he was the fun, loving, caring father. Then he would get downright mean and verbally abusive. The whole family [she has two younger step-brothers] walked on egg shells to avoid setting him off. He [her dad] was never physically abusive towards us, but we didn't know if and when he would become violent. He was an IN YOUR FACE mad, drunk!
>
> When I was 8-years old I started summer camp, it was a program sponsored by the city for inner-city children. The program really boosted my confidence, academic performance, and I began to enjoy school. I loved school. I got good grades; it [school] was something that I could bury myself in 'cause I was shy and passive. [Her sexual abuse had reportedly occurred around this time.] When I started summer camp the counselors were very nice people, you know they were nice for no reasons and this was odd coming from where I came from. You know, people weren't just nice to you. These counselors had a deep concern and genuine interest in the children, and so, I really grabbed on to that and I soaked it all [meaning the experience] up for what it was worth. Being at camp and around the campus really sparked a fire in me to excel. When I started the program my grades had began to slip, I wasn't performing very well, and I didn't feel good about myself. So, I think the program came just in the nick of time. Going to the program enabled me to leave an abusive home and it coincided with my meeting someone [counselor-fictive kin] who helped me get back on track and helped me believe that I could do anything and be anyone and this helped me a lot. The program and my counselor were definitely a blueprint for me to excel and do something different and be something outside of the 'hood. My counselor inspired me to be the greatest person I could be. When camp ended I kept in touch with my counselor, I still do. My parents gave me permission to spend time with her. I mean we went horseback riding, swimming was my first time swimming—and all that kind of stuff and it was just her showing me that there is more to the world. Because my home was not the best place to me; you know my neighborhood and with parents drinking and low-income, spending time with her [counselor] showed me how things could be better. When I was 10-years old, my counselor convinced my family to let me go to boarding school. I knew that I would miss my family, but it was the best thing to do. My counselor would visit on the weekends and drive me home during holiday and semester breaks. I loved spending time with her [counselor]; my folks even let me spend Christmas with her. I met her family and have maintained a relationship with them too.

This case study illustrates how at-risk children who are competent, have good communication skills, and an external support system can be resilient. Race, class, gender, and socioeconomic status were culturally relevant factors to consider when working with Louise. The client's history of having non-persons of color within her social support enabled her to establish trust and facilitate a therapeutic alliance with other non-persons of color on her treatment team. Louise expressed feelings of abandonment when her parents divorced and described her inability to form a secure attachment relationship with her alcoholic stepmother. Guided by clinical supervision, I continuously addressed objective counter transference (i.e., failure at being the "good enough" mother).

Clinical Implications

The survival of the Black family has been embedded in the adaptive functions of the kinship network. The family is the principal source of socialization and protection against racism. Several authors posit that the kinship network functions as a protective buffer against institutional racism, discrimination, and bigotry for at-risk African-Americans (Billingsley, 1992; Hill, 1999; Hill-Collins, 1997; Logan, 2000; Smith, 2000). Smith (2000) defines the "Black helping tradition" as the independent struggle of Blacks for their survival and advancement from generation to generation (Hill, 1999; Hill-Collins, 1997; McCubbin et al., 1998). Billingsley (1992), Hill (1999), and Hill-Collins (1997) have argued that the whole of African-American families is greater than the sum of its parts. There is a wealth of theoretical and empirical evidence to suggest that the presence of traditional and fictive kin relationships is key to overcoming oppression and fostering resilience for African-American ACOAs. Kin and fictive kin relationships are essentially the glue that holds the family together for ACOAs and non-ACOAs who experience high levels of conflict that break down family communication and cohesion (Hall, 2009).

Although less true now than in the past, the African-American community still maintains a belief that all responsible adults are expected to act in *loco parentis* for children in the community. The presence of an adult has traditionally been enough to deter the young African-American child from too much wrongdoing because the non-parent adult in whose presence the child is acting out usually will comment on or correct the obvious problem behavior (Billingsley, 1992; Hill, 1999). The notion of "loco parentis" is particularly important for ACOAs whose parents (i.e., non-drinking and alcoholic) are unavailable. Things have changed somewhat from the days when a non-parent adult could "take a switch" to the child, but a considerable amount of behavioral observation and advice about appropriate punishment is alive and well in the African-American community. In fact, in Hall's (2008) study of African-American college student ACOAs, most participants stated that only "kin" would physically and/or verbally reprimand them. The majority of ACOAs and non-ACOAs reported that fictive kin generally provided nurturance and/or tangible support.

In a longitudinal study covering more than 40 years, Werner and Johnson (2000) found that the presence of at least one caring person provides support for healthy development and learning. The availability of caring and emotionally supportive family, friends, siblings, teachers, and neighbors mediates stressors. Numerous other researchers have found that in the presence of stressful life events, the odds of child maltreatment decreased as social support increased (Hall, 2005; Masten, 2001; McCubbin et al., 1998). At a time of widespread concern about the demise of the family, the African-American family has much to teach us because mental health professionals need useful conceptual tools as much as techniques to support and strengthen families. McCubbin et al. (1998) found that the knowledge of successful adaptation under stressful life conditions also strengthens the conceptual base needed to frame both treatment and preventive intervention for high-risk youth, families, and especially ethnic minority families. These networks of community-based childcare extend beyond the boundaries of biologically and legally related persons and are commonly known as fictive kin. Even when relationships involve kin or fictive kin, community norms traditionally have been such that neighbors cared for one another's children. The resilience of these networks illustrates how cultural values help people cope with and manage daily struggles. In acknowledging the significance of kin/fictive kin relationships that serve as alternate attachment figures for "at-risk" populations, we have identified a resource that enables children and/or groups to prevail against adversity.

Given these aspects of African-American families it is important that clinicians working with African-American COAs and ACOAs help the client identify the key stakeholders in their support systems. Socioeconomic status, education level, geographic location, and gender will be key factors for treatment and the client's ability to access social support. It is imperative that both the client and clinician define the roles and type(s) of support contributed by identified key stakeholders (i.e., kin and fictive kin). In most cases, the client's social support system is an essential asset for successful goal achievement; hence, it is important that the clinician establishes a partnership with these individuals. Respect is a key factor for building trusting relationships, according to Boyd-Franklin (1989):

> Most therapists spend many years in school, where attitudes and interaction tend to follow along more "casual" lines than they do in many African American families. Students call the professors by their first names and refer to each other informally. When they [therapists] begin to work with families, their natural tendency is to view an informal "first-name basis" style as putting people at their ease. With Black families, particularly older, more traditional family members, this may be a serious error. Although many younger Black families allow children to call adults by their first names, many older or more traditional Black families are offended by this practice, seeing it as a sign of disrespect. The therapist should take his or her cues from the family (p. 109).

The clinician should routinely evaluate how the social support system impacts treatment either negatively or positively. This can be accomplished by asking the client and/or other stakeholders their perspectives regarding goal attainment. Successful treatment will be gauged by the client's ability to implement the skills and resources identified throughout treatment. Hence, the clinician should also utilize the client's social support system in both the discharge and follow-up treatment planning.

Research Implications

Researchers are now beginning to appreciate what many in African-American communities have long known, Black families in their day-to-day living have not acquiesced to the oppression around them (Hall, 2007, 2010; Hill, 1999; Hill-Collins, 1997; Rodney & Mupier, 1999). Values related to family are rooted in African traditions. The tradition of extended family members caring for children was carried on during slavery in plantation communities and today is a dependable source of support for ACOAs. Black mothers, "other mothers," and fathers (fictive kin) play key roles in transmitting an Afrocentric worldview to their children and reliable sources of kinship support for ACOAs. The Afrocentric paradigm proposes that in African culture, humanity is viewed as a collective rather than as individuals, and that this collective view is expressed as shared concern and responsibility for the well-being of others. African-Americans are firmly committed to developing the child's knowledge of his or her kinship and who his or her people/family are (Foster, 1983). As knowledge is instilled, so is a sense of curiosity and caring about family relationships. It is quite rewarding to see a child's first awareness that "Mama's sister" is "my aunt," or that Tammye is "my sister." As children place him/her within this cycle of people they care about and who care about them, their experience of the meaning of family and their sense of belonging is heightened. This sense of "belonging" is vital to African-American ACOAs' and non-ACOAs' adjustment in college (Geisner, Larimer, Neighbors, & Neighbors, 2004; Hall, 2010). Collins (1997) and Hill (1999) contend that the ties that bind the Black community together exist primarily because of vigilant actions of kin/fictive kin networks that shape the culture of survival, and the social organizational framework of local and national expressions of African-American community.

Although times have changed and African-American lifestyles are undergoing tremendous evolution, the extended family is still quite viable for many. Difficult life experiences take their toll on children despite possible avenues of resilience. Kin and fictive kin relationships borne out in the cultural values and traditions of the African-American family serve as pathways for promoting resilience for at-risk populations (e.g., children of alcoholics). Therefore, it is important that researchers focus on the inter- and intrapersonal factors that promote resilience among African-American COAs. In addition, future studies should investigate the long-term effects of social support systems for COAs' resilience.

Conclusion

The importance of the extended family (i.e., kin/fictive kin) as a strength has been clearly documented. Throughout this chapter, I have discussed the importance of African-American family resilience. In most cases, family members rely on the informal support provided by kin and fictive kin relationships when crises occur. African-American families are diverse (e.g., functional/dysfunctional, single-parent, two parent, multigenerational), and most value extended family. At the same time, a word of caution is appropriate: it is imperative that clinicians avoid a cookie-cutter treatment approach. Like most families, African-American families have strengths and weaknesses, and it is important to focus on each unique family as well as the culturally embedded nature of their social support system.

References

Ainsworth, M. D. (1967). *Infancy in Uganda: Infant care and the growth of love*. Baltimore, MD: John Hopkins.

American Psychiatric Association. (2000). *Diagnostic and statistical manual of mental disorders* (4th ed., Text Revised). Washington, DC: American Psychiatric Association.

Amodeo, M., & Griffin, M. L. (1997). Parental alcoholism and other family disruptions: Adult outcomes among sisters. *The American Journal of Orthopsychiatry, 67*(4), 585–593.

Amodeo, M., & Griffin, M. L. (2009). Sibling agreement on retrospective reports of parental alcoholism and other childhood events. *Substance Use & Misuse, 44*(7), 943–964.

Bakermans-Kranenburg, M. J., van IJzenoorn, M. H., & Kroonenberg, P. M. (2004). Differences in attachment security between African-American and white children: Ethnicity or socio-economic status? *Infant Behavior & Development, 27*(3), 417–433.

Billingsley, A. (1992). *Climbing Jacob's ladder*. New York: Simon & Schuster.

Black, C. (2001). *It will never happen to me: Growing up with addiction as youngsters, adolescents and adults*. Denver: M.A.C.

Boyd-Franklin, N. (1989). *Black families in therapy. A multisystems approach*. New York: Guilford.

Boyd-Franklin, N. (Ed.). (2003). *Black families in therapy: Understanding the African American experience*. New York: Guilford.

Bureau of Labor Statistics. (2008). *Employed and unemployed full- and part-time workers by age, sex, race, and Hispanic or Latino ethnicity*. Retrieved December 1, 2010, from http://www.bls.gov/cps/cpsaat8.pdf.

Carter, B., & McGoldrick, M. (Eds.). (2005). *The expanded family life cycle: Individual, family, and social perspectives* (3rd ed.). Boston: Pearson.

Chase, N. D., Deming, M. P., & Wells, M. C. (1998). Parentification, parental alcoholism, and academic status among young adults. *American Journal of Family Therapy, 26*(2), 105–114.

Chassin, L., Carle, A. C., Nissim-Sabat, D., & Kumpfer, K. L. (2004). Fostering resilience in children of alcoholic parents. In K. I. Maton, C. J. Schellenbach, B. J. Leadbeater, & A. L. Solarz (Eds.), *Investing in children, youth, families, and communities: Strengths-based research and policy* (pp. 137–155). Washington, DC: American Psychological Association.

Chen, Y. Y., & Weitzman, E. R. (2005). Depressive symptoms, DSM-IV alcohol abuse and their comorbidity among children of problem drinkers in a national survey: Effects of parent and child gender and parent recovery status. *Journal of Studies on Alcohol and Drugs, 66*, 66–73.

Denby, R. W. (1996). *Resiliency and the African American family: A model of family preservation*. Kansas: Westview.

Dube, S. R., Anda, R. F., Felitti, V. J., Croft, J. B., Edwards, V. J., & Giles, W. H. (2001). Growing up with parental alcohol abuse: Exposure to childhood abuse, neglect, and household dysfunction. *Child Abuse & Neglect, 25*(12), 1627–1640.

Durant, A. (2005). African-American alcoholics: An interpretive/constructivist model of affiliation with alcoholics (AA). *Journal of Ethnicity in Substance Abuse, 4*(1), 5–21.

Flaherty, M. J., Sr., Facteau, L., & Garner, P. (1995). Grandmother functions in multigenerational families: An exploratory study of Black adolescent mothers and their infants. In R. Staples (Ed.), *The Black family: Essays and studies* (pp. 195–203). Belmont, CA: Wadsworth.

Foster, H. J. (1983). African patterns in the Afro-American family. *Journal of Black Studies, 14*, 201–232.

Garcia-Coll, C., Lamberty, G., Jenkins, R., McAdoo, H. P., Crnic, K., Wasik, B. H., et al. (1996). An integrative model for the study of developmental competencies in minority children. *Child Development, 67*(5), 1891–1914.

Geisner, I. M., Larimer, M. E., Neighbors, C., & Neighbors, C. (2004). The relationship among alcohol use, related problems, and symptoms of psychological distress: Gender as a moderator in a college sample. *Addictive Behaviors, 6*, 843–848.

Giglio, J. J., & Kaufman, E. (1990). The relationship between child adult psychopathology in children of alcoholics. *The International Journal of the Addictions, 25*(3), 263–390.

Grant, B. F. (2000). Estimates of US children exposed to alcohol abuse and dependence in the family. *American Journal of Public Health, 90*, 112–126.

Greer, T. W., & Chwalisz, K. (2007). Minority-related stressors and coping processes among African American college students. *Journal of College Student Development, 48*, 388–404.

Haight, W. L. (1998). "Gathering the Spirit" at First Baptist Church: Spirituality as a protective factor in the lives of African American children. *Social Work, 43*(3), 213–221.

Hall, J. C. (2004). An exploratory study of the role of kinship ties in fostering resilience among African American adult children of alcoholics. *Dissertation Abstracts International, 65*, 10, 3991 (UMI No. 3152224).

Hall, J. C. (2005). An *exploratory study of the role of kinship ties in fostering resilience among African American adult children of alcoholics*. Doctoral dissertation, ProQuest Dissertations and Theses database. (UMI No. 3152224).

Hall, J. C. (2007). An exploratory study of the role of kinship ties in promoting resilience among African American adult children of alcoholics. *Journal of Human Behavior in the Social Environment, 15*(2–3), 61–78.

Hall, J. C. (2008). The impact of kin and fictive kin relationships on the mental health of Black adult children of alcoholics. *Health and Social Work, 33*(4), 259–266.

Hall, J. C. (2010). Childhood perceptions of family, social support, parental alcoholism, and later alcohol use among Black college student. *Journal of Substance Use, 3*(15), 157–165.

Hatchett, S. J., & Jackson, J. S. (1999). African American extended kin systems: An empirical assessment in the national survey of Black Americans. In H. P. McAdoo (Ed.), *Family ethnicity: Strength in diversity* (2nd ed., pp. 171–190). Thousand Oaks, CA: Sage.

Haughland, B. S. (2005). Recurrent disruptions of rituals and routines in families with paternal alcohol abuse. *Family Relations, 54*(2), 225–241.

Hill, R. B. (1999). *The strengths of African American families: Twenty-five years later.* Lanham, MD: University Press of America.

Hill-Collins, P. (1997). The meaning of motherhood in Black culture and Black mother/daughter relationships. In M. M. Gergen & S. N. Davis (Eds.), *Toward a new psychology of gender* (pp. 325–340). New York: Routledge.

Hussong, A. M., Zucker, R. A., Wong, M. M., Fitzgerald, H. E., & Puttler, L. I. (2005). Social competence in children of alcoholic parents over time. *Developmental Psychology, 41*(5), 747–759.

Jackson, J. F. (1993). Multiple caregiving among African Americans and infant attachment: The need for an emic approach. *Human Development, 36*(2), 87–102.

Jaeger, E., Hahn, N., & Weinraub, M. (2000). Attachment in adult daughters of alcoholic fathers. *Addiction, 95*(2), 267–276.

Kelley, M. L., French, A., Bountress, K., Keefe, H. A., Schroeder, V., Steer, K., et al. (2007). Parentification and family responsibility in the family of origin of adult children of alcoholics. *Addictive Behaviors, 32*(4), 675–685.

Ksir, C., Hart, C. L., & Ray, O. (2008). *Drugs, society, and human behavior* (12th ed.). New York: McGraw-Hill.

Kumpfer, K. L., & Bluth, B. (2004). Parent/child transactional processes predictive of resilience or vulnerability to "substance abuse disorders". *Substance Use & Misuse, 39*(5), 671–698.

Logan, S. L. M. (Ed.). (2000). *The Black family: Strengths, self-help, and positive change.* Boulder, CO: Westview.

Masten, A. (2001). Ordinary magic: Resilience processes in development. *The American Psychologist, 56*(3), 227–238.

McCubbin, H. I., Fleming, W. M., Thompson, A. I., Neitman, P., Elver, K. M., & Savas, S. A. (1998). Resiliency and coping in "At Risk" African-American youth and their families. In H. I. McCubbin, E. A. Thompson, A. I. Thompson, & J. A. Futrell (Eds.), *Resiliency in African-American Families* (pp. 287–328). Thousand Oaks, CA: Sage.

McCubbin, H. I., Thompson, E. A., Thompson, A. I., & Futrell, J. A. (Eds.). (1998). *Resiliency in African-American families.* Thousand Oaks, CA: Sage.

Mulia, N., Yu, Y., Greenfield, T. K., & Zemore, S. E. (2009). Disparities in alcohol-related problems among White, Black, and Hispanic Americans. *Alcoholism Clinical and Experimental Research, 33*(4), 654–662.

Mupier, R., Rodney, H. E., & Samuels, L. A. (2002). Difference in parenting style between African American alcoholic and nonalcoholic parents. *Families in Society, 83*(5–6), 604–610.

National Institute on Alcohol Abuse and Alcoholism. (2007, February). Retrieved November 18, 2009, from http://www.niaaa.nih.gov/FAQs/General-English/.

Porter, S. R., & Pryor, J. (2007). The effects of heavy episodic alcohol use on student engagement, academic performance and time use. *Journal of College Student Development, 48*, 455–467.

Rodney, H. E. (1994). What differentiates ACOAs and non-ACOAs on a Black college campus? *Journal of American College Health, 43*(2), 57–63.

Rodney, H. E. (1996). Inconsistencies in the literature on collegiate adult children of alcoholics: Factors to consider for African Americans. *Journal of American College Health, 45*(1), 19–25.

Rodney, H. E., & Mupier, R. (1999). The impact of parental alcoholism on self-esteem and depression among African-American adolescents. *Journal of Child and Adolescent Substance Abuse, 8*(3), 55–71.

Scharff, J. L., Broaida, J. P., Conway, K., & Yue, A. (2004). The interaction of parental alcoholism, adaptation role and familial dysfunction. *Addictive Behaviors, 29*, 575–587.

Smith, H. Y. (Ed.). (2000). *Building on the strengths of Black families: Self-help and empowerment* (2nd ed.). Boulder, CO: Westview.

Stack, C. (1974). *All our kin: Strategies for survival in a black community.* New York: Harper & Row.

Stack, C., & Burton, L. M. (1993). Kinscripts. *Journal of Comparative Family Studies, 24*(2), 157–170.

Substance Abuse & Mental Health Services Administration. (2005). *The national survey on drug use and health report: Illicit drug use among lifetime nondrinkers and lifetime alcohol users.* Retrieved January 13, 2011, from http://www.oas.samhsa.gov/2k4/alcDU/alcDU.pdf.

Veronie, L., & Fruehstorfer, D. B. (2001). Gender, birth order and family role identification among adult children of alcoholics. *Current Psychology, 20*(1), 53–67.

Walker, J. P., & Lee, R. E. (1998). Uncovering strengths of children of alcoholic parents. *Contemporary Family Therapy, 20*(4), 521–538.

Werner, E. E. (1985). Resilient offspring of alcoholics: A longitudinal study from birth to age 18. *Journal of Studies on Alcohol, 47*(1), 34–40.

Werner, E. E. (1999). Can we apply resilience? In M. D. Glantz & J. L. Johnson (Eds.), *Resilience and development: Positive life adaptations, longitudinal research in the social and behavioral sciences* (pp. 2259–2268). New York, NY: Kluwer Academic/Plenum Publishers.

Werner, E. E., & Johnson, J. L. (2000). *The role of caring adults in the lives of children of alcoholics* (Children of Alcoholics: Selected Readings, Vol. 2). Rockville, MD: National Association for Children of Alcoholics.

Werner, E.E. & Johnson, J. L. (2004). Therole of caring adults in the lives of children of alcoholics. Children of Alcoholics: Selected readings, (Volume 2). National Association for Children of Alcoholics. Rockville, MD.

West, M. O., & Prinz, R. J. (1987). Parental alcoholism and childhood psychopathology. *Psychological Bulletin, 102*(2), 204–218.

Wilson, M. N. (1989). Child development in the context of the Black extended family. *The American Psychologist, 44*(2), 380–385.

Wilson, M. N., & Tolson, T. F. (1990). Familial support in the Black community. *Journal of Clinical Child Psychology, 19*(4), 347–355.

Kim M. Anderson

Introduction

In this Chapter I build on my prior qualitative and quantitative inquiries regarding psychological recovery for females who as children witnessed their mothers being abused by an intimate partner (Anderson & Bang, 2012; Anderson & Danis, 2006; Anderson, Danis, & Havig, 2011). Previous findings underscored how adult daughters can recover from childhood exposure to domestic violence and, against formidable odds, exhibit resilience. However, more research on child witnesses is necessary to further delineate the connection between childhood protective factors and adult hardiness. Additional attention needs to be given to children's specific cognitive, emotional, and behavioral responses along with familial and external support in response to inter-parental conflict. Keeping this in mind, I examine here the retrospective reports of adult daughters ($N=68$) regarding the range of protective strategies employed during childhood and how they may relate, if at all, to adult functioning (i.e., resilience, posttraumatic stress disorder [PTSD]).

Significance of the Topic

When traumatic events occur during childhood they are more likely to be a part of one's identity, serving as a developmental basis for perceiving, thinking, and reacting to life circumstances (Tedeschi & Calhoun, 1995). Herman's (1997) "dose–response" curve implies that the more one is exposed to traumatic effects, the more severe the symptoms will be, and, consequently, the more difficulty one has with recovery. Associated with the intensity of symptomatology for child witnesses are the frequency, severity, and chronicity of violence in the home and the child's relationship with his or her mother and the male who batters her (Edleson, et al., 2007; Mohr & Tulman, 2000; Murrell, Merwin, Christoff, & Henning, 2005). Additionally, exposure to multiple concurrent factors (e.g., child abuse as well as domestic violence) is often more predictive of maladaptation than the presence of any of such factors alone (Edleson, 1999; Mohr & Tulman, 2000; Morgolin & Gordis, 2004). A number of additional factors may influence the degree to which exposure to adult domestic violence may affect

K.M. Anderson (✉)
School of Social Work, University of Missouri,
705 Clark Hall, Columbia, MO 65211-4470, USA
e-mail: andersonki@missouri.edu

D.S. Becvar (ed.), *Handbook of Family Resilience*,
DOI 10.1007/978-1-4614-3917-2_28, © Springer Science+Business Media New York 2013

a child's development, including a child's age (Mabanglo, 2002), gender (Reynolds, Wallace, Hill, Weist, & Nabors, 2001), and parental mental health problems and substance abuse (Anderson & Bang, 2012).

Traumatic responses vary for each individual; yet, several studies show that children who are exposed to acts of violence between their parents or parental figures are found to be more maladjusted when compared to individuals from nonviolent families (Dehon & Weems, 2010; McFarlane, Groff, O'Brien, & Watson, 2003). Findings suggest that there is a connection between domestic violence exposure and the development of symptomatology for children including behavioral problems such as conduct disorder, physical aggression, hyperactivity, inattentiveness, impulsivity, destructiveness, and noncompliance (McFarlane et al., 2003; Meltzer, Doos, Vostanis, Ford, & Goodman., 2009; Osofsky, 2003; Wolfe, Crooks, Lee, McIntyre-Smith & Jaffe, 2003). Social adjustment difficulties include poor peer relationships, academic problems, a lack of adaptive interpersonal attachments, and an increased likelihood that a child will become either a victim or a perpetrator of violence later in life (Clements, Oxtoby, & Ogle, 2008).

Child victims may blame themselves for their mothers being abused and feel helpless to change their family situation, creating internalizing problems such as depression, anxiety, low self-esteem, and somatic complaints (Hughes, 1988; Kitzmann, Gaylord, Hold & Kenny, 2003). Morgolin and Gordis (2004) underscore the increased risk of emotional and mood disorders, particularly posttraumatic stress symptoms such as numbing, an exaggerated startle response, nightmares, flashbacks, and emotional detachment from others. Thus, standing by and witnessing violence involving people who are close to them often carries a psychological price for children (Von Steen, 1997).

Exposure to domestic violence also influences parent–child intimacy and the cohesiveness of the child's self-image. The level of the father's aggression toward the mother impacts not only adolescents' perceptions of their parents but of themselves as well (Winstok, Eisikovits, & Karnieli-Miller, 2004). For instance, in cases of mild aggression, adolescents are more likely to identify with their fathers than their mothers. However, as the severity of aggression increases, youth are more likely to distance themselves from their fathers and identify more with their mothers because they have more difficulty separating the abuser from the act of violence. Additionally, more aggression is associated with the adolescent forming more negative perceptions of himself or herself and of his or her parents.

Children of abused women often have conflicted feelings toward both their abusive and victimized caregivers that may linger into adulthood. These feelings may range from empathy to resentment and often these children are not able to share such feelings with their parents. Additionally, they perceive their parents to be less caring and supportive and thus may physically and emotionally distance themselves (Dick, 2005; Henning, et al., 1997; Moon, 2000). Other problematic familial relationships include bonds with siblings that may serve as triggers of the past, or, having assumed particular roles such as being a caregiver, may expect them to continue in that role.

Adults who still carry the childhood scars of witnessing parental violence are beginning to receive more attention, as is empirical research on the long-term effects. In comparison to nonexposed individuals, adult children of abused women experience greater depression (Forstrom-Cohen & Rosenbaum, 1985; Russell, Springer, & Greenfield, 2010), anxiety (Henning, Leitenberg, Coffey, Turner, & Bennett, 1996), psychological distress (Silvern et al., 1995), lower self-esteem (Moon, 2000), and posttraumatic stress (Feerick & Haugaard, 1999). Although research indicates that witnessing inter-parental violence as a child is related to long-term consequences, there remains a dearth of knowledge in regard to adult psychosocial outcomes for this population, particularly regarding the dynamics of resilience (Anderson & Bang, 2012).

Literature Review

Resilience Research

Recognition that not all children exposed to adverse conditions develop adult pathologies has led to the emergence of research on resilience (Fraser, 1997; Masten, 2001; Wolin & Wolin, 1993). Much of this research focuses on uncovering those attributes that help at-risk children resist stress. Such protective factors evolve from the adaptive changes that occur when children *successfully* cope with stress. Research on resilience recognizes a complex interaction among individual attributes (e.g., internal locus of control, problem solving), family milieu (e.g., a safe and secure adult connection, parental stability), and social interactions (e.g., positive adult and peer relations) in promoting well-being (Fraser, 1997; Masten, 2001; Nicolotti, El-Sheikh, & Whitson, 2003).

As inquiry on the consequences of children's exposure to domestic violence has progressed, it has become evident that adaptation varies for each individual and, in fact, some exposed children show no greater problems than nonexposed children (Graham-Bermann & Edleson, 2001). Although not as well studied compared to research on the effects of exposure to domestic violence, some children are resilient relative to such exposure (Graham-Bermann, DeVoe, Mattis, Lynch, & Thomas, 2006). The commonalities across different studies on coping and resilience, including my prior research (Anderson & Bang, 2012; Anderson & Danis, 2006; Anderson et al., 2011), are presented in an attempt to address how some children exposed to domestic violence engage with risk factors and remain competent or develop capacities despite significant stressors in their lives.

Individual Protective Factors

Resilient children have several positive attributes that contribute to their successful engagement with risk factors related to exposure to domestic violence. Ways of coping include trying to make sense of the violence, creating a psychological or physical safe space, keeping siblings safe, being vigilant, attempting to intervene and summon help, and expressing their anger to their parents about the violence (Anderson & Danis, 2006; Humphreys, 2001; Mullender, Hague, Imam, Kelly, Malos, & Regan, 2002). Additionally, attributing the cause of violence to the abuser rather than to the victim or to the self is associated with positive adjustment in children (Grych, Fincham, Jouriles, & McDonald, 2000). Other protective factors include developing an internal locus of control (i.e., insight about what they can and cannot control) and positive self-esteem within at least one area of the child's life such as school, home, or peers (Martin, 2002).

To truly understand resilience, the context of adverse conditions—from which resilience emanates—needs further explication in resilience research and trauma theory. There is minimal if any detail given to how resilience is forged within a particular context of oppression. The term *adverse* is used to describe difficult or even traumatic family environments; yet, the context for these conditions often is stripped or minimized (Cowger, Anderson, & Snively, 2006). Thus, I set out to address this contextual issue in a qualitative study of resilient adult daughters ($N=12$, M age$=37$ years ± 9, European American, $n=9$) that documented how as children they used a variety of protective strategies to "withstand" and "oppose" a sense of powerlessness due to the batterer's oppression of their mothers and of themselves (Anderson & Danis, 2006).

Strategies of "withstanding" were used in relationship to protecting themselves so they could endure exposure to the violence perpetrated on their mothers and included: (1) creating physical and mental escapes; (2) attempting to understand (i.e., make sense of) what was going on in the family; (3) building support networks; and (4) trying to create order within familial chaos. Strategies of "opposing" the abuse that were used in relationship to preventing or stopping the violence perpetrated on their mothers included: (1) developing and executing safety plans; (2) intervening with the batterer; and (3) protecting and comforting their mothers and siblings. All participants used a combination of both "withstanding" and "opposing" strategies that varied depending upon the circumstances of their childhood adversity. Although these acts of resistance began as spontaneous reactions to their mothers', and consequently their own subjugation, they were reshaped into adaptive strategies that were used throughout their lives.

Environmental (Family and External Support) Protective Factors

Childhood exposure to a mother's battering creates a unique set of circumstances (e.g., a family environment characterized by fear, control, and powerlessness), which cannot be minimized in understanding a child's way of coping with such adversity. Mediating environmental protective factors include a strong and secure attachment to the nonviolent parent (usually the mother) or other significant caregiver (Holt, Buckley, & Whelan, 2008). Indeed, having support from a caring individual or a supportive network has been found to be a significant factor in children's adjustment, healing, and recovery from domestic violence. Often the family environment is chaotic; nevertheless, there is usually one adult caretaker who provides stability in the child's life. Positive adult–child relationships provide the child with support as well as models of appropriate social behavior (Anderson & Bang, 2012).

Positive maternal mental health (e.g., low levels of anxiety and depression) is also associated with positive adaptation in children. In other words, a child's coping is influenced by parental functioning (Graham-Bermann, Gruber, Howell, & Girz, 2009). Additionally, a nonabusive parent's ability to problem solve and parent (e.g., provide structure, limit setting, appropriate discipline and support) under stressful circumstances also are associated with children's well-being (Grych et al., 2000; Margolin, Gordis, & Oliver, 2004). Positive sibling relationships also have been shown to buffer the effects of exposure to inter-parental violence (Graham-Bermann et al., 2009).

In addition to evaluating familial support, assessing other positive adult role models and mentors (e.g., teachers, coaches, clergy, friends' parents) in the child's life may be significant in determining additional protective factors that mediate the effects of childhood exposure to domestic violence (Fraser, 1997). Resilient children have many interests and are involved in extracurricular activities that provide opportunities to connect with supportive adults and get away from family problems (Humphreys, 2001). These activities, such as being involved in church or sports, serve as opportunities to acquire safety, guidance, and compassion. Additionally, parents who seek external support and safety through domestic violence agencies find such services are beneficial to their children as well (Bancroft & Silverman, 2002; Clements et al., 2008; Mullender et al., 2002).

My quantitative study (Anderson & Bang, 2012) examined 68 females who as children were exposed to domestic violence to more fully explore environmental risk and protective factors during childhood and their relationship to adult levels of PTSD and resilience. In this inquiry, we addressed the context of witnessing domestic violence (i.e., duration, type of violence, abuser's use of weapons, the child's relationship to the abuser). Additional risk factors included experiences of child abuse and exposure to parental mental health problems, substance abuse, and unemployment. Protective factors were comprised of available childhood resources including access to domestic violence services, mental health counseling, and police intervention.

Our findings (Anderson & Bang, 2012) indicated that higher resilience scores were significantly correlated with lower levels of PTSD in adult functioning. Participants whose mothers had full-time steady employment had significantly higher resilience than those with mothers who did not work or worked inconsistently. Childhood risk factors, particularly mother's mental health problems and police involvement, were significantly associated with more PTSD symptoms in adulthood. Thus, children who experienced mothers with mental health problems and police intervention related to domestic violence had significantly higher PTSD scores. The participants had minimal contact with domestic violence shelters (4.6%) and services (9.5%) or mental health counseling (19%) during childhood and, consequently, such supports were not a significant contributor to functioning in adulthood. This study's findings provided evidence of concurrent victimization as 63% of participants experienced both childhood exposure and child maltreatment. Yet, there were no significant differences on outcomes (perhaps due to small sample size) between participants who had experienced child abuse and those who had not. The findings of this study highlight how adult resilience is possible despite childhood exposure to domestic violence, yet more research on child witnesses is necessary to further delineate the connection between childhood protective factors and adult hardiness and distress.

Current Issues: The Present Study

As noted earlier, in my most recent study I set out to build on my previous inquiries by further analyzing adult daughters' (N=68, Anderson & Bang, 2012) protective strategies employed during childhood and how they may relate, if at all, to adult functioning (i.e., PTSD and resilience). Although previous domestic violence studies continue to deepen our understanding of children's responses to witnessing domestic violence, absent is a measure to evaluate children's use of such strategies. Consequently, I developed the Children's Protective Strategies Index (CPSI) to address this need and apply it in the study. The CPSI is the first measure of its kind to highlight the nature and extent of children's responses to domestic violence in a systematic manner.

Methods

Data Collection

The participants were adult females (N=68) who during childhood were exposed to their mother's abuse by an intimate male partner. Although domestic violence also includes abuse by women against men and same-sex partners, the focus of this study was on the experience "in which most children exposed to domestic violence find themselves, in a home where a man is committing a pattern of violence against an adult woman, who is most often the child's mother" (Edleson et al., 2007, p. 963). Patterns of violence included physical, verbal, sexual, and financial abuse. Childhood exposure was defined as being within sight or sound of the violence or witnessing the aftermath of the violence (e.g., mother's injuries, property destruction, police intervention to remove the abuser, moving to a domestic violence shelter) (Edleson et al., 2007; Meltzer et al., 2009).

After final approval by a university internal review board, participants were recruited through local community and university newspaper advertisements (hardcopy and electronic). Advertisements directed potential participants to contact the researcher (via telephone or e-mail), who then discussed the purpose of the study, explained the consent form, and explored each person's interest in the project. Convenience sampling criteria were used to include women who were (1) 21 or older, (2) did not reside in their parents' homes, (3) had experienced (during childhood) their mothers being battered by intimate male partners, and (4) were able to differentiate between exposure to their mothers' abuse vs. any violence directed personally at them. Of 120 inquiries, 111 met sampling criteria and 19 of those declined to participate in the study. Of 92 questionnaire packets distributed, 68 completed packets were returned along with signed participant consent forms.

Measures

CPSI. The CPSI consists of 75 protective strategies drawn from the author's qualitative findings in the earlier study with adult daughters (Anderson & Danis, 2006) and are organized around themes of "withstanding" ($n=48$ strategies) and "opposing" ($n=27$ strategies) a sense of powerlessness due to the batterer's oppression of their mothers and of themselves. Strategies of "withstanding" the violent environment included creating physical and mental *escapes* (16 items), attempting to *understand* family dynamics (12 items), building *support* networks (9 items), and creating *order* within familial chaos (11 items). Strategies of "opposing" the abuse included developing and executing *safety* plans (8 items), *intervening* with the batterer/diverting violence (9 items), and *protecting* and comforting mother and siblings (10 items).

Each item response is on a 5-point Likert scale in regard to frequency of use: 1=never, 2=rarely, 3=occasionally, 4=frequently, and 5=very frequently. Participant responses for all items are summed to create a total score, with higher scores representing greater strategy use. In addition to capturing the frequency of strategy use, each of the 75 items was recoded on the CPSI to create a dichotomous variable for the occurrence of each individual item (scores of 1 were recoded to 0= "never happened" and scores of 2–5 recoded to 1= "happened"). This recoded variable resulted in a measure of the number of types of strategies used, with a possible range of 0–75.

Cronbach's alpha coefficients for total strategies were 0.89. Cronbach's alpha coefficients for protective strategies related to "withstanding" the violent environment included escapes=0.72, understand=0.41, support=0.71, and order=0.70. Cronbach's alpha coefficients for protective strategies related to "opposing" the violent environment included safety=0.68, intervene=0.84, and protect=0.78. Cronbach's alpha coefficients were acceptable but not high regarding consistency levels; thus, more item analysis was conducted through exploratory factor analysis, which is discussed more fully in the section on results.

Adult psychosocial functioning: *PTSD.* PTSD was measured by the PTSD Checklist Version for Civilians (PCL-C). The PCL-C is a 17-item, self-reporting rating scale used to assess symptom clusters (i.e., intrusion, avoidance, arousal) experienced within the past 30 days (Blanchard, Jones-Alexander, Buckley, & Forneris, 1996). Responses range from 1 (not at all) to 5 (extremely). Symptomatic responses range between "3" and "5" (total scores ranging from 51 to 85), and nonsymptomatic responses include a "1" or "2" (total scores ranging from 17 to 34). The PCL-C corresponds to diagnostic criteria B, C, and D as specified in the *Diagnostic and Statistical Manual of Mental Disorders* (DSM-IV-TR; American Psychiatric Association, 2000) and has demonstrated strong internal consistency in female samples of sexual assault and domestic violence survivors with Cronbach's alphas of 0.96 (Kocot & Goodman, 2003) and 0.97 (Avdibegovic & Sinanovic, 2006). Cronbach's alpha coefficients (0.93, 0.82, 0.82, and 0.86 for the PCL-C total, intrusion, avoidance, and arousal clusters, respectively) were indicative of high internal consistency in the current sample.

Adult psychosocial functioning: *Resilience.* The Connor Davidson Resilience Scale (CD RISC; Conner & Davidson, 2003) is a 25-item scale designed to address resilience displayed in the last month. A factor analysis of the CD-RISC indicates a multistructural nature of resilience. Factor 1 corresponds to personal competence, high standards, and tenacity (8 items). Factor 2 relates to trust in one's instincts, tolerance of negative affect, and the strengthening effects of stress (7 items). Factor 3 reflects a positive acceptance of change and having secure relationships (5 items). Factor 4 corresponds to personal control (3 items), while factor 5 relates to spiritual influences (2 items).

Response options are based on a 4-point Likert scale (0=not true at all, 1=rarely true, 2=sometimes true, 3=often true, and 4=true nearly all the time). Participant responses for the 25 items are summed to create a total resilience score that ranges from 0 to 100, with higher scores representing greater levels of resilience. For instance, scores of "3" or "4" for each of the 25 items yield a range of (75–100) and demonstrate a relatively high level of resilience. The CD-RISC has been tested in the general population as well as in clinical samples and has demonstrated sound psychometric properties (Conner & Davidson, 2003). The mean score for the general population is 80.4 ($\pm$ = 12.8), for primary care outpatients it is 71.4 ($\pm$ = 18.4), for psychiatric outpatients it is 68 ($\pm$ = 15.3), for generalized anxiety disorder (GAD) patients it is 62.4 ($\pm$ = 10.7), and for PTSD patients it is 47.8 ($\pm$ = 19.5). Cronbach's alpha for this study was 0.93.

Results

Demographic Statistics

Study participants (N=68) ranged in age from 19 to 64 years old (M=37, SD=11.5) (See Anderson & Bang, 2012, for a more detailed account of demographics). Fifty-one participants (75%) were European American. Fifty-four participants (79.4%) were employed either full-time or part-time, and 34 respondents (50%) had children. Highest level of education included 20 (29.4%) participants who reported a GED/high school diploma, three (4.4%) had vocational/technical training, six (8.8%) had associates' degrees, and 39 participants (57.4%) had earned undergraduate (n=24) or graduate degrees (n=15). Thirty-six participants (52.9%) were married or living with a significant other at the time of the study and 10 (14.7%) were divorced. Thirty-three (48.5%) respondents reported experiencing intimate partner violence in adulthood.

Thirty-seven participants (54.4%) were exposed as children to the abuser's violence for 11 or more years, with 10 (14.7%) reporting that the violence was 20 or more years. The most frequently reported types of abuse exposure were physical and emotional abuse (n=30, 44.1%) and physical, emotional, and financial abuse (n=16, 23.5%). Nine individuals (13.2%) discussed being exposed to all four patterns of abuse. Abusers included primarily fathers (n=44, 64.7%) and stepfathers (n=14, 20.6%), while ten (14.7%) reported their mothers had multiple abusive partners. Twenty-four participants (35.3%) reported the abuser used weapons including guns, knives, and/or automobiles. Additionally, 53 participants (63%) reported that the abuser also abused them.

Exploratory Factor Analysis of the Children's Protective Strategies Index

In this study, I conducted an exploratory factor analysis of the CPSI using a VARIMAX rotation. Analysis of data from participants yielded 72-items and four factors whose eigenvalues were, respectively, 7.17, 6.90, 5.94, and 5.23. Table 28.1 CPSI, column 1, provides all factors and strategies presented in descending order of eigenvalues. These factors could be roughly interpreted in the following manner. Factor 1 reflects attempts to make sense and physically escape the violence along with promises to self to end its cycle when they become adults. Factor 2 corresponds to diverting, preventing, and mediating the violence. Factor 3 relates to problem solving and control, accessing social and spiritual support, and finding meaning in adversity. Factor 4 relates to avoiding and normalizing the violence along with engaging in isolative activities. Chronbach's alpha coefficients for total strategies and factors 1–4 of the revised CPSI, respectively, were 0.90, 0.85, 0.83, and 0.76, indicating high levels of internal consistency.

Occurrence/Type of Protective Strategy

When examining the occurrence of strategic responses (refer to Table 28.1 CPSI, column 2), there was no one individual strategy used by all participants. However, two strategies from factor 3 (i.e., problem solving, social support, finding meaning) were used by 99% (n=67) of the participants: "I kept busy" and "I had someone in my life that cared about me." Nineteen strategies were used by 91% or more of the sample (refer to Table 28.1 CPSI where an *=91% or more), with factor 1 (i.e., making sense,

Table 28.1 Children's protective strategies index

Factor/Strategy	% who used strategy	Mean	SD
Factor 1			
I wanted my mom to leave my dad	87 ($n=59$)	3.95	1.44
I wondered why my parents stayed together	88 ($n=60$)	3.94	1.40
I knew I was in a situation beyond my control*	93 ($n=63$)	3.94	1.23
I wanted to grow up and be different from my parents*	97 ($n=66$)	4.47	0.98
I wondered why the violence continued*	93 ($n=63$)	4.00	1.20
I questioned why no one would intervene*	91 ($n=62$)	3.06	1.26
I made a plan to escape	72 ($n=49$)	2.47	1.29
I was hyper-vigilant to signs of violence.	82 ($n=56$)	3.55	1.52
I believed my dad was the cause of the violence*	91 ($n=62$)	4.03	1.23
I told my mom to leave my dad	74 ($n=50$)	3.14	1.59
I just wanted the violence to end*	96 ($n=65$)	4.64	0.92
I found places to hide from the violence	88 ($n=60$)	3.17	1.34
I rebelled	59 ($n=40$)	2.30	1.38
I would stay at someone's house to get away from the violence	62 ($n=42$)	2.14	1.40
I saw friends' families where violence did not occur*	96 ($n=65$)	3.94	1.12
I liked things calm and quiet*	96 ($n=65$)	3.91	1.12
I liked structure where you knew the rules*	94 ($n=64$)	3.71	1.19
I talked to someone about the violence	62 ($n=42$)	1.86	0.90
I sought out friends	77 ($n=52$)	2.97	1.45
I stayed away from home as much as possible	87 ($n=59$)	3.27	1.41
I decided when I grew up to not have violence in my life*	94 ($n=64$)	4.50	1.13
I promised myself that when I grew up and had children that they would not be exposed to violence	93 ($n=63$)	4.42	1.64
Factor 2			
I verbally intervened between my parents	71 ($n=48$)	2.85	1.45
I physically intervened between my parents	62 ($n=42$)	2.45	1.43
I stood up to my dad	62 ($n=42$)	2.36	1.34
I argued with my dad to divert the violence	72 ($n=49$)	2.79	1.41
I was the mediator, the go between my parents	53 ($n=36$)	2.29	1.48
I asked my dad to stop the violence	59 ($n=40$)	2.39	1.51
I was sociable	87 ($n=59$)	3.15	1.37
I recognized cues in my dad that alerted me to danger	79 ($n=54$)	2.41	1.58
I would lock my father out of the house	21 ($n=14$)	1.41	1.01
I would stay with a relative or friend to escape	79 ($n=54$)	2.95	1.43
I told my mother the violence isn't right	71 ($n=48$)	2.67	1.50
I reached out to others for help	60 ($n=41$)	1.89	0.93
I helped my mom to physically leave my dad	41 ($n=28$)	2.06	1.50
I called the police or 911	19 ($n=13$)	1.45	1.10
I watched TV to get away from the violence	77 ($n=52$)	2.62	1.25
Factor 3			
I made plans for my future*	91 ($n=62$)	3.71	1.33
I did well in school*	91 ($n=62$)	3.88	1.33
I used writing as an escape	66 ($n=45$)	2.70	1.56
I felt there was something outside of myself (e.g., God) that loved me	77 ($n=52$)	3.05	1.63
I learned to be self-reliant*	91 ($n=62$)	4.03	1.27

(continued)

Table 28.1 (continued)

Factor/Strategy	% who used strategy	Mean	SD
I read a lot as a child	82 (*n* = 56)	3.44	1.54
I believed I could make things happen	81 (*n* = 55)	2.89	1.41
I was an organizer	77 (*n* = 52)	3.09	1.56
I prayed/asked God for help	81 (*n* = 52)	3.21	1.52
I believed things happen for a reason	85 (*n* = 58)	3.00	1.32
I was involved in extracurricular activities	85 (*n* = 58)	3.24	1.48
I kept important phone numbers I could use for help	32 (*n* = 22)	1.52	0.98
I gathered my siblings to hide them	54 (*n* = 37)	2.67	1.67
I kept busy*	99 (*n* = 67)	3.92	1.10
I sought out teachers, coaches, or other adults as role models or mentors	68 (*n* = 46)	2.52	1.40
I searched out answers for life's problems	81 (*n* = 55)	2.92	1.32
I was protective of my siblings	79 (*n* = 54)	3.67	1.56
I connected with nature and or pets	87 (*n* = 59)	3.64	1.42
I had someone in my life that cared about me*	99 (*n* = 67)	3.77	1.17
I believed that I was worthwhile	84 (*n* = 57)	2.82	1.30
Factor 4			
I thought the violence was normal	57 (*n* = 39)	2.56	1.54
I would think about other things during the violence	63 (*n* = 43)	2.42	1.40
I learned to not show emotions	88 (*n* = 60)	3.64	1.38
I would clean up the house after the violence	63 (*n* = 43)	2.55	1.48
I did not show fear*	91 (*n* = 62)	3.17	1.21
I believed it was my mom's fault	60 (*n* = 41)	2.18	1.15
I had a lot of family responsibility	87 (*n* = 59)	3.62	1.38
I acted like nothing (i.e., violence) was happening	84 (*n* = 57)	3.08	1.29
I ran away from home	37 (*n* = 25)	1.70	1.15
I escaped into nature or the outdoors	71 (*n* = 48)	2.77	1.51
I raised myself and my siblings	59 (*n* = 40)	2.59	1.62
I escaped through the use of art, music, and/or humor	87 (*n* = 59)	3.52	1.33
I sought out quiet structured places (e.g., church, library)	71 (*n* = 48)	2.52	1.29
I tried to not think about the violence*	93 (*n* = 63)	3.73	1.10
I would act like everything was okay in the family*	96 (*n* = 65)	3.91	1.12

escape, promises to self) having the most. Of the 19 protective strategies used, 17 were psychological, 10 were cognitive, 6 were behavioral, 1 was emotional, and 2 were related to social support. Factor 2's strategies (i.e., diverting, preventing, mediating the violence) were used the least by participants.

Frequency of Protective Strategy Use

When examining each individual strategy (using the full range of 1–5 for each) (see Table 28.1 CPSI, columns 2 & 3), the most used were cognitive responses in factor 1 (i.e., making sense, escape, promises to self) ranging in means from 4.00 to 4.65, indicating these strategies were used frequently or very frequently: "I just wanted the violence to end" (M = 4.65, SD = 0.91); "I decided when I grew up to not have violence in my life" (M = 4.51, SD = 1.11); "I wanted to grow up and be different from my parents" (M = 4.49, SD = 0.97); "I promised myself that when I grew up and had children that they would not be exposed to violence" (M = 4.44, SD = 1.15); "I believed my dad was the cause of the violence" ($M=4.00$, SD, 1.25); and "I wondered why the violence continued" ($M=4.00$, SD, 1.20). Additionally, "I learned to be self-reliant" ($M=4.00$, SD=1.30) from factor 3 (i.e., problem solving, social support, finding meaning) was used frequently. As previously noted, these strategies also were used by 91% of participants. Thus, a majority not only used them but used them frequently.

Individual strategies that were not used or were used rarely were from factor 2 (i.e., diverting, preventing, mediating the violence) and included: "I would lock my father out of the house" ($M=1.41$, SD=0.97), and "I called the police or 911" ($M=1.50$, SD=1.13). Others rarely used included "I kept important numbers I could use for help" ($M=1.54$, SD=0.98, factor 3), and "I ran away from home" ($M=1.69$, SD=1.14, factor 4).

CPSI and Psychosocial Functioning: PTSD and Resilience

As previously noted, participants were largely asymptomatic for PTSD and demonstrated high levels of overall resilience (see Anderson & Bang, 2012). For the current study, childhood protective strategies (including total and frequency) were not significantly correlated with total levels of resilience or PTSD. However, factor 3 was positively associated with total resilience ($r=0.38$, $p=0.01$). This indicates that during childhood the more one problem solved, developed control, accessed social and spiritual support, and found meaning in adversity the more resilient one was in adulthood. Additionally, factor 3 was positively associated with four factors from the resilience scale: personal competence ($r=0.50$, $p=0.01$), trust in one's instincts ($r=0.36$, $p=0.01$), acceptance of change ($r=0.47$, $p=0.01$), and personal control ($r=0.42$, $p=0.01$). In regard to PTSD symptom clusters, factor 4 (e.g., avoiding and normalizing the violence, isolative activities) was positively associated with intrusion symptoms ($r=0.28$, $p=-0.05$), while factor 3 was positively associated with arousal symptoms ($r=0.48$, $p=0.01$).

The following individual strategies from factor 3 were associated both with an increase in resilience and a decrease in PTSD: "I believed I was worthwhile" (resilience: $r=0.43$, $p=0.000$; PTSD: $r=-40$, $p=0.001$); "I had someone in my life that cared about me" (resilience: $r=0.32$, $p=0.01$; PTSD: $r=-0.239$, $p=0.05$); and "I felt there was something outside of myself (e.g., God) that loved me" (resilience: $r=0.52$, $p=000$, PTSD: $r=-0.26$, $p=0.05$).

Additionally, the following individual strategies from factor 3 were associated with positive increases in resilience only: "I used writing as an escape" ($r=0.24$, $p=0.05$); "I prayed/asked God for help" ($r=0.32$, $p=0.01$); "I searched out answers to life's problems" ($r=0.27$, $p=0.05$); "I believed I could make things happen" ($r=0.32$, $p=0.01$); "I made plans for my future" ($r=0.44$, $p=0.000$); "I kept important numbers I could use for help" ($r=0.26$, $p=0.05$); and "I gathered my siblings to hide them" ($r=0.25$, $p=0.05$). Two strategies from factor 2 also were associated with higher levels of resilience: "I helped my mom to physically leave my dad" ($r=0.24$, $p=0.05$), and "I would lock my father out of the house" ($r=0.25$, $p=0.05$).

Negatively associated with resilience was the strategy from factor 4 (avoiding and normalizing the violence, isolative activities): "I believed it was my mom's fault" ($r=-0.25$, $p=0.05$). Thus, believing it was her mom's fault was associated with lower levels of resilience in adulthood. A strategy from factor 4 positively associated with PTSD included "I ran away from home" ($r=0.26$, $p=0.05$). Thus, the more frequently one ran away from home, the more PTSD in adulthood.

Clinical Implications

The study presented here identifies attributes of daughters of battered women as well as of their support systems that mediated the challenges of a childhood impacted by domestic violence. The interaction between these protective mechanisms demonstrated how resourceful participants were as children and forged a pathway to adult resilience. These findings are further discussed in regard to clinical implications for each of the four factors of the CPSI. Such a conceptual framework may allow practitioners, and the abused mothers they serve, to better understand the responses of children exposed to inter-parental violence.

Factor 1: Making Sense, Promises to Self, and Escape

Factor 1's protective strategies reflect children's attempts to make sense of the violence, promises to self to end its cycle, and to physically escape. Participants used these protective strategies frequently during childhood (particularly cognitive coping), yet they were not significantly associated with adult psychological hardiness or distress. Attempts at "making sense" of their childhood exposure to domestic violence engaged questions such as: "Why does the violence continue?" ($n=93\%$), "How come my mom did not leave my dad when I wanted her to ($n=87\%$) and told her to do so?" ($n=74\%$), "Why did my parents stay together?" ($n=88\%$), and "Why did no one intervene?" ($n=91\%$). Participants' responses underscore how there is much about domestic violence that is paradoxical and difficult to understand, particularly from a child's point of view. Consequently, creating a safe and trusting environment for the child to explore such questions with the nonoffending parent would be an important element of any clinical intervention along with psycho-education regarding the nature and dynamics of domestic violence. Making sense of adverse experiences also involves forming certain kinds of causal attributions: "Attribution theory states that the behavioral and emotional consequences of an event are determined by the way we explain the event, or, in other words, by the causal attributions we make" (Feinauer & Stuart, 1996, pp. 32–33). For participants in the current study, accurate appraisal of their situation became an important distinguishing element of their coping.

Even during childhood, most were able to realize that the violence was beyond their control ($n=93\%$) and attributed the cause of it to their fathers ($n=91\%$). These findings highlight the importance of assessing children's attributions for accuracy (e.g., not blaming themselves for the violence) to reduce guilt, shame, and blame during childhood and foster resilience later in life.

During childhood, participants told themselves that they would get away from the abuse someday and that their futures would be violence free ($n=94\%$) for themselves and their children ($n=93\%$). Thus, they promised themselves they would not perpetuate the cycle of violence or family dysfunction when they grew up ($n=97\%$). Planning for their futures provided participants with hope and a mental escape from their childhood circumstances. Thus, helping children plan for their futures, including breaking the cycle of violence, is an important clinical component to consider with children exposed to domestic violence as it underscores how their fate does not need to replicate their parents' circumstances.

Despite a familial environment of chaos and confusion, participants figured out what they needed in their lives to survive and, consequently, sought out or created structure, rules ($n=94\%$), and calmness ($n=96\%$) during childhood. Additionally, they used a variety of methods to physically escape ($n=72\%$) by being vigilant to signs of violence ($n=82\%$) and thus finding places to hide ($n=88\%$), by getting away from home as much as possible ($n=87\%$), and by staying with friends ($n=77\%$), particularly places where violence did not occur ($n=96\%$). These findings suggest that it is important for helping professionals to assist children in the development of safety plans inclusive of their needs along with people and places that provide safety from the violence.

Factor 2: Diverting, Preventing, and Mediating the Violence

In examining Factor 2, items reflect protective strategies that directly impacted the violence by diverting, preventing, or mediating it. Overall, such protective strategies were used the least compared to those associated with the other factors. Childhood attempts to influence the violence included physically (n=62%) and verbally (n=71%) intervening with the abuser, diverting (n=72%) and challenging the abuser (n=62%), mediating between one's parents (n=53%), or summoning help (n=60%). Surprisingly, two strategies (related to protecting their mothers) were associated significantly with overall levels of resilience, yet few participants actually engaged in such activities: "I helped my mom to physically leave my dad" (41%, n=28), and "I would lock my father out of the house" (21%, n=14).

Factor 2's findings underscore the importance of developing safety plans to enhance children's self-efficacy and preparedness but excludes them from intervening in incidents of violence where the potential of harm and injury is high. Consequently, the nonoffending parent and the child may develop child appropriate safety plans for when there is parental fighting and in the case of emergencies. These safety plans may include recognizing cues in their fathers that alert them to danger along with developing a code word the nonabusing parent may use during emergencies to alert the child to take such action as escaping the premises. Another important aspect of safety planning is to develop a protocol of how to summon help during an emergency, such as calling 911 or the police. Few participants (n=19%) actually utilized this latter strategy, perhaps because they did not have a plan of what to say or do given such circumstances.

Factor 3: Problem solving, Accessing Support, and Finding Meaning

Factor 3 was the only one associated with overall resilience in adulthood. Therefore, participants, who during childhood actively problem solved, accessed support, and searched for meaning, were more resilient later in life, particularly in the areas of competence, trusting one's instincts, acceptance of change, and personal control. Helping children exposed to domestic violence strengthen such protective strategies shows promise for fostering adult resilience. Interestingly, factor 3 was also related to PTSD arousal symptoms, indicating a need to address children's physiological responses and to teach skills of self-comfort, calm, and relaxation.

As factor 3 is related both to resilience and PTSD arousal symptoms, this may indicate how psychological hardiness and distress are not necessarily mutually exclusive but instead are inextricably linked in adaptation to adversity (Saakvitne, Tenne, & Affleck, 1998). This link is also noted in three childhood protective strategies that were associated with both increases in resilience and decreases in PTSD: believing oneself as worthwhile (n=84%), having someone in their life who cared about them (n=99%), and believing that God or something outside themselves loved them (n=77%). These three protective strategies may serve as the foundation for protecting children exposed to domestic violence and thus, if supported and enhanced, may be key to cultivating resilience in adulthood. Additional childhood protective strategies related to adult resilience (and not PTSD) included keeping important numbers that could be used for help (n=31%) and gathering siblings to hide them during the violence (n=54%). These findings highlight additional elements for children's safety plans, including vital phone numbers (in addition to 911 or the police) for summoning help and, for those with siblings, creating strategies to hide and protect them from the violence as well.

Participants viewed their childhood selves as successful in school (n=91%), avid readers (n=82%), self-reliant (n=91%), and organized (n=71%). Perhaps because they believed they were worthwhile and/or successful in solving problems, as children they also believed they could make things happen for themselves (n=81%) and their futures (n=91%). Thus, having an internal locus of control and a sense of personal efficacy were important factors for these adult daughters in overcoming their childhood adversity. Clinical implications include the relevance of helping children develop competence by learning skills to be an effective problem solver. This might involve having children concentrate on a problem they have control over, analyze it, and come up with a solution. In doing so, they may come to believe that their actions and decisions can determine outcomes in their lives.

Developing personal resources, such as competence and agency, did not occur in a vacuum for these participants who, in fact, had a strong and diverse social network. Almost all ($n=99\%$) participants reported having someone in their life during childhood who cared about them. The significance of having one supportive adult in one's life has previously been highlighted in resilience research because of the many functions that these relationships provide: being a role model for appropriate behavior, offering affirmation, providing safety, and reinforcing the idea that the individual deserves to be loved (Werner & Smith, 1992). My study's findings demonstrate the power of relationships in overcoming childhood exposure to domestic violence and the significant role of nonabusive caretakers, most often mothers, in the child's world. A clinical intervention that builds upon this bond and supports mothers in their parenting roles appears essential for children's ability to heal from domestic violence exposure.

The majority of participants kept themselves busy ($n=99\%$) and were involved in extracurricular activities ($n=85\%$) that opened up avenues to connect with teachers, coaches, friends' parents, or other adults as role models or mentors ($n=68\%$). These adults may have helped them think positively about themselves, reinforced the idea that they were worthwhile, and provided them with guidance, support, and the possibility of a life free from violence. Resilience research indicates that children often work toward developing alternative families, or at least seek out role models, from whom they can get their needs fulfilled. They enjoy the relative normality and safety of these interactions, which are helpful to them even though they may not disclose family violence (Wolin & Wolin, 1993). Clinical implications include the importance of connecting children with activities outside of the home and fostering relationships with safe adults who they may come into contact with as a result of such experiences.

Having a connection to God or some other type of spiritual influence ($n=77\%$) provided another avenue of support for participants during childhood. These spiritual influences may have helped them to have faith in their ability to prevail until they could reach a point when their lives would get better. The help of caring individuals, such as religious mentors or teachers, may have assisted them in being able to have faith in their abilities and may have provided meaning to their lives. Prayer, deemed an important activity by many participants ($n=81\%$), may have afforded opportunities to express what was happening to them and to ask for help in getting through their troubles. Many participants sought to find meaning in their adversity ($n=85\%$) and actively searched for answers to life's problems, including exposure to domestic violence ($n=81\%$). Resilience research indicates that spiritual beliefs, activities, and supports are important in giving a sense of purpose to individuals' lives and their childhood adversity in a manner that frees them from guilt and shame (Valentine & Feinauer, 1993). Clinical implications include the importance of exploring and enhancing children's spiritual activities and supports while also addressing the existential and spiritual questions regarding the reasons for life's problems and suffering.

Factor 4: Avoiding and Normalizing the Violence, Isolative Activities

Protective strategies in factor 4 related to avoiding ($n=93\%$) and normalizing the violence ($n=63\%$) along with thinking about other things during the violence ($n=63\%$). A strategy associated with lower levels of resilience for participants included attributing the cause of violence to the victim mother ($n=60\%$). During childhood, believing that the violence was her mother's fault was associated, consequently, with lower levels of resilience in adulthood. Additionally, running away from home ($n=37\%$) was positively associated with PTSD in adulthood. Factor 4 also included strategies of *not* reaching out for help including *not* showing emotions ($n=88\%$), particularly fear ($n=91\%$), *not* letting anyone know what was happening in the family ($n=96\%$), and *not* letting on that anything was wrong ($n=84\%$). Additional protective strategies included isolative activities such as artistic pursuits

($n=87\%$), being in nature or the outdoors ($n=71\%$), and being in quiet structured places ($n=71\%$). These activities may have provided solace but not necessarily connections to others. Factor 4 also highlights how children exposed to domestic violence may have significant family responsibilities ($n=87\%$), including raising themselves and their siblings ($n=59\%$).

These findings suggest the importance of approaching rather than avoiding cognitive processing of trauma experiences. It also includes helping children understand the connection between their thoughts, feelings, and behaviors. For example, if a child avoids thinking about what is happening, this may cause her to internalize feelings such as fear, causing depression and anxiety. Also, if a child shuts down emotionally, then she may need to learn to expand her range of feelings so that she is less emotionally constricted. Avoiding feeling or thinking about the violence also may generalize to other aspects of the child's world and prevent involvement in activities, places, and events (e.g., birthdays) that serve as trauma reminders. Clinical implications include gradually exposing the child to trauma processing by developing a narrative comprised of one's exposure to domestic violence and incorporating the nonoffending parent's support and guidance during its creation.

Because traumatic experiences and their consequences are overwhelming, many children exposed to domestic violence may lose sight of their resources and aspirations. Thus, helping professionals may use the CSPI to prompt children to recognize the many ways they defended themselves and thus provide a different view of themselves as being resourceful, courageous, and determined. In rediscovering these strengths, a dialogue between children, their nonoffending caregivers, and practitioners then may evolve into addressing children's present problems and whether or not these protective strategies are still useful, need to be modified, or should be retired.

Research Implications

Resilience research recognizes a multifaceted process inclusive of individual attributes, family milieu, and social interactions in promoting well-being. Yet, missing from this research is a systematic way to gather such information for children exposed to domestic violence. Thus, the CPSI provides a means of investigating strategy use in a methodical manner that can be replicated with additional study to determine pattern use and how it may vary based on demographics (e.g., age, gender) and the child's exposure to domestic violence (e.g., frequency, duration, types). Although the continued study of the negative consequences of abuse exposure is important, by focusing only on the negative consequences, we may miss a more complete picture of the impact that exposure has on children, that of their ability to cope with abusive environments. We need to further take into account children's abilities to adapt, reorganize, and regenerate. At the same time, the focus on protective factors and resilience should not inadvertently serve to direct attention away from the serious issues of domestic violence. Children should not continue to live in dangerous familial environments and be expected to "bounce back" from such exposure, yet there is much to be learned from individuals who are not presenting or reporting developmental problems in the aftermath of childhood exposure to domestic violence.

Case Example

The following case example demonstrates how the CPSI may be used to assess coping, inform treatment, and enhance Trauma-Focused Cognitive Behavioral Therapy (TF-CBT) for children with emotional and behavioral difficulties associated with violence exposure (Cohen & Mannarino, 2008; Cohen, Mannarino, & Deblinger, 2006). TF-CBT is an evidence-based intervention where children and nonabusing parents receive psycho-education on violence and build skills in problem solving, cognitive restructuring, stress reduction, emotional regulation, and safety planning while gradually being exposed to trauma processing. Areas assessed in the CPSI align with TF-CBT's core components and help to individualize it to the unique needs of child witnesses and their nonabusing parents.

Rain is a 7-year-old girl in the first grade who enjoys school recess, being outside, camping, and swimming. Her mom, Darla, is 43 years old and was formerly in an abusive relationship with Rain's father, Alan. Darla has been separated from Alan for a year, but continues to have contact with him regarding parenting and visitation matters. Although he has not perpetrated violence since the separation, he and Darla often argue about raising Rain. Darla has worked with the local domestic violence and sexual assault center and has received services including advocacy, crisis intervention, and case management. In a conversation with her advocate, Darla expressed her concerns regarding Rain's emotional and behavioral problems, including her anger outbursts, difficulty concentrating, distractibility, and over-sensitivity to parental correction and discipline. She reported that Rain was tested for attention-deficit hyperactivity disorder (ADHD) and that the results were negative.

Darla believes Rain's current difficulties are a result of being exposed to domestic violence for the first 6 years of her life. Rain often witnessed her father threatening, swearing, and screaming at her mother. On occasion she also was exposed to her father's property destruction and physical abuse toward her mother. Police were involved intermittently and in such domestic violence incidents her father was often asked to leave the home. In the past, Rain's father was also emotionally and verbally abusive to her.

Darla's advocate recommended that she and Rain participate in the agency's TF-CBT services—a counseling program for children and nonabusing parents that is provided free of charge by a licensed clinical professional. TF-CBT is typically delivered in 16–20 weekly 90 minute sessions (45 minutes with the child, 30 minutes with the parent). The core components of TF-CBT make up the acronym PRACTICE and occur in the following sequence: psycho-education, relaxation, affective modulation, cognitive coping and processing, trauma narrative, in vivo mastery of trauma reminders, conjoint child–parent sessions, and enhancing future safety (Cohen & Mannarino, 2008; Cohen et al., 2006). Each component is covered in one to two sessions, except for the trauma narrative, which may take up to six sessions. Generally, at each session the therapist first meets with the child to work on the components of the PRACTICE model. Then, the therapist meets with the parent to summarize the child's session and discuss with the parent ways to support the child's progress between sessions.

Upon following up with the counseling referral, Darla and Rain both met with the TF-CBT project coordinator for an intake session, who further explained TF-CBT services and the components of the PRACTICE model. The project coordinator met with Rain to complete the CPSI. Additionally, Darla completed a psychosocial history on the family, including the intensity, frequency, and duration of Rain's exposure to domestic violence. Gathering intake information helped to understand Rain's current psychosocial functioning and coping along with providing guidelines of how to shape the PRACTICE model in a way that was specific to her needs.

Rain is personable, creative, talkative, and makes friends easily. She likes art, music, and being organized. She does well in school, works hard at her homework, and enjoys reading. Rain searches out answers to her problems and copes by trying to think of the good things in her life. She is quite connected to nature and likes being outdoors. She likes calm and quiet places. Additionally, Rain has a supportive social network (e.g., parents, relatives, friends, teachers). Rain reports that her parents care about her and she views herself as a worthy person. She has a close relationship with her mother and a positive relationship with her father. Rain indicated that prayer and a relationship with a Higher Power were not a strong presence in her life at this point, yet she does question the purpose of adversity such as why some kids have parents who fight and hurt each other while others do not.

Rain angers easily mostly when corrected or disciplined by her parents. She has difficulty calming herself down when she is upset and at bed time, as evenings were often when the domestic violence occurred. In general, she is on the "look out" for bad things to happen, which often leaves her feeling tired and alone. She remains hyper-vigilant to signs of violence (e.g., cues in her father's behavior), particularly when her mother and father argue over parenting issues and visitation schedules. Rain does not blame her mother for the violence but at times believes she was at fault since some of their arguments were about her. She also thinks that she could have done more to stop the violence as she felt responsible for her mother but helpless to protect her, which prevented her from intervening during incidents of parental fighting. She often wondered why her mother and father stayed together since there was so much anger toward each other. Rain learned to not show emotions, particularly fear, and would act like nothing was going on in her family. She would often try to not think about it and would think about other things when her father was harming her mom. She reported not having a safety plan or knowledge of how to call 911/the police in case of emergencies. Rain expressed a desire for breaking the cycle of violence when she got older and to live a life free of violence. Rain stated that she wants to be different from her mother and father when she grows up and does not want her children to go through what she experienced.

The aforementioned intake information from the CPSI helped in adapting the PRACTICE model to the specific needs of Rain and her mother, Darla. The involvement of nonabusing parents is integral to TF-CBT services as they learn the skills along with their children and thus can reinforce them outside of sessions. (Note: The domestic violence and sexual assault center does not serve domestic violence offenders and thus Alan was not involved in TF-CBT services). Included were the following interventions:

- Psycho-education content related to the prevalence, causes, and nature of domestic violence. As Rain enjoyed reading, bibliotherapy was selected as the medium for delivering psycho-education and prompting a dialogue between Rain and Darla on the topic of domestic violence.
  - The text, "No More Hitting! A Child's Story of Domestic Violence" (Lynne, 2009) addressed the nature and dynamics of domestic violence. This also provided an avenue for Rain to raise questions with her mother regarding why Darla and Alan stayed together even though they were fighting and why they eventually decided to separate. It also provided clarity about why and how often domestic violence occurs. The book also allowed for undoing lessons that are part and parcel of an abusive environment: violence is unacceptable, violent behavior is a choice, and children are not responsible for parents' aggression and violence.
  - The text, "Straight Talk About PTSD: Coping with the Aftermath of Trauma" (Porterfield, 1996) addressed the connection between violence exposure and violence reactions. This prompted a discussion regarding the link between Rain's past exposure to domestic violence and her present posttrauma symptoms of hyper-vigilance, anger outbursts, distractibility, difficulty sleeping, and problems with calming herself. It was discussed how TF-CBT services would focus on these areas in order to reduce and hopefully eliminate them.
  - Both aforementioned texts also opened up a conversation between Rain and her mom regarding breaking the cycle of violence when she grows up. This process engaged questions regarding the differences between Rain and her parents and any similarities that she found concerning, such as her anger outbursts. It allowed for further discussion of how TF-CBT would help Rain to understand the connection between her thoughts, feelings, and behaviors, and how to manage them.
- Relaxation and stress management involved Rain learning self-comfort, calming, and relaxation skills to reverse any physiological changes as a result of experiencing trauma. As Rain found nature and the outdoors to be a safe place and thus relaxing, it was important to integrate these into her relaxation skills.
  - Guided imagery was used to help Rain access a safe place in her mind where she could go for self-comfort when feeling anxious and upset. Rain's safe place was a particular river bank where she often went camping with her parents. She remembered it as being calm and peaceful.

- Deep breathing was taught as a skill for Rain to calm herself and to do progressive muscle relaxation. Rain learned how to scan her body to "breathe" out tension areas.
- A relaxation CD was made that included Rain's choice of song and verbal cues by the therapist to help her and Darla practice deep breathing, guided imagery, and progressive muscle relaxation between sessions.

• Affective expression and modulation skills included Rain learning ways to address unpleasant and uncomfortable subjective experiences. As Rain enjoyed art and music, both were used for learning to express and regulate her feelings.

- A feeling card was created in which Rain assigned different colors to different emotions. This helped her to learn a range of emotions, both positive and negative. It also helped her to separate out her anger from sadness, disappointment, and fear.
- A gingerbread person was created to represent Rain, with which she could assign different emotions from her feeling card to where she felt them in her body. This helped her to understand the connection between her feelings and cues in her body.
- A CD of Rain's favorite songs was created to show the connection between stimuli and emotions. During the session, Rain would listen to a song briefly and then identify the feeling on her card. This exercise helped Rain to better understand how feelings can be induced and how easily they can be changed. So if she was feeling sad and wants to change her mood, she could pick a song to listen to that would make her feel happy. Additionally, the volume button was used as a metaphor for modulating her feelings by turning them up, down, or off.

• Cognitive coping and processing skills involved Rain learning the connection between thoughts, feelings, and behaviors. It also included addressing any cognitive distortions that developed as a result of her childhood exposure to domestic violence, such as Rain blaming herself for not doing enough to protect her mother.

- The "Talking, Feeling, and Doing" game by Creative Therapeutics was used to help Rain understand the connection between thoughts, feelings, and behaviors. This game included a deck of cards containing different scenarios of talking, feeling, and doing in everyday situations along with more difficult areas (e.g., parents fighting). Rain and her therapist took turns drawing cards and acting out the scenarios.
- Using positive talk was encouraged when Rain was having an unpleasant or distressing thought. Rain made a list of the good things in her life to substitute when she was having a troubling thought.
- Thought stopping was used with Rain for intrusive memories of her father harming her mother. When such images occurred, Rain would envision a large, red STOP sign to block them along with using her deep breathing and relaxation skills.
- Rain's interest in searching out answers to her problems also was supported. Such problem-solving skills were used to figure out new ways of behaving and interacting in everyday situations and in times of distress.
- Cognitive distortions were discussed as unhelpful ways in which Rain thinks about her circumstances, such as feeling guilty and blaming herself for not doing enough to protect her mother from her father's abuse. After processing with Rain the pros and cons of her cognitive distortion, she was then asked to give it a name. She chose "Clueless Candy," who is clueless about what she can and cannot control in her life. The fictitious character was then further discussed in regard to what parts of Rain's life she can impact (e.g., her thoughts, feelings, behaviors) and what parts she cannot (e.g., how her parents interact with each other).

• Trauma narrative development focused on Rain creating a story about her life including her exposure to domestic violence. As Rain enjoyed reading, writing, and drawing, these talents were drawn upon to create her story.

- In order for the therapist to introduce story structure and form to Rain, she was asked to bring her favorite book to the session. Upon reading the story, Rain and her therapist reviewed the following story elements: What is the story about (plot)? Is there a beginning, middle, and end? Who are the characters in the story? Is there a protagonist/central character? Is there an antagonist/enemy? Does the story have a message?

- After addressing the form and structure of a story, Rain was given art materials to create a story she titled, "A Story About Me." She was initially excited about it and worked steadily on it until the third narrative session when she began processing her most difficult memory of the abuse. At that point, Rain ceased working on it because she no longer wanted to think about it. Rain was encouraged to remember all the skills she had learned and how they had helped her with other problems in her life. In the fourth session, she figured out that it would help if she created her story's ending—her current situation. In doing so it gave her more control over the story process and provided her the strength and courage she needed to approach the most difficult aspect of her past.

- In vivo mastery of avoidance behaviors included approaching Rain's trauma-related cues (e.g., feeling anxious) associated with bedtime.
  - The therapist and Rain created a plan for bedtime that included the following: turning on a nightlight, doing deep breathing and progressive muscle relaxation, thought stopping, and listening to her music. Rain practiced her bedtime protocol several times in vivo (in session) with the lights turned down low. She then used her plan at home during bedtime.

- Conjoint parent–child sessions focused on Rain sharing her trauma narrative directly with her mother.
  - Darla had been exposed to the trauma narrative throughout its creation and was comfortable reviewing it again with Rain. In doing so, it allowed them to overtly process the trauma narrative together and address any ongoing concerns, such as Rain being uncomfortable with her parents continued arguing.

- Enhancing personal safety plans involved figuring out how Rain could better manage her reactions to her parents' disagreements. Although the domestic violence had ended between Darla and Alan, Rain continued to get distressed regarding their arguing.
  - Rain was reassured that she was not responsible for protecting her mother, and Darla reinforced with her that she was not to physically or verbally intervene between her parents. Rain was reminded of what she had control over in her life, consequently, a plan was made in regard to how to better manage her reactions. This included physically or mentally getting away from the arguing such as going outside to her backyard, listening to music, drawing, or reading.
  - Rain and her mother also developed a safety plan in case of emergencies. Her mother and Rain determined a code word that could be used to indicate an emergency. Additionally, their safety protocol included how to make a 911 call and what to say. Darla also provided a list of phone numbers of safe people (e.g., neighbors, relatives, friends) for Rain to contact in the event of an emergency.

Rain graduated from the TF-CBT program after 16 sessions. Rain and her mother noted considerable improvement in her psychosocial functioning and in interactions with her parents.

Conclusion

Traumatic experiences incapacitate one's normal mechanisms for coping and self-protection; therefore, one often resorts to extraordinary measures in order to survive physically and psychologically (Wade, 1997). The pain and suffering children experience from exposure to domestic violence should not be minimized. Yet, standing alongside the entire range of debilitating effects of trauma, many children display a stunning capacity for survival, perseverance, and resilience.

References

American Psychiatric Association. (2000). *Diagnostic and Statistical Manual of Mental Disorders* (4th ed., Text Revision). Washington, DC: Author.

Anderson, K. M., & Bang, E. (2012). Assessing PTSD and resilience for females who during childhood were exposed to domestic violence. *Child and Family Social Work, 17*(1), 55–65.

Anderson, K. M., & Danis, F. S. (2006). Adult daughters of battered women: Resistance and resilience in the face of danger. *Affilia, 21*(4), 419–432.

Anderson, K. M., Danis, F. S., & Havig, K. (2011). Adult daughters of battered women: Recovery and posttraumatic growth following childhood adversity. *Families in Society, 92*(2), 154–160.

Avdibegovic, E., & Sinanovic, O. (2006). Consequences of domestic violence on women's mental health in Bosnia and Herzegovina. *Croatian Medical Journal, 47*, 731–741.

Bancroft, L., & Silverman, J. G. (2002). *The batterer as parent: Addressing the impact of domestic violence on family dynamics.* Thousand Oaks, CA: Sage.

Blanchard, E. B., Jones-Alexander, J., Buckley, T. C., & Forneris, C. A. (1996). Psychometric properties of the PTSD Checklist (PCL). *Behaviour Research and Therapy, 34*(8), 669–673.

Clements, C. M., Oxtoby, C., & Ogle, R. L. (2008). Methodological issues in assessing psychological adjustment in child witnesses of intimate partner violence. *Trauma Violence & Abuse, 9*(2), 114–127.

Cohen, J. A., & Mannarino, A. P. (2008). Trauma-focused cognitive behavioural therapy for children and parents. *Child and Adolescent Mental Health, 13*(4), 158–162.

Cohen, J. A., Mannarino, A. P., & Deblinger, E. (2006). *Treating trauma and traumatic grief in children and adolescents.* New York: Guilford.

Conner, K. M., & Davidson, J. (2003). Development of a new resilience scale: The Connor Davidson resilience scale (CD-RISC). *Depression and Anxiety, 18*(76), 76–82.

Cowger, C., Anderson, K. M., & Snively, C. (2006). Assessing strengths: The political context of individual, family, and community empowerment. In D. Saleebey (Ed.), *The strengths perspective in social work practice* (pp. 93–113). Boston, MA: Allyn & Bacon.

Dehon, C., & Weems, C. F. (2010). Emotional development in the context of conflict: The indirect effects of interparental violence on children. *Journal of Child and Family Studies, 19*, 287–297.

Dick, G. (2005). Witnessing marital violence as children: Men's perceptions of their fathers. *Journal of Social Service Research, 32*(2), 1–24. *JAMA, 286*, 3089–3096.

Edleson, J. L. (1999). The overlap between child maltreatment and woman battering. *Violence Against Women, 5*(2), 134–154.

Edleson, J. L., Ellerton, A. L., Seagren, E. A., Kirchberg, S. L., Schmidt, S. O., & Ambrose, A. T. (2007). Assessing child exposure to adult domestic violence. *Children and Youth Services Review, 29*, 961–971.

Feerick, M. M., & Haugaard, J. J. (1999). Long-term effects of witnessing marital violence for women: The contribution of childhood physical and sexual abuse. *Journal of Family Violence, 14*(4), 377–398.

Feinauer, L. L., & Stuart, D. A. (1996). Blame and resilience in women sexually abused as children. *American Journal of Family Therapy, 24*(1), 31–40.

Forstrom-Cohen, B., & Rosenbaum, A. (1985). The effects of parental marital violence on young adults: An exploratory investigation. *Journal of Marriage and the Family, 47*, 467–472.

Fraser, M. (1997). *Risk and resilience in childhood: An ecological perspective.* Washington, DC: NASW Press.

Graham-Bermann, S. A., DeVoe, E. R., Mattis, J., Lynch, S., & Thomas, S. (2006). Ecological predictors of traumatic stress in Caucasian and Ethnic Minority children exposed to domestic violence. *Violence Against Women, 12*(7), 662–692.

Graham-Bermann, S., & Edleson, J. (2001). *Domestic violence in the lives of children: The future of research, intervention, and social policy.* Washington, DC: American Psychological Association.

Graham-Bermann, S., Gruber, G., Howell, K. H., & Girz, L. (2009). Factors discriminating among profiles of resilience and psychopathology in children exposed to intimate partner violence (IPV). *Child Abuse & Neglect, 33*, 648–660.

Grych, J. H., Fincham, F. D., Jouriles, E. N., & McDonald, R. (2000). Interparental conflict and child adjustment: Testing the meditational role of appraisals in the cognitive-contextual framework. *Child Development, 71*(6), 1648–1661.

Henning, K., Leitenberg, H., Coffey, P., Turner, T., & Bennett, R. T. (1996). Long-term psychological and social impact of witnessing physical conflict between parents. *Journal of Interpersonal Violence, 11*, 35–51.

Henning, K., Leitenberg, H., Coffey, P., Bennett, T., & Jankowski, M. (1991). Long-term psychological adjustment to witnessing interparental physical conflict during childhood Child Abuse & Neglect, 21(6), 501–515.

Herman, J. (1997). *Trauma and recovery.* New York: BasicBooks.

Holt, S., Buckley, H., & Whelan, S. (2008). The impact of exposure to domestic violence on children and young people: A review of the literature. *Child Abuse & Neglect, 32*, 797–810.

Hughes, H. M. (1988). Psychological and behavioral correlates of family violence in child witnesses and victims. *The American Journal of Orthopsychiatry, 58*(1), 77–90.

Humphreys, J. C. (2001). Turnings and adaptations in resilient daughters of battered women. *Journal of Nursing Scholarship, 33*(3), 245–251.

Kitzmann, K. M., Gaylord, N. K., Hold, A. R., & Kenny, E. D. (2003). Child witnesses to domestic violence: A meta-analytic review. *Journal of Consulting and Clinical Psychology, 71*(2), 339–352.

Kocot, T., & Goodman, L. (2003). The roles of coping and social support in battered women's mental health. *Violence Against Women, 9*(3), 323–346.

Lynne, C. (2009). *No more hitting! A child's story of domestic violence.* Self-published.

Mabanglo, M. (2002). Trauma and the effects of violence exposure and abuse on children: A review of the literature. *Smith Studies in Social Work, 72*(2), 231–245.

Margolin, G., Gordis, E. B., & Oliver, P. H. (2004). Links between marital and parent–child interaction: Moderating role of husband-to-wife aggression. *Development and Psychopathology, 16*, 753–771.

Martin, S., Moraccoa, K., Garrod, J., Tsuia, A., Kupperd, L., Chasea, J. & Campbell, J. (2002). Domestic violence across generations: findings from northern India International Journal of Epidemiology, 31 (3): 560–572.

Masten, A. S. (2001). Ordinary magic: Resilience processes in development. *The American Psychologist, 56*(3), 227–238.

McFarlane, J. M., Groff, J. Y., & O'Brien, J. A. (2003). Behaviors of children who are exposed and not exposed to intimate partner violence: An analysis of 330 Black, White, & Hispanic children. *Pediatrics, 112*(3), 202–207.

Meltzer, H., Doos, L., Vostanis, P., Ford, T., & Goodman, R. (2009). The mental health of children who witness domestic violence. *Child and Family Social Work, 14*, 491–501.

Mohr, W. K., & Tulman, L. J. (2000). Children exposed to violence: Measurement considerations within an ecological framework. *Advances in Nursing Science, 23*(1), 59–68.

Moon, M. (2000). Retrospective reports of interparental abuse by adult children from intact families. *Journal of Interpersonal Violence, 15*(12), 1323–1331.

Morgolin, G., & Gordis, E. B. (2004). Children's violence exposure in the family and community. *Current Directions in Psychological Science, 13*, 152–155.

Mullender, A., Hague, G., Imam, U., Kelly, L., Malos, E., & Regan, L. (2002). *Children's perspectives on domestic violence.* Newbury Park, CA: Sage.

Murrell, A. R., Merwin, R. M., Christoff, K. A., & Henning, K. R. (2005). When parents model violence: The relationship between witnessing weapon use as a child and later use as an adult. *Behavior and Social Issues, 14*, 128–133.

Nicolotti, L., El-Sheikh, M., & Whitson, S. M. (2003). Children's coping with marital conflict and their adjustment and physical health: Vulnerability and protective functions. *Journal of Family Psychology, 17*(3), 315–326.

Osofsky, J. D. (2003). Prevalence of children's exposure to domestic violence and child maltreatment: Implications for prevention and intervention. *Clinical Child and Family Psychology Review, 6*(3), 161–170.

Porterfield, K. M. (1996). *Straight talk about posttraumatic stress disorder: Coping with the aftermath of trauma.* New York: Checkmark Books.

Reynolds, M. W., Wallace, J., Hill, T. F., Weist, M. D., & Nabors, L. A. (2001). The relationship between gender, depression, and self esteem in children who have witnessed domestic violence. *Child Abuse & Neglect, 25*, 1201–1206.

Russell, D., Springer, K. W., & Greenfield, E. A. (2010). Witnessing domestic abuse in childhood as an independent risk factor for depressive symptoms in young adulthood. *Child Abuse & Neglect, 34*, 448–453.

Saakvitne, K. W., Tenne, H., & Affleck, G. (1998). Exploring thriving in the context of clinical trauma theory: Constructivist self-development theory. *Journal of Social Issues, 54*(2), 279–299.

Silvern, L., Karyl, J., Waede, L., Hodges, W. F., Starek, J., Heidt, E., et al. (1995). Retrospective reports of parental partner abuse: Relationships to depression, trauma symptoms, and self-esteem among college students. *Journal of Family Violence, 10*(2), 177–202.

Tedeschi, R. G., & Calhoun, L. G. (1995). *Trauma & transformation: Growing in the aftermath of suffering.* Newbury Park, CA: Sage.

Valentine, L., & Feinauer, L. (1993). Resiliency factors associated with female survivors of childhood sexual abuse. *American Journal of Family Therapy, 21*(3), 216–224.

Von Steen, P. G. (1997). Adults with witnessing histories: The overlooked victims of domestic violence. *Psychotherapy, 34*(4), 478–484.

Wade, A. (1997). Small acts of living: Everyday resistance to violence and other forms of oppression. *Contemporary Family Therapy, 19*(1), 23–39.

Werner, E., & Smith, R. (1992). *Overcoming the odds: High risk children from birth to adulthood.* Ithaca, NY: Cornell University Press.

Winstok, Z., Eisikovits, Z., & Karnieli-Miller, O. (2004). The impact of father-to-mother aggression on the structure and content of adolescents' perceptions of themselves and their parents. *Violence Against Women, 10*(9), 1036–1055.

Wolfe, D. A., Crooks, C. V., Lee, V., McIntyre-Smith, A., & Jaffe, P. G. (2003). The effects of children's exposure to domestic violence: A meta-analysis and critique. *Clinical Child and Family Psychology Review, 6*(3), 171–187.

Wolin, S. J., & Wolin, S. (1993). *The resilient self.* New York: Villard Books.

Wood, G. G., & Roche, S. E. (2001). Representing selves, reconstructing lives: Feminist group work with women survivors of male violence. *Social Work with Groups, 23*(4), 5–23.

Family Resilience and Sexuality

Tina M. Timm

Introduction

Individuals and families are confronted with issues related to sexuality whether they like it or not. A topic of high significance, sexual experiences can entail pleasure and/or pain. Throughout this book there are many conceptualizations and definitions of resilience. For the purpose of this chapter, resilience is framed within the ecological literature. Canadian ecologist Holling (1973) was the first to describe resilience within ecological systems. He and his colleagues later defined ecological resilience as the capacity of a system to absorb disturbance and reorganize while undergoing change so as to still retain essentially the same function, structure, identity, and feedbacks (Walker, Holling, Carpenter, & Kinzig, 2004).

Families are ecological systems and it is inevitable that families will have events or disturbances transpire along the way that require adaptation and in some cases reorganization. When these occur, be they predictable or unpredictable, families will work to regain their structure and identity. The more resilient the family, the smoother these transitions will go. In this chapter, I focus on sexual resiliency in families, essentially asking the questions, "What do sexually healthy families look like?" "What can be done to promote this status?" and "How can families overcome both predictable and unpredictable events related to sexuality?". The overarching conceptualization of sexual resilience is that families should not only survive developmental and situational stressors related to sexuality, but are also able to grow in positive ways in the process. I define "family" broadly and include caregivers with children, or couples. In addition, sexuality is looked at across the lifespan, operating on the notion that sexuality is relevant from the "cradle to the grave."

Theoretical Perspectives

In their book, *The Expanded Family Lifestyle*, Carter and McGoldrick (1999) provide a framework for understanding families when they describe them as organized on a vertical as well as a horizontal axis, both of which have application to sexual development and sexual well-being. The vertical axis includes family history and patterns of interaction passed down through the generations. Relative to sexuality it includes rules and values, both spoken and unspoken, related to the boundaries and expressions of

T.M. Timm (✉)
School of Social Work, Michigan State University, East Lansing, MI, USA
e-mail: timmtm@gmail.com

D.S. Becvar (ed.), *Handbook of Family Resilience*,
DOI 10.1007/978-1-4614-3917-2_29, © Springer Science+Business Media New York 2013

sexuality. For example, this includes what is talked about and what is not, patterns of affection and intimacy between family members, what has been modeled, familial values, and what is expected. Sexual histories of families include sexual secrets (e.g., pregnancies before marriage, abortions, sexual trauma), sexual beliefs (e.g., religious messages), and non-secret events laden with traumatic or shameful narratives (e.g., infidelities, sexual offenses). The sociocultural environment is also an important part of the vertical axis. Gender roles relative to sexuality can dictate both how males and females should behave in general and what acceptable sexual behaviors are. It includes stereotypes, issues of power and oppression, and legacies of trauma (e.g., stereotypes of certain groups being "more sexual" than others, heterosexism, rape being used to oppress and dominate in times of war). From a multicultural perspective, there are numerous expressions of sexuality within some cultures that may not be accepted in other cultures. These cultural beliefs, attitudes, and behaviors may affect a family's resilience in handling developmental changes and/or non-normative stressors (e.g., having more secrecy or shame around sexual issues).

The horizontal axis captures how the family moves through time and copes with both predictable and unpredictable changes relative to sexuality. In a long-term relationship, either heterosexual or same sex, there are predictable changes that occur over time, the most obvious of which are related to sexual development (e.g., bodies aging, menopause for women, a longer refractory period between erections for men). These cannot be avoided. If children are added to the family, they also undergo predictable stages that need to be negotiated (e.g., puberty, sexual decision making).

In addition to the predictable developmental challenges, any number of events and issues related to sexuality can arise within the life of a family that are unexpected, for example, illnesses or injuries, questioning of orientation or gender identity, infidelity, and sexual abuse, to name a few. The responses to these events will vary greatly depending on the individual family members, age of family members, parental subsystem, and the family dynamics. In addition, the sociocultural environment of the horizontal axis includes the current events and social policies that affect families (e.g., the development of medications to treat erectile dysfunction, current laws about who is allowed to get married and who is not, federal funding focused exclusively on abstinence-only sexuality education).

Some factors may have an influence on both the vertical and the horizontal axes. There may be intergenerational family attitudes and beliefs about what are acceptable behaviors or beliefs (vertical axis) that coincide with the current cultural climate in which the family lives (horizontal axis). Issues relative to sexuality that fall within this category could be abortion, acceptance of same sex relationships, awareness of sexual abuse, and flexibility of gender roles.

Assessing both the vertical and horizontal axes can be helpful in the attempt to understand how a family might react to issues of sexuality. In addition, the ecological resilience of the system and the resilience of each individual within the system will play a part in how well the family handles events as they unfold over the generations and within the developmental lifespan of each family. Unfortunately, the family history cannot be changed (although discussing it openly can promote change in meaning and behavior in the present). Sociocultural factors do change, but these changes often take a great deal of time. Families can prepare for the predictable changes, but the unpredictable ones are always a wild card, and often come at the most unexpected times. That said, resilience in families related to sexuality can and should be encouraged, especially as families face events that are painful, unexpected, or out of their comfort zones.

Significance of the Topic

Fostering resilience relative to sexuality is important given that individuals and families are confronted with issues of sexuality across the lifespan. Despite this fact, very little has been written about resilience and sexuality and even less about resilience in families relative to sexuality. A case could be made that "sexual resilience" has significant overlap with "healthy sexuality." Healthy sexuality in families could potentially prevent things such as early sexual initiation, sexually transmitted infections (STIs/HIV), unplanned pregnancy, severe effects of sexual trauma, and sexual dysfunction, to name a few. In some instances, it could even prevent suicide. However, resilient sexuality also entails the ability of the system to absorb disturbances that inevitably result from sexual development and life events, and to reorganize effectively while undergoing change.

Literature Review

The literature on sexuality, sexual development, and problematic sexual behaviors is expansive. In this literature review, my goal is to focus on a number of sexual issues relative to sexuality, making a case for how sexual resilience may prevent or help individuals and families cope more effectively if such issues were to arise.

Unpredictable Sexual Difficulties

Sexually Transmitted Infections/HIV

Although there is more information than ever before about how to prevent sexually transmitted infections (commonly known as STIs), more than 19 million STIs are estimated to occur in the United States every year. Roughly half of those afflicted are between the ages of 15 and 24 (Center for Disease Control and Prevention, 2009). Specific populations such as lesbians deem themselves at very low risk for STIs despite the fact that research says otherwise (Marrazzo et al., 2002; Marrazzo, Stine, & Wald, 2003). There are over 55,000 new HIV infections per year (Center for Disease Control and Prevention, 2008), with young people, African Americans, and Hispanic/Latinos bearing a disproportionate burden of these diagnoses. Not only is this a public health crisis, being diagnosed with an STI or HIV is a significant stress for individuals, their partners, and their families. Resilient individuals are able to address the crisis and hopefully reach a place of resolution and healthy interaction with partners and themselves.

Unplanned Pregnancy

Unintended pregnancies account for approximately half of all pregnancies in the United States (Eaton et al., 2010). Unfortunately, the rates of unplanned teenage pregnancies are again on the rise after a decade of being relatively stable. Unplanned pregnancies can be related to a number of factors including lack of accurate information about sexuality, inadequate skills to communicate about sexuality, inaccessible contraception, family history, etc. Comprehensive sexuality education has been shown to be more effective than abstinence-only programming; yet the popularity of the latter is widespread. Unplanned teenage pregnancies present a crisis for many families. Often there is confusion and even shame associated with the pregnancy. The reaction of the families hinges on many things—religious beliefs, values, community standing, availability of social support, and circumstances around the pregnancy. Families need to make decisions related to issues such as keeping the child, putting the child up for adoption, or terminating the pregnancy. Families also need to be able to counsel their child, inform friends and family, and in many cases prepare their child to be a parent. Resilient families are more likely to negotiate the unplanned pregnancy and support the teenager, her child, or other family members.

Childhood Sexual Abuse

Although the rates vary, in a geographically stratified, random sample of adults ($n=935$), 14.2% of men and 32.3% of women reported childhood experiences that met the criteria for sexual abuse (Briere & Elliott, 2003). Over two decades of research suggests with relative unanimity that childhood sexual abuse (CSA) has a wide number of psychological sequelae. Among these are low self-esteem, anxiety, depression, anger and aggression, posttraumatic stress, dissociation, substance abuse, sexual difficulties, somatic preoccupation and disorder, self-injurious or self-destructive behavior, and most of the various symptoms and behaviors seen in those diagnosed with borderline personality disorder (Berliner & Elliott, 2002). Factors that may determine the severity of these effects include age at the time of abuse (greater risk=younger), length of time the abuse occurred (greater risk=continuous abuse across developmental levels), who the abuser was (greater risk=close, trusted relationship), severity of abuse (greater risk=penetration with violence), and protection post-disclosure (greater risk=not believed and/or not protected) (Conte & Schuerman, 1987). There are individual, internal characteristics of resilience that may influence symptomatology, as well as family characteristics and the ability to respond. The risk of a child being sexually abused increases when variables such as physical abuse, having a mother who was mentally ill, not having someone to confide in, and being socially isolated are present (Fleming, Mullen, & Bammer, 1997). Knowing this, sexual resilience can be fostered by addressing any of the factors listed above. The more resilience in the child and the family, the more likely it would be that CSA could be prevented, or if it happened, the length of the abuse would be shorter and the type of abuse less involved.

The most positive outcomes post-disclosure are for the child to be believed, protected, and given emotional support. Research has indicated that these parental reactions to disclosure are an important factor in the child's ability to successfully cope with the experience of sexual abuse. For example, Johnson and Kenkel (1991) found that among adolescent incest victims, nonsupportive reactions by mothers were rated as highly stressful and that this stressor was a highly significant predictor of self-reported emotional distress. Furthermore, both individual and family therapies are recommended to promote healing.

Sexual Dysfunction

Sexual difficulties and/or dysfunctions occur in the general population at alarming rates. According to Laumann, Gagnon, Michael, and Michael (1994), as many as 31% of men and 43% of women reported having a sexual difficulty in the previous year. Issues can include lack of desire, arousal problems, sexual pain, or the inability to have an orgasm (mostly for women, but also occurs in men) to name a few. It can be a complex puzzle to assess the combination of factors contributing to any one of these issues. What is clear is that resilience relative to sexuality could have positive implications for addressing any one of them.

Suicide

One of the most serious possibilities relative to sexuality and family dynamics is the risk of suicide. The likelihood of suicide attempts is increased in gay males and lesbians, as well as bisexuals of both sexes when compared to their heterosexual counterparts (Silenzio, Pena, Duberstein, Cerel, & Knox, 2007). Unfortunately, this is due in large part to being disproportionately subjected to anti-gay attitudes, leading to increased isolation and loneliness for these youth. Families that have fostered resilience relative to sexuality would have a much stronger foundation for communicating about these painful issues. Research has demonstrated that families who reject their son or daughter after the disclosure of being gay/lesbian increase their children's risk of taking their lives (Ryan, Huebner, Kiaz, & Sanchez, 2009).

Predictable Sexual Development Issues

Sexual Initiation

Families can have an important influence on the age at which adolescents become sexually active. Age of sexual initiation is an important risk consideration because of the implications it may have for future sexual decision making. Research indicates that adolescents who are "early sexual initiators" are more prone to engage in sexual risk behaviors (O'Donnell, O'Donnell, & Stueve, 2001; Sandfort, Orr, Hirsch, & Santelli, 2008). Conversely, initiating sexual activity at older ages may have a protective effect. In a meta-analysis of 35 longitudinal studies investigating the onset of heterosexual intercourse, Zimmer-Gembeck and Helfand (2008) found that the majority of the research suggested that those adolescents initiating sex after age 16 (considered middle to late initiators according to their criteria) engaged in fewer sexual risk behaviors and were more likely to use condoms consistently than those who initiated sex at 16 or younger. From this research, it is evident that later sexual initiation in terms of age serves as a protective factor for sexual risk.

Current Issues

Sexual Minorities Being Marginalized

Currently there are several contextual/cultural issues that are affecting families and sexuality in the United States. One of these is the ongoing marginalization of sexual minorities. This includes the debate about whether or not same sex couples should be allowed to marry. Although attitudes are slowly beginning to change as a handful of states now allow same-sex marriage or civil unions, many states have passed specific legislation defining marriage as only being between a man and a woman. The overall heterosexist climate creates a hostile environment for individuals, couples, and families who comprise the sexual minority.

Support of sexual minorities has come from a variety of professional organizations, most notably, the American Psychological Association (APA), which convened a six-person task force to examine the efficacy of the so-called "reparative therapy" or sexual orientation change efforts (SOCE). The task force reviewed journal articles from 1960 to 2007 ($n=83$). Based on this review of the literature, the APA adopted a resolution stating that mental health professionals should avoid telling clients that they can change their sexual orientation through therapy or other treatments. The resolution advises that parents, guardians, young people, and their families avoid sexual orientation treatments that portray homosexuality as a mental illness and instead seek affirmative therapeutic interventions (American Psychological Association, 2009).

With regard to same sex parenting, Crowl, Ahn, and Baker (2008) conducted a meta-analysis of 19 studies examining outcomes for children raised in gay and lesbian households and concluded that the development, adjustment, and well-being of children being raised in families with same sex parents do not differ markedly from children being raised in the context of heterosexual marriage. Despite the research evidence, there continue to be stereotypes, lack of tolerance, overt oppression, and in some cases acts of violence against sexual minorities. For these reasons, it is all the more important that we support resilience in non-traditional families.

Sexuality and Technology

Families are often struggling to catch up with the ways in which sexuality and technology intersect. This is an excellent example of the unexpected aspects of sexuality for which families are not always prepared. The explosion in the usage of graphic sexual content on the internet is due in part to what is known as the Triple-A Engine—anonymity, accessibility, and affordability (Cooper, Delmonico, & Burg, 2000). Such a context makes it enticing for people who would otherwise not seek out sexually explicit material in a more public way. The pornography industry's venture into the Internet has been hugely successful. It is estimated that the Internet pornography's annual revenues range from 5 to 30 billion dollars. All told, pornographic websites offer 260 million pages of online pornography and 1.6 million pornographic URL websites. "Type 'XXX' into Google.com and 106 million pages arise" (Paul, 2005, p. 60). While the prevalence of internet pornography is potentially problematic for adults, there is very little information about the consequences of exposure to developmentally inappropriate sexual material for children and teenagers.

In addition to the volume of sexual content on the internet, there is also the serious issue of sexual perpetrators using the internet to prey on vulnerable youth. Children, especially adolescents, are sometimes curious about sexuality and sexually explicit material. Because they may be curious, they may turn to the Internet to access such materials. Sex offenders targeting children will use and exploit this developmental stage. Children often do not recognize the common grooming techniques of an offender, for example, using attention, affection, kindness, or even using gifts to establish a secretive, "trusting" relationship. They often do not fully understand or recognize the potential danger of giving out personal information or having contact with an individual met online (Federal Bureau of Investigation, 2010). This can lead to devastating consequences, including molestation, rape, and abduction.

In less extreme, but nonetheless in potentially devastating ways, the issue of adolescents engaging in what is commonly known as "sexting" is more and more common. Sexting includes the transmission of sexual comments or images to another person, typically using a cell phone. This obviously can be done using conventional computer systems as well. Adolescents, with their underdeveloped cognitive functioning, sometimes engage in these behaviors without thinking about the consequences. When there is misplaced trust in the people to whom the information is sent and this trust is violated, embarrassment and humiliation can occur. According to the Family Online Safety Institute (FOSI), explaining the consequences of posting inappropriate material online and monitoring the child's mobile phone usage is essential these days. Additional safety guidelines for parents are available at the FOSI website (2011).

Sexuality Education

The former surgeon general of the United States, Dr. Joycelyn Elders, says it best: "The best contraceptive in the world is a good education. A population that is well-educated and informed about sex, sexuality, and sexual health concerns, through age-appropriate, scientifically-based universal sexual education across the lifespan is necessary" (2010, p. 249). Since 1997, over $1.5 billion has been spent on abstinence-only sexuality education, despite the lack of demonstrated efficacy (Hampton, 2008). The foundation of sexual resilience is accurate information and open communication across the lifespan.

Aging Population

We are moving into an unprecedented time of having the largest aging population in history. The number of people worldwide 65 and older is estimated at 506 million as of mid-2008; by 2040, that number will hit 1.3 billion. Thus, in just over 30 years, the proportion of older people will double from 7 to 14% of the total world population (Kinsella, & Wan, 2009). In the United States, this is due in part not only to the aging of the baby boomers—an estimated 76 million American children were born between 1945 and 1964—but also because people are living longer. Consequently, people who wish to remain sexually active are doing so well into their golden years. As stated in the introduction, sexual resilience is a topic that is relevant across the lifespan. As people age, sexual behaviors and meanings may change, but they still need to be able to negotiate the predictable and unpredictable changes that life presents. This includes physical changes and potential difficulties in mobility, the possibility of chronic illnesses, and related medications. Couples (defined as a family in this chapter) need to continue to foster resilience together as they face these challenges.

Clinical Implications

In her book, *Strengthening Family Resilience*, Walsh (2006) describes three key processes for family resilience: belief systems, organizational patterns, and communication processes. All these areas provide the potential for both prevention and intervention relative to sexuality in families, and are used as a guiding framework to discuss the clinical implications and structure the case examples to follow.

Clinicians are in a powerful position to help families prepare for the trials and tribulations relative to sexuality. Clinicians can help families create a sex-positive environment, which will help them weather both the vertical and the horizontal issues that inevitably affect families as they move through time.

Belief Systems

Belief systems include three components: meaning making, positive outlook, and transcendence/spirituality. Essentially, they describe how the family "makes sense of things." One potentially helpful response on the part of the clinician thus would be to normalize and contextualize issues of sexuality in the family. This may be particularly useful relative to the predictable lifespan events on the horizontal axis. The more families know about what is developmentally appropriate and what is factually accurate, the more resilience they can evidence.

A belief system that is relationally based vs. located within individuals also will allow for more support during difficult times. With this stance, the family views themselves as a team, instead of sending one member out into the world by himself or herself. This may be particularly important when couples present for a sexual problem. Often, they will state that one partner is "the problem" and it is that person who needs treatment. A systemically trained therapist quickly educates the couple on the relational aspects of the problem and works to get them both fighting against the issue vs. seeing it as an individual problem. In narrative therapy, this would be captured by the idea of externalization (White & Epston, 1990).

Couples who come in maintaining a positive outlook that sexuality is important and change is possible are likely to demonstrate more resilience. However, there are times when chronic illnesses or genetic abnormalities affect sexuality in ways that cannot be changed. The powerful part of resilience is that clients have control over what it means to them. In the words of the serenity prayer, "accepting things that cannot be changed" also can contribute to resilience related to sexuality.

The final component of the resilient belief system is transcendence and spirituality. This is broadly defined and, although it includes organized religion, is also about values, purpose, and growth from adversity. Many times people who have had negative sexual experiences go on to share their experiences with others. It becomes their purpose in life to educate others by bringing the topic out into the open and promoting dialog. Similarly, some do not ask the question, "Why me?" but rather, "Why not me?". This is a valuable shift in the belief system that can contribute to resilience. Strong values and beliefs can help individuals make good decisions about sexuality and relationships as long as they are not packaged in fear and shame.

Organizational Patterns

The organizational patterns that contribute to resilience include areas of flexibility, connectedness, and social and economic resources. Flexibility captures the idea that families need to be able to "bend, not break." They can maintain stability in the face of disruption. They can rebound and reorganize as needed. This is often facilitated by a more authoritative (vs. authoritarian or passive) style of parenting as well as egalitarian couple dynamics. Adolescence is characterized as a time when sexuality becomes more prominent. This is the period in which puberty, potential dating, and for some, decision making about intimacy and sexual activity occurs. Some parents handle this more effectively than others. The authoritarian style of parenting that is characterized by rigidity related to sexuality may backfire as some adolescents rebel and others are just left with negative messages and a lack of information with which to make decisions. The opposite type of parenting, being passive and/or "too open," certainly also has dangers. For example, lack of supervision has been associated with early sexual initiation (Borawski, Ievers-Landis, Lovegreen, & Trapl, 2003).

Connectedness, as the name would imply, encourages cooperation and collaboration. If relationships are damaged in some way, individuals would seek to repair them. Connectedness also includes a respect for others and their differences, as well as appropriate boundaries. The concept of appropriate sexual boundaries is complex because, of course, all families have a different idea about what appropriate boundaries should be within a family. Families vary greatly on stances related to children bathing together (if ever, or until what age), nudity, or degree of affection between parents. The list goes on and on. It is most useful to move away from "right and wrong" and "black and white" thinking. The core resilience concept is about respect for others. If you combine this with the idea of flexibility, you get families who easily adapt when a 7-year-old who previously would streak through the house naked suddenly insists on closing the door when getting dressed.

Lastly, it comes as no surprise that families are often more resilient if they have access to social and economic resources. Relative to sexuality this would include access to information about sexuality (e.g., having a computer), institutional supports if there was a concern or problem (e.g., doctors, mental health professionals), and social networks to offer support and/or guidance (e.g., churches, extended family).

Communication Processes

Communication processes set a norm for the family that has important implications for sexuality. Walsh (2006) organizes communication processes into the following categories: clarity, open emotional expression, and collaborative problem solving. As the name would imply, clarity is clear communication and lack of ambiguity between words and actions. There is a seeking of accurate information. Parents providing accurate, developmentally appropriate sexuality information would be a hallmark of this aspect of resilience. For some, this is more difficult than others. The Sexuality Information and Education Council of the United States (SEICUS, 2002) strongly advocates for parents to communicate about sexuality with their kids. In a study by Miller, Kotchick, Dorsey, Forehand, and Ham (1998) in which youth were asked about who or what most influenced their actual sexual decision making, parents were most commonly identified (38%), friends were second-most commonly identified (32%), and only a small percentage identified the media (4%). Unfortunately, parents sometimes misjudge the timing of when to have the talk about the "birds and the bees" with their child(ren) and menstruation has already started or sexual activity has begun. It is also quite common for parents, as a result of their discomfort, to avoid having the conversation at all (perhaps deferring exclusively to the school to educate about this topic) or try to "dodge the bullet" by saying that the child is too young to know and they will explain it when they are older, or as I have heard parents describe, "I told him I would answer the question after dinner, and then fortunately he forgot about it and I did not have to." Fortunately, there are many approaches available to increase parent–child communication about sexuality (SEICUS).

It is a well-known premise of communication theory that one "cannot not communicate" (Watzlawick, Beavin, & Jackson, 1967). This is abundantly clear related to issues of sexuality. By NOT talking about something, families are saying volumes. Clinicians can investigate these spoken and unspoken "rules" by encouraging families to talk about not just the current state of family functioning, but ways that the topic of sex was handled in previous generations as well. Parents will often tell poignant stories of the communication that did or did not happen when they were growing up. One way to facilitate this process is by completing a sexual genogram (Hof & Berman, 1986), which includes the basic structure of a family genogram with specific questions asked to illuminate issues of sexuality through the generations.

Open emotional expression means that individual family members take responsibility for identifying and discussing their feelings. Furthermore, they are encouraged to have a wide range of feelings. Sharing of emotions is characterized as pleasurable, not dreaded, and may also involve humor. Although it would perhaps be rare to find children who "enjoy" talking to their parents about sex, due to the inherent feelings of discomfort associated with parents being confronted with their child's sexual potential and children being confronted with the possibility of their parents being sexual, it is a sign of resilience in families that when the conversation is started, or the "tough questions" get asked, families can stay with it.

Lastly, there is collaborative problem solving. This would include a proactive stance to actually prevent problems before they happen. If that were not possible (i.e., if it was a non-normative event), then resourcefulness and creativity characterize responses. There could be shared decision making and negotiation. Perhaps a family could set concrete goals and build on success and learn from failure. An example to illustrate this is the issue of unplanned teenage pregnancy. This can be approached in many different ways, but if this model is to be followed, the teenager and caregivers would discuss the options, and see what solutions there might be. Regardless of the "solution," resources would be explored and a plan would be developed together.

Assessment

The key to assessing sexual resilience is to be knowledgeable about what it looks like, and to ask good questions to discern where those areas might be. This is similar to a strength-based approach where the clinician looks for what the family is doing well, not just the areas in which they are struggling. Once this information is gleaned, the clinician can inform intervention—pointing out the areas of strength and coaching around the areas where resilience is harder to find. As mentioned above, this may include doing a genogram specifically focused on sexuality across the generations.

Another helpful resource for individuals to reflect on the effects of their family of origin on their sexual development is the book *Sex Smart: How Your Childhood Shaped Your Sexual Life and What to Do About It* (Zoldbrod, 1998). Self-assessments are included within every chapter to investigate what was modeled and taught in the family as well as the effects this has had on sexuality. Topics include everything from touch, trust, and body image to masturbation and violence.

Building Resilience Through Prevention

Professionals can be instrumental in helping to coach parents (this word is meant to be inclusive of any primary caregiver) to foster sexual resilience in children. This begins with the concept of attachment.

The earliest proponent of attachment theory, Bowlby (1969) discovered that interactions with early caregivers establish what are called internal working models. These models determine the level of safety and comfort found in close relationships when distressed, the probable availability and responsiveness of attachment figures in attending to the distress, and the individual's perception of his or her own worthiness to receive sensitive, loving care from attachment figures. Decades of research into infant attachment consistently show that babies thrive mentally, socially, and emotionally in direct relation to having a secure attachment.

Hazan and Shaver (1987) were the first to propose that romantic love is an attachment process, meaning that bonds formed by adult lovers replicate the affectional bonds of infants with their caregivers. They believed that individuals' early experiences in close relationships shape the nature and development of subsequent relationships in adulthood. This theoretical perspective is significant relative to sexuality in families because investigations exploring the link between adult attachment and risky sexual behaviors make a strong case for securely attached individuals being the least likely of all the attachment styles to be susceptible to these activities and their consequences (Feeney & Raphael, 1992; Kalichman et al., 1993; Rubenstein, 1990). Insecure attachments also can lead to a number of child sexual behavior problems (Friedrich, 2007).

Building and maintaining a secure attachment between a caregiver and an infant can be facilitated by what is commonly known as "attunement" (Haft & Slade, 1989). Examples of attunement behaviors include:

- Holding and touching your infant frequently, including skin-to-skin contact.
- Becoming a careful observer of your child and learning how to interpret his or her needs and bids for attention.
- Responding sensitively to your baby's cries. This builds trust that you will be responsive to his or her needs.
- Maintaining eye-to-eye contact at close range.
- Encouraging the child to imitate your facial expressions and gestures.

These behaviors and skills come naturally and easily to some parents. However, they can be disrupted by environmental stressors, post-partum depression, or lack of knowledge about the importance of attachment and bonding. What is clear is that secure attachment is connected to healthier sexual outcomes in adulthood, the equivalent of sexual resilience. Consequently, attachment should be a part of any conversation related to fostering resilience.

Building on a secure attachment, parents continue to shape their children through what is known as sexual socialization. The key elements of sexual socialization are: (1) recognition and acceptance of pleasure, (2) consistent socialization for privacy and responsibility (i.e., appropriate time, place, and person), (3) continuing education about sexuality (see below for more information), (4) building self-esteem, and (5) supporting the child to be in charge of his/her body and all its functions (Calderone & Johnson, 1981).

Parents should be encouraged to teach children the correct terms for ALL body parts. Children should know, and be able to talk about, what is informally called their "private parts." Using proper terminology sends a message that these are no different than other parts of the body, therefore decreasing the spoken and unspoken messages about them being dirty, or so hidden in secrecy that we cannot even acknowledge them. Comfort with this most basic level lays a solid foundation for all that is to come down the road. It also facilitates the "good touch, bad touch" conversations that help children to sort out who should and should not be touching them. Furthermore, if anything inappropriate did happen to the child, she or he could accurately report it to responsible adults. When children have "pet names" for genitalia, adults may not understand what the child is trying to convey. One particularly sad example of this was a child who was taught to call her vulva a "purse." When she decided to tell an adult what was happening, she reported that someone was touching her "purse." Consequently, the adult did not think anything of it, which left the girl unprotected longer than necessary.

Sexuality education should happen "early and often." The better the family does in the formative years, the fewer problems the children will have as teenagers and adults. Parents should not just be open to the questions that children ask; they should be actively looking for "teachable moments" or opportunities to give developmentally appropriate information to children. Accurate information builds sexual resilience down the road.

The use of books, or what is commonly known as bibliotherapy, is another way for parents to feel more confident to share developmentally appropriate information about sexuality. Starting in pre-school, books can be used to teach the correct names for body parts. This is followed by teaching about what kind of touching is acceptable and differentiating between "good" secrets—ones that make you feel good and are time limited (e.g., the present you got mom for her birthday)—vs. "bad" secrets—ones that make you feel bad and are supposed to be kept forever (e.g., someone touching you in a way that makes you feel uncomfortable). As puberty approaches there are many resources for both boys and girls to help make this time less confusing.

Creating a Sex-Positive Environment

A sex-positive environment is neither embarrassed by sexuality or consumed with it, meaning there is balance—couples or families do not over-focus on it, do not under-focus on it. Sexuality is integrated into the family life and conversation in open, factual ways. Parents strive to teach critical thinking skills in order for kids to make good decisions about sexual activity and behavior. Most importantly, children are taught to respect themselves and their bodies. Sexuality education is provided in the home, but not to the exclusion of other sources (e.g., sex education in school). It includes factual information that is grounded in family values, but not in oppressive ways. Children become knowl-edgeable about puberty BEFORE it starts, and both mothers and fathers are involved in this process. Indeed, daughters have reported that they wanted more open communication about sexuality with their fathers (Hutchinson & Cedarbaum, 2011).

In The Intimate Circle, parents in a sex positive environment are categorized as "Sex Expressive Parents" (Ehrenberg & Ehrenberg, 1988). This environment includes having appropriate boundaries in the house. Although the type of boundaries may vary from house to house (e.g., comfort with nudity), it would be important to provide at least basic respect for individual choices (e.g., someone wanting privacy to change clothing) and family members would be able to say no to unwanted touch.

Related to gender, ideally there would be flexibility in gender roles and no objectifying of women. Ideally, non-traditional gender behavior would be supported, but at the very least tolerated vs. discour-aged, shamed, or even met with hostility. Families must understand two important things: (1) non-conforming gender behavior does not MAKE someone gay or lesbian, and (2) if the child is in fact questioning gender identity or sexual orientation, negative comments and attitudes serve to isolate the child, which often leads to depression and anxiety over time.

To facilitate a sex-positive environment, parents would also model affection and intimacy. It is good for children to see mom and dad kissing, hugging, holding hands, and going on dates. How children see their parents treating each other sets a template for the child's future relationships.

Lastly, a sex-positive environment is related to the overall atmosphere of the household. In general, are the child's feelings taken into consideration? Do they feel "heard?" Are they free to talk about difficult things without fear of reprisal? This is an atmosphere that is set over time.

Research Implications

National representative samples about sexuality give us valuable information about individual sexuality and behaviors. Two examples of this include the National Health and Social Life Survey (NHSLS) (Laumann et al., 1994), and more recently, the National Survey of Sexual Health and Behavior (NSSHB) (Herbenick et al., 2010). However, there is less information about family sexuality. Some of what is available details when it does not go well (e.g., incestuous families) (Maddock & Larson, 1995). There is much less known about when it goes "right." Certainly, there are a lot of resilient families who are doing well when encountering points of transition and non-normative events, sexual and otherwise. Research on non-clinical populations is essential to begin to identify what they do well. Furthermore, research needs to investigate how race, ethnicity, culture, and religion potentially contribute to resilience relative to sexuality. It would also be helpful to know more about what goes well in non-traditional families—single parents, same sex parents, step-families, etc.

As discussed above, technology is growing exponentially. This easy access to sexual content, the way it affects families and relationships, and the effect on children's sexuality are essential research topics. Questions such as, "How is the meaning of sexuality and relationships altered and passed down through the generations?" should be asked. Families struggling with issues of sexual compulsion/addiction (e.g., internet pornography) have few resources for empirically validated treatment for adults and certainly not for adolescents and young adults.

Case Examples

There are many examples of family resilience relative to sexuality. Fortunately, most families negotiate issues of sexuality quite well and never need outside intervention. The two examples highlighted below are ones in which therapy was sought: one family demonstrated minimal signs of resilience and the other had many more indicators of resilience.

The first case is an example of a family who had trouble negotiating a predictable stage of sexual development. The parents would be a classic example of the "Sex Repressive Parents" as described by Ehrenberg and Ehrenberg (1988). Such parents tend to believe that sex is inherently immoral and send consistent messages that sex is dirty and evil. There are rigid rules and belief systems in place to prevent sexual thoughts and behavior of the children—even natural sexual development.

Case Example #1: Difficulty Negotiating Adolescent Sexuality

The Carter family called because their daughter Alison, age 16, was "out of control." They reported that she was skipping school, not doing her homework, and breaking curfew on a regular basis. The family reported attending church regularly. Alison was the oldest of five children. Both parents worked full-time. During the family assessment, Alison was withdrawn and offered limited information. It wasn't until the therapist met with her alone that she started to open up about the difficulties she was facing. She reported that ever since she hit puberty her dad had become increasingly controlling. Where previously they had had a close relationship and shared many common interests, now they were hardly speaking. It started with her dad telling her what she could and could not wear, but doing so in an accusatory, demeaning way, for example, "You're not leaving the house in that," and "You look like a street walker." Both of her parents were relentless in telling her that they would disown her if she got pregnant. When she requested privacy, they accused her of hiding something and removed the door from her room. She was not allowed to go to friends' houses because of the suspicion that there would be boys there. Alison denied dating anyone and reported a firm conviction to remain sexually abstinent until married. The lack of resiliency relative to sexuality was related to:

- A family environment that did not support the expression of emotions
- Virtually no sexuality education except for the negative consequences of having sex
- A rigid belief system around sexuality and gender roles
- A lack of understanding about normal adolescent development
- Isolation from friends and social support

These factors were making it particularly difficult for the family to navigate the teenage years of the daughter. Given that she was in trouble most of the time and being accused of things she was not doing, she stated that she "might as well break the rules." Doing a genogram revealed that both parents were raised in conservative families where sex was not discussed. The only message Alison's mom ever received about sex was on her wedding day from her own mom and it was, "It's a wife's duty to have sex with her husband once a week. Just lay there and get it over with." Alison's dad had a lot of shame about the fact that his older sister got pregnant as a teenager and was "sent away" so no one would know about it. It made sense, given the combination of these two histories, that Alison's parents would have a negative view of sex and have difficulty negotiating this developmental stage.

In the beginning phase, it was imperative that the therapist be respectful of the belief systems of the parents, thereby not alienating the parents and causing an early termination. It would have been easy to get polarized regarding the extreme behaviors the daughter was reporting. Maintaining the therapeutic alliance with all members of the family was essential if change was to occur. Additionally, as with many parents, they were initially coming in to change their daughter's unacceptable behavior, not to be confronted with their own contribution to the problem. Family therapy thereby proceeded cautiously with the goal of increasing family resilience in the following ways:

- Educating about what is developmentally appropriate during adolescence
- Discussing the potential benefits
- Building on a belief system that is focused on the importance of relationships and the common goals (i.e., abstinence)
- Encouraging connectedness by fostering respect of others
- Advocating for more open communication about the family sexual history
- Supporting the expression of feelings
- Finding ways to facilitate collaborative problem solving

The parents were able to become less extreme when they realized that Alison was not doing anything dangerous and she was still embracing the values with which she was raised. Building safety to discuss difficult topics was essential to expressing emotions, opinions, and sharing family history. When the family ended treatment, they had embraced many new aspects of sexual resilience that eliminated the behavioral issues that prompted treatment and gave the parents new skills to handle the younger children as they approached adolescence.

Case Example #2: Dealing with Sexual Abuse

The following is an example of a family that faced an unpredictable situation related to sexuality and handled it quite well. The Thomas family presented for therapy within a week of their son David (age 10) disclosing that he had been sexually assaulted by a neighborhood boy. The parents, Judy and Bob, were confused about how to proceed but knew that they needed help for their son, who was showing initial signs of post traumatic stress disorder including flashbacks, hypervigilance, increased anxiety, and avoidance. They were a middle class, Caucasian family with traditional gender roles:

Bob working outside of the home and Judy was a stay-at-home mom. They also had an older son Michael, age 14, who was aware of what had happened to David. There were clear signs of family resilience already present at the time of the assessment:

- They believed David immediately and took action to protect him
- They did not keep it a secret
- They rallied as a parental unit and a family to "make it better"
- They had a belief system that this was an obstacle they could overcome
- There was a supportive extended family on the maternal side
- They were emotionally expressive

They were acutely aware that this was an issue that was affecting all of them and instead of wanting help only for David, they requested family therapy. A genogram was completed during the assessment phase with a particular focus on issues of sexuality within the family history. It was discovered that Bob also had been molested as a child by a family friend on several occasions. Unfortunately for him, this was not handled well in his family of origin and there were still many unresolved issues. This added additional emotional intensity to the current situation because he was processing both the trauma of what happened to his son and also recalling his own abuse. The disclosure of this to his wife and his son resulted in more connectedness and compassion. In therapy, additional steps were taken to build resilience:

- Normalizing the feelings of all involved.
- Providing education within session and recommending books to read.
- Predicting and helping to prepare for future challenges.
- Creating positive interactions so that the abuse would not take over all of the family life.

Therapy progressed with David attending weekly individual therapy, and after four family therapy sessions during the crisis stage, the frequency decreased to every other week and then moved to "as needed." The dad also decided to seek treatment so he could finally deal with his own victimization.

Conclusion

There are many things that families can do to build resilience through both prevention and intervention. This book is part of a growing body of literature that supports such a goal. Key factors related to resilience can and should be applied specifically to sexuality. Sexuality is an ever present force in the lives of families—in terms of individual and relational development and the context in which they live. The more resilient families are, the better they will be able to negotiate the known and unknown challenges throughout their lives.

References

APA Task Force on Appropriate Therapeutic Responses to Sexual Orientation. (2009). *Report of the task force on appropriate therapeutic responses to sexual orientation.* Washington, DC: American Psychological Association.

Berliner, L., & Elliott, D. M. (2002). Sexual abuse of children. In J. E. B. Myers, L. Berliner, J. Briere, C. T. Hendrix, T. Reid, & C. Jenny (Eds.), *The APSAC handbook on child maltreatment* (2nd ed., pp. 55–78). Newbury Park, CA: Sage.

Borawski, E. A., Ievers-Landis, C. E., Lovegreen, L. D., & Trapl, E. S. (2003). Parental monitoring, negotiated unsupervised time, and parental trust: The role of perceived parenting practices in adolescent health risk behaviors. *Journal of Adolescent Health, 33*(2), 60–70.

Bowlby, J. (1969). *Attachment and loss: Vol. I. Attachment.* New York: Basic Books.

Briere, J., & Elliott, D. M. (2003). Prevalence and symptomatic sequelae of self-reported childhood physical and sexual abuse in a general population sample of men and women. *Child Abuse & Neglect: The International Journal, 27,* 1205–1222.

Calderone, M. S., & Johnson, E. (1981). *The family book about sexuality*. New York: Harper and Row.

Carter, B., & McGoldrick, M. (1999). *The expanded family lifestyle: Individual, family, and social perspectives* (3rd ed.). Boston: Allyn & Bacon.

Center for Disease Control and Prevention. (2008). *HIV/AIDS annual surveillance report, 20*. Atlanta, GA: Center for Disease Control and Prevention.

Center for Disease Control and Prevention. (2009). *Sexually transmitted disease surveillance*. Atlanta, GA: Center for Disease Control and Prevention.

Conte, J. R., & Schuerman, J. R. (1987). Factors associated with an increased impact of child sexual abuse. *Child Abuse & Neglect, 11*(2), 201–211.

Cooper, A., Delmonico, D. L., & Burg, R. (2000). Cybersex users, abusers, and compulsives: New findings and implications. *Sexual Addiction and Compulsivity: The Journal of Treatment and Prevention, 7*, 5–29.

Crowl, A. L., Ahn, S., & Baker, J. (2008). A meta-analysis of developmental outcomes for children of same-sex and heterosexual parents. *Journal of GLBT Family Studies, 4*(3), 385–407.

Eaton, D. K., Kann, L., Kinchen, S., Shanklin, S., Ross, J., Hawkins, J., et al. (2010). Center for Disease Control and Prevention. Youth risk behavior surveillance—United States, 2009. *MMWR Surveillance Summary, 59*, 1–142.

Ehrenberg, M., & Ehrenberg, O. (1988). *The intimate circle: The sexual dynamics of family life*. New York: Simon and Schuster.

Elders, M. J. (2010). Sex for health and pleasure throughout a lifetime. *The Journal of Sexual Medicine, 7*(5), 248–249.

Family Online Safety Institute. (FOSI). (2011). *Top internet safety tips for parents*. Retrieved from http://www.fosi.org/images/stories/resources/fosi-parent-tips.pdf.

Federal Bureau of Investigation. (2010). *A parent's guide to Internet safety*. Federal Bureau of Investigation, Cyber Division, Innocent Images National Initiative. Retrieved June 20, 2012 from www.fbi.gov/stats-services/publications/parent-guide.

Feeney, J. A., & Raphael, B. (1992). Adult attachments and sexuality: Implications for understanding risk behaviours for HIV infection. *The Australian and New Zealand Journal of Psychiatry, 26*, 399–407.

Fleming, J., Mullen, P., & Bammer, G. (1997). A study of potential risk factors for sexual abuse in childhood. *Child Abuse & Neglect, 21*(1), 49–58.

Friedrich, W. N. (2007). *Children with sexual behavior problems: Family-based attachment-focused therapy*. New York: W.W. Norton & Company.

Haft, W. L., & Slade, A. (1989). Affect attunement and maternal attachment: A pilot study. *Infant Mental Health Journal, 10*(3), 157–172.

Hampton, T. (2008). Abstinence-only programs under fire. *Journal of American Medical Association, 299*, 2103–2105.

Hazan, C., & Shaver, P. R. (1987). Romantic love conceptualized as an attachment process. *Journal of Personality and Social Psychology, 52*, 511–524.

Herbenick, D., Reece, M., Schick, V., Sanders, S. A., Dodge, B., & Fortenberry, J. D. (2010). Sexual behavior in the United States: Results from a national probability sample of men and women ages 14–94. *The Journal of Sexual Medicine, 7*(5), 255–265.

Hof, L., & Berman, E. (1986). The sexual genogram. *Journal of Marital and Family Therapy, 12*, 39–47.

Holling, C. S. (1973). Resilience and stability of ecological systems. *Annual Review of Ecology and Systematics, 4*, 1–23.

Hutchinson, M. K., & Cedarbaum, J. A. (2011). Talking to daddy's little girl about sex: Daughters' reports of sexual communication and support from fathers. *Journal of Family Issues, 32*(4), 550–572.

Johnson, B. K., & Kenkel, M. B. (1991). Stress, coping, and adjustment in female adolescent incest victims. *Child Abuse & Neglect, 15*, 293–305.

Kalichman, S. C., Sarwer, D. B., Johnson, J. R., Ali, S. A., Early, J., & Tuten, J. T. (1993). Sexually coercive behavior and love styles: A replication and extension. *Journal of Psychology and Human Sexuality, 6*(1), 93–106.

Kinsella, K., & Wan, H. (2009). *U.S. Census Bureau, international population reports, P95/09-1, an aging world: 2008*. Washington, DC: U.S. Government Printing Office.

Laumann, E. O., Gagnon, J. H., Michael, R. T., & Michael, S. (1994). *The social organization of sexuality: Sexual practices in the United States*. Chicago: The University of Chicago Press.

Maddock, J. W., & Larson, N. R. (1995). *Incestuous families: An ecological approach to understanding and treatment*. New York: W.W. Norton & Company.

Marrazzo, J. M., Koutsky, L. A., Eschenbach, D. A., Agnew, K., Stine, K., & Hillier, S. L. (2002). Characterization of vaginal flora and bacterial vaginosis in women who have sex with women. *Journal of Infectious Diseases, 185*, 1307–1313.

Marrazzo, J. M., Stine, K., & Wald, A. (2003). Prevalence and risk factors for infection with herpes simplex virus type-1 and -2 among lesbians. *Sexually Transmitted Diseases, 30*, 890–895.

Miller, K. S., Kotchick, B. A., Dorsey, S., Forehand, R., & Ham, A. Y. (1998). Family communication about sex: What are parents saying and are their adolescents listening? *Family Planning Perspectives, 30*(5), 218–225.

O'Donnell, L., O'Donnell, C. R., & Stueve, A. (2001). Early sexual initiation and subsequent sex-related risks among urban minority youth: The reach for health study. *Family Planning Perspectives, 33*(6), 268–275.

Paul, P. (2005). *Pornified: How pornography is transforming our lives, our relationships, and our families*. New York: Henry Holt and Company.

Rubenstein, R. (1990). Antecedents of prostitution: Flawed attachment and early sexual experiences. In K. Pottharst (Ed.), *Research explorations in adult attachment* (pp. 269–299). New York: Peter Lang.

Ryan, C., Huebner, D., Kiaz, R. M., & Sanchez, J. (2009). Family rejection as a predictor of negative health outcomes in white and Latino lesbian, gay, and bisexual young adults. *Pediatrics, 123*(1), 346–352.

Sandfort, T. G. M., Orr, M., Hirsch, J. S., & Santelli, J. (2008). Long-term health correlates of timing of sexual debut: Results from a national US study. *American Journal of Public Health, 98*(1), 155–161.

Sexuality Information and Education Council of the United States (SIECUS). (2002). *Innovative approaches to increase parent–child communication about sexuality; Their impact and examples from the field*. Washington, DC: Sexuality Information and Education Council of the United States.

Silenzio, V. M., Pena, J. B., Duberstein, P. R., Cerel, J., & Knox, K. L. (2007). Sexual orientation and risk factors for suicidal ideation and suicide attempts among adolescents and young adults. *American Journal of Public Health, 97*(11), 2017–2019.

Walker, B., Holling, C. S., Carpenter, S. R., & Kinzig, A. (2004). Resilience, adaptability and transformability in social-ecological systems. *Ecology and Society, 9*(2), 5.

Walsh, F. (2006). *Strengthening family resilience* (2nd ed.). New York: Guilford Press.

Watzlawick, P., Beavin, J., & Jackson, D. D. (1967). *Pragmatics of human communication*. New York: Norton.

White, M., & Epston, D. (1990). *Narrative means to therapeutic ends*. New York: W.W. Norton and Company.

Zimmer-Gembeck, M. J., & Helfand, M. (2008). Ten years of longitudinal research on U.S. adolescent sexual behavior: Developmental correlates of sexual intercourse, and the importance of age, gender and ethnic background. *Developmental Review, 28*(2), 153–224.

Zoldbrod, A. P. (1998). *Sex smart: How your childhood shaped your sexual life and what to do about it*. Oakland, CA: New Harbinger Publications.

The Community as Family: Resilience in Older Women Religious Sexually Abused in Early Life

Gary U. Behrman

Introduction/Background

The horrific events of September 11, 2001, traumatized all of our communities to various degrees. The enormous ramifications and pervasive consequences that these traumatic events are having on our way of life are evidenced in our airports, postal services, workplaces, schools, and homes. Our sense of safety from terrorist attacks and our previously unshakable belief that such devastation could not happen here have been severely eroded. The resulting anxieties, fears, and apprehensions about the future have permeated our daily lives and are potent ingredients for discord, disconnection, and disharmony among communities, families, and individuals. Much is at stake when individuals and communities are traumatized, and a "community as family" approach is offered here as one way to enhance resilience relative to the chronic conditions that trauma often entails.

Trauma following crisis events occurs in national, communal, familial, and personal domains. Whether trauma is associated with a cancer diagnosis, a household fire, sexual abuse, or terrorist acts, the responses to a particular crisis are nuanced and varied. In my research with aging Catholic nuns (heretofore referred to as women religious) who suffered early life sexual abuse, I addressed trauma from a "community as family" approach. In this chapter, I describe the application of symbolic interaction theory when interpreting the strengths that helped these participants mitigate the unwelcome effects that they associate with their sexual abuse.

The 12 participants in this study were recruited from an original study conducted by Saint Louis University School of Medicine to determine prevalence rates of sexual abuse among Catholic women religious (Chibnall, Wolf, & Duckro, 1998). Participants in the follow-up study were sexually abused before the age of 18 and at the time of the study were over the age of 65, with a mean age of 74. I explored the variety of later life responses that they associated with early life sexual abuse and their self-reported resilience as aging women religious living in community (Behrman, 2009).

G.U. Behrman (✉)
BSW Program, Lindenwood University, St. Charles, MO, USA
e-mail: GBehrman@lindenwood.edu

D.S. Becvar (ed.), *Handbook of Family Resilience*,
DOI 10.1007/978-1-4614-3917-2_30, © Springer Science+Business Media New York 2013

Significance of This Topic

Because 9/11 transformed our collective experience of trauma there is a pressing need to reevaluate and reassess resilience theories and clinical approaches to healing individuals and communities following trauma (Kaltman & Bonanno, 2003). Working with scarce resources and seeking common ground amidst polarized social, economic, and religious factions, mental health professionals, along with physicians, nurses, teachers, law enforcement officers, and firefighters, share a common goal of serving traumatized individuals, families, and communities and helping them to achieve and maintain resilience when traumatic events intrude into their lives.

It is both imperative and opportune to be asking, "What are the potential strengths that exist in our communities when facilitating resilience among individuals and families, and how do we recognize and activate these strengths when serving those whose lives are disrupted by trauma?" Such questions are addressed in this chapter by presenting the scaffolding for a "community as family" posttrauma intervention approach. This approach is based upon my professional training and experiences providing critical incident stress debriefings (CISD) (Everly & Mitchell, 1997), clinical work as a licensed social worker, and subsequent research. As the stories of these women religious indicate, sometimes human service providers overlook strategic community approaches to scaffolding resilience when serving persons with histories of trauma.

Literature Review

Research on resilience has proliferated since World War II (Figley, 1985; Saigh & Bremner, 1999; Walsh, Zauta, & Hall, 2010). Identifying individual and environmental strengths over a lifespan that sustain resilience is an immensely complex process (Rigsby, 1994). That is, "Like stress and coping research, resilience research looks for factors which maintain and protect health" (Bengel, Strittmatter, & Willmann, 1999, p. 58). A broad variability exists on individual and community levels in terms of what is needed to be resilient following trauma (Kaplan, 1999; Kemmis & McTaggert, 2000). Defining resilience is both an empirical and a political challenge, with the goal of discovering what lowers the risk of undesirable outcomes following trauma without unjustly or irresponsibly diagnosing persons as pathological who do not fit scientific, cultural, religious, or professional standards of what constitutes successful outcomes. According to Masten (1994), "resilience implies a qualitative evaluation of functioning based substantially on normative expectations for adaptations that vary according to age and environmental contexts" (p. 19). Indeed, paying attention to the community context in which the client/family is located is critical when assessing trauma and interpreting resilience.

Crisis events categorized as having the potential to create traumatic effects generally have been defined in a variety of ways, but many social scientists utilize the "trilogy definition" (Kanel, 1999): a highly unexpected event, perceived by the individual (or group) as physically, socially, psychologically, or spiritually life threatening, which overwhelms available coping methods and resources. During the past 50 years, the process of measuring, recognizing, and diagnosing postcrisis bio-psycho-social-spiritual effects as traumatic has shifted and expanded as indicated in the revisions of the Diagnostic and Statistical Manual of Mental Disorders (DSM) IV-R (American Psychiatric Association, 2000). Both the related literature and the DSM indicate a deeper understanding of the complexity and multiple nuances in measuring, assessing, and diagnosing maladaptation as traumatic following a crisis event. Research findings on trauma resulting from a crisis event in the areas of epidemiology, phenomenology, neurobiology, and treatment are summarized in McFarlane and Yehuda (2000).

Studies consistently report that trauma influences individual development in myriad ways depending upon particular environments and available resources (Alaggia & Michalski, 1999; Bell, 2003; Black

& Jeffreys, 1993; Graham, 1993; Greenburg & Keane, 1997; Levine, 2001; Pomeroy, Kiam, & Green, 2000). The levels of trauma associated with the effects of sexual abuse are related to the situation of the person who is abused. Environmental context, including available resources, family and professional supports, and the general health condition of the person, influences both manifested effects and treatment outcomes (Kaplan, 1999).

In this study I did not measure the effects of early life sexual abuse in later life nor was there an attempt to diagnose for trauma. Rather, what is recorded is what the participants identified as unwelcome consequences in old age that they associate with their early life sexual abuse. It is important to understand that early life sexual abuse generally meets criteria as a crisis event with the potential to create a continuum of effects varying in degree of severity. Whether the effects reported by this study's participants can be assessed as traumatic is a topic for future studies. The scarcity of research regarding the effects of childhood sexual abuse in old age calls for further investigation.

In summary, trauma is a complex and disabling process, which has the potential to create detrimental effects on self-awareness and relationships with others (McFarlane & Bookless, 2001). What is important is both understanding how and why people thrive following a crisis and what constitutes resilience for persons who report successful adaptation. Garmezy (1993), a founder of contemporary research on resilience, states that "resiliency is the extension of competencies in a variety of adaptive behaviors despite a background of high stresses" (Rolf, 1999, p. 7). According to Rutter (1990), resilience refers to "maintaining adaptive functioning in spite of serious risk hazards" (p. 209). For Masten (1994), resilience relates to "how effectiveness in the environment is achieved, sustained or recovered despite adversity" (p. 4). As a concept, resilience "is explicitly, if not tacitly implicit, in almost all explanatory models of behavior ranging from biological to social" (Glantz & Sloboda, 1999, p. 110).

Understanding resilience as the individual's ability to interact and relate effectively in his/her particular environment assumes that no a priori definition of resilience exists separate from the individual's environmental context and his/her relationships within that context. Indeed, the complexity and diversity of community cohorts and the plurality of social, cultural, and religious structures interact to create subjective interpretations of what qualifies as resilience. However, according to Ungar (2005), a "broad developmental perspective on resilience that can fully account for how (individuals) become resilient in multiple contexts and across cultures has yet to be fully articulated" (p. xvii). Some researchers recommend abandoning any definition for resilience, yet "some aspects of resilience are so ubiquitous as to appear universal" (Ungar, p. xix). These essential elements of resilience surface in global studies on health, such as the ability to maintain meaningful relationships and perform essential tasks that enable individuals to transfer from one developmental stage to another (Luthar, 2003).

How one adapts to trauma within his/her environmental context is at the heart of understanding resilience through the lens of the "community as family" approach. The theoretical framework I utilize views resilience more as a verb (relationship) than a noun (characteristics of the person or the environment). The focus is upon relationships between the individual and her environment that have been disrupted by the trauma rather than each examined in isolation from the other. Consistent with a strengths perspective, I understand resilience as "a continuing growth and articulation of capacities, knowledge, insight, and virtues derived through meeting the demands and challenges of one's world" (Saleebey, 1997, p. 9).

An immense amount of research on postchildhood sexual abuse, especially relative to children and adolescents, has been conducted (Glantz & Johnson, 1999; McFarlane, 2000; McFarlane & Yehuda, 2000; Walsh, 1998). The prevalence and characteristics of childhood sexual abuse are discussed by Finkelhor, Hotaling, Lewis, and Smith (1990). Polusny and Follette (1995) provide a review of the literature on the consequences of childhood sexual abuse, and Moeller, Bachmann, and Moeller (1993) report the effects of childhood sexual abuse for women in adulthood. A review of the long-term effects of child sexual abuse also can be found in Beitchman et al. (1992).

Much of this research focuses on the immediate negative developmental impact and/or the impact during adolescence, and early or middle adulthood. Research that is relevant to my study is provided by Moeller et al. (1993), who report a marked loss of hope and meaning among women following childhood sexual abuse that leads to various forms of depression and anxiety in later life. Other studies indicate that there may be a prevalence of destructive behaviors that are harmful to self and society, such as a propensity for enduring and engaging in abusive relationships, various types of substance abuse, and an inability to remain faithful to commitments (Greenwood, Tangolas, & Maruta, 1990). All of these symptoms could be the results of early life sexual abuse (Nash, Hulsey, Sexton, Harralson, & Lambert, 1993). In addition to the behavioral and social outcomes of childhood sexual abuse, the spiritual effects may be a diminished belief in a Divine Presence and a mistrust of people in authority in adulthood (Rossetti, 1995; Sipe, 1990).

The finding of various research studies is consistent in suggesting that childhood sexual abuse has the potential to create a wide range of responses during adulthood consisting of (1) emotional dysfunction characterized by depression, poor impulse control, and anxiety disorders; (2) somatic dysfunction such as eating disorders, sleep disturbance, chronic pain, and sexual maladjustment; and (3) social problems such as substance abuse, addictions, violent behaviors, and disrupted relationships (Caplan, 1961; Cole, Benore, & Pargament, 2004; Finkelhor, 1994; Hall, Sachs, Rayens, & Lutenbacher, 1993; Moeller et al., 1993; Parad, 1965; Parad & Miller, 1963; Polusny & Follette, 1995).

Theoretical Framework

Linking practice with theory is imperative for being effective when serving individuals and communities who are traumatized (Bengston, Burgess, & Parrott, 1997). Theory and practice are inexorably connected (Turner, 1996), and the theories we hold within our professional disciplines deeply influence how we interpret data, explain behavior, and design our interventions (Guba & Lincoln, 1986). Three perspectives comprise the foundation for this discussion of resilience following trauma, including the person in environment (PIE), a strengths perspective, and symbolic interaction theory.

The PIE perspective suggests that resilience is deeply embedded in the person's ability to interact effectively and efficiently with his/her environment. People will evidence different coping behaviors based upon environmental factors that both impede and enhance resilience (Compton & Galaway, 1989). Thus the focus of assessment and intervention is on the interaction of the person with his/her environment, not the individual in isolation from his/her environment, or vice versa. Accordingly, consideration is given to cultural, economic, and religious/spiritual characteristics in both the individual and the community that may enhance or diminish a person's resilience

Paying attention to strengths in the environment shifts understandings and interpretations of resilience beyond the individual to include the community as a part of the healing process (Becker, 1997). Sometimes community strengths are concealed and submerged due to harsh economic disparities that diminish transparent strengths. Some socioeconomic structures create environments that make it extremely demanding for individuals and families to be resilient following trauma (Marshall, 1995). Further, the use of binary diagnostic labels that divide people and communities into either resilient or nonresilient categories may pathologize individuals and communities, both diminishing and dismissing their strengths following trauma. This may occur when perceived strengths are solely measured and narrowly defined within normative categories based upon community expectations (Becker). Indeed, the process of identifying strengths is influenced by who decides what constitutes healthy outcomes and why some behaviors are considered successful adaptation (Garmezy, 1993). These biases are not wrong or necessarily detrimental unless they overlook ethnic, cultural, religious, socioeconomic, and age factors by narrowly labeling nonnormative behaviors as psychopathology (Kaplan, 1999). Nonnormative behaviors are not necessarily pathological, and potentially they could be a sign of resilience.

Third, connecting resilience with how a person interacts with his/her community is consistent with a core principle of symbolic interaction theory that creating and maintaining meaning within a particular environment is central to all human relationships (Blumer, 1969; Stryker, 1980). Accordingly, persons and their environments cannot be understood independent of one another. For example, how the participants in my study interpret who they are as Catholic women religious who were sexually abused does "not arise simply from intra-psychic or physiological processes. Rather, they develop through the process of interaction and are shaped, in part, by the views and attitudes that others hold about us" (Robbins, Chatterjee, & Canda, 1998, p. 269). The cultural expectations regarding how they self-identify and what resilience should look like play a significant role in their coping responses following trauma.

It is essential when assessing and designing interventions to facilitate resilience that the environment's impact on the individual, as well as the reverse, is considered. According to symbolic interaction theory, people are actively engaged with their environment when interpreting trauma and making choices to resolve problems that they associate with this crisis (Longress, 2000). They are interpreting the trauma through the lens of their community's beliefs about what it means to be resilient and what roles people must assume in order to be considered resilient. A community that overtly values work as a primary role will claim that a person is being resilient when he/she returns to work.

The concept of role is central to symbolic interaction theory (Longress, 2000). According to Robbins et al. (1998, p. 269), "A role is a social category or position with a set of expected behavior patterns. Roles do not exist in isolation and are defined by their relationship to one another." Persons who experience trauma often undergo tremendous changes in their roles that shape how they interpret themselves in relationship to others. In order to be resilient, individuals re-negotiate and re-interpret what a crisis event means within their communities when faced with the task of maintaining or creating new roles following the trauma (Becker, 1997). When utilizing symbolic interaction theory, attention is given to the subjective interpretation of an event within particular environments. Noticing what the community and the individual believe and value about resilience are paramount to designing assessments and shaping interventions (Stryker & Stratham, 1985).

A crisis event such as sexual abuse has the ability to disrupt meaningful relationships, and subsequently there can be fragmentation of self and alienation from the person's roles in the community (Becker, 1997). In order to be resilient, individuals must re-negotiate and re-interpret what this event means within the order established by community norms. Each is faced with the task of maintaining or creating new roles that will enhance the possibilities for experiencing life in a holistic and meaningful way. Key to mastering this challenge is the capacity to successfully create new relationships with self (identity) and with others (roles) in order to craft meaning and significance within religious, cultural, and social environments (Behrman & Reid, 2002). When this is not possible, often people will remove themselves from those situations and institutions that are obstacles in maintaining or creating meaningful relationships with self and others. In environments where leaving is perceived as being not an option, people will sometimes succumb to various types of disruptive and in some cases, destructive relationships with self and others (Becker, 1997).

Research Findings

An analysis of my study data revealed reports by the participants that they are living in a unique cultural and religious environment, and that the trauma of sexual abuse had an impact upon their identities as well as their relationships with their community. What was expected of them in order to claim resilience was clearly defined by the community (Behrman, 2009). The cultural, social, and religious coping behaviors reported by these women religious following early life sexual abuse were organized around a set of beliefs and expectations that were established by the community, which each person identified. Together with her community, each Sister engaged in psycho-social, familial, and spiritual rituals, creating meaning through shared behaviors that made sense within her religious community. Whether it was through prayer, novenas, spiritual direction, or yoga, these women and their communities named the trauma, interpreted the impact, and designed coping behaviors that each believed would enhance resilience based upon her unique culture. Problems surfaced when interpretations and expectations conflicted.

Some of the other members of the various religious communities questioned participants' strategies for being resilient when they perceived these strategies to be nonnormative and not what was expected of a member of the particular religious community given their unique interactions with each other (Behrman, 2009). Such perceptions are shaped by what is meaningful or what "makes sense" in a given context: "Meaning and social interaction are interdependent; meaning is shaped in and by interaction, and meaning shapes the course of the interaction" (Stryker & Stratham, 1985, p. 321). Thus, one of the first tasks following trauma is to examine and redefine social roles and what is expected of the individual whose role is prescribed by her community.

Social roles are not the only relationships that are negotiated following trauma, according to symbolic interaction theory, as "individuals also negotiate their own identities with the situation, that is, how they present themselves. Two working agreements must be reached, one with the self and one with the others in the situation" (Longres, 2000, p. 398). Many of the Sisters reported an identity crisis in adulthood when their religious faith and community no longer could provide the language needed to make sense of their childhood sexual trauma as religious women (Behrman, 2009).

Further, "an important additional implication is that a totally determinant explanatory model of social interaction is not possible…neither interaction nor meaning can be taken as unilateral cause and effect…reciprocal rather than unidirectional causal models are essential" (Stryker & Stratham, 1985, p. 322). This reciprocal relationship is at the heart of symbolic interaction theory, which guides and informs this "community as family" approach. The roles that a person assumes following trauma and the attempts to create a new personal identity are interacting and informing each other as the individual attempts to create new ways of relating and being with others.

Many of the Sisters spoke about their struggle in their adult lives to find meaning in their histories of sexual abuse (Behrman, 2009). Trauma is a crisis of meaning (Becker, 1997). Our relationships, and the environments in which we function, contain constructed meanings, with both assigned social roles and agreed upon mutual responsibilities. When an unexpected, life-threatening event occurs, overwhelming coping strategies and resources, these roles and constructed meanings shift, and often identities are permanently disrupted. Experiences such as becoming a widow, being unemployed, or being diagnosed with cancer can leave people vulnerable, overwhelmed, frightened, mistrustful, resentful, and fragmented. A significant majority of participants reported that such reactions surfaced for them in adulthood (Behrman, 2009).

In the case of these women religious, their identities as victims of early life sexual abuse and their social roles as educated, professional women had to be renegotiated as both their own and their community's interpretations of childhood sexual abuse changed significantly over time. New ways of being contemporary women religious coincided with the dramatic shifts associated with the reforms of the Catholic Church that took place during the 1960s and 1970s (O'Sullivan, 2002). Gradually, and in some situations dramatically, immense changes were introduced that dynamically altered the environments of community religious life and subsequently their social interactions and identities. The outward gestures of removing medieval garb and replacing it with contemporary clothing is just one of many symbols of the inward reinterpretation of what it means to be a Catholic woman religious in the twenty-first century. What is more, there now existed a safe platform from which to speak about their sexual abuse experiences, and there were new opportunities to integrate and heal some of the lingering effects that they identified as being associated with their early life trauma (Behrman, 2009). When exploring resilience following trauma, we are investigating what both the person and her community have determined to be expected developmental, orderly levels of functioning, which are being inhibited and thwarted by the trauma. As reported by the participants, these community and individual expectations radically shifted for them following the changes of Vatican II, and this had an immense positive impact on their ability to be resilient.

Indeed, the human ability to create symbols that convey meaning is another key feature of symbolic interaction theory (Blumer, 1969). The symbols that are utilized by persons are chosen within environmental contexts that make sense to a particular community. Accordingly, paying attention to the metaphors participants used when describing trauma and resilience informed my methodology and is recommended in the assessment process in clinical contexts as well. What metaphors describe the effects that the trauma is having upon the person and her relationships with her community, and which metaphors depict the ideal outcome that is being sought? Metaphors are pervasive in communicating what we believe to be important and vital in maintaining our community identity and subsequent roles in that community. They are the fundamental structures when trying to make sense of our trauma, embody cultural expectations, and keep life unified and understandable (Lakoff & Johnson, 1980). Studies bear out the role of metaphor in naming trauma and how language is used in attempts to create meaning out of chaos and disorder (Becker, 1997).

People symbolically represent their experiences of trauma by selecting metaphors familiar to them. Through metaphor, people reinterpret the crisis event in order to recreate meaningful relationships and to socially construct new identities in the community that will usher in a sense of order following trauma's devastating chaos (Becker, 1997). To the degree that they are able to realign their interpretation of what is expected of them in their community they will be identified as resilient and roles will be restored and/or new ones created. The use of narrative and metaphor assist in grasping the complexity of identifying and understanding resilience. How people represent their experiences of trauma through metaphor is a critical component of the "community as family" approach in understanding what is needed to be resilient (Behrman, 2009).

Current Issues

America's population is aging at a rapid pace. In 2008, Americans over the age of 65 numbered 38.9 million, an increase of 4.5 million or 13.0% since 1998; one in every eight, or 12.8% of the population, is an older American (Administration on Aging, 2010). Because of this expanding aging population it is imperative for mental health professionals to re-examine and challenge prevalent assumptions about what social roles and identities are most important to people during the later years of life. It is opportune to be identifying resources and approaches that are effective in sustaining and increasing resilience for aging populations (Walker & Salt, 2006).

The participants' stories in my research offer a critical window into the lives of early twentieth-century women, not because of their unique religious status, but because their early life sexual abuse experiences are perhaps representative of other women of that time (1930s–1950s). My approach can deepen and broaden our understanding of aging populations with histories of sexual abuse. Although these women religious served in many public and professional capacities, their personal stories of sexual trauma, like those of other women of their era, demanded silence. Ecclesial as well as socio-political-economic-familial structures defined the limitations of women's voices in telling their stories, and patriarchal structures limited how and whether women could address, interpret, and speak about their sexual abuse (O'Sullivan, 2002).

These women's stories of self-reported resilience are potential references for others who struggle within their environments to recreate social roles and identities, which connect their lives with others in meaningful ways. As they interpret both their trauma and their resilience in their own language, the capacity to experience wholeness and meaningful relationships in life can be enhanced.

Summary of Participants' Self-Reported Resilience

All of the participants reported personal strengths in later life in dealing with unwelcome effects of sexual abuse. For most, they gained personal strength by breaking the silence that surrounded their abuse (Brown & Gilligan, 1991). Most participants would concur with what the following participant believed is central to resilience:

> But through the years I've gotten a voice. I mean, I don't really have anything to be ashamed of. When I was going through my traumatic experience of depression and anxiety, the anxiety I haven't quite conquered but I had depression, is pretty capped. My therapist said to me, "You have a good mind." It's probably the most important thing she has ever said to me.

For participants, claiming their personal authority and identifying strengths as they created new roles within their communities, were critical when addressing their trauma. By acknowledging that she has a "good mind" this Sister was assuming responsibility for interpreting what sexual abuse means to her today and what she believes are the lingering effects, rather than having the community craft this claim for her. This metaphor, "I've gotten a voice" resonated with most participants when describing how they confronted institutional structures, whether familial, religious, or cultural, according to which they were expected to remain silent:

> You know, the effects of alcoholism and child abuse on keeping secrets and not trusting and being isolated are probably the hardest things. And once you can get into a 12 step program or once you can break the silence and it takes enormous, enormous strength … I'm beyond some of that now, you know. Now, I say again, that I don't go from total keeping secrets to total blabbermouth, but that there's a middle road and I've chosen that. And I get nothing but affirmation for this.

Finding their voices means discerning what new roles they must create in their communities in order to tell their stories. This breaking the silence is the first step to challenging institutional structures that silence them and prevent them from speaking in their own voice, and trusting that they will be heard with respect and safety. In one participant's words, this step is "mind blowing":

> It's like, God, was my whole life a waste? But it's just all a part of the process in my healing, so I know I have come through and survived and it's been very, very hard. But the hardest part for me was, you know, being isolated and not knowing I could trust people with this story…I had spoken to about forty of my friends in our congregation, all of whom, you know, have just loved me, you know, which blows my mind. 'You love me anyway?' And everyone has said the same thing, 'Thank you for trusting me. I'm sorry this happened to you.'

Trusting people in authority who have power over them was an issue that many of the participants carried with them into adulthood. By breaking the silence and receiving positive affirmation and protection against further abuse, participants found agreement with their community in interpreting what sexual abuse means and how to approach this together:

> It was very hard for me to break this secret the first time I told it was a small gathering (Sisters she lived with) where none of us were professional counselors in that sense. But I decided it's time for me to break the silence. And so I told them and I was weeping. And I got all kinds of sympathy, compassion, affirmation and there were some other parallel disclosures from people saying, 'well I too…' So I know that disclosure invites more disclosure. And so each time I share it, which isn't easy, cause I do it only with trusted people, because I'm protecting myself psychologically in terms of what I tell, who I tell and when I tell.

In general, all participants in this study who reported their histories of sexual abuse to religious leaders, spiritual directors, and fellow Sisters in their communities experienced overwhelming support and affirmation. However, all were reticent to disclose their sexual abuse nondiscriminately to community members. Each Sister defined her own boundaries of who should know and who needs to know. This circle of confidents varied considerably among the Sisters, but all echoed the value of telling their stories in their own voices.

It appears from the data that members of religious communities will respond to a community member who was sexually abused in a variety of supportive ways. As indicated in the data, a majority of the participants have chosen not to disclose their histories of abuse to members at large, but have been selective in confiding in religious superiors, spiritual directors, and friends within their communities.

All of the participants presented with remarkable strengths in later life, demonstrating a personal authority that is able to negotiate social roles to varying degrees of competency and self-assuredness. A strengths perspective suggests that, with appropriate environmental resources, individuals can create helpful change for themselves and others (Henderson, 2007; Saleebey, 1997). All participants reported positive change in their current lives that they attribute to their religious communities functioning as families that enhanced their personal strengths:

> When it was time, God put the right people there to ask the question and to say 'share the secret.' You know, the more courageous I get, the more breaking silence with trusted people like this encounter, (our interview). I've been able to mentor other women. It's very helpful.

When analyzing the data I intentionally listened for changes in the Sisters' relationships with others and what they identified as resilience according to their interpretations. I was also curious about how effective professional therapists were for these women religious. Most spoke of how long it took to find an effective therapist:

> I have told several people…when you get into therapy, don't go to a generalist. You go to someone without specialized training, they don't get it. They miss it and I've suffered through that, when I think of it, money and time spent, and I, you know, I was dancing as fast as I could, so the spiritual piece comes last, they don't all have the training, and the woman that I went to in the end was very, very good. She had training in bio-spirituality that you can use in spiritual direction.

Through the metaphor, *I was dancing as fast as I could*, this Sister is interpreting her experience of ineffective therapy that did not give her a voice in telling her story and she wasn't getting better and going nowhere:

> Twenty, twenty five years ago generalists didn't have a clue (about sexual abuse recovery), and so I stopped being angry with them, but I went through a time when I was very angry, you know that people were not helping me the way I needed to be helped, and even my own community said we don't know what you need but go get it. I mean who do you go to? Who'll believe you? But, but this is a very, very hard nut to crack, you know.

The metaphor, "hard nut to crack," describes her trauma, hidden beneath a hard surface of years of repression and secrecy.

What was significant is that most participants reported how integral professional help was for achieving resilience once they found a knowledgeable therapist. Adding a trained spiritual director to their bio-psycho-social medical treatment plan shifted their self-understanding:

> So you can get healed psychologically, you know sexually and psychologically, but spiritual healing is the last piece. So what I've learned is that you don't talk about spirituality to somebody who is on the front end coming in to it, first time breaking silence and telling the stories. You bring them through the process, like in spiritual direction, and then, finally you're looking at spiritual healing. Most people don't go through spiritual direction for sexual abuse, until they've healed the psychological thing because it's the last piece to be taken care of.

This aspect of spiritual resilience following sexual abuse was the most significant factor for these participants. Without spiritual resilience they believed that their lives as women religious were not whole and integrated. Because of their religious environment, spiritual direction is an expected and normative relationship for these participants. All reported that their spiritual director served as a noteworthy platform in learning how to find their voice and be resilient.

When therapists missed combining psychological services with spiritual insights, a significant lapse was reported by all of the participants:

> I was doing much spiritual direction towards the end, but also what helped me make the jump from psychological to spiritual was I had that wonderful theological re-framing from that protestant woman therapist on the west coast. She was able to say, in non-clinical terms, a framework that I was comfortable with theologically, what was going on, and she's brilliant with this.

This points to the value of surfacing what the client values as most integral for resilience based upon her unique cultural meanings. For a Hindu male client who lost his prestigious job, a Jewish woman who has been raped, an agnostic widower, each client is seeking to be connected to what is most meaningful in his/her life and what roles and relationships need to be restored and/or recreated following the trauma. Framed in this way, spirituality is an essential strength in scaffolding resilience in the community as family approach.

It is crucial for the therapist to nurture a capacity for self-awareness of his/her own biases that each brings to the professional relationship. We may not believe that certain religious rituals, or options such as complementary and alternative medicine (CAM) (Behrman & Tebb, 2009), are helpful, but we need to be open to what the client names as meaningful and helpful in being resilient.

Clinical Implications

The application of PIE, strengths-based, and symbolic interaction perspectives to the "community as family" approach to the systematic study of resilience following trauma is based upon the following seven assumptions about human identity and interactions:

> First, human beings act toward things on the basis of the meanings that the things have for them. Second, meaning arises in the process of interaction between people. Third, meanings are handled in and modified through an interpretative process used by the person in dealing with things he/she encounters. Fourth, individuals are not born with a sense of self but develop self concepts through social interaction. Fifth, self concepts provide an important motive for behavior. Sixth, individuals and groups are influenced by larger cultural and societal processes. Seventh, it is through social interaction that individuals work out the details of social structure (LaRossa & Reitzes, 1993, pp. 143–144).

These assumptions influenced data gathering and analysis in this study of women religious and the subsequent development of the "community as family" approach to clinical assessment and intervention. We now look at practical ways in which resilience is assessed and scaffolded, utilizing the theoretical perspectives presented as well as various metaphors to illuminate the stories of trauma and resiliency in the voices of the study participants.

The Community as Family Approach

1. Welcoming/building trust
Without trust, the client/family members will not feel safe to speak with their own voices nor will they find the courage to interpret the trauma and attempt to remain resilient in ways that are consistent with what they believe to be meaningful, important, and essential. Rituals and a comfortable therapeutic setting add to the trust that the client will feel towards the practitioner. I recommend asking, "Do you have any questions or concerns that need to be addressed before we engage in this helping relationship?"
2. Identifying sources of authority
Who are the influential voices in the clients' lives that have the authority to interpret their story of trauma and to whom they tend to listen either consciously or unconsciously? Who provides credence

and credibility to their interpretations of their crisis experiences (family members, peers, professionals, government, schools, and/or religion)? It is important to understand the power these institutions have in defining clients' identity following trauma, and how much influence they currently exert on shaping clients' roles in their environments. By examining the ways in which these sources of authority may be discrediting their experiences and/or interpretations of their experiences. The following are questions that might be asked in this regard: Who is the person(s) you turn to when you want to know what to do in a difficult situation? Who do you trust when you have questions about what is most important in life? Who are the people that you can rely upon to guide and instruct you? What religious commandments/leaders are reliable sources of knowledge for you?

3. Recognizing multiple sources of authority

Often there are conflicting sources of authority competing for prominence in clients' reinterpretation of a new or renewed identity following trauma. Where do these sources of authority resonate and are in harmony, where do conflicts exist, and how much bio-psycho-social-spiritual discomfort is this creating? It is important to be aware of issues at each of these levels:

Bio: Stomach problems and headaches, changes in appetite, sleep patterns, sexual drive, etc.

Psycho: Levels of anxiety, depression, agitation, guilt, shame and resentments;

Social: Alienation from others, isolating from primary support persons, disengagement and/or enmeshment.

Spiritual: What is most meaningful in their lives? What needs to be restored first? How has belief (lack of) in God changed, and does he/she pray? Why or why not? Does the person attend religious services, cultural events, why or why or not?

4. Listening for social roles

Here I consciously listen for the language clients use when describing the relationships that are meaningful to them, and I especially pay attention to the roles that have changed dramatically because of the trauma: "The underlying premise of symbolic interactionism is that the subjective aspects of experience must be examined because the meanings people assign to things ultimately organize their behavior" (Stryker & Stratham, 1985, p. 320). All persons engaged in social interaction are actors, creating meaning together through shared symbols and metaphors that make sense within their context and influence how they behave in their assigned roles. I may ask, "What roles changed because of your trauma immediately following the trauma, later on, and today?" Additional questions may include the following: "I would like to ask you about your relationships with others who you claim to be a part of your community." "Who are the most important people in your life and why?" "What relationships remain stable today?" "What relationships have dramatically changed and/or were disrupted?" "What comforts and strengthens you in managing the trauma?" "What role (if any) does God play in your ability to be resilient?"

I suggest listening closely to how each person makes sense of this event. Notice the nuances that are unique to this person, while considering the environmental context he/she is interacting with and the sources of authority who may be interpreting his/her story for him/her. I then proceed to a second set of questions: "What helps you today to integrate your trauma into your life and make sense of what happened to you?" "I realize that trauma has many effects, but I am interested in finding out from you what you have noticed are the effects in your relationships with others." Some people remember this vividly and are reminded of it often, while others do not think about this much, so I say, "Please answer the questions the best that you can." "How does this trauma influence your life today?" "How has this trauma influenced your relationships with God?" "What effects of the trauma are most troubling today?" "What effects of the trauma have surprised you or caught you off guard?"

Applying symbolic interaction theory to understanding the roles that were disrupted, changed, and/or permanently lost as a result of the trauma, I ask: "What has changed?" "Which roles provided the most meaning prior to the trauma, which ones were burdensome and disconnecting?" Making a list of these roles can assist in visually grasping how much the trauma has disrupted the person's life. Teaching the person how to grieve these losses and working through the anger, sadness, and remorse can be helpful. In addition, which roles will be missed, which ones need to be released according to the client? What new roles might enhance growth and healing in line with the client's priorities and values?

5. Surfacing identity issues

I want to understand what it means to be a woman religious, an electrician, a parent, a marathon runner, etc., based on each person's lived experiences. Each client is given the opportunity to explore how he/she self-identifies. For example, using this particular study I could begin by asking clients about their lives today as women religious: "What is it like for you to be a Catholic religious Sister today?" "What do you appreciate most about being a religious Sister?" "What is most meaningful in your life today?"

Along with such questions I also invite the client to describe her identity through metaphor. For example, "If you could select a tree that captures the essence of your religious life today, what tree would that be and why?" My intent is help the person name how the trauma has disrupted her sense of identity within her community. Many of the primary losses following trauma are losses of identity: Who am I now that I am widowed, orphaned, unemployed, or disfigured following a particular trauma?

Involved here is a grieving process that can be discussed with the client to assist him/her in letting go of the past in order to create a better future (Carnes, 1993). Identifying and listening for the metaphors used to describe losses as the result of a trauma paints a picture for each person to examine and explore. Within a given cultural context the roles are interpreted and the meanings behind these metaphors and phrases are expanded. Exploring metaphors that appear on the surface can lead to a depth of understanding with which the clinician and client may work.

6. Naming strengths

The following questions explore the internal and external strengths that have been most helpful according to the client: "I want you to focus upon how your trauma affects you today in any way. I realize that this is difficult but I am here with you and we will not go beyond your capacity to remember how this trauma has changed you and your relationships. Who or what helps you the most today when you remember the trauma? What environments, circumstances, resources or rituals have been most helpful in managing the effects of your trauma? Can you identify in particular what helps you with some of the effects you named earlier?"

7. Managing triggers

The following questions open the door for clients to tell their story in their own voice, owning what has been most difficult, consistently pointing out where they have been resilient when recovery was painful and confusing: "How often do you remember the trauma?" "Where does this memory show up the most frequently?" "What situations or people seem to trigger memories of the trauma?" "What has been most hurtful for you?" "What troubles you the most about this event?" "What seems unfinished and remains painful and disruptive?" "What strategies get you through this?" "What gives you hope?" "Could you describe this time in your life as if you were describing the weather. What season, what type of day/night would you be in currently?"

It is important to respect what is most meaningful to the person. What does the person believe is most important for him/her to focus upon and why? Be open to details that seem insignificant initially but may be the source of his/her triggers with the trauma. Once the triggers are identified then techniques for managing them should be provided.

8. Identifying community resources

It is critical to identify community influences that are potent sources of strength for clients as they journey through the trauma. Who and what can they rely upon in an emergency as well as consistently during the everydayness of each step they take? These resources need to be meaningful, accessible, and available. Focus on hobbies, relaxation techniques, volunteer opportunities, exercise avenues, spiritual rituals, social networking, and more. Together, prioritize what needs to be put in place immediately and what may be a long-term goal. Sometimes purchasing tennis shoes and encouraging walking comes before recommending gym membership. Simply walking in a soothing environment each day may be a beginning in getting through difficult days and months.

9. Logging changes

It is critical to point out growth in the client that is accessible and tangible. This may include losing/gaining weight, how often he/she is exercising, hours sleeping, number of nightmares, telephone calls for support, books read, volunteer work, etc. Once again, it is essential that the client recognizes growth and change from a strengths perspective. In the midst of the posttrauma event, often it feels like no progress is being made for the emotions can cloud changes (Carnes, 1993).

Keeping a log with the client can diminish the tendency to slip into despair and the feeling that this will never get better. Thus, it is important to determine base line behavior prior to the trauma and at the time the person initiates professional services. This is an ongoing assessment that requires attentiveness to fluctuations and variations: "What used to work in managing stress?" "What is no longer working?" "What would you like to try?" "What have you tried that did not work?" The client must co-create these activities and explore new options.

10. Closing the professional relationship

It is important to remember that a strengths-based assessment focuses on assisting the client in creating new meaning, renewed relationships, and revitalized roles. When concluding, be aware of assumptions about what constitutes resilience and inquire into the client's own assessment of progress or lack of it. What will be used to measure change and growth and who will determine which instrument to be used? What criterion is used to determine that the professional work is complete (for now) and what follow up plan is in place? Keep in mind that alcohol, drug, and lethality assessment takes place throughout this process.

Case Study

The following case study illustrates the "community as family" approach. Data are derived from the study in which I sought to identify strengths in later life among the women religious and how their experiences of sexual abuse affected their lives in their own words, always listening for metaphors that would enlarge my understanding of their experiences. It is important to embrace what these participants identify as furnishing their lives with resilience in later life and what intensely disrupted and threatened their lives when the trauma occurred. I listened for strengths amidst their pain and confusion and how the effects of sexual abuse remain with them today.

Metaphor

The following is an example of the use of metaphor taken verbatim from the interview data as one participant describes her experience of sexual trauma:

> I must have been alone because he kissed me, and I thought the weather, it was like a lightning bolt. I thought what in the hell; I couldn't imagine what was happening. I had nobody to tell, nobody to run to I was so young. I was just amazed; you know just, I don't know how to describe it.

She continues to describe, through metaphor, how traumatized she was by the sexual abuse, enabling me to empathize with her and to deeply understand what her experience means to her. She continues,

I don't know if it is the abuse, but the fact that I was like afraid of adults. I have an expression, 'I always felt half-baked.' Like I was never a real mature adult. I do not know. The fact that I was angry, always fussing at something. I am never really at peace. I myself cannot see how the connection is there, but there must have been something. I took the courses, I got the degree but, I just never felt really, really comfortable…and then the tree, my early life is the thorns, and right now during the fall across the street was the most beautiful maple tree. It was so red and so beautiful, and there was one on this property, too. I just picked this off as a reminder that I think in my later life, not that I am beautiful, but that I am at peace (*she shows me the red maple leaf*). Because all during my life I was filled with anger. I talked to different priests and psychologists and so forth. There was always like a civil war within me fighting within myself, but not just the civil war, the Vietnam War because in Vietnam they could not tell the enemy, he looked the same, the same as the good guys. So I did not know what the heck I was fighting.

By linking together key phrases and stories with each metaphor, categories begin to emerge and individual metaphors take on new meaning when clustered. The above participant uses powerful metaphors to describe the effects of her sexual abuse, a *civil war* in which she did not know who the enemy was, thus she could not trust nor identify with adults. Her metaphor, of being *half baked*, describes a person who is becoming what she is intended to be, but she is not there yet. She continues by further interpreting her metaphor of the *Vietnam War*:

It is the fact that now in my older season that I am more at peace like the beauty of the red maple. I am not fighting the Civil War. I am not fighting the Vietnam War any longer.

Process

It is recommended that all questions, both research and clinical, be open ended, with no questions posing "yes or no" responses. This enables the participant to take the question wherever he/she values the most. Yet, the questions do lead the participant in a direction that seeks to meet the purpose of a study or the goals of therapy.

Other participants reported similar gratitude for religious community resources:

I had to come to believe through a lot of therapy and a lot of good people, I couldn't tell you how many people reached out to me to help me and would go on walks with me and take me someplace to get ice cream or go to dinner or ride with me. So probably all of that has some bearing on the abuse that I had as a child. It certainly gave me a sense of guilt and shame until someone did tell me, 'You know, you were a child and you didn't have the power to resist that.'

What became apparent was how helpful the new relationships within their communities were:

Definitely. I said, if I don't have friends I will die. I will die of loneliness, you know not physically die but you just die, you know. I've got to do something about this (sexual abuse), so then I started connecting with people. I've been blessed by good friends and they help a lot. It's the tangibles and so God puts people in our lives to help us get through. So, I am really grateful that I came through it.

Many reported that the leaders in their religious communities were helpful:

I've had very good general superiors, very good ones, and each of them has been so very, very generous to me in my life. There was never a time in my life that they've said, 'now, I think you've had enough therapy. But they've never done that. They were just very giving women, you know, so I'm very, very, I'm a very grateful person for that.

Their religious communities provided them with the healthcare and support they needed to address their sexual abuse in a confidential and professional setting:

The gift is the community. I got the best of help. I got great doctors. I am grateful for the many religious experiences; there are many benefits of which I am grateful. It's like a marriage I guess. You have to learn to live together, that's it. I don't know how else to put it. Then you have to talk, you have to keep on talking. The gift is the community.

Other participants reported similar strengths in their community life:

The first word that comes into my mind is the security, I guess. Part of the community charism or spirituality is based on this sense of family and you know being there for each other, that sense of community. That's what drew me to the congregation in the first place when I was a little girl in, like the 3rd grade.

Just the whole culture of being in a Catholic religious community and, you know, being able to practice the religion and have that common shared understanding of looking at the world. Yes, and I got all kinds of sympathy, compassion, affirmation.

The most meaningful thing to me is that I have a religious community whom I call on for support, with whom I belong and with whom I interact. Of course, my very best friends are Sisters. Most of them have known me almost all of my life or at least almost all of my religious life. And our congregation is a very loving and caring group.

I love being here. I love the Sisters. I love the life. I love everything about it. I am in a good space right now, a really good space. I like being identified with them.

The greatest enjoyment I have is the grassroots and the community.

They're wonderful ladies (religious sisters) and I like being with them.

It's the relationships that are very pleasurable and meaningful to me but certainly not the institution.

These women religious self-reported that it is "community as family" that has facilitated resilience and given them the hope for meaningful relationships in later life.

Research Implications

The findings of my study both confirm and expand the data generated in the Chibnall et al. (1998) study and will be valuable for women religious communities that are committed to providing healthy environments for their members. Whether any of the findings of my study can be applied to other aging populations would require significant further investigation. However, a critical component of this study is that it raises awareness of the need to revisit theoretical understandings and clinical assumptions about the trauma of sexual abuse among aging populations who present with difficulties coping in later life. What does it mean to be resilient in later life for those with childhood histories of sexual trauma? Telling these stories of tragedy and suffering, hope and resilience has the potential to connect research participants with the members of other aging populations who suffer from sexual abuse and/or perhaps other forms of trauma.

Many of the spiritual resources that the Sisters reported as assisting them with resilience are supported in popular literature (Breaszeale, 2009). Data from empirical research indicates that religion and spirituality play an important protective factor in well-being and health in aging populations (Miller & Thoresen, 2003). The scientific evidence for incorporating spirituality in our clinical approach to scaffolding resilience is reviewed and discussed in over 800 studies presented in the Koenig compilation (Koenig, 2000). My findings support the value of nurturing spiritual resources and religious identity in later life.

Conclusion

My intention was to identify both shared meanings and unique interpretations of what trauma and resilience meant to the study participants, and what holds most meaning for them as they live today as women religious. However, one does not have to be a woman religious who was sexually abused in early life to find common meaning with their experiences of loss and vulnerability when listening to their words. These participants' interpretations can create meaningful connections and encourage women from diverse cultures to initiate the process of interpreting their own stories in their own voices.

To be resilient often involves a quest for transformation amidst harsh environments that threaten our identities and relationships. Each of us has experienced this to varying degrees and at different points in our lives. We strive to create a language for these experiences through song, poetry, and prayer. We seek understanding and enlightenment in order not to be destroyed by the trauma but rather to be transformed because of it. One Sister sums up what it means to her to be resilient:

> Hope is what most survivors cling to. It's not faith because sometimes faith has gone out the window, but it's the virtue of hope. There's something resilient in the hope that there's something good going to happen. But you can't see it yet…you don't know it. And when somebody is in tears in front of you because they can't see it, but down here, what keeps them coming back is that hope.

I began my research in order to unravel what it means for elderly women religious to have been sexually abused at a young age, how sexual abuse manifests in their lives today, and to identify the strategies and resources they utilize to remain resilient. During these interviews I listened to their struggles to address the trauma of sexual abuse and to painfully negotiate what is required to be resilient. What I heard is that claiming one's own authority in this process is both painful and transforming. Each story portrays a woman who has carved a new personal identity for herself within her religious community and is engaged in the dynamic process of creating new relationships. Each voice holds hope for those who struggle with trauma in all of its multiple manifestations.

References

Administration on Aging. (2010). *Profile of older Americans*. Washington, DC: Administration on Aging. Retrieved October, 2010, from www.aoa.gov/aoa/stats/profile/default.htm.

Alaggia, R., & Michalski, J. (1999). The use of peer support for parents and youth with the trauma of child sexual abuse. *Journal of Child Sexual Abuse, 8*(2), 57–76.

American Psychiatric Association. (2000). *Diagnostic & statistical manual of mental disorders* (4th ed., text revision). Washington, DC: Office of Publishing Operations, American Psychiatric Association.

Becker, G. (1997). *Disrupted lives: How people create meaning in a chaotic world*. Berkeley, CA: University of California Press.

Behrman, G. (2009). Exploring the effects of early life sexual abuse among aging Catholic nuns. *Critical Social Work, 10*(1), 38–51.

Behrman, G., & Reid, W. (2002). Post traumatic interventions: Essential tasks. *Brief Treatment & Crisis Intervention, Special Issue, 2*(1), 39–48.

Behrman, G., & Tebb, S. (2009). The use of complementary & alternative interventions as a holistic approach with older adults. *Journal of Religion & Spirituality in Social Work, 28*, 1–2.

Beitchman, J., Zucker, K., Hood, J., DeCosta, G., Akman, D., & Cassavia, E. (1992). A review of the long term effects of child sexual abuse. *Child Abuse & Neglect, 16*, 101–118.

Bell, H. (2003). Strengths and secondary trauma in family violence work. *Social Work, 4*(48), 513–522.

Bengel, J., Strittmatter, R., Willmann, H. (1999). What keeps people healthy? The current state of discussion and the relevance of Antonovsky's salutogenic model of health. HYPERLINK "http://www.worldcat.org/search?qt=hotseries&q=se%3A%22Research+and+practice+of+health+promotion%22" \o "Search for other items in this series" Research and Practice of Health Promotion, Vol. 4. Expert report commissioned by the Federal Centre for Health Education. [Ed.: Stephan Blümel ; Katharina Salice-Stephan. Transl. by Debbie Johnson]. Cologne: FCHE.

Bengston, V., Burgess, S., & Parrott, D. (1997). Theory, explanation and a third generation of theoretical development in social gerontology. *Journal of Gerontology: Social Sciences, 2*(52B), 72–88.

Black, P., & Jeffreys, D. (1993). Personal history of psychosocial trauma in the early life of social work and business students. *Journal of Social Work Education, 29*(2), 171–181.

Blumer, H. (1969). *Symbolic interactionism: Perspective and method*. Englewood Cliffs, NJ: Prentice-Hall.

Breaszeale, R. (2009). *Duct tape isn't enough: Survival skills for the 21st century*. Portland, ME: BBUSA.

Brown, L., & Gilligan, C. (1991). Listening for voice in narratives of relationship. In M. Tappan & M. Packer (Eds.), *Narrative and storytelling: Implications for understanding moral development* (pp. 43–62). San Francisco: Jossey-Bass.

Caplan, G. (1961). *An approach to community mental health*. New York: Grune & Stratton.

Carnes, P. (1993). *A gentle path through the twelve steps: The classic guide for all people in the process of recovery.* Center City, MN: MN Hazelden Educational Materials.

Chibnall, J., Wolf, A., & Duckro, P. (1998). A national survey of the sexual trauma experiences of Catholic nuns. *Review of Religious Research, 40*(2), 142–155.

Cole, B., Benore, E., & Pargament, K. (2004). Spirituality and coping with trauma. In S. Sorajjakool & H. H. Lamberton (Eds.), *Spirituality, health, and wholeness* (pp. 49–76). New York: Haworth Press.

Compton, B. A., & Galaway, B. (1989). *Social work processes* (4th ed.). California: Wadsworth.

Everly, G. S., & Mitchell, J. T. (1997). *Critical incident stress management. An operations manual for the prevention of traumatic stress among emergency services and disaster workers* (2nd ed.). Ellicott City, MD: Chevron Publishing Corporation.

Figley, C. (Ed.). (1985). *Trauma and its wake.* New York: Brunner/Mazel.

Finkelhor, D. (1994). Current information on the scope and nature of child sexual abuse. *The Future of Children, 4*(2), 31–53.

Finkelhor, D., Hotaling, G., Lewis, I. A., & Smith, C. (1990). Sexual abuse in a national survey of adult men and women: Prevalence, characteristics and risk factors. *Child Abuse & Neglect, 14*(1), 19–28.

Garmezy, N. (1993). Vulnerability and resilience. In D. C. Funder, R. D. Parke, C. Tomlinson-Keasey, & K. Widaman (Eds.), *Studying lives through time* (pp. 377–397). Washington, DC: American Psychological Association.

Glantz, M., & Johnson, J. (Eds.). (1999). *Resilience and development: Positive life adaptations.* New York: Plenum Publishers.

Glantz, M., & Sloboda, Z. (1999). Analysis and reconceptualization of resilience. In M. Glantz & J. Johnson (Eds.), *Resilience and development: Positive life adaptations* (pp. 109–126). New York: Plenum Publishers.

Graham, T. (1993). Beyond detection: Education and the abuse student. *Social Work Education, 15*(4), 197–207.

Grcenburg, H., & Keane, A. (1997). A social work perspective of childhood trauma. *Social Work Education, 19*(1), 11–23.

Greenwood, C., Tangolas, E., & Maruta, T. (1990). Prevalence of sexual abuse, physical abuse, and concurrent traumatic life events in a general medical population. *Mayo Clinic Proceedings, 65*(8), 1067–1071.

Guba, E., & Lincoln, Y. (1986). Research, evaluation, and policy analysis: Heuristics for disciplined inquiry. *Policy Studies Review, 5*(3), 546–551.

Hall, L., Sachs, B., Rayens, M., & Lutenbacher, M. (1993). Childhood physical and sexual abuse: Their relationship with depressive symptoms in adulthood. *The Journal of Nursing Scholarship, 25*(4), 317–323.

Henderson, N. (Ed.). (2007). *Resilience in action: Practical ideas for overcoming risks and building strengths.* Ojai, CA: Resiliency in Action.

Kaltman, S., & Bonanno, G. (2003). Trauma and bereavement: Examining the impact of sudden and violent deaths. *Journal of Anxiety Disorders, 17*(2), 131–147.

Kanel, K. (1999). *A guide to crisis intervention.* Pacific Grove, CA: Brooks/Cole.

Kaplan, H. (1999). Toward an understanding of resilience: A critical review of definitions and models. In M. Glantz & J. Johnson (Eds.), *Resilience and development: Positive life adaptations* (pp. 17–84). New York, NY: Plenum Publishers.

Kemmis, S., & McTaggert, R. (2000). Participatory action research. In N. Denzin & Y. Lincoln (Eds.), *Handbook of qualitative research* (2nd ed., pp. 567–605). Thousand Oaks, CA: Sage.

Koenig, H. (2000). Religion, well being and health in the elderly: The scientific evidence for an association. In J. Thorsen (Ed.), *Perspectives in spiritual well-being and aging.* Springfield, IL: C.T. Thomas.

Lakoff, G., & Johnson, M. (1980). *Metaphors we live by.* Chicago: University of Chicago Press.

LaRossa, R., & Reitzes, D. (1993). Symbolic interactionism and family studies. In P. G. Boss, W. J. Doherty, R. LaRossa, W. R. Schumm, & S. K. Steinmetz (Eds.), *Sourcebook of family theories and methods: A contextual approach* (pp. 135–162). New York: Plenum Press.

Levine, J. (2001). Lessons from holocaust survivors. *Social Work, 46*(4), 350–361.

Longres, J. (2000). *Human behavior in the social environment* (3rd ed.). Itasca, IL: Peacock Publishers.

Luthar, S. (2003). *Resilience and vulnerability: Adaptation in the context of childhood adversities.* Cambridge, UK: Cambridge University Press.

Marshall, C. (1995). Social models of aging. *Canadian Journal on Aging, 14*(1), 12–34.

Masten, A. S. (1994). Resilience in individual development: Successful adaptations despite risk and adversity. In M. C. Wang & E. W. Gordon (Eds.), *Educational resilience in inner-city America* (pp. 3–25). Hillsdale, NJ: Erlbaum.

McFarlane, A. (2000). Posttraumatic stress disorder: A model of the longitudinal course and the role of risk factors. *The Journal of Clinical Psychiatry, 61*(Suppl 5), 15–23.

McFarlane, A., & Bookless, C. (2001). The effect of PTSD on interpersonal relationships: Issues for emergency service workers. *Sexual and Relationship Therapy, 16*(3), 261.

McFarlane, A., & Yehuda, R. (2000). Clinical treatment of posttraumatic stress disorder. Conceptual challenges raised by recent research. *The Australian and New Zealand Journal of Psychiatry, 34*(6), 940.

Miller, W., & Thoresen, C. (2003). Spirituality, religion and health. *American Psychologist, 58*(1), 24–35.

Moeller, T., Bachmann, G., & Moeller, J. (1993). The combined effects of physical, sexual, and emotional abuse during childhood: Long-term health consequences for women. *Child Abuse & Neglect, 17*(5), 623–640.

Nash, M., Hulsey, T., Sexton, M., Harralson, T., & Lambert, W. (1993). Long-term sequelae of childhood sexual abuse: Perceived family environment, psychopathology, and dissociation. *Journal of Consulting and Clinical Psychology, 61*(2), 276–283.

O'Sullivan, M. (2002). *101 Questions and answers on Vatican II*. New York. Paulist Press.

Parad, H. J. (1965). *Crisis intervention: Selected readings*. New York: Family Services Association of America.

Parad, H. J., & Miller, R. (Eds.). (1963). *Ego-orientated casework: Problems and perspectives: Papers from the Smith College School for Social Work*. New York: Family Services Association of America.

Polusny, M., & Follette, V. (1995). Long term correlates of child sexual abuse: Theory and review of the empirical literature. *Applied and Preventative Psychology, 4*(3), 143–166.

Pomeroy, E., Kiam, R., & Green, D. (2000). Reducing depression, anxiety, and trauma of male inmates: An HIV/AIDS psychoeducational group intervention. *Social Work Research, 24*(3), 156–168.

Rigsby, L. C. (1994). The Americanization of resilience: Deconstructing research practice. In M. C. Wang & E. W. Gordon (Eds.), *Educational resilience in inner-city America* (pp. 67–96). Cambridge: Cambridge University Press.

Robbins, S., Chatterjee, P., & Canda, E. (1998). *Contemporary human behavior theory: A critical perspective for social work*. Boston: Allyn & Bacon.

Rolf, J. (1999). Resilience: An interview with Norman Garmezy. In M. Glantz & J. Johnson (Eds.), *Resilience and development: Positive life adaptations* (pp. 5–16). New York: Plenum Publishers.

Rossetti, S. (1995). The impact of child sexual abuse on attitudes toward God and the Catholic church. *Child Abuse & Neglect, 19*(12), 1469–1481.

Rutter, M. (1990). Psychological resilience and protective mechanisms. In J. Rolf, A. S. Masten, D. Cicchetti, K. H. Nuechterlein, & S. Weintraub (Eds.), *Risk and protective factors in the development of psychopathology* (pp. 181–214). New York: Cambridge University Press.

Saigh, P., & Bremner, J. (Eds.). (1999). *The history of posttraumatic stress disorder*. Needham Heights, MA: Allyn & Bacon.

Saleebey, D. (Ed.). (1997). *The strength's perspective in social work practice* (2nd ed.). New York: Longman.

Sipe, A. W. (1990). *A secret world: Sexuality and the search for celibacy*. New York: Brunner & Mazel.

Stryker, S. (1980). *Symbolic interactionism: A social structure version*. Merlo Park, CA: Benjamin Cummings.

Stryker, S., & Stratham, A. (1985). Symbolic interaction and role theory. In G. Lindzey & E. Aronson (Eds.), *The handbook of social psychology* (pp. 311–378). New York: Random House.

Turner, F. (1996). *Social work treatment* (4th ed.). New York, NY: The Free Press.

Ungar, M. (Ed.). (2005). *Handbook for working with children and youth: Pathways to resilience across cultures and contexts*. Thousand Oaks, CA: Sage.

Walker, B., & Salt, D. (2006). *Resilience thinking: Sustaining ecosystems and people in a changing world*. Washington, DC: Island Press.

Walsh, F. (1998). *Strengthening family resilience*. New York: Guilford Press.

Walsh, J., Zauta, A., & Hall, J. (2010). *Handbook of adult resilience*. New York: The Guilford Press.

Index

A

ABCX model, 5–6
Acceptance and commitment therapy (ACT), 447
ADHD. *See* Attention-deficit/hyperactivity disorder
  (ADHD)
Adult children of alcoholics (ACOAs)
  African-American risk and resilience factors,
    486–487
  alcoholism and African-American alcoholics,
    484–485
  attachment relationships, 487–489
  chaotic family life, 491
  clinical implications, 491–493
  commitment, 487–489
  family resilience, 489
  homicidal/suicidal ideations, 490
  kin/fictive kin relationships, 490
  middleclass culture, 489
  parental alcoholism, 483
  research implications, 493
  risk factors, 485–486
  shared values, 487–489
  social support, 489
Affordable Care Act, 391
Aging
  biological resilience, 349
  contexts, 343
  cumulative adversity, 342
  emotional resilience, 352
  families, 348–349
  healthy aging, 347
  life course and resilience, 348
  narrative gerontology, 354–355
  older adults, 348–349
  psychological resilience, 350–351
  recovery/resolution, 342
  resilience
    contexts, 343
    end of life, 353–354
    meaning of, 341–342
    metaphor, 355
    modern standards, 356

  older ages, 343–345
  practice-based definition, 343–345
  religious resources, 356
  social resilience, 351
  spiritual resilience, 352–353
  strengths perspective, 345–347
  successful and positive aging, 347–348
  Alcohol abuse. *See also* Adult children of alcoholics
    (ACOAs)
  healthy aging, 347
  Korean families, 262–263
  Native American family resilience, 207–208
Alzheimer's disease, 289
Ambiguous loss theory
  cautions, 295–296
  definition, 288
  development of, 288–289
  origin, 288
  physical disappearance, 287
  resilience
    discovering hope, 294–295
    family resilience, 290–291
    find meaning, 292–293
    history of, 290
    normalizing ambivalence, 294
    psychology, 290
    research implications, 295
    research updates, 291–292
    revising attachment, 294
    sociology, 290
    stress perspective, 289
    tempering mastery, 293
  therapy and intervention, 292
  tolerance, 287
Applied behavior analysis (ABA), 412
A relational invitational sequence for engagement
    (ARISE) intervention
  abuser, 474
  invitational intervention, 473
  recovery, 473–474
  SSTAR, 474–475
  supporting treatment and early recovery, 473

Traumatic brain injury (TBI), 118
Traumatic events
   ADHD, 511
   affective expression and modulation skills, 513
   avoiding and normalizing, 509–510
   clinical implications, 506–507
   cognitive coping and processing skills, 513
   CPSI, 501
      frequency, 505–506
      PTSD and resilience, 506
      type, 503–505
   demographic statistics, 503
   enhancing personal safety plans, 514
   environmental protective factors, 500–501
   individual protective factors, 499–500
   methods
      data collection, 501–502
      measures, 502–503
   PRACTICE model, 511–512
   PTSD arousal symptoms, 508–509
   relaxation and stress management, 512–513
   research implications, 510
   resilience research, 499
   self and escape, 507
   TF-CBT, 510
   trauma narrative development, 513–514
   violence, 507–508

W
World Health Organization (WHO), 390

Y
Youth at risk and family resilience
   atypicality, 146–147
   case study, 151
   clinical implications, 149–150
   complexity, 147–148
   cultural relativity, 148–149
   decenter, 144–146
   family environment, complexity of, 143–144
   horizontal and vertical stressors, 140–141
   research implications, 150
   social ecological definition, 141–142
   strengths/assets, 142 143

Made in the USA
Columbia, SC
20 September 2021